Privacy Rights in the Digital Age

Second Edition

Privacy Rights in the Digital Age

Second Edition

EDITORS
Jane E. Kirtley, JD
Michael Shally-Jensen, PhD

Grey House
Publishing

Cover photo: Digital fingerprint. By ktsimage (via iStock).

PRESIDENT: Richard Gottlieb
PUBLISHER: Leslie Mackenzie
EDITORIAL DIRECTOR: Laura Mars
PROJECT EDITOR: Mary Donovan
PRODUCTION MANAGER: Kristen Hayes
MARKETING DIRECTOR: Jessica Moody
Grey House Publishing, Inc.
4919 Route 22
Amenia, NY 12501
518.789.8700; Fax 845.373.6390
www.greyhouse.com
books@greyhouse.com

Publisher's Cataloging-In-Publication Data
(Prepared by The Donohue Group, Inc.)

Names: Kirtley, Jane E., editor. | Shally-Jensen, Michael, editor.
Title: Privacy rights in the Digital Age / editors, Jane E. Kirtley, JD [and] Michael Shally-Jensen, PhD.
Description: Second edition. | Amenia, NY : Grey House Publishing, [2019] | Includes bibliographical references and index.
Identifiers: ISBN 9781642650778 (hardcover)
Subjects: LCSH: Privacy, Right of--United States--Encyclopedias. | Electronic surveillance--United States--Encyclopedias. | Computer security--United States--Encyclopedias. | Data protection--United States--Encyclopedias. | Electronic government information--Access control--United States--Encyclopedias. | LCGFT: Encyclopedias.
Classification: LCC KF1263.C65 P75 2019 | DDC 342.730858--dc23

First Printing
PRINTED IN CANADA

Table of Contents

Publisher's Note

Grey House Publishing is pleased to publish the second edition of *Privacy Rights in the Digital Age*. Its comprehensive reach discusses the practical, political, psychological, and philosophical challenges faced by society, and as individuals, as advances in technology redefine our notions of privacy. This volume presents a current, balanced, and reliable collection of material that enables the reader to navigate the emerging privacy rights terrain through a series of articles and essays, written by an impressive collection of scholars and experts with corporate and technical expertise.

Privacy Rights in the Digital Age includes an introduction written by Jane Kirtley, the Silha Professor of Media Ethics and Law at Northwestern University, as well as an essay on cross-cultural perspectives on privacy rights by Julie Ann Embler, an instructor of Law School Admission Test Preparation classes at the University of South Florida. The 227 entries that follow investigate the laws, legal cases, events, organizations, individuals, and technologies that affect our privacy rights as the world becomes more and more connected. It provides background and context for privacy issues ranging from privacy of our own bodies to privacy in the workplace.

Coverage is detailed and far-reaching. Entries include social media such as Twitter, Instagram, and Snapchat; amendments in the Bill of Rights most relevant to privacy rights, the First, Fourth, and Fourteenth; and significant Supreme Court cases. Just as important are entries that discuss the theoretical and philosophical basis for our understanding of the concept of privacy, from the writings of Aristotle to Edward Snowden. Coverage also explores more contemporary aspects of privacy rights through topics such as WikiLeaks, Julian Assange, sexting, and e-mails.

Many entries include photographs and illustrations, including cartoons by Herbert Block, an American editorial cartoonist and author known for his commentaries on national domestic and foreign policy.

Following the A to Z entries is a selected bibliography for further reading. The backmatter continues with a reprint of the Privacy Rights Act of 1974, a chronology of privacy rights, a glossary of terms, two valuable tables listing court cases and statutes related to privacy rights, and an index.

Grey House Publishing extends its appreciation to all involved in the development and production of this work. The entries have been written and signed by scholars and experts in the areas of constitutional law, legal history, philosophy, and business as well as other disciplines related to privacy rights. Without these expert contributions, a project of this nature would not be possible. A full list of contributor's names and affiliations follows this Publisher's Note.

Privacy Rights in the Digital Age, as well as all Grey House Publishing encyclopedias, is available in print and as an e-book. Please visit www.greyhouse.com for more information.

Contributors

Maureen Halliden Anderson, LLM, MLS, JD
Associate Professor, University of Dayton School of Law

Ashley Baker, JD
Legal intern, Pernod Ricard, USA

Daniel Berens, JD
JD candidate, University of Alabama Law School

Jesse Bowman, MLS, JD
School of Library and Information Science
JD, Creighton Law School
Librarian, Northwestern Pritzker School of Law

Jill Bronfman, JD
Adjunct Professor, University of California at Hastings College of the Law

Shaunté Chácon, MPA
Independent Researcher

Sandra F. Chance, JD
Professor, University of Florida

Paula Collins, JD
Teacher, New York Public Schools

Joe Custer, MBA, MLIS, JD
Associate Professor, Case Western Reserve University School of Law

Amber R. Dickinson, PhD
Oklahoma State University

Steven L. Danver, PhD
Walden University

Myra Din, JD
JD candidate, Brooklyn Law School
Teaching and Research Assistant, Brooklyn Law School

Eric B. Easton, JD, PhD
Professor of Law, University of Baltimore

Julie Ann Embler, JD
Instructor at Educational Testing Consultants

J. Lyn Entrikin, MPA, JD
Professor of Law, University of Arkansas at Little Rock

Mary E. Ernhart, JD
University of Arkansas

Ethan P. Fallon, JD
Judicial Law Clerk at U.S. District Court for the Eastern District of New York

Lawrence M. Friedman, JD, LLM
Professor of Law, New England Law, Boston

Reuben Fuller-Bennett, JD
Staff Attorney, Housing Unit at Legal Services NYC

Harold W. Fuson Jr., MS, JD
Director, First Amendment Coalition

Melissa A. Gill, JD
Instructor of Law, David A Clarke School of Law, University of the District of Columbia

Ursula Gorham-Oscilowski, MLS, MPM, JD, PhD
Lecturer, Information Studies, University of Maryland

Sarah Green, MLS
Project Manager, IPLP, LAC Group

Stuart A. Hargreaves, JD, SJD
Assistant Professor of Law, LLB Programme Director
Assistant Dean (Undergraduate Studies), The Chinese University of Hong Kong

Kimberly A. Harper, MPA
Master Certificate of Cybersecurity Technology, University of Maryland University College
Professor, University of the District of Columbia Community College

Katharina Hering, MLS, MA, PhD
Project Archivist for the National Equal Justice Library, Georgetown Law

W. Wat Hopkins, MA, PhD
Professor, Virginia Tech, Department of Liberal Arts and Human Sciences

Lydia A. Jones, JD, LLM
Adjunct Professor of Law, Vanderbilt Law School

RonNell Andersen Jones, JD
Associate Dean of Academic Affairs & Research, Brigham Young University Law
Professor of Law, Brigham Young University Law

Rachel Jorgensen, MLS, JD
Information Literacy and Reference Librarian, University of the District of Columbia

Sandra Jowers-Barber, MA, PhD
Division Director for Humanities at University of the District of Columbia Community College

John W. Klinker, JD
Loyola University Chicago School of Law

Tomasz Kolodziej, MA
Legislative Analyst, Hogan Lovells, Washington, DC

Crystal N. Le, JD
Intellectual Property Fellow, Thomas Jefferson School of Law

Raleigh Hannah Levine, JD
Professor of Law, William Mitchell College of Law

Frank LoMonte, JD
Executive Director, Student Press Law Center

Rebecca Lutkenhaus, MLS, JD
Associate Professor and Reference Librarian, Drake University Law Library

Charles E. MacLean, MBA, JD
Associate Professor of Law, Indiana Tech Law School

Nancy McCormack, MA, MLIS, JD, LLM
Associate Professor of Law, Queen's University

Douglas B. McKechnie, JD
Assistant Professor, United States Air Force Academy

Eric Merriam, JD, LLM
Associate Professor, University of Central Florida

Daniel J. Metcalfe, JD
Adjunct Professor of Law, American University Washington College of Law
Founding Director, United States Department of Justice, Office of Information and Privacy

Gretchen Nobahar
Senior Human Resources Information Analyst, Washington Area Metropolitan Transit Authority (WMATA)

Savanna L. Nolan, JD
Digital Services Assistant, Catholic University of America, Columbus School of Law

Mary M. Penrose, JD, LLM
Professor of Law, Texas A&M University School of Law

Lauren Perelli, MLIS
IP Research Analyst, Landon IP

Michael J. Puniskis, MSc, PhD
Visiting Lecturer, Midddlesex University, UK

Julie E. Randolph, JD
Associate, Schnader Attorneys at Law

Paul Riermaier, MLIS, JD
Research & Information Specialist, Montgomery McCracken Walker & Rhoads

Eric P. Robinson, MA, JD
Co-Director, Press Law and Democracy Project

Stephanie Romeo, JD
Loyola University Chicago School of Law

Lowell Rudorfer, MLIS, JD
Research assistant, Georgetown Law Library

Scott Russell, JD
Postdoctoral Fellow, Indiana University – Maurer School of Law Center for Applied Cybersecurity Research

Ana Santos Rutschman, JD, SJD, LLM
Lecturer and Visiting Professor of Intellectual Property, Uppsala University
Co-Director, Global Health Innovation Alliances, Duke University

David A. Schulz, MA, JD
Senior Research Scholar and Floyd Abrams Clinical Lecturer, Yale Law School
Partner, Levine Sullivan Koch & Schulz, LLP

Tania Sebastian, LLM
Assistant Professor of Law, Gujarat National Law University

Joy M. Shoemaker, MLS, JD
Branch Law Librarian, Ninth Circuit Court of Appeals, Pasadena, California

Carey Sias, MLS
Reference Librarian, Jenkins Law Library

Drew Simshaw, JD, LLM
Clinical Teaching Fellow at Georgetown University Law Center

Noëlle Sinclair, MLS, JD
Head of Special Collections, University of Iowa Law Library

Lissa N. Snyders, MLS
NIH Library, Division of Library Services, Office of Research Services, National Institutes of Health

Donald A. Watt, PhD
Middletown, Idaho

Nic Weber, Phd
Research Associate, University of Washington Information School

Sonja R. West, JD
Associate Professor of Law, University of Georgia Law

Linda M. Wright, JD
Senior Research Counsel, Canadian Imperial Bank of Commerce

Śimal Efsane Yalçin, LLB
Istanbul Institute of Social Sciences, Istanbul Turkey

Editor's Introduction

What do you think of when you hear the term "privacy"? Does it mean that you should be able to keep information about yourself secret such as where you go with your friends for fun on Saturday night, whether you ever drink alcohol or use illegal drugs, what books or movies you read or watch, what grades you earn in school, or how much money you make? Does it mean you should have a right to know whether and how law enforcement officers monitor your electronic communications when you use your tablet or smartphone to post to Facebook or Twitter? Does it mean you should be able to control what kind of information an online retailer collects about your purchasing or browsing history? Does it mean that you should be able to seek medical care without the government learning about the choices you make?

"Privacy" in the twenty-first century means all these things, and more. The advent of the digital has created unprecedented opportunities to share and access information about each one of us. This makes it simpler and quicker than ever to obtain a store credit card, to pay bills online without ever writing a check, and to publish our ideas and thoughts to the world. But it also gives both government and the private sector unprecedented opportunities to keep an eye on our movements, our interactions with others, and in some ways, our thoughts and ideas.

This is the paradox of privacy. On the one hand, we benefit from the easy exchange of personal information through digital communications. On the other, we give up some degree of control about what happens to that information. Is that an appropriate trade off? Is it worth it?

It may surprise you to learn that privacy is a relatively new concept. In 1890, an American attorney named Louis D. Brandeis was fed up with what he saw as the excesses of the popular press in Boston, Massachusetts. Gossip columns in the newly-emerging "penny press" regaled ordinary readers with insolent and insinuating details about the doings of Mabel, the socially prominent wife of Brandeis's law partner, Samuel D. Warren. The stories were not outright lies, so she could not sue for libel. Such lawsuits are limited to situations where someone has published false information that harms an individual's reputation. To make matters worse, the invention of smaller cameras allowed photographers to take pictures with a snap of the shutter. Although the cameras manufactured by companies such as Eastman Kodak would seem cumbersome to us today, they were a significant advance over the clunky, slow-exposure cameras used only a few years earlier by Matthew Brady and other Civil War photographers. The pictures these photographers captured ended up in the mass circulation Sunday rotogravure magazines, sold for only a few cents a copy. Worse still, inventors like Thomas Edison were working on cameras that would produce *moving* pictures. Moreover, there was nothing the law could do to stop them.

So Warren and Brandeis wrote a scholarly article about the situation that they found so appalling, and published it in the *Harvard Law Review*, the scholarly journal produced at Harvard Law School. They wrote:

> The press is overstepping in every direction the obvious bounds of propriety and decency. Gossip is no longer the resource of the idle and of the vicious, but has become a trade, which is pursued with industry as well as effrontery. To satisfy a prurient taste the details of sexual relations are spread broadcast in the columns of the daily papers. To occupy the indolent, column upon column is filled with idle gossip, which can only be procured by intrusion upon the domestic circle.

However, Warren and Brandeis were not bothered only by the intrusions into their personal lives when the press published the "gossip" about them. They were also worried that these articles degraded the readers as well.

Each crop of unseemly gossip, thus harvested, becomes the seed of more, and in direct proportion to its circulation, results in the lowering of moral standards and of morality. Even gossip apparently harmless, when widely and persistently circulated, is potent for evil...When personal gossip attains the dignity of print, and crowds the space available for matters of real interest to the community, what wonder that the ignorance and thoughtless mistake its relative importance.

Thinking like the lawyers they were, Warren and Brandeis concluded that the best solution would be to create a new legal theory, a "right to be left alone," to be recognized by judges, which would allow individuals to sue others for money damages if they believed that their privacy had been violated.

Brandeis and Warren were not the only ones who thought that the press was going too far using new-fangled "mechanical devices" that could record conversations and cameras that produced "instantaneous" pictures. Lawsuits in England had already prevented the exhibition and distribution of copies of photographic portraits without the subject's consent. Nor did the law partners invent the concept of "privacy." They acknowledged that France already had recognized the right to "*la vie privée*" in its 1868 press law.

Nevertheless, U.S. courts were slow to embrace this new right, and the legal liability that would accompany it. Congress did nothing to enact laws addressing the issue, and most legislative action in the states was limited to protecting an individual's right to safeguard his name and image from commercial exploitation through advertisements.

With one law review article, this pair of Boston lawyers—one of whom would later become a Justice of the Supreme Court of the United States—began a discussion that continues to the present day. What is the right to privacy? How much control should we have over our personal information? When do freedom of the press and freedom of speech outweigh the individual's right to be left alone? When do national security concerns justify the government's monitoring of our electronic communications? How much of our personal data are we prepared to give away or "trade" in exchange for making consumer transactions like shopping or traveling faster and easier?

Several international human rights declarations and conventions created after the Second World War recognize that privacy—traditionally defined as a person's private life, home, and correspondence—is a fundamental right. This means that the preservation of privacy is seen as essential to personal fulfillment, and to functioning within a democratic society. Inevitably, the equally "fundamental" right of the news media to gather and report news and to inform the public collides head on with this "fundamental" right of privacy.

However, the right to privacy has never been elevated to this level in the United States. The Fourth Amendment to the Constitution guarantees citizens the right to be "secure in their persons, houses, papers, and effects" and to be protected from the government conducting unreasonable searches and seizures of people and their property. This is a powerful statement supporting individual autonomy. In recent years, it has been interpreted by the Supreme Court not only to limit how law enforcement conducts criminal investigations, but to curb the power of government to control or intrude into intimate aspects of our lives, such as the right to obtain contraception and abortion. As important as the Fourth Amendment is, it says nothing about invasions of privacy committed by non-governmental actors like corporations or the press.

In fact, the First Amendment right of the press to report on newsworthy matters has been vigorously protected by rulings of the Supreme Court. The high court has been reluctant to curtail the news media when they choose to report on subjects that are considered newsworthy and of legitimate public interest, even if they involve such controversial matters as the identities of crime victims. The idea that journalists could be punished for simply telling the truth seems to violate those constitutionally-guaranteed rights.

And so there seemed to be a stalemate. Although a few skirmishes between proponents of these seemingly irreconcilable interests cropped up during the years immediately after the Warren and Brandeis article appeared, the conflict did not come to a head until roughly a hundred years later. By that time, a growing debate, driven by new incarnations of the factors that had so upset the two lawyers, prompted courts and legislatures to begin rethinking the concept of privacy. Many argued that sensational media who profited from salacious stories about the rich and powerful, and who utilized sophisticated equipment to capture their subjects in embarrassing and compromising situations, needed to be reined in. Laws to make it a crime to use surreptitious surveillance devices such as hidden cameras were enacted, and both federal and state law prohibited wiretapping of telephone conversations. Courts began to recognize a right to protect one's personal information from disclosure by others, at least in cases where it would be highly offensive to a reasonable person. A few states allowed individuals to sue for invasion of privacy when someone described or depicted them in a "false light"—for example, by publishing an accurate photograph with a misleading caption that distorted reality.

However, it was not until 1997, following the death of Diana, Princess of Wales, in a car crash in a Paris tunnel while she and her companions were attempting to dodge a pack of *paparazzi*, that public support for new restrictions on reporting about individuals took off. Using Diana's death as a pretext, the European Parliament scheduled an "emergency" debate on strengthening privacy laws, and its Culture and Media Committee asked the European Commission to launch a comparative study of existing legislation with the aim of developing an international "code of conduct" for the news media. The Press Complaints Commission in the United Kingdom declared that British newspapers should stop buying *paparazzi* photographs obtained "illegally or unethically."

In the United States, legislators introduced bills in Congress and in several states to invent a new federal crime of "harassment," create buffer zones around famous people, and authorize official inquiries into journalistic behavior. Celebrities testified about how the media were making their lives, and those of their families, miserable. Although much of the initial hysteria about intrusive news coverage eventually died down, new and growing privacy concerns have continued to fuel new efforts to restrict both newsgathering and reporting.

One example is the increasing use of drones by the general public and by businesses. This particular technology, which at one time was limited to use by the military and law enforcement, has become comparatively inexpensive and readily available for a variety of recreational and commercial uses. However, drones also raise legitimate privacy concerns. The Federal Aviation Administration and several states have considered measures to restrict the use of drones.

The *Los Angeles Times* reported on August 16, 2014, that the Paparazzi Reform Initiative, described as "a group representing celebrities and others," persuaded Assemblyman Ed Chau to introduce a bill in the California legislature that would prohibit the use of aerial drones to collect video, photos, and audio of celebrities. The newspaper also reported that a drone had taken photographs of singer Miley Cyrus in her backyard. The photographs were offered for sale to a "major photo broker" who declined to purchase them, although he did tell the *Times* that he would use drones to take photographs of celebrities' homes "as long as no individuals can be seen in the pictures to raise personal privacy issues." Laws and regulatory initiatives like these illustrate the difficulty of striking the appropriate balance between competing rights of privacy and freedom of expression.

The digital age has only complicated these issues. As we utilize computer technology for our everyday communications, we are creating a digital profile that can be tracked by the government and the private sector to create elaborate dossiers about our habits, our health, our preferences in food and entertainment, and much more. Although often this is done transparently, the exact parameters of collection of personal data by retail merchants, social media sites like Facebook, and other digital service providers are often buried in complicated "Terms of Service" which consumers rarely read in full before clicking a box to signify their consent. Most people agree to share their personal information without giving much thought to the consequences. Moreover, if the most significant consequence of sharing data is that the consumer receives targeted emails or other electronic communications tailored to her preferences, is that a big deal? Isn't it a benefit to patients if their health care providers can access digitized medical records? Doesn't the existence of reports that compile our financial history make it easier to obtain loans and other forms of credit?

By contrast, when the government conducts the surveillance, the consequences can be a very big deal indeed. Although law enforcement, including the FBI, has long had the authority to observe and record individuals' communications, that authority was limited by strict legal requirements that search warrants or court orders be obtained, often in advance, from judges. Oversight of the executive branch by the judiciary helped to keep overzealous investigations in check. However, after the 2001 terrorist attacks on the World Trade Center in New York and the Pentagon in Washington, DC, the intelligence community demanded—and was given by Congress in the USA PATRIOT Act—legal authority to conduct much more extensive surveillance than had been authorized previously. They argued that some suspension of the Fourth Amendment protections was necessary to protect the public from similar terrorist attacks in the future. Many Americans accepted this as a necessary bargain "to keep us safe."

But even those who were prepared to go along with expanded government powers to keep tabs on "the bad guys" were shocked to learn just how extensive surveillance was when, in 2013, a former defense contractor named Edward Snowden disclosed classified documents detailing how the intelligence community monitored the communications of millions of ordinary American citizens. He revealed details about how the National Security Agency (NSA) and its counterparts in other countries intercepted phone records, text and email messages, video chats, and locational data. Even people who had believed that they had nothing to fear as long as they "weren't doing anything wrong" began to question whether the government's actions prying into so many details of their personal lives actually infringed on their fundamental civil liberties.

In response to outcries from their citizens, the U.S. Congress, as well as other legislatures around the world, has been forced to confront the difficult question of how to balance safety and security against privacy. Even under ideal circumstances, drafting new digital privacy laws is a challenge. Putting aside the inevitable and constant political squabbles, evolving technology moves much faster than any legislative body can. The intelligence community, having acquired the ability to conduct massive surveillance, is reluctant to surrender it. Moreover, countless consumer data breaches launched by hackers—often based outside the United States—have repeatedly compromised personal information held by credit card companies, retailers, and health providers, and the law seems powerless to stop them. It hardly seems possible to encrypt or secure digital systems quickly enough to prevent their exploitation by criminals, and consumers understandably worry about financial fraud and identity theft.

Legitimate as these concerns are, however, they can lead to unintended consequences. For example the federal Freedom of Information Act (FOIA), which provides the public with access to executive branch documents, is an important tool to allow citizens to keep an eye on "what the government is up to," as a Supreme Court Justice once wrote. Of course, before computers, these records were kept in paper form, in file drawers, and it took some doing to find them. However, converting these documents to digital form, and making them accessible online, changed everything. Now anyone, anywhere in the world, at least theoretically, could look at whatever government documents he chose. The sheer quantity of personal information that governments collect, coupled with the ease of access to this information, has led the Supreme Court to permit agencies to withhold otherwise public documents claiming that disclosure would constitute an "unwarranted invasion of personal privacy." The Court's rulings have included denying access to computerized "rap sheets" that compile someone's criminal history, photographs taken at a crime scene, and even arrest records—which traditionally have been open to the public. The high court has determined that whatever the legal history may have been during the era of parchment and paper, the digital age has changed the rules. Combine privacy with post-9/11 security concerns, and the net result is that the public's access to government information is under serious threat.

Ultimately, the concept of privacy is really about control. Should individuals, through the instrumentalities and often with the complicity of the government, have the power to control the content of news reporting? Should public officials be able to hide the facts from the public in the name of protecting privacy? Should legislatures and international bodies restrict the collection, retention, and distribution of "personal" data by businesses in the name of protecting privacy?

An example from Europe helps to illustrate this. The European Union's 1995 Data Protection Directive grants "data subjects" the right to exercise dominion over information that uniquely identifies them, including physical, economic and cultural characteristics such as race, ethnicity, religion, or political affiliation. Among other things, the Directive requires "processors" of data to notify individuals of how they will use information collected about them, as well as give the subjects the right to approve or veto those uses, gain access to databases containing the information, and demand copies, corrections, or deletions. Although the Directive deals only with the personal information of EU citizens, it prohibits the transfer of that information into other countries that have less protective laws, which has significant consequences for international trade and business. The United States entered into a "Safe Harbor" agreement that allowed domestic companies to certify that they would comply with the EU rules, even though these practices were not required under United States law. However, less than 20 years after the Directive took effect, the European Union has declared that the Safe Harbor provides inadequate protection, and new negotiations to try to reach a compromise are ongoing.

As far-reaching as the impact of the Data Protection Directive has been, a new idea out of Europe threatens to be even more significant. The "Right to be Forgotten" (RTBF) has been discussed and debated by European policymakers and privacy advocates since about 2010, but first formally appeared in a proposal to reform the Data Protection Directive issued in January 2012. It is based on a right to privacy, or personality, enshrined in Article 8 of the European convention on human rights, which provides that "Everyone has the right to respect for his private and family life, his home and his correspondence." However, the RTBF goes far beyond mere "respect" for privacy. Driven initially by concerns about data harvesting by search engines like Google, and exacerbated by the Snowden revelations, the RTBF elevates privacy interests to a new level. As Viviane Reding, vice-president of the European Commission stated in 2012, "I want to explicitly clarify that people shall have the right—and not only the 'possibility'—to withdraw their consent to the processing of the personal data they have given out themselves." The RTBF would allow record subjects to control personal data that they consider to be "irrelevant or outdated," regardless of whether they affirmatively chose to place it in the public domain initially.

Many would argue that teenagers should have the power to "erase" ill-advised photographs of themselves that they impetuously posted online without considering the consequences in the longer term. California enacted a law, effective in 2015, that does just that. However, the RTFP goes far beyond shielding youthful indiscretions from public scrutiny. Not only journalists, but historians and archivists also fear that the RTFP could wipe out their primary source materials. Should individuals be able to decide for themselves when accurate information about them is "no longer relevant" and consign it to oblivion? A former concentration camp guard in his nineties who now lives quietly in retirement in Germany as a model citizen might argue that the record of his affiliation with the Nazi death camps is "no longer relevant." However, even elderly alleged war criminals could still face prosecution, which supports the counterargument that archives like these should be maintained in perpetuity, no matter what the record subject prefers.

In the classic 1938 drama, *Our Town*, the character of the Stage Manager describes the mythical American town of Grover's Corners: "In our town we like to know the facts about everybody." And he is right. We *do* want to "know the facts" about our friends, neighbors, and colleagues. The news media report facts they deem newsworthy about government officials, celebrities, and ordinary individuals. Government files reveal many facts about individuals and their interactions with government, which in turn tell us a lot about how the government functions. The commercial sector collects information about its customers to "serve them better"—and to increase its profits.

Some of these practices are beneficial. Others have the potential to harm. The difficulty lies in deciding where the public interest stops and privacy interests prevail. That is the privacy paradox that this encyclopedia explores.

Privacy is a subjective, and therefore, elusive, concept. Invoking it can create unlimited opportunities for mischief and genuine damage to public welfare. Ignoring it can undercut the individual's right to determine for herself what her identity and destiny will be.

How much is your privacy worth to you? Are you willing to give it up for convenience, for access to information, or for safety and security? Do you think that privacy is an outdated idea? Does privacy even matter anymore?

How would you resolve the "privacy paradox"?

—*Jane E. Kirtley, JD*

Cross-Cultural Perspectives on Privacy

"Differences in culture and tradition, in short, have made for palpable differences in law."

Professor James Q. Whitman,
The Two Western Cultures of Privacy: Dignity Versus Liberty

As computers became more regularly used to store and search governmental and corporate data in the 1960s-1970s, so did concerns about privacy protection of personal information; that concern continues to grow to this day, and in some cultures, concern has even heightened to the level of fear. Views on the importance of privacy differ between countries in large part because of cultural differences between regions. However, as Justice Stephen Breyer observed in his book *The Court and the World: American Law and the New Global Realities*, about one-fifth of cases heard by the United States Supreme Court now deal with international law, a count that is up dramatically from the time when Justice Breyer first took the bench. As we move into a global economy, understanding and reconciling differences in laws of national origin but with international effects becomes increasingly important. Justice Elena Kagan suggests that, because many threats to privacy cannot and do not respect national borders, we must seek out and employ helpful ideas related to privacy protection wherever we can find them. This is especially true with respect to the privacy laws that govern the electronic data that has become indispensable in international transactions.

The world's first data privacy statute was passed in Hesse (a German "lander" or state) in 1970; the United States followed suit shortly thereafter when it included privacy protections in the Fair Credit Reporting Act, 84 Stat. 1127 (1971). The first comprehensive national legislation on data protection came from Sweden in 1973; those laws became a model for not just European countries, but also countries around the world. Since then, privacy laws to protect online data have been passed across the globe, some of which have international implications. The approaches taken by the country implementing the laws, however, differs according to the culture to which that country subscribes. One of the reasons for this, according to Katiza Rodriguez, the international rights director of the Electronic Frontier Foundation, is that the majority of countries view data protection privacy as a fundamental right, written into a comprehensive law, such as a constitution. This is true of the European Constitution (as a constitutional example) as well as the Japan, with its Japanese Act Concerning Protection of Personal Information. By contrast, at the time of writing, the United States has no such comprehensive universal foundational legislation (although the Obama administration has attempted to change that). Such differences create difficulties for companies attempting to follow the law while working across borders, which has become common-place in today's global society. Like many issues in the global economy, there is a trade-off between unifying to make things simpler while moving forward into the international community, while honoring the cultural perspectives that keep a nation unique.

Multiple theories have been posed as to why privacy rights, laws, and concerns differ among different cultures. Suggested by Steven Bellman, Eric J. Johnson, Stephen J. Korbin, and Gerald L. Lohse in *International Differences in Information Privacy Concerns: A Global Survey of Consumers* are the following: the differences relate to differences in cultural values as described by other research; the differences reflect different Internet experiences; the differences reflect different goals of the underlying political institutions (without reflecting differences in privacy presences of actual users of the Internet). Soumitra Dutta, William H. Dutton, and Ginette Law (*Faculty & Research Working Paper: The New Internet World —*

A Global Perspective on Freedom of Expression, Privacy, Trust and Security Online) suggest that what a user shares online depends on how long the users' home country has had access to the Internet, drawing a divide between "full integration of the Internet" and "older Internet nations," the latter still feeling a "certain wariness" about disclosing personal information online due to a recollection of a time when such information was much less secure. This author suggests that several other considerations come into play when considering cultural differences within privacy rights and protections, including a nation's view of property rights as well as freedom of speech.

Perhaps the easiest way to understand the cultural ramifications upon privacy protections is to look at *how* and *where* these differences exist. The following entry first examines the Western World (including but not limited to the European Union and some member countries, and former British colonies having Anglo legal and cultural traditions, such as Canada, Australia, and New Zealand). Next the article looks at privacy laws in Russia and Eastern European, Central Asian nations formerly under Russia's direct or indirect control, East Asia (including China, Hong Kong, Japan, and North- and South Korea) and South Asia (including India- Pakistan, Bangladesh, and Afghanistan). Finally, it considers the Middle East, as defined broadly, (including Israel and Turkey); Sub-Saharan Africa (including South Africa and Zimbabwe); and South and Latin America, (including Mexico and Argentina). It is important to note that the countries examined are meant to highlight cultural differences rather than be an exhaustive survey of international law. It is also important to note that this article focuses on data protection, but privacy protections cannot be divorced from criminal law, where a number of our protections originated and which are examined throughout this book. Finally, because the focus of this encyclopedia is privacy in the United States, much of the comparisons examined compare other cultures to that of the United States.

The European Union

The European Union's Data Protection Directive: Adopted in 1995, the European Union's comprehensive Data Protection Directive brought global attention to privacy issues and technology. Like all European Union Directives, it is not self-executing and instead requires Member States to pass synchronized national legislation to enact the terms (a few of such laws are examined below). It is organized around key principals of information use, including notice, consent (or "unambiguous consent"), consistency, access, security, further transfers, and enforcement. Additionally, Article Twenty-Eight sets forth the role of a Data Protection Authority to oversee compliance with each country's data protection legislation.

While this comprehensive piece of legislation contains many important provisions, the Safe Harbor Provision is particularly notable. For international legal actions, like recent actions of the United States, European Union governments encourage self-regulations with deference to nongovernment programs to enforce appropriate standards for participating countries. This model puts some control back into the hands of consumers to choose which countries with which to do business, depending on the participation of such companies. The European Union has set up the Safe Harbor Agreement for optional participation by the United States (and other non-European Union companies) to ensure compliance with the European Union's standards. For participation, United States' companies receive U.S. jurisdiction in most legal actions brought by European Union citizens against those companies.

Article 8 of the European Convention for the Protection of Human Rights and Fundamental Freedoms: Europe has created an obligation for governments to secure privacy values within communities. Under this view, governments are expected to protect human rights, and thereby by its own directives privacy, within all aspects of life, not just when the government is involved. This type of approach is not the typical view in the United States, where most privacy implications are realized in *negative* terms (*i.e.,* what a government cannot do) but rather, what a government must do to ensure privacy protection.

Member Countries of the European Union

Finland: Article Six of the Constitution of Finland states, "Every Finnish citizen shall be protected by law as to life, honour, personal liberty and property," and Article Twelve further states, "The secrecy of postal, telegraphic and telephonic communications shall be inviolable unless exceptions are provided by law." Thereby, the roots of privacy protection in Finland can be found in the constitution. Finland has also enacted The Personal Data Act, with the stated objectives of, "implement[ing], in the processing of personal data, the protection of private life and the other basic rights which safeguard the right to privacy, as well as to promote the development of and compliance with good processing practice." (Int'l. Information Security & Privacy § 5:1). This law has inherent international implications and provides specific directives for information being transferred both within and outside of the European Union.

France: Privacy is a paramount value in France. A public opinion survey conducted in 1975 found that financial and sexual privacy were considered the most important privacies. Still, data protection is recognized as an important issue and has been since the beginning of the technological revolution. The Safari affair (1974) highlights the view of the French on this topic; when the press identified an administrative plan that would link all personal files, the huge public concern for privacy prompted a halt to the project. The Safari system was stopped, and the Minister of Justice set up a commission to ensure personal data would be protected in the public, semi-public and private sectors alike.

Following a comprehensive report by this commission, a data protection law was developed in 1978. The data protection law consists of five basic principles, the first of which established the above-mentioned commission (Commission Nationale de l'Informatique et des Libertés' or "the Commission") as an independent body with a defined role. Under the second principle, a method of licensing and registering data processing systems was established. The third principle established a general right of subject access and rectification. The fourth principle (most likely prompted by the failed Safari system) regulated name-linked data. The fifth principle outlined the successive phase-in of the Commission's powers. Today, the regulations are very similar to most other European data protection laws.

In complying with the European Union Data Protection Act, French law provides that its Act is applicable in two specific ways when international law in concerned: (one) "the data controller is established on French territory. The data controller who carries out his activity on French territory within an establishment, whatever its legal form, is considered established on French territory;" and (two) "the data controller, although not established on French territory or in any other Member State of the European Union, uses means of processing located on French territory, with the exception of processing used only for the purposes of transit through this territory or that of any other member State of the European Union."

Germany: Germany's Basic Law speaks to "human dignity" and "personal honor" without explicit mention of privacy or a privacy provision. Still, the privacy interests in German law and culture have been considered more readily protected in Germany than in the United States. Sometimes this difference is strictly cultural rather than legal. For example, employers in Germany are less likely to engage in surveillance of their employees, even for legitimate ends. Furthermore, electronic "snooping" (video surveillance, listening in on phone calls) is explicitly illegal in Germany. Germany has enacted a Privacy Act in compliance with the European Union's Privacy Directive.

Former British colonies having Anglo legal and cultural traditions

Australia: Unlike other former colonies of Western nations, Australia has no equivalent to such guarantees of basic rights as the United States' Bill of Rights or the incorporation of the European Convention. Furthermore, privacy is not an express right in the federal constitution or any of the state constitutions. Much like the United Kingdom, privacy protections are found in individual statutes at the federal and state level.

Canada: The Supreme Court of Canada has emphasized that the "reasonable expectation of privacy," is a normative standard rather than an empirical one. In *R. v. Tessling* (2004 3 S.C.R. 432, 452, paragraph 42 (Can.), Justice Binnie explains that as technology advances, "…ordinary people may come to fear (with or without justification) that their telephones are wiretapped….Suggestions that a diminished *subjective* expectation of privacy should automatically result in a lowering of constitutional protection should, therefore, be opposed…the expectation of privacy is a normative rather than a descriptive standard." This relative difference can be observed utilizing the specific example of privacy and whether it is tethered with property ownership, as it is in the United States (see *United States v. Jones*, 132 S.Ct. 945 (2012)), highlighting the coupling of ownership to privacy, and as Justice Anthony Scalia explains, the United States' Fourth Amendment jurisprudence is connected to common-law trespass theory). By contrast, in Canada, one can claim a constitutional privacy interest in data that is found on a computer owned by the government, an idea that is impossible within the United States legal framework.

New Zealand: Originally, New Zealand's data protection law was the only one in the world that was directed only and specifically at regulating information about law enforcement. As of 1993, the comprehensive Privacy Act set forth a broad privacy management system with twelve fundamental principles. Interestingly, this law sets forth that whenever possible, private information is to be collected directly from the source—the subject of the data. Like European nations and unlike the United States, New Zealand's Privacy Act sets forth a positive obligation for any governmental agency to have a privacy officer. The privacy officer becomes the direct contact when complaints are received alleging breach of the Privacy Act. New Zeeland also employs a Privacy Commissioner with the power to implement specific rules of practice for specific agencies as well as specific activities. The Privacy Commissioner investigates complaints of wrong-doing by agencies with respect to privacy protection.

Russia and Eastern European and Central Asian nations formerly under Russia's direct or indirect control

When the Union of Soviet Socialist Republics was still in existence, it ratified the United Nations' Covenant on Civil and Political Rights as well as the Covenant on Economic, Social, and Cultural Rights. The right to privacy was guaranteed by Article Fifty-Six of the federal Constitution (1977), specifically stating that, "the privacy of citizens, of correspondence, telephone conversations, and telephonic messages shall be protected by law."

Modern-day Russia still provides for the protection of privacy and it could be argued that privacy is respected more today than ever before. Federal Law of 27 July 2006 N 152-FZ on Personal Data provides "This Federal Law regulates activities related to the processing of personal data by federal, regional and other state agencies (hereinafter, "state agencies"), municipal and other local authorities (hereinafter, "municipal authorities"), legal entities and individuals, both automatically and manually, provided that manual data processing is by its nature similar to automatic data processing. (Int'l. Information Security

& Privacy § 11:2). The law provides for an exception for previously archived information. Violations of the law can carry civil and criminal penalties, as well as administrative remedies.

East Asia

China (People's Republic of China): China has very limited privacy protection. There has been an affirmation that the personal dignity of citizens is inviolable, yet privacy is protected on a sporadic basis, at best. Interestingly, in a survey done in conjunction with *Faculty & Research Working Paper: The New Internet World – A Global Perspective on Freedom of Expression, Privacy, Trust and Security Online*, researchers found that in China, a very high percentage of people were willing to share private information in exchange for a trade-off (like opening a bank account or finding a job). Forty-six percent of people were prepared to make this trade-off in China, whereas only twenty-eight percent were in the United States (China's was the second-highest percentage on this statistic, beat only by India, whereas the United States was the third lowest, followed by a tie between Spain and France).

Therefore, the attitude towards privacy in China is unique. Despite how little privacy data is protected, people are very willing to share private information. This highlights the cultural differences on how individuals approach privacy and how those differences are reflected in the law. Should people not consider privacy as strong of a virtue, perhaps laws to protect privacy are less important. Of course, arguably, if one has never had his or her privacy protected, he or she would inherently find the protection of privacy less important due to little experience with such protections.

Japan: The Personal Information Protection law governs privacy in Japan in conjunction with four related bills that helped the law take immediate effect and enforcement. Originally, The Personal Information Protection law only protected information in the public sector, however, in 2005, the reach of the law extended to the private sector as well. In 2004, the law was amended to handle privacy violations on the Internet specifically, as well as disclosure of personal information or other incidents that could result in human rights violations. Unfortunately, no law was tight enough to prevent the loss of millions of pieces of personal information by Yahoo! JAPAN and as a result, the Ministry of Public Management, Home Affairs, Posts, and Telecommunications reformed their guidelines relating to the privacy responsibilities of telecom carriers.

North Korea (People's Republic of Korea): Personal privacy is not respected in North Korea. State surveillance of private life is common to ensure there are no anti-nationalistic sentiments expressed by any one, at any time, in any way. While there are laws on the books that suggest there is privacy protection, many have suggested that such laws in North Korea are a façade to cover up the massive human rights violations that take place in North Korea on a daily basis. The Kirby Commission, an inquiry lead by Michael Kirby of the United Nations, has found that privacy protections are comprehensively breached in North Korea.

South Korea (Republic of Korea): "The privacy of no citizen may be infringed," reads South Korea's Constitution at Article Seventeen. Perhaps to add further guidance as to what types of privacy are protected and what an infringement might look like, South Korea also has enacted comprehensive privacy legislation in the Act on the Protection of Personal Information Managed by Public Agencies of 1994. The Act required that governmental agencies limit the amount of data protected and who can access such data, as well as ensuring the security of the data and that it is only used for the purpose for which it was collected. Additional sectoral legislation governed medical information, telecommunications, and e-commerce. Now, data protection is regulated under the comprehensive Personal Information Protection Act which was designed to consolidate all of the competing privacy laws in one place, but many sectoral laws still work in conjunction with the Act (such as laws regulating the use of information held by credit card companies.)

South Asia

India: The right to privacy is not mentioned in the Indian Constitution, but the courts have found an implicit constitutional right to privacy, similar to the history of the privacy jurisprudence in the United States. Unlike the United States, however, India does not recognize invasion of privacy or defamation as torts. Much of the regulation of privacy is done at the state level utilizing legislation or administrative rules. However, this operates to protect information in the hands of the government as opposed to blanket protections of privacy. In 2000, India passed the Information Technology Act, which deals with privacy and data protection. The Act was drafted as an attempt to utilize data protection ideas from countries with mature, long-standing data-protection laws.

Pakistan: The Constitution of Pakistan guarantees a right to privacy. Additionally, Pakistan has signed multiple international treaties that recognize the right to privacy as a fundamental right. There is no federal law, however, that addresses cyber security or data protection. Thus, the non-government organization, "Bytes for All," reports that privacy rights in practice are in conflict with the Constitution and calls for Congress to implement a privacy act. The group covers government surveillance, well as to what extent the government may invade the private lives of the citizens by use of the Internet.

Afghanistan: Because of the current state of affairs in Afghanistan, the future of data protection regulation remains uncertain. Afghanistan has not experienced peace since 1978. The country utilizes extensive surveillance of citizens. Identification cards with microchips are set to replace the standard identification cards citizens are required to carry.

The Constitution of 2004 establishes a combination of civil law and Islamic law. It establishes many specific rights for citizens that deal with privacy (such as "liberty and dignity") without expressly granting a right to privacy. A draft "Access to Personal Information" law was prepared with the help of outside nations in 2011, but there has not been much progress since then as data protection is understandably not high on the nation's agenda.

The Middle East

Israel: Privacy is a basic right in Israel, a country that has perhaps the most privacy protections of any nation. The Protection of Privacy Law requires that database owners (of databases of a specific size) must register with the Registrar of Databases. The Registrar has the authority to investigate violations of the Protection of Privacy Law. Furthermore, certain activities that impinge on the right to privacy are flatly prohibited.

Turkey: Although Turkey does not have a general data protection law, The Turkish Constitution of 1982 grants rights to privacy as well as the secrecy of communication. If these rights are violated, a citizen may seek injunctive relief. Turkey has signed the Convention for the Protection of Human Rights and Fundamental Freedoms as well as the Council of Europe's Convention for the Protection of Individuals with Regard to Automatic Processing Personal Data, but has yet to ratify the latter.

Sub-Saharan Africa

South Africa: Both a right to privacy and a right of access to information held by the state are protected in the South African Constitution. In November of 2013, a comprehensive data protection privacy law (known as the Protection of Personal Information Act) was passed after years of deliberations. Much like any western countries (excluding the United States) the law establishes a centralized authority for privacy issues: the Information Regulator. The Information Regulator has the power to: authorize a specific breach (exception) of the processing of personal information; issue regulations without prior approval; and issue enforcement notices (some of which carry criminal implications.) South Africa also recognizes invasion of privacy as a tort.

Zimbabwe: In 2002, Zimbabwe enacted the Access to Information and Protection of Privacy Act. Combining these topics is notably a smart tactic as many countries have found regulations in these two areas to conflict with one another and thus leave issues to be resolved by the courts. The law includes a provision for a Media and Information Commission headed by a commissioner. However, since the law was enacted, the government has had strict control over the media, thus making it difficult to report on the true status of privacy protections in Zimbabwe.

South America and Latin America

Argentina: In Argentina, the Constitution provides for a special judiciary remedy for the publishing of personal data: *habeas data*. Thus, the right to privacy is a fundamental one in Argentina. Furthermore, The Personal Data Protection Act went into effect in 2001. Despite its location, Argentina seems to have responded to the data exporting restrictions that the European Union Directive had established, adopting many of the provisions word-for-word. The European Union has acknowledged Argentina's Personal Data Protection Act as being "substantially similar" to Article Twenty-Five of the European Union Directive. However, some of the provisions of the Act seem to be even more stringent than the European Union Directive. This is true when it comes to the security of personal information; Argentina requires a responsible party or user of the data to use whatever technical measures necessary to guarantee security of the data and detect and alterations of the data. While the European Union Directive encourages similar measures, it does so with qualifications. Finally, the Regulation established a National Directorate for the Protection of Personal Data.

Mexico: The Mexican Constitution recognizes an individual's right to privacy as one of the most fundamental human rights and is in accordance with Article Twelve of the Universal Declaration on Human Rights and Article Eleven of the American Convention on Human Rights. Persons' basic privacy protections with respect to themselves, family, home, papers, possessions, private communications and correspondences sent through the postal services are laid out in Article Sixteen of the Mexican Constitution. While the privacy rights are broad, there is no specific article of the constitution or a specific privacy law that relates to data protection specifically.

Still, the Federal Consumer Protection Act, the Federal Transparency and Pubic Governmental Information Act as well as the Geographic Statics and Information Law and the Law for Regulating Credit Information Companies are all nation-wide laws that protect privacy in the private sector in some way. Additionally, the Mexican E-commerce Law (which is not a single law as the name implies but rather a reform of the Federal Civil Code, the Federal Code of Civil Procedure, the Code of Commerce and the Federal Consumer Protection Act) works to accommodate electronic documents into the country's online consumer protection legal scheme. In 2004, four years after the passage of the Mexican E-commerce

Law, the Federal Consumer Protection Act was amended again to incorporate even stronger privacy protections for consumers. There are several other laws that regulate privacy indirectly by protecting confidential information (such as the Federal Telecommunications Act).

Conclusion

When looking at several cultures in the aggregate, one might notice more similarities than differences in privacy protections across the globe. Where major differences do exist, it is often in conjunction with political unrest and instability within a nation at war. Thus, in addition to the previously mentioned factors that help shape privacy laws, political stability should also be considered.

Beyond data protection, privacy is also inherently intertwined with criminal law and criminal justice systems, which are beyond the scope of this article but not beyond the scope of this encyclopedia. Readers are encouraged to think about the implications of the privacy within an individual country's framework while learning how the United States handles certain criminal matters.

It is important to remember that the United States does not have an explicit right to privacy in her constitution. Still, most citizens of the United States hold privacy as a very strong virtue. Thus, while law and culture are inherently related, one does not create a definitive impact on the other as a number of considerations go into the development of the law; certainly the least of which is not culture.

Further Reading

Bellman, Steven, Eric J. Johnson, Stephen J. Kobrin, and Gerald L. Lohse. "International Differences in Information Privacy Concerns: A Global Survey of Consumers." *The Information Society*: 313-24.

Cate, Fred H. *Privacy in the Information Age*. Washington, D.C.: Brookings Institution Press, 1997.

Dutta, Soumitra, William H. Dutton, and Ginette Law. "Faculty & Research Working Paper: The New Internet World: A Global Perspective on Freedom of Expression, Privacy, Trust and Security Online." *Insead* 2011/89/TOM.

Michael, James. *Privacy and Human Rights*. Paris: United Nations Educational, Scientific and Cultural Organization and Dartmouth Publishing Company Limited.

Sarat, Austin. *A World without Privacy: What Law Can and Should Do?* New York, New York: Cambridge University Press.

Westby, Jody R., ed. *International Guide to Privacy*. Chicago, IL: ABA Pub., 2004.

A

Abortion

Identification: A woman's right to abortion is recognized as a fundamental constitutional privacy right. *Roe v. Wade,* 410 U.S. 113 (1973).

In *Roe,* the Supreme Court held that the constitutional right of privacy "is broad enough to encompass a woman's decision whether or not to terminate her pregnancy." This seven to two decision invalidated the Texas anti-abortion statute and rendered unenforceable similar laws in most every other state. The essential holding in *Roe* has been upheld by the Supreme Court in several subsequent decisions.

After *Roe* was decided, a woman's right to abortion became defined in terms of her right to privacy. In other words, the constitutional right to reproductive privacy is articulated in terms of autonomy, or freedom from governmental interference in that decision. The woman's decisional privacy became the starting point for the conception of privacy associated with reproductive choice.

Although the right of "privacy" is not explicitly stated in the United States Constitution, the courts now recognize a sphere of intimate personal conduct that is constitutionally protected from governmental interference. In *Griswold v. Connecticut,* 381 U.S. 479 (1965), its first explicit recognition of this constitutional right the U.S. Supreme Court invalidated a state law restricting the use of contraceptive devices and articulated the right to reproductive privacy. Developing since the *Griswold* case, courts have recognized the right of privacy in cases involving personal choices involving sex, reproduction, and end-of-life medical decisions.

To determine whether women had a fundamental right to decide to have an abortion, the *Roe* Court balanced the pregnant woman's privacy rights as opposed to "important state interests" in regulation. The state interests identified as legitimate included the interests in maternal health and in protecting prenatal life. In terms of the state's interest in maternal health, abortion in the early stages of pregnancy is safer than childbirth, therefore the state has no genuine interest in maternal health that would be furthered by laws prohibiting or regulating abortion. At the point when abortion becomes more dangerous than its alternative, childbirth at "approximately the end of the first trimester," the state may regulate abortion "in ways that are reasonably related to [protection of] maternal health."

The Court spent more time discussing the state's interest in protecting prenatal life. The state argued in *Roe* that a fetus is a "person" under the Fourteenth Amendment, whose "right to life" is protected under the due process clause. The Court reviewed the contexts in which the word "person" is used in the Constitution and concluded that the Fourteenth Amendment was not intended to apply to the unborn. Even as "potential human life," the fetus was still entitled to some state protection. The issue was this: when does the state's interest in protecting the fetus become compelling? The Texas statute totally prohibited abortion, thus implying that the state had designated that time as conception. The Court, however, concluded that "the unborn have never been recognized in the law as persons in the whole sense." The Court chose viability as the time in which the state could assert its interest in this regard. In the Court's balancing test, the fundamental privacy rights of the pregnant woman outweigh the state's interest in protecting fetal rights until the fetus has acquired the capacity for independent life (i.e., viability). At this point, the state's interest is no longer distinguishable from its general interest in preventing the killing of human life. Abortion in such instances, thus, becomes virtually recognized as infanticide.

The state's interest, thus, outweighs the pregnant woman's rights, so as to justify regulation or even prohibition of abortion, *except* when necessary to preserve the life or health of the mother. Similarly, the state's health interest increases in weight throughout the rational analysis, supported by legal precedent and responsive to the complex issues it seeks to address. Lacking in sufficient clarity on these points, however, *Roe* has been often criticized by individuals who refuse to accept *Meyer v. Nebraska*, 262 U.S. 390 (1923) and *Griswold* as valid applications of substantive due process in privacy cases.

The dissenting opinions in *Roe* sharply disagreed with the majority's view on recognizing the constitutional privacy under the facts of the case. Justice Byron White wrote that the Court "simply fashions and announces a new constitutional right for pregnant mothers and, with scarcely any reason or authority for its action, invests that right with sufficient substance to override most existing state abortion statutes." He, thus, concluded that the *Roe* decision was an "exercise of raw judicial power," and an "improvident and extravagant exercise of the power of judicial review." Justice William Rehnquist also characterized the Court's application of the right of privacy as a "right to abortion,"

thus effectively separating *Roe* from its connections in *Meyer* and *Griswold*. In addition, Justice Rehnquist interpreted "constitutional privacy" as having the same meaning as "privacy" in the standard dictionary sense, which entails concepts of secrecy and seclusion. He then criticized the majority for recognizing the right, which does not comport with the dictionary definition.

One may question the Court's choice of the word "privacy" to identify a right that has at least as much to do with personal autonomy as it does with secrecy or seclusion; however, it seems unwise to criticize the right because the phraseology is perceived as inappropriate.

The right of privacy, no matter what it is called, would still face objections by those opposed to applying it to abortion cases. Justice Rehnquist focused his attack by characterizing the majority opinion as granting constitutional protection to abortion itself, i.e., that *Roe* is a right-to-abortion case. It is not the abortion itself, however, but the women's decision to have an abortion that is the issue. *Eisenstadt v. Baird*, 405 U.S. 438, 453 (1972), quoted in *Roe*, 410 U.S. at 169–70 (Stewart, J., concurring). "From this language in Eisenstadt to the abortion decisions is neither so that is shielded both from public view and from public interference. That decision is private, even in the dictionary sense of secrecy and seclusion. The distinction between the right to abortion and the right to make the abortion decision is crucial to the definition and scope of the right. A right to abortion would protect the pregnant woman only if she decided to have an abortion. Protecting the decision also protects her right not to have an abortion."

The term "privacy" fits in this context because it identifies a common characteristic of the types of activities that are protected in its name. Activities relating to marriage, procreation, contraception, and family relationships all involve intimate aspects of an individual's personal life. They are concerned with the individual's private, as opposed to public, life. It is in this area that government interference is most intrusive and least justified. The more complicated and the more urbanized our social and economic structure becomes, the more difficult it becomes to attain physical seclusion, and the more the individuals within that structure need the emotional seclusion that is provided by keeping their private lives truly private. The constitutional right of privacy recognizes that need and protects it from intrusion by government. This is a logical and necessary extension of the concept of liberty embodied in the U.S. Constitution.

Nowhere is the need for protection from government intrusion more important than it is in the abortion decision. "A woman's decision to have or forego an abortion is perhaps more than any other she makes an intimate one, expressive of both her identity and her autonomy." In 1923, *Meyer* recognized recognized the significance as well as the personal intimacy of the abortion decision:

> Certainly the interests of a woman in giving of her physical and emotional self during pregnancy and the interests that will be affected throughout her life by the birth and raising of a child are of a far greater degree of significance and personal intimacy than the right to send a child to private school . . . or the right to teach a foreign language . . . .

Justice Byron White, in his dissent, refers to the woman's interest as mere "convenience." Since "substantive due process" analysis entails weighing the relative interests of the pregnant woman and the state in the abortion decision, trivializing the woman's interest shifts the balance in the state's favor. Thus, when Justice White analyzed the case, weighing the "convenience of the pregnant mother" against the state's interest in preserving fetal life, the outcome could not be much of a surprise.

Some women endured a significant burden by laws prohibiting abortion, resulting in a large number of illegal abortions prior to 1973. It is

highly unlikely that so many women would have been willing to risk pain, disability, and even death for "trivial reasons." Under the pre-*Roe* abortion laws, however, a pregnant woman who was not physically, emotionally, or financially able to devote the next twenty years of her life caring for a child had only one realistic legal alternative: placing the child up for adoption. Thus, it is understandable that so many women instead chose to have illegal abortions. For many women, despite the hazards, an illegal abortion seemed to be the least negative of the few highly negative alternatives.

The pregnant woman's side of the balance receives added weight from certain First Amendment values, entailed in the right of privacy. Abortion laws are morals legislation. The state issues a moral judgment, based on strong moral and religious beliefs held by many of its constituents, and enforces that judgment on all pregnant women, despite their individual moral and religious beliefs. Thus, many pro-choice advocates argued that these anti-abortion statutes represented the same type of enforcement of official belief that the Court rejected in *West Virginia State Board of Education v. Barnette*, 319 U.S. 624 (1943) and *Wooley v. Maynard*, 430 U.S. 705 (1977). Other first amendment values can be invoked as well, notably associational rights and the free exercise and establishment themselves to account for the autonomy aspects of the right of privacy.

Only the notion of liberty in the due process clause itself is broad enough to encompass the full scope of the right of the individual to conduct her *private* life without undue government interference. First Amendment rights grant additional support to that right, but the Court has not adequately defined or explained them.

In articulating certain general principles that guide its abortion-related jurisprudence, the Supreme Court has repeatedly articulated the view that the right of a woman to an abortion is based on the due process clauses of the Fourteenth and Fifth Amendments. In earlier cases, the Court has identified the right as specifically within the realm of liberty-related privacy; the Court, in its more current jurisprudence, while consistently maintaining that the right to an abortion is within those freedoms protected by substantive due process liberty, has increasingly distanced itself from the right's specific identification with privacy. The Court has created certain limitations on a woman's right to terminate her pregnancy, recognizing that the state has certain legitimate, countervailing interests: the interest in the protection of potential life, and in the protection of the health of pregnant women.

Abortion remains a controversial issue and the right to reproductive freedom remains a controversial issue. Opponents of abortion have fought unsuccessfully for a constitutional amendment that would ban abortion. They, however, have successfully persuaded several state legislatures several laws to make it more difficult and costly for a woman to obtain an abortion. The lower federal courts have invalidated many of these laws as unconstitutional, while others have been allowed to go into effect. Most of this legislation has been based on model laws written by national anti-abortion groups, such as the National Right to Life. These state laws have included mandating invasive ultrasounds on women seeking abortions, preventing health insurance coverage, closing women's health clinics, restricting methods for medical abortions, requiring abortion providers to have admitting privileges at hospitals, requiring abortion clinics to become certified surgical centers, and prohibiting abortions at or after twenty weeks gestational age.

Opponents of these anti-abortion statutes, such as Planned Parenthood, challenge the legitimacy of the reasons provided by proponents justifying this legislation. Opponents contend that lawmakers have drafted these laws as a pretext for the elimination of abortion as a real-world option for women, especially poor women. Proponents are making abortions more difficult to obtain and providing legal cases that eventually will have to be addressed by the Supreme Court.

With a more conservative Supreme Court, there may be the possibility it may endorse some of these approaches and may even overturn *Roe v. Wade.*

Common law privacy right to an abortion

In seeking to exercise their right to seek an abortion, many patients have been photographed and harassed outside the clinics. Anti-abortion protestors have posted some of those photographed on the Internet. While there is much uncertainty and debate as to what constitutes the common law of privacy, one possible formulation is that privacy is identified as an independent value and defined in terms of autonomy. One persuasive argument is that limiting access of anti-abortion protestors to prospective clinic patients protects women's privacy, as does making it unlawful to disclose and individual's abortion as an invasion of privacy tort, for the purpose of promoting reproductive autonomy.

Further Reading

Colker, Ruth. *Abortion; Dialogue Pro-choice, Pro-life, and American Law.* Bloomington: Indiana University Press, 1992.

Garfield, Jay L. *Abortion, Moral and Legal Perspectives.* Amherst: University of Massachusetts Press, 1984. Garrow, David J. *Liberty and Sexuality: The Right to Privacy and the Making of Roe v. Wade.* 1994

Hull, N. E. H. *The Abortion Rights Controversy in America: A Legal Reader.* Chapel Hill: University of North Carolina Press, 2004.

Lassieur, Allison. *Abortion.* San Diego, Calif.: Lucent Books, 2001. Lee, Ellie. *Abortion Law and Politics Today.* Houndmills, Basingstoke, Hampshire: Macmillan Press, 1998. McClellan, Grant S., ed. *The Right to Privacy.* New York:

H.W. Wilson, 1976. Merino, Noe. *Abortion.* Farmington Hills, MI: Greenhaven Press, 2013. Murphy, Paul L. *The Right to Privacy and the Ninth Amendment.* New York: Garland Publishing. O'Brien, David M. *Privacy, Law and Public Policy.* New York: Praeger, 1970.

Powers, Meghan. *The Abortion Rights Movement.* Detroit: Greenhaven Press/Thomson/Gale, 2006.

Reagan, Leslie J. *When Abortion Was a Crime Women, Medicine, and Law in the United States, 1867–1973.* Berkeley: University of California Press, 1997.

Westin, Alan F. *Privacy and Freedom*. New York: Athenaeum, 1970. Williams, Mary E. *Abortion*. Detroit: Greenhaven Press, 2007.

See also: Body, Privacy of the; Griswold v. Connecticut; Legal Evolution of Privacy Rights; Meyer v. Nebraska; Personal Autonomy; Right to Privacy; Supreme Court of the United States; Unenumerated Constitutional Rights

Administrative searches

Identification: Administrative searches are a Fourth Amendment shortcut developed in the context of heavily regulated industries, given expansive new life in post-9/11 America.

The starting point for every nonconsensual search of a nonpublic place by government agents is the Fourth Amendment, which requires either a warrant supported by a showing of probable cause to believe that the search will yield evidence of a crime, or some judicially recognized substitute (for instance, that a warrantless search is necessary for the safety of officers at the scene of an arrest). Among the more obscure and little-understood of these judicial workarounds is the administrative search.

An administrative search takes place in a setting—an airport terminal, a school building—in which courts have recognized a heightened interest in public safety and/or a reduced individual expectation of privacy such that neither a warrant nor a showing of probable cause is required. In these contexts, a search will be constitutional as long as it is found to be reasonable in scope and duration.

In its earliest applications, the doctrine was understood to apply to health and safety inspections of heavily regulated industries. But increasingly, the government relies on the administrative search doctrine to legitimize collecting information about average citizens as both anxiety about national security and the technological ability to gather data with minimal discernible intrusion

have increased. Most controversially, the administrative search rationale has been advanced to support the federal government's clandestine (but now publicly disclosed) regime of warrantless wiretapping of those suspected of terrorist involvement after the attacks on the World Trade Center and Pentagon of September 11, 2001.

Administrative searches originate in the Supreme Court's 1967 ruling in *Camara v. Municipal Court*, 387 U.S. 523, involving municipal inspectors' routine warrantless entries into private homes in search of housing code violations. In that case, the Court crafted a relaxed Fourth Amendment standard applicable to noncriminal investigations for the purpose of enforcing health and safety codes. The Court explained that "area inspections" of entire neighborhoods were the only recognized way of effectively enforcing minimal housing code standards and that requiring an individualized showing of probable cause before entering each dwelling would make such inspections as a practical matter impossible. Rather, the Court concluded, the inspection program could itself supply its own probable cause—admittedly, on an area level and not an individual level—by applying reasonable standards to identify the neighborhoods requiring attention (for example, because of the age of the structures). The Court thus conflated reasonableness with probable cause in the context of municipal code enforcement.

The principle recognized in *Camara*—that inspectors may lawfully enter private property with neither a warrant nor the owner's consent merely by showing reasonable grounds to check for safety code violations—was subsequently applied to industries including junkyards (*New York v. Burger*, 482 U.S. 691, 712 [1987]), funeral homes (*Heffner v. Murphy*, 745 F.3d 56, 66 [3d Cir. 2014]), horse-racing tracks (*Shoemaker v. Handel*, 795 F.2d 1136, 1141 [3d Cir. 1986]) and firearms dealers (*United States v. Biswell*, 406 U.S. 311, 316 [1972]), even where the investigation is for the enforcement of criminal rather than purely regulatory codes. These cases rested on the notion that industries with a history of significant government oversight forfeited some expectation of privacy by virtue of the nature of that relationship. Conversely, in *Free Speech Coal., Inc. v. Attorney Gen'l*, 787 F.3d 142 (3d Cir. 2015), the Third Circuit found no such long-established history of regulation over adult entertainment that could legitimize a statute permitting the warrantless search of adult filmmakers for unlawful pornographic images of children.

Once it is found that a business is closely regulated and thus subject to an administrative search, courts will still evaluate the constitutionality of the search with regard to whether the intrusion is necessary to further the government's legitimate regulatory interests and whether the intrusion is part of a regularized inspection program, giving it some degree of reliability and predictability.

Civil-libertarian critics have questioned the post-1970s judicial expansion of the administrative search doctrine beyond so-called dragnet searches of entire industries or neighborhoods into the individualized search of criminal suspects. A major landmark case was the Supreme Court's 1976 ruling in *United States v. Martinez-Fuerte*, 428 U.S. 543, which upheld the use of warrantless highway checkpoints to detect the smuggling of undocumented aliens over the border. The ruling dispensed with the notion that warrantless administrative searches are permissible only for the enforcement of noncriminal regulatory codes in heavily regulated industries. Rather, the opinion rested on the nature of the intrusion—what Justice Lewis Powell termed the "minor interference with privacy" of a brief highway stop to inquire about the citizenship of the passengers. A vigorous dissenting opinion by Justice William Brennan called the *Martinez-Fuerte* ruling a "defacement" of the Fourth Amendment that "permits search and seizure to rest upon 'nothing more substantial than inarticulate hunches.'"

The administrative search rationale has been extended to legitimize schools' warrantless drug screening of student-athletes (*Board of Education v. Earls*, 536 U.S. 822, 837 [2002]) and even of students engaged in nondangerous extracurricular activities (*Vernonia School District 47J v. Acton*, 515 U.S. 646, 665 [1995]). But even in a setting where the government's security concerns are heightened and the citizen's privacy interests are reduced, a search can be unconstitutional if it is unreasonably intrusive compared with the harm the government seeks to avert. Thus, in *Safford Unified School District v. Redding*, 557 U.S. 364 (2009), the Supreme Court found that a warrantless strip-search of a 13-year-old schoolgirl by school authorities was excessive because the information on which it was based—an unverified tip that the student might be carrying an over-the-counter painkilling tablet—was neither sufficiently reliable nor of sufficient urgency to justify the invasiveness of the search.

Frank LoMonte

Further Reading

Lee, Cynthia, ed. *Searches and Seizures: The Fourth Amendment: Its Constitutional History of Contemporary Debate.* Amherst, NY: Prometheus Books, 2011.

Morgan, John S. "Comment, The Junking of the Fourth Amendment: *Illinois v. Krull* and *New York v. Burger*." *Tulane Law Review* 63, no. 2 (December 1988): 335–378.

Primus, Eve Brensike. "Disentangling Administrative Searches." *Columbia Law Review* 111, no. 2 (March 2011): 254–312.

Schulhofer, Stephen J. *More Essential Than Ever: The Fourth Amendment in the Twenty First Century.* New York: Oxford University Press, 2012.

See also: Fourth Amendment to the U.S. Constitution; Search warrants

Airport security systems

Identification: Contribute to the continuing debate over the balancing of privacy rights and providing passenger security through airport security systems, in which privacy rights play a major role.

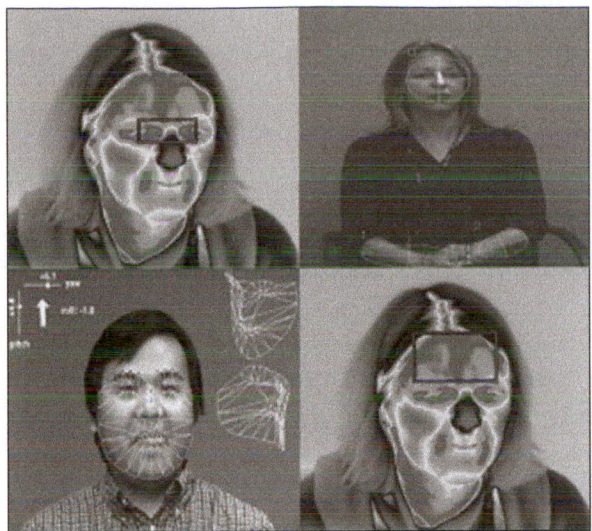

A demonstrative image for "Project Hostile Intent." By DHS Project Hostile Intent - Department of Homeland Security website.

From the invention of the world's first successful airplane in 1903 to the present, the progress of civil aviation has continuously accelerated along with globalization. Since the air travel has been widely accepted because of its time savings, its cost effectiveness, and increasing convenience, there has been a corresponding need for comprehensive airport security.

The world's busiest airport, Atlanta International Airport, serves more than 150 U.S. destinations and more than 60 international cities in 50 countries with more than 2,500 daily flights. With such a large number of passengers, the unique risks of air travel, and high-profile terrorist attacks, a wide range of airport security systems have been put into place.

In recent decades, various different security measures have been used in civil aviation. Several terrorist attacks have demonstrated the defects in security systems and practices. On December 22, 2001, the "shoe bomber" attempted to detonate explosives that were hidden in the heel of his shoes. This failed bombing led some nations to use specific measures to monitor shoes of passengers. In 2006, there was an attempt to detonate several bombs on board aircraft over the Atlantic Ocean by using liquid explosives. This

attempt led to the prohibition of liquids on passenger aircraft in several countries.

Undoubtedly, airport security precautions have become a topic of heated debate, particularly after the 9/11 attacks. On September 11, 2001, terrorists hijacked four passenger airliners and then used the planes to destroy the World Trade Center in New York and attack the Pentagon in Washington, DC. Shortly after that tragic incident, several nations reviewed and enhanced their security measures for civil aviation.

Following the 9/11 attacks, the United States and European Union Countries have enhanced security precautions and implemented various different security systems to secure passengers.

If you visit the United States, you will be asked to walk through a metal detector to determine whether you are carrying metal objects. If a metal detector is activated, you will be asked to remove metal objects and pass through the detector again. Afterward, you may be asked to pass through a body scanner. This scanner allows Transportation Security Agency (TSA) security officials to detect metallic or non-metallic objects or explosives carried by passengers. If, however, you refuse to pass through body scanners, security officials will pat you down. Aside from those technological security measures, you may also be a subject of behavioral profiling by examining facial expressions, eye contact, and other behaviors.

If you visit an EU member nation, you may be faced with similar precautions as the ones previously mentioned. You will be monitored on body scanners. If you refuse to be screened, you will be screened by hand search. Behavioral profiling, however, is not a common practice in EU countries.

Governments present legitimate reasons for using advanced security measures; however some privacy rights may be infringed while operating security systems. Growing numbers of passengers have been complaining about security precautions. Most of them found such measures humiliating, and an invasion of privacy.

Some of the privacy rights impacted through various airport security measures include:

1. Right to Respect for Privacy

   Monitoring parts of the human body may infringe human dignity and right to privacy. For instance, transgender passengers and passengers with prosthetic limbs may not prefer to undergo intrusive screening and such preference may also arise from religious belief, or ethnic, and traditional culture. So, being subject to screening violates the cultural norms of the passenger. Where such threats occur to an individual's privacy, then infringement of privacy rights or even discrimination concerns may arise.

2. Rights to Freedom of Movement and Thought

   The use of body scanners or pat-downs could interfere right to freedom of movement since individuals who refuse to go through body scanners, or pat downs may be prohibited from the flight. Also, an individual should not be forced to decide between not being able to fly or violating his or her religious or cultural beliefs and traditions. Forcing a passenger to make this choice would violate that passenger's freedom of thought or conscience.

3. Right to Equal Treatment

   Airport security measures could discriminate against passengers based on factors such as nationality, race, color, religion, language, previously visited countries, name similarity, and political opinions if airline companies share personal data of passengers to airport security agencies.

4. Protection of Personal Data

   The images obtained from body scanners may constitute personal data if the face of a person is not obscured, or the name of an individual appears on the image or somehow any person may identify the passenger. Moreover, if body scanners

create personal data, then this data must be deleted. Through this procedure, the use of body scanners would not infringe protection of personal data.

The delineation in balancing privacy rights and the government interest in public safety has been evolving by court cases, statutes, and regulations. For instance, passenger privacy rights are protected by the European Convention for the Protection of Human Rights ("ECHR"), Charter of Fundamental Rights of European Union ("CFREU") and International Covenant of Civil Rights ("ICCPR") in EU states, the U.S. Bill of Rights, and the Universal Declaration of Human Rights.

Regardless of the different legal protections, the Ninth Circuit Court of Appeals held that consent on screening does not affect the validity of the security procedures. *United States v. Aukai*, 497 F.3d 955 (9th Cir. 2007). Nonetheless, airport security precautions must both effectively ensure public safety while also providing screening options that ensure fundamental privacy rights of all passengers.

Şimal Efsane Yalçın

Further Reading

Hoff, Jessica, *Enhancing Security While Protecting Privacy: The Rights Implicated by Supposedly Heightened Airport Security*, 2014 *Michigan State Law Review*. 1609 (2014)

Rotenberg, Marc, *Body Scanners, Pat Downs Violate Law And Privacy*, November 19, 2010, http://edition.cnn.com/2010/OPINION/11/17/rotenberg.scanners.privacy/

See also: Body, Privacy of the; Consent; Fourth Amendment; Right to Privacy; Terrorism

Amazon

Identification: An e-commerce business that was founded in 1995 by Jeff Bezos.

In its initial permutation, Amazon was an online retailer of books. However, throughout the 1990s and into the first decades of the 21st century, Amazon steadily increased the products it offered so that it is now a general retailer and a direct competitor of bookstores, electronics retailers, drugstores, and department stores. It is also an aggregator of third party retailers.

In 2007 Amazon introduced the Kindle, a hand-held electronic book reader made exclusively for the United States market. The Kindle created a market for electronic books in the United States. By 2009, the sale of electronic books had exceeded that of physical books on Amazon. However, Amazon has continually redeveloped the Kindle into a hand-held wireless entertainment tablet that can stream movies, television shows, and music. In 2014 Amazon released the Amazon Alexa, a virtual assistant that is embedded into Amazon's smart speaker, the Echo. The Alexa was developed by Amazon Lab126, the research and development division of Amazon, which also developed the Kindle. In addition, Amazon launched its cloud computing services, incorporated as Amazon Web Services, in 2002 with a reluanch in 2006. The National Institutes of Standards and Technology (NIST) defines cloud computing in NIST Special Publication 800-145 as "a model for enabligh ubiquitous, convenient, on-demand network access to shared pool of configurable computing resources (e.g., networks, servers, storage, applications and services)..." Amazon Web Services are utilized by large corporations, as well as smaller companies world-wide.

A consequence of Amazon's business model is the mass accumulation of customers' data. Amazon collects a myriad of information from each customer interaction. This data includes the customer's IP address, computer and connection information, including time zone, browser, browser plug-ins and versions, operating system, and operating platform. Amazon also collects a customer's purchase history, clickstream information, cookies, as well as all ordering and payment information, including the addresses of third parties that a customer had merchandise sent to. Third party advertisers also collect

data, such as the user's IP address. Many privacy rights proponents criticize Amazon for not allowing a customer to cancel his account and delete all data gathered by Amazon. While Amazon does not sell the data it collects, it does form relationships with other companies, which they refer to as "affiliated," or "co-branded," businesses. At the current time Amazon states that it does not share a customer's Amazon purchase history with these third-party companies.

Amazon.com has had numerous breaches and lapses of its security, compromising customers' data. In 2018 Amazon.com disclosed customers' names and emails and erroneously released transcripts of private conversations that had been recorded by an Amazon Echo to the incorrect person. In January of 2014 the hacker activist group Anonymous gathered customer's credit card information, passwords, and user names from Amazon.com, which they subsequently published on the website Ghostbin. Amazon Web Services have had multiple breaches of security that have released information from individual companies, as well as on companies' clientele and customers.

Amazon's business practices also provided a strong impetus for the development of the personalized web. The personalized web presents information or advertising targeted to the individual user. This individualization is accomplished by tracking such things as a person's past searching behavior, geographic location, time of year, and social data. Many scholars and industry analysts are exploring the conflict between the benefits of the personalized web with the privacy concerns caused by companies tracking individual data in order to provide targeted information or advertisements. In addition, state, local, and the Federal government are passing legislation to protect an individual's privacy while using the internet. Amazon's current privacy policy does allow customers to opt out of providing personal information; however, by doing so, a customer loses much of the functionality that creates a seamless buying experience. A customer is able to choose to not see personalized ads while on Amazon; however, opting out of seeing advertisements does not prohibit Amazon from collecting personal data.

Amazon released its initial biannual transparency report in 2015 and has continued to release reports since then. This report provides information on governments' requests for data. However, Amazon has been criticized for the reports' brevity and lack of detail, particularly as to how the company administers data gathered from Alexa and the Amazon Echo.

Rachel Jorgensen

Further Reading

Bleich, Holger. "Alexa, Who has Access to My Data?" *c't Magazin.* (Dec. 20, 2018) https://www.heise.de/newsticker/meldung/Amazon-reveals-private-voice-data-files-4256015.html

Brandt, Richard L. *One Click: Jeff Bezos and the Rise of Amazon.* New York: Portfolio/Penguin, 2011.

Kumar, P. and P. Herbert Raj, P. Jelciana. "Exploring Data Security Issues and Solutions in Cloud Computing. *Procedia Computer Science* 125 (2018): 691-697.

Nash, Richard. "Publishing 2020," *Publishing Research Quarterly* 26, no. 2 (June 2010): 114-118.

Newcombe, Chris and Tim Rath, Fan Zhang, Bogdan Munteanu, Marc Booker, Michael Deardeuff. "How Amazon's Web Services Uses Formal Methods." *Communications of the ACM* 58, no. 4 (April 2015): 66-73.

Stone, Brad. *The Everything Store: Jeff Bezos and the Age of Amazon.com.* New York: Little Brown and Company, 2013.

Van Loo, Rory. "Helping Buyers Beware: The Need for Supervision of Big Retail." *University of Pennsylvania Law Review* 163, no. 5 (April 2015): 1311-1392.

See also: Apple, Inc.; Cloud Computing; Foreign Intelligence Surveillance Court (FISC); National Security Agency (NSA); PRISM

American Civil Liberties Union (ACLU)

Identification: One of the oldest and most widely recognized civil rights and liberties organizations in the United States.

The ACLU's mission is to protect the individual rights and liberties that the U.S. Constitution's Bill of Rights guarantees, including speech and religious liberty, due process, and privacy rights. Headquartered in New York City, the nonprofit, nonpartisan ACLU comprises two separate corporate entities: the American Civil Liberties Union, which engages in legislative lobbying, and the ACLU Foundation, the tax-exempt arm that conducts the organization's litigation efforts. The ACLU currently has approximately 500,000 members, 200 staff attorneys, and thousands of volunteer attorneys, with staffed affiliate offices in every state.

The ACLU was officially established in 1920 after the Palmer Raids, in which U.S. Attorney General Mitchell Palmer rounded up and deported thousands of suspected communists, arresting them without regard to Fourth Amendment protections against unreasonable searches and seizures. In its early years, the ACLU focused on protecting trade unionists' free speech rights. Indeed, several of its founders, including Roger Baldwin, Elizabeth Gurley Flynn, and Helen Keller, were members of militant labor organizations. The young ACLU made headlines during the 1925 Scopes "Monkey Trial" for supporting biology teacher John T. Scopes, who had violated a Tennessee law banning the teaching of evolution. The organization also received national attention in 1933, for defending James Joyce's *Ulysses* against obscenity charges, and in 1954, when the Supreme Court decided *Brown v. Board of Education*, 347 U.S. 483 (1954), striking down the "separate but equal" doctrine in response to the ACLU's and the NAACP's joint challenge to racial segregation in public schools.

Privacy has always been one of the ACLU's foremost concerns. Initially, the ACLU focused on privacy as a component of the constitutional ban on warrantless searches and seizures. Beginning in the 1960s, the organization embraced a new, expanded view of constitutionally protected privacy, encompassing the rights to marry, procreate, and engage in consensual adult sexual activity. In its landmark 1965 ruling in *Griswold v. Connecticut*, 381 U.S 479 (1965), the U.S. Supreme Court explicitly recognized that the Constitution guarantees these bodily and behavioral privacy rights, also known as penumbral privacy rights. At the ACLU's instigation, the *Griswold* Court struck down Connecticut's prohibition against the provision or use of contraceptives, deeming it an unconstitutional violation of privacy. The ACLU similarly supported the petitioner in *Roe v. Wade*, 410 U.S. 113 (1973), the historic 1973 decision in which the U.S. Supreme Court held that the constitutional right to privacy protects a woman's choice to abort her pregnancy. In 2003, in *Lawrence v. Texas*, 539 U.S. 558 (2003), the ACLU helped to persuade the Supreme Court to expand on the privacy rights that *Griswold* and *Roe* recognized by striking down a Texas law that criminalized sexual intimacy between same-sex couples. The organization played the same pivotal role in *Obergefell v. Hodges*, 135 S.Ct. 1039 (2015), the 2015 U.S. Supreme Court case that held that the Fourteenth Amendment guarantees same-sex couples the right to marry.

The ACLU has also long championed the right to informational privacy (privacy of personal data and communications). It protested in the 1980s when President Ronald Reagan's administration authorized the Central Intelligence Agency (CIA) to collect information on citizens within the United States, and the Federal Bureau of Investigation (FBI) to open domestic security investigations of any persons or groups it suspected of advocating criminal activity. Its objection was not shared by the American public, which was largely convinced that the threat of terrorism required such surveillance. The ACLU's opposition to governmental surveillance practices has only heightened since the September 11, 2001, terror attacks, as the organization works to strike an appropriate balance between national security and privacy interests. In 2006, the ACLU challenged the federal government's warrantless wiretapping program in federal court, arguing that the National Security Agency (NSA) had violated Americans' First and Fourth Amendment privacy rights by monitoring their telephone calls and emails without first securing warrants. The case was eventually dismissed on the ground that the plaintiffs had no standing to sue because they could not prove that the NSA had wiretapped them. Since then, the ACLU has continued to press the courts and Congress to stop the NSA's mass collection of citizens' telephone records, on the ground that such metadata—details about the maker, recipient, time, and length of calls—reveal intimate, constitutionally protected information about individuals' private lives. It has similarly sought to curtail the NSA's mass interception and searching of Americans' international Internet communications, including emails and web searches. The organization has achieved some success on this front with the passage of the USA Freedom Act, 29 Stat. 268 (2015), which prohibits the bulk collection of Americans' call records. At the same time, the ACLU has advocated—as yet unsuccessfully—before Congress, the executive branch, and the courts for access to the proceedings of the Foreign Intelligence Surveillance Court (FISC, also called the FISA Court), which oversees, without public review, the government's surveillance activities.

Technological advances have outpaced privacy protections in many instances, so the ACLU is now focusing its informational privacy efforts on three fronts: litigation, lobbying, and working with private companies to protect individual privacy against technological incursion. To date, the ACLU's efforts have included attempting to secure a warrant requirement for law enforcement access to electronic information, working to bring greater transparency to the government's surveillance practices, and promoting privacy-protective technologies.

Raleigh Hannah Levine

Further Reading

American Civil Liberties Union. *Privacy and Surveillance.* https://www.aclu.org/issues/national-security/privacy-and-surveillance.

American Civil Liberties Union. *Privacy & Technology*. https://www.aclu.org/issues/privacy-technology.

Cottrell, Robert C. *Roger Nash Baldwin and the American Civil Liberties Union*. New York: Columbia University Press, 2000.

Walker, Samuel. *In Defense of American Liberties: A History of the ACLU*. 2nd ed. Carbondale: Southern Illinois University Press, 1999.

See also: First Amendment to the U.S. Constitution; Foreign Intelligence Surveillance Court; Fourth Amendment to the U.S. Constitution; *Griswold v. Connecticut*; *Lawrence v. Texas*; National Security Agency; Obscenity; September 11; USA Freedom Act; Wiretapping

Anonymity and anonymizers

Identification: Anonymity and anonymizers are concepts that have taken on a new significance in the digital age. While anonymous communication is protected by the First Amendment of the U.S. Constitution, complete anonymity, particularly when communicating on the Internet, is difficult to achieve for the average person. Anonymizers can be used to accomplish nearly complete anonymity in digital communication.

In *Talley v. California*, 362 U.S. 60 (1960), the U.S. Supreme Court determined that the First Amendment's free speech clause protects anonymous speech. Long before digital communication existed, a City of Los Angeles ordinance prohibited the distribution of a leaflet or handbill unless it identified the name and address of its publisher. A leafleter was arrested for failing to comply with the ordinance and argued that the requirement that he identify himself by name and address violated his constitutional right to freedom of speech. The Court agreed. The Court reasoned that anonymous communication has historically played an important part in the development of society and social change. For example, the Court pointed to various instances in U.S. history where colonists who supported the revolution and the Founding Fathers themselves engaged in anonymous speech. The Court

Protesters outside a Scientology center on February 10, 2008, donning masks, scarves, hoods, and sunglasses to obscure their faces, and gloves and long sleeves to protect them from leaving fingerprints. (By David Shankbone.)

determined that prohibiting anonymous speech would have a chilling effect on speech and, in particular, would lessen the distribution of literature critical of government. The Court has affirmed this protection of anonymous speech in cases such as *McIntyre v. Ohio Elections Commission*, 514 U.S. 334 (1995).

The Internet has provided the appearance of facilitating anonymous communication. Users are able to access digital communication platforms and contribute to the discussion of ideas without revealing much, if any, information about themselves. Whether through social networks, email, blogs, or chatrooms, users can create fabricated persona, or no persona at all, and engage in an exchange of ideas without revealing their true identity—thus retaining anonymity. Many scholars argue that this anonymity provided by the Internet democratizes communication and thus increases the exchange of ideas that the First Amendment was intended to protect. Others argue that anonymous communication through the Internet results in more caustic, hurtful speech and disconnects speakers from the emotional injury they may cause. Anonymous speech may simply provide protection for people who engage in illegal threats and intimidation.

Many people access the Internet through an entity, such as a private company, that acts as an Internet service provider. The Internet service provider connects its users to the Internet and thus often has access to its customers' information. While most Internet service providers allow their customers to engage others on the Internet anonymously, the Internet service provider nevertheless retains the customer's name and other personally identifiable information. As a result, when users have anonymously communicated via the Internet and the communication is the basis for legal action, courts have been asked to order Internet service providers to reveal the identity of the anonymous user. Because of the constitutional commitment to protect anonymous speech, courts have struggled to articulate the proper standard for when to require Internet service providers to reveal their users' identities. Moreover, the U.S. government has allegedly accessed users' identity and data through Internet service providers' records regardless of users' attempts to remain anonymous.

Because a user may not want his or her Internet use to be traceable, he or she may use an anonymizer to try to accomplish complete anonymity. Anonymizers are tools that protect a user's personally identifiable information by masking his or her Internet protocol address—the way a computer and its user is identified on an Internet service provider's network. Masking the Internet protocol address makes it difficult to trace a user's Internet usage, thus ensuring his or her privacy.

There are two basic forms of anonymizers: networked anonymizers and single-point anonymizers. Networked anonymizers transfer the user's communication or other Internet traffic through a network of Internet server computers before it arrives at its destination website. The destination website then routes its information back to the user through the same network. The path the information takes between the original sources is thus obscured and difficult to map, and the user's Internet protocol address is not associated with having visited a particular website, where he or she may have shared information or communicated. These sorts of anonymizers are generally considered more secure because of the multiple connections through which the information must travel. A single-point anonymizer is a website through which a user can surf the web. The anonymizer website communicates on behalf of the user and sends a request to the destination website for the user. The destination website then sends information back to the anonymizer website, which then encrypts the communication and provides it to the user seeking anonymity. As with any technology, anonymizers are used by people with both good and ill intentions. They can be used to engage in debate and criticism without the threat of being exposed and retaliated against for one's beliefs. At the same time, however, anonymizers can be used by people with nefarious goals, such as Internet-related crime.

Anonymity has long been recognized as a valuable tool for communicating fringe, minority, or unpopular views without the threat of retaliation. Online anonymity has extended that benefit to millions of people while at the same time providing protection for those that might abuse it. Although true online anonymity is difficult to achieve, technology such as anonymizers allow those who seek anonymity to protect their identity from those who may want to reveal it.

Douglas B. McKechnie

Further Reading

Barrett Lidsky, Lyrissa. "Silencing John Doe: Defamation and Discourse in Cyberspace." *Duke Law Journal* vol. 49, no. 4 (2000): 855–946.

Kizza, Joseph Migga. *Ethical and Social Issues in the Information Age.* 4th ed. London: Springer, 2010.

Payton, Theresa, and Theodore Claypoole. *Privacy in the Age of Big Data: Recognizing Threats, Defending Your Rights, and Protecting Your Family.* Lanham, MD: Rowman & Littlefield Publishers, Inc., 2014.

See also: Email; First Amendment to the U.S. Constitution; Social networking technologies

Anti-Forensics

Identification: The means by which individuals attempt to hide their digital activity from of forensic analysis by investigators.

Forensic investigations can be undertaken as part of criminal or civil judicial cases, as well as by private firms seeking information about unauthorized use of corporate data. Forensic searches can be geared to finding specific electronic items or be broader in scope. Those in possession of illegal, illegally obtained, or electronic items obtained without authorization usually attempt to hide them to make it difficult for the computer forensic analyst to recover the data. Communications regarding illegal, or unauthorized, actions or data are also the focus of forensic investigation as well as anti-forensic efforts. Just as throughout history in the physical world there has been an ever changing struggle between law enforcement and criminals, the same is true in the electronic venue. The extent of the steps taken to thwart forensic analysis depends on the resources available to the person/group establishing the anti-forensic barriers and the value of keeping the information hidden.

Some anti-forensics tools are versions of programs used by legitimate sites, such as encryption. The difference is in the intent of the action. Originally based on physical systems of encryption, which have existed for thousands of years, the encryption of electronic data has become more and more elaborate, based on the extensive capabilities of current computing systems. However, as is evident from the number of "secure" corporate sites that get hacked each year, systems of decryption can be developed for any system of encryption. Depending on how elaborate the encryption program used, the time and computing power needed to break the encryption could be beyond some law enforcement/corporate budgets. Encryption does offer security from a non-analyst using the computer or network.

Another way of hiding data from a non-analyst is Steganography, which is the insertion of data into another type of file. Thus, a large file, such as a JPEG for a photo, could have other bits of data put into it that are totally unrelated to the JPEG image. Once this is seen as a possibility, however, the forensic analyst can usually get the data without major problems.

The basic operating systems and programs used on a computer generally keep copies or indicators of what has been run on the computer, which many users forget. Those seeking to block forensic searches of their computers or networks try to change aspects of these programs, in order to hide the trail that might lead to the hidden data. Virtual disks are created as part of many legitimate computer programs, but as part of an anti-forensic effort a more elaborate system of virtual disks can be created to hinder an analyst's efforts to find the hidden data. Similarly, the file system of a computer, or network, can be altered to keep the existence of files hidden. Programs undertaking related tasks, such as those that indicate when files were created, can be altered in such a fashion as to render the information useless to anyone attempting to find files created during a certain time period.

In certain situations the destruction of the hardware that has been used to store data is the means of choice to keep it from being uncovered by forensic analysis. Experts agree that this is the only full-proof means for securing data. While many of the electronic defenses are formidable, there is the possibility of failure. By destroying the hardware upon which the data is kept, its contents cannot be resurrected. However, this is true for both the forensic analyst and for the individual who originally compiled the data. While explosives have been used to destroy computers, it has not been done as often as it appears in the movies. In the past few years, physical covers for disk drives have been created that can be remotely triggered, with the result that the disk is shredded or crushed. For older hard drives and floppy disks, degaussing a hard drive, by passing it through a strong magnetic field, was reliable; however, this may not be effective on modern drives. On a smaller scale, a special file deletion or disk wiping program may be used, although these are not always reliable.

Communications regarding illegal/unauthorized activities between individuals using electronic devices is subject to forensic analysis. However, depending on the device, there are privacy laws that do offer some protection, even for those engaged in criminal activities. In addition to these laws, individuals communicating from one computer to another can take steps to keep the communication confidential. One form is called tunneling. In this, both computers run the same program in which the message is encapsulated into what seems to be a normal data packet. Often, additional encryption is added to the special packet. Although it goes through the normal internet, the tunnel established between the two computers does not allow it to be intercepted. A second common method is using "onion routing," named for a system created by U.S. Navy researchers. In this, the data is encrypted numerous times by being sent through numerous routers, rather than taking as direct a route from sender to recipient as possible. The result is that encrypted files are themselves encrypted, multiple times, making this is a very effective means of communicating covertly. As with any encrypted file, a set of "onion" files could be decrypted by a forensic analyst; however, the time and computing power necessary to decrypt would be much greater than a simple encrypted file.

In terms of malicious software, the use of viruses that exist only in a computer's memory is becoming more common. Because these programs are never themselves written to disk, the code they run is not available for later examination. However, log files or other records on the computer may still record the activity carried out by the virus.

Only in recent years have systems been put in place, as part of anti-forensic efforts, to extensively use programs to attack the efforts of a forensic analyst, rather than to just resist the analyst's efforts to find or break into the trove of hidden data. Investigative agencies and corporations use a small selection of disk or memory forensic tools for analysis, which allows anti-forensic practitioners to designed tools or data payloads that attempt to break features in forensic tools or otherwise provide skewed results. Another change in the forensic/anti-forensic balance has been the now common use of the cloud for data storage. While the cloud itself is not a barrier to forensic investigation, it offers new possibilities in anti-forensic efforts to evade detection.

Donald A. Watt and Nathan A. B. Watt

Further Reading

Afonin, Oleg, Danil Nikolaev, and Yuri Gubanon. "Countering Anti-Forensic Efforts – Part 1" and "Countering Anti-Forensic Efforts – Part 2." *Forensic Magazine.* (September 3 and 16, 2015).

Fahey, Ryan. "Computer Forensics: Anti-Forensic Tools & Techniques." *Infosec Institute.* resources.infosecinstitute.com/category/computerforensics/introduction/areas-of-study/digital-forensics/anti-forensic-tools-techniques/#gref

Littlefield, Ryan. "Anti-Forensics and Cryptography: An insight into how offenders disrupt cyber crime investigations." *Medium* (August 6, 2017). littlefield.co/anti-forensics-and-cryptography-an-insight-into-how-offenders-disrupt-cyber-crime-investigations-e44637513709

Strickland, Jonathan. "How Computer Forensics Works: Anti-Forensics." *HowStuffWorks.* computer.howstuffworks.com/computer-forensic3.htm

See also: Cloud computing; Computers and privacy; Cybersecurity; Dark web; Hacking, computer; Law enforcement; Metadata; Online privacy and protection

APEC Cross Border Privacy Rules System

Identification: Statement of principles to which APEC member economies may aspire

The road to adoption of the APEC Cross Border Privacy Rules System (CBPRS) began in

1998 following the adoption of the Blueprint for Action on Electronic Commerce by the 27 APEC (Asian-Pacific Economic Cooperation) member economies. That Blueprint led to the development of the APEC Privacy Framework; the CBPRS is an extension of that Framework and therefore it is necessary to begin with a brief overview of the latter. Finalized in 2005, the Framework is largely based upon the OECD Fair Information Principles (FIPs) that form the basis of a variety of data protection regimes. However, the focus of the Framework is on protecting privacy as a means of facilitating commerce rather than something fundamentally connected to human dignity. Its preamble, for instance, notes that excessive regulation in the area of privacy may have "adverse implications for global business."

This conservative approach reveals itself most starkly on the questions of implementation and enforcement. The Framework is best understood as a statement of principles to which APEC member economies may aspire, rather than a binding international treaty. There is no mechanism, for instance, that allows one member economy to force another member to uphold their commitments under the Framework. Moreover, member economies are not required to implement the provisions of the Framework into their domestic legislation. Even if they choose to do so, nothing in the Framework requires the creation of independent national authorities or direct enforcement in the local courts. Part IV of the Framework makes clear that judicial enforcement of the principles contained within it is optional for member economies. They are given significant leeway in how they may choose to implement the principles, including the use of central authorities, multi-agency enforcement bodies, self-regulation or co-regulation by industry, etc. This stands in stark contrast to the rigorous enforcement mechanisms in fully-fledged data protection regimes, which invariably require a quasi-autonomous national commissioner to supervise the relevant laws, ultimately backed by force of law to ensure compliance.

This pro-industry approach to privacy is likewise reflected in the CBPRS, which is a voluntary extension of the Framework; at the time of this writing, eight member economies had joined the CBPRS – the United States, Mexico, Canada, South Korea, Japan, Singapore, Australia, and Taiwan. Once a member has joined the scheme, companies that operate in that jurisdiction may become 'certified' as adhering to that data privacy principles found in the Framework. Personal information may then flow freely between those organizations without the need for any further approval or inclusion of particular contractual clauses, regardless of the jurisdiction in which they were certified. This allows for a level of interoperability, commercially speaking, between different privacy regimes within APEC, making cross-border transfers of personal data easier.

Certification is done by third-party (non-government) bodies in each jurisdiction known as "Accountability Agents." An APEC-wide "Joint Oversight Panel" makes recommendations as to whether an "Accountability Agent" should be recognized as such, though final approval rests with the member economy. The Panel is also responsible for determining whether an applicant member economy meets the participation requirements. Those requirements include the establishment of a regulatory authority capable of supervising organizations that join the scheme for ongoing compliance and to provide a forum for resolution of complaints. However, nothing in the CBPRS requires member economies to provide consumers with resort to the judicial system to enforce the privacy rules.

It has been suggested that the CBPRS may in the future include interoperability with the European Union's General Data Protection Regulation (GDPR), specifically its Binding Corporate Rules (BCR). The lack of judicial redress is one of several reasons a jurisdiction with a privacy regime based upon the Framework is unlikely to ever be considered 'adequate' by the European Data Protection Board (EPB) under Art. 45 of the GDPR (such a finding would allow the free flow of personal data between an EU and non-EU jurisdiction). However, large multinational organizations with branches both inside and outside the EU can adopt BCR that allow them to easily transfer personal information between its various branches, even if one branch is located in a jurisdiction with an inadequate privacy regime from the perspective of the EDPB. If the EDPB were to recognize the CBPRS as functionally equivalent the BCR, however, then a large multinational certified under the former would not have to go through the time-consuming and expensive process of being recertified by the EDPB. Of course, this would still only allow it to easily transfer personal data between its various EU and non-EU branches, rather than with other EU organizations. Thus, at least as currently conceived, the CBPRS is not a panacea for all challenges related to international flows of personal data.

Stuart Hargreaves

Further Reading

Greenleaf, Graham. "Five Years of the APEC Privacy Framework: Failure or Promise?" *Computer Law & Security Report* 25 (June 2009), 28-43.

Kenyon, Andrew T., and Megan Richardson, eds. *New Dimensions in Privacy Law: International and Comparative Perspectives.* New York: Cambridge University Press, 2006.

See also: Data protection regimes; General Data Protection Regulation

Apple, Inc.

Identification: Apple, Inc., formerly Apple Computer, Inc., is a multinational corporation

Apple, Inc. designs, manufactures, and markets mobile communication and media devices, personal computers, and portable digital music players, and sells related software, services, peripherals, networking solutions, and third-party digital content and applications. The company's products and services include iPhone; iPad; Mac; iPod; Apple TV; consumer and professional software applications; the iOS and OS X operating systems; iCloud; and accessory, service, and support offerings. The company also sells and delivers digital content and applications through the iTunes Store, App Store, iBook Store, and Mac App Store. Steve Jobs formed Apple Computer with Steve Wozniak.

Today, Apple sells its products worldwide through its retail stores, online stores, and direct sales force, as well as through third-party cellular network carriers, wholesalers, retailers, and value-added resellers. In addition, the company sells a variety of third-party iPhone-, iPad-, Mac-, and iPod-compatible products, including application software and various accessories through its online and retail stores. The company sells to individuals; small and midsize businesses; and education, enterprise, and government customers.

The company successfully introduced the iPod music player in 2001 and iTunes Music Store in 2003. Apple established itself as a leader in the consumer electronics and media sales industries, leading it to drop "Computer" from the company's name in 2007. The company is now also known for its iOS range of smartphone, media player, and tablet computer products that began with the iPhone, followed by the iPod Touch and then iPad. As of 2012, Apple is the largest publicly traded corporation in the world by market capitalization, with an estimated value of $26 billion (USD) as of September 2012. Apple Inc.'s market cap is larger than that of Google and Microsoft combined. Apple's worldwide annual revenue in 2010 totaled $65 billion (USD), growing to $127.8 billion (USD) in 2011 and $156 billion in 2012.

In recent years, Apple Inc. has been involved in the following high-profile privacy controversies concerning the company's policies and its products.

Privacy litigation involving Apple, Inc.

In *In re* iPhone/iPad Application Litigation, forty-eight various plaintiffs sought class action certification for a case against Apple Inc. and other tracking defendants alleging, among other things, that the defendants, without the plaintiffs' knowledge, collected precise home and workplace locations and "current whereabouts" of the plaintiffs by using certain features of iPhone and iPad operating systems and applications. The district court granted motions to dismiss the complaint with leave to amend on the ground that the plaintiffs failed to allege sufficient facts to establish the court's Article III standing. The court noted that it "does not take lightly Plaintiffs' allegations of privacy violations" but that, "[d]espite a lengthy Consolidated Complaint, Plaintiffs do not allege injury in fact to themselves."

The plaintiffs filed their amended complaint, and the defendants filed a new motion to dismiss. The court granted the other tracking defendants' motion to dismiss along with all counts against Apple relating to the Stored Communications Act, the Wiretap Act, the Computer Fraud and Abuse Act, and the California Constitution. The court allowed only two counts against Apple to proceed, but those counts concern misrepresentations rather than a right of privacy regarding geolocation.

Congressional testimony—2011

Google Inc., Apple Inc., and Facebook Inc. defended their privacy practices to lawmakers considering how to update privacy laws to include more protections for Internet users.

At a Senate hearing on mobile privacy issues Thursday, lawmakers grilled technology executives on their policies and how they share consumer information with other companies. The hearing comes amid recent revelations that Apple's iPhone and Google's Android phones routinely collect information about the location of consumer cellphones. Apple has since limited the data it collects.

"I know you can shut off your location services but that doesn't do the trick because we want to use them," said Sen. John Kerry (D-MA.), who introduced a privacy bill along with Sen. John McCain (R-AZ), which would establish consumer online privacy rights.

The Kerry-McCain legislation is among at least five legislative proposals introduced in 2011 by House and Senate lawmakers. The bills would update existing privacy laws and set new rules for broadband and mobile applications, such as creating requirements that companies allow consumers to decline online tracking.

Technology executives defended their practices, saying that their companies have privacy policies and aren't responsible for the actions of software developers that may not have such policies and don't face rules on how they can collect or share consumer information.

Ios4 lawsuit

In 2012, Amanda Ladas filed a suit under the Class Proceedings Act in Supreme Court of British Columbia alleging that Apple Inc. has violated the privacy and security rights of users of mobile devices running the software operating system iOS4, including the iPhone, iPad, and iPod.

> "It's clear that Apple routinely and automatically collects sufficient information such that they can identify the real-world identity of the registered user of an iOS4x device, as well as the device's physical location, at an update frequency of now less than once every six hours."—Eric Smith, Information Security, Networking and Systems Administration Expert, whose report is included in the filings.

The claim alleged that Apple has violated the privacy and security rights of users of its products by the design, production, distribution, and/or operation of iOS4, and has engaged in deceptive acts or practices that have the capability, tendency, or effect of deceiving or misleading class members and that these practices entitle members of the class to aggravated, punitive and/or exemplary damages.

Ladas is concerned that, without her permission, anyone with moderate computer knowledge can find out where she's been. She considers the comings and goings of herself and her family to be personal and sensitive information. She has retained legal counsel Ganapathi and Company of Vancouver and a number of leading experts in digital forensics examination, information security, networking and systems administration, geographic profiling, and clinical and forensic psychology. These experts' extensive reports have been filed together with the certification materials.

Digital forensics expert Francis Graf examined Ladas's iPhone and desktop computer and found that her location data, going back approximately one year, was easily accessible using free tools readily available on the Internet. Graff's investigation found that iOS4x stores specific location-based data in unencrypted form, including dates and times, associated to geographic location coordinates. That data is copied onto any computer to which the devices are connected when they are backed up. Each successive backup file contains new location data for approximately one year prior to the date of that backup, thereby increasing the aggregate location-based data stored in unencrypted form.

Apple uses privacy as a marketing device

In increasingly blunt and pointed remarks, chief executive Tim Cook says Apple handles user information differently than rivals like Google Inc. and Facebook Inc., which employ the data to sell targeted advertising. "We don't build a profile based on your email content or web browsing habits to sell to advertisers," Mr. Cook wrote in a letter posted on Apple's website last week. "We don't 'monetize' the information you store on your iPhone or in iCloud. And we don't read your email or your messages to get information to market to you."

But Apple does sell targeted advertising. Its iAd unit allows advertisers to reach users on Apple mobile devices based on their age, gender, home address, iTunes purchases, and App Store downloads. It works with data broker Acxiom Corp. to supplement that information and help advertisers target its users more precisely. And it installs an "advertising identifier," similar to a browser cookie, on iPhones and iPads; the identifier tracks users' activity on the devices.

Apple says that its system is less intrusive because it gives users more control over the use of their data and lets them opt out. It also doesn't target advertising based on users' locations as they move with their devices. As Apple moves into more sensitive areas, it says that it won't have access to—and therefore cannot make money from—data from its new Apple Pay mobile-payment service and HealthKit for storing medical and fitness information.

Students of digital advertising say that these distinctions aren't clear cut. "There are aspects of Apple's activities that are admirable from a privacy standpoint," said Joseph Turow, a University of Pennsylvania professor who studies privacy and digital advertising. "At the same time, there are areas where Apple shows the kind of conflict that it and other companies have in monetizing users' data."

Beyond its own advertising network, Apple benefits from ads that others place on its devices, particularly ads that encourage users to download apps. An Apple user who sees such an ad and installs King Digital Entertainment PLC's "Candy Crush Saga" may later buy items within the game. In a revenue split with the developer, 30 percent of the money from those in-game purchases goes to Apple.

What most distinguishes Apple's targeted advertising program from its rivals, Turow and others say, is that Apple is less aggressive pushing boundaries on data collection. In part, that's because it doesn't have to be. Google and Facebook rely on advertising for the bulk of their revenue. Apple will get the vast majority of its projected $180 billion in revenue in the fiscal year ending September 27, 2014, selling hardware—iPhones, iPads, and Mac computers.

In 2015, Apple CEO Tim Cook warned of "dire consequences" if tech companies can't protect the privacy of those who use their products. "Giving up our privacy to digital technologies exposes us to greater risks than just identity theft and financial losses," Cook said in a brief speech at a cybersecurity summit in Silicon Valley. "History has shown us that sacrificing our right to privacy can have dire consequences. We still live in a world where all people are not treated equally," he said, "where too many people do not feel free to practice their religion or express their opinion or love who they choose, a world in which that information can make the difference between life or death."

He may have been alluding to oppressive regimes that punish citizens for political beliefs or sexual orientation. But speaking to an audience that includes U.S. policymakers, Cook's remarks are also a reminder of the government's need to protect privacy as it conducts its digital surveillance campaigns.

"If those of us in positions of responsibility fail to do everything in our power to protect the right of privacy, we risk something far more valuable than money. We risk our way of life," he said.

Cook spoke at the White House Summit on Cybersecurity and Consumer Protection, where President Barack Obama signed an Executive Order to encourage the development of Information Sharing and Analysis Organizations, making it easier for the government to share sensitive information about cyber-threats with the private sector.

Google, Microsoft, and other big tech companies sent representatives to the summit, but Apple was the only one that sent its CEO, possibly reflecting divisions between Silicon Valley and the U.S. government over its surveillance programs.

Cook spoke for only twelve minutes but crammed a lot in. He took a jab at compa-

nies like Google and Facebook whose business models are based largely on personal data they collect about their users. "We have a business model that focuses on selling the best products and services in the world, not on selling your personal data," Cook said. "Apple's products are built with security in mind from their inception," he said.

Still, Apple has been far from perfect in protecting privacy. iCloud was hacked in 2014 and nude photographs of dozens of celebrities were stolen and posted on the Internet. Apple had to strengthen its security afterward to try to prevent a repeat.

Apple and privacy rights

U.S. law enforcement authorities have criticized Apple for the security of iOS 8. U.S. Deputy Attorney General James Cole claimed in 2014 that Apple was marketing to criminals and that its technology would one day lead to the death of a child because police would not be able to get the data they needed from an iPhone. In particular, iOS 8 is designed to encrypt iPhone and iPad data automatically, but Apple has no access to encryption keys, so the firm cannot produce someone's data even when pressured by intelligence agencies or when served a subpoena.

On June 5, 2015, National Security Agency (NSA) contractor and whistleblower Edward Snowden praised Apple for being an industry leader on privacy issues. Snowden wrote, "Basic technical safeguards such as encryption were once considered esoteric and unnecessary and are now enabled by default in the products of pioneering companies like Apple, ensuring that even if your phone is stolen, your private life remains private."

Snowden's leaked documents revealed a Central Intelligence Agency (CIA) program to crack the security of iOS, OS X, BitLocker, and other platforms. The extent that U.S. intelligence may have compromised iOS 8, earlier versions of iOS have been cracked by law enforcement.

Snowden had said earlier that he would not use an iPhone because it "has special software that can activate itself without the owner" that will collect data. The statement from Snowden's attorney did not expand on whether that meant deep-level spyware or just general data tracking for device diagnostics.

In the aftermath of the Snowden revelations, tech companies, such as Apple, were forced to show that they were doing all they could to protect users' privacy. Apple, like other major tech companies, uses end-to-end encryption. The messages are encrypted on both ends of the conversation. Apple doesn't store copies of the messages unless users upload them to the iCloud, where messages are not encrypted, so data cannot be transferred to authorities unless it is stored in iCloud.

In September 2015, the U.S. Department of Justice and Federal Bureau of Investigation (FBI) discussed suing Apple after the tech giant refused to turn over text messages between suspects using iPhones. Leading law enforcement officials said that the confrontation was a natural reaction by companies such as Apple, Microsoft, and Google, which adopted tougher encryption following leaks of classified documents by Edward Snowden. Apple told the officials that its iMessage service was fully encrypted and that it was unable to comply.

The issue became even more contentious when Apple refused to help the FBI access information contained in the iPhone 5C belonging to one of the shooters involved in the December 2015 San Bernardino, California, terrorist attack. In February 2016, a judge filed an order directing Apple to assist the FBI in accessing the data, which Apple opposed. On March 21, 2016, the FBI withdrew the request, as it had contracted with a third party to access the data on the phone.

Apple, others "winning" public relations fight

The FBI and Justice Department officials are often frustrated that the technology companies are winning the public relations fight and that the White House has failed to move quickly. Washington is yet to come up with a public response to the argument that the government's victory in the Microsoft case would give countries like Russia and China a way to access servers in the United States.

The Justice Department wants Apple, Google, and other companies using end-to-end encryption to comply with wiretap orders, just like telecom carriers do. Law enforcement officials argue that consumers wouldn't mind investigators getting wiretaps in the digital world if it helped solve crimes. Officials told the *New York Times* that a legal battle against Apple was still pending, though it would be a long shot.

Apple and artificial intelligence

Apple might not be able to compete in the rapidly progressing field of artificial intelligence because of its strict stance on privacy, which will ultimately lead to undermining its ability. Apple makes serious efforts to ensure that the data of its users is protected, for which it imposes certain constraints on the analysis of its users' behavior. Rather than sending the data of iPhone users to the cloud, Apple relies on analyzing data on individuals' own devices. This way it is not able to study the data alongside information from millions of others.

Safe Harbor

In 2015, the European Union (EU) rejected a Safe Harbor agreement with the United States that allowed 3,000 U.S. companies, including Apple Inc., and other tech companies, to bring home European personal data. The tension exposed sharp differences between the United States and the European Union on strong data protection and strong trade ties.

Apple continues to market its products as being secure, especially in comparison to the data-handling practices of other ubiquitous high-tech firms like Google and Facebook. Some of this is because of Apple's diffuse business model, which relies less on advertising revenue from its own apps and software, leaving the advertising to independent developers who create the apps people use on their devices. The fact that Apple does not control how developers profit from their apps means that Apple can claim that they do not make use of customers' data for profit in the way that others do, but looked at another way, Apple appears to be simply passing that part of the business model on to others, over whom they do not exercise control.

Gretchen Nobahar

Further Reading

Angelelli, L. *Steve Paul Jobs.* Computer Science Department NSF-Supported Education Infrastructure Project. 2008. http://ei.cs.vt.edu/~history/Jobs.html.

Boddie, J. "Has Apple Hit the Right Disruptive Notes?" *Strategy & Innovation* (July–August, 2005): 3–4.

Deutschman, A. *The Second Coming of Steve Jobs.* New York: Broadway Books, 2000. Kahney, L. *The Cult of Mac.* San Francisco, CA: No Starch Press Inc., 2004.

Frier, S. "Is Apple Really Your Privacy Hero?" *Bloomberg Businessweek* (August 8, 2018). https://www.bloomberg.com/news/articles/2018-08-08/is-apple-really-your-privacy-hero.

Hawkins, D. "The Cybersecurity 202: Apple's latest security fix is deepening divisions over FBI access." *Washington Post* (June 15, 2018). https://www.washingtonpost.com/news/powerpost/paloma/the-cybersecurity-202/2018/06/15/the-cybersecurity-202-apple-s-latest-security-fix-is-deepening-divisions-over-fbi-access/5b2251121b326b6391af0a12/?utm_term=.ddcf18820b1f.

Kahney, L. *Inside Steve's Brain.* New York: Penguin Books Ltd., 2008. Linzmayer, O. W. *Apple Confidential: The Real Story of Apple Computer, Inc.* New York, 2004.

Mark, K., and M. Crossan. *Apple Computer, Inc.: iPods and iTunes.* Ivey Case Studies, Richard Ivey School of Business, Ivey Publishing, 2005, 1–14.

Moisescot, R. *Steve Jobs: A Biography by Romain Moisescot. All About Steve Jobs.* 2008. http://www.romain-moisescot.com/steve/home/home.html.

Morrow, D. (1995). *Oral History Interview with Jobs.* April 20, 1995.

Wozniak, S., and G. Smith. *iWoz: Computer Geek to Cult Icon: How I Invented the Personal Computer, Co-Founded Apple, and Had Fun Doing It.* New York: W.W. Norton & Co., 2006.

Yoffie, D. B., and M. Slind. *Apple Inc., 2008.* Harvard Business School Case Studies (708–480). Cambridge, MA: Harvard Business School Publishing, February 2008, 2–32.

Young, J. S., and W. L. Simon. *iCon Steve Jobs: The Greatest Second Act in the History of Business.* Hoboken, NJ: John Wiley and Sons, 2005, 35.

See also: Cellphones; Computer Fraud and Abuse Act; Electronic surveillance; Google; Safe Harbor Agreement; National Security Administration (NSA); Smartphones; Snowden, Edward: Social networking technologies; Wiretapping

Apps

Identification: Apps, or applications, are collections of code or software designed to run on a particular device. Common usage includes mobile apps that are formulated to be downloaded and run on mobile devices or to be used exclusively for a particular type or brand of mobile device. Apps are also being developed for wearable devices, unmanned aerial vehicles (UAVs), and biometric devices. Software platforms for app development use similar tools, called application programming interfaces (APIs), within the platform to design and run the apps.

One of the unique features of apps versus computer software, in general, is that apps are focused on the individual user, a specific function, or both. There are apps that offer simple services or provide the user with a stream of unanalyzed information (for example, streams regarding sports statistics, current weather, stock market ups and downs, directions, and traffic updates). At the other end of the complexity spectrum, some apps, such as gaming or social media apps, offer a complete experience within the app. Between these two types, a variety of apps, such as calendaring and communication functions, offer services that accept some input from the user but maintain the essence of their programmed structure. Most users access these apps from a mobile device, whether the apps come preloaded when the user purchases the device or are individually selected and downloaded from an app store.

Apps have provided a broader platform than conventional computer software for nontechnical designers to approach the market and develop innovations. Several app-creation languages offer simpler functionality than traditional software languages, allowing an individual to translate a business idea into an app design. Usually, apps are brought to market much more rapidly than are new computer programs. An app store, or the marketplace for apps on any given device, is broken down into two primary platforms: one for Apple devices and one for devices that run on the Android platform. Other app markets include those operated by Amazon, Facebook, Google, Hewlett-Packard, Microsoft, and Research In Motion. The introduction of the Apple iPhone in 2007 marked a transition from app provision by carriers to app provision by device manufacturers. When the Apple app store opened in 2008, just a few hundred apps were available, with a significant percentage of free apps offered. In more recent years, Apple and Android app stores have each offered more than a million apps. Apple strictly controls access to its market, and it is considered more difficult to enter than the Android market.

The user experience in operating apps is considered one of the main factors that drives the success or failure of any given app. Mobile app designers pay particular attention to the appearance—or graphical user interface (GUI)—of the app as well as the app's actual function. Components of the user experience include ease of download, cost, sensitivity of data input, look and feel of the screens shown to the user, number of screens or clicks required to complete transactions, accuracy of information provided, and number of push or automated notifications. The next front in the development of new apps is to move from high-touch, separate functionalities, such as entering an event into a calendar, to lower-impact background functionalities such as passive check-ins for location and display of card format information.

The Federal Trade Commission (FTC) is the agency that generally issues privacy regulations governing app design and information collection. Apps that utilize healthcare data are also regulated under the Health Insurance Portability and Accountability Act of 1996 (HIPAA), 110 Stat. 1936 (1996). The payment card industry (PCI) governs apps that involve financial transactions using credit cards. The FTC closely monitors whether each app marketer makes promises about what the app can do and whether the app actually provides those benefits. Generally, the app's promises to protect privacy appear in the app's privacy policy statement, but they may appear elsewhere in the marketing materials or security assurances. The FTC and other regulatory advice encourage privacy by design. Under this principle, privacy may be considered during the design phase, or at the onset of app programming, rather than after the new app is released to and used by consumers.

Because the U.S. government is concerned about the amount and type of data collected from children under the age of thirteen, Congress enacted the Children's Online Privacy Protection Act (COPPA) in 1998, 112 Stat. 2681 (1998). COPPA's restriction on data about children applies to apps, and a large number of children interact with mobile devices and tablets in the highly accessible app format. Once an app is downloaded, often the only barrier to children's access is that they must touch or click on it to open it, and it is not necessary for them to log in to start the app. Thus, children can access apps easily, and many apps are designed and marketed with children as the primary target, such as educational and gaming apps.

Apps are also different from other methods of electronic collection of personal data because they frequently continue running and collecting data even when the user is not actively engaged with the app. Also, apps may gather data that does not directly relate to the primary function of the app, such as apps that note the user's physical location, peruse photos, or mine personal contacts on the mobile device even if these activities are not strictly necessary for the app's operation. In one example, an app that converted the light-emitting diode (LED) flash from a phone's camera operation into a consistent flashlight function also happened to collect location data when the app was running. Following the collection of the user's personal data, apps can process it, sell it, or upload it to the Internet.

The collection and sale of personal data from apps has become a significant market. One of the best ways to ascertain whether an app is collecting personal data for use beyond the functioning of the app is to look at the price for downloading the app. If the app is free to the user, there's a good chance that the app will capture user data for sale to third-party advertisers. Otherwise, the app could not turn a profit. Even if the app has a fee associated with a download, there's a possibility that the app could capture data from users that is not required for the app to function as promised.

Often, it is much more difficult for mobile app users to determine whether they are being tracked by an app than whether they are being tracked by a website in a traditional online environment. Apps track their users by identification codes such as the device's serial number; the Unique Device Identifier (UDID); or the carrier's identification number for that phone's customer of record, the International Mobile Station Equipment Identity (IMEI). Unlike cookies, which are used to track an individual's use of webpages online, these unique identifiers cannot be controlled by the individual user. However, mobile device operating systems usually have a settings menu that includes a privacy setting for apps, which allows the user to adjust the collection and location tracking settings for individual apps or for all apps on that device.

A notice on personal data collection by mobile apps may be issued on the carrier, device, or platform level, but ultimately it is the respon-sibility of the app company itself to notify its customers. The app may offer broad notices in its privacy policy about the type of data it collects and how it uses this data, which ideally should be related to the provision of the stated services and not for ancillary revenue. The app could also provide just-in-time notices informing the app user that a certain point of data, such as automatic location tracking, is about to be collected either affirmatively from user input or behind the scenes without additional action on the part of the user. The app, in addition to offering notice, must also obtain customer consent before proceeding with the data collection. To institutionalize increased methods of ensuring consent, mobile app customers could use a do-not-track tool to prevent tracking of their location and usage across the board. This would be similar to the Do Not Call database that allows consumers to halt calls to their residential telephone numbers.

The collection of users' personal data by apps is particularly problematic given questions surrounding mobile app security. While this security is enhanced by the closed nature of mobile systems vis-à-vis Internet systems, apps nevertheless remain vulnerable to hacks and viruses. As app markets mature, multiple points of access mean multiple points of entry for security threats. Also, as individual users allow more and more of their personal data to be housed on mobile devices, this big data becomes extremely valuable to hackers intent on accessing this information to commit fraud or identity theft, or introduce malware to control the device remotely.

Jill Bronfman

Further Reading

BinDhim, Nasser F., and Lyndal Trevena. "Health-Related Smartphone Apps: Regulations, Safety, Privacy and Quality." *BMJ Innovations* 1, no. 2 (2015): 43–45.

"Consumer Watchdog Calls California 'Apps' Privacy Agreement a Step Forward, but Says Do Not Track Legislation Is Necessary to Protect Consumers." *Marketing Weekly News*, March 10, 2012.

Engdahl, Sylvia. *Mobile Apps*. Detroit, MI: Greenhaven Press, 2014.

"FTC Report Raises Privacy Concerns on Mobile Apps for Children." *Entertainment Close-Up*, February 26, 2012.

Martínez-Pérez, Borja, Isabel De La Torre-Díez, and Miguel López-Coronado. "Privacy and Security in Mobile Health Apps: A Review and Recommendations." *Journal of Medical Systems* 39, no. 1 (2014): 181.

Melson, Brent. "Protecting Privacy and Security in Software and Mobile Apps: How to Take Precautions to Keep Your Data Secure." *Wireless Design & Development*, July 1, 2015.

Mohapatra, Manas, Andrew Hasty, et al. *Mobile Apps for Kids Current Privacy Disclosures Are Disappointing.*

Washington, DC: U.S. Federal Trade Commission, 2012.

Shema, Mike. "Browser & Privacy Attacks," in *Hacking Web Apps: Detecting and Preventing Web Application Security Problems.* Boston, MA: Syngress, 2012.

Sweatt, Brian, Sharon Paradesi, Ilaria Liccardi, Lalana Kagal, and Alex Pentland. "Building Privacy-Preserving Location-Based Apps," in 2014 Twelfth Annual International Conference on Privacy, Security and Trust, Toronto, Ontario, Canada, July 23–24, 2014. New York: IEEE/Wiley, 2014.

See also: Big data; Cellphones; Children's Online Privacy Protection Act (COPPA); Do Not Track Legislation; Email; Federal Communications Commission (FCC); Federal Trade Commission (FTC); Health Insurance Portability and Accountability Act of 1996 (HIPAA); Mobile devices; Social networking technologies; Telephones; Wearable technology

Assange, Julian

Identification: Founder of WikiLeaks, a whistleblowing website that exposes the secrets of governments, corporations, and large organizations.

Julian Assange was the winner of *Time* magazine's popular vote for "Person of the Year" in 2010, called "one of the best-known and most well-respected human beings on Earth" by Robert Mann in *The Monthly*, and known to Vice President Joe Biden as "a high-tech terrorist." He has garnered both respect and disdain in recent years.

At first, little was known of Assange's childhood, a subject that he rarely discussed. Assange's parents parted when he was an infant; Assange did not meet his father until he was about twenty-five years old. Assange is named after his stepfather, Brett Assange, whom Assange has called a decent man, despite calling him an alcoholic. His mother separated from him when Assange was about eight years old. While only sixteen years old, Assange met and soon married his girlfriend.

This happened as the computer hacking subculture was on the rise in Melbourne, Australia, where Assange lived. Now known to be the anonymous hacker Mendax, Assange formed a close-knit group with two other hackers and called themselves The International Subversives. Motivated by adventure and curiosity, the group developed something of a creed that highlighted their anti-establishment politics, and they refused to profit from their work.

With a program that Assange wrote, the group was able to infiltrate the U.S. military. This attack was facilitated through a Canadian telecommunications company that ultimately led to the capture of Mendax (Assange) by the Australian federal police. Ultimately, Assange received a $5,000 good behavior bond and was required to pay a $2,100 fine, but he received no prison time. The arrest and trial, however, shaped Assange's life and politics immensely.

While awaiting trial, Assange, assisted by his mother, fought for custody of Assange's young son (his wife had left him and taken the child). This experience led him to form the activist group Parent Inquiry into Child Protection, a small group that received much public support. This continued what was emerging as a theme in Assange's life: to take something important to him and transform it to benefit the masses.

Soon, Assange met other like-minded thinkers and joined a new hacking group: the Cypherpunks. They firmly believed in an individual's right to privacy because, as they said, "privacy is necessary for an open society in the electronic age," yet they thought that "governments, corporations, [and] other large, faceless organisations" could not be counted on to grant that privacy. The association with the Cypherpunks brought Assange together with an American architect, John Young, who set up Cryptome, a website dedicated to exposing "government impropriety" and that attracted the attention of the U.S. National Security Agency (NSA). After helping Young from the sidelines, Assange began formulating the platform for Leaks.org.

WikiLeaks, a whistleblowing website exposing the secrets of governments, corporations, and large organizations, was launched in 2006. Assange explained to the British Broadcasting Company, "[in order to] keep our sources safe, we . . . spread assets, encrypt everything, and move telecommunications and people around the world to activate protective laws in different national jurisdictions."

For further protection, Assange never lived in one place for long. WikiLeaks won international infamy when in 2010 it released footage of U.S. soldiers shooting down civilians from a helicopter in Iraq (a release facilitated by the then soldier Chelsea Manning). Also in 2010, Assange was detained in the United Kingdom because Swedish police had issued an international arrest warrant based on an alleged sexual assault. Assange sought political asylum, seeking refuge in the Ecuadorian embassy in England. While Ecuador granted Assange political asylum, England refused Assange safe exit from the country, claiming it was necessary to uphold the extradition order. Later that year, Assange turned himself in. In August 2015, the Swedish police dropped the molestation charge, but the more serious rape allegation, which will not be time barred until 2020, remains; Assange continues to deny all allegations.

Despite early positivity, Assange's public image has become somewhat fraught .In 2016, during the lead up to the British referendum to leave the European Union, Assange endorsed the Leave campaign, criticizing David Cameron's

government. Additionally, Assange met with Nigel Farage, leader of the pro-Brexit U.K. Independence Party (UKIP). Also in 2016, Assange and WikiLeaks became the subject of scrutiny after leaking emails from John Podesta, an advisor in Hillary Clinton's campaign for president.

Assange reportedly had his internet access limited after WikiLeaks tweeted in support of the October 2017 independence referendum in the Spanish autonomous region of Catalonia, a perennial flashpoint in Spanish politics. Because of this, some have posited that Spain may have pressured Ecuador into muzzling Assange.

In response to negative press and allegations ranging from bad hygiene to mistreatment of his "Embassy cat," in January of 2019 WikiLeaks released a list of 140 "false or defamatory" things to not report about Assange. The list was sent to media organizations in an email marked "confidential… not for publication." It was of course quickly published and derided on social media. While some of the items on the list are patently absurd, others relate to his alleged meetings with political figures and involvement with collaboration between WikiLeaks and the Russian government.

The influence of Julian Assange and WikiLeaks cannot be overstated. After exposing documents that led to the collapse of Icelandic banks, Assange helped draft a proposal that was ultimately adopted for the regulation of such banks. Assange and WikiLeaks now work directly with news organizations to get stories to the masses in an organized fashion. Assange has helped expose documents concerning the National Aeronautical Space Agency (NASA), the Church of Scientology, the U.S. detention camp at Guantanamo Bay, Sarah Palin's private email (it was allegedly used to circumvent U.S. disclosure-of-public-officials laws), censored websites, and much more. Whether he should be regarded as a hero or a villain is a question of a different order.

Julie Ann Embler and J. N. Manuel

Further Reading

Fowler, Andrew. *The Most Dangerous Man in the World: The Explosive True Story of Julian Assange and the Lies, Cover-Ups and Conspiracies He Exposed.* New York: Skyhorse Publishing, 2011.

Mann, Robert. "The Cypherpunk Revolutionary: On Julian Assange." *The Monthly*, March 1, 2011.

"Profile: Wikileaks Founder Julian Assange—BBC News." BBC News. August 13, 2015. Accessed September 1, 2015.

Reuters. "WikiLeaks tells reporters 140 things not to say about Julian Assange," *Reuters*, January 6th 2019, https://www.reuters.com/article/us-britain-ecuador-assange/wikileaks-tells-reporters-140-things-not-to-say-about-julian-assange-idUSKCN1P00NN

Rovira, Adria. "L'Equadorprohibeixparlar de Catalunya a Assange," *El Nacional*, August 6th 2018, https://www.elnacional.cat/ca/politica/equador-prohibeix-catalu-nya-assange_294696_102.html

Katchadourian, Raffi. "Julian Assange, a Man Without a Country," *The New Yorker*, August 21st 2017, https://www.NewYorker.com/magazine/2017/08/21/julian-assange-a-man-without-a-country

See also: Hacking, computer; Law enforcement; Public morality; WikiLeaks

Automated teller machines (ATMs)

Identification: automated machines that use a consumer banking card with a magnetic strip to complete financial transactions.

ATMs are almost inescapable in our digital economy. The protection of your private ATM banking and credit card information is becoming increasingly difficult every time the magnetic strip is swiped at an ATM. The amount of possibilities for criminals to access banking information is endless and confusing for most consumers. There are more than 150 banks or credit unions in the United States according to a 2010 report from American Banker. Of those that provide ATMs, some of the largest are JP Morgan Chase, Bank of America, Wells Fargo, Citigroup, PNC, HSBC, Suntrust, and Capital One. Thousands of ATMs provide consum-

ers access to their banking funds or credit lines for transactional purposes. The growing usage of transactional dispensing of bank funds, has increased the funds' vulnerability to fraud and theft. It is critical for consumers to mitigate and lower the potential exposure to fraud and theft by understanding the ways to protect their privacy and to increase awareness of ways criminals can access banking and credit card information for fraudulent purposes.

Consumers can protect banking and credit card information from criminal activity in various ways, including tracking financial and credit report information, using trusted sources for ATM usage, and becoming watchful of their ATM or financial transactions. ATM cards or credit cards are proof of a financial relationship that the consumer has with the banking institution to secure and gain access to funds or lines of credit and banks have insurance to protect their financial relationship. Consumers need to educate themselves on protecting their funds and lines of credit provided by the financial institutions that also provide convenient access via ATMs. Cybercriminals are less likely to be able to poach consumers' ATM information if consumers educate themselves on how they can protect their privacy. Tracking all financial transactions is one way consumers may begin to increase the financial security of their banking information. Accessing banking and financial institution information to track purchases and transactions should be done as often as this information is used or exchanged in person or online. Tracking all financial transactions confirms the initial use and arrival at the targeted or intended source. This may include cash transactions because the usage of an ATM card at a financial institution makes the consumer vulnerable to physical tampering. According to a Verizon Report from 2012 titled "ATMs May Be Top Targets for Crime":

More than half of intrusions in the financial industry involved tampering with

ATMs. Overall 61% of security threats involved physical tampering, including the installation of skimming and camera devices on ATMs to capture magnetic strip data and PINs (Personal Identification Numbers). Roughly one in four threats involved malware that captures usernames and passwords. Another 22% involved hacking.

Consumers can decrease criminals' accessibility to physical tampering by ensuring that they use confirmed financial institutional ATMs for cash dispensary. If the ATM appears sketchy or unauthorized by a commercial bank or credit union, then consumers should select another location for cash withdrawals to minimize exposure to the fraudulent use of funds.

Consumers can also protect their ATM card information by adding or participating in multilayered authentication offered by financial institutions that may include, but may not be limited to: encrypted passwords, one-time passcodes with time expiration, personal identification questions, or card code data verification required prior to banking access. These additional ATM card defense measures increase privacy protection and minimize the likelihood of financial theft. If these methods are used properly to authenticate each transaction, they make it harder for criminals to duplicate this information because the added layer is a unique identifier of characters, words, or symbols that the consumer must possess to confirm his or her identity as it relates to the ATM card.

Fraud prevention for consumers begins with increasing awareness through education on ways criminals can access ATM banking information. The ATM financial information used for consumer purchases can be accessed by cybercriminals via online transactions, check electronic payments, electronic funds transfers (EFTs), physical tampering through ATMs, and credit/debit transactions. All transactional use of an ATM card opens a potential pathway to fund-ing that a criminal may follow to gain fraudulent access to consumers' finances. Therefore mitigating this risk is an integral part of fraud prevention in the use of ATMs.

Relief may not be too far away for consumers to maintain fraud prevention at ATMs. Technological advancements widely used in other areas by financial institutions are being applied to ATMs. According to *American Banker Magazine,* biometrics in banking is becoming increasingly used: Automated teller machines featuring fingerprint readers have been used in South Africa since 1996. Brazil today boasts more than 55,000 ATMs that integrate biometrics technology into the authentication process. United States banks have been using biometrics since the mid-2000s to facilitate secure self-service access to safe deposit boxes for consumers.

Advancements are not guaranteed because of limitations in cost, implementation, efficiency, and social acceptance. Once the fingerprint information has been duplicated or fraudulently obtained by criminals, there would be no measure to prevent the user from accessing the funds. Passwords can be changed, verified, and authenticated at an ATM; therefore, this information can safeguard funds much more easily for financial institutions and consumers.

A new wave of privacy protection amounts to either a multilayered approach for consumers to gain access to ATM banking and credit card information (i.e., added one-time password, secret question, or biometric authentication) or a limitation on consumer interaction with ATMs. Consumer awareness about the fraudulent use of ATM privacy information in this digital economy should reduce overall exposure to cyber-thefts. After working hard to earn funds or credit, it is an injustice for an unknown person to take advantage of those fiscal rewards by silently stealing them from an ATM. The protection of privacy at ATMs is not impossible, but it is inevitable that the advances in criminal activity to breach privacy protections are increasing faster than preventative measures.

Shaunté Chácon

Further Reading

Browdie, Brian. "ATMs May be Top Targets for Crime: Verizon Report." *Payments Source* (October 25, 2012).

Heun, David. "Pealing Back Layers of Fraud Protection." *Payments Source* (March 14, 2012)

Natoli Jr., Frank. "Biometrics in Banking: Overcoming the Barriers." *American Banker Magazine* (June 2014)

Taylor, Simon. "Fraud and Security." *European Voice*. January 15, 2015. www.europeanvoice.com.

See also: Consumer privacy; Credit and debit Cards; Financial information, privacy right to

B

Background checks

Identification: Investigations by employers intended to verify the representations made by a job applicant regarding his or her background.

Employers may conduct background checks on employees either prior to employment or, less commonly, after they have been hired. Because so many people misrepresent aspects of their backgrounds and credentials, employers believe it is a vital part of the hiring process to conduct a background check to determine whether the applicant has made truthful statements about his or her background. Employers justify background checks as a means of providing insight into an individual's behavior, character, reliability, and integrity.

Employers most often conduct background checks to verify that the job applicant or employee has not been involved in any immorality, physical violence, theft, or financial misconduct, or whether the individual has ever been convicted of a crime. Employers also use background checks to determine if the applicant is indeed qualified for the job or has some personality trait or pattern of behavior that may be problematical for the employer if the person were hired.

Employers must obtain the employee's (or prospective employee's) written permission before conducting a background check. This requirement varies by state law and is also subject to federal law. Some states require only a general signed release. Other states, however, require disclosures and strict written consent.

The Fair Credit Reporting Act (FCRA), 84 Stat. 1114–2 (1970), regulates how employers can collect and use certain information in the hiring or promotion process. The FCRA requires that a consent form be completed, that the prospective employee be notified if an adverse employment action results from information in the report (for example, that the individual did not get the job because of a felony conviction), and that the prospective employee be informed of which reporting agency provided the information so that the prospective employee may challenge the findings.

One reason why employers conduct a background check is that the employer can be held liable if it negligently hires someone with a criminal record, if it fails to become aware of an employee's unfitness for a particular position, or if it subsequently fails to take any corrective action—such as training, reassignment, or discharge—to remedy the problem once the issue has been discovered. The elements of the tort of negligent hiring are: (1) the existence of an employment relationship between the employer and the employee, (2) the employee's unfitness, (3) the employer's actual or "constructive" knowledge of the employee's unfitness (failure to investigate can lead to a finding of constructive knowledge), (4) the employee's act or omission causing injuries to a third person, and (5) the employer's negligence in hiring the employee was most likely the cause of the third party's injuries. Employers must also conduct background checks to avoid being judged arbitrary and capricious, which could then make the employer legally liable for damages to the applicant.

Potential risks of background checks include the receipt of information that is irrelevant, taken out of context, or inaccurate. During the employee selection process, requesting or using information that is irrelevant or unrelated to the job may be illegal and may place the employer at risk for litigation. To avoid such legal issues in conducting background checks; employers should do the following: Create a written policy on background checks; make applicants aware of the employer's policy on these background checks; and explicitly state that the employer reserves the right to disqualify applicants based on the results of a background check. Such a policy should list the criminal convictions that automatically disqualify an applicant. Relevant factors that may influence the hiring decision include seriousness of an offense, how long ago the conviction occurred, and evidence of rehabilitation.

Once the policy takes effect, it must be fairly implemented and impartially enforced. All qualified candidates should be interviewed and their references checked. In certain circumstances, undisclosed references should be contacted based on the applicant's information.

The employer should perform the background check only after the initial interview and after the applicant has been informed about the background check and provided the signed disclosure agreement. The applicant should be informed of the result within the time prescribed by law or in a reasonably timely manner if the statute is silent on the matter.

Background checks may have a broad range of information that an employer may use to make employment-related decisions. Certain types of information cannot be reported, however, and a background check with this information may violate federal law. Such information includes: incomplete information; records of dismissed charges or other nonconvictions occurring more than seven years earlier; records of criminal convictions, dismissals, arrests, or other nonconvictions that have been expunged; records of arrest(s) occurring more than seven years earlier; records of noncriminal traffic offenses occurring more than seven years earlier; records of bankruptcies occurring more than ten years earlier; records of evictions that occurred more than seven years earlier; and other adverse information documenting events that occurred more than seven years earlier.

Credit reports

A credit history report on a job applicant includes information such as the applicant's address, Social Security number, bankruptcies, tax liens, judgments, child support obligations, loans, and the names of other employers who have checked the applicant's credit. Credit reports do not provide information on previous income, college degrees, bank accounts, personal investments, criminal history, or medical history.

The FCRA provides the applicant with several privacy rights when a background check is conducted for employment purposes. Under the FCRA, the employer must obtain an employee's written consent before seeking an employee's credit report. The employer must clearly and accurately explain what a credit report contains. If an employer decides not to hire or promote an individual based on information in the credit report, the employer must provide a copy of the report and inform the applicant of his or her right to challenge the report under the FCRA.

Before an employer acts to terminate an individual or deny that individual a job or promotion based on information from a background check, it must: (1) provide the individual with a copy of the background report and contact information of the company that prepared the report, (2) provide the individual with a summary of his or her rights under the FCRA, and (3) inform the individual of his or her right to dispute the accuracy of the report in a reasonable amount of time to make this challenge.

The FCRA also prohibits companies that provide background checks from reporting information that is considered misleading or inaccurate. Such information may include information on the wrong person, debts that have been discharged in bankruptcy, and inaccurate reporting of criminal records (such as a dismissed charge as a conviction or reporting an incorrect offense title or date). The same charge may not appear several times on the same report.

A credit background check is used by 60 percent of employers in hiring decisions and is frequently justified as a reliable indicator of both an individual's financial aptitude and overall integrity. The use of credit information to consider the character of job applicants is increasingly being criticized because often otherwise fiscally responsible individuals experience financial difficulties caused by circumstances outside their control. Thus, some states and equal opportunity organizations are challenging the use of credit backgrounds checks. While legal in most states, some states, such as Hawaii and Washington, have prohibited the use of credit background checks for most employment decisions.

Criminal records

The extent to which a private employer may consider an applicant's criminal history in making hiring decisions varies from state to state. Employers usually conduct criminal background checks on applicants who will be bonded because of access to money or valuables; carry a weapon; drive a vehicle; have access to drugs or explosives; have access to master keys; have a great deal of contact with patients, children, and other vulnerable people; or will be filling a position that requires a criminal records check under state law.

Both federal civil rights law and state law regulate the use of criminal records checks. If there is an adverse impact on minority applicants, the employer may violate antidiscrimination law. Therefore, if there is such an adverse impact, the employer must determine whether the record check is related to the performance of the job or some other business necessity, and, if there is a business necessity, whether there is another way to investigate the applicant's background to avoid the adverse impact.

Lie detector tests

The Employee Polygraph Protection Act, 102 Stat. 646 (1988), prohibits most private employers from using lie detector tests, either for preemployment screening or during the course of employment. The statute includes the exceptions that apply to businesses that provide armored car services or alarm or guard services, or those that manufacture, distribute, or dispense pharmaceuticals.

Even though there is no federal law specifically prohibiting the employer from using a written honesty test on job applicants, these tests frequently violate federal and state laws that protect against discrimination and violations of privacy.

Medical records

Under the Americans with Disabilities Act, 104 Stat. 327 (1990), employers cannot discriminate based on a physical or mental impairment or request an employee's medical records. Businesses can inquire, however, about an applicant's ability to perform specific job duties. Some states also have stronger laws protecting the confidentiality of medical records.

Bankruptcy records

Bankruptcies are a matter of public record and may appear on an individual's credit report. The Federal Bankruptcy Act prohibits employers from discriminating against applicants if they have declared bankruptcy. Bankruptcy is not a valid reason to deny employment.

Military records

Military service records may be released only under limited circumstances, and consent is generally required. However, the military may disclose name, rank, salary, duty assignments, awards, and duty status without the service member's consent.

School records

Under the Family Educational Rights and Privacy Act (FERPA), 88 Stat. 571 (1974) and similar state laws, educational records such as transcripts, recommendations, and financial information are confidential and cannot be released by the school without a student's consent.

Workers' Compensation records

Workers' compensation appeals are a matter of public record. Information from a workers' compensation appeal may be used in a hiring decision if the employer can show the applicant's injury might interfere with his or her ability perform required duties.

Social networking searches

Social networking searches should not be part of a routine background check because simply viewing an applicant's social networking site has the potential to provide subjective information on off-duty behavior that is not job related and may unduly influence a hiring decision. Social networking sites may reveal embarrassing information on an applicant that is not related to the job. It is also often difficult to determine what information is true, exaggerated, or totally false.

Firearm sales

One of the most politically contentious areas in which background checks are used – and many would like to see their use expanded – is in the sale of firearms. While some supporters of the National Rifle Association (NRA) see the use of background checks for gun sales as an infringement of citizens' Second Amendment rights, a vast majority of the American public – between 90 and 97 percent depending on the poll – support the idea of universal background checks for gun sales. Although federal law mandates background checks for commercial gun sales, the sale of firearms between people – which, importantly, includes gun shows – is not subject to background checks. The main reason that lawmakers have not demonstrated the political will to mandate universal background checks is the political power wielded by the NRA.

Discriminatory use of background checks

Over the years, several large companies have been found to have violated the law in conducting background checks on employees and job applicants. Several companies, including Kmart, Home Depot, Wal-Mart, and Domino's Pizza, have been sued by employees and job applicants for failing to comply with federal law on background checks because they did not follow certain procedures in conducting the background check or used background checks improperly in making employment decisions.

While many employers conduct background checks to determine whether someone should be hired or promoted, employers may not use background check information to discriminate against an employee or job applicant based on race. The U.S. Equal Employment Opportunity Commission (EEOC) has been reviewing its position on the use of arrest records during the hiring process in view of concerns that African Americans and Hispanics face discrimination under blanket hiring policies that exclude applicants with past convictions.

Several employers have been sued because their hiring policies were allegedly discriminatory. For example, a lawsuit against Pepsi resulted in a $3.13 million settlement to resolve claims that the company discriminated against African Americans in its background checks. The EEOC found that Pepsi disproportionately excluded African American applicants because the company's hiring policy did not permit those who had been arrested to be hired for permanent jobs, even if they were never actually convicted of any crime.

In California, which has very strict laws governing employers' procurement of background checks without the consent of the prospective or current employees, the state supreme court issued a unanimous decision on August 20, 2018, in the case of *Connor v. First Student* 2018 WL 3966434 (Cal. S. Ct. 2018). The plaintiffs, a group of bus drivers, won their case because the defendant (their employer) only included a check box indicating consent through the requesting of a copy of the employee's background check. This was deemed insufficient to meet the law's mandate of "written authorization." The case drew into sharp focus the need for extreme care by all parties requesting background checks on individuals to protect their privacy to the full extent mandated by federal and state laws.

Further Reading

Hubbartt, William S. *The New Battle over Workplace Privacy: How Far Can Management Go? What Rights Do Employees Have?: Safe Practices to Minimize Conflict, Confusion, and Litigation.* New York: AMACOM, 1998.

Jacoby, Nicolle L., Melissa Bergman Squire, and Bureau of National Affairs. *Employee Background Checks: Balancing the Need to Hire Wisely with Employees' Right to Privacy.* Workforce Strategies 29, no. 4 (2011).

Larence, Eileen Regen. *Firearm and Explosives Background Checks Involving Terrorist Watch List Records.* Washington, DC: U.S. Government Accountability Office, 2009.

Manchester, Julia. "Poll: 97 percent support background checks for all gun buyers." *The Hill*, February 20, 2018. https://thehill.com/blogs/blog-briefing-room/news/374692-poll-97-percent-support-background-checks-for-all-gun-buyers

Muller, Max. *The Manager's Guide to HR Hiring, Firing, Performance Evaluations, Documentation, Benefits, and Everything Else You Need to Know,* 2d ed. New York: American Management Association, 2013.

Quackenboss, Robert T., Evans, Karen Jennings, and Brown, Jason P. "California Supreme Court's Clarification of 'Background Check' Laws" *The Recorder*, October 5, 2018. https://www.law.com/therecorder/2018/10/05/california-supreme-courts-clarification-of-background-check-laws/

Richey, Warren. "Supreme Court: NASA's Intrusive Background Checks OK." *Christian Science Monitor*, January 19, 2011.

Townsend, Katherine Novak. *Employee Privacy Challenges & Solutions: Electronic Monitoring, Health Information, Personnel Files, and More.* Brentwood, TN: M. Lee Smith Publishers, 2008.

Western, Bruce. "Criminal Background Checks and Employment among Workers with Criminal Records." *Criminology & Public Policy* 7, no. 3 (August 2008): 413–417.

Wugmeister, Miriam. *Global Employee Privacy and Data Security Law.* Arlington, VA: BNA Books, 2009.

See also: Consent; Credit Reporting Agencies; Fair Credit Reporting Act; Fair Information Practice Principles; Family Educational Rights and Privacy Protection Act of 1974; Health Information Portability and Accountability Act; Medical Confidentiality; Workplace, Privacy in the

Bartnicki et ano v. Vopper, et al., 532 U.S. 514 (2001)

Identification: Case addressing the recurring problem of how courts should resolve the conflict between the First Amendment's guarantee of free speech and the protection of other constitutional values.

The case of *Bartnicki et ano v. Vopper, et al.* specifically addressed a conflict between speech and privacy. It considered whether the First Amendment prevents Congress from attempting to protect the privacy of telephone calls by imposing punishment on anyone who discloses the contents of a telephone conversation they know to have been intercepted illegally. *Bartnicki* is significant for the widely conflicting views expressed by the highly divided Court about the scope of First Amendment protection and for the narrow legal standard it finally adopted to protect the free discussion of true, newsworthy information by people who did nothing wrong to obtain it.

Bartnicki arose out of a protracted labor dispute involving the teachers at the Wyoming Valley West High School in Pennsylvania. For the better part of two school years, the teacher's union and the school board engaged in negotiations that were both highly contentious and the subject of a great deal of local media attention. In May 1993, the union's chief negotiator, Gloria Bartnicki, used her cellphone for a lengthy call with the union president, Anthony Kane. During that call, they discussed the status of the ongoing negotiations, the timing of a possible strike, the school board's intransigence, and the need for a dramatic response. At one point, union president Kane said to his chief negotiator, "[I]f they're not going to move for 3%, we're going to have to go to their, their homes . . . To blow off their front porches, we'll have to do some work on some of those guys" (532 U.S. at 519).

Months later, the teacher's union and the school board accepted the proposal of an arbitrator that was generally favorable to the teachers and ended their dispute. In this context, someone sent a tape recording of the telephone conversation between Bartnicki and Kane to a local activist who had opposed the teacher's union. The activist did not know who sent him the unmarked recording, but he recognized the voices and shared the recording with various local media outlets.

Several news organizations reported the contents of the recorded call in their coverage of the school board's settlement with the union, and a local radio commentator, Frederick Vopper, played the recording several times on his public affairs talk show. The reporting on their secretly recorded telephone call led Bartnicki and Kane to sue Vopper and others, asserting that it was illegal to reveal the contents of their private telephone conversation, even in a news report.

Bartnicki and Kane sought statutory and punitive damages under state and federal eavesdropping laws that had long made it illegal for anyone to "willfully disclose" the contents of an electronic communication "knowing or having reason to know" that the information was obtained through an illegal wiretap or an unauthorized intercept of a wireless communication (18 U. S. C. § 2511(1)(c); 18 Pa. Cons. Stat. § 5703). When Vopper and the other defendants moved to dismiss the claims, asserting a constitutional right under the First Amendment to discuss true, newsworthy information, the government intervened to defend the constitutionality of the federal statute. When the case arrived at the Supreme Court, it presented "a direct conflict between interests of the highest order—on the one hand, the interest in the full and free dissemination of information concerning public issues, and, on the other hand, the interest in individual privacy and, more specifically, in fostering private speech" (532 U.S. at 518).

In a long line of earlier cases, the Supreme Court had consistently refused to allow civil or criminal punishment to be imposed upon the press for disseminating true, newsworthy information. In *Smith v. Daily Mail Publishing Co*, 443 U.S. 97 (1979), and *Oklahoma Publishing Co. v. District Court, Oklahoma Cty.*, 430 U.S. 308 (1977), the Court prohibited punishment for the accurate disclosure of the name of a juvenile charged with a crime; in *Florida Star v. B.J.F.*, 491 U.S. 524 (1989), and *Cox Broadcasting Corp. v. Cohn*, 420 U.S. 469 (1975), the Court struck down laws making it illegal to publish the name of a rape victim; and in *Landmark Communications, Inc. v. Virginia*, 435 U.S. 829 (1978), it prohibited punishment for truthful reporting on the confidential proceedings of a commission reviewing the conduct of a state judge. In each of these cases, the Court accepted the proposition that the First Amendment prohibits the press from being punished for the publication of "truthful information about a matter of public significance" absent a need to further a state interest "of the highest order" (*Daily Mail*, 443 U.S. at 103). Vopper argued that the claims against him should be dismissed under this same principle.

In each of these earlier cases, however, the Supreme Court had refused to adopt as a fixed constitutional principle that the First Amendment always precludes punishment for the publication of true newsworthy information. Rather, its holdings "carefully eschewed reaching this ultimate question, mindful that the future may bring scenarios which prudence counsels our not resolving anticipatorily" (*Florida Star*, 491 U.S. at 532). Furthermore, none of the earlier decisions involved a situation where the true, newsworthy information that was published by the press had been obtained illegally. In this case, someone clearly violated the law in recording the telephone call between Bartnicki and Kane, even if the individual defendants themselves did nothing wrong and innocently received copies of the recording.

Given these distinctions, Bartnicki argued that a different line of Supreme Court authority should control. The Court previously had adopted the principle that a content neutral regulation does not violate the First Amendment as long as it (a) furthers some important government interest unrelated to the suppression of speech, and (b) any incidental restriction imposed on speech is no greater than necessary to further that important interest (see, for example, *Turner Broadcasting System*, 512 U.S. at 662). A "content neutral regulation" is one that does not seek to limit speech on any particular topic or to limit any specific point of view. Bartnicki contended that protecting the privacy of telephone calls and other electronic communications is an important government interest and that laws prohibiting the knowing dissemination of an illegally intercepted telephone call were content neutral laws with only an incidental impact on free speech. These laws did not violate the First Amendment, she argued, because their incidental impact on the speech of others was no broader than necessary to protect the privacy of the participants in the illegally intercepted telephone call.

The critical question facing the Court in *Bartnicki* was which of these approaches properly resolved the conflict between privacy and speech when illegal eavesdropping has occurred. Writing for a plurality of four judges, Justice Stevens acknowledged that the laws prohibiting the dissemination of illegally intercepted telephone calls were indeed content neutral regulations that would typically be subject to minimal scrutiny by the courts:

> The statute does not distinguish based on the content of the intercepted conversations, nor is it justified by reference to the content of those conversations. Rather, the communications at issue are singled out by virtue of the fact that they were illegally intercepted—by virtue of the source, rather than the subject matter. (532 U.S. at 526)

Although the illegally intercepted communication was content neutral, however, the punishment imposed for the subsequent disclosure of illegally intercepted communications was a "naked prohibition" on speech. This aspect of the eavesdropping statutes did not punish the wrongful interception of a call but its subsequent discussion by others. Because this provision, if enforced in this case, would punish the *publication* of truthful information of public concern, not the wrongful *conduct* of the eavesdropper, Justice Stevens concluded that the *Daily Mail* line of cases should control. Accordingly, he turned to the interests served by the statutes to see if they could justify the direct restrictions they imposed on speech.

The government advanced two interests in defense of the eavesdropping laws: First, it asserted that punishment of those who disseminate illegally intercepted information was necessary to remove the incentive to intercept illegally in the first place. The government contended that individuals who eavesdrop on the calls of others would routinely pass the information along to third parties for public dissemination to avoid criminal prosecution, as happened in this case. Without a specific prohibition on the dissemination of the intercepted material *by anyone,* the wiretapping and eavesdropping laws could not effectively meet their objective of protecting the privacy of electronic communications. Second, the government asserted that the prohibition on dissemination is needed to minimize the harm that would otherwise be inflicted on those whose privacy is invaded by the secret and illegal interception of their communications.

Justice Stevens rejected the government's first rationale as constitutionally inappropriate, finding that "it would be quite remarkable to hold that speech by a law-abiding possessor of information can be suppressed in order to deter conduct by a non-law-abiding third-party" (532 U.S. at 529). He also pointed to the number of individuals who have been criminally prosecuted for intercepting electronic communications and questioned the factual basis for the government's claim that further deterrence was required.

Justice Stevens agreed with the government, however, that privacy of communications is an important interest that Congress has a legitimate reason to protect, and found the government's second justification "considerably stronger." He quoted a presidential commission report from 1967 making the point:

> In a democratic society, privacy of communication is essential if citizens are to think and act creatively and constructively. Fear or suspicion that one's speech is being monitored by a stranger, even without the reality of such activity, can have a seriously inhibiting effect upon the willingness to voice critical and constructive ideas. (532 U.S. at 533, quoting President's Commission on Law Enforcement and Administration of Justice, *The Challenge of Crime in a Free Society,* 202 (1967))

Acknowledging the important interests on both sides of the equation, the four justices led by Justice Stevens nonetheless concluded that the desire to protect privacy did not justify restricting speech on a newsworthy topic by someone who did nothing wrong. Following the *Daily Mail* line of cases, Justice Stevens's opinion concludes that the First Amendment protection of true, newsworthy speech must carry the day on the facts presented. The result would be different, he stressed, in a case against someone disseminating a company's illegally intercepted trade secrets or the entirely personal affairs of a private individual, but protecting speech on a matter of public concern is a core purpose of the First Amendment (532 U.S. at 534).

Chief Justice Rehnquist disagreed strenuously. Writing for three judges in dissent, he concluded that the *Turner Broadcasting* principle squarely applied. In his view, the eavesdropping laws imposed a content neutral regulation that the Court should sustain because it furthers a substantial government interest, and the incidental impact on speech is no greater than essential to further that interest effectively. The Chief Justice saw the restrictions against subsequent disclosures of illegally obtained information as a deliberate and necessary step toward the legitimate goal of safeguarding the privacy of electronic communications. He stressed that ensuring the privacy of electronic communications enables "frank and uninhibited" conversations, "not cramped by fears of clandestine surveillance and purposeful disclosure" (532 U.S. at 543). He found the *Daily Mail* line of cases entirely unpersuasive because, in those cases, unlike this one, the information for which disclosure was being punished had been lawfully obtained and was already public to some extent. Punishing the publication of information in that context would promote self-censorship, a concern not addressed by the restrictions in the eavesdropping laws. Chief Justice Rehnquist would not apply the *Daily Mail* test, however, and would allow Bartnicki to proceed with her claims. So far, the count was 4–3. This left the deciding votes to the two remaining justices, Breyer and O'Connor.

In an opinion written by Justice Breyer, these two justices agreed with the outcome reached by the Stevens's opinion but disagreed with its broad reading of the protection given to true, newsworthy information. Justice Breyer articulated a more nuanced and constrained view of the First Amendment's protection of speech in this context. First, he found the type of "strict scrutiny" applied in the *Daily Mail* line of cases, which applies a strong presumption against the constitutional validity of any restriction on true, newsworthy speech, to be inappropriate where competing constitutional interests are directly at stake. Justice Breyer then highlighted the speech-enhancing aspects of the statutory ban on disseminating intercepted material. Protecting the privacy of electronic communications *promotes* private speech, he explained, by assuring individuals that their conversations will not be intercepted and repeated by others. In his view, "the Federal Constitution must tolerate laws of this kind because of the importance of these privacy and speech related objectives" (532 U.S. at 537–38).

Justice Breyer nevertheless agreed that, as applied to the circumstances of this case, the statutory restrictions on speech "do not reasonably reconcile the competing constitutional objectives" (532 U.S. at 538). He believed that punishing the dissemination of the intercepted Bartnicki conversation would "disproportionately interfere" with freedom of speech and freedom of the press. Justice Breyer reached this conclusion based on the facts that: (1) there was no misconduct by any of the media defendants, (2) the participants in the conversation had "little or no legitimate interest" in maintaining the privacy of communication that was disseminated, (3) the law in many other contexts recognizes a privilege to disclose threats to public security such as the one made on the intercepted telephone call, and (4) the speakers on the intercepted call were essentially limited-purpose public figures in connection with the school labor controversy. On these facts, Justice Breyer agreed that Vopper had a constitutional privilege to disclose the unlawfully intercepted conversation. He also underscored, however, that this holding did not create any broad "public interest" exception to the privacy protections in the eavesdropping and wiretapping statutes.

The tension between free speech and other objectives resolved in *Bartnicki* arises in many contexts beyond privacy, such as with restrictions on speech in the Espionage Act that are intended to protect national security (18 U.S.C. § 793) or restrictions on hate speech or student conduct codes designed to promote civility and lawful behavior (see, for example, *R.A.V. v. St Paul*, 505 U.S. 377 (1992) (striking down hate crime ordinance); *Morse v. Frederick*, 551 U.S. 393 (2007) (upholding school code prohibiting messages that promote drug use)). When these conflicts arise, we expect the courts to resolve them in ways that achieve a proper balance among competing interests. How the Court will apply the constrained approach to the First Amendment adopted in Justice Breyer's *Bartnicki* opinion remains an open question.

David A. Schulz

Further Reading

Easton, Eric B. "Ten Years After: *Bartnicki v. Vopper* as a Laboratory for First Amendment Advocacy and Analysis." *University of Louisville Law Review* 50 (2011): 287. Halstuk, Martin E. "Shielding Private Lives from Prying Eyes: The Escalating Conflict between Constitutional Privacy and the Accountability Principle of Democracy." *Communications Law Conspectus* 11 (2003): 71.

Hunt, Jennifer Nichole. "*Bartnicki v. Vopper*: Another Media Victory or Ominous Warning of a Potential Change in Supreme Court First Amendment Jurisprudence?" *Pepperdine Law Review* 30 (2003): 367.

Paradis, Daniel P. Paradis. "*Bartnicki v. Vopper*: Cell Phones and Throwing Stones." *New England Law Review* 37 (2003): 1117.

Richards, Neil. *Intellectual Privacy: Rethinking Civil Liberties in the Digital Age.*, 2015, 60 –78.

See also: Cell Phones; First Amendment to the U.S. Constitution; *Sorrell v. IMS Health Inc*

Beliefs, privacy of

Identification: Commitments that an individual really holds as true, that a person is willing to defend against criticisms and objections, and that one uses to base assumptions.

Like the definition of religion, there has been no complete consensus on how to define belief. The German sociologist, Georg Simmel, wrote that the concept of belief first appeared as an "interrelationship between human beings." In the earliest period of the history of humanity, belief was a form of social relationship. When belief first appeared as a concept, it was not influenced by religion. It was, instead, a pure form of spiritual relationship between individuals. Later, belief became associated with the relationship between deities and human beings.

In the modern era, peoples throughout the world value both the freedom of belief and privacy of belief as a crucial part of their humanity. In other words, the right and privacy of belief, like the right to life, is self-evident and a value that all people are entitled to enjoy. Legal confirmation of citizens' right of privacy of belief began with the Edict of Toleration and the Edict of Milan was concluded jointly by Roman leader Constantine and Licinius in BC 313. For the first time, it stipulated that believers in different religions enjoyed the same freedoms and would not be discriminated against or persecuted. In the twentieth century, the freedom of belief was recognized as a universal principle. Article 18 of the Universal Declaration of Human Rights adopted by the UN General Assembly in 1948 states: "Everyone has the right to freedom of thought, conscience and religion; this right includes freedom to change his religion or belief, and freedom, either alone or in community with others and in public or private, to manifest his religion or belief in teaching, practice, worship and observance." Moreover, the Declaration on the Elimination of All Forms of Intolerance and on Discrimination Based on Religion or Belief, passed by the UN General Assembly in November 1987 provides:

"No one shall be subject to coercion that would impair his freedom to have a religion or belief of his choice. Freedom to manifest one's religion or belief may be subject only to such limitations as are prescribed by law and are necessary to protect public safety, order, health or morals or the fundamental rights and freedoms of others."

Privacy of belief – the American context

The First Amendment is the preeminent source of privacy rights in the United States, and it guarantees the freedom of belief. By its explicit terms, the First Amendment prohibits Congress from interfering with the free exercise of religion, abridging free speech or freedom of the press, interfering with the right of peaceful assembly, or restricting the right to petition the government for redress of grievances. In other words, it provides robust protections for the privacy of belief.

The first part of the First Amendment includes the two religion clauses: the establishment clause and free exercise clause. They provide that the government is forbidden from establishing a national religion and that the government may not legally prefer one religion to another. The "No Establishment Clause," in addition to forbidding an established church, also means that the government may not enforce its observance by law, nor compel any citizen to worship in a manner contrary to his or her conscience. The Free Exercise of Religion Clause is intended to prohibit a government from restricting a citizen's free exercise of his religion. It is designed to prevent the state from restraining a citizen's unfettered choice to believe in the tenets of his faith and to worship in accordance with his or her conscience.

While the First Amendment secures the free exercise of religion, most privacy cases on religion rely on the Fourteenth Amendment, to prohibit discrimination on the basis of religion. The First Amendment also guarantees freedom of the press and forbids the government from controlling what is published.

Invasions of privacy of belief

The Supreme Court has rejected state-sponsored efforts to impose an official belief. The Court has held that when the state issues a moral judgment, based on strong moral and religious beliefs held by many of its constituents, and enforces that judgment on others despite their individual moral and religious beliefs, that this is unconstitutional. *West Virginia State Board of Education v. Barnette*, 319 U.S. 624 (1943) and *Wooley v. Maynard*, 430 U.S. 705 (1977). Both cases involved members of the Jehovah's Witnesses.

In *Barnette*, the West Virginia Board of Education adopted rules that required that all public school students salute the flag and recite the Pledge of Allegiance. Students who did not participate could be expelled, and their parents could lose custody of them. Several Jehovah Witness families challenged the West Virginia law on First Amendment grounds. They argued that the compulsory flag salute clashed with their religious beliefs against idol worship and graven images, and, therefore, violated their free exercise of religion and freedom of speech rights under the First Amendment.

By a 6–3 vote, the Supreme Court held that school officials had violated the First Amendment by compelling students to salute the flag and recite the Pledge of Allegiance. The court reasoned that the First Amendment prohibits the government officials from compelling individuals to speak or espouse certain beliefs that conflict with their conscience and values. "There is no doubt that, in connection with the pledges, the flag salute is a form of utterance." The court ruled that the purpose of the First Amendment is to ensure that individuals have an individual sphere of freedom of thought and belief that the government cannot invade. "Authority here is to be controlled by public opinion, not public opinion by authority." Justice Robert Jackson wrote that, "If there is any fixed star in our constitutional constellation, it is that no official, high or petty, can prescribe what shall be orthodox in

politics, nationalism, religion, or other matters of opinion or force citizens to confess by word or act their faith therein."

Jackson's opinion was based not so much on religious freedom grounds, as on the broader freedom of belief and conscience. "Struggles to coerce uniformity of sentiment in support of some end thought essential" have been waged by good and by evil men throughout history, Jackson wrote, and the battle over "what a doctrine and whose program public educational officials shall compel youth to unite in embracing" is but one example. The "coercive elimination of dissent," he cautioned, soon devolves into "exterminating dissenters."

Justice Felix Frankfurter, writing in dissent, said, "An act compelling profession of allegiance to a religion, no matter how subtly or tenuously promoted, is bad. However, an act promoting good citizenship and national allegiance is within the domain of governmental authority and is, therefore, to be judged by the same considerations of power and of constitutionality as those involved in the many claims of immunity from civil obedience because of religious scruples."

George Maynard and his wife were Jehovah's Witnesses who lived in New Hampshire. The law in that state required them to display license plates, which contained the motto "Live Free or Die." The Maynards objected to the motto as violative of their moral, religious, and political beliefs. For this reason, they covered up the motto on the license plates of their automobiles. In late 1974, George Maynard received a citation for violating the state statute forbidding the obscuring of the state motto. The Supreme Court, in a six to three decision, held that the state's requirement that its citizens display the state motto on their license plates was unconstitutional. Chief Justice Burger, writing for the Court, found that the statute mandated state residents to utilize "their private property as a 'mobile billboard' for the State's ideological message." The Court further ruled that the

State's interests in requiring that the motto being displayed did not outweigh free speech principles under the First Amendment, including "the right of individuals to hold a point of view different from the majority and to refuse to foster ... an idea they find morally objectionable." The state's interest in motor vehicle identification, thus, was achievable by "less drastic means," and its interest in generating state pride did not outweigh the Maynard's First Amendment rights.

During the 1950s, the Supreme Court acknowledged that compelled disclosure, in itself, can seriously infringe on privacy of association and belief guaranteed by the First Amendment: and that the invasion of privacy of belief may be as great when the formation sought concerns the giving and spending of many as when it concerns the joining of organizations. In *Nat'l Ass'n for Advancement of Colored People v. State of Ala. ex rel. Patterson*, the Supreme Court upheld an NAACP's right to keep the names of its members secret for their protection. The court held The right of expressive association recognizes the right of the people to come together to advocate for religious, political, fraternal, or any other reasons related to the liberty interest. For example, the government cannot prohibit an individual from affiliating with particular political causes, however offensive others may consider those groups.

Further Reading

Cappel, James J. "A Study of Individuals' Ethical Beliefs and Perceptions of Electronic Mail Privacy." *Journal of Business Ethics J Bus Ethics*: 819–27.

Duda, Nancy Lee. *The Intersection of Privacy Concern and Trust: Beliefs of Privacy Orientation Groups*. 2004.

Johnson, Johna Till. "Privacy Discussion Overdue." *Network World*, August 28, 2006. "Justice Scalia Challenges Privacy Rights at Conference." *Church & State*, March 2009.

Lerner, Natan. *Religion, Beliefs, and International Human Rights*. Maryknoll, N.Y.: Orbis Books, 2000.

Lever, Annabelle. *On Privacy*. New York: Routledge, 2012.

Li, Han, Rathindra Sarathy, and Jie Zhang. "The Role of Emotions in Shaping Consumers' Privacy Beliefs about Unfamiliar Online Vendors." *Journal of Information Privacy and Security*: 36–62.

Lin, Zhen Owen. "Genomic Research and Human Subject Privacy." *Science*, July 9, 2004

McThomas, Mary. *The Dual System of Privacy Rights in the United States*. Hoboken: Taylor and Francis, 2013.

Notturno, Mark Amadeus. *Privacy and Privacy Rights*. Parkersburg, WV: Interactivity Foundation Press, 2005.

Watkins, Tamara E. "Privacy, the Individual, and the 'Good' Society. (Philosophy)." *Michigan Academician*, March 22, 2002.

Wolfe, Alan. "The Politics of Privacy, Right and Left." *Harper's Magazine*, May 1, 1993.

See also: First Amendment; Legal evolution of privacy rights in the United States; Philosophical basis of privacy; Private sphere; Supreme Court of the United States.

Big data

Identification: A massive volume of intricate and jumbled data-sets generated and output every second of every day, and subsequently subject to analysis.

The actual, quantifiable measurements of big data are not yet known. The Intel Corporation has suggested that any company produces data that is Big when it generates, per week, a median of 300 terabytes of data (Ward et al. 2013). In one of a series of White House reports issued concerning big data, the authors (2014) note that data created worldwide has either reached, or exceeded, 4 zettabytes. A 2011 article featured in UK magazine *The Guardian*, titled "What's a Zettabyte? By 2015, the Internet Will Know, says Cisco," equates a zettabyte to roughly the virtual storage space occupied by 250 billion DVDs. However, this degree of data, incredible though it seems, represents only the "very nascent stage" of the digital revolution. In essence, big data are quantities of data so large and complex, customary database systems cannot yet withstand the capacity. But with the advent of cloud computing, the internal infrastructure of

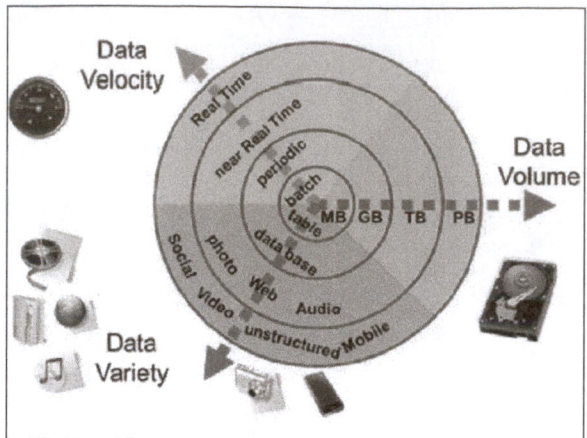

Shows the growth of big data's primary characteristics of volume, velocity, and variety. (By Ender005.)

companies, housed in the cloud, can document and mostly regulate data being transmitted via social media, mobile devices, GPS, any machines with readable Internet signals, and telecommunication channels. As a result, data mining or analytics, data-intensive computing, individual autonomy, consumer protection and how each relates to privacy are concepts dominating current public discourse.

Different individuals and organizations access big data for different purposes. This, in part, explains why multiple definitions arise in discussions and analyses on the topic. A commonly quoted definition, though, is credited to research firm Gartner, Inc., which linked the "3 Vs" model with big data. Since then, Volume, Variety, and Velocity—better known as the 3 Vs—has come to signify a quick and dirty rundown of big data. In previous years analytics tools for big data existed, but at an exorbitant fee. However, as technology continues to advance at breakneck speed, big data analytics has become an achievable goal for many companies, directly impacting consumers. Concerns related to differential pricing—three types of price discriminations that affect consumers—prompted the White House to report on the subject, the steps they are putting into place to protect consumers from unfair price discrimination, as well as the steps consumers can take to protect their fami-

lies and themselves. Yet, for business leaders who choose to use big data justly, the insights revealed by the data have the power to innovate industry like never before. The medical and scientific communities have also taken note of the unparalleled results obtained through synthesis of big data. For example, a study conducted by British researchers assessed a big data set of Autism-Spectrum Quotient (AQ) questionnaires completed by 450,394 persons (*Ruzich et al. 2015*). The findings, extracted from the largest set of AQ scores to date, establish invaluable statistics on the sex and careers of individuals who are diagnosed with autism or display autistic traits.

The investment in big data now outweighs the cost, and the future promises to deliver more tightly refined, efficient resources to the main players in the big data community—namely businesses, governments, medical and health sectors. Consequently, the need for data scientists and other professionals versed in statistics, computer science, and mathematics will only increase. Time will tell, however, if these advancements will also increase the threat to individual civil rights, and freedom of speech.

Lauren Perelli

Further Reading

Barker, Adam and Jonathan Stuart Ward, "Undefined By Data: A Survey of Big Data Definitions," *arXiv preprint arXiv:1309.5821*, 2013. http://arxiv.org/abs/1309.5821.

Brehm, Robert P. "What CIOs and CTOs Need to Know About Big Data and Data Intensive Computing." PhD diss., University of Oregon, 2012.

De Mauro, Andrea, Marco Greco, and Michele Grimaldi. "What is Big Data? A Consensual Definition and a Review of Key Research Topics." *AIP Conference Proceedings* 1644, no. 97 (2015). doi: 10.1063/1.4907823.

Dumbill, Edd. Volume, Velocity, Variety: What You Need to Know About Big Data. Forbes, January 19, 2012. http://www.forbes.com/sites/oreillymedia/2012/01/19/volume-velocity-variety-what-you-need-to-know-about-big-data/.

Executive Office of the Presiden*t. Big Data: Seizing Opportunities, Preserving Values*. The White House. May 1, 2014. https://www.whitehouse.gov/sites/default/files/docs/big_data_privacy_report_may_1_2014.pdf.

Executive Office of the President. *Big Data and Differential Pricing.* The White House. February 2015. https://www.whitehouse.gov/sites/default/files/docs/Big_Data_Report_Nonembargo_v2.pdf.

President's Council of Advisors on Science & Technology. *Big Data and Privacy: A Technological Perspective.* The White House. May 1, 2014. https://www.whitehouse.gov/sites/default/files/microsites/ostp/PCAST/pcast_big_data_and_privacy_-_may_2014.pdf .

Ruzich, Emily, Carrie Allison, Bhismadev Chakrabarti, Paula Smith, Henry Musto, Howard Ring, and Simon Baron-Cohen. "Sex and STEM Occupation Predict Autism-Spectrum Quotient (AQ) Scores in Half a Million People." *PLoS One* 10, no. 10 (2015): e0141229.

Tanner, Adam. Different Customers, Different Prices, Thanks To Big Data. *Frobes,* April 14, 2014. http://www.forbes.com/sites/adamtanner/2014/03/26/different-customers-different-prices-thanks-to-big-data/.

Yan, Jean. "Big Data, Bigger Opportunities - Data.gov's Roles: Promote, Lead, Contribute, and Collaborate in the Era of Big Data." 2012 President Management Council Inter-Agency Rotation Program, Cohort 2, April 9, 2013. http://www.meritalk.com/pdfs/bdx/bdx-whitepaper-090413.pdf.

See also: Computers and privacy; Data Harvesting; Data Science; Global Positioning Systems: Social Media

Bioethics

Identification: An interdisciplinary field of study that analyzes the ethical and philosophical implications of medical and scientific research, policy, and practice.

Bioethics is a relatively new field of study, having taken shape in the 1960s in response to unprecedented advances in medicine and technology as well as international events that required the development of internationally recognized medical ethics. It is generally understood to comprise three primary subdisciplines: medical ethics, animal ethics, and environmental ethics. Additional subfields within bioethics include research ethics, clinical ethics, population ethics, ethics of new technologies, neuroethics, and global ethics. Common issues that bioethicists examine include gene manipulation, abortion, euthanasia, reproductive technology, natural resources, allocation of healthcare resources, cloning, human and animal testing, organ transplantation, artificial life, eugenics, pollution, and the moral status of animals. Bioethicists may have professional training in medicine, law, genetics, philosophy, public health, sociology, anthropology, and other related fields.

The origins of bioethics as a distinct academic discipline can be traced to Van Rensselaer Potter's seminal book, *Bioethics: Bridge to the Future*, and Dan Callahan's 1973 article, "Bioethics as a Discipline." In particular, Callahan pushed for the academy to develop bioethics as an independent field of study and its disciplinary standards, criteria of excellence, and clear pedagogical and evaluative norms. Callahan also founded and directed the Institute for Society, Ethics and the Life Sciences (now the Hastings Center). In addition to Potter and Callahan's influence, the Rose Kennedy Center for the Study of Human Reproduction and Bioethics (now the Kennedy Institute of Ethics) was established in 1971, which was a concerted effort among scholars to promote the examination of medical dilemmas by engaging with moral philosophical standards.

Once established, the bioethics discipline was primarily associated with medical ethics, and the environmental and animal ethics subfields developed at a much later date. The demand for a robust set of medical ethics emerged from certain historical events that presented new moral and ethical dilemmas in the medical field.

The first major international event that hastened the need to develop a standard of medical ethics occurred during World War II. During Germany's occupation of Europe, Nazi scientists and doctors conducted extensive human research experiments that led to many deaths or severe disabilities. Nazi doctors used prisoners as test subjects—without their consent—to experiment with drugs, diseases, head injuries, hormone therapy, and other physically invasive research. Though many of the Nazi experiments are now considered to have been medical torture, at the time no set of medical ethics had been developed to place recognized limits on doctors for conducting scientific tests on human life.

After World War II ended, the United States conducted a series of twelve military trials for war crimes committed by Nazi leaders. In particular, the Doctor's Trial focused on the Nazi scientists and doctors involved with the human experimentation of prisoners. As a result of the trials, a set of ten medical research principles were produced, later known as the Nuremberg Code. In addition to the Nuremberg Code, the World Medical Association, in 1964, developed its own set of ethical principles regarding human experimentation and research, known as the Declaration of Helsinki. The declaration was particularly noteworthy because its creation was the medical community's first major internal attempt to regulate human research.

In the United States, the Tuskegee Syphilis Study served as another significant impetus for establishing a widely recognized set of medical ethics. The study, executed by the U.S. Public Health Service between 1933 and 1972, was aimed at researching and better understanding the natural progression of untreated syphilis in African American men. The men were provided with medical care, meals, and burial insurance for their participation, but none of them were notified if they were in fact infected with the disease. Despite the advent of penicillin—an effective treatment for the disease—in the 1940s, doctors failed to treat any of the men and instead continued to monitor the progression of syphilitic patients without informing them of an accurate diagnosis. Ultimately, as a result of the study, several men died, many wives of the participants were infected, and dozens of children were born with congenital syphilis.

The widespread exposure and ethical failings of the Tuskegee Syphilis Study led to significant changes in U.S. law and medical ethics regulation generally. In 1974, the U.S. Congress enacted the National Research Act, which established the National Commission for the Pro-

tection of Human Services of Biomedical and Behavioral Research. The commission published the *Belmont Report* in 1979, which was a major blueprint for advanced ethical principles and guidelines involving human research and experimentation. The *Belmont Report* established three fundamental ethical principles: (1) respect for persons, (2) beneficence, and (3) justice. These three principles remain the basis for protecting and regulating human subject research in the United States and abroad.

The U.S. Department of Health and Human Services established the Office for Human Research Protections, which continues to serve as an ethical oversight of clinical research conducted in the United States. The office regulates institutional review boards (IRBs), which serves as a formal review of the institutional procedures for proposed studies on human subjects. IRBs regulate institutional procedures and protect research participants by ensuring the ethical and fair treatment of patients. IRBs continue to rely on the *Belmont Report*'s principles in evaluating proposed scientific and medical studies.

Ultimately, a broad range of ethical and practical problems has arisen as a result of rapid development and progress in science, technology, medicine, and globalization. The objective of bioethics is to guide and establish a set of ethical limits and best practices as technological advances trigger new inventions and treatments related to the human body, the environment, and animals.

Ethan P. Fallon

Further Reading

Baker, Robert. "A Theory of International Bioethics: The Negotiable and Non-Negotiable." *Kennedy Institute of Ethics Journal* 8, no. 3 (1998): 233–273.

Callahan, Daniel. "Bioethics as a Discipline." *Hastings Center Studies* 1 (1973): 66–73.

Holland, Stephen. "The Virtue Ethics Approach to Bioethics." *Bioethics* 25, no. 4 (2011): 192–201.

Jonsen, Albert R. "The History of Bioethics as a Discipline." *Philosophy and Medicine* 78 (2004): 31–51.

Jonsen, Albert R. *A Short History of Medical Ethics*. New York: Oxford University Press, 2008.

Pellegrino, E. "Toward a Virtue-Based Normative Ethics for the Health Professions." *Kennedy Institute of Ethics Journal* 5, no. 3 (1995): 253–277.

Pence, Gregory. *Elements of Bioethics.* New York: McGraw-Hill, 2007.

Potter, Van Rensselaer. "Bioethics: The Science of Survival." *Perspectives in Biology and Medicine* 14, no. 2 (1970): 127–153.

Singer, Peter. *Animal Liberation: A New Ethics for Our Treatment of Animals.* New York: Random House, 1975.

See also: Body, privacy of the; End-of-life care; Fair Information Practice Principles (FIPPs); Genome sequencing

Biometric Center of Excellence

Identification: Established in 2007 by the Science and Technology Branch of the Federal Bureau of Investigation (FBI) to explore, advance, and develop the use of new and enhanced biometric technologies, capabilities, standards, and policies, for integration into operations.

The overall mission of the Biometric Center of Excellence (BCOE) is to strengthen criminal investigative capability and enhance national security. Stemming from a need to approach and manage the growing biometric activities and priorities of the FBI more efficiently, the BCOE is essentially a consortium of the services and expertise of three divisions—the Criminal Justice Information Division, Laboratory Division, and Operational Technology Division—intended to foster collaboration, improve information sharing, and advance the adoption of optimal biometric and identity solutions.

This collaboration helps to eliminate a major challenge—the capability gap—by providing available biometric capabilities while assessing future needs. Outside the FBI, the center regularly works with the Office of the Director of National Intelligence, Department of Homeland Security, Department of Defense, and Department of Justice, as well as other law enforcement agencies and national security communities. The BCOE also sponsors research, evaluates technologies, develops training, establishes standards, and certifies biometric products. The BCOE addresses privacy and procedural and policy issues related to the use of biometric systems while working in compliance with privacy laws, policies, and regulations.

The center is located in Clarksburg, West Virginia, and engages in a wide range of biometric projects and initiatives. In 2014, the new Next Generation Identification (NGI) system became fully operational, replacing the FBI's Integrated Automated Fingerprint Identification System (IAFIS), which was implemented in 1999. The new upgrade provides faster and more advanced biometric identification services through multimodal functionality, such as the Advanced Fingerprint Identification Technology (AFIT), which improved processing and accuracy of fingerprinting services from 92 percent to 99.6 percent; the Repository for Individuals of Special Concern (RISC), which is a rapid search facility allowing officers to screen individuals against a repository of wanted individuals and persons of interest; the Interstate Photo System (IPS), which is an expansive database of front-facing photos used in facial recognition searches; the Latents and National Palm Print System (NPPS), which contains millions of searchable palm prints; and Iris Recognition (IR), which is a new tool to determine identity based on eye characteristics quickly and accurately.

In addition, other emerging biometric modalities include footprint and hand geometry and handwriting collection, gait recognition, speech and voice recognition, and the Combined DNA Index System (CODIS), which contains nearly 11.5 million offender DNA profiles. In 2012, the center began working with a range of experts in academia and the private sector to create a tattoo database, which also includes other body marks, scars, and blemishes, as well as graffiti and other symbols used by offenders. In 2015, the BCOE hosted the Tattoo Recognition Challenge in partnership with the National Institute for Standards and Technology. Programmers developed algorithms using surveillance technologies to identify individuals digitally based on scans of tattoos; offenders are more likely than other people to have such body artwork.

Undoubtedly, the use of biometric technology has provided law enforcement agencies and intelligence services with many capabilities over the years. For more than a century, police have relied on fingerprints to solve crimes, and over decades, forensic DNA profiling has become an invaluable technique for bringing offenders to justice, as well as exonerating those wrongly accused. Today, biometric technologies such as facial identification and speech and voice recognition are regarded as crucial for combating terrorism, transnational crime, and other serious offenses. Despite the security benefits these technologies afford society, however, their widespread use also entails serious issues, including technological challenges and concerns for individual citizens' rights of privacy.

Many forms of identification, such as driver's licenses, passports, and other identity cards, are increasingly being combined with biometric information. This wealth of personal information will require more advanced data protection measures, encryption technologies, and other safeguarding measures, both to encourage their acceptance and use by the civilian population and to keep this vital information from falling into the wrong hands. Still, biometric data may be used by governments in many ways. Critics such as the American Civil Liberties Union (ACLU) are concerned that such power may be easily abused for unethical purposes. While biometric technologies have advanced rapidly, they are still prone to technological shortcomings, such as computer errors and glitches, which can misidentify individuals, leak sensitive personal data, and lead to other privacy-related issues.

Michael J. Puniskis

Further Reading

Hossain, S. M. E., and G. Chetty. "Human Identity Verification Using Physiological and Behavioral Biometric Traits." *International Journal of Bioscience, Biochemistry and Bioinformatics* 1, no. 3 (2011): 199–205.

Probhakar, S., S. Pankanti, and A. K. Jain. "Biometric Recognition: Security and Privacy Concerns." *IEEE Security and Privacy* 2, no. 1 (2003): 33–42.

Vacca, John R. *Biometric Technologies and Verification Systems*. Boston, MA: Butterworth-Heinemann/Elsevier, 2007.

See also: American Civil Liberties Union (ACLU); Biometrics; Integrated Automated Fingerprint Identification System (IAFIS), Next Generation Identification (NGI); Repository for Individuals of Special Concern (RISC)

Biometric Optical Surveillance System

Identification: A system with the capacity to recognize faces and match them with personal identification information.

Government agencies and federal, state, and local law enforcement developed Biometric Optical Surveillance System (BOSS) to store and utilize this data legally, as needed. Government agencies, particularly public safety agencies, are major collectors of data. The U.S. government operates some of the largest biometric identification systems in the world. The Department of Homeland Security (DHS) maintains automated biometric identification systems (IDENT) that have a database of more than 126 million records and conducts 250,000 biometric transactions per day averaging 10 seconds or less per transaction. BOSS can perform real-time facial recognition and also capture the iris data from 10 meters away while a person is in motion.

Even though American citizens have an expectation of privacy, this right is balanced against the needs public for safety and national security. Personal information is stored, linked, and shared among law enforcement agencies to ensure public safety, but this use may involve some trade-offs in terms of individual privacy. Cyber-tampering is a real risk based on how much and how often this information is used and secured. Inadequate security may allow criminals to access this information and allow personal identification information to be compromised.

The Federal Bureau of Investigation (FBI) has invested over $1 billion in facial recognition technology (FRT). The technology was used initially to collect information of known criminals or terrorists, but the use of facial recognition data was expanded in DHS, FBI, and other law enforcement organizations. The same storage of information was later expanded to driver's license images. Combined efforts of collection with funding increases the surveillance of video images and also introduces the risk to the personal identification information attached to that record. Citizen concerns arise from the fact that no specific permission was required either because the images were captured in public areas from surveillance cameras or because the consumers were unaware that their driver's license photos would be used for these purposes. Law enforcement and government officials are free to use the image information collected when they decide it is necessary for public safety reasons.

Whether the risk involved with using FRT is worth the protection or public safety also must be considered. The theft of the data either from transmission, during collection, or while it is being used within BOSS presents a real threat to private personal information. Law enforcement commonly uses this information to track down criminals, so it also makes information vulnerable to capture by criminals. BOSS makes the personal images and personal identification information available to its users for public safety reasons, but it cannot guarantee protection of personal information to citizens, who have never authorized their information to be utilized in this way. Law enforcement officials argue it is worth the risk for public safety purposes. Some privacy advocates express concern that the risk is not worth what they view as weak guarantees of protection.

The aggregation of data from several different sources can pose a serious privacy threat.

The theft of biometric information could facilitate criminal access to bank accounts and credit cards. There is a danger of data creep, where information voluntarily provided to one law enforcement agency may be transferred without permission to another government agency, then linked with other data or applied to a new and unauthorized purpose. At the same time, the unregulated scope of data collection, sharing, linking, and storing could invite misuse. Law enforcement officials are aware of the risks involved in the usage of BOSS. They trust that the government surveillance is necessary in these instances and requires support.

How should BOSS be regulated so that the legitimate privacy rights of U.S. citizens are not violated? One proposal is to limit access to BOSS as much as possible. Two policies are necessary to provide adequate parameters for BOSS. First, facial recognition databases should be populated only with images of known terrorists and convicted felons. Driver's license photos and other images of innocent people should never be included in a facial recognition database without the knowledge and consent of the public. Second, access to databases should be limited and monitored. Police officers should be given access only after a court grants a warrant. The access should be tracked and audited. The authorities should have to record publicly what databases are being mined and provide aggregate numbers on how often they are used.

These policy measures will not prevent all information theft, but regulation will ensure that it is less likely to occur. Responsibly tracked and audited use of BOSS ensures that the database is used for the purposes for which it is intended. Involving the judicial system in determining whether the information obtained is necessary adds an impartial and legal element to BOSS's usage that should protect the rights of citizens. Judicial oversight also reduces the danger that this information will be accessed for improper purposes. Tracking the usage of the information will ensure greater accountability for users of the system. For example, if the information is used for improper purposes, then proper corrective actions can be taken Auditing may add an increased amount of efficiency to its use: The information and why it is being accessed will be tracked, and its effectiveness in maintaining public safety will be clear. Limiting the use and requesting permission prior to use can be added measures taken by law enforcement and government to protect the personal identification information or privacy of citizens, whether or not they are aware of BOSS. These policies do not discourage the funding already invested in the program, but they can assure the public that the use of personal identification information is not freely or secretly operated within BOSS.

Public awareness that BOSS is being used can be helpful in deterring crime, assure citizens that they are being protected, and encourage law enforcement to continue to implement new and innovative methods in the digital age.

Shaunté Chácon

Further Reading

Cooper, Candance. "Preparing for Biometrics and Drones in the 'Post Privacy' Era". *Corporate Legal Times* (November 2014).

McCall, Ginger. "The Face Scan Arrives." *New York Times* (August 30, 2013).

Shelton-Mason County Journal Staff. "Codewords, Secrecy Become Clearer." *Shelton-Mason County Journal* (August 2013).

See also: Biometrics; Department of Homeland Security; Facial recognition technology; Law enforcement

Biometrics

Identification: A term derived from the Greek words *bios* ("life") and *metrikos* ("measure"), any personal physical feature unique to an individual, such as fingerprints, iris scans, DNA, and facial geometry.

Biometrics are unique data markers. They identify using intrinsic physical or behavioral characteristics, which include face prints (facial recognition-ready photographs), iris scans, palm prints, voice prints, wrist veins, and a person's gait. Behavioral biometrics are nonbiological or nonphysiological features such as distinctive and unique mannerisms (signature or keystroke patterns, habitual behaviors). The concept of identifying individuals using unique biometric features goes back centuries. The ancient Egyptians and Babylonians used fingerprints for the same purpose they are used today. While fingerprints have been collected for generations, the newest biometrics technology provides real-time capture of considerably more biometric data and advances in digital storage technology. This enables the permanent storage of large amounts of very detailed data.

Biometrics are used mostly for authentication and identification by governments, employers, and various service providers. Data collection is easily done and does not require cooperation or awareness of the target. Government agencies, particularly law enforcement agencies, are the largest data collectors. The U.S. government operates some of the largest biometric identification systems in the world. The Department of Homeland Security (DHS) maintains an automated biometric identification system (IDENT). IDENT maintains a database of more than 126 million records and conducts about 250,000 biometric transactions, averaging 10 seconds or less per transaction, every day. The DHS Biometric Optical Surveillance System (BOSS) performs real-time facial recognition and can capture iris data from a target 10 meters away even while the individual is moving.

As biometric technology has expanded, the capacity to store and disseminate the collected data has increased dramatically. Most local and national law enforcement agencies seek to make the communication between their various databases seamless and responses to inquiries quick and accurate. The ability to integrate and store information from many different databases has dramatically increased the value of biometric data to organizations. However, it also has dramatically increased the risks that come with collecting and maintaining it.

Privacy advocates expressed their great concern about the use of biometrics in law enforcement. With the combined use of surveillance tools such as facial recognition technology, many fear that the United States is entering a regime of pervasive, all-encompassing surveillance. The use of biometrics does entail various and serious privacy risks, including identity theft, function creep, and government surveillance.

There is greater safety and convenience in using biometrics rather than older forms of personal recognition. In some cases, biometrics may be used to replace or supplement the existing technology. In others, biometrics is the only viable approach given the circumstances.

Biometrics is better than traditional recognition in several different cases. In some applications, it either replaces or supplements existing technologies; in others, biometrics is the only reasonable approach to personal recognition. As the infrastructure for reliable automatic personal recognition continues to be developed along with the ability to associate an identity with other personal behavior, privacy advocates express increasing concern that this information might violate individual privacy rights.

A human physiological or behavioral trait may be a biometric characteristic if it meets the following features: (1) the trait must be universal (each person has the characteristic) and (2) distinctive (the characteristic is unique for each person), and the trait must be (3) permanent (the characteristic should be sufficiently invariant; that is, it must match the criterion over a certain period of time), and (4) collectible (the characteristic should be quantitatively measurable). To be practical, a functioning biometric system must reach acceptable levels of performance, acceptability, and circumvention. It must also be sufficiently strong to withstand various fraudulent methods and attacks.

A biometric system uses pattern recognition to recognize a particular person based on a specific physical or behavioral characteristic possessed by a particular person. Depending on the application context, a biometric system typically operates in one of two modes: verification mode or identification mode. In the verification mode, the system confirms the person's identity by comparing the captured biometric characteristic with the individual's biometric template, which is stored in the system database.

Biometrics raises several concerns:

1. *Unintended functional scope.* Because biometric identifiers are biological in origin, collectors might glean additional personal information from the biometric measurements.

2. *Unintended application scope.* Strong biometric identifiers such as fingerprints allow for possibly unwanted identifications

3. *Covert recognition.* A biometric sample, such as a person's face, may be retrieved without the target person knowing it. This means that individuals who seek to maintain their anonymity could have their privacy rights violated by biometric recognition.

Possible abuse of biometric information (or its derivatives) can be prevented or mitigated through several methods:

1. *Government legislation and regulation.* The European Union (EU) has adopted legislation against sharing biometric identifiers and personal information.

2. *Assurance of self-regulation.* A group of biometric vendors could join to agree to be bound by ethical guidelines in their operations.

3. *Autonomous enforcement* by independent regulatory organizations, such as a central biometrics agency.

Many business functions require highly reliable personal recognition. Because conventional processes and token-based processes rely on surrogate representations of a person's identity to ensure personal recognition, any system that assures reliable positive personal recognition must use a biometric module. In fact, a sound personal recognition system design must incorporate many biometric and nonbiometric components.

Biometric-based systems have limitations, however, that may adversely affect their performance. The accuracy of existing biometric systems is not perfect. Sophisticated spoofing may attack a certain biometric system. As biometric technology develops and improves, these limitations most likely will be overcome. But foolproof personal recognition systems are nonexistent. Security is defined as risk-management strategy, which seeks to identify, control, eliminate, or minimize uncertain events that may adversely affect system resources and information assets. A system's security requirements depend on the application's requirements (the threat model) and the cost-benefit analysis. If properly implemented, biometric systems should be effective deterrents to perpetrators.

The use of biometrics indeed raises several serious privacy concerns. A just and equitable trade-off between security and privacy might be necessary. Such an arrangement should be entered into only if it is possible to enforce collective accountability and acceptability standards through legislation. Supporters of the technology claim that biometrics can provide the protections needed to safeguard individuals' right to privacy.

Despite all the claims that biometrics would include privacy safeguards, the use of biometrics is increasingly the subject of lawsuits based on privacy concerns. Frederick William Gullen initiated a class action lawsuit against Facebook, charging that the defendant had violated the Illinois Biometric Information Privacy Act (BIPA). The U.S. District Court, Northern District of Illinois, heard the case.

Gullen argued that the Illinois statute was specifically enacted to prevent private entities from obtaining or having a person's biometrics without explicit permission. Gullen specifically claimed that Facebook had engaged unlawfully in collecting, storing, and using the biometric identifiers and biometric information of individuals without consent, in violation of BIPA. Gullen also alleged that Facebook was doing these actions without notifying the public or informing the public of its data retention procedures. Ironically, Gullen, the plaintiff in the lawsuit, does not have a Facebook profile himself.

Privacy is understood as freedom from unauthorized intrusions. Over time, the concept has transformed from a physical place to include information space. Developments in modern technologies are forcing privacy law to continue to evolve as society seeks to formulate new standards, practices, and perhaps even a fundamental redefinition of privacy itself.

Aggregations of data from several sources into one megadatabase can give rise to serious privacy threats. Biometric information could be stolen, which could allow unauthorized access to a customer's bank accounts and credit cards. Also, data creep is a distinct risk (data creep occurs when information voluntarily transferred to one recipient may be sent without authorization to a second recipient, and then aggregated with other data or used for an unauthorized purpose). In this situation, the unregulated scope of data collection, sharing, linking, and storing could facilitate further misuse.

Further Reading

Bleumer, Gerrit. "Biometric Yet Privacy Protecting Person Authentication." *Information Hiding Lecture Notes in Computer Science*, 99–110.

Booth, Phil. "The UK Should Take Note of the U.S. Biometric Security Projects Says Privacy Advocate." *Computer Fraud & Security* (2007): 7.

Feng, Yicheng, and Pong C. Yuen. "Biometric Template Protection: Towards A Secure Biometric System." *Handbook of Pattern Recognition and Computer Vision.* 455–476.

Galbally, Javier, Julian Fierrez, Javier Ortega-Garcia, and Raffaele Cappelli. "Fingerprint Anti-spoofing in Biometric Systems." *Handbook of Biometric Anti-Spoofing Advances in Computer Vision and Pattern Recognition*, 35–64.

Gelenbe, Erol. *Information Sciences and Systems 2013: Proceedings of the 28th International Symposium on Computer and Information Sciences.*

Jain, Anil K., and Karthik Nandakumar. "Biometric Authentication: System Security and User Privacy." *Computer* 11, no. 45 (2012): 87–92.

Linnartz, Jean-Paul, and Pim Tuyls. "New Shielding Functions to Enhance Privacy and Prevent Misuse of Biometric Templates." *Lecture Notes in Computer Science Audio- and Video-Based Biometric Person Authentication*. 393–402.

Liu, Chengjun, and V. K. Mago. *Cross Disciplinary Biometric Systems*. Berlin: Springer, 2012.

Liu, Yue. "Rational Concerns about Biometric Technology." *Computer Security, Privacy and Politics: Current Issues, Challenges and Solutions* (2008): 94–134.

Marcel, Se. *Handbook of Biometric Anti-spoofing: Trusted Biometrics under Spoofing Attacks.*

Mckenna, Brian. "Privacy Advocate Warns Biometric Industry to Stay Clear of Government." *Computer Fraud & Security* 11 (2004): 3.

Wirtz, Brigitte. "Technical Evaluation of Biometric Systems." *Computer Vision—ACCV'98 Lecture Notes in Computer Science*. 499–506.

Woodard, Damon L., and Patrick J. Flynn. "Finger Surface as a Biometric Identifier." *Computer Vision and Image Understanding* 100, no. 3 (2005): 357–384.

See also: Biometric Optical Surveillance System (BOSS); Department of Homeland Security; DNA; Law enforcement

Blockchain technologies

Identification: Emerging technologies allowing for decentralized, semi-anonymous, and pseudonymous exchanges, whether of information or of financial or other assets.

This essay will explain the general design elements of a blockchain and then address its implications for privacy.

Design of a blockchain

A blockchain is a decentralized database that uses encryption to verify digital transactions made across a computer network. Although the technical details of a blockchain may seem overwhelmingly complex, the basic design elements are quite simple. The four most basic design elements in a blockchain are nodes, public ledgers, blocks, and chains. Nodes are individual computers, or clients, that connect to one another through a blockchain protocol. Public ledgers record all transactions made over the blockchain protocol. Blocks are a list of verified transactions that will be added to a public ledger. Chains connect blocks of verified transactions by linking them to one another in the public ledger.

A bitcoin transaction may serve as one example of a real-world application of a blockchain, illustrating how these different elements interact. On the bitcoin blockchain, the individual nodes are computers connected to one another as a secure network. When two nodes exchange information over the secure network, they complete a bitcoin transaction. If Mary logs on to the bitcoin network and sends Peter a bitcoin, their transaction is a simple example of a bitcoin transaction.

In a blockchain network, all transactions are recorded in what we may think of as a public ledger. This is similar to an accounting ledger, wherein the same information is recorded for each transaction that is made. So when Mary pays Peter a bitcoin, the public ledger is updated to reflect who was paid, when the person was paid, and for what amount.

The recording in a public ledger begins with the very first transaction made between two nodes, and the public ledger is continually updated to reflect each new transaction. In practice, this means that a copy of the public ledger for every transaction ever completed on the bitcoin blockchain is stored for every node connected to the bitcoin network.

In every blockchain application, a network of nodes is involved in making and recording transactions, as well as verifying that a transaction is credible. This verification step ensures that fraudulent activity is prevented. For example, on the bitcoin blockchain, how do we know Mary has enough bitcoin to pay Peter? Or what if Mary actually paid Peter and Paul the same bitcoin at the same time? A blockchain is designed to prevent this by requiring that transactions be verified *before* they can be completed. Each attempted transaction will be checked against the public ledger to verify whether the transaction is credible.

Simultaneously verifying each transaction, recording it, and then updating a public ledger would be incredibly expensive computationally if it required every node on the network to perform these actions simultaneously. Instead, a blockchain gets some nodes in the network to perform these tasks by rewarding them with new bitcoins. So in exchange for handling the computational burden of verifying a transaction, bitcoin nodes can earn as well as spend digital currency. In practice, this is achieved when individual transactions—which are cryptographically encoded—are solved by being decoded. As individual nodes become more certain about the credibility of a transaction, such transactions are grouped into blocks. A simple analogy is that blocks are like a page in a ledger. When a big enough of a block has been assembled, it can be distributed rapidly to all of the other nodes in the network. Nodes in the bitcoin network then update their public ledger by adding a new block of verified transactions.

By requiring nodes to verify transactions against all existing public ledgers, blocks enable a kind of "double entry accounting." This ensures that no other node in the network can defraud another node. This double-entry accounting is made possible because blocks of transactions are connected by a "chain" that also verifies each new block is connected to all previous blocks. We can think of chains as the binding of a public ledger securely keeping many pages (blocks) in a correct order so that a full history of transactions is securely maintained.

In summary, a bitcoin blockchain consists of a network of nodes making transactions.

These transactions are verified when other nodes in the network solve a cryptographic code. As these nodes solve more and more codes, the transactions that are verified as credible are then assembled into blocks. The blocks are sent out to every node connected to the blockchain network to update its public ledger. Blocks are connected to one another in the ledger through chains to verify that the correct order and history of verified transactions has been preserved.

Immutability and decentralization

A unique design aspect of a blockchain is that public ledgers are immutable; they can be updated only by recording new transactions. This also means that public ledgers can never be appended or modified to change previous transactions. In some sense, this immutability is what allows for authority, validity, and trust to be decentralized in a blockchain. Because a blockchain relies on an entire network of double-entry verification, it is very hard for individual nodes to perform fraudulent transactions against the network. The system of peer-to-peer trust enabled by a blockchain is radically different than—for instance—current approaches to banking that rely on a centralized, or single-point, transaction verification. In a centralized verification system, only one node must be convinced that a fraudulent transaction is credible.

Although this decentralized design is difficult to defraud, critics rightly point out that, in the current blockchain architecture, there are exploitable features of how transactions are combined into blocks. When blocks are assembled too quickly, there is a risk of accepting fraudulent transactions in favor of speeding up network performance. In contrast, slowing down a network by creating a higher threshold of verification creates latency in processing individual transactions. This latency could in turn prohibit broad adoption of a payment system like bitcoin. These vulnerabilities pose a major design challenge for future applications of the blockchain and of decentralized verification systems more generally.

Current applications

The most popular current application of a blockchain is to verify financial transactions such as the bitcoin example described above. Yet any form of verification, registration, confirmation, or contract may be viewed as being a potential application of the blockchain. Examples of future applications may include an improved identification process for individuals moving between countries (passports), a set of smart contracts that require authentication of many individuals (digital signatures), or even a way to authenticate the origin of rare items such as diamonds (certificates of authenticity).

Blockchain and privacy

One of the major design advantages of a blockchain is that it allows for pseudonyms to be used in place of personally identifying information. For instance, the bitcoin blockchain uses an encrypted public key address—a randomly generated twenty-seven- to thirty-two-digit alphanumeric string—to identify individual nodes that participate in a transaction. Obtaining a public key address can be done through several identity-masking channels, each of which allows an individual to decouple their real-life identity from the transactions they make through a blockchain. Blockchain applications such as bitcoin can therefore be semi-anonymous in the sense that the identity of the person who creates a bitcoin account is not necessary to verify transactions that he or she makes as a node in a blockchain network.

For digital privacy advocates, the blockchain represents an exciting experiment in both semi-anonymous, and pseudonymous information exchange. A decentralized blockchain technology can be applied to many facets of contemporary life, including those currently used by centralized transaction systems in the banking and insurance industries. Even though a decentralized architecture can provide many advantages over a more traditional centralized approach to verification, the two systems can and should coexist.

Nic Weber

Further Reading

Antonopoulos, Andreas M. "Bitcoin Neutrality." Bitcoin 2013 Conference, May 18, 2013, San Jose, CA. YouTube, June 10, 2013. https://www.youtube.com/watch?v=BT8FXQN-9-a.

Omohundro, Steve. "Cryptocurrencies, Smart Contracts, and Artificial Intelligence." *AI Matters* 1, no. 2 (December 2014): 19–21.

Sigal, Mark. "You Say You Want a Revolution? It's Called Post-PC Computing." Radar (O'Reilly), October 24, 2011. http://radar.oreilly.com/2011/10/post-pcrevolution.html.

Swan, Melanie. *Blockchain: Blueprint for a New Economy.* Sebastopol, CA: O'Reilly Media, 2015.

See also: Anonymity and anonymizers; Financial information, The Right to Privacy; Social networking technologies

Body, privacy of the

Identification: The constitutional right enjoyed by all Americans under the Fourth Amendment to the U.S. Constitution to be free from unreasonable searches and seizures of our bodies.

Technologies have advanced much faster, however, than legislatures and courts can respond, and all of our bodily privacy rights have been diminished in the digital age. And that diminishment will only accelerate as the digital age progresses. This essay addresses the privacy of our bodies' externally visible characteristics, of the material our bodies cast off or leave behind, and of our bodies' internal and thus invisible characteristics.

To understand the privacy of our bodies, we must bear in mind that we should logically have very different expectations of privacy for different parts of our bodies. Externally visible characteristics, on the one hand, can be seen by those around us without any need to search, seize, or intrude upon privacy at all. The color of our hair or eyes, our approximate height, weight, facial freckling, dominant-handedness, and so on, are available for all to see; those externally visible characteristics are not really private at all. Evidence that is cast off from our body is deemed abandoned by us, and thus we enjoy no privacy in that cast-off evidence, such as saliva, fingerprints, blood, semen, or urine. But our thoughts, internal disease processes, genetic makeup or predispositions, drug concentrations, alcohol percentages, and the like, are not visible without intrusion or without our consent or other exigency. In other words, those internal body characteristics are private. So the degree of privacy to which our bodies are entitled depends largely on where a body's particular physical characteristic falls on that continuum from externally visible to internal and thus invisible.

The digital age has seriously eroded even the minimal privacy of our bodies' externally visible characteristics by multiplying the kinds and quality of information that can be extracted from otherwise externally visible characteristics. For example, retinal-imaging and facial recognition software allow a person's identity to be remotely and instantaneously ascertained without need for notice, contact, or interview. A person's face has always been externally visible, but in the digital age, a person's face, when coupled with facial recognition software, now tells us much more and with far more specificity and certainty than it ever did before.

The substances and artifacts our bodies leave behind generate a great deal of information and potential evidence about largely or entirely invisible physical characteristics with or without our knowledge or consent. A fingerprint left at a crime scene can be used to identify a perpetrator. A biological specimen—say, from blood, semen, or hair—can yield DNA evidence that can sometimes identify a perpetrator with a billion-to-one probability or even higher.

The advent of touch DNA has further eroded our previous rights to bodily privacy. *Touch DNA*

is the term used to describe how even the slightest and shortest physical touch or presence can leave enough DNA material behind to allow reliable DNA testing of that infinitesimally small sample. In the 1980s, the earliest era of forensic DNA evidence in criminal cases (so-called random fragment length polymorphism [RFLP] DNA testing), a DNA identification could not be obtained without a nondegraded specimen, say, blood, that was about the size of the circumference of a quarter. Today's much more robust DNA testing protocols and approaches (such as polymerase chain reaction-short tandem repeat [PCR-STR] mitochondrial DNA testing, and single nucleotide polymorphisms [SNPs]) allow DNA identifications to be extracted from a biological specimen smaller than an unaided human eye can see. As technology advances, our bodily privacy erodes.

The privacy of what is inside our bodies, hidden from view, has also eroded and will continue to erode in the digital age. A few examples will suffice. Ordinarily, a biological specimen found at a crime scene can be compared against known DNA profiles in the FBI's nationwide CODIS DNA database to identify a match— a person in the database with the same unique DNA profile as the biological specimen at the crime scene. The DNA profiles in the database were previously extracted from persons convicted (or even arrested) for serious crimes, so the law considers those convictees and arrestees less entitled to privacy in their internal DNA profiles. Using what is known as familial DNA, criminal investigators can identify a person as a suspect even through that person has never been convicted or even arrested for a serious crime. Investigators accomplish this by taking advantage of the fact that biological family members, particularly family members of the same gender, share many common DNA features. In this way, the investigators identify first the family of the person who left the DNA at the crime scene, then search for the true perpetrator by examining the family tree. Though the investigators never seized a DNA specimen from the true perpetrator, they were able to look inside to see the unseen DNA profile of the true perpetrator.

Similarly, many other digital age techniques allow investigators to observe unseen invisible bodily characteristics. Investigators can use computerized pharmaceutical databases to determine who is purchasing and ingesting illicit drugs. They use drug recognition protocols to examine externally visible cues to determine the types of drugs contained within a suspect's body. An investigator can use a computerized voice stress analyzer or a polygraph to observe the unseen by determining what a suspect is thinking. At airports, Transportation Safety Administration officers use digital imagery and other nitrate detectors to ascertain whether a person trying to board a plane is carrying or has recently carried weapons or explosives. Border patrol agents use remote imaging devices to determine whether vehicles at or near the border contain hidden persons trying to enter the country illegally.

Even now, in the relatively early stages of the digital age, technology has already dramatically curtailed our bodily privacy. Some have argued that, rather than leave our bodily privacy in the digital age to whatever devices and techniques the engineers can invent, perhaps the only solution is to have Congress draw, in the digital age, the privacy thresholds those engineers and investigators cannot cross.

Charles E. MacLean

Further Reading

Abeyratne, Ruwantissa. "Full Body Scanners at Airports—the Balance between Privacy and State Responsibility." *Journal of Transportation Security*: 73–85.

Hall, John Wesley. *Search and Seizure,* 3rd ed. Charlottesville, VA: LEXIS Law, 2000.

Keizer, Garret. *Privacy.* New York: Picador, 2012.

Klitou, Demetrius. "Body Scanners: A Strip Search by Other Means?" *Information Technology and Law Series Privacy-Invading Technologies and Privacy by Design*: 71–111.

Laws, Joseph, and Yang Cai. "A Privacy Algorithm for 3D Human Body Scans." *Computational Science—ICCS 2006 Lecture Notes in Computer Science*: 870–77.

McKinney, K. D. "Space, Body, and Mind: Parental Perceptions of Children's Privacy Needs." *Journal of Family Issues* (1998): 75–100.

Mironenko, Olga. "Body Scanners versus Privacy and Data Protection." *Computer Law & Security Review*: 232–44.

Panos, Linda. "Privacy in Schools: Dogs, Lockers, Bodies, and Backpacks (Human Rights Law)." *LawNow*, March 1, 2009.

See also: Airport Security Systems; Biometrics; DNA Databases; Genome Sequencing; Home, Privacy of the; Privacy Laws, Federal

Border Security, Immigration Reform, and Privacy

Identification: Illegal immigration to the United States has declined significantly since its peak in the mid-1990s. Yet with some 11 million undocumented immigrants currently residing in the United States, border security and immigration reform have become two of the most partisan and polarizing political issues in the United States today.

President Donald Trump ran on the issue of "building a wall" along the U.S.-Mexican border (i.e., extending the current wall or barrier). Two years into his presidency, after having done little to address the issue, Trump sent troops to the border (October 2018) to dramatize the topic in the context of approaching midterm elections. Two months later he forced a closure of the government over the matter during a budget impasse involving the newly empowered Democratic opposition in the U.S. House of Representatives. Meanwhile, the Trump administration was subjected to intense criticism over its policy of separating young children from their parent(s) at the border, placing them with U.S. caretakers for weeks or even months at a time. The courts, too, found that the recordkeeping in these cases was shoddy, making reunifications of child and parent, or the further processing of their cases, difficult.

Over the years, there have been several efforts at comprehensive immigration reform. All of these more current efforts would have significant privacy implications. By a vote of sixty-eight to thirty-two, the U.S. Senate passed the Border Security, Economic Opportunity, and Immigration Modernization Act of 2013 (S. 744) on June 27, 2013. If enacted, it would have provided stringent enforcement and deportation measures, and it would have enhanced workplace enforcement by mandating that employers use an electronic employment eligibility verification system (E-Verify). In short, it would have been the most important reform of the U.S. immigration system in more than twenty-five years, providing a path to American citizenship for perhaps as many as 11 million illegal immigrants, allocating additional funding for securing the southern border, and restructuring the family immigration system.

In November 2013, however, then–House Speaker John Boehner (R-OH) announced that the House would not consider the legislation in that session of Congress. Immigration reform was dead, and no serious efforts at immigration reform have been made since. The Obama administration and many congressional leaders were committed to legalizing the status of unauthorized migrants, but they also agreed to strengthen border security and immigration control. During the Obama administration, immigration enforcement activity has dramatically increased, including a sharp increase in deportations. State, local, and private entities have also become involved in indirectly enforcing immigration law by regulating access to rights, benefits, and services—including employment, social services, driver's licenses, transportation services, and education—based on citizenship or immigration status. The criminal justice system has also been used increasingly to help enforce immigration policy.

New, increasingly transformative surveillance and dataveillance technologies have been used for immigration enforcement. As in many other areas of government action, immigration control is increasingly becoming an information- centered and technology-driven enterprise. In almost every stage of the immigration process, or even while traveling within the United States, both noncitizens and U.S. citizens are now subject to collection and analysis of extensive quantities of personal information for immigration control and other law enforcement and national security purposes. This information is aggregated and stored by government agencies for extended retention periods in networks of interoperable databases and shared among a variety of public and private entities, both inside and outside the United States, with little transparency, oversight, or accountability. Despite the growing concern about surveillance and data mining in other contexts, the development of surveillance in the context of immigration has been largely ignored. Immigration control, directed primarily against noncitizens at the southern border, is increasingly part of a system of migration and mobility surveillance, with no geographical boundaries, affecting both citizens and noncitizens alike.

Legalization also reinforces immigration surveillance. Like many other aspects of immigration governance, legalization programs (even those providing straightforward amnesty rather than the more rigorous earned legalization) now being proposed necessarily require identification, screening, and authorization of individuals to determine whether they meet certain eligibility criteria and to confer formally the legal status that they seek.

The earned-legalization approaches in many of the comprehensive reform proposals are considerably more complicated and involve stringent initial eligibility criteria and long probationary periods during which applicants must satisfy a series of continuing obligations to "earn" legal status. For example, under the initial eligibility criteria in the Senate's 2013 immigration reform bill, applicants not only must satisfy a durational residence requirement but also must not have convictions for specified offenses; pay an application fee, a penalty, and any back taxes; submit biometric and biographic data; and successfully complete national security, criminal law, and immigration background checks. After extended periods of time in this provisional status, individuals may adjust to permanent resident status if they continue to satisfy the initial eligibility criteria; successfully complete a second set of background checks; and meet a series of additional prospective criteria, such as obtaining employment, satisfying minimum income requirements, remaining physically present in the United States continuously, registering for the military draft, meeting English-language proficiency and civics knowledge requirements, and others.

To implement and monitor compliance with these requirements, authorities most likely use the techniques and technologies of immigration surveillance—collecting, storing, analyzing, and disseminating vast quantities of information on millions of eligible noncitizens, on a continuous basis, to identify and ascertain who qualifies for legalization and ultimately for adjustment to lawful permanent resident status. In a world in which the availability of more information is almost always assumed to be better, the likelihood of long retention periods and secondary use of that data for purposes not contemplated at the time of collection is quite high.

Not every unauthorized migrant will be able to regularize his or her status. Those who cannot meet these requirements and remain undocumented will remain even more deeply in the shadows than current undocumented immigrants. They will also confront an array of enforcement practices, processes, and penalties, which would include intrusive mechanisms of surveillance and control.

Whether as part of comprehensive immigration reform or in some other form, any legalization program that Congress ultimately might adopt would invariably require similar but increasingly intrusive processes of data collection, processing, storage, and dissemination of personal information. While legalization usually is discussed in terms of advancing justice, compassion, and human dignity, advocates and policymakers increasingly characterize legalization as a means of achieving objectives closely connected to immigration surveillance. For example, some legalization advocates emphasize the social harms that arise from a large "underground shadow population" and the benefits that legalization would bring by enabling authorities to "know the names and addresses of the nation's inhabitants." Especially since the 9/11 attacks, increasing the presence of the surveillance state had been justified in the name of national security and public safety.

Some provisions of the Border Security, Economic Opportunity, and Immigration Modernization Act seek would have curtailed the employment of undocumented immigrants through the use of a photo tool. This tool would have involved the creation of a national biometric database of almost every adult living in the United States in what privacy advocates claimed would lead to a national identification system administered by the Department of Homeland Security. The database would contain the names, ages, Social Security numbers, and photographs of every person in the United States with a driver's license or other state-issued photo ID. The act would also implement a mandatory electronic employment eligibility verification system (E-Verify), which every U.S. employer would be required to use to search every new hire in the database to verify that each prospective employee matched his or her photo. The legislation would have required the database to be used only for employment purposes. Privacy advocates warn, however, that such restrictions may relax over time. The Social Security card, for example, was created solely for individuals to track their government retirement benefits. Today, the Social Security card is necessary to purchase health insurance. Privacy advocates believed that a slippery slope would emerge; the requirement to show proof of legal status could extend, for example, to renting an apartment, opening bank accounts, or even attending sporting events.

As of this writing (mid-January 2019), however, it remains to be seen whether Republican and Democratic leaders in Washington will arrive at any agreement regarding border security and immigration reform or the issue will continue to go unaddressed except through expressions of mutual distrust and hostility.

Further Reading

Associated Press. "Border Security" (news feed). https://www.apnews.com/Bordersecurity Borjas, George J. *Immigration Economics.* Cambridge, MA: Harvard University Press, 2014.

Bruno, Andorra, et al. *Immigration Legislation and Issues in the 112th Congress.* Washington, DC: Congressional Research Service, September 30, 2011. https://www. fas.org/sgp/crs/homesec/R42036.pdf.

Felderer, Bernhard. "Can Immigration Policy Help to Stabilize Social Security Systems?," in *Economic Aspects of International Migration,* ed. Herbert Giersch. Berlin: Springer-Verlag, 1994.

Gonzales, Alfonso. *Reform without Justice: Latino Migrant Politics and the Homeland Security State.* New York: Oxford University Press, 2014.

Lee, Ronald, and Timothy Miller. "Immigration, Social Security, and Broader Fiscal Impacts." *American Economic Review* 90, no. 2 (2000): 350–354.

Nowrasteh, Alex Cole. "Open the Gates." *USA Today,* November 1, 2013. Parsons, Kimberly D. *Immigration Policy Proposals and Potential Budgetary Effects.* New York: Nova Science, 2015.

"Real Estate Roundtable Urges Pro-Growth Immigration Reform with Flexible Visa Caps." *Real Estate Weekly News,* May 10, 2013.

Roewe, Brian. "Bill Proposes Sweeping Immigration Reform." *National Catholic Reporter,* April 26, 2013. Winters, Michael Sean. "Push for Immigration Reform: Negotiation, Compromise Lead to Senators' New Proposal." *National Catholic Reporter,* May 10, 2013.

See also: Background Checks; Big Data; Criminal Justice; Electronic surveillance; Employment eligibility verification systems; Homeland Security, U.S. Department of (DHS); Migrants and refugees in the United States, privacy rights of

Bots

Identification: An autonomous software application that runs automated tasks over a network, often the internet. Typically performed at a much faster rate than that which would be possible for a human, the tasks are simple and repetitive.

By some estimates, bots make up more than half the traffic on the internet. Bots fit broadly into four categories: social, commercial, malicious, and helpful—which can at times overlap. Most scholars also include automated personal assistants like Amazon's Alexa, Apple's Siri, and Google Assistant in discussions of bots.

Some scholars trace the origin of bots to Alan Turing and the Turing Test. In 1964 Joseph Weizenbaum at the MIT Artificial Intelligence Laboratory created the ELIZA, a social or chat bot programmed to respond to a number of keywords. Though incapable of "learning" through interaction alone, ELIZA caused several participants in the experiment to become emotionally attached to it during their "conversations." As Weizenbaum noted at the time, "extremely short exposures to a relatively simple computer program could induce powerful delusional thinking in quite normal people."

Modern "chat bots" are far more adaptive than ELIZA and employ natural language

Wikimedia Commons Bots icon.

processing systems to relate keywords and patterns from a database and formulate their responses. Companies will often employ chatbots as a first layer of customer service on a website. Chatbots can also be routed through third-party platforms, such as WeChat, or Facebook Messenger.

Another form of social bot is a fraudulent account on social media. This type of bot came to prominence during the 2016 American presidential election cycle. Often, these accounts feature profile images and details that make them appear as if they are real people. However, they interact on social media at a rate that no human possibly could. In a 2018 article for *Wired* magazine, Paris Martineau gave the example of a Twitter bot account that had tweeted more than 2,000 times in three days, averaging 660 retweets and seven original tweets per day.

This type of social bot is often referred to as a "troll" due to its programmed behavior, usually political. A well programmed bot of this variety can be very difficult to discern from an actual person, even for social media companies themselves. Two prominent platforms for bots of this variety, Facebook and Twitter, have both launched campaigns to rid themselves of bots following bad press in the aftermath of the 2016 presidential race.

These types of social bots are widely regarded as malicious; however, some function as news aggregators and might retweet articles that feature certain keywords. Others are used to archive threads on social media (e.g. Thread Reader App), or for parody (e.g. Think Piece Bot, HaikuBot), and can be helpful or even commercial. Helpful or commercial bots, however, usually disclose that they are bots. Malicious social bots attempting to impersonate genuine accounts typically will not disclose this.

Another variety of malicious bot is represented by BotNets, a portmanteau of "Robot" and "Internet." BotNets are comprised of a number of internet-connected devices, each of which is running a particular bot application. Devices can be part of a BotNet without their users knowing. The BotNets can then be used to perform a variety of tasks including Distributed Denial of Service (DDoS) attacks, cryptocurrency mining, and data mining.

Computers compromised by a BotNet are often referred to as "zombie computers." Their users may have no idea that they are being employed for malicious purposes. Often, computers are infected via spam email or fraudulent downloads. They can also be infected by visiting an infected website, or by exploited vulnerabilities in a web browser. The decentralized nature of BotNets makes them difficult to quarantine after a number of machines have been infected. Moreover, after zombie computers have reconnected to the BotNet's "home," malicious software download packets often delete themselves, leaving little visible evidence of the BotNet's presence on the zombie machine.

Legally, there is not much precedent for bots or BotNets. Until 2016, many gaps existed in the Federal Rules of Criminal Procedure, creating substantial obstacles both for prosecuting the creators of BotNets and also when attempting to de-infect zombie computers. With the new regulation, which went into effect on December 1, 2016, investigators are allowed to bring a single warrant to search infected computers to one federal court rather than being required to craft identical warrants in up to 94 jurisdictions. Previously, individual warrants had to be issued for each computer, regardless of whether or not they were in the same jurisdiction, making the process slow and ineffectual.

The State of California passed a law that goes into effect in July 2019 requiring chatbots to identify themselves as not being human. While most commercial chatbots already do this, the law's author, State Senator Robert Herzberg, said that the measure was particularly targeted at "deceptive commercial and political bots." Some legal scholars have questioned whether or not this might constitute "compelled speech," either from the bot, its programmer, or the company that owns it. Moreover, as the law is state-level, it is unclear whether or not it will have the intended effect. Companies that do not already have their bots disclose that they are not human will likely simply reprogram their bots to do so in order to do business within California. However, malicious bots are unlikely to comply regardless of the legislation.

More legislation is likely to center on bots particularly as "home assistants" like the Amazon Alexa, Google Assistant, and Apple's Siri become more prevalent. Questions have already been raised about the potential for Alexa to surveil its users in order to gain marketing information on them. At present, however, most users seem to privilege the convenience of such bots over their potential negative side effects. Moreover, data protection laws in the United States have been tepid in keeping pace with technology.

J. N. Manuel

Further Reading

Shah, H., K. Warwick, J. Vallverdú, and D. Wu. "Can Machines Talk? Comparison of Eliza with Modern Dialogue Systems". *Computers in Human Behavior* 58 (2016): 278–295.

Weizenbaum, J. *Computer Power and Human Reason: From Judgement to Calculation*, London: W. H. Freeman & Co., 1976.

Gershgorn, Dave. "A California law now means chatbots have to disclose they're not human," BotLaw, *Quartz*, October 3, 2018. https://qz.com/1409350/a-new-law-means-californias-bots-have-to-disclose-theyre-not-human/

Sacharoff, Laurent. "Do Bots Have First Amendment Rights?," The Big Idea, *Politico*, November 27, 2018. https://www.politico.com/magazine/story/2018/11/27/bots-first-amendment-rights-222689

Swaine, Jon. "Twitter admits far more Russian bots posted on election than it had disclosed," January 19, 2018. https://www.theguardian.com/technology/2018/jan/19/twitter-admits-far-more-russian-bots-posted-on-election-than-it-had-disclosed

Matineau, Paris. "What is a Bot?," Business, *Wired*, November 16, 2018. https://www.wired.com/story/the-know-it-alls-whats-is-a-bot/

www.justice.gov/archives/opa/blog/ensuring-botnets-are-not-too-big-investigate

See also: Amazon; Apple; Election interference; Facebook; Hacking, Computer; Social media technology; Twitter

Boundless Informant

Identification: A big data analytical and data visualization tool that the National Security Agency (NSA) developed and used for national security intelligence purposes.

Boundless Informant was a powerful tool used for recording and analyzing where NSA intelligence originated from. It summarized NSA's worldwide data collection activities by counting metadata on calls routed through Verizon. The tool counted and categorized metadata (the records of communication) rather than the content of an email or instant message. Metadata itself consists of which phone numbers called which other numbers, and how long the calls lasted. Thus, the data collected by the NSA included which phone numbers called which other numbers, how long the calls lasted, and the locations where the calls were made and received. Boundless Informant recorded no conversation, and the government will never be able to obtain a recording of the actual conversation. If a number called is associated with a suspected terrorist, however, either in the United States or another country, or to someone whose calling patterns or call locations are deemed suspicious, the NSA, Federal Bureau of Investigation (FBI), or other agency would be able to obtain a warrant, based on probable cause. This warrant would authorize monitoring conversations from a particular number.

The Boundless Informant program was intended to allow the NSA to monitor the intelligence coverage the agency had on a specific country in close to real time via the signals intelligence infrastructure. The tool allowed the NSA to select a nation and determine the metadata volume and select details from the collections from that nation. The program also summarized data records from more than 500 separate Dial Number Recognition (DNR; metadata collection) and Digital Network Intelligence (DNI; content collection) sources, or SIGADS (signal activity designators that identify signals intelligence).

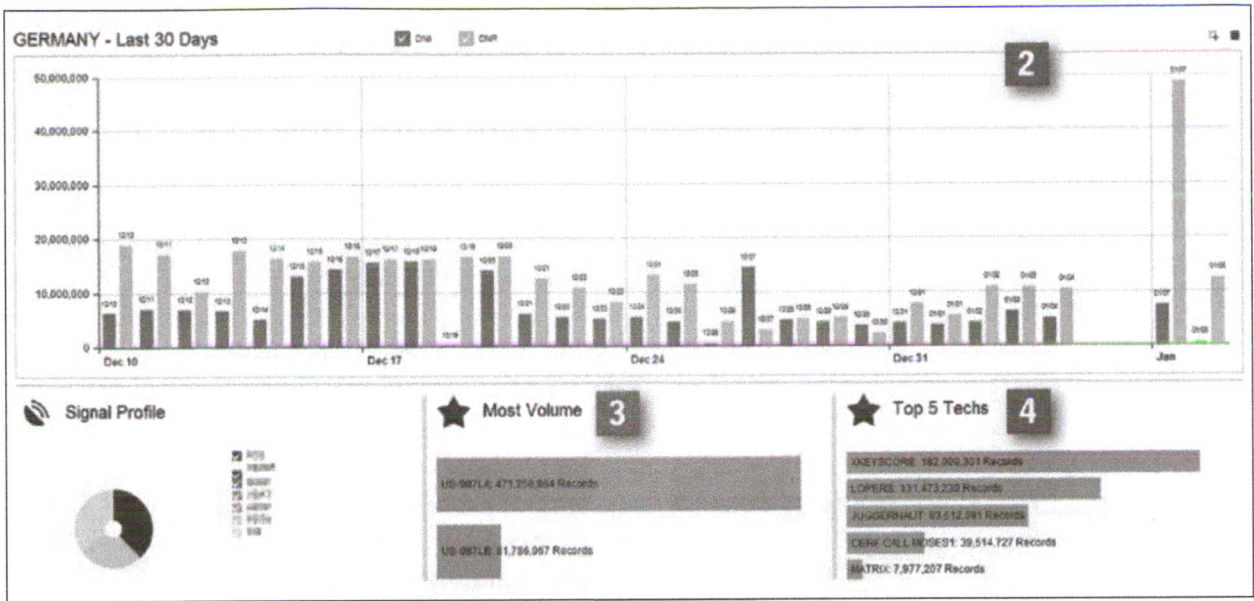

Screenshot from the BOUNDLESSINFORMANT tool, showing charts with different details about data collection related to Germany. The upper chart shows internet (dark gray bars) and telephony (light gray bars) data, the bottom center chart mentions two SIGADs and the most important "tech" in the bottom right section is the XKeyscoreprogram. (By NSA.)

The existence of Boundless Informant was revealed by documents leaked by Edward Snowden, an NSA contractor employed by Booz Allen Hamilton. The general public became aware of the program on June 8, 2013, after Snowden leaked the documents to the *Guardian,* a British newspaper. Subsequent revelations included charts and details that the NSA gathered from a number of European nations from December 10, 2012, to January 8, 2013.

Snowden claimed that the program had collected more information on Americans within the United States than on Russians in Russia. Specifically, the NSA obtained nearly 3 billion data items from within the United States from February 2013 through March 2013.

Snowden claimed that he reported his concerns to his supervisors at the NSA Threat Operations Center regional office in Hawaii and to his supervisors at the NSA Technology Directorate in October 2012. Snowden also claimed that he followed the appropriate NSA internal procedures.

The Snowden revelation occurred when a Senate committee was investigating whether the NSA was illegally monitoring the communications of Americans within the United States. The Snowden revelation contradicted NSA representations to Congress that the agency does not collect data on Americans, and that it lacked the capacity to monitor effectively all the surveillance it gathers on American communications.

NSA has long maintained global mining projects. The revelations of programs of intelligence gathering and analysis that included data gathered from within the United States were particularly facilitated by amendments to U.S. surveillance law enacted by President Bush and renewed by President Obama in December 2012.

Programs such as Boundless Informant provide early warning of significant national security dangers that the United States could be confronting. Programs that use tools with powerful capacities, along with increasingly ubiquitous surveillance camera; photo recognition software; the development of rapid recognition DNA analysis; drones that can spy or kill; and DNA, fingerprint, photo and other searchable digital databases, could very well be abused and curtail vital liberties, including the right to privacy. In other words, these advanced surveillance technologies may potentially enable a small group of powerful individuals to control and restrict the freedoms of whole nations. This is a sobering scenario for anyone concerned with the future of democracy and essential privacy rights.

Further Reading

Birnbaum, Michael. "Europeans Seek to Learn Extent of U.S. Agencies' Data Collection." *Washington Post,* June 11, 2013.

Handley, John. "Prism and Boundless Informant: Is NSA Surveillance a Threat?" *American Diplomacy,* July 17, 2013.

Ignatius, David. "Rules for Spying." *Washington Post,* November 3, 2013.

Keane, Tom. "Assessing Snowden, Six Months Later." *Boston Globe,* December 29, 2013.

Steininger, Michael. "In Return to Berlin, Obama Finds a Cooler Germany." *Christian Science Monitor,* June 19, 2013.

See also: Data Science; Electronic Surveillance; National Security Agency (NSA); Snowden, Edward

Brain-computer interfacing (BCI)

Identification: A direct communication link between the brain and an external device.

Brain-computer interfacing also known as BCI:

"Represent[s] a direct communication link between the brain and an external device. By using the measured brain signals for communication, BCI's allow for non-verbal communication between a user and a device. Based on the observations that the BCI devices provide an access to our unique brain wave patterns, which allow others to make inferences about our memory, intentions, conscious and unconscious interests, as well as about our emotional reactions, we conjecture the impact of exploiting, or even mishandling BCI devices will be severe and far

reaching . . . . privacy issues arising from the use of BCI deserves . . . . attention."

Based on its widespread growth and technological use in neurological advancements, BCI provides medical professionals and information technology (IT) development professionals with unrestricted and unregulated access to the brain. This cranium access may pose an increasing risk to individual privacy rights or private thoughts.

This entry discusses various concerns on the privacy of BCI such as "brain spyware" or malware, financial institution information, extraction of private information for commercial gain, and a lack of regulations or laws to protect unauthorized intrusion of brain activity during BCI.

"Brain spyware" is a risk when BCI is used via computer applications or software. This makes the information communicated a risk to the medical or education professionals who are observing, monitoring, or researching the brain activity. For example, the software or computer application may include a tracking of information that is processed such as likes, dislikes, interests or disinterests of an individual who is participating in an educational study. This information collection and tracking is done without the knowledge or awareness of the participant whose brain is being measured to track the accuracy of the software or computer application. The information collected may be sold and used for something other than the researcher and participant originally intended. This example can be possible in the development of the software and used maliciously to extract information or predict the participant's personal preferences. This constitutes a potential risk to the individual privacy for invasive or non-invasive BCI.

Another potential risk to individual privacy is using BCI may make the participant's personal financial institution information vulnerable to fraudulent and unauthorized financial transactions. When BCI is used and games, surveys, or simulated realities are created via computer software that the brain is controlling, this opens exposure to manipulation or extraction of personal information such as home address, Personal Identification Numbers (PIN), and banking information that may be a part of the simulation created to invoke natural responses from the brain. Scientists at the Laboratory of Adaptive Intelligence commented that BCI leaves the mind open to hacking and allows researchers to *"secretly extract sensitive information from the brain."* Brain hacking is a risk that makes the private information that is used in participants everyday vulnerable when using BCI.

Extracting this information is clearly something that can be utilized for commercial gain if financial institution information is extracted and sold to criminals who use it for fraudulent financial transactions. However, businesses may want the information to enter the minds of consumers and discover what things they can sell consumers that they are guaranteed to buy. This makes the extraction of BCI information a business of pirating private information from the mind of its users. Howard Chizeck, professor of electrical engineering at the University of Washington told Geekwire.com:

> "You could see that a game would be just the ideal way to collect information, and if it was tied into, say, a large Internet marketing company or search engine company, they could very quickly learn brand preference and send you targeted advertisements. This is the kind of privacy that we're concerned about protecting."

The use of BCI is a privacy invasion of individual thoughts, even when playing what seems to be a game, profitable to brain hackers. Private information and protecting that privacy is a risk that has and will continue to be big business.

As BCI expands, it become almost impossible for the government to regulate to protect privacy. Just like the educated use of the Internet and information that individuals protect by controlling what is posted, searched, and used the same can be exercised as BCI is used for a variety of purposes. An educated participant makes for a participant that should be responsible for protecting what is explored in their minds to the extent possible. Harmless information may be extracted that does not necessarily give a tremendous amount of insight into the individual's private thoughts, however, just as a targeted group that does not make their private financial information at risk. In other words, limiting and policing use BCI may assist in how much harm or how much private information may be extracted and individual judgment of the line of private information can be drawn voluntarily.

Shaunté Chácon

Further Reading

Bonaci, T. and H. Chizack. Privacy by Design in Brain-Computer Interfaces. University of Washington, Department of EE. website: www.ee.washington.edu/ techsite/papers/documents/UWEETR-2013–0001 http://www.geekwire.com/2014/geekwire-radiobrain-computer-interfaces-future-personal-privacy/

Luber B, Fisher C, Appelbaum PS, Ploesser M, Lisanby SH. Lisanby. Non-invasive Brain Stimulation in the Detection of Deception: Scientific Challenges and Ethical Consequences. *Behavioral Sciences & the Law*, 27(2):191–208, 2009.

Martinovic, Ivan, Doug Davies, Mario Frank, Daniele Perito, Tomas Ros, and Dawn Song. On the Feasibility of Side-Channel Attacks with Brain-Computer Interfaces. In *the Proceedings of the 21st USENIX Security Symposium*. USENIX, 2012.

See also: Beliefs, Privacy of; Body, privacy of; Computers; Fourth Amendment of the U.S. Constitution; Invasion of Privacy; Neurology

Brandeis, Louis Dembitz

Born: November 13, 1856
Died: October 5, 1941
Significance: Known as the father of privacy law in the United States; practiced law in Boston,

Massachusetts, and served as an associate justice of the Supreme Court of the United States from 1916 to 1939.

Brandeis began attending Harvard Law School at age eighteen without a college degree. He subsequently graduated in 1877 with the highest grade point average in the law school's history, and later helped to found the *Harvard Law Review* in 1886. As a Supreme Court Justice, he focused on societal implications, privacy and free speech, and individual dignity.

In 1890, Brandeis co-authored a law review article entitled "The Right to Privacy," which is one of the most significant legal works in American history. The authors explained that it was their "purpose to consider whether the existing law affords a principle which can properly be invoked to protect the privacy of the individual; and, if it does, what the nature and extent of such protection is." After discussing the common law origins of the right, Warren and Brandeis describe six major limitations of the right to privacy and two main legal remedies for an invasion of the right to privacy. The article prescribed an outline for the entire body of privacy law. For decades, the article was regarded as a personal response to the publicity experiences of the Warren family; however, that theory was later proven wrong. Warren and Brandeis were the first to articulate fully what Thomas Cooley described "the right to be let alone." The publication of their article resulted in the emergence of an entirely new area of privacy law.

Throughout his career, Brandeis continued to advocate for the rights of individuals and small communities to be able to retain control over their affairs. He joined the American Zionist movement, even accepting a leadership position in 1914 because he believed so fervently in individual development and control of his own life (in that case, advocating for the case of the Jewish people to be in control of their destiny in their ancestral homeland).

While serving on the Supreme Court Justice, Brandeis explained his views on the right to pri-

Louis Dembitz Brandeis. (Photography by Harris & Ewing.)

vacy most famously in his dissent in *Olmstead v. United States,* 277 U.S. 438, 471 (1928), in which he emphasized the importance of "the right to be let alone" as follows:

The makers of our Constitution undertook to secure conditions favorable to the pursuit of happiness. They recognized the significance of man's spiritual nature, of his feelings and of his intellect. They knew that only a part of the pain, pleasure and satisfactions of life are to be found in material things. They sought to protect Americans in their beliefs, their thoughts, their emotions and their sensations. They conferred, as against the government, *the right to be let alone* [emphasis added]—the most comprehensive of rights and the right most valued by civilized men. To protect that right, every unjustifiable intrusion by the government upon the privacy of the individual, whatever the means employed, must be deemed a violation of the Fourth Amendment.

Brandeis viewed warrantless wiretaps as unreasonable search and seizure under the Fourth Amendment. However, the majority of the Court did not agree. Three other justices also dissented in *Olmstead*. It was not until 1967, however, in *Berger v. New York*, 388 U.S. 41 (1967), and then in *Katz v. United States*, 389 U.S. 347, 352 (1967), that the Court recognized Brandeis's view as legitimate and overturned *Olmstead*: "although a closely divided Court supposed in *Olmstead* that surveillance without any trespass and without the seizure of any material object fell outside the ambit of the Constitution, we have since departed from the narrow view on which that decision rested." Almost forty years after his dissent, Brandeis's view of privacy in Fourth Amendment search and seizure law became the law of the land.

The legacy of Justice Brandeis includes a clear belief in the right of an individual to privacy. His legal scholarship and jurisprudence on the Supreme Court have had an enduring impact on the development of this area of American law.

Joy M. Shoemaker

Further Reading

Paper, Lewis J. *Brandeis:* Prentice-Hall, 1983. Symposium, *The Right to Privacy One Hundred Years Later. Case Western Reserve Law Review* 41 no. 643 (1991)

Urofsky, Melvin. *Louis D. Brandeis: A Life.*, 2009.

See also: Constitutional law; Fourth Amendment to the U.S. Constitution; *Katz v. United States*; *Olmstead v. United States*; Right to be left alone

C

Caller ID

Identification: Also known as caller identification, a service based on a telecommunications technology that passes the caller's telephone number and/or name to the recipient of the call via a caller ID stand-alone device, or through the phone itself. The number or name appears after the first ring.

Calling Party Number (CPN) technologies became generally available in the U.S. telephony market with the advent of out-of-band signaling services such as SS7. It is important to note that caller ID services only identify the telephone number of the calling telephone and the customer of record for that telephone rather than the actual person calling, and would not identify, for example, a visitor calling from someone else's home. Names associated with telephone numbers and other identifying information about telephone subscribers are kept in databases owned by the telecommunications carriers, and the owners of this data may charge caller ID providers a fee for database lookup. The phone number itself, however, is transmitted with the call necessarily as a method of determining where the call terminates and so does not require a separate lookup or fee in order to provide it as part of caller ID service.

Caller ID service was deployed by telecommunications carriers in the 1990s after the service was deemed in the public interest by the Federal Communications Commission (FCC) in FCC 47 CFR Part 64 [CC Docket No. 91–281, FCC 95–187]. The FCC order specifically preempted state regulations on this issue that would interfere with the federal order, although the FCC only has jurisdiction over interstate, not intrastate, calls. If the call was completed using SS7 technology, then the number must be transmitted, although consumers were permitted to block individual numbers using *67, effectuating a caller's request for privacy for that call (*82 unblocks a call from a blocked line). The FCC also required telecommunications companies to educate and inform their customers about the new service and its privacy-protective alternatives.

Caller ID was launched as a paid service and is now a ubiquitous feature on many landline telephones and nearly all mobile phones. Looking at caller ID, we may find a useful case study for the application of a new technology to existing privacy and telecommunications protocols. The advocates both for and against caller ID argued that they stood for the protection of individual privacy. Those supporting caller ID offered the new technology as a return to previous expectations of privacy before the innovation of telecommunications, that is, the knock on the front door before one opened the door to let in a friend, a salesperson, or even a stranger. Those against caller ID included not only supporters of the ability to make anonymous calls for political or fundraising purposes but also those who were particularly concerned about the safety of abused women who made calls from secret locations and women's shelters. Of course, telemarketers advocated for vociferously banning caller ID because it would reduce their ability to conduct business anonymously or possibly completely if the call recipient saw the incoming number and decided not to answer the call.

To volley back, technology is also available to prevent the sent telephone number from appearing on the call recipient's device: caller ID block. This service solves some of the problems raised by the opponents of caller ID but makes the service less privacy-protective for the recipient subscriber to caller ID services. As is possible with all telephone calls, the recipient of the call may choose not to answer an unidentified call, to block unidentified calls, and/or to allow the call to go to voicemail or an answering service. There is also caller ID available as a feature of call waiting service, allowing incoming calls during a preexisting call to be identified by telephone number or name. The same advantages and disadvantages to privacy apply to these mid-call interruptions, perhaps even more so as the stakes may be higher when the call recipient must choose between two available calls.

Both the Federal Trade Commission (FTC) and the FCC have weighed in on whether telemarketers should be required to use caller ID to identify their calls for the public. The FTC said yes, telemarketers must use caller ID for the telephone number and, if available, for the name of the calling party, in FTC Order, 68 Fed. Reg. at 4623. Telemarketing companies continued to argue the order thereafter, with a particular emphasis on the technical limitations on their ability to comply with the order.

The FCC agreed with the FTC's reasoning that caller ID protected consumers in the FCC's 2003 order, FCC 03–153 CG Docket No. 02–278 at paragraph 179 et. seq. The FCC cited numerous privacy and consumer-friendly benefits to caller ID, even for call recipients who do not subscribe to the paid caller ID service who can use

the *69 feature on their phones to find out who just called them and return the call if desired.

The government agencies especially mentioned the potential use of caller ID to identify, track, and prosecute perpetrators of consumer fraud. Consumers could also use the identified number to request that they be placed on a Do Not Call Registry for the calling company. The FCC noted that the many technical objections that telemarketers made citing their inability to transmit the calling number was eliminated when they were required to pass on at least the billing number, which every call contained to route and bill the call to the calling party. To effectuate its intent fully, the FCC noted that telemarketers could not comply with the order to transmit the number and then subscribe to the caller ID blocking service to block the numbers. The ruling specifically did not apply to tax-exempt non-profits, who may still call consumers to solicit donations, memberships, and the like, without complying with the FCC order to transmit their calling numbers.

Congress also responded to concerns about caller ID fraud, also known as caller ID "spoofing," by enacting the Truth in Caller ID Act of 2009 (S. 30, Public Law No: 111–331), which prohibited companies from falsifying caller ID data. Significant monetary fines may be imposed for violation of this act. The FCC adopted rules implementing the act in 2011.

Jill Bronfman

Further Reading

Caller ID and My Privacy: What Do I Need to Know? San Diego, CA: Center for Public Interest Law, University of San Diego, 1996.

Lee, Laurie Thomas. *U.S. Telecommunications Privacy Policy and Caller ID: A Study of Anonymity and Solitude Interests in Conflict.* Location of Publisher: Publisher's Name: 1993.

Lee, Laurie Thomas, and Robert Larose. "Caller ID and the Meaning of Privacy." *The Information Society*: 247–265.

Lesk, Michael. "Caller ID: Whose Privacy?" *IEEE Security & Privacy*: 77–79. Moore, Adam D. *Information*

Ethics: Privacy, Property, and Power. Seattle: University of Washington Press, 2005.

Noll, A. Michael. "An Inquiry into the Privacy Aspects of Caller-ID." *Telecommunications Policy*: 690–693.

Pattison, Scott. "Restricting 'Caller ID.'" *Consumers' Research Magazine*, May 1, 1992.

Toth, Victor J. "Telephone Privacy—How to Invade It (Caller Identification and Automatic Number Identification) (Washington Perspective)." *Business Communications Review*, April 1, 1994.

See also: Federal Communications Commission; Federal Trade Commission; Mobile Devices; Telephones

Cantrell v. Forest City Publishing Company, 419 U.S. 245 (1974)

Identification: An eight to one decision, with a majority opinion by Justice Potter Stewart, in which the U.S. Supreme Court ruled that a tort action brought under the theory of "false light" invasion of privacy may proceed against a newspaper that knowingly or recklessly published falsehoods. The decision is notable as one of only two Supreme Court decisions that directly address "false light," a theory more talked about than actually employed and more akin to libel than to that touchstone of privacy, the "right to be let alone."

The case of *Cantrell v. Forest City Publishing Company* arose out of a 1968 feature article by Joe Eszterhas in the Sunday magazine of the *Cleveland Plain Dealer,* a newspaper whose corporate owner was Forest City Publishing Company. The article concerned the aftermath of a notorious 1967 bridge collapse in West Virginia that killed 44 people. Eszterhas had covered the tragedy at the time of the incident and then returned to the scene several months later to do the feature article for the magazine. Eszterhas later became highly successful as a Hollywood screenwriter and his bridge collapse feature reflected both his powerful writing skills and his active imagination.

The article provided a dramatic account of the tragedy's impact on surviving family members. The circumstances of the plaintiffs, the bridge widow Margaret Cantrell and her children, were at the heart of Eszterhas's account. Unfortunately, the story of the Cantrells contained numerous factual errors and, most important, a false representation that Eszterhas had met and spoken with Cantrell in her home. In fact, Mrs. Cantrell was not present when Eszterhas interviewed her children and observed conditions inside the home with a photographer, who took fifty pictures.

When the opposing parties in civil litigation are from different states (the Cantrells were citizens of West Virginia and the defendants were in Ohio), the plaintiffs may bring their lawsuit either in state court or, because of the "diversity" of citizenship, in federal court. The Cantrells chose federal district court in Ohio, contending, as their counsel later told the Supreme Court, "This is an invasion of privacy and may I respectfully suggest that it's an invasion of four types of privacy in one continuous event or series of events."

Indeed, there were contentions made—intrusive entry, publication of intimate family details, false portrayals, and commercial appropriation—that smacked of all four categories of invasion of privacy that William Prosser's influential writings had derived from the case law of many states. By the time the Supreme Court considered the case, however, the legal theory as summarized by Justice Stewart had been narrowed to just one of Prosser's categories, "false light," which turned on whether "publishing the false feature story about the Cantrells and thereby making them the objects of pity and ridicule" had caused the Cantrells "to suffer outrage, mental distress, shame, and humiliation." A jury found for the Cantrells, awarding them $60,000 in compensatory damages.

The trial judge dismissed a punitive damages claim, finding no evidence that the publication "was done maliciously within the legal definition of that term." Punitive damages, as the name suggests, are intended to punish bad conduct, may be awarded without regard to the actual injury suffered, and require a heightened level of culpability (often labeled as "malice" or "actual malice"), whereas compensatory damages are limited to measurable harm and may be awarded even when the defendant had no intent to cause injury.

The trial court had found and the federal Court of Appeals had agreed—though, as Justice Stewart noted, without much analysis—that both Ohio and West Virginia had adopted a "legally protected interest in privacy." Justice Stewart acknowledged, citing Prosser, that "(p)ublicity that places the plaintiff in a false light in the public eye is generally recognized as one of the several distinct kinds of invasions actionable under the privacy rubric." The Supreme Court thus accepted the existence of a false light tort, the details of which were a matter of state law.

The court of appeal reversed the award of compensatory damages, pointing to the trial judge's statement about the absence of evidence that the publication "was done maliciously," reading the statement to mean that there was no evidence that the defendants knowingly or recklessly published falsehoods under the constitutional standard that the Supreme Court had set in *New York Times v. Sullivan*, 376 U.S. 254 (1964). In its only other false light ruling, the Supreme Court had said that the *New York Times* standard applied in such cases and that no recovery could be had without a showing of knowing or reckless falsity. (*Time, Inc. v. Hill*, 385 U.S. 374 (1967))

Justice Stewart disagreed with the court of appeals conclusion, stressing that a finding of "malice" or "actual malice," as those terms were used in tort law, often as synonyms for intent to cause harm, was not the same as the standard set forth in Justice William J. Brennan's holding in *New York Times*: Proof that a "statement was made with 'actual malice'—that is, with knowledge that it was false or with reckless disregard of whether it was false or not." In fact, the Supreme Court held in *Cantrell* that the award of compensatory damages should stand because the record showed that the falsehoods in the article had been knowing or reckless under *New York Times*.

The sole dissenting vote was cast by Justice William O. Douglas, who cited the dissent of his late First Amendment collaborator Justice Hugo Black in *Time, Inc v. Hill:* "The words 'malicious' and particularly 'reckless disregard of the truth' can never serve as effective substitutes for the First Amendment words: '. . . make no law . . . abridging the freedom of speech, or of the press.'"

Harold W. Fuson Jr.

Further Reading

Doyle, Michael. "False Light, Camera, Action: The Story Joe Eszterhas Forgot to Share." *Slate,* February 25, 2004. Accessed August 29, 2015. http://www.slate.com/articles/news_and_politics/jurisprudence/2004/02/false_light_camera_action.html.

Emerson, Thomas I. "The Right of Privacy and Freedom of the Press," in vol. 1 of *Privacy,* 2 vols., ed. by Raymond Wacks. New York: New York University Press, 1993. Faculty Scholarship Series. Paper 2776. Available at http://digitalcommons.law.yale.edu/fss_papers/2776.

Zimmerman, Diane. "False Light Invasion of Privacy: The Light That Failed." *New York University Law Review* 64, no. 2 (May 1989): 364–453.

See also: Douglas, William Orville; *New York Times v. Sullivan*; Privacy laws,state; Privacy torts; Prosser, William Lloyd

Cellphones

Identification: Mobile communications devices originally used for verbal communications but now providing a full range of multimedia communications options.

The United States Supreme Court has recognized that modern cellphones are essentially mini-computers storing photographs, text messages, emails, bank records, and other highly personal items. Because of this, cellphones, smartphones and pagers are covered by Fourth

Evolution of mobile phones, to an early smartphone. (by Anders.)

Amendment protection against governmental searches. There has been increased development of legal and privacy rights relating to cellphones, smartphones and pagers or other devices capable of sending digital messages. The U.S. Supreme Court has issued three noteworthy opinions in this area.

The first case, *City of Ontario, California v. Quon*, 560 U.S. 746 (2010), discussed the limits on governmental employers reading the contents of one's text messages sent and received on a work pager. *Quon* was a 9–0 opinion decided by the Roberts Court. Justice Anthony Kennedy, writing for the Court, found that the Fourth Amendment provides some measure of protection for governmental employees against certain searches. Relying on the Rehnquist Court's decision, *O'Connor v. Ortega*, 480 U.S. 709 (1987),

the Roberts Court extended *Ortega*'s holding that governmental employees retain certain Fourth Amendment protections from searches in the workplace.

Jeff Quon was a SWAT officer for the Ontario Police Department. In 2001 the City of Ontario purchased pagers for its officers to send and receive text messages. These pagers were intended to be used so that officers could respond to official police business, including emergency situations. Although the city maintained a computer usage, Internet, and email policy advising its employees of the rights and obligations relating to their city computer usage, this policy did not directly address text messages sent or received via pagers. The city's computer usage, Internet and email policy advised city employees that they had no expectation of privacy in their computer usage because the city actively monitored it.

The City of Ontario used an outside entity, Arch Wireless, to provide the capabilities to send and receive text messages on the city-issued pagers. Text messages being sent on city-issued pagers were neither using nor retained on the city computer servers. In 2002, the city advised its employees that it considered these text messages to be indistinguishable from email and therefore covered by the broader city computer usage policy. Jeff Quon was made aware of this at both a staff meeting and via written memorandum. Shortly after the pagers were provided, Quon ran over his allotted text usage. Quon's supervisor reminded him of the city's computer usage policy but indicated that he would rather have Quon pay the overage than begin looking through his text messages. Quon, and other employees who had also exceeded their monthly allotment, paid overage fees to the city. The overages continued, and Quon continued to pay for his overage fees.

The City of Ontario became concerned that it was underestimating its need for text data and sought to discern whether the overages were due to work-related text messages or personal messages being sent via the work pagers. A city employee requested the text message transcripts from Arch Wireless for a two-month period. The city reviewed the transcripts and found that, of the 456 messages Quon sent during work hours in August 2002, only fifty-seven were work-related. Of the non-work-related text messages, some were sexually explicit. The city eventually disciplined Quon.

The Supreme Court found that, because the city sought the text message transcripts for work-related, noninvestigatory purposes (essentially, to discern whether city employees were being given adequate text message allotments for work purposes), the Fourth Amendment had not been violated. The Court applied the two-part *Ortega* test that evaluated (1) whether the search was based on a noninvestigatory, work-related matter, and, if so, (2) whether the search was reasonable in its scope, going no further than necessary to answer the noninvestigatory, work-related matter. Because the Court found that both components of the test were satisfied—the goal of the search was to ensure that city employees had sufficient text allowances, and the city sought only two months of overages for consideration, a narrow search— the search was found to be reasonable.

A more important outcome from the *Quon* case, however, was the Court's directive that issues on technology should be narrowly decided. Justice Kennedy wrote, "[t]he Court must proceed with care when considering the whole concept of privacy expectations in communications made on electronic equipment owned by a government employer. The judiciary risks error by elaborating too fully on the Fourth Amendment implications of emerging technology before its role in society has become clear."

While *Quon* did not involve cellphones per se, the case provides important insight into why the Supreme Court has been reluctant to rule expansively on the privacy aspects relating to cellphones. In 1979, the Court held that the numbers that an individual dials from his or

her landline (or from a traditional telephone) are not subject to Fourth Amendment protections because an individual has no reasonable expectation of privacy in the phone numbers that he or she dials. The case, *Smith v. Maryland*, 442 U.S. 735 (1979), was a 5–3 ruling issued by the Burger Court. Justice Harry Blackmun, the author of *Roe v. Wade*, 410 U.S. 113 (1973), wrote the Court's opinion in *Smith*. While the modern Supreme Court has nine justices, and all nine justices ordinarily participate in a case, Justice Lewis Powell did not participate in this particular decision, leaving the Court with a 5–3 majority opinion.

With *Smith* holding that individuals have no Fourth Amendment expectation of privacy in the numbers they dial, a search issue will only arise when the government attempts to use the content of one's phone conversation or messages. In fact, *Katz v. United States*, 389 U.S. 347 (1967), was the first case in which the Court found that individuals have a reasonable expectation of privacy in the contents of a phone conversation that occurred in a closed telephone booth. *Katz*, decided by the Warren Court and written by Justice Potter Stewart, famously distinguished that the Fourth Amendment protects people, not places. *Katz*, the case responsible for establishing constitutional search rules by analyzing reasonable expectations of privacy, remains one of the foremost Fourth Amendment decisions. Not until *Riley v. California*, 134 S. Ct. 2473 (2014), did the Supreme Court address the reasonable expectations of privacy relating directly to cellphones. In an opinion written by Chief Justice John Roberts, the Court actually evaluated two separate instances in which criminal prosecutions were based on information obtained from criminal defendants' cellphones, secured without a warrant. The two cases, *Riley v. California* and *United States v. Wurie*, 724 F.3d 255 (1st Cir., 2013), were consolidated on appeal before the Supreme Court. Both cases involved warrantless searches of the defendant's cellphone made incident to a lawful arrest. The Court has long recognized that warrantless searches, subject to a few clearly defined exceptions, are generally unconstitutional.

One of the well-established exceptions is the "search incident to arrest" exception first established in *United States v. Robinson,* 414 U.S. 218 (1973). Search incident to arrest exceptions are permitted to protect officer safety and prevent the destruction of evidence by securing all evidence directly on the arrestee's person at the time of arrest. This exception also permits warrantless search of the area within the arrestee's "immediate control" provided that the search occurs contemporaneous with the arrest (*Chimel v. California,* 395 U.S. 752 (1969)). *Riley* dealt with the issue of whether a cellular smartphone recovered during a warrantless search incident to arrest falls within the broader search incident to arrest exception under either *Robinson* or *Chimel.* Two different criminal defendants had cellphones taken during an otherwise lawful search incident to arrest, and the contents were searched. In the first case, Riley was pulled over when officers noticed that his vehicle registration tags had expired. The officer then learned that Riley's driver's license had been suspended. During the search incident to arrest, an officer found what was believed to be gang-related items. A cellular smartphone was also found in Riley's clothing. The officer began accessing Riley's text messages and contacts list, noticing additional indications of gang activity. Without first securing a search warrant, the officer then had a detective with gang specialization review the phone for evidence. This search yielded videos and photographs that implicated Riley in a gang-related shooting. Riley filed a motion to suppress the evidence found on his phone. The trial court denied his motion. Riley was found guilty of three shooting-related crimes, including attempted murder, and sentenced to a prison term of fifteen years to life. All of Riley's appeals to the California state courts were denied.

The second case involved a drug arrest of Brima Wurie. Officers witnessed Wurie par-

ticipating in an alleged drug deal and arrested him. Two cellphones were taken from Wurie when he arrived at the police station. Unlike Riley's cellular smartphone, Wurie's phone at issue was a flip phone, one the Court indicated generally has fewer features than the modern cellular smartphone. Wurie's flip phone repeatedly rang immediately after Wurie arrived at the station. The calls all came from a number identified as "my house" when the call came in. The officers opened Wurie's phone and saw a picture set as Wurie's screen saver that was later used to associate Wurie with a particular apartment. Using the information gleaned from the flip phone, officers sought and obtained a search warrant for the apartment. During the search, officers found a large quantity of cocaine, marijuana, drug paraphernalia, weapons, and money.

Like Riley, Wurie sought unsuccessfully to suppress the information obtained from the phone. In Wurie's case, if the information gathered from the phone without a warrant had been suppressed, the search warrant issued for the apartment would have been invalid and all the evidence obtained therein would have been inadmissible. Wurie was tried and convicted for distributing cocaine and sentenced to 262 months in federal prison. The federal appellate court for the First Circuit agreed with Wurie that the motion to suppress should have been granted and reversed his conviction.

The Supreme Court consolidated Riley's and Wurie's appeal under the single case name, *Riley v. California.* Justice Roberts's opinion found that cellular smartphones have "vast quantities of personal information," distinguishing modern cellphones from other physical items routinely uncovered during a warrantless search incident to arrest. The typical reasoning supporting search incident to arrest, officer safety and prevention of the destruction of evidence, do not readily arise with cellphone searches. Instead, modern cellphones are used to make phone calls, send emails, send text messages, keep calendars, surf the Internet, and host a variety of applications (apps) providing a wealth of information about its user. In many regards, modern cellphones are minicomputers that enable people to carry enormous amounts of information about their daily lives, finances, hobbies, and family with them at all times.

In neither Riley's nor Wurie's case was there any evidence that exigent circumstances provided the police with a basis to conduct a warrantless search of the cellphones. California and the U.S. government sought to expand search inci- dent to arrest to permit warrantless searches of all cellphones when the phone was discovered during a search incident to arrest.

Justice Roberts found that a cellphone found during a warrantless search incident to arrest could still be evaluated to ensure that it poses no physical safety risk to the officer, thus permitting the officer to remove any protective cover to discover hidden articles capable of being used as a weapon. Once it is clear the phone poses no physical threat, however, the phone may not be further evaluated for evidence without first securing a search warrant. The Court was unwilling to place cellphones in the same category of other physical evidence typically uncovered during a search incident to arrest. In other words, cellphones are unique to each individual and contain far too much private information to permit warrantless searches.

Riley holds, excepting unusual cases, that cellphones found during other valid warrantless searches require an independent search warrant to evaluate the contents of the phone, including photos, videos, and contact lists. It does not hold that officers are prohibited from reviewing the contents of a cellular smartphone. Rather, *Riley* reminds that warrants are ordinarily required before private items are searched by government officials. The case did not involve any issue on cellphone passwords or other potential Fifth Amendment questions. Cellphones, following *Riley*, are entitled to strong Fourth Amendment protection.

Most recently, the Supreme Court held that police must secure a search warrant to track the digital signal cellphones omit that track movement. *Carpenter v. United States*, announced in 2018, held that acquiring one's cellphone location records violates a person's reasonable expectation of privacy, constituting a search. Chief Justice Roberts wrote the opinion for a 5-4 divided court. The majority opinion explained that the Fourth Amendment protection against search and seizure protects both physical trespass and reasonable expectations of privacy. Chief Justice Roberts began the opinion by noting there are more 70 million more cellphone accounts in the United States than people (396 million cellphone accounts and only 326 million people).Because cellphone use continually increases, cellphone providers have increased the ability to service—and track—cellphone usage.

As the Court explained:

Cellphones continuously scan their environment looking for the best signal, which generally comes from the closest cell site. Most modern devices, such as smartphones, tap into the wireless network several times a minute whenever their signal is on, even if the owner is not using one of the phone's features. Each time the phone connects to a cell site, it generates a time-stamped record known as cell-site location information (CSLI). . . .

While carriers have long retained CSLI for the start and end of incoming calls, in recent years phone companies have also collected location information from the transmission of text messages and routine data connections. Accordingly, modern cellphones generate increasingly vast amounts of increasingly precise CSLI.

Police sought the cell-site locations for Carpenter. Without seeking a search warrant, the police sought 159 days' worth of Carpenter's CSLI from his two cellphone carriers. The carriers, in turn, produced 127 days of CSLI data, which provided nearly 13,000 location points. The cell-site data was central to the government's case against Carpenter. Carpenter filed a

Motion to Suppress reliance on the CSLI information. The Motion was denied. During trial, the government used the CSLI information to show that Carpenter was physically present near four robberies at the exact time each occurred. Carpenter was convicted and sentenced to over 100 years in prison.

Carpenter appealed his conviction. The intermediate Circuit Court denied his appeal. The Supreme Court then accepted the case for review. Carpenter challenged that such sustained surveillance constituted a search under the Fourth Amendment. The majority agreed, holding that the lengthy, extensive tracking of a person's movement violates their reasonable expectations of privacy. The majority disagreed that simply because individuals transfer their CSLI to third parties (their cellphone carriers), they lose their reasonable expectation of privacy in tracking their physical location. Thus, police seeking to collect CSLI from cellphone carriers must generally secure a search warrant.

Chief Justice Roberts' opinion noted the serious law and privacy issues that arise as technology develops. The Court found that CSLI gives "deeply revealing" information about an individual's movements. In closing, the Court quoted Justice Brandeis's famous dissent in *Olmstead v. United States* to remind us that technological advances must not be used to erode Fourth Amendment protections. Instead, when the "progress of science" gives police new tools, courts must jealously guard against government encroachment. The opinion was a victory for privacy rights.

Mary M. Penrose

Further Reading

Bagley, Ian. "Constitutional Law—Search-Incident-to-Arrest Exception to Prohibition against Warrantless Searches Inapplicable to Cell Phone Searches—*Smallwood v. State*." *Suffolk University Law Review* (2014).

Bedi, Monu Singh. "Fourth Amendment Doctrine Mash-Up: The Curious Case of Cell Phone Location Data." *SSRN Electronic Journal SSRN Journal*.

Clancy, Thomas K. *Cyber Crime and Digital Evidence: Materials and Cases*. New Providence, NJ: Lexis-Nexis, 2011.

"Constitutional Law—Fourth Amendment—First Circuit Holds That the Search-Incident-to-Arrest Exception Does Not Authorize the Warrantless Search of Cell Phone Data." *Harvard Law Review* (2013).

"Criminal Procedure—Fourth Amendment—Florida Supreme Court Holds That Cell Phone Data Is Not Subject to the Search Incident-to-Arrest Exception." *Harvard Law Review* (2014).

"Fourth Amendment—Search and Seizure—Searching Cell Phones Incident to Arrest." *Harvard Law Review* (2014).

Friedland, Steven. "Cell Phone Searches in a Digital World: Blurred Lines, New Realities and Fourth Amendment Pluralism." *SSRN Electronic Journal SSRN Journal*.

Johnson, Emily M. *Legalities of GPS and Cell Phone Surveillance*. New York: Novinka, 2012.

Reardon, Conor M. "Cell Phones, Police Recording, and the Intersection of the First and Fourth Amendments." *Duke Law Journal* (2013).

Silk, Jennie Vee. "Calling Out *Maryland v. King*: DNA, Cell Phones, and the Fourth Amendment." *SSRN Electronic Journal SSRN Journal*.

Thompson, Richard M. *Governmental Tracking of Cell Phones and Vehicles: The Confluence of Privacy, Technology, and Law*. Washington, DC: Congressional Research Service, 2011.

Thomson, Aimee. "Cellular Dragnet: Active Cell Site Simulators and the Fourth Amendment." *SSRN Electronic Journal SSRN Journal*.

See also: Criminal justice (criminal procedure); Fourth Amendment to the U.S. Constitution; *Katz v. United States*; Law enforcement; *Ontario v. Quon*; *Riley v. California*; Search warrants; Smartphones

Center for Democracy and Technology (CDT)

Identification: A Washington, DC–based organization formed in December 1994 as a 501(c) (3) nonprofit public policy organization dedicated to promoting democracy on the Internet. The organization's mission is to develop and implement public policies to protect and advance civil liberties and democratic values in new interactive media. Its mission is guided by six principles:

(1) the unique nature of the Internet, (2) freedom of expression, (3) privacy, (4) surveillance, (5) access, and (6) democratic participation.

Americans have greatly valued privacy, and even more so because of events of privacy invasion throughout U.S. history. This value of individual privacy is so strong that the Founding Fathers created clauses in the Constitution that would uphold this right. The creators of the Constitution were correct in protecting our right to privacy because it is essential in a democracy where citizens need to be autonomous and free thinking to ensure self-government.

Groups such as the American Civil Liberties Union (ACLU), the Electronic Frontier Foundation (EFF), the Electronic Privacy Information Center (EPIC), Computer Professionals for Social Responsibility, the United States Privacy Council, and the Privacy Rights Clearinghouse are responsible for much of the privacy that still exists in the United States. These institutions monitor encroachments on privacy, lobby against such encroachments, and maintain a network to alert the public to new developments.

CDT has been involved in work such as analyzing constitutional, legal, and enforcement issues presented by the Exxon bill (aka Communications Decency Act of 1995), with which the Department of Justice (DOJ) agreed; expert testimony for the Senate Judiciary Subcommittee on Terrorism and Technology on free speech issues posed by the availability of bomb manuals on the Internet; monitoring the implementation of the Digital Telephony Bill; and studying the alternatives to the so-called clipper chip.

CDT pursues its mission through research and public policy development in a consensus-building process based on working groups comprised of public interest and commercial representatives of divergent views. These working groups lie in the areas of online privacy, digital security, and free expression (e.g., Interactive Working Group, and Digital Privacy and Security Working Group). Because working groups are educational in nature, they do not take formal positions on legislation.

CDT promotes policy positions on American issues as well as foreign and international issues through public policy advocacy, online grassroots organizing with the Internet user community, public education campaigns, litigation, and the development of technology standards and online information resources.

CDT is supported by contributions from industry and foundations. Most supporters join and fund one or more working groups, activities, and projects. Working group and special project participants attend CDT-coordinated forums on policy issues and are kept informed through the center's email, online policy posts, issue briefs, and reports.

Shaunté Chácon

Further Reading

Arterton, F. Christopher. *Teledemocracy: Can Technology Protect Democracy?* Newbury Park, CA: Sage Publications; 1987.

"High Tech, Media Seek Possible Compromise. (Center for Democracy and Technology)." *The Online Reporter*, December 2, 2002.

Li, Joyce H. *The Center for Democracy and Technology and Internet Privacy in the U.S.: Lessons of the Last Five Years.* Lanham, MD: Scarecrow Press, 2003.

MacKinnon, Rebecca. *Consent of the Networked: The World-wide Struggle for Internet Freedom.* New York: Basic Books, 2012.

The Net Democracy Guide: Politics and the Internet. Washington, DC: Center for Democracy and Technology, 2006.

Northouse, Clayton. *Protecting What Matters: Technology, Security, and Liberty since 9/11.* Washington, DC: Computer Ethics Institute:, 2006.

Privacy Recommendations for the Google Book Search Settlement. Washington, DC: Center for Democracy and Technology, 2009.

"Regardless of Frontiers": The International Right to Freedom of Expression in the Digital Age. Version 0.5, discussion draft ed. Washington, DC: Center for Democracy and Technology, 2011.

Weil, Nancy. "CDT to File FTC Complaint on Pentium III. (Center for Democracy and Technology)." *Network World*, March 1, 1999.

See also: American Civil Liberties Union (ACLU); Computers and privacy; Constitutional law; Electronic Privacy Information Center (EPIC); Electronic surveillance

Central Security Service

Identification: A United States Defense agency formed in 1972. Prior to this reorganization, Service Cryptologic Elements (SCE) had been under the direction of the various branches of the U.S. military.

With the creation of Central Security Service (CSS), functions such as tactical signals intelligence, cryptology, and information assurance were placed under the direction of the National Security Agency (NSA).

The NSA/CSS is considered the U.S. government's official cryptographic agency. Its role is to protect U.S. national security systems and to produce foreign signals intelligence information. Signals intelligence comprises communications intelligence and electronics intelligence. Communications intelligence consists of foreign communications passed by radio, wire, or other electromagnetic means. Electronics intelligence consists of foreign electromagnetic radiations such as emissions from a radar system.

Tactical military intelligence had been gathered historically by specially trained members of the military stationed throughout the world. During the Vietnam War, for example, each of the military services had their own cryptologic units, supported by the NSA, which had separate signals intelligence (SIGINT) support groups (SSGs). With demands for enhanced cryptologic standards, the defense SIGINT systems were modernized and unified. This accompanied the integration of the NSA and the Service Cryptologic Agencies (SCAs) into a new unified command, with NSA now taking over the SCA functions.

Originally, The NSA/CSS was proposed to be a distinct service along with the other military branches (army, air force, marines, and navy). Due to opposition by the existing branches, the CSS became an inter–service agency within the Defense Department. President Richard Nixon issued a presidential directive that created the CSS in February 1972. The new agency was charged with facilitating cooperation between the NSA and the SCEs of the various branches of the military services.

The NSA/CSS organization was credited with increasing performance standards and training. It also helped centralize NSA and the various military groups with cryptologic responsibilities and capabilities.

The CSS directs all SIGINT-related activities. The NSA director is the chief of CSS and directs its activities. In other words, the NSA director is responsible for overseeing the entire U.S. signals intelligence system, which includes the cryptologic elements of the military services, which is known as the CSS. The various cryptologic groups receive logistical and administrative support from the respective branches of the U.S. military. The secretary of defense, in consultation with the Joint Chiefs of Staff, may direct other CSS SIGINT–related military units and resources.

The CSS is responsible for capturing enemy signals (radar, telemetry, radio/satellite communications) through the means provided by military branch involved with the operation.

In the current environment, most U.S. intelligence is devoted to counterterrorism, hard targets, and support to military operations that originate from the NSA. The U.S. government has long stressed that it is vital to national security that NSA have cryptographic superiority to protect the United States and its citizens. U.S. national security officials argue that the United States is fighting a war against foreign foes in cyberspace. Thus, they argue, warrantless surveillance of international Internet traffic is essential to national security. They stress that the NSA has a critical role in protecting national security and that this effort does not violate the privacy rights of Americans.

NSA surveillance has created controversy several times, including its spying on prominent anti–Vietnam War leaders or economic espionage. A balance between national security and privacy rights was reached in the 1970s due to congressional inquiries into controversial NSA operations that allegedly violated the privacy rights of Americans. Those investigations led to the creation of the present oversight and legal structure in the executive, legislative, and judicial branches. After the September 11, 2001, attacks, the American public and lawmakers again deliberated where to delineate between legitimate national security concerns and essential privacy rights. Specifically, in the case of CSS, this involved when and how the agency should gather and use SIGINT without violating the privacy rights of Americans.

In 2013, the extent of the NSA's secret surveillance programs was revealed to the public by Edward Snowden, a contractor working at the NSA. According to the leaked documents, NSA intercepts the communications of over 1 billion people worldwide and tracks the movement of hundreds of millions of people using cellphones. It has also created or maintained security vulnerabilities in most software and encryption, leaving the majority of the Internet susceptible to cyberattacks from the NSA and other parties. In addition to the various data-sharing concerns that persist, research has pointed to the NSA's ability to surveil the domestic Internet traffic of foreign countries through boomerang routing.

Further Reading

Greenwald, Glenn. *No Place to Hide: Edward Snowden, the NSA, and the U.S. Surveillance State.* New York: Metropolitan Books/H. Holt, 2014.

Landree, Eric, et al. *A Delicate Balance: Portfolio Analysis and Management for Intelligence Information Dissemination Programs.* Santa Monica, CA: RAND, 2009.

National Security Agency. *The Origins of NSA.* Fort George G. Meade, Md.: Center for Cryptologic History, 1996.

Pincus, Walter. "NSA Reform Should Proceed Cautiously." *Washington Post*, November 7, 2013.

Ransom, Harry Howe. *Central Intelligence and National Security.* Cambridge, MA: Harvard University Press, 1958.

Sternstein, Aliya. "NSA to Crack Codes with Big Data (National Security Agency)." *NextGov.com*, March 30, 2012.

Wanlund, Bill. "Intelligence Reform: Are U.S. Spy Agencies Prepared for 21st-century Threats?" *CQ Researcher* 25, no. 2 (May 29, 2015).

See also: Cellphones; Electronic surveillance; National Security Agency (NSA); Snowden, Edward

Children's Online Privacy Protection Act, 15 U.S.C. §§ 6501–6508

Identification: An act signed into law on October 21, 1998, by President William J. Clinton. In October 1999, the Federal Trade Commission issued the Children's Online Privacy Protection Act Rule (the "COPPA Rule") (15 C.F.R. Part 312), which became effective on April 20, 2000. The Federal Trade Commission (FTC) administers and enforces the Children's Online Privacy Protection Act (COPPA).

Purpose and requirements of COPPA

The FTC's 1998 report, *Privacy Online: A Report to Congress,* contained findings related to its study of the practices of websites directed toward children. Among other pertinent findings, the report revealed that, while 89 percent of websites collected personal information directly from children, only 10 percent of these sites offered any mechanisms for parental control over the collection and use of such information. Based on these findings, the FTC recommended that Congress pass comprehensive legislation that would provide parents with greater control over the collection and dissemination of children's personal information.

According to the lead sponsor of COPPA, Senator Richard Bryan (D-NV), Congress had four related aims in creating this legislation: (1) to enhance parental involvement in children's online activities as a way to protect children's privacy, (2) to protect children's safety when they engage in online activities, (3) to maintain the security of children's personal information collected online, and (4) to limit the collection of personal information from children without parental consent. Toward that end, COPPA initially imposed requirements on two groups of operators of commercial websites and online services: operators or websites and online services that are directed to children under the age of thirteen that collect, use, or disclose personal information from children, *and* operators of web-sites and online services intended for a general audience but who have actual knowledge that they are collecting, using, or disclosing personal information from children under the age of thirteen. "Personal information," as broadly defined under COPPA, incudes an individual's name, physical address, email address, telephone number, and social security number, as well as any other identifier (as determined by the FTC) that permits an individual to be contacted in person or online. Excluded from the definition of "operator" are nonprofit websites and personal homepages. In determining whether a website is "directed to children," the FTC considers factors including subject matter, visual or audio content (including use of animated characters), age of models, and language.

Key requirements imposed on covered operators include the provision of an effective notice as to its data use and collection policies with regard to children, the receipt of verifiable parental consent prior to collection of information, the disclosure to parents of information collected with respect to their children, procedures for parents to revoke consent and have information deleted, and limitations on the use of games and prizes directed toward children. Requirements of "effective notice" include the clear labeling and prominent placement of links to the privacy policy on the homepage. Also, the policy must provide the contact information of website operators collecting and maintaining information, indicate whether the information is disclosed to third parties, and specify how such information is used. "Verifiable parental consent" requires operators to use a consent method

that is reasonably calculated, in light of available technology, to ensure that the person providing consent is the child's parent.

The COPPA rule has a safe harbor provision, whereby industry groups can seek FTC approval of self-compliance programs that implement protections of the COPPA rule. Under this provision, the FTC must act within 180 days of the request. Since 2000, the FTC has approved the safe harbor programs offered by the Entertainment Software Rating Board; Aristotle International, Inc.; the Children's Advertising Review Unit of the Council of Better Business Bureaus; PRIVO, Inc.; TRUSTe; kidSAFE; and iKeepSafe.

Enforcement

Congress delegated all enforcement duties to the FTC, granting it the power to bring forward adjudicatory actions against websites and the power to levy fines for violations. The FTC is authorized to treat a violation of the COPPA rule as a violation of a rule defining an unfair or deceptive act or practice prescribed under section 18(a)(1)(B) of the Federal Trade Commission Act. COPPA does not provide parents or children with a private right of action. It does, however, grant states and certain federal agencies the authority to enforce compliance with respect to entities over which they have jurisdiction. To date, only Texas and New Jersey have brought COPPA enforcement actions. Violators of COPPA are liable for civil penalties of up to $16,000 per violation. By 2010, the FTC had collected $3.2 million through fourteen COPPA enforcement actions. Notable COPPA enforcement actions were filed against Xanga.com in 2006 (a $1 million civil penalty) and Sony BMG Music Entertainment ($1 million civil penalty) in 2008.

Recent developments

Pursuant to COPPA and § 312.11 of the COPPA rule, the FTC was required to initiate a review no later than five years after the rule's effective date to evaluate the rule's implementation. After initiating this review in April 2005, the FTC considered extensive public comment on the COPPA rule, ultimately reaching a decision in March 2006 to retain the COPPA rule without change. In March 2010, however, the FTC sought public comment on whether it was necessary to reexamine the COPPA rule given ongoing changes in the online environment—notably, children's increasing use of mobile technology to access the Internet.

The COPPA rule was amended effective July 1, 2013. The amended rule takes into account technological developments, including mobile devices, interactive gaming, and social networking, that alter how children use and access the Internet. Thus, under the revised rule, COPPA now applies to third-party service, including ad networks and plug-ins, that collect information from users of a website or online service directed to children under the age of thirteen. It now also applies to mobile apps that send or receive information online and Internet-enabled gaming platforms. In addition, the amended COPPA rule adds four new categories of information to the definition of "personal information": geolocation information, photographs and video files containing a child's image as well as audio files containing a child's voice, a screen or username that reveals an individual's email address or a similar identifier that enables direct online contact with an individual, and persistent identifiers that may be used to recognize a user over time or across different websites or online services.

With the revelations of privacy lapses among the large social media companies like Facebook and Google during the late 2010s, the question of the sufficiency of COPPA's provisions have resurfaced. In an April 2018 congressional hearing on privacy for children and teens, Senator Ed Markey (D-MA) proposed a "privacy bill of rights" for teenagers that would cover the gap between COPPA, which covers children up to age 13, and adult privacy laws. Facebook CEO Mark Zuckerberg argued against such additional laws, calling them unnecessary. The timing of this assertion was difficult, as it came close upon the heels of the controversy Facebook faced due to the sharing of information on 87 million

users with Cambridge Analytica, a social media consulting firm hired by Donald J. Trump's 2016 presidential campaign. During that same month, the video sharing site YouTube, which is owned by Google, faced charges by consumer advocacy groups that they did not comply with COPPA in the way they handled children's data.

Ursula Gorham

Further Reading

Boyd D., Hargittai E., J. Schultz, and J, Palfrey J. (2011). "Why Parents Help Their Children Lie to Facebook about Age: Unintended Consequences of the 'Children's Online Privacy Protection Act.'" *First Monday* 16, no. 11.

Davis, J. J. "Marketing to Children Online: A Manager's Guide to the Children's Online Privacy Protection Act." *S.A.M. Advanced Management Journal* 67, no. 4 (2002), 11–21.

Delaney, E. (2012). "The Children's Online Privacy Protection Act and Rule: An Overview." *Journal of Civil Rights and Economic Development*, 16, no. 3 (2101): 641–648.

Madden, M., S. Cortesi, U. Gasser, A., Lenhart, and M. Duggan. *Parents, Teens, and Online Privacy*. Pew Internet & American Life Project, 2012.

Maheshwari, S. "YouTube Is Improperly Collecting Children's Data, Consumer Groups Say." *The New York Times*, April 9, 2018. https://www.nytimes.com/2018/04/09/business/media/youtube-kids-ftc-complaint.html

Stanaland, A. J. S., M. O. Lwin, and S. Leong, (2009). "Providing Parents with Online Privacy Information: Approaches in the U.S. and the UK." *Journal of Consumer Affairs* 43 no. 3 (2009): 474–494.

Whittaker, Z. "At hearing, Facebook's Zuckerberg rejects law to protect privacy of children." *ZDNet*, April 10, 2018. https://www.zdnet.com/article/at-hearing-zuckerberg-rejects-law-to-protect-the-privacy-of-children/

See also: Children's right to privacy; Federal Trade Commission (FTC); Mobile devices; Online privacy and protection; Social networking technologies

Children's right to privacy

Identification: A right that emanates from natural rights and the legal rights of children that have evolved over the past two centuries.

The natural rights of children were codified in 1924 by the League of Nations under the *Geneva Declaration of the Rights of the Child*. This declaration identified five rights of the child, including the right to have normal physical and spiritual development, the right to not be hungry and the right to care, to be relieved of distress, and to not be exploited. In 1990 the United Nations adopted 41 articles under the Convention on the Rights of the Child. This convention elaborated upon the five natural rights of the child, as defined by the *Geneva Declaration*, and defined the role of the state in protecting children from harm and insuring physical, mental, and emotional sustenance. A child's legal rights have grown from these natural rights. These rights include the prohibition of child labor and physical and emotional abuse, as well as the right to attend school. However, the volitional rights of children have been continually limited by their status as minors. For example, children are not allowed to enter into contracts, to marry, to hold a driver's license, or to buy alcohol until they reach the age of majority, typically at 18. Today there exists a tension between a child's volitional rights to explore and participate in the world and the right to be protected from harm. This tension is exacerbated by the fungible nature of the right to privacy in the United States.

There is no Constitutional protection of privacy in the United States. The "right to privacy" as a legal right was first described in 1890 by Samuel D. Warren and Louis D. Brandeis in their seminal article "The Right to Privacy" published in the *Harvard Law Review*. Warren and Brandeis defined the right to privacy as the right to "be left alone." Due to the lack of an explicit right, the United States Supreme Court has repeatedly defined and redefined the legal concept of privacy for adults. However, the United States Supreme Court has used the Constitutional guaranty of "liberty" to attempt to address the questions raised in cases concerning a person's privacy. In so doing, the Court

has continued to balance the liberty interests of individuals with the state's desire to impinge upon a person's right to privacy. However, the concept of a child's right to privacy has only been expressly delineated in law in specific areas, such as education and health care. Currently there are three Federal laws that protect the privacy rights of children —the Family Educational Rights and Privacy Act (FERPA), the Children's Online Privacy Protection Act (COPPA), and the Heath Insurance Portability and Accountability Act (HIPAA).

The FERPA is a Federal law that was enacted in 1974 and that controls the accessibility of educational records. These rights originate with the child's parents or guardians and is transferred to the child at the age of 18, or when the child attends a school beyond the high school level. The child who has attained this status are known as "eligible students." FERPA gives parents and guardians the right to inspect their child's education records and to request corrections to the records. It also limits the ability of educational institutions to release any individual student's records to third parties, with these exceptions: school officials with a legitimate educational interest; schools to which the child is transferring; for authorized audits or evaluations; appropriate third parties administering financial aid; accrediting organizations. FERPA also allows the release of information in the extenuating circumstances of a court order or subpoena, in the context of health or safety emergencies, or to the juvenile justice system, pursuant to specific State law.

The Children's Online Privacy Protection Act (COPPA) was enacted in 1998 and became effective in 2000. It was last amended in 2012. It allows the Federal Trade Commission to enforce regulations that protect children's on-line privacy. The rule applies to commercial websites and online services and mobile applications that are directed to children who are 13 years of age or younger, as well as to federal government websites. Foreign websites must also comply to COPPA if the website collects information from children in the United States. The rule also applies to websites who have actual knowledge that personal information is being collected from a third party website that is directed to children who are 13 years or younger. COPPA allows educational institutions to give consent in order to allow their students to use online educational resources, such as homework help sites, learning modules, and testing sites.

The Children's Online Privacy Protection Act requires these operators to: 1) provide a clear and comprehensive privacy policy; 2) provide direct notice to parents and obtain parental consent before collecting information from a child; 3) give parents to the right to prohibit the transference of their child's information to a third party; 4) provide parental access to a child's information and the ability of the parent to edit or delete the information; 5) give the opportunity to the parent to prevent further use or collection of a child's information; 6) maintain the confidentiality, integrity, and security of the child's information; 7) limit the maintenance of a child's information to the extent necessary for the purpose; 8) delete a child's information using methods that will protect unauthorized or third party use.

Under COPPA, a child's personal information includes her name, address, contact information, screen or user name, telephone number, social security number, a persistent identifier, photograph, video or audio recording, geolocation information, or any other information that could lead to a person being able to identify the child. This regulation on information is restricted to that *collected from the child*, and does not apply to information collected about the child from a parent or adult. Websites can proactively comply to COPPA regulations by participating the Act's Safe Harbor Program, which requires the website company to comply with the self-regulation process on an annual basis.

The Health Insurance Portability and Accountability Act (HIPAA) was enacted in 1996. It provides privacy protection to children in

three ways: 1) protecting medical records of children who consent to care, and were the parents' consent is not necessary for the child to receive the care; 2) when a child receives medical treatment at the direction of a court, or at the direction of a court-appointed person; 3) or where the parent consents to a confidential relationship between a child and a health care provider. However, if a state or local law gives a parent the right to access their child's medical records the state or local law takes precedence. These rights can be circumnavigated if the health care provider has a reasonable belief based on her professional judgment that the child has been, or will be, subjected to abuse, neglect, domestic violence, or if a parent's knowledge of the medical treatment could endanger the child. HIPAA also protects a child's individually identifiable health record, whether it is an electronic, written, or oral record from disclosure.

The increasing amount of time that children spend on social media and the internet has necessitated the consideration of a child's right to participate and interact with the digital world, while maintaining the child's safety. The discussion of children's right to actively participate in the online world is further complicated by a child's status as a legal minority. This status prohibits children from participating in certain activities and restricts their access to certain types of materials. A fundamental aspect of a right to privacy is the concept of being left alone, which is inherently impossible for children. Therefore, many argue that the concept of "children's privacy" is fundamentally different from that of adults.

The United Nations Convention on the Rights of the Child adopted a comprehensive resolution that includes two articles that pertain to children's privacy rights and rights of expression. Article 13 of the Convention states that a child has "the right to freedom of expression; this right shall include freedom to seek, receive and impart information and ideas of all kinds, regardless of frontiers, either orally, in writing or in print, in the form of art, or through any other media of the child's choice." Article 13 continues "[t]he exercises of this right may be subject to certain restrictions, but these shall only be such as are provided by law and are necessary." Article 16 of the convention states that "[n]o child shall be subjected to arbitrary or unlawful interference with his or her privacy, family, or correspondence, nor to unlawful attacks on his or her honour and reputation" and "[t]he child has the right to the protection of the law against such interference or attacks."

The rights articulated in Article 16 are increasingly being addressed in "cyberbullying" or "cyberharrassment" laws. Cyberbullying is defined as threatening or harassing emails, instant messaging, blog entries, or the development of websites with the sole purpose of tormenting an individual. Many of these laws were enacted in response to high-profile cyberbullying cases, such as the death of Megan Meier. Megan Meier committed suicide in 2006 after having been subjected to harassment through her Myspace account. Cyberbulling can result in depression and anxiety in the victim, as well as isolation and health problems. Decreased academic achievement has also been found in children who have been cyberbullied.

The Center for Disease Control conducted a geographically comprehensive surveillance study of students in grades 9 - 12. Published in 2013, the study found that 14.8 percent of children who participated in the study had experienced electronic bullying. In 2011, the United States Department of Education published the results of the School Crime Supplement to the National Crime Victimization Survey. The survey reported that 2,198,000 students had reported being cyberbullied. Of that 1,073,000 had received unwanted contact by text message, and 884,000 had had hurtful information posted on the internet.

State and local cyberbullying laws define the specific prohibited conduct and the sanctions and punishments incurred when a person is convicted for such behavior. Twenty-two states currently have cyberbullying laws. Three states have proposed cyberbullying legislation. However, not all state laws require criminal sanction for bullying. All but one state, Wyoming, requires a school policy. Of the 22 states with cyberbullying laws, only 15 include harassment that is conducted off of the school's campus.

There are no direct Federal cyberbullying laws; however, cyberbullying can overlap with existing Federal prohibitions, such as discriminatory harassment. Federally funding public educational institutions are obligated to resolve issues of harassment of students. Harassment is defined for this purpose as severe, persistent or pervasive behavior that is based on a student's race, color, national origin, sex, disability, or religion that creates a hostile environment and interferes or limits a student's ability to participate or benefit from the services, activities, or other opportunities offered by the school. In 2009, a cyberbullying law was proposed by Representative Linda Sanchez of the 39th congressional district of California. Named the Megan Meier Cyberbullying Prevention Act (H.R. 1966). This act defined cyberbullying as the transmission "in interstate or foreign commerce any communication, with the intent to coerce, intimidate, harass, or cause substantial emotional distress to a person, using electronic means to support severe, repeated, and hostile behavior." The punishment imposed if convicted of cyberbullying is a fine, up to two years' imprisonment, or both. This bill, however, was not passed by Congress.

An aspect of children's rights not adequately reflected in the laws created to protect children from violation of their privacy are the rights of children to maintain privacy within the family. The United Nations Convention on the Rights of the Child does not recognize the right of a child to have privacy apart from her parents or guardians. Additionally, the United States Supreme Court ruled in *Hodgson v Minnesota*, 497 U.S. 447 (1990), that there is a realm of privacy within the family, but that privacy right extends to intrusion from outside of the family by third parties, not intra-familial. The tension rises from the inherent need of children to be dependent on his or her parent or guardian and the concurrent need for children to be able to have volitional expression —children have personhood, interests, and individual needs. This individualism is increasingly being expressed in the online world.

The majority of children under the age of eight have a smartphone, and a little under half own a tablet, with just more than a quarter having an iPad touch or something similar. Nearly three quarters of children 8 years or younger use some type of mobile media or applications on a device. In a survey of 802 teenagers, the Pew Research Center found that there has been steady growth of teenagers throughout the early 21st century. Of those surveyed, 91% post photos of themselves, 71% post their school name, 71% post the town or city where they live, 53% post their email address, and 20% post their phone number. In addition, 92% use their real name, 82% post their birth date, and 24% post videos of themselves. The study also found that 70% of teenagers who use Facebook are friends with their parents, 76% are friends with brothers and sisters, and 91% are friends with extended family members.

The use of social media by children, as defined as any child under the age of 18, exemplifies the conflict between protecting a child's right to self-expression from inhibition, both from inside of the family and from without, and the need to ensure the safety of the child. In the United States there are very few legal protections for a child's right to self-expression. For example, the Children's Online Privacy Protection Act (COPPA) attempts to regulate the collection of personal data from children under the age of 13. However, the right of enforcement is given to the parents or guardians of the child, not the child herself. The Family Educational Rights and Privacy Act (FERPA) similarly gives the right of protection to the parents, not the child. In these two instances the child and parent are considered

as one entity, indistinguishable. Two examples of policies that protect the individual privacy of the child are the American Library Association's (ALA) policy regarding a child's use of the library and certain aspects of the Heath Insurance Portability and Accountability Act.

The ALA is the primary professional body that sets and defines best practices for library management. The ALA Library Bill of Rights stipulates that library policies and procedures should not restrict a child's "equitable access" to all library facilities, materials, and services. Furthermore, the ALA's position on the role of parents and guardians encourages the parent's active participation in the child's library usage, rather than having the library act as a supplemental guardian who proactively restricts the child's use of facilities, materials, and services in anticipation of probable parental objections. In addition, the ALA Library Bill of Rights strongly encourages libraries to not restrict access to information technology, and emerging technologies, based on age. In fact, the ALA sees a child's right to access and interact with the digital world as an extension of the minor's First Amendment rights, as well as being an integral part of the child's learning process. Finally, the ALA Code of Ethics protects "each library user's right to privacy and confidentiality with respect to information sought or received and resources consulted, borrowed, acquired or transmitted." As the ALA makes no distinction between a child and an adult patron, this provision protecting the privacy and confidentiality of information or resource use applies equally to children as it does to adults.

In 2000 Congress passed the Children's Internet Protection Act (CIPA). The Children's Internet Protection Act requires any public school or library that receives discounts through the E-rate Program to have an internet safety policy, which includes technological blocking systems, in place. The E-rate Program provides discounts to schools and libraries in order to obtain affordable broadband access. The safety policies must block or filter specific obscene pictures, pictures of child pornography, or pictures that are harmful to minors. In order to receive the E-rate discounts, schools and libraries must be able to demonstrate that their internet safety policy monitors online activity of minors and that there are educational programs in place that inform minors of appropriate online behavior and cyberbullying. The internet safety policy must address: 1) minor's access to inappropriate materials; 2) safety and security of minor's using email, chat, and any other form of direct online communications; 3) unauthorized use of online systems, such as through hacking; 4) unauthorized disclosure or use of a minor's personal information; 5) systems in place to restrict access to harmful material. However, CIPA does not require tracking of a minor's use of the internet.

The Health Insurance Portability and Accountability Act (HIPPA) creates certain privacy rights that provide children with the ability to control access to confidential information. Emancipated minors have the same privacy rights as adults. In specific circumstances, un-emancipated minor children can maintain their individual right to privacy, which precludes the parents or guardians from acting as the representative of the child. These circumstances are: 1) when the child consents to care under a state's minor consent law; 2) where a child can legally receive care without the consent of the parent; 3) when parents or guardians consent to their child or minor receiving confidential care. In all three of these circumstances the parent is no longer the representative of the child and cannot have access to the child's medical records. Additionally, where state law does not require a physician to disclose the medical records of a child to a representative adult, the physician can use her discretion as to granting the request for access.

There are two instances wherein a healthcare provider can refuse to release the information of an un-emancipated child to a representative parent or guardian. In the first, a healthcare provider can refuse to provide information about the child if the provider has a reasonable belief that the parent has subjected the child to abuse or neglect, or when providing the information could endanger the child. In the second, a health care provider can also deny information to a representative parent or adult if providing the information could result in harm to the child, or to another person. Conversely, a health care provider can release the medical information of a child if by doing so prevents or diminishes an imminent threat to a person's or the public's health or safety.

Rulings of the United States Supreme Court have had an impact on the status of children as individuals who maintain Constitutional rights. In *In re Gault*, 387 U.S. 1 (1967), the Court reasoned that any juvenile facing a criminal charge in a delinquency court has a right to due process under the XIV amendment, establishing Constitutional parity between juveniles in delinquency proceedings and adults in criminal proceedings. The Supreme Court ruled in *Tinker v Des Moines Independent Community School District*, 393 U.S. 503 (1969), clarified the First Amendment right to freedom of speech by students on school property. The Court also ruled that schools can only suppress student speech when the speech would "materially and substantially" interfere with the operation of the school. In Planned Parenthood *of Central Missouri v Danforth*, 428 U.S. 52 (1976), the Court ruled that states cannot require parental consent for an unmarried minor under the age of 18 to have an abortion. The Court reasoned that requiring approval from the minor's parents could not trump the right of a minor to have an abortion under *Roe v Wade* and that such a requirement was insufficiently supported by the state's desire to protect family unity. Danforth, therefore, establishes a right of privacy for minors with regard to abortion that is separate from the family. However, children do not have a clearly defined right to privacy under the Constitution, nor under statute.

Rachel Jorgensen

Further Reading

Gutnick, Aviva Lucas. and Michael Robb, Laurie Takeuchi, Jennifer Kotler. *Always Connected: The New Digital Media Habits of Young Children*. New York: The Joan Ganz Cooney Center at Sesame Workshop, 2011.

Keiter, Robert B. "Privacy, Children, and Their Parents: Reflections on and Beyond the Supreme Court's Approach," *Minnesota Law Review* 66 (November 1981): 459-468.

Shin, Wonsun and Hyunjin Kang. "Adolescents' Privacy Concerns and Information Disclosure Online: The Role of Parents and the Internet. *Computers in Human Behavior*. 54 (January 2016): 114-123. https://doi.org/10.1016/j.chb.2015.07.062

Shmueli, Benjamin and Ayelet Blecher-Prigat. "Privacy for Children," *Columbia Human Rights Law Review* 42, no. 3 (Spring 2011): 759 - 795.

Souris, Renee N. "Parents, Privacy, and Facebook: Legal and Social Responses to the Problem of 'Over-Sharing' in Navin A. Cudd (ed.) *Core Concepts and Contemporary Issues in Privacy*. Cham, Switzerland, Springer, 2018.

Teens, Social Media, and Privacy. Washington, DC: Pew Research Center, 2013.

van der Hof, Simone and Bibi van den Berg, Bart Schermer. *Minding Minors Wandering the Web: Regulating Online Child Safety,* Information Technology and Law Series. The Hague, The Netherlands: T.M.C. Asser Press, 2014.

Zero to Eight: Children's Media Use in America 2013. San Francisco: Common Sense Media, 2013.

See also: Children's Online Privacy Protection Act (COPPA); Family Educational Rights and Privacy Act of 1974 (FERPA); Federal Trade Commission (FTC); Health Insurance Portability and Accountability Act of 1996 (HIPAA); The Right to Privacy

City of Ontario, Cal. v. Quon, 506 U.S. 746 (2010)

A unanimous decision, with a majority opinion by Justice Anthony Kennedy, in which the U.S. Supreme Court ruled that a city's review of an officer's text messages was reasonable and did not violate the Fourth Amendment.

In this case, Jeff Quon, a police officer employed by the City of Ontario, received a government-issued alphanumeric pager capable of sending and receiving text messages. The city purchased twenty such pagers to assist members of its SWAT team, of which Quon was a member, to mobilize and respond to emergency situations more efficiently. Each pager was allotted a limited number of characters that could be sent or received each month, and if a pager exceeded that predetermined limit, the city would be charged an overage fee.

Prior to receiving a pager, Quon had signed a computer policy agreement that acknowledged the city reserved a right to monitor and log all network activity, including email and Internet use, without notice. The agreement also stated that users should have no expectations of privacy or confidentiality when using city computer resources.

Although the agreement contained no provision specifically mentioning the monitoring of text messaging, the city communicated with Quon that it would treat text messages the same way it treated emails.

Within the first or second billing cycle, Quon exceeded his monthly text-messaging character allotment. At the suggestion of his superior, Quon reimbursed the city for the overage fee. In the following months, Quon exceeded his character limit three or four additional times, and he subsequently paid for those extra charges as well. Quon's consistent overage charges led the chief of police to investigate whether the character limits were sufficient for the officers. As part of his investigation, the chief acquired the transcripts of Quon's text messages from the pager service provider. It was discovered that some of Quon's text messages were non-work-related, including many that were sexually explicit in nature.

Quon was subsequently referred to an internal investigation unit to determine if he had violated any police department rules. The investigation concluded that the vast majority of Quon;s text messages were non-work-related, and Quon was subsequently disciplined.

Quon filed suit against the city, alleging that it violated federal and state law, including his

Fourth Amendment rights. The district court determined that Quon had a reasonable expectation of privacy in his text messages but that the audit of his messages would be reasonable if the intent behind the search was for a legitimate, work-related purpose. After a jury determined that the intent of the audit was to determine the efficacy of the character limits, the district court held that Quon's Fourth Amendment rights were not violated.

The U.S. Court of Appeals for the Ninth Circuit reversed in part, holding that the search of the text messages was not reasonable in scope.

The U.S. Supreme Court granted review of the case so that it could consider the issue of whether the city violated Quon's Fourth Amendment rights by reading his text messages.

Justice Kennedy first explained that the Fourth Amendment applied even where the government acts as an employer, discussing the majority and concurring opinions in *O'Connor v. Ortega*, 480 U.S. 709 (1987). The Court acknowledged that the *O'Connor* decision left unclear the proper analytical framework for evaluating Fourth Amendment claims against government employers because no majority rationale prevailed in deciding the case. For the purposes of deciding Quon's case, Justice Kennedy explained that the Court did not need to decide which rationale in *O'Connor* applied. Here, he noted, both approaches would lead to the same result.

The Court next discussed whether Quon had a reasonable expectation of privacy in his text messages, acknowledging that rapid technological changes have made privacy expectations uncertain in modern times. The Court proceeded with caution and simply assumed that Quon had a reasonable expectation of privacy in his text messages. The Court also assumed two additional propositions: First, that the city's review of Quon's text messages constituted a search within the meaning of the Fourth Amendment, and, second, that the principles that apply to a government employer's search of an employee's physical office would

apply with at least the same force where the intrusion occurs in the electronic sphere.

Justice Kennedy explained that, even if Quon had a reasonable expectation of privacy in his text messages, the city's acts may not have necessarily violated the Fourth Amendment. As a general matter, warrantless searches are per se unreasonable under the Fourth Amendment, but the Court has recognized a few exceptions to this rule. In this case, Justice Kennedy concluded that the special needs of the workplace justified the search of Quon's text messages. Thus, because the search of the text messages was for a work-related purpose—namely, whether the predetermined character limits for the pagers were sufficient—the city had reasonable grounds to inspect the transcripts. In addition, the search was not excessively intrusive, and therefore the scope of the city's search was permissible. Thus, the Court held that the city did not violate Quon's Fourth Amendment rights. The judgment of the court of appeals was reversed.

While the Supreme Court unanimously concluded that Quon's Fourth Amendment rights were not violated, Justices John Paul Stevens and Antonin Scalia wrote separate concurrences.

It is evident in *Quon* that the justices struggled to apply Fourth Amendment standards to the circumstances of this case. Rather than decide whether Quon had a reasonable expectation of privacy in the content of his text messages, the Court simply assumed that he did and rejected his Fourth Amendment claim by citing an exception to the general prohibition against warrantless searches. The Court's trepidation to decide the issue indicates a growing uncertainty of how traditional Fourth Amendment legal principles apply to emerging technologies.

Ethan P. Fallon

Further Reading

Bentzen, Sheila A. "Safe for Work? Analyzing the Supreme Court's Standard of Privacy for Government Employees in Light of *City of Ontario v. Quon*." *Iowa Law Review* 97, no. 4 (May 2012): 1283-1304.

Fishman, Clifford S. "Electronic Privacy in the Government Workplace and *City of Ontario, California v. Quon*: The Supreme Court Brought Forth a Mouse."

Mississippi Law Journal 81, no. 5 (May 2012). "Fourth Amendment-Reasonable Expectation of Privacy." *Harvard Law Review* 124 (2010): 179–188.

See also: Constitutional law; Criminal justice (criminal procedure); Fourth Amendment to the U.S. Constitution; Search warrants; Supreme Court of the United States

City of Sherman v. Otis Henry, 928 S.W.2d 464 (1996)

Identification: A unanimous decision of the Texas Supreme Court, with a majority opinion by Justice Greg Abbott, in which the court held that a police officer's rights of privacy under the U.S. Constitution and Texas Constitution were not violated when he was denied a promotion because of a sexual affair with another officer's wife. This decision narrowly interprets the Texas Constitution and allows employers to consider off-duty behavior when making employment decisions.

The U.S. Constitution does not explicitly recognize the right of privacy. The U.S. Supreme Court has, however, found that the Constitution implies two distinct types of privacy interests. The first protects an individual's interest in avoiding the disclosure of personal information from governmental intrusion. It is a fundamental "right to be let alone." The second is the right to make decisions on marriage, procreation, contraception, family relationships, child rearing, and education.

The Texas Constitution does not expressly guarantee a right of privacy. The Texas Supreme Court, however, has determined that there is an implied right of a person to be free from unreasonable intrusion. The Texas Constitution also provides greater safeguards for personal freedoms than the U.S. Constitution. For the government to infringe on this right to privacy, the government must show that a compelling government objective may not be achieved by any less intrusive means. Under the Texas Constitution, a person who believes his rights have been violated bears the burden of proving that his conduct gives a right to privacy protection. Once a right of privacy is found, the burden shifts to the state to demonstrate a compelling government interest.

Patrol officer Otis Henry was next in line for a promotion to the rank of sergeant. He had the highest level of eligibility points and was named "outstanding officer of the year" for the prior year. The City of Sherman was required by law to promote Henry unless there was a valid reason to deny his promotion. Following an investigation, the City of Sherman police chief denied Henry the promotion because Henry was having a sexual affair with a fellow police officer's wife. The woman was a police dispatcher for the City of Sherman. Henry was unaware that the other officer and the dispatcher were married to each other. When Henry discovered that she was married, he ended the relationship. Henry's relationship with the dispatcher resumed only after the other officer filed for divorce.

The Fireman's and Police Officers' Civil Service Commission of the City of Sherman upheld the decision, finding that the police chief had valid reasons for not promoting Henry. Henry appealed to the district court. The district court held that the basis of the police chief's decision violated Henry's right to privacy under the U.S. and Texas Constitutions and was not a valid reason for denying his promotion. Consequently, Henry was promoted with back pay plus attorney's fees. The City of Sherman appealed.

Chief Justice Thomas, for the Dallas Court of Appeals, determined that the issue was "whether a public employee's private, legal sexual conduct is protected under the Texas Constitution." The Court of Appeals held that the Texas Constitution protects Henry's right to privacy. The court found that the City of Sherman offered no evidence to prove that other officers would refuse to work for Henry, nor did it have any written guidelines on officers' off-duty sexual behavior. Consequently, the City of Sherman failed to show a compelling government interest that could be achieved by no less intrusive, more reasonable means. The City of Sherman then appealed the decision to the Texas Supreme Court.

The Texas Supreme Court ruled in favor of the City of Sherman. The state supreme court focused its analysis on Henry's conduct rather than on the governmental intrusion. The court concluded that the sole issue for review was "whether conduct involving an affair by one police officer with the wife of another officer is a fundamental, constitutionally protected right." The court did not address the issue of whether Henry could have maintained an action against the City of Sherman for unreasonably scrutinizing his private affairs.

The court held that adultery, like homosexuality, was not a fundamental right protected by the U.S. or Texas Constitutions. A right to engage in adultery was not either implicit in the concept of ordered liberty or deeply rooted in the nation's history and tradition. The court concluded that the U.S. Constitution did not include the right to maintain a sexual relationship with the spouse of someone else. Recognized privacy rights were limited to child rearing and education, family relationships, procreation, marriage, contraception, and abortion.

Justice Abbott explained that just as the U.S. Supreme Court held in *Bowers v. Hardwick*, 478 U.S. 186 (1985) that there is no fundamental right to engage in homosexual sodomy, adultery is not a fundamental right protected by the U.S. or Texas Constitutions. He stated that adultery, by its very nature, undermines the marital relationship and often destroys families. Moreover, while adultery is no longer illegal in Texas, the state did not cloak it with constitutional protection.

Justice Rose Spector concurred with the majority but expressed concern that the Texas Constitutional right to privacy was shrinking to the point that most personal aspects of a person's life were the government's business. She also challenged how the majority framed the issue of Henry's conduct to come to a conclusion it wanted. According to Justice Spector, the City of Sherman interfered with Henry's right of privacy when the chief of police ordered an investigation into Henry's private, off-duty affair, and when the chief thereafter denied Henry the promotion based on the affair. Nevertheless, she concurred with the majority opinion because, despite the fact that Henry's right to privacy was violated, the City of Sherman had a compelling interest in denying the promotion.

Justice Priscilla Owen also concurred with the majority but focused on the state's right as an employer. Henry's behavior was disruptive within the police department and put his authority in jeopardy. While she concluded that the City of Sherman was justified in denying the promotion, she felt that the majority opinion was too broad.

In Texas, as a result of *City of Sherman v. Otis Henry*, the constitutional right to privacy has been narrowly construed to allow employers to consider off-duty adulterous behavior when making employment decisions. The right to make fundamental decisions on marriage and family does not protect extramarital affairs. As a result, Officer Henry had no privacy claim against the city. Texas employers currently have the unusual right to take an employee's personal life into consideration when making employment decisions, but these employers may not engage in intrusive investigations into the sexual practices of its employees.

Maureen Halliden Anderson

Further Reading

Notestine, Kerry E. *Fundamentals of Employment Law*. Chicago: American Bar Association, 2000.

Skeen, Shelly L. "Note & Comment: City of Sherman v. Henry: Is the Texas Constitutional Right of Privacy Still a Source of Protection for Texas Citizens?" *4 Tex. Wesleyan L. Rev. 99* (1997) 99–122.

See also: Right to be let alone

Cloud computing

Identification: A recent trend in computing in which data hardware and software work in unison over a virtual network to deliver on-demand self-service to users anywhere around the globe at competitive rates.

Cloud computing is a web of intersecting parts that are challenging to define. In 2011, the National Institute of Standards and Technology (NIST) issued "The NIST Definition of Cloud Computing," which guides users through the main points of the topic. According to the document, the cloud-computing model embodies five characteristics: on-demand self-service, rapid elasticity, broad network access, measured service, and resource pooling. Through on-demand self-service, users autonomously manage their personal cloud accounts. This saves costs and time for both users and providers. In addition, rapid elasticity acts as a metaphorical accordion, allowing cloud users to increase or decrease their storage space as needed, just as providers can allocate, amplify, or reduce provisions in the cloud. The hallmark

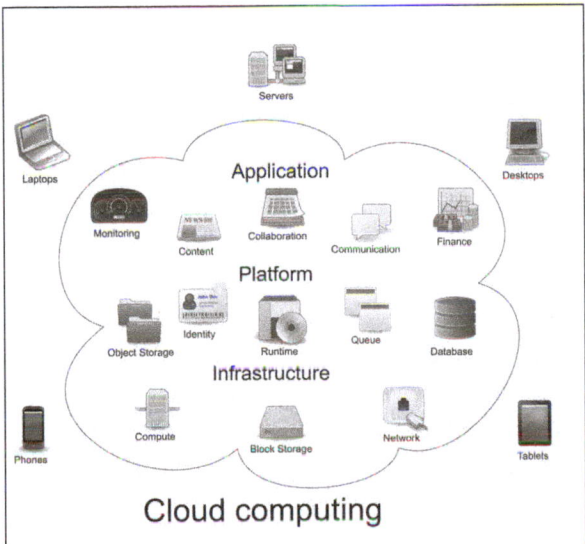

Cloud computing metaphor: the group of networked elements providing services need not be individually addressed or managed by users; instead, the entire provider-managed suite of hardware and software can be thought of as an amorphous cloud. (By Sam Johnston.)

of rapid elasticity is its seamless process. Broad network access or ubiquitous network access epitomizes the ability to connect to a variety of applications and platforms. Measured service is comparable to services rendered and billed by electrical, gas, or phone companies; cloud-computing providers meter the usage of their systems and invoice users as appropriate. In other words, the larger the meter reading, the more dynamic the cloud program requested by and deployed for the user, and the higher the costs incurred for this functionality. Resource pooling refers to the shared pool of the cloud's resources among different users in what is known as a multitenancy. A cyberattack on a multitenant cloud environment could lead to widespread damage because of the nature of the cloud's framework. Consequently, much stock is placed in cloud-computing infrastructures as it defends against and mitigates the risks and consequences of hacks.

Cloud-computing architecture is essentially composed of three layers: the physical, the virtual, and the cloud. The physical layer is the hardware sustaining cloud computing, such as central processing units (CPUs), memory, bandwidth, servers, data centers, and Data Center Networks (DCNs), while the virtual layer is a the virtualized infrastructure consisting of the virtual machine (VM) and the virtual network, input/output virtualization, and software tools. The final component, the cloud-computing layer, handles the cloud distribution system enabled by cloud service models, deployment models, and big data. The three primary service models are infrastructure as a service (IaaS), platform as a service (PaaS), and software as a service (SaaS); examples of each are Amazon Web Services (public IaaS), OpenStack (private IaaS), Microsoft Azure (PaaS), and Google Mail or Gmail (SaaS). Cloud systems can be either public or private, which speaks to the system's deployment model. Numerous providers choose to establish a hybrid environment, combining private back-end resources with public front-end services. In general, only large companies employ a private cloud-computing model to keep the IT infrastructure internal to the organization. Overall, the demands of big data drive the need for state-of-the-art cloud computing. At the rate which big data is being produced, it is currently impossible to filter, analyze, and index it all.

Different cloud environments provide different services and interfaces to users. Therefore, it should be emphasized that users have as much choice in what cloud-computing infrastructure they subscribe to as they do when deciding which automobile to buy. Of fundamental importance to the selection process are cost constraints, speed, performance, storage volume, usability, usage frequency, and moving costs. The ratio of the storage volume compared to the processing speed marks the performance of the cloud system. Many consumers hope to obtain the most out of cloud configurations for the least money. For certain services, however, skimping on costs can lead to a mediocre product. Therefore, the user must identify and prioritize the issues that the resource will address at a personal or organizational level. Typically, these metrics relate to storage volume, usability, usage frequency, and moving costs. And above all, confidentiality and data integrity rise above these concerns because cloud providers are responsible for guaranteeing the safety of the data they manage.

Privacy is a major issue in the cloud because control of information stored and transmitted is never actually in the user's possession. Instead, any one cloud is, at any given moment, controlled by its provider. Consequently, issues of trust and reputation factor heavily into the success of cloud service providers such as Dropbox, Google Drive, Microsoft OneDrive, and Apple iCloud, among others. Privacy concerns still present one of the largest obstacles to the proliferation of the cloud, and many researchers, companies, and computer scientists continually test and implement methods to strengthen the security of their software. Recently, the con-

cept and practice of remote data auditing has received much attention for its capacity to ensure data security. Much like the auditing of financial accounts, providers engage third-party auditors to sample sets of data in the cloud and test it against criteria that reveal the provider's reliability. Software advances various protocols of outsourced data encryption, such as L-EncDB, attribute-based encryption, geoencryption, and identity-based encryption, have been proposed, yet such methods could also expose users to privacy threats regarding identity, tracking, collusion attacks, and dynamic attribute cheating. These present high-stake losses for individual users, who lack the support of a company IT department. Instead, these individuals must remain vigilante and careful with the data they outsource. On the other hand, companies employ IT teams to monitor sensitive data stored in the cloud to anticipate breaches before they occur or to act quickly if one does.

The basic lack of control over the data is one aspect of cloud computing that worries privacy advocates. From the user perspective, cloud providers have concentrated on ease of access, and the details of the data migration and storage are not readily apparent. As has been discussed, encryption is key to the security of data transmission by providers. But the availability of providers to be audited by consumer advocates is also a necessary step. The security of the data, the location of the data, who has oversight over the data, and who can control the uses of the data are each areas where additional security may be necessary. In an era where data breaches by all manner of institutions has become commonplace, the large amounts of data that users put into cloud storage services are especially attractive to hackers. Much like the development of the Internet itself, the exponential growth of cloud computing has often meant that growth has outstripped efforts to ensure security.

A 2018 law, the Clarifying Lawful Overseas Use of Data Act, or CLOUD Act (18 U.S.C. §2713), requires that:

A provider of electronic communication service or remote computing service shall comply with the obligations of this chapter to *preserve, backup, or disclose the contents of a wire or electronic communication* and any record or other information pertaining to a customer or subscriber within such provider's *possession, custody, or control,* regardless of whether such communication, record, or other information is located within or outside of the United States. (emphasis added)

The law thus closes a loophole that companies and organizations previously had been able to exploit by storing data overseas and claiming that said data was not therefore subject to examination by U.S. authorities.

Lauren Perelli

Further Reading

Buyya, R., Pandey, S. and Vecchiola, C. "Market-Oriented Cloud Computing and the Cloudbus Toolkit." In *Large Scale Network-Centric Distributed Systems,* edited by H. Sarbazi-Azad and A. Y. Zomaya, 319–358. Hoboken, NJ: John Wiley & Sons, Inc., 2013.

Catlett, Charlie. *Cloud Computing and Big Data.* Amsterdam: IOS Press, 2013. Ceruzzi, Paul E. *Computing: a concise history.* Cambridge, Mass: MIT Press, 2012.

Chee, Brian J. S., and Curtis Franklin. *Cloud Computing: Technologies and Strategies of the Ubiquitous Data Center.* New York: CRC, 2010.

Durga Priya, G., and Soma Prathibha. "Assuring Correctness for Securing Outsourced Data Repository in Cloud Environment." In *2014 IEEE International Conference on Advanced Communications, Control and Computing Technologies,* 1745–1748. IEEE, 2014.

Grandinetti, Lucio, Ornella Pisacane, and Mehdi Sheikhalishahi. *Pervasive Cloud Computing Technologies: Future Outlooks and Interdisciplinary Perspectives.* Hershey, PA: Information Science Reference, 2014.

Karimi, Hassan A. *Big Data: Techniques and Technologies in Geoinformatics.* Boca Raton, FL: CRC Press/Taylor & Francis Group, 2014.

Kayastha, Nipendra, Dusit Niyato, Ping Wang, and Ekram Hossain. " Applications, Architectures, and Protocol Design Issues for Mobile Social Networks: a Survey." *Proceedings of the IEEE* 99, no. 12 (2011): 2130–2158.

Li, Fei, YogachandranRahulamathavan, Mauro Conti, and MuttukrishnanRajarajan. "Robust Access Control Framework for Mobile Cloud Computing Network." *Computer Communications* 68 (2015), 61–72.

Li, Jin, Zheli Liu, Xiaofeng Chen, FatosXhafa, Xiao Tan, and Duncan S. Wong. " L-encdb: a Lightweight Framework for Privacy-Preserving Data Queries in Cloud Computing." *Knowledge-Based Systems* 79 (2015): 18–26.

Mahmood, Zaigham. *Cloud Computing: Methods and Practical Approaches.* London: Springer, 2013.

Murray, Jim. *Digital Forensics for Network, Internet, and Cloud Computing: A Forensic Evidence Guide for Moving Targets and Data.* Burlington, MA: Syngress, 2010.

Takabi, H., Joshi, James B.D., and Ahn, G-J. "Security and PrivacyChallenges in CloudComputing Environments." *IEEE Security and Privacy Magazine,* 24-31. January 2011.

Talia, Domenico, Paolo Trunfio, and Fabrizio Marozzo. *Data Analysis in the Cloud: Models, Techniques and Applications.* Elsevier, 2015.

Tsai, Wei-Tek, Guanqiu Qi, and Yinong Chen. "Choosing Cost-Effective Configuration in Cloud Storage." In *2013 IEEE Eleventh International Symposium on Autonomous Decentralized Systems (ISADS),* 1–8. IEEE, 2013.

Wang, C., Wang, Q., Ren, K., and Lou, W. "Privacy-Preserving Public Auditing for Data Storage Security in Cloud Computing." In *2010 IEEE International Conference on Advanced Communications, Control and Computing Technologies.* IEEE, 2010.

Zheng, Zibin, Jieming Zhu, and Michael R. Lyu. "Servicegenerated Big Data and Big Data-As-a-Service: an Overview." In *2013 IEEE International Congress on Big Data (BigData Congress),* 403–410. IEEE, 2013.

See also: Amazon; APEC Cross Border Privacy Rules; Apple, Inc.; Big data; Computers and privacy; Data collection; Data protection regimes; General Data Protection Regulation; Google

Computer Fraud and Abuse Act (CFAA)

Identification: As amended in 1994, an act that allows a private party who suffers damages or loss as a result of hacking, or unauthorized computer access, to bring a civil action and obtain compensatory damage, injunctive relief, or other equitable relief.

The U.S. Congress enacted the first version of the CFAA in 1984. It was originally entitled the Counterfeit Access Device and Computer Fraud and Abuse Act. This act imposed criminal sanctions on hackers and other criminals who accessed computers without authorization. Ratified during the dawn of the Internet era, the statute prohibited hacking of certain types of information, such as matters concerning national security, foreign relations, and financial credit.

In 1986, the act was renamed the Computer Fraud and Abuse Act (CFAA). In 1994, the CFAA underwent a notable expansion and established a private right of action for individuals harmed by certain violations of the CFAA. But for an individual to be exposed to civil liability, the individual's actions must meet one of at least six additional factors listed in the statute.

The six bases for civil liability include: loss aggregating to at least $5,000 in value; the modification or impairment, or potential modification or impairment, of the medical examination, diagnosis, treatment, or care of one or more individuals; physical injury to any person; a threat to public health or safety; damage affecting a computer used by or for the U.S. government to further the administration of justice, national defense, or national security; or damage affecting ten or more protected computers during any one-year period.

CFAA claims are most often brought under 18 U.S.C. §1030(a)(2), §1030(a)(4), and §1030(a)(5). Each of these sections includes either the phrase "without authorization" or the phrase "exceeds authorized access." While the phrase "exceeds authorized access" is defined in the statute as "to access a computer with authorization and to use such access to obtain or alter information in the computer that the accessor is not entitled to so obtain or alter," the term *authorized* is never defined. Consequently, courts in different federal circuits have used varying definitions of the term *authorized*.

The different interpretations of the term *authorization* are relevant because, under a broad interpretation, more conduct constitutes a federal crime. Under a narrow interpretation, only a small subset of conduct that meets that definition is prohibited. In federal circuits that adopt a broad definition of authorization, employers have been able to bring lawsuits under the CFAA for conduct such as unfair competition and trade secret misappropriation. However, in circuits that had adopted a narrow definition, less conduct has qualified as lacking or exceeding authorization, and fewer types of lawsuits have been successful.

The Fourth and Ninth Circuits have adopted a narrow definition of authorization. Under this definition, only a *technical* breach of access is deemed to lack or exceed authorization. The reason behind this narrow view is discussed at length in the seminal Ninth Circuit case *United States v. Nosal*, 676 F.3d 854 (9th Cir. 2012). In that case, current employees of an executive search firm used their employer-granted access to the company database to obtain and pass along confidential information to a former employee who was setting up a competing business. The Ninth Circuit held that, because the current employees had logged into the firm database with their valid log-in credentials, they had proper authorization and did not violate the CFAA, despite the fact that their ultimate use of the information breached the company's policies. The court also found that only a narrow interpretation of authorization matched the plain meaning of the statute. It stated that any other meaning would turn a serious federal criminal hacking statute into "sweeping Internet-policing mandate" and "make criminals of large groups of people who would have little reason to suspect they are committing a federal crime."

In contrast to these circuits, the First, Fifth, Eleventh, and DC Circuits have adopted broad definitions of authorization. To do so, they have creatively adapted agency theories, contract theories, and use-based theories to find CFAA liability in situations in which computer users had been given technical access but were violating an employment contract or company policy. For example, the duty of loyalty theory provides that authorization implicitly ends as soon as an employee proves disloyal to an employer, even if the employee still has technical authorization. Thus, in the case *Shurgard Storage Centers, Inc. v. Safeguard Self Storage, Inc.*, 119 F. Supp. 2d 1121 (W.D. Wash. 2000), the District Court held that the plaintiff lost authorization and breached the CFAA when he became an agent of a direct competitor and used his former employer's proprietary information in a way that damaged his former employer.

The contract-based understanding of authorization provides that if an individual acquires or utilizes information in breach of a written policy, such as a confidentiality agreement, workplace rules of conduct, or a terms-of-service agreement, then even technically authorized use constitutes unauthorized use under the CFAA. Therefore, in the case of *EF Cultural Travel BV v. Explorica, Inc.*, 274 F.3d 577 (1st Cir. 2001), the First Circuit held that the company Explorica likely violated the CFAA when it used a computer robot to glean information from its competitor EF Cultural Travel. The court reasoned that the breach of a confidentiality agreement between the vice president of Explorica and EF Cultural Travel constituted a breach of authorization under the act.

The Fifth and Eleventh Circuits have both employed an "intended use" analysis. These courts looked at the underlying purpose of certain company policies to determine whether an employee breached or exceeded technically authorized access. This theory resembles contract theory but is broader because it considers how employees used the information they attained, even if there was no direct contradiction of a written policy or contract. Thus, in *United States v. John*, 597 F.3d 263 (5th Cir. 2010), the Fifth Circuit held that an employee violated the statute when she used data from Citigroup's internal computer system to attain customer account information, which she then shared with others in order to engage in fraudulent activities. The court reasoned that such use

was *unlikely* to be what the company intended when it granted her access.

The circuit split over critical language in the CFAA is problematic for courts and individuals. The lack of a single definition makes it difficult for judges to comply consistently with Congress's true intent, and it makes it more likely that potential violators will not be given sufficient notice that they are in danger of violating a federal criminal act. Although the circuit split is unresolved, the CFAA remains a viable statute for many data-breaching cases, especially those that involve a technical breach of authorization. As society's dependency on computers continues to grow, there is a growing need for the judiciary to offer clearer guidance for applying this statute.

Myra Din

Further Reading

Bernescu, Laura. "When Is a Hack Not a Hack: Addressing the CFAA's Applicability to the Internet Service Context." *University of Chicago Legal Forum* (2013): 633.

Kerr, Orin S. "Cybercrime's Scope: Interpreting 'Access' and 'Authorization' in Computer Misuse Statutes." *New York University Law Review* 78 (2003): 1596.

Kerr, Orin S. "Vagueness Challenges to the Computer Fraud and Abuse Act." *Minnesota Law Review* 94 (2010): 1561.

Murray, Ryan Patrick. "Myspace-ing Is Not a Crime: Why Breaching Terms of Service Agreements Should Not Implicate the Computer Fraud and Abuse Act Written February 2, 2009," *Loyola of Los Angeles Entertainment Law Review* 29, no. 3 (June 2009): 475.

Olivenbaum, Joseph M. "Ctrl-Alt-Delete: Rethinking Federal Computer Crime Legislation." *Seton Hall Law Review* 27 (1997): 574.

Patterson, Kelsey T. "Narrowing It Down to One Narrow View: Clarifying and Limiting the Computer Fraud and Abuse Act." *Charleston Law Review* 7, no. 3 (March 2013): 489.

Rosen, David J. "Limiting Employee Liability under the CFAA: A Code-Based Approach to 'Exceeds Authorized Access.'" *Berkeley Technology Law Journal* 27 (2012): 737.

Schieck, Glenn R. "Undercutting Employee Mobility: The Computer Fraud and Abuse Act in the Trade Secret Context." *Brooklyn Law Review* 79, no. 2 (2014): 831.

See also: Computers and privacy; Data breaches; Hacking, computer

Computer harvesting

Identification: The practice of extracting and collecting large amounts of personal and commercial data, mostly from Internet websites.

Data harvesting (also known as web harvesting, data scraping, data aggregation, or data mining) is the process of digitally compiling large amounts of information such as search results, purchasing preferences, commercial offerings, product prices, and demographic data from the Internet. Data harvesting is usually done through the use of magnetic robots known as web harvesters or screen scrapers that collect data, filter inappropriate content, and present it to consumers in easy-to-use formats, such as graphs, tables, and indexes.

Businesses, banks, credit card bureaus, and even certain public-sector agencies often hire experts to design sophisticated web harvesters to collect data that is hard to retrieve manually. Indeed, most web harvesters can translate various computer languages, such as HyperText Markup Language (HTML), JavaScript, and PHP: Hypertext Preprocessor (PHP), among others. Experts at web harvesting are highly sought after by businesses because they can engage in data collection and data translation at warp speeds. Most web harvesters can retrieve several pages on a server simultaneously and can automatically access target websites repeatedly throughout the day. As such, web harvesting allows businesses to create reports, presentations, and profiles about individuals and groups of consumers quickly.

Because many web harvesters are quite inexpensive and can be accessed easily through a basic Internet search, many individuals engage in web harvesting as well. The use of web harvesters has recently grown so much that Internet users frequently interact with harvesters without even knowing that they are doing so. Common examples of web harvesters that consumers frequently come into contact with include: search engines, business advertisers, auction compilers, price aggregators, real estate listing services, financial data aggregators, financial money management applications, and social media websites.

The websites that are targeted by web harvesting are usually referred to as data hosts.

Whether web harvesting is a socially beneficial or harmful activity often depends on the collateral damage that the web harvester causes to a data host. For example, certain web harvesters, such as price amalgamators and targeted advertisers, cause minimal or no damage to data hosts and allow businesses to match consumer needs with commercial offerings efficiently. In fact, web harvesters such as price amalgamators and targeted advertisers often benefit both consumers and data hosts because, in addition to causing the data hosts at most minimal harm, they increase the visibility of the data hosts' products and services.

Another example of a web harvester that Internet users frequently interact with is a search engine. These web harvesters are almost universally lauded for the benefits they provide to end-users through constant accessing of thousands of websites, pulling bits of information from these websites, and presenting the data in the form of easily readable search engine results. Search engines are also particularly useful web harvesters because they can collect archived data that is stored on a system but that can no longer be accessed due to the incompatibility of an old system or Internet website with newer computer hardware or software.

On the other hand, web harvesting can also cause extensive damage to data hosts. If a web harvester is designed to overcome a technical barrier such as a password or other code barrier, the web harvester may end up undercutting a competing business's revenue, gaining access to confidential company information, or damaging the physical infrastructure of the data host. Indeed, some web harvesting has caused data hosts to suffer extensive damage, such as increased bandwidth usage, system crashes, the need to purchase anti-spam devices, the need to erect technical barriers, the need to clear up consumer confusion, and damage to reputation.

Because of some of the negative effects caused by web harvesting, it is not surprising that there have been many lawsuits involving web harvesting and data scraping in recent years.

In addition to the prevalent use of web harvesters, a primary reason for these lawsuits is that many websites are poorly equipped to fend off web harvesting and want to deter web harvesters from gaining unfettered access to their data.

For example, in *eBay v. Bidder's Edge,* 100 F. Supp. 2d 1058 (N.D. Cal. 2000), a federal lawsuit that was litigated in Northern California in 2000, eBay complained that Bidder's Edge (BE) was unlawfully compiling eBay's auction listings and copying eBay's auction format on its own website without incurring any of the investment and operating costs that eBay incurs. eBay showed the court that it had unavailingly tried to block BE's data scrapers through telephonic and written communications and by trying to block BE's IP addresses. The court sided with eBay and held that BE was liable for aggregating data from eBay's servers without attaining prior authorization and that BE was free-riding on the time, effort, and money that eBay had invested in its system.

A similar situation was litigated the following year in *EF Cultural Travel BV v. Explorica, Inc.,* 274 F.3d 577 (1st Cir. 2001). In this case, EF Cultural Travel BV (EF), a company that offered tour guides for groups of teenagers, complained that Explorica was unlawfully scraping information about EF's tour prices in order to undercut EF from the teenage tour market. The First Circuit sided with EF and approved an injunction against Explorica to prohibit further scraping that would be to EF's detriment.

Because of the ubiquity of web harvesters, and in light of the numerous benefits that they provide, it is critical for users of web harvesters to become familiar with the laws governing web harvesting. Again, many uses of web harvesting are considered harmless to data hosts and beneficial to consumers. Such uses are unlikely to lead to legal disputes. But given that some data hosts are opposed to unknown web harvesting, it is critical for users of web harvesters to know what types of web harvesting may expose them to liability. Similarly, it is important for data hosts that are opposed to web harvesting to stay abreast of the capabilities of web harvesters so that they can erect technical barriers and other sophisticated blockades to protect their data.

Myra Din

Further Reading

Fibbe, George H. "Screen-Scraping and Harmful Cyber-trespass after Intel." *Mercer Law Review* 55, no. 1011 (2004).

Gladstone, Julia Alpert. "Data Mines and Battlefields: Looking at Financial Aggregators to Understand the Legal Boundaries and Ownership Rights in the Use of Personal Data." *Journal of Marshall Computer and Information Law* 19, no. 313 (2001).

Hirschey, Jeffrey Kenneth. "Symbiotic Relationships: Pragmatic Acceptance of Data Scraping," *Berkeley Technical Law Journal* 29, no. 897 (2014).

Rubin, Aaron. "How Website Operators Use CFAA to Combat Data-Scraping." *Law360.* http://www.law360.com/articles/569325?utm_source=rss&utm_medium=rss&utm_campaign=articles_search.

What Is a Screen Scraper? wiseGEEK. http://www.wise-geek.com/what-is-a-screen-scraper.htm.

Wierzel, Kimberly L. "If You Can't Beat Them, Join Them: Data Aggregators and Financial Institutions." *North Carolina Banking Institute* 5, no. 457 (2001):.

See also: Big data; Computers and privacy; Credit and debit cards; Data collection; Marketing; Search engines

Computers and privacy

Identification: Concern about unauthorized release of personal information through computers and similar devices.

Computers and other digital mobile devices bring a whole world of information into users' homes, while at the same time dramatically reducing our privacy. With this massive paradigm shift comes a wide variety of privacy issues, including electronic surveillance, the unauthorized release of personal information, cookies and spyware, and workplace monitoring. With the increasing ubiquity of smartphones, computers, and Internet access through devices not previously thought of as loci of user information, the privacy issues involved in computer technology are likely to continue to grow as privacy continues to diminish, as technological innovations continue to flourish and offer even more and better ways to stay connected with each other.

Privacy, according to Brandeis and Warren, is the right to be left alone. Among other things, privacy means freedom from surveillance and unreasonable personal intrusions. "Information privacy" means the right to determine when and to what extent information about oneself may be communicated to other parties. This assertion of privacy applies to individuals, groups, and institutions. Privacy is capable of a variety of interpretations, which contributes to the debate on privacy expectations and the availability of personal information.

Privacy is a broad, all-encompassing concept that includes many different human concerns about many various forms of intrusive behavior, including wiretapping, physical surveillance, and mail interception. Individuals claim a right of privacy for many various issues from reproductive rights to maintaining the confidentiality of financial information.

In every developed country, the right of privacy is not absolute. This right must be balanced against social needs. In many nations, the public's right to know takes precedent over the individual's right of privacy. Achieving this balance may make it difficult to investigate and enforce privacy regulations.

Electronic surveillance

Electronic surveillance involves monitoring people with technology, usually without user consent. Common electronic surveillance methods include photography, video recording, and audio recording. Electronic surveillance is regularly conducted at businesses such as banks, and retail stores. Almost everyone is likely to be subject to some form of electronic surveillance on a regular basis. Many localities, for example, use video surveillance to enforce traffic ordinances. Customers may be recorded on video when they shop or do their banking. Individuals may live in an apartment building or are employed at a workplace that is equipped with video surveillance to deter crime and assist in investigating crimes after they occur.

Personal information

Increasingly, it is possible to retrieve an incredible amount of personal information by even the most casual of Internet searches, and sometimes even more so, then methods such as going to government offices to check for documents, interviewing acquaintances, and other such approaches.

As computer technology becomes ever more advanced and sophisticated, it is relatively easy to find personal information on almost anyone. A large amount of information on individuals is retained in a variety of databases. These databases retain personal information such as those relating to social security, personal finance, employment, and health and medical condition. Many organizations retain robust databases of all those that they do business with. This gives rise to issues including: whether or not they should be collecting this type of information, what they do with this information, how secure the information is, the accuracy of the information, and who can the information be sold to or shared with. Personal data is also becoming more readily available in online databases and accessible by search engines.

Many privacy advocates have expressed concern about how much and what kind of personal information should be readily available to the public. The availability of personal information online continues to accelerate at a quickening pace. Government entities at all levels, including courts, are increasingly placing public records online. This raises concerns that sensitive personal information could be now freely available on the Internet. In a bankruptcy case, for example, the petitioner must provide their Social Security number, financial information, and information on their family members.

One major issue is that personal information made available online increases opportunity for identity theft risks. Identity theft has been growing at an alarming rate. A person engages in identity theft by misappropriating another person's Social Security number, credit card number, or other similar personal information to borrow money, make purchases, and incur debts. Identity thieves also are able to withdraw money directly from a victim's bank accounts. Even the major credit bureaus, such as Equifax, once thought to be impenetrable bastions of security, have seen data breaches that exposed the personal information of over 100 million users. Because many private and government entities retain information about individuals in accessible databases, identity thieves may easily be able to retrieve and misuse it.

Cookies, malware, and spyware

Websites of all types are able to very easily monitor consumer behavior without knowledge or consent. Vendors may track the movements of consumers through cookies. Cookies are small data files that are written and retained on a user's hard drive by a website after a user visits the site. Cookies provide information within the website on pages visited, items examined, times of visits, and passwords. This information is retained in the cookie and transmitted to the company.

Spyware is an even more intrusive type of technology. It is a small computer program, which installs itself on the user's hard drive, which gathers information on user habits and transmits that information to a third party, all without user consent. Spyware may monitor websites the user visits, while cookies are spe-

cifically tied to a specific website. Spyware may install itself after a user downloads particular software, especially certain types of freeware or shareware.

The relentless advances in technology mean that it is becoming increasingly intrusive in all aspects of our personal lives. Personal information on individuals is constantly being gathered by both public and private entities, usually without their knowledge or consent. Users depend on technology to maintain contacts, calendar, personal messages to friends and colleagues, and other important information. With such wide use, there are risks and downsides that users must be aware of. Users must be constantly vigilant regarding security and privacy issues.

In 2016, many of the leading cyber security companies, such as Kaspersky, McAfee, Microsoft, Symantec, and Trend Micro, and others, collaborated on standards for safe PC apps. Around the same time, many app developers collaborated on the creation of CleanApps.org, which creates a standard for software companies. As the presence of computer-based information devices does nothing but increase, the need for this type of cooperation to prevent malware and security breaches is clear.

Storage of personal information

With the increased presence of personal information on the Internet, users are becoming attuned to the increased need for care as they increasingly store personal information (such as financial information or Social Security numbers) on their devices. Even information stored on a home computer is not completely secure from hackers or even physical thieves who might steal a device simply for the data stored upon it. Even deleted information may be recovered. Password protection is only a first step toward keeping data secure. Websites are increasingly using stronger security measures, such as multi-factor authentication, requiring "strong" passwords that have a combination of numbers, letters, and special characters, and even scans of users thumbs or eyes. Users should also access personal information on encrypted websites. These sites code user information to confirm that hackers are not able to access it.

Location tracking

Location tracking is available on almost every mobile device and app being sold. Google uses it to provide turn-by-turn directions. Social media sites such as Facebook and Instagram use it to tag a user's location and camera to map where photos were taken. When companies like these and many others use location tracking to sell items or to make determinations about personal preferences, some privacy advocates see trouble. Using such features can compromise user privacy and allows corporations or governments to know the user's location at all times.

Tracking online activity

In addition to tracking user location, devices also track the online behavior of users through tracking cookies, or data transmitted from a website and saved to the user's Web browser. These cookies create a log of websites a person has visited and may even contribute—using third-party cookies —to personalized advertisements on various websites. Cookies may even be able to save such personal information as user addresses, credit card numbers, and passwords for certain websites.

Conclusion

Computer technology in many different forms is becoming more pervasive and integrated into the personal and work lives of its users. It is a part of everyday life and continues to be more so. The number of individuals who own various high technology gadgets such as smartphones, laptops, tablets, and even information systems in automobiles continues to rise dramatically. As users become more familiar and comfortable with such mobiletechnology they run the risk of becoming more lax and not as conscious of security matters as they need to be.

It is vital that users of computer technology realize the risks involved in such technology and take affirmative action to protect their privacy. This is why all users should be highly cautious about what information is stored on their devices and how these devices and Web browsers use the information provided them. Caution, knowledge, and awareness are vital user attributes to protect user habits to maintain user privacy in the digital era.

Gretchen Nobahar

Further Reading

Agre, Philip. *Technology and Privacy the New Landscape.* Cambridge, Mass.: MIT Press, 1997.

Andrews, Lori B. *I Know Who You Are and I Saw What You Did: Social Networks and the Death of Privacy.* New York: Free Press, 2012.

Caloyannides, Michael A., and Michael A. Caloyannides. *Privacy Protection and Computer Forensics.* 2nd ed. Boston: Artech House, 2004.

Cate, Fred H. *Privacy in the Information Age.* Washington, D.C.: Brookings Institution Press, 1997. Garrett, Brandon. *The Right to Privacy.* New York: Rosen Pub. Group, 2001. Kallen, Stuart A. *Are Privacy Rights Being Violated?* Detroit: Greenhaven, 2006.

Fleishman, Glenn. "Equifax Data Breach, One Year Later: Obvious Errors and No Real Changes, New Report Says." *Fortune,* September 8, 2018. http://fortune.com/2018/09/07/equifax-data-breach-one-year-anniversary/

Levmore, Saul. *The Offensive Internet: Speech, Privacy, and Reputation.* Cambridge, Mass.: Harvard University Press, 2010.

Lyon, David. *Computers, Surveillance, and Privacy.* Minneapolis: University of Minnesota Press, 1996.

Raskin, Sarah Bloom. "Cyber security firms show how to bring the rule of law online." *Financial Times,* February 20, 2019. https://www.ft.com/content/9a3adb9a-2e1e-11e9-80d2-7b637a9e1ba1

Solove, Daniel J. *The Future of Reputation Gossip, Rumor, and Privacy on the Internet.* New Haven: Yale University Press, 2007.

See also: Amazon; Apple, Inc.; Cloud computing; Consumer privacy; Cookies; Facebook; General Data Protection Regulation; Google; Identity theft; Malware; Online privacy and security; Right to be left alone; The Right to Privacy; Spam; Spyware

Confidential informants

Identification: An informant, by definition, is any individual who provides law enforcement with crime-related information, which might simply be a citizen who has some knowledge of a situation. A confidential informant (CI), however, is usually somebody who provides information, often over a prolonged period of time, in return for either monetary gain or the hope that law enforcement will not prosecute their own criminal activity. In some cases, an individual will become an informant after they have been arrested, in the hope of receiving a lighter sentence.

Due to the nature of informing, which requires the individual to give information about their associates, often without their knowledge, informers are often at risk of repercussion from their former associates. As a result, many are protected, often by inclusion in a witness protection program.

Famous, or perhaps infamous, examples include James "Whitey" Bulger, who ran the Winter Hill gang in Boston while simultaneously acting as a CI for the FBI; and Henry Hill, whose testimony against New York organised crime was the direct inspiration for the film *Goodfellas*.

A representative from the U.S. State Department congratulates and offers a partial payment to a fully disguised informant, whose information led to the neutralization of a terrorist in the Philippines. (By Troy Latham.)

The United States Witness Protection Program, or "WITSEC," is operated by the U.S. Marshals Service and seeks to protect the identity and safety of confidential informants. Some states, along with Washington, D.C., have their own protection programs for crimes not covered under the federal program. WITSEC began in 1970, under the Organized Crime Control Act, and since that time over 8,000 witnesses have been protected.

In terms of legal importance, the area in which this type of individual often has the greatest impact is in regard to the Fourth Amendment to the US Constitution, which states that "The right of the people to be secure in their persons, houses, papers, and effects, against unreasonable searches and seizures, shall not be violated, and no Warrants shall issue, but upon probable cause, supported by Oath or affirmation, and particularly describing the place to be searched, and the persons or things to be seized."

Typically, informants may give information that leads to police being able to obtain a search warrant. Historically, evidence recovered by law enforcement, even without a search warrant, was often used against defendants in court. However, the Supreme Court, in the case of *Weeks v. United States* (1914), adopted the "exclusionary rule," which states that, under most circumstances, evidence obtained through an illegal search and seizure (i.e. one without a search warrant) could not be admissible evidence in a criminal trial, as it breached the fundamental constitutional rights of the defendant.

This led to a rise in defence lawyers seeking to prove that search warrants were invalid, thus rendering any evidence found inadmissible. However, there were no strict guidelines in place defining the legality of a search warrant, especially in regard to information received through a confidential informant.

In the 1960s, the Supreme Court developed the Aguilar-Spiller test, which established a two-prong requirement for evaluating the validity of a search warrant or warrantless arrest made on information received through an informant or anonymous tip. The two parts to the test were that, when law enforcement was seeking a search warrant, the magistrate signing the warrant:

- must be informed of the reasons to support the conclusion that such an informant is reliable and credible; and
- must be informed of some of the underlying circumstances relied on by the person providing the information.

These two factors would allow the magistrate to make an independent evaluation that probable cause existed that a crime had been, or would be, committed.

In the case of a warrantless arrest, the same tests were applied and law enforcement was required to show that both elements had been met prior to any trial, or else the judge could dismiss the case for lack of probable cause.

However, the Supreme Court subsequently abandoned this rule in Illinois v. Gates (1983). In this case, the majority opinion, written by Justice Rehnquist, held that:

The rigid "two-pronged test" under Aguilar and Spinelli for determining whether an informant's tip establishes probable cause for issuance of a warrant is abandoned, and the "totality of the circumstances" approach that traditionally has informed probable-cause determinations is substituted in its place.

In this case, the police department in Bloomingdale, Illinois, received an anonymous letter containing details of claims that a local couple, the Gates', were involved in drug trafficking and drug dealing from Florida to Illinois. Working with the U.S. Drug Enforcement Agency, the police were able to identify that the details of the alleged travel arrangements outlined in the letter were consistent with information they were able to identify about the couple's movements. Law enforcement signed an affidavit detailing the information they had identified, along with

the anonymous letter, and received a search warrant. Upon searching the couple's house and car, a large amount of marijuana was recovered.

The Illinois Circuit court, citing the Aguilar-Spinelli test, held that the search was unlawful, finding that the affidavit did not provide enough evidence to establish probable cause, thus excluding evidence received from that warrant. This ruling was upheld by both the Illinois Appellate Courts and the Supreme Court of Illinois.

The U.S. Supreme Court, in overturning the rulings of the Illinois Courts, agreed that the letter alone probably would not have provided probable cause, but that there was more evidence than just the letter indicating that the couple was involved in the drug trafficking. The Court also held that, under the Aguilar-Spinelli test, the reliability of an anonymous tip would be extremely difficult to ever be satisfied on its own and therefore held that this test should be abandoned, stating that

We agree with the Illinois Supreme Court that an informant's "veracity," "reliability" and "basis of knowledge" are all highly relevant in determining the value of his report. We do not agree, however, that these elements should be understood as entirely separate and independent requirements to be rigidly exacted in every case... [T]hey should be understood simply as closely intertwined issues that may usefully illuminate the common sense, practical question whether there is "probable cause" to believe that contraband or evidence is located in a particular place.

In dissent, Justices Marshall and Brennan argued that the Aguilar-Spinelli test remained effective, did not need to be replaced, and felt that the Court did not show any persuasive opinion for rejecting the test, writing that:

Words such as *practical*, *nontechnical*, and *common sense*, as used in the Court's opinion, are but code words for an overly permissive attitude towards police practices in derogation of the rights secured by the Fourth Amendment.

The dissent argued that the two prongs of the test, namely, the reliability of the informant and the basis of knowledge, were more likely to be protective of the rights of a citizen under the Fourth Amendment, as they were less likely to allow for a warrant to be issued based on the claims of an unreliable informant.

Indeed, while it has been replaced on the federal level by *Illinois v. Gates*, a number of states, including Alaska, Massachusetts, and New York, have rejected the Gates argument and retained Aguilar-Spinelli as the test in their state laws.

Melissa A Hale

Further Reading

Aguilar v. Texas, 378 U.S. 108 (1964).

Earley, Pete, Gerald Shur. *WITSEC: Inside the Federal Witness Protection Program.* New York: Bantam Books, 2002.

Fitzpatrick, Robert, and John Land. *Betrayal: Whitey Bulger and the FBI Agent Who Fought to Bring Him Down.* New York: Forge Books, 2011.

Illinois v. Gates, 462 U.S. 213 (1983).

Organized Crime Control Act of 1970 (Pub.L. 91–452, 84 Stat. 922) October 15, 1970.

Spinelli v. United States, 393 U.S. 410 (1969).

Weeks v. United States, 232 U.S. 383 (1914).

Confidential Information Protection and Statistical Efficiency Act of 2002

Identification: A federal law(Pub.L. 107–347, 116 Stat. 2899, 44 U.S.C. § 101) that sets out confidentiality protections for information collected by U.S. government agencies for statistical purposes. It permits data sharing among agencies while also establishing confidentiality protocols.

Although a primordial version of the internet existed in the 1960s, during the 1990s changes in hardware, software, and user expectations resulted in the transformation of electronic communications via the computer. This meant that data, which at one time would have been difficult and expensive to obtain, could be shared at virtually no cost with a few keystrokes. Although various federal laws existed that protected some information, there was no comprehensive guarantee of the confidentiality of information collected for statistical research. In the pre-computer era, this was not as much of an issue, as paper files took greater effort to distribute. The combination of digital records and the internet caused great concern for the privacy of individuals' responses and data sets. Although originally an independent bill, the Confidential Information Protection and Statistical Efficiency Act (CIPSEA) was incorporated into the E-Government Act of 2002, which passed on December 17, 2002.

Confidentiality

As indicated by its name, the purposes of CIPSEA are for both personal privacy and governmental efficiency. For the general public, CIPSEA was included to ensure that statistical research information given to government researchers under a promise of "confidentiality" would be used only for statistical analysis, and that anyone reading the publicly distributed results of the study would not be able to identify the respondents or associate them with the data they had submitted. Within the law, there was a broad definition of what research was covered. It applies to agencies and employees of the government, and also to "agents" of the government. "Agents" are individuals involved in the research, ranging from for-profit contractors and their employees to individuals affiliated with institutions of higher education who participate in the collection or analysis of the statistical data. All such "agents" are prohibited from inappropriately sharing information collected, whether from individuals or corporate entities. The Director of the Office of

Management and Budget was given the authority to oversee the implementation of this section of the law and to make any necessary "rules or provide other guidance to ensure consistent interpretation of this title."

In various sections of CIPSEA, it was made clear that this did not replace others laws that mandated stricter confidentiality for specific types of data. Similar to other confidentiality laws, CIPSEA specifically stated that research/survey data obtained for programs covered by this law could not be "used against such individuals or organizations in any agency action." Similarly, since the information was obtained for use in "statistical research" it could not be used for any other purpose, including law enforcement. In addition, a provision was included in the law to identify which individuals in the government, or its contractors, had access to the information in the data set, in the event that some information was illegally made public. It also contained provisions for those found guilty to face up to five years in prison and/or a fine of $250,000. The only exceptions to the confidentiality provision was if the individual respondent consented to making the information public or if public notice was given that the data sought would be made public.

Efficiency

The second goal of the law was to enable government agencies to more effectively undertake research. The three agencies that are mentioned in this law are the Bureau of the Census and the Bureau of Economic Analysis, both in the Department of Commerce, and the Bureau of Labor Statistics in the Department of Labor. CIPSEA allows these agencies to share statistical information with the goal of assisting government officials to develop better public policy. Prior to the enactment of this law, there were times when each of these three agencies had independently conducted research to obtain the same data. CIPSEA made it clear that these agencies could share data, thus reducing research costs.

It also allowed government officials using reports from these three agencies to develop public policy to know that the information given them by each agency was based upon the same data. Thus, although each agency has been charged with analyzing different aspects of the data set, the government official can be certain that differences in what the three agencies might state were not due to different data sets, but rather from differences in what the agency has been charged to consider in its analysis. Thus the law not only was implemented to "reduce reporting burden and cost imposed on the public" but also "to improve the quality and reduce the cost of statistical programs."

Although the provisions related to confidentiality were the central focus of most members of the public, the push for greater government efficiency was not lost on them. Because twenty-first century governmental data was compiled and processed digitally, it could not only be processed with greater ease but it could be transmitted or surreptitiously taken more easily than when paper files were the norm. CIPSEA was one step toward balancing governmental needs with privacy.

Donald A. Watt

Further Reading

Bureau of Labor Statics. "Public Law 107-347 'E-Government Act'."*United States Department of Labor,* (2002). https://www.bls.gov/bls/cipsea.pdf.

Office of Management and Budget. "Implementation Guidance for Title V of the E-Government Act." *Office of the Federal Register Volume 72,* (June 15, 2007.) www.govinfo.gov/content/pkg/FR-2007-06-15/pdf/E7-11542.pdf

Superintendent of Documents. "Public Law 107-347—Dec. 17, 2002." *United States Government Printing Office.* (December 17, 2002). www.govinfo.gov/content/pkg/STATUTE-116/pdf/STATUTE-116-Pg2899.pdf.

Wallman, Katherine K. and Brian A. Harris-Kojetin. "Implementing the Confidential Information Protection and Statistical Act of 2002." *Chance.* Vol. 17, n3. pp. 21–25. (2004).

See also: Big data; Data protection regimes; General data protection regulation; Health care information

Consent

Identification: Is classically defined as valid only if the consent was knowing, intelligent, and voluntary, and consent is classically applicable only to those matters that fall expressly within the specific consent granted.

In the digital age, consent is more accurately defined as waivers of adhesion where computer and cellphone service providers present interminable, opaque, and confusing "privacy waivers" to their users in a take-it-or-leave-it format wherein users are obliged to consent to erosion of their data privacy when they click through those one-sided privacy waivers that are not susceptible of amendment by the user. If the user wants to use that computer or cellphone service, the user cannot do so without waiving the user's privacy rights. That is not knowing, intelligent, and voluntary consent; it is coerced consent.

Consent, to be effective in most areas of the law, must be voluntarily given in an exercise of free will by an informed party, and coerced consent is not really consent at all. Consent is only freely given if the party granting the consent would also have been free to either withhold consent or grant consent but to a limited degree or with a limited scope. Thus, a person asked by a law enforcement officer to consent to search of the person's car must be free to consent, to withhold consent, or to consent to a limited degree or scope – such as "you may search the passenger compartment only" – or it would not be a valid consent.

Consent and e-commerce

Consent in the digital age has lost much of its luster and much of its previous legal robustness and logical underpinnings. Clear and consistent explicit consent and expressed contractual assent principles have been supplanted by digital age pseudo-consent and implied consent principles, such as shrink-wrap, clickwrap, and browse-wrap agreements wherein assent – particularly to waivers of consumer privacy rights – are not expressed, but are merely implied whether or not the on-line consumer ever intended to consent, assent, or waive the consumer's privacy rights. Before the digital age, contracts borne of unequal bargaining posture where the powerful party controlled all the terms of the contract and the weaker party had no power to modify those terms, were called contracts of adhesion, and in most circumstances were unenforceable. In the digital age, on-line contracts of adhesion and on-line waivers of adhesion drafted and controlled by the powerful on-line purveyors and completely unamenable to modification by the consumer, are a dime a dozen, and so far have been upheld as enforceable at most every turn.

In shrink-wrap agreements, common with purchased software where the disk is sealed in shrink-wrap, the user is deemed to have agreed to all terms – all of which were written by the manufacturer – as soon as the user opens the shrink-wrap. Of course, these are all-or-nothing, take-it-or-leave-it "agreements" where the user has no power whatever to modify the terms of those agreements. The user only has one choice: to accept the terms or forgo purchasing and using the software.

In clickwrap agreements, common with online purchases of goods and services of many kinds, a consumer surfs various sites for the target item then, when ready to purchase, is confronted with a large clickable icon labeled "Click Here" or "I Agree" – by clicking that button, the on-line consumer is deemed to have agreed to, consented to, or assented to all the terms of the agreement – terms that virtually none of the prospective buyers has ever read, let alone understood. And, like the purchaser opening the shrink-wrap and being thereby bound by all the terms of the shrink-wrapped agreement, the consumer clicking the "I Agree" button has thereby agreed to be bound by all the unread terms. Here too, the consumer has only one choice to make – either accept all terms or forgo the purchase; consumers have virtually no power to negotiate or modify any of the clickwrap agreement's terms. Clickwrap "consent" is not knowing, intelligent, or even voluntary; it is an illusion.

In browse-wrap agreements, the "agreement" is classic fine print. At the bottom of the on-line merchant's homepage will be a tagline in small print indicating variously: "Use of this Site Constitutes Acceptance of Its Terms and Conditions," or more simply, "Terms of Use," or "Conditions of Use," and the like. When the consumer clicks through to subsequent pages on that merchant's website, the consumer is deemed bound by those terms and conditions – often without having even noticed the fine print, without having read the terms and conditions themselves, without understanding all those terms and conditions, and obviously without any power or right to reject, negotiate, or amend any of those terms or conditions that were drafted by and overwhelmingly favor the merchant. In the pre-digital age, these were largely unenforceable contracts of adhesion. In the digital age, this is the way of e-commerce.

Where contracts traditionally required a meeting of the minds between the parties to the contract as to all its principle terms, e-contracts (sometimes labeled "licenses") don't require any meeting of the minds on any of the contract terms; indeed, the consumer need not have ever understand or even read the terms to be deemed bound by them in e-commerce. This lenient approach by the courts and legislatures is largely grounded on a fear that requiring more consumer protections, notice, and power could dampen the economic benefits that flow from e-commerce. However, if the courts and legislatures fail to protect the consumers and rely on merchant self-regulation instead, the weaker party, the consumer, suffers in the digital age.

Of course, not all digital age contracts suffer from these clickwrap, shrink-wrap, and browse-wrap infirmities. Contracts for most good and services today still must demonstrate a meeting of the minds and valid consent. Only e-commerce and other digital age products, such as CDs, DVDs, and boxed computer software, seem to be exempted from these traditional contract law protections.

Consent principles as applied to e-commerce are out of step with traditional contract law principles requiring eyes-open, meetings of the mind, and true mutual assent to agreed-upon terms before any contract is deemed enforceable. Perhaps one day the favored position now enjoyed by e-commerce merchants will fade as traditional contract law principles are once again applied to buying and selling on the Internet.

Consent and consumer data privacy

When cellphone users activate a phone to make a call, are the users aware that they have thereby transmitted their precise geospatial locations to the phone service provider? Do cellphone users remember when they eyes-open consented to that?

When a user posts a photograph on the user's Facebook page, does the user realize that the photograph is accompanied by metadata, including the exact time and location of when and where the photograph was taken? Do Facebook users remember when they freely consented to that?

When a consumer surfs on Google or Amazon or eBay looking for, say, just the right textbook on privacy in the digital age, and soon begins seeing popups from those and other vendors offering a panoply of related textbooks, does that consumer remember intelligently, knowingly, and voluntarily consenting to those Big Data firms freely sharing the consumer's Internet browsing and buying history with other vendors or other data aggregators?

On the contrary, in the digital age, virtually none of these consumers consented in any traditional sense to any of these privacy invasions. Rather, in the digital age, the government's efforts to aid on-line merchants and the government's willingness to look the other way, have emboldened those merchants and data aggregators to secure consumer "consent" – or more aptly those merchants and data aggregators have been empowered to obtain consumers' "pseudoconsent." By some accounts, just seven percent of all computer and cellphone users "always" read all privacy policies – that is, privacy waivers or consents – and the rest of the consumers might be split into two camps: (1) those who are unaware that privacy waivers were ever extracted from them; and (2) those who are vaguely aware of these pseudo-waivers, but have given up, because they are aware that they have no power to negotiate or modify those waivers. Their consent has been obtained by subterfuge and sheer unequal bargaining power buoyed up by the government's complicity in the charade.

It seems clear that even if consumers in some ethereal sense have privacy rights, those rights can be cavalierly waived and their consent can be unfairly obtained by sleight of hand enabled by the technological advancements of the digital age.

Consent and electronic surveillance

In the digital age, all of the following electronic surveillance occurs every minutes of every day, all without the consent of the subjects of that surveillance:

- Facial recognition software tracks people at airports searching for known terrorists;
- Unmanned speed sensors pick up motor vehicle speeders and issue tickets by mail;
- Every ATM transaction is tracked numerically and by video camera;
- Service stations, other commercial and industrial buildings and grounds, and a growing number of residences have outdoor motion-activated security video cameras;
- Many stores have installed indoor security video cameras;

- Employees are subject to tracking of business computer, telephone, and vehicle use, and movement in, out, and through company buildings;
- Cellphone service providers track all your incoming and outgoing calls and text messages, and track the phone's physical location in real time;
- Proprietary websites provide ground-level photography of residences, buildings, and homes across the country and around the globe;
- The National Security Agency intercepts and stores a huge proportion of all domestic U.S. cellphone conversations and other metadata details;
- Persons seeking to board an airplane submit to metal detection as do people entering many courthouses and other government buildings;
- Internet service providers track your online activity and sell the details to retailers and data aggregators – for a price; and
- Travelers crossing into the United States are subject to have their cellphones seized and searched without a warrant, probable cause, or even reasonable suspicion.

These are just a very few of the ways all of us are being surveilled daily – usually without our knowledge, and always without our express and voluntary consent. What has become of consent in the digital age?

Consent and the third party doctrine

Finally, and in a sense the most devastating legal principle leading to diminished privacy in the digital age, is the irrelevance of consent in the face of the third party doctrine. That doctrine provides that when an individual "voluntarily" discloses information to a third party (whether a person or an entity), the individual no longer has a reasonable expectation of privacy in the disclosed information and cannot contest further dissemination of those data by that third party. Thus, when that third party intentionally or inadvertently disseminates that information to anyone or everyone else, the individual has no privacy rights in those data and thus no cause of action to pursue.

By way of example, when a cellphone user discloses cellphone location and calling history to the cellphone service provider (a third party) for the purpose of placing cellphone calls, the user cannot contest when the government seeks to obtain those data from the service provider. The service provider has no standing to vicariously assert the phone user's privacy rights and the user has no privacy right remaining in the voluntarily disclosed cellphone data. But did the cellphone user really "voluntarily" disclose those cellphone data to the service provider and the cellphone towers? The cellphone user only had one choice: either disclose those cellphone data and your cellphone location to the service providers and cell towers or you must refrain from using a cellphone. That is no choice at all, and that is not valid and voluntary consent. The third party doctrine should be held inapplicable in the digital age, because it obviates the individual's right to freely consent or freely withhold or limit consent.

Opt-out, do-not-track and related approaches fall far short of reviving individuals' rights. Consent in the digital age, as the law currently stands, no longer need be intelligent, knowing, and voluntary. Rather, it can be hidden in interminable privacy policies, or shrink wraps, or "I agree" buttons, or "terms and conditions" fine print, and consent can even be inferred from acquiescence to service providers' one-sided waivers of adhesion. In the final analysis, in the digital age, consent is hardly required at all.

Charles E. MacLean

Further Reading

Hotaling, A. (2007). Protecting personally identifiable information on the internet: Notice and consent in the age of behavioral targeting. CommLaw Conspectus.

Lamparello, A. (2015). Online Data Breaches, Standing, and the Third-Party Doctrine. Cardozo Law Review de Novo 119–129.

Looijen, D. (2010). Time for a Change: The Schema of Contract in the Digital Era. Journal on Telecommunications & High Technology Law 8: 547–570.

See also: Privacy Laws, Federal; Fourth Amendment to the U.S. Constitution; Smartphones; Electronic Surveillance; Big Data; Cookies

Constitutional law

Identification: Protects the individual against certain government action that may violate that person's right to privacy, as guaranteed in the Bill of Rights. The Bill of Rights refers to the original first ten amendments to the United States Constitution.

As this entry explains, the First, Third, Fourth, Fifth, Sixth, Fourteenth, and (very broadly) the Ninth Amendments provide specific guarantees of personal privacy rights, which the U.S. Supreme Court interprets and applies at the federal level. Also, several state constitutions include specific provisions that expressly protect individual privacy. Those states include Alaska, Arizona, California, Florida, Hawaii, Illinois, Louisiana, Montana, South Carolina, and Washington. Courts in other states have interpreted their Constitutions to implicitly protect privacy rights. These rights, however, vary among the states. Some state courts have interpreted state constitutions to provide expanded privacy protections to individuals beyond the privacy rights guaranteed by the federal constitution.

Both federal and state constitutions prohibit only the government from violating personal privacy rights. In some instances, a person may bring a lawsuit against state or local government officials who act "under color of state law," meaning that the official violated an individual's federal constitutional rights while acting to or pretending to carry out his or her official duties. See, for example, 42 U.S.C.

§ 1983. Constitutional law generally does not apply in cases where private persons or corporations violate an individual's personal privacy. These are generally considered as private wrongs, which an individual must pursue as a privacy tort in a civil action.

Constitutional privacy rights distinguished from state common law and statutory rights

Constitutional privacy protections differ from state laws that allow individuals to file civil claims against private parties (rather than government officials) for violating individual privacy rights. In a civil claim against a private company or individual, the legal remedy is not based on constitutional law. Instead, most states recognize a personal right of privacy by common law or state statute.

Those state laws allow a person who suffers emotional distress or other injury as a result of an invasion of privacy to file a civil action, known as a tort claim, against another private party to assert that right. A person who claims that his or her privacy rights have been violated may ask a court for compensation from the other party for injuries caused by the invasion of privacy. Some state laws allow the court to order the infringing party to stop the conduct that has resulted in the invasion of privacy. Referred to as an injunction, this type of order may serve either as an alternative to a court award of money, known as compensatory damages, or as an additional remedy. As its name suggests, a court award of money damages is intended to compensate the individual for injuries resulting from the invasion of privacy.

The Bill of Rights as the foundation of personal privacy

In the United States, the constitutional right of privacy is based on several provisions of the Bill of Rights. While the Constitution does not expressly state a right of privacy, the United States Supreme Court has interpreted the First, Third, Fourth, Fifth, Sixth, Ninth, and Fourteenth Amendments as providing various types of constitutional privacy rights. The Court has declared that each of these Amendments includes a "penumbra" (term metaphorically used to describe "space") from which personal privacy rights originate. (*Griswold v. Connecticut*, 381 U.S. 479 (1965)).

The most established constitutional privacy protection in the United States is derived from the Fourth Amendment's guarantee against unreasonable searches and seizures. The Fourth Amendment states:

> The right of the people to be secure in their persons, houses, papers, and effects, against unreasonable searches and seizures, shall not be violated, and no warrants shall issue, but upon probable cause, supported by oath or affirmation, and particularly describing the place to be searched, and the persons or things to be seized.

In 1914, the United States Supreme Court ruled for the first time that "the Fourth Amendment bar[s] the use of evidence secured through an illegal search and seizure" in a criminal prosecution in federal court. (*Weeks v. United States*, 232 U.S. 383 (1914)).

> [The Fourth Amendment] took its origin in the determination of the framers of the Amendments to the Federal Constitution to provide for that instrument a Bill of Rights, securing to the American people, among other things, those safeguards which had grown up in England to protect the people from unreasonable searches and seizures, such as were permitted under the general warrants issued under authority of the government, by which there had been invasions of the home and privacy of the citizens, and the seizure of their private papers in support of charges, real or imaginary, made against them."

The Court later explained in *Wolf v. Colorado*, 338 U.S. 25 (1949), that the exclusionary rule (which prevents the government from using most evidence collected in violation of the U.S. Constitution) "was not derived from the explicit requirements of the Fourth Amendment; it was not based on legislation expressing Congressional policy in the enforcement of the Constitution. The decision was a matter of judicial implication."

While the Constitution's Framers originally focused on protecting the home against unreasonable searches, the Court has since recognized that Fourth Amendment protects certain fundamental privacy interests. The Court has found that the Fourth Amendment's primary purpose is to protect privacy rather than property. For that reason, the Court has "increasingly discarded fictional and procedural barriers rested on property concepts." (*Warden, Md. Penitentiary v. Hayden,* 387 U.S. 294 (1967)).

Over the last two centuries, the federal courts have defined the constitutional right of privacy primarily by interpreting the Fourth Amendment in both federal and state criminal cases. For example, in the case of *Mapp v. Ohio,* 367 US 643(1961), the Court ruled evidence gathered in violation of the Fourth Amendment is inadmissible in a court of law. The purpose of the Fourth Amendment is to protect citizens against the types of general and arbitrary searches that English customs officials regularly conducted during the colonial period. (*Steagald v. United States,* 451 U.S. 204 (1981)).

However, the Fourth Amendment does not prohibit all searches. It prohibits only *unreasonable* government searches. A government search is presumed to be reasonable, and, therefore, constitutional, if a judge has first issued a search warrant to law enforcement officers based on a finding of "probable cause." Before issuing a warrant, a neutral judge or magistrate must first decide that the facts provided by a law enforcement officer under oath demonstrate probable cause to believe that the search or seizure

will yield evidence of criminal activity. Even if the magistrate finds probable cause, the search warrant must specifically describe the place to be searched, and it must identify any person whom officers may arrest or the particular things they may seize. If the facts provided by the law enforcement officer are sufficient to support probable cause, the judicial officer may issue a search warrant. The warrant represents the neutral magistrate's judgment that the government's interest in searching for evidence of criminal activity outweighs the personal right of privacy implicated by the search.

The Supreme Court has recognized several exceptions to the warrant requirement of the Fourth Amendment, primarily because the fundamental prohibition is against *unreasonable* searches. Thus, some searches are reasonable even if law enforcement officers do not first obtain a search warrant. Generally, these exceptions to the warrant requirement reflect the Court's efforts to balance the privacy interests of the individual against the legitimate need of the government to protect public safety.

For example, the Court has recognized a broad exception to the warrant requirement for evidence seized by law enforcement officers incident to an otherwise lawful arrest. (*Arizona v. Gant,* 556 U.S. 332 (2009)). A related exception applies to automobile searches when a driver has been lawfully stopped for a traffic violation. That exception, however, is primarily designed to protect officer safety and, to a lesser extent, to prevent the destruction of evidence. Therefore, a warrantless vehicle search incident to a traffic stop is generally limited in scope to areas within reach of the driver. Another example of an exception to the warrant requirement is a search conducted with the consent of someone who has a possessory interest in the place searched. (*Georgia v. Randolph,* 547 U.S. 103 (2006)).

The Court has specifically held that students in a public school setting have Fourth Amendment rights to be free from unreasonable searches and seizures. (*New Jersey v. T.L.O.,* 469

U.S. 325 (1985)). School officials, however, do not need a search warrant or even probable cause to search a student. Given the government's important interest in maintaining an appropriate and safe learning environment, the Court held that school officials must only have reasonable suspicion, not probable cause, that a student has violated either a law or a school disciplinary rule to conducting a warrantless search. The Court, however, has held that a school may constitutionally require students to consent to random drug testing as a condition for participating in extracurricular activities, such as athletics, music, or academic competitions.

The United States Supreme Court has devised a judicial remedy for unreasonable searches to deter police misconduct. If law enforcement officers seize evidence of criminal activity in a constitutionally unreasonable search, the trial court will refuse to admit the evidence against the person whose Fourth Amendment rights were violated. While this judge-made rule of evidence is known as the exclusionary rule, the Court has emphasized that the rule is based on the Fourth Amendment. (*Mapp v. Ohio*, 367 U.S. 643 (1961)).

When the Court first announced the exclusionary rule more than a century ago, it applied only to federal criminal cases. (*Weeks v. United States*). Since then, the Court has extended the exclusionary rule to state criminal cases, because the Due Process Clause of the Fourteenth Amendment incorporates the privacy protections guaranteed by the Fourth Amendment to the states. The Court explained,

> Since the Fourth Amendment's right of privacy has been declared enforceable against the States through the Due Process Clause of the Fourteenth, it is enforceable against them by the same sanction of exclusion as is used against the Federal Government.

In this case, the Supreme Court required state courts to apply the exclusionary rule in state criminal prosecutions to exclude evidence obtained by local law enforcement officers in violation of the privacy protections guaranteed by the Fourth Amendment.

Privacy penumbras of the Bill of Rights

As explained above, the federal constitutional right to privacy was historically based on the Supreme Court's interpretation of the Fourth Amendment. Over the last half century, the United States Supreme Court has interpreted various other Amendments in the Bill of Rights to support a more comprehensive constitutional right of privacy that is much broader in scope. The boundaries and scope of the constitutional right remain unclear, and they continue to evolve.

In 1964, the Supreme Court considered the constitutionality of a state law that prohibited anyone, even married couples, from using contraceptive drugs or devices. The lawsuit was filed by individuals who had been convicted as accessories to the criminal offense for providing information to married couples about contraception, and by prescribing contraceptives. The Court held the statute unconstitutional because it violated the "right of marital privacy" protected by the "penumbras" surrounding specific guarantees in the Bill of Rights.

Chief Justice Douglas explained the Court's reasoning as follows:

> [S]pecific guarantees in the Bill of Rights have penumbras, formed by emanations from those guarantees that help give them life and substance. Various guarantees create zones of privacy. . . . We have had many controversies over these penumbral rights of "privacy and repose." [T]he right of privacy which presses for recognition here is a legitimate one.

For the first time, the Supreme Court recognized a constitutional right of privacy that protects an individual's freedom to make decisions about private, intimate matters, without government interference. Just three years later in 1967, the Supreme Court addressed whether a person has a constitutional right of privacy even while using a pay telephone inside a glassed-in public telephone booth. Historically, the Court interpreted the Fourth Amendment based on principles of property ownership or possession, reasoning that the government could not intrude into a person's home or other private location. Thus in *Katz v. United* States, 389 U.S. 347 (1967), the government argued that the caller waived any right to privacy when he voluntarily made a telephone call in a public telephone booth rather than in the privacy of his home or another private place. The Supreme Court disagreed, holding for the first time that "the Fourth Amendment protects people, not places."

Thus, beginning in the mid-1960s with *Griswold* and *Katz*, the Supreme Court recognized that the constitutional right of privacy was not limited to personal conduct or conversations occurring outside public view or hearing. The Court has since followed the same reasoning to recognize a constitutional privacy right that far exceeds the original interpretation of the right to protect against government intrusions into a person's home or another private place.

In 1972, the Court extended to unmarried couples the constitutional right of privacy to make personal decisions about procreation, striking down a state law that restricted contraceptives to married couples. (*Eisenstadt v. Baird,* 405 U.S. 438 (1972)). Just one year later, in *Roe v. Wade*, 410 U.S. 113 (1973), the Court struck down a Texas statute that prohibited women, in consultation with their personal physicians, from terminating their pregnancies, using privacy as the fundamental basis for the decision.

The First Amendment is another significant source of privacy rights. By its explicit terms, the First Amendment prohibits Congress from interfering with the free exercise of religion, abridging free speech or freedom of the press, interfering with the right of peaceful assembly, or restricting the right to petition the government for redress of grievances. In the late 1960s, the Supreme Court began interpreting these protections to include several aspects of the constitutional right of privacy.

In 1969, the Supreme Court struck down a statute that allowed the state to convict an individual merely for possessing films that law enforcement officers considered obscene. (*Stanley v. Georgia, 384 U.S. 557 (1969)*). While the government may regulate the sale and distribution of obscene materials, the government may not prohibit a person from possessing and viewing literature or media in the privacy of his own home that others might characterize as offensive. The Court held that the First Amendment protects private thoughts, including the right to read or watch whatever one pleases.

As the Court observed,

Fundamental is the right to be free, except in very limited circumstances, from unwanted governmental intrusions into one's privacy. Defendant has a right to be free from state inquiry into the contents of his library. Mere categorization of these films as "obscene" is insufficient justification for such a drastic invasion of personal liberties . . . [in] the privacy of one's own home...[A] state has no business telling a man, sitting alone in his own house, what books he may read or what films he may watch. Our whole constitutional heritage rebels at the thought of giving government the power to control men's minds.

In 1990, however, the Supreme Court upheld a similar state criminal law that prohibited possession of child pornography, reasoning that the state's compelling interest in protecting children from exploitation outweighed the privacy interests of individuals, even when viewing materials in the privacy of the home. "Given the gravity of the State's interests in this context...[the government] may constitutionally proscribe the possession and viewing of child pornography." (*Osborne v. Ohio*, 495 U.S. 103 (1990)).

The Court has also interpreted the First Amendment to protect a person's right to use a pseudonym or remain anonymous while engaging in the constitutional right of free expression. (*McEntyre v. Ohio Elec. Comm.*, 514 U.S. 334 (1995)). For example, the government may not punish a person who authors or distributes anonymous handbills or pamphlets. Requiring an author or speaker to self-identify would tend to discourage the exercise of free speech, and, therefore, would violate the First Amendment. The Court observed that anonymous advocacy for political causes reflected "an honorable tradition of advocacy and of dissent" in the United States. More recently, the Delaware Supreme Court has held that even when posted on the internet, anonymous speech warrants First Amendment protection. (*Doe v. Cahill*).

First Amendment rights, however, protect more than freedom of speech and freedom of thought. The Court has interpreted the First Amendment's freedom of peaceful assembly to protect an important penumbral privacy right known as "expressive association."

> [T]he Court has recognized a right to associate for the purpose of engaging in those activities protected by the First Amendment—speech, assembly, petition for the redress of grievances, and the exercise of religion. The Constitution guarantees freedom of association of this kind as an indispensable means of preserving other individual liberties.

The right of expressive association recognizes the right of the people to come together to advocate for religious, political, fraternal, or any other reasons related to the liberty interest. For example, the government may not prohibit an individual from affiliating with particular political causes, however, offensive others may consider those groups.

It is beyond debate that freedom to engage in association for the advancement of beliefs and ideas is an inseparable aspect of the "liberty" assured by the Due Process Clause of the Fourteenth Amendment, which embraces freedom of speech…Of course, it is immaterial whether the beliefs sought to be advanced by association pertain to political, economic, religious or cultural matters, and state action that may have the effect of curtailing the freedom to associate is subject to the closest scrutiny. (*Nat'l Ass'n for Advancement of Colored People v. State of Ala. ex rel. Patterson*, 357 U.S. 449 (1958)).

More recently, in 2011, the Court relied on the First Amendment right of expressive association to reverse a multi-million dollar judgment against a church and its members for picketing the funeral of a young soldier to protest matters of concern "to society at large." (*Snyder v. Phelps*, 562 U.S. 443 (2011)). Writing for the Court, Chief Justice John Roberts explained, "While these messages may fall short of refined social or political commentary, the issues they highlight—the political and moral conduct of the United States and its citizens, the fate of our Nation, homosexuality in the military, and scandals involving the Catholic clergy—are matters of public import." Those constitutional rights outweighed the interests of the soldier's grieving father, protected by state law, to avoid intrusive interference with his son's funeral procession.

To a lesser extent, the Court has cited other amendments in the Bill of Rights as the basis for penumbral privacy rights. The Third Amendment prohibits the government from requiring citizens to quarter soldiers in their homes in times of peace without their consent, or in wartime except as prescribed by law. The Fifth Amendment prohibits the government from compelling an individual "to be a witness against himself," which creates a "zone of privacy which the government may not force him to surrender to his detriment." The Fifth Amendment also prohibits the federal government from interfering with an individual's liberty. (*United States v. Windsor, 133 S.Ct. 2675 (2013)*). Moreover, even the Court has even acknowledged the Ninth Amendment as a potential source of residual privacy rights in a more broad context. It provides, "The enumeration in the Constitution of certain rights shall not be construed to deny or disparage others retained by the people."

The Fourteenth Amendment is another significant and extensive source of the constitutional right of privacy, both alone and along with other provisions of the Bill of Rights. In addition to the right of expressive association protected by the First Amendment, the Court has recognized a constitutional right of intimate association, a "fundamental element of personal liberty" guaranteed by the Fourteenth Amendment. This right guarantees the "formation and preservation of certain kinds of highly personal relationships a substantial measure of sanctuary from unjustified interference by the State." (*Roberts v. U.S. Jaycees*, 468 U.S. 609 (1984)).

In conjunction with the right of intimate association, which involves private decision-making on personal family matters, the Court has recognized a broad privacy right as part of the Fourteenth Amendment's guarantees of liberty and due process. In 1990, for example, the Supreme Court held that an individual has a right to refuse medical treatment. "[T]he Due Process Clause protects an interest in life as well as an interest in refusing life-sustaining medical treatment." (*Cruzan v. Missouri Dep't of Health*, 497 261 (1990)). In 1997, however, the Court refused to extend that right to include the right to assisted suicide. (*Washington v. Glucksberg*, 521 702 (1997)).

In 2003, the Court relied on the Fourteenth Amendment right of intimate association to strike down a state law prohibiting intimate sexual activity between consenting adults, including gay and lesbian individuals. (*Lawrence v. Texas*, 539 U.S. 558 (2003)). That decision was a significant shift in the Court's constitutional jurisprudence because the decision reversed the Supreme Court's holding issued just seventeen years earlier in *Bowers v. Hardwick*, 478 U.S. 186 (1986). In that 1986 decision, the Court had upheld a state criminal statute prohibiting sodomy as applied to a same-sex couple.

As societal norms shifted and the public has become more accepting of homosexuality, the Court's constitutional interpretation has followed. In 2013, in *United States v. Windsor*, the Court relied on a related provision in the Fifth Amendment to strike down a federal statute known as the Defense of Marriage Act (DOMA), 110 Stat. 2419, enacted in 1996, that had expressly defined "marriage" for purposes of federal law to mean "a legal union between a man and a woman." The Court held that "DOMA . . . violates basic due process and equal protection principles applicable to the Federal Government."

The Fourteenth Amendment's Due Process Clause has been the source of judicial decisions recognizing relational or family privacy rights involved with the death of a loved one. In *National Archives & Records Administration v. Favish*, 541 U.S. 157 (2004), the Court held that the statutory right of family members to prevent the disclosure of photographs outweighed the right of a person who sought access to them under the federal Freedom of Information Act, 80 Stat. 250 (1967) The United States Court of Appeals for the Ninth Circuit has relied on that decision, as well as the Fourteenth Amendment's Substantive Due Process Clause, to hold that close family members have a constitutional right of privacy on the disclosure of death images of a loved one. (*Marsh v. Cnty. of San Diego*, 680 F.3d 1148 (9th Cir., 2012)).

The long-standing tradition of respecting family members' privacy in death images partakes of both types of privacy interests protected by the Fourteenth Amendment. First, the publication of death images interferes with "the individual interest in avoiding disclosure of personal matters…"

Second, a parent's right to control a deceased child's remains and death images flows from the well-established substantive due process right to family integrity.

It remains to be seen whether the United States Supreme Court will hold that the right of family privacy with respect to the death of a family member is "so ingrained in our traditions that it is constitutionally protected," as the Ninth Circuit squarely held in 2012," *Marsh v. Cnty. of San Diego,* rather than longstanding tradition acknowledged in state and federal statutes, as acknowledged by the Supreme Court in *Favish.*

Recent developments in privacy law

Most recently, the Supreme Court has issued two significant decisions on the constitutional right of privacy. In *Riley v. California,* 134 S.Ct. 2473 (2014), decided in June 2014, the Court unanimously held that police may not, generally, search the contents of a cellphone seized during a warrantless search incident to a lawful arrest for a traffic violation. The police must first secure a warrant specifically authorizing the search. In reaching its conclusion, the Court acknowledged the unprecedented intrusiveness of a law enforcement search of the contents of an arrestee's cellphone:

> Cellphones differ in both a quantitative and a qualitative sense from other objects that might be kept on an arrestee's person. The term "cellphone" is itself misleading shorthand; many of these devices are in fact minicomputers that also happen to have the capacity to be used as a telephone. They could just as easily be called cameras, video players, rolodexes, calendars, tape recorders, libraries, diaries, albums, televisions, maps, or newspapers.

In June 2015, the Court issued a landmark decision striking down state laws and constitu-

tional provisions that did not recognize same-sex marriage. (*Obergefell v. Hodges,* 135 S.Ct. 2071 (2015)). Justice Kennedy, writing for the majority, relied on several constitutional rights implicating privacy, including the "concept of individual autonomy" to make personal decisions about marriage; the fundamental right of marital privacy recognized in *Griswold*; the right of intimate association protected by the Fourteenth Amendment; the fundamental right to marry "as a matter of history and tradition"; and the Equal Protection Clause of the Fourteenth Amendment. Justice Kennedy concluded:

> [T]he right to marry is a fundamental right inherent in the liberty of the person, and under the Due Process and Equal Protection Clauses of the Fourteenth Amendment couples of the same-sex may not be deprived of that right and that liberty. The Court now holds that same-sex couples may exercise the fundamental right to marry. No longer may this liberty be denied to them.

Recent cases interpreting the constitutional right of privacy, indicate that the right continues to evolve due to changing social norms, as well as contemporary expectations on privacy in an increasingly technological age. It is not unreasonable to assume that as society's attitudes shift and technology continues to advance, changes in the interpretation of privacy rights will ensue.

J. Lyn Entrikin

Further Reading

Ball, Howard. *The Supreme Court in the Intimate Lives of Americans: Birth, Sex, Marriage, Childrearing, and Death.* New York: New York UP, 2002. Print.

Bartee, Alice Fleetwood. *Privacy Rights: Cases Lost and Causes Won before the Supreme Court.* Lanham, MD: Rowman & Littlefield, 2006. Print.

Farber, Daniel A. *Retained by the People: The "Silent" Ninth Amendment and the Constitutional Rights Americans Don't Know They Have.* New York: New York: Basic Books. 2007.

Johns, Fran Moreland. *Perilous Times: An inside Look at Abortion Before- and After- Roe v. Wade*. N.p.: n.p., n.d. Print.

Shaman, Jeffrey M. *Equality and Liberty in the Golden Age of State Constitutional Law*. New York: Oxford UP, 2008. Print.

Solove, Daniel J., and Paul M. Schwartz. *Privacy Law Fundamentals*. Portsmouth, NH: International Association of Privacy Professionals, 2011. Print.

Urofsky, Melvin I. *Lethal Judgments: Assisted Suicide and American Law*. Lawrence, Kan.: U of Kansas, 2000. Print.

Wacks, Raymond. *Privacy: A Very Short Introduction*. Oxford: Oxford UP, 2010. Print.

See also: First Amendment to the U.S. Constitution; Fourth Amendment to the U.S. Constitution; Fourteenth Amendment to the U.S. Constitution; *Griswold v. Connecticut; Katz v. United States; Lawrence v. Texas;* Legal evolution of privacy rights; *Mapp v. Ohio; Riley v. California;* Search warrants; *Stanley v. Georgia*

Consumer privacy

Identification: A mirage in the digital age.

Marketers place cookies and keylogging software on consumers' computers to largely surreptitiously track those consumers' purchase and browsing activities. Why do marketers do that? Because the digital age makes it pitifully easy to technologically accomplish, and marketers can turn that captured user data into more sales and a saleable commodity. In essence, they do it because they can and because there is money to be made doing it.

If a customer entered a brick-and-mortar store and the clerk told the customer, "I will let you look around our store and even buy an item or two, but only if you agree to disclose to us every website you visit for the next several years along with your physical locations in real-time, your friends' identities and photographs, and all on-line purchases you make during that same period." Any reasonable customer would turn around and walk right out of that store. However, in the Internet era, virtually all on-line

marketers gather exactly those data and much more from all visitors and customers to their online stores. We have allowed ourselves – and our privacy – to be victimized by marketers empowered by the latest computer gadgetry. As President Barack Obama's White House released in 2012 when it proposed a Consumer Privacy Bill of Rights, "it is incumbent on us to do what we have done throughout history: apply our timeless privacy values to the new technologies and circumstances of our times."

Nonetheless, when the Obama administration released a revised Consumer Privacy Bill of Rights Act in February 2015, data privacy advocates universally objected to its blurry definition of consumer data, insufficient protections, and lax enforcement regime. In essence, that Act straddled the line between some protection of private consumer data on the one hand and enabling consumer data collection and sale on the other hand, the idea being that sharing consumer data can have a positive effect on the U.S. economy. Such a laissez-faire, even cavalier, approach to consumer data protection illustrates the government's conflicted approach to consumer data privacy. To the extent that enhanced consumer data privacy will impede sales by any American company, the government is loathe to protect the consumer data.

Moreover, once a consumer has more-orless willingly turned over to online marketers the keys to their privacy kingdom, along with the credit card and bank account numbers, Social Security numbers, and mothers' maiden names, the online marketers are just the first entities to possess these private data, certainly not the last. has already happened." In that study of Ameri- Many online marketers sell their caches of private consumers:

vate consumer data to other marketers. Indeed, one can hopefully differentiate between first-party data gatherers, who have a direct relationship with the tracked user, and third-party data gatherers, who purchase consumer data from first-party gatherers and mine the

Internet for dozens more data points about those same users. Users' private data, including health records, pregnancy status, HIV status, credit scores, assets, debts, purchase and browsing history are all readily available from third-party consumer data vendors. Perhaps more disturbing is that all these heretofore private data on consumers are susceptible to domestic and foreign hackers and other unintended dissemination and sharing of private facts about American consumers.

The rationale for such large-scale collection and dissemination of private consumer data is largely ex-post rationalization. The theory goes that allowing marketers to track all this private consumer data has the allegedly salutary benefit of allowing those marketers to better target its advertisements to users who are likely to be genuinely interested in the advertised products. That is why once a user engages in online cost comparisons for baby strollers, that user is subsequently inundated with popup ads from one vendor or another advertising strollers and other baby-related items. However, is that modest shopping convenience really worth the cost of all that privacy erosion? Are American consumers and their elected representatives willing to wade into the Internet and take back their consumer privacy rights?

It may be too late for that, for now, at least, because American consumers believe – and act as if they believe – that they are powerless to stem the tide of personal consumer data collection by online marketers. As one 2015 study notes, "Americans believe it is futile to manage what companies can learn about them . . . [the majority] do not want to lose control over their information but also believe this loss of control

- 49% incorrectly believed a supermarket must obtain the consumer's permission before selling information about the consumer's purchases to other companies;
- 69% inaccurately thought a pharmacy must have your permission before selling

to others information about the over-the-counter products you have purchased;

- 65% falsely believed that if a company has a "privacy policy," that means the company will not share consumer data with others without consumer permission;
- 91% believed it is not fair for business to collect consumer data without their knowledge;
- 71% felt it was not fair for businesses that provide free in-store Wi-Fi to collect surfing and use data from consumers using the service;
- 64% wrongly believed that clearing cookies on a cellphone prevented marketers from tracking the user;
- 84% want to be empowered to control what data business collect from them online; but
- 65% report that they have come to accept that they have little control over what marketers can learn about on-line consumers; and
- only 18% of all Internet users have activated a "do not track" feature to prevent online marketers from tracking and logging their consumer information and activity.

If one examines these results, it appears that those consumers who are more aware of the depth and breadth realities of online data collection by marketers are the most resigned to the inevitability of that data collection. The most informed have given up.

As the *Wall Street Journal* reported in 2010, "One of the fastest-growing businesses on the Internet... is the business of spying on Internet users." Moreover, why not? It is, after all, big business indeed. Recent studies suggest that buying and selling otherwise private consumer data mined from the Internet will soon top $60 billion in annual revenue in the United States alone.

We ought not to blame the Internet marketers, first-party data gatherers, third-party data gatherers, and those who purchase consumer data from them. They are just following a free market model: they are simply entering a profitable market. In reality, the regulators and legislators are the ones to be blamed. For example, the Federal Trade Commission (FTC), the federal agency most broadly charged with consumer protection, and which talks a good game ("In today's world . . . companies are collecting, storing, and sharing more information about consumers than ever before . . . they should not do so at the expense of consumer privacy"), and has some solid policy stances (such as, "The Commission now also calls on Congress to consider enacting baseline privacy legislation and reiterates its call for data security legislation"), has largely served as the chief apologist and enabler of data privacy erosion, focusing on industry self-regulation rather than on top-down legislated limits on consumer data privacy erosion.

Even the FTC's data privacy enforcement actions have been largely ineffective. When the FTC compelled Google and Facebook to more clearly disclose to consumers the private consumer data they were capturing and selling to others, the result was not more consumer protection but merely more dense and indecipherable privacy disclosures that most users simply click-through without reading them – and certainly without understanding them – and therefore, without truly consenting to the data privacy erosion.

To compound the problem, all of this consumer data privacy erosion is largely irreparable and likely irreversible. Once data resides on the Internet, it is very difficult or impossible to erase.

Firms routinely take snapshots of the Internet that yield the cached webpages that turn up on your browser searches. Immense amounts of these data can be stored in a very small physical space and thus easily transported, shared, and stolen. Hackers have successfully targeted data stored in banks, hospitals, stores, and even government computers. According to one source, the Pentagon and the National Security Agency each repelled approximately ten million attempted cyber-intrusions per day in 2014. Some one million new malware threats were unleashed each day of 2014 alone. In 2014, private data concerning 110 million consumers was stolen from Target, another 83 million from J.P. Morgan Chase, and another 56 million from Home Depot. The consumer data stolen from Target earned the cyber-thieves at least $53.7 million on the black market and cost Target at least $148 million. More recently, large data breaches were reported by Equifax (2017) and Marriot International (2018). And the resultant downstream consequences in cybercrime, identity theft, and even extortion based on stolen consumer data, are skyrocketing.

The digital age has ushered in an age of privacy erosion unparalleled in history. Perhaps the closest analog occurred in the nineteenth century when photography and the growth of newspapers combined to put on the front page what once was hidden in the parlor. Louis Brandeis, destined to become an Associate Supreme Court Justice twenty-six years later, wrote in 1890 about this last era of privacy erosion. En route to recommending broad adoption of a right to privacy, later-Justice Brandeis and his co-author presaged the digital age:

Recent inventions and business methods call attention to the next step that must be taken for the protection of the person, and for securing to the individual . . . the right "to be left alone." . . . Of the desirability – indeed of the necessity – of some such protection, there can, it is believed, be no doubt. . . . The intensity and complexity of life, attendant upon advancing civilization, have rendered necessary some retreat from the world, and man, under the refining influence of culture, has become more sensitive to publicity, so that solitude and privacy have become increasingly essential to the individual; but modern enterprise and invention have, through invasions upon his privacy, subjected him to mental pain and distress. . . . The common law secures to each individual the right of determining, ordinarily, to what extent his thoughts, sentiments, and emotions shall be communicated to others [and each individual] generally retains the power to fix the limits of publicity that shall be given them. . . . The common law has always recognized a man's house as his castle, impregnable, often, even to its own officers engaged in the execution of its commands. Shall the courts thus close the front entrance to constituted authority, and open wide the back door to idle or prurient curiosity?

Similarly, in the digital age, when heretofore private consumer data – through the wide open "back door" – is so freely captured, used, resold, reused, and more, for profit alone, and largely without the consent of the consumer who is the subject of the data, our right to privacy has been eroded almost beyond repair. It is past time for the FTC, other agencies, the executive branch, and Congress to step in and control this torrent of purloined consumer data. Opaque privacy waivers that consumers merely click through without understanding are no substitute for real and substantive consumer privacy protections in the digital age.

Charles E. MacLean

Further Reading

Federal Trade Commission Report (March 2012). Protecting Consumer Privacy in an Era of Rapid Change.

Federal Trade Commission Staff Report (Jan. 2015). Internet of Things: Privacy & Security in a Connected World.

Tobias, Sharon (Dec. 31, 2014). 2014: The Year in Cyberattacks. Newsweek.

Turow, J., Hennessy, M., & Draper, N. (June 2015). The Tradeoff Fallacy: How Marketers are Misrepresenting American Consumers and Opening Them Up to Exploitation (University of Pennsylvania, Annenberg School for Communication).

Warren, S. D. & Brandeis, L. D. (1890). The Right to Privacy. Harvard Law Review 4(5), 193–220.

White House Press Release (Feb. 23, 2012). We Can't Wait: Obama Administration Calls for a Consumer Privacy Bill of Rights for the Digital Age. Retrieved from: https://www.whitehouse.gov/blog/2012/02/23/we-cant-wait-obama-administration-calls-consumer-privacybill-rights-digital-age.

See also: Privacy laws, federal; Cookies; Big data

Cookies

Identification: Small text files that some websites place on an individual's computer, typically containing a small string of numbers that can be used to identify a computer.

Cookies are stored in a computer's browser, and they collect information about the pages an individual views and the activities an individual engages in on the site. Cookies enable a site to "remember" an individual's information between pages or visits and to transmit the information back to the website's computer (or server), which generally is the only computer that can read it. Cookies are often used for log-in, remembering preferences, tracking visitors, and more. Advertisers install cookies to track user browsing history and to display targeted ads to users. For example, if the individual searches for "automobiles" on Google, cookies track the visit. Later in the day, on another website, Google may target car ads at the user because the cookies enable Google to remember the identity of the user.

Single-session cookies assist in navigation on the website. They record information only temporarily and are erased when the user quits the session. They are enabled by default to provide the smoothest navigation experience possible. Persistent (or multisession) cookies remain on the computer and record information every time the individual visits some websites. They are stored on the hard drive of an user's computer until that user deletes them manually from a browser folder, or until they expire, which can be months or years after they were placed on the computer.

Some cookies also collect data across many websites, which creates behavioral profiles of individuals. These profiles can then be used to decide what content or advertisements to show the user. The privacy problem from cookies comes from the aggregation of tracking across different websites into profiles and from attempts at linking this profile to the user's identity. By tracking these identifiers across websites that users visit, advertisers can infer a user's interests, perhaps sensitive ones, such as medical conditions, political opinions, or sexual interests.

A user can set his or her Web browser to warn him or her about attempts to place cookies on the computer or to limit the type of cookies to be allowed. While users may be able to avoid some tracking by blocking cookies, this approach assumes that advertisers will respect individual choices and that advertisers will not use alternative methods for tracking.

By requiring websites to inform and obtain consent from visitors, laws such as the European Union (EU) Directive on Privacy seek to grant web users more control over their online privacy. The EU law on cookies is intended to protect computer users. It requires websites to obtain consent from visitors to store or retrieve any information on a computer, smartphone, or tablet. This law was intended to protect online privacy by alerting consumers to how their personal information is being collected and used online, and by giving them the option to allow it or not. Website owners in the EU are required to comply with the law or face enforcement actions and perhaps a fine. Consumers may be presumed to prefer to avoid engaging with websites that they believe might compromise their privacy.

The law on cookies began as an EU directive that granted individuals the right to refuse cookies. All EU countries adopted the directive in May 2011. All websites owned in the EU or targeted toward EU citizens are required to comply with the law. Most small websites track visitors to their website through a tool such as

Google Analytics, and they use social media plug-ins such as Facebook-like buttons. This EU law appears to outlaw these devices as well.

In the United States, cookies have been the subject of multi-million-dollar litigation. In 2013, Google agreed to pay $17 million to 37 states and the District of Columbia in a settlement over tracking consumers online without their knowledge. The case involved Google's bypassing of privacy settings in Apple Safari browsers in 2011 and 2012 to use cookies to track users' online activities and show them targeted advertisements. Google claimed that it discontinued circumventing the settings early in 2012, after this practice was disclosed, and stopped tracking Safari users and sending them ads based on their profiles. The penalty, however, is a small fraction of the billions that Google earns in advertising revenue each year.

The case against Google represented just one of many government investigations, lawsuits, and punishments regarding Google's practices relating to privacy matters. The government based its position on the argument that consumers should know whether their online habits are being tracked, and by tracking millions of people without their knowledge, Google violated not only consumers' privacy but also their trust.

Since the Google case began being litigated, however, tracking technology moved beyond cookies, particularly on mobile devices that do not use cookies in apps. Regulators and industry groups have attempted to develop standards for digital tracking but have not been able to keep up with technological changes. For example, Google was considering an anonymous identifier, connected to users of its Chrome browser, that advertisers would use instead of cookies to target ads. It also introduced new tools such as one to track consumers across devices and to inform marketers whether a consumer makes a purchase on a computer after researching an item on a phone.

Gretchen Nobahar

Further Reading

Ayenson, Mika, Dietrich James Wambach, Ashkan Soltani, Nathan Good, and Chris Jay Hoofnagle. "Flash Cookies and Privacy II: Now with HTML5 and ETag Respawning," July 29, 2011. http://ssrn.com/abstract=1898390.

Brazhnik, Tatiana. "Cookies in E-Commerce: Balancing Privacy and Business." *SSRN*, April 29, 2013.http://ssrn.com/abstract=2366262.

Harvey, Trevor. "Cookies Part II—Privacy Pirates or Useful Utilities?" *British Journal of Healthcare Management* 5, no. 8 (August 1999): 323.

Hormozi, Amir M. "Cookies and Privacy." *Information Systems Security* 13, no. 6 (2005): 51–59.

Mayer-Schönberger, Viktor. "The Internet and Privacy Legislation: Cookies for a Treat?" *Computer Law & Security Review* 14, no. 3 (May 1, 1998): 166–174.

Mitchell, Ian D. "Third-Party Tracking Cookies and Data Privacy." April 25, 2012. http://ssrn.com/abstract=2058326.

Popoli, Anna Rita. "Cookies and Electronic Commerce: A Survey About Actual Knowledge of the Issues Concerning Privacy." December 10, 2012. http://ssrn.com/abstract=2187496.

Sipior, Janice C., Burke T. Ward, and Ruben A. Mendoza. "Online Privacy Concerns Associated with Cookies, Flash Cookies, and Web Beacons." *Journal of Internet Commerce* 10, no. 1 (2011): 1–16.

See also: Computers and Privacy; Mobile Devices; Smartphones

Cox Broadcasting Corporation v. Cohn, 420 U.S. 469 (1975)

Identification: A landmark U.S. Supreme Court case involving the right to privacy and freedom of speech and of the press. Justice Byron White wrote the majority opinion striking down a Georgia statute that made it a misdemeanor to broadcast the name of a rape victim.

In this important case, which pitted the right to privacy against the protections of the First Amendment, the U.S. Supreme Court ruled that the First Amendment protected the television reporter's right to publish accurately a rape victim's name, which had been obtained from judicial records open to the public and part of a public prosecution.

The U.S. Supreme Court had to weigh two competing fundamental rights. While recognizing the importance of an individual's right to privacy and the "right to be let alone," which protects private information, the U.S. Supreme Court held that the First Amendment right to attend and report on criminal trials is a fundamental right in the United States. This right protects the dissemination of a rape victim's name.

The 17-year-old victim was raped and later died. Six young men were initially charged with rape and murder. Despite intense media interest, the victim's name was not publicized initially because of the Georgia statute that made it unlawful for the news media or any person to print and publish, broadcast, televise, or disseminate the name or identity of any female who may have been raped or sexually assaulted. Any person or corporation that violated the law would be charged with a misdemeanor. The murder charges were dropped, and the six defendants ultimately pled guilty to rape. There was intense media interest in the case, and a television reporter, covering the sentencing hearing, revealed the victim's name during an evening broadcast.

The victim's father, Martin Cohn, sued the reporter and the television station, WSB, for publishing his daughter's name. Mr. Cohn claimed that they violated the Georgia statute and his common-law right to privacy. The Georgia trial court agreed and rejected the media's First Amendment claim. The Georgia Supreme Court also ruled that the statute was intended to protect a rape victim's name and that, as a matter of public policy, was not a matter of concern.

Cox Publishing Corp., owner of the television station, urged the U.S. Supreme Court to rule that the First Amendment protected the press from criminal or civil liability for publishing information that was accurate, even if it damaged someone's reputation or "individual sensibilities."

In its opinion, the U.S. Supreme Court discussed the First Amendment protections for publishing truthful information in the ground-breaking defamation case of *New York Times Co. v. Sullivan*, 376 U.S. 254 (1964). The U.S. Supreme Court, however, refused to extend First Amendment protection to cover the publication of all truthful information, regardless of how embarrassing that information might be. In its decision, the U.S. Supreme Court narrowed its ruling to the First Amendment right to publish information contained in judicial records available to the public and press. The Court, referring to the "sphere of collision between claims of privacy and those of the free press," focused on the issue of whether a state can punish the accurate publication of a rape victim's name when the victim's name is obtained from public court records as part of a public trial. The U.S. Supreme Court ruled that a state may not.

The Court was concerned that allowing the media to be punished for publishing truthful information from court records would lead to censorship and the suppression of important information. The public depends on the press to report on the operation of the government and its public officials, including the judiciary. In his decision Justice White referred to the case of *Sheppard v. Maxwell*, 384 U.S. 333 (1966), in which the Court said that the press helps guarantee a fair trial. Justice White also referred to the precedential case of *Craig v. Harney*, 331 U.S. 367 (1947), wherein the Court asserted that a "trial is a public event. What transpires in the court room is public property. . . . Those who see and hear what transpired can report it with impunity." As a result, the reporting on the commission and prosecution of crimes, including judicial proceedings, are, without question, matters of legitimate concern to the public.

In his concurring opinion, Justice William O. Douglas would have extended First Amendment protections. "There is no power on the part of government to suppress or penalize the publication of 'news of the day,'" Justice Douglas wrote.

While the U.S. Supreme Court's decision in *Cox v. Cohn* held that the First Amendment protected the right to publish truthful information contained in public court records, most members of the media choose not to publish the names of rape or sexual assault victims. In addition, news organizations such as the Society of Professional Journalists and the Radio Television Digital News Association have professional codes of ethics that encourage journalists to adhere to these standards, which include reporting with integrity, honesty, and fairness. The guidelines also recommend ways to handle sexual assaults, emphasizing the importance of dealing with victims with respect and dignity.

Sandra F. Chance

Further Reading

Alderman, Ellen, and Caroline Kennedy. *The Right to Privacy*. 1995; reprint, New York: Vintage Books, 1997. Blasi, Vincent. "The Checking Value in First Amendment Theory." *Am. B. Found. Res. J.* 00, no. 00 (1977): 521.

Chemerinsky, Erwin. "Narrowing the Tort of Public Disclosure of Private Facts." *Chapman Law Review* 11 (2008): 423–433.

Denno, Deborah W. "The Privacy Rights of Rape Victims in the Media and the Law: Perspectives on Disclosing Rape Victims' Names." *Fordham Law Review* 61 (1993): 1113–1131.

"Developments in the Law—The Law of Media: III. Prosecuting the Press: Criminal Liability for the Act of Publishing." *Harvard Law Review* 120 (2007): 1007–1019.

Johnson, Michelle. "Of Public Interest: How Courts Handle Rape Victims' Privacy Suits." *Communications Law and Policy*, 4 no. 201 (1999): 000–000.

Sheinkopf, Cheryl M. "Balancing Free Speech, Privacy and Open Government: Why Government Should Not Restrict the Truthful Reporting of Public Record Information." *UCLA Law Review* 44 (1997): 1567–1612.

Spurlock, Jefferson Tarter. "The Effects of the *Cox Broadcasting Corp. v. Cohn* Decision: Almost Four Decades Later." *Communications Law Review* 14, no. 00 (0000): 48–62.

See also: First Amendment to the U.S. Constitution; *New York Times Co. v. Sullivan;* Supreme Court of the United States; The Right to Privacy

Credit and debit cards

Identification: Plastic payment cards that can be used to purchase goods or services electronically, or without cash on hand.

Each credit and debit card features a unique number, usually up to sixteen digits long and embossed on the front of the card. In the United States, the back of a credit or debit card has traditionally featured a magnetic stripe. This stripe stores digital data about the credit or debit account, including the account number; the card-holder's name; the card's expiration date; and an encrypted numeric code known as a card verification value (CVV1), which the merchant's card reader uses to verify that the card is valid. Transactions during which a consumer's card is swiped through a merchant's card reader are known as card present transactions. In card not present transactions, such as purchases made online or over the phone, the consumer gives to the merchant the card number and other information, including the card's expiration date, the consumer's address on file for the card, and the three- or four-digit CVV2 number printed on the back of the card. The CVV2 serves the same purpose as a CVV1, and may also be called a card security code (CSC) or card verification code (CVC, depending on the credit card company.

Some card issuers are incorporating alternatives to the magnetic stripe in their cards, including contactless or tap-and-go cards that use a radio frequency identification (RFID) chip that can be read by the merchant's card reader from a short distance away. Some credit cards are incorporating EMV microchips, which require the consumer to verify the transaction with either a personal identification number (PIN) or a signature. ("EMV" refers to Europay, Master-Card, and Visa; these three companies were the creators of the standard.) Debit cards always require either a PIN or a signature. A single card could contain multiple methods for proving a card present transaction; for example, contact-less cards are a fairly recent development, and many contactless RFID chip cards also have a magnetic stripe so that the card can be used regardless of the type of card reader provided by the merchant. Merchants have also begun to accept m-payments (mobile payments), a process by which the consumer can use a credit or debit card to pay for goods or services either through a smartphone app or by tapping the mobile device itself against a card reader if the mobile device contains an RFID chip.

Credit versus debit

Credit transactions and debit transactions differ practically and legally. In a credit transaction, the consumer is paying with money borrowed from the bank that issued the card. The bank issuing the card sets a credit limit, and the consumer can use the card to borrow up to the credit limit. If a consumer's credit limit has been reached, the card issuer declines to process the transaction when a consumer next uses the card, and the consumer must find an alternative method of payment. If the consumer does not pay the balance of the card by the end of the billing cycle, the card issuer can charge an interest rate on the remaining amount in accordance with the terms and conditions of the card.

In contrast, debit transactions are a form of electronic fund transfer where the consumer pays for goods or services with money in the consumer's checking account. If there is not enough money in the consumer's checking account to cover the purchase, the transaction does not go through.

In a credit transaction, the order to pay the merchant is given by the consumer. In a debit transaction, the order to pay the merchant comes from the merchant. These differences mean that credit and debit transactions are governed by different laws, with credit transactions governed by the Truth in Lending Act, 82 Stat. 146 (1968), and debit transactions governed by the Electronic Funds Transfer Act, 92 Stat. 3641 (1978). The Truth in Lending Act offers much more protection than the Electronic Funds Transfer Act for consumers who have their cards stolen or used fraudulently. Under the Electronic Funds Transfer Act, a consumer can be liable for part or all of the fraudulent charges, depending on when the consumer notifies the bank of the loss or theft of a card or any irregular transactions. In contrast, the Truth in Lending Act limits consumer liability to $50.00 for unauthorized transactions, regardless of whether the consumer reported the card as stolen or missing.

EuroPay, MasterCard, and Visa (EMV)

In the beginning of 2014, news broke that major retailers Target and Neiman Marcus had been the victims of data breaches that allowed hackers to access customers' credit card information, including home addresses and names. These hacks were extensive, with the Target hack affecting up to an estimated 70 million customers.

In light of these massive data breaches, major credit card companies EuroPay, MasterCard, and Visa jointly developed the EMV standard, which incorporates the use of EMV microchip cards without magnetic stripes. When read, EMV chips create a unique, transaction-specific number to verify the account with the bank instead of using a card number, or CCV (card code verficiation). This is a major advance over magnetic stripe technology, where thieves can capture the security information permanently embedded in the magnetic stripe simply by swiping the card through a device called a skimmer.

EMV technology has already been implemented in much of the rest of the world, with one of the major examples being the chip-and-pin machines of the United Kingdom. The United States has been slow to adopt EMV technology, particularly because of the cost incurred: Merchants will have to pay for new card readers, and individuals will have to have new cards issued.

With EMV technology now available and incidents like the Target breach a reality, most major American credit card companies announced that they would shift liability for fraudulent payments as of October 1, 2015. Prior to that date, card issuers were liable for fraudulent purchases made with magnetic stripe cards. After September, the liability fell either to the merchant or the card issuer, whichever party failed to implement EMV technology. This liability shift gave an incentive to merchants to purchase new EMV card readers and to card issuers to distribute new EMV cards to their customers.

Card metadata and privacy

While the loss of personal data in events like the Target data breach are obvious breaches in privacy because of the unique combination of purchases a consumer makes, an individual could be identifiable even in a dataset that has had personal information—like a name, date of birth, address, or credit card number—removed. These types of scrubbed datasets are frequently used by companies to hone algorithms that allow the company to market more efficiently to an individual. Anonymous credit card metadata are also used regularly to determine credit scoring and to detect fraud. Massachusetts Institute of Technology (MIT) researchers have recently discovered that they could uniquely identify 90 percent of individuals from a dataset comprising 1.1 million people and three months of credit-card data if they knew the dates and locations of four of the individual's purchases through outside information like receipts or social media updates. The study also found that, even when the data was coarse and used ranges instead of precise dates or locations, individuals could still be readily identified. With both coarse data and standard data, the chance of identification increased if the researchers had more confirmed pieces of data using outside information. For example, even with fairly coarse data, the researchers found a 40 percent chance of identification if four data points were known and an 80 percent chance of identification if ten data points were known.

Savanna L. Nolan

Further Reading

Barker, Katherine, Jackie D'Amato, and Paul Sheridan. "Credit Card Fraud: Awareness and Prevention." *Journal of Financial Crime* 15 (2008): 398.

Gray, Dahli, and Jessica Ladig, "The Implementation of EMV Chip Card Technology to Improve Cyber Security Accelerates in the U.S. Following Target Corporation's Data Breach." *International Journal of Business Administration* 6 (2015): 60.

Peretti, Kimberly Kiefer. "Data Breaches: What the Underground World of 'Carding' Reveals." *Santa Clara Computer and High Technology Law Journal* 25 (2009): 375.

See also: Apps; Credit and debit cards; Data breaches; Fair Credit Reporting Act; Federal Trade Commission; Smartphones

Credit reporting agencies (CRAs)

Identification: Defined by the Fair Credit Reporting Act (FCRA) as "any person which, for monetary fees, dues, or on a cooperative nonprofit basis, regularly engages in whole or in part in the practice of assembling or evaluating consumer credit information or other information on consumers for the purpose of furnishing consumer reports to third parties, and which uses any means or facility of interstate commerce for the purpose of preparing or furnishing consumer reports." The third parties that receive the credit reports generated by CRAs are generally businesses, including lenders, employers, landlords or residential real estate management companies, banks, insurance companies, or utility companies. Note that the definition of a CRA in part hinges on the definition of a consumer report, which the FCRA defines as "any written, oral, or other communication of any information by a consumer reporting agency bearing on a consumer's creditworthiness" for personal credit or insurance purposes, employment purposes, or any other purposes authorized by the statute. This means the definitions of a CRA and a credit report are circular, with each depending in part on the other.

Congress enacted the Fair Credit Reporting Act (FCRA), 15 U.S.C. § 1681 (1970), in part because it found that consumer reporting agencies (CRAs), colloquially called credit reporting agencies, had "assumed a vital role in assembling and evaluating consumer credit and other information on consumers." The banking system had grown and depended on fair and accurate credit reporting, and Congress thus found that CRAs had a twofold responsibility to provide fair and impartial credit information while also respecting the consumer's right to privacy.

In the United States, the most recognized CRAs are the three major credit bureaus: Experian, Equifax, and Transunion, which are also referred to as the Big Three. Smaller, specialty CRAs compile information on specific types of transactions, such as apartment rental payments, car insurance claims, or medical payments. Because of the FCRA's broad definition of a CRA, many types of companies and individuals can be considered CRAs. For example, the Federal Trade Commission (FTC) has held that entities like Lexis Nexis, tenant screening services, or employment background screening companies that collect and assemble or evaluate publicly available information, including criminal records, are CRAs. There is currently debate about whether online data brokers, including search engines and social media platforms, should be considered CRAs.

Obligations of CRAs

Congress amended the FCRA when it passed the Fair and Accurate Credit Transactions Act (FACTA), 117 Stat. 1952 (2003), as a way to prevent identity theft and the misuse of consumer data while simultaneously increasing consumer awareness about credit information. Under FACTA, a consumer has the right to request a credit report from each of the Big Three nationwide CRAs once a year. Under certain state laws, a consumer may be entitled to additional annual reports. Many individuals choose to receive one report every four months, allowing them to monitor any changes in their credit. Reports cannot be requested directly from the CRAs, but individuals can request reports by visiting www.annualcreditreport.com or by calling (877) 322–8228.

On May 20, 2015, Ohio attorney general Mike DeWine announced that he and thirty other state attorneys general had reached a settlement with the Big Three CRAs. Highlights of the agreement include requiring CRAs to maintain information about entities that provide inaccurate data; requiring CRAs to implement an escalated process for particularly complex cases—such as those involving identity theft; and limiting CRAs from placing medical debt on a credit report until 180 days after the account is reported, which will allow consumers time to work out any billing issues with their insurance company.

Savanna L. Nolan

Further Reading

Consumer Financial Protection Bureau, *List of Consumer Reporting Agencies*. Washington, DC: 2015. http://files.consumerfinance.gov/f/201501_cfpb_list-consumer-reporting-agencies.pdf.

Fair Credit Reporting. Boston, MA: National Consumer Law Center, 2013. www.nclc.org/library.org.

Schmitz, Amy J. "Secret Consumer Scores and Segmentations: Separating the 'Haves' from 'Have-Nots.'" *Michigan State Law Review* (2014): 1411.

See also: Background checks; Credit and debit cards; Employment eligibility verification systems; Fair Credit Reporting Act (FCRA); Federal Trade Commission (FTC)

Criminal justice (criminal procedure)

Identification: A system by which a society maintains order and public safety by detecting; investigating; prosecuting; defending; trying; and, where appropriate, punishing or supervising those who violate criminal laws enacted to protect health, life, public safety, and property. In the criminal justice system, the government steps in and stands in the shoes of all citizens to preserve the peace and protect public order. In contrast, the civil justice system is a set of laws and procedures by which individuals can seek compensation or satisfaction on their own behalf.

The criminal justice system is composed of many interrelated parts, each serving a unique and indispensable role. Law enforcement detects and investigates crime and charges, by ticket, less serious offenses. Prosecutors, aided in some states by grand juries, decide what cases should be brought and what charges should be filed. Defense attorneys represent criminal defendants to ensure a fair trial and due process. Judges protect the criminal justice process, ensuring that search warrants are providently issued and constitutionally executed; charges are lawfully filed; trials are conducted with due process; exhibits and testimony at trial are limited to relevant and material evidence; and sentences are measured, lawful, and proportional to the severity of the offense and the characteristics of the offender. Each part of the criminal justice system is simultaneously independent of and dependent on every other. This essay explores some of the highlights of the criminal justice system, focusing on due process and the respective roles of the key players.

Legislative function

The criminal law arose many years ago out of the common law, a body of judge-made law that grew and evolved over time as each new case was decided. For many decades now, the criminal law has been codified, in what are known as criminal codes, and thus reduced to writing as enacted by the legislature and approved by the chief executive for each jurisdiction. The criminal codes must be clear and precise, and must properly grade both the severity of the crime and its maximum possible punishment. The codified criminal law forms the backbone of the criminal justice system.

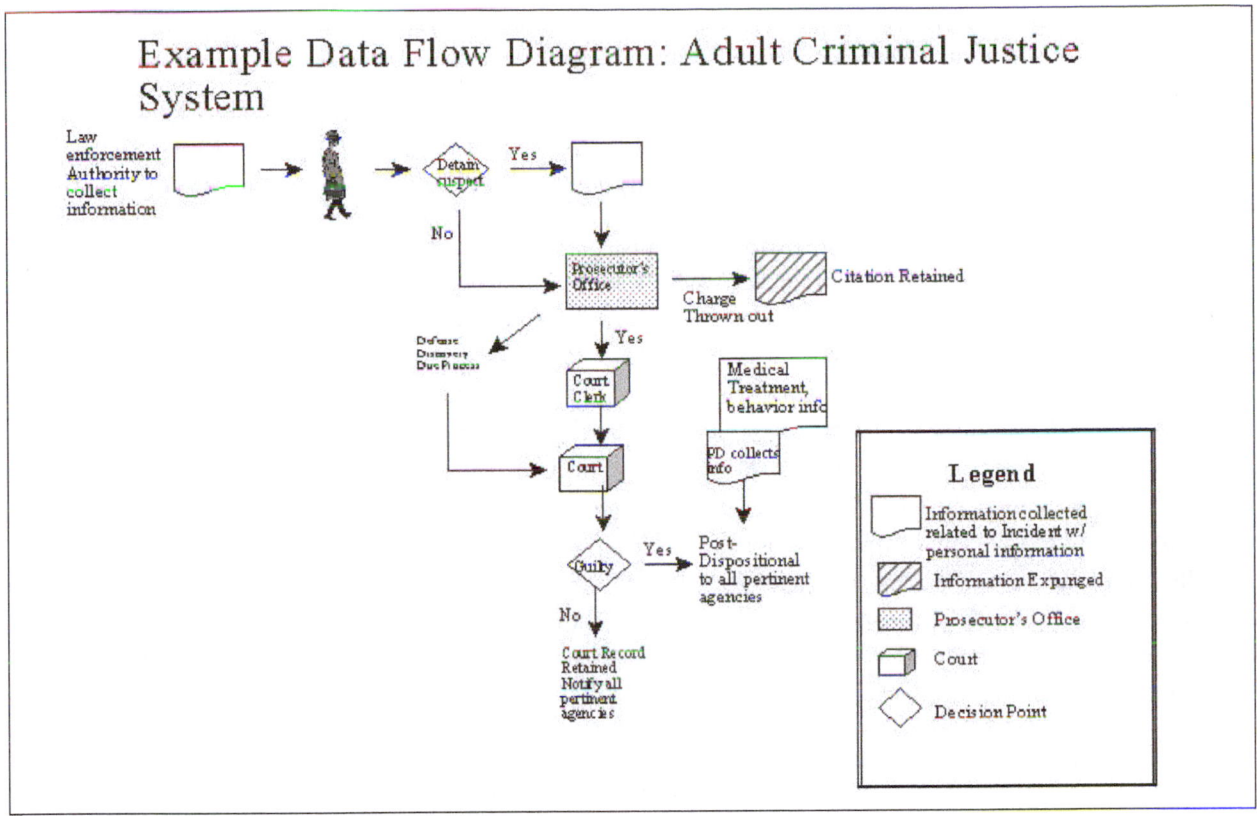

This image shows the procedure in the criminal justice system. From: Privacy Impact Assessment for Justice Information Systems Working paper August 2000, US Department of Justice.

The criminal codes reflect the federalist structure of the United States, with each jurisdiction—the federal government and every state, county, city, and so on—adopting its own, largely independent criminal code. This independence means that, even though all states, except Louisiana, derived their criminal codes from the common law, every state is free to define its crimes and punishments uniquely subject to the requirements and limits imposed by the U.S. Constitution and each state's constitution. In other words, Georgia and Minnesota are free to define the crime of murder differently, and they do.

Law enforcement function

Those criminal codes, and public safety and order more generally, are enforced through the law enforcement function of the criminal justice system. Each jurisdiction with a criminal code has at least one law enforcement agency or contracts with another jurisdiction to provide law enforcement services. At the federal level are the Federal Bureau of Investigation (FBI); the U.S. Secret Service; the U.S. Postal Service Investigation Branch; the Bureau of Alcohol, Tobacco, and Firearms; the U.S. Marshals Service; the U.S. Homeland Security Department, and dozens of others, each with responsibility and authority nationwide to enforce all or a subset of the federal criminal code. At the state level are state bureaus of investigation, state highway patrols, and others. At the county level are county sheriff or county police agencies. At the city level are police departments. These agencies' officers serve on the front line, some call them the thin blue line, in our cities and towns, preserving the peace and serving victims in particular and society in general.

Constrained by constitutional and statutory privacy rights, these law enforcement agencies detect and investigate crimes and protect public safety. For example, law enforcement officers have the power to stop a motor vehicle if they have reasonable suspicion that its occupants are committing or have committed a crime. Officers can search and seize items in plain view when they see the items from a lawful vantage point where they had a right to be. They can execute warrants issued by neutral and detached magistrates upon a showing of probable cause—a showing higher than reasonable suspicion—to search people and their houses, papers, and effects. They have a right to patrol and observe and to approach citizens to investigate crimes even on as little as an educated hunch. They also have a right to arrest suspects for crimes committed in the officers' presence and for serious crimes committed outside the officers' presence, but only if the officers have probable cause to believe the suspect committed those serious crimes.

For less serious offenses, law enforcement officers are authorized to issue tickets, sometimes called citations, to suspects, The tickets compel those suspects to pay a fine or appear in court to contest the ticket or fine. For more serious offenses, including all felonies, officers must conduct investigations and prepare reports, which they then forward to the relevant prosecuting agency for possible charging.

Prosecution function

Each jurisdiction also serves a prosecution function through elected or appointed prosecutors whose role is to seek justice using the reports submitted to them by law enforcement and sometimes by the public. They review those reports and decide which suspects will be charged criminally and with what crimes. At the federal level, the prosecutors are the U.S. Attorney General and all of the U.S. attorneys and their subordinates, who prosecute in each of the federal judicial districts. At the state level, the prosecutors are the state attorneys general and their assistants. At the county level, the prosecutors are county attorneys or district attorneys, and at the city, the prosecutors are typically call

city attorneys. Each jurisdiction's prosecutors are responsible for pursuing crimes committed within or affecting the geographic region controlled by each jurisdiction. Thus, Florida's attorney general has the power to prosecute all serious state crimes occurring or affecting persons or property located within Florida's boundaries. County prosecutors handle serious cases within the county, and city attorneys typically prosecute less serious offenses.

The standard for prosecution is notably higher than for law enforcement. As you will recall, law enforcement can approach a person when the officer has merely an educated hunch, can stop a motor vehicle upon reasonable suspicion, can arrest with probable cause, and can search with a warrant. On the other hand, prosecutors, to charge a person with a crime, must have both probable cause plus a substantial probability of success at trial where the standard of proof is higher yet—proof beyond a reasonable doubt. Sometimes prosecutors convene a grand jury of the jurisdiction's citizens to make the charging decisions in a case. If the grand jury finds sufficient probable cause and likelihood of conviction at trial, it will return an indictment; that is, the grand jury will indict the suspect. If the grand jury decides there is insufficient evidence to indict, the grand jury will issue a no bill. Once a prosecutor brings criminal charges or once a grand jury returns an indictment, the extensive adjudicative process begins.

Adjudicative function

In the United States and all its jurisdictions, each person charged with or indicted for a crime is presumed innocent, and that presumption remains with the person until and unless the person is found guilty in a court of law beyond a reasonable doubt—the highest burden of proof in the law. The process of determining guilt beyond a reasonable doubt plays out in the adjudicative function—that is, the judicial function—of the criminal justice system. The quest of the adjudicative function is to ensure that all criminal defendants receive due process—not a perfect trial, but a fair one.

Each state jurisdiction and the federal jurisdiction maintain its own judicial function and system of courts. Typically, each court system has three tiers: the trial courts, the intermediate courts of appeals, and the supreme court. All criminal cases are eligible to be tried in a trial court. Federal criminal cases are heard in federal trial courts, called federal district courts, and state criminal cases are heard in state trial courts, variously called state district courts, state circuit courts, and others.

In general, the criminal court process begins with a first appearance of the charged person (known as the defendant) in court, often also treated as a bail hearing. That first appearance must occur quite soon after the defendant is arrested or charged. In almost every criminal case in the United States, a criminal defendant has the right to have an attorney present to represent the defendant at the defendant's own expense. But if the defendant is facing possible incarceration upon conviction and cannot afford adequate representation, that defendant is entitled to have the court appoint a defense attorney to represent the defendant at no or at a reduced cost to the defendant.

At any time after criminal charges are filed, the prosecutor and the defendant (or defense attorney) can seek to resolve the matter through plea bargaining or plea negotiations. In that process, the parties seek to agree on which charge or charges the defendant will plead guilty and on the sentence or other consequences. More than 90 percent of all criminal cases are resolved pretrial through plea bargaining or when the defendant simply pleads guilty. If the parties cannot resolve the matter through plea bargaining, the matter proceeds toward trial.

Criminal defendants have a constitutional right to a trial by jury. Each defendant is free, however, to waive a jury trial and have the matter tried solely by a judge, which is known as a bench trial.

Whether facing a jury trial or a bench trial, the criminal defendant is presumed innocent before the trial begins and can be convicted only if the evidence makes the defendant's guilt clear beyond a reasonable doubt. In a bench trial, the presiding judge's final ruling is termed a decision. In a jury trial, the jury's decision is termed its verdict. A jury's criminal verdict must be unanimous.

If the trial results in a finding or verdict of not guilty, that is, results in an acquittal, the defendant, by virtue of the double jeopardy clause of the U.S. Constitution, is free from ever being tried again for that criminal event. If the trial results in a finding or verdict of guilty, the matter proceeds to sentencing. Sentencing, almost always, even in jury trials, is in the sole purview of the judge. In brief, the sentence for a criminal conviction should be commensurate with the severity of the crime of conviction and specific, relevant characteristics of the defendant, such as remorse, criminal history, other cooperation, and so on. Irrelevant defendant characteristics that cannot be lawfully considered at sentencing include the defendant's gender, employment, socioeconomic status, race, and ethnicity.

After conviction and sentencing, criminal defendants are free to appeal to a higher court for relief. In almost every jurisdiction, the first appeal—to the intermediate court of appeals—is always permitted. That is termed as "appeal as of right." Appeals thereafter to a higher court—a supreme court—are not automatic. Those are termed discretionary appeals. Appeals must be timely brought or they are waived. If new evidence arises, however, even long after the trial and any appeals are complete, criminal defendants may bring a post-conviction relief petition to the original trial court seeking a new trial or other remedy.

The adjudicative process has undergone some recent evolution, including notably, the rise of alternative processes, such as sentencing circles, restorative justice, and pretrial diversion. Courts have also begun to explore the benefits of creating specialized courts, sometimes called problem-solving courts, to address specific types of offenders or offenses. Drug courts and veterans courts are just two examples of problem-solving courts.

Corrections function

If the sentencing judge commits the defendant to serve jail time of up to one year, that time is usually served in a county jail. If the defendant is sentenced to incarceration of more than one year, that time will be served in a state penitentiary. Other conditions are often imposed at sentencing in addition to or instead of incarceration. Those other conditions could include chemical dependency treatment, mental health counseling, restitution to victims, criminal fines, day reporting, home arrest, ongoing alcohol or drug testing, no-contact orders to protect victims, and the like.

If the sentence includes a period of supervision outside incarceration, that is usually referred to as probation or community supervision. If that supervision time commences only after release from prison, that supervision time is often called parole. Probation sentences usually include conditions to which the probationer must adhere and that are intended to protect public or victim safety or prevent future criminal behavior.

In any ordered society, a criminal justice system protects public safety and maintains the peace. In the United States, the criminal justice system, handling more than 20 million criminal cases per year, coordinates the simultaneously interdependent and independent legislative, law enforcement, prosecution, adjudication, and corrections functions to strive toward due process for all criminal defendants.

Charles E. MacLean

Further Reading

Braswell, Michael, John Fuller, and Bo Lozoff. *Corrections, Peacemaking, and Restorative Justice: Transforming Individuals and Institutions.* Cincinnati, OH: Anderson, 2001.

Cole, George F., and Marc G. Gertz, *The Criminal Justice System: Politics and Policies,* 10th ed. Belmont, CA: Belmont-Cengage, 2012.

Decker, Scott H., Leanne Fiftal Alarid, and Charles M. Katz, eds. *Controversies in Criminal Justice: Contemporary Readings.* New York: Oxford University Press, 2002.

Dreisbach, Christopher. *Ethics in Criminal Justice.* New York: McGraw-Hill, 2008.

Lab, Steven G., et al. *Criminal Justice: The Essentials,* 3d ed. New York: Oxford University Press, 2012.

Maguire, Mary, and Dan Okada, eds. *Critical Issues in Crime and Justice: Thought, Policy, and Practice.* Los Angeles: SAGE, 2015.

Parry, John T., and L. Song Richardson, eds. *The Constitution and the Future of Criminal Justice in America.* New York: Cambridge University Press, 2013.

Pollock, Joycelyn M. *Ethical Dilemmas and Decisions in Criminal Justice,* 8th ed. Belmont, CA: Wadsworth, 2014.

Schmalleger, Frank. *Criminal Justice Today,* 13th ed. Boston, MA: Pearson, 2015.

Siegel, Larry J., and John L. Worrall. *Essentials of Criminal Justice,* 9th ed. Stamford, CT: Cengage Learning, 2015.

Strang, Heather, and John Braithwaite, eds. *Restorative Justice and Civil Society.* New York: Cambridge University Press, 2001.

See also: Fifth Amendment to the U.S. Constitution; Fourth Amendment to the U.S. Constitution; Law Enforcement; Supreme Court of the United States

Cruzan v. Director, Missouri Department of Health, 497 U.S. 261 (1990)

Identification: A Supreme Court opinion analyzing whether the U.S. Constitution's Due Process Clause creates a freestanding constitutional "right to die."

Chief Justice William Rehnquist authored the majority opinion in a split decision for the Rehnquist Court. The Court held that, while there is a legal right to refuse unwanted medical treatment, such right does not extend to an unconscious person seeking to withdraw life-sustaining medical treatment. Substantive due process, through either the privacy or liberty line of cases, does not include a constitutional "right to die." Rather, the majority upheld the State of Missouri's heightened evidentiary requirement that an unconscious individual's surrogates must demonstrate, through clear and convincing evidence, that the individual would, if competent, seek to withdraw the life-sustaining treatment. There is no freestanding constitutional "right to die."

Nancy Cruzan was involved in a single car accident that left her in a permanent vegetative state. To ensure that Nancy received adequate nutrition, a gastric feeding tube was inserted, and she began receiving nutrition and hydration through artificial means. Nancy's parents wanted the life-sustaining treatment withdrawn, indicating that Nancy would not have wanted to endure the treatment. The hospital refused to accede to the Cruzans' requests without court intervention. So the Cruzans sued.

The trial court found in favor of the Cruzans, based largely on a former housemate's testimony that Nancy had indicated in conversations that she would not want to live in a vegetative state. The Missouri Supreme Court reversed. The Missouri Supreme Court found the housemate's trial testimony insufficient to prove Nancy's intent to withdraw life-sustaining nutrition and hydration. It also found that Nancy's parents could not substitute their judgment for their now unconscious daughter. In reaching these findings, the court emphasized Missouri's interest in preserving life.

The Cruzans sought permission to appeal to the U.S. Supreme Court by filing a petition for writ of certiorari. The Supreme Court granted their petition and accepted the appeal.

Justice Rehnquist's opinion begins by confirming that, at common law, there was a legal right to be free from unwanted touching. Any unconsented touching, both at common law and modernly, amounts to a battery. From this basic premise of unwanted touching stems the right to require informed consent for all medical procedures. If a doctor were to perform a medical test or operation on a patient who failed to consent, the doctor commits battery.

Because no medical procedures can take place without informed consent, the Court stated that the logical extension of this right was a legal right to refuse unwanted medical treatment. The Court cited the famous "right to die" case, *In re Quinlan*, 355 A.2d 647 (1976), as the beginning of state court decisions addressing the legalities of who had the legal right to substitute the decision to refuse unwanted medical care for an incompetent person and how that right could be implemented.

Karen Ann Quinlan, much like Nancy Cruzan, was in a permanent vegetative state. Karen's parents, like Nancy's, sought to have the life-sustaining treatment, a respirator and nasal feeding tube, removed to allow Karen to die naturally. *In re Quinlan*, 348 A.2d 801 (1975). Karen's mother, sister, and friend all testified that Karen indicated she would not want to be kept alive solely through extraordinary medical treatment. The family's request was opposed by the hospital, the doctors, the guardian ad litem appointed to represent Karen, and, the State of New Jersey. The trial court found no "right to die" based on the privacy line of cases, such as *Griswold v. Connecticut*, 381 U.S. 479 (1965), and *Roe v. Wade*, 410 U.S. 113 (1973).

The Supreme Court of New Jersey disagreed, finding a constitutional right of privacy to avoid unwanted, extraordinary medical treatment. "Although the Constitution does not explicitly mention a right of privacy, Supreme Court decisions have recognized that a right of personal privacy exists and that certain areas of privacy are guaranteed under the Constitution." *In re Quinlan*, 355 A.2d 647 (1976). In addition to the seminal *Griswold* case, the New Jersey Supreme Court also relied upon *Eisenstadt v. Baird*, 405 U.S. 438 (1972) and *Stanley v. Georgia*, 394 U.S. 557 (1969), to buttress its privacy finding. While the New Jersey Supreme Court was not convinced by the testimony of those conveying Karen's alleged wishes were she to be confronted with this situation, the court nonetheless allowed her parent/guardian to exercise derivatively Karen's right to privacy.

Cruzan is a good example of judicial restraint, where the federal courts yield to the legislative process. Justice Rehnquist underscored the importance of judicial restraint in following an 1897 case, *Twin City Bank v. Nebeker*, 167 U.S. 196, admonishing that when deciding "a question of such magnitude and importance . . . it is the [better] part of wisdom not to attempt, by general statement, to cover every possible phase of the subject." Thus, the *Cruzan* court issued a narrow opinion focused solely on the question of whether the State of Missouri's heightened evidentiary standard violated Nancy Cruzan's constitutional right to privacy or liberty.

Cruzan was not the final word on a constitutional right to die. Seven years later, the Rehnquist Court again considered whether there is a constitutional "right to die" in *Washington v. Glucksberg*, 521 U.S. 702 (1997). *Glucksberg*, a 9–0 opinion written by Justice Rehnquist, held there is no constitutional privacy or liberty right to assisted suicide. Emphasizing that substantive due process rights, such as privacy and liberty, require an analysis of the nation's historical practices and traditions, the Court easily found that laws have consistently outlawed the practice of assisting suicide. In fact, suicide itself was long considered criminal. To hasten another's death, even if that person is terminally ill, remains criminal in most states.

Glucksberg's holding, much like the holding in *Cruzan*, allows individual states to craft the parameters of any so-called "right to die." If state legislatures want to permit surrogates to make end-of-life decisions, such as removing life-sustaining treatments, states are free to do so. If state legislatures want to legalize assisted suicide, states are free to do so. *Cruzan* and *Glucksberg* simply remind that, to have a recognized, enforceable right to privacy or liberty under the Constitution, that right must generally have a historical pedigree where the right, narrowly construed, has received protection or accept-

ance in the past. Because most end-of-life issues are modern creations resulting from scientific advancements, no constitutional "right to die" has yet been recognized by the Supreme Court.

Mary M. Penrose

Further Reading

Annas, George J. "Nancy Cruzan and the Right to Die." *New England Journal of Medicine* 323, no. 10 (September 6, 1990): 670–673.Arthur, John. *Morality and Moral Controversies*. 5th ed. Upper Saddle River, N.J.: Prentice Hall, 1999.

Capron, Alexander Morgan. "Medical Decision-making and the Right to Die after Cruzan." *The Journal of Law, Medicine & Ethics J Law Med Ethics*: 5–8.

Colby, William H. *Long Goodbye: The Deaths of Nancy Cruzan*. Carlsbad, Calif.: Hay House, 2002.

Halper, T. "Privacy and Autonomy: From Warren and Brandeis to Roe and Cruzan." *Journal of Medicine and Philosophy*, 1996, 121–135.

Monagle, John F. *Health Care Ethics: Critical Issues*. Gaithersburg, Md.: Aspen Publishers, 1994.

Urofsky, Melvin I. *Lethal Judgments: Assisted Suicide and American Law*. Lawrence: University Press of Kansas, 2000.

See also: Constitutional Law; *Stanley v. Georgia;* Supreme Court of the United States; Unenumerated Constitutional Right, Privacy as an; *Washington v. Glucksberg*

Customer proprietary network information (CPNI)

Identification: Information collected by telecommunications services such as local, long-distance, and wireless telephone companies about their subscribers. CPNI data include the time, date, duration, and destination number of each call; the type of network a consumer subscribes to; and any other information that appears on the consumer's telephone bill. CPNI is not a customer's name, address, or telephone number (when used in phone books and directory listings/publishing services) or aggregate information, that is, data that is lumped together and is not specific to a single customer, such as reports containing total counts, number of subscribers selecting various long-distance carriers, and customer premise.

Telemarketers working for telecommunications companies who seek either to win back a customer or sell a customer additional services must first ask the customer's consent before accessing billing information or before using that information to offer an sell or any change of services. Usually, this is done at the beginning of a call from the telemarketer to the telephone subscriber.

CPNI was first regulated after AT&T was broken up into several different companies. The Telecommunications Act of 1996, 110 Stat. 556, had formal requirements regarding CPNI that applied not just to the Bell operating companies but to all telecommunications carriers. The U.S. Telecommunications Act also grants the Federal Communications Commission (FCC) regulatory power over how CPNI may be used and to enforce related consumer information privacy provisions. The rules in the 2007 FCC CPNI Order further restrict CPNI use and create new notification and reporting requirements.

On February 14, 2006, the FCC released a notice of proposed rulemaking seeking comments on what action, if any, it should take to further protect CPNI from unauthorized disclosure to third parties. The FCC's notice was a response to a petition from the Electronic Privacy Information Center (EPIC) expressing concern that current telecommunications carrier practices were insufficient to protect CPNI.

The FCC found CPNI to be highly sensitive personal information obtained by a telecommunications carrier in the course of providing service to its customers. The FCC acknowledged its statutory duties under the Telecommunications Act to protect CPNI from improper use and dissemination, and it had already imposed rules and restrictions on telecommunications carriers. The FCC, for example, had already issued regulations requiring telecommunications carriers to obtain a customer's knowledge and consent before using or disclosing CPNI. The FCC had

also already required telecommunications carriers to instruct and train their employees on all the circumstances under which they were and were not allowed to disclose CPNI. Also, the FCC stipulated that telecommunications carriers must maintain records of all instances in which CPNI was disclosed, and they must certify, annually and publicly, their compliance with the carrier's CPNI requirements.

The Telecommunications Act, along with regulations and decisions from the FCC, generally prohibits the use of CPNI without customer permission, even to market other services to the consumers. In the case of customers who switch to other service providers, the original service provider may not use CPNI in attempts to lure the customer back. CPNI includes information such as optional services subscribed to, current charges, directory assistance charges, usage data, and calling patterns.

The FCC's CPNI rules do not prohibit the gathering and publishing of aggregate customer information or the use of customer information for the purpose of creating directories.

The rules promulgated in the 2007 CPNI Order:

- *limit* the information that carriers may provide to third-party marketing firms without first securing the affirmative consent of their customers.
- *define* when and how customer service representatives may share call details.
- *create* new notification and reporting obligations for carriers (including identity verification procedures). The verification process must match what is shown with the company placing the call.

As long as an affiliate is "communications" related, the FCC has ruled that CPNI must follow an opt-out approach (that is, CPNI may be shared without the explicit permission of a customer unless the customer has opted out). A phone company may sell all information on the customer, such as numbers the customer has called, when the customer called them, where the customer was when the customer called them, or any other personally identifying information. CPNI would normally require a warrant for law enforcement agencies yet can be freely sold to "communications"-related companies. (One can verify this by checking rule 64.2007(b) (1) and footnote 137 in the 2007 CPNI Order.)

One may contact a phone company and opt out by requesting that the phone company does not share CPNI information. In the case of Verizon Wireless, for example, the company states, on the one hand, "Your privacy is an important priority at Verizon Wireless," and, on the other hand, that Verizon shares CPNI "among our affiliates and parent companies (including Vodafone) and their subsidiaries unless you advise us not to." Verizon Wireless adds that it shares "URLs (such as search terms) of websites you visit when you use our wireless service, the location of your device ('location information'), and your use of applications and features" as well as other "information about your use of Verizon products and services (such as data and calling features, device type, and amount of use), as well as demographic and interest categories (such as gender, age range, sports fan, frequent diner, or pet owner)" with other nonaffiliated companies. Verizon Wireless does allow customers to request, via an online form, that such sharing not be done, but it is unclear whether Verizon considers some or all such "online" requests to be about CPNI or as legally binding as "call-based" requests about CPNI.

The 2007 CPNI Order did not revise all CPNI rules. For example, the rule revisions adopted in the order do not limit a carrier's ability to use CPNI to perform billing and collections functions, restrict CPNI use to effect maintenance and repair activity, or affect responses to lawful subpoenas.

Fines for failure to comply with CPNI rules can be substantial. The FCC may impose fines of up to $150,000 for each rule violation or each day of a continuing violation up to a maximum of $1.5 million for each continuing violation. The rules adopted in the order are effective either six months after the order is published in the *Federal Register* or on receipt of Office of Management and Budget (OMB) approval of the new rules, depending on which event is later.

In June 2013, the FCC ruled that telecommunications carriers must follow the safeguards for CPNI for information stored on mobile devices. "When a telecommunications carrier collects CPNI using its control of its customers' mobile devices, and the carrier or its designee has access to or control over the information, the carrier is responsible for safeguarding that information," the FCC wrote. Acting Chair Mignon Clyburn stated that "[p]rotecting consumer privacy is a key component of our mission to serve the public interest," while Commissioner Jessica Rosenworcel asked the commission to be aware of the increasing "market incentives to keep our data and slice and dice it to inform commercial activity."

In September 2014, Verizon agreed to pay the FCC a $7.4 million fine to settle claims that the company violated the privacy rights of nearly 2 million consumers. The FCC found that Verizon failed to inform consumers of their privacy rights, including how to prevent their personal information from being used for marketing purposes. At the time, the Verizon case was the largest consumer privacy settlement in FCC history.

In April 2015, the FCC settled an enforcement action against AT&T for the company's massive consumer privacy violations. The FCC found that employees at AT&T call centers in Mexico, Columbia, and the Philippines accessed the CPNI of nearly 280,000 U.S. customers without their permission. Then AT&T employees, without authorization, distributed that information to traffickers of stolen cellphones. As a condition of the settlement, AT&T was ordered to pay a $25 million penalty, which surpassed the 2014 Verizon settlement as the FCC's largest ever data security action.

The FCC continues to regard the protection of CPNI to be of paramount importance because CPNI includes some of the most sensitive personal information that carriers have about their customers, which is a result of their business relationship (such as phone numbers of calls made and received; frequency, duration, and timing of such calls; and any services purchased by the consumer, such as call waiting and voicemail). The FCC continues to issue and enforce rules to protect the privacy of CPNI and to ensure that CPNI is adequately protected from unauthorized access, use, or disclosure.

Further Reading

Dudley, Christie. "Statutory (Re) Interpretation of CPNI: Protecting Mobile Privacy." February 14, 2013. http://ssrn.com/abstract=2217524.

Duffy, Gerard J. "The New CPNI Rules." *Rural Telecommunications,* March 1, 2008.

Figliola, Patricia Moloney. *Wireless Privacy and Spam Issues for Congress.* Washington, DC: Congressional Research Service, Library of Congress, 2006.

Henry, Anna. "The Fight to Protect CPNI." *Rural Telecommunications*, November 1, 2009.

Johnson, Kenneth C. "Beast of Burden: Regulatory Compliance and the Small Carrier." *Rural Telecommunications*, January 1, 2008.

Karas, Stan. "Privacy, Identity, Databases: Toward a New Conception of the Consumer Privacy Discourse." *American University Law Review* 52 (December 2002). http://ssrn.com/abstract=340140.

Klitou, Demetrius. "Technological Threats to Privacy." Part II of *Privacy-Invading Technologies and Privacy by Design.* The Hague: T.M.C Asser Press, 2014.

Knowles, Jeffrey, and Ronald Jacobs. "FCC's CPNI Rule Limits Telecoms." *Direct Marketing News*, May 21, 2007.

Kulesza, Joanna. "International Law Challenges to Location Privacy Protection." *International Data Privacy Law* 3, no. 3 (2013): 158–169.

Leonard, Peter. "Customer Data Analytics: Privacy Settings for 'Big Data' Business." *International Data Privacy Law* 4, no. 1 (2014): 53–68

"10 Steps to Cyber Security." Cheltenham, UK: Communications-Electronics Security Group (CESG)/National Technical Authority for Information Assurance and Department for Business, Innovation & Skills, 2012. Updated January 16, 2015. https://www.gov.uk/government/publications/cyber-risk-management-aboard-level-responsibility.

Tharp, Marye C. *Transcultural Marketing: Building Customer Relationships in Multicultural America.* New York: Routledge, 2014.

See also: Cybersecurity; Federal Communications Commission (FCC); Mobile devices; Telemarketing

The Cyber Intelligence Sharing and Protection Act (CISPA) H.R. 3523 (112th Congress), H.R. 624 (113th Congress), H.R. 234 (114th Congress)

Identification: Proposed amendments to the National Security Act of 1947, 61 Stat. 495, which currently lacks provisions on cybercrime. CISPA, as introduced in the U.S. Congress, would: 1) facilitate the sharing of information relating to Internet information between the U.S. government and technology and manufacturing companies and remove obstacles to such sharing; and 2) enhance the U.S. government's ability to investigate cyber threats and ensure the security of networks against cyberattacks. Privacy advocates opposed the bill all three times it was introduced citing privacy concerns.

CISPA defines "cyber threat intelligence" as "information in the possession of an element of the intelligence community directly pertaining to a vulnerability of, or threat to, a system or network of a government or private entity, including information pertaining to the protection of a system or network from either "efforts to degrade, disrupt, or destroy such system or network."

Much of CISPA focused on information sharing between agencies. CISPA authorizes the Director of National Intelligence to issue rules and regulations that would allow intelligence agencies to share cyber threat intelligence with private-sector entities and encourage the sharing of such intelligence.

Rep. Michael Rogers (R-MI), chair of the House Intelligence Committee, introduced the first CISPA bill (HR 3523) during the 112th Congress, on November 30, 2011. C.A. "Dutch" Ruppersberger (D-MD), ranking Democratic member of the Intelligence Committee, also joined Rogers, and over 111 co-sponsors, in supporting the bill. The legislation passed in the House of Representatives on April 26, 2012. The Senate, however, did not act on the legislation.

The Obama administration opposed the bill, arguing that CISPA lacked adequate confidentiality and civil liberties safeguards. The President further vowed he would veto the legislation if it passed Congress.

Largely unchanged, CISPA was reintroduced in the 113th Congress in February 2013 as H.R. 624. An amended version passed the House on April 18, 2013. As what happened previously, the Senate did not act on the legislation. Two similar bills on information sharing were introduced in the 114th Congress. The House version was a revised version of CISPA, and the Senate version was known as the Cybersecurity Information Sharing Act. The Obama administration was involved in the process, by both sending proposed legislation and issuing an executive order on information sharing. In January 2015, the bill was reintroduced in the House and referred to the House Committee on Intelligence.

Corporations and pro-business advocacy groups such as Microsoft, Facebook, AT&T, IBM, Apple Inc. and the U.S. Chamber of Commerce all supported CISPA, arguing that it would authorize straightforward and effective mechanisms to share crucial cyber threat information between the private sector and the government. The business community regarded CISPA as necessary so that companies could protect themselves against global cybersecurity threats. The legislation would create a voluntary information-sharing framework, and would impose no new federal mandates on either private individuals or businesses.

Bill supporters argued that CISPA would protect the privacy of individuals, by prohibiting the government from forcing private companies to surrender personal information while encouraging companies to anonymize the information that they do share. Further, supporters of the bill argued that the legislation would meet the needs of businesses to receive targeted information necessary to protect their computer networks and customers' personal data. They stressed that businesses needed timely and actionable information to oppose advanced and sophisticated attacks coming from organized criminal gangs and foreign governments. Also, voluntary information-sharing with federal agencies, such as the U.S. Department of Homeland Security, would improve the government's capacity to protect itself and the business community against foreign cyberthreats.

Some commentators agreed that the bill would help fight those who would attempt to illicitly obtain private information or potentially disrupt infrastructure networks. Business would also benefit by being provided the certainty that cybersecurity information shared with the government would be provided safe harbor.

Effective and efficient information sharing in the name cybersecurity is crucial for protecting information systems from unauthorized access. Commentators have argued that undue barriers to information sharing on threats, attacks, and vulnerabilities is a significant weakness to effective cybersecurity, especially regarding critical infrastructure, such as the financial system and the electric grid.

Private-sector entities have stated that they are reluctant to share such information among themselves because of issues including legal liability, potential misuse of information, such as trade secrets and other proprietary information. Perceived barriers to sharing with the government include concerns about risks of disclosure and the ways governments might use the information it receives.

The provision on information-sharing, however, gave rise to serious privacy and civil liberties. The issues, in this case, involve understanding the risks to privacy rights and civil liberties of individual citizens associated with sharing different types of cybersecurity information, and what are the best ways to protect these rights.

Privacy concerns, especially those related to the protection of personal and proprietary information and uses of shared information, imperiled the bill from the beginning. Although the legislation had provisions that sought to reduce risks of inappropriate sharing and misuse of such information, some observers argued that privacy-related information is seldom required in sharing cybersecurity information, suggesting that privacy concerns may be limited and relatively easy to address. Various factors made the process more complicated, including potential impacts of advances in data analytic capabilities (which is commonly known as "big data"). A presidential advisory panel reported that "By data mining and other kinds of analytics, nonobvious and sometimes private information can be derived from data that, at the time of their collection, seemed to raise no, or only manageable, privacy issues." There are many potential sources, unrelated to the information-sharing activities addressed in the bills, from which an individual's personal information in cyberspace could be identified and acquired by various entities.

While CISPA opponents acknowledged that certain national security threats are genuine, also stressed the need to balance security concerns with those of individual privacy. Several security experts, engineers and other industry experts told Congress, expressed strong concern for national security, but added that, effective computer and network security does not mean that Internet users should have to surrender their liberties. They argued, then, not whether Internet security should be improved or better monitored, but rather, that the original CISPA bill lacked sufficient privacy protections for those it seeks to

protect. For example, the bill was prefaced with "Notwithstanding any other provision of law," which suggested to some privacy advocates that CISPA was intended to abolish or limit privacy protections or limitations on government access to private or personal information. Additionally, another section grants immunity to private entities for sharing information that would have previously required a warrant. This provision would protect parties liable for the sharing of network data (this was one of issues in the AT&T wiretapping incident in 2006). While CISPA does not explicitly legalize warrantless wire tapping such as that in the AT&T incident, it appears to allow private companies such as AT&T to share that same type of data with the government without liability. The legislation also explicitly limits oversight, stating that any information shared with a federal agency, is not required to comply with the Freedom of Information Act (FOIA), 80 Stat. 250 (1967).

CISPA was criticized by several Internet privacy and civil liberties, such as the Electronic Frontier Foundation, the American Civil Liberties Union, as well as various conservative and libertarian groups including the TechFreedom, FreedomWorks, and the American Conservative Union. These groups argue CISPA inadequately restricted the government regarding how and when the government would be allowed monitor a private individual's Internet browsing information. Additionally, they expressed concerns that as such the government would use its powers under the act for general surveilliance on Americans, rather than to pursue hackers.

Some critics argued that provisions included in CISPA were another attempt to protect intellectual property after Congress stopped action on the Stop Online Piracy Act in the face of opposition to that legislation. At first, provisions on the theft of intellectual property were included in the bill as possible justifications for sharing Web traffic information with the government. These provisions, however, were struck from subsequent drafts.

Promoted to enhance network security, privacy advocates expressed concerns that CISPA was overly vague and would erode individual privacy rights. Some critics of the bill claimed that if CISPA passed, private sector companies could engage in surveillance on the electronic communications of millions of Internet users and then share this information with the government with no oversight. They criticized the fact that no guidelines were developed for companies on the scope of data to be collected and transferred. Further, they were concerned that the bill offers companies broad immunities if they act in "good faith," granting them exemption from liability for all "decisions made" based on "cyberthreat information"—a term the bill did not adequately define.

In addition to civil liberty groups, the Obama administration opposed the legislation, and criticized CISPA, asserting that any cybersecurity bill "must include robust safeguards to preserve the privacy and civil liberties of our citizens." The administration further said it would oppose any bill that would "sacrifice the privacy of our citizens in the name of security."

Due to strong opposition to CISPA, the cosponsors offered to amend the bill to address many privacy-related concerns, including limiting the bill's coverage to more restricted types of cyber-threats, and stating that the "theft of intellectual property" refers to the theft of research and development. Also, the bill was amended to impose fines if private companies or the government misappropriates data from CISPA for purposes not related to cyberthreats.

Privacy advocates, however, were not appeased. Many of them argued that the proposed amendments fell short in remedying the civil liberties threats posed by the bill. They continued to oppose CISPA. Rainey Reitman, of the Electronic Frontier Foundation (EFF), claimed that the bill's sponsors dismissed serious concerns on how the bill could adversely affect the privacy rights of Internet users. While acknowledging that some positive changes were made to the legislation, Kendall Burman of the Center for Democracy and Technology (CDT) said that none of the changes reached addressed the core "privacy concerns" of privacy advocacy groups. The CDT and other privacy rights groups actively opposed CISPA and supported a competing House bill sponsored by Rep. Dan Lungren (R-CA).

In opposing CISPA, the ACLU said it "would create a cybersecurity exception to all privacy laws and allow companies to share the private and personal data they hold on their American customers with the government for cybersecurity purposes….Beyond the potential for massive data collection authorization, the bill would provide no meaningful oversight of, or accountability for, the use of these new information-sharing authorities."

CISPA also faced opposition from conservative groups such as the American Conservative Union because they believed that the legislation would greatly increase federal power, interfere with free enterprise, and harm U.S. competitiveness.

Media groups such as Reporters Without Borders opposed the legislation, arguing that in the name of fighting cybercrime, CISPA would authorize the government and private companies to use harsh measures to monitor and perhaps censor Internet traffic. The group also suggested that the government would be granted the power to shut sites that publish classified files or information.

Further Reading

Chander, Anupam. *Securing Privacy in the Internet Age.* Stanford, Calif.: Stanford Law Books, 2008.

Kostopoulos, George K. *Cyberspace and Cybersecurity.* Boca Raton, Fl.: CRC Press, 2013.

Lee, Newton. *Counterterrorism and Cybersecurity: Total Information Awareness.* New York: Springer, 2013.

See also: American Civil Liberties Union (ACLU); Center for Democracy and Technology (CDT); Computers and privacy; Cybersecurity; Electronic surveillance; Federal Freedom of Information Act (FOIA)

Cybersecurity

A critical and necessary component of computer systems, implemented to protect computer users and networks from threats from nefarious cyber actors, to protect them from computer disruptions that are intended and unintended, as well as to prepare for unpreventable natural disasters.

Cybersecurity provides security against threats to data that resides on computer architecture, hardware, software and networks connecting in cyberspace. The Internet—also known as cyberspace or simply connecting online—has become a ubiquitous part of global world interconnectedness. The virtual world of cyberspace allows human activity to take place in the same manner as conducting life in the material world. Nation-states, governments, corporations, and individuals conduct daily activities online that once required personal human contact.

Cybercrime does not have a current definition that distinguishes it from traditional crime. What is clear, however, is that cybercrimes involve computers, online networks, or some other form of illegal cyberactivity. The U.S. Department of Defense has added cyberspace to land, sea, space, and air as the fifth war domain. The scale and magnitude of protecting cyberspace has become so critical that the Obama administration regards technology issues and policy as a major priority to "ensure that cyberspace is reliable, trustworthy and secure for all users." The

U.S. Department of Homeland Security has taken the lead in securing nonsecurity digital technology. The U.S. Department of Defense defends the nation against threats of looming cyberwar.

At risk

Public- and private-sector cybernetworks represent the critical infrastructure of the United States, and those cybernetworks are vital to the functions of the economy, security and health of the United States. According to the U.S. Department of Homeland Security, sixteen sectors that are computer-, network-, and cyber-regulated require supervisory control and data acquisition (SCADA) systems to provide remote signals and information for airports, electric companies, heating and gas systems, and other large facility type systems. Confidential personally identifiable information (PII) data resides in cyberspace, and the confidentiality, integrity, and accessibility of PII on networks owned and managed by governments, corporations, and individuals are always at risk of a potential data breach. Governments and corporations suffer losses in the billions, loss of financial records, and loss of consumer confidence when systems suffer from a data breach. Securing what now is termed *data* from cybercriminals has become a chief aim of policy and lawmakers. Compromised PII across digital platforms and computers can result in identity theft, loss of intellectual property, or cyberwar. A massive cyber-breach of the U.S. Federal Office of Personnel Management computer systems in the summer of 2015 compromised the PII of approximately 21.5 million government employees and government contractors. Data breaches affecting transnationals and major corporations are often reported. Home Depot, Target, Sony Studios, and Wal-Mart are only some of the corporations in the United States that have been targeted, costing billions in the theft of consumer data. Any person, business, or government is continually at risk for a cyber-breach that has the potential to create financial chaos. Computer scientists were unaware of the security required for the data of the future during the early invention and design of personal computers (PCs) and networks. Technology is developed at such a fast pace that it is difficult for those seeking security measures to keep up with the technology. The phenomenon of the Internet of things (IoT) is defined as an ecosystem that houses all shared data through networking and other wireless technologies (Wi-Fi). IoT includes all technology that can connect to and interact with the cyberspace environment. Internet technologies include, but are not limited to, computers, laptops, tablets, digital cameras, smartphones, smart TVs, and game consoles. The U.S. Federal Trade Commission (FTC) estimates that 50 billion devices will connected in cyberspace by 2020.

How cyberspace works

Cyberspace is located and travels through submarine fiber optic cables located at the bottom of the ocean floor. The late nineteenth century ushered in the first submarine cables across the English Channel to carry written telecommunications. Today's transatlantic sea cables are only three inches thick and house fiber optic cables that stretch 550,000 miles and circle the earth twenty-two times. The architectural design of the Internet allows cyber-technologies to communicate through the vast cyberspace network of fiber optic cables. Data travels through cyberspace as individuals log in to computers, phones, and other Internet technologies. Email exchange, information processing, banking, and all other cyberactivities must travel through a set of Internet Protocols. Internet Protocols called Transmission Control Protocol/Internet Protocols (TCP/IPs) direct interchange and transmission of communication through cyberspace, routing each communication to a specific destination. Internet protocols direct Internet data packets (traffic) through four layers by splitting and routing packets to their final destination. Those four layers include the application link, transport layer, network layer, and data link layer.

1. *Application layer*: guides and directs packets based on application protocols such as HyperText Transfer Protocol (HTTP), File Transfer Protocol (FTP), and others.

2. *Transport layer*: transports data packets that are split into different sizes to process across the network to their target destinations.

3. *Network layer*: sends data packets through routers throughout the network while organizing packets as they travel.

4. *Data link*: transfers data packets to physical components such as driver devices and network interfaces.

Cybercriminals are aware of the weaknesses at each layer most susceptible to a data breach.

Cyberweapons

Cyberweapons used to commit cybercrimes consist of any physical tool and/or cyber-related malware used in the effort to attack, harm, disrupt, or destroy computers and/or networking operations. Malicious actors in cyberspace such as hackers spend countless hours discovering threats and vulnerabilities within the cyber ecosystem for identity theft and other nefarious purposes. Threats to a technology are defined as any probable cause leading to an incident resulting in harm to a system. Vulnerabilities are weaknesses in the system that can be exploited through existing probable threats within a system. Common types of tools used in cybercrime include:

- *Distributed denial-of-service attacks* threaten a network with efforts of making a domain unavailable. The attack floods a website with requests from botnets, which results in overloading the server and thus bringing down the website. The website becomes unavailable, unreachable, and inaccessible for business. There are documented cases of such attacks perpetrated by governments against other governments.
- *Malware* is short for "malicious software code," which is used to exploit and or attack the threats and vulnerabilities within computers and networks. Malware presents itself as inconspicuous, harmless, and useful software. All malware has the objective of modifying a computer program to attack the system.
- *Viruses* are malware found on a system that replicate themselves by attaching to executable code. When the executable

file is run unknowingly by a user, a virus spreads and infects other files on contact. Viruses are identified by their ability to reproduce and spread through a system.

- *Worms* are more advanced than viruses. They penetrate the computer system and networks, and replicate without the requirement of human interaction to initiate the process. Once a worm has penetrated a system, it does not require attachment to an executable file.
- *Backdoor malware* bypasses all security controls and allows open access for hackers to come in and out of systems at any time. Compromised systems allow intruder(s) to place malware.
- *Trojan horses*, unlike worms and viruses, do not replicate themselves. They are software programs appearing to have a harmless function. Trojans trick users because they appear as useful software or applications. Once a Trojan is installed, hidden tasks direct unscrupulous exploits throughout the system.
- *Spyware* spies on users' activities and records keystrokes and visited software applications, allowing for unauthorized monitoring.
- *Rootkits* are typically Trojan backdoor malware that hides. Rootkits are difficult to find, and they alter the kernel of the operating system. Once the system is compromised, the actual functions of the computer may be altered, leaving the user unaware of changes.
- *Botnets*, also called zombie computers, are identified as several members that compose a network. Botnet malware has the ability to shut down government and business networks. Botnets can attack in small numbers or in the thousands without leaving a trace of origination, allowing the crime to cross borders. Botnets are responsible for spam, spyware, denial-of-service attacks, click frauds, and several other malware cybercrimes.
- *Phishing attacks* generally show up in an email appearing to be from a legitimate source. The objective of a phishing email is to access PII data for the use of bank fraud, identity theft, and other crimes of theft by falsely using another person's information.
- *Card scanning* is the act of stealing a credit card and/or bank card information and duplicating the card. Many techniques are used in card scanning, which is often committed in the presence of the victim.

Goal of cybersecurity

The goal of cybersecurity is to protect cyberspace and society against potential threats that can cause harm to a nation, government, business, or individual. Cybersecurity does not rely on a particular device to protect computers, networks, and other digital technologies but is a set of procedural mechanisms, controls, and processes. Home networks are different from large business and government entities. Home networks should always be secured with firewalls and tools provided by Internet service providers (ISPs). For cybersecurity to be effective in personal networks, it is important to use every available security measure. This includes consistently updating passwords, updating antivirus software, and guarding personal computers while logging into free Wi-Fi computer networks. Critical to home network Wi-Fi is securing Internet access at home to avoid wardriving, which is defined as the act of driving through neighborhoods in search of unsecured home networks. Locking home Wi-Fi networks to protect against cyber-crime has become the equivalent of locking a home or car while away, and it is important because PII is accessible on home devices, which can lead to identity theft and other crimes.

Current best practice methods for large entities include following:

1. *Implement security and access controls.* Only give access to authorized users. Access controls limit and monitor network and computer access.

2. *Implement a security policy.* Security policies are directives on how to handle incidents. This includes natural disasters as well as cybersecurity breaches.

3. *Evaluate threats and vulnerabilities often.* Any person in or out of an organization is a threat. Make sure that background checks are made on all employees. Training for employees should be ongoing and create a culture of cybersecurity.

4. *Use all available built-in operating system (OS) applications and software.* Firewalls and other security features are built into most OSs.

Monitor network traffic continually. Use third-party services or special software for network intrusion.

Conclusion

The future of cybersecurity rests on a commitment to keeping cyberspace safe. In the United States, lawmakers are working to make cyberspace safe and available for everyone. Awareness of cybersecurity measures assists in keeping computer and network owners safe from potential cybercrimes. The new cyber-domain has similarities to the physical world because criminals exist in both domains. Safety is a priority when traveling through cyberspace, which makes cybersecurity comparable to security in the physical world.

Kimberly A. Harper

Further Reading

Hastedt, G. P. *Reading in American Foreign Policy: Problems and Responses.* Lanham, MD: Rowman & Littlefield, 2016.

Hills, J. "Regulation, Innovation and Market Structure in International Telecommunications: The Case of the 1956 TAT1 Submarine Cable." *Business History* 49, no. 6 (2007): 868–885.

Johnson, T. A. *Cybersecurity: Protecting Critical Infrastructures from Cyber-Attack and Cyber Warfare.* Boca Raton, FL: CRC Press, 2015.

See also: Background checks; Data breaches; Federal Trade Commission; Hacking, Computer; Identity theft; Malware; Spam

D

Dark web

Identification: As the name suggests, a section of the internet that is not easily seen.

People using the most common software tools and browsers to search or conduct business on the internet do not normally encounter the dark web. Although news accounts focus on the dark web's sinister aspects and controversial sites, of which there are many, some uses of and sites on this area the internet do not fit that description. Since communications undertaken on the dark web are not easily intercepted by any person, company, or government (hence its use as a venue for illegal activities), any individual, government, or group not wanting others to have easy access to their communications can make use of the dark web. It does not differentiate between someone placing an order for illegal drugs or weapons and another person sending a grocery list for items to be purchased at a regular grocery store, although the former would be a much more likely use of the dark web. In addition to the dark web's common use for illegal commerce, it is also used for political ends by terrorist, revolutionary, and opposition groups desiring to evade governmental restrictions. Ironically, the initial development of many dark web tools was for all diplomatic, military, and other governmental security forces to have a secure form of electronic communication.

Brief History

In the mid-1960s the first long-distance, two-computer network allowed digital communications between the machines via normal telephone wires. As what eventually became known as the internet grew, advances in both the hardware and software used in the system began to allow a virtually unlimited number of computers to communicate via the web. Early in this process it was recognized that not all information should be available to every computer and user, resulting in systems of encryption being developed and put into use in the 1970s. Originally established to secure military and civilian governmental data and computer systems, private companies expanded their computer networks and needed to secure their data as well. The spread of encryption was the foundation for what is called the deep web: sites and information not available to the general user. (It is estimated that significantly less than ten percent of the World Wide Web is visible to internet users via popular browsers or search engines.) Encryption of the deep web is the foundation for internet commerce, as the encryption keeps data, such as credit card numbers, safe from those seeking to steal this type of information. However, given the type of encryption and security necessary for commerce and deep web communication, it was only a small step to strengthen the encryption and "bury" sites deeper, to create the dark web.

The dark web is generally seen as beginning in the 1990s with not only the explosion of internet availability and usage, but also the development of new, relatively easy-to-use, free programs for the encryption and decryption of data. The two major systems/programs developed during the 1990s were Freenet and The Onion Router (TOR). Freenet was established as an alternative to the mainstream internet, as an attempt to allow uncensored, private communication among its users. The amount of security and anonymity one has depends on whether one uses the open or the darknet mode, with the latter being the most secure. For many ordinary purposes, the separation from other, larger sections of the internet makes this mode less useful, yet many users find that it meets certain needs. Nevertheless, bridges to the mainstream internet have been developed, and these tend to negate much of the security available using Freenet.

TOR was developed by the U.S. Navy as a means for secure communication, with it becoming available to the general public in the early twenty-first century, although still partially funded by the American and Swedish governments. TOR can work within the general internet, but it strengthens its encryption by sending information through several routers/relays that encrypt/decrypt the information several times before it reaches the desired destination. Having multiple layers of encryption (hence the onion analogy in its name) makes breaking the security of any given transmission through the system, as well as finding the physical location of the sender, extremely difficult. In addition to the network aspects of TOR, it can be used to create generally inaccessible websites (which have a .onion suffix) that can only be reached using the TOR browser.

More recently, I2P has gained popularity among those attempting to avoid government surveillance, especially in light of some governmental success against selected TOR dark websites and malware released into the system. As with TOR, I2P uses multiple intermediary points where the information is encrypted and decrypted, making it difficult to intercept or locate the origin of the information. While the general internet can be reached using I2P, some functions such as email are secure only when sent between two computers that are both running I2P. As with TOR, I2P has its own section of the internet that uses the .i2p suffix.

Uses

Although most people do not think too much about it, general use of the internet results in records to which government agencies, as well as internet providers, browser owners, and operators of search engines have access. Thus, there is a small segment of people obsessed with privacy who go to the extreme of using the dark web for what most people would see as mundane purposes. They are not intentionally using the web for any illegitimate or illegal purposes; they only want complete privacy if possible, when accessing the internet. Such users make up a relatively small portion of dark web users, yet they often complain loudly when any government or international action is contemplated regarding possible dark web restrictions.

While the deep web is an area in which many secretive yet legitimate/legal communication/data files are located, the dark web appeals to those seeking even greater security along with those seeking to conduct illicit activities. The main purpose for which the U.S. Navy developed TOR, namely, secure communications between government entities, still exists; secure electronic communications between people in Washington, D.C. and various agents of the government, whether military or civilian, is still needed and conducted on part of the dark web. Additionally, some private commercial interests have similar needs and make use of the dark web for these purposes.

Reliable statistics regarding dark web usage do not exist, and yet many experts agree that illegal, or at least illicit, activities seem to be its greatest use. This would principally be divided between politics and commerce, although there is an overlap on sites dealing with weapons or weapon technology. Terrorist groups and other extremis, organizations make extensive use of the dark web for internal communications as well as recruitment. While obviously a recruitment ad on a general internet site would reach more people, it would quickly be shut down and the site owner located with relative ease. Thus, in addition to coded ads on the general internet, these organizations make more explicit information available to individuals drawn to their message on the dark web.

Dark web commerce incorporates all manner of illegal product and service offerings. Illegal drugs, almost any type of gun or tactical weapon, illegal forms of pornography, stolen goods (including numbers for credit cards, banks, or the totality of a person's ID), and other things that require the transaction being outside government surveillance are found on the dark web. Services that must be discreetly arranged, whether sexual, or a wide range of illegal or violent acts, are on dark web sites. The first iteration of Silk Road, one of the earliest large-scale dark web marketplaces, ran for about two years. It has been estimated that over $1 billion passed through the site during this period. Numerous other sites, large and small, also operated during this time with an unknown amount of money changing hands.

In addition to encryption techniques and basic legal protections such as the right to privacy, the development that has done the most to boost dark web commerce is the reliance on cryptocurrencies such as bitcoin. As with many other things associated with the dark web, cryptocurrencies are not illegal but they do make illegal transactions easier. Bitcoins, and other cryptocurrencies, can be transferred in such a manner as to conceal the identity of the sender, thus making it ideal for dark web transactions. Using markets like Silk Road has proved beneficial to both buyers and sellers, in that the market acts as a kind of intermediary entity that holds

the cryptocurrency and guarantees to the seller that adequate funds are available, and then sends it to the seller once the buyer has acknowledged that the goods or service has been delivered. (The method is similar to PayPal, although the currency is different and there is no bank involved.)

Although efforts by a variety of law enforcement agencies around the world have diminished the illegal activities occurring on the dark web in recent years, human ingenuity has allowed many criminal entrepreneurs to transform their operations and continue exploiting the less well known recesses of the internet.

Donald A. Watt and Nathan A. B. Watt

Further Reading

Choudhury, Saheli Roy and Arjun Kharpal. "Beyond the Valley: A Look Inside the Mysteries of the dark web." *CNBC*. (September 6, 2018.) www.cnbc.com/2018/09/06/beyond-the-valley-understanding-the-mysteries-of-the-dark-web.html.

Gehl, Robert W. *Weaving the dark web: Legitimacy on Freenet, Tor, and I2P*. (The Information Society Series) Cambridge MA: The MIT Press, 2018.

Patterson, Dan. "dark web: A Cheat Sheet for Business Professionals." *TechRepublic*. (October 26, 2018.) www.techrepublic.com/article/dark-web-the-smart-persons-guide/

Porolli, Matias. "Cybercime black markets: dark web services and their prices." *welivesecurity by eset*. (January 31, 2019.) welivesecurity.com/2019/01/31/cybercrime-black-markets-dark-web-services-and-prices/

Retzkin, Sion. *Hands-On dark web Analysis: Learn what goes on in the dark web, and how to work with it*. Birmingham UK: Packt Publishing, 2018.

See also: Anonymity and anonymizers; Anti-forensics; Cybersecurity; Law enforcement; Online privacy and protection; Pornography; Search engines

Data Breach Notification Laws

Identification: Laws that address disclosure to customers and clients that their personal information has been, or may have been, compromised as a result of a malicious data breach or an inadvertent leak.

The legislative trend toward implementing some kind of mandatory reporting regime for data breaches has continued. Since 2018 mandatory breach notification laws now exist in multiple jurisdictions including all states in the United States, the nation states of the European Union, Canada, Australia, and the United Kingdom.

In jurisdictions that do have data breach notification laws, the legislation customarily (but not always) includes provisions that set out who is governed by the law (e.g. private and/or government entities), what is defined as "personal information" (e.g. name, date of birth, home phone number, social insurance number, driver's license number, credit card number), what is defined as a "data or security breach" (e.g. the loss, unauthorized access to, or disclosure of personal information), what is defined as "harm" , (e.g. significant harm, serious harm), the notice requirements (e.g. the timeframe and method for giving notice and the identification of who must be notified), any exemptions (e.g. encrypted information, immaterial breach, criminal investigation), and any penalties or remedies (e.g. fines or the right of private action) for non-compliance.

The following sections describe data breach notification laws in specific countries and geographic areas:

United States: While no federal mandatory reporting standard yet exists, as of March 2018, all 50 States have mandatory breach notification laws. The District of Columbia, Guam, Puerto Rico and the Virgin Islands have enacted security breach notification laws that require businesses or government to notify consumers or citizens if their personal information is breached. California passed additional privacy laws in July 2018 (in effect January 1, 2020). The *California Consumer Privacy Act of 2018* will give consumers several new rights in addition to the private right of action for individuals. The National Conference of State Legislatures (NCSL) has compiled a comprehensive list of security breach notification laws. As of the date of this publication,

these laws were accessible on the NCSL website, current to September 29, 2018.

Canada: Following a lengthy legislative process, Canada has enacted a federal mandatory privacy breach notification regime under the *Personal Information Protection and Electronic Documents Act*, SC 2000, c 5 (PIPEDA).

The federal regime's data breach reporting requirements came into effect on November 1, 2018 and:

1. requires organizations to notify certain individuals and organizations of certain breaches of security safeguards that create a real risk of significant harm and to report them to the Privacy Commissioner;

2. requires organizations to keep and maintain a record of every breach of security safeguards involving personal information under their control;

3. creates offences in relation to the contravention of certain obligations respecting breaches of security safeguards (fines up to $100,000 per offence).

The federal regime will apply to all private sector organizations except those that operate entirely in Alberta, British Columbia, or Quebec. These provinces have their own private sector privacy statutes which will apply to private sector organizations operating within their jurisdiction, but not to federally regulated organizations. In addition, the health privacy statues in Ontario, New Brunswick, Newfoundland & Labrador, and Nova Scotia will apply to private health providers operating within those provinces; however, PIPEDA continue to apply to all other private sector activity in these provinces.

European Union: In 2016, the *General Data Protection Regulation* (Regulation (EU) 2016/679) ("GDPR") came into force and following a two-year transition period, became law in all member states of the European Union on May 25, 2018. A data breach must be reported to the Supervisory Authority within 72 hours after discovery, unless the risk to individuals is low. In certain circumstances, it may also be necessary to report the breach to the affected individual, depending on the level of risk. All breaches must be recorded. The fines for failing to give notice of a personal data breach can be up to EUR 10,000 or 2 percent worldwide annual turnover, whichever is higher.

United Kingdom: The GDPR, which came into effect on May 25, 2018, and the updated *Data Protection Act 2018*, set out the framework for data protection. Personal data breaches must be reported to the Supervisory Authority (Information Commissioner's Office) within 72 hours after discovery. In certain circumstances, it may also be necessary to report the breach to the affected individual, depending on the level of risk. All breaches must be recorded. The fines for failing to report a data breach are much higher under the GDPR than under the DPA 2018.

Australia: As of February 22, 2018, Australian law now has a mandatory breach notification scheme in place. Australia's recently-passed data breach notification legislation, the Privacy Amendment (Notifiable Data Breaches) Act 2017, requires any organization affected by a serious data breach to notify all individuals whose information has been unlawfully accessed or disclosed. A failure to report the data breach could result in fines up to $2.1 million.

In our increasingly wired and connected world, the need to protect data in a meaningful way continues to grow. The legislative trend toward implementing and refining mandatory reporting regimes for data breaches will also continue.

Linda M. Wright

Further Reading

Baker & McKenzie, *Global Data Breach Notification Guide,* https://globaltmt.bakermckenzie.com/data-security<accessed February 22, 2019>

DLA Piper, Data Protection Laws of the World, Breach Notification, https://www.dlapiperdataprotection.com/index.html?t=breach-notification&c=CA&c2=GB<accessed February 22, 2019>

General Data Protection Regulation (Regulation (EU) 2016/679), https://eur-lex.europa.eu/legal-content/EN/TXT/?uri=celex:32016R0679<accessed February 22, 2109>

Information Commissioner's Office, United Kingdom, *Data Breach Reporting*, https://ico.org.uk/for-organisations/report-a-breach/personal-data-breach/<accessed February 26, 2019>

National Conference of State Legislatures, *Security Breach Notification Laws*, September 29, 2018. http://www.ncsl.org/research/telecommunications-and-information-technology/security-breach-notification-laws.aspx#1 , accessed February 25, 2019>

Norton Rose Fulbright, Parker Chatbot, Data Privacy in Canada, https://www.nortonrosefulbright.com/en-ca/knowledge/publications/8a6e467e/canada-data-breach-reporting-new-regulations<accessed February 26, 2019>

Norton Rose Fulbright, Parker Chatbot, Does the GDPR apply to your non-EU business, https://www.nortonrosefulbright.com/en/knowledge/publications/dfff365a/does-the-gdpr-apply-to-your-non-eu-business<accessed February 26, 2019>

Office of the Australian Information Commissioner, *Data breach preparation and response — A guide to managing data breaches in accordance with the Privacy Act1988* https://www.oaic.gov.au/agencies-and-organisations/guides/data-breach-preparation-and-response,accessed February 8, 2019>

Office of the Privacy Commissioner of Canada, *Privacy Breaches,*https://www.priv.gc.ca/en/privacy-topics/privacy-breaches/<accessed February 22, 2019>

Supra., *What you need to know about mandatory reporting of breaches of security safeguards*, https://www.priv.gc.ca/en/privacy-topics/privacy-breaches/respond-to-a-privacy-breach-at-your-business/gd_pb_201810/<accessed February 22, 2019>

Supra., *Respond to a Privacy Breach at Your Business,*https://www.priv.gc.ca/en/privacy-topics/privacy-breaches/respond-to-a-privacy-breach-at-your-business/gd_pb_201810/<accessed February 22, 2019>

See also: Data breaches; General Data Protection Regulation; Hacking, computer; Identity theft

Data breaches

Identification: Events in which information deemed valuable, sensitive, personal, or otherwise secure has been accessed by an unauthorized individual or group. The information subject to the breach may have been viewed, processed, or sold to a third party as an element of the breach. A lesser category of data breach is the security incident, in which data may have been released but did not reach any unauthorized users. Encrypted data released to the public may be considered as part of a data breach because encryption is not a complete guarantee that the data may never be unencrypted and viewed.

Companies are concerned about the loss or leak of data that belongs to them and also about the loss of the personal data with which they have been entrusted. Corporate data includes trade secrets, such as the formula for a soft drink; proprietary information, such as customer lists and sales data; intellectual property still in development; employment and employee data; and business processes that are the essence of the corporation's success. The types of personal data at issue in a data breach situation include medical data that may be protected under the Health Insurance Portability and Accountability Act (HIPAA), 110 Stat. 1936 (1996), that is, protected health information (PHI); personally identifiable information (PII) that could be used for identity theft or other financial fraud; and other sensitive information, including social security number (SSN), religion or political affiliation, or sexual activity. The types of information that are considered personal vary by state, country, or sectorial regulation.

Breaches may occur as the result of an affirmative attack during which an individual or group of individuals intentionally breaks into a network to capture data in transit or into a database to capture data at rest, and view, destroy, or steal the data. Data breaches may also occur due to negligence or mistake, such as when an employee of the company leaves a laptop in a taxi on the way to a meeting or introduces a data-mining virus into his or her home network from a USB drive picked up on the way out of that meeting. Breaches that result from employee malfeasance or accidental leaks are called insider threats.

Regardless of how the breach originates, companies may take certain measures

to reduce the likelihood of a data breach, to reduce or mitigate the impact should one occur, and to help customers recover from a data breach that involves their personal information. While physical and network security protocols have been developed to reduce the incidence of data breaches, most companies now realize that no network or database is invulnerable to a data breach.

As a result, companies preparing for a data breach first create a data map showing how data are collected; what type of data is stored and in transit (paying special attention to the secure transmission and storage of sensitive personal data); and where the data are housed, including with third-party vendors. Ideally, the amount of data collected should be the minimal amount of data necessary to conduct business, following the principle of data minimization. The company's attorneys may examine the contracts it has with third-party vendors such as cloud storage and network service providers, and determine if the company has adequately protected itself with flow downs of its security provisions, or at least collect reassurances that the other companies that touch its data have followed industry standards in protecting that data. The company may then take its data map and shore up protections, and examine where improvements are needed.

The time to rally an incident response team is before a breach occurs, in anticipation of a potential data breach. The team may include cybersecurity lawyers; information technology (IT) personnel; executives; security professionals; privacy professionals; marketing and public relations, government relations, and customer-care and call-center managers; human relations (HR) officers for employee communications and other employee issues; risk management and cyberinsurance contacts; and possibly law enforcement or government contacts. This team can be utilized to run simulations to prepare a reaction if a data breach occurs.

When a breach does occur, the first step is to alert the incident response team and begin to investigate the cause of the breach and the nature of the compromised data. To the extent possible, the point of attack must be re-secured and any leaks must be sealed. Companies without the resources to maintain full-time breach response teams may hire contractor forensic companies to perform these services. Under most state laws, the company that stores or processes the breached data must notify affected customers. State laws vary considerably on the requirements for the notices, including different minimum number of customers and types of data affected to trigger notification requirements; timing for the notices; and whether law enforcement, government agencies, or the media must also be notified of the breach. Several federal laws have been proposed that would require a coordinated response to a data breach on a national level, also with varying factors triggering notification. Some of the federal laws would preempt state laws, and some would not. Also, many of the federal laws proposed would carve out exceptions for existing data breach regulation under HIPAA for health-care-related data breaches and for financial data breaches already covered under other regulation.

Data breaches have grown in number, scope, and magnitude in recent years, most likely because of the increasing value of electronic information about individuals and companies, and also to the increasing concentration of this information into big-data storage in databases. Media attention centers on the immediate costs to the company of notifying customer and defending against class action lawsuits and fines. The long-term consequences of a data breach for companies involved in the breach may include costs associated with new research and development and product redesign to meet updated security needs and standards; hiring new employees for call centers and security monitoring; employee time and education; and purchasing new security services, including diagnostic, testing, and forensic services.

Jill Bronfman

Further Reading

Anandarajan, M., R. D'ovidio, and A. Jenkins. "Safeguarding Consumers against Identity-Related Fraud: Examining Data Breach Notification Legislation through the Lens of Routine Activities Theory." *International Data Privacy Law* 00, no. 00 (2012): 51–60.

Belangia, David. "Data Breach Preparation." Master's thesis, SANS Technology Institute, Los Alamos National Laboratory, 2015. https://www.sans.org/reading-room/whitepapers/dlp/data-breach-preparation-35812.

Chander, Anupam. *Securing Privacy in the Internet Age.* Stanford, CA: Stanford Law Books, 2008.

Dhasarathan, Chandramohan, Vengattaraman Thirumal, and Dhavachelvan Ponnurangam. "Data Privacy Breach Prevention Framework for the Cloud Service." *Security and Communication Networks* 8, no. 6 (April 2015): 982–1005.

Ezor, Jonathan. *Privacy and Data Protection in Business: Laws and Practices.* New Providence, NJ: LexisNexis, 2012.

Herold, Rebecca. "Privacy Breach Incident Response," in *Information Security Management Handbook,* 6th ed., ed. Harold F. Tipton and Micki Krause. Boca Raton, FL: Auerbach Publications, 2007.

Hutchins, John P. *U.S. Data Breach Notification Law: State by State.* Chicago, IL: American Bar Association, Section of Science & Technology Law, 2007.

Kennedy, Charles H. *The Business Privacy Law Handbook.* Boston, MA: Artech House, 2008.

Kostopoulos, George K. *Cyberspace and Cybersecurity.* Boca Raton, FL: CRC Press, 2013.

"Patent Issued for Healthcare Privacy Breach Prevention through Integrated Audit and Access Control." *Computer Weekly News,* April 2, 2015.

Stalla-Bourdillon, Sophie, Joshua Phillips, and Mark D.Ryan. *Privacy vs. Security.* New York: Springer, 2015. Springer Briefs in Privacy and Security series.

See also: Cybersecurity; Data breach notification laws; Federal Trade Commission (FTC); Medical confidentiality, privacy right to; Social Security numbers (SSNs)

Data brokers

Identification: As defined by the Federal Trade Commission (FTC), "companies that collect information, including personal information about consumers, from a wide variety of sources for the purpose of reselling such information to their customers for various purposes, including verifying an individual's identity, differentiating records, marketing products, and preventing financial fraud." Well-known data brokers include Acxiom, Experian, Datalogix, and Epsilon, but in actuality, these are just a few of the many data brokers in existence. A list of 270 companies is provided by Privacy Rights Clearinghouse via its *Online Data Vendors* database (https://www.privacyrights.org/ online-information-brokers-list).

According to a May 2014 FTC report entitled *Data Brokers: A Call for Transparency and Accountability* (hereinafter *Data Brokers*), data brokers acquire their information from a wide variety of outlets, including federal, state, and local government records; the Internet and social media; commercial sources; consumer self-reporting; and other data brokers. Government-sourced information may include U.S. census records; federal and state court filings; real property and county tax assessor data; occupational licenses; and, depending on the jurisdiction, voter and driving records. Meanwhile, individuals' profiles on social media sites such as Facebook, Twitter, and LinkedIn, particularly when restrictive privacy settings have not been enabled, can provide data such as age, gender, location, educational background, and interests and dislikes. Commercial sources, such as brick-and-mortar and online retailers, may provide data brokers with information on the purchasing habits of individuals, including the date, cost, and category of purchases made, as well as the method of payment. Consumer self-reporting, via website signups, marketing surveys, sweepstakes entries, and product warranty registrations, may provide data such as demographic information, household income levels, and health-related concerns. Data brokers may purchase information from other data brokers to supplement their collection efforts. The result is the creation of a sizable data file on hundreds of millions of Americans. For example, in its 2013 annual report, data broker Acxiom claims to possess "over 3,000 propensities for nearly every U.S. consumer" and to have information on more than ten percent of the world's population.

According to Privacy Rights Clearinghouse's *Fact Sheet 41: Data Brokers and Your Privacy*, the customer base for data brokers is extensive and may include "financial institutions, insurance companies, the hospitality industry, cable and telecommunications companies, political campaigns, retail stores, and even government entities and law enforcement agencies." These purchasers acquire information from data brokers primarily for marketing, risk mitigation, and people-search purposes. For marketing purposes, data brokers may, for example, provide a retailer with a list of individuals who possess certain characteristics, such as an interest in high-end clothing, which the retailer can then use to market their product more effectively. Meanwhile, data brokers help companies mitigate risk by supplying information to help confirm individuals' identities and detect fraud attempts. For example, a company may work with a data broker to ensure that personal information submitted by a customer matches the information contained in the data broker's file. Finally, individuals and companies use data brokers' people-search products for "tracking the activities of executives and competitors, finding old friends, researching a potential love interest or neighbor, networking, or locating court records."

As explained in a December 18, 2013, staff report for Chairman John D. Rockefeller IV prepared by the U.S. Senate's Committee on Commerce, Science, and Transportation, entitled *A Review of the Data Broker Industry: Collection, Use, and Sale of Consumer Data for Marketing Purpose*, the collection and sale of information by data brokers is highly controversial. First, privacy concerns exist because the data is compiled without consumers' knowledge. As such, consumers have little opportunity to assess the accuracy of the information and are often unaware of how it is being used. Next, because data brokers store vast amounts of personal information, they are particularly susceptible to data breaches. Finally, the compiled data may be used for illicit practices. One particularly troublesome example, reported by the *New York Times* in its May 20, 2007, story *Bilking the Elderly, with a Corporate Assist*, involved the sale of information by data broker InfoUSA. According to the story, InfoUSA sold lists of names, including headings such as Elderly Opportunity Seekers, Suffering Seniors, and Oldies but Goodies, to purchasers, who in turn used the information to defraud senior citizens.

The Government Accountability Office (GAO) released a report in September 2013 entitled *Information Resellers: Consumer Privacy Framework Needs to Reflect Changes in the Technology and the Marketplace)*, which concluded that data brokers are, by and large, exempt from federal privacy laws. According to the report, existing federal laws "generally do not provide individuals the universal right to access, control, or correct personal information that resellers and private-sector companies use for marketing purposes." Drawing on the GAO report, Privacy Rights Clearinghouse states that the data brokers become subject to greater regulation *if* they fall under the purview of the Fair Credit Reporting Act (FCRA), 84 Stat. 1114–2 (1970). This occurs if the information provided by data brokers "is used by issuers of credit or insurance, or by employers, landlords, and others in making eligibility decisions affecting consumers." Most data brokers, however, are exempt from the FCRA. Recognizing this lack of federal regulation, the FTC has recommended that Congress pass legislation requiring data brokers to operate with more transparency. In response, Senator Edward Markey (D-MA) introduced Senate Bill 668, the *Data Broker Accountability and Transparency Act of 2015*, but no Congressional action was taken on that bill or any other at the federal level, as of early 2019. However, two states have implemented laws directly affecting data brokers. Effective in January, 2019, Vermont mandates the registration of data brokers whose files include citizens of that state and make available to the public information about the types of information they hold and insure that it is not used for illegal purposes. In a similar, although less direct, move California has created new laws regarding personal privacy, which includes provisions for California citizens to bar any company from selling their data. This law takes effect in January, 2020. Thus, while these laws (and any other passed in the near future) might have a dramatic impact upon data brokers, it is too soon to tell if that will come to pass. In Europe, the General Data Protection Regulation (GDPR) was adopted by the European Union giving its citizens strong control over their personal data (if they desire) including the right to "be forgotten." The GDPR makes the default choice "opt out of data collection" instead of what has been the norm that everyone desires inclusion in these massive data bases. As with the laws in the United States, even though it would seem that this regulation would drastically change the way data brokers do business in Europe, it is too soon to know the full effect this regulation will have.

Jesse Bowman and Donald A. Watt

Further Reading

Burt, Andrew. "States Are Leading the Way on Data Privacy." *The Hill.* August 21, 2018. thehill.com/opinion/technology/402775-states-are-leading-the-way-on-data-privacy.

Pasquale, Frank. "The Dark Market for Personal Data." *New York Times*, October 17, 2014.

Roderick, Leanne. "Discipline and Power in the Digital Age: The Case of the U.S. Consumer Data Broker Industry." *Critical Sociology* 40, no. 5 (2014): 729–746.

Singer, Natasha. "A Data Broker Offers a Peek behind the Curtain." *New York Times*, September 1, 2013.

Wayne, Logan Danielle. "The Data Broker Threat: Proposing Federal Legislation to Protect Post-Expungement Privacy." *Journal of Criminal Law and Criminology* 102, no. 1 (Winter 2012): 253–282.

See also: Data breaches; Fair Credit Reporting Act (FCRA); Federal Trade Commission (FTC); Marketing; Social networking technologies

Data harvesting

Identification: The practice of extracting and collecting large amounts of personal and commercial data, mostly from Internet websites.

Data harvesting (also known as web harvesting, data scraping, data aggregation, or data mining) is the process of digitally compiling large amounts of information such as search results, purchasing preferences, commercial offerings, product prices, and demographic data from the Internet. Data harvesting is usually done through the use of magnetic robots known as web harvesters or screen scrapers that collect data, filter inappropriate content, and present it to consumers in easy-to-use formats, such as graphs, tables, and indexes.

Businesses, banks, credit card bureaus, and even certain public-sector agencies often hire experts to design sophisticated web harvesters to collect data that is hard to retrieve manually. Indeed, most web harvesters can translate various computer languages, such as HyperText Markup Language (HTML), JavaScript, and PHP: Hypertext Preprocessor (PHP), among others. Experts at web harvesting are highly sought after by businesses because they can engage in data collection and data translation at warp speeds. Most web harvesters can retrieve several pages on a server simultaneously and can automatically access target websites repeatedly throughout the day. As such, web harvesting allows businesses to create reports, presentations, and profiles about individuals and groups of consumers quickly.

Because many web harvesters are quite inexpensive and can be accessed easily through a basic Internet search, many individuals engage in web harvesting as well. The use of web harvesters has recently grown so much that Internet users frequently interact with harvesters without even knowing that they are doing so. Common examples of web harvesters that consumers frequently come into contact with include: search engines, business advertisers, auction compilers, price

aggregators, real estate listing services, financial data aggregators, financial money management applications, and social media websites. The websites that are targeted by web harvesting are usually referred to as data hosts.

Whether web harvesting is a socially beneficial or harmful activity often depends on the collateral damage that the web harvester causes to a data host. For example, certain web harvesters, such as price amalgamators and targeted advertisers, cause minimal or no damage to data hosts and allow businesses to match consumer needs with commercial offerings efficiently. In fact, web harvesters such as price amalgamators and targeted advertisers often benefit both consumers and data hosts because, in addition to causing the data hosts at most minimal harm, they increase the visibility of the data hosts' products and services.

Another example of a web harvester that Internet users frequently interact with is a search engine. These web harvesters are almost universally lauded for the benefits they provide to end-users through constant accessing of thousands of websites, pulling bits of information from these websites, and presenting the data in the form of easily readable search engine results. Search engines are also particularly useful web harvesters because they can collect archived data that is stored on a system but that can no longer be accessed due to the incompatibility of an old system or Internet website with newer computer hardware or software.

On the other hand, web harvesting can also cause extensive damage to data hosts. If a web harvester is designed to overcome a technical barrier such as a password or other code barrier, the web harvester may end up undercutting a competing business's revenue, gaining access to confidential company information, or damaging the physical infrastructure of the data host. Indeed, some web harvesting has caused data hosts to suffer extensive damage, such as increased bandwidth usage, system crashes, the need to purchase anti-spam devices, the need to erect technical barriers, the need to clear up consumer confusion, and damage to reputation.

Because of some of the negative effects caused by web harvesting, it is not surprising that there have been many lawsuits involving web harvesting and data scraping in recent years. In addition to the prevalent use of web harvesters, a primary reason for these lawsuits is that many websites are poorly equipped to fend off web harvesting and want to deter web harvesters from gaining unfettered access to their data.

For example, in *eBay v. Bidder's Edge,* 100 F. Supp. 2d 1058 (N.D. Cal. 2000), a federal lawsuit that was litigated in Northern California in 2000, eBay complained that Bidder's Edge (BE) was unlawfully compiling eBay's auction listings and copying eBay's auction format on its own website without incurring any of the investment and operating costs that eBay incurs. eBay showed the court that it had unavailingly tried to block BE's data scrapers through telephonic and written communications and by trying to block BE's IP addresses. The court sided with eBay and held that BE was liable for aggregating data from eBay's servers without attaining prior authorization and that BE was free-riding on the time, effort, and money that eBay had invested in its system.

A similar situation was litigated the following year in *EF Cultural Travel BV v. Explorica, Inc.,* 274 F.3d 577 (1st Cir. 2001). In this case, EF Cultural Travel BV (EF), a company that offered tour guides for groups of teenagers, complained that Explorica was unlawfully scraping information about EF's tour prices in order to undercut EF from the teenage tour market. The First Circuit sided with EF and approved an injunction against Explorica to prohibit further scraping that would be to EF's detriment.

During the 2016 U.S. election, a major scandal involving data harvesting became headline news when a company named Cambridge Analytica harvested personal data from millions of people's Facebook profiles without their knowledge or consent. The campaigns of U.S. Senator Ted Cruz (R-TX) and presidential candidate Donald Trump both used Cambridge Analytica's data to target their campaign efforts. Eventually, Facebook CEO Mark Zuckerberg was called to testify before Congress about the compromising of the privacy rights of over 80 million users.

Facebook was once again in the news for data harvesting in 2019, when a virtual private network (VPN) app they owned named Onavo, was revealed to actually be collecting user data rather than protecting it, which is the entire purpose of a VPN. VPNs are gateways through which users' Internet traffic goes in order to protect the identity of the user. But rather than protecting the user, it was used by Facebook as a source of information concerning users' web and app use habits.

Because of the ubiquity of web harvesters, and in light of the numerous benefits that they provide, it is critical for users of web harvesters to become familiar with the laws governing web harvesting. Again, many uses of web harvesting are considered harmless to data hosts and beneficial to consumers. Such uses are unlikely to lead to legal disputes. But given that some data hosts are opposed to unknown web harvesting, it is critical for users of web harvesters to know what types of web harvesting may expose them to liability. Similarly, it is important for data hosts that are opposed to web harvesting to stay abreast of the capabilities of web harvesters so that they can erect technical barriers and other sophisticated blockades to protect their data.

Myra Din

Further Reading

Chadwick, Paul. "How Many People Had Their Data Harvested by Cambridge Analytica?" *The Guardian*, April 16, 2018. https://www.theguardian.com/commentis-free/2018/apr/16/how-many-people-data-cambridge-analytica-facebook

Feldman, Brian. "Even If Facebook Stops Aggressively Collecting Data, Developers Will Still Supply It." *New York Magazine*, February 22, 2019. http://nymag.com/intelligencer/2019/02/why-facebooks-data-collection-practice-is-so-messy.html

Fibbe, George H. "Screen-Scraping and Harmful Cyber-trespass after Intel." *Mercer Law Review* 55, no. 1011 (2004).

Gladstone, Julia Alpert. "Data Mines and Battlefields: Looking at Financial Aggregators to Understand the Legal Boundaries and Ownership Rights in the Use of Personal Data." *Journal of Marshall Computer and Information Law* 19, no. 313 (2001).

Hirschey, Jeffrey Kenneth. "Symbiotic Relationships: Pragmatic Acceptance of Data Scraping," *Berkeley Technical Law Journal* 29, no. 897 (2014).

Rubin, Aaron. "How Website Operators Use CFAA to Combat Data-Scraping." *Law360.* http://www.law360.com/articles/569325?utm_source=rss&utm_medium=rss&utm_campaign=articles_search.

What Is a Screen Scraper? wiseGEEK. http://www.wise-geek.com/what-is-a-screen-scraper.htm.

Wierzel, Kimberly L. "If You Can't Beat Them, Join Them: Data Aggregators and Financial Institutions." *North Carolina Banking Institute* 5, no. 457 (2001):.

See also: Big data; Cambridge Analytica; Computers and privacy; Credit and debit cards; Data collection; Facebook; Marketing; Online privacy and security; Search engines; Social networking technologies

Data protection regimes

Identification: Comprehensive legislative frameworks designed to govern the collection, use, and transfer of personal information by all organizations within a jurisdiction.

Globally, there are two broad approaches taken to the protection of personal information. One approach may be generally described as "sectoral" in nature: there are various legislative regimes that create standards and rules in discrete areas of the economy. Beyond those areas, privacy protection is left purely to the free market: if people desire privacy, then they can (in theory) pay for it. Different jurisdictions regulate different areas, and at different levels of protection. The United States, for instance, has legislated privacy protections in various areas—including, but not limited to, telecommunications, health information, credit reporting, and websites aimed at children—but there is little

consistency as to the kind of privacy protection offered in each area. Vietnam has also adopted a sectoral approach, choosing to regulate only e-commerce and consumer transactions. India goes further (or has gone nowhere, depending on your perspective), having no data privacy regulation whatsoever. Proponents of a sectoral or free-market approach argue that excessive privacy laws impose costs on business and are therefore a threat to technological innovation and economic growth.

But the sectoral model is a global outlier. Critics argue that it leaves gaps in the law and creates confusing inconsistencies. Leaving privacy protections to the free market in those gaps is ineffective since there are great disparities in bargaining power between individuals and large organizations that seek to profit off their personal information. As a result, the approach adopted by much of the rest of the world is to legislate a single data protection regime applicable to all organizations that seek to collect, use, or disclose personal information. Broad state involvement through data protection regimes is justified because privacy is understood as a human right connected to individuality, dignity, and autonomy; while there may be economic costs to robust privacy rights, they are justified because of the values at play.

The origin of comprehensive data protection regimes may be found in the 1980 Organisation for Economic Co-operation and Development (OECD) Privacy Guidelines, the core of which was the adoption of eight "fair information practice principles" (FIPPS) intended to give direction to the collection, use, and disclosure of personal information. Though having jointly developed the OECD Guidelines, the United States and Europe went in two different directions regarding their applicability in the years that followed. The United States saw them as a framework of "useful guidelines" that could be freely adopted by industry if they so chose, while in Europe they were gradually strengthened and made directly enforceable. This strengthening culminated in the passage of the EU Data Protection Directive. In one form or another, an enforceable version of the FIPPS can be found in all other modern data protection regimes, such as Canada's Personal Information & Protection of Electronic Documents Act, Hong Kong's Personal Data (Privacy) Ordinance, South Africa's Protection of Personal Information Act, and so on.

Because of this common ideological heritage, data protection regimes typically share some general features. These include a usually wide definition of "personal information" (such as any information that can lead to an identifiable individual) and of activities that count as "data processing" (both manual and automatic). Data protection regimes place a heavy emphasis on the knowledge of and/or consent to collection of personal information by the data subject and a strict limitation on the purposes to which collected information can be put. In other words, an individual must generally be informed at the time of collection of her or his information as to the purpose of the collection, and any new purpose must receive new consent.

Generally speaking, under a data protection regime, *all* organizations that collect, use, or disclose personal information will be subject to the same rules; this is in clear contrast to the sectoral approach. Some jurisdictions, however, may choose to have two separate regimes for public and private organizations. Likewise, while all data protection regimes grant exemptions for data processing or collection in specified areas such as journalism, statistical research, or public security, only some may grant exemptions to all noncommercial or personal use of information. Finally, while the definition of "personal information" tends to be broad, some regimes treat certain classes of information as particularly sensitive (for example, medical information, financial records, and political opinions) and thus deserving of additional protections, while others do not.

Data protection regimes are also typically supervised by an independent commissioner, though the exact power of that commissioner may vary. Canada's Privacy Commissioner, for instance, lacks the power to issue fines directly to violators of the relevant law, while under the EU General Data Protection Regulation (adopted in 2016 and implemented in 2018) national data protection authorities are granted the power to issue sanctions to organizations found to be in noncompliance of up to 2 percent of their worldwide turnover. Beyond sanctioning, other powers that may vary across regimes include the possibility of an independent lawsuit absent public complaint, compelling reporting of data breaches, strength of independence from government, and so on.

Further shared features most data protection regimes include a right of individual access to information held about them, and the right to seek erasure or correction of information where it is incorrect. However, differing interpretations of this basic principle (drawn from the FIPPS) can be found in the recent discussion over the right to be forgotten—whether individuals can request online sources to remove information about them. Interpretation of the Data Protection Directive by the European Court of Justice has found such a right to exist. In *Google Spain v. Gonzalez* (2014) C-131/12, the Court found that existing provisions that granted the data subject the right to erasure of "irrelevant" data could support the right to be forgotten and required the well-known search engine to delete links to a news story regarding the complainant's financial difficulties from some fifteen years prior. The current General Data Protection Regulation explicitly recognizes and expands the application of this right. But no other jurisdiction with data protection regimes has yet announced any intention to introduce similar amendments or recognized such a right in its courts, arguing that as long as the information is true, forcing its deletion is incompatible with the right to free expression.

Indeed, the debate over the right to be forgotten is indicative of a new set of challenges that data protection regimes face. The FIPPS were developed in the 1970s in response to a particular set of privacy issues relevant at the time. In 2019, we live in age of "always-on" Internet-connected devices that are carried voluntarily in our pockets, and an economy the lifeblood of which is information. There are thus disputes about whether data protection regimes can be adapted (or need to be adapted) to respond to these changes. In the coming years, we may a split within data protection regimes over some of these issues, just as the 1980s saw a split between interpreting the FIPPS as "useful guidelines" (the free market/sectoral approach) and as the basis for directly enforceable laws (the data protection regime approach).

Stuart A. Hargreaves

Further Reading

Bygrave, Lee A. "The Place of Privacy in Data Protection Laws." *University of New South Wales Law Journal* 24, no. 1 (2001): 277–283.

Bygrave, Lee A., *Data Privacy Law, an International Perspective.* Oxford: Oxford University Press, 2014.

Cate, Fred. "The Changing Face of Privacy Protections in the European Union and the United States." *Indiana Law Review* 33 (1999): 173–232.

Koops, Bert-Jaap, "The Trouble with European Data Protection Law." *International Data Privacy Law* 4, no. 4 (2014): 250–261.

Levin, Avner, and Mary Jo Nicholson. "Privacy Law in the United States, the EU, and Canada: the Allure of the Middle Ground." *University of Ottawa Law & Technology Journal* 2, no. 2 (2005): 357–395.

Mantlero, Alessandro. "The EU Proposal for a General Data Protection Regulation and the Roots of the 'Right to Be Forgotten.'" *Computer Law & Security Review* 29, no. 3 (June 2013): 229–235.

Shoenberger, Allen. "Privacy Wars." *Indiana International & Comparative Law Review* 17 (2007): 355–393.

Whitman, James Q. "Two Western Cultures of Privacy: Dignity versus Liberty." *Yale Law Journal* 113, no. 6 (April 2004): 1151–1221.

See also: APEC Cross Border Privacy Rules; Credit Reporting Agencies; Fair Information Practice Principles; Financial Information, Privacy Right to; General Data Protection Regulation; Global Data Privacy; Mobile Devices; Right to Be Forgotten

Data science

Identification: The use of information or data collected used to predict the decision and behavior of an individual or a group of targeted individuals.

Data science is: "......*powerful new approach to making discoveries. By combining aspects of statistics, computer science, applied mathematics, and visualization, data science can turn the vast amounts of data the digital age generates into new insights and new knowledge.*"

The lines of privacy are blurred for an individual's privacy rights when so much data gathering is a part of almost every facet of our everyday lives; Internet searches, emails, text messaging applications, or even financial transactions, are made online. Data can be tracked then used to predict private decisions, and companies continue to obscure the lines of what data is collected for a variety of purposes without regulation. The essence of data science is based on the information that is able to be collected during this digital age. Information is commonly requested, exchanged, and inputted on a regular basis, but data science can be used to help make decisions including what to buy. Decisions made are analyzed to compare and expand the knowledge of how people purchase a variety of things; eventually this data is valuable because consumer spending patterns can be targeted and strategically marketed to for financial gains.

Data science is being increasingly regulated as its use affects all consumers and the data is used for different purposes than even most users are aware. On September 25, 2012, for example, the Federal Trade Commission (FTC) released a statement on data collection for the improper use of data, which amounted to an invasion of personal privacy by several rent-to-own private companies. The FTC announced a regulatory settlement with seven rent-to-own companies because they improperly monitored consumers using the web cameras installed in the computers.

Seven rent-to-own companies and a software design firm have agreed to settle Federal Trade Commission charges that they spied on consumers using computers that consumers rented from them, capturing screenshots of confidential and personal information, logging their computer keystrokes, and in some cases taking webcam pictures of people in their homes, all without notice to, or consent from, the consumers.

The software design firm collected the data that enabled rent-to-own stores to track the location of rented computers without consumers' knowledge according to the FTC complaint. The settlements bar the companies from any further illegal spying, from activating location-tracking software without the consent of computer renters and notice to computer users, and from deceptively collecting and disclosing information about consumers. 'An agreement to rent a computer doesn't give a company license to access consumers' private emails, bank account information, and medical records, or, even worse, webcam photos of people in the privacy of their own homes,' said Jon Leibowitz, Chairman of the FTC. The FTC orders today will put an end to their cyber spying. There is no justification for spying on customers. These tactics are offensive invasions of personal privacy...

This breach of personal privacy amounts to an illegal use of data science to obtain information for purposes other than the consumer and private company originally intended. Information that is shared or provided by a consumer for its intended purpose is important to establishing individual privacy rights and maintaining a standard for all consumers. Using data science to predict consumer purchases, track financial information and obtaining a consumer's mother's maiden name, are just a few examples of the pervasiveness involved with collecting data and analyzing it. Filtering through data obtained from consumers to extract specific information or reselling the information to another company can all be improper practices of the use of data science that put private information at an increased risk of getting into the wrong hands for the wrong purposes.

Consumer information obtained by companies must reflect the freedom and right for each individual to make free choices. Once legitimate privacy rights have been violated through misuse of data science that inappropriately disseminates private consumer information, then there is an invasion of privacy that must be remedied and deterred. Legal standards for appropriate use of data science as a tool are promulgated by agencies such as the Federal Trade Commission, which investigates consumer complaints when the consumer believes that their right to privacy has been violated. The FTC then investigates these complaints. For the freedom to establish the societal lines to protect private information, this means individuals must help to establish the lines that private companies may not violate in their use of data science. Clear privacy standards must be promulgated so that companies may follow data science practices that fairly respect individual expectations of privacy.

Shaunté Chácon

Further Reading

Federal Trade Commission: https://www.ftc.gov/newsevents/press-releases/2012/09/ftc-halts-computer-spying

O'Neill, Cathy and Rachel Schutt, *Doing Data Science: Straight Talk from Frontline.* O'Reilly Media Inc., 2013.

Payton, Theresa and Ted Claypoole, *Privacy in the Age of Big Data: Recognizing Threats, Defending Your Rights and Protecting Your Family.* Rowman & Littlefield, 2014.

Provost, Foster and Tom Fawcett, *Data Science for Business: What you need to know about data mining.* O'Reilly Media Inc., 2013.

See also: Computers and privacy; Consumer privacy; Federal Trade Commission (FTC); Right to privacy

Debt collection

Identification: In some cases, when an individual or a business is owed money by a debtor, along with possible interest, the creditor hires a debt collection agency to collect the money for the creditor.

A creditor has certain rights to collect money that is owed by a consumer. There are, however, legal protections put in place to protect consumer rights. This entry reviews the overall goal of debt collection, laws related to debt collections that protect consumers' privacy, and how the laws are implemented to protect private or personal information used to collect a debt.

The overall goal of debt collection is to work cooperatively with consumers to obtain the money owed to the creditor, which sometimes includes interest. During difficult economic times, more consumers are in debt, have problems paying their debt, and debt–collection agencies are more often hired to contact the debtor to make arrangements for the payments. The information on the consumer debt, therefore, would be transferred to two companies, the original creditor and the debt collection company. This consumer information would include some personal identification information of the creditor to track the debt for the creditor. The debt–collection process begins after the original creditor made unsuccessful efforts to collect the outstanding debt and the debt collection company was hired to make the collection efforts. Debt–collection companies specialize in contacting the consumer and seek to convince the customer that payment is required immediately.

There are several laws and regulations in force to ensure that debt collection agencies follow debt collection practices to protect consumers' personal information that include, but are not limited to, financial information obtained to collect the debt. The Fair Debt Collection Practices Act (FDCPA) is the most important law that regulates debt collection practices. The following describes the Congressional intent behind the statute.

Congressional findings and declarations of purpose [15 USC 1692]

(a) There is abundant evidence of the use of abusive, deceptive, and unfair debt collection practices by many debt collectors. Abusive debt collection practices contribute to the number of personal bankruptcies, to marital instability, to the loss of jobs, and to invasions of individual privacy.

(b) Existing laws and procedures for redressing these injuries are inadequate to protect consumers.

(c) Means other than misrepresentation or other abusive debt collection practices are available for the effective collection of debts.

(d) Abusive debt–collection practices are carried on to a substantial extent in interstate commerce and through means and instrumentalities of such commerce. Even where abusive debt collection practices are purely intrastate in character, they nevertheless directly affect interstate commerce.

(e) It is the purpose of this title to eliminate abusive debt–collection practices by debt collectors, to insure that those debt collectors who refrain from using abusive debt collection practices are not competitively disadvantaged, and to promote consistent State action to protect consumers against debt collection abuses.

The FDCPA places strict guidelines for communications, enforcement, and fraudulent activities by debt collectors used towards consumers to collect a debt. Consumers should understand their rights within the law and what debt collectors are legally able to do while collecting a debt. Understanding these restrictions are important so that the behavior of debt collectors can respect the privacy information obtained to collect funding from consumers. The regulations do not necessarily prevent inappropriate debt collection activities but they can encourage and promote the goal of debt collection while providing consumer protection. The National Consumer Law Center (NCLC) succinctly describes the intent of fair debt–collection laws as: ". . . federal and many states' laws require that financially distressed consumers not be abused, deceived, lose their privacy, or be treated unfairly."

The Federal Trade Commission (FTC), the nation's leading consumer protection agency, enforces fair debt–collection laws to ensure the protection of consumers, including protection of their personal information. Congress delegated this power to the FTC through the FDCPA. If a consumer experiences unfair, deceptive or inappropriate treatment from a creditor, lawyer or debt collector, they may contact the FTC, their state's Attorney General, or the Consumer Financial Protection Bureau for enforcement of the FDCPA. The Consumer Financial Protection Bureau works to educate, enforce, and study consumer activities specifically

"protect consumers by carrying out federal consumer financial laws. Among other things, we: write rules, supervise companies, and enforce federal consumer financial protection laws, restrict unfair, deceptive, or abusive acts or practices, take consumer complaints, promote financial education, research consumer behavior, monitor financial markets for new risks to consumers, and enforce laws that outlaw discrimination and other unfair treatment in consumer finance."

Enforcement of these fair debt–collection laws is necessary to ensure that the financial laws are properly followed by all creditors or debt collectors to protect consumers. An opportunity to report and actively assist regulators consumers can work in conjunction with state and federal enforcement to keep them aware of changing

practices during the ever changing digital age and continue to protect their private information.

Shaunté Chácon

Further Reading

Public Law 104–208,110 Stat. 3009 (September 30, 1996). 15 USC 1692 www.nclc.org/issues/debt-collection.html

Debt Collection, Privacy, Fair Credit Reporting & Consumer.

Conference on Consumer Finance Law, 2000 Bankruptcy. www.debt.org/credit https://www.ftc.gov/enforcement/rules/rulemaking-regulatory-reform-proceedings/fair-debt-collectionpractices-act-text http://www.consumerfinance.gov/ the-bureau/

See also: Consumer privacy; Federal Trade Commission (FTC); Financial information, privacy right to.

Defence and Security Media Advisory Committee (DSMA Committee)

Identification: Formerly known as the Defence, Press and Broadcasting Advisory Committee, a body that oversees the voluntary code observed by the news media and British government departments responsible for national security.

The Defence, Press and Broadcasting Advisory Committee (DPBAC) used the Defence Advisory (DA) Notice System to assist the media in preserving national security. The Defence and Security Media Advisory (DSMA) Committee, the successor entity, retained the role of overseeing the voluntary code. The British government continues to use this system to inform media organizations when certain news stories could threaten national security, although the communications are now known as security advisory notices. The DSMA system is intended to "prevent inadvertent public disclosure of information that would compromise UK military and intelligence operations and methods, or put at risk the safety of those involved in such operations, or lead to attacks that would damage the critical national infrastructure and/or endanger lives," according to the DSMA Committee's statement of objectives.

In June 2014, the Permanent Secretary of the Ministry of Defence sponsored an independent review to examine the purpose and effectiveness of the DPBAC and the DA Notice System from the perspectives of the British government, the media, and the general public. The independent inquiry, which was completed in March 2015, came after the *Guardian* newspaper released information about mass surveillance by security services based on leaks from Edward Snowden. The review found that the system still played a useful role and validated its work. The review also produced several recommendations reflecting "evolving social, media and security challenges," the most important of which were adopted effective July 2015. Among them was the change of name to Defence and Security Media Advisory Committee.

Although covered by the Freedom of Information Act 2000 or the Freedom of Information (Scotland) Act of 2002, the DSMA Committee is committed to a policy of maximum disclosure of its activities consistent with the effective conduct of business and the need to ensure that it honors any obligations of confidentiality to the people and organizations with which it conducts business.

While the DSMA Committee stresses the importance of advising the British media on whether the reporting of certain information could inadvertently endanger national security, it also acknowledges that rapid changes in worldwide information collection, storage, and dissemination, particularly those related to the Internet, have resulted in major changes in the public availability and accessibility of information. These changes have also raised the possibility of very different interpretations of the term "widely available." On one hand, information may be obtained from a very wide variety of sources, each of which is readily available to the general public. On the other, information may exist somewhere on the Internet, but it may

be limited to a single source and be capable of being found only after prodigious effort and ingenuity. Between these two positions, a range of potentially valid interpretations of "widely available" exists.

In clarifying its understanding of the term, the DSMA Committee concluded that the DSMA Notice System will consider prior publication or broadcast by major newspapers, broadcast networks, and high-profile magazines; prior distribution by internationally networked news, picture, and television agencies; and prominence on major Internet search engines or widely used webcast channels. When providing DSMA Notice advice, the committee's secretary will make a decision on a case-by-case basis if some form of prior publication or broadcast is involved.

The DSMA Committee acknowledges that worldwide information collection, storage, and dissemination are continuing to evolve rapidly. In cases where the rebroadcast or republication of certain information could inadvertently damage national security, the DSMA Committee seeks to ensure that the advice it provides to the British media continues to reflect changing realities.

The Security Notice system remains a voluntary, nonstatutory arrangement. Recently, more representatives from the news media have been added to DSMA. Currently, fifteen of the twenty members are journalists. The committee has also been increasingly focused on counterterrorism and intelligence rather than on matters of national defense.

Further Reading

The Defence Advisory Notices: A Review of the D Notice System. London: Ministry of Defence, 1993.

Gill, Peter. *Policing Politics: Security Intelligence and the Liberal Democratic State.* Hoboken, NJ: Taylor and Francis, 2012.

Shorts, Edwin. *Civil Liberties: Legal Principles of Individual Freedom.* London: Sweet & Maxwell, 1998.

Wilkinson, Nicholas. *Secrecy and the Media: The Official History of the D-notice System. Government Official History Series.* New York: Routledge, 2009.

See also: Electronic surveillance; Snowden, Edward

Descartes, René

Born: March 31, 1596

Died: February 11, 1650

Identification: A French philosopher, mathematician, and scientist. Commonly viewed as the father of modern philosophy, Descartes rejected the traditional Scholastic-Aristotelian philosophy widely accepted in his time. He developed and promoted the new, mechanistic sciences. Descartes believed that the Scholastic method was prone to doubt because of its reliance on sensation as the source of all knowledge. He also sought to replace the Scholastic scientific causal model of scientific explanation with a mechanistic approach.

Descartes attempted to address the former issue through his method of doubt. His basic strategy was to consider false any belief that was

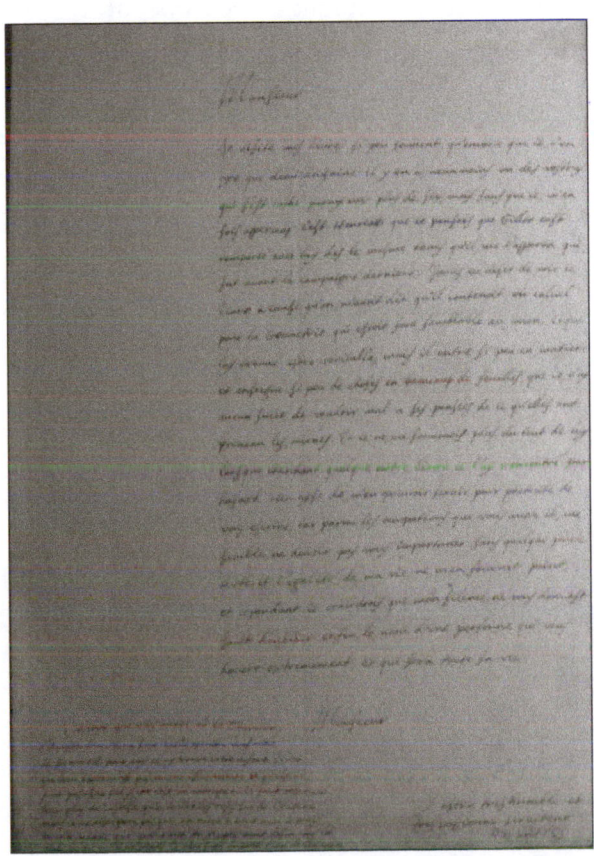

Handwritten letter by Descartes, December 1638. (By PHGCOM.)

subject to even the slightest doubt. This hyperbolic doubt then allowed for what Descartes called an unbiased search for truth. This removal of established beliefs then placed him in a state of *tabula rasa* ("blank state"). From this state, Descartes sought to discover something transcending doubt. He concluded that "I exist" is impossible to doubt and is therefore absolutely certain. Starting at this point, Descartes proceeded to demonstrate that God exists. This, in turn, established the certainty of all that is clearly and distinctly understood and provided the epistemological foundation that Descartes sought to establish.

Once he reached this conclusion, Descartes proceeded to construct his system of previously dubious beliefs on this absolutely certain foundation. These beliefs, which are reestablished with absolute certainty, include the existence of a world of bodies external to the mind, the dualistic distinction of the immaterial mind from the body, and his mechanistic model of physics based on the clear and distinct ideas of geometry. This points toward his second, major break with the Scholastic-Aristotelian tradition: Descartes intended to replace that system based on final causal explanations with his system based on mechanistic principles. Descartes also applied this mechanistic framework to the operation of plant, animal and human bodies, sensation, and the passions. All of this eventually culminated in a moral system based on the notion of generosity.

Rationalist (e.g., Cartesian) philosophy, religion, and perhaps common sense assume that the individual is essentially indivisible. In other words, a person is a person through time. The person is an adult who was once a child. The person changed, but it is the same person who has changed, so the person persists through time. The integral personality is usually based philosophically on some account of the soul, or on pure reason.

The concept that the mind is largely private became a leading part of the Cartesian concept of the self, a concept that is no longer accepted, for several reasons. Descartes not only held that human thoughts were private, he believed they were transparent. However, all thoughts were also conscious. Sigmund Freud disproved this. Descartes also believed that the only way for "special access" to a person's thoughts was to consider thoughts to be composed of a different sort of material than a person's body to take human minds, to be nonphysical, as opposed to the brain. Modern neuroscience and psychology have disproved this part of Cartesian thought.

Descartes's ideas on the connection between privacy and the self continue to be sound. To be an autonomous person is to be capable of having privileged access to information on your own psychological state, such as your hopes, dreams, beliefs, and fears. The capacity for privacy is necessary for autonomous personhood.

If another person could somehow read all your conscious and unconscious thoughts and feelings, he or she could know about them in as much detail as you; and if you could not, in any way, control access of other people, you do not share your thoughts with others; others take them from you. This would give others tremendous power over you. You would not be able to conceal yourself from others. They would instantaneously know a significant amount about how the outside world affects you, what frightens you, what causes you to act the way you do. Others would know what you think and could also control, to a large extent, control what you do.

Political concerns and anxieties about the loss of privacy and freedom are not theoretical. Google's targeted ad programs track Internet searches to transmit ads that reflect a person's interests, and these programs are able to create complicated psychological profiles—especially when an individual searches for emotional or personal advice information. If the government or some entity requests, based on national security concerns, the identity of those who have searched for certain subjects,

such requests could open the door to thought control on a large scale.

What makes an individual's thoughts his or her thoughts is based largely on the philosophical concept of privileged access to them. This entails both that (1) the individual provides access to these thoughts in a way that others cannot (others cannot know what the individual feels in the same way that the individual can), and (2) others can, at least sometimes, control what the individual knows about his or her thoughts. The individual may either hide his or her true feelings from others or let others have the key to his or her heart and soul.

The loss of privacy does not just threaten political freedom. In our example above, the position of the knower would dramatically increase, and the position of the individual as a distinct person would dramatically decrease. The relationship between the two would be so uneven that there might cease to be, at least to the knower, anything subjective about the individual. As the knower learns about the individual's reactions to stimuli, the individual becomes merely another object to manipulate and therefore becomes dehumanized.

The nexus between the loss of privacy and dehumanization is well established. It is used throughout the world in prisons and detention camps. It forms the basis of interrogation methods that strips prisoners, literally and figuratively, of all they own. Prisoners might hide their resentment or bravely resist torture for a while, but when they lose the very capacity to have privileged access to their psychological information, especially the capacity for self-knowledge, they in fact lose themselves.

Further Reading

Ariew, Roger, and Marjorie Grené, eds. *Descartes and His Contemporaries: Meditations, Objections, and Replies.* Chicago, IL: University of Chicago Press, 1995.

Broughton, Janet. *Descartes's Method of Doubt.* Princeton, NJ: Princeton University Press, 2003. Descartes, René. *Philosophical Essays and Correspondence.* 2000.

Dicker, Georges. *Descartes: An Analytical and Historical Introduction.* Oxford, England: Oxford University Press, 1993.

Frankfurt, Harry. *Demons, Dreamers and Madmen: The Defense of Reason in Descartes' Meditations.* Indianapolis, IN: Bobbs-Merrill, 1970.

Garber, Daniel. *Descartes' Metaphysical Physics.* Chicago, IL: University of Chicago Press, 1992. Gaukroger, Stephen. *Descartes: An Intellectual Biography.* Oxford, England: Clarendon Press, 1995.

Kenny, Anthony. *Descartes: A Study of His Philosophy.* New York: Random House, 1968.

Marshall, John. *Descartes's Moral Theory.* Ithaca, NY: Cornell University Press, 1998.

Rodis-Lewis, Genevieve. *Descartes: His Life and Thought,* translated by Jane Marie Todd. Ithaca, NY: Cornell University Press, 1998

Rozemond, Marleen. *Descartes's Dualism.* Cambridge, MA: Harvard University Press, 1998.

Secada, Jorge. *Cartesian Metaphysics: The Late Scholastic Origins of Modern Philosophy.* Cambridge, England: Cambridge University Press, 2000.

Skirry, Justin. *Descartes and the Metaphysics of Human Nature.* London: Thoemmes-Continuum Press, 2005.

Verbeek, Theo. *Descartes and the Dutch: Early Reactions to Cartesian Philosophy 1637–1650.* Carbondale: Southern Illinois University Press, 1994.

See also: Beliefs, privacy of; Natural law of privacy; Philosophical basis of privacy; Theoretical basis of privacy

DNA databases

Identification: Deoxyribonucleic acid (DNA) carries all of the genetic information about an individual and can be retrieved from skin, tissue, organs, muscle, brain cells, bone, teeth, hair, and fingernails, as well as bodily fluids, including saliva, mucus, perspiration, urine, and feces.

A single strand of DNA contains even more information than a medical record, because DNA contains information about potential future medical aliments and/or otherwise unknown medical conditions; information that cannot be found anywhere but in DNA. Therefore, individuals interested in keeping their health records private are most certainly interested in privacy rights related to their DNA. Growing concerns over how this data will be protected, and what this data will ultimately be used for have many questioning the collection and storage of individual DNA. While DNA from a medical perspective may provide positive benefits, the storage of that type of information certainly causes some to question a potential privacy rights issue.

In addition to the potential health-related uses of DNA, this type of information may be used in other areas connected to individual rights and liberties. Because each person's DNA is unique, it is immensely useful for law enforcement in identifying perpetrators of crimes. As more and more DNA is stored in databases that can be searched to find matches used to identify culprits of crimes, more individuals have lost an unprecedented aspect of their privacy. Because of the advancement in DNA technology and use, there are increasing questions about the efficiency and effectiveness of DNA testing in relation to individual privacy rights.

Peter Budowle of the FBI has said, "One attorney . . . had a position that thousands of innocent people are in jail because of DNA typing. That same attorney has this position—thousands of innocent people are in jail because of no DNA typing." The New York State's Division of Criminal Justice Services conducted a research study of New York's use of DNA databases and found that, over an eighteen-month period, thirty-three matches made were in cases in which police had no suspects and had exhausted every possible lead. If DNA databases were not useful for the criminal justice system, they would not be so widely employed. Like many things in the technological revolution, with significant advances come great trade-offs. For example, evidence has been found to suggest that DNA evidence found at a crime scene is not always indicative of an individual's guilt in the crime. So, while technology may indicate a person's guilt, the flaws in this type of evidence may not be accurate. Furthermore, the collection of DNA from an individual to prove or disprove guilt in a crime certainly brings privacy rights into question.

Governing law

Each state has a statute or statutes authorizing the use of DNA databases. One type of DNA database has the DNA of individuals who have been convicted of certain crimes, for example, sex crimes. Another contains the DNA of crimes, including those that are left open and classified as unsolved. The types of DNA databases a statute authorizes depends on each state's enacting language. For example, New York utilizes a database containing all persons convicted of a set list of offenses committed on or after the effective date of the state DNA law. Any person who falls into this category is required to provide a DNA sample. Because of confidentiality and security concerns implicated by privacy issues surrounding the use of DNA databases, most states have privacy provisions that impose sanctions for certain specified unauthorized uses of DNA samples.

Common law also governs the use of DNA evidence. For example, the U.S. Supreme Court has held that DNA evidence is "non-testimonial" in nature; therefore, it does not implicate the Fifth Amendment's prohibition of self-incrimination (*Schimerber v. California*, 384 U.S. 757 (1966)). The Supreme Court has also held that if an officer makes an arrest supported by probable cause, taking a cheek swab for DNA evidence from a suspect while that suspect is being detained and booked is not unlike fingerprinting or other routine police business and thus does not violate the Fourth Amendment. See *Maryland v. King*, 133 S. Ct. 1958 (2013). The Court did determine that swabbing a cheek for DNA is a search within the protections of the Fourth Amendment, but the outcome of the case turned on the Court's balancing of the interests, and the "minimally invasive" cheek swab did not violate Fourth Amendment protections, especially because the court determined that the DNA test did not reveal sensitive personal information. Thus, the state is allowed to collect DNA from a person arrested, but not yet convicted, of a serious crime. The underlying Maryland statute at issue in *King* provided that, should the individual be cleared of the underlying charges, his or her DNA sample must be destroyed.

In courtrooms across the country, DNA evidence has been deemed admissible under both the *Frye* standard (from *Frye v. United States*, 293 F. 1013 (D.C.Cir., 1923)) and the *Daubert* standard of admissibility for scientific evidence (from *Daubert v. Merrill-Dow Pharmaceuticals*, 43 F.3rd 1311 (9th Cir., 1995)). The true ramification of this precedent will unfold over time.

History of DNA in criminal justice

Human forensic identity testing, of which DNA testing is a form, can be traced to the late nineteenth century when different individuals in Argentina and Europe noticed the utility of recognizably unique fingerprint patterns to forensic science. The first modern use of DNA in a criminal investigation took place in 1987. Rather than use a DNA database, which had not yet been established, a technique known as dragnet was employed. The DNA pulled from a large set of people that share a common attribute linked to the crime, such as residents of a town, employees of a company, or owners of a certain car, would voluntarily give their DNA for comparison against DNA retrieved from the crime scene. Should a person refuse, as stated by the chief deputy in West Baton Rouge as well as several other individuals, it was often considered indicative of guilt. If samples obtained for use in a DNA dragnet are not truly voluntary, there is the potential for Fourth Amendment implications.

As the use of DNA evidence became more integrated into the criminal justice system, the first DNA databases were established in 1990. These databases grew in number rapidly in part due to the passage of the 1994 DNA Identification Act. This act ensured police officers could make lawful arrests based on DNA evidence. Today, all fifty states have at least one DNA database as well as Combined DNA Index System (CODIS), the national database in the United

States maintained by the Federal Bureau of Investigation (FBI). The commonplace nature of these databases and the potential rights' ramifications they may have make DNA testing and data storage a contentious issue.

Privacy concerns with DNA databases

While cases such as *Rise v. Oregon* (59 F.3d 1556 (9th Cir. 1995), *cert. denied* 517 U.S. 1160 (1996)) once provoked a general fear that DNA databases statutes would allow for DNA samples to be taken from any mere suspect, state legislatures by and large have not taken that route. While some may argue DNA information should be seriously guarded, others, such as Hugh Miller III, argue genetic information deserves no more protection than does any other protected healthcare information. This issue centers on the issue of whether DNA is fundamentally different from other types of medical records. If it is not considered fundamentally different the same privacy protections currently in place will protect genetic information. When debating this argument, one should consider the nature of DNA and the information it provides, and the fact that information not otherwise revealed in a medical record could be revealed through DNA. The benefits of DNA information, for some, may be worth the potential costs.

Most states have addressed privacy concerns associated with DNA profiles and samples utilizing prohibition clauses complete with consequences for infractions. However, some states have not codified clear rules regarding the fate of a DNA sample after testing. The statute will often prescribe that the profile is to be filed with the DNA database, but the statute is silent about what is to be done with the actual sample. Other states' statutes suggest that the DNA samples should be stored with the state indefinitely. The longer a state retains control of the DNA sample, the greater an individual's risk to privacy.

CODIS

CODIS was established by the FBI after Congress granted the FBI the express power to establish a DNA index in 1994 as part of the DNA Identification Act. CODIS uses data resulting from the analysis of thirteen short, tandem, repeat analysis loci. These specific loci are used because of high degrees of both polymorphism and discrimination potential. Thus, an accurate and reliable match can be established from a profile in the database and a profile from a sample obtained from a crime scene. Because the CODIS loci include the loci used by European and South American databases, CODIS is compatible with those systems; in other words, DNA from CODIS can be searched in the European and South American databases, and vice versa.

There are two separate CODIS indexes (just as many states employ two similar systems at the state level): the Convicted Offender Index, with profiles of those who have been convicted of violent crimes, and the Forensic Index, with DNA profiles derived from samples obtained from crime scenes. In addition to the profile, CODIS has information on the original specimen, the laboratory that processed the DNA, and the names of laboratory employees that handled the specimen. Such information is useful should a breach of privacy be alleged. The genetic profiles themselves are protected because only authorized individuals have access to them. Still, privacy concerns surrounding a national database remain.

To abate the same privacy concerns that surround state databases mentioned above, the DNA Identification Act of 1994, 108 Stat. 2065, authorizes a fine of no more than $100,000 for knowingly improper disclosure or unauthorized acquisition of individually identifiable information from CODIS. If a criminal justice agency does not implement certain measures that are designed to protect privacy, that agency's access to CODIS may be canceled.

Conclusion

When the government begins collecting DNA and retains the file on that DNA sample in a database, many privacy implications arise, as do many benefits for the criminal justice system. To best protect privacy, enabling statutes should be narrowly drafted and narrowly construed. Protecting the fate for the samples from which profiles are derived is also crucial to ensure civil liberty protections. Both courts and legislatures, as well as voters, will have important key roles in ensuring that privacy is protected as the use of DNA databases becomes more standard and widely used.

Julie Ann Embler

Further Reading

Kobilinsky, Lawrence F., Thomas F. Liotti, and Jamel Oeser-Sweat. DNA: *Forensic and Legal Applications*. Hoboken, NJ: Wiley-Interscience, 2005.

Murphy, Erin E. *Inside the Cell: The Dark Side of Forensic Data*. New York, NY: Nation Books, 2015.

Lazer, David, *ed. DNA and the Criminal Justice System: The Technology of Justice*. Cambridge, MA: MIT Press, 2004.

Webster, Warren R., Jr. "DNA Database Statutes & Privacy in the Information Age." *Health Matrix: Journal of Law-Medicine* 10, no. 1 (Winter 2000): 119. *Academic Search Premier*, EBSCOhost (accessed September 26, 2015).

See also: Background Checks; Health Information; National Instant Criminal Background Check System (NICS)

Do-not-track legislation

Identification: A series of legislative efforts to give Internet users the option to choose not to have their online behavior tracked by third parties.

Regular Internet use involves constant interaction between the user and various entities, including large corporations such as Google and Facebook. During these interactions, the Internet users provide identifying information to third parties. This information, such as IP addresses and browsing history, can be used to track and profile the online behaviors of the user. For example, many websites store a piece of data, called a cookie, on the user's computer. From these cookies, advertising services can determine what websites the user has visited. This record can be used to build a profile of that user's potential interests. In turn, this behavior profile can be used to display targeted ads to which the user is more likely to respond.

Cookies were first used in 1994 as a way for a website to remember session history between user visits. The creation of the cookie was responsible for many modern Internet features, such as virtual shopping carts and persistent logins. Third-party cookie usage was quickly identified as a consumer privacy problem, drawing the attention of the Federal Trade Commission (FTC). Subsequently, Internet privacy advocates have attempted to respond to this threat by proposing cookie management policies that limit or prevent the storage of cookies on a web user's computer. Many web browsers have implemented features specifically designed for cookie control. Successive cookie-like technologies, however, such as the local shared objects stored by Adobe's Flash, have been developed to circumvent advances in privacy controls.

Privacy concerns arising from using this type of online behavioral tracking in social networking, advertising services, and web page analytics have resulted in international legislative efforts to protect a web user's ability to choose not to participate in such tracking. In March 2011, the FTC recommended that Congress impose restrictions on web behavior tracking, including the implementation of a uniform do-not-track mechanism for web browsers. Since 2011, a series of bills have been introduced in the United States based on the issue of behavioral tracking.

The Do Not Track Me Online Act of 2011, proposed to authorize the FTC to promulgate regulations that would require companies to abide by opt-out settings. The act would have enabled the FTC to impose fines on services that continue to track users who have chosen the do-not-track setting, while allowing exceptions for websites using such information for their own website analytics, websites serving less than 10,000 visitors per year, and websites belonging to the government. The FTC would have been authorized to enforce these regulations through random audits (H.R. 654, 112th Cong. (2011)).

The similarly titled Do Not Track Online Act of 2011 proposed that the FTC establish standards by which a user could indicate whether he or she wished to opt out but excepted information necessary to provide services requested by the user. Under this act, the FTC would be obligated to enforce compliance with the do-not-track standards (S. 913, 112th Cong. (2011)). This act was reintroduced in 2013 (S. 418, 113th Cong. (2013)).

Also proposed in 2011 was the Consumer Privacy Protection Act of 2011, which proposed to balance consumer and business interests by requiring a notice and an opt-out mechanism for third-party use of personally identifiable information for targeted advertising. The FTC would have been charged with creating a safe harbor program, which would have individually accepted entities with privacy practices with substantially the same notice and data collection practices as those required by the act (S. 799, 112th Cong. (2011)).

The Commercial Privacy Bill of Rights Act of 2011 would have required websites to provide clear notice to the users and give them the opportunity to opt out or opt in to their information being collected. This act incorporated an exception for companies that collect data but are conspicuous and visible to the users and have preexisting relationships with the user. This proposal limited protection to a user's more sensitive data such as medical, financial, and religious information (S. 799, 112th Cong. (2011)).

Subsequently, the Commercial Privacy Bill of Rights Act of 2014 was proposed. The first portion of the act targeted companies that collect, use, transfer, or store personally identifiable information, requiring them to provide increased notice to the customer of their data usage and means to access and correct stored information. As with the Commercial Privacy Bill of Rights Act of 2011, tracking services must provide opt-in or opt-out opportunities. The second part of the act was an amendment to the Children's Online Privacy Protection Act of 1998, 112 Stat. 2681– 728, referred to as the Do Not Track Kids Act of 2014. It was intended to expand the prohibition on collecting information about children from websites and online services to online and mobile applications (S. 2378, 113th Cong. (2014)).

The Obama administration released a draft legislation of a Consumer Privacy Bill of Rights Act of 2012 in February 2012. This proposal sought to provide additional protection for the customer by addressing the commercial uses of personal data and information. This proposal incorporated several concepts from earlier acts, including mandating the secured handling of customer data and ensuring a user's ability to access and correct stored data. This draft legislation was reintroduced in 2015 as the Consumer Privacy Bill of Rights Act of 2015, along with the companion bill, the Data Security and Breach Notification Act of 2015. This bill expanded on the original draft by proposing to permit services and industries to create their own regulatory standards, subject to approval by the FTC (S. 1158, 114th Cong. (2015)).

Although no Federal general do-not-track legislation has been enacted, California managed to enact Assembly Bill AB 370 in 2013. This legislation amended a section of the California Business and Professions Code and required websites that collect personally identifiable information about California residents to provide explicit privacy policies that clearly identify which types of personal information they are collecting. The bill also mandated that websites and services describe how they respond to do-not-track signals or other actions that indicate a user's tracking preference.

Beyond legislative efforts, the FTC has worked with the advertisement industry to provide a private solution to unwanted behavior tracking. For example, the Digital Advertising Alliance promoted a self-regulatory solution that would permit users to opt out of targeted ads, and most of the major web browsing platforms incorporate tracking control features.

Some privacy advocates have noted a retreat from do-not-track efforts since the legislative push of 2011-2012. Though sporadic efforts were made in the U.S. Congress, such as the Do Not Track Kids Act in 2015 and the Do Not Track Act in 2016, both failed to get a vote. In February 2019, Apple announced that it would be removing a "do not track" option from its Safari browser. Much of the difficulty with "do not track" initiatives, whether from legislative or corporate sources, revolves around the fact that compliance by websites with these user preferences is voluntary. Some efforts have been made to introduce "plug-ins" for browsers that prevent cookies from tracking user activity and to notify users whether or not the website they are accessing has agreed to honor their privacy requests. However, these efforts cannot truly prevent tracking, and are mainly information for users so that they can make decisions for themselves as to how they would like to proceed.

Mary E. Ernhart

Further Reading

Campbell, James, et al. "Privacy Regulation and Market Structure." *Journal of Economics & Management Strategy* 24 (2015): 47–73. http://ssrn.com/abstract=1729405.

Chmielewski, Dawn. "How 'Do Not Track' Ended Up Going Nowhere." *Recode.* January 4, 2016. https://www.recode.net/2016/1/4/11588418/how-do-not-track-ended-up-going-nowhere

Garbin, Brigette, et al. "Tracking Legislative Developments in Relation to 'Do Not Track' Initiatives." *In Uberveillance and the Social Implications of Microchip Implants: Emerging Technologies*, edited by M. G. Michael and Katina Michael. Hershey, PA: Information Science Reference, 2014.

Garcia, Ahiza. "What Apple killing its Do Not Track feature means for online privacy." *CNN*, February 13, 2019. https://www.cnn.com/2019/02/13/tech/apple-do-not-track-feature/index.html

Kristol, David M. "HTTP Cookies: Standards, Privacy, and Politics." *ACM Transaction on Internet Technology* 1, no. 2 (2001).

Soltani, Ashkan, et al. "Behavioral Advertising: The Offer You Cannot Refuse.", *Harvard Law & Policy Review* 6, no. 273 (2012)

See also: Anti-forensics; Children's Online Privacy Protection Act (COPPA); Cookies; Data Breaches; Federal Trade Commission (FTC); General Data Protection Regulation; Privacy Laws, Federal; Privacy Laws, State; Right to be forgotten

Douglas, William Orville

Born: October 16, 1898
Died: January 19, 1980
Identification: The longest serving U.S. Supreme Court justice. Not surprisingly, Justice Douglas authored more opinions than any other justice in U.S. history. Douglas became best known for his civil liberties jurisprudence and was a reliable liberal voice throughout the entire Warren Court era. Douglas wrote the opinion of the Court in one of the most significant cases addressing privacy rights, *Griswold v. Connecticut*.

William Orville Douglas was born in 1898 in Maine, Minnesota, but spent most of his childhood in Yakima, Washington. According to Douglas, childhood illness encouraged him to be active outdoors, establishing a deep appreciation of the environment that informed his work as an early environmentalist. Douglas attended Whitman College and was a high school teacher for two years before entering Columbia University Law School. After briefly practicing law, Douglas joined the Columbia law faculty, later teaching at Yale Law School in 1928. Douglas's reputation as an academic was superb; University of Chicago president Robert Maynard Hutchins referred to

Douglas as "the most outstanding law professor in the nation."

In 1934, President Franklin Roosevelt appointed Douglas to the newly formed Securities and Exchange Commission (SEC), and in 1937 appointed him as chair. In the wake of the Great Depression, Douglas earned a reputation for being a liberal crusader at the SEC. In 1939, Roosevelt nominated him as an associate justice to succeed the retiring Louis D. Brandeis, a nomination that drew little opposition.

Justice Douglas was one of Roosevelt's final two potential running mates to join him on the Democratic ticket in 1944, but Roosevelt ultimately selected the other, Harry Truman. Douglas, whose personal ambition for the presidency was well known, was stung by the slight. Roosevelt's death and Truman's rise to the presidency bothered Douglas even more, and he refused Truman's later offer to accept a vice presidential nomination.

Justice Douglas's notable jurisprudence largely focused on individual rights, especially those protected by the First Amendment. His appointment to replace Justice Brandeis was especially remarkable because Brandeis, along with Professor Samuel Warren, is widely credited with first articulating a constitutional right to privacy. Douglas would eventually author the majority opinion in *Griswold v. Connecticut,* in which the Court clearly articulated a right to privacy, at least in the context of marriage. In a brief opinion, Douglas asserted that various guarantees in the Bill of Rights contained "emanations" that formed "penumbras" creating a zone of privacy. Only one other justice— Thomas C. Clark— joined Douglas's opinion without also issuing a separate concurrence finding the right affected by Connecticut's contraception ban elsewhere in the Constitution. Though Douglas's word choice has been derided extensively, the greater failing of his majority opinion is that it was unpersuasive and unsupported, resulting in an articulation of a right to privacy that has rarely been cited in subsequent cases. For instance, *Griswold* is often understood as enabling *Roe v. Wade.* Even the majority in *Roe,* however, did not rely on Douglas's *Griswold* rationale.

Justice Douglas's opinions have been widely criticized by scholars, and even fellow jurists, as sloppy and ill-supported. One former clerk reported Douglas often drafted opinions hastily ("many were drafted in 20 minutes") and published without meaningful revision. Some jurists and scholars who agree with Douglas's inclinations and conclusions lament his weak opinions, which ultimately had little precedential power and were easy to ignore. Even fellow liberal Justice William J. Brennan Jr. complained about the "slovenliness" of Douglas's opinions.

Ultimately, Justice Douglas's jurisprudence seems to have fallen short of the intellectual capacity and energy he demonstrated as a student and professor, though scholars disagree about the cause of Douglas's unrealized potential as a justice. Some have argued that Douglas's sloppy jurisprudence was consistent with, or even caused by, his personal failings, including notorious womanizing (over a thirteen-year span, Douglas was married four times and openly flouted extramarital affairs) and problems with alcohol. Another legal theorist has asserted that, although Douglas was sure of his convictions, they were, the theorist thought, a product of his biases rather than universal truth, and thus Douglas had no right or responsibility to convince others. Some have also suggested that Douglas's extrajudicial writing—he wrote thirty books while on the Court—left him with little time to focus on his work as a Supreme Court justice. Finally, some scholars have contended that Douglas's disappointment at not achieving the presidency caused him to be uninterested in his jurisprudential responsibilities.

Following a stroke in 1975, Justice Douglas reluctantly retired from the bench. He died in Washington, DC, in 1980.

Eric Merriam

Further Reading

Douglas, William O. *The Court Years*. New York: Random House, 1980.

_____. *Go East, Young Man: The Early Years*. New York: Random House, 1974.

Murphy, Bruce. *Wild Bill: The Legend and Life of William O. Douglas*. New York: Random House, 2003.

Rosen, Jeffrey. *The Supreme Court: The Personalities and Rivalries That Defined America*. New York: Times Books, 2006.

Simon, James F. *Independent Journey: The Life of William O. Douglas*. New York: Harper & Row, 1980.

See also: Brandeis, Louis Dembitz; *Griswold v. Connecticut*; The Right to Privacy; Supreme Court of the United States; Warren, Earl

Doxing

Identification: (Also spelled doxxing or doxing), the sharing of someone's personal information on the Internet without their consent. Information shared in doxing is personal, such as cellphone numbers and work or home addresses. Sometimes it includes more sensitive material, such as Social Security numbers, personal messages, and photos.

The word "dox" derives from having someone's documents, or information, which was shortened to "docs" and then to "dox." It is an abbreviation of "dropping dox," a revenge tactic used on hacker bulletin boards in the 1990s. As much of hacker culture depended on anonymity, disclosing someone's personal information (or PI) was a way to retaliate against them in an argument, show them to be vulnerable, and open them up to harassment or prosecution if they were breaking any laws. While initially doxing mostly revealed user profile information, the tactic expanded as the Internet grew.

In 2006, a YouTube channel called Vigilantes was created. Its mission was to locate and publish the personal information of other YouTube channels that posted what Vigilantes deemed to be hateful or racist content. In January 2007, the head of the Vigilantes group was doxed by members of Encyclopedia Dramatica. The information included her name, address, and personal posts she made to a newsgroup.

At this point in time, the hacker collective Anonymous and associated groups, such as Chan Enterprises LLC and Lulzsec, began to use doxing in targeted campaigns. One of the first documented doxing campaigns focused on white nationalist and radio host Hal Turner. Turner shared the telephone numbers of prank callers that phoned in to his radio show in December 2006. In response, Anonymous members calling themselves Chan Enterprises LLC began a doxing investigation that discovered Turner's criminal record, home address, and phone number, which they posted. Turner filed several lawsuits against the online forums and websites that posted his dox, such as 4chan, eBaums World, and 7chan, in January 2007. However, all the cases were dismissed by December of that year.

Forums like 4chan and 7chan are similar to Reddit, except that they have no user names and few rules. They are considered to be the antithesis of social media, where people anonymously say and post whatever they wish with few or no consequences. These forums are often hosts to doxing campaigns or other anonymous postings. For instance, 4chan was blamed for the leaks of many female celebrity nudes.

In January 2008, anonymous hackers started Project Chanology, a doxing campaign that targeted members of Scientology. The hackers published the personal information of high-ranking members and internal memos from the church. This doxing campaign received international coverage.

By 2008, the term "doxing" had become more widely known and was added to Urban Dictionary, which defined it as personal information leaked by a third party. Wikitionary added a "doxing" definition in 2011. Today, the term appears in mainstream dictionaries such as the Oxford British and World English Dictionary, which added the term in 2015.

The definition of doxing is generally perceived to be negative, as it violates privacy and was historically used for retaliation. However, there is some debate about whether doxing is, at times, warranted, when the goals achieved outweigh a person's privacy and anonymity. There are a wide variety of motives for doxing someone.

Internet vigilantism often uses doxing, where those who disagree with an individual's actions publish the person's personal information so that they are subject to harassment and criticism. Groups on both the left and the right of the political spectrum have employed this technique. It is not just political or hacker groups that use doxing. In July 2015, newspapers reported that Cecil the Lion was illegally killed by a hunter from Minnesota. *The Telegraph*, a British newspaper, identified the hunter as a dentist from Minnesota. His address, website, work, and vacation homes were vandalized and he received death threats and protests.

Doxing can serve as a tool for protest or exposing corruption. Government corruption in China was the target of the "Human Flesh Search Engine," a group of Internet citizens who search for and publish information about government wrongdoing. One of their doxes exposed government officials using public funds for recreational trips.

Sometimes doxing is used to expose perceived wrongdoing. In 2015, a group of hackers called the "Impact Team" breached the Ashley Madison database. The online dating site catered to married people wishing to have affairs. The hackers demanded that the site shut down permanently or they would dox the information they obtained. When the site remained up, the hackers released 30 million user email addresses and profiles. The doxing led to several suicides, extortion attempts, and general embarrassment.

Certain types of investigative journalism can have the effect of doxing, such as the disclosure of the identity of the presumed Bitcoin inventor, Satoshi Nakamoto. This has spurred debate about where the line between investigative journalism and doxing lies, and whether and when it might be acceptable to disclose the names of individuals that are making efforts to remain anonymous.

Doxing is most commonly understood to be a means of harassment or a form of cyberbullying. It is intended to threaten someone and make them feel vulnerable. In the worst cases, it is used in "cyber-stalking" and makes someone fearful for their safety or life to the point where they need to go into hiding.

A Pew Research Center survey in 2014 stated that 40 percent of adult Internet users have experienced some form of harassment and 7 percent have experienced "sustained" periods of harassment. Since information on the Internet is difficult to erase, a dox may haunt the targeted person both personally and professionally for years. All one has to do is enter the person's name into a search engine for the material to come back up.

Due to the difficult task of fighting this sort of harassment, numerous groups have formed to offer support to victims of doxing. For instance, Crash Override Network is "a crisis helpline, advocacy group and resource center for people who are experiencing online abuse." The group was formed by two victims of doxing during "Gamergate," a 2014-2015 campaign of online harassment against women gamers, developers, and videogame critics.

Since the launch of the service, they have assisted over 400 clients. They offer the assistance of social workers, lawyers and computer security professionals. Doxing is the most frequent sort of harassment they encounter, as it is relatively easy to find information about someone on the Internet and it has a strong impact. The harasser is also able to rationalize doxing actions as benign and deny responsibility for other's actions, even though the intention is to violate another's personal space and sense of security.

As the Internet has evolved, opportunities to share personal data have increased in myriad ways, such as through social media, online shopping, and other means. Doxing, through its use and misuse, highlights the challenge of balancing online interconnection with anonymity and privacy, both personally and in relation to others.

Noëlle Sinclair

Further Reading

Citron, Danielle Keats. *Hate Crimes in Cyberspace*. Cambridge, MA: Harvard University Press, 2014.

Crash Override Network. "So You've Been Doxed: A Guide to Best Practices." Crashoverridenetwork.com. Last modified February, 2019. http://www.crashoverridenetwork.com/soyouvebeendoxed.html

Douglas, David M. "Doxing: A Conceptual Analysis." *Ethics and Information Technology* 18, no. 3 (2016): 199-210.

Harcourt, Bernard E. *Exposed: Desire and Disobedience in the Digital Age*. Cambridge, MA: Harvard University Press, 2015.

Li, Lisa Bei. "Data Privacy in the Cyber Age: Recommendations for Regulating Doxing and Swatting."*Federal Communications Law Journal* 70, no. 3 (2018): 317-328.

Pew Research Center. "The Future of Free Speech, Trolls, Anonymity, and Fake News Online, 2017." Elon. edu. Last modified February, 2019. http://www.elon. edu/docs/e-web/imagining/surveys/2016_survey/ Pew%20and%20Elon%20University%20Trolls%20 Fake%20News%20Report%20Future%20of%20 Internet%203.29.17.pdf

See also: Data protection regimes; Email; Hacking, computer; Identity theft; News leaks; Plame affair; Private sphere

Driver's Privacy Protection Act of 1994 (DDPA), 18 U.S.C. 2271–2725

Identification: Enacted by the U.S. Congress, a federal statutory scheme that regulated the disclosure of driver information in states' motor vehicle department records.

The Driver's Privacy Protection Act of 1994 (DPPA) was passed as part of the Violent Crime Control and Law Enforcement Act of 1994, 108 Stat. 2102, and became effective on September 13, 1997. Generally, DPPA instituted a regulatory scheme that restricted the use of drivers' personal information that was collected for state motor vehicle records. DPPA provided a limited number of acceptable uses of drivers' information; some disclosures were allowed without restriction and others required a driver's consent.

Two factors largely spurred the enactment of DPPA: (1) a majority of the states allowed any individual to pay for access to state motor vehicle department records, and (2) criminal activity related to the use of information obtained from motor vehicle records appeared to be increasing. In particular, criminals used vehicle license plate numbers to obtain drivers' home addresses. Using that information, criminals committed thefts, stalking, and violent crimes. Women were especially targeted. The most infamous of these cases involved the murder of actress Rebecca Shaeffer in 1989, in California. Schaeffer's killer obtained her unlisted home address through California state motor vehicle records.

Broadly, DPPA restricts the disclosure of personal information collected in connection with a state motor vehicle record, which includes "an individual's photograph, social security number, driver identification number, name, address (but not the five-digit zip code), telephone number, and medical or disability information" (18 U.S.C. 2725[3] [2012]). DPPA provides a number of exceptions to the disclosure restriction. Generally these exceptions are triggered when the information is used in the course of federal or state government functions or for public safety purposes.

DPPA generally prohibits the disclosure of information, but states may release a driver's personal information to private parties with a driver's consent. When it was originally enacted, DPPA provided that drivers' consent to the release of their information was presumed as long as the driver was given the opportunity to opt out of disclosure and had not done so. DPPA was amended shortly after its effective date, however, to remove the implied consent clause, and it instead required that states obtain a driver's express consent to disclosure of personal information.

Individuals who violate DPPA may be subject to criminal fines. States that violate DPPA may be subject to a $5,000 penalty for each day of noncompliance. If an individual obtains a driver's personal information unlawfully, the driver may bring a civil suit against the individual.

Several states perceived DPPA as an unconstitutional overreach that amounted to the U.S. Congress governing the behavior of state and local authorities. Private entities, including those that had benefited from using drivers' information for marketing purposes, also objected to DPPA on similar grounds. As a result DPPA's constitutionality was challenged several times in federal court. Initially, the result of those challenges was mixed: DPPA was held unconstitutional (*Pryor v. Reno*, 171 F.3d 1281 [11th Cir. 1999]); yet other jurisdictions determined that it was constitutional (*Travis v. Reno*, 163 F.3d 1000 [7th Cir. 1998]); *Oklahoma ex rel. Okla. Dep't of Public Safety v. United States*, 161 F.3d 1266 [10th Cir. 1998]).

Ultimately, following a constitutional challenge initiated by South Carolina and its attorney general, the U.S. Supreme Court resolved the constitutionality of DPPA in *Reno v. Condon*, 528 U.S. 141 (2000), concluding that DPPA did not violate Tenth Amendment federalism principles. At the time of the suit, South Carolina had enacted its own legislation governing the sale of drivers' information, and the state believed that DPPA infringed upon its sovereignty in violation of the Tenth Amendment to the U.S. Constitution. Notably, South Carolina had passed its legislation partially in response to uproar caused by the state's sale of driver's license pictures to a private company.

After the U.S. Court of Appeals for the Fourth Circuit agreed with the U.S. District Court for the District of South Carolina that DPPA was unconstitutional, but prior to the Supreme Court's review of the case, Congress amended DPPA. In part, Congress's amendment conditioned state compliance with DPPA on receipt of federal transportation funds (113 Stat. 986).

DPPA's civil and criminal penalties for noncompliance remained in force. Congress stated that DPPA was enacted pursuant to its U.S. Constitution commerce clause powers and, in light of the transportation fund provision, its spending clause powers. Following this amendment, the case proceeded to the Supreme Court. Before the Supreme Court, the parties in *Reno* argued over the effect of the claimed spending clause authority for DPPA. Yet the Court ultimately focused on whether DPPA was a constitutional exercise of Congress's authority under the commerce clause, and it found that DPPA was constitutional.

Since the Supreme Court's ruling in *Reno*, courts have further outlined the strictures of permissible uses of personal information under DPPA. For instance, a Pennsylvania state court determined that the receipt of funds from the federal Department of Transportation by the Pennsylvania Department of Conservation and Natural Resources caused it to fall under the strictures of DPPA. Consequently, information collected in relation to the registration of snowmobiles was subject to DPPA disclosure restrictions (*Hartman v. Dep't of Conservation and Natural Resources*, 892 A.2d 897, 901–902 [Pa. Commw. Ct. 2006]). The U.S. Supreme Court revisited DPPA in *Maracich v. Spears*, 133 S. Ct. 2191 (2013), wherein the Supreme Court held that DPPA's permissible use exception for information that is used in anticipation of litigation did not extend to attorneys seeking to solicit clients for a class action suit against car dealerships.

Paul Riermaier

Further Reading

Berg, Candace D. "Widening the Lane: An Argument for Broader Interpretation of Permissible Uses under the Driver's Privacy Protection Act." *Notre Dame Law Review* 90, no. 2 (2014): 847–873.

Buckman, Deborah F. "Validity, Construction, and Application of Federal Driver's Privacy Protection Act, 18 U.S.C.A. §§ 2721 to 2725." *American Law Reports, Federal* 183 (2003).

Davis, Michelle R., and Wilson, David L. "S.C. Ranks Worst in Guarding Residents' Privacy—Journal

Study Gave State Only Negative Score in U.S." *The Charlotte Observer* (Charlotte, North Carolina), October 6, 1999.

Maginnis, Maureen. "Maintaining the Privacy of Personal Information: The DPPA and the Right of Privacy." *South Carolina Law Review* 51 (2000): 807–822.

See also: Constitutional Law; Privacy Laws, Federal; Privacy Laws, State; *Reno v. Condon*; Stalking; Supreme Court of the United States

Drones

Identification: Unmanned aerial vehicles (UAVs).

While unmanned aircraft have been part of the history of aviation from the early days of the industry, the word *drone* was initially associated with sizable military unmanned flying devices. Recently, the concept has expanded to include a multitude of unpiloted flying machines, from small devices used for leisure to prototypes developed for potential use in commerce, to surveillance drones designed for law enforcement, to small- and large-scale models currently employed by the military.

There are two main types of drones: law enforcement and civil drones. Drones are already in use for law enforcement purposes in the United States and several other countries. Apart from hobbyist drones which are small and used for recreational purposes, civil drones have not yet been authorized to fly in the United States—although proposals to regulate this matter are currently under review. Europe, on the other hand, has an estimated 2,500 civil drone operators of small proportions, which surpasses the number of civil drones in use in the rest of the world. This landscape could change quickly; the number of entities that will receive authorization to fly drones in the United States is set to increase rapidly, with the Federal Aviation Administration (FAA) estimating that that number might be around 30,000 by 2020.

In accordance with the FAA Modernization and Reform Act of 2012, 126 Stat. 11, the

The RQ-16 T-Hawk, a Micro Air Vehicle (MAV), flies over a simulated combat area during an operational test flight. (By United States Navy; photo by Mass Communication Specialist 3rd Class Kenneth G. Takada)

FAA is currently considering several proposals that would set requirements for, and allow the use of, civil unmanned flying devices. In addition to regulating the use of civil drones, the act also made the licensing process for law enforcement drones less cumbersome. In 2012, the Electronic Frontier Foundation sued the FAA under the Freedom of Information Act, 80 Stat. 250 (1967), seeking the disclosure of the identity of entities that had requested authorization to use drones. As a result, the FAA disclosed the names and details regarding drone license applications from sixty public entities and twelve private drone manufacturers interested in flying drones in the United States. In addition to bringing the 2012 lawsuit, the Electronic Frontier Foundation partnered with collaborative news organization MuckRock to conduct a drone census by making available forms anyone can use to request public records from police agencies regarding drone-based surveillance and related protection of privacy rights.

Both law enforcement and civil drones raise significant privacy issues. In the United States, as in the rest of the world, privacy law has yet to develop to encompass the concerns that widespread use of drones entails. In the case of law enforcement drones, existing case law is insufficient to deal with the nuances of drone surveillance, particularly in matters related to warrantless surveillance and the boundaries of long-term surveillance. As far as civil drones are concerned, it is likely that many of these drones will record or gather personal information unrelated to the tasks they are authorized to perform. In the United States, a regulatory framework dealing with these and other issues is expected to emerge soon.

In addition to privacy concerns regarding the gathering and use of personal information, the use of drones and their regulation also triggers privacy-related concerns in connection with the First and Fourth amendments to the United States Constitution. For example, the question of whether or not drones will be considered a means of unreasonable search and seizure (which we are protected against in the Fourth Amendment) will more than likely arise. Recently developed technology allows drones to collect information from increasingly greater distances without loss of accuracy, a development that raises significant concerns regarding privacy rights and expectations of privacy. For instance, drones can be placed on public property and nonetheless be used to conduct unreasonable searches without physical contact ever occurring.

Most drones are equipped with an extensive range of sensors; global positioning systems and imaging, image-intensification, and acoustic and radio technology rank among the most common features. Other features may include thermal imaging, which provides the ability to observe targets with or without illumination, or electronic olfaction, through which a drone can electronically detect and recognize odors. Discrete technologies currently being employed by or tested on drones are often combined with one another and may be combined with other surveillance-enhancing technology, such as statistical analysis functions to enable crossing of data.

While many of these technologies are routinely used in other areas, most complex forms of technology capable of being used in drones, such as highly sensitive imaging radars, are not available for civil use. Even if the FAA authorizes use of civil drones, it will not be possible to use military technology in civil drones. The United States Munitions List of the Code of Federal Regulations, 22 C.F.R. § 121.1, classifies drones that "are specifically designed, modified, or equipped for military purposes" as restricted "munitions." According to federal law, drones may also be considered "defense articles" if they possess "significant military or intelligence applicability." Nevertheless, manufacturers of civil drones are increasingly exploring the development and incorporation of several technologies that were first developed by or for the military, or that are still commonly used in the military field. This is the case with positions-tracking technology or a wide array of different kinds of imaging systems.

The incorporation of different kinds of potentially intrusive technology into drones, including for use in civil drones, combined with their ability to operate pervasively from a distance without being noticed creates new challenges in adapting existing privacy laws. One currently evolving issue is interpretation of the Fourth Amendment as applied to the use of law enforcement drones. There have been technology-specific decisions that shed some light on certain features commonly adopted by drone manufacturers. For instance, the *Kyllo v. United States* case, 533 U.S. 27 (2001), established that thermal imaging of a private home constitutes a search for purposes of the Fourth Amendment and therefore requires a warrant. There have also been cases dealing broadly with remote technology, such as the decision in *Katz v. United States*, 389 U.S. 347 (1967), in which the Supreme Court held that the Fourth Amendment protects people not merely from physical intrusions but also from electronic or remote forms of government intrusion. Both technology-specific decisions and other generic privacy case law are helpful in delineating privacy rights vis-à-vis the Fourth Amendment and function as the likely starting point in building a body of law applicable to use of law enforcement drones. They are unlikely to accommodate all the nuances, however, that the current fast-paced development of drones is poised to bring about. For instance, several of the technological features that can be incorporated into a drone may call into question the meaning of "plain view" for purposes of the plain view doctrine. Under certain conditions, this doctrine allows the police to perform seizures without a warrant if officers are lawfully present in a location otherwise protected from intrusions by the Fourth Amendment. Because drones enable observation and surveillance in unprecedented ways, the scope and boundaries of plain view will likely need to be reevaluated. Similarly, drones have the ability to stretch the temporal limits of warrantless long-term observation and surveillance to unheard-of levels, and therefore a new body of case law will likely be needed to set standards in this field.

The interplay between types of information collected by military drones employed on a specific mission and the plain view doctrine is also poised to come under closer scrutiny. Data transmitted or recorded during a military mission may include extraneous information that may be relevant in a different context. This information, if sought by law enforcement agents, is likely to fall outside the scope of the plain view doctrine, which is certainly a privacy concern.

The imminent approval of the use of civil drones in the United States is also likely to challenge many current legal standards that affect privacy. For instance, the legal concept of trespassing will likely need to be reexamined as drones start permeating civil channels, as incorporation of multiple technologies leads to a blurring of the boundaries between physical and remote or electronic contact. Widespread use of civilian drones—particularly if the use of drones in commerce becomes common—is

also likely to push the boundaries of the concept of reasonable expectation of privacy because the drones will fly across both public and private spaces.

Impending civil drone privacy regulation may clash with the First Amendment to the U.S. Constitution as well because it has the potential to intersect with freedom of expression. One of the areas in which challenges have occurred is photography; some states have introduced or sought to introduce legislation that would ban or criminalize drone photography of certain places, such as bridges or highways. Privacy drone legislation might also affect freedom of the press, which is also shielded by the First Amendment, particularly through the establishment of no-fly zones to prevent media coverage. That was the case during the Ferguson, Missouri, protests of 2014, in which the FAA banned low-flying aircraft over an area where riots had been taking place.

In addition to the state level, debate surrounding regulation of the privacy implications of drones in the United States has also occurred at the federal level. The Preserving American Privacy Act (H.R. 637), introduced in the 113th Congress (2013–2014), sought to regulate extensively the use of drones by both law enforcement agencies and private parties, but it did not pass. The development of drone technology and impending laws that will increase the presence of drones will certainly bring about legal questions that will need to be answered in an attempt to uphold privacy rights in the United States.

Ana Santos Rutschman

Further Reading

Calo, M. Ryan. "The Drone as Privacy Catalyst." *Stanford Law Review* 64 (2011): 29–33. Carter, Stephen. "A Battlefield of Drones and Privacy in Your Backyard." *Chicago Tribune*, August 3, 2015.

New York Times Editorial Board. "Regulating the Drone Economy," February 19, 2015.

Schlag, Chris. "The New Privacy Battle: How the Expanding Use of Drones Continues to Erode Our Concept of Privacy and Privacy Rights." *Pittsburgh Journal of Technology Law and Policy* 13, no. 2 (Spring 2013).

See also: Electronic Frontier Foundation; Federal Freedom of Information Act (FOIA); First Amendment to the U.S. Constitution; Fourth Amendment to the U.S. Constitution; Global Positioning Systems; *Katz v. United States*; *Kyllo v. United States*

Drug and alcohol testing

Identification: Substances that can affect a human's biological and neurological states. They may be organic, such as the chemical tetrahydrocarmabinol (THC), which occurs naturally in marijuana; or synthetic, such as amphetamines or sedatives, which are manufactured in laboratories.

Drugs can be swallowed, injected with a needle, applied to the skin, taken as a suppository, or smoked. Narcotics are any drugs that dull the senses and commonly become addictive after prolonged use. Authority to regulate drug use rests foremost with the federal government, derived from its power to regulate interstate commerce. Federal law prohibits and punishes the manufacture, possession, and sale of illegal drugs from marijuana to heroin, as well as some dangerous legal drugs.

The war on drugs originated in the 1960s when illicit drugs were becoming increasingly popular. The increase in drug use led the administration of President Richard Nixon to introduce comprehensive anti-drug legislation in what he called the War on Drugs.

Prior to the mid-1980's, employee drug testing was a non-issue because only a very small proportion of the workforce was subjected to such testing. During the 1980's several factors coalesced to make drug testing a major workplace issue. Increases in drug-related urban crime lead to an intensified "war on drugs" in the United States, which shifted its focus somewhat from attacking supply to attacking demand. Concerns were raise regarding public safety as the possible threat of "on-the-job impairment" especially in the transportation sector—was raised. Such testing was also justified in the name of enhancing employee productivity, and reducing the likelihood of employee theft to support drug habits.

A perennially controversial issue is who should be drug tested: job applicants, employees, workers in industries regulated by government, athletes, applicants for benefits, and in what circumstances: pre-employment, post-accident, with cause to suspect impairment, without cause, at random, or some combination.

The prevailing drug testing method of choice is urinalysis. After President Reagan Reagan's announced his War on Drugs, the use of urinalysis drug testing in the employment setting exploded. Proponents of workplace drug testing through urinalysis argued that this was the most efficient means to resolve the problems of employees who use drugs. Urinalysis, however, cannot measure impairment on the job.

Privacy advocates argued that drug testing profoundly infringes on personal privacy in a profound sense. Drug testing is intrusive of the individual's right to privacy. Such testing is especially intrusive when imposed randomly and without "reasonable suspicion." Many employees forced to go through this process complained of the humiliating and degrading nature of the process.

Urinalysis testing can result in the collection of highly sensitive personal information, including whether a person may have consumed the drug or drugs being tested for during the recent past, and even from some time prior to this.

Drug testing also has the potential to affect more than only those who use illicit drugs. Urinalysis testing may also reveal medical conditions, such as epilepsy or pregnancy. Test subjects could be required to disclose use of legal drugs (such as prescription drugs and over-the-counter inhalants) that could, themselves, cause a positive result.

Widespread drug testing became politically popular as a simple, expeditious solution to a complex social issue. Privacy advocates questioned whether treating difficult social and workplace issues such as stress, inadequate employee counseling and the continuing failure to treat substance abuse as a health issue as opposed as a criminal matter, was the correct approach to the issues at hand.

Despite these concerns, both private and public sectors in the United States adopted urinalysis testing. Following President Reagan's Executive Order, the use of drug testing in the private sector expanded rapidly. By 1987, nearly 58 percent of the largest U.S. employers had drug testing programs. Some of these firms were compelled to adopt drug testing programs because of new federal regulations mandating testing in industries such as railroads and trucking. Many others began to implement drug testing programs voluntarily, moved by the example of the federal government or the exhortation of political leaders.

U.S. corporations with testing programs said they adopted them to help curtail illegal drug traffic. They also said they implemented such programs to help enhance workplace performance through reducing accidents and improving productivity

Concern over the "pervasive" use of illicit drugs and seeking to reduce the demand for drugs led President Ronald Reagan to issue the executive order, "Drug-free Federal Workplace" in 1986, which required the leader of each executive agency to establish a drug testing program to detect illegal drug use by federal employees in sensitive positions. The executive order also authorized testing for all applicants to a federal executive agency. Simultaneously, the U.S. Department of Transportation issued regulations requiring drug testing for public transportation workers.

On April 11, 1988, the U.S. government adopted Mandatory Guidelines for Federal Workplace Drug Testing Programs. The guidelines apply to the following: certain executive agencies, the Uniformed Services (but excluding the Armed Forces) and any other employing unit or authority of the federal government. The guidelines do not apply to drug testing conducted under legal authority other than the executive order. The guidelines do not, for example, cover testing of persons in the criminal justice system, such as arrestees, detainees, probationers, incarcerated persons or parolees.

Current federal government drug testing policy: 1) provides for testing of government employees under a wide range of justifications; 2) provides for universal testing of applicants for government jobs; 3) obliges, not merely permits, government agencies to test for some drugs, and permits testing for others; 4) tests for certain illegal drugs only and does not apply to alcohol; and 5) the executive order and guidelines cover testing in the federal workplace only.

For any drug testing program, crucial issues that need to be resolved are what types of drugs are being tested for and what is the "threshold" concentration of each drug that will lead to calling a test result positive. Another issue is what type of testing method should be implemented: blood, urine, hair, saliva, psychological, breath. A third issue is that it must be determined what the testing is seeking to identify: present use, present use and present impairment, past use, or past use and past impairment. Fourth, it must be determined what the results of positive test results would be: dismissal, treatment, discipline, prosecution, refusal of benefits, or, denial of eligibility to participate in sporting events. Fifth, the decision maker must understand the scientific limitations of the testing method and carefully determine the precise goals of the testing program are prerequisites to any decision as to the effectiveness of a drug testing program.

In a case where the testing program that does not confirm positive results from screening, tests will be unacceptable because they generate many false positives. Urinalysis to confirm impairment would not be useful, even with the proper confirmatory tests, since urinalysis can show past use only. It cannot show either present use or present or past impairment. Finally, even a properly designed test intended to confirm drug use may nonetheless be unacceptable because of

Fourth Amendment protections against unreasonable search and seizure.

To protect the rights of those required to take drug tests, several states have enacted employee or job applicant testing laws, which cover both government and private sector employers and employees. They extend the constitutional restrictions imposed on public sector employers to private employers. Some of the statutes were patterned after a model bill drafted by the American Civil Liberties Union (ACLU). No state has prohibited drug testing in the workplace. Various state laws require an employer to have some form of either "probable cause" or a "reasonable suspicion" to test an employee for the presence of drugs; restrict pre-employment testing; require a job offer before pre-employment testing; and restrict random testing.

Protecting health and promoting safety are often put forth as objectives of testing programs. These objectives have five aspects. First, protecting the safety of persons being tested when these persons might be injured through impairment (examples might include impaired driving or operating machinery in a factory). Testing drivers for blood alcohol is perhaps the best known example of drug testing. Second, protecting the safety of co-workers by detecting an impaired worker who might cause injury or death. Military service members, police officers, firefighters, train and aircraft crews are examples of those who could be endangered by impaired colleagues. Third, protecting the public safety by detecting impairment, or risk of impairment, in anyone whose impairment could harm the public—such as a truck driver, pilot, or train engineer Testing to detect blood alcohol levels is often justified using the public safety argument. Fifth, protecting the health of the person being testing. Test results could signal the need to help the person who tested positive. The use of certain drugs (nicotine, alcohol, cocaine, for example) can result in serious health problems.

Privacy rights advocates criticize the impact that drug testing has on personal autonomy.

Drug testing coerces conformity and restricts autonomy. The issue of drug testing raises the basic issue of to what extent should governments or employers be allowed to use the coercive power of drug tests to restrict the consumption of substances? Is it sometimes right to coerce (to prevent impaired driving, for example), and sometimes wrong (to regulate the simple consumption of substances away from the workplace in situations that create no danger for others)?

Drug testing, many privacy rights advocates argue, supposes an employer's (or government agency's) right to exercise substantial control over individuals and to intrude into some of the most private parts of their lives. The technology of drug testing, privacy rights advocates argue, been allowed to shape the limits of human privacy and dignity.

In the mid-1980's, as employers began implementation of drug testing programs, employees or their representatives instituted a number of court cases challenging these policies. Because much of the early testing was undertaken by public employers, or as the result of federal mandates, the early cases most often raised constitutional challenges, alleging that the testing violated workers' Fourth Amendment rights to be free from unreasonable searches. This early litigation produced mixed results regarding the constitutionality of workplace drug testing; however, courts generally agreed that the testing implicated important privacy interests.

Critics of workplace drug testing framed their concerns primarily in terms of the threat to personal privacy and autonomy, identifying a number of ways in which the process of urinalysis drug testing infringed upon workers' interests. First, they argued that the process of collecting urine samples implicates workers' interest in their bodily privacy.

In 1989, the U.S. Supreme Court heard two cases that addressed the constitutionality of drug tests under the Fourth Amendment, i.e. *Skinner v. Railway Labor Executives' Ass'n*, 489

U.S. 602 (1989) and *National Treasury Employees Union v. Von Raab*, 489 U.S. 656 (1989). *Skinner* involved a challenge to the constitutionality of regulations promulgated by the Federal Railroad Administration (FRA) requiring drug and alcohol testing of railroad employees involved in a major train accident. *Von Raab* addressed the United States Customs Service's policy of requiring all employees transferred or promoted to certain positions to undergo urinalysis drug tests. Covered positions included those directly involved in drug interdiction, those requiring the incumbent to carry firearms, and those that entailed handling of "classified" material.

The Supreme Court in *Skinner* unambiguously recognized that the drug tests implicated significant privacy interests. It held that both the physical intrusion entailed in obtaining a blood sample, and the visual or aural monitoring of the act of urination required under the regulations infringed "expectations of privacy that society has long recognized as reasonable." Because testing bodily fluids "can reveal a host of private medical facts about an employee, including whether he or she is epileptic, pregnant, or diabetic," the Court found that the ensuing chemical analysis constituted a further invasion of privacy, and concluded that these intrusions "must be deemed searches under the Fourth Amendment." The Court observed, however, that the Fourth Amendment proscribes only unreasonable searches and seizures. Emphasizing the safety-sensitive nature of the railroad workers' jobs and the pervasive regulation of the railroad industry to ensure safety, the Court held that the government's "compelling" interest in testing without individualized suspicion outweighed the workers' interests in privacy.

The Court reached a similar conclusion in *Von Raab*, referring to a "veritable national crisis" caused by the smuggling of illegal drugs, and finding that the Government had a compelling interest in ensuring that "front-line interdic-

tion personnel are physically fit, and have unimpeachable integrity and judgment."

Despite the clear recognition of a privacy interest in *Skinner* and *Von Raab*, those decisions made it more difficult for workers to challenge drug testing policies under the Fourth Amendment by accepting as compelling justifications the employers' asserted interests in safety in *Skinner* and in the "integrity" of the Customs Service in *Von Raab*. Prior to those decisions, published federal courts of appeals' decisions on Fourth Amendment challenges to workplace drug testing were evenly split. In contrast, in the years following the Court's decisions in *Skinner* and *Von Raab*, the courts of appeals overwhelmingly upheld government drug policies in the face of Fourth Amendment challenges.

Although the issue of drug testing may be largely settled as a legal matter, conflicts between employers' exercise of control in the workplace and employees' interests in privacy and autonomy continue to reoccur. New technologies offer an increasing number of ways to monitor worker activities both on and off the job, and the incentives for employers to use these technologies are significant.

Further Readings

Cornish, Craig M. *Drugs and Alcohol in the Workplace: Testing and Privacy*. Wilmette, Ill.: Callaghan, 1988. Craig, John D. R. *Privacy and Employment Law*. Oxford: Hart, 1999. Fay, John. *Drug Testing*. Boston: Butterworth-Heinemann, 1991.

Gilliom, John. *Surveillance, Privacy, and the Law: Employee Drug Testing and the Politics of Social Control*. Ann Arbor: University of Michigan Press, 1994.

Karch, Steven B. *Workplace Drug Testing*. Boca Raton: CRC Press, 2008. Liu, Ray H. *Handbook of Workplace Drug Testing*. Washington, DC: AACC Press, 1995.

Tunnell, Kenneth D. *Pissing on Demand Workplace Drug Testing and the Rise of the Detox Industry*. New York: New York University Press, 2004.

See also: Body, privacy of the; Fourth Amendment to the U.S. Constitution; Right of Privacy; Workplace, privacy in the

E

Economic arguments for privacy rights

Identification: The view that although there are economic benefits to the disclosure of information, including personal information, there are many economic benefits to protecting personal privacy.

The U.S. Supreme Court has defined the right to private personal information, as the right to "control of information concerning an individual's person" (U.S. *Department of Justice v. Reporters Committee for Freedom of the Press*, 489 U.S. 749, 763 (1989)). Personal information is any data on an individual that is identifiable to that individual, ranging from his or her genetic code, sexual preference, or eye color to video preferences, credit history, or income. Such information—like all information—is property. Often courts are asked to answer: Who owns the property rights to such information? Is it the individual involved, is it the person who obtains the information, or is ownership shared in some fashion?

Many economists have argued that, in terms of privacy in personal information and with other factors being equal, more information is better, and thus more disclosure is preferable for reasons of economic efficiency, as opposed to the information remaining private.

The same economic factors that drive search behavior by employers and consumers might also drive investments in obtaining and in protecting private information. This issue is a beginning point for analyzing the economic impact of privacy. It is costly to assimilate a great deal of information, much of it of little relevance to determining whether to hire or otherwise enter into a business transaction with a given individual. This may be a persuasive argument against any rule requiring full disclosure of negative personal information, such as what is required by securities laws or the Truth-in-Lending Act. It does not, however, state a case for granting legal protection to a person's private information. It also may be unlikely that the failure to create such rights encourages individuals to spend significant resources on protecting the confidentiality of their personal information.

The common law generally disfavored privacy claims. Beginning in the 1960s, legislatures began to enhance privacy rights in personal information. Some economists criticized such legislation. The "law and economics" school of legal academics began questioning the efficacy of privacy rights legislation starting in the late 1970s. Leading members of this school, including Judge Richard Posner, argue that restricting information to protect personal privacy generally does not maximize social wealth because restrictions inhibit decision making, increase transaction costs, and encourage fraud. Judge Posner summed up his position by saying that the "privacy legislation movement remains a puzzle from the economic standpoint."

There is, however, an economic case for privacy that extends beyond the individual preference for privacy, and the economic benefits of privacy should be considered in issues concerning the unrestricted disclosure of personal information.

When personal information is obtained in voluntary transactions, and sometimes when it is obtained without consent, one important issue is whether a rule permitting subsequent disclosure is preferable, as a default rule, over a rule requiring privacy. Which rule is more efficient depends on the nature of the commercial transaction and the nature of the information. It is debatable whether a persuasive case can be made to support a general disclosure default rule.

The distinction between voluntary and non-voluntary transactions is the salient issue in privacy law. Common law protection from disclosure of personal information collected outside a voluntary or contractual relationship (such as by the media) largely no longer exists. Privacy protection for information given in the context of a contractual relationship has been enhanced both in the case law and in statutory law. Such protections are often not rules preventing disclosure but rather default rules that parties may contract with each other voluntarily, which negates many of the economic arguments given against privacy protections.

Many economists argue that it is in a person's economic interest to share information about him- or herself because such information reduces search costs for the individual and others, whether in the market for a car or a mortgage. Not only is information willingly shared but it is inevitably how American society functions.

Why would a person want to prevent the disclosure to others of true information about him- or herself? One answer given by economists is the intent to commit fraud. Every individual has a reputation, which he or she consciously seeks to enhance, either by downplaying or concealing "bad" facts or by accentuating "good" facts. Also, some individuals present different faces to different people at different times. An individual may wish to conceal information on his or her credit history because he or she does not want to be pegged as a poor credit risk. Such restriction could have significant costs because it could facilitate individuals who default on consumer credit.

Thus, some privacy claims are efforts at reputation protection. When the only interest is in reputation protection, economists argue it is usually inefficient to limit disclosure of available information. Those who consider whether to transact business with an individual depend on such information to determine whether and to what extent they should transact business with that person. The more accurate the information that is available, and the less expensive that information is to obtain, the more beneficial economic transactions will occur. In the commercial world, constricting the disclosure of information would force the decision about with whom to transact business to be made either with inferior information or with information obtained at a higher cost. In other words, constricting the flow of accurate information would result in an efficiency loss, whether that loss is in increased transaction costs, a cross-subsidization of "undesirable" activity, or a decrease in the number of mutually beneficial transactions.

The economic argument does not mean, however, that all limits on disclosure of personal information are inefficient. First, the costs of restricting disclosure must be considered against the benefits. The principal benefit is the usefulness to the individual of the privacy preference itself. To the extent that the privacy preference is based on a reputational interest, it may often be viewed as the utility derived from deception. In these instances, the cost of restricting disclosure will likely outweigh the gain.

Reputation protection is, of course, not the only reason people seek to protect their privacy. The desire to avoid embarrassment and the desire for peace and solitude or for modesty may motivate different privacy preferences in what many people generally view as private conduct.

Under the utility calculus, emotional issues still matter. Limiting disclosure of information may be appropriate when an individual values his or her privacy highly, for any reason other than to deceive. It is irrelevant whether the information is considered as "objectively" private information, although, if the reason for the preference appears to be to protect a reputation, it is less likely that limiting disclosure will be perceived as legitimate. It is the "pure" privacy preference that is relevant. The fact that a particular individual's preference for privacy may be difficult to understand does not necessarily mean that the person is deceitful.

The amount of information available to be disclosed does not necessarily remain the same. When disclosure diminishes the quantity or quality of information being produced, prohibiting disclosure may be positive in the final analysis. This is one of the key reasons for trade secret and copyright protection. With personal information, there is the potential that disclosure will diminish the extent to which people engage in the underlying activity. This may be beneficial if society wants to discourage the underlying activity. The recent leak of the names of customers of the website Ashley Madison, for example, may discourage people from seeking affairs through various websites.

One persuasive view that effectively balances the needs to disclose and the needs to protect individual privacy is that the disclosure of personal information may be permitted if and only if (1) the value of the information, when disclosed, exceeds the value of the pure privacy preference of the individual, and (2) allowing disclosure would not distort or eliminate the information in future commercial transactions.

One benefit is simply the utility derived from privacy, where that utility is not merely instrumental to reputation enhancement. There are also benefits to a legal system that protects privacy, including the willingness of people to engage in certain activities that they would not engage in if the information was revealed, the reduction of expensive extralegal precautions, and the reduction of wasteful expenditures on reputation enhancement needed to correct misleading impressions resulting from the disclosure of accurate but incomplete information.

Privacy rules are often implied contractual terms. To the extent that information is produced through a voluntary business transaction, imposing nondisclosure obligations on the recipient of the information may be the best approach for certain types of information. The value that information has is of secondary importance. The primary issue is identifying the efficient contractual rule. Courts increasingly impose an implied contractual rule of nondisclosure for many types of business transactions, such those with lawyers, physicians, bankers, and accountants. Many statutes can also be analyzed from default privacy rules. Thus, a persuasive argument can be made for the efficiency of a privacy default rule in many business transactions between a merchant and a consumer.

Most Americans agree that privacy is a basic human right. Both civilized society and commerce cannot exist without privacy. The concept of privacy, like the concept of property, is widely understood to be what is one's own.

Privacy affects how companies and organizations retain their trade secrets, conduct their operations, and protect themselves against the leak of insider information. Information almost always has actual value. Because property rights protection does not cover much of this information, this information must be protected under a privacy theory. To permit easy access to this information would necessarily lead to a diminished production of such information.

Privacy in the business setting may also increase economic risk taking. Certain investments may not occur if the identity of the investors were disclosed. In that sense, privacy may encourage investment. An obvious downside is that privacy protection may also facilitate illegal transactions.

The absence of privacy may contribute to inefficient information transfers. Without privacy, people use various types of devices to conceal or reduce the transmission of information.

Privacy definitely has a vital role in commerce in the digital era. For example, the U.S. government fought attempts to make computer encryption technology commercially available based on national security grounds. This effort failed in part because many of the largest corporations in the United States insisted on strong encryption technology to conduct business around the world. Commercial privacy also became a major issue in the European Union after European companies claimed that they lost contracts because of a lack of data security against.

U.S. competitors

Further Reading

Inness, Julie C. "The Threatened Downfall of Privacy: Judith Jarvis Thomson's 'The Right to Privacy' and Skepticism about Privacy." In *Privacy, Intimacy, and Isolation*. New York: Oxford University Press, 1996.

Jentzsch, Nicola. *The Economics and Regulation of Financial Privacy: An International Comparison of Credit Reporting Systems*. [Electronic resource.] Heidelberg : Physica-Verlag, 2006.

Moore, Tyler. *Economics of Information Security and Privacy*. New York: Springer, 2010.

Odlyzko, Andrew. "Privacy, Economics, and Price Discrimination on the Internet." In *Proceedings of the Fifth International Conference on Electronic Commerce—ICEC,* edited by Norman M. Sadeh et al. New York: ACM Press, 2003. http://ssrn.com/abstract=429762.

Posner, Richard A. "Orwell versus Huxley: Economics, Technology, Privacy, and Satire." University of Chicago Law School, John M. Olin Law & Economics Working Paper No. 89 (November 1999). http://ssrn.com/abstract=194572.

Posner, Richard A. *The Economics of Justice*. Cambridge, MA: Harvard University Press, 1981. Posner, Richard A., and Francesco Parisi. *The Economics of Private Law*. Cheltenham, UK: Edward Elgar, 2001. Schneier, Bruce. *Economics of Information Security and Privacy III*. New York: Springer, 2013.

Solove, Daniel J. *The Future of Reputation Gossip, Rumor, and Privacy on the Internet*. New Haven, CT: Yale University Press, 2007.

See also: Consent; Credit Reporting Agencies; Data Protection Regimes; Financial Information, Privacy Right to; Global Data Privacy; *U.S. Department of Justice v.*

Reporters Committee for Freedom of the Press, 489 U.S. 749 (1989); Reputation Management

Education Data Exchange Network (EDEN)

Identification: A digital repository of U.S. state education data for grades Kindergarten through 12.

Generally referred to as EDEN, and synonymous with Ed*Facts*, the Education Data Exchange Network is an offshoot of the policies mandated by the No Child Left Behind Act. The database was created and afterward officially launched between 2003 and 2004. Shortly thereafter, EDEN and its accompanying tools were renamed ED*Facts*. In total, ED*Facts* consists of three data programs: the EDEN Submission System (ESS), the EDEN Survey Tool (EST), and the EDEN Staging database. All three work in tandem to collect and report aggregate data provided by state education agencies (SEA), local education agencies (LEA), and sometimes schools themselves. In addition, the ED*Facts* Metadata and Process System (EMAPS) supports the State Submission Plan and data designed for a webpage interface. The Education Data Exchange Network has evolved into a centralized source of key education statistics concerning the U.S. public school system. Navigating Ed*Facts* procedures, data submission policies, and a series of transitions, local, state, and federal government personnel worked together to unify education data across the United States.

In 2003, the United States Department of Education implemented the Performance-Based Data Management Initiative (PBDMI) to address and improve the means through which each state facilitated the collection of education statistics. The purpose of the initiative was two-fold: to reduce the data collection efforts exhausted by each state, and to streamline the process to allow both the federal government and states access to the same uniform data sets.

The outcome of the initiative was the Education Data Exchange Network. At first voluntary, on January 25, 2007 the Federal Register published a compulsory regulation directing all states to submit data to EDEN according to file specifications outlined by the Department of Education. SEAs faced fines if they failed to do so. Enforcing these requirements, however, boosted the current storehouse of information included in EDEN, and the government also extended technical assistance to smooth the transition. Additionally, between 2008 and 2010, the government funded the MSIX Data Quality program, the goal being to support state-level methods of recording migrant student data.

Each state has a designated SEA contact, also known as the EDFacts Coordinator, who submits the state's data to the EDEN/ED-Facts Submission System. The submission of the data is summarized in the EDFacts Submission System (ESS) User Guide, supplemented by a detailed EdFacts workbook that is revised approximately every school year. Four reports help the SEA contract track the timeliness and accuracy of the data they enter into the ESS. Firstly, the Transmittal Status Report displays the status of recent files transmitted to the system and errors identified in these files, if any. Secondly, the Submission Error Report retrieves all submitted files with errors later found. The Submission Error Report can be limited or expanded to include one or more school years from 2007–2008 or sooner. Next, the Submission Progress Report allows the SEA contact to gage their progress for the current school year, and they can filter the results to view the numbers submitted at the state, local, or school level. Lastly, mirroring a practice the National Center for Education Statistics (NCES) applies to their Common Core of Data (CCD), the Match Error Report ensures the directory listing of each school remains consistent by comparing the current and previous school year entries to CCD.

Beyond the reports, all data submitted by SEAs are subjected to a scrupulous, two-step edit, conducted first by the Education Data Exchange Network and then NCES statisticians assisted by the U.S. Census Bureau. Once the statistics are verified and published, two main outside sources analyze them. Professional researchers funded typically by the federal government or private sector organizations may either generate or evaluate EDEN data to serve the needs of specific projects and studies. On the other hand, private foundations—including private schools—not only refer to U.S. Department of Education data for their own uses, but also they generate data that will support the goals of their individual organizations. Although the various applications of EDEN data may appear endless, only just over 100 data groups represent the figures delivered to the Education Data Exchange Network. Data categories further define data groups. Among these groups are specific counts of students, ages 6 through 21, with disabilities who are enrolled in special education courses and Individualized Education Plans (IEP). This data speaks directly to the Individual with Disabilities Act, which has established explicit rules regarding the types of data to collect. Other data groups feature information on schools receiving Title I funding, graduation and dropout rates, teacher quality, homeless students, student performance in science, and math proficiency—to name a few. Data, however, is never submitted on individual students.

Though the U.S. Department of Education spearheaded the EDEN initiative, it transformed into collaboration between the Department, state and local education agencies, NCES, and most importantly schools. Today, the EdFacts website lists four overarching objectives: to inform policy and decision making; to alleviate the data collection burden shouldered by states; to enhance state software and tools which obtain and stockpile data records; and to deliver freely available, concise data to the local, state, and federal government. In short, the creation of the Education Data Exchange Network altered the course of U.S. education data and it will continue to play an essential role in present and future education issues.

Lauren Perelli

Further Reading

Ahearn, Eileen M. "Special Education in the New National Educational Data System." *Communication Disorders Quarterly* 29, no. 4 (2008): 236–238.

Kanstoroom, Marci and Eric C. Osberg, Ed. *A Byte at the Apple: Rethinking Education Data for the Post-NCLB Era*. Washington D.C.: Thomas B. Fordham Institute Press, 2008.

Liss, Jerald M. "Creative Destruction and Globalization: The Rise of Massive Standardized Education Platforms." *Globalizations* 10, no. 4 (08/01; 2015/10, 2013): 557–570.

See also: Big data; Data collection; Educational setting, Privacy in an

Educational setting, privacy in an

Identification: The challenge of securing students' and educators' private information, particularly in today's online educational environment. The age of technology has greatly benefitted education. It has also presented new challenges as technology has advanced and been embraced by a generation of students, many of whom are ready to relegate notebooks and pencils to the past.

Traditional students, adult learners, participants in continuing education classes, online learning communities, and hybrid classes are affected by the use of technology. For some, the ability to gain new knowledge would be out of reach without it. Digital access makes it possible for traditional long-distance learning to become immediately accessible. No longer is there a time lag between wanting to know something and knowing it. The process of receiving new information, facts, and ideas can be as swift as the speed of your laptop. The use of Blackboard and other platforms make it possible for knowledge to be attained from anywhere. Massive open online courses (MOOCs) have made access to college courses a more democratic process. All that is needed is a computer or access to a computer. Being able to gain new knowledge without cost presents an exciting opportunity. Persons struggling to secure tuition and other related higher education costs can access college-level courses at no cost. Adult learners, persons interested in isolated courses, workers needing training or retraining in an industry, or life-long learners seeking to explore a new field of scholarship all have the ability to do so without much difficulty.

Students in traditional brick-and-mortar classrooms use laptops, iPads, cellphones, tablets and other electronic devices to gain new knowledge, compose essays, conduct research, and write papers. Teachers accept homework submitted by email, and faculty members in many schools are mandated to use Blackboard to provide students with the syllabus, class assignments, and other course-related information. Students form learning communities using Google and other applications.

The digital era has made the acquisition of new knowledge less restrictive and elitist. The democratic focus of MOOCs has created a new population of online learners who are not interested in a degree but who want the exposure to a new subject, often with well-known faculty. Interested learners search for their subject matter and sign on. MOOCs do not confer degrees to those enrolled, but they do allow for exploration of various topics offered in institutions of higher learning without the cost.

Nevertheless, the element of privacy in an educational setting in the digital arena has become an issue of concern. Grades given for submitted work no longer reside in the instructors' roll book. Final papers and other original work submitted in higher education are uploaded on Blackboard or some similar platform. The grade for the work is retrieved from the same platform. What level of privacy is in place to ensure that the grade is not accessed? How do students know that their grades will not be accessed by sources outside the academic environment? What are the responsibilities of the institution to ensure that the records of students remain private? What does that privacy cover? Is it only student grades? Are other academic experiences, such as allegations of plagiarism or other offenses that may have triggered a grievance, protected as well? How do students discover that information may be on their record that they may want to challenge, and what are their rights to do so? Are these issues different for students in high school or elementary school? Where do parents and guardians fit into the picture? Some of these issues were present before recent technological advancements, but with the digital environment, the demand for information has grown and with it come the risks of securing it.

In 1974 Congress enacted the Family Educational Rights and Privacy Act (FERPA), 129 Stat. 437, codified as, 20 U.S.C. § 1232g. It is a federal statute that applies to all institutions receiving federal funding. FERPA works on several academic levels. It provides parents of students under the age of eighteen the ability to access their records and, more important, to inspect information contained within those records. Students who are eighteen are able to self-advocate and request access to their own educational files. This statute provides a level of protection for students from outside agencies that are not eligible to view information contained within their educational records. To provide academic privacy, FERPA created restrictions on what individuals and entities can access student information. It also details what information may be given to authorized agents. The digital age adds a threat even to those restrictions because of the vulnerability of computers to external access from hackers.

Books, articles, and websites have been devoted to the threat to educational privacy.

The twentieth century produced FERPA in the pre-digital age. In the digital-driven twenty-first century, there has been an explosion of cyberattacks on educational, governmental, and commercial websites. As the digital age of technology becomes part of the educational environment, opportunities for invasion of privacy increases. There may be a need to create a digital form of FERPA that acknowledges that educational records are vulnerable to cyberattack. What is known is that the maintenance of privacy is challenging in an educational environment that uses cyberspace as a file cabinet. Congressional action may be needed to create new federal laws that are more relevant in this new century where technology brings significant benefits and major concerns.

Sandra Jowers-Barber

Further Reading

Borgman, Christine L. *Scholarship in the Digital Age: Information, Infrastructure, and the Internet.* Cambridge, MA: MIT Press, 2010

Protecting the Security of Educational Records. https://www.digicert.com/news/2009–10–13-digicert-education-white-paper.pdf

Student Data Protection in an Era of Education Technology Innovation. http://www.duanemorris.com/alerts/student_data_protection_education_technology_innovation_0815.html

Suber, Peter. *Open Access.* Cambridge, MA: MIT Press, 2012.

United States Institute of Peace. "Cyberterrorism: How Real Is the Threat?" December 2004. http://www.usip.org/sites/default/files/sr119.pdf

See also: Computer; Cybersecurity; Data Breaches; Email; Family Educational Rights and Privacy Act of 1974 (FERPA); Google; Hacking

Electoral interference and privacy

Identification: Also known as election meddling, this has been around for a long time and raises a number of privacy issues. From 1946 to 2000, the

United States and Russia alone tried to influence foreign elections 117 times using both overt and covert methods.

Events leading up to the 2016 U.S. presidential election showed that the old electoral interference tactics had fully transferred to the digital age. According to one of President Donald Trump's informal strategic advisors, Roger Stone (indicted in 2019), it was not Russian operatives who hacked the Democratic National Committee (DNC) in 2015 but rather a lone hacker that went by the name Guccifer 2.0. Stone's assertion has since been shown to be false; in fact, the hackers were identified by investigators as twelve Russian intelligence officers working to undermine the 2016 election.

The Russian hackers used the pseudonym Guccifer 2.0 to post documents obtained through network intrusions into a variety of Democratic Party entities to influence the election. According to federal indictments announced in February 2018, the Guccifer persona had been operated by Russian military intelligence (GRU). On July 13, 2018, Special Counsel Robert Mueller, charged with investigating the matter, indicted the twelve GRU agents for allegedly perpetrating the cyberattacks; Mueller also looked into various Trump associates, many of whom have been indicted for crimes both related to and unrelated to electoral activities.

The team of Russian intelligence officers stole damaging information including emails between high-level DNC staff highly critical of presidential candidate Bernie Sanders and offering ways to discredit him. Shortly after Sanders declared his support for the Democratic frontrunner and eventual nominee Hillary Clinton, the critical emails were publicly disclosed, turning many Sanders supporters against Clinton. Not long afterward, there was a similar stream of unflattering emails stolen from Clinton campaign chairman John Podesta's email account and leaked by WikiLeaks. U.S. intelligence agencies alleged that all of this supported the Kremlin's efforts to interfere with the 2016 election,

apparently in order to hinder Clinton's chances and facilitate the election of Trump.

The extent of the election interference in 2016, and subsequent Russian efforts at meddling, are unprecedented in the United States, although they do echo efforts undertaken by Russia earlier in Ukraine. Agents distributed false or damaging information directly to voters via social media sites and also attempted to interfere with voters' privacy rights through hacking into voter registration databases and electronic voting machines. Unfortunately, U.S. laws have not yet caught up to the ever-changing technology and changes in social media. Once a tool used to expand freedom of expression, social media has now also become a tool for the spreading of misinformation, doubt, and suspicion. Ads, for example, are manipulated on social media to target users in such a way as to sway their thinking, including their political preferences.

The largest social media company, Facebook, has been less than forthcoming when it comes to describing its efforts to protect the privacy of its users and ensuring the integrity of its product. In 2010, Facebook executives wanted to make the company indestructible to competitors, so they formed partnerships with other companies such as Netflix, Amazon, and Microsoft and gave them access to its user data. Facebook took its data and placed it on other social media sites. In doing so, the company did not ask its users for permission. It reasoned that it could make use of the data because most users had, when signing up for Facebook, indicated that Facebook could access their lists of friends to display them on personal homepages. Facebook rationalized this on the basis that users had relinquished their privacy rights. The company contended that it ended this practice in 2015, yet questions remain and further revelations act to dispute this.

After a tumultuous year in 2016, Facebook CEO Mark Zuckerberg went on a "listening tour" to meet and hear from people in all 50 states. Nevertheless, it was reported in March 2018 that the political data firm Cambridge

Analytica, which had been hired by the Trump campaign, had gained access to and misappropriated data from tens of millions of Facebook users without their knowledge before the 2016 election. The data accessed included users' identities, friends, and "likes." The idea at Cambridge Analytica was to create "personality maps" based on what people liked and then use that information to target them and others like them with digital ads.

Appearing before the Congress on April 11 and 12, 2018, Zuckerberg stressed that Facebook had been working to prevent interference in future elections after Russian-linked accounts spread untruths across the platform to vast swaths of the country. He said that Facebook was using artificial intelligence methods to uncover fake accounts, yet allowed (as reported by Arjun Kharpal for CNBC Tech, April 12, 2018) that "as long as Russia has people who are employed, who are trying to perpetuate this kind of inference, it will be hard for us to guarantee that we're going to fully stop everything."

In June 2018, when users were still reeling from the Cambridge Analytica debacle, it was reported by *The New York Times* that Facebook had also reached deals with Apple, Microsoft, Amazon, and Blackberry to share Facebook users' data. In July 2018, Facebook revealed that, following the April 2018 hearings, it gave dozens of companies users'" friend" data, even after publicly stating that it had shut off access to such companies in 2015.

One of the companies to which Facebook extended its data was a Russian internet giant, Mail.ru, which has ties, through a wealthy Russian investor, Alisher Usmanov, to Russia's president Vladimir Putin. A November *New York Times* article alleged that Facebook covered up Russian interference on the platform during the 2016 election and voted against specifically naming Russia in an April 2017 white paper that Facebook published on foreign interference. In December 2018, the *Times* also made clear that

there was far more private data turned over to other major social media companies than previously stated in the April 2018 Congressional hearings. As of this writing, Facebook seems still to be working through the issue and the company's approach to it.

It seems likely that without the adoption of tighter regulations, election interference by means of social media platforms will continue. Facebook proclaims itself a self-regulator, but this does not appear to have produced any concrete results as of early 2019. So, what are social media users to do? There are very few laws on the books now that directly protect a user's privacy on social media. Current law is limited to requiring providers to post notices of policies and work to adhere to them. The availability of personal information on social media, however, allows businesses access to information that they could not otherwise acquire directly from those who post the data. As things stand, most any data a user makes available on social media cannot be expected to receive full privacy protection, precisely because the user has made it available.

Joseph A. Custer

Further Reading

Dance, Gabriel J.X, LaForgia, Michael, and Confessore, Nicholas, *As Facebook Raised a Privacy Wall, It Carved an Opening for Tech Giants*, New York Times (December 18, 2018).

_____, *Facebook Gave Device Makers Deep Access to Data Users and Friends*, New York Times (June 3, 2018).

Frenkel, Sheera, Confessore, Nicholas, Kang, Cecilia, Rosenberg, Matthew, and Nicas, Jack, *Delay, Deny and Deflect: How Facebook's Leaders Fought through Crisis*, New York Times (November 14, 2018).

Glaser, April, *What the Latest Mueller Indictment Reveals About Guccifer 2.0, the "Lone Hacker" Who Was Really a Group of Russian Agents*, Slate (July 13, 2018).

Granville, Kevin, *Facebook, and Cambridge Analytical: What You Need to Know as Fallout Widens*, New York Times (March 19, 2018).

Guyun, Jessica, *Mark Zuckerberg's 2017 Resolution: Meet more Americans*, USA Today (Jan. 3, 2017).

Hackett, Roger, *Clinton Foundation Denies Hacking Claims*, FORTUNE (Oct. 4, 2016).

Kharpal, Arjun, *Mark Zuckerberg's Second Day in Congress: Here are the Points You Need to Know*, CNBC Tech (April 12, 2018).

Khrennikov, Ilya, *Usmanov Drops Mail.ru Control in Move Seen Spurred by Sanctions*, Bloomberg Business (October 22, 2018).

Levin, Don H., *When the Great Power Gets a Vote: The Effects of Great Power Electoral Interventions on Election Results*, 60 INT'L STUD. Q. 189 (2016).

Shackelford, Scott, J. *Managing Cyber Attacks in International Law, Business, and Relations: In Search of Cyber Peace*. New York, NY: Cambridge University Press (2014).

See also: Bots; Cambridge Analytica; Cellphones; Facebook; Online privacy and security; Social media; Social networking technologies; Twitter; WikiLeaks

Electronic Communications Privacy Act (ECPA), 18 U.S.C. § 2510 et seq.

Identification: An act passed by Congress in 1986 that expanded the protections of the Fourth Amendment to new forms of communication and data storage. With the passage of ECPA, Congress intended to afford privacy protection to electronic communications. Title I of ECPA amended the federal Wiretap Act, which previously addressed only wire and oral communications, to "address . . . the interception of . . . electronic communications" (S. Rep. No. 99–541 at 3 (1986)). Title II of ECPA created the Stored Communications Act (SCA), 18 U.S.C. §§ 2701–2712, which was designed to "address . . . access to stored wire and electronic communications and transactional records" (18 U.S.C. § 2701(a)). A third title was added in 2001 and is discussed below.

The intersection of these two statutes composing ECPA "is a complex, often convoluted, area of the law" (*Konop v. Hawaiian Airlines, Inc.*, 302 F.3d 868, 874 (9th Cir.2002)). The labyrinth is compounded by the fact that ECPA was written

prior to the advent of the Internet and the World Wide Web. The original act addressed the interception of conversations using hard telephone lines. It did not apply to interception of computer and other electronic and digital communications.

Later legislation clarified and modernized ECPA to add more protections as new technologies and communication methods have evolved. ECPA was first significantly amended by the Communications Assistance to Law Enforcement Act (CALEA) in 1994 (47 U.S.C. §§1001–1010 (1994)). The most important change brought by CALEA was making it illegal to intercept communications over cordless telephones.

With the enactment of the Communications Decency Act (CDA) of 1996 (47 U.S.C. § 230), protections were granted to Internet service providers (ISPs). CDA granted ISPs immunity from liability for defamation and similar actions by prescribing that "[n]o provider or user of an interactive computer service shall be treated as the publisher or speaker of any information provided by another information content provider" (47 U.S.C. § 230(c)(1)).

The USA PATRIOT Act of 2001, Pub. L No. 107–56 (2001), often called the PATRIOT Act, stripped away much of the privacy protections of ECPA and CDA. Under the PATRIOT Act, an Internet service provider can disclose an electronic communication to a "law enforcement agency" voluntarily—even without the consent of the user or any request by the agency—as long as the ISP "in good faith, believes that an emergency involving danger of death or serious physical injury to any person requires disclosure without delay of communications relating to the emergency" (28 U.S.C. § 2702(b)).

In addition, under the PATRIOT Act of 2001, the ISP may disclose customer records to a "governmental entity"—again, voluntarily without consent of the user or any request by the agency— if the ISP "reasonably believes that an emergency involving immediate danger of death or serious physical injury to any person justifies disclosure of the information . . . " (18 U.S.C. § 2702(c)). The PATRIOT Act goes even further, stating the ISP may disclose customer records voluntarily "to any person other than a governmental entity"— meaning, to anyone without restriction (18 U.S.C. § 2702(c)(6)). Clearly, the privacy protection for ISPs offered by ECPA and CDA regarding Internet communications and subscriber records have been eroded by the PATRIOT Act of 2001.

A third title was also added to ECPA in 2001 legislation: the Pen Register Act, 18 U.S.C. § 3121 et seq. The Pen Register Act allows law enforcement officers, through their use of devices, to intercept "dialing, routing, addressing, or signaling information" (Title 18 U.S.C. § 3127(3)) but not the actual content of any such information. Ironically, the addition of the Pen Register Act essentially led to the monitoring of actual content of electronic information on a laptop or other mobile electronic device through the use of the previously established titles of ECPA, the Wiretap Act, and SCA. The Wiretap Act covers surveillance of electronic communications "in transmission" while the SCA covers surveillance of communications that are in "electronic storage."

The next act that significantly amended ECPA was section 102(a) of the USA PATRIOT Improvement and Reauthorization Act of 2006. This act made permanent fourteen sections of the previous PATRIOT Act of 2001 that affected both ECPA and FISA acts. ECPA applies in the context of domestic criminal investigations, while FISA applies in the context of foreign intelligence gathering. The sections directly amending ECPA in the USA PATRIOT Improvement and Reauthorization Act of 2006 are Section 201 (Electronic Communications Privacy Act wiretapping in certain terrorism investigations), Section 202 (ECPA wiretapping in computer fraud and abuse investigations), Section 204 (pen register order amendments, including extension to electronic communications, for example, Internet use), Section 209 (seizure of stored voicemail by warrant rather than ECPA order), Section

212 (communications providers' emergency disclosures of communications content or related records to authorities), Section 217 (law enforcement access to computer trespassers' communications within the intruded system), Section 218 (FISA wiretap or search orders with an accompanying law enforcement purpose; removal of "the wall" of separation between criminal catchers and spy catchers), Section 220 (nationwide service of court orders directed to communication providers), and Section 223 (civil liability and disciplinary action for certain ECPA or FISA violations).

In summary, ECPA has become much more defined through amendments from later legislation such as CALEA, CDA, the PATRIOT Act of 2001, the USA PATRIOT Improvement and Reauthorization Act of 2006, and the FISA Amendment of 2008, H.R. 6304 (2008), in which Congress included ECPA in consideration of conducting foreign-intelligence surveillance. It protects oral, wire, and electronic communications while those communications are stored on computers or other mobile devices, while those communications are being made, or while they are in transit. The act now applies to telephone conversations, electronically stored data, and email.

Joe Custer

Further Reading

Doyle, Charles. *Wiretapping and Electronic Surveillance: The Electronic Communications Privacy Act and Related Matters*. Washington, DC: Congressional Research Service, Library of Congress, 1992.

Easttom, Chuck, and Jeff Taylor. *Computer Crime, Investigation and the Law*. Boston, MA: Course Technology Publishers, 2011.

Haul, Marissa G. *Electronic Communications Privacy Act: Overview and Issues for Consideration*. New York, NY: Nova Publishers, 2014.

Jasper, Margaret C. *Privacy and the Internet: Your Expectations and Rights under the Law*, 2d ed. Dobbs Ferry, NY: Oceana Publications, 2009.

Jennings, Laurel, and Richard M Eastman. *Wiretaps and Electronic Eavesdropping: Federal Law and Legal Ethics*. New York: Nova Publishers, 2013.

Martin, James P., and Harry Cendrowski. *Cloud Computing and Electronic Discovery*. Hoboken, NJ: Wiley, 2014.

See also: Electronic Surveillance; Foreign Intelligence Surveillance Act (FISA); Stored Communications Act (SCA); USA PATRIOT Act, Pub. L. No. 107–52; Wiretapping

Electronic Frontier Foundation

Identification: A United States–based and donor-funded U.S. § 501(c) (3) nonprofit digital rights group that defends civil liberties in the digital world.

Electronic Frontier Foundation (EFF) was established in 1990 to promote user privacy, freedom of expression, and innovation. The organization engages in impact litigation, policy analysis, grassroots activism, and advisory work and litigation on the surveillance of individuals and protection of privacy rights.

In defending privacy rights, EFF focuses its efforts in informing the general public of their privacy rights, as well as educating citizens about ways to keep their personal information private. Additionally, the organization works to help citizens protect themselves from government and law enforcement intrusions. EFF's privacy-related education work encompasses the following areas: international privacy standards; locational privacy (personal privacy rights concerning data gathered through use of the Global Positioning System [GPS] incorporated into cellphones and other media); mass surveillance technologies and cybersecurity legislation. The EFF's education work also addresses mandatory data retention, which imposes obligation on Internet and telecom service providers to collect and store information documenting the online activities of users; online behavioral tracking, as well as do-not-track mechanisms to protect Internet users from behavioral advertising; open wireless networks; social media, data collection, and government surveillance; National Security Agency (NSA) surveillance; and medical privacy.

To further citizen protections, the EFF has also launched the Surveillance Self-Defense Project, which offers background information on government surveillance, as well as briefings and tutorials on several privacy-related questions. This work is largely animated by a how-to philosophy; example topics include "How Strong Encryption Can Avoid Online Surveillance," "An Introduction to Threat Modeling," "Protecting Your Device from Hackers," and "Attending Protests in the United States and Abroad." The Surveillance Self-Defense Project offers information ranging from password protection and encryption options to instructions on how to download free and open source software. There are also instructions about applications to encrypt group, text, picture, and video messages, among other. The organization has created tutorials for privacy protection on social networks; choice of virtual private networks (VPNs); and protection against malicious software. EFF has also issued several research papers on privacy issues such has locational privacy, biometrics, open wireless, digital books, and best practices for online service providers.

In terms of impact litigation, the EFF has taken action resulting in directly addressing privacy concerns founded on the basis of guaranteed constitutional protections. The EFF filed an amicus brief in *USA v. Pen Register* (W.D. Tex., 2014), in which a Texas federal district court ruled the government was not allowed to track the location of cellphone users without probable cause. The organization also filed an amicus brief on litigation in New York that involved the real-time collection of cell data under the Pen-Trap Statute, 18 U.S.C. §§ 3121–3127, and the Stored Communications Act, Title III, 100 Stat. 1848 (1986), advising the court that search warrants should be required before the collection of information.

The EFF has been especially active in opposing several activities conducted by NSA. In 2006, former AT&T employee Mark Klein provided EFF with whistleblower evidence that telecommunications company AT&T was providing NSA access to extensive amounts of personal communications. According to Klein, AT&T allowed NSA to gather Internet backbone traffic through an interception facility in San Francisco, known as room 641A, therefore enabling large-scale surveillance. The data collected referred to both domestic and international activities of AT&T customers in a manner which, Klein argued, certainly violated citizens' rights. EFF filed a class action lawsuit against AT&T (*Hepting v. AT&T*, C-06– 672 VRW (N.D. Cal., 2009)), for violation of the privacy rights of its customers. EFF alleged violations of the Foreign Intelligence Surveillance Act (FISA), 92 Stat. 1783 (1978); the Wiretap Act, codified as 18 U.S.C. § 2510–2522; the Electronic Communications Privacy Act, 100 Stat. 1848 (1986); the Stored Communications Act, Title III, 100 Stat. 1848 (1986); and the Fourth and First Amendments to the U.S. Constitution. The lawsuit was dismissed in 2009 after AT&T was granted retroactive immunity by the 2008 FISA Amendments Act, 122 Stat. 2436. In 2012, the Supreme Court denied certiorari in *Hepting v. AT&T*.

Moving forward, the EFF will continue to serve an important watchdog role in helping to preserve the individual privacy rights of citizens, especially as technology continues to advance.

Ana Santos Rutschman

Further Reading

Klein, Mark. *Wiring Up the Big Brother Machine—and Fighting It.* Charleston, SC: BookSurge, 2009.

McCandlish, Stanton. *EFF's Top 12 Ways to Protect Your Online Privacy.* https://www.eff.org/wp/effs-top12-ways-protect-your-online-privacy

Timberg, Craig. "Try as It Might, Anti-Surveillance Group Can't Avoid Washington." *Washington Post*, October 11, 2013.

See also: Biometrics; Cybersecurity; Electronic Communications Privacy Act (ECPA); Electronic Surveillance; Foreign Intelligence Surveillance Act (FISA); Foreign Intelligence Surveillance Court; First Amendment to the U.S. Constitution; Fourth Amendment to the U.S. Constitution;

National Security Agency (NSA); Social Media; Stored Communications Act (SCA); Whistleblowers; Wiretapping

Electronic Privacy Information Center (EPIC)

Identification: A privacy rights watchdog organization.

The Electronic Privacy Information Center (EPIC) is a nonprofit organization that addresses privacy rights and constitutional issues through research and advocacy. The organization comprises a small staff; a board of directors; and an advisory board with experts in technology, law, and public policy. EPIC is independent from the government and does not have any clients, customers, or shareholders. EPIC is headquartered in Washington, DC.

Formed in 1994, EPIC was created at the convergence of two movements: the long-standing legal effort to recognize privacy as a fundamental right to be protected, and the swift emergence of technology, which has a great impact on users' privacy. As a result, EPIC strives to "protect privacy, freedom of expression, democratic values, and to promote the Public Voice in decisions concerning the future of the Internet." EPIC accomplishes its goals through multiple avenues, such as educating the public about privacy issues, advocating for privacy rights reform, and participating in litigation to change existing privacy rights programs and laws.

In particular, EPIC promotes awareness by providing easily accessible information on privacy rights to the public. EPIC details its initiatives on two privacy websites: epic.org and privacy.org. The websites provide information on a wide range of privacy topics, including government surveillance, drones, and search engines. EPIC also publishes a biweekly electronic newsletter, *EPIC Alert*, with current privacy rights updates as well as longer semiannual reports, which provide an overview of privacy issues and laws in the United States and in different countries. For example, EPIC published *Privacy & Human Rights 2006*, an annual report with Privacy International, and also the *Consumer Law Sourcebook* and the *Privacy Law Sourcebook*. The publications are aimed at educating the public on privacy rights issues and laws. EPIC also organizes conferences and participates in international projects; coalitions; and forums, including The Public Voice Project, the Global Internet Liberty Campaign, and the Internet Democracy Project, to collaborate and share information. Thus, as demonstrated by its written and oral communication efforts, EPIC is committed to promoting awareness on a national and international scale.

In addition to public education, EPIC engages in strong advocacy efforts. EPIC regularly presents to Congress on emergent privacy and civil liberty issues. EPIC also files amicus court briefs in support of privacy rights cases. For example, EPIC filed an amicus brief in *Riley v. California,* 134 S.Ct. 2473 (2014) (where the U.S. Supreme Court held search warrants must be obtained to search cellphones even during lawful searches) and *FTC v. Wyndham,* No. 14–3514,__ F.3rd ___ (3rd Cir., Aug. 25, 2015) (where the U.S. Third Circuit Court of Appeals reaffirmed the Federal Trade Commission's authority to regulate data security standards).

EPIC also supports the advocacy efforts of others. In 2004, EPIC established the Champion of Freedom Award "to recognize individuals and organizations that have helped safeguard the right of privacy, promote open government, and protect democratic values with courage and integrity." The first Champion of Freedom Award was presented in 2004 to Senator Patrick Leahy (D-VT), who was at the forefront of technology issues in Congress. Other past winners include judges, congressional representatives, and journalists, among others.

EPIC directly shapes the privacy rights arena by challenging companies over their use of data. EPIC has participated in major privacy rights lit-

igation, including actions involving federal agencies and large corporations. EPIC frequently relies on the Freedom of Information Act (FOIA) to obtain government surveillance and privacy policy information. For instance, EPIC has used FOIA to challenge the Department of Homeland Security and Transportation Security Administration over body scanning methods and the Department of Homeland Security over social media content monitoring and data collection. EPIC has also filed many complaints with the Federal Trade Commission, such as filing a complaint against Google's Buzz application as being deceptive toward users, who were provided with no opt-out option for the application, and against Facebook's deceptive practice of gathering users' private information for a Facebook study without their consent. Those complaints, as well as others, have led to major rulings by the Federal Trade Commission and new privacy protections.

Through its public education, advocacy, and litigation efforts, EPIC has served as a watchdog organization over governmental and corporate actions. EPIC has championed numerous privacy rights and constitutional issues and has provided the public with substantial access to privacy issues and past and pending privacy cases. EPIC's legitimacy is further enhanced through its partnerships with other privacy organizations and collaborative events. By engaging in outreach and preventative enforcement measures, EPIC has established a dynamic presence in the national and international privacy rights arena.

Stephanie Romeo

Further Reading

"Case Study: Electronic Privacy Information Center (EPIC)." *The Public Voice.* Accessed

August 1, 2015. http://thepublicvoice.org/events/EPIC_Case_Study2.pdf.

Electronic Privacy Information Center. *Epic.org.* https://www.epic.org/.

Electronic Privacy Information Center and Privacy International. *Privacy & Human Rights: An*

International Survey of Privacy Rights and Developments. United States: EPIC, 2006.

Rotenberg, Marc, Harry A. Hammitt, Ginger McCall, John A. Verdi, and Mark S. Zaid, eds. Electronic Privacy Information Center.

Litigation under the Federal Open Government Laws (FOIA) 2010. Washington, DC: EPIC, 2010.

See also: Constitutional Law; Email; Facebook; Federal Freedom of Information Act; Federal Trade Commission; Global Data Privacy; Homeland Security, U.S. (DHS), Department of; *Riley v. California*; Wiretapping

Electronic surveillance

Identification: Approaching ubiquity in the digital age. Places and activities that were private and protected, shielded from prying eyes in the pre-digital age – the workplace, in stores, at home, in your car, in your doctor's office, on the phone, at the bank – are now pierced by people, businesses, hackers, criminals, and even our own government using an array of electronic surveillance techniques. And these privacy intrusions occur regardless of whether the subject has consented to or is even aware of the intrusions.

Electronic surveillance, in the workplace

Employers are permitted to track the comings and goings of employees both as they arrive at work and leave and within the workplace; track and intercept telephone calls on work phones; intercept and read entries on work computers; track websites visited and keystrokes logged; track the physical locations of work vehicles; use keycard, iris, fingerprint and other recognition software to identify and track employees and their locations and activities; administer personality tests; require alcohol and drug testing pre-employment and in some positions, post-employment; require a medical or psychological examination; and

Charles Harvey monitors contacts from the "Van." It is possible to monitor a large area through the use of multiple Mobile Sensor Platforms (MSP). (All Hands, September 2003, pg. 26) (Photo by PH1 Shane T. McCoy.)

some employers routinely track employees' banking, credit, and social media records and footprints. These are just a small subset of the ways employers spy on their employees.

Furthermore, when employees, to save their "minutes," use work Wi-Fi to access the Internet and personal emails via their smartphones, all of these activities may be tracked and recorded by employers, because the company's equipment enabled it. But the question should not end with "What can we track given the current state of technology?" The question should be, in this society, "What employee activities should we protect as private and which can we decide as a society ought to be susceptible to or free from employer surveillance?" Employees presumably want complete privacy, but employers have an interest in safeguarding the workplace, property, other employees, and customers or clients, so the proper place to delineate privacy rights is controversial. But disputes of this nature, in our society, are put up to a vote – in our legislatures. Most legislation to date has focused on requiring data aggregators to keep data safe from unauthorized intrusions and to keep children's data private, and regulators have engaged in some enforcement actions to ensure employer compliance with data protection safeguards. These employee data protections are far from fool-proof, for example, the 2015 data breach involving U.S. workers overseas; perhaps most importantly, as more and more private employee data is gathered and retained by more and more employers, the risk of unauthorized access and hacking will continue to exponentially increase in the future. However, when the issues related to employee data privacy has been weighed against employers' right to intercept and record employee activity, especially on or using employer property, the scales have, so far, tipped almost entirely in favor of employers.

Electronic surveillance, at the marketplace

Card swipes at Target checkout lines, securities records at J.P. Morgan Chase, and Sony Corporation's internal and personal emails are just a few commercial examples of electronically stored personal data that were hacked and stolen in 2014. On a smaller scale, many of us, lured by in-store discounts, have used our grocery key cards to identify ourselves at the store and get the "member" discounts. Our grocery purchases are captured by use of those key cards, and then are stored, sold, and re-sold to other vendors – and we are deemed to have "consented" to release of all that private data even though we only agreed to use those key cards to obtain a discount on our groceries. At a grander scale, Amazon and eBay have become among the largest consumer data aggregators and they both routinely sell those data (such as purchases, searches, IP and addresses) to other vendors – for a price. We are deemed to have consented to that surveillance by browse-wrap agreements of which most of us are not fully aware, hidden as they are behind unassuming banners denominated "terms and conditions" or "I agree." Security cameras are everywhere at the mall, capturing your presence there and shopping habits under the assumption that you have impliedly "consented" to those security camera videos capturing your image and activi-

ties simply because they happened in the mall – that is, in a public place. Common wisdom is that American consumers have steeled themselves to the allegedly inevitable loss of privacy; however, other countries have been much more active in appropriately reining in consumer data collection in the absence of clear, explicit, and voluntary consent by the consumers whose data are to be gathered.

Electronic surveillance, in your home

If your ex-wife or your boss chooses to record a phone conversation with you – even when you are using the phone in your own home – each can do so with impunity in most states and under federal law. The so-called one-party rule provides that so long as one party to a phone conversation consents to interception and recording of the telephone conversation, the recording need not be disclosed to the unaware parties (although there are some exceptions, such as attorneys and telephone marketers, who must disclose when they are recording a telephone call). Law enforcement frequently use the one-party consent doctrine to place surreptitiously recorded telephone calls from a cooperating and consenting victim or accomplice to a suspect to extract recorded admissions from that suspect.

Law enforcement may obtain a home's electric use records to identify whether the home's high electric use masks a marijuana grow operation. Users' cellphones send "pings" to cellphone towers, which disclose the phone's exact geophysical position, even from within a home.

Those same cellphones operated from inside the users' home interact with cellular service providers who thereby obtain dialed numbers, incoming call numbers, durations of calls, and so on, and then law enforcement can quite simply obtain those call records from the cellular service providers without a search warrant under the third party doctrine.

Electronic surveillance, in your car

Just a few examples will illuminate that electronic surveillance of motor vehicles is happening in many ways, often without the subject's explicit consent. If a cellphone user places a call using that phone while in a car, the car's (and phone's) location is captured in real time and stored for a long time.

Across New York, cameras mounted to squad cars and in fixed locations photograph tens of millions of license plates as the vehicles bearing those plates travel around New York. The photograph's metadata simultaneously record the date, time, and exact places where the license plate was located when it was photographed. Those license plate data are accessible to Homeland Security (U.S. federal law enforcement) officers and to law enforcement officers across New York State. Nine or more New York counties store those records for the long term.

In areas of the United States near international borders, using a Z Backscatter Van, basically a truck-mounted remote x-ray device, border patrol agents inside the territorial United States are able to x-ray nearby moving vehicles to ascertain whether they contain hidden compartments and individuals. No search warrant is obtained prior to those searches.

In a critically important United States Supreme Court case from 2012, *United States v. Jones*, 132 S.Ct. 945, the Court limited at least extensive global positioning system (GPS) tracking of motor vehicles. In that case, officers surreptitiously (and without a warrant) placed a GPS tracking device on a subject vehicle. The officers then tracked that vehicle's location second-by-second for weeks. The Court's interestingly held that such extensive tracking was an unconstitutional violation of the Fourth Amendment, however, the individual Justices reached that same conclusion through different reasoning. Most of the majority Justices deemed that extensive tracking to have violated the vehicle operator's reasonable expectation of privacy,

that is, the vehicle operator's reasonable expectation that the vehicle would not be tracked so extensively in real time, even though it was tracked on only public roads. The other majority Justices deemed the warrantless placement of the GPS device on the vehicle as an illegal trespass, and thus, held the GPS and its tracking to have violated the vehicle operator's property right to be free from trespasses. Nonetheless, the Court's decision notably restricted law enforcement's previous tactic to place a warrantless GPS device on a subject vehicle and track it for as long as necessary.

Electronic surveillance, in your doctor's office

Along with the rapid increase of the percentage of care providers and other allied medical companies to maintain their medical records electronically, known as electronic health records (EHRs), law enforcement has seen a huge growth in medical identity fraud and theft and misuse of others' EHRs. Although there are undeniable benefits of maintaining EHRs rather than paper medical records, the risks are just as obvious. EHR thefts have increased close to 25 percent per year since 2010, victims of EHR theft and fraud can expect to pay up to $13,500 to close the privacy gap, up to 89 percent of EHR theft and fraud victims felt their reputations had been damaged by release of private health records, and almost one-fifth felt they lost career prospects and opportunities as a result of EHR theft and fraud. The convenience and value-added of EHRs certainly comes at a heavy price.

Electronic surveillance, on your telephone

Your placed calls and incoming calls, their durations, and your physical locations when you place those calls are all captured by your cellular service provider, and have been routinely also provided directly to the National Security Agency (the "NSA"). These data have been stored for an indeterminate time, and those records retained by the NSA have been searched without a warrant. The NSA's on-again, off-again cellular telephony metadata collection program has been whipsawed of late by competing court cases and legislative enactments, but at the time this book went to press, the NSA was again, at least temporarily, authorized to collect and store all of that telephone data, although there was some indication the NSA was resolved to purge all of the bulk-collected phone records obtained to date. That NSA program, created by the FISA and USA PATRIOT Acts detailed elsewhere in this volume, was supported by both legislation and an order issued by a secretive FISA court, but not through a typical targeted wiretap warrant. Suffice to say, your cellular telephone is constantly subject to electronic surveillance, whether supported by wiretap orders, search warrants, your consent, or none of the above.

Electronic surveillance, online

Virtually every click, keystroke, website visit, and online purchase is subject to electronic surveillance, and the data gathered through that surveillance are big business in America. Indeed, two entirely new industries, big data and data aggregation, both were born of the sheer volume and monetary value of consumer and other data gleaned from users' Internet activities. The real magic – and risk – of data aggregation is that these companies can cobble together a detailed portrait of every individual who goes online by connecting disparate data points (purchase activities, browsing history, banking records, real estate ownership information, wedding and birth registers, etc.) and attaching them all to common data points, such as a computer's IP address or the user's name and date of birth. These online user profiles are then sold to retailers and others for a profit.

The tragedy of electronic online surveillance is that the surveillance is conducted only on the thinnest pseudo-consent. Online users are deemed to consent to this private data collection by various less than clear means; the overt "I consent to you capturing and selling my personal information to whomever you wish" consent alternative is almost unheard of online. Rather, user consent, that is, user privacy waiver, is usually passive at best, implied in the main, or imaginary in the worst case. Just by using some websites, users are deemed to have consented to capture and resale of all their private online activity on that website. Yet, truth be told, an exceedingly small percentage of all online users have a full appreciation and awareness of the personal data privacy they lost just by using the Internet. That seems like an unfair and even misleading expedience aimed predominantly at supporting and enabling the Big Data and data aggregation industries.

Electronic surveillance – proceeds remain ad infinitum

All these data captured through electronic surveillance come to have lives of their own, and those lives sometimes last forever. Some of those private records are sold and transmitted on the black market. Some are bartered or exchanged for other information. Some are used to bombard a user with targeted advertisements to sell various goods and services.

And all those data live on in data repositories that are never purged from Internet "wayback" servers, or in cached webpages, or on hard drives around the world. It seems, at times, there is no way to get that data genie back in the bottle. Or perhaps it seems to some that since we cannot stop the privacy erosion, the best we can strive for is to manage it.

The privacy erosion occasioned by electronic surveillance seems inevitable, but perhaps we should consider following the decisions taken in the European Union and other nations that have legislated a higher level of data privacy than the Untied States. The Congress and other states may also benefit by reviewing existing electronic privacy legislation in Maine and Utah along with the recent California legislation (known as CalECPA, the California Electronic Communications Privacy Act), all of which dramatically tighten the procedures that must be followed before law enforcement can search digital content, especially contained within cellular telephones. We need not sit idly by and be victimized by the digital age. Instead, we can, should, and must proactively limit the privacy carnage through legislatures and the courts.

Charles E. MacLean

Further Reading

California Senate Bill No. 178, California Electronic Communications Privacy Act (signed into law by California Governor Jerry Brown on October 8, 2015). Retrieved from: http://leginfo.legislature.ca.gov/faces/billNavClient.xhtml?bill_id=201520160SB178.

Friedersdorf, C. (Oct. 19, 2015). The NYPD Is Using Mobile X-Ray Vans to Spy on Unknown Targets. Atlantic Monthly. Retrieved from: http://www.theatlantic.com/politics/archive/2015/10/the-nypd-is-using-mobile-xrays-to-spy-on-unknown-targets/411181/.

Grabell, M. (Jan. 27, 2012). Drive-by Scanning: Officials Expand Use and Dose of Radiation for Security Screening. ProPublica. Retrieved from: http://www.propublica.org/article/drive-by-scanning-officials-expand-use-and-dose-of-radiation-for-security-s.

McCann, E. (June 17, 2015). Medical identity theft hits all-time high. Healthcare IT News. Retrieved from: http://www.healthcareitnews.com/news/medical-identity-theft-hits-all-time-high.

Orr, S. (July 28, 2014). New York knows where your license plate goes. USA Today. Retrieved from: http://www.usatoday.com/story/news/nation-now/2014/07/28/New-York-archiving-license-surveillance-data/13261679/.

See also: Privacy Laws, Federal; Fourth Amendment; Smartphones; Big Data; Cookies; Workplace, Privacy in the; Metadata; Home, Privacy of the; Consent; Consumer Privacy; USA PATRIOT Act; Wiretapping

Email

Identification: Messages that are transmitted electronically from the sender's computer to one or more recipients by way of a network.

Users may often view email as private conversations with another person, in which no one else is participating; however, email is one of the least secure methods of communication available. In contrast, phone calls typically aren't recorded and stored. Even if they were, your employer and law enforcement would have to go to court to gain access to them. Emails are stored at several different locations: on the sender's computer, the Internet service provider's (ISP) server, and on the receiver's computer. Deleting an email from an inbox doesn't mean there aren't multiple other copies of it in existence. Emails are also vastly easier for employers and law enforcement to access than phone records. And because of their digital nature, they can be stored for very long periods of time.

Email privacy concerns include issues of unauthorized access of electronic mail. Unauthorized access of an individual's email may occur while an email is in transit, when it is stored on email servers, or when it is stored on a user's computer.

In the United States, Americans have a constitutional guarantee of the secrecy of correspondence. It is a matter of considerable debate as to whether email should receive the same kind of legal protection as paper letters sent through the postal service and under what circumstances. The very nature of email influences whether it should receive legal protection from any and all types of eavesdropping. These issues are increasing in importance as email continues to be such a popular means of communication.

Certain technological processes help curtail the unauthorized access to email. Because email messages are often transmitted through different nations that may have wide array of different regulations and restrictions pertaining to the access of other people's email, the user should be aware of the laws, practices, and realities of the countries through which their email is transmitted.

Email at the workplace
The general rule is that employees have no reasonable expectation of privacy when using email

at their workplace. If an employer is using email at work, the employer is legally entitled to monitor it. Employers, unlike law enforcement, largely have an unfettered right to search through the email of their employees. Employers typically believe that sending email through their equipment could affect their business, which justifies searching and monitoring employee email.

Many employers require their employees to sign and acknowledge an employer computer and email use policy. This document may explicitly state that email may be used for work purposes, the computer system is the employer's property, email may be monitored, and the employee has no reasonable expectation of privacy in email use. Once signed by an employee, this policy gives the employer a contractual right that it can rely on if it wants to monitor an employee. Also, if a dispute arises over monitoring of email, the employer can point to the signed statement to show that it was unreasonable for the employee to think that email was private.

Even if a written policy does not exist, the employer may still monitor its employees' email. Courts have rarely found that the employee had a reasonable expectation of privacy to his or her email at work for several reasons. Some courts have held that email at the workplace is part of the work environment, similar to a fax or copy machine, in which the employee doesn't have a reasonable expectation of privacy. Other courts have found that emailing to colleagues at work was inherently work-related, and thus there could be no reasonable expectation of privacy.

Employers are concerned about misuse of email, including the fact that employees should be supposed to be working. Employers' monitoring of work email is a way to ensure that employees are using email appropriately.

Many employers are concerned about liability. If the employer is ever a party in a lawsuit, the opposing litigants may be entitled to review employee email. Employers are also concerned about workplace harassment claims. One way that employers protect themselves against law-

suits is to monitor email and prevent or deter computer-related harassment at the workplace. Many employers have software on their networks that seek emails that might be problematic.

The other main concern with liability is that old emails could be used years down the road in a lawsuit. What an employee says can be preserved for years, and unless the company has an established, reasonable practice of purging its emails, those emails can be a gold mine for anyone suing the company. Emails can be especially devastating because of the informal way that people write and send them, saying things in emails that they never would in professional correspondence.

Most public-sector employees have even less privacy rights in their email than most private-sector employees. Under different public records statutes and the Freedom of Information Act (FOIA), the public may gain access to much of the communications of a public employee. Also, because of the nature of public employees' jobs, courts are reluctant to hold that government employees have a reasonable right to privacy in workplace email.

Email from home and personal accounts

Unlike work emails, personal email from one's personal email account and computer is more likely to be protected because there is a much more reasonable expectation of privacy. But even personal emails may not be fully protected. Anonymous hackers may be intercept private accounts.

Because emails are stored locally, at the ISP, and on the receiving end, hackers or law enforcement can gain access to them at multiple points. While it may be difficult for law enforcement to gain legal access to one's personal computer and local copies of saved emails in one's personal computer, they may be able to get them easily from the ISP. Law enforcement officials with a warrant are permitted to seize electronic correspondence of those suspected of a crime. Under some circumstances, ISPs are legally able to scrutinize the email of individuals.

ISPs are also increasingly imposing end-user service agreements that users must agree to. These agreements reduce any expectation of privacy. They also often include terms that grant the ISP the right to monitor the network traffic or give records at the request of a government agency. For example, the service agreement for one popular ISP states: "Service Provider has no obligation to monitor the Service, but may do so and disclose the information regarding the use of the Service for any reason if Service Provider in its sole discretion believes that it is reasonable to do so, including to satisfy governmental or legal requests."

While sending personal email only from home greatly protects your privacy more than using email at work, the individual's email is vulnerable to interception by hackers. After the email leaves the sender's home, it goes over several online services and open networks before it reaches the recipient.

Legal protections for email privacy

Email privacy is derived from the Fourth Amendment to the U.S. Constitution and is governed by the "reasonable expectation of privacy" standard. Considering the open nature of email, the expectation of privacy may be less for email, especially work email, than for other forms of communication.

The Fourth Amendment provides that "the right of the people to be secure in their persons, houses, papers, and effects, against unreasonable searches and seizures, shall not be violated." The Fourth Amendment is often envied to protect privacy rights against government activities.

The courts have found varying degrees of Fourth Amendment protections of email. In *O'Connor v. Ortega*, 480 U.S. 709 (1987), the administration at Napa State Hospital, after placing Dr. Magno Ortega on administrative leave during an investigation into possible misconduct, searched Ortega's office. Dr. Ortega sued the hospital, claiming that the search violated his Fourth Amendment rights. Both the federal district court and the circuit court found that the search did violate Ortega's Fourth Amendment rights. The U.S. Supreme Court disagreed. The Court based its decision on two factors: (1) whether Dr. Ortega had a reasonable expectation of privacy and (2) whether the search of Dr. Ortega's office was reasonable. The Court held that because Dr. Ortega had a private office, he had a reasonable expectation of privacy. However, the Court also found the search of his office was reasonable because it was work-related. The government's need to ensure efficient operation of the workplace, therefore, outweighs an employee's expectation of privacy, even if the privacy expectation is reasonable. Because work environments vary, a public-sector employee's expectation of privacy must be determined on a case-by-case basis. The court considered factors such as: (1) notice to employees, (2) exclusive possession by an employee of keys to a desk or file cabinet, (3) the government's need for access to documents, and (4) the government's need to protect records and property.

After the *Ortega* decision, the extent of constitutional protection afforded to emails is unclear. Unlike a locked desk or file cabinet, emails are not locked. The employer has access to all messages on the system.

In addition to Fourth Amendment protection of email privacy, federal statutory law provides additional protection. Interception of email transmission, capturing the email while it is sent from sender to recipient, is a criminal violation under the Electronic Communications Protection Act (ECPA), 100 Stat. 1848 (1986), codified as 18 U.S.C.A 2517(4). Although ECPA originally set up protections (such as a warrant requirement) to protect email, those protections have been weakened in many instances by the PATRIOT Act, 115 Stat. 272 (2001). ECPA also permits an ISP to search through all stored messages. Some ISPs temporarily store all messages that go through the system. In most cases, ECPA generally prevents the ISP from disclosing the messages to others. Law enforcement officials, with warrants or administrative subpoenas, may collect information about users from ISPs and also obtain access to the content of stored messages. Also, ECPA does not protect against hackers intercepting the message at the recipient's mailbox.

Email covered by ECPA loses its status as a protected communication in 180 days, meaning that a warrant is no longer necessary and the emails of individuals may be accessed by a simple subpoena instead of a warrant to order to access email from a provider. If the emails are stored on a user's personal computer instead of a server, those emails would still require the police to obtain a warrant first to seize the contents. This part of ECPA been criticized as obsolete. At the time ECPA became law, infinite storage at webmail servers was not available. In 2013, some members of Congress first proposed reforming the law.

The Email Privacy Act, HR 1852, 113th Cong. (2013), HR 699, 114th Cong. (2015), would amend ECPA to prohibit a provider of remote computing services or electronic communication services to the public from knowingly divulging to any governmental entity the contents of any communications that are in electronic storage or otherwise maintained by the provider. The Email Privacy Act also would have provisions under which the government may require, pursuant to a warrant, the disclosure by such a provider of the contents of such communications. It eliminates the different requirements depending on whether such communications were stored for fewer than, or more than, 180 days. It also requires a law enforcement agency, within ten days after receiving the contents of a customer's communication, or a governmental entity, within three days, to provide the customer with a copy of the warrant and a notice that such information was requested by, and given to, the law enforcement agency or government entity. The U.S. House of Representatives has passed the bill

for the act more than once, but the Senate has yet (as of early 2019) to vote in favor of it.

Although the ECPA bill has been brought up a number of times by its sponsors, to date (2019) it has not garnered sufficient support in the Senate to win authorization.

State constitutional protection of emails

State constitutions in at least ten states (Alaska, Arizona, California, Florida, Hawaii, Illinois, Louisiana, Montana, South Carolina, and Washington) recognize the individual's right to privacy. Some of these state privacy protections reflect Fourth Amendment protections. The state constitutions, however, have more references to privacy. Courts have interpreted general constitutional provisions in other states without specific privacy provisions to have established privacy rights of various types. Similar to the rights granted by the U.S. Constitution, the privacy rights under state constitutions usually extend to protection from state government actions and do not cover the actions of private entities. However, an important exception to these laws exists: provider exception. Under the provider exception, these laws do not apply to "the person or entity providing a wire or electronic communications service." This exception, for example, allows various free email providers (Gmail, Yahoo Mail, etc.) to process user emails to display contextual advertising.

Email sent by employees through their employer's equipment has no expectation of privacy; the employer may monitor all communications through its equipment. According to a 2005 survey by the American Management Association, about 55 percent of U.S. employers monitor and read their employees' email. Even attorney-client privilege is not guaranteed through an employer's email system; U.S. courts have rendered contradictory verdicts on this issue. Generally speaking, the factors that courts use to determine whether companies can monitor and read personal emails in the workplace include:

(1) the use of a company email account versus a personal email account and (2) the presence of a clear company policy notifying employees that they should have no expectation of privacy when sending or reading emails at work, using company equipment, or accessing personal accounts at work or on work equipment.

Common law protection of email

Various parties have asserted email privacy protection under privacy common law arguments in various state court cases. Thus, state law governing email privacy has been evolving. Under the common law, email privacy is protected under the tort of invasion of privacy and the causes of action related to this tort. Four distinct torts protect the right of privacy: (1) unreasonable intrusion upon the seclusion of another, (2) misappropriation of another's name and likeliness, (3) unreasonable publicity given to another's private life, and (4) publicity that unreasonably places another in a false light before the public. Of these, the tort of "unreasonable intrusion upon the seclusion of another" is the most relevant to the protection email privacy.

Global surveillance

The documents leaked by ex-NSA contractor Edward Snowden indicated that many governments have programs for monitoring and intercepting communication, including email, on a massive scale. The legality, ethics, and propriety of these programs continue to be debated. As part of this mass surveillance, the email of many innocent individuals with no terrorist connections have been intercepted and stored. Whistleblower and former National Security Agency (NSA) employee William Binney claimed that NSA has intercepted over 20 trillion communications, including many email communications, representing one aspect of NSA's warrantless surveillance efforts.

The American Civil Liberties Union (ACLU) and other privacy and civil liberties organizations have alleged that Verizon illegally granted the U.S. government unrestricted access to its entire Internet traffic without a warrant and that AT&T had a similar agreement with NSA. While the Federal Bureau of Investigation (FBI) and NSA claim that all their activities were and are legally sanctioned, Congress passed the FISA Amendments Act of 2008 (FAA), granting AT&T and Verizon immunity from prosecution.

Maintaining email privacy

Unless the user takes affirmative steps to encrypt messages (a process by which sophisticated software uses cryptographic algorithms to garble the words in a message and then allows the recipient to unscramble and read the message, provided that the recipient has the correct digital key to reconstitute it), email cannot be regarded as a confidential method of transmitting information. Thus, encryption is the only way to ensure a high degree of privacy for email messages. In a notable recent case, the 2016 Democratic presidential nominee Hillary Clinton faced questions on the campaign trail because, while serving as Secretary of State, she used a private email server rather than more secure equipment maintained by the federal government, thus potentially exposing classified information to hackers.

Commonly used public key technology has two keys: one that is unique and private, and one that is public and freely distributed to all users of a particular system. These keys work only when they are matched: What one scrambles, only the other can undo. These techniques can also verify the integrity of the data (that it wasn't altered) and authenticate it (ensure that the stated creator is the person who sent the message).

Gretchen Nobahar

Further Reading

Gelman, Robert B., and Stanton McCandlish. *Protecting Yourself Online: The Definitive Resource on Safety, Freedom, and Privacy in Cyberspace.* New York: HarperEdge, 1998.

Kent, Stephen T. *Who Goes There? Authentication through the Lens of Privacy.* Washington, DC: National Academies Press, 2003.

Levmore, Saul. *The Offensive Internet: Speech, Privacy, and Reputation*. Cambridge, MA: Harvard University Press, 2010.

Macdonald, Lynda A. C. *Tolley's Managing Email and Internet Use*. Croydon: LexisNexis UK, 2004.

Merkow, Mark S., and Jim Breithaupt. *The E-Privacy Imperative: Protect Your Customers' Internet Privacy and Ensure Your Company's Survival in the Electronic Age*. New York: AMACOM, 2002.

Mills, Jon L. *Privacy: The Lost Right*. Oxford Scholarship Online, 2008.

Sin, Yvonne Pui Man. *Email Privacy: Legal and Ethical Implication of Workplace Surveillance and Monitoring*. Auckland, New Zealand: Department of Management Science and Information Systems, University of Auckland, 2002.

Wugmeister, Miriam. *Global Employee Privacy and Data Security Law*. Arlington, VA: BNA Books, 2009.

See also: Computers and privacy; Constitutional Law; Electronic Communications Privacy Act (ECPA); Fourth Amendment of the U.S. Constitution; Home, Privacy of the; Law enforcement; USA PATRIOT Act; Workplace, privacy in the

Employment eligibility verification systems

Identification: Systems intended to ensure that individuals holding jobs are authorized to work in the United States.

U.S. law requires companies to employ only individuals who may legally work in the United States: U.S. citizens, or foreign citizens who have the necessary authorization. The diverse U.S. workforce contributes greatly to the vibrancy and strength of the U.S. economy, but that same strength also attracts unauthorized employment. As such, programs like E-Verify are crucial in identifying violations of U.S. law.

E-Verify is an Internet-based employment eligibility verification system allowing businesses to determine the eligibility of their employees to work in the United States. E-Verify is easy to use and is one of the best ways employers can ensure a legal workforce. The E-Verify program allows employers to confirm the immigration status of new hires by checking their identity data against government databases. While not without controversy, E-Verify is widely accepted as a useful immigration enforcement tool, making companies accountable for employing only those who are authorized to work in the United States.

After several years of debate about unauthorized immigration to the United States, Congress enacted the Immigration Reform and Control Act (IRCA) of 1986. In 1986, there were an estimated 3.2 million unauthorized immigrants (sometimes referred to as illegal aliens) in the United States. IRCA combined legalization programs for some unauthorized immigrants with provisions to deter future unauthorized immigration by reducing the attraction of employment. These latter provisions reflected a belief, widely held then and now, that most unauthorized aliens enter and remain in the United States to find work. To reduce the attraction of employment, IRCA amended the Immigration and Nationality Act (INA) with Section 274A to make it unlawful to knowingly to hire, recruit, or refer for a fee, or continue to employ, an unauthorized alien. This act requires all employers to examine documents presented by new hires to verify identity and work authorization and to complete and retain employment eligibility verification (I-9) forms. These INA Section 274A provisions are sometimes referred to collectively as employer sanctions.

Employers and civil libertarians successfully lobbied to weaken the bill's verification provisions as part of the broader IRCA negotiations. It is also worth noting that neither the national ID card nor the call-in system provisions were included in IRCA. As a result, compliance with IRCA is based on the I-9 form, upon which workers attest they are authorized to work in the United States and employers record information about the documents the worker presents. This document-based system has proven to be highly unreliable, primarily because IRCA's passage sparked a large market for fraudulent green cards and other fake forms of identification.

The law requires employers to check workers' documents, but it also undermines their ability to do so. In an effort to prevent discrimination and facilitate the process for legal workers, IRCA established a long list of documents acceptable for proving work authorization. It also prohibited employers from questioning the authenticity of documents that "appear to be genuine" and seem "to relate to the employee." A delicate balance between the protection of liberties and adherence to the law was certainly taking place.

The IRCA provisions did not deter illegal immigration. After declining eligible unauthorized aliens status to an estimated 1.9 million in 1988, the unauthorized population began to increase. By the early 1990s, illegal immigration had surpassed pre-IRCA levels. The I-9 process was effectively undermined by the availability of genuine-looking fraudulent documents.

From its voluntary pilot testing and first use in 2004 by very small numbers of employers, E-Verify has expanded significantly. Since 2006, more than fifteen U.S. states have implemented some type of E-Verify mandate, either through legislation or executive order. The Supreme Court recently upheld, through *Chamber of Commerce v. Whiting,* the states' right to make participation in E-Verify mandatory for all employers. An executive order requiring all federal contractors and subcontractors to use E-Verify, signed by President George W. Bush in 2008, went into effect in September 2009.

E-Verify has since experienced dramatic growth both in terms of use among employers and the number of queries processed, partly as a result of these mandates. As of January 2011, over 243,000 employers had registered to use the system, up from 9,300 in June 2006, according to U.S. Citizenship and Immigration Services (USCIS). And overall use of the program increased eightfold between 2006 and 2010, from 1.7 million to 13.4 million queries, covering about one out of four people hired in the United States in 2010.

Certain changes were also made to increase the effectiveness of the program. E-Verify was the new name given in 2008 to a basic pilot program. The program included an automatic flagging system that prompts employers to double-check the data entered into the web interface for those cases that are about to result in a mismatch. This change reduced data entry errors and initial mismatches by approximately 30 percent.

The launch of E-Verify also marked the addition of photo matching. Photo matching is the first step in incorporating biometric data into the web interface. Photo matching was developed for employees presenting a permanent resident card or employment authorization document, and allows an employer to match the photo on an employee's document with the photo in USCIS records. State workforce agencies were encouraged to use E-Verify to confirm the employment eligibility of any worker referred to an employer in response to an H-2A job order.

USCIS has taken a number of steps since 2005 to strengthen E-Verify, but some aspects of the program remain contentious. Security experts worry that it is not perfectly reliable (in particular the use of biometric facial recognition software), business groups see it as costly, and labor and immigration advocates are concerned about the negative effects of E-Verify on some legal workers.

The House Judiciary Committee, which has authority on immigration matters, held a hearing on E-Verify in February 2011. At least six new bills related to E-Verify were introduced in the House in spring 2015, and the Secure America Through Verification and Enforcement (SAVE) Act (HR 2000), which would require mandatory E-Verify participation by all U.S. employers, was reintroduced in late May. Although a mandatory E-Verify bill may pass in the House this session, such a bill's prospects in the Senate are uncertain. In May 2011, USCIS launched I-9 Central, a site dedicated to making guidance for form I-9, employment eligibility verification, more accessible and user-friendly. I-9 Central provides one online location to keep employers and workers up to date with the information needed to complete form I-9 properly.

Under E-Verify, the information on the I-9 form is checked against information in Social Security Administration and Department of Homeland Security databases. The system detects certain types of document fraud, such as when a new hire presents counterfeit documents with information about a non-work-authorized or nonexistent person. E-Verify currently has limited ability to detect other types of document fraud and identity fraud.

In the future, E-Verify may be able indirectly to deter unauthorized employment by increasing the cost of securing that employment. As unauthorized workers learn more about E-Verify, presumably some of them will increasingly seek to obtain counterfeit, borrowed, or stolen documents with information about work-authorized persons or will use fraudulent documents such as birth certificates to obtain "legitimate" documents. As it becomes more difficult to obtain fraudulent documents that E-Verify cannot detect, the cost of such documents will increase. Therefore, E-Verify may result in some reduction of the unauthorized workforce.

E-Verify could make it too difficult for unauthorized aliens to obtain legitimate employment. One possible result is that they may instead end up working "under the table" or "off the books," thereby increasing the risks of worker exploitation. In the end, E-Verify will not limit the number of jobs. It will simply encourage workers to move underground, where they will be more vulnerable to abuse and less likely to pay taxes.

For an electronic employment eligibility verification system to reduce unauthorized worker employment yet not deprive legal workers of job opportunities, it must respond to queries correctly—that is, it must confirm the employment eligibility of individuals who are in fact authorized to work and not confirm the employment eligibility of individuals who lack work authori-

zation. To be most effective, the system must also be efficient.

Proposals to expand E-Verify, particularly proposals to make the system mandatory for all employers, have increased the concerns of some groups about employee privacy. In his April 26, 2007, House testimony, Jim Harper of the libertarian Cato Institute argued that a nationwide electronic employment verification system would have serious privacy consequences. He sharply distinguished between a paper-based I-9 system, in which employee information "remains practically obscure," and a web-based electronic system, in which the entered information is very easy for participating agencies to access, copy, and use. Harper added:

> Unless a clear, strong, and verifiable data destruction policy is in place, any electronic employment verification system will be a surveillance system, however benign in its inception, which observes all American workers. The system will add to the data stores throughout the federal government that continually amass information about the lives, livelihoods, activities, and interests of everyone—especially law-abiding citizens.

In January 2013, E-Verify released a new, searchable database that enabled the public to find employers enrolled in E-Verify. The database replaced the list of E-Verify employers and federal contractors. It allows users to filter, sort, and export employer results.

In 2013, Congress considered proposals to convert E-Verify into a mandatory tool, requiring employers to check legal status with both documents and photos stored in the system. Some observers have characterized it as a national database on every authorized worker in the United States. Privacy advocates again expressed their concerns. Success in passing a bill depended on the ability to balance, effectively and persuasively, tighter security standards with personal rights, including the right to privacy.

The American Civil Liberties Union (ACLU) expressed concerns about what it perceived as threats to privacy posed by a mandatory E-Verify system. The ACLU said in a statement submitted to the House Judiciary Committee during the E-Verify hearing in February 2013:

> Nationwide, E-Verify would create a virtual national ID and would lay the groundwork for a possible biometric national ID system, thereby imposing significant privacy and civil liberties costs on all Americans, including lawful workers, businesses, and taxpayers.

The ACLU also objected to a mandatory E-Verify system because it believed it would create a whole new level of intrusive government oversight of daily life—a bureaucratic "prove yourself to work" system that would hurt ordinary people. Also, the organization said, E-Verify's inaccuracies could create obstacles to employment for hundreds of thousands of citizens. The scope of private information housed in the system would create enormous privacy and security risks. Finally, the ACLU also argued that mandatory E-Verify would essentially make employers law enforcement agents who would police the workforce.

Supporters of E-Verify claim that the privacy concerns were overblown; the fact that the federal government seeks to establish a database for all authorized workers does not necessarily mean that the primary motive for such a database is to establish a national identification system. While employment information will be centralized through a government process, procedural safeguards through amendments to the Senate bill would be sufficient to ensure user privacy.

E-Verify was introduced as part of the Border Security, Economic Opportunity, and Immigration Modernization Act on April 16, 2013. The legislation sought to harmonize two immigration reform goals: increased border security and the legalization of undocumented immigrants. On June 27, 2013, the Senate approved the bill on a 68–32 vote. The bill then went to the House of Representatives. On November 2013, then–House Speaker John Boehner (R-OH) said that the House would not consider immigration reform in that session of Congress. At this writing, use of E-Verify remains a nonmandatory system for all employers nationwide. Should the use of E-Verify expand to include suggested advances for moving forward, there is no doubt privacy advocates will continue to challenge the scope and authority of the E-Verify system.

Gretchen Nobahar

Further Reading

Employment Systems Review Guide to the Audit Process: Employment Equity. Ottawa: Employment Equity Branch, Canadian Human Rights Commission, 2002.

Lapets, Andrei. "Machine Involvement in Formal Reasoning: Improving the Usability of Automated Formal Assistance and Verification Systems." Ph.D. diss., Boston University, 2011.

Nichols, Randall K., and Daniel J. Ryan. *Defending Your Digital Assets against Hackers, Crackers, Spies, and Thieves*. New York: McGraw-Hill, 2000.

Vermaat, Misty, and Susan L. Sebok. *Discovering Computers 2016: Tools, Apps, Devices, and the Impact of Technology*.

See also: American Civil Liberties Union (ACLU); Border Security, Economic Opportunity, and Immigration Modernization Act; Migrants and Refugees in the United States, Privacy Rights of; The Right to Privacy

End-of-life care

Identification: Choosing treatment, or refusing treatment, at the end of one's life is inevitably a sensitive decision and one that an individual would want to keep private for several reasons. As with all health-related issues, most people naturally prefer that they (each individual) should be the one to decide when and with whom conversations about end-of-life care should be had. End-of-life care decisions also carry consequences, many of which are psychological in nature, and an individual may wish to spare his or her family from the full effect of those consequences. Therefore, there are important privacy considerations in end-of-life care.

The right-to-die cases

The first case involving the right to die was the case of *Karen Ann Quinlan* (70 N.J. 10; 355 A.2d 647 (1976)) and involved a twenty-one-year-old woman who fell into a coma after a party. Because Quinlan had expressed to her family (after witnessing a car accident) that she would not want to remain alive by artificial means, her family asked that her artificial breathing machine be removed. The hospital refused. The Quinlans went to court with their request, and the case ultimately made it to the Supreme Court of New Jersey. With *Roe v. Wade*, 410 U.S. 113 (1973), decided only three years earlier, the court reasoned that every person has a right to privacy regarding medical decisions and that to protect that right to privacy, Quinlan's wishes needed to be honored.

When the issue made it to the U.S. Supreme Court, in the case of *Cruzan v. Missouri Department of Health*, 497 U.S. 261 (1990), the right to privacy was not necessary for the Court to decide that a person has a right to decide to refuse medical treatment and to choose a healthcare surrogate (now known as a healthcare power of attorney) to make decisions on his or her behalf should he or she become incapacitated. Therefore, the current status of the law does not implicate the right to privacy in right-to-die cases. *Quinlan* and *Cruzan*, as well as a few cases involving Jehovah's Witnesses refusing blood transfusions, paved the way for recent cases that have enthralled popular culture, including the case of Terry Schiavo.

Privacy and end-of-life documents

The Health Insurance Portability and Accountability Act (HIPAA), 110 Stat. 1936 (1996), pro-

tects all information in an individual's medical files from being disclosed without a waiver by the person holding the protection. Therefore, HIPAA ensures that medical information is kept private. Because living wills, do-not-resuscitate orders, and related documents are part of an individual's medical file, they are necessarily ensured by law to be kept private. The two most common ways in which one waives his or her HIPAA protections are by explicitly doing so in writing (in order to share private information with a friend, family member, or attorney, for example) or by initiating a malpractice claim against a medical provider in which the medical provider would need to reveal information in the medical file in order to establish a defense. Another situation in which there might be disclosure without a waiver by the individual holding the protection under HIPPA would be if the state has a required disclosure law more stringent than the HIPAA law. Other than these waivers and exceptions, all end-of-life-care documents in the individual's medical file are protected as private.

If an individual employs an attorney to aid in the drafting of such documents, that attorney is guided by state ethics rules to keep the documents confidential (i.e., private). While the rules for attorney ethics vary by state, the American Bar Association publishes *The Model Rules for Professional Conduct*, which provides guidance about how each individual state's attorney confidentiality rules may function.

Model Rule 1.6 states that "[a] lawyer shall not reveal information relating to the representation of a client unless the client gives informed consent, the disclosure is impliedly authorized in order to carry out the representation or the disclosure is permitted by [the rules]" and further provides that "[a] lawyer shall make reasonable efforts to prevent the inadvertent or unauthorized disclosure of, or unauthorized access to, information relating to the representation of a client." Because any document an attorney drafts on behalf of a client has "information relating to the representation" of that client, a do-not-resuscitate order, living will, or advanced directives document would automatically be protected and kept private, regardless of whether the client explicitly asked his or her attorney to do so. While the rules allow disclosure in some situations, these situations are finite and include situations such as the following: "to prevent reasonably certain death or substantial bodily harm;" "to prevent the client from committing a crime . . . that is reasonably certain to result in substantial injury to the financial interests . . . of another and in furtherance of which the client has used or is using the lawyer's services;" "to secure legal advice about the lawyer's compliance with these Rules;" "to establish a claim or defense on behalf of the lawyer in a controversy between the lawyer and the client . . . " and "to comply with other law or a court order[.]"

While legally these documents must be kept private, it may not be practical for an individual to keep the documents entirely private. For example, if a person has a living will that he or she keeps in a file in a locked drawer at home (in addition to the copies kept on file with the attorney and one with the individual's primary doctor) and that person is in a traumatic accident while on vacation, the hospital has no way of knowing that the document exists, let alone what it says. Therefore, it is helpful to inform a close family member or friend of the existence and placement of end-of-life documents if at all possible.

Living will

Living wills, sometimes called advanced directives, or directives to physicians, are used to explain an individual's preferences for treatment should the individual be unable to speak on his or her own behalf in the case of serious or terminal illness. Many states have laws regarding specific requirements necessary to make a living will valid (such as witnesses to the signature, or specific language). In most states, this document does not choose a healthcare surrogate (or healthcare power of attorney) to make decisions on behalf of the individual but instead lists the actual desires of the patient should the patient be faced with certain decisions but is incapacitated and thus unable to communicate these desires. A living will can become problematic, however, because it forces a person to attempt to document the way that he or she might handle a variety of imagined situations. The document can easily be under-inclusive or, in the case of an unusually cautious individual, over-inclusive.

Do-not-resuscitate orders

Healthcare providers have an obligation to attempt to restart a heartbeat or respiration should an individual's heart stop beating or the person become unable to breathe; a do-notresuscitate (DNR) order relieves the healthcare provider of that obligation. Unfortunately, many people do not contemplate a situation in which they stop breathing or their heart stops beating until after a DNR order becomes necessary. Therefore, it is often family members who make the decision to sign a DNR on behalf of an incapacitated loved one. This is often a difficult and traumatic decision for the family, who is already experiencing excessive grief. To relieve loved ones of this decision, an individual should contemplate drafting a DNR order before it becomes a relevant decision.

Healthcare power of attorney

Rather than have the court or hospital choose a healthcare surrogate to make decisions on behalf of an incapacitated person, which will happen should there be no healthcare power of attorney on file, an individual may draft a healthcare power of attorney to designate the person that individual would prefer to make decisions on his or her behalf in the event of incapacitation. Many states have statutes designating the specific requirements for this document, such as the documents discussed in this essay, and should no healthcare power of attorney exist (or be able to be located), most states have a preferential list of family members who become the healthcare surrogate, if necessary. For example, a state may list a spouse as the healthcare surrogate, should it be necessary, but if there is no spouse, then a parent, and if there is no parent, a sibling, and so on.

Conclusion

While end-of-life decisions have many privacy implications, the Court has chosen not to use the right to privacy to establish one's decision-making powers at the end of life. The documents that outline these decisions are further complicated with privacy implications, and a delicate balance of the practical and preferential is necessary to ensure the best result for the patient at issue because, if privacy is not properly protected, or wishes are not honored at the onset, it could be the most public of forums—a court of law— where any issues are resolved.

Julie Ann Embler

Further Reading

Cantor, Norman L. *Advanced Directives and the Pursuit of Dying with Dignity.* Bloomberg: Indiana University Press, 1993.

Caplan, Arthur L., James J. McCartney, and Dominic A. Stisi. *The Case of Terri Schiavo: Ethics at the End of Life.* Amherst, NY: Prometheus Books, 2006.

Weir, Robert F., ed. *Ethical Issues in Death and Dying*, 2nd ed. New York: Columbia University Press, 1986.

See also: Constitutional Law; Health Care Information; Philosophical Basis of Privacy

The Enlightenment

Identification: Also known as the Age of Enlightenment, a philosophical movement prominent in the eighteenth century that was marked by a "restless spirit of inquiry" in which many traditional beliefs, especially those related to the church or state, were scrutinized and criticized because they lacked a reasonable basis.

During the Enlightenment, reason, a concept based on logic (as opposed to "revelation," religious faith, or allegiance to traditional powers) came to prominence. The Enlightenment challenged metaphysical ideas and any attempts to explain human existence outside reason. Enlightenment philosophy transformed human understanding and greatly influenced the American Founding Fathers, the men who wrote the Constitution of the United States. Thus the Enlightenment profoundly shaped American jurisprudence from the beginning of the Republic.

The Enlightenment defies easy periodization, and scholars use different dates to define the Enlightenment. Isaac Newton, René Descartes, John Milton, and Thomas Hobbes wrote during the beginning of the Enlightenment. Philosophers such as John Locke, David Hume, Charles de Montesquieu, Voltaire, Jean-Jacques Rousseau, Cesare Beccaria, Adam Smith, Immanuel Kant, and Jeremy Bentham all wrote during the apex of the Enlightenment.

Many Enlightenment philosophers discussed and developed the principles that form the basis of modern privacy ideas, including the idea that governments and societies should allow a degree of freedom from the scrutiny of others, whether it be the state or other individual people. Enlightenment philosophers also argued that individuals needed a certain autonomy in making decisions affecting aspects of individual life. Despite some similarities, the various Enlightenment philosophers viewed autonomy in significantly different ways.

In *The Leviathan,* Thomas Hobbes criticized many of the actions of the English monarchy. Hobbes focused on the individual's power and right to preserve his or her life. He viewed the state of nature (the primitive condition of human society before the establishment of government) as "a state of pure liberty" where there was pure lawlessness and each individual person had unlimited freedom to preserve his life and maximize his happiness, even if exercising such freedom came at the expense of the life and happiness of others. Life in the state of nature, Hobbes said, was "solitary, poor, nasty, brutish, and short." Hobbes wrote that government was the answer to the anarchic state of nature. Being rational, man surrenders his unlimited liberty, autonomy, and privacy to the sovereign in a "social contract" in which the government exists to preserve the lives of its citizens and thereby serve the common good. According to Hobbes, the social contract established the sovereign's power. Hobbes did not recognize a place for the privacy of the individual. Later Enlightenment philosophers strongly rejected the Hobbesian idea that humans had the moral obligation to obey the sovereign unconditionally.

Locke, for example, believed that all people were endowed with inalienable rights from nature, which included individual autonomy to act to preserve life. Locke's *Two Treatises of Government* (1689) remains an influential work that shaped political philosophy and provided a basis for later political thought, and was later ennunciated in both the Declaration of Independence and the U.S. Constitution. *Two Treatises of Government* places sovereignty in the hands of the people. Locke's fundamental argument is that people are equal and invested with natural rights in a state of nature in which they live free from outside rule. People then exchange some of their natural rights to enter into society with other people and to be protected by common laws and a common executive power to enforce the laws. Locke sees personal liberty as the key component of a society that works toward the individual's and the state's best interests.

Enlightenment philosophers developed their ideas based on the work of their predecessors and thus expanded ideas pertaining to the rights to life, liberty, and property. Like Locke, Rousseau and Kant broadened the concept of liberty through their development of concepts of autonomy to be one's "self" or one's own "person." In the early nineteenth century, John Stuart Mill used these ideas to form the basis of his concept that "individuality" was a core element of well-being.

During the late eighteenth century, American revolutionaries relied heavily on Enlightenment ideas. In *Common Sense*, Thomas Paine insisted that the law recognize certain rights from the time when the United States was established, stressing that "[s]ecuring freedom and property" for all men should be core values of a free nation. Paine's works, like the writings of the Enlightenment philosophers, greatly influenced the American Founding Fathers' views of the rights of the individual. These ideas are reflected in the Declaration of Independence and the U.S. Constitution, both of which rely heavily on the work of Enlightenment philosophers.

Further Reading

Blatterer, Harry. *Modern Privacy Shifting Boundaries, New Forms*. New York: Palgrave Macmillan, 2010.

Grayling, A. C. *Liberty in the Age of Terror: A Defence of Civil Liberties and Enlightenment Values*. London: Bloomsbury, 2009.

Im Hof, Ulrich. *The Enlightenment*. Tr. by William E. Yuill. Cambridge, MA: Blackwell, 1994.

Israel, Jonathan I. *Democratic Enlightenment: Philosophy, Revolution, and Human Rights 1750–1790*. New York: Oxford University Press, 2011.

MacCormick, Neil. *Enlightenment, Rights, and Revolution: Essays in Legal and Social Philosophy*. Aberdeen, UK: Aberdeen University Press, 1989.

Michael, John. *Anxious Intellects: Academic Professionals, Public Intellectuals, and Enlightenment Values*. Durham, NC: Duke University Press, 2000.

Slote, Michael A. *From Enlightenment to Receptivity: Rethinking Our Values*. New York: Oxford University Press, 2013.

See also: Constitutional Law; Descartes, René; Legal Evolution of Privacy Rights; Locke, John; Privacy, Right of

Espionage Act

Identification: Legislation intended to punish and criminalize actions that interfere with U.S. foreign relations, foreign commerce, and intelligence activities while also enhancing the enforcement of U.S. criminal law, especially during wartime.

"U.S. Charges Snowden with Espionage" was the breaking news transmitted around the world in late June 2013. The U.S. government had charged Edward Snowden, an ex-contractor with the U.S. National Security Agency (NSA), with violating the Espionage Act of 1917, 40 Stat. 217 (1917) because he leaked confidential information on NSA surveillance. The Snowden affair, with the 2010 incident of the WikiLeaks revelation of confidential documents through its organization, its website, and the editor-in-chief Julian Assange, all brought much attention to the statute.

The Espionage Act, from its inception, was intended to punish and criminalize actions that interfere with U.S. foreign relations, foreign commerce, and intelligence activities while also enhancing the enforcement of U.S. criminal law, especially during wartime. The purpose of the statute concerned the perceived threat of German espionage immediately prior to the U.S. entry into World War I. The act also represented efforts to prohibit and punish certain hostile actions sponsored by enemy powers against the United States during wartime. These efforts included provisions to prevent insubordination in military recruitment and operations.

Previously, the Sedition Act of 1798 punished acts of espionage by foreign powers against the United States. The Sedition Act expired in the spring of 1801, however, and as World War I drew closer, lawmakers sought to promulgate a new statute. The Defense Secrets Act of 1911, 36 Stat. 1804 (1911), is the predecessor of the Espionage Act and refers to certain provisions of the former statute. The main purposes of the Defense Secrets Act were also used to justify the Espionage Act.

The Espionage Act was introduced as the Webb-Overman bill and represented the Wilson administration's efforts to punish treasonous activity, thereby deterring activities that could potentially interfere with American wartime efforts. A special session of Congress in February 1917 reviewed what the Senate had passed.

Congress adjourned before approving the bill. The bill was reintroduced, however, after the United States declared war on Germany. Congress seemed particularly motivated to pass the legislation after revelations that the German government had disseminated a German War Book that was intended to encourage German Americans to sabotage the American war effort.

The Espionage Act became effective on June 15, 1917. It prohibited "obtaining information respecting the national defense with intent or reason to believe that the information to be obtained is to be used to the injury of the United States, or to the advantage of any foreign nation" (Section 1) and is specific to central aspects of the defense including information regarding navy vessels, submarines, aircraft, forts, and so on. The person charged is to be punished with a fine up to $10,000 or with an imprisonment term for not more than two years, or both.

Section 2 of the act imposes the punishment of death or imprisonment of thirty years or less if a person acts "with intent or believes" that such action can cause "injury to the U.S." or can be used to "the advantage of a foreign nation" and is for communication of information privy to the defense by means of the written word, a code, photographs, or other instruments. This provision need not apply only during a time of war.

The provisions restricted First Amendment freedom of speech (Section 3) by stating that, during a time of war, a punishment "by a fine of not more than $10,000 or imprisonment for not more than twenty years, or both" shall be imposed if a person willfully makes or conveys "false reports or false statements" that interferes or with an intention to interfere "with the success of the military or naval forces of the U.S." or otherwise "to promote the success of the enemies." The statute criminalizes actions wilfully causing or attempting to cause "insubordination, disloyalty, mutiny, refusal of duty in the military or naval forces" of the United States or wilfully obstructing recruitments or enlistments for serving the United States during wartime.

Congress rejected the original press censorship provision by a majority vote, and a considerably watered-down substitute version of Section 3 was proposed that excluded any type of press censorship.

Title 12 of the act granted unlimited power to the U.S. Postmaster General to check mails and remove postage material considered "treasonable or [having an] anarchistic character." It is most commonly known as the non-mailability provision. Congressional opposition led to the watering down of this section of the act to mail "containing any matter advocating or urging treason, insurrection or forcible resistance to any law of the United States." The remaining sections prescribe punishments for conspiracy, and for harboring or concealing person(s) who have committed an offense under the Espionage Act.

During the passing of the act in the Congress, other constitutional objections raised related to the denial of a trial by jury (as required in the U.S. constitution) and the delegation of power of legislation to the president, which is again is unconstitutional.

The Espionage Act has been controversial from 1917 to the present, beginning with *Masses Publishing Co v. Pattern*, 244F 535 (SD NY 1917), revd, 246F 24 (2d Cir 1917) (also known as the *Masses Publishing* case). In that case, Judge Learned Hand, while not holding the act unconstitutional, addressed the importance of freedom of speech as being the cornerstone of the long-standing tradition and history of the nation, and stressed the compelling understanding of the fact that Congress would not unnecessarily curb free speech without "an equivocal statement of its purpose to that end."

Section 3 of the act was amended to include punishing the use of profanity and abusive language against the United States. Nine indictments have been brought under the Espionage Act since 1917.

Tania Sebastian

Further Reading

"The WikiLeaks Story and Criminal Liability under Espionage Law." Reuters, August 26, 2010. http://blogs.reuters.com/great-debate/2010/08/26/the-wikileaks-story-and-criminal-liability-under-the-espionage-laws/.

Bivins, Amy E. "United States: Privacy—House Judiciary Explores Espionage Act's Application to Wikileaks' Net Posts." *World Communications Regulation Report* 6, no. 1 (2011): 16–18.

Carroll, Thomas F. "Freedom of Speech and of the Press in War Time: The Espionage Act." *Michigan Law Review* 17, no. 8 (1919): 621–665.

Cogen, Marc. *Democracies and the Shock of War: The Law as a Battlefield*. New ed. Burlington, VT: Ashgate, 2012.

Estlack, Russell W. *Shattered Lives Shattered Dreams: The Disrupted Lives of Families in America's Internment Camps*. Springville, UT: Bonneville Books, 2011.

Finn, Peter, and Sari Horwitz. "U.S. Charges Snowden with Espionage." *Washington Post*, June 21, 2013. https://www.washingtonpost.com/world/national-security/us-charges-snowden-withespionage/2013/06/21/507497d8-dab1–11e2-a016–92547bf094cc_story.html.

Greenwald, Glenn. "On the Espionage Act Charges against Edward Snowden." *Guardian* June 22, 2013. http://www.theguardian.com/commentisfree/2013/jun/22/snowden-espionage-charges.

Manz, Willaim H., ed. *Civil Liberties in Wartime: Legislative Histories of the Espionage Act 1917 and the Sedition Act of 1918* (vol. 1, Documents 1–57). Buffalo, NY: William S. Hein & Co., Inc., 2007.

Nelles, Walter, ed. *Espionage Cases: With Certain Others on Related Points*. New York: National Civil Liberties Bureau, 1918.

Post, Robert. 2000. "Reconciling Theory and Doctrine in First Amendment Jurisprudence." *California Law Review* 88, no. 6 (2000): 2353.

Shane, Scott. "Ex-Contractor Is Charged in Leaks on NSA Surveillance." *New York Times* June 21, 2013. http://www.nytimes.com/2013/06/22/us/snowden-espionage-act.html?_r=0.

Stone, Geoffrey R. "Judge Learned Hand and the Espionage Act of 1917: A Mystery Unraveled." *University of Chicago Law Review* 70, no. 1 (2003): 335–358.

See also: Assange, Julian; Constitutional Law; First Amendment to the U.S. Constitution; Law Enforcement; National Security Agency; Snowden, Edward Joseph; Whistleblowers; WikiLeaks

F

Facebook

Identification: Created in 2004 by Harvard University student Mark Zuckerberg. It was based on the concept of the university's "facebook" — a directory of student names with a picture, typically organized by graduating class year.

In its first iteration, Facebook was a program called Facemash, which Zuckerberg developed, that allowed Harvard students to rank photographs of their classmates according to attractiveness. Zuckerberg obtained the photographs by hacking into Harvard's database of student identification images. Harvard University administration shut down the site a few days after Zuckerberg began disseminating it. However, a few months later Zuckerberg began development of the thefacebook.com. Thefacebook.com was launched in February 2004 and only allowed Harvard University students to join. In March of 2004, thefacebook.com expanded to Columbia University, Stanford University, and Yale University. At this time Eduardo Saverin, Dustin Moskovitz, Andrew McCollum, and Chris Hughes joined Zuckerberg in the development and management of the website. Very quickly, thefacebook.com expanded to include Ivy League universities and Boston-area colleges. It continued to expand and by 2006 Facebook was available to anyone over the age of 13. By 2012, Facebook announced it had reached its one-billionth user. Facebook is now a publicly-traded company that has a net worth in the billions of dollars. Its primary source of revenue is through advertising, with a small amount of additional revenue coming from fees and payments for virtual services, such as games.

In many ways, Facebook has become the symbol for the contradictory nature of an online social network. One facet of Facebook is its ability to assist people in maintaining social connections that extend beyond the sphere of everyday life. Conversely, Facebook is a publicly-traded company with responsibilities to its shareholders to maintain a certain level of profitability. Also, its primary source of revenue is advertising. Advertising, by its nature, must respond to its audience. Facebook, must, therefore, be able to define the characteristics of its users. This tension between the use of Facebook as a personal mode of expression, as well as a generator of revenue, informs the question of privacy and Facebook.

The impact on the privacy of individuals using Facebook has been an issue from its initial iteration as Facemash. When the Harvard University administration shut it down one of the reasons they gave was the privacy concern of disseminating students' pictures without their consent. This concern has persisted, despite Facebook's continued effort to assure its users that the information they generate by using Facebook is adequately protected.

It was reported that Facebook has participated in lobbying for the passing of the Cybersecurity Information Sharing Act (CISA) of 2015.

This act allows companies to share cybersecurity threat information with federal agencies such as the Federal Bureau of Investigations and the National Security Agency. Privacy advocates argue that the definition of a cybersecurity threat under CISA is too broadly defined and will allow companies to actively monitor users without a warrant. This information could then be provided to various federal agencies.

In 2018 Facebook faced multiple questions regarding its protection of users' personal information, security structures, and dissemination of information to third parties. Most notably, *The New York Times* reported that Cambridge Analytica, a voter-profiling company, acquired the personal information of 50 million Facebook users without users' permission in order to create a national "psychographic profile" that would be used in its work for the Trump presidential campaign. Facebook later stated that the personal information of 87 million users had been accessed without the users' permission. Facebook did make changes to the accessibility of the privacy controls as a result; however, Mark Zuckerberg and Facebook continue to be criticized for security breaches and third-party access to personal information.

Rachel Jorgensen

Further Reading

Cohen, Julie E. "Inverse Relationship Between Secrecy and Privacy." *Social Research* 77.3 (Fall 2010): 883–898.

Hoefflinger, Mike. *Becoming Facebook: The 10 Challenges that Defined the Company That's Disrupting the World*. New York, AMACON, 2017.

Newton, Lee. *Facebook Nation: Total Information Awesomeness*. New York: Springer, 2014.

Rosenberg, Matthew and Nicholas Confessore, Carole Cadwalladr. "How Trump Consultants Exploited the Facebook Data of Millions." *The New York Times*. March 17, 2018. https://nyti.ms/2GB9dK4

Rubenstein, Ira S. and Nathaniel Good. "Privacy By Design: A Counterfactual Analysis of Google and Facebook Privacy Incidents." *Berkeley Technology Law Journal* 28.2 (Fall 2013): 1333–1413.

Trottier, Daniel. *Identity Problems in the Facebook Era*. New York, Routledge, 2014.

See also: Computers and privacy; Cyberspace Information Sharing Act (CISA); Data collection; Marketing; Social media

Facial recognition technology

Identification: A biometric technology that identifies people by measuring and analyzing their physiological or behavioral characteristics.

Biometric technologies were developed to identify people through characteristics such as their faces, fingerprints, hands, eye retinas and irises, voice, and gait. Unlike conventional identification methods, including a card to gain access to a space or a password to log on to a computer system, biometric technologies determine characteristics that are unique to each person and would be difficult to alter.

There has been strong opposition to the commercial use of facial recognition technology (FRT). Google removed facial recognition apps and services. Europe ordered Facebook to discontinue the use of facial recognition for photo tagging. When he was in office, Senator Al Franken (D-MN) raised concerns about NameTag. Franken wrote to an app developer, calling for the delay of the app's release until best practices are established. Some leading privacy groups recommended that FRT be suspended until adequate safeguards were implemented.

An FRT system has four basic parts: a camera to capture an image, an algorithm to create a faceprint (also known as a facial template), a database of stored images, and an algorithm to compare the captured image to the database of images or a single image in the database. The quality of these components determines the effectiveness of the system. Also, the more similar the environments in which the images are compared—such as the background, lighting conditions, camera distance, and size and orientation of the head—the better a facial recognition technology system will perform.

FRTs are able to perform several functions, including (1) detecting a face in an image;

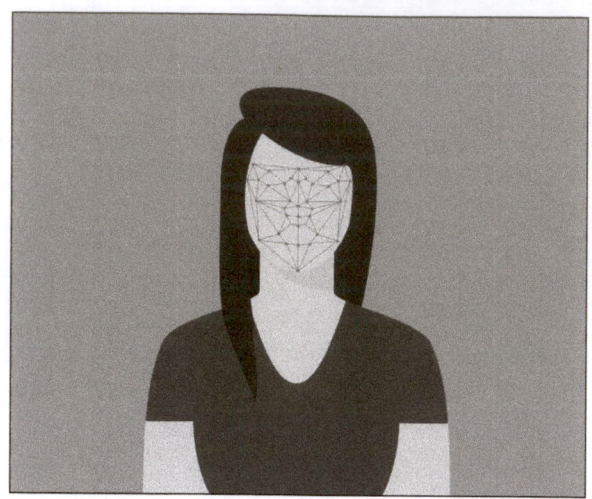

Flat Recognition Facial Face Woman System. (By teguh-jatipras.)

(2) estimating personal characteristics, such as an individual's age, race, or gender; (3) verifying identity by accepting or denying the identity claimed by a person; and (4) identifying an individual by matching an image of an unknown person to a gallery of known people. FRT systems can generate two types of errors—false positives (reporting an incorrect match) or false negatives (not reporting a match when one exists). Studies of FRT algorithms have indicated that this technology has improved over time. Error rates continue to decline, and algorithms are getting better at identifying individuals from images of poor quality or that are captured under low light. Also, certain controlled tests have indicated that facial recognition algorithms surpassed humans in accurately identifying whether pairs of face images, taken under different lighting, were images of the same person or of different people.

Various federal agencies, privacy and consumer organizations, and some industry representatives have raised serious issues regarding the commercial use of FRT, including the technology's ability to identify and monitor individuals in public spaces without their knowledge, and around the collection, use, and sharing of personal data associated with the technology. FRT proponents argue that the technology has raised no new privacy risks or that such risks can be reduced.

Despite these concerns, FRT continues to improve rapidly in accuracy. Individuals continue to upload billions of pictures to social networking and other Internet sites, which develop a large repository of facial images. These images in turn are often linked to names or other personal information. The combination of these two trends may make it feasible to soon identify almost any individual in several public spaces. Privacy organizations, who have expressed concerns about the commercial application of facial recognition technology, have generally focused on (1) how it affects the ability of individuals to remain relatively anonymous in public; (2) the capacity to track individuals across locations; and (3) use of facial recognition without the individuals' knowledge or consent.

In rebuttal, FRT supporters have argued that

(1) individuals should not expect complete anonymity in public (individuals effectively relinquish some of their anonymity when they make their faces public);

(2) privacy and anonymity are not synonymous and that relinquishing complete anonymity is not the total abandonment of privacy (they also argue that capturing a facial image or faceprint in public does not necessarily infringe on an individual's anonymity because it does not directly reveal a name, Social Security number, or any other similar personal information);

(3) surveillance is already present in ordinary American life (commercial entities already routinely install security cameras) and that facial recognition does not increase their use;

(4) privacy advocacy organizations may have exaggerated the capabilities of FRT systems because cameras usually are not interconnected and it is not practical to implement commercial applications that would use multiple

cameras to track individuals' movements; and

(5) consumers seem willing to exchange some privacy for the security supposedly provided by surveillance technology.

Generally, FRT supporters assert that there are trade-offs between some loss of privacy and the benefits that new technologies give to consumers and businesses, and to economic growth that such technology supposedly creates.

Many FRT supporters also argue that (1) consumers' expectations and ideas of privacy have evolved because of technological innovation (for example, consumers have reportedly demonstrated their willingness to share private information in public settings—such as by posting to social networking sites to obtain benefits such as photo sharing and management; (2) the need for consent should depend on the context (i.e., the context in which FRT is used should have a bearing on issues of consumer consent); and (3) FRT should not be singled out because the privacy issues associated with FRT are largely identical to those of any biometric technologies, including voice or gait recognition, which also can identify individuals from some distance without their knowledge. Several FRT technology companies have said that lawmakers should protect personal information gathered from all biometrics, not only FRT. In addition, they argue that businesses that use the security technology should not be required to obtain consent before the technology is used because obtaining consent is not required for social networking sites, which have repositories of facial images that can be used to identify individuals more broadly.

Several government, industry, and privacy organizations have proposed or are developing privacy guidelines governing the commercial use of FRT, including describing how commercial organizations collect, use, and store data. FRT is found in several different consumer and business applications, but the extent of its current use in commercial settings is still largely unknown. The technology is commonly used in software that manages personal photographs and in social networking applications to identify friends. Also, several companies use FRT instead of a password to provide secure access to computers, phones, and gaming systems. FRT may have applications for customer service and marketing; however, in the United States, use of the technology for such purposes appears to be largely for detecting characteristics (such as age or gender) to tailor digital advertising rather than identifying unique individuals. Some security systems in retail stores, banks, and casinos incorporate facial recognition technology.

Many, including privacy groups and government agencies, have asserted several privacy concerns on the commercial use of FRT. They claim that, if FRT use became widespread, it could allow businesses or individuals to identify almost everyone in public without their knowledge or consent and to monitor the locations, movements, and associates of individuals. They have also expressed concerns that information collected or associated with FRT could be used, shared, or sold in ways that consumers do not understand, anticipate, or want to consent to. Some stakeholders disagree that the technology presents new or unusual privacy risks, again citing that individuals should not expect absolute anonymity in public and that some privacy loss is offset by the benefits that the technology gives to consumers and businesses.

Many government, industry, and privacy organizations have proposed voluntary privacy guidelines for commercial FRT use. Suggested best practices vary, but most call for disclosing the technology's use and obtaining consent before using it to identify someone from anonymous images.

No federal privacy law expressly regulates commercial uses of facial recognition technology, and laws do not fully address key privacy issues raised by stakeholders, such as the circumstances under which the technology may be used to identify individuals or track their whereabouts and companions. Laws governing the collection, use, and storage of personal information may potentially apply to the commercial use of facial recognition in specific circumstances, such as information collected by healthcare entities and financial institutions. Also, courts have interpreted the Federal Trade Commission Act to require companies to abide by their stated privacy policies.

Face recognition data can be accessed without an individual's knowledge. With commercial uses of FRT increasing and replacing older access methods such as password log-ins, the technology continues to raise vexing privacy questions.

Facebook first started using FRT by licensing technology from another company, Face.com, which it acquired in 2012. Facebook then introduced a new app, known as Moments, using the same technology as in tag suggestions, which groups photos in a user's smartphone based on the faces identified. Photos can then be shared with specific friends as opposed to uploading them to Facebook. When a person is identified in a picture on Facebook, the biometric software remembers the face so it can be tagged in other photographs. Its current system (since 2016) is known as DeepFace.

Facebook Inc. claims that FRT enhances the user experience. However, privacy advocates argue that the company's technology, which was halted in Europe and Canada after privacy concerns were raised, should be implemented only with explicit permission or consent. In Europe, strict privacy laws forced Facebook in 2012 to delete data collected for its tag-suggestion feature following a probe by Irish authorities. Canadian authorities forced Facebook to turn off its tag suggestions in that country.

Facebook was sued for its FRT policy and practices in Illinois, which has one of America's strictest biometric privacy laws. The plaintiffs alleged that Facebook failed to notify users that the service was collecting facial data on users tagged in photos. The photo publishing site Shutterfly Inc. was sued in Illinois over that company's photo tagging feature.

Facebook attempted to defend its use of FRT, which develops a unique faceprint and which may be used to identify someone when he or she has already been identified through tagging. The technology powers a photo feature called tag suggestions, which is automatically turned on when users sign up for a Facebook account. The suggestions are made only to a user's friends. Tag suggestions make it easy for friends to tag each other in photos. When someone is alerted that he or she has been tagged in a photo, it is easier to take action, whether it is commenting, contacting the person who shared it, or reporting it to Facebook. Users can opt out at any time. However, this requires that they change their settings.

Privacy activists complained that the U.S. government's approach to regulating the use of face data by companies is insufficient in protecting privacy because face recognition data may be collected without a person's knowledge. These activists further argue that facial recognition is one of those categories of data where a very clear consent is necessary.

Some business leaders have opposed requiring prior consent. They argue that fears that facial data may be used to track people have been exaggerated because the technology supposedly reveals less information about a person's habits than most customers would reveal by using a mobile phone that also tracks and shares location data.

Privacy advocates have provided examples companies that obtained proper consent for FRT implementation. Google, for example, provides users of its Google app with the option to use face identification by turning on the "find my face" feature. Companies such as Microsoft Corporation, which was placing FRT into Windows 10, and MasterCard, which had plans for selfie verification for online payments, require the download of an app or the purchase of hardware.

Industries using FRT have generally agreed that a code of conduct should be implemented that would require companies using facial recognition to be transparent about their use of the technology. A notice or a sign might be the answer, but how much information would be required and through what means to gain consent of those being surveilled by FRT remain a hotly disputed issue.

Gretchen Nobahar

Further Reading

Cackley, Alicia Puente. *Facial Recognition Technology: Commercial Uses, Privacy Issues, and Applicable Federal Law: Report to the Ranking Member, Subcommittee on Privacy, Technology and the Law, Committee on the Judiciary, U.S. Senate.* Washington, DC: United States Government Accountability Office, 2015.

Denham, Elizabeth. *Investigation into the Use of Facial Recognition Technology by the Insurance Corporation of British Columbia.* Victoria: Office of the Information and Privacy Commissioner for British Columbia, 2012.

Dumas, M. Barry. *Diving into the Bitstream: Information Technology Meets Society in a Digital World.* New York: Routledge, 2012.

Kallen, Stuart A. *Are Privacy Rights Being Violated?* Detroit, MI: Greenhaven, 2006.

Laptop Computer–Based Facial Recognition System Assessment. Oak Ridge, TN: Oak Ridge Y-12 Plant, 2001.

Lee, Newton. *Facebook Nation: Total Information Awareness.* New York: Springer, 2013.

Li, Stan Z., and Anil K. Jain. *Handbook of Face Recognition,* 2nd ed. London: Springer London, 2011.

Mago, V. K. *Cross-Disciplinary Applications of Artificial Intelligence and Pattern Recognition Advancing Technologies.* Hershey, PA: Information Science Reference, 2012.

Marks, Murray K. *Computer-Graphic Facial Reconstruction.* Burlington, MA: Elsevier Academic Press, 2005.

What Facial Recognition Technology Means for Privacy and Civil Liberties: Hearing before the Subcommittee on Privacy, Technology and the Law of the Committee on the Judiciary, United States Senate, One Hundred Twelfth Congress, Second Session, July 18, 2014.

See also: Apps; Biometrics; Computers and privacy; Consumer privacy; Facebook; Google; Next Generation Identification

Fair Credit Reporting Act

Identification: Fair Credit Reporting Act (FCRA), Public Law No. 91–508, of 1970. An act that created new standards for credit reporting agencies (CRAs) to protect the privacy of consumers in credit reporting.

The Fair Credit Reporting Act (FCRA) fundamentally changed the way CRAs interact with businesses and the general public. Not all companies disseminating information are governed by the FCRA, but typically for-profit entities distributing information about private individuals do have to follow FCRA requirements. To enforce these new rights and responsibilities, the FCRA provides private rights of action for citizens alleging violations of the FCRA. The Federal Trade Commission (FTC) may also begin criminal actions for deceptive or unfair trade practices. In addition, the FCRA statutorily exempted CRAs from certain common law torts.

A CRA is an entity that, broadly speaking, gathers, organizes, and disseminates information about consumers to help evaluate their credit. Normally this information is in the form of a credit report. CRAs facilitate the movement of credit from lenders to borrowers by providing information to lenders concerning the credit history of borrowers. Credit history is strongly predictive of future borrower behavior, so lenders use this information to match borrowers to loans, interest rates, and other terms of the transaction. CRAs are vital because they gather and collate cost-effectively more information than a lender, such as a bank, could gather about a borrower. CRAs also play a vital role in changing borrower behavior because the prospect of a negative credit report provides inducement for borrowers to engage in responsible practices. The three major CRAs in the United States are Equifax, Experian, and TransUnion.

The FCRA was the result of consumer concerns about the scope of privatized data banks and the personal information that these banks held and gave to third parties. Before the FCRA, consumers had to rely on traditional common law remedies for protection, such as defamation, negligence, slander, libel, or "invasion of privacy." Despite these common law remedies, CRAs often escaped legal penalties because they enjoyed what was called conditional privilege. The remedies for consumers varied from state to state, making it difficult to find out whether CRAs had broken the law.

The FCRA changed the credit reporting landscape in three major areas. The act increases the accuracy of information held by CRAs and ensures that they transfer consumer reports responsibly and accurately. Second, the FCRA provides a framework for consumers to challenge and correct the information in their credit reports. Third, it removes some of the secrecy of the credit reporting process, at least the part between the CRAs and the consumer.

The FCRA first created minimum standards of accuracy concerning consumer information. CRAs must avoid sending credit reports to ineligible recipients and have a general duty of "following reasonable procedures to assure maximum possible accuracy" of information. The "maximum possible accuracy" standard is a high one because CRAs must strive not only for technical accuracy in collecting and entering data but also must actively seek to give the "whole picture" of a consumer's credit. For example, in *Pinner v. Schmidt*, the Fifth Circuit found that a consumer report was inaccurate because it indicated "litigation pending" when the consumer was the one bringing a suit. While technically accurate, the report could be interpreted as a consumer being the one sued instead of the one bringing suit, thus giving a negative picture of the consumer's credit.

Any time a creditor denies a loan or takes an adverse action because of a CRA's credit report, the creditor must notify the consumer and give specific grounds for the action. *Safeco Insurance Co. of America v. Burr* held this adverse action could be something as minimal as a higher rate for an insurance policy compared to a rate that would have applied if the lender not seen the credit report. If a consumer finds certain information inaccurate in the credit report, he or she may challenge the erroneous entry. The CRA then conducts another investigation. The CRA then examines the accuracy of the information on file for a specific consumer. Once the CRA has conducted its reinvestigation, it must notify the consumer within five days of its findings and give the consumer a copy of the revised credit report. If the reinvestigation shows the CRA could have detected the inaccuracy if it had engaged in an investigation itself, the CRA may be liable to the consumer under the FCRA.

Significant for consumers is the fact that the FCRA creates multiple causes of action for consumers who feel CRAs have mishandled their information. If the CRA has negligently or willfully ignored their duty to consumers, then the consumer may recover damages, costs, attorney's fees, and even punitive damages. In this way the FCRA gives those with the greatest incentive to ensure accurate data, the consumers, the greatest ability to ensure responsible CRA practice.

A number of amendments have changed the scope of the FCRA since 1970. Some are small, such as the Ted Weiss Child Support Enforcement Act of 1992, which requires CRAs to report a consumer's failure to pay certain child support in any credit report passed to a creditor. Other amendments, such as the Consumer Credit Reporting Reform Act of 1996, accomplished more fundamental changes in credit reporting. The reform act allowed CRAs to sell lists of prescreened consumers who met certain criteria for lenders. Lenders can use these lists to send offers to consumers for their services. Creditors may use prescreened lists, however, only if they meant to make a "firm offer of credit" to the consumers on the list. In *Cole v. U.S. Capital, Inc.*, the Seventh Circuit held the "firm offer of credit" cannot be a solicitation or advertisement because creditors should have no access to consumer's records under a prescreened list unless the consumer stood to derive some benefit as well. Instead the "firm offer of credit" must be an actual offer for a service that consumers can accept.

The Fair and Accurate Credit Transaction Act of 2003 (FACTA) further amended the FCRA to help consumers fight against the growing specter of identity theft. Identity theft is a fraud committed using the identifying information of another person. If a consumer believes that he or she is a victim of identity theft, FACTA allows the consumer to file a fraud report with a CRA. There are two fundamental types of fraud reports that consumers may give. The consumer may contact a CRA at any time and inform the CRA that he or she consumer wishes to remove the fraud report.

The first type of fraud report, a one-call fraud report, allows consumers to alert CRAs if they have a good-faith suspicion that they have been or are about to become a victim of fraud or a related crime, including identity theft. If the consumer files such a report, the CRA must

(1) add such a fraud alert to any credit report for the consumer in the next ninety days and

(2) transmit the fraud alert to other CRAs. The CRA must also inform the consumer that he or she may receive a credit report within three days.

The second type of fraud report is an extended report. As the name implies, this report lasts longer—for up to seven years—and removes the consumer from prescreened lists for the next five years. Like the one-call report, the extended report requires CRAs to notify other CRAs. The extended report informs creditors that the consumer did not allow issuance of new credit cards and plans, and requires users of credit reports to contact the consumer via telephone to verify, to a reasonable level of certainty, that the consumer actually requested the user's service.

FACTA also requires CRAs to provide consumers with a free copy of their credit report every twelve months. Consumers may further request a CRA to provide their credit score and the metrics used to calculate the score, including the major negative factors leading to a negative score. FACTA also increases the amount of time during which consumers may opt out of prescreened lists. While it may appear that CRAs got the short end of the stick, FACTA increases the amount of CRAs' protection from state laws that provide ways for consumers to sue. FACTA preempts states from passing a whole gambit of laws concerning consumer credit reports.

Daniel Berens

Further Reading

Gardner, Steven. "Privacy and Debt Collection Implications of the Fair Credit Reporting Act and the 2003 Fact Act." *Consumer Finance Law Quarterly Report* 58, no. 46 (2004).

Griffith, Elwin J. "Credit Reporting, Prescreened Lists, and Adverse Action: The Impact of the Fair Credit Reporting Act and the Equal Credit Opportunity Act." *California West Law Review* 46, no. 1 (2009)

Maurer, Virginia, and Roger D. Blair. "Statute Law and Common Law: The Fair Credit Reporting Act." *Missouri Law Review* 49, no. 289 (1984)

Pinson, Chad M., and John B. Lawrence. "FCRA Preemption of State Law: A Guide Through Muddy Waters." *Journal of Consumer and Commercial Law* 15, no. 47 (2012)

Schein, David D., and James D. Phillips. "Holding Credit Reporting Agencies Accountable: How the Financial Crisis May Be Contributing to Improving Accuracy in Credit Reporting." *Loyola Consumer Law Review* 24, no. 329 (2012).

Weinstein, Donald D. "Federal Fair Credit Reporting Act—Compliance by Lenders and Other Users of Consumer Credit Information." *Banking Law Journal* 89, no. 410 (1972)

See also: Credit and debit cards; Credit reporting agencies (CRAs); Data protection regimes; Federal Trade Commission (FTC); Financial information, privacy rights in

Fair information practice principles

Identification: A set of practices that address how personal information should be collected, used, retained, managed, and deleted.

The Fair information practice principles (FIPPs) have taken many forms, both within the United States and internationally, and aim to serve as a foundational framework within both the public and private sectors to protect the privacy and integrity of personally identifiable information.

The FIPPs originated in a 1973 report issued by the Advisory Committee on Automated Personal Data Systems of the U.S. Department of Health, Education, and Welfare, the precursor to the Department of Health and Human Services, entitled *Records, Computers, and the Rights of Citizens*. In examining advancements in record-keeping systems, the committee called for a code of fair information practices that would diminish arbitrary and abusive record-keeping practices that were believed to harm personal privacy. These articulated practices would become the core principles of the FIPPs and serve as the foundation of many privacy laws throughout the 1970s, including the Privacy Act of 1974, 88 Stat. 1896.

The FIPPs were articulated in perhaps their most influential form in guidelines adopted by the Organisation for Economic Co-operation and Development (OECD) in 1980. The *Guidelines on the Protection of Privacy and Transborder Flows of Personal Data* were developed with the goal of harmonizing the national privacy laws of OECD member countries in order to facilitate the international flow of data during the rise of automatic data processing while still protecting privacy interests. Although the guidelines did not use the term FIPPs, the OECD's articulation relied on the original U.S. statement of the principles and would subsequently become the most widely cited version of the principles following its adoption. The OECD guidelines pertain to personal data, defined as any information relating to an identifiable individual, known as the data subject. The specific principles, which were reaffirmed by the OECD in 2013, are collection limitation, data quality, purpose specification, use limitation, security safeguards, openness, individual participation, and accountability.

The principle of collection limitation promotes limits to the collection of personal data. It states that personal data should be obtained only by fair and lawful means and, when possible, should be obtained only with the knowledge or consent of the data subject. The principle of data quality states that personal data should be accurate, complete, and kept up-to-date to the extent necessary for relevant use. Under the principle of purpose specification, the purpose of collection should be specified no later than the time when the data is collected, and subsequent uses of those data should be consistent with the original purpose. Under the principle of use limitation, personal data should be used, disclosed, or made available only for purposes that have been specified in accordance with the principle of purpose specification unless the data subject consents or the law authorizes other uses. The principle of security safeguards promotes reasonable safeguards for personal data against risks of loss, unauthorized access, destruction, use, modification, and disclosure. The openness principle encourages general policies of openness about developments, practices, and policies regarding personal data. The principle of individual participation prescribes to individuals certain rights of access and control over data pertaining to them. The accountability principle states that data controllers should be accountable for complying with measures that give effect to these principles.

The OECD principles would serve as a major influence on both national and sector-specific privacy laws and on international agreements and general best practices developed over the ensuing decades. Despite frequent praise from privacy advocates, the FIPPs have also been widely criticized over the years. For instance, some critics believe that the collection limitation principle relies too heavily on consent procedures, which impose burdens on data subjects more than on data custodians. Nevertheless, the OECD's principles remain to this day the quintessential and most frequently relied upon rendition of the FIPPs.

Recent years have seen the emergence of FIPPs-based frameworks that attempt to modernize the principles in light of new technologies. For instance, during the Obama Administration, the proposed consumer privacy bill of rights and the Federal Trade Commission's privacy framework in the White House report, *Protecting Consumer Privacy in an Era of Rapid Change: Recommendations for Businesses and Policymakers*, emphasized practices focusing on the context of data transactions and the sensitivity of the data involved, allowing increased flexibility for companies to determine proper data collection, use, and retention practices in light of new technologies. More recently, some have advocated for the FIPPs to be codified in federal legislation to protect personal information privacy.

The OECD also revised its guidelines in 2013 to address changes in technologies, markets, and user behavior, but it left the eight fundamental principles unchanged. Instead of amending the core principles, the revised guidelines introduced additional concepts, including stronger accountability in which a data controller should provide notice, when appropriate, to authorities and data subjects if there has been a significant security breach affecting personal data. The revised guidelines also describe the type of privacy management program that a data controller should have in place, as well as national privacy strategies. The 2013 revisions were the subject of much criticism, including the lack of revision of the core principles, believed by some to be out of date. For instance, some believe that a renewed focus on disclosure and consent requirements leaves companies subject to criticism for either failing to provide to consumers an exhaustive list of possible data collection, use, and retention practices, or for describing their practices with overly broad terminology.

Because many areas of emerging consumer technology are not subject to specific privacy regulations, the FIPPs will continue to influence how companies, policymakers, and privacy advocates evaluate the adequacy of data collection, use, and retention practices. However, as new technologies, including wearables, mobile apps, and robotics, evolve in ways that pool, share, and reuse data in unprecedented new ways, the adequacy and applicability of the FIPPs will continue to be challenged.

Drew Simshaw

Further Reading

Cate, Fred H. "The Failure of Fair Information Practice Principles." In *Consumer Protection in the Age of the "Information Economy,"* new edition, edited by Jane K. Winn. Burlington, VT: Ashgate, 2006.

Federal Trade Commission. *Protecting Consumer Privacy in an Era of Rapid Change: Recommendations for Businesses and Policymakers,* 2012. https://www.ftc.gov/reports/protecting-consumer-privacy-era-rapid-change-recommendations-businesses-policymakers.

Gellman, Robert. *Fair Information Practices: A Basic History*. February 11, 2015. http://ssrn.com/abstract=2415020 and at http://bobgellman.com/rgdocs/rg-FIPShistory.pdf. (2013).

White House. *Consumer Data Privacy in a Networked World: A Framework for Protecting Privacy and Promoting Innovation in the Global Digital Economy*. Reprinted in *Journal of Privacy and Confidentiality* 4, no. 2 (2013). http://repository.cmu.edu/jpc/vol4/iss2/5.

See also: Data breaches; Data protection regimes; Federal Trade Commission (FTC); Privacy laws, federal

Family Educational Rights and Privacy Act

Identification: Family Educational Rights and Privacy Act (FERPA), 20 U.S.C. § 1232g. A federal statute regulating educational records and protecting their confidentiality.

The Family Educational Rights and Privacy Act FERPA was enacted by Congress in 1974, a time of great concern over schools' increasing collection and computerization of records that might be used to students' detriment, perhaps without students even knowing that the records existed or having a chance to challenge their veracity. The measure was a by-product of

Watergate-era skepticism about the trustworthiness of government, a skepticism that also produced the federal Privacy Act of 1974, which entitles citizens to inspect and correct federal records pertaining to themselves.

Ironically, a statute birthed as a government-accountability measure has evolved into a perpetual source of conflict between educational institutions and transparency advocates, who question the institutions' propensity to categorize records as confidential when they contain unflattering information about school employees or policies.

The statute contains both a rights provision and a privacy provision. The rights provision guarantees a student (or, in the case of a minor attending a K–12 school, the parent or guardian) the opportunity to inspect his or her own education records maintained by an educational institution, to submit corrective or supplemental information if the records are misleading, and to demand a hearing if the corrective material is rejected.

The privacy provision is the subject of much debate. It provides that educational institutions may be declared ineligible for federal education funding if they do not enforce policies safeguarding against the release of education records to unauthorized eyes outside those within the institution with a legitimate business reason to need access.

FERPA originated as a Senate floor amendment by senators James Buckley of New York (hence its shorthand name, the Buckley amendment) and Claiborne Pell of Rhode Island. As a floor amendment, it lacks extensive history of committee debate illuminating how the sponsors understood it to work. In recent years, however, Buckley has spoken out about the widespread misclassification of documents as education records for purposes of concealing scandal and has urged Congress to rewrite the law to curb abuses.

The act defines education records as "those records, files, documents, and other materials which (i) contain information directly related to a student; and (ii) are maintained by an educational agency or institution or by a person acting for such agency or institution." In other words, there are two essential criteria for a document to be confidential under FERPA: It must be "directly related" to a student, and it must be "maintained" by the institution. The law explicitly exempts several types of documents from the definition of education records, including teachers' notes and records of nonstudent employees.

The U.S. Department of Education is delegated exclusive enforcement authority over FERPA, which provides no right of action for a person aggrieved by a violation to take the educational institution to court. The department has enacted regulations elaborating on the consequences of violating FERPA, which make clear that no institution will be penalized unless, after receiving a notice from the department, it refuses to enact corrective measures to avoid repeat infractions. To date, no educational institution has ever been sanctioned under FERPA.

The statute recognizes a class of benign directory information that may lawfully be released without invading privacy, including a student's name, address, phone number, honors and awards, and other such routinely disclosed information as might be found in the program at a graduation ceremony or a sporting event. Schools must tell students, or the parents of minor students, what will be disclosed and give them an opportunity to opt out of disclosure even of this basic demographic information.

Significantly, Congress amended FERPA in 1992 expressly to remove privacy protection for records created by a police or campus security agency "for the purpose of law enforcement." The amendment resulted from a successful lawsuit brought by a college student editor, Traci Bauer, aggrieved that her college, Southwest Missouri State University, blacked out names from campus police reports before providing them to journalists. Congress further amended FERPA in 1998 to remove any impediment to the release of college disciplinary records where a campus judicial board concludes that a crime of violence or a sex crime occurred.

The U.S. Supreme Court has rarely had the opportunity to interpret FERPA because litigation involving the public's access to records almost invariably arises under state rather than federal law. In one of the rare exceptions, the Supreme Court decided in *Owasso Independent School District v. Falvo,* 434 U.S. 429 (2002), that an Oklahoma school did not violate FERPA by allowing students to grade each others' quiz papers during class because the papers had not yet become part of the children's centrally maintained education records that would thus fall within FERPA:

> The word "maintain" suggests FERPA records will be kept in a filing cabinet in a records room at the school or on a permanent secure database, perhaps even after the student is no longer enrolled. The student graders only handle assignments for a few moments as the teacher calls out the answers. It is fanciful to say they maintain the papers in the same way the registrar maintains a student's folder in a permanent file.

In the *Owasso* case, the Department of Education supported the school's position that quiz papers are not protected by FERPA, noting that none of the usual access rights associated with FERPA would apply to a quiz—the family would have no right to insert corrective information into the quiz or to demand a hearing to challenge its accuracy. This is significant because the statute is often misapplied to records that parents could logically have no right to challenge or correct, such as videos of altercations on school buses.

Similarly, the Department of Education has interpreted FERPA to be a statute about the integrity of records and not an overall secrecy statute, so that schools are free to discuss facts about students derived from personal observation. In a 2006 interpretation issued to the Montgomery County, Maryland, school district, the Department of Education explained:

> FERPA applies to the disclosure of tangible records and of information derived from tangible records. FERPA does not protect the confidentiality of information in general, and, therefore, does not apply to the disclosure of information derived from a source other than education records, even if education records exist which contain that information. As a general rule, information that is obtained through personal knowledge or observation, and not from an education record, is not protected from disclosure under FERPA.

In the absence of Supreme Court guidance, state courts have varied in their willingness to second-guess schools' invocation of FERPA to withhold otherwise-public records. In a highly deferential application of the statute, the Ohio Supreme Court refused to order Ohio State University to turn over records about a football scandal—including emails between the head football coach and a booster—all of which the university categorized as education records. Conversely, Maryland's highest court rejected the University of Maryland's position that parking tickets issued to athletes and coaches could be withheld under FERPA, concluding: "The federal statute was obviously intended to keep private those aspects of a student's educational life that relate to academic matters or status as a student."

Because of the statute's confusing wording and the unpredictability of interpretations from the courts and the Department of Education, FERPA is prone to mistaken application and, at times, conscious misuse. Among some of the most notable cases of FERPA-aided concealment include the following:

- Oklahoma State University refused to tell anyone, even the police, about a known serial sex offender at large on the campus until a tip to the student newspaper alerted the campus police chief. Administrators claimed that FERPA forbade disclosing the findings of a campus disciplinary inquest, an interpretation the university later admitted was faulty.

- An Arizona school district tried unsuccessfully to use FERPA to block the release of a settlement agreement in the case of Savana Redding, whose nationally publicized challenge to an unlawful school strip-search went all the way to the U.S. Supreme Court. School attorneys insisted that the dollar amount paid to resolve the lawsuit was an education record. A judge disagreed.
- The University of Virginia forced a student rape victim to sign a waiver—under threat of disciplinary action—agreeing never to discuss her case with anyone, insisting that the form was necessary to comply with FERPA. In November 2008, after receiving a complaint about the practice, the Department of Education instructed universities to refrain from imposing such gag orders.

Widespread anxiety over the proliferation of databases with student performance data accessible to school technology vendors led to a flurry of proposed legislation tightening FERPA during 2015, including a bill proposed by the Obama administration. These proposals were intended to restrict the use of student data for commercial marketing purposes and to place third-party school contractors, vendors, and researchers under the same stringent confidentiality obligations that already apply to educational institutions themselves.

The Supreme Court's 2012 ruling on the constitutionality of President Obama's healthcare reforms, *NFIB v. Sebelius*, 567 U.S. 1, cast considerable doubt on the popular understanding of FERPA. In striking down a key Affordable Care Act (ACA) provision that required states to expand the scope of Medicaid coverage, the Court concluded that the penalty

for noncompliance—revocation of all federal healthcare subsidies—rendered the statute unconstitutionally coercive. The penalty associated with violation of the ACA is legally indistinguishable from the penalty accompanying a violation of FERPA— forfeiture of all federal education funding, which at the college level would include ineligibility to accept life-sustaining federal student aid. In the event that the Department of Education ever attempted to bring a FERPA enforcement proceeding, imposition of the "financial death penalty" would be vulnerable to challenge under *Sebelius*.

Frank LoMonte

Further Reading

Buchanan, Sarah Alix. "An Evaluation of the FERPA (1974) on Student Records Management and Access." MA thesis, University of California at Los Angeles, 2009.

Carr, Peter F. *Lawfully Managing Student Records without Violating Privacy Rights*. Eau Claire, WI: National Business Institute, 2013.

"Family Educational Rights and Privacy Act (FERPA)." *Journal of Empirical Research on Human Research Ethics* 2, no. 1 (March 2007): 101.

Gluck, Elizabeth Brody. "An Act Worth Balancing: Privacy and Safety on Today's College Campuses." *University Business* 11, no. 11 (November 2008).

Graham, Richard, Richard Hall, and W. Gerry Gilmer. "Connecting the Dots . . .: Information Sharing by Post-Secondary Educational Institutions under the Family Education Rights and Privacy Act (FERPA)." *Education and the Law* 20, no. 4 (2008): 301–316.

Humphries, Stephanie. "Institutes of Higher Education, Safety Swords, and Privacy Shields: Reconciling FERPA and the Common Law." *Journal of College and University Law* 35, no. 1 (2008): 145.

Jones, Kyle M. L. "Learning Analytics & FERPA: Issues of Student Privacy and New Boundaries of Student Data." *Proceedings of the American Society for Information Science and Technology* 50, no. 1 (2013): 1–5.

Murphy, Daniel Robert. *Educational Records: A Practical Guide for Legal Compliance*. Lanham, MD: Rowman & Littlefield, 2009.

Norlin, John W. *Confidentiality in Student Testing: Access and Disclosure Requirements under FERPA and the IDEA*. Horsham, PA: LRP Publications, 2008.

Shear, Bradley. "Ed Tech Must Embrace Stronger Student Privacy Laws." *T H E Journal* (April 2015).

THE *Journal* Staff. "Keeping Student Data Private: Five CTOs Discuss Their Data Privacy Concerns and Reveal How They Are Working with Teachers, Students and the Community to Safeguard Student Information." *T H E Journal* (March 2014): 22–30.

See also: Affordable Care Act; Educational Setting, Privacy in a; Law Enforcement; Privacy Act of 1974; Privacy Laws, State; Privacy Laws, Federal

Federal Communications Commission

Identification: An independent U.S. government agency that regulates radio, television, wire, satellite, and cable communication. Overseen by Congress, the FCC is charged with the regulation of interstate and international communications in all states, the District of Columbia, and territories of the United States.

The Federal Communications Commission (FCC) was created by the Communications Act of 1934, 48 Stat. 1064, which then had jurisdiction over radio licensing from the Federal Radio Commission and over telecommunications from the Interstate Commerce Commission. The act has been amended several times to address problems and respond to changes in technology and market conditions. As an independent federal agency, the FCC is directed by five commissioners who are appointed by the president and serve five-year terms. No more than three commissioners may belong to the same political party as the president, and all must be confirmed by the Senate. The FCC is composed of seven bureaus: Consumer and Governmental Affairs; Enforcement; International; Media; Wireless Telecommunications; Wireline Competition; and Public Safety and Homeland Security.

Over the years, Congress and the FCC have addressed the privacy concerns of consumers resulting from the invasiveness of new technologies. In 1991, Congress passed the Telephone Consumer Protection Act (TCPA), 105 Stat. 2394, which restricts, among other things, unsolicited telemarketing calls and commercial faxes to consumers' homes. Under this law, the FCC joined the Federal Trade Commission (FTC) in establishing the national Do Not Call list. Telemarketers are prohibited from calling the home or mobile phone numbers of consumers on the list unless the consumer gives prior express permission or has an established business relationship with the company. The FCC has also passed Caller ID rules enabling consumers to protect their privacy by blocking the visibility of their telephone number when placing a call. The rules require telephone companies to make available free and simple procedures for consumers to block the transmission of their number on all interstate calls.

The FCC has also established rules that require the protection of certain customer information by all telephone companies, including providers of local, long-distance, wireless, and Voice over Internet Protocol (VoIP) services. These rules apply to information such as what numbers are called, the times the calls are made, and the types of services used, including voicemail and call forwarding services. With regard to this Customer Proprietary Network Information (CPNI), companies may use, disclose, or permit access to such information only with customer approval, if required by law, or in providing the services from which the information is obtained. Companies must maintain accurate records of disclosures and customer approvals, and must submit annual certifications to the FCC about compliance with the rules and documentation of all complaints received by consumers.

Privacy was also a focus of the Cable Television Consumer Protection and Competition Act of 1992, 106 Stat. 1460 (the Cable Act). Customers of cable television services are protected by certain FCC rules governing information such as the customer's address, services subscribed to, and pay-per-view transactions. Cable companies must notify customers about what personally identifiable information is collected, including the purpose of the collection, how long the information will be retained, and how customers may access the information and enforce any limitations placed on the cable operator on the collection and disclosure of such information. Also, customers must be afforded reasonable opportunities to correct errors contained within the information held by the company. Customers may sue cable providers who violate these requirements in federal court.

The FCC encourages consumers to file complaints if they believe their personal information has been disclosed by a telephone company without permission, or in cases where consumers receive unwanted telemarketing calls, fax advertisements, or commercial messages on wireless devices. Consumers may also file complaints with the FCC against their cable companies for violating rules on the protection of personally identifiable information.

Some believe that the FCC has not been active enough in protecting privacy in recent years. Some members of Congress spoke out in 2006 when the FCC declined to investigate whether several large phone companies broke the law by aiding the National Security Agency (NSA) in wiretapping customers. The FCC became more active in protecting privacy during the Obama Administration under Chairman Tom Wheeler. In 2014 the commission brought privacy actions against TerraCom, Inc., and YourTel America, Inc., for violating laws protecting the privacy of personal information of phone customers, which resulted in $10 million in fines. Following the commission's 2015 Open Internet Order, which reclassified Internet Service Providers(ISPs) as common carriers under Title II of the 1996 Telecommunications Act, 110 Stat. 56, the commission sought to regulate the privacy practices of ISPs with rules passed in 2016.However, the 2015 "net neutrality" order was repealed under the commission's new leadership following the 2016 presidential election, and the 2016 "broadband privacy" rules were overturned by a Congressional Review Act measure signed by President Trump in early 2017.

Drew Simshaw

Further Reading

Brinson, Susan L. *The Red Scare, Politics, and the Federal Communications Commission, 1941–1960*. Westport, CT: Praeger, 2004.

Craig, Terence, and Mary Ludloff. *Privacy and Big Data*. Sebastopol, CA: O'Reilly Media, 2011.

Dorr, Dieter, and Russell L. Weaver, eds. *The Right to Privacy in the Light of Media Convergence: Perspectives from Three Continents*. Berlin: De Gruyter, 2012.

Huber, Peter W. *Law and Disorder in Cyberspace: Abolish the FCC and Let Common Law Rule the Telecoms*. New York: OxfordUniversity Press, 1997.

Information Privacy Law Sourcebook. Chicago, IL: American Bar Association, 2012.

Jung, Donald J. *The Federal Communications Commission, the Broadcast Industry, and the Fairness Doctrine, 1981–1987*. Lanham, MD: University Press of America, 1996.

See also: Caller ID; Customer proprietary network information (CPNI); Federal Trade Commission (FTC); Mobile devices; National Security Agency (NSA); Telemarketing; Telephones

Federal Communications Commission v. AT&T Inc., 562 U.S. 397 (2011)

Identification: A 2011 U.S. Supreme Court decision (562 U.S. 397) that unanimously rejected an attempt to have corporations regarded as "persons" entitled to personal privacy protection under the Freedom of Information Act (FOIA).

Arising in an a typical procedural posture, *Federal Communications Commission v. AT&T Inc.* began with a relatively routine decision by the Federal Communications Commission (FCC) that Freedom of Information Act (FOIA)'s law enforcement privacy protection of information the disclosure of which "could reasonably be expected to cause an unwarranted invasion of personal privacy," does not protect the interests of a corporation or any other "artificial entity," such as AT&T.

AT&T managed to obtain direct judicial review of that administrative decision in the U.S. Court of Appeals for the Third Circuit as if it were a purely regulatory matter, without adjudication first at the district court level as ordinarily would be the case in FOIA litigation. Even more remarkably, AT&T managed to persuade the Third Circuit Court of Appeals that, because it is deemed a "person" for litigation claims purposes under a general statute called the Administrative Procedure Act (APA), information submitted by it to the government therefore is entitled to broad "personal privacy" protection (not just narrower "business information" protection) under FOIA.

The appellate court ruling that AT&T won was unprecedented and was extremely broad in its potential ramifications. It also held serious practical complications for the uniform administration of FOIA. Under it, for instance, any corporation registered in the state of Delaware could have brought a "reverse" FOIA lawsuit within the Third Circuit's geographic bounds and authoritatively argued that information submitted by it for regulatory purposes was entitled to broad privacy protection under FOIA Exemption 6 or under its law enforcement record counterpart Exemption 7(C), not just protection from ordinary competitive harm under FOIA Exemption 4, to block FOIA disclosure. This was the basis for what was perhaps the most important step in the case: the solicitor general's decision to seek Supreme Court review even in the absence of any direct conflict in the circuit courts of appeals on the issue.

AT&T's position before the Supreme Court was one of very basic statutory interpretation. It argued that, because the law often includes corporations in the definition of *personhood,* such as in the word *person* as defined within the APA, and because FOIA was enacted by Congress as part of the APA, that "must mean" that the word *personal* in FOIA's "personal privacy" exemptions, Exemption 6 and the later-enacted Exemption 7(C), "*necessarily*" includes AT&T and other corporations (emphasis in original). Like the Third Circuit, as described below, it advocated a simplistic, if not unduly syllogistic, approach to the legal question it raised in the case.

The Supreme Court rejected this position, however, because of its total failure to take cognizance of "the difference between 'person' and 'personal.'" Emphasizing that FOIA's privacy exemptions use the latter adjectival term, not the former noun, and that adjectives do not "always" mean the same as their "corresponding nouns," the Court examined "the ordinary meaning of 'personal'" and found that it "ordinarily refers to individuals." Even further removed from the legal term *person,* the Court focused on the entire language used by Congress in both Exemption 6 and Exemption 7(C) and thus considered "the ordinary meaning of the phrase 'personal privacy.'" Most significantly, it also recognized that Congress first used that phrase in 1966 in enacting the language of Exemption 6, where it "importantly defines the particular subset of . . . information Congress sought to exempt." And because "personal privacy" has always been properly understood to mean an "*individual*'s right of privacy" in that earlier exemption (emphasis added), that fact provided the key "context" for the Court to decide that "personal privacy" was intended by Congress to mean the same thing when it amended FOIA to create Exemption 7(C) eight years later in 1974. So the Third Circuit's aberrational privacy decision was reversed.

Notably, the author of the Court's opinion, Chief Justice John G. Roberts, Jr., did not use the case to address the limits of corporate personhood in the immediate wake of the Court's controversial decision in *Citizens United v. Federal Election Commission* the year before. Rather, his opinion explicitly eschewed any consideration of constitutional privacy, stating that the statutory construction issue raised by the Third Circuit's novel FOIA interpretation "does not call upon us to pass on the scope of a corporation's 'privacy' interests as a matter of constitutional or common law." And almost as notably, Chief Justice Roberts resoundingly concluded his opinion with the following ringing message: "We trust that AT&T will not take it personally."

Daniel J. Metcalfe

Further Reading

Hartman, Scott. Note in "Privacy, Personhood, and the Courts: FOIA Exemption 7(C) in Context." 120 *Yale Law Journal*, no. 379 (2010). http://papers.ssrn.com/sol3/papers.cfm?abstract_id=1684498.

Huggins, Maeve E. Note in "Don't Take It Personally: Supreme Court Finds Corporations Lack Personal Privacy under FOIA Exemptions." *Catholic University Journal of Law & Technology* 19, no. 481 (2011). http://commlaw.cua.edu/res/docs/09-v19-2-Huggins-Final.pdf.

See also: Constitutional law; Freedom of Information Act (FOIA)

Federal Trade Commission

Identification: A federal regulatory agency that protects consumers and oversees businesses.

The Federal Trade Commission (FTC) seeks to protect consumers from unfair or fraudulent practices as well as to encourage competition among businesses. The FTC is headquartered in Washington, DC, and has regional offices that oversee seven regions throughout the United States. The FTC was created by the Federal Trade Commission Act (FTC Act) in 1914, which was signed into law by President Woodrow Wilson. Prior to the FTC, the Bureau of Corporations was an early federal effort to address the abuses of large businesses and trusts. This agency, however, could not pursue administrative cases. Consequently, the FTC's creation occurred during the growing antitrust debate and to answer the need to curb trusts. The FTC's authority eventually expanded to include consumer protection by preventing unfair or deceptive practices.

Currently, the FTC is led by a chair and four other commissioners. The five commissioners are appointed by the president and approved by the Senate for seven-year terms. The FTC is comprised of several bureaus that pursue the agency's mission of protecting consumers by inhibiting anticompetitive, deceptive, or unfair business practices and informing consumers of choice and competition. The Bureau of Competition enforces antitrust laws and strives to prevent anticompetitive business practices and mergers. The Bureau of Consumer Protection enforces congressional consumer protection laws and FTC rules to protect consumers from unfair, fraudulent, or deceptive business practices. The Bureau of Economics conducts economic analysis research to assist with rulemaking and investigating antitrust and consumer protection cases. The FTC is also comprised of ten administrative and support offices to enable the FTC to function effectively and efficiently.

Besides creating the FTC, the FTC Act serves as the primary authority for FTC decisions. Section 5 of the FTC Act, in particular, is broad and is used as a means of prohibiting unfair and deceptive business practices. Under the FTC Act, unfair practices "are practices that cause or are likely to cause consumers substantial injury that is neither reasonably avoidable by consumers no[r] offset [by] any countervailing benefit to consumers or competition." The test for deception is generally based on "the likelihood of deception or the capacity to deceive" as opposed to actual deception, and intent to deceive, common law fraud, or deceit need not be established. *Montgomery Ward & Co. v. F.T.C.*, 379 F.2d 666, at 670 (7th Cir., 1967). Section 5 of the FTC Act may be used to oversee anticompetition matters, including the creation of monopolies and price fixing, as well as consumer concerns of misbranding, false advertising, and other unfair and deceptive practices. (*Consolidated Book Publishers v. F.T.C.*, 53 F.2d 942 at 945 (7th Cir., 1931.)) Thus, the FTC Act is a fundamental source for consumer protection and competition regulation.

The FTC exercises its enforcement powers by proceeding on its own or in accordance with an outside complaint and investigating the allegations. After the investigation, if an unfair or deceptive act is believed to have occurred, the FTC will issue a complaint to the business, listing the charges and providing a notice of hearing. (15 U.S.C. §45(b.)) If a violation is also found at the hearing, a cease and desist order will be issued against the business. Afterward, the final decision may be appealable to the U.S. Court of Appeals, and any violations of the final cease and desist order may result in penalties. Besides enforcement actions, the FTC can seek short-term relief through temporary restraining orders or preliminary injunctions as well as withhold enforcement if it is in the best public interest to settle cases through consent orders and stipulations.

Under its unfair and deceptive policing authority, the FTC enforces companies' privacy policies. The FTC relies especially on Section 5 of the FTC Act to fight unfair and deceptive claims that businesses make on the security of consumers' personal information. The FTC has also challenged businesses over a number of privacy issues involving social networking, spam, spyware, advertising, and peer-to-peer file sharing. In the process of enforcement, the FTC has created a common law on privacy issues.

Besides regulating unfair and deceptive practices, the FTC also protects consumers and data security and privacy through several other means. Beginning with one of the first laws with privacy provisions, the Fair Credit Reporting Act, the FTC has been charged with enforcing over seventy other sector-specific laws, including the Children's Online Privacy Protection Act and the Truth in Lending Act. The FTC also hosts workshops, roundtable events, and town halls to address emerging consumer privacy issues. The FTC issues policy recommendations and regulations as well as consumer education materials to promote awareness of security topics. In addition, the FTC participates in international efforts to regulate E-commerce, such as joining with other Organization for Economic Cooperation and Development countries to develop new E-commerce guidelines in 2016. The commission has a great impact on consumer and privacy rights.

The FTC has a long history of successfully opposing unethical business practices and protecting consumers. Through the FTC Act and the FTC's various enforcement measures, competitors and consumers are protected against unfair and deceptive practices. The FTC's means and overseen sectors are broad and diverse, however. For example, the FTC also engages in rule-making, public education, and advocacy. When taken together, the FTC has a substantial role in the functioning of the marketplace and other industries and in the realm of privacy rights.

Stephanie Romeo and Donald A. Watt

Further Reading

Federal Trade Commission. *Federal Trade Commission: Protecting America's Consumers*. https://www.ftc. gov/.

_____. *Privacy & Security Update: 2017*. (January, 2018.) www.ftc.gov/system/files/documents/reports/privacy-data-security-update-2017-overview-commissions-enforcement-policy-initiatives-consumer/privacy_and_data_security_update_2017.pdf

Johnson, Arthur M. "Theodore Roosevelt and the Bureau of Corporations." *The Mississippi Valley Historical Review* 45, no. 4 (March 1959): 571–590. http://www.jstor.org/stable/1888711.

Solove, Daniel J., and Woodrow Hartzog. "The FTC and the New Common Law of Privacy." 584 *Columbia Law Review* 114 (2014): 583–676.

Stevens, Gina. *The Federal Trade Commission's Regulation of Data Security under Its Unfair or Deceptive Acts or Practices (UDAP) Authority*. 2014.

Taufick, Roberto. "Understanding the Federal Trade Commission—An Overview." *Revista de Direito da Concorrência* 14 (2008): 69–106. http://ssrn.com/abstract=2479703.

Wayleith, Paulus R., ed. *Data Security: Laws and Safeguards*. New York: Nova Science Publishers, Inc., 2008.

See also: Children's Online Privacy Protection Act; (COPPA) Credit and debit cards; Credit reporting agencies (CRAs); Data breach notification laws; Electronic Privacy Information Center (EPIC); Right to be let alone; Spyware

Financial information, privacy rights in

Identification: The delimited right to privacy in financial information under U.S. federal law. How much you earn, how much you borrow, how much you spend, and how your credit score fares. These are personal questions, and one might think the answers are not for public consumption. But what rights to privacy actually exist when it comes to financial information?

When the first U.S. federal law addressing consumer privacy was passed decades ago, it was specifically designed to address privacy rights in financial information. Yet, over time, privacy rights in personal financial information have been diluted. And in recent years these rights have been even further diluted with the passage of the USA PATRIOT Act, enacted after the attacks on the United States on September 11, 2001.

Today, the level of privacy afforded to financial information depends on who *has* possession of the information and who wants to gain *access* to the information. Also, why the financial information is being disclosed, to whom, and for what purpose oftentimes alter the level of privacy afforded to the information.

This entry examines privacy rights in financial information under U.S. federal law within the context of three scenarios: (i) the government's authority to access financial information; (ii) a financial institution's right to use and share consumer financial information; and (iii) a private person's or entity's right to obtain someone else's financial information.

The government's authority to access financial information

In *United States v. Miller*, 425 U.S. 435 (1976), the U.S. Supreme Court held that individuals did not have a reasonable expectation of privacy in their records at financial institutions, because such records contain information that the individuals voluntarily gave to the financial institutions in the ordinary course of business, which in turn gave the financial institutions the authority to give such information over to the government. (*Miller*, 425 U.S. at 442-44.)

The *Miller* court based its ruling on what is currently known as the "third party doctrine." Under this doctrine, privacy rights against

government access to private information may be forfeited when the information is voluntarily passed to a third party. This doctrine has, however, been questioned and under some circumstances rejected.

In response to the *Miller* case, Congress attempted to limit the federal government's power to access financial records by enacting the Right to Financial Privacy Act (RFPA). The RFPA prohibits banks and other financial institutions from disclosing certain customer personal data to the government absent customer authorization or a valid subpoena, summons, search warrant, or other appropriate written request that meets certain statutory requirements. (12 U.S.C. §§ 3401-3422.)

The Right to Financial Privacy Act: Under the RFPA, no government authority may have access to, or obtain copies of, the information contained in the financial records of any customer from a bank or other financial institution unless the financial records are reasonably described, and at least one of the following is true: (1) the customer authorizes access; (2) there is an appropriate administrative subpoena or summons; (3) there is a qualified search warrant; (4) there is an appropriate judicial subpoena; or (5) there is an appropriate written request under the RFPA. (12 U.S.C. § 3402.)

Within the RFPA, however, there are numerous exceptions and limitations. For example, disclosure of information to the federal government by a financial institution is allowed without authorization of the customer, subpoena, summons, or warrant in the following circumstances:

- Disclosure of information that does not identify a particular customer. (12 U.S.C. § 3413(a); *Donovan v. National Bank of Alaska*, 696 F.2d 678 (9th Cir. 1983));
- Disclosure that serves the financial institution's specified business-related interests, such as disclosure to perfect the institution's security interest, or a disclosure

incident to administering a government-insured loan. (12 U.S.C. § 3403(d));

- Disclosure of an account holder's name and suspected illegal activity. (12 U.S.C. § 3403(c));
- Disclosure in connection with a supervisory agency's investigation of the financial institution. (12 U.S.C. § 3413(b));
- Disclosure authorized under other federal laws or rules, such as the Internal Revenue Code or the rules of procedure governing litigation subpoenas. (12 U.S.C. § 3413(c) (f)); and
- Disclosure to federal agencies for certain protective, national security, or intelligence functions. (12 U.S.C. § 3414).

In addition to these exceptions, the federal government has the authority to access financial information under The Bank Secrecy Act.

The Bank Secrecy Act of 1970: The Bank Secrecy Act of 1970, formally known as The Currency and Foreign Transactions Reporting Act of 1970, (BSA), requires financial institutions to assist federal agencies in detecting and preventing criminal activity such as tax evasion and money laundering. (31 U.S.C. §§ 5311-5332.)

Since the passage of the BSA, financial institutions have been required to keep records and file reports "[d]esigned to help identify the source, volume, and movement of currency and other monetary instruments transported or transmitted into or out of the United States or deposited in financial institutions[.]" (http:// www.fincen. gov/news_room/aml_history.html.) For example, financial institutions must keep records of cash transactions that exceed a daily aggregate amount of $10,000. (31 C.F.R. §§ 1010.300-1010.370.)

The BSA as amended by The USA PATRIOT Act: In 2001, the BSA was amended by the USA PATRIOT Act to "increase the strength of United States measures to prevent, detect, and prosecute international money laundering and the financing of terrorism[.]" (Public Law 107-56, 115 Stat. 272, 297, § 302(b)(1) (2001).)

Under the BSA as amended, financial institutions are now required to keep certain records and make certain reports to the federal government if such records or reports would have "a high degree of usefulness in...the conduct of intelligence or counterintelligence activities, including analysis, to protect against international terrorism." (31 U.S.C. § 5311.)

The amendments also provide legal protections and immunities to financial institutions and employees for reporting suspicious transactions indicating possible violations of laws or regulations, and prohibit financial institutions and employees from notifying customers that a transaction in which they have been involved has been reported as suspicious. (Public Law 107-56, 115 Stat. 272, 320-21, § 351 (2001); 31 U.S.C. §§ 5318(g)(2)-5318(g)(3).)

By requiring financial institutions to identify and report suspicious transactions to the government, and by authorizing the government to obtain personal information about a financial institution's customer—each without the customer knowing or having any right to be informed that a suspicious activity report was made or requested—the BSA and the USA PATRIOT Act have effectively eroded what little privacy rights against government access existed in financial information in the first place.

A financial institution's right to use and share consumer financial information

Consumers must provide personal information such as name, address, phone number, income, Social Security number, etc. to a bank or other financial institution in order to apply for or obtain financial products and services. And as the relationship between the consumer and a financial institution grows, so too does the amount of disclosed personal financial information, such as account numbers, loan or deposit balances, credit or debit purchases and the like.

Under The Gramm-Leach-Bliley Act, also known as the Financial Modernization Act of 1999, a financial institution may share this ever-growing consumer financial information with other entities in order to serve its interests in expanding business and consumer opportunities, so long as certain requirements are met.

Since a financial institution may share most of this information, are there any privacy rights that affect, or even trump, a financial institution's right to use and share consumer financial information?

Yes, there are. But they are limited, for the most part, to rights to receive notices of information sharing, rights to opt out of some (but not all) information sharing, and requirements that financial institutions protect financial information from unauthorized access (by hackers, for example) by implementing data security measures.

The Gramm-Leach-Bliley Act: The Gramm-Leach-Bliley Act (GLBA) requires that financial institutions (meaning companies that offer consumers financial products or services like loans, financial or investment advice, or insurance) comply with what are known as the Privacy Rule and the Safeguards Rule. (15 U.S.C. §§ 6801-6809.)

The Privacy Rule requires financial institutions to issue annual privacy notices to their customers (and any other consumers whose information is shared with nonaffiliates) and to notify them of their right to opt out of certain information sharing. (15 U.S.C. § 6803.) In contrast, the Safeguards Rule stipulates that financial institutions implement security programs to protect its customers' nonpublic personal information from unauthorized access, including by cybercriminals. (15 U.S.C. § 6801(b).)

With some exceptions, the Privacy Rule applies to consumers' nonpublic information (NPI), which is defined under the GLBA as personally identifiable financial information that a financial institution collects about an individual, including for example in connection with

providing a financial product or service, unless that information is otherwise publicly available. (15 U.S.C. § 6809(4).)

Under the Privacy Rule, financial institutions must provide privacy notices to their customers annually in written, electronic, or other approved form. These notices must include a clear and conspicuous description of the financial institution's information collection and sharing practices and policies. (15 U.S.C. § 6803.)

Privacy notices must also include an opt-out notice for certain kinds of information sharing. For example, if a financial institution shares its consumers' NPI with non-affiliates (meaning any company outside of those companies the financial institution controls, is controlled by, or with which the financial institution shares common control), the financial institution must provide those consumers with an "opt-out" notice explaining consumers' rights to prohibit the financial institution from sharing their NPI with non-affiliates. (15 U.S.C. §§ 6802-6809.)

Note, however, that the GLBA does not allow consumers to opt out of the financial institution's sharing of NPI with non-affiliates "to perform services for or functions on behalf of the financial institution, including marketing of the financial institution's own products or services, or financial products or services offered pursuant to joint agreements between two or more financial institutions…if the financial institution fully discloses the providing of such information and enters into a [confidentiality] agreement with the third party…." (15 U.S.C. § 6802(b)(2).)

Other exceptions to the opt-out rule are found in Section 502 of the GLBA, which include allowing disclosure of NPI when it is legally required (15 U.S.C. § 6802(e)(8)) and when financial institutions are reporting suspected financial abuse of the elderly to law enforcement. (15 U.S.C. § 6802(e)(3), 15 U.S.C. § 6802(e)(5), and 15 U.S.C. § 6802(e)(8), as interpreted by the 2013 *Interagency Guidance on Privacy Laws and Reporting Financial Abuse of Older*

Adults, found at https://www.fdic.gov/news/news/press/2013/Interagency-Guidance-on-Privacy-Laws-andReporting-Financial-Abuse-of-Older-Adults. pdf?source=govdelivery.)

Further, the Privacy Rule does not prohibit a financial institution from sharing NPI with its affiliates, meaning any company that the financial institution controls, or that the financial institution is controlled by, or that is under common control with the financial institution. (15 U.S.C. § 6809(6).)

Nor does the Privacy Rule prohibit the sharing of NPI where such NPI has been de-identified, meaning it is being shared in aggregate form or in blind data form that does not contain personal identifiers, such as account numbers, names or addresses. (12 C.F.R. § 1016.3(q)(2)(ii)(B).)

Under the Safeguards Rule, financial institutions must develop procedures to "protect the security and confidentiality of [their] customers' nonpublic personal information." (15 U.S.C. § 6801(a).)

For example, financial institutions must implement a written security program, containing specific elements, that describes how they protect the security and confidentiality of customers' information. The program must designate at least one employee to coordinate the institution's information security program, provide for the implementation of safeguards that are regularly tested, and make the institution's information security program relevant to the institution's particular size and circumstances. (15 U.S.C. § 6801; 16 C.F.R. § 314.)

A private person's or private entity's right to obtain someone else's financial information

When neither the government nor a financial institution's rights to access financial information is at issue, does a private party or entity have the right to obtain another party's financial information without the consent of, or over the objection of, the person(s) who may be identified in the information? Yes, they do.

The Fair Credit Reporting Act: Under the Fair Credit Reporting Act (FCRA), a consumer reporting agency may provide an individual's credit report—without the consent of the individual—to private parties with a valid need such as creditors, insurers, and landlords. (15 U.S.C. §§ 1681 *et seq.*)

Also under FCRA, however, individual consumers do have the right, among other things, to know what is in their credit report files (15 U.S.C. § 1681g(a)); dispute inaccurate information (15 U.S.C. § 1681i(a)); have inaccurate information corrected (15 U.S.C. § 1681i(a)(5)); opt out of prescreened offers (15 U.S.C. § 1681s-3); and require consent for their reports to be provided to employers (15 U.S.C. § 1681b(b)).

Federal Rules of Civil Procedure: In furtherance of the judicial system's interest in full and fair resolution of legal disputes, under the Federal Rules of Civil Procedure, a private party in civil litigation may obtain another's financial information by issuing what is called a "discovery request" to another party in the litigation or by issuing a subpoena to a financial institution or other third party.

For example, if one sues another party or is sued by someone, either party may issue interrogatories, document requests, or deposition notices to any other party requesting disclosure of the party's private financial information to the extent it is relevant to the case. (Rules 30-34, Fed. R. Civ. P.)

By way of another example, if an individual has been a party to a lawsuit, has a judgment rendered against him or her, and fails to pay that judgment, the prevailing party may inquire through a discovery request (usually in the form of a debtor's examination) into the owing party's finances to determine how the judgment may be paid. (Rule 69, Fed. R. Civ. P.)

Similarly, a party to a lawsuit may also issue a subpoena for another party's financial records from a third party, so long as the information being sought is relevant and necessary. (Rule 45, Fed. R. Civ. P.) Sometimes financial information may be subpoenaed from a third party that is not a financial institution, such as an employer. In other cases, the financial information may be subpoenaed from a financial institution. In the latter instance, the GLBA will apply, but the financial institution generally still must comply with the subpoena.

Conclusion

Some rights to privacy in financial information exist. But as the federal laws explored in this entry show, those rights are in tension with, and therefore have been balanced against, several competing interests. Those interests include the government's interests in investigating and deterring crime and in protecting national security, the financial institutions' interests in expanding business and consumer opportunities, certain private parties' valid needs to obtain consumers' credit reports, and the judicial system's interest in full and fair resolution of legal disputes.

Further Reading

Nizan Geslevich Packin & Yafit Lev Aretz, *Big Data and Social Netbanks: Are You Ready to Replace Your Bank?*, 53 Houston Law Review __ (forthcoming 2016)

Daniel J. Solove & Paul Schwartz, *Information Privacy Law* (2015)

M. Maureen Murphy, *Privacy Protection for Customer Financial Information*, Congressional Research Service (2014)

Francesca M. Brancato, *Fourth Amendment Right to Privacy with Respect to Bank Records in Criminal Cases*, 29 Touro Law Review 1241 (2013)

See also: Big data; Consumer privacy; Credit reporting agencies (CRAs); Fair Credit Reporting Act; GrammLeach-Bliley Act; Subpoenas

First Amendment to the U.S. Constitution

Identification: A cornerstone of the Bill of Rights protecting against government action that unduly restricts the fundamental American freedoms of speech, press, religion, assembly, and the right to petition the government for redress.

The right to oppose government policies without retribution by speaking, writing, or organizing was not universally honored in the English common law on which U.S. law is grounded. The common-law charge of "seditious libel" enabled government officials to prosecute critics who incited public discontent, regardless of whether the criticism was truthful. A turning point came with the trial of publisher John Peter Zenger in 1735. Zenger was prosecuted for newspaper columns critical of the administration of New York governor William Crosby's administration, but he was acquitted by a jury despite the judge's instructions that the truth of Zenger's accusations was no defense to seditious libel. The spectacle of a journalist put on trial for editorial commentary on the performance of government officials provoked widespread outrage. The year after the Zenger trial, Benjamin Franklin wrote in *The Pennsylvania Gazette*: "Freedom of speech is a principal pillar of a free government; when this support is taken away, the constitution of a free society is dissolved, and tyranny is erected on its ruins." Reflecting on the trial's significance decades later, one of the Constitution's principal drafters, Gouverneur Morris, wrote: "The trial of Zenger in 1735 was the germ of American freedom, the morning star of that liberty which subsequently revolutionized America."

In colonial America, publications played a significant role in stirring public sentiment behind the Revolution. Newspapers even provided coverage of the debate between Federalists and Anti-Federalists over whether a Bill of Rights would be included in the Constitution. The *Aurora*, a Philadelphia-based newspaper operated by Benjamin Franklin's grandson, was instrumental in building support for the Anti-Federalists' position that, to constrain the powerful new federal government against abusing its authority, the Constitution should enumerate foundational individual rights that may not be denied or abridged.

The First Amendment's five freedoms had antecedents in statutory and common law. By the time the framers signed the Constitution in 1787, nine of the thirteen states already had their own constitutional protections for freedom of the press. The right to petition the government traces its origins back centuries earlier, with roots in the venerated Magna Carta. Yet it took considerable political bloodletting to arrive at the ten constitutional amendments that, in 1789, became the Bill of Rights. Federalists, led by Alexander Hamilton, argued that enumerating individual rights in the Constitution would actually devalue those rights by implying that without explicit constitutional constraints the government would have limitless authority over individuals' lives. In the end, skepticism over the power of centralized government prevailed, and in 1791 the Bill of Rights attained the two-thirds margin of states necessary for ratification.

While it purports to constrain only Congress, the First Amendment has more modernly been applied equally to speech-restrictive actions by the executive and judicial branches; for instance, in *Snyder v. Phelps,* 562 U.S. 443 (2011), the Supreme Court held that the judiciary could not constitutionally render a civil judgment against protesters whose antigay hate speech outside a military funeral was not audible at the funeral and caused emotional distress only when viewed afterward on television.

The First Amendment functions today as a muscular check on the authority of government, vastly more well-developed than a century ago when Justice Oliver Wendell Holmes Jr. wrote the speech clause was intended to prevent only prior restraints on publication and not after-the-fact punishment. The Court never invalidated a law under the First Amendment until 1931, and commercial speech was not recognized as a protected category until decades later.

The First Amendment's speech clause is implicated when government action is directed at a speaker's content or message. Underlying the First Amendment is the philosophical judgment that the remedy for offensive or misleading speech is not government sanction but counter-speech, which will prevail in the marketplace of ideas. As Justice Louis Brandeis explained it in *Whitney v. California,* 274 U.S. 357 (1927): "If there be time to expose through discussion the falsehood and fallacies, to avert the evil by the processes of education, the remedy to be applied is more speech, not enforced silence."

Once a government action is found to have the intent or effect of restricting speech based on content, courts will review it skeptically. To justify such a restriction, the government must demonstrate it is necessary to accomplish a compelling objective and that no less restrictive method will suffice—a legal standard known as strict scrutiny. Speech addressing issues of public concern is valued especially highly, and restraints on political speech are especially difficult to defend. Regulations that burden or advance only one side of a contested issue are particularly disfavored. Once a government action is found to be viewpoint discriminatory, it is almost invariably struck down as unconstitutional.

Much less rigorous judicial scrutiny applies to a content-neutral regulation that merely restricts the time, place, or manner in which speech is delivered, regardless of its message. Noise ordinances are classic examples of content-neutral speech restrictions, applying not to the content of the speech but its method of presentation. A content-neutral restriction on the time, place or manner of speech will be overturned as unconstitutional only if it lacks a rational basis, a heavy burden for anyone attempting a legal challenge. Such a regulation is constitutional even if it has the side effect of making it harder for a particular speaker to deliver his or her message successfully, so long as the government was not motivated by an intent to silence that speaker. Thus, the Supreme Court has upheld ordinances restricting outdoor camping in public spaces (*Clark v. Community for Creative Non-Violence*, 468 U.S. 288 (1984)) and amplified music at a Central Park bandshell (*Ward v. Rock Against Racism*, 491 U.S. 781 (1989)), even though those ordinances interfered with speakers' planned political demonstrations. Even a regulation that is neutral on its face, however, is subject to constitutional challenge if it is designed or enforced in a way that discriminatorily affects only certain speakers.

The most noxious and disfavored of all restrictions on speech is the concept of prior restraint. While some government regulations penalize harm-causing speech after it is uttered, prior restraint prevents speech from ever being disseminated and reaching its intended audience. Because prior restraint is considered the most drastic form of regulating speech, it is presumed to be unconstitutional absent the most compelling of justifications. In its landmark ruling in *Near v. Minnesota*, 283 U.S. 687 (1931), the Supreme Court interpreted the First Amendment to mean that "every man shall have a right to speak, write, and print his opinions upon any subject whatsoever, without any prior restraint," and consequently struck down a Minnesota law enabling the government to obtain a court order prohibiting the distribution of any publication with a history of speech that is "obscene, lewd and lascivious" or "malicious, scandalous and defamatory."

The First Amendment protects not only against direct prohibitions on speech but on indirect constraints that would inhibit the exercise of free expression—often referred to as the chilling effect. Thus, in the case of *United States v. Rumely*, 345 U.S. 41 (1953), the Supreme Court overturned the contempt conviction of a political activist who refused to disclose to Congress the names of people who had purchased books from his organization, which was suspected of engaging in illegal lobbying activities. Justice William O. Douglas, one the Court's fiercest champions of the First Amendment, wrote that exposing book buyers to congressional inquiry would discourage intellectual curiosity: "If the lady from

Toledo can be required to disclose what she read yesterday and what she will read tomorrow, fear will take the place of freedom in the libraries, bookstores, and homes of the land."

Even otherwise-permissible regulations on speech may be struck down if they are vague or overly broad; failing to give those affected by the regulation fair notice of whether their conduct is legal. First Amendment champion Justice William Brennan said it most clearly in *NAACP v. Button,* 371 U.S. 415 (1963), striking down a Virginia ordinance that prohibited civil rights lawyers from advertising for potential clients: "Because First Amendment freedoms need breathing space to survive, government may regulate in the area only with narrow specificity." What Justice Brennan was saying is that, if a regulation is ambiguous or unclear, the speaker must be given the benefit of the doubt. Otherwise, the speaker will censor him- or herself for fear of stepping over an indistinct line of legality. To use a baseball analogy, when it comes to regulating speech, the tie goes to the runner.

The First Amendment applies regardless of the value or merit of the speaker's message. Because constitutional rights are integral in protecting minority viewpoints against silencing by the power of the majority, extremist fringe messages receive full constitutional protection. Even speech that is hateful or offensive—burning a cross to express racial hatred (*Virginia v. Black*, 538 U.S. 343, (2003)), displaying a Nazi symbol while parading down a public street (*National Socialist Party v. Skokie*, 432 U.S. 43 (1977)), burning a flag to criticize American policies (*Texas v. Johnson*, 491 U.S. 397 (1989)), displaying an antiwar slogan containing harsh profanity (*Cohen v. California*, 403 U.S. 15 (1971))—cannot be banned or prosecuted. While these ideas may be offensive they are still protected under the constitutional provision of free speech and expression.

A narrow few categories of speech are entirely unprotected, including realistic threats of violence, obscenity, and the incitement of others to imminent lawless action. The latter category was outlined in Justice Holmes's oft-quoted "shouting fire in a crowded theatre" opinion in *Schenck v. United States*, 249 U.S. 47 (1919), in which he wrote: "The question is whether the words are used in such circumstances and are of such a nature as to create a clear and present danger that they will bring about the substantive evils that Congress has the right to prevent." These unprotected categories of speech may be subject to prior restraint and even criminalized. A few other categories of speech, such as defamation, exist in a legal gray area. While defamatory speech may be punished post-publication, a court may not prevent a speaker from distributing speech that is anticipated to be defamatory. Rather, the remedy is for a person whose reputation has been falsely maligned to sue for civil damages after the fact.

There are other areas in which speech has been deemed limited by the government. The Supreme Court has recognized a diminished level of protection for speech disseminated over federally licensed public airwaves. In a case involving stand-up comic George Carlin's profanity-laden monologue, "Filthy Words" (*FCC v. Pacifica Foundation*, 438 U.S. 726 (1978)), the Court upheld the Federal Communications Commission's (FCC's) authority to penalize speech that is merely "indecent" even if not legally "obscene." The rationale for singling out over-the-air broadcasting for differential regulation is that speakers are using a scarce public resource uniquely accessible to children. Yet the proliferation of alternative distribution systems for audio and video content—cable and satellite subscription services, and Internet-based streaming services—has called into question the scarcity rationale underpinning the FCC's authority. A federal appeals court struck down the FCC's indecency enforcement regime on First Amendment grounds in *Fox Television Stations, Inc. v. FCC*, 613 F.3d 317 (2d Cir. 2010). Nevertheless, the Supreme Court decided the case on narrow due process grounds and vacated

the First Amendment holding, *FCC v. Fox Television Stations Inc.*, 132 S.Ct. 2307 (2012), leaving continued uncertainty about the extent to which the FCC can constitutionally penalize fleeting displays of nudity or profanity.

The Court has declined attempts to categorize the Internet as, like broadcasting, a uniquely intrusive and accessible medium justifying heightened government regulation on content. In *Reno v. ACLU*, 521 U.S. 844 (1997), the Court struck down Congress's attempt to extend the prohibition on "indecent" speech from the broadcast airwaves to the Internet. The *Reno* ruling invalidated key portions of the federal Communications Decency Act of 1996, which criminalized the transmittal of indecent or "patently offensive" material over the Internet knowing that the recipient of the material was under 18.

No line of First Amendment cases have been more contentious in recent times than the Court's series of rulings regarding campaign finance jurisprudence. In the foundational case of *Buckley v. Valeo*, 424 U.S. 1 (1976), the justices decided that capping the amount a donor could contribute to a political candidate involves the First Amendment because limiting donations "necessarily reduces the quantity of expression by restricting the number of issues discussed, the depth of their exploration, and the size of the audience reached." Expanding on that rationale, the Court decided its most controversial campaign finance case, *Citizens United v. Federal Elections Commission*, 558 U.S. 310 (2010). In *Citizens United*, a bitterly divided Court, overruling its own recent precedent, declared unconstitutional a federal statute banning corporations from making direct contributions to candidates for federal office or from making independent expenditures advocating the election or defeat of a candidate through public communication. The opinion was roundly denounced as empowering big-business interests to pour limitless resources into buying elections; First Amendment scholar Erwin Chemerinsky wrote that the 5–4 ruling was "a stunning example of judicial activism . . . to advance the traditional conservative ideological agenda."

When a speaker seeks to use public property rather than privately owned property as the conduit to deliver a message, the government's ability to control or even prohibit speech is heightened. Whether a speaker may insist on using a government vehicle—the commons of a college campus, the sidewalk outside a military base, the side of a city bus—to convey speech depends on whether the property is categorized as a "public forum" that, by historical practice or by express designation, is open for citizens' expressive use. The public forum doctrine recognizes not all public property is equally suited to wide-open communicative use, however, and where property functions as a public forum, the government may neither regulate the content of speech nor give preferential access to speakers based on their message. The doctrine was set forth most fully in the case of *Perry Ed. Assn. v. Perry Local Educators' Assn.*, 460 U.S. 37 (1983), involving a union's demand for access to teachers' school mailboxes. The Court determined that, because the mailboxes were not by tradition or practice held open as a forum for unfettered public use—rather, they were restricted by their nature and purpose to official communication in furtherance of school business—outsiders had no right to insist on using the mail system for their own communications. Only a very limited category of public property (sidewalks and parks) has ever been recognized as categorically a public forum. Other property may, situation by situation, take on the heightened First Amendment protection of a public forum if it is "designated" for expressive use by its government owners.

Two classes of citizens—public employees and students—present special challenges, leading the courts to fashion compromises that recognize a heightened level of government interest in restricting speech that interferes with the government's ability to function. In *Pickering v. Board of Education*, 391 U.S. 563 (1968), the Supreme Court confronted the case of a school teacher disciplined for criticizing his school district's financial stewardship in a letter published in his local newspaper. The Court determined that a public employee could not be fired for the content of speech addressing a matter of public concern without first balancing his interests as a citizen in contributing to the public discourse versus the government employer's interest in minimizing disruption to the workplace. This approach is now known as the *Pickering* balancing test. The Court somewhat narrowed this legal protection in the 1983 case of *Connick v. Myers*, 461 U.S. 138, ruling that a government employee could be punished more freely for speech that is primarily about a personal workplace grievance (in that case, whether a state prosecutor treated his employees fairly). When the employee speaks in the course of official duty, the First Amendment may not apply at all. The Supreme Court ruled in *Garcetti v. Ceballos*, 547 U.S. 410 (2006), when a public employee is carrying out a work assignment—giving a presentation, writing a memo—that speech is "government speech" for which the employee receives no First Amendment protection.

Courts have struggled to define the boundaries of students' right to speak without restraint or punishment by their schools, never more than in the social media era, in which students have access to costless publishing platforms that defy easy categorization as "in school" or "out of school." The Court memorably declared in the landmark case of *Tinker v. Des Moines Independent Community School District*, 393 U.S. 503 (1969), that "it can hardly be said that students or teachers leave their First Amendment rights at the schoolhouse gate." The case validated the rights of student antiwar protesters to wear black armbands to school because the school was unable to demonstrate that a "material and substantial disruption" of school functions occurred or was imminent. In decades since, courts have applied the *Tinker* disruption standard in a relatively deferential way, hesitating to second-guess school authority figures on matters implicating school safety. Thus, in a 2014 ruling the Supreme Court declined to review, a federal appeals court found no First Amendment violation when a California school prohibited students from displaying American flags on a day designated for the celebration of Latino pride for fear the competing displays would provoke violence. When students seek to use a school-provided medium for speech that is part of the school's curricular offerings, their free speech rights greatly decrease. In *Hazelwood School District v. Kuhlmeier*, 484 U.S. 260 (1988), the Supreme Court determined that student speech in a class-produced newspaper could be freely censored as long as administrators could identify a reasonable educational purpose for the censorship, a standard that has since been applied to graduation speeches, musical, and theatrical performances.

In contrast to its approach to student speech in K–12 schools, the Court has sided unfailingly with college students when their institutions seek, even indirectly, to control speakers' messages. Thus, the Court has held that a college may not discipline a college student for distributing offensive political cartoons with depictions of rape and mockery of police (*Papish v. Board of Curators of University of Missouri*, 410 U.S. 667 (1973)) or withhold funding from a student-produced publication merely because it espouses a religious viewpoint (*Rosenberger v. Rectors & Visitors of University of Virginia*, 515 U.S. 819 (1995)).

Regardless of the long history of rulings and the movements towards both protecting and regulating speech, social media has made interpreting the provision of freedom of speech in schools extremely complicated. The Supreme Court did not even use the word *Facebook* in a published opinion until 2015 (*Elonis v. United States*, 135 S.Ct. 2001, brought by a man convicted of making terroristic threats based on social media postings he claimed were jokes or experimentation with song lyrics), and its First Amendment jurisprudence has lagged behind

the explosive growth of speech on Twitter and other social media platforms. In the absence of guidance from the Court, lower courts have struggled to decide the extent to which a school or college might punish students for the content of speech created and distributed outside school using personal resources. In a particularly extreme case widely condemned by legal scholars, the New York–based Second Circuit decided [*Doninger v. Niehoff*, 527 F.3d 41 (2008)] that a Connecticut high school student disciplined for using a crass word on an off-campus blog to refer to school administrators in the context of a disagreement over a school policy decision did not have an actionable First Amendment claim. Other courts have been warier, however, about extending punitive school authority to speech beyond the proverbial schoolhouse gate merely because the speech is about the school. Most notably, the federal Third Circuit decided in *J.S. v. Blue Mountain School District*, 650 F.3d 915 (2011) that a Pennsylvania middle school lacked authority to punish a student who cruelly mocked her principal on an off-campus MySpace social media page that was neither viewed at school nor caused a disturbance beyond the principal's own distress.

As an adjunct to the First Amendment right to speak, courts have recognized a First Amendment right to receive information as well. In a 1982 ruling, *Board of Education, Island Trees School District v. Pico*, 457 U.S. 853, the Court recognized First Amendment rights of students are "directly and sharply implicated" when a book is removed from a school library. Therefore, a decision to remove a book will be unconstitutional if it is shown the motive was to deny students access to ideas with which the decision maker disagrees. This now-established proposition—that the First Amendment necessarily includes a right to read that gives the reader, and not just the speaker, a legal claim against the censor—represents a significant conceptual expansion of the right to speak. More recently, the Court again reasserted the listener's right to receive information in *Brown v. Entertainment Merchants Association*, 131 S.Ct. 2729 (2011), which invalidated a California law making it a misdemeanor to sell videogames depicting realistic acts of graphic violence to minors.

Perhaps second only to speech issues, issues of government endorsement of—or constraints on—religious observance are the richest vein of First Amendment litigation. The First Amendment contemplates both a prohibition on government action that unreasonably burdens religion (the free exercise clause) and on the use of government resources to advance religiosity or a particular faith (the establishment clause).

In its earliest application, *Reynolds v. United States*, 98 U.S. 145 (1879), the free exercise clause was interpreted as covering only religious beliefs, not religious practices violating neutrally enforced criminal laws (in that case, a ban on polygamy). The *Reynolds* case stands for the principle that the government may enforce generally applicable laws in a way that has the effect of burdening religious practices as long as the law has a legitimate religion-neutral purpose. During the 1970s and 1980s, however, the free exercise clause was reinvigorated. Courts became more willing to require exemptions to laws that in their text do not hinder or favor religious practice, in cases such as *Wisconsin v. Yoder*, 406 U.S. 205 (1972), involving a law of general application requiring school attendance of all children until age 16. The Court held the law could not be enforced against members of an Amish order that sought to withdraw their children from school after the eighth grade because their religion required being sheltered from worldly cultural influences.

In applying the Establishment Clause, courts have distinguished between government acts merely placing religious organizations on equal footing with nonreligious ones versus acts expressing a preference for a religion or for religiosity in general. Government is expected to tolerate religious expression on public property but not to organize or promote it. School requirements that students open the day with a prayer, learn creation science alongside evolution, pause for a moment of silent prayer-like reflection, or vote on a prayer to be read at football games have all been overturned on Establishment Clause grounds. But, there was no establishment clause violation when a New York school merely allowed a Christian community group to use meeting space after school hours on the same terms as nonreligious organizations [*Good News Club v. Milford Central School*, 533 U.S. 98 (2001)]. Government-funded displays of religious messages typically have been vulnerable to establishment clause challenge. Deviating from its traditional skepticism, however, the Court decided in *Van Orden v. Perry*, 545 U.S. 667 (2005), that the state of Texas did not violate the establishment clause by displaying a privately donated monument reproducing the stone tablets of the biblical Ten Commandments on the grounds of the state capitol. Because the monument was part of a larger display of historical images, and its reference to religion was historical and therefore not reasonably seen as an endorsement of religion, the majority held.

Frank LoMonte

Further Reading

Cate, Fred H. *Privacy in the Information Age.* Washington, DC: Brookings Institution Press, 1997.

Cogan, Neil H., ed. *The Complete Bill of Rights: The Drafts, Debates, Sources, and Origins.* New York: Oxford University Press, 1997.

Epstein, Richard A. "Privacy, Publication, and the First Amendment: The Dangers of First Amendment Exceptionalism." *Stanford Law Review* 52 (2000): 1003–1048.

Forer, Lois G. *A Chilling Effect: The Mounting Threat of Libel and Invasion of Privacy Actions to the First Amendment.* New York: Norton, 1987.

Hudson, David. *Let the Students Speak!: A History of the Fight for Free Expression in American Schools.* Boston, MA: Beacon Press, 2011.

Lewis, Anthony. *Freedom for the Thought That We Hate.* New York: Basic Books, 2009.

"Privacy in the First Amendment." *Yale Law Journal* 82, no. 7 (June 1973): 1462–1480.

Sack, Robert D. "Protection of Opinion under the First Amendment: Reflections on Alfred Hill, 'Defamation and Privacy under the First Amendment.'" *Columbia Law Review* 100, no. 1 (January 2000): 294–330.

Steinberg, Robert A. "Defamation, Privacy and the First Amendment." *Duke Law Journal*, no. 5 (December 1976): 1016–1050.

Stern, Seth, and Stephen Wermiel. *Justice Brennan: Liberal Champion,* 2010. Reprint, Lawrence: University Press of Kansas, 2013.

Tunick, Mark. *Balancing Privacy and Free Speech: Unwanted Attention in the Age of Social Media.* New York: Routledge, 2015.

See also: Constitutional Law; Educational Setting, Privacy in an; Legal Evolution of Privacy Rights; Philosophical Basis of Privacy; Supreme Court of the United States

Florida Star v. B.J.F., 491 U.S. 524 (1989)

Identification: A landmark U.S. Supreme Court case, where the Court considered two fundamental and conflicting constitutional rights, the right to privacy and the First Amendment. In this case, the Court considered the conflict between an individual's right to privacy and the First Amendment protections for reporting the names of crime victims, including the names of sexual assault victims.

In a series of cases, the U.S. Supreme Court considered the tension between the First Amendment and various state statutes and common law doctrines that protect a person's right not to have even truthful information about her or him published. In *Florida Star*, the U.S. Supreme Court applied the reasoning in one of these cases, *Smith v. Daily Mail Publishing Co.,* 443 U.S. 97 (1979), in its 6–3 decision, a ruling that the First Amendment protects the right to publish lawfully obtained information on a matter of public concern, absent a compelling state interest of the highest order, but emphasizes that the ruling applies to the facts of this case. The media had argued that the Court should find that the First Amendment protects the press from civil or criminal penalties for publishing the truth.

The U.S. Supreme Court emphasized that, while prior U.S. Supreme Court rulings have upheld the right of the press to publish, the Court has also emphasized that the decisions were limited to the facts of each of the cases and refused to rule that the press could never be punished for publishing the truth. In *Daily Mail,* the U.S. Supreme Court said, "[I]f a newspaper lawfully obtains truthful information about a matter of public significance, then state officials may not constitutionally punish publication of the information, absent a need to further a state interest of the highest order."

B.J.F. was robbed and sexually assaulted one night in Jacksonville, Florida. The sheriff's department prepared a crime report, which included her full name, and placed this report in the department's press room for reporters who write about crimes in the city, a matter of public significance. The *Florida Star*'s trainee-reporter copied the police report verbatim, and the story ran in the newspaper, although the paper had a policy not to print rape victims' names. In fact, the account mentioning B.J.F. was one of fifty-four police items that appeared in the weekly paper. The newspaper had never before printed a rape victim's name. Unfortunately, B.J.F.'s attacker saw her name in the paper and called her house, threatening to rape her again.

B.J.F. sued the *Florida Star* and the sheriff's department, claiming that the paper violated a Florida statute that made it unlawful to "print, publish, or broadcast . . . in any instrument of mass communication" the names of sexual assault victims and imposed civil penalties on the newspaper. She also sued the sheriff's department, which settled. The paper lost a jury verdict of $75,000 in compensatory damages and $25,000 in punitive damages. Florida's First District Court of Appeal affirmed the decision, and the Florida Supreme Court refused to hear the case.

The U.S. Supreme Court, in reversing the lower court's decision, did not declare Florida's law criminalizing the publication of a rape victim's name unconstitutional. It said that it was unconstitutional in this case, where the newspaper had lawfully obtained B.J.F's name and the details of the case from publicly available police reports. The Court said that application of the law in this case would result in "self-censorship" by the media, who routinely rely on government news releases.

Justice Thurgood Marshall, writing for the majority in the *Florida Star* case, discussed the clash between the First Amendment and privacy rights. Justice Marshall explained that, when the media obtain information about a matter of public concern from the government, the government may not then punish the media, absent a "compelling state interest of the highest order."

The Court decided that imposing liability on the newspaper did not serve a compelling state interest of the "highest order." While the Court conceded that protecting the privacy and safety of sexual assault victims and encouraging victims of sexual assault to report the crimes were certainly significant and important, the Court nonetheless ruled that the statute, which imposes automatic liability for publishing the information the government disseminates violates the First Amendment. The Court also observed that the government released the information to the press and that the government could have and should have taken measures to protect the victim's privacy. According to Justice Marshall's opinion, when a state passes a statute that punishes truthful publication of information of public concern in the name of privacy, "it must demonstrate its commitment to advancing this interest by applying its prohibition even-handedly, to the smalltime disseminator as well as the media giant."

Sandra F. Chance

Further Reading

Alderman, Ellen and Kennedy, Caroline, *The Right to Privacy,* Vintage; Reprint edition (September 29, 2010).

Beattie, James R., Jr. "Privacy in the First Amendment: Private Facts and the Zone of Deliberation." *Vanderbilt Law Review* 44 (1991): 899–923.

Blasi, Vincent. "The Checking Value in First Amendment Theory." *American Bar Foundation Research Journal* 2, no. 3 (1977): 521.

Brandeis, Louis D., and Warren, Samuel D. "The Right to Privacy." *Harvard Law Review* 4, no. 193 (1890)

Chemerinsky, Erwin. "Narrowing the Tort of Public Disclosure of Private Facts." *Chapman Law Review* 11 (2008): 423–433.

Denno, Deborah W. "The Privacy Rights of Rape Victims in the Media and the Law: Perspectives on Disclosing Rape Victims' Names" *Fordham Law Review* 61 (1993): 1113–1131.

"Developments in the Law—The Law of Media: III. Prosecuting the Press: Criminal Liability for the Act of Publishing." *Harvard Law Review* 120 (2007): 1007–1019.

Keeton, W. Page, et al. *Prosser and Keeton on the Law of Torts* § 117, at 85, 5th ed., 1984. Levy, Leonard. *Freedom of the Press from Zenger to Jefferson.* Carolina Academic Press, 1996.

Meiklejohn, Alexander. *Free Speech and Its Relation to Self-Government.* The Lawbook Exchange, Ltd., 2011.

Prosser, William L. "Privacy." *California Law Review* 48, no. 383 (1960).

Sheinkopf, Cheryl M. "Balancing Free Speech, Privacy and Open Government: Why Government Should Not Restrict the Truthful Reporting of Public Record Information." *UCLA Law Review* 44 (1997): 1567–1612.

See also: First Amendment to the U.S. Constitution; The Right to Privacy; Supreme Court of the United States.

Foreign Intelligence Surveillance Act of 1978

Identification: Foreign Intelligence Surveillance Act of 1978 (FISA), 92 Stat. 1783, 50 U.S.C. ch. 36. Enables the United States government to conduct electronic surveillance on foreign intelligence within the United States.

The Foreign Intelligence Surveillance Act of 1978 (FISA)was enacted after many decades of uncertainty and controversy regarding the constitutionality of electronic surveillance conducted by the Executive Branch. FISA has been significantly amended since its enactment by the Intelligence Authorization Acts of 1995 and 1998, the Uniting and Strengthening America by Providing Appropriate Tools Required to Intercept and Obstruct Terrorism Act of 2001 (USA PATRIOT Act) and the USA PATRIOT Additional Reauthorization Amendments Act (2006), as well as the Foreign Intelligence Surveillance Act Amendments Act of 2008, and by the FISA Sunsets Extension Act of 2011. In 2015 the USA Freedom Act was passed, amending procedures of surveillance outside of the United States.

The Foreign Surveillance Intelligence Act and the subsequent amendments codified the authorization procedures for electronic surveillance, physical searches, searches of records, and the use of pen registers and trap and trace devices. It established the Foreign Surveillance Intelligence Court, and the Foreign Surveillance Intelligence Court of Review, both of which have sole jurisdiction over activities conducted within FISA guidelines. Surveillance under FISA targets two general groups —foreign powers and agents of foreign powers. An agent of a foreign power can include United States citizens who knowingly participate in secret intelligence gathering for a foreign power that violates United States criminal statutes, as well as any United States citizen who knowingly participates in acts of sabotage or acts of terrorism for a foreign power. A foreign power is defined as any government outside of the United States. This includes a foreign government's diplomat or representative or an employee of a foreign government, as well as any faction or entity that is acknowledged, directed, or controlled by a foreign government, or any group engaged in international terrorism or activities in preparation for international terrorism. A United States person, for purposes of FISA, is any citizen of the United States, an alien lawfully admitted for permanent residence, or a United States corporation.

Until the terrorist attacks of September 11, 2001, FISA was not the subject of much popular controversy. The primary intellectual debate concerning the powers given to the Executive Branch under FISA were centered on the distinction between surveillance done in furtherance of a criminal investigation and that done for national security. This distinction became to be known as "the wall." The wall was codified in the separation of criminal and national security investigations into discrete groups in agencies such as the Federal Bureau of Investigations. After September 11, investigations were conducted into the investigation practices of the FBI in order to ascertain weaknesses in the collection and processing of intelligence on national security threats. This investigation highlighted the lack of communication, which was caused by the "wall," which lead to failures to detect and address terrorist threats. The subsequent amendments made to FISA after the September 11 attacks attempted to address these failures.

Such amendments arose out of the USA PATRIOT Act, which expanded the ability of the government to conduct surveillance under FISA. Specifically, it relaxed the standard of showing that the government had to meet from "primary purpose" to "significant purpose." With regard to business records, section 215 of the USA PATRIOT Act expanded the ability of the government to amass information by allowing the collection of all "tangible things," as well as overriding the existing standard that required "specific and articulable facts giving reason to believe that the person to whom the records pertain is a foreign power or an agent of a foreign power." The new standard under section 215 simply requires that these "tangible things" are being "sought for an authorized investigation… to protect against international terrorism or clandestine intelligence activities."

The government's use of the powers given to it under FISA, as amended by the USA PATRIOT Act, has spawned multiple controversies. One example of this is the PRISM program. PRISM is administered by the National Security Agency and governed by section 702 of FISA. Its existence was made public by Edward Snowden and journalists Ewan Macaskill, Glenn Greenwald, Laura Poitras, and Barton Gellman in 2013. Through PRISM the National Security Agency was able to tap directly into the systems of large internet companies and providers, including Google, Facebook, Skype, Apple, Youtube, and Yahoo. Through PRISM the NSA was able to collect data directly from the servers of these companies, including audio and video chats, photographs, emails, documents, and data logs that allowed analysts to track targets.

Multiple lawsuits have been brought against the NSA that challenge its activities and procedures. The NSA argues that all programs and actions are allowed under FISA. The United States Supreme Court has heard one case on the constitutionality of FISA, but the majority of adjudication of FISA-related questions has occurred in multiple Federal Circuit Courts and Federal Courts of Appeal. The overriding issue of these cases is the constitutionality of FISA with regard to the Government's searching and seizure of various types of information owned and metadata generated by United States citizens. The Constitutional questions raised in these cases emanate from the Fourth Amendment's requirement of a warrant supported by probable cause and particularity, as well as a defendant's Sixth Amendment right to a public trial, confrontation of the witnesses against her, and assistance of counsel.

With regard to Fourth Amendment questions, Federal Circuit Courts have ruled that FISA strikes an appropriate balance between the Government's need to insure national security and an individual's constitutional rights and that a person's Fourth Amendment rights are not violated by the information gathering procedures defined by FISA. In addition, the Circuit Courts have ruled that the probable cause requirement of the Fourth Amendment does not apply to international surveillance, as actions

taken for national security are not analogous to criminal prosecutions. Lastly, the Fourth Amendment's requirement for particularity, the courts have ruled that FISA's requirement for a general description of the information being sought is sufficiently particular.

Another argument that has been brought to challenge the Constitutionality of FISA is the issue of standing. A person must have "standing" to be able to bring a case against the Government in Federal Court. Standing is defined by Article III, section 2 of the Constitution. It states: "The judicial power shall extend to all cases, in law and equity, arising under the Constitution, the laws of the United States...to controversies to which the United States shall be a party..."Between 2009 and 2013 the question of standing, as it relates to Government actions performed under authority of FISA, was adjudicated in Federal court. In 2009 the district court for the Southern District of New York ruled in *Amnesty International United States. v John McConnell*, 646 F. Supp. 2d 633, that the plaintiffs did not have standing because they could not show that they had been surveilled under FISA; i.e., there case lacked a "controversy." Amnesty International appealed this decision to the United States Court of Appeals for the Second District and it was heard under *Amnesty International USA v Clapper*, 638 F.3d 118 (2011). The Second District reversed the Southern District's decision and remanded the case. The Second District reasoned that the plaintiffs have shown injuries in fact; i.e., controversies, under the "established rules of standing, the plaintiffs here have alleged that they reasonably anticipate direct injury...because they engage in legitimate professional activities that make it reasonably likely that their privacy will be invaded and their conversations overheard." In turn, the defendants petitioned the United States Supreme Court for writ of certiorari. This writ was granted in 2012 and the Court heard the case as *Amnesty International United States v Clapper*, 133 S. Ct. 1138(2013).

The Court reversed the ruling of the Second District in a 5-4 decision. Justice Alito authored the majority opinion, stating that the respondents do not have standing under Article III of the Constitution for the following reasons: 1) that potential injury is insufficient to be an injury in fact; 2) that an "objectively reasonable likelihood" that the respondents' communications with foreign contacts will be monitored by the Government acting within its powers under §1881a is insufficient; 3) that ongoing injuries due to the increased cost and burden of insuring privacy of the respondents' communications from potential surveillance under §1881a is insufficient; 4) the respondents' arguments that their definition of injury and standing are supported by adjudication in prior Supreme Court decisions is incorrect. With this ruling, the Supreme Court restricted the argument for standing to any party who is a stated target of surveillance or a party who can demonstrate an in fact injury due to government actions under FISA.

In June, 2015 the USA Freedom Act was approved by Congress. This Act modified many sections of the USA PATRIOT Act. It limits some of the bulk collection programs performed by the National Security Agency, including the collection of telecommunications metadata of citizens by United States intelligence agencies. It also declassifies FISA Court opinions that contain significant legal analysis, or, if declassification is not possible it requires a summary of the Court's decision. The Freedom Act implemented the requirement of an *amicus curiae* panel to represent the public's interest in cases of new or significant legal questions. Additionally, it extends section 215 of the Patriot Act to 2019. In 2017, FISA was reauthorized until 2023 through the FISA Reauthorization Act.

Rachel Jorgensen

Further Reading

Atkin, Michelle Louise. *Balancing Liberty and Security: An Ethical Study of U.S. Foreign Intelligence Surveillance, 2001-2009*. Security and Professional Intelligence Education Series. Lanham, MD: Rowman & Littlefield Publishers, 2013.

Doyle, Charles. *Terrorism: Section by Section Analysis of the USA PATRIOT Act*. Congressional Research Service Report for Congress. Washington, D.C.: Library of Congress, 2001.

Harper, Nick. "FISA's Fuzzy Line between Domestic and International Terrorism" *The University of Chicago Law Review* 81, no. 3 (Summer 2014): 1123-1164.

Korjus, Markus. *The Foreign Intelligence Surveillance Act*. Intelligence and Counterintelligence Studies Series. New York: Nova Science Publishers, 2013.

Posner, Steve C. *Privacy Law and the USA PATRIOT Act*. LexisNexis, 2015.

Richards, Neil M. "The Dangers of Surveillance" *Harvard Law Review* 126, no. 7 (May 2013): 1934-1965.

See also: Electronic Surveillance; Foreign Intelligence Surveillance Court (FISC); Fourth Amendment to the U.S. Constitution; Greenwald, Glenn; Metadata; National Security Agency (NSA); Poitras, Laura; PRISM; Search Warrants; September 11; Snowden, Edward Joseph; Supreme Court of the United States; Terrorism and Privacy; USA FREEDOM Act; USA PATRIOT Act

Foreign Intelligence Surveillance Court

Identification: A court created with the enactment of the Foreign Intelligence Surveillance Act in 1978.

The power of the Foreign Intelligence Surveillance Court (FISC) emanates from chapter 36, "Foreign Intelligence Surveillance," of chapter 50, War and National Defense, of the United States Code. The court is located in Washington, D.C. and is administered under the Federal Court system and is comprised of 11 federal district court judges who are appointed by the Chief Justice of the United States Supreme Court. The judges must represent at least seven of the federal court districts. The judges preside on the court on a rotating basis, with each rotation lasting one week. At least three of the judges must reside within 20 miles of Washington, D.C. The court holds jurisdiction over applications for electronic surveillance of foreign powers, or agents of foreign parties, in the United States.

The Court has purview over four categories of electronic surveillance. The first is wire or radio communication that targets "a particular, known United States person who is in the United States." The second category is wire communications made to or from a person in the United States. The third category pertains to radio communications if both the sender and all intended recipients are in the United States. The fourth category includes electronic monitoring to obtain information that is not wire or radio communications.

Electronic communications have radically changed since 1978, which has had an impact on the Court's ability to have jurisdiction over a wider array of modern communications, including email and internet-based voice and video communications. Additionally, in the aftermath of September 11, 2001, Congress passed the Patriot Act. Section 215 of the Patriot Act expanded the types of materials the government could collect to gather intelligence on terrorism. Under section 215 the government must show that "there are reasonable grounds to believe that the tangible things sought are relevant to an authorized investigation . . . to obtain foreign intelligence information not concerning a United States person or to protect against international terrorism or clandestine intelligence activities."

Since 2001 the Court has interpreted section 215 as giving the government the right to conduct mass surveillance programs. Subsequently, the National Security Agency received authorization from the Court to conduct bulk collection of metadata from telephone calls in 2006. This metadata included time of the call, the call length, and the telephone numbers of the caller and the recipient. In 2011 the Court approved the collection of metadata on internet use. In neither instance did the Court approve the collection of content. However, the Court's power to approve the mass collection of metadata on telephone and internet use came under

sharp public scrutiny after Edward Snowden, a computer specialist contractor working for the National Security Agency, provided documentation of the government's mass surveillance program to journalists Glen Greenwald, Laura Poitras, and Ewan MacAskill, who subsequently published articles in *The Guardian* and *The Washington Post*.

This reporting set off a backlash against the Court, with particular criticism of the Court's lack of transparency and adversarial procedure. In turn, these criticisms have raised questions of the Court's constitutionality, particularly under Article III and the Fourth Amendment. Article III stipulates that "judicial power shall extend ...to *controversies* to which the United States shall be a party..."Many have argued that the movement to mass surveillance and bulk collection, by its very nature, lacks the requisite element of controversy, as the United States cannot have an adversarial relationship with the millions of people from whom metadata is being collected. The Fourth Amendment protects the people from unreasonable searches and seizures. The government has argued that foreign intelligence and the "incidental collection" of the metadata generated by non-target persons is not protected by the Fourth Amendment. Additionally, the Court has reasoned that the government's surveillance falls under the "special needs" doctrine, which allows for warrantless searches under the theory that the substantial public interest inherent in preventing terrorist acts overcomes a person's individual privacy rights.

The Court's decisions are classified and, unlike standard judicial procedure, the United States Government is the only party allowed to argue and present evidence to the court. The hearing itself is also classified and not open to the public. However, passage of the USA Freedom Act (2015) did mandate some reform of the Court. Section 401 of the Act created a role for *amici curiae*– five individuals or organizations who will provide assistance with the Court's consideration of novel or significant legal questions. Section 402 requires the Director of

National Intelligence to "conduct a declassification review of each decision order, or opinion" issued by the Court. There is an appeals court, the Foreign Intelligence Court of Review, which is comprised of three Federal judges, also selected by the Chief Justice of the United States Supreme Court. These review hearings are also classified.

Rachel Jorgensen

Further Reading

Declan, Keara. *Foreign Intelligence Surveillance Courts: Background, Issues, and Proposals.* New York: Novinka, 2014.

Donohue, Laura K. "Bulk Metadata Collection: Statutory and Constitutional Considerations." *Harvard Journal of Law and Public Policy* 37 (Summer 2014), 757- 900.

Privacy and Civil Liberties Oversight Board. *Report on the Telephone Records Program Conducted under Section 215 of the USA PATRIOT ACT and on the Operations of the Foreign Intelligence Surveillance Court.* Washington, DC, 2015. https://www.pclob.gov/library/215-Report_on_the_Telephone_Records_Program.pdf

U.S. Library of Congress, Congressional Research Service, *Reform of the Foreign Intelligence Surveillance Courts: Procedural and Operational Changes,* by Andrew Nolan and Richard M. Thompson II. R43362. 2014.

See also: Electronic surveillance; Foreign Intelligence Surveillance Act of 1978 (FISA) Greenwald, Glenn; National Security Agency (NSA); Poitras, Laura; Snowden, Edward Joseph

Fourth Amendment to the U.S. Constitution

Identifcation: The provision from the Bill of Rights of the U.S. Constitution that prohibits unreasonable searches and seizures.

The Fourth Amendment means that for a government actor, typically a police officer, to search your home, or anywhere it is thought that you have a right to privacy, the actor must obtain a search warrant or have a well-established and recognized exception to the search warrant requirement. James Madison wrote the Fourth Amendment in 1789 in response to the perceived abuse of the "writ of assistance," which was a general warrant used by British soldiers prior to the American Revolution. The Fourth Amendment was passed in December 1791. Thomas Jefferson, then secretary of state, announced its adoption in March 1792.

Specifically, the amendment states: "the right of the people to be secure in their persons, houses, papers, and effects, against unreasonable searches and seizures, shall not be violated, and no Warrants shall issue, but upon probable cause, supported by Oath or affirmation, and particularly describing the place to be searched, and the persons or things to be seized."

History

Most U.S. law has its roots in English common law. The Fourth Amendment is no exception. Sir Edward Coke, a seventeenth-century English barrister, judge, and politician, once wrote, "The house of every one is to him as his castle and fortress, as well for his defence against injury and violence as for his repose" (*Semayne's Case* [1604] 5 Coke Rep. 91). This recognized that the king did not have unlimited authority to search his subjects but could conduct searches only when the purpose was lawful and a warrant had been obtained. By 1765, English common law had established that warrants needed probable cause and that they could not be overly broad, meaning, they had to specific about what they were searching for and where the item was to be found.

The same rights, however, were not extended to England's colonies. In fact, legislation was specifically written to allow the enforcement of British revenue-gathering policies on customs, leaving authorities able to search almost anything, at almost any time, with little to no oversight. Specifically, the Excise Tax of 1754 gave tax collectors the ability to use the general "Writ of Assistance" allowing them to search colonists' homes and seize any prohibited or undocumented goods. To combat this, in 1756,

Massachusetts enacted legislation that specifically banned the use of general warrants. The governor rejected the legislation, however, finding that it conflicted with English law.

Also, the Virginia Declaration of Rights of 1776 specifically forbade the use of general warrants. Eventually, this led to the Fourth Amendment ban on unreasonable searches and seizures being included when the Bill of Rights was written and proposed.

Government actor

The Fourth Amendment specifies that the government shall not commit an unreasonable search and seizure, which means that it does not bar private individuals from committing searches.

Trespassing laws, or specific laws against invasions of privacy, prevent nongovernment actors from committing searches; however, it is not a Fourth Amendment issue if a government actor is not involved. Initially, the Fourth Amendment applied only to the federal government, but in 1961, *Mapp v. Ohio* (367 U.S. 643 [1961]) ruled that through the Due Process Clause of the Fourteenth Amendment, the Fourth Amendment applies to state government as well.

Though the Fourth Amendment is not applicable to private individuals, if the private individual is acting on behalf of the government, she or he can be treated as a government actor for purposes of the Fourth Amendment. For example, if your neighbor takes it upon him- or herself to search your house, finds something incriminating, and gives it to the police, that is not a violation of the Fourth Amendment because your neighbor is not a government actor. However, if the police ask your neighbor to search your house and your neighbor agrees to work with the police, that is a Fourth Amendment issue.

Right to privacy

Before the Fourth Amendment applies, it must be established that the place being searched is, in fact, something protected by the Fourth Amendment. If there is no right to privacy, then there

has not been a "search" and thus, no violation of the Fourth Amendment. The meaning of the right to privacy has changed over the years. Currently, most courts agree that a right to privacy is established if there is both a subjective expectation of privacy and that society as a whole recognizes that expectation of privacy (*Smith v. Maryland*, 442 U.S. 735 [1979]).

Early case law focused on the physical intrusion into one's home, such as "persons, houses, papers, or effects" and ruled that things like wiretaps, or general police surveillance, were not searches (*Olmstead v. United States*, 277 U.S. 438 [1928]). In *Katz v. United States*, 389 U.S. 347 (1967), however, the Court significantly expanded Fourth Amendment protections. In *Katz*, the Court held that a government wiretap was indeed an intrusion into one's privacy and constituted a Fourth Amendment search. Specifically, Katz involved the government wiretapping a telephone booth by using a microphone attached to the outside of the glass.

The Court held that even though there was no physical intrusion into the booth, Katz had entered the booth and shut the door behind him; thus, he exhibited his desire to keep his conversation private. Also, the Court felt that it was a privacy expectation that society as a whole grants. Furthermore, Justice Potter Stewart said, "The Fourth Amendment protects people, not places." He went further to clarify the right to privacy protects the right to be let alone by other people. Also, the Court does not dispute that the government could have obtained a warrant to search, via wiretap, the phone booth. Without a warrant, however, the search was unconstitutional.

The Court has stopped short of granting an expectation of privacy to those instances where information is freely given to a third party. In *Smith,* the Court held that there is no expectation of privacy in phone numbers dialed because the numbers are being freely given to the telephone company when dialed. The Court made no distinction between giving the number to a human operator or to a mechanical switchboard.

The right to privacy was further expanded in cases such as *United States v. Jones,* 132 S. Ct. 945 (2012), where law enforcement agents had attached a Global Positioning System (GPS) device on a car's exterior without Jones's knowledge or consent. The Court concluded that, because the purpose of the GPS was obtaining information, it was a Fourth Amendment search. Justice Antonin Scalia authored the majority opinion, stating any physical trespass into a protected area, with the intent to obtain information, constitutes a search under the Fourth Amendment.

Also, the Court used a similar reasoning in 2013 to determine that bringing a drug-sniffing dog to the front door of a home was a search. In *Florida v Jardines,* 569 U.S. 1 (2013), police received a tip that marijuana was being grown in a home. They led a drug-sniffing dog to the front door of the house, where the dog alerted officers to contraband. Justice Scalia again wrote the majority opinion, basing the decision less on the expectation of privacy and more on a citizen's property rights. They used their reasoning in *United States v. Jones,* focusing on the fact that the use of a drug-sniffing dog to sniff at a front door is a physical intrusion with the intent of gathering information. Prior cases have held that drug-sniffing dogs that were put to work at vehicle checkpoints or to sniff luggage were constitutional (*United States v. Place,* 462 U.S. 696 (1983); *City of Indianapolis v. Edmond,* 531 U.S. 32 (2000)). Prior cases held that actions such as luggage sniffs and vehicle checkpoints were mere "Terry stops" (see below), which do not violate the Fourth Amendment.

In addition to having an expectation of privacy in one's home, that protection is extended to the curtilage, which is considered to be the area intimately surrounding the home. In deciding whether something is curtilage, the Court has decided that "curtilage questions should be resolved with particular reference to four factors: the proximity of the area claimed to be curtilage to the home, whether the area is included

within an enclosure surrounding the home, the nature of the uses to which the area is put, and the steps taken by the resident to protect the area from observation by people passing by" (*United States v. Dunn,* 480 U.S. 294 (1987)). The Court has also ruled things left beyond the curtilage, such as trash left on a curb, is not covered by the Fourth Amendment (*California v. Greenwood,* 486 U.S. 35 (1988)). The Court felt that, even though trash is hidden in opaque bags, it is common knowledge to reasonable people that trash left out is accessible to animals and scavengers, and left out specifically so that a stranger, the trash collector, could take it. Therefore, there is no expectation of privacy.

Technology has also changed the way we view an expectation of privacy and the Fourth Amendment. In *Kyllo v. United States,* 533 U.S. 27 (2001), the Court held that using thermal imaging to monitor heat from a house, constitutes a search under the Fourth Amendment, even if the device is being used from a public vantage point. In the majority opinion, Justice Scalia reasoned that there is no difference between "off the wall" and "through the wall" surveillance. The Court also made the distinction that if the technology is not available to the general public, use of that technology can constitute a search.

As technology, and the way we use it, changes, we continue to think about how that impacts privacy. For example, cellphones, with GPS trackers, are further changing the way we think about privacy and the fourth amendment. In the recent case of *Carpenter v. United States* (2018), the Supreme Court dealt with privacy and cellphone location records. Prior to *Carpenter,* there was no warrant needed for police to request cellphone location records. The reasoning was largely based on cases like *Smith v Maryland,* which are based on landlines and dialing numbers . The majority in Carpenter determined that the third-party doctrine applied to telephone communications in Smith could not be applied to cellphone technology and ruled that the government must obtain a warrant in order to access historical cellphone records. Chief Justice Roberts argued that technology "has afforded law enforcement a powerful new tool to carry out its important responsibilities. At the same time, this tool risks Government encroachment of the sort the Framers [of the US Constitution], after consulting the lessons of history, drafted the Fourth Amendment to prevent." The majority went on further to add, "[S]eismic shifts in digital technology … made possible the tracking of not only Carpenter's location but also everyone else's, not for a short period but for years and years. Sprint Corporation and its competitors are not your typical witnesses. Unlike the nosy neighbor who keeps an eye on comings and goings, they are ever alert, and their memory is nearly infallible. There is a world of difference between the limited types of personal information addressed in *Smith* and *Miller* and the exhaustive chronicle of location information casually collected by wireless carriers today." However, it should be noted that the Court's decision was relatively narrow, and did not expand to include all cellphone related information.

Plain view and fields

If something is left in plain view, that is, generally out in the open, it is not protected by the Fourth Amendment because, if individuals leave something in a space where people can generally view it, it is thought that they did not express a desire to keep something private. In *Coolidge v. New Hampshire*, 403 U.S. 443 (1971), the court ruled that, "if an officer is lawfully present, he may seize objects in plain view." It must be immediately apparent, however, without a further search or inquiry, that the item in question is contraband. Similarly, things in places such as open fields, pastures, open waters, and woods are considered to be in plain view and thus not subject to privacy rights. Specifically, in *Hester v. United States*, 265 U.S. 57 (1924), the Court stated, "[T]he special protection accorded by the Fourth Amendment to the people in their persons, houses, papers and effects is not extended to open fields. This is true even if the Govern-

ment Actor in question was trespassing and ignoring 'no trespassing' signs" (*Oliver v. United States*, 466 U.S. 170 (1984)). In *Florida v. Riley*, 488 U.S. 445 (1989), the court further clarified that even if a law enforcement agency is using a plane to observe something in the open field, it does not constitute a Fourth Amendment search.

Seizure

A seizure of property occurs when there is "meaningful interference with an individual's possessory interest in that property" (*United States v. Jacobsen*, 503 U.S. 540 (1992)). The Fourth Amendment also protects against individuals being seized, including a brief detention or arrest. The courts have held that a person has been seized for purposes of the Fourth Amendment if a reasonable person would not feel free to leave, specifically if there is a restraint on freedom of movement, and/or a show of physical force or authority (*United States v. Mendenhall*, 466 U.S. 544 (1980)).

The law does not consider it a seizure, however, when an officer briefly questions a person in a public place. The Court has ruled that questioning is merely a "citizen encounter" and not a seizure if the police do not convey a message that compliance with their questioning is required (*Florida v. Bostik*, 501 U.S. 429 (1991)). *Bostik* specifically addressed the question of when a reasonable person feels free to leave and ruled that, although Bostik was not free to leave due to the bus schedule, his freedom was not curtailed by any showing of authority by the police and therefore, it was not a Fourth Amendment seizure.

Warrant

The Court has held that searches conducted without a warrant are per se unreasonable. This means that there is a presumption toward the search being unreasonable, with the burden on the state to prove that there was an exception to the warrant requirement. The Fourth Amendment requires a judicially sanctioned warrant, and for such a warrant to be granted, and considered reasonable, it must be supported by probable cause and must be limited in scope as to who or what can be searched, and what is being searched for.

The question becomes what exactly is "probable cause"? The government has probable cause to make an arrest when "the facts and circumstances within their knowledge and of which they had reasonably trustworthy information" would lead a reasonable and prudent person to believe the individual in question had committed, or was in the process of committing, a crime (*Beck v. Ohio,* 379 U.S. 89 (1964)). Also, the probable cause must exist before the arrest is made, so evidence obtained after the arrest may not apply retroactively to justify the arrest (*Johnson v. United States,* 333 U.S. 10 (1948)).

As for a search, the police must show that they have probable cause to believe that the search will uncover criminal activity or contraband. In a 1925 case, the Court ruled that probable cause is a flexible and "common sense" standard (*Carroll v. United States,* 267 U.S. 132 (1925)). In *Aguilar v. Texas,* 378 U.S. 108 (1964), the court set forth the Aguilar-Spinelli Test to evaluate the validity of a warrant. The Court established a two-prong test, stating "[T]he magistrate must be informed of some of the underlying circumstances relied on by the person providing the information and some of the underlying circumstances from which the affiant concluded that the informant, whose identity was not disclosed, was credible or his information reliable."

In *Illinois v. Gates,* 462 U.S. 213 (1983), however, the Court abandoned the two-prong test, for a general totality of the circumstances test. Chief Justice Rehnquist wrote in his opinion:

"We agree with the Illinois Supreme Court that an informant's 'veracity,' 'reliability' and 'basis of knowledge' are all highly relevant in determining the value of his report. We do not agree, however, that these elements should be understood as entirely separate and independent requirements to be rigidly exacted in every case[. . .] [T]hey should be understood simply as closely intertwined issues that may usefully illuminate the common sense, practical question whether there is 'probable cause' to believe that contraband or evidence is located in a particular place."

Some states, including Alaska, Massachusetts, New York, Tennessee, Vermont, and Washington, still use Aguilar-Spinelli as their basis for probable cause.

Exceptions

While searches conducted without a warrant are considered per se unreasonable, there are some exceptions to this rule. These exceptions apply "[o]nly in those exceptional circumstances in which special needs, beyond the normal need for law enforcement, make the warrant and probable cause requirement impracticable" (*New Jersey v. T.L.O.,* 469 U.S. 325 (1985)).

Stop-and-frisk. Courts have ruled that some things fall short of being considered a Fourth Amendment search. For example, in *Terry v. Ohio,* 392 U.S. 1 (1968), the Court held that, if law enforcement has a "reasonable suspicion" of criminal activity, an officer may perform a search on an individual. This means the officer does not need probable cause. Terry specified, however, that the officer must believe that "criminal activity may be afoot," and that a suspicious person has a weapon and is posing a danger to the officer or others. To do this, the officer must point to "specific articulable fact." In determining reasonable suspicion, the Court uses a totality of the circumstances test, much like probable cause.

If this occurs, an officer may perform a "pat down" on the outer layer of clothing, to search for weapons. This means that an officer may not do things like empty pockets, or search inner layers of clothing. If an officer feels something that he or she recognizes as illegal based on touch alone, he or she may seize it. This is referred to as the "Plain Feel" doctrine, and searches such as these are known as "Terry stops." Though police officers must believe the individual to be armed, or posing a danger, this often gets construed quite broadly.

Consent. If an individual consents to the search, the police search of that individual is not considered a Fourth Amendment violation and no warrant is required. One must determine if the person had the authority to consent, whether the consent was freely given, and what the scope of the consent is. In contrast to the Fifth Amendment rule that rights must be explained to the individual in question, however, the Court has held that consent may be considered to be freely given even if the individual was not informed of her or his right to refuse a search (*Schneckloth v. Bustamonte*, 412 U.S. 218 (1973)). Also, the person conducting the search need not be identified as a law enforcement officer but can be working undercover or as an informant and the evidence is still admissible.

The issue becomes who has authority to give consent. One may consent if she or he has possession of the premises. This includes cotenants, who may consent to any common areas or shared areas. A co-tenant may grant consent, however, only to areas that he or she has control over, for example, his or her own bedroom, but not a roommate's bedroom.

In addition, a search made with consent can be considered valid as long as the officers relied on apparent authority; that is, they believed in good faith that the party had authority to consent, even if it was later discovered the individual consenting lacked the necessary authority. For example, in *Illinois v. Rodriguez,* 497 U.S. 177 (1990), the Supreme Court held that a search was valid if the police reasonably believed that the party giving consent had actual authority over the premises but were later proved incorrect in their belief. The Court stressed that the touchstone of the Fourth Amendment is not consent but reasonableness. This means that one does not judge consent but actual authority; what a reasonable police officer would know, or have reason to know, at the time.

Search incident to lawful arrest. Another exception to the rule requiring warrants is a search incident to a lawful arrest. The key to this exception is that the arrest be "lawful," meaning the officer had a warrant to arrest the individual or that the arrest was done with probable cause. This exception allows the police officer to search an arrested person without a warrant in the interest of officer safety as well as public safety. The officer can search the area within the arrestee's immediate control, often referred to as the person's "wingspan." Specifically, in *Chimel v. California,* 395 U.S. 752 (1969), the court stated that an officer can search the arrestee's immediate control, but not the entire house, "in order to remove any weapons that the [arrestee] might seek to use in order to resist arrest or effect his escape" and to prevent the "concealment or destruction of evidence."

If an arrest occurs in a car, the officer may search the vehicle's passenger compartment but not the trunk. In *Arizona v. Gant,* 556 U.S. 332 (2009), the court further clarified this by stating that the officer may only continue to search the vehicle that was recently occupied by the arrestee if it is reasonable to believe that the arrestee might still be able to access the vehicle at the time of the search. Specifically, in *Gant,* the arrestee was already secured in the police car while the search took place, and the court ruled this goes beyond the automobile exception.

Automobile exceptions. There is also an exception for automobiles. This does not mean that there is no expectation of privacy in a vehicle. It means that if an officer has probable cause that evidence or contraband is in the vehicle, she or he can search the vehicle without a warrant. The policy behind this rule is that evidence in a car is mobile, and taking time to get a warrant may lead to the evidence no longer being accessible.

This exception was established through *Carroll v. United States,* 267 U.S. 132 (1925). The Court stressed that there is a difference between buildings and vehicles, and it is not practical to get a warrant for vehicles, where contraband can be quickly moved out of the jurisdiction. The scope of the search is limited, however, to the area that the officer has probable cause to believe contains contraband. This can extend to the entire vehicle, however, including the trunk. The exception doesn't apply just to motor vehicles but to anything that can be easily moved, such as motor homes, boats, and airplanes. The Court has drawn distinctions, however, between readily movable mobile homes, which can be searched, and parked mobile homes, which cannot. An example of a parked mobile home would be one on blocks. The Court has reasoned that if it is not readily able to be moved, it is not a vehicle.

Checkpoints. Courts have held that, as long as society's need is great, and there are no other available or effective means of meeting the need, and the intrusion is minimal, discretionless checkpoints may be used to detain motorists briefly. For example, the government can employ immigration checkpoints or sobriety checkpoints (*United States v. Martinez-Fuerte*, 428 U.S. 543 (1976); *Michigan Department of State Police v. Sitz*, 496 U.S. 444 (1990)). Vehicle checkpoints are only allowed as long as the officers do not have discretion. For example, every vehicle, or every fifth vehicle, must be stopped. The officers cannot choose which cars to stop. The Supreme Court has also held that checkpoints that are very general, for instance, to search for any instance of a crime, are not allowed.

Exigent circumstances. Another warrant exception is exigent circumstances, where police officers may enter a residence without a warrant if people are in imminent danger, evidence faces immediate destruction, or there is a chance of escape. Unfortunately, there is no one test to determine when an exigent circumstance exists.

Courts have established general factors, however, such as clear evidence of probable cause, the likelihood of the destruction of evidence, the seriousness of the offense, clear indications of exigency (or emergency), and limitations on the search to minimize the intrusion only to prevent the destruction of evidence. In exigent circumstances, it should be stressed, officers may only seize what is in plain view.

Exclusionary rule

The remedy for a government violation of the Fourth Amendment is excluding evidence that was found during the illegal search, otherwise known as the exclusionary rule. In *Elkins v. United States*, 364 U.S. 206 (1960), the Court states that the purpose of this rule is "is to deter—to compel respect for the constitutional guaranty in the only effectively available way—by removing the incentive to disregard it." This rule was originally adopted in 1914, in *Weeks v. United States*, 232 U.S. 383 (1914). Prior to this case, all evidence, even if obtained in violation of the Fourth Amendment, would be admitted.

Also, the Court has held that if an illegal search led to other evidence, that evidence too would be excluded. This is referred to as the "fruit of the poisonous tree" doctrine (*Nardone v. United States*, 308 U.S. 338 (1939)). Those that favor the exclusionary rule argue that there is no other effective way to deter Fourth Amendment violations, while those who oppose the rule argue that it allows criminals to walk free on technicalities. With modern technology, what constitutes an expectation of privacy is constantly evolving. Moreover, some commentators would argue that in voluntarily providing information to companies such as Facebook, Apple, Google, Twitter, and more, not to mention the constant use of GPS devices on phones and cars, there is a slow erosion of the Fourth Amendment.

Melissa A. Gill

Further Reading

Carpenter v. United States, 38 S. Ct. 2206, 2018.

Clancy, Thomas K. *The Fourth Amendment: Its History and Interpretation.* Durham, NC: Carolina Academic Press, 2008.

Greenhalgh, William W. *The Fourth Amendment Handbook: A Chronological Survey of Supreme Court*

Decisions. Chicago: Criminal Justice Section, American Bar Association, 1995.

Lee, Cynthia. *The Fourth Amendment: Searches and Seizures: Its Constitutional History and the Contemporary Debate*. Amherst, N.Y.: Prometheus Books, 2011.

Maclin, Tracey. *The Supreme Court and the Fourth Amendment's Exclusionary Rule*. New York: Oxford University Press, 2013.

McInnis, Tomas N. *The Evolution of the Fourth Amendment*. Lanham, Md.: Lexington Books, 2009.

Schulhofer, Stephen J. *More Essential Than Ever: The Fourth Amendment in the Twenty-First Century*. New York: Oxford University Press, 2012.

Slobogin, Christopher. *Privacy at Risk: The New Government Surveillance and the Fourth Amendment*. Chicago, Ill.: University of Chicago Press, 2007.

Solove, Daniel J. *The Digital Person: Technology and Privacy in the Information Age*. New York: New York University Press, 2004.

Taslitz, Andrew E. *Reconstructing the Fourth Amendment: A History of Search and Seizure, 1789–1868*. New York: New York University Press, 2006.

Victory! Supreme Court says Fourth Amendment Applies to Cell Phone Tracking, Crocker, Andrew and Jennifer Lynch, Electronic Frontier Foundation, June 22nd, 2018. https://www.eff.org/deeplinks/2018/06/victory-supreme-court-says-fourth-amendment-applies-cell-phone-tracking

Vile, John R. *Encyclopedia of the Fourth Amendment*. Thousand Oaks, Calif.: CQ Press, 2013.

Worrall, John, and Craig Hemmens. *Criminal Evidence: An Introduction*. Los Angeles: Roxbury, 2005.

See also: Consent; Constitutional law; Criminal justice (criminal procedure); Electronic surveillance; Fifth Amendment to the U.S. Constitution; HIV testing; *Katz v. United States; Kyllo v. United States;* Law enforcement; Legal evolution of privacy rights in the United States; *Mapp v. Ohio; New Jersey v. T.L.O.; Olmstead v. United States;* The Right to Privacy; Search warrants; Stop-and-frisk policy; Supreme Court of the United States; *United States v. Jones;* Wiretapping

Freedom of Information Act

Identification: Freedom of Information Act (FOIA), 5 U.S.C. § 552 (1966); an openness-in-government or "government access" statute that was enacted by the U.S. Congress in 1966.

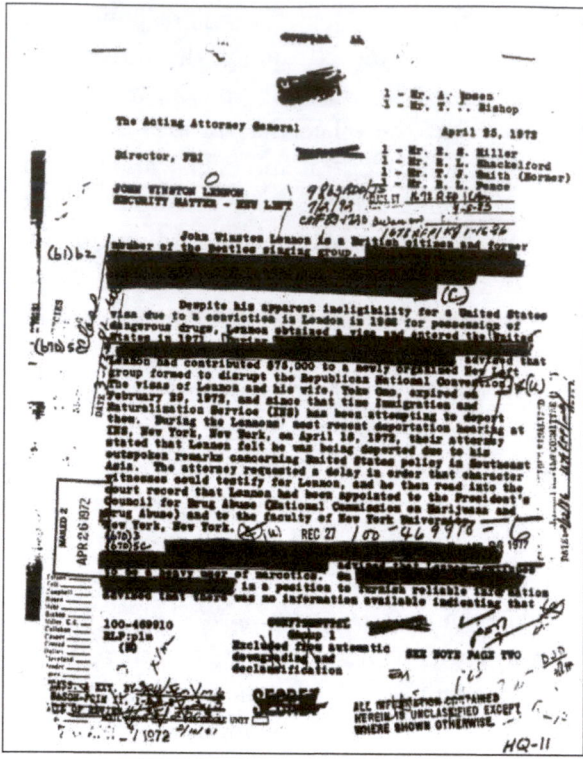

In the early 1970s, the US government conducted surveillance on ex-Beatle John Lennon. This is a letter from FBI director J. Edgar Hoover to the Attorney General. After a 25-year Freedom of Information Act Request battle initiated by historian Jon Wiener, the files were released. Here is one page from the file. This first release received by Wiener had some information missing—it had been blacked out presumably with magic marker—or what is termed "redacted." A subsequent version was released which showed almost all of the previously blacked-out text.

The Freedom of Information Act (FOIA) took effect on July 4, 1967, the American Independence Day, and became only the third such law in the world, after one that was enacted in Sweden (and later devolved to Finland) exactly 200 years earlier. The U.S. FOIA allows the American public (or even "any person" in the world, with only limited exceptions for "intelligence community" files) to request access to any record or information maintained by any agency of the executive branch of the federal government (that is, not including Congress or the federal judiciary), except for (due to constitutional reasons) the records of the "inner White House" (that is, those of the president and his or her closest advisers).

If a FOIA "requester" is not satisfied with the agency's response to his or her request, he or she (or it) may file a lawsuit in federal court to enforce this right. There have been an estimated 10,000 such FOIA lawsuits filed thus far, with thirty-two of them ultimately adjudicated through decisions issued by the U.S. Supreme Court. The most significant of these is the Supreme Court's landmark *Reporters Committee* decision (489 U.S. 749), issued in 1989, which established several key principles for the balancing of personal privacy interests against the public interest in disclosure under FOIA's two privacy exemptions, Exemptions 6 and 7(C), which by far are the exemptions most frequently invoked (that is, in more than 53 percent of cases between the two). Most recently, in 2011, the Supreme Court's decision in *Milner v. Department of the Navy* (562 U.S. 562 [2011]) flatly rejected the broad interpretation of Exemption 2 that had prevailed for nearly three decades, leaving that exemption effectively eviscerated and the government unable to protect some information of particular homeland security sensitivity.

Most fundamentally, FOIA has become a key foundation for the democratic form of government, fostering democracy by allowing Americans to be more aware of "what their government is up to" and thereby to become a more informed electorate. It also promotes government accountability to its citizenry, indirectly supports the freedom-of-the-press mandate of the First Amendment to the U.S. Constitution, and in recent years has become an increasingly vital tool in combating government corruption. In fact, while other nations were slow to embrace the freedom-of-information principle (for instance, only two more countries had such laws by the time of FOIA's fifteenth anniversary), today more than 100 nations of the world have followed the United States's example in enacting and effectively implementing their own FOIA-type laws—thus creating a vibrant, worldwide openness-in-government community and establishing "transparency" (a term

imported to the United States from Europe in the mid-2000s) as an important new societal norm. And in the United States, similar laws exist for the records of all states and many government localities as well.

The operation of FOIA is relatively simple: A FOIA requester sends a letter (or an email message or a website submission, where permitted) to an agency of the federal government seeking access to identifiable records that exist within that agency's control in either paper or electronic (for example, database or email) form. (In 1996, Congress enacted the Electronic Freedom of Information Act Amendments, which in effect brought FOIA into the twenty-first century by updating its provisions for the electronic age.) The requester's obligation is only to "reasonably describe" the records sought so that they can be located efficiently. Under the law, an agency is not required to create a record in order to satisfy a request (though agencies sometimes do so, as a matter of administrative discretion), nor is an agency required to comply with any request framed in the form of a question or without respect to existing records or information at that agency.

Apart from that—and the possible payment of applicable fees for the direct costs of record searches, duplication, and (for commercial requesters) document review—the burden is entirely on the agency to do what is necessary to satisfy the request, usually by mailing the disclosed records in paper form but sometimes in requested electronic form. In the United States, hundreds of thousands of FOIA requests are filed with the approximately 100 federal departments and agencies each year, at an annual cost that now exceeds $500 million. Almost since its inception, however, FOIA generally has been underfunded by Congress, resulting in large backlogs of pending FOIA requests at many agencies, particularly those with law enforcement, national security, or international responsibilities; this alone can be the cause of considerable, seemingly intractable conflict between requesters and agencies.

Beyond FOIA's procedural aspects—which include a basic response deadline of twenty working days, special provisions for media requesters, automatic "electronic reading room" disclosure, and the right to appeal administratively to a higher-level agency official any "adverse determination"—the heart of FOIA lies in its exemptions to required disclosure, which have been the greatest focus of dispute, policy interpretation, amendment, and litigation over the years. FOIA's exemptions, which total fourteen (nine enumerated ones, with one comprised of six subparts), encompass certain types of records (or portions thereof) that hold particular sensitivity under the U.S. legal system.

These exemptions cover:

(1) classified national defense and foreign relations information;

(2) information related to internal agency personnel rules and personnel practices;

(3) information that is prohibited from public disclosure by another federal statute;

(4) trade secrets and other confidential or privileged commercial or financial information submitted from the private sector;

(5) interagency or intra-agency communications that are routinely protected by recognized legal privileges such as the deliberative process privilege, the attorney work-product privilege, and the attorney-client privilege;

(6) information about identifiable individuals involving matters of personal privacy in which there is no overriding public interest in disclosure;

(7) records or information compiled for law enforcement purposes the disclosure of which (a) could reasonably be expected to interfere with an ongoing or prospective law enforcement proceeding, (b) would deprive a person of a right to a fair trial, (c) could reasonably be expected to constitute an unwarranted invasion of an identifiable individual's personal privacy, (d) could reasonably be expected to disclose the identity of and/or information provided by a confidential source, (e) would disclose techniques, procedures, or guidelines for law enforcement investigations or prosecutions, but in the latter case only if that could reasonably be expected to risk circumvention of the law, or (f) could reasonably be expected to endanger the life or physical safety of any individual;

(8) information relating to the supervision of banks and other financial institutions; and

(9) geological information on wells.

In addition, FOIA was amended by Congress in 1986 to include three special record "exclusions" for matters of exceptionally acute law enforcement or national security sensitivity. The language of FOIA's exemptions has been amended five times, most recently in 2016, and its exact contours have been shaped greatly over the years by authoritative judicial decisions as well. An example of the latter, and a case to watch, is *Food Marketing Institute v. Argus Leader Media,* a non-FOIA case that nevertheless offers the Supreme Court the opportunity, for the first time, to interpret the terse language of FOIA's fourth exemption (oral arguments presented April 22, 2019).

FOIA is administered throughout the federal government on a decentralized basis. In other words, each federal agency, as well as major subagencies of the fifteen federal departments (for example, the Federal Bureau of Investigation, which is part of the U.S. Department of Justice), handles its own FOIA requests, with the authority for adjudicating administrative appeals vested in each agency head. Overall, less than 2 percent of FOIA requests proceed to the administrative appeal stage, and only 0.1 percent of FOIA requests become the subject of litigation. Traditionally, the responsibility for overseeing and guiding FOIA's government-wide administration rests with the Attorney General, who discharges this responsibility (and also is responsible for defending FOIA lawsuits in court) through the Justice Department's Office of Information Policy (OIP), which was created in 1981. An additional government-wide office, called the Office of Government Information Services (OGIS) and located within the National Archives and Records Administration, holds partly overlapping responsibilities and came into existence in 2009.

Attorneys General also traditionally issue major guidance memoranda setting general FOIA implementation policy for an incoming presidential administration. The one still currently in effect, issued by Attorney General Eric H. Holder, Jr. on March 19, 2009, most significantly calls on all federal agencies to employ a "foreseeable harm" standard and concomitantly to make discretionary disclosures in applying FOIA exemptions. (Such disclosures are *not* permitted, however, for any information about U.S. citizens that is protected by the Privacy Act of 1974.) This policy replaced the policy that prevailed during the George W. Bush administration, which was less inclined toward disclosure, and it served to reinstate the exact same policy standard originally established by Attorney General Janet Reno for the Clinton administration in 1993. Although President Barack Obama created exceedingly high expectations when he first took office in promising to have "the most transparent administration in history," by nearly all accounts those expectations were far from met; no small part of this appears to be the increasing difficulty of achieving optimal federal government transparency in a post-9/11 world, especially in related areas of public controversy.

Remarkably, no such major FOIA policy memorandum—nor any other substantive FOIA policy guidance, for that matter—has been issued by the Department of Justice during the entire first two years of the Donald J. Trump administration. Instead, under Trump, FOIA denials have increased, FOIA litigation has skyrocketed, and agencies such as the Department of the Interior have been allowed by the Justice Department to blatantly flout the law.

While journalists make up only a surprisingly small percentage of FOIA requesters (the vast majority of FOIA requesters are commercial entities or individuals seeking records about themselves), the most striking use of FOIA is when it contemporaneously compels the disclosure of records pertaining to matters of government "scandal," including the files of internal investigations, where controversy over the very handling of a FOIA request itself can "add fuel to a fire." This was so during the Clinton administration, and the subsequent administrations of George W. Bush, Barack Obama, and Donald Trump have been plagued by disclosure controversies as well. More than anything else, the steps taken by the United States in the wake of 9/11 have spawned intense FOIA activity at, and subsequent criticism of, many federal agencies.

In summary, FOIA is a vital and continuously developing government disclosure mechanism that over the past half century has served as a pillar of democracy. With refinements over time to accommodate both technological advancements and society's maturing interests in transparency, it has truly enhanced, and will continue to enhance, the American way of life.

Daniel J. Metcalfe

Further Reading

American University. *Web Site of the Collaboration on Government Secrecy*, edited by Professor Daniel J. Metcalfe. Washington, DC: Washington College of Law, 2014. https://www.wcl.american.edu/lawandgov/cgs/.

Dashboard Insights. "Supreme Court Grants Cert. in Case that May Redefine Scope of FOIA Exemption 4..." (Jan. 29, 2019).

Freedominfo.org. "Alphabetical and Chronological Lists of Countries with FOIA Regimes (Sept. 28, 2017).

Hammitt, Harry A., et al., eds. *Litigation under the Federal Open Government Laws.* Washington, DC: Electronic Privacy Information Center, 2010. http://epic.org/bookstore/foia2010/.

Metcalfe, Daniel J. "*Amending the FOIA: Is It Time for a Real Exemption 10?*" *Administrative and Regulatory Law News* 37, no. 16 (Summer 2012). https://www.wcl.american.edu/faculty/metcalfe/ABA.article.2012.pdf.

———. "Hillary's E-Mail Defense Is Laughable." *POLITICO Magazine,* March 16, 2015. http://www.politico.com/magazine/story/2015/03/hillaryclinton-email-scandal-defense-laughable-foia-116116.html#.VXw6lvlViko.

Metcalfe, Daniel J. "The History of Transparency," in *Research Handbook on Transparency*, edited by Padideh Ala'i and Robert G. Vaughn. Northampton, MA: Edward Elgar, 2014.

Metcalfe, Daniel J. "*The Nature of Government Secrecy.*" *Government Information Quarterly* 26, no. 305 (2009) https://www.wcl.american.edu/faculty/metcalfe/nature.pdf.

ThinkProgress. "Post-shut down, an ocean of outrage greets Interior's proposed changes…" (Jan. 30, 2019). thinkprogress.org

United States Department of Justice. *Department of Justice Guide to the Freedom of Information Act.* 2009. http://www.justice.gov/oip/doj-guide-freedom-information-act-0\.

United States Department of Justice. "OIP Gives FOIA Implementation Advice to Other Nations." *FOIA Post, December 12, 2002.* http://www.justice.gov/archive/oip/foiapost/2002foiapost30.htm.

See also: Electronic Communications Privacy Act; First Amendment to the U.S. Constitution; Legal Evolution of Privacy Rights; Privacy Act of 1974; The Right to Privacy; September 11, Supreme Court of the United States

G

Genome sequencing

Identification: The process of determining the precise order of the base pairs in an entire strand of DNA.

Every cell in our bodies contains deoxyribonucleic acid (DNA) that codes for externally visible characteristics, health profile, disease predisposition, and to some extent personality traits. That DNA, which forms in a double helix and is combined into just twenty-three chromosomes, contains a series of base nucleotide pairs composed entirely of different combinations of just four nucleotide bases (guanine, cytosine, thymine, and adenine). A human body's entire complement of DNA has about 3 billion of those nucleotide base pairs, which together are called the human genome.

Genome sequencing is critical for many purposes, including diagnosis of genetic diseases; development of new medicines, treatments, and vaccines; identification of the source of biological material; forensic investigations; anthropological studies; paternity determinations; and so on. It is the precise order of these base pairs that makes us all unique, except for identical twins, who share the same DNA profile. The Human Genome Project completed the first-ever sequencing of the entire human genome in 2003. To allow maximum benefit from that sequencing effort, all of the project's human genome results were publicly released at that time.

Privacy concerns. A good deal of discussion relevant to genomics has revolved around personal privacy and each person's right not to know. For example, should insurance companies be allowed to conduct genetic testing and determine rates or insurability based on a person's disease predisposition profile? Or should a prosecutor be allowed to compel a criminal defendant to submit to a genetic test to determine whether the defendant has intermittent explosive disorder or compulsivity, and then use that evidence to seek a longer sentence due to the allegedly higher risk the defendant poses to public safety? Or, conversely, should all young couples approaching parenthood be compelled to undergo genetic testing to determine the presence of high-transmissibility genetic diseases they could pass on to their children? Or, on the other hand, do people simply have a right not to know?

Medical uses. As the Centers for Disease Control and Prevention (CDC) noted, as of 2013, genetic tests have been developed to diagnose thousands of diseases, some obvious and long known (such as sickle cell anemia), some in the news more recently (such as the BRCA1 and BRCA2 genetic mutations that predispose sufferers to breast and ovarian cancers), and some much closer to the cutting edge (such as BRAF testing for metastatic melanoma). The CDC assigns each genetic test to a different tier based on its reliability and robustness as a genetic marker for the disease. Some genetic markers directly indicate the presence of disease, while other, less robust genetic markers merely indicate a potential predisposition for disease.

Psychiatric uses. Some genetic tests detect mutations and other genetic characteristics that indicate predisposition for obsessive-compulsive disorder, depression, hyperactivity disorders, schizophrenia, insomnia, and other personality disorders and psychiatric diagnoses. Such tests can inform healthcare providers on treatment paths that would be more likely to ease or manage symptoms or modify behaviors.

Anthropological uses. Genomics has often been used to assess and track ancient anthropological shifts and migrations through the transfer of genetic material around the world and from one subpopulation to another. It is now possible, for less than $100, to submit some saliva to any of several genetic testing firms that will report your ancestral profile, that is, what percentage of your DNA profile is likely to have come from ancestors in various geographic regions around the globe.

Agricultural uses. Genomics are instrumental in designing new strains of crops and farmed animals. Genetic testing reveals the profile of potential mates, and scientists design the combinations most likely to yield the desired physical and nutritional makeup. This type of genetic engineering has helped improve agricultural yields worldwide.

Sports enhancement. Some parents of young athletes have turned to genomics to assess the strength profiles of their children in an effort to best direct their nutrition and thus highlight their genetic strengths and overcome genetic weaknesses.

Missing persons. In World War II, for example, when a soldier died in battle, his comrades took his dogtags from around his neck and wedged them between his teeth. The information on those dogtags allowed fallen soldiers to be identified. Nonetheless, for the unidentifiable bodies fallen in war, they erected a Tomb of the Unknown Soldier; now, there is almost no need for such a tomb. Soldiers provide DNA specimens early after enlistment, and they are used to identify their remains. Similarly, missing persons are often identified by genomic testing that allows identification even in the absence of dental records or other identification.

Forensic genotyping uses. Since the mid-1980s, genomics has been used to identify the source of biological material left by a perpetrator at a crime scene. That approach is known as DNA genotyping. It presupposes that scientists develop a DNA profile from the unknown crime scene sample and then compare it against a database of known DNA samples taken from persons arrested for or convicted of violent crimes. In the early days of forensic DNA profiling, the crime scene sample had to be quite large because the testing approaches were not able to amplify and identify the DNA in smaller samples. With today's DNA genotyping approaches, valid DNA profiles of crime scene samples can be obtained from biological material almost smaller than the eye can see.

Familial DNA forensics. When the crime scene DNA genotyping sample fails to reveal an exact match in the DNA profile database, investigators sometimes turn to familial matching, a hotly contested approach. In familial matching, forensic scientists take advantage of the fact that many genetic features are shared by many members of a biologically related family. The investigators take the crime scene profile and query the DNA profile database for near-matches. The nearest matches often turn up to be close relatives of the actual perpetrator. Thus, investigators can find perpetrators who are not yet in the database by instead finding near-matches to the perpetrator's family members who do have their DNA profiles in the database. DNA offers a great deal of detail about its sources, which calls into question the limits of privacy in a forensic community so driven to use DNA results to fight crime. ***Forensic phenotyping uses.*** Where there is no known DNA sample to compare it against, a crime scene biological specimen can be tested using forensic phenotyping, which uses DNA analysis to identify the likely physical characteristics of the person who left the specimen at the crime scene. Although this approach is still in its infancy, it has already been used to solve some cases where there are no eyewitnesses and no other leads. Given the current state of DNA phenotyping, there are already tests that have been shown to identify reliably whether the source of the crime scene sample was male or female, had blond or red hair, and had light or dark skin tone. Future DNA phenotyping developments could allow investigators to determine from a crime scene sample whether the offender had a cleft chin, dimples, freckling, or a detached or attached earlobe. It may one day be able to discern the offender's dominant hand, general face morphology, and full adult height. Imagine the benefits of such information. Perhaps one day, through forensic DNA phenotyping, scientists and investigators will be able to generate a wanted poster using only DNA data derived from an unidentified crime scene sample. Although DNA phenotyping results are unlikely ever to be admitted into evidence in a criminal case, those results can be extremely valuable at the investigation stage.

A case study. In 1951, a doctor at Johns Hopkins University, treating a woman with cervical cancer, cut out a small piece of the woman's cervix and retained it for testing purposes. That woman, who later died, was Henrietta Lacks. The specimen, removed from Ms. Lacks without her knowledge or consent, was cultured for years, allowing its use in countless scientific and medical studies. Specimens grown from that cervix were sent into space to test their reaction to weightlessness. As a result of the work of a British lab, Ms. Lacks's specimen ultimately yielded its entire genome (the HeLa genome), which was released publicly to be used by scientists for laboratory work around the world. Ms. Lacks's family was unaware of this until twenty years after Ms. Lacks died, and the appropriation and use of Ms. Lacks's specimen raises a number of troubling ethical questions. Of course, that genome discloses a great deal about Ms. Lacks, but it also discloses a great deal of private medical and psychological information about her family members, who are still living. The Lacks family supports the use of Henrietta Lacks's genome for scientific study but hopes that techniques can be developed to permit the scientific study while simultaneously protecting their genetic privacy.

In a sense, we have moved through the looking glass on genetic testing. Its power and the quantity and clarity of information it yields are almost unimaginable. Scientific studies based on genetics are exploding exponentially. But society's management of that process lags decades behind. What are the rights that all people have in their individual genetic information and genome sequence? What use can we allow scientists, doctors, criminal investigators, and snoopy neighbors to make of that genetic data, and how can we allow use of such information while safeguarding each individual's genetic privacy rights?

In the digital age, in genetics and genomics as much as in surveillance technologies, our reach exceeds our grasp and our abilities exceed our wisdom. There are clear roles here for scientific advisory groups, legislatures, courts, and others to help contain the privacy erosion sure to come as we open yet wider Pandora's genomics box.

Charles E. MacLean

Further Reading

Ayday, Erman, Emiliano De Cristofaro, Jean-Pierre Hubaux, and Gene Tsudik. "Whole Genome Sequencing: Revolutionary Medicine or Privacy Nightmare?" *Computer*: 58–66.

Centers for Disease Control and Prevention, Genetic Testing: Genomic Tests and Family Health History by Levels of Evidence, http://www.cdc.gov/genomics/gtesting/tier.htm.

Damon, Joseph P. *Whole Genome Sequencing: Privacy and Security in an Era of Genomic and Advancements.*

"Genome Sequencing." *Bioinformatics* (2006): 1–23.

MacLean, Charles E., and Adam Lamparello, *Forensic DNA Phenotyping in Criminal Investigations and Criminal Courts: Assessing and Mitigating the Dilemmas Inherent in the Science*, 8(2) Recent Advances in DNA & Gene Sequencing 104–112 (2014). http://www.eurekaselect.com/128392.

National Human Genome Research Institute, The Human Genome Project Completion. https://www.genome.gov/11006943.

"Privacy Protection in Whole-Genome Sequencing." *Cancer Discovery* (2012): 1070.

Rees, Mark I. *Challenges and Opportunities of Next-Generation Sequencing for Biomedical Research.* Amsterdam: Elsevier/Academic Press, 2012.

"Report on Whole-Genome Sequencing Concerns Issued; Presidential Commission Worries About Privacy." *Biotechnology Law Report*: 579.

Skloot, Rebecca. *The Immortal Life of Henrietta Lacks.* Broadway Books 2011.

See also: Body, privacy of the; Criminal justice (criminal Procedure); DNA databases; Fourth Amendment to the U.S. Constitution; Law enforcement; Medical confidentiality, privacy right to

General Data Protection Regulation

The General Data Protection Regulation (GDPR) is a regulation within European Union (EU) law designed to safeguard the storage and use of an individual's data. Its scope covers "data controllers" (companies and organizations which collect and store data), "data processors" (an individual or organization which possesses data on behalf of the controller), and "data subjects" (individuals) based in the EU, giving the regulation's theoretical application a reach far beyond the EU's physical borders. Notably, GDPR does not apply to individuals who collect data privately, or for a "purely personal or household

activity and thus with no connection to a professional or commercial activity." Law enforcement and national security organizations are also exempt, and exceptions exist for scientific research and employee-employer relationships.

For the purposes of GDPR, the European Commission has stated that personal data is considered, "any information relating to an individual, whether it relates to his or her private, professional or public life. It can be anything from a name, a home address, a photo, an email address, bank details, posts on social networking websites, medical information, or a computer's IP address." In remarks given in May of 2018, prior to GDPR going into effect, Pierre Nicolas Schwab, chairman of the Big Data Initiative of the European Broadcasting Union, noted that even requesting an email address of an EU citizen for a paperless credit card receipt had the potential to create issues of compliance with GDPR for US-based companies.

GDPR consists of 99 articles, grouped within 11 chapters. Additionally, there are 171 "recitals" and explanatory remarks. An EU-wide data reform effort was first proposed in January of 2012. The GDPR was adopted by the EU Parliament and the Council of the European Union in April of 2016. It went into effect for member states in May of 2018, and in July GDPR became valid in all European Economic Area countries.

The goal of GDPR is to simplify data protection for individuals and safeguard the data rights of individuals providing them with greater "control" over the collection and use of their data. Companies that collect and store data would be required to attain an affirmative consent regarding what kind of data is collected and what it is intended to be used for. Additional protections exist for individuals under the age of 16, requiring someone of "parental responsibility" to opt into data collection on a minor's behalf. Companies would also be required to inform individuals of a data-breach within 72 hours of their becoming aware of it.

For individuals, GDPR guarantees more safeguards on data usage and rights to personal data. Included in this is the right to see data a company may have collected, the right to opt out of data collection, and the right to have data deleted. For companies, GDPR mandates safeguards such as pseudonymization, restricting the transfer of data to a third (non-EU) country, and acquiring informed consent to data collection and usage from individuals. Further, it is incumbent on "data controllers" (the company or organization collecting the data) that any partner organizations with access to data ("data processors") are also GDPR compliant.

The penalty for being found in violation of GDPR is 4 percent of a company's annual global turnover, or 20 million Euros, whichever number is higher. In theory, both a "data controller" and "data processor" found to be in violation of GDPR could be penalized. Violations are enforced by the data regulation ministry of each member state, meaning that if a company is based in France and is found in violation of GDPR, it is up to the Commission nationale de l'informatique et des libertés (CNIL) to enforce the regulation and collect any pursuant fines. Companies can also appeal alleged violations.

While some have criticized the GDPR for having unclear compliance standards and creating burdensome requirements of companies that handle data, most data experts have agreed that the GDPR is necessary for both companies and consumers. Facebook creator Mark Zuckerberg said in May of 2018, "A lot of the philosophy that is encoded in regulation like GDPR is really how we've thought about a lot of this stuff for a long time." The regulation has also been praised by whistleblower Edward Snowden and several consumer-protection organizations including the European Consumer Organization. Zuckerberg, however, declined to implement Facebook's GDPR compliance standards globally.

Critics of the regulation have also argued that although GDPR guarantees access to data, many individuals will have trouble understanding and contextualizing the data collected on them.

Though companies had two years (from April 2016 to May 2018) to prepare for GDPR, many noted that individuals were informed haphazardly with emails regarding data policy changes arriving en masse between April and May of 2018. Moreover, the exact changes in policy were often hard to parse and the barrage of notifications led some user to describe the roll out as "notification fatigue." Some even argued that the GDPR notifications may have violated the EU's own anti-spam laws.

After the implementation of GDPR, some U.S. companies, including the *Chicago Tribune* and *Los Angeles Times,* began blocking EU-based users altogether. Others, like National Public Radio, redirected EU-based users to pared down versions of their websites, often with fewer data-driven advertisements, in an effort to comply with the regulation. A non-profit also sued Facebook within hours of the GDPR going into effect over its "all or nothing" consent policies, believing it to be in violation of the GDPR's "particularized consent" model. As of January 2019, Google has been fined 50 million Euros by the French CNIL for having unclear data consent notifications in violation of GDPR. German Bundeskartellamt anti-monopoly regulators have also warned Facebook against combining information gathered through Facebook, Instagram, and Whatsapp (all of which are owned by Facebook), in violation of GDPR data consent regulations.

On 29 March 2019, barring an extension, the United Kingdom is expected to leave the European Union (a process popularly known as Brexit). Some have speculated as to whether or not Brexit will have an impact on British companies' data protection practices. Due to the interconnectedness of British and European businesses, it is expected that GDPR-like regulations will be folded into British law to ensure as seamless a transition as possible.

J. N. Manuel

Further Reading

Brandom, Russell. "Everything you need to know about GDPR," Web, *The Verge*, May 25, 2018. https://www.theverge.com/2018/3/28/17172548/gdpr-compliance-requirements-privacy-notice

Brandom, Russell. "Facebook and Google hit with $8.8 billion in lawsuits on day one of GDPR," Tech, *The Verge,* May 25 2018.https://www.theverge.com/2018/5/25/17393766/facebook-google-gdpr-lawsuit-max-schrems-europe

Cunnane, Yvonne. "Why We Disagree With the Bundeskartellamt," Facebook Newsroom (blog), February 7, 16, 2019.https://newsroom.fb.com/news/2019/02/bundeskartellamt-order/

Hern, Alex. "What is GDPR and how will it affect you?," Tech, *The Guardian*, May 21, 2018.https://www.theguardian.com/technology/2018/may/21/what-is-gdpr-and-how-will-it-affect-you

Hern, Alex. "Privacy policies of tech giants 'still not GDPR-compliant'," Tech, *The Guardian*, June 4, 2018. https://www.theguardian.com/technology/2018/jul/05/privacy-policies-facebook-amazon-google-not-gdpr-compliant

Porter, Jon. "GDPR makes it easier to get your data, but that doesn't mean you'll understand it," Apple, *The Verge*, January 27, 2019.https://www.theverge.com/2019/1/27/18195630/gdpr-right-of-access-data-download-facebook-google-amazon-apple

See also: Big data; Data protection regimes; Facebook; Google; Online privacy and security; Right to be forgotten

Global positioning system (GPS) tracking

Identification: Location-tracking mobile devices that can detect, store, and broadcast their physical location. Such devices raise major privacy issues, such as those involving the legitimate user's expectation of privacy in public and private spheres.

Many users of GPS tracking technology use it to locate services, nearby acquaintances, and recommended restaurants; receive promotions; and obtain current traffic reports.

GPS law has been evolving with court cases and Federal Trade Commission (FTC) regulations. The regulation about geolocational privacy is concerned with the use of tracking or locating technology that reveals a person's location.

A mobile device or a beacon with GPS may be used for tracking. Smartphones offer several ways of tracking their holders, including GPS, triangulation of cell towers, and Wi-Fi pickups, and law enforcement regularly requests both realtime and historical information on a cellphone's location from phone companies, generally (since 2018) after obtaining a warrant (see below).

Many cars have tracking technology from a manufacturer or insurance company. Cameras at intersections and buildings may be used for geolocational tracking because they show the time that a certain person entered the camera's view, and security cards and toll booth E-Z Pass and fast passes clock a time and location.

A major U.S. Supreme Court case involving geolocational privacy occurred in the context of a criminal conviction based on GPS technology. In *United States v. Jones*, 132 S.Ct. 945 (2012), the Court could have addressed the issue of whether constant monitoring of a person's location was a violation of a person's expectation of privacy; however, the Court decided the case on narrower grounds. In *Jones,* a drug dealer was convicted based partly on information sent from a GPS tracking device that was placed on the defendant's car without a warrant. The device reported the suspect's location every ten seconds for twenty-eight days. The appellate court overturned the conviction, concluding that law enforcement is required to obtain a warrant prior to using a GPS tracking device for such an extended period. The U.S. Supreme Court found that, while a person has no expectation of privacy on public roads and highways, a "reasonable person does not expect anyone to monitor and retain a record of every time he drives his car, including his origin, route, destination, and each place he stops and how long he stays there. Instead, he expects each of these movements to remain 'disconnected and anonymous.'"

Prior to *Jones*, some courts, in restricting GPS technology in criminal cases, relied on the reasoning from *Department of Justice v. Reporters Committee for Freedom of the Press*, 816 F. 2d 730 (DC Cir., 1987). In that case, the DC Circuit Court ruled that:

[a] person who knows all of another's travels can deduce whether he is a weekly church-goer, a heavy drinker, a regular at the gym, an unfaithful husband, an outpatient receiving medical treatment, an associate of particular individuals or political groups—and not just one such fact about a person, but all such facts.

One such case was *United States v. Maynard*, 615 F.3d 544 (D.C. Cir. 2010). In that case, the Federal Bureau of Investigation (FBI) installed a GPS tracking device on Antoine Jones's car while it was parked in a public parking lot. The FBI then used the device to track his vehicle's movements over a one-month period. The discovery that Jones conspired to distribute cocaine was partially based on the location data generated by the GPS device. The U.S. Court of Appeals for the DC Circuit reversed Jones's conviction, The court found that the warrantless GPS tracking was a search and violated the Fourth Amendment. The court did not address whether the GPS device's warrantless installation also constituted a search under the Fourth Amendment.

The Seventh Circuit, in *United States v. Cuevas-Perez*, 640 F.3d 272 (7th Cir., 2011), refused to apply the precedent in *Reporter's Committee* to a case in which law enforcement tracked a defendant's car for sixty hours as it traveled through New Mexico, Texas, Oklahoma, Missouri, and Illinois. In the last state, the GPS battery began failing. Immigration and Customs Enforcement (ICE) agents then asked the Illinois state police to follow the car and stop him for any traffic violation possible. The police complied with this request and stopped the defendant for a minor traffic violation. This stop allowed the police to search his vehicle. Nine pounds of heroin was seized, and the defendant was then arrested for possession with intent to distribute heroin.

The defendant sought to suppress the drug evidence, based on grounds of invasion of privacy, which was based on the court's holding in *Maynard*. Both the trial court and the U.S. Court of Appeals rejected the defendant's argument.

The Seventh Circuit ruled that *Maynard* specifically did not apply to a single trip, reasoning that "the chances that the whole of Cuevas-Perez's movements for a month would actually be observed is effectively nil—but that is not necessarily true of movements for a much shorter period."

In *Jones*, the Supreme Court ruled that law enforcement must obtain a warrant before placing a tracking device on a suspect's car and electronically tracking movements of the car. The justices disagreed, however, about whether the warrantless search, in this case, was an invasion of the defendant's reasonable expectation of privacy, as articulated in *Katz v. United States*, 348 U.S. 347 (1967). Five justices believed that the police trespassed on the suspect's car when they place the tracking device on it. The majority thus viewed this as an unreasonable search of the defendant's car, which was in violation of the Fourth Amendment. The majority added that this "trespass" made it unnecessary to resolve the issue of whether the *Katz* "reasonable expectation of privacy" test was met under the facts of this case.

Four justices agreed with the outcome but believed that the Court should have answered some of the most important issues in *Jones*, including whether the Fourth Amendment allows the electronic monitoring of a suspect for twenty- eight days without a warrant. The minority believed that the court should have been found that the government had violated the Fourth Amendment because the defendant had a reasonable expectation that his movements would not be electronically monitored every ten seconds for four consecutive weeks.

Justice Sonia Sotomayor, who voted with the majority, also issued a concurring opinion in which she agreed with Justice Alito "that, at the very least, 'longer term GPS monitoring in investigations of most offenses impinges on expectations of privacy.'" She added that awareness of government surveillance "chills associational and expressive freedoms."

In his concurrence, Judge Alito observed how technological advances could endanger privacy rights; he wrote that "the greatest protections of privacy were neither constitutional nor statutory, but practical. Traditional surveillance for any extended period of time was difficult and costly and therefore rarely undertaken. . . . Devices like the one used in this present case, however, make long-term monitoring relatively easy and cheap."

In *United States v. Arrendondo,* C#2:11-CR-63-FTM-29DNF (M.D., Fla, 2012), which was decided after *Jones,* a federal district court denied a motion to suppress evidence gathered pursuant to a warrant using a GPS tracking device that was installed in a package. Ultimately, the GPS device tracked the defendant's package while it was in a truck that was moving in public places. The court reasoned that there was no Fourth Amendment violation because, unlike the Jones case, "no law enforcement officer trespassed on the defendant's vehicle to install a tracking device" because the package was placed in the truck by the defendant.

In *Carpenter v. United States* (16-402; 585 U.S.__ [2018]), the U.S. Supreme Courtruled that it was a violation of a criminal suspect's Fourth Amendment protection against unreasonable searches for law enforcement officials to obtain location data concerning the suspect from cell-phone companies without first obtaining a warrant. The ruling disrupted longstanding law enforcement practices that relied on ready access to such data, yet it was hailed by civil libertarians as a victory for the rights of the individual.

Further Reading

Johnson, Emily M. *Legalities of GPS and Cell Phone Surveillance.* New York: Novinka, 2012.

Kuhn, Betsy. *Prying Eyes: Privacy in the Twenty-first Century.* Minneapolis, MN: Twenty-First Century Books, 2008.

Leipnik, Mark R. *GIS in Law Enforcement Implementation Issues and Case Studies.* London: Taylor & Francis, 2003.

Rabbany, Ahmed. *Introduction to GPS: The Global Positioning System.* Boston, MA: Artech House, 2002.

Rengel, Alexandra. *Privacy in the 21st Century.* Leiden: Martinus Nijhoff Publishers, 2013.

Swire, Peter P. *Privacy and Surveillance with New Technologies.* Thibault, Edward A., and Lawrence M. Lynch. *Proactive Police Management,* 9th ed. Boston, MA: Pearson, 2015.

Thompson, Richard M. *Governmental Tracking of Cell Phones and Vehicles: The Confluence of Privacy, Technology, and Law.* Washington, DC: Congressional Research Service, 2011.

See also: Electronic surveillance; Federal Trade Commission (FTC); Fourth Amendment of the U.S. Constitution; *Katz v. United States*

Godkin, Edwin Lawrence (1831–1902)

Born: October 2, 1831
Died: on May 21, 1902
Identification: A journalist, publisher, and lawyer. He is best known for founding *The Nation,* an influential American magazine of opinion and commentary.

Godkin was born in Ireland to English parents, on October 2, 1831. His father was a minister and a journalist who shared his passion for the American Revolution with his son. Godkin attended Queen's College in Belfast, leaving in 1851 to study law in London.

Once in London, he wrote for various magazines and newspapers. He first worked for *The Workingman's Friend.* His articles on the Hungarian struggle for independence from Austria became the basis of his first book, *The History of Hungary and the Magyars*. Published in 1853, it was a popular success. Godkin also wrote for the *London Daily News*, traveling in Turkey and Russia from 1853 to1855 as a Crimean War correspondent.

In 1856, Godkin moved to the United States. He toured the Southern states on horseback and authored a series of articles about slavery and American culture that was published in the *London Daily News*. He then moved to New York City and studied law under David Dudley Field, an influential judge and legal reformer. Godkin was admitted to the New York bar in 1858, although he practiced law infrequently.

Godkin returned to Europe in 1860 due to poor health. By 1862, however, he had returned to the United States. He continued to write for the *London Daily News* and the *New York Times* through the end of the Civil War. In 1865, he and nearly forty investors raised enough money to found the *Nation*, a magazine that contained opinion, literature, art, and politics. In 1866, Godkin bought out all but two of the stockholders and remained editor-in-chief. *The Nation* under Godkin's editorship never had a large formal circulation—it was about 10,000 at its peak—but it had an estimated 50,000 readers. While its circulation and readership were small, it was influential in forming American opinion. Politicians, academics, and writers, including Ralph Waldo Emerson, were among its readers. Godkin, as editor, advocated for several political and social causes, including civil service reform and reduced government expenditures, and against political corruption.

On July 1, 1881, the *Nation* merged with a daily paper, the *New York Evening Post*, owned by Henry Villard. *The Nation* continued as the paper's weekly edition. Godkin became the *Post*'s editor-in-chief in 1883 and served as such until he retired, due to ill health, in 1900. Again, while he was not a popular success and the *Evening Post*'s net circulation under his editorship was never above 25,000, Godkin continued to appeal to the intellectual and political elite.

Many scholars believe that privacy law originated from the 1890 publication of Samuel D. Warren and Louis D. Brandeis's *Harvard Law Review* essay "The Right to Privacy." Six months before Warren and Brandeis published "The Right to Privacy," however, Godkin had published an article on the same subject in *Scribner's Magazine* [E. L. Godkin, "The Rights of the Citizen: IV. To His Own Reputation," *Scribner's Magazine* 8 (July 1890): 58]. Though Warren and Brandeis denied that it was Godkin's specific article that inspired them to write about privacy, Godkin's influence remains apparent in many ways.

The end of the nineteenth century saw the rise of a new type of journalism. Events and interactions that had previously been private became fodder for yellow journalism focusing on gossip and lurid stories of crime and misfortune. Godkin was critical of the muckraking, scandal-filled newspapers and supported legal reforms to prevent gossip and sensationalist journalism from being published as news. He believed their publication was indicative of a decline in morality in publisher and reader alike. Godkin believed that publications should shape, inform, and educate public opinion (E. L. Godkin, "Opinion-Moulding," *The Nation*, August 12, 1869) rather than pander to prying gossip. The tension between these two types of reporting is where ideas of privacy, the right to be let alone, began to crystallize.

Godkin reprinted much of Warren and Brandeis's article in *The Nation*, along with his commentary. He stated: "When personal gossip attains the dignity of print, and crowds the space available for matters of real interest to the community, what wonder that the ignorant and thoughtless mistake its relative importance? . . . Triviality destroys at once robustness of thought and delicacy of feeling"

Godkin passed away in England on May 21, 1902, at the age of 71.

Noëlle Sinclair

Further Reading

Armstrong, William M. *E. L. Godkin: A Biography.* Albany: State University of New York Press, 1978.

Coyle, Erin K. "E. L. Godkin's Criticism of the Penny Press: Antecedents to a Legal Right to Privacy." *American Journalism* 31, no. 2 (2014): 262–282.

Glancy, Dorothy J. "The Invention of the Right to Privacy." *Arizona Law Review* 21, no. 1 (1979): 1–39.

Godkin, Edwin Lawrence. *Life and Letters of E. L. Godkin.* Edited by Rollo Ogden. New York: Macmillan, 1907.

Godkin, Edwin Lawrence. *The Gilded Age Letters of E. L. Godkin.* Edited by William M. Armstrong. Albany: State University of New York Press, 1974.

Rhodes, James Ford. "Edwin Lawrence Godkin." In *Historical Essays,* 1909. Reprint, Port Washington, NY: Kennikat Press, 1966.

Richie, Donald A. *American Journalists: Getting the Story.* Oxford: Oxford University Press, 1997.

Villard, Oswald Garrison. "Edwin L. Godkin, Master of Comment and of Style." In *Some Newspapers and Newspaper-Men.* New York: Alfred A. Knopf, 1923.

See also: Brandeis, Louis Dembitz; Right to Be Forgotten; "The Right to Privacy"

Gonzaga University v. Doe, 536 U.S. 273 (2002)

Identification: An important case centered on the Family Educational Rights and Privacy Act of 1974 (FERPA). Chief Justice William Rehnquist delivered the majority opinion in the 7–2 decision. FERPA prohibits the federal government from funding educational institutions that release educational records to unauthorized persons, but the Supreme Court held that there is no private right that is enforceable.

The plaintiff was a student at Gonzaga University who planned on becoming an elementary school teacher after graduation. Under Washington State law, all new teachers require an affidavit of good moral character from the graduating college. Robert League, an employee of Gonzaga and a teacher in charge of certifying such affidavits, overheard a student, Julia Lynch, tell another student that "Jane Doe" was in obvious physical pain after the plaintiff raped her. Because of this overheard conversation, League launched an investigation into the matter and refused to certify the affidavit. In addition, he contacted the state agency responsible for teacher certification, identified the plaintiff by name, and discussed the allegations against the plaintiff with the agency. The plaintiff did not learn of these allegations, the investigation, or the discussion with the agency until much later, when he learned he would not be receiving the certification necessary to be a public school teacher. The plaintiff, "John Doe," subsequently sued Gonzaga University and Robert League for defamation and violation of FERPA.

FERPA prohibits "the federal funding of educational institutions that have a policy or practice of releasing education records to unauthorized persons." Congress enacted FERPA under its spending power because it conditioned federal funding on compliance with the act. The act specifies that the secretary of education enforce the act's spending conditions and requires that the secretary establish an office and review board within the Department of Education for "investigating, processing, reviewing and adjusting violations of the Act." (§1232 of the Act.)

The plaintiff argued that the statute confers upon any student enrolled at an applicable school the right to enforce the act, and specifically to seek damages under the act, under §1983. Section 1983 is also known as 42 U.S. Code §1983, or A Civil Action for Deprivation of Rights. It confers on individuals a right to bring civil suits against those that have violated their civil rights. In 1980, six years after Congress enacted FERPA, the Court agreed that §1983 actions may be brought against the state in order to enforce rights created by federal statutes as well as the Constitution. Specifically, the Court held that plaintiffs could recover payments that were wrongfully withheld by a state agency, in violation of the Social Security Act (*Maine v. Thiboutot*, 488 U.S. 1). A year later, however, the

Court held that the Developmentally Disabled Assistance and Bill of Rights Act of 1975 conferred no such right to private action, stating, "In legislation enacted pursuant to the spending power, the typical remedy for state noncompliance with federally imposed conditions is not a private cause of action for noncompliance but rather action by the Federal Government to terminate funds to the state" (*Pennhurst State School and Hospital v. Halderman*, 451 U.S. 1 [1981]). The court reasoned that this does not grant any personal rights to enforce under the civil rights provisions of §1983 because the statute addresses only federal funding. Essentially, the Court has found that unless Congress has specifically, and unambiguously, given a private right, federal funding provisions alone do not provide such a right. The Court determined in *Blessing v. Freestone*, 520 U.S. 239, that there were three factors to use when determining if a statute confers a private right: (1) Congress must have intended that provision to benefit the plaintiff, (2) the plaintiff must demonstrate that the asserted right is not so vague that "its enforcement would strain judicial competence," and (3) the provision granting the asserted right must be set forth in mandatory terms.

This Court stressed that they shall not "permit anything short of an unambiguously conferred right to support a cause of action brought under §1983." It emphasized that Section 1983 provides remedies only for the deprivation of rights, privileges, or immunities under the Constitution and laws of the United States. The Court stated that there is a difference between rights and benefits and that here FERPA only confers a benefit.

The Court also stated that §1983 only provides a mechanism for enforcing rights secured elsewhere and that one cannot go into court and claim only a violation of §1983. The Court felt that, because FERPA speaks only in broad terms and directs the secretary of education to act, there is no private right.

Justice John P. Stevens and Justice Ruth Bader Ginsburg dissented, arguing that FERPA did, in fact, create private rights. The dissenting justices pointed to the fact that FERPA included ten subsections that not only created rights for parents and students but also detailed procedures for enforcing those rights. The justices felt that the statute clearly met the standards set forth in *Blessing*.

The American Civil Liberties Union (ACLU) filed an amicus brief that essentially agreed with the dissent, stating that the statute is clearly intended to benefit students and their families and that "[t]he right of confidentiality is expressed in concrete terms that are not so vague and amorphous as to strain judicial competence." The ACLU also stressed that the obligation for schools to maintain confidentiality is mandatory, not optional. The ACLU also felt that the right of confidentiality for school records is important enough to provide a private cause of action and that such a cause of action is completely consistent with Congress' goals in enacting FERPA.

Some scholars believe that the effect of this ruling is that it erodes rights under §1983. In addition, most believe that the Court in *Gonzaga* leaves too much ambiguity in interpreting §1983 cases, and some believe that the Court should rely more on legislative history when deciding if the statute has conferred a private right.

Melissa A. Gill

Further Reading

Horner, Annie M. Gonzaga v. Doe: *The Need for Clarity in the Clear Statement Test*, 52 S.D.L.Rev 537 (2007).

Mank, Bradford. *Suing under §1983: The Future after* Gonzaga v. Doe (2003). Faculty Articles and Other Publications. Paper 123. http://scholarship.law.uc.edu/fac_pubs/123.

See also: American Civil Liberties Union (ACLU); Educational setting, privacy in an; Family Educational Rights and Privacy Act of 1974 (FERPA); Supreme Court of the United States

Google

Identification: A corporation founded in 1998 that dominates the Internet with its products and services.

Google remains the most widely used search engine around the globe, and many of the company's communication and publishing tools and services continue to be among the market leaders, including its email service Gmail, video-sharing service YouTube, blogging platform Blogger, social media network Google+, and file-sharing service Google Drive. As Google—which set out to "organize the world's information and make it universally accessible"—rose to become one of the world's most powerful technology companies, concerns about the company's protection of privacy also began to rise. While Google's web crawlers have been caching and indexing billions of web pages, the company has also been storing vast amounts of personal information on its servers. In 2007, the watchdog organization Privacy International rated Google as "hostile" to privacy in a report that ranked Internet companies by how they handle the protection of personal data.

In 2004, in response to the launch of Gmail, thirty-one privacy and civil liberties organizations wrote a letter to Google's cofounders urging them to suspend the Gmail service until the company clarified its privacy protection policies and made its practices more transparent. The signers were concerned about Google's plan to scan the text of all incoming messages so that companies could place targeted ads based on keywords. In addition, they warned about the risks of misuse posed by the unlimited period for data retention. In 2004, the Online Privacy Protection Act, Cal. Bus. & Prof. Code §§ 22575–22579 (2004), became effective in California. The initial bill prohibited the provider of electronic mail to scan email without the consent of all parties. Google, however, had initiated a public relations and lobbying campaign against the proposed bill and was ultimately successful in convincing lawmakers to remove the major consent provisions. Gmail was implemented as planned.

Google Street View, introduced in 2007 as a feature of Google maps, has been particularly controversial. Street View allows users to view panoramic photographic images of locations and to zoom in and out on specific locations. Google has been collecting these images by dispatching a fleet of assorted vehicles equipped with specialized surveillance cameras to the areas that have been mapped. After being uploaded to the Internet, the photos are merged to create seamless panoramic views. Street View, initially introduced in a few U.S. cities, was quickly expanded and is now available for locations around the globe. The controversies surrounding Street View also highlight the challenges of confronting Google's data-collecting practices while establishing and affirming international safeguards for the protection of privacy.

Lauren H. Rakower, an expert in technology law, has argued that Street View violates the international right to privacy as stated by the Universal Declaration of Human Rights and the International Covenant on Civil and Political Rights. Several European countries, as well as Australia, temporarily banned the implementation of Street View, and citizens in several countries formed grassroots campaigns against dispatching Google's Street View fleet in their neighborhoods. Protests increased after a European data protection agency discovered that Google has been collecting vast amounts of Wi-Fi data in addition to collecting images for Street View. In response, privacy advocates called for a Federal Communications Commission (FCC) investigation into whether Google's practices violated the federal Wiretap Act.

Subsequently, more than twelve countries investigated Google's practices, and the company was ultimately charged with violating privacy laws in at least nine countries. In the class action suit *Joffe v. Google, Inc.*, 729 F.3d 1262 (9th Cir. 2013), Google was sued for intercepting private communications from millions of users on unencrypted networks. The U.S. Ninth Circuit Court of Appeals affirmed the ruling that intercepting unencrypted Wi-Fi broadcasts violates the Wiretap Act. Google attempted to appeal to the U.S. Supreme Court. The Court declined to hear the case, however, affirming the lower court's decision. The company reached a $7 million settlement with the attorneys general of thirty-eight states and the District of Columbia over the Street View collection from unprotected Wi-Fi networks.

Defending its practices, Google claimed that it collected the data by accident, yet it also admitted that it did not adequately protect the privacy of consumers. While Google stopped collecting Wi-Fi data through its Street View fleet, concerns about the company's data collection practices have not been alleviated. Indeed, the privacy issues are closely linked to the very nature of Google's operation and mission: The company "makes money because it harvests, copies, aggregates, and ranks billions of Web contributions by millions of authors," according to Siva Vaidhyanathan. Google collects information when users use its services; it copies and disseminates information about people that has been published on the Internet; and it continues to collect images for Street View, potentially exposing private views to the public. While Google has made it easier to control one's privacy settings by introducing a central portal under the "my account" settings, controlling the information that the company retains about individual users remains daunting. Google's privacy policies frequently change as the company evolves and develops new features such as Google Glass, opening up new privacy concerns.

Significant recent challenges to Google's data collection and retention practices have come from European courts and policymakers. In *Google Spain v. AEPD,* (May 13, 2014) (Case C-131/12), the European Court of Justice ruled that European citizens have a right to request that commercial search firms, such as Google, that gather personal information for profit should remove

links to private information when asked, provided the information is no longer relevant. The decision affirmed the "right to be forgotten," which has been developed and implemented in the European Union (EU) and Argentina for the past decade. Subsequently, Google has had to respond to tens of thousands of requests to remove personal information from its index.

Privacy advocates have been calling for establishment of the right to be unlinked in the United States as well. The movement to establish international regulations to safeguard the protection of privacy by Google and other companies that collect vast amounts of user data continues to gain ground.

Katharina Hering

Further Reading

Bennett, Colin J. *The Privacy Advocates: Resisting the Spread of Surveillance.* Cambridge, MA: MIT Press, 2008.

Electronic Privacy Information Center. Ben Joffe v. Google, Inc. https://epic.org/amicus/google-street-view/.

Rakower, Lauren. "Blurred Line: Zooming in on Google Street View and the Global Right to Privacy." *Brooklyn Journal of International Law* 37, no. 1 (2011): 317–347.

Sarpu, Bridget A. "Google: The Endemic Threat to Privacy." *Journal of High Technology Law* 15, no. 1 (2014): 97–134.

Vaidhyanathan, Siva. *The Googlization of Everything (And Why We Should Worry).* Berkeley: University of California Press, 2011.

"31 Privacy and Civil Liberties Organizations Urge Google to Suspend Gmail." *Privacy Rights Clearinghouse,* posted April 6, 2004. https://www.privacyrights.org/ar/GmailLetter.htm.

See also: Data protection regimes; Email; Federal Communications Commission (FCC); Right to be forgotten; Wearable technology

Government Communications Headquarters (GCHQ)

Identification: A British security and intelligence organization, in order to protect the national security of the United Kingdom, formerly known as the Government Communications Headquarters. The GCHQ is the British version of the National Security Agency (NSA) and collaborates with British security services such as the Secret Intelligence Service (SIS) and MI5.

The GCHQ's predecessor agencies provided intelligence to the British government since 1919. A major highlight of the agency's history occurred during World War II, when GCHQ agents known as the "Bletchley Park Code Breakers" broke the code to the Axis communications systems, which greatly assisted the Allied war effort.

Claiming to use the most innovative tools in modern technology, the GCHQ continues to gather intelligence in a challenging and ever-changing communications environment. Among its current objectives, GCHQ works to help prevent the proliferation of chemical, biological and nuclear weapons. The agency also provides intelligence to the British military throughout the world.

The GCHQ justifies the secrecy of its operations because the Internet can be both a haven and a tool for terrorists and criminals, and because Britain's adversaries also operate in secret. Despite this secrecy, the GCHQ, like the MI5 and the Secret Intelligence Service, is covered by stringent legal requirements. The government disclosed the extent of GCHQ's work to Parliament in 1983. The GCHQ is currently governed by the Intelligence Services Act of 1994. The Foreign Secretary and other senior Cabinet Ministers direct the agency; while agency activities are monitored through the Parliament's Intelligence and Security Committee, two independent Commissioners, and High Court judges. This oversight ensures that GCHQ activities are always lawful, necessary and proportionate.

During the Cold War Era from 1945 through 1991, the Soviet military was the most significant military threat to Great Britain. The main focus of GCHQ's signals intelligence efforts, thus, were directed against the Soviets. Since 1946,

GCHQ has provided intelligence and information assurance support to military, diplomatic and law enforcement agencies of the British Government and its Allies. Also, since World War II, the GCHQ has shared its signals intelligence with the United States, Canada, Australia and New Zealand.

Since World War II, the dynamic and changing communications environment presenting GCHQ with formidable technical challenges while it seeks to follow its targets. In 1973, GCHQ achieved a major accomplishment in secure communications in 1973 when Cliff Cocks, James Ellis and Malcolm Williamson developed what became known as public key cryptography. They made this discovery several years before it was independently discovered by Whitfield Diffie and Martin Hellman in the United States.

The Internet has been the most significant technology innovation since World War II era. GCHQ's targets heavily use the same digital technologies that the general population does. The immense volume and vast diversity of the contemporary communications environment continues to be a major challenge for the GCHQ.

After the Warsaw Pact dissolved in 1991, GCHQ turned to a different range of global targets. The more unpredictable nature of newly emergent threats demanded both that the GCHQ act in a more agile manner and that it develop new areas of expertise. The agency increasingly made counter-terrorism, counter-proliferation and cybersecurity a more important part of its mission. In recent years, GCHQ has provided intelligence support to British forces deployed in Iraq (2003–2011) and Afghanistan (2001-present).

In 2013, former NSA contractor Edward Snowden leaked documents, subsequently published in the British newspaper, the *Guardian*, in June of that year, which revealed the Tempora Program. In Tempora, the GCHQ had placed data interceptors on 200 fiber-optic cables that transmit Internet data entering or leaving Great Britain. The GCHQ did this with the secret cooperation, voluntary or coerced, of companies that operate the cables. This allowed the GCHQ to directly access to ten gigabits of data a second, or twenty-one petabytes a day. Approximately 300 GCHQ and 250 NSA agents sifted through the data, which can be stored for up to three and thirty days for content and metacontent respectively.

These agents used a method called Massive Volume Reduction (MVR), which helps reduce the volume of data by 30 percent. They also were able to use specific searches, which are related to trigger words, email addresses of interest, or targeted persons and phone numbers. GCHQ and the NSA have identified 40,000 and 30,000 triggers respectively.

The GCHQ shared this data with the NSA. The *Guardian* reported that 850,000 NSA contractors had access to the data. Critics charged that American and British intelligence agencies cooperated with each other to circumvent restrictions on intelligence gathering their respective nations, i.e., the NSA is not covered by British restrictions on surveillance of British citizens and the GCHQ is not restricted by U.S. restrictions on surveillance of U.S. citizens.

Under Britain's Regulation of Investigatory Powers Act of 2000 (RIPA), defined targets can be tapped if the GCHQ receives a signed warrant. The Home or Foreign Secretary, however, must sign the warrant. Paragraph four of section eight of RIPA, however, provides an exception allowing the Foreign Secretary to certify broad interception of categories of communications relating to areas such as terrorism or organized crime. GCHQ could have been using that provision to justify the broad interception of web traffic. GCHQ, for its part, claims that its agents acted lawfully, and complied with relevant statutes including the Human Rights Act. This statute states that searches must "be necessary and proportionate." GCHQ also claimed that it does not spy on ordinary citizens, but focuses its efforts on terrorists and criminals, and asserted that Tempora has prevented terrorist attacks in Britain itself.

Further Reading:

Aldrich, Richard J. *GCHQ: The Uncensored Story of Britain's Most Secret Intelligence Agency.* London: HarperPress, 2010.

Government Communications Headquarters (GCHQ): New Accommodation Programme : Report. London: Stationery Office, 2003.

Hinsley, F. H. *Codebreakers: The inside Story of Bletchley Park.* Oxford: Oxford University Press, 1993.

McKay, Sinclair. *The Secret Life of Bletchley Park: The History of the Wartime Codebreaking Centre by the Men and Women Who Were There.* London: Aurum, 2010.

Smith, Michael. *Station X: The Codebreakers of Bletchley Park.* London: Channel 4 Books, 1998.

West, Nigel. *The SIGINT Secrets: The Signals Intelligence War, 1900 to Today: Including the Persecution of Gordon Welchman.* New York: W. Morrow, 1988.

See also: Electronic surveillance, National Security Agency (NSA), Tempora.

Gramm-Leach-Bliley Act

Identification: Gramm-Leach-Bliley Act (GLBA) of 1999, 113 Stat. 133. Enacted by Congress on November 4, 1999, to both reform the financial services industry and address issues of consumer financial privacy.

Congress passed the Gramm-Leach-Bliley Act (GLBA) by a large bipartisan majority. GLBA supporters argued that the legislation would modernize U.S. finance, and make the U.S. competitive with the rest of the world. GLBA came after two decades of United States on the nature of financial competition and regulation.

At the time, privacy issues in the financial sector were the subject of heated debate and were leading. Before the GLBA's passage, there were distinct barriers between insurance companies that retained the individual's health records, the bank that mortgaged the individual's house, and the stockbroker that traded in the individual's stocks. If these companies were to merge, they could consolidate, analyze and sell the personal details of their consumers.

Combining several financial services in one company provides expanded opportunities for cross-selling. The large firms that either had recently merged or were contemplating a merger viewed the proposed new regulations as impediments. The firms argued that they could take advantage of significant efficiencies, greater scale, and provide better product information if they were allowed to freely merge and freely use the information from the merging companies. At the same time, there was widespread and increasing concern about how personal information would be used.

Supporters of the GLBA argued that it would stimulate competition in providing all types of financial services. They claimed that the likely benefits of the Act would include the following: the array of products would increase, become obtain, and perhaps less expensive. Larger businesses would benefit from being able to receive all their financial services from one provider, while smaller businesses and individuals may benefit from some economies of transactions. That could result in lower prices for some services for individual consumers. Consumer groups, however, expressed concern that some changes could lead to higher prices to consumers for checking accounts and small loans.

In the guise of modernizing the U.S. financial system, the GLBA would abolish the *Glass-Steagall Act*, which prohibited banks and securities firms affiliating with each other, and the *Bank Holding Company Act*, which prohibited banks and insurance companies from affiliating with each other. As a result, the GLBA was widely viewed as the most important banking legislation in sixty years.

The GLBA's privacy provisions

The GLBA is very complex and addresses a broad range of issues. This entry focuses on those matters relating to privacy. The GLBA requires the Federal Trade Commission (FTC) and other government agencies that regulate financial institutions to implement the regulations to implement the GLBA's financial privacy provisions. The GLBA required that covered businesses be in full compliance by July 1, 2001.

The GLBA's privacy protections only regulate financial institutions (those engaged in banking, insuring, stocks and bonds, financial advice, and investing). These financial institutions, whether they wish to disclose their personal consumer information or not, must develop precautions to ensure the security and confidentiality of customer records and information, to protect against any anticipated threats or hazards to the security or integrity of such records, and to protect against unauthorized access to or use of such records or information that could result in substantial harm or inconvenience to any customer.

Subtitle A: The GLBA Safeguarding Rule

Because of privacy risks due to mergers of financial institutions, the GLBA included three requirements to protect the personal data of individuals. Under Subtitle A, banks, brokerage companies, and insurance companies must securely store personal financial information; advise the customers of their policies on sharing of personal financial data; and, provide consumers the choice to opt out of sharing of personal financial information.

Subtitle A governed the disclosure of nonpublic information. Under the GLBA "Safeguards Rule," financial institutions under the FTC's jurisdiction are required to develop and implement appropriate safeguards to protect nonpublic consumer information, including within an organization's security plan. The rule provided that the financial institutions must designate one or more employees to coordinate the safeguards, identify and access the risks to consumer information in relevant areas of operations; design, implement, and regularly monitor a safeguards program; hire appropriate service providers and contract with them to implement the safeguards; and evaluate and adjust the program as needed.

The Act delegates to agencies such as the FTC the responsibility for issuing standards for financial institutions safeguards that: 1) ensure the security and confidentiality of customer records and information; and 2) protects against hazard so unauthorized access to such information.

For a financial institution to disclose the nonpublic information of its customer to a non-affiliated third party, it must comply with the GLBA's consumer notification provisions, which requires, that the financial institution would provide the following to the consumer: 1) a clear and conspicuous disclosure that its customers' information may be disseminated to third parties and 2) the opportunity for consumers to prevent such disclosures.

Financial institutions must establish privacy policies and disclose them when a customer relationship is formed and send update policies not less than annually after that. These policies disclose how the institutions share information with affiliates as well as with third parties.

With some exceptions, these institutions are prohibited from disclosing nonpublic personal information (NPI) to nonaffiliated third parties unless they have given consumers the opportunity to "opt out." Under the opt-out provision, the consumer would direct the financial institution not to share information with unaffiliated companies.

The GLBA also prohibited a financial institution from disclosing a consumer's account numbers, access number or code to a nonaffiliated third party for use through any marketing effort through any medium to the consumer. The enforcement of Subtitle A of the statute rests with certain designated federal agencies, state insurance authorities, and the FTC.

Financial institutions must provide their consumers with a notice of their information sharing policies when a person first become a customer, and annually after that. That notice must inform the consumer of the financial institution's policies on: disclosing nonpublic personal information (NPI) to affiliates and non-affiliated third parties, disclosing NPI after the customer relationship is terminated, and protecting NPI. "Nonpublic personal information" means all information on applications to obtain financial services (credit card or loan applications), account histories (bank or credit card) and the fact that an individual is or was a customer. This interpretation of NPI makes names, addresses, telephone numbers, Social Security numbers and other data subject to the GLBA's data sharing restrictions.

Consumers have no right under the GLBA to prevent sharing of NPI among affiliates. An affiliate is any company that controls, is controlled by, or is under common control with another company. The individual consumer has absolutely no control over this kind of "corporate family" trading of personal information.

The GLBA has several exemptions that would permit information sharing despite objections of consumers. If a financial services company chooses to do transactions with an another company, it is within its rights to transfer its customer's personal information to that second company on the basis that such data is necessary to for the second company to be able to perform its services. It is allowable for the financial institution, for example, to share its customer's private information to a marketing firm to promote new products or services or jointly offered goods or services. Once the unaffiliated third party has a customer's personal information, they may legally share it with their "corporate family." However, they cannot likewise transfer the information to other companies through this exemption.

Also, financial institutions may disclose the consumer's information to credit reporting agencies, financial regulators, if a business is sold, in compliance with laws or regulations governing the transaction, if the buyer requests such information.

Financial institutions may not disclose, except to consumer reporting agencies, certain information to any nonaffiliated third party for marketing. The significance of this is even if a consumer does not "opt out" of a financial institution's information transfers, his or her credit card numbers, and other such information may not be sold.

Subtitle B: Protection Against Pretexting

Subtitle B of the GLBA addresses fraudulent access to financial information and establishes guidelines about a financial institution's customer information. Violations of these prohibitions are subject to FTC enforcement actions, as well as civil and criminal penalties. This general prohibition, however, does not apply under certain circumstances, including when law enforcement agencies were acting under proper legal authority.

The GLBA also strengthened prohibitions on pretext calling (obtaining customer information by false pretenses). Pretexting is the practice of collecting personal information under false pretenses. Pretexters often pose as authority figures (such as law enforcement agents, social workers, and potential employers) and develop false stories to obtain personal information on the victim.

The GLBA also prohibits the use of false, fictitious or fraudulent statements or documents to get customer information from a financial institution or directly from a customer of a financial institution; the use of forged, counterfeit, lost or stolen documents to get customer information from a financial institution or directly from a customer of a financial institution; and asking another person to get someone else's customer information using false, fictitious, or fraudulent documents or forged, counterfeit, lost or stolen documents.

Proposals to undo the GLBA

Over the past ten years, there have been efforts to undo some of the provisions of the GLBA, because of a series of high-profile cases involving banks selling consumer information with customers suffering losses due to marketing, credit fraud, and identity theft.

The privacy risks from mergers in the financial services industry became apparent after a series of international and domestic events. In 1995, the European Union (EU) enacted its Data Protection Directive, which requires that data exchanges transmitting te personal data of EU citizens provide the equivalent degree of protection as their home country would grant them. Thus, U.S. companies became required to ensure that when they use the personal data of citizens of EU nations, which these citizens be given the same level of protection that they would have within the EU. The EU expressed concerns with both the self-regulatory approach to privacy and absence of federal privacy legislation in the United States. Despite the "Safe Harbor proposal" (since struck down by an Irish court) between the United States and the European Union, which had allowed companies to regulate themselves while being subject to oversight by the FTC, the financial services sector was not included in the agreement.

In the aftermath of the financial crisis in 2008, several issues were raised in connection with GLBA: Is it prudent to let banks get too big in the first place? How big is too big to fail? To what extent will the government intervene when a financial services industry participant begins to melt down? Many observers began to question the deregulatory policies that underlay Gramm-Leach-Bliley and to urge reform of the banking regulatory system with more robust constraints on the activities and affiliations of financial institutions. Many liberal economic experts argue the repeal of Glass-Steagall encouraged the conditions that led to the financial crisis and that the Dodd-Frank Act was not sufficient to restore safety to the banking industry.

Reform and repeal efforts drew support during the Obama years, with liberal reformers such as Senators Bernie Sanders (I-VT) and Elizabeth Warren (DMA) proposing that it be replaced by a banking system with fire-walls between banking, securities, and insurance activity as existed under Glass-Steagall. But in the wake of the 2016 presidential race and the election of Donald Trump, the reformers saw themselves drowned out by voices calling for a loosening of financial regulations and the abandonment of Dodd-Frank. With Democratic control of the U.S. House of Representatives, as of January 2019, the reformers were emboldened; yet with the Senate remaining in the hands of Republicans, the likelihood of major new financial legislation being written seemed dim.

Further Reading

Benson, Kenneth R. *Financial Services Modernization: GLBA of 1999: Law and Explanation.* Chicago, Ill.: CCH, 1999.

Dunham, Wolcott B. *After the Gramm-Leach-Bliley Act: A Road Map for Insurance Companies.* New York, N.Y.: Practicing Law Institute, 2000.

Examination of the GLBA Five Years after Its Passage: Hearing before the Committee on Banking, Housing, and Urban Affairs, United States Senate, One Hundred Eighth Congress, Second Session, on the GLBA(P.L. 106–102), T. Washington: U.S. G.P.O. :, 2006.

"Financial Data Safeguards. (GLBA Regulates Financial Institution Security)." *Security Management,* September 1, 2002.

Financial Modernization after Gramm-Leach-Bliley. Newark, NJ: LexisNexis, 2002.

Financial Services Modernization: Analysis of the GLBA of 1999. New York, N.Y.: Matthew Bender, 2000. "Gramm-Leach-Bliley Act: Creating a New Bank for a New Millennium." *SpringerReference.*

The Gramm-Leach-Bliley Act: Financial Services Modernization: Hearings before the Committee on Banking, Housing, and Urban Affairs, United States Senate, One Hundred Sixth Congress, First Session, on Legislative Proposals, Culminating in the Enactment of the Gramm-Leach-Bliley Act. Washington: U.S. G.P.O.: 2000.

Grant, Joseph Karl. "What the Financial Services Industry Puts Together Let No Person Put Asunder: How the GLBA Contributed to the 2008–2009 American Capital Markets Crisis." *Albany Law Review,* 2010.

Hassan, M. Kabir, and Abdullah Mamun. "Global Impact of the Gramm-Leach-Bliley Act: Evidence from Insurance Industries of Developed Countries." *Financial Market Regulation,* 2010, 63–77.

Natter, Raymond. "The Reasons for the Gramm-Leach-Bliley Act." *SSRN Electronic Journal SSRN Journal.*

Sorokina, Nonna. "Long-Term Impact of GLBA on the Financial Industry." *SSRN Electronic Journal SSRN Journal.*

See also: Consumer privacy; Data protection regimes; Federal Trade Commission (FTC); Financial information, privacy right to

Greenwald, Glenn (1967–)

Born: March 6, 1967
Identification: An American journalist and lawyer instrumental in the criticism and exposure of U.S. secret surveillance programs conducted by the George W. Bush and Barack Obama administrations. Working with whistleblower Edward Snowden and other journalists, Greenwald published articles in the British newspaper the *Guardian* revealing, for the first time, the intricacies and breadth of the U.S. government's collection of its citizens' electronic data.

Born March 6, 1967, in Queens, New York, Greenwald moved with his family to Florida at a young age. As a child he became politically aware in great part due to his grandfather's influence and experience as a city councilman in Florida. Greenwald's grandfather instilled in him the drive to challenge authority. That drive led Greenwald to hone his rhetorical skills as a state champion on his high school debate team and to become socially active by running for city council at the age of seventeen. In addition, the discrimination he witnessed and encountered as a homosexual teenager had a formative effect on his disposition to question institutional power.

Greenwald attended George Washington University and, after graduating, enrolled in New York University School of Law. While a law student, he organized a successful drive to ban Colorado law firms from recruiting on campus because of Colorado's voter-approved referendum prohibiting the state from recognizing homosexuals as a protected class. After law

Miranda (left) and Greenwald (right) speak at the National Congress of Brazil in the wake of the 2013 mass surveillance disclosures. (by Elza Fiúza / Agência Brasil)

school, Greenwald initially worked for a large, corporate law firm. During his short time practicing corporate law, Greenwald discovered the opportunity to engage in political and policy debates via the Internet. He joined an Internet forum hosted by conservative-leaning organizations and brought his debate skills to bear. Quickly becoming disillusioned with representing rich and powerful clients, Greenwald began his own legal practice in 1996 focused on First Amendment cases and representing disadvantaged clients. At the same time, he continued developing his presence on the Internet as a critic of the U.S. reaction to the 9/11 terrorist attacks. After six years of managing his legal practice, Greenwald began a business consulting firm with a friend in 2002. Greenwald's role in the company was that of in-house counsel, but after a short stint with the company, he sold his interest and visited Brazil with the intent to take time off and reevaluate his career path.

While in Brazil, Greenwald met his life partner, David Miranda, and soon thereafter he moved to Brazil to be with him. Unable to practice law in Brazil, Greenwald began blogging in October 2005. His first major splash in the blogosphere came with popular blog posts about the then-recent indictment of I. Lewis ("Scooter") Libby, Vice President Dick Cheney's chief of staff. He then launched his journalism career with critiques of the National Security

Agency's warrantless wiretapping that had been authorized by the Bush administration. Within months, major online news outlets were citing his blog, *Unclaimed Territory*. Two years later, in 2007, he began writing for the online news website *Salon* and appearing as a guest on cable news shows. In 2012, Greenwald left *Salon* to work for the British newspaper the *Guardian*, where he continued his critique of secret government surveillance and data collection.

Less than a year into his tenure with the *Guardian*, Greenwald was contacted by an anonymous source attempting to begin an encrypted email conversation. That anonymous source was former Central Intelligence Agency (CIA) employee and security contractor Edward Snowden. The source was vague about the information he possessed, and Greenwald was unfamiliar with the encryption protocols the source demanded, so he soon gave up on the potential source. Six months later, in May 2013, Greenwald's friend, filmmaker Laura Poitras, showed him encrypted emails from Snowden, who remained anonymous and had contacted Poitras. Intrigued by the emails, Greenwald began an encrypted conversation with Snowden and soon asked him to demonstrate his authenticity. Snowden provided evidence of secret U.S. surveillance programs that enabled the government's mass collection of personal data.

Greenwald, along with Poitras and Ewen MacAskill, another journalist from the *Guardian*, flew together to Hong Kong, where Snowden had rented a room and awaited their arrival. Over the course of two weeks, Greenwald interviewed Snowden about the classified evidence of U.S. surveillance and data collection programs he had gathered while working for the U.S. government. (Poitras filmed these encounters and assembled the edited footage for her film *Citizenfour* [2014]; the film won an Academy Award for that year's best documentary.) Greenwald published his first series of articles exposing the programs in June 2013. The first article described a secret court order requiring telephone companies to release customer data to the U.S. government. The subsequent articles described various programs, such as PRISM, run by the U.S. government and shared with the British government's Government Communications Headquarters (GCHQ). These programs enabled both governments to access bulk Internet data such as emails and search histories. In 2013, Greenwald left the *Guardian*. A year later he teamed up with Poitras and Jeremy Scahill, another well-known investigative reporter, and the three began First Look Media. With funding from eBay founder Pierre Omidyar, First Look Media began publishing its first online news magazine, the *Intercept*. The magazine's stated mission is to focus on investigative articles exposing government secrecy, civil liberties violations, and public corruption. Greenwald's 2013 *Guardian* articles, along with his other work on government surveillance and data collection, have earned him numerous awards and acclaim as a journalist and author.

Because of his exposure of government programs that facilitated the secret gathering of massive amounts of information, Greenwald has been labeled by some an enabler of espionage and by others a herald of illegal government action. Nonetheless Greenwald played a key role in sparking domestic and international debate about government transparency as well as the appropriate limitations on government surveillance and bulk data collection in the digital age.

Douglas B. McKechnie

Further Reading

Bernstein, Fred. "Glenn Greenwald: Life Beyond Borders." *Out Magazine*, May 2011.

Greenwald, Glenn. *No Place to Hide: Edward Snowden, the NSA, and the U.S. Surveillance State*. New York, N.Y.: Metropolitan Books, 2014.

Keller, Bill. "Is Glenn Greenwald the Future of News?" *New York Times*, (New York, NY) Oct. 27, 2013. Poitras, Laura, dir. *Citizenfour*. 2014. New York: Radius-TWC, 2015. Streaming Video.

See also: Electronic Surveillance; National Security Agency (NSA); Poitras, Laura; PRISM; Snowden, Edward; Whistle-blowers; Wiretapping

Griswold v. State of Connecticut 381 U.S. 479 (1965)

Identification: A 7–2 ruling, with the majority opinion written by Justice William Douglas, in which the Supreme Court ruled that the state could not restrict married couples from using contraception. This was a landmark case in which the Supreme Court recognized there was a right to privacy. This was considered a new right at the time, and the ruling set the groundwork for subsequent cases like *Roe v. Wade*, 410 U.S. 113 (1973).

Griswold v. State of Connecticut centers on the Connecticut Comstock Act of 1879. This law provided that "[a]ny person who uses any drug, medicinal article or instrument for the purpose of preventing conception shall be fined not less than fifty dollars or not less than sixty days nor more than one year or be both fined and imprisoned." In addition, it provided that "[a]ny person who assists, counsels, causes, hires or commands another to commit any offense may be prosecuted and punished as if he were the principal offender." In general, the Comstock Law was a federal act passed in 1873 that criminalized the usage of items such as erotica, contraceptives, sex toys, and anything else that might be considered obscene or immoral. The law was named after its leading proponent, Anthony Comstock, whose ideas of what were obscene were quite broad. In fact, some anatomy textbooks were prohibited from being sent to medical students under this act.

Historically, physicians tended to avoid publishing materials on birth control methods. They might advise married patients, but the topic was largely taboo and mostly illegal. The Connecticut Birth Control League, which would eventually develop Planned Parenthood clinics, sought to challenge these laws. Over the years, many challenges were made and failed, largely due to technical grounds such as standing. These cases focused on using the birth control pill for contraceptive use rather than health-related matters because, in 1918, Margaret Sanger, an early advocate for birth control, was successful in establishing a doctor's right to promote, discuss, or provide contraceptives for the use of preventing and curing illness and disease.

In 1961, Estelle Griswold, who was the executive director of the Planned Parenthood League of Connecticut, and C. Lee Buxton, who was a licensed physician and professor at the Yale Medical School and also served as medical director for the league at its center in New Haven, sought to challenge the law. They opened a birth control clinic in New Haven, Connecticut, and Griswold and Buxton gave information, instruction, and medical advice to married couples on preventing conception. Typically, they would examine the wife and prescribe the best contraception device or material. Shortly after the clinic opened, Griswold and Buxton were arrested and found guilty as accessories under the Comstock Act, and were both fined $100.

Unlike prior cases, the Court established that here there was standing and, specifically, that the appellants had standing to raise the constitutional rights of the married people with whom they had a professional relationship. This was a significant change from prior challenges. The Court also felt that this statute presented questions under the due process clause of the Fourteenth Amendment.

The Court began its opinion by explaining that many things are not specifically mentioned in the Constitution but are nonetheless protected: "The foregoing cases suggest that specific guarantees in the Bill of Rights have penumbras, formed by emanations from those guarantees that help give them life and substance." For example, the Court explained that, logically, the First Amendment's right to free speech not only protects the right to utter or print speech but also, by extension, the right to distribute, the right to receive, the right to inquire, the right to freedom of thought, the right to teach, and the right to read. Because of this, the Court reasoned that the U.S. Constitution guarantees a

"zone of privacy" and that this statute violated that zone.

The Court focused on the use and advice, rather than the manufacture, asking, "Would we allow the police to search the sacred precincts of marital bedrooms for telltale signs of the use of contraceptives? The very idea is repulsive to the notions of privacy surrounding the marriage relationship." The Court focused on the idea of marriage being "intimate to the degree of being sacred" and older than the Bill of Rights.

This was significant because the Court was stating that, although the Constitution does not specifically mention a right to privacy, it is implicit in various amendments, including the First, Third, Fourth, Fifth and Ninth, as well as the due process clause of the Fourteenth Amendment. The Court defined a right to privacy as protection from governmental intrusion.

Justice Goldberg and Chief Justice Brennan concurred, stressing the importance of the Ninth Amendment, and stating that "the concept of liberty protects those personal rights that are fundamental, and is not confined to the specific terms of the Bill of Rights." The Ninth Amendment specifically states, "The enumeration in the Constitution, of certain rights, shall not be construed to deny or disparage others retained by the people."

Justice Hugo Black and Justice Potter Stewart dissented. Justice Black specifically argued that the Constitution does not mention or provide for a right to privacy and also critiqued the majority opinion interpretations of the Ninth and Fourteenth Amendments.

While Griswold focused much of the opinion on married couples, the right was later extended to all persons in *Eisenstadt v. Baird*, 405 U.S. 438 (1972). The logic in *Eisenstadt* was that it would be a violation of the equal protection clause to extend the right of privacy only to married couples.

Griswold's legacy is significant because it paved the way for cases such as *Roe v. Wade*, which extended the right of privacy to abortion, and *Lawrence v. Texas* 539 U.S. 558 (2003), which extended the right of privacy to homosexual acts. These cases and more extend the penumbra of privacy to well beyond birth control. The importance of *Griswold v. Connecticut* for women cannot be underestimated because the case is conventionally understood to have secured crucial liberty rights for women on the most intimate of matters.

Melissa A. Gill

Further Reading

Bailey, Martha J. " 'Momma's Got the Pill': How Anthony Comstock and *Griswold v. Connecticut* Shaped U.S. Childbearing." *American Economic Review* 100, no. 1 (2010): 98–129.

Franklin, Cary. "Griswold and the Public Dimension of the Right to Privacy." *Yale Law Journal Forum* 124, 332.

Garrow, David J. "Human Rights Hero: The Legal Legacy of *Griswold v. Connecticut*." *Human Rights* (2011): 26–25.

Johnson, John W. Griswold v. Connecticut: *Birth Control and the Constitutional Right of Privacy*. University Press of Kansas, 2005.

Siegel, Neil S., and Reva B. Siegel. *Contraception as a Sex Equality Right*. *Yale Law Journal Forum* 124, 349.

See also: Constitutional law; Douglas, William Orville; *Lawrence v. Texas;* Privacy laws, state; Privacy laws, federal; The Right to Privacy

Hacking, computer

Identification: Using programming knowledge to illegally access a computer or network.

The word *hack* by most accounts originated at the Massachusetts Institute of Technology (MIT), where the Tech Model Railroad Club (TMRC) was founded in 1946. The members of the club created automated model trains that operated using telephone relays; they used the word *hack* to mean a creative way of solving a problem. A second meaning of *hack,* also in use at MIT, was "an ingenious, benign, and anonymous prank or practical joke, often requiring engineering or scientific expertise and often pulled off under cover of darkness."

This sense of hacking as a creative solution with an element of humor or mischievousness has remained steady through time. Like the multiple meanings within the etymology of the term *hack,* the various meanings of computer hacking have evolved as our technological world has evolved.

Origins

In 1961, MIT purchased the first PDP-1. While it was a large computer that filled much of a room and cost (at the time) a whopping $120,000, it was compact and inexpensive compared to the hulking mainframe computers previously available. The members of the TMRC were fascinated with the new computer, and many of the club members formed MIT's computer science department. These students spent a great deal of time exploring and expanding the PDP-1's capabilities. They developed programming tools for it, composed and played music on it, and even played chess on it. In 1962, they created the very first videogame, called *Spacewar!*

The precursor to today's Internet, ARPAnet, appeared in 1969. Built by the U.S. Defense Department as an experiment in digital communications, ARPAnet was the first transcontinental high-speed computer network. It linked universities, contractors, and labs, providing students and researchers a place to communicate with each other without regard to geographical boundaries. A hacker community formed through these networks, sharing hardware and software "hacks" and developing a shared vocabulary.

The earliest hackers were known as phreakers and explored the telephone system. The term *phreakers* comes from the combination of *phone* and *freak*. In 1971, John Draper discovered that a prize whistle from Cap'n Crunch cereal (the origin of his nickname) could reproduce the 2,600-hertz tone needed to access AT&T's long-distance system in "operator mode." This allowed phreakers to explore proprietary aspects of the system, as well as make free calls. Draper was arrested many times over the following few years for phone tampering.

In 1975, two members of the Homebrew Computer Club in California started selling blue boxes, tone producers based on Draper's discovery, to allow people to make free long-distance phone calls. Their names were Steve Wozniak and Steve Jobs, who would go on to start Apple Computers in 1977.

While exploring the phone system was not illegal, stealing long-distance telephone service was. In spite of the involvement of the Federal Bureau of Investigation (FBI) at this point, hackers continued exploring new technologies without much legal or law enforcement interference.

When hackers were prosecuted, they were often given probation and a small fine. Hackers often sought to share what they discovered, either through publication or online bulletin boards, much to the chagrin of companies whose security flaws or functions were discovered. As technology advanced at a rapid pace, hacker knowledge and ability to locate weaknesses in systems outpaced the law. This somewhat antiauthoritarian spirit of exploration and sharing of knowledge would remain in the nuances of hacking's definition, although the technological universe was about to change.

Personal computing revolution

The early 1980s saw the first personal computers: The IBM PC, running MS-DOS, appeared in 1981, and Apple's Macintosh appeared in 1984. These computers sold for as low as $1,500, a fraction of the cost of the mainframe or PDP computers of the past. Computers were no longer confined to universities and laboratories— they were affordable enough for people have them in their homes. ARPAnet was still in service, so these desktop computers (instead of whole-room computers) could be hooked up to the telephone network and talk with each other.

The potential universe for hackers to explore grew exponentially. The demand for new software applications and faster computers continued to grow. Computer software companies sprung up. People could now explore the new technology easily on the desktop computers.

The hacker community grew, and online bulletin-board systems thrived where groups could meet to share tips. With the growth of the computer and software industry, many security flaws could be found, and hackers were interested to see what they might unlock.

In 1983, the movie *War Games,* starring Matthew Broderick, was released. He played a teenage hacker who accesses a Pentagon supercomputer and narrowly avoids starting a nuclear war. The computer is named WOPR (War Operation Plan Response), supposedly a pun on an early NORAD computer that was called BRGR. While the idea of teenager starting a nuclear war was perhaps far-fetched, it illustrated a growing concern about what these new technologies and the information they controlled might do should they be compromised.

In a case of life imitating art, that same year the FBI arrested six teenagers in Milwaukee who referred to themselves as the 414s, after the city's area code. They were accused of breaking into over sixty computer networks, including the Los Alamos National Laboratory. One hacker received immunity for testifying against the others; the rest received probation.

Hackers already had a tradition of publishing and sharing their discoveries, and in 1984 a hacker magazine, *2600: The Hacker Quarterly,* began publication. The magazine's name comes from the 2,600-hertz tone that John Draper used to hack into AT&T's operator mode. The editor, Eric Corley, goes by the pen name Emmanuel Goldstein, a reference to the narrator in George Orwell's *1984.* The magazine publishes articles on a variety of topics, including privacy issues, computer security, and the digital underground.

By the mid-1980s, repeated break-ins into government and corporate databases and networks forced Congress to respond. The Counterfeit Access Device and Abuse Act (18 U.S.C. § 1030) was passed in 1984. It was the first federal law designed specifically to prosecute computer crimes. It focused on prosecuting computer activity that accessed government information protected for national defense or foreign relations, financial information from financial institutions, and government computers. In 1986, the Computer Fraud and Abuse Act (CFAA) amended the Counterfeit Access Device and Abuse Act and expanded the law's coverage from a "federal interest computer" to *any* "protected computer."

The first known computer virus, called Brain, appeared in 1987. It infected MS-DOS systems and was released through the Internet. It was benign compared to the viruses we see today: The virus simply put a small file on the computer's hard drive with business card information for Brain Computer Services in Pakistan.

Hackers were not just limited to computers; changes in hardware and software on media players and game consoles could allow these devices to use media that was homemade, pirated, or free. In 1988, the Digital Millennium Copyright Act (DMCA) was passed; it criminalized the creation and distribution of hardware and software that disabled copyright protections on digital media.

In 1988, twenty-three-year-old Cornell University graduate student Robert Morris created the Internet's first worm. The son of a National Security Agency (NSA) computer security expert, he wrote ninety-nine lines of code and released them to the Internet as an experiment. The self-replicating software multiplied more quickly than anticipated and wound up infecting more than 6,000 systems. Almost one-tenth of the entire Internet at the time was affected, and the network was out of service for days. The first person tried under the CFAA, Morris was arrested and sentenced to three years of probation, 400 hours of community service, and a $10,000 fine. He later formed an Internet startup, Viaweb, which he sold in 1998 for almost $49 million.

A hacker named The Mentor published what is now a classic treatise on hacking, *The Conscience of a Hacker,* in 1989. The last line reads: "You may stop this individual, but you can't stop us all."

The rise of the Internet

In the late 1980s and early 1990s, commercial Internet service providers (ISPs) began to emerge. They replaced ARPAnet, the first Internet, which was decommissioned in 1990. Online retailers began to appear, such as Amazon.com in 1995. Personal information began flowing through the Internet—hackers noticed. Enthusiasm for the growing Internet led to more serious hacks, some just for exploration, and some for criminal gain.

Four hackers calling themselves the Legion of Doom were arrested in 1990 for stealing technical information on BellSouth's 911 emergency telephone network. While they did not do anything with it, the information could have disabled 911 service for the entire country. Three of the hackers were found guilty and received prison sentences ranging from fourteen to twenty-one months, along with almost $250,000 in damages.

In 1990, the Secret Service and Arizona's organized crime unit joined forces to create Operation Sundevil, a crackdown on "illegal computer hacking activities." It resulted in three arrests and the confiscation of computers, the contents of electronic bulletin board systems (BBSs), and floppy disks. The arrests and following court cases resulted in the creation of the Electronic Frontier Foundation (EFF), which focuses on defending civil liberties issues affected by technology.

The 1990s also saw the first hacker breach of big banking. In 1994, Russian hacker Vladimir Levin had Citibank's computers transfer an estimated $10 million to his accounts; Citibank recovered all but $400,000 of what was stolen. In January 1998, Levin pled guilty in federal court to charges of conspiracy to commit bank, wire, and computer fraud. He admitted using passwords and codes stolen from Citibank customers to make the transfers. Levin was sentenced to three years in prison and was ordered to pay Citibank $240,000.

The first Defcon hacker conference was held in Las Vegas, Nevada, in 1993 and continues as an annual event. The term comes from the movie

War Games and references the U.S. armed forces defense readiness condition (DEFCON). In the movie, Las Vegas was selected as a nuclear target. It also references DEF, the letters on the number 3 on a standard phone, with *con* meaning conference.

Defcon and the other big hacker conferences (such as Black Hat or RSA) focus on so-called ethical hacking. There are demonstrations of security flaws, such as an 11-year old child hacking into a replica of Florida's election website and changing votes in under 10 minutes in 2018, or the takeover of a Jeep's computer system while it was driving (which led to a recall of over 1 million cars). Bug bounties are offered by companies large and small (such as Facebook, Microsoft, and the Justice Department) for hackers that turn in security flaws. Shame boards list those who attend and find themselves hacked, as well as an award for the most epic fail. In 2018, some of the contenders were Under Armour's MyFitnessPal for compromising personal information for over 150 million people, and the Facebook website hack, that exposed "access tokens" affecting the accounts of 29 million people.

Despite the CFAA, hackers continued to break into government computers. In 1996, the General Accounting Office reported that hackers tried to break into Defense Department files more than 250,000 times in 1995; about 65 percent of the attempts succeeded. In August, hackers added swastikas and a picture of Adolph Hitler to the U.S. Department of Justice website and renamed it the Department of Injustice. The next month, hackers broke into the Central Intelligence Agency's (CIA's) website and changed the department's name to Central Stupidity Agency.

By 1998, the Symantec AntiVirus Research Center estimated that 30,000 computer viruses were circulating on the Internet. That same year, federal prosecutors charged a juvenile for the first time with computer hacking after a boy shut down an airport communications system in Massachusetts. No accidents occurred and his name was not released; however, he pled guilty and was sentenced to two years of probation, 250 hours of community service, and restitution to Bell Atlantic for $5,000.

A hacker think tank called L0pht (pronounced "loft") testified before Congress in 1998 that it could shut down the Internet in half an hour. (The congressional hearings were about software and Internet security flaws.) With the government, retailers, and financial institutions utilizing the Internet, more personal and financial data than ever before had become accessible to hackers who had an interest in finding it.

Hacking today

Verizon's *2018 Data Breach Investigations Report*, the best-known annual study of data breaches, indicated that the majority of the breaches, about three out of every four attacks, were due to criminals looking to steal money in some fashion.

Thieves use more than payment systems to steal money. In 2017, the use of ransomware increased, accounting for 40 percent of malware incidents. Ransomware locks a victim's data and then threatens to erase or publish it if money, or a "ransom" is not paid. Ransom demands in 2017 averaged about $500.

Information is also a valuable commodity to thieves. For instance, in August 2015, nine people were charged in the largest known computer hacking and securities fraud scheme to date. They stole over 150,000 press releases from three major newswire companies about publicly traded companies and made insider stock trades, which generated over $30 million, based on the information. The defendants were in Ukraine and various locations in the United States In addition to stealing information and money, sometimes hacks cost money simply because of their disruption. As of 2000, a new computer virus was created every hour, according to the Symantec AntiVirus Research Center. In 2017, denial-of-service (DDoS) attacks continued to be the leading cause of security breaches. DDoS attacks overwhelm a server with requests so that it cannot accept more traffic and sometimes crashes.

While large attacks tend to make the news, such as the February 2000 DDoS attack on Yahoo, eBay, CNN, Amazon.com, and E*Trade, even short-lived smaller attacks can cause security issues. The FBI estimated that such attacks cost about $1.7 billion in lost business and other damages. To counteract this trend, in 2003, Microsoft started a $5 million bounty on hackers attacking Windows. It continues a bug bounty program to this day. These bounties provide balance to the black market for unpatched bugs because members of organized crime and others are willing to pay well for these access points.

Viruses and malware have also shown that they can wreak havoc on systems ranging from phones to appliances, to nuclear power plants. These systems are managed and maintained by computers and Internet connections. For example, between 2009 and 2010, Iran's nuclear program was infected by a virus named Stuxnet. This virus was unlike any other because it caused physical destruction of the equipment controlled by the computers. Stuxnet targeted the rotation speeds of centrifuges and caused one-fifth of them to destroy themselves, which delayed the progress of Iran's nuclear program.

The attackers also took over the facilities' workstations and blasted "Thunderstruck" by AC/ DC at highest volume. It is suspected that the virus was developed by the U.S. and Israeli governments, but in the digital realm, reliable attribution of any hack is very difficult.

Hacking has also taken on social and political purposes (this kind of hacking is called hacktivism). Hactivists sometimes work alone, like The Jester, who takes down Islamic jihadist websites. Some work in loose groups, such as Anonymous and Lulz Security (abbreviated to LulzSec). Their targets have been varied, ranging from the Church of Scientology to PayPal.

There is no defined leadership for such groups, and sometimes their actions are condemned by others within the group. Quinn Norton of *Wired* wrote of Anonymous in 2011:

> . . . [Y]ou're never quite sure if Anonymous is the hero or antihero. The trickster is attracted to change and the need for change, and that's where Anonymous goes . . . And when they do something, it never goes quite as planned. The internet has no neat endings.

The hacker fascination with pushing boundaries of all sorts has been around as long as we have had access to computers. In fact, that fascination has played a major role in the advancement of technology. As our virtual worlds become more intricately intertwined with our physical worlds, these explorations will likely continue to provoke the tensions between security and the convenient and free flow of information.

Noëlle Sinclair

Further Reading

Carlin, John P. *Dawn of the Code War: America's Battle Against Russia, China, and the Rising Global Cyber Threat.* New York: Hachette Book Group, 2018.

Coleman, E. Gabriella. *Coding Freedom: The Ethics and Aesthetics of Hacking.* Princeton, NJ: Princeton University Press, 2013.

Goldstein, Emmanuel. *Best of 2600: A Hacker Odyssey.* Indianapolis, IN: Wiley Publishing, 2008.

Greenberg, Andy. *Sandworm: A New Era of Cyberwar and the Hunt for the Kremlin's Most Dangerous Hackers.* New York: Doubleday. 2019

Lapsley, Phil. *Exploding the Phone: The Untold Story of the Teenagers and Outlaws who Hacked Ma Bell.* New York: Grove Press, 2013.

Levy, Steven. *Hackers: Heroes of the Computer Revolution— 25th Anniversary Edition.* Sebastopol, CA: O'Reilly Media, 2010.

Mitnick, Kevin. *Ghost in the Wires: My Adventures as the World's Most Wanted Hacker.* New York: Little, Brown and Company, 2011.

Olson, Parmy. *We Are Anonymous: Inside the Hacker World of LulzSec, Anonymous, and the Global Cyber Insurgency.* New York: Little, Brown and Company, 2012.

Peterson, T.F., Institute Historian. *Nightwork: A History of Hacks and Pranks at MIT* (updated edition). Cambridge, MA: MIT Press, 2011.

Smith, Jeremy N. *Breaking and Entering: The Extraordinary Story of a Hacker Called "Alien."* New York: Eamon Dolan / Houghton Mifflin Harcourt, 2019.

Zetter, Kim. *Countdown to Zero Day: Stuxnet and the Launch of the World's First Digital Weapon.* New York: Broadway Books, 2014.

See also: Cellphones; Computers and privacy; Cybersecurity; Data breaches; Data harvesting; Identity theft; Malware; Online privacy and protection; Security flaws, computers; Spam; Spyware

Harassment

Identification: On social media, a form of behavior targeting, embarrassing, threatening, or otherwise exposing an individual to ridicule, shame or bodily harm via email, text messages, Instagram photo-sharing, Twitter, Facebook, or other digital platforms.

Harassment generally requires some pattern of continuing behavior. A single, egregious act— particularly one that is shared repeatedly by others—can also constitute harassment. Harassment does not require sexual exploitation, but such exploitation is increasingly becoming a common form of harassment through sexting, the sharing of sexually graphic photos and information not intended to be shared with a wider audience. Sexual exploitive harassment can also be called "revenge porn." With the advent of social media, and constant advancements in technology, harassment has become a serious issue for schools, parents, and employers. Another phrase used to describe digital harassment, particularly when a child or minor is targeted, is cyberbullying.

Not all forms of harassment are unlawful. Many social media campaigns target individuals— and companies—by depicting (and forwarding, or sharing) a particular story to cause humiliation or to bring about change. This type of harassment can be hurtful and damaging to an individual. In response, many schools, including colleges, and employers have enacted social media or online harassment policies to minimize disruptions at school and work. Such policies may be subject to First Amendment challenge for stifling free speech and expression; however, the First Amendment only applies to governmental actors. Private schools and private employers have broad ability to sanction speech without breaching the First Amendment. When harassment is severe or pervasive, there can be legal—even criminal—consequences.

Several high-profile cases of cyberbullying have resulted in teen suicides. These tragedies have helped shape state legislation regarding harassment and cyberbullying. Two notable cases include the deaths of Megan Meier, a Missouri adolescent who hung herself after being bullied through a fake MySpace account, and Tyler Clementi, a Rutgers University freshman who jumped to his death after his roommate secretly filmed him kissing another man and then discussed the episode via Twitter. Both cases resulted in criminal prosecutions and garnered significant media and legislative attention. The line between criminally sanctionable conduct and free expression in a technologically advancing world is sometimes difficult to discern, and the legal landscape in this area keeps evolving.

Another high-profile harassment claim that resulted in criminal prosecution is the case of Michelle Carter. Carter's case was profiled by CBS on its criminal news show, *48 Hours*. The episode is titled "Death by Text: The Case Against Michelle Carter."

Massachusetts prosecuted Carter for urging her then boyfriend to commit suicide through a series of text messages and phone calls. The victim, Conrad Roy, had unsuccessfully attempted suicide several times. During their mostly long-distance relationship, Roy shared details about his suicidal thoughts with Carter. Roy researched and shared potential suicide methods with Carter. In response, Carter helped Roy plan the how, when, and where of his final suicide attempt. n the days leading up to his death, Roy and Carter exchanged numerous text messages. Carter taunted Roy for his indecisiveness and delay in killing himself. Prosecutors argued the text messages incited Roy to act:

Defendant: "You're gonna have to prove me wrong because I just don't think you really want this. You just keep pushing it off to another night and say you'll do it but you never do" . . .

Defendant: "SEE THAT'S WHAT I MEAN. YOU KEEP PUSHING IT OFF! You just said you were gonna do it tonight and now you're saying eventually. . . ." . . .

Defendant: "But I bet you're gonna be like 'oh, it didn't work because I didn't tape the tube right or something like that' . . . I bet you're gonna say an excuse like that" . . .

Defendant: "Do you have the generator?"

Victim: "not yet lol"

Defendant: "WELL WHEN ARE YOU GETTING IT"

Defendant: "You just need to do it Conrad or I'm gonna get you help"

Defendant: "You can't keep doing this everyday"

Victim: "Okay I'm gonna do it today"

Defendant: "Do you promise"

Victim: "I promise babe"

Victim: "I have to now"

Defendant: "Like right now?"

Victim: "where do I go?"

Defendant: "And u can't break a promise. And just go in a quiet parking lot or something" (emphasis added).

In seeking criminal charges against Carter, prosecutors claim that her harassing text messages and phone calls drove Roy to his death. Roy told Carter he was going to use a carbon monoxide pump and push toxic air into his truck. On the day of his death, Roy called Carter letting her know he couldn't go through with it. Carter, however, urged Roy on. Carter instructed Roy to get back into the truck. Carter apparently listened on the phone as Roy took his own life. Later, Carter emailed a friend claiming she was responsible for Roy's death, even noting that she encouraged him to go back into the truck. At no time during the exchange did Carter seek medical attention for Roy, contact the authorities or alert his family. The State of Massachusetts charged Carter with involuntary manslaughter.

Carter was convicted in a juvenile hearing and sentenced to 15 months in custody. She appealed her conviction on various grounds, including the First Amendment. The Massachusetts Supreme Court denied Carter's appeal, finding that her text messages and encouragement were not merely "speech" but unlawful conduct. The court found Carter's conduct persuading Roy to get back into the car and kill himself "reckless and wanton." It had previously found that such reckless and wanton conduct could qualify as involuntary manslaughter when done through "pressuring text messages and phone calls, preying upon well-known weaknesses, fear, anxieties and promises, that finally overcame the willpower to live of a mentally ill, vulnerable, young person, thereby coercing him to commit suicide." The Massachusetts court affirmed Carter's conviction.

As these modern cases prove, not all speech receives protection under the First Amendment. For example, speech that defames, libels, is obscene, or threatens has been ruled low-value speech by the U.S. Supreme Court and is not protected. Individuals can be sued civilly for monetary damages if they defame or libel another individual. Defamation and libel generally require a false statement of fact, not an opinion, that is published (which can mean merely spoken to another person) that causes injury to that person's reputation. Public figures, such as political leaders and certain entertainers, have less protection than ordinary individuals under defamation and libel laws. Violations against public figures require actual malice. In contrast, an ordinary factual misstatement published on social media (or reposted on social media) can constitute defamation or libel.

In addition to civil penalties, harassment can lead to criminal penalties. The federal government criminalizes "any communication containing any threat . . . to injure the person of another," 18 United States Code § 875 (c). The Supreme Court recently clarified the parameters of this statute in *Elonis v. United States*, 135 S.Ct. 2001 (2015). The decision, issued in 2015 by the Roberts Court, analyzed the criminal conviction, and nearly four-year prison sentence, of a man who had used Facebook to communicate what he characterized as rap-style lyrics. Anthony Douglas Elonis, writing under the pseudonym "Tone Dougie," posted several communications with violent undertones. Elonis allegedly targeted his coworkers, ex-wife, Federal Bureau of Investigation (FBI) agents, and an unknown elementary school with his posts. The case recounted several of Elonis's posts.

Elonis's posts regarding his wife, including a satirical posting about killing his wife, resulted in her receiving a protective order against Elonis. Thereafter, Elonis posted the following:

> Fold up your [protection-from-abuse order] and put it in your pocket
> Is it thick enough to stop a bullet?
> Try to enforce an Order that was improperly granted in the first place
> Me thinks the Judge needs an education on true threat jurisprudence
> And prison time'll add zeros to my settlement. . .
> And if worse comes to worse I've got enough explosives to take care of the State Police and the Sheriff's Dept.

At the bottom of this post was a link to the "Freedom of Speech" article on Wikipedia. A later post suggested that Elonis was willing to attack an elementary school:

> That's it, I've had about enough
> I'm checking out and making a name for myself

> Enough elementary schools in a ten mile radius to initiate the most heinous school shooting ever imagined
> And hell hath no fury like a crazy man in a Kindergarten class
> The only question is . . . which one?

Following reports of Elonis's posts to police, the FBI began monitoring Elonis's Facebook account. After the school posting appeared, FBI agents went to Elonis's home to talk with him. Once the agents left, Elonis made another violent post:

> You know your s***'s ridiculous when you have the FBI knockin' at yo' door
> Little Agent lady stood so close
> Took all the strength I had not to turn the b**** ghost
> Pull my knife, flick my wrist, and slit her throat
> Leave her bleadin' from her jugular in the arms of her partner
> So the next time you knock, you best be serving a warrant
> And bring yo' SWAT and an explosive expert while you're at it
> Cause little did y'all know, I was strapped wit' a bomb
> Why do you think it took me so long to get dressed with no shoes on?
> I was jus' waitin' for y'all to handcuff me and pat me down
> Touch the detonator in my pocket and we're all goin'
> [BOOM!]
> Are the pieces comin' together?
> S***, I'm just a crazy sociopath that gets off playin' you stupid f**** like a fiddle
> And if y'all didn't hear, I'm gonna be famous
> Cause I'm just an aspiring rapper who likes attention who happens to be under investigation for terrorism cause y'all think I'm ready to turn the Valley into Fallujah
> But I ain't gonna tell you which bridge is gonna fall into which river or road

And if you really believe this s*** I'll have some bridge rubble to sell you tomorrow [BOOM!] [BOOM!] [BOOM!]

Based on these and other postings, the federal government prosecuted Elonis under the federal statute prohibiting communications threatening another. Elonis was charged with five felony counts of violating the federal statute and convicted on four counts. He appealed based on the trial and appellate court's failure to require proof of specific intent—or mens rea—that Elonis's posts were intended to communicate an actual threat. The Supreme Court overturned Elonis's conviction but did not clarify whether the required mens rea is recklessness (that the defendant knew or should have known the language communicated an actual threat) or actual knowledge. *Elonis* nevertheless is a reminder that online harassment, even if packaged as satire or music, can result in criminal prosecution and, possibly, jail time. *Elonis* is the first Supreme Court case addressing criminal culpability for digital harassment.

The Court did not address the First Amendment's applicability as a defense to digital harassment statutes. State courts have analyzed such statutes under the First Amendment, often finding that legislatures have gone too far in suppressing speech despite their laudable desire to protect individuals against harassment. One notable example is *People of New York v. Marquan M.*, 24 N.Y.3d 1 (2014), 19 N.E.3d. 480 (2014), which was decided by the New York Court of Appeals in July 2014. The court, in striking down Albany County's antibullying statute, noted that the "problem of bullying continues, and has been exacerbated by technological innovations and the widespread dissemination of electronic information using social media sites." Nonetheless, and despite recording its disdain for the defendant's bullying tactics, the court found the county's legislation facially invalid due to its overbroad application.

In contrast, a North Carolina appellate court upheld a cyberbullying statute against a First Amendment attack, distinguishing conduct of a criminal nature from the expression of ideas. In *State of North Carolina v. Robert Bishop*, 774 S.E.2d 337, 2015 N.C. App. LEXIS 522 (2015), the North Carolina Court of Appeals analogized the North Carolina statute criminalizing "use of a computer or computer network to '[p]ost or encourage others to post on the Internet private, personal or sexual information pertaining to a minor' with 'the intent to intimidate or torment a minor' to harassment using a telephone. Both statutes targeted conduct, not speech. Thus, the North Carolina statute and the defendant's conviction (resulting in a suspended jail sentence and forty-eight months of probation) were both upheld.

Legislatures wanting to protect individuals against digital harassment must be cautious in the drafting process to ensure that enacted criminal statutes do not offend the First Amendment. Harassment may be wrong, and it may be hurtful, but it is not always illegal.

Mary M. Penrose

Further Reading

Baker, Patricia. "Sexual Harassment: High School Girls Speak Out." *Canadian Review of Sociology and Anthropology* 34, no. 1 (February 1997): 114.

Cullina, Matt. "Broadband Bullies: Homeowners Insurers Are Being Asked to Pay Damages for Social Media Harassment." *Best's Review*, November 1, 2013.

Laer, Tom Van. "The Means to Justify the End: Combating Cyber Harassment in Social Media." *Journal of Business Ethics* 123, no. 1 (August 2014): 85–98.

Levmore, Saul. *The Offensive Internet: Speech, Privacy, and Reputation.* Cambridge, MA: Harvard University Press, 2010.

"Mainstream Neglect of Sexual Harassment as a Social Problem." *Canadian Journal of Sociology* 21, no. 2 (March 22, 1996): 185–203.

Volokh, Eugene. "Freedom of Speech, Cyberspace, Harassment Law, and the Clinton Administration." *Law and Contemporary Problems* 63, nos. 1 and 2 (Winter/Spring 2000): 299–335.

See also: First Amendment to the U.S. Constitution; Obscenity; Sexting; Social media

Health care information

Identification: Healthcare records of patients that are retrievable by personal identifiers such as a name, Social Security number, or other identifying number or symbol. Most Americans believe that medical and other health information is private and should be protected, and most want to know who has this information. An individual's health care information is protected by the following major federal laws: the Privacy Act of 1974, the E-Government Act of 2002, and the Health Insurance Portability and Accountability Act (HIPAA).

The Privacy Act of 1974, 88 Stat. 1896, as amended at 5 U.S.C. 552a, protects health care information. Individuals are entitled to access to their health records and to request correction of these records under certain circumstances.

The Privacy Act prohibits disclosure of these records without the written consent of the individual patient to whom the records pertain unless one of the twelve disclosure exceptions in the act applies. The Privacy Act applies only to federal agencies and covers only records possessed and controlled by federal agencies.

The Privacy Act requires that agencies create and maintain, as necessary, system of records notices (SORNs), as defined in the Privacy Act. This system of records consists of any item, or collection of information on an individual, where the records are retrievable by the name of the individual or by some other type of identifier unique to the individual.

The E-Government Act of 2002, 116 Stat. 2899 (2002), requires federal government agencies to assess the impact on privacy for systems that collect personally identifiable information in privacy impact assessments (PIAs). All Department of Health and Human Services (HHS) PIAs can be found online.

The privacy provisions of the federal Health Insurance Portability and Accountability Act (HIPAA), 110 Stat. 1936, apply to health information created or maintained by health-care providers who engage in certain electronic transactions, health plans, and healthcare clearinghouses. The Department of Health and Human Services issued the regulation "Standards for Privacy of Individually Identifiable Health Information," which applies to entities covered by HIPAA. The Office for Civil Rights (OCR) is responsible for implementing and enforcing the HIPAA privacy regulation.

The HIPAA Privacy Rule, 45 C.F.R. § 164.500, provides federal protections for individually identifiable health information held by covered entities and their business associates, and gives patients an array of rights with respect to that information. At the same time, the Privacy Rule is balanced so that it permits the disclosure of health information needed for patient care and other important purposes. The Security Rule, 45 C.F.R. § 164.302, specifies a series of administrative, physical, and technical safeguards for covered entities and their business associates to use to ensure the confidentiality, integrity, and availability of electronic protected health information.

The Privacy Rule grants the individual rights with regard to his or her health information and sets rules and limits on who may access an individual's health information. The Privacy Rule applies to all forms of individuals' protected health information, whether electronic, written, or oral. The Security Rule requires security for health information in electronic form.

The information covered in this law includes information that doctors, nurses, and other healthcare providers place in a medical record; conversations a doctor has about the patient's care or treatment with nurses and others; information about the patient in a health insurer's computer system; and billing information about the patient at a clinic.

Most other health information about you is held by those who must follow these laws. Organizations not covered by these Privacy and Security Rules include life insurers, employers, workers' compensation carriers, most schools and school districts, many state agencies like child protective services, most law enforcement agencies, and many municipal offices. Entities covered by the law must implement safeguards to protect individual health information and ensure that they do not use or disclose individual health information improperly. Covered entities must reasonably limit uses and disclosures to the minimum necessary to accomplish their intended purpose; they must have procedures in place to limit who can view and access the health information of individuals as well as implement training programs for employees on how to protect health information.

State privacy laws in many states can be as important as HIPAA. In some states, state privacy and security law either doesn't exist or is identical to HIPAA. In most states, however, the differences between HIPAA and state privacy law require the individual to be aware of both federal and state law.

Gretchen Nobahar

Further Reading

Carroll, Jamuna. *Privacy*. Detroit, MI: Greenhaven Press, 2006.

Donaldson, Molla S. *Health Data in the Information Age: Use, Disclosure, and Privacy*. Washington, DC: National Academy Press, 1994.

HIPAA in Practice: The Health Information Manager's Perspective. Chicago, IL: AHIMA, 2004.

Hosek, Susan D., and Susan G. Straus. *Patient Privacy, Consent, and Identity Management in Health Information Exchange: Issues for the Military Health System*.

US Government Printing Office. *Protecting Our Personal Health Information, Privacy in the Electronic Age: Hearings before the Committee on Labor and Human Resources, United States Senate, One Hundred Fifth Congress, First Session Examining Standards with Respect to the Privacy of Individuals*. Washington, DC: Author, 1998.

See also: Data protection regimes; Fair Information Practices Principles (FIPPs); Health Insurance Portability and Accountability Act (HIPAA); HIV testing; Privacy Act of 1974; Privacy laws, federal; Privacy laws, state

Health Insurance Portability and Accountability Act

Identification: Health Insurance Portability and Accountability Act (HIPAA), 110 Stat. 1936. A federal statute that aims in part to protect individually identifiable health information.

Though its original primary focus was on the issues of fraud and computerization of information within healthcare, Health Insurance Portability and Accountability Act (HIPAA), is now widely recognized as the preeminent federal health information privacy law. Often heralded by privacy and patients' rights advocates, the law is nevertheless frequently misunderstood by both patients and providers. Although its reach has expanded in recent years with the passage of the Health Information Technology for Economic and Clinical Health Act (HITECH Act), 123 Stat. 115 (2009), advances in health information technology are swiftly expanding to areas not currently covered by HIPAA, causing some to question its ability to protect health information adequately in the coming years.

HIPPA requires healthcare providers, healthcare organizations, and their business associates to ensure the confidentiality and security of protected health information. The protections prescribed in the law apply to individually identifiable health information that is transferred, received, handled, or shared by these entities. HIPAA does not provide the means for individuals to sue covered entities for violations of its provisions, but it does allow individuals to file complaints with their provider or health insurer, or with the federal government. The law's rules that place duties on covered entities and their business associates are enforced by the U.S. Department of Health and Human Services's Office for Civil Rights (OCR), as well as state attorneys general.

Congress passed HIPAA in 1996. Its main purpose was to simplify and reduce administrative costs in healthcare, and to allow individuals to transfer and continue their health insurance coverage when they change or lose their job. Because these changes would result in increased use of information technology, Congress added the Privacy and Security Rules, which address the use and safeguarding of personally identifiable health information. The HIPAA Privacy Rule governs the confidentiality of protected health information, whether electronic, written, or oral, by prescribing limits on its use and disclosure without patient authorization. The Privacy Rule also gives patients the right to examine, obtain a copy of, and request corrections to their health records. The HIPAA Security Rule, 45 CFR Part 160 and 45 CFR subparts A and B, specifies certain administrative, physical, and technical safeguards that aim to ensure the confidentiality, integrity, and availability of electronic protected health information.

There are many misconceptions about HIPAA, particularly regarding who is covered by the law, with whom information can be shared, and for what reasons it can be shared. Contrary to popular belief, most employers, schools, and state and local law enforcement agencies are not considered covered entities and therefore are not subject to HIPAA. Many patients, and even healthcare providers, also do not know that the law permits disclosure of otherwise protected information for certain public health, law enforcement, and research uses.

HIPAA underwent significant changes with the passage of the HITECH Act as part of the American Recovery and Reinvestment Act of 2009 (ARRA), 123 Stat. 115. These laws contain incentives for healthcare providers to adopt electronic health records (EHRs). With the resulting expansion of electronic personal health information, HIPAA accordingly now provides for more potential liability for noncompliance and enables more enforcement by OCR, including requiring the U.S. Department of Health and Human Services (HHS) to conduct audits of covered entities and their business associates. HITECH also requires notification by covered entities to patients of any data breach involving unauthorized use or disclosure of unsecured personal health information. The law now contains increased potential civil penalties for violations, with a maximum penalty of $1.5 million per year. HITECH also now authorizes state attorneys general to enforce HIPAA.

Perhaps most notably, through HITECH, HIPAA now extends its privacy and security requirements directly to contractors, subcontractors, and other business associates who are not employees of covered entities but who nevertheless provide services that require access to patient information. Before HITECH, these business associates were only responsible for complying with HIPAA through required contracts with covered entities. Now, these business associates are directly liable under the law, greatly expanding its reach.

Even though HIPAA's reach has expanded in recent years through HITECH, many question whether its protections are keeping up with the privacy challenges presented by technological advances in healthcare. Although HIPAA's rules account for the disclosure practices of identifiable health information held by covered entities and their business associates, many other custodians of health information now operate outside HIPAA's domain. Currently, smartphone apps, wearables (for example, Fitbit), and other platforms and devices that are part of the quantified self-movement, are not subject to HIPAA. As a result, agencies beyond HHS may soon become involved in the regulation of health information. The White House's 2015 draft consumer privacy bill of rights, for example, suggested the extension of oversight by the Federal Trade Commission (FTC) into healthcare by including certain medical data in the categories of information that the Obama Administration believed should be protected by the FTC. Despite several proposals in recent years, Congress has not enacted a privacy bill of rights.

Calls have also been made to reform HIPAA to allow for more research that utilizes health information, especially research that makes secondary use of existing data. Although data that have undergone certain "de-identification" are exempt from HIPAA, many believe that such information is of limited value because the identifiable information provides essential context to researchers. Even if HIPAA does not explicitly prohibit certain uses, some researchers avoid or abandon studies as a result of the perception of the law as a burden and a barrier to effective research. If HIPAA is to serve as a means of protecting health information in the coming years, it must account for rapid technological innovation, the extension of healthcare outside the traditional hospital setting, and the resulting challenges to privacy and security.

Drew Simshaw

Further Reading

Blumenthal, David. "Launching HITECH." *New England Journal of Medicine* 362 (February 2010): 382–85.

Buckman, Deborah F. "Validity, Construction, and Application of Health Insurance Portability and Accountability Act of 1996 (HIPAA) and Regulations Promulgated Thereunder." *American Law Reports Annotated.* 194 (2004) Fed. 133.

Denison, Charles M. *Transforming Healthcare with Health Information Technology.* New York: Nova Science Publishers, 2011.

Herold, Rebecca, and Kevin Beaver. The Practical Guide to HIPAA Privacy and Security Compliance, 2d ed. Boca Raton: Auerbach Publications, 2014.

Klosek, Jacqueline. *Protecting Your Health Privacy: A Citizen's Guide to Safeguarding the Security of Your Medical Information.* Santa Barbara, CA: Praeger, 2011.

Leo, Ross. *The HIPAA Program Reference Handbook.* Boca Raton: Auerbach Publications, 2005.

Nass, Sharyl J., Laura A Levit, and Lawrence O Gostin. *Beyond the HIPAA Privacy Rule Enhancing Privacy, Improving Health through Research.* Washington, DC: National Academies Press, 2009.

Sobel, Richard. "The HIPAA Paradox: The Privacy Rule That's Not." *The Hastings Center Report,* July 1, 2007.

Terry, Nicolas P. "Protecting Patient Privacy in the Age of Big Data." *University of Missouri Kansas City Law Review* 81, no. 2 (2012): 1–31.

Tilden, Samuel J. "Health Research and the HIPAA Privacy Rule." *JAMA* 299, no. 11 (March 19, 2008): 1259.

Wu, Stephen S. *Guide to HIPAA Security and the Law.* Chicago: ABA Section of Science & Technology Law, 2007.

See also: Data breaches, Federal Trade Commission (FTC); Medical confidentiality; Wearable technology

HIV testing

Identification: Medical testing that detects the antibodies that are developed after exposure to the human immunodeficiency virus (HIV). Americans largely became aware of acquired immunodeficiency syndrome (AIDS) and HIV beginning in the early 1980s. In an atmosphere that was largely fearful and hostile toward those with HIV, AIDS and HIV-infected people were reticent to disclose their condition to their employers and others because they feared employment discrimination and the stigma associated with the disease.

AIDS is a group of diseases or conditions that indicate severe immunosuppression related to infection with HIV. HIV degrades the body's immune system by invading white blood cells, which reduces the ability of the cells to combat infection. A blood test indicates this condition along with HIV antibodies and symptoms such as fever, sudden weight loss, chronic diarrhea, or swollen glands. A person with the HIV virus will also develop antibodies to the virus.

Although HIV tests with a positive result indicate that an individual may be infected with the HIV virus, the test merely detects the antibodies that develop after exposure to the virus. A positive test result does not necessarily mean that a person will develop AIDS. These tests, however, when used together, are almost 100 percent reliable.

HIV is never transmitted through casual contact, such as by sitting next to or attending meetings with an HIV-infected coworker. HIV is found in the blood, semen, or vaginal secretions of AIDS-infected patients. HIV is most commonly transmitted through sexual contact and through sharing intravenous drug needles.

Because HIV-infected people face possible discrimination if their condition is disclosed, many of them may get tested and treated for HIV only if they are guaranteed that their results remain confidential. Both federal and state law protect the confidentiality of an individual's HIV status. The Health Insurance Portability and Accountability Act (HIPAA), 100 Stat. 1936 (1996), protects the privacy of personal health information, including HIV status. Some states have confidentiality of HIV-related information statutes forbidding the release of HIV test results without written consent, except under very limited circumstances. HIPAA thus ensures that the privacy of individuals' health information is protected while ensuring access to care. Not all HIV testing sites, however, are covered by HIPAA restrictions.

The U.S. Department of Justice Office for Civil Rights (OCR) enforces HIPAA privacy rules. HIV/AIDS patients who believe that their health information privacy rights have been violated may file a complaint with OCR.

If an individual's HIV test is positive, the testing site must report the results to the state health department so that public health officials may monitor HIV cases in a given jurisdiction. Federal and state funding for HIV/AIDS services is often allocated to areas where the need is the greatest. The state health department also removes all of personal information from the test results.

Many jurisdictions have partner-notification laws, which require HIV-positive individuals (or their healthcare providers) to inform any sex or needle-sharing partner(s). In some jurisdictions, HIV-positive individuals who do not inform their partner(s) may be committing a crime. Some health departments require healthcare providers to report the name of the patient's sex and needle-sharing partner(s) if their identity is known. Some states have duty-to-warn statutes that require clinic staff members to notify a third party if they believe that person has a significant risk for HIV exposure from a patient that the staff member knows is HIV-infected.

The HIV status of incarcerated persons may be disclosed under the Occupational Safety and Health Administration's (OSHA's) Standard for Occupational Exposure to Bloodborne Pathogens. State or local laws may also require that an individual's HIV status is reported to public health authorities, parole officers spouses, or sexual partners.

An employee may sue the employer for disclosing his or her HIV or AIDS status under various tort causes of action or under relevant state statutory law. Over the past few decades, many lawsuits have been brought alleging the unauthorized disclosures of HIV- and AIDS- related information in the employment context. Also, several states have enacted statutes addressing the issue of confidentiality of communicable disease information and confidentiality of HIV test results.

Disclosure of an employee's AIDS status may result in emotional harm to the employee and perhaps in threatened or actual violence. The unauthorized disclosure of an employee's HIV status has frequently resulted in hostile and sometimes intimidating reactions by coworkers. These incidents led to a dramatic increase in privacy-related litigation and legislation that sought to protect worker privacy or allow limited employer information gathering.

HIV-infected employees also have sued alleging various privacy tort law violations in cases where they alleged that the employer has breached a right to privacy of medical information.

Invasion of privacy claims, in the context of disclosure of HIV-related information in employment, are generally categorized as intrusion into solitude or seclusion and public disclosure of private facts.

Invasion of privacy

The U.S. Supreme Court has often invoked the constitutional right to privacy to protect individuals from public disclosure of private information. The courts have also recognized a privacy right in medical information that an employer had disclosed in the workplace. Whether a disclosure constitutes an invasion of privacy may depend on the existence or nonexistence of a person's "legitimate expectation of privacy." Courts often balance an individual's right to privacy against the right to discover relevant facts. In the employment area, this is often in balancing the plaintiff's right of privacy against the defendant's legitimate business interests. The court recognized an invasion of privacy claim asserting an "unreasonable publicity given to the life of another" in *Borquez v. Ozer*, 923 P.2d 166 (Colo. Ct. App., 1995). In *Borquez*, the employee alleged that his employer invaded his privacy when it disclosed his HIV status. The court held that the information that defendant disclosed was "not a matter of legitimate concern to the public," was "inherently private," and could "be disclosed only under narrowly specified circumstances." The court also held that it was "appropriate to recognize the tort of invasion of privacy . . . where private information was unreasonably disseminated to fellow employees who had no legitimate interest therein."

Intrusion into solitude or seclusion. To establish the tort of intrusion into solitude or seclusion, the plaintiff must prove that the defendant "intentionally intruded" into his "private affairs or concerns," and that the "intrusion would be highly offensive to a reasonable person." An inquiry about a person's HIV status or the taking of an unauthorized HIV test would likely be "highly offensive to a reasonable person" because it would "provide knowledge of the most vital details of one's present health and in some cases allow inferences about one's intimate behavior."

Public disclosure of private facts. An employee may also bring a cause of action against an employer for disclosure of private facts. To establish a claim of public disclosure of private facts based on an individual's HIV status, a plaintiff must show that private information on an individual's status was disclosed and that this disclosure would be offensive and objectionable to a reasonable person. "The information published must be private and not part of a public record and must not be information which the plaintiff has consented to have published."

In *Cronan v. New England Telephone Co.* (Mass. Super. Ct., Sept. 16, 1986), the Superior Court of Massachusetts held that the plaintiff's allegations, that his supervisor published his AIDS status to other company employees, set forth a claim that his privacy right was breached. The plaintiff alleged that defendant's disclosure was "not reasonably necessary to safeguard substantial or legitimate business interests of the Company." Following the disclosure, the plaintiff received threatening phone calls from employees promising that he would be attacked when he came back to work. The plaintiff claimed that he did not return to his job because he feared for his well-being and that the physical threats and violation of his privacy caused him severe anxiety, which substantially aggravated his physical condition.

Cronan alleged that defendants breached his right to privacy in violation of Massachusetts civil rights law. Subsequently, the parties settled out of court and the plaintiff returned to his job at New England Telephone Co., which agreed to implement an AIDS education program.

Intentional infliction of emotional distress. A plaintiff may bring a claim against his or her employer for intentional infliction of emotional distress when his or her HIV status is disclosed without his or her consent. A plaintiff must prove that the employer "intentionally committed an extreme or outrageous act" to establish a case of intentional infliction of emotional distress.

In *Sullivan v. Delta Air Lines, Inc.*, 52 Cal. Rptr. 2d 662 (Cal. Ct. App., 1996), the plaintiff sued his employer for invasion of privacy after he was terminated one year after he told a supervisor that he was infected with HIV. A jury "found that Delta had invaded Sullivan's privacy by placing his name on a roster of employees who were HIV positive" and was liable for emotional distress.

When confidential medical information about HIV/AIDS may generally be disclosed

Disclosure of HIV- and AIDS-related information may occur more commonly in certain areas of employment than in others. In the healthcare industry, for example, disclosure of an employee's HIV or AIDS status may be necessary to protect the health and safety of both healthcare workers and patients. In cases involving disclosure in the healthcare industry, a balancing approach has been used by courts, by which the healthcare workers' rights are weighed against the patients' rights. In *Estate of Behringer v. Medical Center at Princeton*, 592 A.2d 1251 (N.J. Super. Ct. Law Div. 1991), disclosure to patients that a surgeon had AIDS was held to be proper because of the nature of the relationship between the surgeon and his patients. Nevertheless, the hospital was found to have "breached its duty of confidentiality" to the surgeon by failing to take "reasonable precautions" to prevent the surgeon's medical records containing his AIDS status from becoming "a matter of public knowledge." The court decided that, while a hospital can require an AIDS-afflicted surgeon to obtain informed consent from his patients prior to performing surgery, the surgeon had a privacy interest in his HIV test results and a hospital must take "reasonable precautions" to prevent the diagnosis from becoming "a matter of public knowledge."

The court held that the medical center should have given advisory instructions to its employees about the confidentiality of HIV results, and access to the plaintiff's diagnosis should have been limited to those people who were involved in treating the plaintiff. The holding in *Behringer* established a "standard of confidentiality" for HIV tests, which makes hospitals and other healthcare employers both recognize the physician's right to privacy and enforce a patient's right to be fully informed as to any risks to which he or she may be exposed by agreeing to surgery.

In *Urbaniak v. Newton*, 277 Cal. Rptr. 354 (Cal. Ct. App. 1991), a patient's reasonable expectation of privacy in his HIV-positive status was held to have been violated where this information "had limited relevance to [his] . . . medical examination." This holding reflects the beliefs of many courts that individuals should be encouraged to disclose their HIV-positive status, which may be crucial for healthcare workers to take the necessary safety precautions. The holdings in *Estate of Behringer* and *Urbaniak* illustrate how courts balance the privacy rights of individuals with HIV/AIDS and the need for disclosure.

Many Americans continue to fear that contact with an HIV-positive individual could result in transmission. This is especially true when employees have jobs that are deemed high risk. High-risk jobs involve a high probability of AIDS transmission, unlike jobs involving casual contact. Employees have almost no rights to be informed about a coworker's HIV infection in low-risk jobs involving "casual social contact." Even in high-risk jobs, when extensive precautions are taken, there are few requirements to notify other employees that a coworker has AIDS. Precautions must be in place to maintain a safe workplace for employees and to maintain an HIV-infected employee's privacy. In most workplace situations, there is almost no chance of a transmission of AIDS. Therefore, if an employer determines that an employee is "physically able to perform the job" and concludes that the HIV/AIDS does not pose a risk to others, there is no duty to notify other employees.

If an employer becomes aware that one of its employees is HIV-positive, the employer must consider whether there exists a need to inform the employee's coworkers. If the employer chooses to disclose an employee's HIV-positive status, the employer will likely risk violating that employee's privacy rights and be subject to legal liability.

HIV testing programs

Employers who feel compelled to establish HIV testing programs for employees who perform invasive procedures or who are otherwise at risk of contracting and/or transmitting AIDS in the workplace must ensure that test results will be disclosed in a legal manner and to the fewest possible persons who need to be informed. The privacy of such results is essential because, without a guarantee of confidentiality, many individuals may not seek HIV testing and counseling.

Some employer-required HIV testing may "an intrusion and a search and seizure within the meaning of the Fourth Amendment." Mandatory AIDS testing of employees may be valid, however, if the group of employees involved was at a high risk of contracting and/or transmitting AIDS to the public. The employer must demonstrate that universal precautions and voluntary testing will not prevent the contracting and/or spread of AIDS by high-risk employees or professionals.

In *Glover v. Eastern Nebraska Community Office of Retardation,* 686 F. Supp. 243 (D. Neb. 1988), the court ruled that mandatory HIV testing for workers in a state government facility was an unreasonable search and seizure after applying "the standard which requires that 'both the inception and the scope of the involuntary intrusion into the body must be reasonable.'" The court held that the testing policy was not justified because the risk of anyone being infected with HIV was almost nonexistent.

Further Reading

Bove, Victor M. "HIV Testing of Health Care Workers. (AIDS)." *Physician Executive* 18 (May 1, 1992): 000–000.

Espejo, Roman. *AIDS.* Detroit, MI: Greenhaven Press, 2012.

Etzioni, Amitai. "HIV Testing of Infants: Privacy and Public Health." *Health Affairs* 17, no. 4 (July/August 1998): 170–83.

Etzioni, Amitai. *The Limits of Privacy.* New York: Basic Books, 1999.

Greene, Kathryn, Valerian J. Verlega, Gust A. Yep, and Sandra Petronio. *Privacy and Disclosure of HIV in Interpersonal Relationships: A Sourcebook for Researchers and Practitioners.* New York: Routledge, 2003.

Hamblen, J. W. "Preservation of Privacy in Testing." *Science* 151, no. 3715 (March 11, 1966): 1174.

Jasper, Margaret C. *Healthcare and Your Rights under the Law.* Dobbs Ferry, NY: Oceana Publications, 2002.

New South Wales Privacy Committee. *Private Lives and Public Health: Privacy Guidelines for HIV Testing.* Sydney: Committee, 1993.

Repa, Barbara Kate. *Your Rights in the Workplace,* 9th ed. Berkeley, CA: Nolo, 2010.

Rothstein, Mark A. *Genetic Secrets: Protecting Privacy and Confidentiality in the Genetic Era.* New Haven, CT: Yale University Press, 1997.

See also: Fair Information Practice Principles (FIPPs); Invasion of Privacy; Medical confidentiality; The Right to Privacy; Privacy torts

Home, privacy of the

Identification: The right enshrined in the Fourth Amendment to the U.S. Constitution to a home generally free of governmental intrusion. The Framers of the Constitution, wary of a strong central government and committed never again to allow the sorts of general warrants that were commonplace under British rule, carefully crafted the Constitution's Fourth Amendment:

The right of the people to be secure in their persons, houses, papers, and effects, against unreasonable searches and seizures, shall not be violated, and no warrants shall issue, but upon probable cause, supported by oath or affirmation, and particularly describing the place to be searched, and the persons or things to be seized.

The fifty-four words of the Fourth Amendment make clear the sanctity of the home, but the U.S. Supreme Court, except for a few missteps along the way, has always protected the privacy of the home more than the privacy of any other property. As will be illuminated later in this essay, the technologies available in the digital age have eroded some of the protections the Framers intended to protect the home.

It stands to reason that the home would be the most private and constitutionally protected space. The home is where we live our private lives, engage with our spouses and other family member, retain our personal papers, safeguard our cherished heirlooms and mementoes. The colonists and Framers wanted what we enjoy, a home generally free of governmental invasion in the absence of a judicially issued search warrant or another emergency justifying immediate warrantless entry.

A warrant to search a home is lawful only if it is issued by a neutral judge and is supported by a sworn statement containing probable cause to believe that specifically enumerated relevant evidence is inside that home. Thus, a warrant cannot be issued by a police officer acting alone and cannot be supported by whim or curiosity. Rather, a warrant to search a home must contain enough evidence in the sworn statement to lead a reasonable judge to believe the relevant criminal evidence is inside.

Unless there is an immediate danger to officers or danger of destruction of evidence known to the issuing judge, a warrant to search a home must be preceded by a knock at the front door by the officers and an announcement of their presence and purpose. The knock must be followed by an appreciable time to allow those inside to open the door for the officers. An entry without a knock is known as a no-knock entry, and a warrant preauthorizing the officers to enter without knocking is known as a no-knock warrant. Entry without a required knock violates the rule but does not typically result in suppression of the subsequently seized evidence.

Even without a no-knock warrant issued by the judge, officers at the scene can determine that a no-knock entry is required for their safety or to prevent destruction of evidence. For example, if officers executing a cocaine warrant knock and announce, and then hear those inside running to the bathroom and flushing the toilet repeatedly,

the officers can enter without any additional delay to safeguard that evidence from destruction. In another example, if officers preparing to execute a knock-and-announce warrant on a home see the main suspect entering the home with two sawed-off shotguns, the officers need not knock and announce their purpose before entering with that warrant.

Nonetheless, a close reading of the Fourth Amendment reveals that warrantless searches, even of a home, can be constitutional as long as they are reasonable. A couple of examples should suffice to sketch out the boundaries of this area. Suppose an officer walks up to a home to investigate a missing child and hears a child screaming inside, "Please help me!" It would certainly be unreasonable for the officer to drive to the police station and draft a search warrant; indeed, it would be reasonable for the officer to enter the home immediately, without a warrant, to check on the welfare of that child inside. In another example, suppose an officer walks up to a home, sees that it is engulfed in flames, and hears a neighbor saying that there are two children trapped inside. Again, it would be unreasonable to wait for a warrant and it would be reasonable to enter immediately without the warrant. These are two examples of emergencies, often referred to as exigencies, that officers can use in proper circumstances to enter a home without a warrant. Other exceptions to the warrant requirement include hot pursuit of a suspect into a home, voluntary consent to enter the home, and search of the areas in the immediate vicinity of an arrestee inside a home if the search was for officer safety or to prevent the destruction of evidence.

Of course, the definition of a home has changed somewhat since the Constitution was ratified. People live in homes of all kinds: single-family dwellings, townhouses, apartments, mobile homes on blocks, and even mobile homes on wheels. With a few minor exceptions, the law and the Constitution treat all these as homes for Fourth Amendment protection from unreasonable searches.

What is included in the home protected by the Constitution is also critical. In short, the home includes the interior of the residence; an attached garage; and the home's curtilage, that is, the area immediately surrounding a home where people are deemed to engage in private and personal activities. Law enforcement searches of any of these areas require a warrant or an exigency discussed above, unless the law enforcement observations were made of items in plain view of the officer's own senses. Officers may seize items in plain view if they are standing where any officer has a right to be and can discern the incriminating nature of the items immediately and without moving or manipulating them first. Therefore, if a homeowner invites an officer into the home and the officer sees cocaine in plain view on the table just inside the door, the officer can seize that cocaine without a warrant; the officer would know immediately that it was contraband and had a right to be inside the house where he or she saw the cocaine because the homeowner had invited the officer inside. Indeed, items viewed in a home through open windows are in plain view. And odors emanating from inside a home and out into a public space are not protected by the Fourth Amendment; the odors, once emanated, are no longer in the home and are no longer in a place of any description that might be deemed private.

The ability of officers to fly over a home has reduced the privacy of the home and its curtilage to a substantial degree. At the time of publication of this essay, the current law holds that anything that can be seen in plain view, even inside the curtilage of a home, does not require a search warrant. This is really an extrapolation of the "reasonable expectation of privacy" doctrine. In essence, that doctrine holds that no one has a right to privacy except as to those items in which one has both a subjectively and objectively reasonable belief it is private. Thus, anything in your yard that can be seen by your neighbor, someone on the adjacent sidewalk, or an officer in an airplane overhead is not private because it

is not reasonable to believe that such items are private. As more technologies intrude on privacy and as our belief in the extent of privacy declines with every new surveillance technology innovation, the Supreme Court may have to abandon the reasonable expectation of privacy doctrine.

In a related sense, people do not have a reasonable expectation of privacy in items they have abandoned. The paradigm example of this is a bag of garbage from inside a home placed out on the curb or in a container by the curb to be picked up by sanitation workers. That bag of garbage, if placed on public land and off the home's curtilage, is deemed abandoned. Officers take advantage of that by riding in garbage trucks to observe the garbage being picked up from suspect homes. Once the garbage from the suspect home is picked up by the sanitation workers, the officers ask to have the garbage turned over to them. The officers then inspect the contents looking for evidence of drug dealing or other crimes. That evidence then is written up into a search warrant as probable cause to enter the home itself pursuant to that warrant based on evidence from abandoned garbage.

Consent issues have muddied the law of warrantless searches of homes. For example, what if two persons share residency of a home, and one consents to the search and the other person objects? If one cotenant has previously refused to consent to the search, must the officers inform the other cotenant of that previous refusal to consent? Or what if cotenants each have separate lockable bedrooms in a shared residence with shared spaces for the bathroom, kitchen, and living room? In each of these circumstances, courts will strive to honor the constitutionally mandated sanctity of the home but must also balance that against each cotenants' right to admit or exclude whomever they wish from their home. It is a muddy area. The current rules allow a present cotenant to refuse entry even over another present cotenant's consent to enter, but an absent cotenant's refusal is overridden by a present cotenant's consent.

Similarly, any cotenant can consent to entry into common areas but cannot consent to entry into their cotenants' locked bedrooms. Parents, however, can consent to entry of their children's bedrooms in the parental home.

What if officers engage in a subterfuge and represent themselves as, say, electricians and ask to be allowed inside; is that valid consent? That issue is more straightforward. Consent, to be valid, must be knowing, intelligent, and voluntary. Subterfuge pierces all three requirements.

In the digital age, the privacy of the home has come under some attack. If occupants of a home use a cellphone, that cellphone is sending signals out of the home to "ping" cell towers. Using those signals, officers can triangulate the location of an unseen person holding that cellphone inside the home to an amazing degree of specificity. Heat-sensing devices can remotely determine where a person's body heat signature is inside the home. Electrical use readings can allow officers to discern whether an illicit drug-growing operation is in the home. Perhaps Congress will have to legislate the boundaries of privacy in the digital age. If we leave the boundaries of privacy to whatever technology allows, technology will eventually erode privacy out of existence when we all come to believe, subjectively, that nothing is private anymore.

Even more troubling in the digital age is that we carry with us, in our cellphones, much of what we used to leave in our homes and protected in the warm embrace of the Fourth Amendment. In our cellphones, particularly our smartphones, we hold our private correspondence, bank records, Internet activity, photographs, local and long-distance telephone history, videos, text messages, voicemails, and so on. However, that data in our cellphones is not as protected as it would be in our homes. If our cellphones are not password-protected, anyone can access the phone's contents. Even if we password-protect our cellphones, it is very easy for an expert to crack or bypass that password. Similar points

can be made about our laptop computers that we carry each day to and from work.

Cellphone emanations from phone calls placed inside a home can be tracked by stingrays, law enforcement–operated cell towers that are used solely and without a warrant to discern locations of suspects in real time. Parabolic listening devices can amplify sounds and voices inside a home that could not otherwise be heard unless one was listening inside the home. The pace of technological surveillance techniques threatens to overtake privacy unless courts and Congress step in.

Charles E. MacLean

Further Reading

Bryson, Kerry J. "The Naked Truth: Fourth Amendment Lessons from the U.S. Supreme Court: A Review of Recent Home-search Cases from the U.S. Supreme Court, including the Rettele Case from May, Where the Court Ruled That Police Didn't Act Unreasonably When They Forced Search." *Illinois Bar Journal* (2007).

Carolan, Eoin. "Surveillance and the Individual's Expectation of Privacy Under the Fourth Amendment." *SSRN Electronic Journal SSRN Journal.* http://ssrn.com/abstract=2178986.

Crocker, Thomas P. "From Privacy to Liberty: The Fourth Amendment after Lawrence." *SSRN Electronic Journal SSRN Journal.*

Ferguson, Andrew Guthrie. "Personal Curtilage: Fourth Amendment Security in Public." *William and Mary Law Review* 55, no. 4 (2014).

Heffernan, William C. "Fourth Amendment Privacy Interests." *Journal of Criminal Law and Criminology* 92, no. 1 (2001).

Jolls, Christine. "Privacy and Consent over Time: The Role of Agreement in Fourth Amendment Analysis." *William and Mary Law Review* 54, no. 5 (2013).

Lewis, Sean M. "The Fourth Amendment in the Hallway: Do Tenants Have a Constitutionally Protected Privacy Interest in the Locked Common Areas of Their Apartment Buildings? (Note)." *Michigan Law Review* (2002).

Mizell, Louis R. *Invasion of Privacy.* New York: Berkley Books, 1998.

"Protecting Privacy under the Fourth Amendment." *The Yale Law Journal* 91, no. 2 (1981): 313.

Rosen, Jeffrey. *The Unwanted Gaze: The Destruction of Privacy in America.* New York: Random House, 2000.

Solove, Daniel J. "Digital Dossiers and the Dissipation of Fourth Amendment Privacy." *SSRN Electronic Journal SSRN Journal.*

See also: Body, privacy of the; Cellphones; Consent; Fourth Amendment to the U.S. Constitution; Privacy laws, federal; Search warrants; Smartphones; USA PATRIOT Act; Wiretapping

Homeland Security, U.S. Department of

Identification: A federal cabinet-level agency created by the Homeland Security Act of 2002, 116 Stat. 2135.

On October 8, 2001, shortly after the terrorist attacks of September 11, 2001, President George W. Bush signed Executive Order (EO) 13228, which established the Office of Homeland Security, headed by the assistant to the president for homeland security. Its mission is to "develop and coordinate the implementation of a comprehensive national strategy to secure the United States from terrorist threats and attacks." Many of the functions of the Office of Homeland Security were transferred from other departments when DHS was established in 2002.

Executive Order 13228 also established the Homeland Security Council. The council is made up of the president; vice president; secretaries of Treasury, Defense, Health and Human Services, and Transportation; the attorney general, the directors of the Federal Emergency Management Agency (FEMA), Federal Bureau of Investigation (FBI), and Central Intelligence Agency (CIA); and the assistant to the president for Homeland Security. The EO was later amended to add the secretary of Homeland Security. Other White House and departmental officials could be invited to attend Homeland Security Council meetings. The council advises and assists the president with regard to all aspects of homeland security.

In November 2002, Congress passed the Homeland Security Act, which established DHS. The act delegated to the new department the mission of preventing terrorist attacks, reducing the vulnerability of the nation to such attacks, and responding rapidly should such an attack occur. To secure the United States, DHS was given key responsibilities in terrorism prevention and protective security, transportation security, border security, immigration enforcement, cybersecurity, and disaster recovery.

The act essentially consolidated within one department twenty-two agencies that had, as part of their missions, domestic security functions including: FEMA, Customs and Border Protection (CBP), Transportation Security Administration (TSA), Immigration and Customs Enforcement (ICE), and the Secret Service. This consolidation created a unified department intended to protect homeland security. The creation of DHS was the largest governmental reorganization of government in more than half a century. DHS also became the third largest federal cabinet agency.

DHS has the mission to ensure a homeland that is safe, secure, and resilient against terrorism and other hazards. Five key concepts form the foundation of the U.S. national homeland security strategy designed to achieve this vision: (1) prevent terrorism and enhance security, (2) secure and manage the borders, (3) enforce and administer immigration laws, (4) safeguard and secure cyberspace, and (5) ensure resilience to disasters.

No federal agency has greater power to develop systems of surveillance and otherwise encroach on the personal privacy of Americans than DHS. Within the enabling legislation that created DHS, the statute also created the DHS Privacy Office.

In fulfilling its mission to safeguard the nation, DHS must ensure that its activities do not illegally violate the right of Americans to their privacy. On a daily basis, law-abiding Americans are subjected to varying degrees of surveillance and other privacy intrusions. The extent of DHS and its component agencies to intrude on Americans' rights to privacy is possessed by few other federal agencies.

This includes activities ranging from screening and patting down travelers at the airport to conducting domestic intelligence and law enforcement operations, to screening Internet traffic to federal agencies' networks.

Since DHS was created, issues have consistently been raised as to whether the agency was sufficiently safeguarding Americans' right to privacy. For example, Americans have questioned the appropriateness of certain screening procedures that have been implemented to mitigate the recognized threat of terrorist attacks against commercial aviation, including TSA pat-downs and the initial deployment of screening technologies that produce revealing images of passengers. There have also been many questions about DHS's domestic intelligence programs, including whether the government was spying and collecting information on its citizens, and whether that information was about activities that are protected under the First Amendment. There have also been questions about whether DHS is adequately safeguarding sensitive and personal information that it maintains to protect the privacy of Americans.

DHS has the challenge of ensuring that proper policies and procedures are implemented to ensure in turn that all programs are operating in a manner that respects the privacy rights of Americans. In 2017, it issued an order to all federal agencies to increase the use of encryption to protect the privacy of American citizens whose records were stored by the agencies.

Internal privacy oversight and monitoring of DHS activities

When DHS was created, Congress formed the DHS Data Privacy and Integrity Advisory Committee to advise the department on issues related to personally identifiable information, data integrity, and other privacy-related matters; to ensure that its programs "do not erode privacy protections;" and to ensure that personal information is "handled in full compliance with fair

information practices as set out in the Privacy Act of 1974, 88 Stat. 1896."

To further ensure that the privacy rights of Americans were protected, Congress also created the DHS Privacy Office, which is charged with implementation privacy related to DHS action. As set out in the DHS Act of 2002 and amended by the 9/11 Commission Act of 2007 (12 Stat. 266), the DHS Privacy Office is responsible for:

1. ensuring that the use of technologies sustain, and do not erode, privacy protections relating to the use, collection, and disclosure of personal information;

2. ensuring that personal information contained in Privacy Act systems of records is handled in full compliance with fair information practices as set out in the Privacy Act of 1974;

3. evaluating legislative and regulatory proposals involving collection, use, and disclosure of personal information by the federal government;

4. conducting a privacy impact assessment of proposed rules of the department or of the department on the privacy of personal information, including the type of personal information collected and the number of people affected;

5. coordinating with the Officer for Civil Rights and Civil Liberties to ensure that

   (A) programs, policies, and procedures involving civil rights, civil liberties, and privacy considerations are addressed in an integrated and comprehensive manner; and

   (B) Congress receives appropriate reports on such programs, policies, and procedures; and

6. preparing a report to Congress on an annual basis on activities of the department that affect privacy, including

complaints of privacy violations, implementation of the Privacy Act of 1974, internal controls, and other matters.

Congress has granted the DHS Privacy Office considerable investigative authority, including access to nearly all documentation relating to DHS, the power to conduct investigations into any program or operation, the power to take sworn affidavits, and the power to issue subpoenas with the approval of the DHS secretary. In recent years, this has been systematized with annual reports on Privacy and Civil Liberties, based on a 2015 executive order, from the departments of Homeland Security, Treasury, Defense, Justice, Health and Human Services, Energy, and the Director of National Intelligence.

Most of the Privacy Office's actions have focused on privacy impact assessment for each DHS action. The DHS Privacy Office is divided into two major functional units: Privacy Compliance, and Departmental Disclosure and Freedom of Information Act (FOIA). The office has focused primarily on privacy impact assessments of privacy-invasive DHS technology acquisitions as opposed to serving as a check on actions that may have a negative impact on privacy.

The Chief Privacy Office has been criticized for failing to challenge DHS programs that many have claimed infringed on privacy rights, including fusion centers and the information-sharing environment; whole body imaging, closed-circuit television (CCTV) surveillance, and suspicionless electronic border searches. Specifically, the Privacy Office was criticized for failing to ensure that the use of technologies did not unlawfully infringe on privacy protections in the use, collection, and disclosure of personal information. DHS critics have also claimed that privacy impact assessments have no real force and have no meaningful control over DHS activities that could jeopardize privacy rights.

The DHS Privacy Office issued its First Quarter Fiscal Year 2012 Report to Congress. The report detailed DHS programs and functions that affect privacy, including privacy impact assessments and system of records notices. The report also summarized the 295 privacy compliance complaints that DHS has received between September 1, 2011, and November 30, 2011.

In 2014, the DHS Security Quarterly Report to Congress covered programs and databases affecting privacy. DHS received 964 privacy complaints between September 1, 2013, and November 30, 2013. Despite these complaints, DHS claims that most of its systems comply with Privacy Act notice requirements. The report also indicated, however, that DHS maintains several databases with personally identifiable information lacking in the required Privacy Act notices.

Examples of alleged DHS privacy violations

The following subsections discuss several specific examples when DHS was accused of privacy act violations or where the agency exceeded its mission by engaging in law enforcement actions outside its statutory mandate. DHS is a powerful department that conducts a wide range of intelligence, investigative, and law enforcement activities. Concern over the department has increased as its mission has grown broader and more amorphous over time. DHS has allegedly exceeded its mission by expanding into areas traditionally governed by state law enforcement, or areas in which government involvement.

Border protection. In 2010, a federal judge ruled against the DHS Customs and Border Protection (CBP) claim that DHS agents could not only search the electronic devices of cross-border travelers without a warrant or even reasonable suspicion, they could also seize the devices indefinitely for more invasive searches. In *United States v. Hanson*, U.S. District Judge Jeffrey White ruled that "[g]iven the passage of time between the January and February searches and the fact that the February search was not conduct[ed] at the border, or its functional equivalent, the court concludes that the February search . . . must be justified by reasonable suspicion."

Cybersecurity. In 2009, President Obama identified the basic challenge that the United States faces in terms of protecting itself from cyberattacks. While most Americans agree the government and private sector must collaborate to defend the nation's infrastructure from cyberattacks, privacy and civil liberties advocates have opposed legislation that could greatly expand DHS collection of Americans' personal information.

DHS's National Cybersecurity Protection System (NCPS) serves as an intrusion detection, analysis, information-sharing, and intrusion prevention system for civilian federal networks and identifies suspicious traffic through analysis and comparison with signatures of known threats. DHS achieves these four objectives in NCPS through three iterations of DHS's Accelerated. In 2014, the DHS inspector general identified serious problems in the development of these systems that included inadequate privacy protections in top secret computer systems. The inspector general also found that DHS's operating procedures for handling individuals' personally identifiable information did not protect that information adequately and that DHS lacked specific instructions for how analysts should handle personally identifiable information, how they should minimize usage of it when it is unnecessary, and how to protect it on a daily basis. Also, the privacy impact assessment that DHS completed on the program overstates the training their analysts received in protecting individuals' privacy. The training itself was poorly documented. It is questionable from DHS's records whether it occurred at all, and the inspector general found that, even if it did, those analysts might be unable to differentiate personally identifiable information from less- or non-sensitive data. They could have been exposed to personal data on almost every American citizen because taxpayers submit their tax returns to the Internal Revenue Service (IRS), retirees receive their Social Security checks, soldiers their salaries, and veterans receive their retirement benefits.

In 2018, cybersecurity efforts were elevated when the Cybersecurity and Infrastructure Security Agency was created within DHS. This new agency includes an officer charged with insuring privacy concerns are considered while various security needs are addressed.

Enhanced Cybersecurity Services (ECS) is DHS's cybersecurity information-sharing service. Through ECS, DHS shares many of the same threat indicators and signatures used in its NCPS with critical infrastructure owners and operators. The ECS also presents a potential privacy concern. It includes a way for private-sector participants to send suspected threat data back to USCERT on an automated basis, for analysis, if they choose. Sending such data back to DHS, however, presents privacy concerns if the data includes individuals' personally identifiable information, such as the names of a participating companies' employees or customers. For example, a local internet service provider or bank might opt in to sending data back to DHS without the consent of its customers whose personal data might be included in the data package.

Transportation safety. In some cases, TSA's technologies were challenged on the basis of privacy concerns. In 2013, TSA announced that it was removing the X-ray scanning systems that had been deployed to airports because the screening systems were producing naked images of passengers and that TSA could not ensure that it was complying with privacy guidelines. DHS had acquired 251 of these machines, which cost more than $41 million. However, these machines were reprogrammed to conform with rulings on this privacy issue, and are once again operational.

CBP was accused of pursuing warrantless searches of general aviation aircraft, and TSA engages in warrantless searches of valet parked cars at airports.

TSA conducted searches at public venues such as rail stations and transit stations, which resulted in arrests for relatively minor offenses such as drug possession. TSA also collaborated with state governments to put checkpoints on highways to perform searches of trucks for drugs and other contraband.

License plate readers and video surveillance systems. DHS provides grants to localities for license plate readers and video surveillance systems. DHS is seeking to gain nationwide access to license plate databases based on the local reader systems.

Drones. DHS provides grants to towns and cities to purchase aerial drones, and it uses a growing number of drones itself.

Stingrays. DHS offers grants to localities to purchase cell-site simulators, or International Mobile Subscriber Identity (IMSI) catchers (also known informally as stingrays because of the wide adoption of the Harris Corporation's StingRay model). Stingrays gather records of every mobile telephone call, text message, and data transfer up to a half-mile from the device. Stingrays are becoming widely used by law enforcement across the nation.

Fusion centers. Fusion centers are jointly operated by DHS and other federal, state, and local agencies. There are more than seventy fusion centers throughout the United States; they are intended to combat terrorism. They generate little useful intelligence yet cost hundreds of millions of dollars a year. These centers gather a large amount of information about Americans that is already in the public domain, and often about citizens involved in lawful political activities. A congressional committee reported in 2012 that fusion centers produced intelligence of "uneven quality—oftentimes shoddy, rarely timely, sometimes endangering citizens' civil liberties and Privacy Act protections, occasionally taken from already-published public sources,

and more often than not unrelated to terrorism." Fusion centers were also criticized for providing very little useful information in terms of opposing terrorism.

Political retribution. There have been several examples of employees at DHS or related agencies attempting to exact political retribution. In September 2015, several Secret Service agents accessed the unsuccessful job application of Representative Jason Chaffetz (R-UT) for a Secret Service job in 2003. The agents did this shortly after Representative Chaffetz, as chair of the House Oversight and Government Reform Committee, began hearings in March 2015 into misbehavior by senior Secret Service agents.

Further Reading

Brown, Cecilia Wright, Kevin A. Peters, and Kofi Adofo Nyarko, eds. *Cases on Research and Knowledge Discovery: Homeland Security Centers of Excellence.* Hershey, PA: Information Science Reference, 2014.

CW Productions, Ltd. *The United States Department of Homeland Security: An Overview,* 2d ed., edited by Richard White, Tina Markowski, and Kevin Collins. New York: Pearson, 2010.

Kettl, Donald F., ed. *The Department of Homeland Security's First Year: A Report Card.* New York: Century Foundation, 2004.

Kimery, Anthony. "As DHS stands up national vetting center, privacy issues persist, assessment says." *Biometric Update.Com.* (December 23, 2018.) biometricupdate.com/201812/as-dhs-stands-up-national-vetting-center-privacy-issues-persist-assessment-says

Marion, Nancy E., Kelley A. Cronin, and Williard M. Oliver. *Homeland Security: Policy and Politics.* Durham, NC: Carolina Academic Press, 2015.

Maxwell, Bruce, ed. *Homeland Security: A Documentary History.* Washington, DC: CQ Press, 2004. Miller, Debra A. *Homeland Security.* Detroit, MI: Green-haven Press, 2009.

Nemeth, Charles P. *Homeland Security: An Introduction to Principles and Practice,* 2d ed. Boca Raton, FL: CRC Press, 2013.

Noftsinger, John B., Jr., Kenneth F. Newbold, Jr., and Jack K. Wheeler. *Understanding Homeland Security: Policy, Perspectives, and Paradoxes.* New York: Palgrave Macmillan, 2007.

Tillman, Bob. "The Changing Political Landscape: The War on Terrorism Delays Congressional Action on Privacy, the Paperwork Reduction Act, and

E-Government. (Capital Edge: Legislative & Regulatory Update)." *Information Management Journal* 36, no. 1 (January–February 2002): 14.

Tillman, Bob. "More Information Could Mean Less Privacy: President Bush Signed the E-Government Act to Enhance Public Access to Information after Authorizing Homeland Security Legislation That May Threaten Privacy. (Capital Edge: Legislative & Regulatory Update)." *Information Management Journal* 37, no. 2 (March–April 2003).

Whitley, Joe D., and Lynne K. Zusman, eds. *Homeland Security: Legal and Policy Issues.* Chicago IL: ABA Section of Administrative Law and Regulatory practice, 2009.

See also: Cybersecurity; Drones; Electronic surveillance; Law enforcement; License plate reader system; Terrorism and privacy

Homeless people, right to privacy of

Identification: Legally defined as "[a] person who: (1) lacks a fixed, regular, and adequate nighttime residence, or (2) lives in a shelter, an institution other than a prison, or a place not designed for or ordinarily used as a sleeping accommodation for human beings" (Stewart B. McKinney Homeless Assistance Act, 108 Stat. 482 (1987)).

Every part of the United States has a homeless population who often live in public areas. Most often, the homeless live at publicly or privately operated shelters, the streets, in doorways, train stations, bus terminals, parks, subways, abandoned buildings, and loading docks. All homeless people do not have a permanent place to live and are destitute. The homeless include persons of all ages, all racial and ethnic backgrounds, the urban and rural working and nonworking poor, displaced and deinstitutionalized individuals, substance abusers, the mentally ill, AIDS victims, physically abused mothers and their children, runaway children, sexually abused adolescents, recent migrants and refugees, and veterans. Homelessness is often caused

A homeless man outside the United Nations building in New York with the American flag in the background. (By C. G. P. Grey.)

by unemployment, shortage of low-cost housing, the closing of state mental hospitals, and lack of public assistance programs.

A problem of defining privacy of the homeless

The common law right of privacy gave very little help to the homeless because it excludes homeless people through its traditional definition of privacy. Traditionally, courts have not recognized that people have a right of privacy for actions in the public sphere, despite the fact that the homeless may be using the street to do the functions that people would do in their homes. Individuals, under the traditional view, would have great difficulty in asserting the right to privacy when their actions occur in plain view and in public. In short, they are said not to have a reasonable expectation of privacy. In many cases, many have argued that a person who chooses to live on the street has willingly forfeited his or her right of privacy.

Although the homeless do not have a traditional home, they often have a home base, which is a distinct single location where one sleeps, eats, and to which one intends to return whenever he or she leaves it temporarily. The homeless may form something of a community based on issues such as weather, food, and security. They also face the daily struggle to protect themselves against the indecencies and indignities they face in their daily lives. They often create communities to safeguard their security. Many of the homeless sleep in parks or on the streets to protect their privacy.

Fourth Amendment protection for the homeless

The homeless have long lacked recognition of the constitutional right to be free from unreasonable government search and seizure of private property. While the Fourth Amendment protects "persons, houses, papers, and effects," the homeless, by definition, do not have a traditional home. Nor do the homeless live in a house as traditionally interpreted by the courts. Under this traditional view, the courts Fourth Amendment using a trespass theory, which combined with privacy rights with property rights. *Katz v. United States*, 389 U.S. 347 (1967), broadened this application by focusing decisively on privacy rights rather than property rights. This provided the homeless with a significant opportunity to assert privacy rights.

To determine whether a person has a legitimate right of privacy, courts generally use the two-part test that Justice John Marshall Harlan II articulated in his concurrence in *Katz*: (1) A person must have an actual subjective expectation of privacy, and (2) society must be prepared to recognize that expectation as objectively reasonable. Both the majority and minority opinion and Justice Harlan's concurrence acknowledge

that the Fourth Amendment protects people, not places. Although the case held that Katz had a reasonable expectation of privacy for a conversation in a public telephone booth, this test has not offered protection for tangible personal items in public. Justice Harlan said, after introducing the two-part test, that "[i]tems exposed to the public, abandoned, or obtained by consent are not protected because an individual does not have a legitimate expectation of privacy in those items." Thus, several courts decided after *Katz* held that homeless people does not have an objectively reasonable expectation of privacy for actions done in public.

One issue is that *Katz* failed to provide a clear standard for establishing legitimate expectations of privacy. *Katz* largely allows society to determine homeless individuals' Fourth Amendment rights based on expectations that it accepts as reasonable. Society deems the behavior of marginalized people as "unreasonable," however, which would deny them Fourth Amendment protection.

Some of the crucial Fourth Amendment issues affecting the homeless are: Does the Fourth Amendment protect these nontraditional homes and the person's possessions within? For example, should homeless persons who build makeshift homes on government-owned land be afforded the expectation of privacy, and subsequent

Fourth Amendment protection, usually associated with a home? Does the individual have a reasonable expectation of privacy in this makeshift home against warrantless searches and seizures?

Connecticut v. Mooney (1991)

One possible breakthrough in terms of the privacy rights of homeless people came in 1991, when the Connecticut Supreme Court decided *Connecticut v. Mooney*, 218 Conn. 85 (1991). *Mooney was* the first case in which a state high court had considered the issue of how the Fourth

Amendment's prohibition of unlawful search and seizure of a home should apply in the case of a homeless individual. In this case, a homeless man created a makeshift home under a secluded bridge abutment. The defendant made an area under the bridge into a living space, where he stored his belongings n a duffle bag and cardboard box. The court considered the issue of whether the defendant had a reasonable expectation of privacy in his makeshift home, such that his belongings, stored within the duffle bag and cardboard box, were protected by the Fourth Amendment. The court decided that Mooney had the same Fourth Amendment right to privacy as the belongings of any house or apartment dweller, even though the defendant's "house" was a public place, where anyone could enter.

The court, splitting on a 4–3 vote, said that police should have obtained a search warrant to open the duffel bag and cardboard box belonging to Mooney, who had lived under a highway in New Haven, Connecticut, until August 1987, when he was arrested on a murder charge. Mooney was convicted of murder in 1989 and sentenced to fifty years in prison. Seeking to rebut the defendant's Fourth Amendment claims, the state had argued that the defendant's possessions should be considered abandoned property and cited several cases as precedent. The Connecticut Supreme Court accepted the case on appeal, to consider the issue of whether the defendant had a reasonable expectation of privacy, recognized by the Fourth Amendment, in his makeshift home under the bridge abutment and in the closed duffle bag and cardboard box located under the bridge abutment.

The court ordered a new trial for the defendant because his personal items should not have been admitted into evidence: Their seizure violated the Fourth Amendment. Associate David M. Borden, writing the majority opinion, said, "The interior of those two items represented, in effect, the defendant's last shred of privacy from the prying eyes of outsiders, including the police. Our notions and of customs and

civility, and our code of values would include some measure of respect for that shred of privacy." The majority opinion did not rule that Mooney's place of residence, which was on public land and belonged to the state, was the equivalent of a home. No search warrant was needed to enter the premises, the court said; however, it maintained that the officer, once under the bridge and among Mooney's private possessions, should not have opened any closed containers in searching for evidence.

The court said that the police could have properly seized the defendant's duffel bag and the carton, and taken both into evidence unopened. A warrant was then required to open the containers. The court reasoned that Mooney demonstrated his intent to return to the bridge, and the area was relatively isolated and concealed by shrubbery, unlike a public restroom or a city sidewalk. Thus, the court believed that Mooney had a "reasonable expectation" that his property would not be disturbed, however, flimsy and lockable (or unlockable) their containers.

In rejecting the majority opinion, Associate Justice Robert Callaghan, wrote, "The majority has allowed the current publicity and concern for the plight of the homeless to create empathy that in turn has created bad Fourth Amendment law. The defendant did not have a reasonable expectation of privacy."

Criminalization of the homeless and privacy

The homeless are often criminalized because of their circumstances rather than any antisocial actions. The public often perceives a need of protection against them; therefore, some localities associate homeless people with crime or equate them with criminals. Many local law enforcement agencies have had a long history and practice of arresting, harassing, and otherwise interfering with homeless people for engaging in basic activities of daily life, including sleeping and eating, in the places where they are forced to live.

Some law enforcement officials would sometimes approach the homeless who are not violating the law to harass them. The police either demand to see their identification, search their belongings, or attempt to remove them from the area. Also, recent local legislation has made it even more difficult by banning camping, sleeping (including in parked cars), and often sitting or lying in public places. The Department of Justice recently issued a document indicating that such prohibitions may be "cruel and unusual punishment" because it is unconstitutional to penalize people for sleeping outside if there are not enough beds available in local shelters.

Homelessness is becoming more visible in local communities, so there is more pressure on local political leaders to take action on this matter. Often, unfortunately, they seek to resolve the social issue through criminal justice solutions. Research has indicated that investing in shelters and affordable housing is more cost-effective than using prison in managing the homeless. Both federal and state governments should invest in affordable housing and decriminalization of homelessness. For example, the federal government should invest in affordable housing at the scale necessary to end and prevent homelessness, and it should have a leadership role in fighting local government criminalization of homelessness and promoting constructive alternatives.

Homeless Person's Bill of Rights and Privacy

Many localities have laws that forbid loitering, vagrancy, sitting or lying on the sidewalk, begging, and similar behavior. Advocates for the homeless assert that these laws disproportionately affect homeless people and violate their right to privacy.

The Homeless Bill of Rights refers to legislation protecting the civil and human rights of homeless people. Among these rights is the right to privacy. States such as Rhode Island, Connecticut, and Illinois have all passed legislation

recognizing bills of rights for the homeless. Other states are considering similar legislation. The Rhode Island law states: "A person experiencing homelessness . . . has the right to a reasonable expectation of privacy in his or her personal property to the same extent as personal property in a permanent residence" (Rhode Island Bill of Rights, 34–37.1–3).

Homeless Management Information System (HMIS)

HMIS is a computerized system intended to collect client data and data on what housing and other services are provided to homeless individuals and families and persons who may become homeless. HMIS programs track recipients of benefits to assess the number of people receiving care and to improve the efficiency of services to the poor. Privacy advocates have complained that the mandatory guidelines for HMIS issued by the Department of Housing and Urban Development (HUD) are highly privacy-invasive. Under the proposed guidelines, federally supported entities that provide support for the poor, or each entity on the Continuum of Care (CoC) must:

1. gather personally identifiable information from all clients, including full legal name, date of birth, Social Security number (SSN), ethnicity and race, gender, veteran status, and the person's residence before he or she entered the program.

2. gather other private information from clients. The HMIS asks several personal questions, tracking where the clients have traveled; the services they have received; their income, benefits, disabilities, health status, pregnancy status, HIV status, behavioral health status, education, and employment; and whether they have experienced domestic violence.

3. report it regularly (at least annually) to central servers (in the state or region).

Privacy advocates argue that the HUD information requirements far exceed its underlying congressional authority and propose an expansive homeless surveillance system that endangers the privacy rights of the homeless. Gathering excessive information on homeless individuals may pose an increased privacy risk to each homeless individual. Thus, balancing the needs to collect and analyze data must be balanced with substantial privacy concerns. Privacy advocates also argue that the homeless are tracked in much the same way criminals are. They further argue that such tracking violates the fundamental rights of individuals to travel, rights to receive benefits, and personal autonomy.

Privacy advocates express concerns that the guidelines would lead to a centralized, nationwide homeless tracking system. Even if a national HMIS database is not created, the CoCs may self-organize and transcend jurisdictional lines. Under the guidelines, CoCs may create statewide or regionwide information-sharing agreements.

SSNs have long had a major role in the tracking, identification, and authentication of Americans in several different ways. To protect individuals' privacy, including the use of the person's SSN, Congress enacted the Privacy Act of 1974, 88 Stat. 1896. The statute made it illegal for a government agency to deny a right, benefit, or privilege solely because someone declines to disclose his or her SSN.

Section 7 of the Privacy Act further provides that any agency requesting an individual to disclose his or her SSN must "inform that individual whether that disclosure is mandatory or voluntary, by what statutory authority such number is solicited, and what uses will be made of it." This provision in the Privacy Act seeks to limit the use of the Social Security number to only those purposes for which legal authorization of Social Security numbers are clearly required.

Another concern of privacy advocates is that a database of SSNs presents privacy and identity theft risks to individuals enrolled in the system.

HUD should employ an alternate identity number for aid recipients. HMIS could exacerbate increasing incidence of identity theft by requiring greater use of SSNs.

Further Reading

Armijo, Lisa Marie. *The Search for Space and Dignity: Using Participatory Action Research to Explore Boundary Management among Homeless Individuals.* 2002.

FERPA and Homelessness: A Technical Assistance Tool for NAEHCY Members. Lever, Annabelle. *On Privacy.* New York: Routledge, 2012. Liebow, Elliot. *Tell Them Who I Am: The Lives of Homeless Women.* New York: Free Press, 1993.

Mooney, Linda A., and David Knox. *Understanding Social Problems,* 6th ed. Belmont, CA: Wadsworth/Cengage Learning, 2009.

Wakin, Michele. *Otherwise Homeless: Vehicle Living and the Culture of Homelessness.* Winegarten, Debra L., and Gisela J. Hinkle. *Women, Homelessness and Privacy.* 1990.

See also: Big data; Drug and alcohol testing; Fourth Amendment to the U.S. Constitution; HIV testing; Invasion of privacy; *Katz v. United States*; Law enforcement; Privacy laws, federal; Privacy laws, state

Hustler Magazine v. Falwell, 485 U.S. 46 (1988)

Identification: A unanimous decision in which the U.S. Supreme Court held that outrageousness was an insufficient test of tort liability when a case involves matters of public concern and that public figures and public officials must prove actual malice to win damages for intentional infliction of emotional distress.

In the 1980s, a political debate began swirling between the Rev. Jerry Falwell of Lynchburg, Virginia, who had achieved national prominence because of the phenomenal growth of his church and his founding of the Moral Majority, and Larry Flynt, the editor and publisher of *Hustler,* one of the country's most obnoxious pornographic magazines. Falwell had initiated a campaign against pornography in the United States, and Flynt had been a natural target. The two public figures sparred until Flynt launched an especially offensive attack at Falwell. In the November 1983 issue of the magazine, Flynt published a parody in which Falwell was featured. The inside back cover of the magazine contained what appeared to be an advertisement for Campari Liquors. The parody followed the style of an advertising campaign focusing on celebrities, in which each celebrity talked about his or her "first time" in an interview format. Double entendre gave the impression that the celebrity was talking about a first sexual experience. Readers learned at the end of each interview, however, that the celebrity was talking about the first time he or she drank Campari Liquor. The parody featuring Falwell purported to have the clergyman report that his first sexual experience was in an outhouse with his mother when they were both drunk.

Falwell learned of the publication when it was called to his attention by a journalist. He sued Flynt and *Hustler* in the U.S. District Court for the Western District of Virginia for libel, invasion of privacy, and intentional infliction of emotional distress. The judge threw out the privacy claim because Virginia does not recognize invasion of privacy as a tort. The jury found for *Hustler* on the libel claim, finding that no reasonable person would conclude that the parody contained statements of fact. The jury found for Falwell, however, on his claim of intentional infliction of emotional distress, awarding him $100,000 in compensatory damages and $100,000 in punitive damages. Both Falwell and *Hustler* appealed the case. The Fourth U.S. Circuit Court of Appeals affirmed the verdict, and the Supreme Court granted certiorari.

Chief Justice William Rehnquist, writing for a unanimous Court (Justice Anthony Kennedy did not participate, and Justice Byron White wrote an opinion concurring in judgment to the effect that *New York Times Co. v. Sullivan,* 276 U.S. 254 (1964), was not applicable to the case), recognized the important role satirists and political cartoonists have played in debates of public importance. "The art of the cartoonist," he wrote, "is often not reasoned or evenhanded, but slashing and one-sided." Cartoonists and other political commentators are often outrageous and act "with motives that are less than admirable." They are, nonetheless, protected by the First Amendment.

"Thus," Rehnquist wrote, "while such a bad motive may be deemed controlling for purposes of tort liability in other areas of the law, we think the first Amendment prohibits such a result in the area of public debate about public figures." The parody published by *Hustler,* the Chief Justice wrote, was "a distant cousin" of the great satirists of political history but was nonetheless part of political and social discourse that deserved the highest degree of protection provided by the First Amendment. In overturning the verdict, therefore, Chief Justice Rehnquist held that public figures and public officials may not recover for the tort of intentional infliction of emotional distress involving a speech-based claim without proving actual malice, that is, knowledge of falsity or reckless disregard for the truth.

While the opinion provided additional protection for speech on matters of public concern, it also raised a definitional issue on the actual malice test. Actual malice became part of tort law with the 1964 decision in *New York Times Co. v. Sullivan.* In that case, Justice William Brennan, writing for a unanimous court, held that public officials could not win libel actions based on criticisms of their public conduct unless they could prove that the publication was made with knowledge of falsity or reckless disregard for the truth. Actual malice, therefore, applied to statements of fact. In later opinions, the Court held that plaintiffs must also prove that statements upon which libel actions are based must be proved by plaintiffs to be false and that a libel action based upon statements of opinion— that is, statements that could not be proved to be either true or false—were not actionable. Therefore, the actual malice test was reserved for tort actions based on knowingly or recklessly made false publications.

Hustler magazine made it clear that the parody did not consist of statements of fact. The table of contents for the issue indicated that the inside back cover contained "Fiction; Ad and Personality Parody," and on the bottom of the page on which the parody appeared, *Hustler* reported, "[A]d parody—not to be taken seriously." The parody was not intended to be passed off as the truth, yet the Court held that for Falwell to win, he would have had to prove that it was false—a proposition that *Hustler* readily admitted.

Despite this fuzziness created around the actual malice rule, the opinion in *Hustler Magazine v. Falwell* provided significant additional protection for speech on matters of public concern, although the speech-based tort of intentional infliction of emotional distress was weakened in the Supreme Court's ruling in *Snyder v. Phelps*, 562 U.S. 443 (2011).

W. Wat Hopkins

Further Reading

Hopkins, W. Wat. "*Snyder v. Phelps* and the Unfortunate Death of Intentional Infliction of Emotional Distress as a Speech-Based Tort." *Journal of Media Law and Ethics* 3, no. 3/4 (Summer/Fall 2012): 1–36.

Post, Robert C. "The Constitutional Concept of Public Discourse: Outrageous Opinion, Democratic Deliberation, and *Hustler Magazine v. Falwell*." *Harvard Law Review* 103 (1990): 601–686.

Smolla, Rodney. "Emotional Distress and the First Amendment: An Analysis of *Hustler v. Falwell*." *Arizona State Law Journal* 20 (January 1, 1988): 423–474.

Smolla, Rodney. *Jerry Falwell v. Larry Flynt: The First Amendment on Trial*. New York: St. Martin's Press, 1988.

See also: First Amendment to the U.S. Constitution; Invasion of privacy; *New York Times Co. v. Sullivan, Abernathy, et al.*; Privacy laws, federal; Privacy laws, state; Privacy torts

Identity theft

Identification: The most frequent consumer complaint reported to the Federal Trade Commission (FTC), a relatively new crime that is often perpetrated through various familiar crimes, such as forgery; counterfeiting; and check, credit, and computer fraud.

Identity theft continues to grow. In 2016, 15.4 million people were victims of identity theft, up from 2015's figure of 13 million, according to Javelin's *2018 Identity Fraud Study*. The losses from identity theft totaled $16.8 billion. Part of this increase is due to some significant changes in data breaches. According to the FTC's *Consumer Sentinel Data Book*, in 2017 almost a third of U.S. consumers were notified of a breach, an increase of 12 percent from 2016. For the first time, Social Security numbers (35%) were compromised more than credit card numbers (30%).

The National Crime Victimization Survey (NCVS) defines identity theft as (1) unauthorized use or attempted use of an *existing* account, (2) unauthorized use or attempted use of personal information to open a *new* account, and (3) misuse of personal information for a *fraudulent purpose*.

The term *identity theft* did not appear in federal laws until 1998. Prior to 1998, crimes related to identity theft were charged under late nineteenth- century "false personation" statutes. False personation refers to impersonating another individual, such as a police officer or

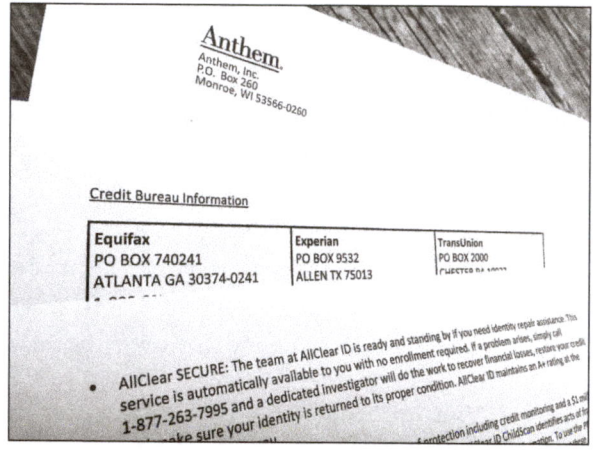

Anthem breach notification. (By Tony Webster from San Francisco, California.)

other official, and does not have the financial connotations that the term *identity theft* now carries. The late 1990s saw a staggering increase in reporting on identity theft. TransUnion, one of the three major national credit bureaus, reported that the total number of identity theft inquiries to its fraud department rose from about 35,000 in 1992 to almost 523,000 in 1997. While these numbers did not indicate what percentage of the inquiries were actual identity thefts, they did indicate a growing concern on the part of consumers. In 1998, Congress responded to these growing numbers and passed the Identity Theft and Assumption Deterrence Act, 112 Stat. 3007, making identity theft a federal crime. It expanded 18 U.S.C. § 1028, "Fraud and related activity in connection with identification documents," to make it a federal crime to "knowingly transfer or use, without lawful authority, a means of identification of another person with the intent to commit, or to aid or abet, any unlawful activity that constitutes a violation of Federal law, or that constitutes a felony under any applicable State or local law."

According to the Office for Victims of Crime, the Identity Theft and Assumption Deterrence Act accomplished four things:

- Identity theft became a separate crime against the person whose identity was stolen. Previously, victims were defined as those who had financial losses, so the emphasis was on banks and other financial institutions rather than on individuals.
- It made the FTC the federal government's point of contact for reporting instances of identity theft by creating the Identity Theft Data Clearinghouse.
- Criminal penalties for identity theft and fraud were increased, providing for up to fifteen years' incarceration as well as substantial fines.
- It closed loopholes so it became a crime to steal another person's identifying information. Previously, it was a crime only to produce or possess false identity documents. The act has been updated several times. The Identity Theft Penalty Enhancement Act of 2004, Pub. L. 108–275 § 1028A, established penalties for aggravated identity theft, which is when a stolen identity is used to commit felony crimes, including immigration violations, theft of another's Social Security benefits, and acts of domestic terrorism.

The Identity Theft Enforcement and Restitution Act of 2008 amended 18 U.S.C. § 3663(b) to clarify that restitution for identity theft cases may include the value of the victim's time spent repairing harm from the identity theft. It also allows federal courts to prosecute even if the criminal and the victim live in the same state.

Under the previous law, federal courts had jurisdiction only if the thief used interstate communication to access the victim's information. In addition to the federal laws, state laws help victims of identity theft. Because most crimes are prosecuted at the state level, the Identity Theft Resource Center has a list of state-specific laws that deal with identity theft.

Evolving targets

Identity thieves continue to target individuals, but in recent years they have also used security flaws to break into retailer and other databases to steal personal and financial information. For instance, in 2017 Equifax, one of the three credit reporting agencies, was breached. As of March 2018, over 148 million people had credit card, driver's license, Social Security numbers and other personal information compromised. The data breach was so massive, the FTC devoted a web page to it: www.ftc.gov/equifax-data-breach. The breach went undetected for 76 days and Equifax waited another six weeks to disclose it.

In May 2018, President Trump signed a bill that made freezing your credit easier and requires the three credit agencies to share fraud reports among themselves. However, a September 2018 report issued by the U.S. General Accounting Office (GAO) which investigated the Equifax breach indicated that there were still many unresolved issues and sensitive data remains at risk.

Selling large collections of account information on the black market to thieves who then use the information has become lucrative. It is extremely difficult to identify the perpetrators in these data breaches; when they then sell the stolen data to third parties, the waters become even more muddied.

For instance, in December 2013, in the final shopping days before Christmas, the department store Target had the credit and debit card information of 40 million customers stolen. While Target's security software set off alarms when the offending malware was uploaded, it was not fully investigated. Because the breach was not identified quickly, additional personal information, including email and mailing addresses, for about 70 million people was compromised. The same Eastern European group that attacked Target is also suspected in breaches at Neiman Marcus and Michaels. Millions of people had to cancel and replace their credit and debit cards; many also became victims of identity theft due to the breach.

In August 2014, the *New York Times* reported that a Russian crime ring had assembled the largest known collection of stolen Internet information, including 1.2 billion username and password combinations and more than 500 million email addresses. So far the information has been used only to send spam, for which the group collects a fee.

Another method identity used by thieves to steal money is tax fraud. The Internal Revenue Service (IRS) publishes an annual list of its so-called dirty dozen tax scams. In 2011, only one involved identity theft. By 2015, about one-quarter of all IRS criminal investigations focused on identity theft.

In 2015, the IRS itself became a victim of an online attack that stole personal information, including Social Security numbers, and diverted tax refunds from over 610,000 taxpayers. The breach occurred through a new online service that provided access to past tax returns. The stolen data was subsequently used to file fraudulent tax returns totaling about $39 million. The IRS believes the identity thieves are part of a criminal group from Russia.

The IRS's attempts to modernize and increase taxpayer convenience with online resources highlight the challenge any business faces—how to outpace criminals, provide online convenience, and still keep data secure. The IRS is an interesting combination of old and new in this respect, and some of its seemingly outdated practices actually serve a protective function. For instance, the IRS communicates with taxpayers only by snail mail; it never initiates any contacts by phone or email. Commissioner John Koskinen acknowledged, at a Tax Policy Center conference, that the agency's database software is so old that hackers do not have the programming knowledge to break in.

Methods of stealing data

Both low- and high-tech methods are used to steal personal information, although recent years have seen growth in scams resulting from our increasing use of computers, including email and the Internet. Low-tech methods include purse snatching or digging through trash, known as Dumpster diving. High-tech methods use technology to acquire information, such as phishing e-mails, spyware, and malware. According to Verizon's annual *Data Breach Investigations Report,* the majority of computer hacks occur because people click on links in emails, companies do not apply patches to software flaws in a timely fashion, and computer systems are improperly configured (which includes failure to install updated security software).

Scams that occur through email are called phishing. Phishing scams target people by sending an email that seems to be from a trustworthy source, such as a well-known store or a bank. It asks the recipient to enter personal information, often indicating that there is a problem with an account, or enticing the recipient with coupons or other gains. Once the phishing target has entered his or her personal information, the scammer can use it to open new accounts or access existing accounts. Emails and pop-up messages that request personal and financial information should be viewed with suspicion; calling a business or contacting it through its official website to verify the request can help keep personal information safe. Many institutions, such as the IRS, have policies where they do not ask for personal information through email. Malware is short for "malicious software."

There are many types of malware, including viruses and spyware, that can steal personal information; use a computer for unauthorized activities, such as sending spam; or cause damage to a computer. Computers without security software are especially vulnerable to malware attacks. Spyware is another type of malware that records your computer use. It is often used to display targeted advertisements, redirect Internet surfing to certain websites, monitor Internet surfing, or record keystrokes to obtain passwords and other personal information. Malware can infect your computer in a variety of ways, and antivirus software is constantly struggling to identify and protect against the most recent malware.

Buying and selling data

An entire industry exists to acquire and sell stolen personal data. The *Christian Science Monitor* reported that black market forums and stores that trade in stolen personal information were increasing. With names like Rescator, Republic of Lampeduza, McDumpals, and Blackstuff, they sell stolen Social Security numbers, bank account information, credit card data, and other personal and financial information. They also offer hardware and malware meant to steal this type of information.

In July 2015, a hacking forum called Darkode, which allowed users to buy and sell cybercrime tools and services such as malware, spam services and other items, was infiltrated by the Federal Bureau of Investigation (FBI) and dismantled. Twenty-eight people were arrested, and twelve were charged as a result of international law enforcement efforts involving twenty countries. Indictments included charges such as authoring and selling malware to steal bank account credentials, selling access to botnets (a group of compromised computers used to send spam and other malware), and money laundering.

The only way to become a member of Darkode was to convince existing members of the value of the abilities or products that an individual could bring to the forum. Membership had to be approved by the other members. Just weeks after the indictments, however, Darkode was ready to reopen with a different domain suffix (Darkode.cc instead of the original Darkode. me). Most of the staff members appeared to be untouched by the arrests, and the forum implemented even more stringent membership requirements to keep out informants.

A report entitled *Markets for Cybercrime Tools and Stolen Data* by RAND Corporation predicts that the future will see an expansion of darknets, in terms of both numbers and activity. It also anticipates that, while greater attention will be paid to encrypting and protecting communications and transactions, the ability to generate successful cyberattacks will likely outpace the ability to defend against them. "Crime will increasingly have a networked or cyber component, creating a wider range of opportunities for black markets; and that there will be more hacking for hire, as-a-service offerings, and brokers."

The report says that there is disagreement on who will be the target of the black market (e.g., small or large businesses, or individuals), what products will be on the rise in the black markets (e.g., fungible goods, such as data records and credit card information; nonfungible goods, such as intellectual property), and which types of attacks will be most prevalent (e.g., persistent, targeted attacks; opportunistic, mass smash-and-grab attacks).

Identity protection services

As the black market that facilitates identity theft grows, so does another market—companies that offer protection against identity theft. The increasing number and size of data breaches causes concern and is fueling a growth in identity protection services from companies such as LifeLock, ezShield, and IdentityForce. In 2015, consumers spent $3.8 billion on identity protection services, an 18 percent increase from the previous year, according to Javelin Strategy & Research. These services may check to see if customer data is being bought and sold on darknets or other places that are difficult for an average person to access. Another possible benefit of such a service may be the remediation services some offer in case of theft. It is a great deal of work to repair the damage once an identity has been stolen. While an individual can do it, having assistance may make a difficult situation easier. Some insurance companies, banks, and employers offer these services for little or no cost.

It appears that the companies that are looking to help prevent identity theft, however, are not without their own problems. In a suit against LifeLock, the FTC asserted that, from 2012 to 2014, the company failed to alert customers as soon as their identities were used by thieves and also failed to protect data with the same high-level safeguards used by financial institutions, both claims the company has made to its customers. The company has since settled the lawsuit with the FTC.

Another concern about identity theft and the need for protection services is that it may not be as dire a problem as it appears in recent news. The *New York Times* reported that it is the type of data stolen that actually determines the seriousness of a data breach. The theft of Social Security numbers can allow thieves the opportunity to open new accounts in the victim's name, a particularly damaging type of identity theft. These types of theft are also difficult to discover and fix before significant damage occurs. Many times, however, large breaches expose data that is available through other, legal means, such as email and home addresses, or information that is shared willingly, such as through social media. The size and surreptitious nature of the breach are alarming and leads to concern, even though breaches of this type of data do not often lead to crimes of identity theft. The *Times* reported that, according to the American Bankers Association, the largest expense that occurred from the 2013 Target breach was the cost of reissuing compromised debit and credit cards and assisting affected customers. Also, merchants and banks, rather than individual consumers, generally bear the financial cost of stolen credit card

numbers. Because of their interest in keeping these losses to a minimum, banks and merchants are investing in better ways to find and prevent fraudulent purchases.

The government is taking the increased reporting of identity theft seriously. An entire FTC website, www.identitytheft.gov, has been created to assist those dealing with identity theft. It offers step-by-step advice on detecting identity theft, as well as how to repair the various types of damage that may be the result. The FTC also provides resources on their website for law enforcement, attorneys assisting victims of identity theft, and businesses trying to prevent future data breaches.

Noëlle Sinclair

Further Reading

Abagnale, Frank W. *Stealing Your Life: The Ultimate Identity Theft Prevention Plan*. New York: Broadway Books, 2008.

Ablon, Lillian, Martin C. Libicki, and Andrea A. Golay. *Markets for Cybercrime Tools and Stolen Data*. Santa Monica: RAND Corporation, 2014. http://www.rand.org/pubs/research_reports/RR610.html.

Bureau of Justice Statistics. "Victims of Identity Theft, 2016." bjs.gov. Last modified February, 2019. https://www.bjs.gov/index.cfm?ty=pbdetail&iid=6467.

Copes, Heith, and Lynne M. Vieraitis. *Identity Thieves: Motives and Methods*. Boston: Northeastern University Press, 2012.

Hastings, Glen, and Richard Marcus. *Identity Theft, Inc.: A Wild Ride with the World's #1 Identity Thief*. New York: The Disinformation Company, 2006.

Hoofnagle, Chris Jay. "Identity Theft: Making the Known Unknowns Known." *Harvard Journal of Law and Technology* 21, no. 1 (2007): 97–122.

McNally, Megan. *Identity Theft in Today's World*. Santa Barbara, CA: Praeger, 2012.

Poulsen, Kevin. *Kingpin: How One Hacker Took Over the Billion-Dollar Cybercrime Underground*. New York: Broadway Paperbacks, 2011.

Verizon. "2018 Data Breach Investigations Report." Verizonenterprise. com. Last modified February, 2019.

See also: Computers and privacy; Consumer privacy; Credit and debit cards; Cybersecurity; Dark web; Data harvesting; Data science; Health care information; Malware; Marketing; The Right to Privacy; Spam; Spyware.

In re iPhone Application Litigation, 844 F.Supp.2d 1040 (E.D. Cal. 2012)

Identification: The consolidated litigation over the collection and use of the personal information of users of Apple Inc.'s iPhone, iPad, and iPod products, or iDevices. The litigation unfolded over the period from 2010 to 2012.

Privacy advocates objected after British computer experts discovered that Apple's iPhones and iPads had been tracking user movements since 2010. A feature on these Apple devices logs Global Positioning System (GPS) coordinates of users to the nearest mobile tower, along with timestamps, in a secret file on the devices, as well as any computer they connect to. Thus, Apple made it possible for anyone to obtain detailed knowledge of the user's movements.

In December 2010, two separate parties of iPhone, iPad, and iPod users sued Apple, alleging that certain Apple software applications were disseminating personal user information to third-party application developers to collect, transmit, and otherwise use personal identifying information from iPhone and iPad users without user consent. The individual cases were consolidated in the U.S. District Court for the Northern District of California, San Jose division, as *In re* iPhone Application Litigation. Courts consolidate cases to eliminate duplicative discovery, prevent inconsistent pretrial rulings, and conserve the resources of the parties and the judiciary. Other defendants, including Google, were joined in the lawsuit. The plaintiffs asked the court to prohibit the dissemination of user information without consent and financial compensation. They asked for damages for breach of privacy, among other claims.

The plaintiffs alleged that Apple designed its devices to let mobile advertising and analytics companies, such as Google, collect personal data through free app downloads. Among the information gathered were user gender, age, and zip code. The plaintiffs argued that, although Apple provided the apps in this case for free, they did pay a price in the sense that Apple-approved apps allowed personal data to be collected from the devices in question. Apple made the somewhat contradictory argument that it took precautions to protect consumer privacy, even while it turned over consumer data to app makers.

In April 2011, Apple agreed to change its developer agreement to prevent user data from being transferred to third-party app developers except if the information was needed in order to ensure the app's functionality. The plaintiffs, however, alleged that Apple failed to implement the agreement meaningfully because it faced opposition from advertisers.

Congress conducted hearings on the device privacy issue. Some members argued that commercial storage and usage of location information without a consumer's express consent was illegal under existing law. Apple responded to congressional concerns by claiming that it was not subject to the same privacy rules as telecommunication carriers, and thus the rule did not cover iPad and iPhone data collection. It also claimed that its voluntary practices met the same standards. Section 222 of the amended Telecommunications Act of 1996, 110 Stat. 56, prevents phone and cable companies from sharing certain user data with third parties, such as marketers.

On May 9, 2011, Apple defended its use of customer tracking. Contradicting earlier statements, Apple representatives claimed that a software glitch had caused iPhones to continue to send anonymous location data to Apple servers, even after the location service had been disconnected.

In September 2011, Judge Lucy H. Koh, for the District Court, dismissed the case because the plaintiffs had failed to state a legally cognizable claim. The court also gave the plaintiffs leave to amend their complaint. The court ruled that, without a showing of damages recognized under existing law, the plaintiffs had not demonstrated that the defendants had in fact injured them. The plaintiffs were prevented from pursuing their claim in the absence of a federal privacy law that allows for compensatory damages for breach of privacy. The victims of data breaches faced a similar dilemma because breaches could not be shown to have inflicted actual damages under existing law. Therefore, under existing federal law at the time, the court found that damages could not be awarded.

Further Reading

Abramson, Shelton, and Mali Friedman. "Key Holdings in the In re iPhone Application Dismissal Order." *InsidePrivacy*, June 18, 2012. http://www.insideprivacy.com/advertising-marketing/district-court-dismisses-stored-commuications-act-and-wiretap-act-claimsagainst-apple-for-iphone-da/.

Balasubramani, Venkat. "Judge Koh Whittles Down iPhone App Privacy Lawsuit—In re iPhone Application Litig." Technology and Marketing Law Blog, July 4, 2012.

Chen, Brian X. *Always On: How the iPhone Unlocked the Anything-Anytime-Anywhere Future—and Locked Us In*. Boston, MA: Da Capo Press, 2012.

Lashinsky, Adam. *Inside Apple: How America's Most Admired—and Secretive—Company Really Works*. New York: Business Plus, 2012.

Smallwood, Robert F. *Information Governance: Concepts, Practices, and Best Strategies*. Hoboken, NJ: Wiley, 2014.

See also: Apple, Inc.; Apps; Data breaches; Global positioning system (GPS) tracking; Google; Marketing; Metadata

Information Awareness Office (IAO)

Identification: An office established within the Defense Advanced Research Projects Agency (DARPA) following the 9/11 terrorist attacks. Adopting the motto *scientia est potentia* ("knowledge is power"), the IAO sought to develop technology that would improve information gathering and analysis, thereby resulting in earlier identification of threats and the prevention of terrorist activities within the United States. It also hoped to enhance the sharing of information and expertise between various governmental and law enforcement agencies.

The IAO began its work in January 2002 under the leadership of John Poindexter, who served as the National Security Adviser during the Reagan administration. Poindexter's appointment as the director of the IAO was controversial because of his role in the Iran-Contra affair in the 1980s, in which sales of arms to Iran were used to finance rebels fighting in Nicaragua. His involvement in the affair resulted in five felony convictions, but all were reversed on appeal in *United States v. Poindexter*, 951 F.2d 369 (D.C. Cir. 1991).

The IAO pursued a variety of initiatives, some of which focused on the gathering and analysis of information, while others focused on data security measures, including Genisys, intended to integrate data from various underlying databases; Genisys Privacy, developed to prevent the unauthorized access and misuse of data through the use of algorithms; Evidence Extraction and Link Discovery, an effort to differentiate between legitimate activities and credible threats based on recognized patterns; MisInformation Detection, launched to identify inconsistencies within data and separate potentially unreliable data and instances of intentional misinformation; Human Identification at a Distance, expected to use facial recognition, gait, and other physical characteristics to identify individuals from up to 500 feet away in assorted weather conditions and circumstances, such as in large groups; and Activity, Recognition, and Monitoring, a program to identify and classify suspicious activity through the analysis of human movement, individually or within crowds.

All of these initiatives supported the IAO's key project, a controversial initiative called Total Information Awareness (TIA). Spokesperson Jan Walker described the program as a "prototype system to revolutionize the ability of the United States to detect, classify and identify foreign terrorists, and decipher their plans, and thereby enable the U.S. to take timely action to successfully pre-empt and defeat terrorist acts." TIA was to rely on the data mining of telephone records, banking transactions, tax and health records, travel documents, email messages, and similar records and activities to identify patterns and relationships.

Proponents argued that TIA would automate low-level analytical functions so that humans could focus on higher level analysis of the threats and patterns TIA identified. Privacy advocates critical of the initiative expressed concerns, however, that it would bypass Fourth Amendment search and seizure protections and result in domestic spying on ordinary U.S. citizens for uses that extended well beyond counterterrorism efforts. Another concern was the possibility that citizens' personal data could be hacked by unauthorized users.

The project was renamed Terrorism Information Awareness in early 2003 in an effort to quell privacy concerns, but criticism persisted, and in May of that year Congress required the IAO to submit a report on the agency's activities. In that report, the IAO addressed concerns by stressing that TIA would operate within the confines of existing federal laws and not expand the types of underlying data to which the government has access, that security measures would be implemented to prevent hacking, and that any agency making use of TIA would need to conduct a predeployment review to ensure that the agency's contemplated use would be consistent with current laws.

On October 1, 2003, President George W. Bush signed the Fiscal Year 2004 Defense Appropriations Act, 117 Stat. 1054 (2003), which eliminated funding for TIA and disbanded the IAO. Four noncontroversial IAO programs remained within DARPA, "two to develop software for wargaming future terrorist attacks and the response to them, a project to speed detection of bioterror attacks, and one to develop software that automatically translates foreign documents and broadcasts." Some of the more controversial IAO programs were not completely dismantled but were instead transferred into the classified intelligence budget.

Rebecca Lutkenhaus

Further Reading

Associated Press. "Pentagon's 'Terror Information Awareness' Program Will End." *USA Today*, September 25, 2003.

Harris, Shane. "TIA Lives On." *National Journal* 38, no. 8 (2006): 66–67.

Lee, Newton. *Counterterrorism and Cybersecurity: Total Information Awareness.* 2nd ed. Cham: Springer, 2015.

Markoff, John. "Pentagon Plans a Computer System That Would Peek at Personal Data of Americans." *New York Times*, November 9, 2002.

Stevens, Gina Marie. *Privacy: Total Information Awareness Programs and Latest Developments.* New York: Novinka Books, 2003. Excerpted from CRS Report No. RL31730.

Stevens, Gina Marie. *Privacy: Total Information Awareness Programs and Related Information Access, Collection, and Protection Laws.* Washington, DC: Congressional Research Service, 2003. CRS Report No. RL31730: http://fas.org/irp/crs/RL31730.pdf.

US Department of Defense. *Report to Congress Regarding the Terrorism Information Awareness Program: In Response to Consolidated Appropriations Resolution, 2003, Pub. L. No. 108–7, Division M, § 111(b).* Washington, DC: Defense Advanced Research Projects Agency, 2003. https://epic.org/privacy/profiling/tia/may03_report.pdf.

See also: Data harvesting; Fourth Amendment to the U.S. Constitution; September 11; Terrorism and privacy

Informative asymmetries

Identification: Relationships in which one party has insider knowledge that the other party (or parties) does not have. This knowledge benefits the first party until it comes to light that he or she has insider knowledge, at which point the other side loses trust or confidence in the relationship.

In economics, the concept of informative asymmetries was first used to describe the phenomenon of insider knowledge and the resulting market collapse that it can cause should the general public begin to suspect the asymmetry. An often-cited example by George Akerlof outlines informative asymmetries in the used car market that are not present in the new car market because neither the buyer nor the seller has experience with the new car. In the used car market, the seller has prior knowledge of the car he is selling and is more likely to retain a "good" car until he can get a good price for it, whereas he will try harder to sell a "bad" car (a lemon) because getting rid of the lemon will increase the average value of the rest of his stock, and he will get a better price for the car than it is worth. Over time, buyers will catch on that there is a chance they might be sold a lemon, and they will be unwilling to pay previously higher prices for any of the used car salesperon's stock. In turn, the used car salesperson will be even less likely to sell good cars because now the price that people will pay is lower than before. The suspicion of dishonesty drives the price down, and as the price is driven down, worse cars replace better cars that are for sale.

Informative asymmetries can be found in numerous relationships beyond buyer-seller transactions, including those between employers and job seekers, health insurers and health insurance purchasers, governments and their citizens, small entrepreneurs and crowdfunders, and myriad others. Whenever a person has advantageous knowledge that other people do not have, an information asymmetry exists. The dynamic can be and often is present in any relationship in which one side values something the other has. Problems occur when one side understands there is a possibility that the other side is not presenting itself honestly, in which case the value of the product, reputation, message, or other unit of value from the questionable side decreases in the view of the other. Because insider knowledge is beneficial to a person for as long as it is generally unknown that he has that knowledge, he might go to great lengths to keep secret the fact that he has insider knowledge. This can be seen in company policies discouraging employees from discussing their salaries, which can uncover pay inequities between employees that were previously unknown to those employees. These kinds of revelations can decrease the trust employees might put into their employers. Inversely,

employers know that employees who are less than qualified for the job would have motivation not to present themselves completely honestly in interviews, which is why employers ask for references and use the Internet to search for more information about applicants.

In situations where an employer is looking to hire a new employee, or an insurance company is evaluating a prospective policyholder, the employers and the insurance companies are aware that there is an information asymmetry benefiting the candidate. More specifically, a job applicant usually knows more about his abilities than the company, and a health insurance candidate usually knows more about his own health than the insurer. Historically, employers, medical insurers, and other organizations that take a risk when contracting with someone have looked for characteristics from which they can generalize about the person, such as where the candidate went to school; whether they smoke; their race, gender, or age; their BMI; and so on. With the existence of the Internet and data-collection companies, it is easier than ever for organizations to gather information about individuals that those individuals did not choose to disclose, giving the organization an advantage for as long as that asymmetry is not known to the candidate. Through social media and other Internet gadgets, people give information about themselves more freely than they used to. The amalgamation of information people release reveals a picture that these people might not have intended to give to anyone. However, the information people give to these sites and via apps can be shared with advertisers, the federal government, hackers, or other groups, enabling yet another, potentially severe information asymmetry.

Some informative asymmetries exist between different socioeconomic classes, enabling better advantaged classes to attain more influential positions in society. Their insider knowledge is kept stratified within their own circles by means of connections between friends and acquaintances, who tend to have similar backgrounds, or through professional organizations, fraternities, alumni associations, clubs, and the like. Those who do not belong to those circles may or may not perceive that people from those circles seem to attain social and economic achievements consistently, such as high positions in government or in corporations. Lightfoot and Wisniewski detail a history of secret societies and the preponderance of their members in positions of power, showing that there has long been a link between secrecy and influence. Many U.S. congressmen and presidents were Freemasons, while the corporate membership group American Legislative Exchange Council (ALEC) that crafted model legislation to benefit corporations was kept under wraps until its exposure in 2013.

Lightfoot and Wisniewski describe how the informative asymmetries model also applies to the totalitarian state, mentioning Eastern Europe before the end of communism as the prime example. In this case, the valued commodity is public opinion; to capture "good" opinions and thus votes, the state officials carefully control the information they release. They exert their influence over press outlets, public schooling, and other influencers of public opinion. More subtle and perhaps more successful are the methods of the United States and other countries in secretly collecting information by going to corporations who routinely collect customer data. The information asymmetry created is huge, and ordinary people are still surprised and dismayed to learn about the ways that data about themselves are collected.

Sarah Green

Further Reading

Akerlof, George A. "The Market for 'Lemons': Quality Uncertainty and the Market Mechanism." *The Quarterly Journal of Economics* 84, no. 3 (1970): 488–500.

Bennett, W. Lance. *News: The Politics of Illusion*, 9th ed. Chicago, IL: University of Chicago Press, 2011.

Goldenberg, Suzanne, and Ed Pilkington, eds. "State Conservative Groups Plan US-Wide Assault on Education, Health and Tax." *Guardian* (New York), December 13, 2013.

Herman, Edward S., and Noam Chomsky. *Manufacturing Consent: The Political Economy of the Mass Media.* New York: Pantheon, 2000.

Lightfoot, Geoffrey, and Tomasz Piotr Wisniewski. "Information Asymmetry and Power in a Surveillance Society." *Information and Organization* 24, no. 4 (2014): 214–235.

Lyon, David. *Surveillance Studies: An Overview.* Malden, MA: Polity, 2007.

Pasquale, Frank. *The Black Box Society: The Secret Algorithms That Control Money and Information.* Cambridge, MA: Harvard University Press, 2015.

Stiglitz, Joseph E. "Information and the Change in the Paradigm in Economics." *American Economic Review* 92, no. 3 (2002): 460–501.

Tomboc, Gmeleen Faye B. "The Lemons Problem in Crowdfunding." *John Marshall Journal of Information Technology & Privacy Law* 30, no. 2 (2013): 253–279.

See also: Consumer privacy; Data harvesting; Data science; Health care information; Marketing

Instagram

Identification: An online social network platform that enables users to take pictures and videos and to share them on a variety of other platforms, such as Facebook, Twitter, Tumblr, and Flickr.

An original identifying feature of Instagram images was a retro look similar to Kodak and Polaroid photos. In August 2015, a new software release permitted users to apply a number of filters and video capture of fifteen seconds in length. This enhanced other Instagram features, such as the ability to edit photos through online sliders and light filters.

Instagram was originally constructed by Kevin Systrom and Mike Krieger. It was released in October 2010 as a free mobile app, available in a variety of platforms, including Android and Apple, and through third-party apps on Blackberry. In 2012, Facebook acquired Instagram for $1 billion in cash and stock. By September 2015, Instagram boasted more than 400 million users.

A key networking feature of Instagram is the use of hashtags to allow users to discover photos

Mike Krieger, CTO and co-founder of Instagram.

and make connections with other people with similar interests. This feature, added in January 2011, is promoted by Instagram's Community Team through a series of photos and hashtags known as the Weekend Hashtag Project.

Two practices of the Instagram user community that have had an impact on popular culture are the practice of throw-back Thursday and the proliferation of selfies. Throw-back Thursday is the practice of posting old photos from users' personal histories, marked with the hashtag #TBT. The trend of taking pictures of one's self and posting a so-called selfie has generated an entire cottage industry of selfie sticks that are designed to facilitate photography of one's own image against a backdrop. The trend has had a psychological impact on certain demographics sufficient to cause social commentators to marvel at the egocentric basis and impact of the selfie on the human psyche.

Innovations to include advertising and other marketing features have been difficult to implement in the Instagram environment. On December 17, 2012, a change in the terms of use would have allowed Instagram to license users' photos in perpetuity. Users revolted and began to

delete accounts. Within twenty-four hours, chief executive Kevin Systrom apologized, saying that it was "our mistake that this language is confusing." In September 2013, Instagram's Emily White announced that the company would begin online advertising. White's strategy was to review every company that had an Instagram account and pay them an in-person visit. The companies spanned a broad swath of the American retail market, ranging from Ford Motor Company to Williams-Sonoma, to Levi Strauss & Company. The risk in introducing advertising was alienation of the user base. After much discussion, the fashion house Michael Kors became the first retailer to advertise on Instagram, on November 1, 2013.

At Blog.business.instagram.com, the company offers potential advertisers tips and support for placing targeted ads to differentiated user demographics. It is interesting to note that, when signing up for the business blog, the Instagram user is directed to the Tumblr site. Driven by the prospect of access to literally millions of users, sorted and targeted according to unique interests, digital marketers have created an entire industry and blogosphere devoted to strategies for marketing via Instagram. In October 2015, a Google search of the topic "marketing on Instagram" generated 305 million hits in 0.55 seconds. In September 2015, the Instagram messaging app known as Direct was overhauled to become much more like a full-featured messaging app. New features allow users to share images from the feed, respond to a photo with a photo, or start a conversation. In 2016, Instagram launched a feature which allowed users to post "stories," using short lived images, photos, stickers, and GIFs. Shortly thereafter, Instagram included a tab which allowed from longer capacity of videos. Films as long as one hour can be launched in an Instagram App called IGTV. The announcement alone caused the value of Facebook shares to jump 2.3 percent in a single day.

In 2013, Instagram acted quickly to respond to a British Broadcasting Corporation (BBC) investigation regarding the role of Instagram in drug trafficking. The BBC's allegation was that users in the United States were posting photos of drugs and completing sales through the Instagram chat and messaging service known as WhatsApp. Instagram has been accused in the press of censorship, after incidents in October 2013 and again in January 2015 in which women displayed photos of themselves in bikinis with pubic hair showing. In both instances, the owners of the accounts were photographers, and their Instagram accounts were deleted. Instagram and other social media platforms continue to frustrate the growing legal marijuana industry by banning advertising by any company or individual who is seeking to promote cannabis-related products.

Nonetheless, the breadth and depth of Instagram's impact in commerce continues to grow, with ad revenue in 2019 expected to reach $10 billion. As of early 2019, Instagram had over 1 billion users who were active at least monthly. Globally, the highest concentration of Instagram users is in the United States (122 million), India (71 million), and Brazil (64 million). Over 60 percent of users log in daily, making it second in popularity (behind Facebook). Males between the ages of 18 and 24 years old represent the biggest category of users, with 60.4 percent of all Instagram users between the ages of 18 and 24. Instagram is credited with influencing 75 percent of all shopping decisions. It continues its influence to include political and social activism, such as the Black Lives Matter movement. Instagram is credited with normalizing personal image and beauty by providing a forum in which more diverse racial and cultural are posted, and in which users feel free to post flaws such as pimples, stretch marks, and scars.

In February 2019, amid growing concern over the role of social media in politics, writer Cass R. Sunstein called for regulation of Facebook, Instagram, Twitter and YouTube. Sunstein cited three distinct reasons: 1) the threat that social media has posed to democracy, following attacks traceable to Russia on elections in the United States and the European Union; 2) the need to protect consumers from privacy violations, such as sale of private data for commercial uses; 3) the monopoly held by Facebook, WhatsApp, and Instagram called for an application of antitrust laws in ways more suitable for the digital age.

Paula Collins

Further Reading

Batty, David. "Instagram Acts after BBC Finds Site Users Are Advertising Illegal Drugs." *Guardian,* November 7, 2013.

Brooks, Aaron. Social Media Today. October 7, 2018. 7 Unexpected Ways Instagram Has Changed the World.

Chaykowski, Kathleen. "Mark Zuckerberg Gains $1.7 Billion After Instagram Announces New 'TV' App, 1 Billion Users". Forbes. June 20, 2018.

Hinde, Natasha. "Did Instagram Ban This Account Because of a Photo Showing Women's Pubic Hair?" *The Huffington Post UK*, January 21, 2015.

Isaac, Mike. "Exclusive: Facebook Deal Nets Instagram CEO $400 Million." *Wired,* April 9, 2012.

McCullagh, Declan. "Instagram Apologizes to Users: We Won't Sell Your Photos." C/net, December 18, 2012.

Miles, Jason G. *Instagram Power: Build Your Brand and Reach More Customers with the Power of Pictures.* New York: McGraw-Hill Education, 2014.

Payne, Bridget Watson, ed. *This Is Happening: Life through the Lens of Instagram.* San Francisco, CA: Chronicle Books, 2013.

Rohrs, Jeffrey K. *Audience: Marketing in the Age of Subscribers, Fans and Followers* Hoboken, NJ: Wiley, 2014.

Rusli, Evelyn. "Instagram Pictures Itself Making Money." *Wall Street Journal,* September 8, 2013.

Setalvad, Ariha. "Instagram Direct Gets a Huge Update Focused on Messaging Your Friends." *The Verge,* September 1, 2015.

Smith, Kit. Brandwatch. 47 Incredible Instagram Statistics. January 7, 2019. https://www.brandwatch.com/blog/instagram-stats/

Sunstein, Cass R. "Regulate Facebook and Twitter? The Case is Getting Stronger." *Bloomberg*, February 14, 2019.

See also: Apps; Facebook; Social media; Twitter

Integrated Automated Fingerprint Identification System (IAFIS)

Identification: A national fingerprint and criminal history repository maintained by the Criminal Justice Information Services (CJIS) division of the Federal Bureau of Investigation (FBI).

The largest fingerprint database in the world, IAFIS contains over 70 million criminal fingerprint records and 34 million civil fingerprint records. More than 18,000 local, state, tribal, federal, and international partners currently use the system. Law enforcement agencies submit criminal records, which include ten-print fingerprints with corresponding criminal histories, mug shots, physical characteristics, and aliases. Civil fingerprint records are acquired from employment and military background checks.

In 1924, the FBI established a central repository for criminal history data. The original collection of over 800,000 fingerprint records consisted of paper cards with ten rolled fingerprint impressions (ten-prints) that were processed and catalogued by technicians. Fingerprint examiners manually compared prints collected at crime scenes (latent prints) against ten-print records on file. As the collection expanded to include criminal and civil files, law enforcement agencies began adopting the small-scale Automated Fingerprint Identification Systems (AFIS) in the 1980s. Automated systems allowed fingerprint examiners to mark features on a scanned fingerprint image, encode data, and search the database for similar prints in a fraction of the time it took to classify and compare prints by hand.

Local and state law enforcement agencies purchased early models of AFIS from proprietary vendors. Software produced by competing vendors was largely incompatible and effectively restricted system communications between neighboring jurisdictions or central state repositories. The FBI implemented IAFIS in 1999, enabling local, state, and federal agencies to access and remotely search the national repository. The system was developed by government defense contractor Lockheed Martin and employs processing algorithms designed by MorphoTrak to extract features and compare prints electronically. IAFIS includes three segments: the Identification Tasking and Networking (ITN) segment for document processing, the Interstate Identification Index (III) segment for storage and retrieval of criminal history records, and the AFIS segment to search the FBI fingerprint repository for fingerprint records. Agencies can submit requests or remotely search IAFIS using Remote Fingerprint Editing Software (RFES) and Universal Latent Workstation (ULW) software. Results of remote searches include a list of potential matches and corresponding fingerprints for manual comparison and verification by forensic experts.

Civil and criminal ten-prints and latent prints are first scanned and processed by local, state, and federal agencies before submission to the repository. Automated feature-extraction algorithms then identify fingerprint ridge singularities, or minutiae points. The American National Standards Institute (ANSI) and National Institute of Standards and Technology (NIST) developed ANSI/NIST-ITL standards defining certain requirements for biometric images and metadata, including fingerprint minutiae. Agencies must also comply with the FBI's Electronic Biometric Transmission System (EBTS) application profile in order to transmit data using the IAFIS interface.

Fingerprint identifications in criminal investigations are generally made by comparing latent prints collected at a crime scene to high-quality ten-prints taken directly from a suspect's fingers. Incomplete or poor-quality latent prints might require additional manual processing by a forensic expert before searching IAFIS for similarities. When an optical image of a latent print is entered, fingerprint-matching algorithms compare minutiae points of the latent print against indexed criminal prints on file to report a list of possible matches and to indicate the level of probability for each. Fingerprint examiners then manually compare images of the latent print against results using the current analysis, comparison, evaluation, and verification (ACE-V) technique. Examiners can report "individualization" if a source is identified, "exclusion" if a suggested match is incompatible with the latent print, or "inconclusive" results.

Automated ten-print searches for criminal identification purposes are highly accurate, but determining the source of latent prints depends on variables such as image clarity, algorithmic accuracy, and the examiner's level of experience and proficiency with a particular system. While ULW software can automatically encode minutiae data for high-quality latent prints, practitioners working with poor-quality latent prints extract the minutiae manually, imparting a subjective element to the process. Examiners often vary images and minutiae to conduct multiple searches in IAFIS and local AFIS repositories. For instance, multiple searches may be necessary if the hand or finger from which the print originated is unknown.

AFIS vendor software and algorithms remain proprietary, requiring latent print examiners to enter minutiae in system-specific ways to enhance search performance. Despite ongoing efforts such as the NIST-sponsored Minutiae Interoperability Exchange (MINEX) Tests to improve performance and interoperability between systems, baseline algorithm standards have not been established. Acceptable FBI error rates allow false positives 0.3 percent of the time and false negatives 1 percent of the time, but accurately measuring system reliability in practice proves difficult. Although an estimated 50,000 suspects are identified each year through IAFIS and AFIS latent searches, there is no national reviewing mechanism to assess system or practitioner errors.

Fingerprint examiners' findings can be affected by cognitive bias, which may result from contextual information about suspects and prior conclusions from biometric specialists. After the Madrid train bombing in 2004, FBI and independent fingerprint examiners identified Brandon Mayfield as the source of a single latent print found at the crime scene, leading to his arrest. After spending over two weeks in custody, Mayfield was cleared when Spanish authorities matched the print to a different suspect. Subsequent review of the investigation determined that the first FBI fingerprint examiner largely influenced conclusions of other examiners. The FBI later admitted wrongdoing and apologized.

The Mayfield case inspired subsequent studies such as the National Research Council and National Academy of Sciences 2009 report, *Strengthening Forensic Sciences in the United States: A Path Forward*. The report stated that the ACE-V test does not guard against bias and does not guarantee reliable and repeatable results. Court cases and articles have challenged latent print evidence on the grounds that findings are fallible. Nevertheless, testimony from fingerprint examiners remains admissible in U.S. courts according to guidelines for scientific evidence set forth in Federal Rule of Evidence 702 and *Daubert v. Merrell Dow Pharmaceuticals, Inc.*, 509 U.S. 579 (1993).

Technological advancements and emerging biometric identification services necessitated improvements to the IAFIS repository and search capabilities. In September 2014, the FBI announced that its Next Generation Identification (NGI) system was fully operational and would replace IAFIS with advanced functionality. The NGI system, also developed by Lockheed Martin, incorporates IAFIS capabilities and offers advanced biometric services including Advanced Fingerprint Identification Technology (AFIT), Repository for Individuals of Special Concern (RISC), Interstate Photo System (IPS), Latents and National Palm Print System (NPPS), Rap Back Service, and Iris Recognition (IR).

Carey Sias

Further Reading

Cole, Simon A. "More Than Zero: Accounting for Error in Latent Fingerprint Identification." *Journal of Criminal Law and Criminology* 95, no. 3 (2005): 985–1078.

Federal Bureau of Investigation. "Fingerprints and Other Biometrics." *FBI.gov.* Accessed August 23, 2015. https://www.fbi.gov/about-us/cjis/fingerprints_biometrics.

Federal Bureau of Investigation. "Integrated Automated Fingerprint Identification System: Five Key Services." *FBI.gov.* Accessed August 23, 2015. https://www.fbi.gov/about-us/cjis/fingerprints_biometrics/iafis/ngi_services.

Holder, Eric Himpton, Laurie O. Robinson, John H. Laub, and National Institute of Justice. *The Fingerprint Source*book. Washington, DC: U.S. Dept. of Justice, Office of Justice Programs, National Institute of Justice, 2011.

McMurtrie, Jacqueline. "Swirls and Whorls: Litigating Post-Conviction Claims of Fingerprint Misidentification after the NAS Report." *Utah Law Review* 2010, no. 2 (2010): 267–297.

National Research Council. *Strengthening Forensic Science in the United States: A Path Forward.* Washington, DC: The National Academies Press, 2009.

See also: Criminal justice (criminal procedure); Fourth Amendment to the U.S. Constitution; Law enforcement

Intellectual property

Identification: The set of rules that governs creations of the mind, including, but not limited to, copyrights and patents. Intellectual property may trigger privacy concerns in connection with aggregation and dissemination of personal information, database protection, freedom of speech under the First Amendment to the U.S. Constitution, and liability of Internet service providers.

Intellectual property rules grant monopolies over intellectual creations. Original works are protected by copyright law, whereas patent law protects inventions. In both cases, the creator or inventor is entitled to a bundle of exclusive rights, enabling him or her solely to control the use and distribution of the work or invention. This monopoly is limited in time, lasting for several decades after the life of the creator, or around twenty years since the invention was patented.

Many of the international agreements that define the global design of current intellectual property regimes have been negotiated in connection with trade agreements. For this reason, many of the intellectual property norms and regulations that affect privacy rights are negotiated in trade arenas and reflect normative and policy choices designed to promote trade goals.

Privacy rights are at stake in situations in which intellectual property directly or indirectly affects access to proprietary information. This is the case of databases, or similar compilations of facts, which contain personal information. Aggregation of personal data can be conducted by private agents, with or without commercial purposes, or by the government. In the case of aggregation of data conducted by private agents, there has been a sharp rise in the economic exploitation of databases over the last two decades. Certain countries, especially in Europe, grant extensive intellectual property rights over databases or other compilations of facts. In the United States, the threshold for the ability to copyright compilations of facts is tied to requirements of minimal originality, which means that acquisition of monopolistic rights over compilations of personal information is subject to slightly more stringent standards.

Control over personal information is therefore affected by laws governing ownership of and access to databases or other compilations. When personal information enclosed in databases or compilations is transmitted, a potential clash might occur between intellectual property–created rights and privacy rights if the person to whom said information pertains is unaware of the transmission or is unable to prevent it. On the other end of the spectrum, intellectual property rights may help strengthen privacy in the sense that they grant ownership over information, making it harder for other parties to access proprietary content. From this viewpoint, the creation of layers of intellectual property protection over data may function as a deterrent against misappropriation of personal information by erecting legal barriers to access and/or use of personal information and nonpersonal information, such as copyrighted content.

The rise of digital technologies has significantly affected the relationship between content or data protection and privacy, especially where exchanges of copyrighted works in the online environment are concerned. Legal mechanisms entitling copyright holders to prevent unauthorized use or distribution of their works tend to require access to and sharing of personal data of individuals. In addition to copyright holders, Internet service providers play a relevant role in this process.

Liability of Internet service providers was regulated following several copyright infringement lawsuits when peer-to-peer technologies enabled the uploading and downloading of copyrighted works at almost no cost. Through peer-to-peer networks, users can easily share digital files containing film, music, or literary works protected by copyright law. When that sharing has not been authorized, copyright holders may request the IP address of the infringing user from the Internet service provider. The IP address, together with user information stored by the Internet service provider, can be used to track and identify the user. In many cases, either the copyright holder or the Internet service provider and the copyright holder jointly send cease and desist letters to reputedly infringing users, asking them to take down the material and informing them of their intention to enforce their rights.

Digital technology has also enabled lawful and unlawful dissemination of copyright works outside peer-to-peer networks, as in the case of personal webpages or social media. Similar user identification issues arise in this context.

Another area in which intellectual property interacts with privacy rights is regulation of freedom of speech, governed in the United States by the First Amendment to the U.S. Constitution.

The First Amendment shields one's ability to convey information without extraneous interference. Intellectual property, in the form of copyright law, protects creative speech through the grant of exclusive rights. For an extended period of time, the author of a copyrighted work possesses a wide array of control mechanisms over that work, including the ability to allow others to copy and distribute the work, with or without compensation, and the ability to prevent them from doing so. Copyright law includes exceptions and limitations, however, that apply to situations in which part of the creative work may be copied regardless of the will of its author. Some of the most common situations include criticism, commentary, or parody. Many countries recognize situations of public interest in access to specific kinds of information as well. Political speech, in particular, or works conveying the personal (and, in some cases, even private) opinions of political figures may override copyright-based monopolies, meaning that parts of the work might be copied, reprinted, or circulated by others. In these and similar situations, privacy expectations and privacy rights may recede in favor of freedom of speech or other copyright-sanctioned goals.

Because of the historical connection between intellectual property and trade, many of the negotiations of privacy-related aspects of intellectual property are connected to sweeping trade agreements. These agreements—which seek, for instance, to impose more stringent sanctions for intellectual property violations, including seizure and destruction of suspected counterfeit or pirated goods—also regulate subjects that may directly affect privacy rights, especially in the case of unlawful uses of copyrighted works in the digital environment.

One of the most salient examples of this was the negotiation process surrounding the Anti-Counterfeiting Trade Agreement (ACTA), a multilateral agreement on enforcement of intellectual property rights that set forth international standards to address the problems raised by piracy and counterfeiting, and regulated *ex novo* the enforcement of intellectual property rights in the digital environment. ACTA was also one of the first instances of international regulation of intellectual property in which privacy and data protection were explicitly mentioned. This is a major departure from classical normative approaches to international intellectual property because neither the Paris Convention on patents nor the Berne Convention on copyrights covered those issues. While one of ACTA's main goals was to promote expeditious identification and disclosure of the identity of Internet users suspected of copyright infringement, it also urged countries to preserve privacy rights. This requirement was generically anchored, however, on observance of fundamental principles, such as the principle of proportionality in implementing ACTA provisions, which does not detract significantly from the core obligations surrounding user identification in the online environment. The emphasis on expeditious identification of the personal information of Internet users is one of the constants around which contemporary regulation of digital intellectual property revolves.

Throughout the twentieth century, international intellectual property agreements allowed exceptions to ensure compliance with privacy laws or regulations. Recent trade-based negotiations over intellectual property enforcement, while still allowing for some exceptions, emphasize and promote the implementation of measures that are likely to affect privacy, especially in the online environment. This is the case for measures that set expedited processes for identification of Internet users by Internet service providers or that require the cross-transfer of personal data between parties.

The association between copyright ownership and the ability to seek and obtain information about the identity of users, an ability that emerged with the democratization of Internet access, may also bring about other kinds of chilling effects that touch on privacy. As laws permit identification of supposedly infringing users of copyrighted content, there might be cases in which the wrong user is identified. Another possibility is that a user might be identified following a request by a copyright holder, but because no determination has been made as to the actual unlawfulness of the use of the copyrighted work, it is possible that the use in question might have been permissible under applicable copyright laws. In addition to peer-to-peer networks, the growth and popularization of social media, among other types of platforms that enable online dissemination of content, has greatly expanded the number of Internet users that may be subject to identification by copyright holders and/or Internet service providers.

Social media are digital platforms, such as Facebook or YouTube, that enable users to share information electronically. Copyright protects a significant amount of content currently shared on social media. When that sharing has not been authorized, the rights holder may request the disclosure of the identity of a specific Internet user through a process similar to the one applicable to peer-to-peer exchanges. Unlike peer-to-peer platforms, whose relevance has faded, the exponential expansion of social media over the last decade has given popular social media an extra incentive to monitor user activity to avoid costly copyright litigation, which in turn raises further concerns about privacy rights in cyberspace.

Ana Santos Rutschman

Further Reading

Marlin-Bennett, Renée. *Knowledge Power: Intellectual Property, Information, and Privacy.* Boulder, CO: Lynne Rienner, 2004.

Moore, Adam, ed. *Information Ethics: Privacy, Property, and Power.* Seattle: University of Washington Press, 2005.

Samuelson, Pamela. *Privacy as Intellectual Property?* In *First Amendment Handbook,* edited by James L. Swanson. New York: C. Boardman, 2002.

Silva, Alberto J. Cerda. "Enforcing Intellectual Property Rights by Diminishing Privacy: How the Anti-Counterfeiting Trade Agreement Jeopardizes the Right to

Privacy." *American University International Law Review* 26, no. 3 (2011): 601–643.

Zittrain, Jonathan. "What the Publisher Can Teach the Patient: Intellectual Property and Privacy in an Era of Trusted Privication." *Stanford Law Review* 52, no. 5 (May 2000): 1201–1250. [Symposium: Cyberspace and Privacy: A New Legal Paradigm?]

See also: First Amendment to the U.S. Constitution; Social media

International Center for Information Ethics (ICIE)

Identification: An academic community that explores the area of information ethics. Information ethics has recently expanded as a discipline in library and information science; however, the field or the phrase has changed over the years. The concept is embraced by many other disciplines.

Information ethics is now understood as a confluence of the ethical concerns of media, journalism, library and information science, computer ethics (including cyberethics), management information systems, business, and the Internet. Information ethics, in the context that ICIE interpets the concept, deals with ethical issues in the areas of digital production and reproduction of phenomena and processes such as the exchange, combination, and use of information

Directed by Rafael Capurro and Jared Bielby, ICIE provides an intercultural exchange of ideas and information on worldwide teaching and research in information ethics, an opportunity to interact with others in the field, and information on current events pertaining to activities by various organizations active in the shared goals of information ethics. ICIE participation and membership is free. ICIE depends on the efforts and participation of group members, and the mutual sharing of related interests and knowledge.

Rafael Capurro founded ICIE in 1999. The organization began as a small group of friends and colleagues but expanded into an international and intercultural group. ICIE now has over 300 members from around the world. ICIE has organized and co-organized symposia since 2001/2002. The group publishes a book series with W. Fink Verlag, Munich-Paderborn (Germany). Since 2004, ICIE has published the *International Review of Information Ethics* (IRIE).

IRIE, the ICIE's journal, facilitates an international and intercultural discussion on the ethical impacts of information technology on human practices and thought, social interaction, and society. IRIE focuses on ethical issues and providing current awareness on key issues. The journal focuses its coverage particularly on ethical issues involving digital devices affecting, through their code and/or content, social interaction as raised (1) on the Internet, (2) in computer science (computer ethics), and (3) in library and information science.

IRIE seeks to provide a general forum for ethical scholarship, research, and discussion in these areas. It seeks contributions providing a critical analysis of issues in information ethics from the following perspectives: (1) the development of moral standards, norms or values; (2) the creation of (new) power structures; (3) information visions and myths; and (4) concealed contradictions and intentionalities in information theories, ethics, and practices. The journal allows for international as well as intercultural discussion among peers.

Further Reading

George, Richard T. *The Ethics of Information Technology and Business*. Malden, MA: Blackwell, 2003.

Gunning, Jennifer, and Law Ethics. *Ethics, Law and Society*. Aldershot, England: Ashgate, 2009.

Himma, Kenneth Einar. *Information Ethics*. Bradford, England: Emerald, 2007.

Quinn, Michael J. *Ethics for the Information Age*. Boston, MA: Pearson/Addison-Wesley, 2005.

Severson, Richard James. *The Principles of Information Ethics*. Armonk, NY: M.E. Sharpe, 1997.

See also: Computers and privacy; data harvesting

Internet cafés

Identification: Also known as cybercafés, retail businesses that rent computers by the hour.

The Internet is a vital communication tool in the twenty-first-century world. One manifestation of the Internet's influence is the Internet café. The first Internet cafés were opened in Europe in the mid-1990s and offered coffee and dessert like a regular coffee shop. Cybercafés may also sell several different kinds of accessories and gadgets. In South Korea, one of the most high-tech-oriented nations in the world, there are thousands of cybercafés, where people use voice and video, and conduct several other computer-related tasks. Computer and Internet access is provided for an hourly or daily fee.

The first cybercafé in the United States was opened in July 1991 in San Francisco, when Wayne Gregori began the SFnet Coffeehouse Network. He built and offered twenty-five coin-operated computer stations in several San Francisco coffee houses. The Binary Café, Canada's first cybercafé, began business in June 1994. Currently, there are thousands of cybercafés throughout the world that provide computer and Internet access.

In some cases, the regulation of Internet cafés has led to tensions between the rights of free speech and privacy, and the duty of government to protect community health and safety. In a leading example, the city of Garden Grove attempted to curtail gang violence at cybercafés operating in that city by requiring cybercafés to install video surveillance systems. The constitutionality of the ordinance was subsequently challenged. A California court of appeal determined that the video surveillance requirement did not violate free speech or privacy protections under either the federal or California constitutions. This decision was immediately criticized by commentators and a dissenting judge as an undue government intrusion into individuals' personal lives.

In January 2004, a California court of appeal for the State of California, in the case of *Vo v. City of Garden Grove*, sought to balance the interests of free speech and public safety. Cybercafé owners challenged the requirement that mandated the installation of video surveillance systems to record patrons. These owners argued that the ordinance violated patrons' rights of free speech and privacy. The court upheld the city ordinance that required cybercafés to implement certain safety measures intended to curtail gang violence. The court concluded that Garden Grove's requirement of video surveillance in cybercafés was a reasonable use of the city's police power and was rationally related to its interest in maintaining safety. The *Vo* majority further held the video surveillance requirements constitutional under the federal right of free speech and the California constitutional right of privacy.

Tips and Warnings for Using Internet Cafés

- While the security provided by many Internet cafés and other similar public access points continues to improve, customers are still required to practice due diligence.
- Mozilla can be downloaded from http://www.lupopensuite.com/, which leaves all
- the temporary files on the flash drive and not on the café's computer.
- To maximize private use, the user should ask for a computer near the back of the establishment or pick a computer that is not surrounded by other computer users.
- If the user is in a public café, he or she should ask staff members to verify that the user has deleted all personal data from the computer.
- Users should never post any personal information in a public place like Myspace, Facebook, or Craigslist.
- Users should use a live boot CD that helps to preserve privacy on a computer. They can use a search engine to find a list of live boot CDs. Booting from a live CD will leave no trace of the user's activities.

Gretchen Nobahar

Further Reading

Bailard, Catie Snow. *Democracy's Double-Edged Sword: How Internet Use Changes Citizens' Views of Their Government.*

Bell, David. *Cyberculture: The Key Concepts.* London: Routledge, 2004.

Berleur, Jacques, and Diane Whitehouse. *An Ethical Global Information Society Culture and Democracy Revisited.*

Horne, Felix, and Cynthia Wong. *"They Know Everything We Do": Telecom and Internet Surveillance in Ethiopia.*

Kgopa, Alfred Thaga. *Information Security Issues Facing Internet Café Users.*

Privacy, Free Speech & the Garden Grove Cyber Café Experiment. Durham, NC: Duke University School of Law, 2004.

See also: Computers and privacy; Facebook; Surveillance cameras.

Internet Service Providers and privacy

Identification: Internet Service Providers (ISPs) are companies or organizations that, at their core, provide access to the Internet to individuals as well as companies and organizations. They may also provide other services, such as e-mail access and website hosting. Typically, ISP services are provided by companies who may offer other services, such as telephones or cable television. Some are owned by larger media companies, such as Comcast/NBC or Time Warner.

Between the late 1960s, when the original ARPAnet was devised, to the late 1980s, Internet access was restricted to government research laboratories and cooperating universities. However, it became clear that there were public and commercial uses to the network that would define its future. With the development of the World Wide Web after 1985, other companies began to form the technological backbone of what would become the Internet. The first large, national ISPs, CompuServe and America On Line, did not offer the type of universal access that

characterizes the Internet today, but rather had carefully curated services and information. But in 1989, an ISP called The World was launched in Brookline, Massachusetts, becoming the first commercial ISP in the United States, and the number of ISPs grew as rapidly as access to the Internet expanded. With the development of higher speed digital subscriber line (DSL) service and cable Internet service, however, the greater access relied upon infrastructure that only established phone and cable companies could provide. This reduced the number of providers to only a few in most markets, creating a situation where a few companies had access to copious amounts of data from a large customer base.

As the main point of contact, ISPs have access to a large amount of customer data that may impact individual users in terms of their applications for employment, applications for credit, and interpersonal relationships. The websites that users visit reflect on their location at particular times, their health or the health of their loved ones, their shopping practices, the types of things they download from the Internet, their personal and ideological preferences in terms of politics and religion, and many other matters that users may not want revealed to coworkers, employers, or even friends or family members. Many businesses have shown a willingness to pay for such information, and in an age where people are often seen by businesses as commodities for sale on the Internet, personal control over such data is becoming increasingly difficult to control.

As the main way that users connect with the Internet, ISPs are a point through which much of a user's data travels. Thus, ISPs are not only points of vulnerability to hacking attacks, but also seen as sources of information that may be for sale to the highest bidder. With the demise under Trump Administration Federal Communications Commission (FCC) chair, Ajit Pai, of the net neutrality rules that had been issued during the Obama Administration, the rules governing ISPs handling of customers' data also were loosened. Regulations restricting the sale of customers' personal information, such as location data, app usage, internet history, financial information, and health data to third parties were repealed, exposing many users to having their personal lives up for sale.

Beyond personal data, corporations have a stake in the discussion as well. Proprietary information and industrial espionage are major concerns for companies in a variety of industries, and their data is just as vulnerable and sometimes an even more enticing target than individual peoples' data.

Websites, such as Facebook, Google, or Amazon track users' data through their accounts. These are governed by terms of service that, in theory, lay out what the company can and cannot do with the data. ISPs are different, in that they see the entirety of a user's Internet activity, making for a more comprehensive view of an individual user or company. Given that high level of access, people and companies need to take care about how they search the Internet. There are a few steps that can be taken.

First, people (and company employees) can search only HTTPS (hypertext transfer protocol secure) sites, rather than insecure HTTP sites. The HTTPS designation means that the sites are encrypted, and ISPs can only see the home domain rather than the specific pages being accessed. This can be enforced through browser plug-ins and by using more secure "private" browsers. Another safeguard feature is the use of SSL (secure sockets layer) encryption, which protects data through creating an encrypted link between the server and the user. Many companies also employ virtual private networks (VPNs), which is an intermediary step through which data must travel before it goes to the ISP. This keeps the data secure by obscuring the source location of the data, making it appear as though it is coming from the VPN's site rather than the user's computer. This makes it very difficult to track the browsing data back to the user. It also encrypts the data that the ISP receives. This protects the users both from their data being used without their consent, as well as from many forms of cyberattacks. Whereas VPNs used to be only for businesses, many are now available for personal use.

Finally, an important step for both business and personal consumers is to check into what their ISP's practices are in terms of securing their data. If the ISP is less than forthcoming about how it protects and whether or not it will sell your data, that is certainly information that savvy consumers can consider when choosing their ISP.

Steven L. Danver

Further Reading

Bode, K. "These Wireless Location Data Scandals Are Going To Be A Very Big Problem For Ajit Pai." *Techdirt*, January 29, 2019.

Frier, S. "Is Apple Really Your Privacy Hero?" *Bloomberg Businessweek*, August 8, 2018. https://www.bloomberg.com/news/articles/2018-08-08/is-apple-really-your-privacy-hero.

Hawkins, D. "The Cybersecurity 202: Apple's latest security fix is deepening divisions over FBI access." *Washington Post,* June 15, 2018.

McCullough, Brian. How the Internet Happened: From Netscape to the iPhone. New York: Liveright Publishing, 2018.

Ryan, Johnny. *A history of the Internet and the digital future*. London: Reaktion Books, 2010.

Whitman, M.E., and Mattord, H.J. *Principles of Internet Security*. Boston: Course Technology/Thomson, 2009.

Wyatt, E. "F.C.C. Backs Opening Net Rules for Debate." *The New York Times*. May15, 2014.

See also: Big data; Federal Communications Commission; Hacking, computer; Net neutrality; Online privacy and security; Search engines; Telephones

Interrogations

Identification: Attempts made by governmental officials, including law enforcement officers, demanding information from an individual that could be incriminating.

Interrogations are most commonly associated with arrest. Many interrogations occur outside the police station and, at times, when an individual is not formally under arrest. For constitutional purposes, interrogations become important under the Fifth Amendment when an individual is in custody, which is legally distinct from arrest. The case most commonly associated with interrogations is *Miranda v. Arizona*, 384 U.S. 436 (1966).

Miranda was decided by the Warren Court, which greatly expanded rights for criminal defendants. Chief Justice, Earl Warren, wrote the majority opinion in this 6–3 decision. *Miranda* involved four consolidated cases—one each from Arizona, New York, and California, and one involving a federal interrogation. The key issue was whether the U.S. Constitution provides an affirmative duty on law enforcement to explain that statements made during a custodial interrogation may be used against a defendant. While the Fifth Amendment's language provides no explicit obligation requiring law enforcement to warn criminal defendants about their constitutional rights, the Warren Court interpreted such a right to exist, implicitly, based on the Fifth Amendment's guarantee against self-incrimination. Because the Fifth Amendment provides that no person "shall be compelled in any criminal case to be a witness against himself," the *Miranda* Court believed that affirmative warnings are constitutionally compelled to protect against involuntary confessions.

The *Miranda* Court's main concern was the psychological pressure that incommunicado interrogation imposes on a criminal defendant. When an individual is placed in legal custody and is separated from family or otherwise isolated, he or she may find that his or her will succumbs to the seriousness of the situation and may make statements that are not entirely reliable. Prior to *Miranda,* the test for determining a confession's admissibility was its literal voluntariness (or was a confession secured by physical violence such as that which occurred in *Brown v. Mississippi*, 297 U.S. 278 [1936]). The *Miranda* Court discussed several police techniques that, though not physically violent, created an oppressive environment conducive to securing a confession regardless of that confession's reliability. The Court observed that interrogations occurring in privacy "results in secrecy and this in turn results in a gap in our knowledge as to what, in fact, goes on in the interrogation room." This belief, warranted or not, led to the creation of the well-known *Miranda* rights.

Miranda requires that before any information gleaned from custodial information is used against a criminal defendant in the prosecution's case-in-chief, the individual must be advised of four distinct rights: (1) you have the right to remain silent; (2) if you waive that right and speak to law enforcement, anything you say during the interrogation can be used against you as evidence in a court of law; (3) you have the right to have an attorney with you during the interrogation by law enforcement; and (4) if you cannot afford an attorney to be with you during the interrogation, the state will provide an attorney for you. If law enforcement fails to provide these warnings or continues to question an individual who has invoked his or her *Miranda* right to remain silent, no statement made by the individual may be used in the prosecution's case-in-chief. Unwarned statements or statements obtained in violation of *Miranda*'s proscriptions, however, may be used to impeach a defendant who provides contrary testimony during trial.

Miranda and the doctrine relating to interrogations are easy to state but somewhat complicated in practice. First, as set forth above, *Miranda* applies only to custodial interrogation situations. Thus, to invoke *Miranda*'s prophylactic (preventive) protections, an individual must be in custody. Custody, while not identical to arrest, requires that a person be either formally arrested or "deprived of his freedom of action in any significant way." Voluntarily speaking with the police will not usually result in a finding of custody. A good example of the Court's interpretation of "custody" for *Miranda* purposes is *Oregon v. Mathiason*, 429 U.S. 492 (1977). Likewise, the ordinary roadside encounter with police usually will not result in a determination that the person is in custody. The issue of *Miranda*'s applicability to driving while intoxicated (DWI) stops is slightly more complicated and was addressed by the Supreme Court in *Pennsylvania v. Muniz*, 496 U.S. 582 (1990).

Miranda's second requirement before its prophylactic protections apply is that the individual be subjected to interrogation by law enforcement or their surrogates. The Supreme Court has defined interrogation to mean "express questioning" and also "any words or actions on the part of the police (other than those normally attendant to arrest and custody) that the police should know are reasonably likely to elicit an incriminating response from the suspect." This definition comes directly from the Court's decision in *Rhode Island v. Innis*, 446

U.S. 291 (1980). In *Innis*, a criminal defendant sitting in a police car (thus, in custody for *Miranda* purposes) voluntarily provided police with the location of a weapon recently used in a crime after police officers in the vehicle discussed among themselves the danger of a gun hidden close to a school where a child might find the gun and injure herself. The *Innis* Court found the defendant's spontaneous confession regarding the location of the gun was not procured through either direct questioning or any police conduct that reasonably would have elicited an incriminating response.

Miranda's prophylactic provisions may result in reliable, relevant evidence being excluded from legal proceedings. Thus, Congress, in response to *Miranda*'s harsh results, passed a federal statute to eliminate the need for *Miranda*'s precise warnings and focus instead on whether a confession had been obtained voluntarily. *See Dickerson v. United States*, 530 U.S. 428 (2000). Prior to *Miranda*, courts—both state and federal—focused on the question of

voluntariness in determining whether a confession was admissible. The Rehnquist Court struck down the federal statute, however, holding that *Miranda* was a constitutional rule and could not be legislatively overruled. *Dickerson*, a 7–2 opinion written by then Chief Justice William Rehnquist, confirmed that *Miranda*'s warnings, while not explicitly appearing in the text of the Constitution, are nonetheless constitutionally compelled.

Miranda and subsequent related rulings continue to generate case law from the Supreme Court. Questions have arisen as to how precisely the warnings must be given (i.e., word for word as set forth by the Court in *Miranda* or more generic expressions that provide the same substance of the warnings); whether an individual that sits without speaking but does not actually invoke his right to remain silent, and later confesses, receives the benefit of *Miranda*'s exclusionary rule; and whether law enforcement dealing with children are required to take the child's age and experiences into account when assessing custody for *Miranda* purposes. See *Florida v. Powell*, 599 U.S. _____ (2010); *Berghuis v. Thompkins*, 560 U.S. 370 (2010; *J.D.B. v. North Carolina*, 131 S. Ct. 2394 (2011).

The most important exception to *Miranda* is the "public safety" exception announced by the Supreme Court in *New York v. Quarles*. 467 U.S. 649 (1984). The Burger Court, in crafting a narrow exception to *Miranda*, found that the social cost of risking an unwarned—though completely voluntary—confession far outweighed *Miranda*'s blanket application to confessions where public safety is at risk. The defendant in *Quarels* was spotted by police in a grocery store after a woman reported being raped by a man matching Quarels's description. Upon spotting the officers, Quarels ran deeper into the grocery. An officer finally apprehended him. Because the female victim had alleged the perpetrator had a gun, the officer patted Quarels down and noticed an empty gun holster. Prior to administering *Miranda* warnings but after handcuffing Quarels, an officer asked where Quarels had put the gun. In response, Quarels nodded to a location and stated, "The gun is over there." The officer immediately went to that location and found the gun. Quarels was ultimately convicted of illegally possessing a weapon. The Supreme Court upheld the introduction of Quarles's confession that the gun was "over there" and the weapon based on the newly created, narrow "public safety" exception to *Miranda*.

Miranda is an unusual case where the Supreme Court clearly sets out four individual warnings deemed constitutionally required—without them being explicitly stated in the Constitution's text—in every case where there is a custodial interrogation. The case, decided during the height of the Warren Court's expansion of criminal procedure rights, has survived many challenges and attempts to limit its application. Still, *Miranda* and its familiar warnings are easily recited by most Americans because television, movies, and popular culture all seem to identify "the right to remain silent" with police questioning.

Currently, conversations between police and those in their vehicles are often recorded on video. Most American police cars are equipped with video and audio devices that record each police stop, including sobriety tests. *Miranda* does not require such recordings. As technology continues to infiltrate our daily lives, however, there is a push toward requiring even more video recordings of police activity, with many individuals calling for police to wear body cameras that record all activity during their entire shift. We can anticipate that, at some point, the use or existence of recording will reshape the *Miranda* doctrine. Until then, the four *Miranda* warnings remain constitutionally required: the right to remain silent, the right to be advised that what you say during custodial interrogation can and will be used against you in court, the right to the presence of an attorney during questioning, and the right to have an attorney

appointed for you to consult during questioning if you are unable to afford one.

Mary M. Penrose

Further Reading

Blair, J. P. "What Do We Know about Interrogation in the United States?" *Journal of Police and Criminal Psychology* 20, no. 2 (September 2005): 44–57.

"Criminal Procedure—Custodial Interviews—Department of Justice Institutes Presumption That Agents Will Electronically Record Custodial Interviews." *Harvard Law Review* 128, no. 5 (March 2015): 1552–1559.

Lassiter, G. Daniel. *Interrogations, Confessions, and Entrapment*. New York: Kluwer Academic/Plenum Publishers, 2004.

Lassiter, G. Daniel. *Police Interrogations and False Confessions: Current Research, Practice, and Policy Recommendations*. Washington, D.C.: American Psychological Association, 2010.

Leo, Richard A. *Police Interrogation and American Justice*. Cambridge, Mass.: Harvard University Press, 2008.

Rodriguez, Joshua I. "Note: Interrogation First, Miranda Warnings Afterward: A Critical Analysis of the Supreme Court's Approach to Delayed Miranda Warnings." *Fordham Urban Law Journal* 40 (March 2013): 1091.

White, Welsh S. "Miranda's Failure to Restrain Pernicious Interrogation Practices." *Michigan Law Review* 99, no. 5 (March 2001): 1211–1247. (Symposium: Miranda after Dickerson: The Future of Confession Law).

White, Welsh S. *Miranda's Waning Protections: Police Interrogation Practices after Dickerson*. Ann Arbor: University of Michigan Press, 2003.

See also: Criminal justice (criminal procedure); Fifth Amendment to the U.S. Constitution; Law Enforcement; Warren, Earl

Invasion of privacy

Identification: A violation of a person's right of privacy. The intrusion into the personal life of another person without just cause may grant the person whose privacy has been invaded a right to pursue a lawsuit for damages against the person or entity responsible for the intrusion.

While there is no constitutional provision articulating a general right to privacy, the U.S. Supreme Court has found an implied right to privacy under several constitutional amendments. There is no one American law that establishes a general right to privacy. The result has been much controversy over where to draw the line between what information on the private individual must remain private and what information can be freely disseminated.

The most authoritative definition of the concept of invasion of privacy is provided by § 652A of the *Second Restatement of Torts*. This section states that "one who invades the right of privacy of another is subject to liability for the resulting harm to the interest of the other." The section then states that an individual's right of privacy is unlawfully invaded by an "unreasonable intrusion, appropriation of another in name or likeness, unreasonable publicity of another's public life, and publicity which places false light before the public." A person is liable to another for invasion of privacy if that person "intentionally intrudes, physically or otherwise, upon the solitude or seclusion of another or his private affairs or concerns . . . if the intrusion would be highly offensive to a reasonable person." In other words, the right to privacy gives a private individual legal redress for any one of four separate acts: (1) an intrusion on his or her solitude or into his or her private affairs, (2) public disclosure of embarrassing private information, (3) publicity that puts him or her in a false light to the public, and (4) appropriation of his or her name or image for personal or commercial advantage.

Generally speaking, public persons may not allege that their privacy has been invaded because they already have placed themselves within the public eye. Details of their activities, even personal and sometimes intimate ones, are considered newsworthy, or of legitimate public interest. The only form of invasion of privacy in the *Restatement* provisions that does not contain a requirement that the act be highly offensive to the reasonable person is the wrongful appropriation of one's name or likeness.

Unlike many torts (private wrongs), invasion of privacy is not derived from English common law. Samuel D. Warren and Louis Brandeis were the primary creators of the concept of invasion of privacy. In 1890, they wrote an article in the *Harvard Law Review* arguing that invasion of privacy should be legally recognized as a tort. They argued that an individual should have full protection in person and property, invoking the concept of the "inviolate personality," which has existed as long as the common law.

Warren and Brandeis believed it was only natural, then, that the law recognizes a right to privacy. They were especially concerned over unauthorized publication of photos and stories by the press. At the time, Warren and Brandeis wrote, "instantaneous photographs and newspaper [enterprises]" thrived on sensationalism; they repeatedly demonstrated a lack of consideration for the "obvious bounds of propriety and decency." Warren and Brandeis stressed that the increasingly hectic pace of modern life made privacy an all the more crucial right. Rather than respecting individual privacy, they believed, the press was irresponsibly satiating an appetite for scandal. This, the authors asserted, harmed society by appealing to the more base part of human nature and distracted attention from more important social and civic concerns. They also proposed that remedies for violating a person's privacy should be monetary damages and, in some cases, an injunction.

Warren and Brandeis based their concept on two types of case law that they believed implicitly recognized the right of privacy. In the first set of cases, courts precluded the publication of works based on intellectual property rights. The second type of cases granted similar protections based on a breach of fiduciary duty. In both types of cases, Warren and Brandeis believed, the outcome was based on the implicit recognition of a right of privacy.

With regard to the first type of cases, Warren and Brandeis believed that intellectual property law, which guarantees the right of an individual to protect the publication value of his or her work, is only an incident of the more general right to be left alone. They addressed cases regarding an author's decision to publish in the first instance. Whether to publish at all is clearly an exclusive right of the artist, yet it is not strictly a property right because there has been no publication that would allow the property laws to control. Therefore they concluded that this right was based on the right to privacy.

In the second type of cases, courts granted injunctions to prevent publication of a plaintiff's work, relying on an implied contract or trust between the plaintiff and the person seeking to publish. Warren and Brandeis believed, however, that the process of implying a trust or a term in a contract was actually a declaration that public morality, private justice, and general convenience demanded the result that the courts reached. Thus, while contract theory may have provided an appropriate way to resolve some cases, this was not the end of the story. Instead, these decisions recognized the legal right of the plaintiff in maintaining his or her right to privacy, which the authors describe as a right to "an inviolate personality," and simply used contract as a method of protecting that right. Warren and Brandeis argued that these lines of cases rested on an implicit privacy right and thus provided precedent for explicit recognition of a right to privacy. Finally, they wrote that both damages and injunctions should be available as remedies for invasions of privacy.

Courts that subsequently considered the issue reached a wide variety of decisions. For several decades, the several state courts either rejected or accepted invasion of privacy as an actionable tort. One reason for the checkered record was that, despite Warren and Brandeis's success in articulating a natural right to privacy (or personality) separated from property rights, the new tort lacked the formal attributes of a property right.

In 1960, William L. Prosser rewrote privacy law when he developed the modern framework for privacy torts, articulating four distinct categories under which a lawsuit could be brought:

(1) intrusion upon seclusion or solitude, or into private affairs; (2) public disclosure of embarrassing private facts; (3) false light publicity; and

(4) appropriation of name or likeness. Prosser also identified limitations of and defenses to the tort, chiefly consent and the privileges of libel and slander.

Prosser's definition was codified in the *Restatement* and assumed its contemporary form in the *Restatement (Second) of Torts* in 1977. The *Restatement* addressed absolute and conditional privileges to the invasion of privacy in defamation. Finally, the *Restatement* generally limits who may bring an invasion of privacy suit to a living individual whose privacy has been invaded.

An example of false light is the publication of a person's photograph beside an article on child abuse, although the person photographed is not a child abuser. The fundamental requirement is that the implication of the statement or picture is false. Like defamation law, false light is intended primarily to protect reputation.

A cause of action for appropriation arises when one individual "appropriates to his own use or benefit the name or the likeness of another," usually for commercial gain. For example, it would be a cause of action for appropriation if a cereal company were to place singer-songwriter Beyoncé's image on its cereal boxes, without Beyoncé's permission, in an effort to sell cereal. This right is similar to copyright in that an individual has a copyright in his or her name and image.

The intrusion tort protects against invasion into someone's personal space. Photographers, for example, are barred from following the singer and actress Jennifer Lopez too closely, even in public. The tort is to protect property, and solitude, and foster informational privacy.

The disclosure tort directly protects informational privacy. One problem is that a would-be plaintiff must prove not merely "publication" (such as in the defamation tort) but also "publicity," meaning widespread dissemination. If there is publicity, however, a defendant might raise the newsworthiness defense (that the incident is "of legitimate concern to the public"), and the courts generally rule in favor of media organizations. Part of this is due to the First Amendment. While the U.S. Supreme Court has not made the tort unconstitutional, it seriously limited its usefulness in *Florida Star v. BJF*, in which the Court held that penalizing a newspaper for publishing a rape victim's name violates the First Amendment.

Currently, most states have either adopted the tort of invasion of privacy through the common law system or explicitly recognized the four-part *Restatement*/Prosser framework (or cited it favorably and explicitly recognized parts of it without rejecting or questioning the others). Other states generally accept the *Restatement* framework yet either explicitly reject or seriously question either or both disclosure or false light, the third and fourth part of the *Restatement*'s definition.

The invasion of privacy tort has grown even more important in the digital age as the contemporary world increasingly continues to "shrink" because of the technological advances of our society. The Internet and social media, serving both information-based needs and communication-based needs of people throughout the world, continue to draw the global community ever closer. In our current information environment, more and more information is being collected on individuals; privacy law has had difficulty keeping up with ever-accelerating technological changes. An infinite amount of information can be easily obtained and that information is becoming more and more accessible. Privacy concerns are growing in tandem as individuals seek greater control over information about themselves, citing the need for privacy as vital for human dignity and intimacy.

The Internet has greatly increased the availability of personal information that can be tracked, recorded, and accessed, giving rise to concerns over the personal invasion of privacy due to Internet monitoring. The evolution of the Internet has greatly changed the workplace and, with it, employee expectations of privacy. Employers have increasingly been monitoring employees and assessing the quality and quantity of their work through advanced technology. Thus, the Internet has dramatically changed the security and supervision of business activities. Employers increasingly have the ability to spy on their employees, intercept electronic communications, and access the information that has been stored on the company's computers.

Several proposals are being discussed to ensure that privacy is not violated by Internet monitoring. Many employers notify their employees about the extent to which they are being monitored at work, that their work laptops are subject to review, and about the employer's acceptable Internet use policy. These rules should be clearly stated and consistently and fairly enforced, and the employer should not abuse its power of oversight over the employee.

It is clear that privacy law must continue to evolve to deal with the changes brought about by the accelerating pace of technology. One effective way of protecting individual privacy is for courts and juries to analyze the transfers of information by businesses to determine if socially shared expectations of privacy have been violated by the transfer. Such scrutiny will force businesses to be more cautious when they transfer information. This is one way to ensure that individual privacy is protected in a manner expected by most Americans.

Further Reading

Barendt, Eric. "Libel and Invasion of Privacy," in *Freedom of Speech*, 2d ed. New York: Oxford University Press, 2007.

Currie, Mary Beth. "Intrusion upon Seclusion: The Tort of Invasion of Privacy." *LawNow* 37, no. 2 (November 1, 2012).

Duffy, D. Jan. "Tortious Invasion of Privacy." *Employment Relations Today* 10, no. 4 (Winter 1983): 381–390.

Horsey, Kirsty, and Erika Rackley. "Invasion of Privacy," in *Tort Law,* 4th ed. New York: Oxford University Press, 2015.

Mizell, Louis R. *Invasion of Privacy*. New York: Berkley Books, 1998.

Price, Ira M. "Torts: Right of Privacy: Invasion of Privacy through Fictional Works." *Michigan Law Review* 45, no. 8 (June 1947): 1064–1066.

Shaughnessy, Perri. *Invasion of Privacy*. New York: Delacorte Press, 1996. Weber, Michael. *Invasion of Privacy: Big Brother and the Company Hackers*. Boston, MA: Premier Press, 2004.

Zelermyer, William. *Invasion of Privacy*. Syracuse, NY: Syracuse University Press, 1959.

See also: Brandeis, Louis Dembitz; *Florida Star v. B.J.F.*; Privacy torts; Prosser, William Lloyd; The Right to Privacy

J

Journalism and the protection of sources

Journalists have used anonymous sources for information for generations. Perhaps the most famous of these sources would be W. Mark Felt, known by the pseudonym Deep Throat, an associate director of the FBI who provided information regarding the Watergate scandal to Washington Post reporters Bob Woodward and Carl Bernstein. Felt's identity was successfully protected until 2005. On a very basic level, information that journalists receive from anonymous sources, as well as the identities of the sources themselves, has been regarded as "reporter's privilege" and has been held as a qualified First Amendment right. However, there have been a number of battles over the years regarding the degree of privilege that reporters retain over confidential sources and whether they can be legally required to release the identity of sources. In the modern, digital era, there are a number of factors that further complicate this debate.

Branzburg v. Hayes

This is a Supreme Court case from 1972, which invalidated the use of the First Amendment as a defence for reporters subpoenaed to appear before a grand jury. The facts of the case revolved around a reporter for the *Louisville Courier Journal*, Paul Branzburg, who in the course of reporting witnessed people both producing and using hashish. Two articles written by him were brought to the attention of law enforcement and Branzburg was subpoenaed to appear before a grand jury regarding both articles and was ordered to name his sources, despite their request to him to remain confidential. Branzburg refused and was held in contempt.

In a 5-4 split, the Supreme Court held that the Press Clause of the First Amendment did not allow for reporter's privilege. Justice White, writing for the majority, held that:

> a number of states have provided newsmen a statutory privilege of varying breadth, but the majority have not done so, and none has been provided by federal statute. Until now the only testimonial privilege for unofficial witnesses that is rooted in the Federal Constitution is the Fifth Amendment privilege against compelled self-incrimination. We are asked to create another by interpreting the First Amendment to grant newsmen a testimonial privilege that other citizens do not enjoy. This we decline to do.

Although finding against the reporter, the Court did acknowledge that the government had to convincingly show "a substantial relation between the information sought and a subject of overriding and compelling state interest." Despite this, however, the ruling did not provide a clear federal precedent regarding the privilege of journalistic sources and the ruling has therefore been interpreted differently by courts over the years. For example, *Branzburg* was cited as precedent by the Federal District Court in 2004, in an opinion denying a motion to quash two grand jury subpoenas issued to reporters in relation to the leak of the identity of CIA operative Valerie Plame. In that opinion, Chief Judge Hogan noted that "because this Court holds that the U.S. Supreme Court unequivocally rejected any reporter's privilege rooted in the First Amendment or common law in the context of a grand jury acting in good faith, this Court denies the motions to quash."

The Judge went on further, adding that:

Whatever extent lower courts around the country have eroded the periphery of the Branzburg opinion, the core of the opinion stands strong. The facts of this case fall entirely within that core – a reporter called to testify before a grand jury regarding confidential information enjoys no First Amendment protection. In the three decades since that opinion was penned, the Supreme Court has chosen not to issue a ruling contradicting that holding. Therefore, neither shall this Court.

Department of Justice Guidelines

The Department of Justice has a set of self-created and self-imposed rules intended to control the use of subpoenas issued against members of the press and to provide some protections for reporters. These rules require that, before any subpoena is issued, the Attorney General must approve it and ensure that the following criteria have been carefully considered:

The government should have unsuccessfully attempted to obtain the information from alternative non-media sources.

The subpoena should not be used to obtain peripheral, nonessential or speculative information.

In criminal cases, there should be reasonable grounds to believe, based on information obtained from non-media sources, that a crime has occurred, and that the information sought is essential to a successful investigation.

In civil cases there should be reasonable grounds, based on non-media sources, to believe that the information sought is essential to the successful completion of the litigation in a case of substantial importance.

Subpoenas should, wherever possible, be directed at material information regarding a limited subject matter, should cover a reasonably limited period of time, and should avoid requiring production of a large volume of unpublished material. They should give reasonable and timely notice of the demand for documents.

However, critics of this system have pointed out that these guidelines do not provide any enforceable right for members of the press and rely solely on the adherence of the Department of Justice, while carrying no substantial punishment for a failure to adhere to them.

Shield Laws

A shield law is a law intended to provide reporters with some legal protection against being forced to disclose their sources. Currently, there are no federal laws governing this area and state laws vary greatly, both in terms of what protection is offered and, indeed, whom it is offered to. Some states provide only qualified protections, while others allow for total privilege. Some states also allow for the privilege to extend further than just the reporter in question including others, such as a newspaper's editor, in the privilege.

Issues regarding confidentiality of sources in the digital age

As technological advances have been made, various issues have arisen in regards to attempts by journalists to protect their sources. In the age of digital reporting, factors such as mass surveillance of means of digital communication by bodies such as the National Security Agency, as well as laws demanding mandatory data retention have meant that journalists face new challenges to ensure protection for their sources. While one method of attempting to do this might take the form of avoiding use of electronic devices and communications, other forms of protection include encrypted data. However, the quickly changing nature of the digital world has meant that previously identified protections have become outdated. A recent UNESCO study concluded that:

unless journalistic communications are recognized, surveillance is made subject to checks and balances (both mass and targeted); data retention laws are limited; accountability and transparency measures (applied to both States and corporations) are improved, confidence in the confidentiality of sources could be seen to be weakened. The result could be that much public interest information, such as that about corruption and abuse, will remain hidden from public view.

The study proposed a series of steps that could be taken to address the problems faced, including ensuring that systems are put in place for transparency and accountability regarding data retention policies and surveillance (including both mass surveillance and targeted surveillance) as well as ensuring that steps are taken by countries to adopt, update, and strengthen source protection laws and their implementation in the digital age.

Melissa A. Hale

Further Reading

Branzburg v. Hayes, 408 U.S. 665 (1972), http://cdn.loc.gov/service/ll/usrep/usrep408/usrep408665/usrep408665.pdf

Department of Justice Guidelines https://www.justice.gov/archive/osc/documents/hogan_07_20_04_opinion.pdf

http://mediashift.org/2017/05/will-take-protect-journalism-sources-digital-age/

https://fas.org/sgp/othergov/doj-media-pol.html

UNESCO Study - "Protecting journalism sources in the digital age" - https://unesdoc.unesco.org/ark:/48223/pf0000248054

See also: First Amendment to the U.S. Constitution; Mass media; News leaks; Plame affair; WikiLeaks

K

Katz v. United States, 389 U.S. 347 (1967)

Identification: A 7–1 decision, with a majority opinion by Justice Potter Stewart, in which the U.S. Supreme Court ruled that the government's activities in electronically listening to and recording Charles Katz's telephone conversations violated his right to privacy and constituted a search and seizure in violation of the Fourth Amendment.

The Court's landmark decision in *Katz v. United States* announced that the Fourth Amendment "protects people, not places." This rationale rejected long-standing precedent whereby the primary Fourth Amendment inquiry was whether the government had committed a physical trespass. Justice John Marshall Harlan II's concurrence would later be used as the touchstone for Fourth Amendment analysis. Following *Katz*, the primary Fourth Amendment inquiry became whether the government intruded upon an individual's reasonable expectation of privacy.

Charles Katz was seen making phone calls in public telephone booths during certain hours of the day and on a nearly daily basis. Federal Bureau of Investigation (FBI) special agents subsequently attached microphones on top of two public telephone booths that Katz was known to frequent. The microphones had wires attached to them that led to a voice recorder. The microphones were capable of recording one end of telephone conversations conducted within the booths.

FBI agents obtained multiple audio recordings of Katz's telephone conversations. The recorded conversations revealed that Katz was placing bets and obtaining gambling information. The FBI then directed an agent to rent a room next to Katz's apartment, where the agent proceeded to listen to conversations through the common wall without the use of any electronic devices. The agent's notes and the audio recordings were used to obtain a warrant to search Katz's apartment. The agents seized items related to materials and instrumentalities involved with placing bets and wagers. Katz was subsequently arrested and charged with an eight-count indictment for violating a federal statute that prohibited the interstate transmission by wire communication of bets or wagers, or information assisting in the placing of bets or wagers by a person engaged in the business of betting or wagering.

At trial, the government sought to introduce into evidence the audio recordings and physical evidence they obtained against Katz. Katz sought to suppress the evidence, arguing that it was obtained from an illegal search and seizure in violation of the Fourth Amendment. The trial court disagreed and convicted Katz on all counts. The Ninth Circuit affirmed the district court, noting that the FBI agents did not physically intrude into the area occupied by Katz in the telephone booth, therefore precluding any possible Fourth Amendment violation.

The U.S. Supreme Court agreed to review the issue of whether the government's electronic surveillance of Katz's telephone conversations violated the Fourth Amendment. As an initial matter, the Court rejected the parties' contention that the proper inquiry should be whether a public telephone booth was a "constitutionally protected area." Rather, the inquiry should be focused on the individual because the Fourth Amendment protects people, not places.

Justice Stewart also noted that the Fourth Amendment cannot be interpreted as a general "right to privacy." Instead, the Fourth Amendment protects individuals from certain types of governmental intrusions, some of which may not implicate privacy concerns at all. The protection of an individual's general right to privacy is largely left to state law.

In analyzing Katz's privacy expectations, the Court stated that an individual in a telephone booth retains the protection of the Fourth Amendment, just as he would at a friend's apartment, in a taxicab, or in a business office. By entering a telephone booth and shutting the door behind him, Katz sought to exclude the "uninvited ear" and rightly assumed that his conversations would not be broadcast publicly. The Court also explained that public telephones played a vital role in private communication.

The government argued that the surveillance technique it used to record Katz did not involve a physical penetration of the telephone booth, thereby foreclosing the possibility of a Fourth Amendment violation. The Court acknowledged that that the absence of a physical intrusion would have normally precluded a Fourth Amendment violation, citing *Olmstead v. United States*, 277 U.S. 438 (1928) and *Goldman v. United States*, 316 U.S. 129 (1942). The Court nonetheless departed from the narrow view that property interests control the right of the government to search and seize and rejected the "trespass" doctrine as articulated in prior cases.

The Court reasoned that, once the proper focus was placed on the person and not the area searched, the Fourth Amendment cannot turn on whether a physical intrusion occurred.

Consequently, the government's surveillance of Katz's telephone conversations violated his privacy and constituted a search and seizure within the meaning of the Fourth Amendment.

The Court nonetheless acknowledged that the investigation of Katz was narrowly confined and noted that a neutral and detached magistrate could have constitutionally authorized, with appropriate safeguards, the surveillance of Katz. Here, however, the agents did not rely on a warrant to record Katz's conversations, and the government could not point to any exigent circumstances justifying the warrantless search. Consequently, the U.S. Supreme Court reversed the Court of Appeals.

While the Supreme Court reversed the Court of Appeals' decision 7–1, three justices wrote separate concurrences and one justice dissented. Most notably, Justice John Marshall Harlan penned a concurrence that would later become the benchmark for Fourth Amendment analysis. Justice Harlan wrote that whether a government search constitutes a search under the Fourth Amendment rests on a two-part test: (1) that the individual had a subjective expectation of privacy and (2) that the individual's expectation of privacy is one that society is prepared to recognize as reasonable. Justice Harlan's "reasonable expectation of privacy" test was explicitly adopted in *Smith v. Maryland*, 442 U.S. 735 (1979), and it remains as the primary inquiry for courts to consider when analyzing Fourth Amendment issues.

Ethan P. Fallon

Further Reading

Kerr, Orin S. "Four Models of Fourth Amendment Protection." *Stanford Law Review* 60, no. 2 (2007): 503–551.

LaFave, Wayne R. *Search and Seizure: A Treatise on the Fourth Amendment,* 5th ed. St. Paul: West Publishing, 2014.

Stuntz, William J. "Privacy's Problem and the Law of Criminal Procedure." *Michigan Law Review* 93, no. 5 (1995): 1057–1062.

Winn, Peter. "Katz and the Origins of the 'Reasonable Expectation of Privacy' Test." *McGeorge Law Review* 40 (2009): 1–9.

See also: Constitutional law; Criminal justice (criminal procedure); Electronic surveillance; Fourth Amendment to the U.S. Constitution; *Olmstead v. United States*; Privacy laws, federal; Privacy laws, state; The Right to Privacy; Supreme Court of the United States; Wiretapping

Kyllo v. United States, 533 U.S. 27 (2001)

Identification: A 5–4 decision, with a majority opinion by Justice Antonin Scalia, in which the U.S. Supreme Court ruled that the use of sense-enhancing technology to obtain information regarding the interior of a home that could not otherwise be available without physical intrusion constituted a search under the meaning of the Fourth Amendment. Applying this rule to the case at hand, the Court held that the use of thermal-imaging technology to measure the heat emanating from inside the home constituted a search within the meaning of the Fourth Amendment.

In *Kyllo v. United States*, agents from the U.S. Department of the Interior became suspicious that marijuana was being grown by Danny Kyllo. Growing marijuana indoors typically requires the use of high-intensity lamps, and the agents sought to determine whether the heat emanating from Kyllo's residence was consistent with the use of such lamps. Thus, the agents used a thermal-imaging device to scan Kyllo's residence. The device was equipped to detect infrared radiation, capable of discerning varying degrees of temperatures.

The scan of Kyllo's home revealed that the roof over the garage and a side wall were relatively hot compared to the rest of the home, as well as being substantially warmer than the neighboring homes. The agents concluded that Kyllo was using high-intensity lamps to grow marijuana in his home. A federal magistrate judge issued a warrant to search Kyllo's home, based on the thermal images, utility bills, and tips from informants. The ensuing search revealed that Kyllo indeed was growing marijuana inside his home, where agents discovered over 100 marijuana plants. Kyllo was subsequently indicted on one count of manufacturing marijuana in violation of federal law.

Kyllo moved to suppress the evidence obtained against him, arguing that his Fourth Amendment rights were violated when agents scanned his home. The district court denied his motion to suppress the evidence, and Kyllo entered into a conditional guilty plea. The Court of Appeals for the Ninth Circuit remanded the case, directing the district court to conduct a hearing regarding the intrusiveness of the thermal-imaging technology.

On remand, the district judge concluded that the thermal-imaging device was a nonintrusive investigative tool and reasoned that the technology did not penetrate walls or windows, nor did it show any intimate details within the home. Accordingly, the district court upheld the validity of the original warrant and reaffirmed its denial of Kyllo's motion to suppress the evidence. The court of appeals affirmed the district court's decision, holding that Kyllo did not demonstrate a subjective expectation of privacy because he did not attempt to conceal the heat emanating from his home. The court of appeals further reasoned that there was no objectively reasonable expectation of privacy because the thermal images did not expose any intimate details.

The U.S. Supreme Court agreed to review the case. The Court first analyzed whether the scan of Kyllo's residence constituted a search within the meaning of the Fourth Amendment. The Court noted that its Fourth Amendment jurisprudence was no longer tied to the concept of trespass but rather that the reasonable expectations of privacy test enunciated in *Katz v. United States*, 389 U.S. 347 (1967), was controlling. Hence, a Fourth Amendment search occurs only where the government violates a subjective expectation of privacy that society recognizes as reasonable.

The Court acknowledged that the degree of privacy secured by the Fourth Amendment had been affected by technological advances. Thus, for the Court, *Kyllo* was a determination on what limits the power of new technologies had on minimizing the realm of guaranteed privacy. In answering this question, Justice Scalia underscored that the inside of a home was a constitutionally protected area where individuals retain a reasonable expectation of privacy. To withdraw protection from this basic expectation of privacy would be to permit new technology to erode the privacy guaranteed by the Fourth Amendment. Thus, the Court concluded that sense-enhancing technology used to obtain information regarding the interior of the home that could not otherwise have been obtained without physical intrusion constituted a search under the meaning of the Fourth Amendment. Applying this standard to Kyllo, Justice Scalia held that the thermal-imaging scan of the interior of Kyllo's home was an intrusion into a constitutionally protected area and was therefore a search within the meaning of the Fourth Amendment.

The government argued, however, that the use of thermal-imaging technology should be permitted because thermal scanning detects only heat radiating from the external surface of the home, asserting that there is a significant distinction between off-the-wall observations and through-the-wall surveillance. The Court rejected this argument, concluding that such mechanical interpretations of the Fourth Amendment were unavailing.

The Court also rejected the government's contention that the thermal scans of Kyllo's home were permissible because they did not reveal private activities occurring in private areas. Justice Scalia clarified that the Fourth Amendment's protection of the home has never been tied to the quality or quantity of the information obtained and that all details within the home are intimate and are held safe from "prying government eyes." Justice Scalia also stated that restricting thermal imaging from gathering intimate details would be impractical in application.

Last, Justice Scalia noted that the Fourth Amendment draws a firm and bright line at the entrance of a home, and that a search of Kyllo's home was presumptively unreasonable in the absence of a search warrant. The judgment of the Court of Appeals was therefore reversed, and the case was remanded to the district court to determine whether the search warrant was supported by probable cause once the thermal images were excluded as evidence.

Justice John Paul Stevens, joined by Chief Justice William Rehnquist, Justice Sandra Day O'Connor, and Justice Anthony Kennedy, dissented from the majority opinion. Justice Stevens opposed the majority's new rule regarding sense-enhancing technology, arguing that it was unnecessary and inconsistent with the Fourth Amendment. Justice Stevens argued that a distinction does exist between through-the-wall surveillance and off-the-wall surveillance. Thus, because the case involved detecting heat emanations off the wall of Kyllo's home, Justice Stevens would hold that no Fourth Amendment search occurred.

Ethan P. Fallon

Further Reading

Kerr, Orin S. "The Fourth Amendment and New Technologies: Constitutional Myths and the Case for Caution." *Michigan Law Review* 102, no. 801 (2004).

McInnis, Thomas N. *The Evolution of the Fourth Amendment.* Lanham, MD: Lexington Books, 2009.

Simmons, Ric. "From Katz to Kyllo: A Blueprint for Adapting the Fourth Amendment to Twenty-First Century Technologies." *Hastings Law Journal* 53 1303 (2002): 000–000.

See also: Constitutional law; Criminal justice (criminal procedure); Fourth Amendment to the U.S. Constitution; *Katz v. United States*; Search warrants; Supreme Court of the United States

L

Law enforcement

Identification: The agencies and officers charged with preventing, detecting, responding to, and investigating crime; housing and caring for inmates accused or convicted of crimes; and maintaining the peace and public order. While serving bravely in meeting these societal needs, some officers occasionally false short of ethical and behavioral ideals. This entry explores these law enforcement agencies and functions, and briefly examines some of the circumstances where a few officers fall short of the mark.

Justifications for law enforcement and punishment are at the heart of both the criminal justice system as a whole and its law enforcement subpart. Every ordered society must have some law enforcement function to protect the populace and maintain public order. And the criminal justice system punctuates those law enforcement efforts by providing graduated and, ideally, proportional punishments to those offenders apprehended by law enforcement. Theoretically, criminal justice system punishments meted out against those whose crimes cause social harm are justified by one or more of the following social goods: (1) general deterrence (consistent and harsh punishment convinces others to refrain from criminal behavior), (2) specific deterrence (incapacitation: at least the incarcerated person will not be able to act criminally during the incarceration), (3) rehabilitation (incarceration and supervision give inmates a chance to improve themselves and reenter society), and (4) retribution (Hammurabi may have called it "an eye for an eye," but today we can think of it as punishment commensurate with and in retaliation for the offender's criminal act).

Law enforcement agencies

Law enforcement agencies, often described as paramilitary in design and operation, serve many critical roles in crime prevention and response and in making our communities safer. Depending on the jurisdiction, law enforcement agencies include the Federal Bureau of Investigation (FBI), the Minnesota Bureau of Criminal Apprehension, the Cook County Sheriff's Office, and the Los Angeles Police Department. The paramilitary structure is mimicked in most law enforcement agencies. The officers hold ranks, not just positions. In a sample law enforcement agency, the top officer may hold the rank of commander. The next in line would be the deputy commander. Then the next tiers, in diminishing rank order, could be lieutenants, sergeants, and patrol officers. When the commander gives work direction, it is an order, in keeping with the paramilitary environment.

Law enforcement agencies are very heavily driven by policies and standard operating procedures (SOPs) contained in policy manuals, and violating an SOP can be treated as insubordination. Those policy manuals often include a general ethics code and the agency's values, mission, vision, creed, and organizational chart.

The policy manuals also guide many of the day-to-day activities of the officers, including case assignment; uniform and weapon requirements; training protocols; use of force and self-defense policies; and policies guiding officer communication, vehicle use, evidence management and control, juvenile detainee protocols, emergency procedures, and administrative procedures.

The extensive policy manuals are necessitated by the reality that law enforcement officers, for most of each day, are not subject to observation by superior officers. Those policies and procedures then give senior management at least the appearance of control over their subordinates.

Hiring, training, discipline, and termination of law enforcement officers is a current focus of much criminal justice research. Each agency's senior officers strive to identify and hire recruits who have the right stuff, or the attributes believed to correlate with ethical decision making, law enforcement mind-set, and officer safety. They train those recruits having the right stuff by following peace officer standards and training procedures, and curricula on ethical decision making, use of force, self-defense, driving skills, drug detection, and many other topics. Training also frequently includes role playing and scenario testing, where new and seasoned officers are immersed into hypothetical ethical or shoot–no shoot dilemmas to test their responses and their internal ethical and moral compasses.

Of course, perhaps most of the real training of new recruits is provided by training officers (TOs), who ride along with and work alongside the recruits as they perform real law enforcement tasks. To the extent that TOs are competent and ethical, those traits are passed on to the recruits as the TOs model competence and ethics in front of the recruits in real time.

Discipline

Discipline is seen in some departments as a no-win situation. Here is the theory. When officers are disciplined for unethical, unsafe, or other behaviors inconsistent with the policy manual and the law, those officers really receive two messages, or one message with two possible officer responses. The disciplined officer (and other officers learning of the discipline meted out to that officer) may either (1) take the discipline as a reminder that the rules are to be adhered to or discipline will result, or (2) take the discipline as a message that, enabled by the fact that so much of police work is solitary, the officer should do a better job of avoiding detection next time. Some even have argued that the interdependence of street-level law enforcement officers on one another, for their shared worldviews and each other's safety, can sometimes breed a conspiracy of silence: Each officer may be willing to "cover" for other officers to avoid discipline for any of the officers.

Termination

Termination is also problematic in many jurisdictions. For example, sometimes civil service regulations may insulate troublesome, intransigent, or unethical officers from serious employment consequences, thus leading at least some superior officers to use lesser discipline, forego discipline all together, or look the other way.

Patrol and crime detection

Patrol and crime detection are important and perhaps the most visible parts of law enforcement's functions. None of us may be happy to be driving too fast only to see the rotating takedown lights of a cruiser right behind us. But none of us would likely shy away from calling 911 if there were a true public safety emergency. Law enforcement officers serve a patrol function, cruising neighborhoods in marked squad cars in an effort to detect and deter crimes. Officers also respond to 911 and nonemergency calls from the public. In point of fact, although officers are key witnesses to many crimes while on patrol, much crime is detected, witnessed, and reported by civilians (by people in our communities), with the officers playing a follow-up and investigative role. Patrol officers are usually assigned to respond to crimes as, for example, first officers on the scene. Follow-up is sometimes handled by those responding patrol officers, but in major cases, follow-up and investigation is referred to detectives.

Investigating major cases consumes a good deal of law enforcement labor, time, and assets, particularly in larger and more urban departments. Although smaller departments tend to have a single all-purpose investigative team, larger departments often have a number of specialized investigation teams, each usually working a different type of crime. A few examples are drug interdiction, white-collar crime, domestic assaults, terrorism, and weapons crimes. In turn, those investigators at the jurisdiction level frequently turn to regional, statewide, or even national investigative laboratories to conduct DNA analysis, fingerprint comparisons, handwriting or voice identifications, tool mark assessments, and firearms testing and comparisons. Those investigative groups and the supporting labs are key elements of law enforcement. (Investigative techniques used by law enforcement in the digital age are examined in other entries in this volume.)

Ethics and corruption

Ethics and corruption seem to be in the news more frequently of late; however, police corruption and intermittent unethical officer behavior have plagued American law enforcement for many decades. Nepotism was rampant in 1800s and 1900s law enforcement in America. During the gangster and bootlegging eras, many officers took bribes to look the other way. Into the late 1900s, more than a few confessions were beaten out of suspects. More recently, law enforcement agencies have strived to erase that history by enhanced pre- and postemployment ethics training; increased educational attainment requirements, IQ testing, and personality testing for recruits; extensive background checks; ethics scenario testing; and improved departmental

racial and gender diversity. Those efforts have borne limited fruit.

Indeed, some commentators believe they have isolated the problem and call it noble cause corruption. In essence, noble cause corruption works in the following way. Recruits self-select based on their interests in law and order. Recruits are tested in ways that may successfully estimate the recruits' preemployment ethical constructs, but those constructs change once the recruit is hired and socialized into the closely knit and interdependent world of street-level law enforcement. As those officers face unpredictable situations on the street daily, they learn to rely absolutely on their fellow officers without question: They have to, they believe; their lives may depend on their trust in each other. Eventually, and some argue, inevitably, these interdependent law enforcement officers, who see themselves as the thin blue line wearing the white hat to protect the vulnerable public from an uncertain and dangerous world, begin to justify internally minor violations of procedure, policy, and even laws in order to "get the bad guy." What may start as the officers' minor violations grows wider and more secretive as these interdependent officers cover for each other for the perceived common good, a good—public safety—the officers believe that only they can deliver. These officers have stooped to corruption in service to a noble cause.

The noble cause corruption theorists believe that it is an intractable problem. That need not be the case. Many ethical law enforcement officers work in America today and in many ethical law enforcement agencies. Thus, those agencies, at least, must have found the key to unlock noble cause corruption. Perhaps it is top-down modeling of ethical behavior from the top officers. Perhaps it is a more flexible civil service approach, allowing more targeted and appropriate discipline and termination. Perhaps it requires training officers who live and work ethically and can serve as the recruits' role models. Or perhaps it requires that oft-told stories around the squad room about long elevator rides, coerced confessions, or falsified officer testimony that was squelched and punished.

Corrections

Law enforcement's corrections role is most obvious in lockups, county jails, and state prisons, which are staffed by law enforcement officers, and probation and parole officers, which in many jurisdictions are staffed by sworn officers. In those correctional facilities, law enforcement officers supervise, protect, and serve the inmates, providing security while also providing bedding, meals, medical care, and haircuts. Some argue that three-strikes laws and life without parole (LWOP) sentences will astronomically increase jail and prison costs astronomically because of higher medical costs alone for aged prisoners.

Excessive force and biased law enforcement

News accounts of officers acting unethically often make news in America with egregious stories of overreaching and overreacting officers, excessive force, racially biased enforcement approaches, falsified officer testimony, and missing evidence. We all remember the horrific police brutality against Rodney King in 1991, in Los Angeles, and Abner Louima, in 1997, in New York City. In 2014 and 2015, excessive force was the primary factor in a number of well-publicized cases:

- Michael Brown, an eighteen-year-old African–American man, was shot and killed by Ferguson, Missouri, police officer Darren Wilson.
- Eric Garner, an African–American man, was killed with an officer's chokehold in New York City.
- Tamir Rice, an African–American boy just twelve years old, was shot and killed by officers in Cleveland (Rice had been holding a BB gun).

- Freddie Gray, an African–American man, died after falling into a coma after his arrest and transport by Baltimore, Maryland, officers, apparently as the result of a spinal cord injury.

Through October 1, 2015, at least 879 Americans had been killed by law enforcement; 1,149 were killed by police in all of 2014. (These statistics, of course, include many instances of justifiable use of force.) These and other such cases in subsequent years led to the growth of the Black Lives Matter movement, which campaigns against racial profiling and police killings of black people.

In 2018, some 998 Americans were killed by law enforcement. This statistic, of course, includes many instances of justifiable use of force; and it represents a slight decline from previous years.

Law enforcement agencies and the public must seek to understand the causes of police excessive force. More important, they must seek solutions. A distrusted law enforcement and criminal justice system is an ineffective one. Even hiring more minority officers, better trained and educated officers, and better vetted officers has not stemmed the tide of unethical police conduct. Law enforcement's role is essential to public safety and public confidence. To rebuild the public's faith in the criminal justice system, the next generation of law enforcement officers and their superiors must find ways to restrain unethical police conduct and excessive use of force by police.

Charles E. MacLean

Further Reading

Balko, Radley. *Overkill: The Rise of Paramilitary Police Raids in America.* Washington, DC: Cato Institute, 2006.

Bender, Lewis G., et al., eds. *Critical Issues in Police Discipline: Case Studies.* Springfield, IL: C. C. Thomas, 2005.

Caldero, Michael A., and John P. Crank. *Police Ethics: The Corruption of Noble Cause,* 3d ed. New York: Routledge, 2010.

Cato Institute. *National Police Misconduct Reporting Project 2010.* http://www.policemisconduct.net/statistics/2010-annual-report/.

Del Carmen, Rolando V., and Jeffrey T. Walker. *Briefs of Leading Cases in Law Enforcement,* 9th ed. New York: Routledge, 2015. [United States Supreme Court cases.]

Doerner, William G., and M. L. Dantzker, eds. *Contemporary Police Organization and Management: Issues and Trends.* Boston, MA: Butterworth-Heinemann, 2000.

Drake, Bruce. "Divide between Blacks and Whites on Police Runs Deep." Washington, DC: Pew Research Center, 2015. http://www.pewresearch.org/facttank/2015/04/28/blacks-whites-police/.

Ebbe, Obi N. I., ed. *Comparative and International Criminal Justice Systems: Policing, Judiciary, and Corrections,* 3d ed. Boca Raton, FL: CRC Press, 2013.

The Guardian. "The Counted: People Killed by Police in the U.S.." http://www.theguardian.com/us-news/ng-interactive/2015/jun/01/about-the-counted. [Ongoing online project.] Holmes, Lesley. *Police Corruption: Essential Readings.* Cheltenham, Gloucestershire, UK: Edward Elgar, 2014.

Kleinig, John. *The Ethics of Policing.* New York: Cambridge University Press, 1996.

Lister, Stuart, and Michael Rowe, eds. *Accountability in Policing.* New York: Routledge, 2015.

Maguire, Mary, and Dan Okada, eds. *Critical Issues in Crime and Justice: Thought, Policy, and Practice,* 2d ed. Los Angeles: Sage, 2015.

Role and Responsibilities of the Police: The Report of an Independent Inquiry Established by the Police Foundation and the Policy Studies Institute. London: The Foundation, 1996.

See also: Criminal justice (criminal procedure)

Lawrence v. Texas, 539 U.S. 558 (2003)

Identification: A 6–3 ruling, with the majority opinion written by Justice Anthony Kennedy, in which the U.S. Supreme Court ruled that a Texas statute making it a crime for two persons of the same sex to engage in certain intimate sexual conduct violated the due process clause of the Fourteenth Amendment.

Lawrence v. Texas was a landmark decision because it not only struck down the sodomy laws in Texas, and invalidated sodomy laws in thirteen other states, but it also overturned the Supreme Court's ruling in *Bowers v. Hardwick,* 478 U.S. 186 1986), therefore making consensual same-sex sexual activity legal in every state. In addition, it is considered a landmark case for civil rights law, and some argue that the case opened the door for legalizing same-sex marriage as well as invalidating other statutes that were based on morality alone. The case also marked a shift from mere privacy to using liberty as a broad spectrum.

In this particular case, officers of the Harris County Police Department, in Houston, Texas, entered John Geddes Lawrence's apartment. The police were dispatched in response to a reported weapons disturbance and, upon entering, found Lawrence and another man engaging in a sexual act. The two men were arrested and charged with violating the Texas statute that stated, "A person commits an offense if he engages in deviate sexual intercourse with another individual of the same sex." This particular sodomy statute was almost never enforced, and it criminalized sex acts only between members of the same sex.

Lawrence challenged the Texas statute as a violation of the equal protection clause of the Fourteenth Amendment; however, this was rejected by the Harris County Criminal Court. The Court of Appeals for the Texas Fourteenth District considered the argument under both the equal protection and due process clauses but rejected the constitutional arguments, indicating that the decision in *Bowers v. Hardwick* was controlling.

The Supreme Court granted certiorari to answer three major questions: First, did the criminal convictions under the law, which criminalized sexual conduct between two men, but not identical conduct between heterosexual couples, violate the equal protection clause? Second, did the convictions violate liberty and privacy interests protected by the due process clause? Third, should *Bowers v. Hardwick* be overruled?

In *Bowers v. Hardwick,* the facts were very similar to *Lawrence,* with a police officer entering a bedroom and observing consensual homosexual conduct that violated state law. In *Bowers,* the Supreme Court ruled that there was no fundamental right to engage in homosexual sodomy and that homosexual acts are not implicit in the concept of liberty. According to *Bowers,* this meant that the state only needed to show a rational basis for the statute. The rational basis meant that the plaintiff needed to prove that the statute was not rationally related to a legitimate government interest. Typically, this was a difficult argument for the plaintiff to prove.

In rendering the majority opinion, Justice Kennedy discussed *Griswold v. Connecticut,* 381 U.S. 479 (1965), which established that the right to make certain decisions on sexual conduct extends beyond the marital relationship. Justice Kennedy quoted *Griswold,* stating, "[I] f the right of privacy means anything, it is the right of the individual, married or single, to be free from unwarranted governmental intrusion into matters so fundamentally affecting a person as the decision whether to bear or beget a child."

The Court felt that *Bowers* construed the issue too narrowly and that it failed to appreciate the extent of the liberty at stake, stating that the statute's penalties and purposes "have far more-reaching consequences, touching upon the most private human conduct, sexual behavior, and in the most private of places, the home." The Court also rejected the idea that prohibiting homosexual conduct has ancient roots, as the Court had stated in *Bowers,* coming to the conclusion that "[a]t the outset it should be noted that there is no longstanding history in this country of laws directed at homosexual conduct as a distinct matter." The Court also focused on the fact that any sodomy laws in the past were directed at preventing predatory acts involving minors and not preventing consenting adults from engaging in private sexual acts.

The Court also acknowledged that many throughout history have condemned homosexual behavior for moral or religious reasons. The Court also stressed, however, quoting *Planned Parenthood of Southeastern Pa v. Casey,* 505 U.S. 833 (1992), "Our obligation is to define the liberty of all, not to mandate our own moral code."

The Court ultimately held *Bowers* invalid, stating in part that *Bowers* had already been eroded by decisions in *Casey* and *Romer v. Evans,* 517 U.S. 620 (1996). *Planned Parenthood v. Casey* was a case that challenged various provisions of a Pennsylvania abortion statute and ultimately upheld a woman's right to an abortion, while stating that the state can restrict the procedure post viability. Even though this placed restrictions on abortion, it upheld the notion of privacy in one's sexual activities. *Romer v. Evans* was the first case since *Bowers* to address homosexuality, where voters approved of a state constitutional amendment that would have prevented homosexuals from being considered a protected class. The Court held that the amendment did not even meet the rational basis test of having a legitimate government concern and was based only on animosity.

The Court also opted to focus on the due process clause versus the equal protection clause, stating that if it were to only focus on the equal protection aspect, courts might hold anti-sodomy laws valid if worded to prohibit sodomy between all couples, not just same-sex couples. The Court reasoned that the state cannot make private sexual conduct between consenting adults a crime. For the state to interfere with private sexual conduct would be an interference with the right to liberty under the due process clause. The Court further reasoned that the Texas statute furthered no legitimate state interest that would justify intrusion into the private sphere.

Justice Antonin Scalia dissented in this opinion, stressing that the Court should not have revisited *Bowers,* and argued that the majority did not respect the doctrine of stare decisis. Scalia also believed that the Court should be prepared to justify laws based on morality; otherwise, the dissent predicted that the majority opinion in *Lawrence* would make state laws against bigamy, same-sex marriage, adult incest, prostitution, masturbation, adultery, fornication, bestiality, and obscenity questionable.

The decision in *Lawrence* is significant not just for the gay community but for all individuals because it holds that morality alone cannot justify an intrusion into the private conduct of any individual. It is also significant because it introduced a large umbrella of rights and privacy, which was a shift from previous courts that only protected activities that the laws themselves protected.

Melissa A. Gill

Further Reading

Andreasen, Kristin. "*Lawrence v. Texas:* One Small Step For Gay Rights; One Giant Leap for Liberty." *Journal of Contemporary Legal Issues* 14, no. 1, (2004): 73–82.

Carpenter, Dale. *Flagrant Conduct: The Story of* Lawrence v Texas: *How a Bedroom Arrest Decriminalized Gay Americans.* W.W. Norton & Company, 2012.

Goldberg, Suzanne B. "Morals-Based Justifications for *Lawrence*: Before and after *Lawrence v. Texas.*" *Minnesota Law Review* 88, no. 5 (2004).

Tribe, Lawrence H. "Lawrence v. Texas: The 'Fundamental Right' That Dare Not Speak Its Name." *Harvard Law Review* 117, no. 6 (2004).

See also: Constitutional law; Supreme Court of the United States

Legal evolution of privacy rights in the United States

Identification: The development of a body of state and federal law determining the application of constitutional provisions for the protection of American freedoms contained in the Bill of Rights, and of privacy tort law.

The right of privacy in the United States is constantly evolving. The courts interpret state and federal constitutions and statutes protecting privacy in various limited respects against government intrusion on individual rights. Most state courts have also recognized the personal right of privacy, at least in some respects, under state statutes or common law. State-recognized civil privacy rights may be enforced by filing a civil lawsuit against another private person who violates those rights in a manner that causes the plaintiff some legally recognized harm.

In 1891, the United States Supreme Court recognized the important common law values giving rise to the personal right of privacy and autonomy in *Union Pacific Railway Company v. Botsford,* 141 U.S. 250. The plaintiff sued the railroad company for personal injuries she suffered in a sleeping car when an upper sleeping berth collapsed and fell on her. Shortly before trial, the defendant railroad asked the court to order a surgical examination of the plaintiff to confirm her diagnosis. The trial court refused to do so, and the Supreme Court agreed, holding the trial court had no authority to require the plaintiff to undergo a surgical diagnostic examination for the benefit of the railroad. The Court reasoned, "No right is held more sacred, or is more carefully guarded by the common law, than the right of every individual to the possession and control of his own person, free from all restraint or interference of others, unless by clear and unquestionable authority of law" (*Botsford*).

In some cases, state common law or statutory privacy rights have been limited by the courts to acknowledge that personal rights must sometimes give way to constitutional rights of free speech and freedom of the press. In that sense, privacy rights continue to evolve by judicial interpretation to balance the personal right of privacy against important governmental interests. The courts also seek to balance the rights of private individuals to exercise their constitutional rights free of restriction by state and federal courts in the process of enforcing personal privacy rights.

Under current law, the right of privacy includes two major types of privacy classifications. The first is generally known as informational privacy, or the right of an individual to control the distribution to others of personal information about oneself. The second has become known as personal autonomy, or the right to make important decisions about one's most intimate relationships, family life, and bodily functions. The common law values the Supreme Court acknowledged in *Botsford* support both major classifications of privacy interests.

Informational privacy is protected by constitutional rights as well as by different federal and state laws. Personal autonomy, however, is protected primarily by judicial interpretation of constitutional privacy rights. Because the right of privacy in the United States was first recognized as a matter of constitutional law, the next section traces the development of federal constitutional privacy rights. In many cases, state courts have interpreted comparable provisions of their respective state constitutions similarly, although some state constitutions provide even more extensive protection for personal privacy.

Constitutional right of privacy. Early in the history of the United States, privacy rights were first recognized as a matter of federal constitutional law, primarily by judicial interpretation of the Fourth Amendment protection against unreasonable searches and seizures by government officials looking for evidence of criminal activity. In fact, the very purpose of adopting the Fourth Amendment to the U.S. Constitution was in part to protect citizens against general warrants then in common use in England, and writs of assistance used in the colonies (*Steagald v. United States*, 451 U.S. 2014 (1981)).

A writ of assistance was a general warrant allowing the British customs official holding it to search any place of his choice and seize any contraband that might be found. Its purpose was to assist customs authorities in enforcing laws against smuggling. British merchants sought

to restrict colonial trade with other countries, and smuggling was commonplace as a means of avoiding duties on imported goods. Law-abiding colonists considered these writs of assistance especially offensive because customs officials could use them indiscriminately against anyone, not just suspected smugglers. The purpose of the Fourth Amendment was to prevent the kinds of abuses by British customs officials that the writs of assistance had authorized. The Fourth Amendment reads in its entirety as follows:

> The right of the people to be secure in their persons, houses, papers, and effects, against unreasonable searches and seizures, shall not be violated, and no Warrants shall issue, but upon probable cause, supported by Oath or affirmation, and particularly describing the place to be searched, and the persons or things to be seized.

While the Fourth Amendment does not expressly state individual citizens have a constitutional right of privacy, the U.S. Supreme Court has consistently interpreted the Fourth Amendment in a manner consistent with its original purpose: to protect individual privacy interests against unreasonable governmental intrusions. For example, in *Johnson v. United States*, 333 U.S. 10 (1948), the Supreme Court acknowledged that when the Fourth Amendment is implicated, the court must balance "the need for effective law enforcement against the [individual's] right of privacy."

The Fourth Amendment does not prohibit all government searches—only unreasonable ones. As a general rule, a neutral judicial officer known as a magistrate, rather than a law enforcement officer, must decide when the government's interest in searching for evidence of criminal activity outweighs the personal right of privacy. If so, the judicial officer issues a search warrant that must specifically identify the place to be searched and the things to be seized.

The law generally presumes a law enforcement search conducted in a manner consistent with a search warrant is a reasonable one, which is all the Fourth Amendment right of privacy requires. However, legal presumption may be rebutted, or overcome, if a criminal defendant establishes the facts presented to the magistrate were legally insufficient to qualify as probable cause. Generally, the term refers to facts available to a law enforcement officer would support a belief by a reasonably cautious person that contraband or evidence of a crime is present in the place to be searched. If the finding of probable cause is challenged, the court considers "the totality of the circumstances" in determining whether the government has met the constitutional standard (*Florida v. Harris*, 133 S.Ct. 1050 (2013))

Historically, a person's home has been considered especially private, so much so the courts routinely hold that government officials should not be permitted to intrude without a very compelling reason. The Supreme Court has often acknowledged a person's home is his castle and has fought to protect privacy rights within the home (*Georgia v. Randolph*, 547 U.S. 103 (2013)). Therefore, in interpreting the Fourth Amendment, the Court has always considered a person's residence and the immediate surrounding area, known as the curtilage, as deserving special protection against unreasonable government searches (*Florida v. Jardines*, 569 U.S. 1 (2013); *Kyllo v. United States*, 533 U.S. 27 (2001)). Traditionally, the courts analyzed the special protections of the home and its surroundings based on the law related to trespassing on private property. For example, if a law enforcement officer spotted unlawful activity by visual observation without trespassing, courts held that the owner's Fourth Amendment right of privacy was not implicated (*United States v. Jones*, 389 U.S. 347 (1967)).

However, in 1967, the Supreme Court held "the Fourth Amendment protects people, not places" (*Katz v. United States*, 389 U.S. 347 (1967)). In *Katz*, the Court held the Fourth Amendment prohibited law enforcement officials from making a warrantless tape recording of a

telephone conversation in a glassed-in public telephone booth. Therefore, the constitutional right of privacy against unreasonable searches and seizures is not limited to places, like the home, in which courts have historically assumed individuals have had a reasonable expectation of privacy.

More recently, the Court has clarified *Katz* expanded the reach of Fourth Amendment beyond the physical areas in which a person has a reasonable expectation of privacy. Therefore, the concept of physical intrusion into a private place, such as the home, continues to be an important basis for Fourth Amendment privacy rights, as well as nonphysical intrusion by visual, auditory, or electronic means, including sense-enhancing technology of the sort that is not in the general public use or readily available to the public (*Kyllo*). As the Court observed in *Kyllo*, "[t]his assures preservation of that degree of privacy against government that existed when the Fourth Amendment was adopted."

Even if the Fourth Amendment does apply the right of privacy it protects can be waived if a person's conduct is inconsistent with an expectation of privacy. "What a person knowingly exposes to the public, even in his own home or office, is not a subject of Fourth Amendment protection" (*Katz*). Thus, an individual can waive Fourth Amendment rights by knowingly making his private affairs public. And if a person voluntarily consents to a search or seizure, the Fourth Amendment is not violated (*Georgia v. Randolph*).

Even if a person does not waive privacy rights or consent to a search, the Supreme Court has carved out many exceptions to the Fourth Amendment warrant requirement. These court-recognized exceptions do not mean the individual does not have a constitutionally protected right of privacy; rather, they acknowledge the government interest advanced by the search outweighs the personal privacy interest at stake.

One important example of an exception to the warrant requirement is a search of the interior of an automobile when lawfully stopped by police for a traffic violation. The purpose of this exception is to protect officer safety and to prevent the destruction of evidence of a crime. For that reason, the search of the car's trunk, or a closed container inside the car not within easy reach of an occupant, is generally not within the scope of the exception. "[A]n automobile search incident to a recent occupant's arrest is constitutional (1) if the arrestee is within reaching distance of the vehicle during the search, or (2) if the police have reason to believe that the vehicle contains 'evidence relevant to the crime of arrest'" (*Davis v. United States*, 131 S.Ct. 2419 (2011)).

Another important exception to the warrant requirement is a search incident to a lawful arrest, which serves the same government interests as the automobile exception: officer safety and preservation of evidence (*Arizona v. Gant*, 556 U.S. 332 (2009)). On the other hand, the Court has imposed limits on the scope of this exception.

In 2014, for example, the Supreme Court held even when a cellphone is seized by law enforcement incident to a lawful arrest, the Fourth Amendment protection against warrantless searches generally extends to the contents of the arrested person's cellphone (*Riley v. California,* 134 S.Ct. 2473). The Court acknowledged cellphones are commonly used by individuals to store a wide variety of private information and the reasons for the warrant exception for searches incident to arrest are not sufficiently served by expanding the scope of that exception to include the contents of cellphones. Therefore, even if police lawfully arrest a driver, they must obtain a search warrant from a neutral magistrate before they can lawfully search the contents of the arrested driver's cellphone.

Even if one of the many judicially recognized exceptions applies and a warrant is therefore not required, the Fourth Amendment requires any search must be reasonable. This fundamental constitutional requirement of reasonableness applies to both the scope of the search and the manner in which it is conducted (*Maryland v. King*, 486 U.S. (1988)). Therefore, even if a law enforcement officer has a search warrant, the search may still be held unlawful if the search exceeds the scope of the warrant's authority or if a court determines that the nature of the search is otherwise unreasonable.

The Court has narrowly defined what qualifies as a Fourth Amendment search in the first place. For example, even if a person has a subjective expectation of privacy in a place to be searched or the information seized, that does not necessarily mean the Fourth Amendment applies. The Supreme Court has interpreted the constitutional protection against unreasonable searches to apply only if the person has an expectation of privacy society recognizes as objectively reasonable (*California v. Greenwood*, 486 U.S. (1988)). If a court determines a particular challenged search does not qualify as a Fourth Amendment search, law enforcement officers are not required to obtain a warrant, nor must the search even be reasonable, as that term is used in the Fourth Amendment.

While the Fourth Amendment restricts only actions by federal officers and agents, the Supreme Court enforces the Fourth Amendment right of privacy against the states through the due process clause of the Fourteenth Amendment (*Mapp v. Ohio*, 367 U.S. 643 (1961)). Federal and state courts both apply the exclusionary rule as a sanction to deter law enforcement from engaging in searches violating the Fourth Amendment. The exclusionary rule is a judge-made rule that refuses to admit evidence at trial against a criminal defendant if evidence was obtained in violation of the Fourth Amendment. Under the fruit-of-the-poisonous-tree doctrine, the exclusionary rule also bars admission of evidence obtained as a direct result of an unlawful search or seizure (*Wong Sun v. United States*, 371 U.S. 471 (1963)).

The Fourth Amendment is not the sole source of federal constitutional privacy rights, and the Fourth Amendment alone does not provide a general right of privacy (*Katz*). The Supreme Court has held privacy protections are primarily the subject of state law rather than federal law:

> [T]he Fourth Amendment cannot be translated into a general constitutional "right to privacy." The Amendment protects individual privacy against certain kinds of governmental intrusion, but its protections go further and often have nothing to do with privacy at all. Other provisions of the Constitution protect personal privacy from other forms of governmental invasion. But the protection of a person's general right to privacy—his right to be let alone by other people—is, like the protection of his property and of his very life, left largely to the law of the individual States (*Katz v. United States*)

In particular, many state constitutions include guarantees against unreasonable searches and seizures, and in some cases the state courts have interpreted those constitutional protections to be broader even than those guaranteed by the U.S. Constitution. The Supreme Court has repeatedly held a state, as a matter of its own law, may impose greater restrictions on law enforcement activities than those imposed by the U.S. Constitution (*Oregon v. Hass*, 420 U.S. 714 (1975)).

Other amendments to the U.S. Constitution provide individuals with limited privacy rights beyond those guaranteed by the Fourth Amendment (*Katz v. United States*). For example, the First Amendment explicitly protects individual privacy with respect to the freedom of association (*Katz v. United States; Nat'l Ass'n for Advancement of Colored People v. State of Ala. ex rel. Patterson*, 357 U.S. 449 (1958)). Also, the Supreme Court has interpreted the First Amendment's freedom of speech as protecting an individual's right to speak anonymously, without revealing one's identity. That freedom extends to protect anonymous advocacy of political causes, as illustrated by the "secret ballot, the hard-won right to vote one's conscience without fear of retaliation" (*McIntyre v. Ohio Elections Comm'n*, 514 U.S. 334 (1995)). As the Supreme Court has often observed, "[T]he First Amendment has a penumbra where privacy is protected from governmental intrusion" (*Griswold v. Connecticut*, 381 U.S. 479 (1965)).

The Third Amendment to the U.S. Constitution prohibits the government from appropriating citizens' homes for quartering soldiers. This protection reflects the strongly held value in protecting the sanctity and privacy of one's home against government intrusion (*Katz*).

Finally, the Fifth Amendment right against compelled self-incrimination in part protects the individual's right to privacy. In *Griswold*, the Court observed, "The Fifth Amendment in its Self-Incrimination Clause enables the citizen to create a zone of privacy which government may not force him to surrender to his detriment."

In 1965, in *Griswold v. Connecticut*, the Supreme Court first recognized the constitutional right of privacy with respect to reproductive decisions. There, the Court held married couples have a constitutional right to decide for themselves whether to use contraceptives, striking down a Connecticut statute prohibiting their use. The Court reasoned the "very idea [of searching the sacred precincts of marital bedrooms for telltale signs of the use of contraceptives] is repulsive to the notions of privacy surrounding the marriage relationship."

> We deal with a right of privacy older than the Bill of Rights—older than our political parties, older than our educational system. Marriage is a coming together for better or for worse, hopefully enduring, and intimate to the degree of being sacred. It is an association that promotes a way of life, not causes; a harmony in living, not political faiths; a bilateral loyalty, not commercial or social projects. Yet it is an association for as noble a purpose as any involved in our prior decisions. (*Griswold v. Connecticut*)

In reaching this conclusion, the Court did not link the ancient right of privacy to any particular constitutional provision, reasoning only the right "concerns a relationship lying within the zone of privacy created by several fundamental constitutional guarantees" (*Griswold*). The Court acknowledged, however, the right of privacy, at least with respect to the marital relationship, is so fundamental it predates even the founding of the United States.

Griswold was the first of many Supreme Court decisions recognizing a constitutional right of privacy related to an individual's personal autonomy to make decisions about private matters, including intimate family relationships. As noted earlier, this important, evolving branch of the right of privacy has become known as the right of personal autonomy. The most important of these decisions involve procreation, intimate relationships, and the right to refuse medical treatment.

In 1973, the United States Supreme Court recognized a constitutional right of privacy with respect to a woman's decision about abortion. The Court held that whether married or unmarried, a pregnant woman has a constitutional right to decide, in consultation with her physician, whether to terminate her pregnancy during the first trimester (*Roe v. Wade*, 410 U.S. 113 (1973)).

In 1990, the Court acknowledged that an individual has a constitutional right of privacy, grounded in the liberty interests protected by the due process clause, to refuse medical treatment, including life-sustaining medical treatment (*Cruzan by Cruzan v. Dir., Mo. Dep't of Health*, 497 U.S. 261 (1990)). This case set the precedent that abortion was a privacy issue, and as such should be protected as a constitutional right.

In 2003, in *Lawrence v. Texas*, 539 U.S. 558 (2003), the Supreme Court held state laws criminalizing sodomy unconstitutional when applied to intimate sexual activity between consenting adults in the privacy of their home. That decision reversed *Bowers v. Hardwick*, 478 U.S. 186 (1986), issued by the Court just seventeen years earlier, upholding a state criminal sodomy statute in a factually similar case. The Court in *Lawrence* recognized adult couples have a constitutional right to privacy with respect to consenting intimate relationships. "Our laws and tradition afford constitutional protection to personal decisions relating to marriage, procreation, contraception, family relationships, child rearing, and education," and that the Constitution demands respect for "the autonomy of the person in making these choices" (*Lawrence*).

Most recently, in 2015, the Supreme Court struck down state laws and constitutional provisions that forbade same-sex marriage (*Obergefell v. Hodges*, 135 S.Ct. 1039 (2015)). While the Court's decision relied primarily on related constitutional concepts of substantive due process and equal protection, it also reasoned the right to marry implicates personal autonomy.

> Like choices concerning contraception, family relationships, procreation, and childrearing, all of which are protected by the Constitution, decisions concerning marriage are among the most intimate an individual can make. Indeed, the Court has noted it would be contradictory "to recognize a right of privacy with respect to other matters of family life and not with respect to the decision to enter the relationship that is the foundation of the family in our society." (*Obergefell v. Hodges*)

By interpreting several specific constitutional provisions as well as the Constitution as a whole, the Supreme Court continues to develop the right of privacy consistent with modern developments in technology and societal norms. A task that has been most difficult given the lack of precedent on these issues not previously dealt with due to technological changes and advancements.

Civil Right of Privacy. The Supreme Court has often recognized a right of privacy existed in common law, even before the adoption of the Bill of Rights as a supplement to the U.S. Constitution (*Griswold*). However, the common law right of privacy in existence then was generally understood to prevent invasions of privacy by government officials and agents. To a limited extent, early common law crimes also recognized a personal right of privacy against other kinds of intrusions by punishing "peeping Toms" who engaged in voyeurism, as well as private individuals who engaged in eavesdropping.

In 1967, for example, the Supreme Court recognized the historical roots of privacy rights with respect to eavesdropping:

> Eavesdropping is an ancient practice that at common law was condemned as a nuisance. At one time, the eavesdropper listened by naked ear under the eaves of houses or their windows, or beyond their walls seeking out private discourse. The awkwardness and undignified manner of this method, as well as its susceptibility to abuse, was immediately recognized. (*Berger v. New York*, 338 U.S. 41 (1967)).

Laws against the crime known at common law as burglary also protected against intrusions into the home. Burglary was committed by a person who engaged in a trespassing by breaking and entering a dwelling of another at night, with an intent to commit a felony inside the home. The common law definition of burglary as a trespassory crime of invasion of another's dwelling echoed the traditional focus on the value of personal privacy with respect to the home.

While the common law generally provided for criminal recourse against peeping Toms, eavesdroppers, and burglars, it did not allow a person whose privacy rights were violated by another to sue in court to recover monetary compensation for the resulting harm. The government itself prosecuted criminal violators, and the individual victim had no direct remedy against the perpetrator for the privacy invasion.

It was not until the last decade of the nineteenth century that scholarly debate addressed what we now know as the common law right of privacy. Since then, the civil right of privacy has evolved primarily as a matter of state common law. However, several states have enacted statutes to supplement, clarify, or limit the scope of the common law right of privacy as a protection against invasions by private persons, including corporations. While most states have judicially recognized the right of privacy in some form, "other common law jurisdictions languish in a quagmire of indecision and hesitancy."

In 1890, an influential law review article published in the *Harvard Law Review* urged the courts to recognize a personal right of privacy of the kind that had never before been recognized at common law. Samuel D. Warren and his former law partner, future Supreme Court Justice Louis D. Brandeis, co-authored an article calling for a new cause of action for invasion of privacy. Cases decided in the early years of the twentieth century debating the existence of a personal right of privacy against other private parties were a direct outgrowth of that law review article. In part, the motivation for the article was the "yellow journalism" common in the late 1800s, as well as the availability of potentially invasive new technologies, including hand cameras and moving pictures.

For example, in one 1890 case, Marion Manola, a comic opera celebrity, successfully sued and obtained a court order to prevent the theater manager from taking flash photos of her performance and distributing the images. By the end of the nineteenth century, photography had become commonplace in the United States. The Kodak box camera was patented by George Eastman in 1888, which made photography available to the general public. Shortly after the turn of the last century, the first Brownie camera could be purchased for just one dollar. The affordability of the portable camera made it possible for many members of the public to engage in surreptitious photography. Private persons who were offended by the taking and publishing of photographs without their consent filed civil lawsuits for violating what the 1909 Rhode Island Supreme Court called "the right of circulating portraits" (*Henry v. Cherry & Webb*, 73 A. 97 (1909)).

In urging courts to recognize a new civil cause of action for invasion of privacy, Warren and Brandeis argued the right was merely a reflection of the "more general right of the individual to be let alone." As discussed earlier, that right had been recognized as a matter of common law, at least in some respects, since before the United States had declared its independence from Great Britain. Warren and Brandeis drew from a legal treatise authored by Professor Thomas Cooley, first published in 1878, that sketched the outlines of a general right of "personal immunity" that would later become known more specifically as the right of privacy. "The right to one's person may be said to be a right of complete immunity; to be let alone."

During the next decade, New York trial courts issued a series of decisions granting court orders, known as injunctions, which prohibited publication or distribution of photographs without the consent of the individual subjects portrayed in them. However, courts in other states refused to recognize the right of privacy urged by Warren and Brandeis. In 1899, for example, the Michigan Supreme Court declared, "We are not satisfied that one has a right of action either for damages or to restrain the possessor of a camera from taking a snap shot at the passer-by for his own uses" (*Atkinson v. John E. Doherty & Co.*, 80 N.W.2d 285)).

In 1902, the highest New York appellate court issued a closely divided opinion rejecting the existence of any common law right of privacy in that state (*Roberson v. Rochester Folding Box*, 171 N.Y. 538). The New York Court of Appeals reversed the trial court's award of money damages to Abigail Roberson. A minor under New York law at that time, Roberson was an 18-year-old young woman whose studio photograph had

been printed and displayed without her consent on 25,000 posters advertising baking flour. The court refused to recognize a common law right of privacy under New York law that would allow Roberson to recover a money judgment for the commercial use of her photograph.

After the New York court had issued its decision reversing the lower court's judgment, the outcome was resoundingly criticized across the country. In 1903, in direct response to the public outcry, the New York legislature enacted a limited statutory right to privacy, the first statute of its kind promulgated by any state. The New York statute was narrowly framed to provide a civil remedy for those whose names or "likenesses," such as Roberson's photograph, were used by anyone for trade or advertising purposes without the person's written consent. A violation of the statute was also defined as a criminal misdemeanor.

Several other state appellate courts followed the New York Court of Appeals, declining to recognize a state common law right to privacy. Many courts were reluctant to declare a new common law right, reasoning state legislatures were better suited to define any new civil right of privacy. A few state legislatures enacted legislation, similar to New York's, that recognized a limited right to recover money damages for certain kinds of privacy invasion. For example, Virginia enacted a statute in 1904 and Utah in 1909.

On the other hand, several other state courts recognized a more sweeping right to privacy. The earliest court to do so, in 1905, was the Georgia Supreme Court. In *Pavesich v. New England Life Insurance Co.*, 122 Ga. 190 (1905), the court held Paolo Pavesich had a valid claim for invasion of his right of privacy because the insurance company used his photograph in a newspaper advertisement without his consent. In recognizing a claim against a private company for invasion of privacy, the court drew from natural law principles as well as state and federal constitutional laws protecting personal liberty interests. The court also relied on a Georgia statute authorizing any court to frame a civil remedy for a violation of any right within the court's jurisdiction. The opinion issued by the Georgia Supreme Court went so far as to predict that one day, the right of privacy would be generally recognized in the United States:

> So thoroughly satisfied are we that the law recognizes, within proper limits the right of privacy, and the publication of one's picture without his consent by another as an advertisement, for the mere purpose of increasing the profits and gains of the advertiser, is an invasion of this right, that we venture to predict the day will come that the American Bar will marvel that a contrary view was ever entertained by judges of eminence and ability . . . (*Pavesich v. New England Life Ins.* Co.).

After the decision in *Pavesich*, other state and federal courts adopted varied positions regarding the state right of privacy. The Rhode Island Supreme Court, following the New York Court of Appeals, rejected the common law right of privacy in 1909, noting it was "unable to discover the existence of the right of privacy contended for" (*Henry*). That same year, the Arkansas Supreme Court acknowledged the issue in a case in which two criminal detainees, not yet convicted of any crime, challenged the use of their photographs in a "rogues' gallery" (*Mabry v. Kettering*, 122 S.W. 115 (1909)). However, the Arkansas Supreme Court decided that law enforcement officers' use of the photographs solely for identification purposes was not improper.

Other state courts followed the trend set by Georgia. In 1911, a Missouri appellate court, relying on *Pavesich,* recognized a five-year-old boy's common law cause of action against a Kansas City jewelry store for using his image in a newspaper advertisement without consent (*Munden v. Harris*, 153 Mo. App. 652 (1911)). Just a year later, a federal district court sitting in Missouri pointedly declined to resolve "the

irreconcilable conflict of opinions and views of courts of last resort in various jurisdictions" (*Vassar Coll. v. Loose-Wiles Biscuit Co.*, 197 F. 982 (WD Mo., 1912)). The court concluded even if a right of privacy did exist, it did not extend to Vassar College, a public educational institution, that asked the court to grant an injunction to prevent a biscuit company from using the college's name and emblems for commercial purposes to promote sales of "Vassar Chocolates." Later courts have agreed the common law right of privacy is a personal right that does not extend to institutions or corporations.

In 1939, the American Law Institute, a non-profit organization of noted scholars and judges, recognized the evolving common law right of privacy when it published the *Restatement of Torts* § 867 (1939). The American Law Institute is highly influential in the development of common law by state appellate courts. According to this first version of the *Restatement*, "[a] person who unreasonably and seriously interferes with another's interest in not having his affairs known to others or his likeness exhibited to the public is liable to the other" (*Restatement of Torts* § 867).

The *Restatement* outlined a single common law right of privacy that could be violated in two different ways: first, by disclosing another person's private affairs to others; and second, by exhibiting another's likeness to the public. To recover money for a violation, a plaintiff needed to convince a court the invasion was an unreasonable and serious interference with the plaintiff's privacy interests. Also, the defendant must have been able to predict the plaintiff would have reason to feel "seriously hurt" by the defendant's conduct. If the plaintiff could prove these elements, it was not necessary to prove physical harm or monetary loss as a result.

Almost immediately, state courts relied on this initial *Restatement of Torts* provision in recognizing a common law remedy for privacy invasions that went well beyond the essential elements outlined by the *Restatement*. For example, in 1941, the Oregon Supreme Court recognized an invasion of privacy when an optical corporation, without consent, signed the plaintiff's name to a telegram lobbying the governor to veto a bill that would have disallowed corporations from dispensing glasses (*Hinish v. Meier & Frank Co.*, 113 P.2d 438). Although the company did not disclose the plaintiff's private affairs to the public and did not exhibit the plaintiff's likeness, the court held that the company unlawfully "appropriated for [its] own purposes [plaintiff's] name, his personality, and whatever [political] influence he may have possessed" (*Hinish v. Meier & Frank Co.*).

In 1960, law school dean William Prosser published a law review article mapping out four related but distinct aspects of the common law right of privacy. The four kinds of privacy invasions proposed in the article included (1) intrusion on seclusion, solitude, or private affairs; (2) public disclosure of embarrassing private facts; (3) publicity casting plaintiff in a false light in the public eye; and (4) appropriation of name or likeness for the defendant's advantage. Each of the four privacy torts protects related but distinct privacy interests. In 1977, the American Law Institute revised the *Restatement of Torts* to incorporate the four distinct kinds of common law invasion of privacy outlined by Dean Prosser in 1960 (*Restatement (Second) of Torts* §§ 652A–652E (1977)). Since then, most states have followed the *Restatement*'s explanation of these four kinds of claims for violation of the common law right of privacy. The American Law Institute is in the process of issuing portions of the *Restatement (Third) of Torts*, but the sections relating to the common law right of privacy have not yet been released.

Over the decades since the American Law Institute last updated the *Restatement of Torts* in 1977, many technological developments, including the Internet, cellphones, electronic surveillance, and drones, have raised difficult new issues implicating personal privacy interests. The common law right of privacy recognized by many states has not addressed these new developments, which raise a host of important new issues that have not yet been resolved. Federal and state statutes have been enacted to address some of these concerns, but in large part the law of privacy in the United States leaves many of these novel issues open for future debate and resolution.

J. Lyn Entrikin

Further Reading

Bratman, Benjamin C. "Brandeis and Warren's The Right of Privacy and the Birth of the Right to Privacy." *Tennessee Law Review* 69, no. 623 (2002): 623–651.

Clancy, Thomas K. "The Importance of James Otis." *Mississippi Law Journal* 82, no. 2 (2013): 487–524. Elder, David A. *Privacy Torts* § 1:1 (2002).

Gajda, Amy. "What If Samuel D. Warren Hadn't Married a Senator's Daughter?: Uncovering the Press Coverage That Led to 'The Right to Privacy,'" *Michigan State Law Review* 2008 35

Glancy, Dorothy J. "Privacy and the Other Miss M." *Northern Illinois University Law Review* 10 401 (1990). Mills, Jon L. *Privacy: The Lost Right*. Oxford University Press, 2008, pp. 5–8. Prosser, William L. "Privacy." *California Law Review* 48 383 (1960).

Richards, Neil M., and Daniel J. Solove. "Prosser's Privacy Law: A Mixed Legacy." *California Law Review* 98 1887, 1924 (2010)

Wacks, Raymond. *Privacy: A Very Short Introduction*. Oxford University Press 2010, pp. 38–50). Warren, Samuel D., and Louis D. Brandeis. "The Right of Privacy." *Harvard Law Review* 4 193 (1890).

See also: Consent; Constitutional law; First Amendment to the U.S. Constitution; Fourth Amendment to the U.S. Constitution: Personal autonomy; The Right to Privacy; Search warrants

License plate reader system

Identification: A technological device typically consisting of a camera that captures images of vehicle license plates, and software that converts the license plate image into machine-readable text.

License plate reader (LPR) systems, or automatic license plate readers (ALPRs), are a form of technology increasingly used by law enforcement and private enterprises to detect, capture, and read vehicle license plates. In the law enforcement realm, once license plates are captured and converted into machine-readable text, they are checked against databases known as hot lists that identify vehicles of interest. For instance, a hot list may be a database of stolen vehicles or vehicles licensed to drivers with outstanding warrants for arrest. When an LPR system is mounted on a police cruiser, license plate information can be captured and checked against hot lists nearly instantly, alerting a police officer if a vehicle of interest is nearby. LPR systems have long been used, but their prevalence is increasing among law enforcement, state transportation departments, and private entities, and the information that is captured is being retained longer and used in more ways.

LPR technology was invented in the United Kingdom in 1976. The technology was widely deployed in London in 1997 through the use of fixed cameras capturing license plates of vehicles entering a security cordon that was established in response to terrorist bombings. Use of LPR systems spread in the United Kingdom, leading to the creation of a national data repository, and by 2010, the repository was receiving around 10 million license plate captures daily from 5,000 cameras.

In the United States, law enforcement agencies have readily adopted and deployed LPR systems. There is no comprehensive study showing exactly how many law enforcement agencies use LPR systems, but a number of studies provide a snapshot of the prevalence of their use. For instance, a 2012 Police Executive Research Forum survey of seventy law enforcement agencies, with an average size of 949 sworn officers, showed that 71 percent of agencies used LPR systems. In response to a series of public records requests made in 2012, the American Civil Liberties Union (ACLU) received 26,000 pages of documents from 293 local police departments and state agencies detailing use of LPR systems.

When deployed, LPR systems can be either fixed or mobile. Fixed LPR systems are permanently installed and continuously monitor the same area. Fixed LPR systems are often attached to roadway infrastructure, such as signs or bridges. Mobile LPR systems are mounted to vehicles, typically law-enforcement vehicles, and capture license plate data as the vehicle drives around.

However they are deployed, all LPR systems generally capture an image of the license plate, a record of the machine-readable license plate number, the time the image was captured, and the location of the vehicle when the image was captured, in the form of global positioning system (GPS) coordinates. An LPR system's effectiveness is based on its ability to capture license plate images, to read those images accurately, and to match license plates against the database records in hot lists. A study of LPR systems in the United Kingdom found that fixed LPR systems correctly read captured license plates 95 percent of the time, while mobile LPR systems read plates correctly 85 percent of the time.

Historically, LPR systems were used in conjunction with hot lists to find stolen vehicles, vehicles registered to individuals with outstanding warrants, vehicles associated with drug purchases, or vehicles associated with Amber Alerts. But as LPR systems proliferate and the cost of data storage decreases, information collected from LPR systems is increasingly being retained for lengthy periods of time and, in some cases, aggregated among regional or national partnerships. Privacy advocates are concerned that as LPR systems move beyond their traditional purpose of looking for vehicles included on hot lists and start collecting, storing, and aggregating data on a vehicle as it travels throughout a network of LPR systems, it will be possible to track an individual's movements.

Private entities are also aggregating information collected from LPR systems. Using this information, companies are compiling regional or national databases of information that can be used to track the entirety of a vehicle's movement as captured by LPR systems. Often these databases are made available to companies that repossess vehicles when owners fail to make payments on car loans; the databases are typically also made available to law enforcement agencies.

The increased prevalence of LPR systems and the growing ease of permanently or semi-permanently saving and aggregating the information gathered has caused concern among privacy advocates. Privacy advocates' concerns derive in part from the limited regulation of the use of LPR systems. A small number of states have passed laws or enacted rules governing the use of LPR systems, and their treatment varies. For example, in New Hampshire, the law generally prohibits the use of LPR systems but provides a few acceptable uses, including investigation of specific crimes. In California, the California Highway Patrol may collect and store LPR information for sixty days, and it may not sell or otherwise make the information available to private entities. As LPR systems proliferate, it is likely that more state legislation addressing the acceptable use of LPR systems will be enacted and that the courts will have more occasion to review the use of LPR systems.

Paul Riermaier

Further Reading

Crump, Catherine, et al. "You Are Being Tracked: How License Plate Readers Are Being Used to Record Americans' Movements." American Civil Liberties Union (July 2013).

Dryer, Randy L., and S. Shane Stroud. "Automatic License Plate Readers: An Effective Law Enforcement Tool or Big Brother's Latest Instrument of Mass Surveillance? Some Suggestions for Legislative Action." *Jurimetrics Journal* 55, no. 2 (Winter 2015): 225–274.

Newell, Bryce Clayton. "Local Law Enforcement Jumps on the Big Data Bandwagon: Automated License Plate Recognition Systems, Information Privacy, and Access to Government Information." *Maine Law Review* 66, (2014): 397–435.

Police Executive Research Forum Staff. "How Are Innovations in Technology Transforming Policing?" Washington, DC: Police Executive Research Forum, January 2012.

Roberts, David J., and Meghann Casanova. "Automated License Plate Recognition Systems: Policy and Operation Guidance for Law Enforcement." Washington, DC: U.S.

Rushin, Steven. "The Judicial Response to Mass Police Surveillance." *University of Illinois Journal of Law, Technology and Policy* 2011, no. 2 (2011): 281–328.

See also: Electronic surveillance; Fourth Amendment to the U.S. Constitution; Law enforcement

Locke, John (1632–1704)

Identification: An English philosopher and the effective inventor of liberalism.

Biography

Locke was born in Wrington, England, in 1632. After completing medical training at Oxford, he came under the patronage of the future Earl of Shaftesbury. He traveled around Europe for reasons both professional and personal: He feared persecution for his writings arguing for religious toleration. After the Glorious Revolution (1688–1689), Locke returned to England for good. Chronically ill, he died in Essex, England, in 1704.

Letter Concerning Toleration

Until nearly the eighteenth century, English subjects did not have religious freedom. The Church of England was the state church, and the government did not tolerate dissent from its dogma. *Letter Concerning Toleration*—which Locke wrote from Dutch exile and got published anonymously in 1689—is one of the first defenses of religious freedom to garner a wide readership. Presaging his argument in the *Second Treatise* (discussed below), Locke asks what a state is for. His answer: It is for protecting "civil interests"—safety for oneself and for one's property—and not for ensuring "the salvation of souls." The state must therefore allow people to believe and practice what they want, excepting such seditious elements as Catholicism.

Essay Concerning Human Understanding

Essay Concerning Human Understanding (1689) is a study of epistemology that has little direct relevance to privacy. But it shares two premises with the *Second Treatise*. First, man's purpose, or "chief end," is to attain "happiness." Second, happiness must be attained as each person understands it, according to his exercise of reason and his inclinations and strengths. It is futile for a ruler to set one standard for "*Summum bonum*," the highest good.

Two treatises of government

Published in one volume (1689), these treatises comprise a defense of a liberal theory, according to which a legitimate government gets its authority by the popular consent of the governed, not directly from God. In the more substantial second treatise, Locke continues to argue for individual initiative and individual freedom. Men naturally enjoy liberty—the freedom to do as they please as long as that does not interfere with anyone else's freedom to do as they please. This liberty extends to property. God gave the world to men in common, but when one person mixes his labor with some part of nature, it becomes his property.

There is a catch, the so-called Lockean proviso: The appropriator must ensure that "enough, and as good, [is] left in common for others." Aside from that, the appropriator may make whatever use he wishes of what is now his property—and is entitled to reap whatever is produced as the fruits of his labor.

Influence

The chief author of the Declaration of Independence, Thomas Jefferson, cited Locke often; the *Second Treatise*'s capsule definition of prop-erty—"life, liberty, and estate"—is echoed in the Declaration's "life, liberty, and the pursuit of happiness."

Today Locke is frequently cited in defense of strong copyright protections. It was largely thanks to his advocacy that the House of Commons in 1695 let lapse England's licensure system. Locke did not elaborate an argument for copyright from first principles; indeed, he may have thought of copyright as less a property right than an expedient trade restriction. Locke was wary of monopolies and argued that anyone should be permitted to print a work that has already been in print for fifty years. Some have argued that the Lockean proviso would exclude copyright protection in the digital world, where little is scarce, after all.

Lowell Rudorfer

Further Reading

Feser, Edward. *Locke*. London: Oneworld, 2007.

Waldron, Jeremy. *God, Locke, and Equality: Christian Foundations in Locke's Political Thought*. Cambridge, England: Cambridge University Press, 2002.

Zemer, Lior. "The Making of a New Copyright Lockean." *Harvard Journal of Law & Public Policy*, no. 3, 29 (2006): 891–947.

See also: The Enlightenment; First Amendment to the U.S. Constitution; Private sphere

M

Magic Lantern

Identification: A software program developed by the Federal Bureau of Investigation (FBI) that is intended to monitor Internet messages by recording every keystroke of people the FBI was seeking to monitor. The FBI was particularly interested in monitoring the keystrokes of encryption passwords. Once installed, Magic Lantern behaved like a Trojan horse program because it could be disguised as a harmless computer file and sent as an attachment to a benign computer email.

Magic Lantern recorded every keystroke, so it could record the contents of documents as they were typed, as well as electronic communications such as email and instant messaging. Hackers and corporate spies often used these programs to obtain secure data, in violation of federal law. Because Magic Lantern was considered a type of spyware, it was eventually referred to as fedware because it was produced by a federal agency.

Prior to Magic Lantern, the FBI used a key logger system, which required both physical entry onto a suspect's property and directly handling a suspect's computers. Magic Lantern did not involve physical contact with persons under surveillance. The FBI had used a key-logging program in the criminal investigation against Nicodemo Scarfo Jr., son of a convicted Philadelphia Mafia boss. FBI agents entered Scarfo's office and installed a key-logging program to capture Scarfo's software encryption key, which later revealed important evidence against the alleged loan shark.

Some observers have compared Magic Lantern to commercial key loggers such as Ghost. One of the significant differences between Magic Lantern and commercial key-logging software is that Magic Lantern is planted as a virus in the suspect's computer. Viruses are sent through infected email.

The FBI disclosed that it was developing the Magic Lantern program on November 21, 2001. This was the first time that the agency introduced a new tool to assist in domestic surveillance. The FBI did so because it needed cooperation from the telephone companies to install the software. The FBI said that Magic Lantern was part of its Cyber Knight program seeking to decrypt Internet messages from white-collar criminals, terrorists, and other wrongdoers operating in cyberspace. The FBI believed that encryption was highly dangerous when used in communications or planning in order to further serious terrorist and criminal activities. Programs including Pretty Good Privacy (PGP) scramble computer files so effectively that it may take a prolonged amount of time for even the most powerful computer to crack them in the absence of the appropriate key. Magic Lantern, the FBI believed, would circumvent this problem by merely copying suspect keystrokes, which may take less than one day.

Although the FBI said that Magic Lantern would be used only "pursuant to the appropriate legal process"—that is, under a court-approved search warrant—privacy and legal experts worried that the program could violate citizens' civil right to be free from unreasonable searches and seizures. Lawyers for Scarfo, for example, have petitioned the courts to review the legality of the evidence gathered by the FBI's previous key-logging program.

Like other Trojan horse viruses, Magic Lantern is detectable by some antivirus programs. Several security software manufacturers announced that they would treat the Magic Lantern bug the same way as any other computer virus. Two U.S. antivirus developers, McAfee and Symantec, however, chose not to include detection for Magic Lantern.

Fedware programs such as Magic Lantern are very controversial. Some commentators believe that the U.S. government should not be writing code that exploits the vulnerabilities of Windows and other operating systems. They further claim that it is an unacceptable use of taxpayer money. Others argue that hackers may benefit from the vulnerabilities revealed and used by U.S. government spyware. The federal government should have an incentive not to use widely available software to conduct its surveillance because such software may already be recognized and defeated by existing anti-spyware and antivirus software.

In 2007, Magic Lantern was renamed the Computer and Internet Protocol Address Verifier (CIPAV). CIPAV, like Magic Lantern and probably most fedware, can be detected by security software.

Further Reading

Donohue, Laura K. "Anglo-American Privacy and Surveillance." *Journal of Criminal Law and Criminology* 96, no. 3 (Spring 2006): 1059–1208.

Etzoni, Amitai. "Seeking Middle Ground on Privacy vs. Security." *Christian Science Monitor*, October 15, 2002: 11.

Kim, Richard S. Y. "Cyber-Surveillance: A Case Study in Policy and Development." Ph.D. dissertation, City University of New York, 2010.

"Magic Lantern Fries Crypto Keys." *Network Security* 2001, no. 12 (December 2001): 2.

"Magic Lantern Snooping Update." *Network Security* 2002, no. 1 (January 2002): 2.

See also: Cybersecurity; Electronic surveillance; Malware

Malware

Identification: Malicious software, or software designed to damage computers or computer networks, or to access information stored within a computer.

Malware can assume many forms, from standard computer viruses to spyware and adware. Individuals may even choose to install malicious software because the malware masquerades as a beneficial program or application. Malware can cause catastrophic damage to a computer's software, The damage malware can do to privacy may not be as obvious but it is equally, if not more, detrimental.

The threat of malware first became a substantial risk to the casual technology consumer when peer-to-peer networks became increasingly popular among those who were not aware of the harms involved. These networks allowed users to access other computers and servers. The networks were often used for the sharing of digital files, such as music. Eventually, malicious individuals discovered that they could disguise harmful software and use the network to corrupt and disable other computers on the peer-to-peer network. One of the first examples of the mass distribution of malware was the music-streaming service Kazaa. Unsuspecting users of the music-sharing networks would inadvertently download files claiming to be MP3 files that were actually malware that would slow down or even destroy their computers. As these threats became more prominent, users became wary of the possibility of downloading malicious software. Today, malware is no longer confined to individuals acting alone on the Internet, nor is it as easy to detect, even for the most perceptive computer users.

```
● ● ●                    READ_FOR_DECRYPT.txt — Edited
Your computer has been locked and all your files has been encrypted with 2048-bit RSA encryption.

Instruction for decrypt:

1. Go to https://fiwf4kwysm4dpw5l.onion.to ( IF NOT WORKING JUST DOWNLOAD TOR BROWSER AND OPEN
THIS LINK: http://fiwf4kwysm4dpw5l.onion )
2. Use 1PGAUBqHNcwSHYKnpHgzCrPkyxNxvsmEof as your ID for authentication
3. Pay 1 BTC (~407.47$) for decryption pack using bitcoins (wallet is your ID for authentication -
1PGAUBqHNcwSHYKnpHgzCrPkyxNxvsmEof)
4. Download decrypt pack and run


---> Also at https://fiwf4kwysm4dpw5l.onion.to  you can decrypt 1 file for FREE to make sure
decryption is working.


Also we have ticket system inside, so if you have any questions - you are  welcome.
We will answer only if you able to pay and you have serious question.

IMPORTANT: WE ARE ACCEPT ONLY(!!) BITCOINS
HOW TO BUY BITCOINS:
https://localbitcoins.com/guides/how-to-buy-bitcoins
https://en.bitcoin.it/wiki/Buying_Bitcoins_(the_newbie_version)
```

Ransomware. (By Palo Alto Networks.)

Consumers may also encounter malware as a result of interacting with major technology companies. In September 2014, Lenovo, a prominent manufacturer of computers, preinstalled Superfish Visual Search software on its computers. The software—named after its parent company, Superfish—was designed to provide targeted advertisements to Lenovo consumers. The software logged every task in which the user of the computer engaged. It also hijacked the computer's security system and allowed for third parties to access easily the data on the individual's computer by altering the security preferences within the user's Internet browsers. Thus, even information transmitted and stored via browsers such as Firefox, which is known for its substantial security, was not entirely secure. Although the practice of developing and disseminating targeted advertisements alone is controversial— if consumers are unaware of and did not consent to the practice—a preinstalled, undisclosed software is even more controversial, especially if it acts as malware to disable a consumer's established computer security.

Because of small-time offenders and the undisclosed activities of corporations such as Lenovo, it seems that users of digital technology must always be aware that, if they are utilizing technology, their information may be at risk. Since the beginning of the digital age, efficiently completing basic tasks, whether at home or work, has become almost impossible without connection to the Internet or technology of some kind. Therefore, privacy activists argue that consumers should be compensated for the destruction of their digital privacy just as if someone violated their privacy in a traditional and tangible fashion. To date, the law has not yet evolved to compensate consumers for the transgressions of malware developers. To combat violations of privacy via court action, potential litigants have no law that promises a chance of success within the courts.

There are only two major technology-oriented laws under which claims involving malware currently have a chance of surviving: the Federal Wiretap Act, 82 Stat. 112 (1968), and the Stored Communications Act, 100 Stat. 1848 (1986), both codified in 18 U.S.C. § 2511. The Wiretap Act is a broadly written but strictly constructed piece of legislation. The first section applies to "any person who intentionally intercepts, endeavors to intercept, or procures any other person to intercept or endeavor to intercept any wire, oral, or electronic communication" (18 U.S.C. § 2511). Under the Wiretap Act, the legal challenge for victims of privacy intrusions as a result of malware is the act's use of the term *intercept*. The act itself does not define the term, and courts have been reluctant to construe it beyond its literal definition. For example, in *United States v. Turk*, 526 F.2d 658, at 659 (5th Cir. 1976), the court interpreted *intercept* to mean that the retrieval of the data must be contemporaneous with the transmission of the data. Thus, for the act to apply, the malware must access the user's data at the very moment the user sends or receive the data. Thus, this standard prohibits claims in regard to most invasions of user privacy on computers because the data accessed is usually stored on the computer rather than in the process of being transmitted. There is a small hope, however, for preserving privacy under the Wiretap Act. In *United States v. Councilman*, 418 F.3d at 13 (1st Cir. 2005), the court held that electronic records, which are not in the state of transmission, would fall under the statute. Yet this trend has not gained momentum because few circuits have decided to adopt this view. Therefore, under the Wiretap Act, distributors of malware have no legal liability.

Malware creators will most likely not be deterred by a claim under the Stored Communications Act, 18 U.S.C. § 2701. This act provides no relief to individuals whose privacy has been negatively affected by malware because the act imposes little in terms of consumer protections. In fact, the act only applies to electronic communication services, which consist only of providers of telephone and email services. Thus, information stored on a personal computer, rather than on a remote server, receives no protection. Therefore, the Stored Communications Act provides no recourse for consumers unless the malware interfered with an email service. Distributors of this harmful software are effectively not deterred

from this practice because consumer protection law in this area is so weak.

Similarly, the Computer Fraud and Abuse Act allows for both criminal and civil actions to be brought against distributors of malware that access "protected computers" (18 U.S.C. § 1030). This language seems to provide some protection to information stored on computers. According to the act, however, the only computers covered under the definition of "protected computers" are computers that are "exclusively for the use of a financial institution of the United States Government, or, in the case of a computer not exclusively for such use, by or for a financial institution or the United States government" 1(8 U.S.C. § 1030 (e)(2)(A)). Therefore, most computer users have no legal protection under federal law from the damage caused by malware.

Although federal law offers little protection against malware, twenty states have passed legislation on malware. The coverage and protection in the twenty states vary, and the statutes grant only criminal causes of action. For example, in New York, the malware statute was codified in the penal code and is written broadly. None of the provisions of New York's Article 156 specifically mention malware or any one of its various forms; rather, Article 156 defines crimes such as "Computer Trespass" in §156.10. Tthe Computer Trespass statute provides that "a person is guilty of computer trespass when he or she knowingly uses, causes to be used, or accesses a computer, computer service, or computer network without authorization and: (1) he or she does so with an intent to commit or attempts to commit or further the commission of a felony; or (2) he or she thereby knowingly gains access to computer material" (NY Penal § 156.10). The sets of broadly written laws in §156 of New York's criminal codes have allowed for successful lawsuits against those who manipulate computers inappropriately with malware (*People v. Puesan*, 973 N.Y.S.2d 121 [N.Y. 2013]).

In contrast, the Consumer Protection Against Computer Spyware Act, a California law, provides for a much more specific protection for consumers against spyware. Most significantly, the Spyware Act protects against software that "collect[s], through intentionally deceptive means, personally identifiable information," Cal. Bus. & Prof. § 22947.2. The act further specifies that software that attempts to prevent the removal of any malicious software or software that "falsely represents that it has been disabled" is prohibited (Cal. Bus. & Prof. § 22974.3). Therefore, computers housed in California are subject to more legal protection than computers within other states.

As the world continuously becomes more digitally oriented, both federal and state laws may evolve, much like California law, to quell effectively the damaging effects of malware upon consumer privacy. As consumers and lawmakers become more aware of the risks associated with various technologies, law and technology will grow in tandem, which will allow for a safer environment in which malicious computer users may not disseminate malware to infringe on privacy rights without retribution.

Ashley Baker

Further Reading

Christodorescu, Mihai, et al. *Malware Detection.* New York: Springer, 2006.

Clancy, Thomas K. "Spyware, Adware, Malware, Phishing, Spam, and Identity-Related Crime," in *Cyber Crime and Digital Evidence: Materials and Cases,* 2d ed. New Providence, NJ: LexisNexis, 2014.

Hyslop, Maitland. *Critical Information Infrastructures: Resilience and Protection.* New York: Springer, 2007.

Iannarelli, John. *Information Governance and Security: Protecting and Managing Your Company's Proprietary Information.* Waltham, MA: Elsevier, 2015.

Kalafut, Andrew, Abhinav Acarya, and Minaxi Gupta. "A Study of Malware in Peer-to-Peer Networks." *Proceedings of the Sixth ACM SIGCOMM Conference on Internet Measurement* (2006): 327–332.

Schwabach, Aaron. *Internet and the Law: Technology, Society, and Compromises.* Santa Barbara, CA: ABC-CLIO, 2014.

Sloan, Robert H., and Richard Warner. *Unauthorized Access: The Crisis in Online Privacy and Security.* Boca Raton, FL: CRC Press, 2013.

Timm, Carl, and Richard Perez. "Malware Attacks," in *Seven Deadliest Social Network Attacks,* tech. ed. Adam Ely. Burlington, MA: Syngress/Elsevier, 2010.

Volonino, Linda, et al. *Computer Forensics: Principles and Practices.* Upper Saddle River, NJ: Pearson/Prentice Hall, 2007.

Wacks, Raymond. *Privacy: A Very Short Introduction.* New York: Oxford University Press, 2015.

See also: Computer Fraud and Abuse Act (CFAA); Spyware; Stored Communications Act (SCA)

Manning, Chelsea Elizabeth

Identification: Was born in Oklahoma on December 17, 1987 to Susan Fox and Brian Manning.

Chelsea Manning was biologically male at birth and was named Bradley Edward Manning. In 2011, Bradley Manning officially changed his gender to female and adopted the name of Chelsea Elizabeth Manning. Ms. Manning's parents divorced in 2000; in 2001 Ms. Manning moved with her mother to Haverfordwest, Wales, United Kingdom. In 2005 Ms. Manning returned to the United States, where she moved in with her father who was living in Oklahoma City with his second wife and child. In September, 2007 Ms. Manning enlisted into the United States Army. Before finishing basic training, Ms. Manning was referred to the discharge unit, but was eventually returned to basic training and graduated the following year. After basic training, Ms. Manning was assigned as an intelligence analyst and rose to the rank of private first class (PFC). As an analyst she received Top Secret/Sensitive Compartmented Information clearance and had access to SIPRNet (Secret Internet Protocol Router Network).

In 2009, Ms. Manning was deployed to Iraq. From 2009 to 2010, Ms. Manning began accessing and downloading classified and sensitive materials from SIPRNet and the Joint Worldwide Intelligence Communications System. Ms. Manning was arrested in early 2010 and charged under article 92, Failure to Obey Order or Regulation, and article 134, a general article for misconduct, under the Uniform Code of Military Justice (UCMJ) on May 29, 2010. The details of the charges made under article 134 include unauthorized possession and dissemination of classified materials to an authorized person, including a video of a military operation that took place in Baghdad in 2007. At the time of the charge, it was reported that PFC Manning had leaked nearly 250,000 classified documents and communications to Wikileaks. Wikileaks did not recognize PFC Manning as the source of the leaked materials. However, the hacker Adrian Lamo, who had had extensive communications through chat and email with PFC Manning, and was the person who notified the Army of PFC Manning's actions, has stated the PFC Manning divulged to Mr. Lamo that he had been the source of the leaks.

Ms. Manning's court martial began in June, 2013. In July, 2013 she was convicted on 20 out of the 22 individual charges, including espionage, and for copying and disseminating confidential and secret documents, but she was acquitted of aiding the enemy. She was sentenced to 35 years in military prison, but will be eligible for parole after serving 7 to 10 years of her sentence. At the time of her sentencing, many argued that Ms. Manning's sentence was harsh, in light of the fact that Ms. Manning's actions were not driven by espionage, but rather by his desire to inform the public of the government's actions.

While she was incarcerated, Ms. Manning became a symbol of the controversies surrounding the government's collection of data, secrecy, and the public's right to access of information. Wikileaks founder, Julian Assange, stated that "Mr. Manning's treatment was intended to send a signal to people of conscious in the US government who might seek to bring wrongdoing to light . . . the Obama administration is demonstrating that there is no place in the system for people of conscious and principle." Many of Ms. Manning's supporters argued that she was a whistleblower who had been unjustly convicted

and who suffered mistreatment while in custody. The government maintained its argument that the sentence imposed on Ms. Manning was insufficient, considering the egregiousness of PFC Manning's actions and the harm it caused to the United States. Ms. Manning's lawyers petitioned for commutation in November, 2016. On January 19, 2017 President Barack Obama granted a commutation; Ms. Manning was released from prison on May 17, 2017.

Rachel Jorgensen

Further Reading

Fishman, Steve. "Bradley Manning's Army of One." *New York*. July 3, 2011. http://nymag.com/news/features/bradley-manning-2011-7/

Maxwell, Lida. "Truth in Public: Chelsea Manning, Gender Identity, and the Politics of Truth-Telling." *Theory & Event* 18, no. 1 (2015) https://muse.jhu.edu/

Poulsen, Kevin and Kim Zetter. "U.S. Intelligence Analyst Arrested in Wikileaks Video Probe." *Wired*. June 6, 2010. http://www.wired.com/2010/06/leak/

Rothe, Dawn L., and Kevin F. Steinmetz. "The Case of Bradley Manning: State Victimization, Realpolitik and WikiLeaks." *Contemporary Justice Review* 16, no. 2 (June 2013): 280-292.

Sangarasivam, Yamuna. "Cyber Rebellion: Bradley Manning, WikiLeaks, and the Struggle to Break the Power of Secrecy in the Global War on Terror." *Perspectives On Global Development & Technology* 12, no. 1/2 (January 2013): 69-79.

Shaer, Matthew. "The Long, Lonely Road of Chelsea Manning." *New York Times*. June 12, 2017. https://www.nytimes.com/2017/06/12/magazine/the-long-lonely-road-of-chelsea-manning.html

True, Michael. „The Passion of Bradley Manning: The Story Behind the Wikileaks Whistleblower." *International Journal On World Peace* 31, no. 3 (September 2014): 84-87

See Also: Assange, Julian; WikiLeaks

Mapp v. Ohio, 367 U.S. 495 (1961)

Identification: A 6–3 decision of the U.S. Supreme Court handed down on June 19, 1961, ruling that, under the Fourteenth Amendment of the U.S. Constitution, evidence obtained from an illegal search is inadmissible in a state court prosecution for a state crime. The majority opinion was written by Justice Tom C. Clark, joined by Chief Justice Earl Warren, and Justices Hugo Black, William O. Douglas, and William Brennan, with separate concurring opinions by Justices Hugo Black, William O. Douglas, and Potter Stewart. Justice John Marshall Harlan, joined by Justices Felix Frankfurter and Charles E. Whittaker, wrote the dissenting opinion.

The Fourteenth Amendment prohibits any state from abridging "the privileges or immunities of citizens of the United States" or depriving "any person of life, liberty, or property, without due process of law." Before *Mapp v. Ohio*, the Supreme Court had ruled illegal the use of evidence seized in violation of the federal Constitution in federal prosecutions but permitted that same evidence to be used in state courts. The result, according to Justice Clark, was that "a federal prosecutor may make no use of evidence illegally seized, but a State's attorney across the street may, although he supposedly is operating under the enforceable prohibitions of the same Amendment."

This inconsistency had its roots in *Weeks v. United States*, 232 U.S. 383 (1914), which established the federal "exclusionary rule." This rule stated that where an individual's papers or possessions had been seized in violation of the Constitution, those materials could not be held and used in evidence against that individual. Otherwise, the Supreme Court noted in *Weeks*, "the protection of the Fourth Amendment, declaring [an individual's] right to be secure against such searches and seizures, is of no value, and, so far as those thus placed are concerned, might as well be stricken from the Constitution."

Thirty-five years later, however, the Supreme Court in *Wolf v. Colorado*, 338 U.S. 25 (1949) decided that the Fourth Amendment's right of privacy is not enforceable against the states through the Due Process Clause of the Fourteenth Amendment. In other words, the Court held that the Fourteenth Amendment does not prevent the admission of evidence obtained by an unreasonable search and seizure in a prosecution in a state court for a state crime.

In light of these two seemingly incongruous decisions, *Mapp v. Ohio* was decided. On May 23, 1957, the police had arrived at Dollree Mapp's house after hearing that an individual wanted for a bombing was hiding there. Mapp refused to allow them entry and called her attorney, who told her that the police must produce a valid search warrant. The police refused to leave the scene and later smashed a glass in the back door, unlocked it, and entered. A piece of paper that was claimed to be a warrant was produced, but Mapp did not retain it, and it disappeared. The police then searched the house. Although the police did not find the individual they were looking for, they found material that they claimed was obscene. Mapp asserted it was the property of a former tenant; nonetheless, she was charged and convicted of being in possession or control of "obscene, lewd, or lascivious" material "of an indecent or immoral nature" in violation of a criminal provision (§ 2905.34) in the Ohio Revised Code.

In his decision, Justice Clark noted that the Supreme Court in 1949 had been very aware of the "'contrariety of views of the States' on the adoption of the exclusionary rule set out in *Weeks*" and had been impressed by the arguments made by the states deeming the "incidence of such conduct by the police too slight to call for a deterrent remedy . . . by overriding the [States'] relevant rules of evidence." The problem was, Justice Clark wrote, that the right to privacy, acknowledged by the Court in *Wolf* twelve years earlier, "could not consistently tolerate denial of its most important constitutional privilege, namely the exclusion of evidence, which an accused had been forced to give by reason of the unlawful seizure. To hold otherwise is to grant the right but in reality to withhold its privilege and enjoyment." The Court decided that the exclusionary rule was an essential part of the Fourth and Fifth Amendments.

Justice Harlan, in dissent, admonished the majority for not following *Wolf* and for their lack of regard for *stare decisis*, which requires courts to observe and respect previous cases that serve as precedent. Unlike the majority, he saw the issue as an inconsistency between the relevant provision of the Ohio Revised Code and the "rights of free thought and expression assured against state action by the Fourteenth Amendment." The majority, he believed, was imposing federal substantive standards of search and seizure and its basic federal remedy, the exclusionary rule (as articulated *Weeks*) on the states. Justice Harlan insisted that the Supreme Court should not fetter the states "with an adamant rule which may embarrass them in coping with their own peculiar problems in criminal law enforcement." The states would find, he believed, their own alternatives to the exclusionary rule to protect the privacy of their citizens.

More than fifty years later, *Mapp v. Ohio* remains controversial for many of the same reasons raised by the dissent and the majority. Nonetheless, it is a landmark case, frequently cited by the courts when considering the Fourteenth Amendment and the prohibition against unreasonable search and seizures under the Fourth Amendment.

The case has also changed the nature of policing in the United States. Before *Mapp v. Ohio*, Supreme Court Justice (then Judge) Benjamin Cardozo had criticized the constitutional exclusionary doctrine, saying, "[t]he criminal is to go free because the constable has blundered" (*People v. Defore*, 242 N.Y. 13, 1926). *Mapp v. Ohio* held that the exclusion was vital because the government cannot be seen to be a lawbreaker. "The criminal goes free," Justice Clark wrote, "but it is the law that sets him free."

Nancy McCormack

Further Reading

Bradley, Craig M. "Reconceiving the Fourth Amendment and the Exclusionary Rule." *Law and Contemporary Problems* 73 (Summer 2010): 211–238.

Curry, Lynne. *Mapp v. Ohio: Guarding against Unreasonable Searches and Seizures.* Lawrence: University Press of Kansas, 2006.

Katz, Lewis R. "Mapp after Forty Years: Its Impact on Race in America." *Case Western Reserve Law Review* 52 (Winter 2001): 471–487.

Zotti, Priscilla H. Machado. *Injustice for All: Mapp v. Ohio and the Fourth Amendment.* New York: Peter Lang Publishing, 2005.

See also: Constitutional Law; Criminal justice (criminal procedure); Fifth Amendment to the U.S. Constitution; Fourth Amendment to the U.S. Constitution; Legal evolution of privacy rights; Supreme Court of the United States

Marketing

Identification: Gathering and analyzing consumer information is important for businesses to be competitive.

Marketing firms develop and use consumer profiles to launch targeted marketing campaigns. Online vendors analyze their shoppers' browsing patterns to provide personalized offers and increase consumer loyalty. Many firms are increasingly able to compile vast amounts of consumer data made possible by advances in storage, networking and data processing technologies. The growing application of data-mining techniques has further fueled the demand for personal information. Thus, collecting consumer information has become the norm for online companies. Almost all commercial Web sites gather personal data. Such a broad scope of gathering and analyzing of consumers' information with or without consumers' awareness have increased online shopper concerns over privacy.

With virtually everything we do, we leave transactional footprints behind. They have value to a business because they can provide businesses a glimpse of a person's life that might indicate his or her receptiveness to products or services that a business may offer.

While each record has some value in and of itself, the information becomes even more valuable and powerful when it is aggregated with each other to create a detailed profile of who the individual is and what he or she does.

This "personality profile" allows marketing companies to make several assumptions about your interests and spending habits, thereby enhancing marketers' ability to target solicitations to those people most inclined to respond. Thus, the same consumer would inevitably find him or herself appearing on several lists that are purchased, borrowed, or sold every day. This particularly applies to persons with specific characteristics. The breadth and specificity of these lists is quite amazing.

Many Americans often believe that these marketing practices violate their privacy rights. Recent cases demonstrate the scope and type of privacy violations emanating from unauthorized dissemination of personal information.

In the current environment, it appears that the only certain way to someone to protect personal privacy is to totally avoid leaving any transactional traces in everyday life. This obviously is exceedingly difficult in a society that is growing increasingly computerized. Many Americans, however, are aware of the increasing unauthorized use of personal information. Americans widely believe that they cannot control information about their personal lives, despite the fact that they believe that they should have the right to control personal information, but that they also are no longer able to control that information. Thus, most Americans seek to gain more control over the dissemination of personal information.

Confronting the consumer is the direct marketing industry. The balance of power between the direct marketing industry and the consumers upon whose information it depends is strongly biased in favor of the marketers. Despite the apparent public concern over unauthorized uses of personal information, it is still legal to disseminate personal information without the consent of the subject of that information. Individuals currently do not have the right to

be informed of the number, names, or types of lists that contain their names, nor do they have a right to have their names removed from these lists. In fact, the direct marketing industry, which has perhaps the largest stake in continued non-regulation of personal information sales, remains completely unregulated.

All types of businesses, whether online or offline, collect and warehouse incredibly vast quantities of personal information on Americans and compile into electronic files to track how these people think and behave. Over a thousand data-mining companies collect and sell data about American consumers. They include large companies like Acxiom (now a part of Interpublic), Experian, and R.L. Polk & Co., which have compiled profiles of almost every American consumer and household. Acxiom's InfoBase profiler collects data from more than 15 million sources and contains demographic information on 95 percent of U.S. households. Experian claims that its databases cover 98 percent of U.S. households and contains more than 1000 data items per household. Polk's "Automotive Profiling System" contains demographic and lifestyle information on more than 150 million vehicle owners and 111 million households.

Online, Internet advertising companies such as DoubleClick track the clickstream of Internet users across the World Wide Web, creating detailed profiles of their behavior. By storing cookies (small text files) on the computers of all visitors to DoubleClick-affiliated sites, the company has collected profiles of more than 100 million individuals.

Other retail companies also engage in consumer profiling, as when online booksellers and other retailers profile customers by tracking the products they view or purchase online. Telephone companies profile customers based on when, how often, and what numbers they call. Grocery stores profile shopping habits by recording and analyzing purchasing information collected through discount or loyalty club cards. Banks and other financial institutions build profiles based on personal financial data. The Gramm-Leach-Bliley Act of 1999 allows users to share customer financial data with affiliated companies on a non-restricted basis and to share it with anyone else if customers do not explicitly choose not to involve themselves in such sharing.

It appears that there are companies, motivated by the belief that "the strategic use of customer information is critical to survival" in a fast, competitive, digitized marketplace, who will seek to exploit their customer data for marketing benefits. Current technology makes it difficult for unrelated businesses to share customer information with other businesses, because their computer systems speak different languages. However, that obstacle may be eliminated by a technology industry initiative known as the Consumer Profile Exchange (CPEX). Working to create standardized XML computer markup language tags that can identify discrete types of personal data, the goal of CPEX is to facilitate the sharing of customer information among different businesses with increasing ease.

"Customer Relationship Management" (CRM), "Business Intelligence" and "Customer Data Integration" are among the euphemisms attached to consumer data profiling. Many observers have researched some of the more unsavory aspects of marketing profiling. Trade articles unintentionally speak volumes about the invasive, dehumanizing, and largely surreptitious nature of profiling for marketing purposes. They talk in terms of capturing, harvesting, and exploiting customer data. The objective, they say, is to "collect intelligence" about the "needs, values, choices and preference" of consumers, thereby allowing businesses to peer into their "identity, attributes, lifestyle and behavior." Competently done, consumer data profiling can result in "a fresh and complete view," an "intelligent profile," "in-depth personalization," and a "complete 360-degree view" of a consumer's life, behavior, and habits.

Concerns over diminishing privacy in a data-driven economy have prompted several proposals from scholars and lawmakers to regulate the field of "information privacy." While all of these proposals have substantial merit, they face potentially insurmountable obstacles.

One approach is to adopt a tort response to address invasive consumer data profiling. Specifically, it would entail that collecting and selling or leasing an extensive consumer data profile without consumer consent should be actionable under the privacy tort of appropriation. Appropriation provides for liability against one who appropriates the identity of another for his benefit, which is nearly always a commercial benefit. Most successful appropriation cases involve situations where the defendant has, without consent, used some aspect of a celebrity's physical likeness, such as a picture or drawing, to promote its product or service.

Consumer data profiles may contain information about some of the most intimate aspects of human life: religion, health, finances, political affiliation, leisure activities, and much more. They constitute the deepest core of a personal identity rather than a mere physical persona. This is true not only because of the massive amount of transactional and other personal information that can be included in a profile but also because of the inferences data miners can draw from that information by applying artificial intelligence to predict the way people might think, feel and behave.

"Data mining" is a broad term that has several definitions. Generally, the term is used to describe the process of sifting through large databases in an attempt to discover patterns and relationships among the data, thereby enabling businesses to make predictive evaluations of consumer behavior. To ferret out these patterns, data-miners rely on a variety of complex automated statistical tools and methodologies.

Data mining a large business that is rapidly growing larger, because consumer information is an extremely valuable commercial asset. Data analytics is a multi-billion-dollar industry today. The revenues of the biggest data-mining companies can exceed $5 billion annually. Experian tells visitors to its website: "Make no mistake about it. Your customer database is your company's most valuable information asset." A leading writer in the field of data mining calls customer information one of the "most important weapons" a company possesses. Some companies reportedly earn more from selling customer lists than from selling their own goods or services. When dot-com businesses fail, their customer data is usually their most valuable asset.

Consumer data collection and analysis yields important benefits for both individuals and society. Acxiom, one of the premier information technology companies, touts these advantages of data mining to consumers: targeted marketing, more efficient catalog and Internet shopping, the ability to locate missing or displaced persons, expedited credit and mortgage transactions, and fraud prevention. Post 9/11, the potential to help identify terrorists may be an added benefit.

While there is room for debate as to the proper balance between the benefits and privacy costs of personal data collection and profiling, the pace of deliberations must move quicker to have any chance of keeping up with the voracious consumption of consumer data. In 2012, global business enterprises stored an estimated 14 million terabytes of data, far exceeding earlier expectations. Plummeting data storage costs make it economical for corporations to warehouse data even if they have not yet determined a use for it. One commentator describes the resulting phenomenon as "data creep," a mentality by which more and more information is sought and retained with the belief it might have some utility in the future.

There is little case law to deter courts from recognizing an appropriation claim in the context of consumer data profiling. More problematic are the several state statutes that appear to limit the remedy for appropriation to situations involving names or likenesses. Essentially, these are right of publicity statutes that ignore the privacy-based component of appropriation.

A few states with appropriation statutes, New York being the premier example, have held that the statutory claim is the exclusive remedy, refusing to recognize a separate common law action. Thus, prevailing on a consumer data profiling claim in such states would require fitting the claim under the statute. Other states, California being the most prominent example, recognize both a statutory and common law claim.

Even states that limit appropriation claims to names or likenesses, either by statute or through common law, a data-profiling appropriation claim could succeed based on the argument that amassing and selling a comprehensive profiled data bank of personal information about a person amounts to an appropriation of the person's "likeness." Courts already have expressed a willingness to stretch the meaning of likeness beyond a person's physical attributes. It is not an unreasonable expansion to argue that a psychographic biography of hundreds of aspects of a person's life constitutes a "likeness" of the person.

Further Reading

Acquisti, Alessandro. *Digital Privacy: Theory, Technologies, and Practices*. New York: Auerbach Publications, 2008.

Garfinkel, Simson. *Database Nation the Death of Privacy in the 21st Century*. Beijing: O'Reilly, 2000.

Grant, Rebecca A. *Visions of Privacy Policy Choices for the Digital Age*. Toronto, Ont.: University of Toronto Press, 1999.

Hemann, Chuck, and Ken Burbary. *Digital Analytics: Making Sense of Consumer Data in the Digital World*. N.p.: Pearson Education, 2018.

Marr, Bernard. "How Much Data Do We Create Every Day?" *Forbes,* May 21, 2018.

Mathieson, Rick. *The On-demand Brand 10 Rules for Digital Marketing Success in an Anytime, Everywhere World*. New York: AMACOM, 2010.

Wertime, Kent, and Ian Fenwick. *DigiMarketing: The Essential Guide to New Media & Digital Marketing*. Singapore: John Wiley & Sons (Asia), 2008.

See also: Brandeis, Louis; Computers and privacy; First Amendment of the U.S. Constitution; Invasion of privacy; Marketing; Privacy torts

Mass media

Identification: Technology intended to reach a mass audience. It is the primary means of communication used to reach much of the general public. The most common platforms for mass media are newspapers, magazines, radio, television, and the Internet. The general public typically relies on the mass media to provide information regarding political issues, social issues, entertainment, and news in pop culture.

The mass media have evolved significantly over time. The newspaper was the original manifestation of the mass media. Newspapers were frequently the only source that provided citizens with the latest news in current events. Once it was invented, the radio superseded the newspaper as the most important source of news and entertainment. Radio became the medium through which most people heard the latest news in politics, social issues, and entertainment. Television eventually replaced radio as the most popular form of mass media. In the current media environment, the Internet has become a major media player and a major source of news for many Americans. With the Internet, the public is able to access news instantaneously instead of having to wait for scheduled programs

Americans indeed value the information and entertainment provided by the mass media. Americans also value privacy. In 1890, Louis Brandeis and Samuel Warren, in "The Right to Privacy," wrote that the citizens' right to be left alone should be protected. "[I]t has been found necessary from time to time to define anew the exact nature and extent of the individual's protections of person and property, and that the scope of such legal rights broadens over time — to now include the right to enjoy life — the right to be let alone." The authors wrote this article, in part, to protest what they considered to be the abuses of a sensationalistic press.

The right to a free press has been defined in the Constitution. What, then, is the definition of privacy? In *Griswold v. Connecticut*, 381 U.S. 479

(1965), Justice Hugo Black once wrote that "'[p]rivacy' is a broad, abstract, ambiguous concept," capable of many different definitions and much in the way of heated controversy. How does the right to privacy interact with the freedom of the press? The right to privacy and freedom of the press, which is enshrined in the First Amendment, are two rights that are always in tension. On the other hand, people are often nervous about the broad, intrusive coverage of modern media, which may disturb their peaceful lives.

The American approach—the reasonable standard of privacy law

In the United States, the media is said to invade the privacy or individuals through one of four means: (1) intrusion upon seclusion, (2) appropriation of name and likeness, (3) publicity that places a person in false light, and (4) publicity of private facts. These are discussed separately in the Restatement (Second) of Torts sections 652B, 652C, 652E, and 652D.

Intrusion

The tort of intrusion upon seclusion usually involves various methods that are used to obtain information. The tort of appropriation involves violating the individual's right in the exclusive use of his or her own identity, represented by his or her name or likeness. The tort of false light publicity concerns the publication of false or misleading information and is similar to defamation.

Appropriation

Appropriation of an individual's name or likeness for commercial purposes without receiving permission from that person is an invasion of that person's privacy. The publication of news and information in any form of media, however, is not a commercial use, even though the mass media companies may make a profit from such publication. Consequently, persons who are named or pictured in news stories or other such material may not sue for tortious appropriation. A news outlet may republish or rebroadcast news stories or photographs that already appeared as news stories in advertising for the mass news organization to promote the quality of the media organization and its work.

A person who seeks to use the name or likeness of an individual for commercial purposes should obtain written consent from that individual. Even written consent may not constitute a sufficient defense in an invasion-of-privacy lawsuit if the consent was given long before publication, if the person who gave the consent is not capable of giving consent, or if the photograph or other material that is used has been substantially changed.

In some instances, courts have recognized the right to publicity cases. Right-to-publicity actions are most often brought by well-known individuals who believe the unauthorized use of their name or likeness deprived them of an opportunity to earn financial gain by selling this right to the user. Some states allow the right to publicity to be passed on to heirs like any other property, meaning that an individual's estate may control the use of his or her name and likeness after the person's death.

False light privacy

It invades someone's privacy to publish false information, which places an individual in a false light. To be tortious, this false information must be considered offensive to a reasonable person, and the plaintiff has the burden of proving that the information was published negligently, with knowledge that it was false, or with reckless disregard for the truth. Most false light cases result from the publication of false information about a person in a news or feature story. Photographs of individuals who are not involved in the news stories that the photographs are used to illustrate also may give rise to false light privacy suits.

Public disclosure of private facts

Courts have recognized that it is an actionable invasion of privacy to publicize private information about another person's life if the publication of this information would be embarrassing to a reasonable person, and the information is not of legitimate public interest or concern. There is no liability for providing further publicity on events already considered public. The news media, for example, may report even embarrassing and sensitive matters available in public records. A reasonable person must consider the publicized information to be offensive for it to be tortious.

Courts use many ways to determine whether information has a legitimate public concern. Stories of great public interest may be considered stories of legitimate public concern. Courts normally view news about both voluntary and involuntary public figures to be of legitimate public concern. When private information is disseminated through the media, there must be a connection that exists between the disclosure of the embarrassing private information and the newsworthy aspects of the story. Embarrassing details about a person's private life cannot be publicized simply to amuse or titillate audiences. News reports that cover past events—including embarrassing details of an individual's life—are normally not considered actionable. Courts usually insist, however, on good reasons for relating embarrassing past events to a person's current life or work.

The *Restatement* defines the public disclosure of truthful information: One who discloses information on the private life of another invades the privacy of another if the matter disclosed is one that (1) would be highly offensive to a reasonable person and (2) is not of legitimate concern to the public.

Apart from the publication of private information in as treated in common law, state and federal statutes prevent the publication of some specific information. For example, Florida law provides statutory remedies for disclosing that a person has AIDS.

The *Restatement* standard deals with three key questions in the case of mass media: (1) What type of media behavior concerning the disclosure of personal information should give rise to civil liability? (2) How does an individual cope with the incompatibility between this liability and the free speech of the First Amendment? and (3) What role should the public interest have?

Publicity

The element of publicity means that an individual, in this case, a member of the mass media or a mass media organization, has publicized a private fact. Where to delineate between the right of privacy and the freedom of the press has long been a contentious matter. The media is in the strongest position to disclose facts.

Highly offensive

The element of disclosure of a private fact is considered highly offensive if "a reasonable person would feel justified in being seriously aggrieved" by the publicity. Again, defining "highly offensive" can be a matter of considerable dispute; however, the *Restatement* provides the most compelling approach. A key issue is how to define a "reasonable person." The Restatement bases its definition based on how it relates to customs of the time and place, in addition to contemporary social values. Courts and commentators elaborate on this definition in their legal analysis in different cases. The difference between the two views may be the way a contemporary reasonable person would feel. Courts consider the "highly offensive" requirement along with the newsworthy test. The two are always considered in conjunction.

The newsworthy test

The newsworthy test of the *Restatement* considers the customs and conventions of a given community. It is again intended to establish a balance between the information that the public is entitled to know and the individual's right to privacy. Even if an individual has not sought publicity or consented to publicity, the newsworthy test is applied to determine whether the person's conduct or the facts in a particular instance makes a particular matter one of legitimate public interest that would thus outweigh the individual's right to personal privacy. In several cases, courts have attempted to strike an appropriate balance between the right of privacy and freedom of the press in matters arising from the tort of public disclosure.

In the *Times-Mirror Co. v. Superior Court*, 813 P.wd 240 (Cal., 1991), the newspaper disclosed the name and address of the plaintiff as a witness in a murder case. The newspaper claimed that the public had a legitimate interest in knowing the witness's identity because she had been involved in a criminal case. The court rejected this argument, distinguishing the newsworthiness of the crime from the public interest in disclosure of the witness's name. In this case, the court found in favor of protecting the witness during a criminal investigation.

Newsworthiness has usually been "broadly construed and liberally applied." In *Walter v. NBC Television Network, Inc.*, 27 A.D. 3d 1070 (4th Dept. 2006), the defendant television network displayed the plaintiff's photograph as part of a televised comedy sketch. Although the sketch was not part of a legitimate news event, the court found a newsworthiness exception in that case.

The balance between personal privacy and a free press on the newsworthiness issue is usually determined by considering the facts in each case. The one thing that all newsworthiness cases have in common is that the decisions involve considerations of freedom of the press. One should always remember that the purpose of the First Amendment is to "preserv[e] an uninhibited marketplace of ideas and [to] foster self-expression free of government restraint." Public debate is essential to American democracy. Courts have long ruled that newsworthy facts, even involving private matters, are indispensable parts of public debates.

Newsworthiness does not entail publicity that is intended to titillate the curiosity of the public; rather, it relates to serious social and political issues. In *Pasadena Star-News v. Superior Court*, 203 Cal. App. 131 (Cal. Ct.

App.1988), for example, journalists identified and located a single mother who abandoned her newborn baby. The court rejected the plaintiff' claim that disclosure of this private and embarrassing fact was tortious because the facts in this case involved issues of unplanned pregnancy, children born to single mothers, adoption, and perhaps even contraception, and abortion.

In terms of protecting facts about public figures, the Restatement suggests that public persons may keep some "intimate details" of their lives private. Many commentators, however, believe that even in an intimate moment, public figures have been "willing accomplices in the creation of a new political culture that sees private aspects of a person's life as politically relevant and that collapses older boundaries between public and private."

Further Reading

Agre, Philip. *Technology and Privacy: The New Landscape.* Cambridge, Mass.: MIT Press, 1997.

Barbas, Samantha. *Laws of Image: Privacy and Publicity in America.* Stanford: Stanford Law Books, 2015.

Freeman, Lee. *Information Ethics Privacy and Intellectual Property.* Hershey, PA: Information Science Pub., 2005.

Gottfried, Ted. *Privacy Individual Right v. Social Needs.* Brookfield, CT: Millbrook Press, 1994.

Hunter, Richard. *World without Secrets: Business, Crime, and Privacy in the Age of Ubiquitous Computing.* New York: Wiley, 2002.

Mills, Jon L. *Privacy in the New Media Age.* Gainseville: University Press of Florida, 2015.

Wacks, Raymond. *Privacy and Media Freedom.* Oxford, England: Oxford University Press, 2013.

Young, John B. *Privacy.* Chichester, England: Wiley, 1978.

See also: Doxing; First Amendment; Fourth Amendment; Invasion of privacy; News leaks; Publicity, right of; Right to be left alone; Right to privacy; Social media;

Medical confidentiality, privacy right to

Identification: An individual's right to keep medical records and information confidential.

During medical treatment, doctors become aware of information concerning their patients through either their diagnoses and observations or what information patients provide. Information intended for medical professionals to treat patients is confidential and must not ordinarily be released to anyone else.

The issue of medical confidentiality arises when information obtained in the course of medical treatment is of interest to others. In such circumstances, two questions must be answered. First, does the doctor have the discretion to disclose the information? If so, then the disclosure of information obtained through the medical treatment is permitted. Second, is the disclosure legally required? For example, law enforcement authorities usually must be informed of cases where the doctor treats a gunshot victim. Health authorities usually must be informed of all HIV-positive carriers.

In the United States, a person is entitled to certain fundamental rights, one of which is privacy. Confidentiality of medical records is recognition of the individual's right to privacy. Not only do individuals benefit from legal protection of their medical confidentiality but society benefits as well. A system of efficient medical treatment may exist if the physician has the maximum amount of relevant information on the patient. In many circumstances, the patient divulges this information only if confidentiality is maintained. The social benefit of having an open exchange of information between doctor and patient may be why physicians have agreed to safeguard the confidentiality of their patients and patient records since the time of the Hippocratic Oath. Despite the fact that the judicial right of privacy has been first legally recognized by the United States beginning in the twentieth century, the doctor's duty to maintain his or her patient's right of confidentiality has existed for at least 2,400 years.

Anglo-American common law did not specifically articulate an obligation by physicians to maintain patient confidentiality. All fifty

American states have enacted legislation, however, creating a duty of confidentiality for physicians. Courts also found a duty of medical confidentiality based on the theories of breach of contract, breach of fiduciary relationship, breach of implied promise of confidentiality, licensing statutes and testimonial privilege that reflect a policy basis for secrecy, and the inherent right of privacy. Whether the duty of medical confidentiality is based on the doctor-patient relationship, on the professional obligations of the doctor as a physician, on the privacy rights of the patient or on the statutes, the scope of this duty of confidentiality is not unlimited. Some of the limitations are specified by statute, while the courts have inferred others.

The most commonly invoked exception is the common law duty of doctors to warn persons who may be endangered by their patients. For example, if a physician fails to warn a person who might be endangered by his or her patient through the spread of disease, the doctor will be guilty of negligence. At a minimum, doctors must exercise reasonable care to advise members of the family and others, who are liable to be exposed to it, of the nature of the disease and the danger of exposure. Notably, this obligation does not extend to unforeseeable victims or the general public. A doctor has no duty to warn persons at large when his or her patient is potentially dangerous to a large segment of the community. There must be a specific victim or a readily identifiable limited class of victims. All states have enacted statutes, however, that require doctors to report certain communicable diseases or infections to public health agencies.

Doctors must also report cases of child abuse, dangerous patients, gun or knife wounds that appear to have been intentionally inflicted, and occupational diseases or injuries. Many states also require doctors to report information on certain prescription drugs, abortions, cancer, and battered adults.

Although most states recognize a doctor-patient testimonial privilege, this privilege is more limited than it appears. In some states, the privilege does not apply in criminal proceedings and when the patient puts his or her condition at issue. The doctor-patient privilege and its exceptions apply only to court proceedings. Outside the courtroom setting, there are other exceptions to physician-patient confidentiality, in addition to the compulsory reporting requirements. These exceptions include medical emergencies, processing health insurance claims, professional peer review, and access by researchers and auditors.

The United States provides relatively few exceptions to the duty of medical confidentiality. In the United States, the obligation of a doctor to maintain confidentiality usually occurs only if he or she was the attending physician. Similarly, the doctor-patient testimonial privilege is limited to communications during treatment.

In contemporary times, growing concerns regarding privacy have made medical confidentiality a major issue. The AIDS epidemic, the increase in genetic testing, the growth of managed healthcare, and electronic record keeping gave rise to serious concerns about patient rights to medical confidentiality.

Several different degrees of protection cover the confidentiality of medical information. On a most basic level, physicians are guided by a professional ethical code to preserve patient confidences. State evidence laws provide protection for medical confidentiality by recognizing a privilege for physician-patient communications. Many states also have confidentiality statutes to restrict disclosure of confidential medical information.

Federal courts have also recognized a constitutional privacy interest in protecting confidential medical information; however, this right is not absolute. Courts have compromised the right to privacy in favor of other constitutional rights. For example, in *United States v. Lindstrom*, 698 F.2d 1154 (11th Cir., 1983), the Court held that the defendant had a right to know private medical information of a witness testifying against her based on her Sixth Amendment rights under the confrontation clause.

Because of the presumption that prisoners surrender some constitutional rights pursuant to their incarceration, the question remains whether inmates possess a constitutional right to medical confidentiality.

In 1996 the Health Insurance Portability and Accountability Act (HIPAA), 110 Stat. 1936, became law. This law has had a great impact on the healthcare industry, including the need for several changes in how medical professionals communicate with their patients, their families, and with each other. HIPAA provides rights to patients and safeguards for employees. It affects all medical professionals and medical staff. The medical profession has stressed how important confidentiality is in all patient matters. The codes of ethics for the various medical professions clearly stress the medical professional's role in promoting and advocating for patient's rights related to privacy and confidentiality. For medical professionals, HIPAA endorses the long-articulated responsibility of medical professionals to their patients.

Because privacy and confidentiality are fundamental rights in U.S. law, safeguarding those rights regarding personal health information is the ethical and legal obligation of medical providers. Maintaining such safeguards is becoming increasingly challenging in the medical environment.

Through and their knowledge, training, and experience, every medical professional understands and respects the need for patient confidentiality. As professionals, their connection to patients and colleagues depends on ensuring such patient confidentiality. Advanced technology and new demands on healthcare—and computer hacking—make it increasingly difficult to keep this promise.

All medical professionals must safeguard the patient's right to privacy. The need for healthcare does not justify unwanted intrusion into the patient's life or affairs. Medical professionals advocate for an environment that provides sufficient physical privacy, including auditory privacy for

discussions of a personal nature, and policies and practices that protect the confidentiality of information.

The medical professional must also maintain confidentiality of all patient information. The patient's well-being could be jeopardized, and the fundamental trust between patient and medical professional could be destroyed by unnecessary access to data or by the inappropriate disclosure of identifiable patient information. The rights, well-being, and safety of the individual patient should be the primary factors in arriving at any professional judgment on the disposition of confidential information received from or about the patient, whether oral, written, or electronic. The standard of healthcare practice and the medical professional's responsibility to provide quality care require that relevant data be shared with those members of the medical team who have a need to know. Only information pertinent to a patient's treatment and welfare is disclosed, and only to those directly involved with the patient's care. Duties of confidentiality are not absolute, however, and may need to be modified to protect the patient, to protect other innocent parties, and in circumstances of mandatory disclosure for public health reasons.

Information used for purposes of peer review, third-party payments, and other quality improvement or risk management may be disclosed only under defined policies, mandates, or protocols. These written guidelines must ensure that the rights, well-being, and safety of the patient are protected. Only that information directly relevant to a task or specific responsibility should be disclosed. When using electronic communications, a special effort should be made to maintain data security.

Medical professionals handle confidential information on a daily basis and must ensure its confidentiality. To emphasize the importance of this duty, all medical professionals must know and understand the privacy requirements of HIPAA and apply this in their work to better protect patient confidentiality.

Health Insurance Portability and Accountability Act (HIPPA)

The Health Insurance Portability and Account-ability Act (HIPAA), 110 Stat. 1936 (1996), was the first federal statute to ensure that the medical insurance information of every patient through-out the United States would be protected. These privacy provisions limit access to a patient's health information and its use. Hospitals and providers may use this information only for treatment, obtaining payment for care, and spec-ified operational purposes such as improving the quality of care. Hospitals and providers must inform patients in writing of how their health data will be used; establish systems to track dis-closure; and allow patients to review, obtain cop-ies, and amend their health information.

HIPAA established standards and require-ments for the electronic transmission of certain health information (eligibility requirements, referrals to other physicians, and health claims). HIPAA protects a patient's rights to the confi-dentiality of his or her medical information and creates federal civil and criminal penalties for improper use or disclosure of protected health information.

Confidentiality protects patient informa-tion, such as the basic identifiers of the patient's past, present, or future physical or mental health conditions, including the provision of health services and payment for those services. Under HIPAA, patients received significant new rights to understand and control how their health information and insurance is used or shared.

In a conceptual framework, a patient's health information record is the collection of all health information in all media generated on the patient under a unique personal identifier and across the continuum of care. The record is created for every patient who receives treat-ment, care, or services at each institution or health network and is maintained for the pri-mary purpose of providing patient care. It is also used for financial and other administrative processes, outcome measurement, research, edu-cation, patient self-management, disease preven-tion, and public health activities. The record has sufficient information to identify the patient, support the diagnosis(es), justify the treatment, document the course and results of treatment, and facilitate the continuity of the patient's care. The health information or data contained in the record belongs to the patient, even though the physical record (either electronic or paper) belongs to the institution.

Establishing and maintaining patients' trust in their caregivers is critical to obtaining a com-plete medical history, obtaining an accurate health record, and implementing an effective treatment plan. If a medical professional fails to protect the patient's privacy, the erosion in the relationship may have dire consequences to the medical professional–patient relationship. At the same time, the reality of the paradigm in which medical professionals practice gives rise to a vari-ety of troubling confidentiality issues. Busy, fre-quently overcrowded hospitals are not conducive environments for guaranteeing confidentiality.

Technology and medical confidentiality

Electronic messaging and new computer tech-nology, though quick and efficient, have major security issues and must be taken into account.

When communicating patient information from one medical professional to another, one must realize that others besides the addressee may view the message, electronic messages may be mistakenly misdirected, electronic commu-nication may be accessed from various loca-tions, or information compiled by one medical professional may be sent electronically to other medical professionals. The Internet does not provide a secure medium for transporting confi-dential information unless both parties are using encryption technologies.

Fax machines are perhaps the least secure technology for transmitting patient information.

Statutory law prohibits certain types of information, including genetic test results, HIV information, and sexual assault counseling, from being faxed outside an institution without appropriate written authorization. All fax cover sheets should contain the standard warning that reads: "The information within this electronic message and any attachments to this message are intended for the exclusive use of the addressee(s) and may contain confidential or privileged information. If you are not the intended recipient, please notify the sender immediately and destroy all copies of this message and any attachments."

All medical professionals have the duty to protect the well-being of those who are entrusted to their care. Protecting the integrity of the medical professional–patient relationship and patient rights is a sacred trust. The issue of medical confidentiality is an essential part of medical practice in the United States. Confidentiality is not just a responsibility of the medical professional but also a right of the patient. Thus, it is the patient, and not the doctor, who may choose to waive this right. Certain exceptions apply where the doctor is not only allowed but required to offer confidential medical information for the social good. Many of the exceptions to medical confidentiality in the United States are based on common law.

In the United States, the right to privacy is frequently implied from common law theories, including contract, fiduciary relationship, implied promise, public policy, and the general right of privacy. The main concept behind medical confidentiality is to encourage a free exchange of information between doctor and patient so that a fully informed physician can provide the best possible treatment. If a patient believes that the information will be kept confidential, the patient is likely to be more forthcoming in his or her discussions with the physician. Thus, in the United States, a physician is not permitted to reveal the medical secrets of his or her patient except in criminal proceedings or where the patient puts his or her condition in issue.

Further Reading

Botkin, Jeffrey R. "Federal Privacy and Confidentiality." *The Hastings Center Report* 25, no. 5 (September-October 1995).

Branscomb, Anne W. *Who Owns Information?: From Privacy to Public Access.* New York: Basic Books, 1994.

Dworkin, Gerald. "Access to Medical Records-Discovery, Confidentiality and Privacy." *The Modern Law Review* 42, no. 1 (1979): 88–91.

Lamberg, Lynne. "Confidentiality and Privacy of Electronic Medical Records." *JAMA* 285, no. 24 (June 27, 2001): 3075.

Laurie, G. T. *Genetic Privacy a Challenge to Medico-legal Norms.* Cambridge, England: Cambridge University Press, 2002.

Lowrance, William W. *Privacy, Confidentiality, and Health Research.* New York: Cambroidge University Press, 2012.

Michalowski, Sabine. *Medical Confidentiality and Crime.* Aldershot, England: Ashgate, 2003.

Nass, Sharyl J., et al., eds. *Beyond the HIPAA Privacy Rule: Enhancing Privacy, Improving Health through Research.* Washington, DC: National Academies Press, 2009.

Rothstein, Mark A. *Genetic Secrets Protecting Privacy and Confidentiality in the Genetic Era.* New Haven, CT: Yale University Press, 1997.

See also: Fair information practices principles; (FIPPs) Health care information; Health Insurance Portability and Accountability Act of 1996 (HIPAA); HIV testing; Privacy laws, state; The Right to Privacy

Metadata

Identification: Documentation of key data that help users locate and put meaning to raw data sets.

Metadata are most commonly described as "data about data." Broadly speaking, this is precisely true. When a photograph, a piece of data, is uploaded to a laptop or computer the information pertinent to the file type, size, resolution, storage location and the upload date/time are all recorded and applied to the saved image file. These fields combined as a whole comprise the metadata—specifically the administrative metadata—for this particular file. Separately, each field represents an individual metadata element.

As this example illustrates, metadata *are* data and are often managed through database registries. When configured within these registries, metadata emerge into specific categories and are organized according to a chosen schema.

Metadata fall into several categories: descriptive, structural, administrative, rights management and preservation—the last two usually grouped with administrative metadata. Examples of each are MARC (Machine-Readable Cataloging) records found in a library's online public access catalog; a digitally scanned box of index cards, sequential grouped and coded according to the schema rules; information necessary to the management and use of files in a digital repository (such as software requirements, etc.) and intellectual property rights data (such as copyright information), respectively. Within these categories, metadata are further delineated at either the item-level or collection-level, forging connections between sets of data known as logical relationships.

These relationships help query coding languages to mine key sources of information from databases. For this reason, metadata must capture a precise depiction of data not only to ensure search results display groups of relevant data, but also to maintain a consistent structure that promotes interoperability and compatibility between metadata registries. A metadata schema, or scheme, facilitates this process of retrieving, sharing, and preserving information by establishing encoding rules for administrative, structural, and other types of metadata. Several widely used schemas are Dublin Core, MODS (Metadata Object Description Schema), METS (Metadata Encoding Transmission Schema), MARC, DOI (digital object identifier), MDDL (Market Data Definition Language), PBCore and CSDGM (Content Standard for Digital Geospatial Metadata), with schemas often based in XML. Depending on the schema, the rules can be organized a number of ways. An authority file may anchor the schema, providing guidelines on how to label elements in a record. For example, the authority file may dictate that "Washington, D.C." always appear with the primary name form of "District of Columbia, the," while variant name forms may list "Washington, DC," "Washington, D.C.," or "The Nation's Capital," etc. Controlled vocabulary such as this bolsters the accuracy of searches as well as semantic interoperability.

Inevitably, discussions of metadata prompt questions concerning what users need to know about the data they seek out to find. Of course, it is undeniable that the sheer volume of metadata necessitate clear standards to maintain order and consistency. The American National Standards Institute (ANSI), the International Electrotechnical Commission (IEC), and the International Organization for Standardization (ISO) are all organizations at the forefront of metadata standards development. Although standards may seem like a secondary issue, in fact they are of primary importance to the entire narrative. The standards create the infrastructure that supports record creation and big data governance, ultimately allowing data to be discoverable. In other words, much of the data we transmit each day—emails, text messages, Google searches, or online transactions—may be lost to the Internet. But as computing technology progresses and standards improve, at some point in time, very little of this data will go undetected.

Lauren Perelli

Further Reading

ANDS Guides. "Metadata: Awareness Level." Australian National Data Service, August 2011.

"Building a Metadata Schema - Where to Start (ISO/TC 46/SC11N800R1)." National Information Standards Organization (NISO), 2014.

Baca, Murtha, and Tony Gill. *Introduction to Metadata.* Los Angeles, CA: Getty Research Institute, 2008. http://www.getty.edu/research/publications/electronic_publications/intrometadata/index.html.

Bargmeyer, Bruce E. and Daniel W. Gillman. "Metadata Standards and Metadata Registries: An Overview." Bureau of Labor Statistics, 2000.

Graybeal, J. "Achieving Semantic Interoperability." In *The MMI Guides: Navigating the World of Marine Metadata*, 2009.

Krishnan, Aishwaria. "Unified Metadata: Key to Reliable, Consistent Information Exchange Between Banks and Regulators." Report, Fintellix Solutions Pvt. Ltd., 2015.

Rousidis, D, E Garoufallou, P Balatsoukas, and M.-A Sicilia. "Metadata for Big Data: a Preliminary Investigation of Metadata Quality Issues in Research Data Repositories."*Information Services and* Use. 34 (2014): 279–286.

Understanding Metadata. Bethesda, MD: NISO Press, 2004.

Zeng, Marcia. "Metadata Basics." Kent State University, 2015.

See also: Computers and privacy; Email; Google

Meyer v. Nebraska, 262 U.S. 390 (1923)

Identification: A 7–2 decision, with a majority opinion written by Justice James Clark McReynolds, in which the U.S. Supreme Court ruled that a Nebraska state law limiting the teaching of foreign languages to children violated the due process clause of the Fourteenth Amendment.

While working as a teacher at the Zion Parochial School in Hampton, Nebraska, Robert T. Meyer ("Meyer") taught Raymond Parpart, a student, how to read in German. On the date in which this lesson occurred, May 25, 1920, Raymond Par-part was ten years old and had not yet successfully completed the eighth grade. Meyer was subsequently charged, by way of an information, with violating a Nebraska statute commonly referred to as "the Siman language law."

The Siman language law consisted of three key provisions. First, no person—including teachers—in any school, was allowed to teach any subject in a language other than English. Second, students could not be taught a foreign language until they had successfully completed the eighth grade. And, finally, violation of the Siman language law would constitute a misdemeanor for those found guilty, and said misdemeanants would be subject to a fine or incarceration.

Meyer was convicted under the Siman language law at the trial court level. The Nebraska Supreme Court subsequently upheld the conviction, reasoning that the Siman language law did not violate the Fourteenth Amendment but was instead a legitimate example of the state's use of police power. The court elaborated that this law was established to instill English as the native language of the children of immigrants, as opposed to the foreign languages brought over to the United States by their parents.

The U.S. Supreme Court agreed to review the issue of whether the Siman language law, as construed and applied against Meyer, improperly infringed upon the liberty guaranteed to Meyer under the Fourteenth Amendment.

Justice McReynolds's opinion delved into a discussion of the liberty afforded to citizens under the due process clause of the Fourteenth Amendment. While stating that liberty in this context cannot be defined exactly, Justice McReynolds did provide an extensive, but nonexhaustive, list of examples of the liberties protected by the clause—included were the freedom from bodily restraint and the right to acquire useful knowledge. In part of his opinion that is salient on privacy matters, Justice McReynolds stated that liberty under the due process clause cannot be hindered by arbitrary legislative action that is disguised as a means to protect the public interest. Also significant to privacy law is Justice McReynolds's assertion that the legislature's approval of matters under its police power are always subject to review by the courts.

Following his general discussion of the due process clause, Justice McReynolds then proceeded to an in-depth discussion of the constitutionality of the Siman language statute itself. Justice McReynolds acknowledged the goal of indoctrinating children with American ideals through the use of English as their native language as a potentially valid one, especially with regard to the usefulness of the children as citizens and the general safety of the public. However, Justice McReynolds stated that, despite their potential validity, these goals may not be achieved through means that conflict with the fundamental rights afforded to citizens under the Constitution. As the Court was unable to observe any potential harm from children knowing languages in addition to English, the majority held that the Nebraska law was arbitrary.

The U.S. Supreme Court reversed the Nebraska Supreme Court's decision and remanded the case for further proceedings. Justice Oliver Wendell Holmes, Jr., and Justice George Sutherland both dissented in this case.

John W. Klinker

Further Reading

Finkelman, Paul. "German Victims and American Oppressors: The Cultural Background and Legacy of *Meyer v. Nebraska*," in *Law and the Great Plains: Essays on the Legal History of the Heartland,* ed. John R. Wunder. Westport, CT: Greenwood Press, 1996.

Ross, William G. "A Judicial Janus: *Meyer v. Nebraska* in Historical Perspective." *University of Cincinnati Law Review 57*, no. 1, (1988): 125–204.

Weinberg, Louise. "The McReynolds Mystery Solved." *Denver University Law Review 89*, no. 1 (January 2011): 133–160.

See also: Constitutional law; Legal evolution of privacy rights

Migrants and refugees in the United States, privacy rights of

Identification: Limited protections covering the personal data of non–U.S. persons.

The Privacy Act of 1974, 5 U.S.C. § 552a, provides statutory privacy rights to U.S. citizens and legal permanent residents, also called U.S. persons. The Privacy Act does not apply to non–U.S. citizens who are not legal permanent residents, also called non–U.S. persons. Privacy advocates have emphasized that the initial

privacy bill, introduced in the Senate by Senator Sam J. Ervin Jr. (D-NC) in 1974, provided privacy protections for non–U.S. citizens as well as for U.S. citizens. The compromise bill that President Gerald Ford eventually signed into law, however, no longer extended to non–U.S. citizens. The Freedom of Information Act (FOIA), in contrast, grants anyone, including non–U.S. citizens, access to the files of federal agencies. While non–U.S. citizens may gain access to their personal files using FOIA, FOIA does not provide the protections of confidential information provided by the Privacy Act.

After the enactment of the Privacy Act, the Office of Management and Budget (OMB), the office responsible for administering the implementation of the act, issued a recommendation that, in cases where agencies maintain "mixed systems of records" (containing information about both U.S. persons and non–U.S. persons). these records should be treated as covered under the Privacy Act.

Following OMB's guidelines more than three decades later, the Department of Homeland Security (DHS), which is the umbrella for the United States Citizenship and Immigration Services (USCIS), in 2007 issued a privacy policy guidance memorandum, which provides that the DHS and all the components under its umbrella, including the USCIS, shall treat personally identifiable information that is held in mixed systems of records in accordance with the fair information practice principles (FIPPs) embodied in the 1974 Privacy Act. Non–U.S. persons thus have the right to access their personally identifiable information collected by the DHS and the right to review and challenge DHS records about themselves.

Specific guidelines regarding third-party disclosure of information contained in or pertaining to asylum applications were initially introduced in the late 1980s following passage of the Refugee Act of 1980, which for the first time created a statutory basis for political asylum in the United States. Based on the 1967 Protocol to the UN Convention Relating to the Status of Refugees, a refugee is defined as a human being who, "owing to a well-founded fear of being persecuted for reasons of race, religion, nationality, membership of a particular social group or political opinion, is outside the country of his nationality, and is unable to, or owing to such fear, is unwilling to avail himself of the protection of that country."

Codified at 8 CFR 208.6., these regulations generally prohibit the disclosure of information "contained in or pertaining to any asylum application, records pertaining to any credible fear determination . . . , and records pertaining to any reasonable fear determination . . . shall not be disclosed without the written consent of the applicant, except as permitted by this section or at the discretion of the Attorney General." This regulation also "safeguards information that, if disclosed publicly, could subject the claimant to retaliatory measures by government authorities or non-state actors in the event that the claimant is repatriated, or endanger the security of the claimant's family members who may still be residing in the country of origin." Based on these regulations, the Board of Immigration Appeals, for example, redacts identifying information about respondents in their precedent decisions published on their website.

While 8 CFR 208.6 offers significant privacy protections, the regulation also includes numerous exemptions threatening the privacy of refugees seeking asylum in the United States. For example, it exempts the disclosure of personal information to any U.S. government investigation in any criminal or civil matter to any federal, state, or local court in the United States, and it also exempts disclosure of information to government officials and contractors who examine information pertaining to asylum adjudications. These exemptions enable a wide circulation of personally identifiable information within the large structure of the DHS, between agencies, and between the DHS and various courts and

law enforcement. The system heightens the risk of mismanagement and security breaches, and leaves many people who have fled wars and persecution particularly vulnerable to violations of their human right to privacy.

Courts establish their own rules to protect privacy, and the regulations vary depending on the jurisdiction and the court. U.S. courts of appeals frequently publish opinions related to asylum applications on the Internet, which contain detailed identifying information about petitioners, including names, medical information, and details about their persecution history. There is no system in place yet that prevents this practice.

While the adjudication of asylum applications is distinct from the regular immigration process in the United States, the patchwork of regulations and the insufficient privacy protections for non–U.S. citizens also expose immigrants seeking legal status in the United States to potential privacy violations. Especially vulnerable are undocumented migrants living in the United States. In recent years, the Electronic Frontier Foundation (EFF) and other advocates have raised particular concerns about the expansion of biometrics collection programs, including the sharing of fingerprints collected by local police with Immigration and Customs Enforcement (ICE), which heightens the risk of deportation. The expansion of international biometricdata-sharing programs poses particular threats for the most vulnerable populations, including refugees and undocumented migrants.

Recent revised regulations of European Dactyloscopy (EURODAC), a European fingerprint database that is a key component of the European asylum system, grant designated law enforcement authorities in European Union (EU) member states as well as Europol access to the database to compare fingerprints. While this access is controlled and intended only for the investigation of serious crimes and terrorism, human rights organizations have been critical because the new regulation contributes to the criminalization of migrants and refugees, and raises the potential for data-processing errors, with potentially grave consequences.

While refugees and migrants are particularly vulnerable to the harm caused by privacy violations, they are caught in a national and international framework that inadequately safeguards their rights, and the human right to privacy.

Katharina Hering

Further Reading

Bloemraad, Irene. *Becoming a Citizen: Incorporating Immigrants and Refugees in the United States and Canada.* Berkeley: University of California Press, 2006.

Boyle, David C. "Proposal to Amend the United States Privacy Act to Extend Its Protections to Foreign Nationals and Non-Resident Aliens." *Cornell International Law Journal* 22, no. 2 (1989): 285–305.

"EURODAC Fingerprint Database under Fire by Human Rights Activists." *Euractiv.com*, July 15, 2015. http://www.euractiv.com/sections/justice-home-affairs/eurodac-fingerprint-database-under-fire-human-rightsactivists-316311.

Hinkle, Robert, David McCraw, Daniel Kanstroom, and Eleanor Acer. Conference on Privacy and Internet Access to Court Files, Panel Two: "Should There Be Remote Public Access to Court Filings in Immigration Cases?" *Fordham Law Review* 79, no. 1 (2010): 25–44.

Kohli, Aarti, Peter L. Markowitz, and Lisa Chavez. "Secure Communities by the Numbers: An Analysis of Demographics and Due Process." Chief Justice Earl Warren Institute on Law and Social Policy, Berkeley Law Center for Research and Administration, October 2011.

Lynch, Jennifer. From Fingerprints to DNA: *Biometric Data Collection in U.S. Immigrant Communities and Beyond.* Special Report for the Electronic Frontier Foundation and the Immigration Policy Center. May 2012.

See also: Electronic Frontier Foundation (EFF); Fair information practice principles (FIPPs); Freedom of Information Act (FOIA); Homeland Security, U.S. Department of (DHS); Privacy Act of 1974

Mobile devices

Identification: Primarily used to describe handheld communications technologies allowing two-way interpersonal communications, may increasingly include a variety of wearable devices and unmanned aerial vehicles (UAVs). Basically, if it can move or be moved from a stationary position, and it permits communications on at least an interpersonal or Machine to Machine (M2M) telephonic or messaging level, it is a mobile communications device.

Mobile communications history began with the onset of radio communications over 100 years ago and continues today with wearable communications and M2M devices. Mobile devices, increasingly in developed countries and often exclusively in developing countries, have become the preferred method for reaching out to other individuals and communications systems like the Internet.

Radio communications allowed telegraph messages to traverse the United States and the Atlantic Ocean in the early 1900s and were used most famously to report the sinking of the *Titanic* in 1912. Besides ship-to-ship and ship-to-shore communications, other early uses of mobile radio were primarily for military communications during World Wars I and II. Domestically, police departments began to use mobile radios and car radios to communicate about pending criminal activity on a live, real-time basis. Still, commercial use of mobile technologies was limited to certain small segments of the population such as Citizens Band (CB) radio aficionados and people who used radio communications for their occupations such as soldiers, police officers, and emergency professionals.

As radio communications proliferated, the need for more bands and more available spectrum, as regulated by the Federal Communications Commission (FCC), became the primary concern for companies offering mobile communications and/or selling mobile devices to customers. In the beginning, the FCC allowed two competing mobile service providers in each geographic area to avoid competing calls on the same portion of spectrum but still to allow some competition to drive down prices and encourage diversity in the features. This carefully constructed balance between pure economic efficiency and public policy continues to drive regulatory decisions today, including spectrum auctions and decisions to approve new services.

Carriers began to build networks of cell-phone towers across the United States to complement and connect with the underground and aboveground telephone wire networks used to provide plain old telephone service (POTS) to customers. For most of the twentieth century, mobile service was viewed as an add-on, even a luxury service, for customers who intended to keep their telephone landlines in service. The first consumer uses of mobile phone devices were often referred to as car phones and were used solely in motor vehicles.

After telegraph messages, voice transmissions through one-way radio, two-way radio, and telephonic communications were the primary application (app) for mobile devices. Text communications began in a nascent form in the early 1990s and began to use more and more mobile device capacity over voice in the following years. Text communications, or Short Message Service (SMS), allows a user to type a brief message of fewer than 160 alphanumeric characters on a device and have it appear on another mobile device or computer. Early text messages were contained in one-way pagers used to alert emergency room doctors on call and other personnel in the field. Nokia was one of the first companies to manufacture mobile devices that had this capacity. In 1997, Nokia produced a mobile device with a full keyboard, easing the ability to text with speed and accuracy. Early texting systems were self-contained. By about 2000, however, interoperability between texting systems allowed the function to become more popular and useful on mobile devices. Mobile devices still use the QWERTY keyboard that typists are familiar with from using typewriters and then computer keyboards. Texting in short messages has changed communications patterns and language customs, especially for the younger generation who grew up using text messages to communicate with friends. Abbreviations and emojis (iconic symbols indicating objects and/or emotional content) have become a new language of communication, parallel to and often supplanting Standard English usage.

Early mobile devices used analog technology, which was later replaced by digital, packet-switched technology. Cellular phones allowed spectrum to be divided into smaller and smaller areas to reduce interference from other spectrum uses, but analog phone calls were notoriously difficult to hear. The primary difference from a user perspective was that analog calls often searched for available frequencies and users would hear static on the line. Digital technology eliminated static, but early digital calls often lost some sounds due to skipped packets of data or calls were dropped entirely when the signal was lost. Digital technology enabled the next generation of mobile devices, which included not only telephonic communications but also access to data-driven services like the Internet. The costly changeover to an entirely different model of transmitting information via mobile devices would eventually make mobile communications less expensive and more expansive. Multiple technical standards still exist internationally, including Time Division Multiple Access (TDMA) and Code Division Multiple Access (CDMA) in the United States, and Global System for Mobile Communications/Groupe Spécial Mobile (GSM) in Europe. Some mobile devices can operate on more than one system, which allows the user to take the device abroad and still use it, although the user will need to engage service in the alternative country, either by subscription or by roaming, a service that allows individual calls, texts, or data usage but charges the user a higher per-use rate.

Apple brought the iPhone to the mobile device market in 2007. The iPhone was unique in the mobile device market because of its Apple-controlled app market and its integrated touchscreen keypad. The touchscreen is now a given in the smartphone market, as is some of the user customization features like the orientation of the screen, choice of applications, and autocorrected text input. When Internet usage became available on mobile devices called smartphones, telephone and text usage was typically metered, with a pay-by-the-minute plan or capped, while data was unlimited. Later, carriers began to offer the lesser-used phone capabilities of smartphones on an unlimited basis and meter and cap the bandwidth-demanding data services for these devices. Recently, many households have opted to become mobile-only customers and have requested disconnection of their landline phones, which has forced providers to create ways to integrate with 911 emergency service systems.

The definition of mobile devices has expanded to include objects that were manufactured previously without any thought to online or communications capabilities. Vehicles have begun to communicate with one another and with networks to transmit location, intention, and emergency alerts, bringing new meaning to the antiquated term *car phone*. The Internet of things (IoT) includes mobile devices capable of communicating with the Internet, including formerly unconnected home appliances, UAVs, automobiles, wearable devices, and nearly any mobile device with a microchip embedded in it. It can be argued that biological and organic matter have become part of the IoT when pets contain microchips (radio-frequency ID [RFID]), and fingerprints are used to identify individuals for password access to mobile devices.

Mobile devices are used simultaneously with other mobile and stationary communications and entertainment portals. Computer tablet devices such as Apple's iPad, Microsoft's Surface, and other tablets, as well as laptop computers, smartphones, and other interactive devices may be used by one individual at the same time, with the user switching her or his attention from one screen to another to watch, download, comment, or communicate with other individuals.

Given the popularity and ubiquity of mobile devices, the amount of data collected by the devices is prodigious. To compound the problem, the data are often personal information connected to the individual user, and, especially in the case of largely unregulated IoT devices, are often not encrypted to enhance user privacy. This information can be resold to advertisers and marketers who can then use the data to sell products and services to the mobile device user. The data may also be used by law enforcement and other government entities to track individuals to monitor terrorists and other individuals. Even when data is created by or collected from a specific user, it is often legally unclear who owns this data and therefore anyone may access, correct, store, or sell it. In many cases, a consumer uses the mobile device, the app on the mobile device, or another related service for free or at low cost and may not realize that his or her data may be sold to support the free product.

Federal and state laws regulate certain uses of mobile devices, but not all uses and users are subject to these regulations. The Children's Online Privacy Protection Act of 2013 (COPPA) protects only children under age thirteen, and the Health Insurance Portability and Accountability Act of 1996 (HIPAA) protects medical and healthcare information but only when such information is kept by a covered entity such as a doctor, insurance company, or hospital. For example, if a doctor prescribes an insulin pump that transmits data about insulin levels to the doctor, the data collected on the mobile device would be regulated by HIPAA. If a consumer buys a fitness monitor online or from a retail establishment and uses it to collect and upload to the Internet various weight, age, gender, global positioning system (GPS) location, and fitness data, the collection and use of that data is far less likely to be regulated or even monitored by any government entity. The Gramm-Leach-Bliley Act (GLBA), the Securities and Exchange Commission (SEC) regulations, and a host of other financial regulations cover the exchange of financial data through mobile devices, including banking transactions, credit card, and mobile app payment systems. In each case, there is still data that may not be encrypted end to end (from the beginning of the transaction until its conclusion). The data then remain accessible on the device and possibly via remote access as well.

Riley v. California, 573 U.S. ___ (2014), a U.S. Supreme Court case, illustrated the legal implications of carrying an extensive database containing all of the user's personal information in a pocket. The police pulled Riley's vehicle over when they noticed his expired vehicle identification license tags, and they conducted a search. Riley also had his cellphone in his pocket; the officers searched the phone and found photos suggesting that Riley belonged to a relevant gang that was suspected in a shooting. Riley was accused of a shooting that occurred out of a motor vehicle. Under the Fourth Amendment to the U.S. Constitution, citizens are protected from unreasonable searches and seizures of their property. The Supreme Court, in the Riley case, found that there was no emergency and the data that the phone contained could wait until a legal warrant was obtained to search the mobile device, similar to a warrant required to search a device located in a person's home. This case may be distinguished from other cases if mobile devices are found to contain weapons or other immediately dangerous objects.

Issues of legal notice and consent for privacy purposes and, more generally, the effective communication of privacy policies, vary extensively by size and type of mobile device. The largest devices have sufficient screens to convey an entire privacy policy document and allow consent via a click-through agreement. Companies can provide thorough privacy policies in this situation, and the policies address all of the potential methods of collecting personal data and all of the foreseeable uses of the data. Smaller devices may have tiny screens that do not lend themselves to reviewing an entire contract or multipage privacy policy. This makes it difficult to obtain consent, either overall for the use of the device or on a use-by-use basis. Some devices, particularly IoT devices and very mobile devices such as UAVs, either do not have screens at all or the screens are not readily available to all affected by the use of such devices. Consumers would not be able to opt in or opt out on a per-use basis without constant access to the screen of the mobile device. Solutions for delivering adequate notice and obtaining valid consent from users are limited in these examples and may have to come from public awareness campaigns directed to all potential users, which, in the case of UAV and drone mobile device use, may be anyone in the vicinity.

Additional security issues that have grown with the exponential proliferation of mobile devices are data leaking, which is the availability of data not through hacking but through poorly-designed apps or user error, phishing attacks, where users are tricked into providing data; poor Wi-Fi security, when users transmit data over unsecured networks; devices becoming out-of-date, which is a particular problem with the IoT; cryptojacking, where hackers use victims' hardware to process cryptocurrency mining operations; the insecure nature of most people's passwords, which are relatively easy for hackers to breach with a brute-force attack; and the simple stealing of or direct hacking into actual devices. Also, the proliferation of cloud data services as the basis for mobile device operation creates an additional need for security in data transmission and storage.

The United States military took action regarding insecure mobile devices in 2018, when it banned smartphones and devices manufactured by Chinese makers ZTE and Huawei. The companies' equipment was banned from being used by American soldiers. The devices were deemed to be vulnerable to efforts by the Chinese government, which owns a large part of the companies, to track American military operations, conducting surveillance or even tampering with communication among military units.

To protect individual privacy on mobile devices, users may begin by reading privacy policies, conducting online research, and looking for third-party trustmarks and/or seals to compare different sites and apps to choose the most privacy-protective service that meets their needs. Next, users can look for privacy options available within each game, social media app, or service on the device to secure their personal data. For example, social media settings often offer users the ability to post selectively to a certain group of recipients, set on a default basis or on a per-use basis. Particularly for young users of social media, those beyond the protection of COPPA but still under the age of majority, these settings should be set to protect the most personal data possible. Beyond individual actions, separate services and privacy-protective apps may be developed to protect privacy across multiple platforms. Trade associations for mobile device manufacturers, mobile communications service providers, mobile app designers, and mobile advertisers each and collectively may design industry standards for the ethical treatment of privacy information collected from mobile users, above and beyond any of the legal requirements imposed on these groups. Any comprehensive federal legislation on data privacy should acknowledge the vulnerability of mobile devices to privacy violations and data breaches.

Security of mobile devices also presents several legal, technical, and ethical concerns. Physical security requires that devices be held by individuals and not shared, lost, or stolen. Mobile devices are especially likely to be shared, lost, and/or stolen and therefore should be protected by encryption and password lockout screens if they are not in use for a set period. Data security issues include the ability to hack the devices and to hack into the apps and services available on the mobile devices. Network security should ensure that the network that connects mobile devices also be prepared for the onslaught of data and people looking to access and use that data, whether for paid advertising purposes or illegal use. Bring your own device (BYOD) means that consumers are bringing their personal devices into the workplace, complicating secure systems designed by engineers for an individual company's needs. Product designers for mobile devices must consider not only the parameters of the physical device and its preloaded software but also the myriad context(s) in which mobile devices may be used. Mobile device designers should incorporate the possibility of software upgrades and patches, and additional uses in the future, even as the generations of devices become shorter and shorter and new devices replace old devices more and more quickly.

Jill Bronfman

Further Reading

"2013 U.S. Consumer Data Privacy Study: Mobile Edition from TRUSTe." https://www.truste.com/resources/privacy-research/us-mobile-privacy-index-2013/.

"Mobile Medical Applications: Guidance for Industry and [FDA] Staff." February 2015. http://www.fda.gov/downloads/MedicalDevices/.../UCM263366.pdf.

Federal Trade Commission (FTC) Staff Report. *Mobile Privacy Disclosures: Building Trust through Transparency.* February 2013.

National Institute of Standards and Technology (NIST). "Guidelines for Managing the Security of Mobile Devices in the Enterprise." June 2013.

Raphael, J.R. "7 mobile security threats you should take seriously in 2019." *CSO*, February 21, 2019.

Woo, S. and Lubold, G. "Pentagon Orders Stores on Military Bases to Remove Huawei, ZTE Phones." *The Wall Street Journal*, May 2, 2018.

See also: Apps; Federal Communications Commission (FCC); Federal Trade Commission (FTC); Smartphones; Telephones

Model legislation on privacy

Identification: Various proposed state statutes designed to protect the right to privacy by providing a statutory remedy in the form of money damages, criminal penalties, or both.

In most states, the civil right of privacy has evolved as a matter of common law developed by the state courts on a case-by-case basis. In a few states, legislatures have enacted statutes providing individuals with a civil claim against others for violating the right to privacy. The earliest of these states was New York, which enacted a statute in 1903 recognizing a civil claim for invasion of privacy. The New York statute also specifies that a violation of the statute is a criminal misdemeanor. The statute was enacted in direct response to widespread public criticism of a 1902 decision of the New York Court of Appeals that refused to recognize a right of privacy under the state's common law (*Roberson v. Rochester Folding Box*, 643 N.E. 442 (NY, 1902)).

Since the early twentieth century, the development of the right of privacy under state common law has been slow and uneven. In states that protect privacy rights by statute, the laws vary significantly with regard to the scope and nature of the right. New York's statute, for example, limits the right of privacy to situations in which a person's name or photograph is used without that person's consent for someone else's benefit. Other state statutes are much broader. Some extend civil remedies for violations of the right of privacy even after the death of the person whose rights are violated. Other states, like California, have enacted privacy statutes that limit certain claims for invasion of privacy while still allowing state courts to develop and expand the right of privacy by common law. The result is a patchwork of statutes and common law that provide substantially different privacy rights from state to state.

Generally, proposals for model legislation on privacy rights seek to make state laws more uniform and standardized. A state legislature may decide to enact model legislation as proposed, it may tailor the model statute by amending it to better suit the policy goals of the legislature, or it can make the law easier to interpret and enforce. Even if a state legislature decides to amend the model legislation in some ways, the result is more likely to be similar to the statutes of other states that have enacted the same model statute. In this way, model legislation is designed to make the laws of various states more uniform and predictable.

The National Conference of Commissioners on Uniform State Laws, more commonly known as the Uniform Law Commission, is a nonprofit organization established in 1892 to develop well-drafted, well-considered model statutes to help clarify critical issues of state law. Its members include lawyers, judges, legislators, legislative staff, and law professors who represent all fifty states, the District of Columbia, and the U.S. territories. The commissioners conduct research and draft model laws to address particular issues of state law for which uniformity is considered desirable and practical. For example, the commission is currently working on drafting uniform laws to protect student online privacy, social media privacy, and employee online privacy.

Another leading organization of legal scholars and judges is the American Law Institute (ALI), formed in 1923 to address the complexity of common law among the states and the absence of agreement from state to state on basic common law principles. The institute was formed in recognition of the fact that the complexity of U.S. law is due primarily to the widely varied ways that state courts address issues of state common law. ALI publishes printed sets known as *Restatements* that propose specific developments in state common law addressing important legal subjects.

Because the ALI is so highly respected, many state courts consult the *Restatements* when considering matters of novel state law that state legislatures have not yet resolved. If a state appellate court decides to follow a *Restatement* provision, it becomes part of the state's common law that other courts in that state will follow when deciding issues involving privacy rights. ALI is currently engaged in a major project drafting Principles of the Law of Data Privacy. The project's goal is to provide a legal framework to govern data privacy and to clarify the legal obligations and best practices for organizations that deal with personal information and data.

One area of recent state legislative activity involves student rights to data privacy. Various nonprofit organizations have proposed model state legislation to address these matters. For example, in 2014, the Electronic Privacy Information Center (EPIC), an independent nonprofit research organization, called for a Student Privacy Bill of Rights for the purpose of ensuring that students have more control over how educational institutions and businesses use their personal information. Similarly, the American Legislative Exchange Council (ALEC) and the Foundation for Excellence in Education have proposed a model Student Data Accessibility, Transparency, and Accountability Act to regulate the collection, use, and distribution of personally identifiable student data. These and other legislative proposals include measures for holding organizations accountable to students for the collection and use of their personal information.

In response to various advocacy efforts, the 2014 California legislature enacted the Student Online Personal Information Protection Act, which took effect on January 1, 2016. The California statute protects the privacy of elementary and secondary students by prohibiting operators of Internet websites, online services, or mobile or online applications from knowingly using personally identifiable information for the purpose of targeting advertising to students or to their parents. The statute also prohibits these operators from selling or sharing student information for prohibited purposes. Operators of online services must protect student information from unauthorized use or disclosure. In addition, upon request by a school or school district, a business is required to delete student information that is within the school's control. On the other hand, the act permits operators to disclose student information for limited purposes, including other provisions of federal or state law

that require the disclosure of personally identifiable student information.

Other state legislatures have followed California's lead by introducing and enacting similar statutes, modified to be consistent with their own policy goals. According to a report by the Data Quality Campaign, a nonprofit national organization, fifteen states passed a total of twenty-eight new student data privacy laws in 2015 alone. Given the dramatic innovations in educational technology, these model state laws are designed to strengthen student rights to allow students to control the use of their private information.

Under the Obama administration legislation was proposed to regulate the collection, storage, management, and use of personal data. The stated purpose of the Consumer Privacy Bill of Rights Act of 2015 was to "ensure that individuals continue to enjoy meaningful privacy protections while affording ample flexibility for technologies and business models to evolve." If such a law were enacted, it would generally preempt any state or local statutes that impose requirements on persons and entities covered by the act regarding the processing of personal data. However, the bill would not preempt state laws designed to protect the privacy of minors or elementary and secondary school students.

J. Lyn Entrikin

Further Reading

The American Law Institute. *Creation.* https://www.ali.org/about-ali/creation/. Data Quality Campaign. *Student Data Privacy Legislation: What Happened in 2015, and What Is Next?* 2015. http://dataqualitycampaign.org/wp-content/uploads/2015/09/DQC-Student-Data-Laws-2015-Sept23. pdf.

Foundation for Excellence in Education. *Building a Trusted Environment: A Snapshot of State Laws on Student Data Use, Privacy and Security.* May 2015.

Foundation for Excellence in Education. *Student Data Accessibility, Transparency, and Accountability Act: Model Legislation.* http://static.excelined.org/wp-content/uploads/Student-Data-Privacy-Accessibility-andTransparency-Act-Model-Legislation-03.2015.pdf.

Uniform Law Commission. "About the ULC." http://www. uniformlaws.org/Narrative.aspx?title=About%20 the%20ULC.

The White House. *Consumer Data Privacy in a Networked World: A Framework for Protecting Privacy and Promoting Innovation in the Global Economy.* February 2012. https://www.whitehouse.gov/sites/default/files/privacy-final.pdf

See also: Educational setting, privacy in an; The Right to Privacy

Moore v. East Cleveland, 431 U.S. 494 (1977)

Identification: A 5–4 decision, with a plurality opinion written by Justice Lewis Powell, in which the U.S. Supreme Court ruled that an ordinance restricting housing to a nuclear family, and thereby excluding extended family from said housing, violated the due process clause of the Fourteenth Amendment and was therefore unconstitutional.

Inez Moore ("Moore") was a resident of the city of East Cleveland. Moore shared her home with her son Dale Moore Sr., as well as with her two grandsons, Dale Jr., and John Moore Jr. Dale Jr. and John Jr. were first cousins. John, Jr. began living in Moore's home after the death of his mother.

In early 1973, Moore received a notice of violation from the City of East Cleveland stating that John Jr. was an "illegal occupant" in Moore's home. The notice called for Moore's compliance with the city's ordinance by removing John Jr. from the home. Moore refused, and the City of East Cleveland responded by filing criminal charges against her. Moore moved for dismissal of the charges, claiming that the ordinance was facially unconstitutional, but the motion was overruled. Moore was subsequently convicted and sentenced to five days in jail and a $25 fine, the conviction was upheld by the Ohio Court of Appeals, and the Ohio Supreme Court denied review of the matter.

The ordinance in question limited the occupancy of homes to a single family. Said limitation was established, in part, to combat an increased number of children moving to East Cleveland in pursuit of better education. According to the ordinance, the term *single family* only applied to nuclear families.

In an attempt to bolster its position, the City of East Cleveland relied heavily on the U.S. Supreme Court decision in *Village of Belle Terre v. Boraas.* In *Belle Terre,* the Court upheld a housing ordinance similar to the one at issue in *Moore;* however, Justice Powell distinguished between *Belle Terre* and the matter at hand based on the fact that the ordinance in *Belle Terre* applied only to unrelated individuals living together. With regard to the ordinance at issue, Justice Powell criticized it for being too intrusive into the lives of private families. Thereafter, Justice Powell proceeded to the heart of his opinion— his discussion of the due process clause.

To begin his discussion of the due process clause, Justice Powell relied heavily on a previous description of the Court's function under the due process clause from Justice Harlan. In this description, Justice Harlan described the liberty afforded by the due process clause as something that cannot be exactly determined through one set formula but instead as something that lies on a vast continuum. This continuum calls for a "freedom from all substantial arbitrary impositions and purposeless restraints" as well as "careful scrutiny of state needs asserted to justify [the] abridgment" of certain interests.

Following his quotation of Justice Harlan, Justice Powell then began his own discourse on substantive due process. This discussion has proven pertinent within the realm of privacy law. Perhaps the most poignant portion of this discussion with regard to privacy law was when Justice Powell stated, "Appropriate limits on substantive due process come not from drawing arbitrary lines but rather from careful 'respect for the teachings of history [and] solid recognition of the basic values that underlie our society.'

" Finally, Justice Powell ended his opinion with a discussion of the merits of child rearing within a home comprising more than just a nuclear family. For these reasons the Supreme Court ruled in favor of Inez Moore and found the East Cleveland law limiting the occupancy of homes to nuclear families to be unconstitutional.

Justice William Brennan penned a concurring opinion to which Justice Thurgood Marshall joined. Justice Brennan used his concurrence to discuss the East Cleveland ordinance's lack of sensitivity with regard to those who are unable to exist as only a nuclear family as well as to criticize the irrationality of a variance for "hardship exceptions" allowed under the law.

Justice John Paul Stevens concurred with the plurality but wrote separately to address his belief that the issue that should have been addressed in this case revolved around an individual's right to use her own property as she sees fit.

Chief Justice Warren Burger dissented from the Court's opinion on the grounds that Moore failed to exhaust adequately her potential remedies before reaching the U.S. Supreme Court and, as such, did not have proper standing before the Court.

Justice Potter Stewart filed a separate dissent that Justice William Rehnquist joined. Justice Stewart argued, largely based on the decision in *Belle Terre*, that the nuclear family limitation in the East Cleveland ordinance was rationally designed to achieve a legitimate government purpose.

Finally, Justice Byron White submitted his own dissent, in which he stated that Moore's equal protection claim should not have been viewed under the strict scrutiny standard because it did not pertain to a fundamental interest or a suspect classification and therefore should have failed.

John W. Klinker

Further Reading

Hersey, Pala. "*Moore v. East Cleveland*: The Supreme Court's Fractured Paean to the Extended Family." *Journal of Contemporary Legal Issues* 14, no. 1, (2004): 57–64.

Jensen, Tamila C. "From *Belle Terre* to *East Cleveland*: Zoning, the Family, and the Right of Privacy." *Family Law Quarterly* 13, no. 1 (Spring 1979): 1–25.

See also: Constitutional law; Legal evolution of privacy rights in the United States; The Right to Privacy; Supreme Court of the United States

Mug shots

Identification: Booking photographs, as they are more formally known, taken by law enforcement authorities upon arrest.

Mug shots can pose unique personal privacy issues under public disclosure laws. Such photographs typically are made available to the public by state and local law enforcement authorities—which is why the most notorious of them (those of actor Nick Nolte, actress Lindsay Lohan, and O. J. Simpson, for example) have been widely disseminated on the Internet and even are available for consolidated public consumption on websites such as (most popularly) thesmokinggun.com. But at the federal government level—that is, for mug shots taken and/or held by the United States Marshals Service (Marshals Service) and the Federal Bureau of Investigation (FBI)—the established policy is to withhold them from the public on grounds of personal privacy.

The nondisclosure policy for federal mug shots is grounded in the law enforcement privacy exemption of the federal Freedom of Information Act (FOIA), 5 U.S.C. § 552(b)(7)(C), which protects law enforcement records that, if disclosed, "could reasonably be expected to constitute an unwarranted invasion of personal privacy." This disclosure exemption is applied through a so-called balancing test: the individual's personal privacy interest in the record in question is balanced against any public interest in its disclosure. If the latter outweighs the former, the record is disclosed under the FOIA; if the privacy interest has greater weight, the record is withheld under FOIA Exemption 7(C).

As a matter of longstanding policy under FOIA, mug shots regularly are withheld from public disclosure on the basis of the significant personal privacy interests in them—the stigma of criminality, regardless of whether the person ultimately is prosecuted and convicted after arrest—and the little if any legitimate public interest in their disclosure. The policy also recognizes that mug shots are taken at what are by definition one of the worst moments of a person's life, with an embarrassing appearance that arrestees invariably would prefer be forgotten—a preference greatly exacerbated by awareness of Internet-era dissemination. The only exceptions to this policy are when a mug shot is used for purposes of capturing a criminal suspect who is at large (a fugitive on a Ten Most Wanted poster, for instance) or where there is an issue about the treatment of the suspect at police hands, in which case the photograph serves an overriding public interest in documenting the suspect's physical condition at the time of arrest.

This established practice at the federal level was disrupted, however, by the first appellate court to consider a mug shot under FOIA. In 1996, in a case entitled *Detroit Free Press, Inc. v. United States Department of Justice*, the Sixth Circuit Court of Appeals ruled that eight indicted persons awaiting trial on federal charges had *no* privacy interest in their mug shots and that, in any event, there were "potential" public interests favoring disclosure under the FOIA (73 F.3d 93, 97–98 [6th Cir. 1996]). Although this was a 2–1 decision, with a strong dissent (see FOIA at 99–100), it was a singular one that received no further judicial review. Mug shot disclosure therefore became required within the Sixth Circuit's geographic boundaries—Kentucky, Michigan, Ohio, and Tennessee—though the federal government did not acquiesce to this ruling elsewhere. This made mug shots the only subject area under FOIA in which a requester would get a different disclosure result according to the state in which he, she, or it was located. Moreover, it led to a common yet no less anomalous

practice of FOIA requesters around the country using surrogates located within those four states (usually cooperating media outlets) to obtain mug shots under the prevailing case law of the Sixth Circuit.

This anomaly persisted for more than fifteen years. During that time, two different circuit courts of appeals considered the issue and explicitly rejected the Sixth Circuit's ruling in *Detroit Free Press*. First, in *Karantsalis v. United States Department of Justice*, the Eleventh Circuit Court of Appeals in 2011 found a strong privacy interest in mug shots, calling them "vivid symbol[s] of criminal accusation" (635 F.3d 497, 503 [11th Cir. 2011]). Then, a year later, in *World Publishing Co. v. United States Department of Justice*, the Tenth Circuit Court of Appeals likewise rejected *Detroit Free Press*, viewing a mug shot as a "vivid and personal portrayal" that warrants protection as a matter of personal privacy (672 F.3d 825, 829 [10th Cir. 2012]). This quickly created a "conflict in the circuits" on the issue, which ordinarily is a strong basis for an issue's resolution by the U.S. Supreme Court. In 2012, however, the Supreme Court declined to accept the *Karantsalis* case for such review, which relegated the issue to potential resolution by the lower courts and left the Sixth Circuit's *Detroit Free Press* precedent intact to yield disparate mug shot results.

This refusal by the Supreme Court finally spurred aggressive action by the government toward resolving what remained the only such anomaly to exist under FOIA. In December 2012, the Justice Department announced that it was no longer going to acquiesce to the *Detroit Free Press* decision within the four states that comprise the Sixth Circuit. Rather, it took the position that the Supreme Court's opinion in an FOIA case entitled *National Archives & Records Administration v. Favish*, 541 U.S. 157 (2004) seriously called into question the reasoning of that aberrational decision and that it should be reconsidered by the full circuit court. Toward that end, the Marshals Service pointedly withheld mug shots from the *Detroit Free Press* itself, leading to a case in which the lower court result was a disclosure order under the Sixth Circuit's precedent.

On August 12, 2015, however, a three-judge panel of the Sixth Circuit issued an opinion in this second *Detroit Free Press* case in which it unanimously "urge[d] the full court to reconsider" the *Detroit Free Press* precedent, declaring that mug shots "convey the sort of potentially embarrassing or harmful information protected by [E]xemption [7(C)]: they capture how an individual appeared at a particularly humiliating moment immediately after being taken into federal custody [and are] an unmistakable badge of criminality" (796 F.3d 649 [6th Cir. 2015]). This inevitably led to a full-court Sixth Circuit ruling (by a vote of 9-7) in which the majority of judges on that court observed that "[t]wenty years ago, we thought that the disclosure of [mug shots] would do no harm. But time has taught us otherwise. The Internet and social media have worked unpredictable changes" since then (329 F.3d 478 [6th Cir. 2016 (en banc)]). The Supreme Court let this ruling stand in mid-2017 (137 S.Ct. 2158 [2017]).

In sum, it now appears most likely that the photographs of arrestees widely known as mug shots will be universally withheld from public view by federal law enforcement authorities even as their counterparts are disclosed, despite considerable privacy concerns, at the state and local levels.

Daniel J. Metcalfe

Further Reading

Frankel, Alison. "Why Is DOJ Fighting to Keep Mug Shots Out of Reporters' Hands?" *Reuters* (August 13, 2015).

Kravets, David. "Mug-Shot Industry Will Dig Up Your Past, Charge You to Bury It Again." *Wired.com* (Aug. 2, 2011).

Messenger, Ashley. "What Would a 'Right to Be Forgotten' Mean for Media in the United States?" *Communications Lawyer* 29, no. 1 (June 2012): 12.

Norris, Cameron T. "Your Right to Look Like an Ugly Criminal: Resolving the Circuit Split over Mug Shots and the Freedom of Information Act." *Vanderbilt Law Review* 66, no. 5 (2013).

Recent Cases. "Freedom of Information Act—Sixth Circuit Holds that Mug Shots May Be Exempt from Disclosure under FOIA Personal Privacy Exemption." *Harvard Law Review* 30, no. 1016 (2017).

United States Department of Justice, U.S. Marshals Service. *Booking Photograph Disclosure Policy* (December 12, 2012).

Wolfe, Gregory Nathaniel. "Smile for the Camera, the World Is Going to See That Mug: The Dilemma of Privacy Interests in Mug Shots." *Columbia Law Review* 133, no. 8 (2013).

See also: Freedom of Information Act (FOIA); *National Archives and Records Administration v. Favish*

N

National Archives and Records Administration v. Favish, 541 U.S. 157 (2004)

Identification: One of the U.S. Supreme Court's most significant Freedom of Information Act (FOIA) decisions ever to deal with matters of personal privacy in a law enforcement context (541 U.S. 157 [2004]).

The decision in *National Archives and Records Administration v. Favish* accepted once and for all the concept of "survivor privacy" under FOIA, which holds that exceptionally sensitive information pertaining to a deceased person (who no longer has a privacy right) can in some situations be properly withheld under a FOIA privacy exemption in order to protect the privacy interests of surviving family members. This privacy protection concept was developed and first applied in 1978 to protect the distinctly acute privacy interests of Coretta Scott King and her children in connection with detailed files compiled by the Federal Bureau of Investigation (FBI) on her deceased husband, Dr. Martin Luther King, Jr.; more than twenty-five years later, in *Favish*, it finally was adopted by the U.S. Supreme Court.

The protection of information about a deceased person was the paramount issue in the *Favish* case; it involved a FOIA request for public disclosure of the "death scene" photographs taken of Deputy White House Counsel Vincent W. Foster Jr. upon his suicide. Exactly six months into the Clinton administration, on July 20, 1993,

Foster casually thanked his secretary for bringing him lunch, left the White House in the middle of the day, drove to Fort Marcy Park on the Virginia side of the Potomac River, and evidently took his own life with an antique firearm that had been in his family for generations. To the shock of his family and coworkers, it turned out that Foster had been suffering from chronic clinical depression, which appeared to have been exacerbated by the first of many Clinton administration scandals (known as Travelgate) in which he had become entangled in the weeks leading up to his death. Almost immediately, multiple conspiracy theories began to circulate about the abruptness and seeming incongruity of his action, fed in no small part by the fact that Foster had been a law partner, close friend, and rumored paramour of First Lady Hillary Rodham Clinton in Arkansas prior to the 1992 presidential election and had been seen by some as personally uncomfortable supporting the depths of her burgeoning White House controversies.

The photographs in question were taken of Foster's body by federal law enforcement officers as it lay on a grassy berm in the park, face up and gun in hand, where it was discovered later that day; several of them showed his full face and, because his mouth was the bullet's point of entry, some blood, but not a profusion of it, was shown as well. The initial investigation into the death was conducted by the U.S. Park Police because it evidently had occurred on federal parkland within its jurisdiction, but ultimately there were no fewer than five additional official investigations conducted as well, including two by Congress and two by successive independent counsels investigating White House–related matters more generally. Each of them found no evidence of foul play.

Many news organizations made FOIA requests for the photographs, among other surrounding investigative files, but the first requester to bring a FOIA case to court was the organization Accuracy in Media (in this case known unfortunately by the acronym AIM), which brought suit in the District of Columbia and lost, on privacy grounds, at the appellate court level. But AIM's counsel, Allan J. Favish, brought another FOIA lawsuit encompassing the same photographs in California. This time, he prevailed at both the district court and appellate court levels, with the federal courts in California ordering disclosure after finding both an insufficient privacy interest and the presence of an overriding public interest in doing so. (The fact that the same records already had been litigated in DC and were found to be exempt under FOIA Exemption 7(C), after a judicious balancing of privacy versus public interests, was of no moment as a legal matter.) The case then proceeded to the Supreme Court, where Favish argued that, first and foremost, disclosure of the photographs was legally compelled by the principle that Foster's privacy rights were extinguished upon his death. (That principle, in and of itself, had been adopted by the U.S. Department of Justice as a matter of government-wide FOIA policy in 1982.) Favish contended that Foster's family (that is, his widow, mother, sister, and minor children), who had been permitted to intervene in the case, had no legally cognizable interest to protect, even with respect to a graphic death-scene photograph. And the fact that Foster in his anguish had chosen to take his life in a public park (rather than in the privacy of his home), where anyone walking nearby the next morning could have seen what the photographs depicted, lent this argument greater force.

But the Department of Justice had established the survivor privacy concept in the late 1970s when it extended FOIA Exemption 7(C) protection to the FBI's detailed recordation (under Di1rector J. Edgar Hoover) of certain intimate details of Martin Luther King's extramarital life. Keenly aware of the impact that disclosure of such details would have on King's widow, as well as on those of her children who were still minors at the time, the Department employed Exemption 7(C) in order to protect their distinct privacy interests in being free from the emotional pain of such publicity, especially as it was then still less than ten years after King's death. The courts accepted this, at both the district court and appellate court levels, in the seminal case of *Lesar v. United States Department of Justice*, and in following years the concept was accepted and applied in a handful of additional cases, including one involving autopsy photographs of President John F. Kennedy and one involving the recorded last words of the crew of the space shuttle *Challenger*—though in some court cases the issue was not entirely free of doubt.

So when the issue was presented to the Supreme Court in the *Favish* case as a potentially dispositive one, it was a question of first impression for the Court, which could have decided that FOIA's exact language (that is, "personal privacy") afforded no room for protecting the interests of survivors—thus leaving it to Congress to amend that language in order to protect survivors or not. The Court unanimously embraced the survivor privacy concept, however, reasoning first that it was not the late Mr. Foster whose interests were being protected but rather those of the surviving Foster family members. The Court observed that they sought "refuge from a sensation-seeking culture for their own peace of mind and tranquility, not for the sake of the deceased." Having thus determined that the Foster family was eligible to have its own privacy interests protected under FOIA, the Court then turned to the nature of their interest in "controlling" the death-scene image of a loved one. Looking to the history of the treatment of the dead, it found a "well-established cultural tradition acknowledging a family's control over the body and death images of the deceased," specifically including "the right of family members to direct and control disposition of the body of the deceased and to limit attempts to exploit pictures of the deceased family member's remains for public purposes." In so finding, the Court was unmistakably influenced by the prospect of inmates jailed for murder plus rape or child molestation being able to obtain raw photographs of their victims for "gruesome" yet potentially stimulating display on the walls of their prison cells—a real-world possibility pointedly emphasized by the government at the Supreme Court level.

Lastly, the Supreme Court used the *Favish* case to set a clear rule about the nature of a public interest that could properly outweigh even such a strong privacy interest under the "balancing" language (that is, "an *unwarranted* invasion of personal privacy") of FOIA Exemption 7(C). Favish had argued, following the public interest finding of the Ninth Circuit Court of Appeals, that public disclosure of the photographs was necessary in order to "show that responsible officials acted negligently or otherwise improperly in the performance of their duties"—that is, that they had carelessly or corruptly investigated the theory that Foster had been murdered elsewhere as Favish suspected. But the Supreme Court ruled that Favish's own personal "doubts" were not "evidence that would warrant a belief by a reasonable person that the alleged [g]overnment impropriety might have occurred." It pointedly declared that "[a]llegations of government misconduct are 'easy to allege and hard to disprove,'" meaning that if any FOIA requester could overcome a privacy interest merely by stating his "bare suspicion" of government wrongdoing, then Exemption 7(C) would have "little force or content" as a "practical" matter.

So by a vote of 9-0, Favish's arguments were rejected on both sides of the Exemption 7(C) balance and the photographs were deemed properly withheld.

Daniel J. Metcalfe

Further Reading

An Act to Improve the National Instant Criminal Background Check System, and for Other Purposes. Washington, D.C.: [U.S. G.P.O.], 2008.

"Congress to Revisit Background Checks for Gun Buyers." *The Christian Science Monitor,* April 23, 2007.

FOIA Post. "Supreme Court Rules for 'Survivor Privacy' in *Favish*" (April 9, 2004).

Gun Control Opportunities to Close Loopholes in the National Instant Criminal Background Check System. Washington, D.C.: U.S. General Accounting Office, 2002.

Gun Control: Options for Improving the National Instant Criminal Background Check System: Report to Congressional Requesters. Washington, D.C.: U.S. General Accounting Office, 2002.

"NICS 10-Year Anniversary: Milestone for FBI's Gun-Buyer Background Check System." *The FBI Law Enforcement Bulletin,* June 1, 2009.

*NICS, National Instant Criminal Background Check System.*Clarksburg, WV: U.S. Dept. of Justice, Federal Bureau of Investigation, Criminal Justice Information Services Division, 1998.

National Instant Criminal Background Check System. Washington, D.C.: U.S. Dept. of Justice, Federal Bureau of Investigation, Criminal Justice Information Services Division, 2004.

See also: Freedom of Information Act (FOIA); Law enforcement; Mug shots; The Right to Privacy

National Instant Criminal Background Check System (NICS)

Identification: A background system that is intended to enhance national security and public safety by providing the timely and accurate determination of a person's eligibility to possess firearms and/or explosives pursuant to federal law.

NICS is housed at the FBI's Criminal Justice Information Services Division in Clarksburg,

West Virginia. It serves federal firearms licensees (FFLs) in thirty states and the District of Columbia. The system was created under the authority of the Handgun Violence Prevention Act of 1993 (Brady Act), 107 Stat. 1536 (1993), to strengthen firearm regulations. The statute was named after former President Reagan's press secretary, James Brady, who was seriously injured during the 1981 assassination attempt on Reagan.

One purpose of the system was to prevent certain designated classes of individuals from obtaining firearms and explosives. Since the passage of the Gun Control Act of 1968, 82 Stat. 1213–2, Section 922 of the act prohibits anyone who fits into any of the following categories from purchasing a firearm:

1. Has been convicted in any court of a crime punishable by incarceration for a term exceeding one year;

2. Is a fugitive from justice;

3. Is an unlawful user of or addicted to any controlled substance;

4. Has been adjudicated as a mental defective or committed to a mental institution;

5. Is illegally or unlawfully in the United States;

6. Has been discharged from the Armed Forces under dishonorable conditions;

7. Having been a citizen of the United States, has renounced U.S. citizenship;

8. Is subject to a court order that restrains the person from harassing, stalking, or threatening an intimate partner or child of such intimate partner;

9. Has been convicted in any court of a misdemeanor crime of domestic violence.

In addition to preventing ineligible individuals from obtaining handguns, the system is also intended to ensure the efficient transfer of firearms to eligible gun buyers. NICS has processed firearm background checks since November 30, 1998. FFLs use the NICS to determine whether the purchaser is eligible to buy firearms or explosives. Before completing the sale, the gun dealer contacts the Federal Bureau of Investigation (FBI) or other designated agencies to ensure that the person is eligible to make a purchase. They do this by running a background check either through the system's toll-free number or electronically on the Internet.

The background checks are usually completed quickly after being requested. If there is no match in any of the checked databases, the dealer may proceed with the sale. Otherwise, the NICS must contact the appropriate judicial and/ or law enforcement agencies for further information. The Brady Act requires that the FBI make its decision to approve or deny the sale within three business days. If the dealer does not receive the decision within that time limit, the sale may proceed. The failure of the FBI to respond within three days was one of the lapses in NICS that allowed Dylan Roof, the perpetrator of the Charleston church shooting in 2015, to purchase a handgun when he was not eligible to do so under the law.

Problems with the NICS screening system were also clear over the years. In 2007, Seung-Hui Cho, a twenty-three-year-old Virginia Tech student, killed thirty-two students and teachers in one of the deadliest shootings in U.S. history. Although a judge had declared Cho mentally ill in 2005, the state of Virginia failed to report its findings to NICS, allowing Cho to pass a background check by a licensed dealer. Jared Lee Loughner, who shot congressional representative Gabby Giffords in Tucson, Arizona, had been expelled from community college for disturbing behavior and denied entrance to the military because of drug abuse. He was still able to buy a firearm and high-capacity ammunition magazines from local licensed dealers.

A would-be purchaser who disagrees with a NICS denial may appeal the decision by either challenging the accuracy of the record used as a basis for the denial or assert that the record used as basis for the denial is invalid or does not pertain to the would-be purchaser. The appellate procedures are in 28 C.F.R. Part 25.10; (Brady Act), Subsection 103 (f) and (g) and Section 104.

The FBI views the privacy and security of information in the NICS as a matter of importance. In October 1998, the Justice Department issued regulations on the privacy and security of the system's information, including the proper use of this information. The NICS website contains this announcement. The NICS website is restricted to agencies that are authorized by the FBI. The NICS is forbidden to establish a federal firearm registry. The NICS destroys information about inquiries about allowed gun sales. See Title 28 C.F.R. 25.9(b)(1), (2), and (3). If a potential purchaser is delayed or denied a firearm and successfully appeals the decision, NICS may not retain a record of the overturned appeal. If the record cannot be updated, the purchaser continues to be denied or delayed, and that individual appeals the decision, the documentation must be resubmitted on every subsequent purchase. For this reason, the voluntary appeal file (VAF) has been established. This process permits applicants to request that the NICS maintain information about themselves in the VAF to prevent future denials or extended delays of a firearm transfer.

See also: Background checks; Computers and privacy

National Security Agency (NSA)

Identification: A U.S. defense agency responsible for government cryptography, intelligence gathering, counterintelligence, and the protection of U.S. government communications. NSA's mission is divided into two categories: Signals Intelligence (SIGINT), the collection, processing, and dissemination of intelligence information; and Information Assurance (IA), the protection of sensitive and classified national security information from foreign adversaries.

President Harry S. Truman created NSA on October 24, 1952, through a classified memorandum revising the National Security Council Intelligence Directive. The intelligence-gathering functions now performed by NSA date back to World War I, with the creation of the Cipher Bureau and Military Intelligence Branch, Section 8 (MI-8). During World War II, these functions were fulfilled by the Signal Security Agency (SSA), which later became the Army Security Agency (ASA). In 1949, prior to the creation of NSA, all U.S. government cryptology was consolidated into the Armed Forces Security Agency (AFSA), to be reorganized three years later with the creation of NSA.

The director of the National Security Agency (DIRNSA) leads NSA and also serves as the chief of the Central Security Service (CHCSS) and commander of the United States Cyber Command (USCYBERCOM). NSA's organizational structure is classified, and much of it is unknown; investigative research, internal leaks, the *Congressional Record,* and partial disclosures obtained through the Freedom of Information Act, 80 Stat. 250 (1974), and other sources, however, show that it is divided into various directorates, each with its own organizational responsibilities. These directorates include, but are not limited to, the Signals Intelligence Directorate, responsible for data acquisition and analysis; the Research Directorate, responsible for research and development of new cryptological techniques; the Information Assurance Directorate, responsible for safeguarding U.S. government communications and other data, and the Technology Directorate, responsible chiefly for implementation and maintenance of the hardware and software used by the various NSA projects and offices throughout the world. In 2012, NSA estimated that it had more than 30,000 employees (it is unclear whether this number included the employees of organizations serving as defense contractors for the agency or only those directly employed by NSA). NSA headquarters are located in Fort George G. Meade,

Maryland, with many other facilities located throughout the United States as well as in each of the Five Eyes (FVEY) nations signatory to the multilateral UKUSA Agreement, a treaty for joint cooperation in signals intelligence: the United Kingdom, Canada, Germany, Australia, New Zealand, and Thailand. NSA has further data-sharing agreements with facilities located in Norway, Denmark, Italy, Greece, Turkey, Austria, Japan, India, Oman, Kenya, Puerto Rico, and South Korea.

NSA has engaged in SIGINT operations chiefly through a network of programs codenamed ECHELON. The ECHELON network obtained foreign and international communications through the use of communications satellites to intercept messages transmitted over the Internet, over telephone lines, and via radio waves. ECHELON was created during the Cold War as an intelligence-gathering tool for use against the USSR and its allies. The U.S. government has never publicly acknowledged ECHELON's existence, so it is known only through internal leaks and other investigative research. Seeking to cast light on the program, the European Parliament established the Temporary Committee on the ECHELON Interception System in July 2000, ultimately issuing a report in 2001, but the U.S. government refused to meet with any representatives of the committee.

Edward Snowden, an information technology professional employed by NSA through defense contractor Booz Allen Hamilton, publicly disclosed the existence of three massive NSA SIGINT operations. The first, called Boundless Informant, granted access to worldwide Internet and telephone metadata from both within the United States and abroad, and provided analytic tools for analyzing it to reveal patterns and connections between callers. One leaked NSA document revealed that 97,111,188,358 pieces of Internet metadata and 124,808,692,959 pieces of telephone metadata were intercepted in March 2013 alone, with 3,095,533,478 collected from users within the United States in that period.

The second program disclosed by Snowden, called XKeyscore, granted access to nearly everything the average user does on the Internet anywhere in the world, including the content of emails, web searches, and websites visited. NSA's account of XKeyscore's capabilities asserts that the program was significantly more limited in scope. In response to Snowden's leaks, an NSA spokesperson stated that XKeyscore was not a data collection tool but rather performed only analytical functions on data that has already been collected using other means, and that the program furthermore had been used only to surveil Internet users outside the United States. NSA used several smaller program to process the massive amounts of data generated by the XKeyscore program into a more usable form: MARINA was a database and an analytic tool used to develop a summary of an individual's Internet behavior for the previous year, whether or not that individual was otherwise made the target of NSA for surveillance; Pinwale was a database used to store and analyze information gathered by XKeyscore and organized by specific search terms; Trafficthief was similar to Pinwale, but it was organized by what one leaked document called a "strong-selector," speculated to refer to a search term such as an email address or phone number.

The third large NSA SIGINT program revealed by Snowden was called PRISM. In the PRISM program, NSA partnered with telecommunications companies such as Google, Yahoo!, Microsoft, Facebook and Verizon to gain direct access to users of those services both inside the United States and abroad. The program was first implemented in 2007, as authorized by the Protect America Act of 2007, 121 Stat. 552, which eliminated the warrant requirement for the targeted surveillance of individuals as long as NSA "reasonably believed" such individuals to be outside the United States. The PRISM program enabled collection of the telephone metadata as well as *both* Internet metadata and Internet content. Under PRISM, the telecommunications partner companies held all of their users' data and would turn over that portion of said data that corresponded with NSA requests targeted at specific individuals and those they contacted using the telecommunications networks. NSA maintained that, although its telecommunications partners were ordered to *store* all their data for NSA's purposes, the agency only *used* the data in this limited way, which complied with U.S. privacy protections in U.S. law. Thus, NSA would identify individuals who had links to terrorism or other activities justifying surveillance (the targets) and would then collect records regarding these individuals as well as any other individual within three "hops" of the target (one hop would be all the individuals with whom the target had direct telecommunications contact; two hops would be all the individuals with whom a one-hop individual had direct telecommunications contract; three hops would be all the individuals with whom a two-hop individual had direct telecommunications contact).

The existence of various smaller NSA intelligence programs, some of which are constitutive of the larger initiatives, is also known. One such program, called Dropmire, was used to gather intelligence through secret surveillance of foreign embassies, including those of U.S. allies. One leaked document listed thirty-eight embassies and missions as targets of Dropmire program surveillance by various techniques, such as the implantation of physical bugging devices, tapping into existing telecommunications cables, and the use of specialized antennas.

Another such smaller program was the decryption program Bullrun. According to leaked documents, Bullrun was able in 2010 to decrypt vast amounts of encrypted Internet data that had been, up until the inception of the program, indecipherable and therefore useless to the intelligence community.

The MYSTIC program had the capability in 2011 of recording and storing both the metadata and content of every cellphone call made in an entire country over a period of thirty days.

Documents leaked by Edward Snowden stated that MYSTIC had been used to collect all telephone metadata from Mexico, the Philippines, and Kenya, as well as all metadata and the content of all cellphone calls in the Commonwealth of the Bahamas and Afghanistan, over a thirty-day period.

MAINWAY was a database containing the telephone metadata mostly for analysis by other NSA programs. It was made known to the public through leaks by anonymous whistleblowers to the *Washington Post* in 2006. It is estimated that MAINWAY contained more than 1.9 trillion telephone metadata records of both domestic and international calls, storing them for at least five years.

The Dishfire program, a joint effort between NSA and the United Kingdom's Government Communications Headquarters (GCHQ), was a database that, according to leaked NSA documents, collected on a daily basis geolocation data corresponding to 76,000 text messages, data containing 110,000 names collected from electronic business cards, data regarding 800,000 online financial transactions, details about 1.6 million individuals crossing international borders, data regarding 5 million missed calls, and 200 million text messages.

Individuals within the United States, as well as U.S. citizens abroad, are protected against unreasonable searches and seizures by the Fourth Amendment. A neutral magistrate must therefore approve any collection of data that is deemed to be either a search or a seizure from such individuals to satisfy the requirements of the Fourth Amendment. To maintain secrecy, NSA submits applications to obtain (search/seize) this data to the Foreign Intelligence Surveillance Court (FISC), a specialized judicial body created by the Foreign Intelligence Surveillance Act (FISA). Rulings and court orders generated by FISC remain secret as a matter of course, so public disclosure of these documents has been gained only by fulfillment of requests under the Freedom of Information Act (FOIA) and through internal leaks.

The Protect America Act of 2007, 121 Stat. 552 (2007), altered the traditional Fourth Amendment analysis as it regarded NSA data collection from individuals within the United States. Although the Fourth Amendment still protected such individuals from being the *direct* target of NSA surveillance, the warrant requirement was eliminated for all subsequent "hops" from a foreign target. Individuals within the United States could therefore still be subjected to surveillance, albeit only by virtue of their telecommunications connections to a primary surveillance target located *outside* the country.

NSA has been made the defendant in numerous cases alleging unlawful and unconstitutional practices as part of its surveillance programs. Most notable among these was the 2013 case *American Civil Liberties Union v. Clapper*, 959 F.Supp.2d 724 (2013), in which the American Civil Liberties Union (ACLU) alleged that NSA's mass surveillance programs had violated both the First Amendment (because of their tendency to chill communications between ACLU and its clients located within the United States, many of whom were likely targets for NSA surveillance) and Fourth Amendment protection against unreasonable searches and seizures. Other similar lawsuits against NSA, such as *Jewel v. NSA*, 673 F.3rd 902 (2011), *Clapper et al. v. Amnesty International et al.*, 133 S.Ct. 1138 (2013) and *ACLU v. NSA*, 493 F.3d 644 (2007), had been dismissed before reaching their merits, with courts finding that the plaintiffs lacked standing because they were unable to prove that they had actually had their telecommunications data surveilled by NSA. *ACLU v. Clapper* was the first of its kind to reach the merits after a finding that the plaintiffs had standing to sue. This was due to the disclosures of Edward Snowden, which showed that NSA had in fact collected data originating from every user of certain telecommunications companies with which NSA had partnered. The district court for the Southern District of New York dismissed the case on December 28, 2013, relying on the holding of the landmark Supreme Court case, *Smith v. Maryland*, 442 U.S. 735 (1979), that the seizure of telephone metadata is not a search and therefore is not entitled to any Fourth Amendment protections, and reasoning that the plaintiff's First Amendment claims were too speculative to be require relief. This judgment was vacated and the case remanded on appeal, however, on May 7, 2015, on statutory rather than constitutional, grounds.

NSA has also been indirectly implicated in civil litigation in several motions made, to FISC, by the telecommunications companies partnered with NSA in the PRISM program. The motions sought to compel FISC to declassify certain information on the companies' involvement in storing and/or sharing its customers' data with NSA. In this context, Google, Facebook, LinkedIn, and Microsoft asked for permission to release previously classified data about the FISC orders it had received, and Yahoo! asked FISC to declassify documents that showed that Yahoo! had objected strenuously to an order compelling it to turn over customer data. All these motions were granted, allowing the documents and data to be publicized.

Following the disclosures made by Edward Snowden in 2013, President Barack Obama convened the President's Review Group on Intelligence and Communications Technologies (consisting of former National Coordinator for Security, Infrastructure Richard C. Clarke; former deputy director of the Central Intelligence Agency (CIA) Michael J. Morell; University of Chicago Law School professor Geoffrey R. Stone; Harvard Law School professor Cass R. Sunstein; and Georgia Institute of Technology professor Peter Swire). This group, on December 12, 2013, issued *The NSA Report: Liberty and Security in a Changing World*. The report acknowledged the unprecedented nature of national security threats in the post-9/11 world and the need to promote U.S. national security and foreign policy interests while safeguarding the right to privacy and the rule of law and promoting U.S. prosperity. The report made several recommendations, including the cessation of bulk metadata collection of individuals within the United States; the curtailing of such collection with regard to individuals outside the United States, absent a showing of specific and compelling needs; the creation of a new process by which surveillance is commenced on foreign nations and their leaders; reform of the position of NSA director to be Senate-confirmed and eligible to civilians; reassigning NSA's domestic programs to other agencies; increasing the efficacy of NSA's Civil Liberties and Privacy Protection Board; creation of the position of public interest advocate to represent the interests of privacy and civil liberties before FISC, while generally increasing the transparency of that court; bolstering Internet security through encryption tools; and safeguarding the government's classified information in a more responsible way.

Reuben Fuller-Bennett

Further Reading

Bamford, James. *Body of Secrets: Anatomy of the Ultra-Secret National Security Agency*. New York: Doubleday, 2001.

Brownell, George A. *The Origin and Development of the National Security Agency*. Laguna Hills, CA: Aegean Park Press, 1981.

Cepeda. Simon. *NSA Intelligence Collection, Leaks, and the Protection of Classified Information: Background and Issues*. New York: Nova Publishers, 2014.

Clarke, Richard A., Michael J. Morell, Geoffrey R. Stone, Cass R. Sunstein, and Peter Swire. *The NSA Report: Liberty and Security in a Changing World*. Princeton, NJ: Princeton University Press, 2014.

Harris, Shane. *@War: The Rise of the Military-Internet Complex*. Boston, MA: Houghton Mifflin Harcourt, 2014.

NSA Director of Civil Liberties and Privacy Office. *NSA's Civil Liberties and Privacy Protections for Targeted SIGINT Activities under Executive Order 12333*.

Office of the Director of National Intelligence, Office of General Counsel. *Intelligence Community Legal Reference Book*, 2d ed. Washington, DC: Office of the Director of National Intelligence, Office of General Counsel/USGPO, 2009.

Washington, DC: NSA Civil Liberties and Privacy Office, October 7, 2014.

See also: American Civil Liberties Union (ACLU); Big data; Boundless Informant; Electronic surveillance; Facebook; Foreign Intelligence Surveillance Act of 1987 (FISA); Foreign Intelligence Surveillance Court (FISC); Fourth Amendment to the U.S. Constitution; Freedom of Information Act (FOIA); Google; Government Communications Headquarters (GCHQ); Metadata; PRISM; Protect America Act; Search warrants; Snowden, Edward Joseph; Whistleblowers

New Jersey v. TLO, 469 U.S. 325 (1985)

Identification: A U.S. Supreme Court opinion establishing the basic Fourth Amendment search rules for public school students. Justice Byron White authored the majority opinion in a 6–3 decision for the Burger Court. Because the Constitution applies only to governmental action and does not have an impact on private activity, *TLO*'s holding does not extend to private schools.

TLO involved simple facts. A fourteen-year-old public high school freshman was accused of smoking in a school bathroom. A Piscataway High School teacher found TLO and a friend smoking cigarettes, which violated school rules, in the girls' bathroom. The teacher escorted both students to the principal's office, where they met with an assistant principal, Mr. Choplick.

TLO's friend admitted she had been smoking; however, TLO denied both that she had been smoking and further that she smoked at all. These denials led Mr. Choplick to look through TLO's purse. Upon opening the purse, Mr. Choplick found a pack of cigarettes as well as cigarette rolling papers. Because Mr. Choplick believed that rolling papers, like those found in TLO's purse, usually indicated marijuana use, he continued looking through TLO's purse. In addition to the cigarettes and rolling paper, Mr. Choplick discovered some marijuana, a pipe, plastic bags, several dollar bills, and writings suggesting that TLO was involved in drug dealing. Mr. Choplick contacted the police and gave them the evidence he found in TLO's purse.

TLO's mother accompanied her daughter to the police station. There, TLO admitted to police what Mr. Choplick feared: TLO had been selling drugs at Piscataway High School. The State of New Jersey relied on the evidence that Mr. Choplick found in TLO's purse and TLO's police station confession to initiate juvenile delinquency proceedings against her.

TLO filed a motion to suppress the evidence from her purse and, relying on the fruit of the poisonous tree doctrine, her confession that occurred only because Mr. Choplick had taken her purse. Her motion was denied and TLO, having been adjudicated a delinquent, was placed on one year's probation. While the lower New Jersey courts found that Mr. Choplick had not violated the Fourth Amendment, the New Jersey Supreme Court disagreed and reversed the suppression ruling. New Jersey then filed a petition for certiorari with the U.S. Supreme Court seeking permission to appeal.

A fourteen-year-old accused of smoking in a high school bathroom was responsible for establishing national search rules in the public school setting, which is exactly what happened when TLO denied smoking cigarettes with her friend. The Supreme Court initially took the case to determine whether criminal evidence found by public school officials during a search was subject to the exclusionary rule—an evidentiary rule that prohibits governmental officials from using items obtained through an illegal search as evidence of an individual's guilt. After hearing arguments on March 28, 1984, however, the Court declined to rule on the exclusionary rule issue and reordered new argument on a different question: whether the Fourth Amendment applies to school officials. That second argument was held on Tuesday, October 2, 1984. Requiring a second oral argument and reframing the issue is highly unusual, but it has happened in other landmark cases, such as *Roe v. Wade*, 410 U.S. 113 (1973).

TLO established two critical rules in criminal procedure. First, the Supreme Court held that the Fourth Amendment does apply to school officials, such as teachers, coaches, and administrators. This holding was later expanded in other cases, discussed below. Because the Fourth Amendment applies to school officials, such as Mr. Choplick, the Court had to determine whether Mr. Choplick's rummaging through TLO's purse constituted a search and, if so, whether the search was reasonable under the Fourth Amendment.

The second critical rule that *TLO* established is that warrants are not usually required in the public school setting. The Court was willing to dispense with the warrant requirement because of the informal nature of school discipline for students, like TLO, violating school rules. Most Americans would not expect a warrant to be issued before a teacher or principal could determine whether a student had been smoking cigarettes in the school bathroom. Instead, the Court found that teachers, coaches, and administrators must be able to impose discipline swiftly to maintain school safety and order.

While these two rules represent the main holding of the case, a third rule actually applying the Fourth Amendment in the school setting may be *TLO*'s greatest legacy. The Fourth Amendment does not outlaw all searches or require that all searches be initiated pursuant to a warrant. Rather, the Fourth Amendment simply requires that all searches be reasonable and that searches conducted pursuant to a warrant be based on probable cause. The plain language of the Fourth Amendment enabled the Court to decline to require a warrant in the public school setting and to empower school officials to initiate a search based on the much lower standard of individualized reasonable suspicion rather than probable cause.

TLO, after balancing the governmental interests against the individual privacy interests at stake, ruled that searches in the public school setting must meet two requirements to be found constitutionally reasonable: First, searches must be justified at their inception, meaning, essentially, that a school official must have reasonable articulable suspicion that someone has violated either a school rule or the law. In this particular case, Mr. Choplick had reasonable suspicion that TLO had violated school rules by smoking in the bathroom. Thus, his initial opening of TLO's purse to look for evidence that she had violated the school rule was reasonable at its inception. Mr. Choplick was informed by a teacher that the two girls had been smoking in the restroom.

Second, to be constitutional, searches by public school officials must be reasonable in scope based on the student's age and gender. This means that a search can only be as broad as the suspicion, or subsequently discovered evidence, justifies. Here, Mr. Choplick found both cigarettes and cigarette rolling papers, something that would suggest possible marijuana use or possession. The discovery of the cigarette rolling papers justified expanding the search to the whole purse, which ultimately proved to be TLO's downfall.

Subsequent public school cases have demonstrated the broad discretion afforded school officials in conducting searches. Two particular cases, *Vernonia School District v. Acton*, 515 U.S. 646 (1995), and *Board of Education v. Earls*, 536 U.S. 822 (2002), decided by the Rehnquist Court, permitted random drug searches to be conducted against public school students involved in extracurricular activities without any showing of individualized suspicion. These cases are unique to the issue of drug testing and do not apply, generically, to traditional searches.

The Supreme Court showed its intolerance for invasive searches of younger students in *Safford Unified School District v. Redding*, 557 U.S. 364 (2009). *Safford*, decided by the Roberts Court, involved the strip search of a thirteen-year-old public school student by a school nurse. The search was prompted by allegations that the student had been giving prescription

strength ibuprofen and over-the-counter naproxen (common medications for light pain, such as headaches or cramps) to other students. The strip search followed an unsuccessful search of the student's backpack and outer clothing. Relying on *TLO*'s two-part reasonableness test, the Court, with Justice David Souter writing, found that the intrusiveness of a strip search, coupled with the relatively mild drugs at issue, violated the student's Fourth Amendment rights. The case was brought as a civil suit, however, and the Court found that the school officials were immune from monetary damages for the indignity they caused the student.

Even today, school searches are governed by *TLO*'s two-part test analyzing the reasonableness of a school search based on whether the search was justified (1) at its inception because of the school official's reasonable suspicion that a student was either violating a school rule or the law, and (as a conjunctive requirement), (2) in its scope, taking into consideration the alleged violation and the student's age and gender.

Mary M. Penrose

Further Reading

Alderman, Ellen M. "Dragnet Drug Testing in Public Schools and the Fourth Amendment." *Columbia Law Review* 86, no. 4 (May 1986): 852–875.

"Constitutional Law. Fourth Amendment. Seventh Circuit Holds That Random Suspicionless Drug Testing of Participants in Extracurricular Activities Does Not Violate the Fourth Amendment. *Todd v. Rush County Schools*, 133 F.3d 984 (7th Cir.), Cert. Denied, 119." *Harvard Law Review:* 112, no. 3 (January 1999): 713–718.

Cuddihy, William J. *The Fourth Amendment*. Oxford University Press, 2009.

"A Fourth Amendment Framework." *The New Government Surveillance and the Fourth Amendment Privacy at Risk:* 21–48.

Jensen, Gary F., and Dean G. Rojek. *Delinquency and Youth Crime,* 4th ed. Long Grove, IL: Waveland Press, 2009.

Leming, Robert S., and Bloomington Education. Indiana v. Jamie L. Curtis: *"The Case of the Questionable Book Bag Search." A Constitution-based Scripted Trial.* Washington, DC: ERIC Clearinghouse, 1992.

Meyers, Martin. "*T.L.O. v. New Jersey:* Officially Conducted School Searches and a New Fourth Amendment Balancing Test." *Juvenile and Family Court Journal* 37, no. 1 (February 1986): 25–37.

Negangard, Richard. *Legal Principles for Guiding School Administrators in the Search and Seizure of Public School Students: Protecting Students' Fourth Amendment Rights and Providing for Safe Schools.* Ph.D Diss. University of Miami, 1988 Torres. Ph.D. Diss. Penn State University, 2003.

Persico, Deborah A. New Jersey v. T.L.O.: *Drug Searches in Schools.* Springfield, NJ: Enslow, 1998.

Rossow, Lawrence F., and Jacqueline Anne Stefkovich. *Search and Seizure in the Public Schools,* 3rd ed. Dayton, OH: Education Law Association, 2006.

Torres, Mario S. *The Impact of Demographics and the Political Environment on the Implementation of Fourth Amendment Law in Schools.* 2003.

See also: Fourth Amendment to the U.S. Constitution

New York Times Co. v. Sullivan, Abernathy, et al., 376 U.S. 254 (1964)

Identification: A watershed decision in which a unanimous U.S. Supreme Court held that, to protect the fundamental First Amendment freedoms of speech and press, a public official who brings a libel action against critics of his or her official conduct can prevail only if there is a showing of "actual malice."

The opinion in the case of *New York Times Co. v. Sullivan, Abernathy, et al.*, authored by Justice William J. Brennan, Jr., offers an important exposition of the inherent tension between defamation law and First Amendment freedoms and the critical role of "uninhibited, wide open, and robust" debate on public issues in our constitutional system. Decades later, the decision continues to shape our understanding of the constitutional protections afforded to speech and the press.

In *Sullivan*, the U.S. Supreme Court analyzed the intersection of the right to recover for harm caused by defamatory falsehood and the right of free expression. Because the publication of false and defamatory statements can damage reputations and even ruin lives, the law has long permitted an individual who believes his or her reputation has been damaged by a false publication to seek redress through legal action. Such a lawsuit, however, punishes a speaker for the content of his or her speech, and thus is at odds with core First Amendment guarantees. In balancing these competing interests, the Supreme Court in *Sullivan* ultimately concluded that the value of free and open public discourse outweighs the dangers posed to the reputation of public officials by injurious falsehoods.

The *Sullivan* case was very much a product of the volatile historical period in which it arose. On March 29, 1960, in the throes of the civil rights movement in the American South, the *New York Times* carried an advertisement that called for donations in support of the student protest movement, the voting rights movement, and the legal defense of Dr. Martin Luther King, Jr. The advertisement recounted the brutal crackdown against student protesters and civil rights leaders in Montgomery, Alabama. Among other injustices, the advertisement alleged that the Montgomery police department had surrounded the Alabama State College campus with armed officers, padlocked the dining hall in order to starve protesting students into submission, and falsely arrested Dr. King on at least seven occasions. The overall gist of the assertions was true, but the details were not. For instance, the Montgomery police, although deployed to the area, did not surround the campus or padlock the dining hall, and Dr. King was arrested only four times.

L. B. Sullivan, who oversaw the police in his capacity as the city's elected commissioner of public affairs, filed a lawsuit against the *New York Times* and the advertisement's authors in Alabama state court, claiming that the advertisement was libelous. Sullivan argued that the advertisement's account of police misconduct was false and that he, as primary supervisor of the local police, was defamed by its publication.

He argued that the factual errors in the advertisement had injured his reputation.

After trial, the jury was instructed that the statements in the advertisement were libelous per se and that falsity was presumed under Alabama state law. This meant that, as long as the jury determined that the advertisement was referring to Sullivan, the defendants would be forced to pay damages. The *New York Times* and the other defendants objected to these instructions, arguing that they violated the freedoms of speech and press guaranteed by the First Amendment. The trial court rejected these arguments and the jury awarded Sullivan $500,000 in damages. On appeal, the Supreme Court of Alabama affirmed the lower court, holding that the First Amendment did not protect libelous statements.

Reversing the judgment of the Alabama Court, the U.S. Supreme Court held for the first time that the constitutional protections for speech and press do limit the ability of state courts to award libel damages against critics of official government conduct. Justice Brennan's majority opinion emphasized the critical importance of an "unfettered interchange of ideas" to the vitality of our constitutional system. Brennan emphasized that enforcement of Alabama's libel law would undermine this interchange by deterring critical discussion of public issues. If an individual speaker or newspaper feared that any statement criticizing a public official and containing even minor errors might result in a lawsuit and a substantial civil penalty, the speaker or newspaper might self-censor, tempering that criticism or avoiding it altogether. In fact, Brennan suggested that the threat of money damages might be even more inhibiting to free speech than a criminal sanction. He said that, even if the law prohibited only critical statements that were false, it could deter legitimate critics of government from voicing their concerns out of fear of accidental error. Thus, the threat of libel judgments prevented potentially valuable criticism from entering the public discourse and eroded First Amendment freedoms.

The Court noted that an elected public official such as L. B. Sullivan enters the public sphere knowing that he or she may well be the subject of "vehement, caustic, and sometimes unpleasantly sharp" attacks but that such an official also enjoys access to many channels of communications for countering falsehood.

Justice Brennan's opinion did not entirely eliminate the ability of public officials to recover damages for libel, but it imposed upon them a burden that has proved to be remarkably difficult. *Sullivan* holds that a public official may recover damages for a defamatory falsehood only if he or she "proves that the [defamatory] statement was made with 'actual malice'—that is, with knowledge that the statement was false or with reckless disregard of whether it was true or not."

Applying this new standard to the statements made in the advertisement, the Court concluded that L. B. Sullivan could not prove that the *New York Times* or the advertisement's authors actually knew that the statements in the advertisement were false or that they showed reckless disregard for the truth of them. At most, the newspaper and the authors negligently failed to double-check their facts. The Court explained that bare negligence—a simple failure to exercise reasonable care—did not rise to the level of "actual malice." Accordingly, the Court reversed the judgment in favor of Sullivan.

Sullivan fundamentally altered libel law in the United States, increasing protections for critics of official conduct and laying a foundation for later cases that would impose additional constitutional limits in defamation cases involving public figures or matters of public concern. More fundamentally, it articulated, as Lee Levine and Stephen Wermiel wrote in *The Progeny: Justice William J. Brennan's Fight to Preserve the Legacy of* New York Times v. Sullivan (2014), a "theory of free expression in a democracy that literally revolutionized the First Amendment's scope and force." *Sullivan* celebrated the goal of unfettered free expression about public matters and privileged it above other interests, giving important substance to the First Amendment's guarantees of free speech and press.

RonNell Andersen Jones

Further Reading

Bollinger, Lee C. *Images of a Free Press*. Chicago, IL: University of Chicago Press, 1991.

Burnett, Nicholas F. "*New York Times v. Sullivan*," in *Free Speech on Trial: Communication Perspectives on Landmark Supreme Court Decisions*, ed. Richard A. Parker, 116–129. Tuscaloosa: University of Alabama Press, 2003.

Hall, Kermit L., and John J. Patrick. *The Pursuit of Justice: Supreme Court Decisions That Shaped America*. New York: Oxford University Press, 2006.

Hopkins, W. Wat. *Actual Malice: Twenty-Five Years After Times v. Sullivan*. New York: Praeger, 1989.

Kalven, Harry, Jr. "The New York Times Case: A Note on 'The Central Meaning of the First Amendment.'" *Supreme Court Review* 1964 (1964): 191–221.

Levine, Lee, and Stephen Wermiel. *The Progeny: Justice William J. Brennan's Fight to Preserve the Legacy of New York Times v. Sullivan*. Chicago, IL: American Bar Association, 2014.

Wilkinson, Francis. *Essential Liberty: First Amendment Battles for a Free Press*. New York: Columbia University Graduate School of Journalism, 1992.

See also: First Amendment to the U.S. Constitution

News leaks

Identification: The use of state secrecy creates dilemmas for a democratic society.

Democratic governance requires public accountability, and public accountability requires public information of what the government is doing. On the other hand, certain activities related to intelligence and national security are, and always have been, cloaked in secrecy and arguably could not function any other way. The scope of that veiled segment of government activity grows as the nation's role in world affairs grows, or as the perceived threats facing the nation grow, and then becomes entrenched in politics and bureaucracy. The latter process suggests that the veiled segment changes in only one direction, growing larger.

Information leaks to the press are an important means by which the public learns of classified activities that are carried out in the name of the people, may have a significant impact on the well-being of the people, but are kept secret from the people. On the other hand, the disclosure of state secrets can potentially have an adverse impact on intelligence and national-security interests intended to protect the people. Advocates for the press will argue that experienced journalists recognize the difference between the rare facts that truly have to be concealed and those that which are important for the people to know. (Often they also seek to verify what their sources tell them and consult with the government before publishing to avoid exposing truly dangerous material.) Intelligence experts will argue that journalists have neither the background nor the awareness of context to do so. Moreover, intelligence agencies argue that hostile foreign powers also read newspapers and news websites and that the public dissemination of classified information can be as damaging as its surreptitious theft.

Classified Information

Leaking information to the media is illegal only if the information is classified, and it can legally be classified only if its disclosure would be detrimental to national security. The three official categories of classification are: confidential (disclosure "reasonably could be expected to cause damage to the national security"), secret (disclosure "reasonably could be expected to cause serious damage to the national security"), and top secret (disclosure "reasonably could be expected to cause exceptionally grave damage to the national security"). In practice, higher categories have been created—such as special access program (SAP) or sensitive compartmented information (SCI)—but these have been sandwiched in as subcategories of top secret (e.g., "TS/SCI"). It is illegal to classify information solely for the purpose of avoiding embarrassment, but that is not to say that it never happens.

Unfortunately, the definitions are extremely vague, and disputes between individuals and among agencies over the appropriate classification (if any) of a particular document are common. One entity, the Interagency Security Classification Appeals Panel (ISCAP), exists solely to address such disputes when the relevant agencies fail to work them out on their own. (Between 1996 and 2012, ISCAP overturned the classification decision of an executive agency in 24 percent of the cases it reviewed and partially overturned the classification decision in another 40 percent.) Moreover, while legal penalties have been laid out for failing to classify information, none exist for classifying information at too high a level. That incentive, added to the ambiguity of the rules and the ambiguity of much of the information itself, means that "overclassification" is rampant. Thus many intelligence specialists will agree, in the abstract, that much information is classified at too high a level and much is classified that should not be classified at all, even if they do not agree as to which information that is. The knowledge that some information is overclassified or should never have been classified, may make it easier in some people's minds to leak classified information to the media.

Motivations for Leaks

Generally speaking, journalists to not find classified information on their own. Rather, it is supplied to them clandestinely by government employees. The motives of those employees may be complex.

The popular image is that of the leaker as whistle-blower, and this is often proclaimed as the motivation even when it is not. The purpose of whistle-blowing is to disclose wrongdoing or mismanagement within government. Not only is it viewed favorably by the public, there are also legally condoned procedures for whistle-blowing and laws to protect whistle-blowers from retaliation. Under U.S. law (5 U.S.C. §2302[b][8]), this relates only to unclassified information that the whistle-blower reasonably believes constitutes evidence of a violation of a law, rule, or regulation or of gross mismanagement, a gross waste of funds, abuse of authority, or a substantial and specific danger to public health or safety. Internal, nonpublic means exist for reporting wrongdoing in classified matters. Beyond the obvious advantages of such whistle-blower reports, they are an often overlooked resource for leaders, containing information about bureaucratic shortcomings or internal turmoil that would otherwise go unnoticed.

The law protecting whistle-blowers, however, is not always effective. Whistle-blowers may face administrative discipline even for divulging unclassified government information, or bureaucratic ombudsmen may be unresponsive or may not agree that wrongdoing is involved. This may lead honest whistle-blowers to avoid the legal path and leak their revelations clandestinely to the media.

In many instances, leaking serves a more self-interested purpose. It may, for example, be used as a tool in bureaucratic infighting. Thus leaks may be intended to shape an internal debate over policy, or even to reverse a policy decision already made, by drawing public opinion into the arena. In such cases, leaking may be highly selective so as to shine a more favorable light on the position being advanced. On the other hand, in certain instances, leaks could be a reaction by bureaucrats to a politician lying to the public about the content of secret information. Apart from that, further possible motivations for leaks are ego, a desire to curry favor with journalists, or a perceived need to settle grudges.

Finally, it should be noted that many apparent unauthorized leaks are in fact authorized disclosures masquerading as leaks. Decision makers may choose to disclose certain bits of information to the public anonymously to shape public opinion, to reveal unfavorable information while avoiding blame, or to test public sentiment before making an official policy announcement.

The relative tolerance for leaks on the part of many administrations may stem from the desire to retain the capacity to leak for themselves.

Legal Aspects

The disclosure of classified information, even if unauthorized, is not always illegal. Congress passed a bill in 2000 that would have made any unauthorized disclosure of classified information a felony, but President Bill Clinton vetoed it. Leaking is criminal in certain circumstances, however, under a variety of specific laws.

Most prominent is the Espionage Act(18 U.S.C. §§793–798), first passed in 1917, which makes it a felony to disclose "national defense information" to those who are not authorized to have it. The Supreme Court, in *Gorin* v. *United States* (1941), determined that conviction under the Espionage Act requires a finding of *scienter*, a legal term indicating bad faith or a knowledge of wrongdoing. Interpreted otherwise, in the Court's opinion, the law would be unconstitutionally vague. Thus, conviction requires proof of intent or a pattern of disclosures sufficient to show intent. A single accidental disclosure would not normally lead to prosecution.

Other laws that have come into play in the prosecution of news leaks relate to the theft of federal property (18 U.S.C. §641), the disclosure of classified information relating to communications activities (18 U.S.C. §798), computer security (18 U.S.C. §1030[a]), or the disclosure of the identity of a secret agent (50 U.S.C. §3121). People may also be convicted of making false statements, perjury, or obstruction of justice(18 U.S.C. §§1001, 1503, 1512, 1623)in the course of a news-leak investigation. Indeed, prosecutors may prefer the latter charges, even if they have evidence of guilt under charges more directly tied to espionage, inasmuch as they are easier to prove and they entail less risk of divulging the underlying classified information in open court.

In addition to laws related to the disclosure of classified information, government employees with authorized access to such information are required to sign nondisclosure agreements as a condition of employment. These agreements require them to keep classified information secret both during and after the term of their employment. They are also obliged to submit all relevant materials that they write for prepublication review to assure that no classified information is divulged. Frank Snepp, a former CIA analyst in South Vietnam, was sued by the CIA for publishing his memoirs, *Decent Interval* (1977), without submitting them for review. The CIA did not claim that the book divulged any secrets, only that it had not been reviewed. The Supreme Court, in *Snepp* v. *United States* (1980), found for the agency, and the CIA seized all proceeds from the book's sale.

The Law and the Press

Prosecutions for news leaks have generally been directed at government employees who have disclosed classified information to journalists. The government has not prosecuted journalists for publishing classified information handed to them, but neither has it fully conceded that it does not have the right to do so.

The main protection for the press comes under the First Amendment: "Congress shall make no law . . . abridging the freedom of speech, or of the press; . . ."Generally speaking, citizens have a right to discuss governmental affairs. The Supreme Court has held that restrictions on speech are allowable only when they are necessary to promote a compelling interest and when they are the least restrictive means to further that interest. On the other hand, the Preamble of the Constitution states that one of the purposes of the government is to "provide for the national defense." The Supreme Court has described national security as a compelling government interest, and that may at times require secrecy.(National security is defined as encompassing both national defense and foreign relations.) It is the job of courts and policy makers to balance these aspects of the law within the constitutional framework. Courts often insist that the government make some showing, beyond the mere fact of classification, that a specific disclosure has a potential to harm national interests, but they do not require prosecutors to prove that the disclosure has already caused a specific harm, and they rarely attempt to second-guess the executive as to what is necessary to protect national security.

With regard to the rights of the press to publish classified information, intelligence agencies and law enforcement sometimes take a strict view. In 1942, after the *Chicago Tribune* published classified details about the Battle of Midway while the battle was still on, the Justice Department's Office of Legal Counsel opined that the government had the right to prosecute the reporter and, depending of the circumstances ,the managing editor, the publisher, and the company as well. No prosecution followed only because the Navy refused to divulge in court exactly which details were the secrets it was trying to conceal.

In practice, although the case did not involve classified information, the principal protection for journalists is the Supreme Court finding, in *Bartnicki* v. *Vopper* (2001), that a reporter who has passively received information is free to publish it, even if the reporter's source obtained the information illegally. The presumption follows, although there is no explicit precedent, that actively soliciting classified information or cooperating with the source prior to the illegal act could land a journalist in legal peril. There is a sizable gray zone here. For example, Barton Gellman, a seasoned journalist in this field, describes a process of gathering information that seems to veer quite close to this. He notes that sources rarely send stories to a journalist out of the blue. Rather, Gellman follows an "iterative" process that begins with hunches and guesses as to who would know whether his hunches are true. He begins with officials with the least at stake in the issue and then works toward the center. He accumulates small facts that collectively lead to larger facts. If it goes well, by the time he arrives at the classified core

of the issue, he can act as if he already knows the answers and is merely seeking confirmation. (Or as Gellman puts it, placing the onus on the potential source: "Hardly anyone in government is comfortable about explicitly crossing the line into classified material. Sometimes a person will rationalize it with the notion that he is saying something I already seem to know.") In 2018 the director of national intelligence expanded the definition of leaks to include the "confirmation" or "acknowledgment" of classified information to an unauthorized person.

Journalists could also be in jeopardy if they knowingly accept information from a hostile foreign intelligence service—even if the information is received passively—rather than a whistleblower or other domestic leaker. If the source is a hostile foreign intelligence service, the journalist will have difficulty relying on a presumption that the source meant to expose wrongdoing for the good of the country. Even then, however, a case might be made if the information does prove to be true and of profound public value.

Journalists do face constraints, however. The Supreme Court, in *Branzburg* v. *Hayes* (1972), the only case that explicitly considers the question of a "reporters' privilege" in testimony, held that the Constitution does not protect journalists any more than other citizens from being compelled to testify before a grand jury, regardless of whether the journalist promised sources confidentiality, if the information sought concerns a matter of overriding and compelling state interest. Consequently, in 2005, Judith Miller of the *New York Times* spent 12 weeks in jail before finally agreeing to tell a grand jury exactly who had revealed to her that Valerie Plame Wilson was an employee of the CIA. Ambiguity persists, however. While Justice Byron White's plurality opinion in *Branzburg* rejected the notion of a reporters' privilege, refusing "to grant newsmen a testimonial privilege that other citizens do not enjoy," Justice Lewis Powell's more hedged concurring opinion, which made it a majority, implied that some sort of reporters' privilege should be recognized, speaking of "striking a proper balance between freedom of the press and the obligations of all citizens to give relevant testimony with respect to criminal conduct." (Notes published years later show that Powell was thinking of "a privilege analogous to an evidentiary one" to be applied on a case-by-case basis, but "we should not establish a constitutional privilege.") Journalists have latched onto a favorable interpretation of Powell's opinion.

The Digital Age

While the general patterns of news leaks have continued into the digital age, modern communications technology and practices have introduced some new aspects. For example, in the digital age, it has become easier to steal and leak classified documents, easier to catch leakers, and easier to leak inadvertently, but harder to identify who is part of the press.

First, technology has made it easier to acquire and leak documents. In 1969, Daniel Ellsberg and Anthony Russo set out to photocopy much of the 7,000-page Pentagon Papers, one page at a time, on a Xerox machine (with occasional help from Ellsberg's 13-year-old son and 10-year-old daughter). It was, needless to say, a tedious and time-consuming operation. In 2013, Edward Snowden could use a commercially available application for making backup files to sweep up an estimated 1.5 million classified computer documents and copy them onto thumb drives that he could fit in his pocket. Technology had not only made it easier to leak but to leak unprecedented amounts of material. Most major newspapers now provide secure drop boxes for the anonymous online transfer of digital information or documents. Some analysts believe that the very anonymity, supportive rationalizations/trivializations (for virtually any act), and abundance of dissemination options made available by the Internet can prime certain personality types to engage in prohibited activities that they otherwise might not have undertaken.

Second, at the same time, technology has made it easier to catch leakers. In 2009, Fox News reported on North Korean plans for nuclear tests (with allusions to a CIA source within North Korea). The story itself had limited news value, and certainly disclosed no wrongdoing, but it alerted North Korea to U.S. knowledge of its activities and intentions and doubtless triggered a manhunt to find the CIA source. Using digital forensics, investigators were quickly able to determine that State Department contractor Stephen Kim had the relevant document on his computer monitor at the exact same time that he was talking to Fox journalist James Rosen on his cellphone. Kim eventually pleaded guilty to a felony account of disclosing classified defense information and was sentenced to 13 months in prison.(Kim's account suggests that Rosen followed Gellman's prescriptions, persisting, flattering his source, and implying that he only needed confirmation for something he already knew.) Rosen, as a journalist, was not arrested, although prosecutors had named him an unindicted coconspirator in order to subpoena his email and phone records. (The latter point became a *cause célèbre* among journalists who saw it as a violation of the First Amendment.)

The availability of such technological investigative tools, along with a growing intolerance for unauthorized leaks, contributed to a sharp increase in leak prosecutions. Prior to the Barack Obama years, there had only been three prosecutions in all. The Obama administration prosecuted eight more, although some of those cases were inherited from the George W. Bush administration. The Donald Trump administration, in the summer of 2017, announced that it would pursue leakers with even greater determination, resulting in two guilty pleas and two indictments in its first 18 months. Journalists understandably decried such measures for their chilling effect, reporting that their past sources were drying up, yet overall it failed to stem the phenomenon of leaking. From 2009 to 2016, despite Obama's legal assault on leakers, the number of leaks reported to the

Department of Justice for possible investigation remained steady at nearly 40 a year.

Third, technology has made it easier to "spill" intelligence. "Spillage" is the term used by intelligence agencies to describe the accidental exposure of classified information. Despite the precautions taken, computerized systems and the Internet have made it possible to divulge things unintentionally by pushing the wrong button at the wrong time or by discussing classified matters on the wrong email system.

Finally, a further complication of the digital age is the rise of "informal" media that fulfill or claim to fulfill the function of journalism. If there is a reporters' privilege that prevents prosecution for publishing leaks, does that privilege extend only to well-established and recognized media corporations or does it include openly partisan websites, independent bloggers, WikiLeaks? The final verdict may not be in, but the standard to date, based on circuit court decisions, seems to be that the intent—the gathering of information for public dissemination—rather than the technology or platform employed is determinative of the journalistic nature of an enterprise.

Concluding Remarks

Given the nature of today's technology, some now believe that information, including classified government information, is simply not controllable. Both government agencies and leakers may be fooling themselves by thinking that it is.

In any event, the issue of news leaks has no simple solution. Some degree of leaking is probably inevitable, and some of those leaks are probably desirable and even necessary for government accountability. Arguably, disclosures should be limited to real wrongdoing with clear and convincing evidence of abuse, and they should be done in ways that minimize potentially adverse effects on national security. That said, definitions of what constitutes real wrongdoing and what is really required for national security will always be contested.

Scott C. Monje

Further Reading

Anonymous. *The Art of Anonymous Activism: Serving the Public While Surviving Public Service.* Washington, DC: Project on Government Oversight, Government Accountability Project, and Public Employees for Environmental Responsibility, [2002]. https://www.peer.org/assets/docs/The%20Art%20of%20Anonymous%20Activism.pdf.

Benkler, Yochai. "Prosecuting WikiLeaks, Protecting Press Freedoms: Drawing the Line at Knowing Collaboration with a Foreign Intelligence Agency." *Just Security,* Nov. 19, 2018, https://www.justsecurity.org/61519/prosecuting-wikileaks-protecting-press-freedoms-drawing-line-knowing-collaboration-foreign-intelligence-agency/.

Bruce, James B. "How Leaks of Classified Information Help U.S. Adversaries: Implications for Laws and Secrecy," in Roger Z. George and Robert D. Kline, eds., *Intelligence and the National Security Strategist: Enduring Issues and Challenges.*Lanham, MD: Rowman & Littlefield, 2006, 399–414.

Fenster, Mark. *The Transparency Fix: Secrets, Leaks, and Uncontrollable Government Information.* Stanford, CA: Stanford University Press, 2017.

Fidler, David P., ed. *The Snowden Reader.* Bloomington, IN: Indiana University Press, 2015.

Gellman, Barton. "Secrecy, Security, and Self-Government: How I Learn Secrets and Why I Print Them." Address to the Woodrow Wilson School, Princeton University, Princeton, NJ, Oct. 9, 2003, https://tcf.org/content/commentary/secrecy-security-and-self-government-how-i-learn-secrets-and-why-i-print-them/.

Moynihan, Daniel Patrick. *Secrecy: The American Experience.* New Haven, CT: Yale University Press, 1998.

Mulligan, Stephen P., and Jennifer K. Elsea. *Criminal Prohibitions on Leaks and Other Disclosures of Classified Defense Information,* CRS Report R41404. Washington, DC: Congressional Research Service, March 7, 2017.https://fas.org/sgp/crs/secrecy/R41404.pdf.

Pozen, David E. "The Leaky Leviathan: Why the Government Condemns and Condones Unlawful Disclosures of Information." *Harvard Law Review* 127, no. 2 (December 2013): 512–635.

Rosenzweig, Paul, Timothy J. McNulty, and Ellen Shearer, eds., *Whistleblowers, Leaks, and the Media: The First Amendment and National Security.* Chicago: American Bar Association, 2014.

Sagar, Rahul. "Against Moral Absolutism: Surveillance and Disclosure after Snowden." *Ethics and International Affairs* 29, no. 2 (Summer 2015): 145–59.

Sagar, Rahul. *Secrets and Leaks: The Dilemma of State Secrecy.* Princeton, NJ: Princeton University Press, 2013.

Walzer, Michael. "Just and Unjust Leaks." *Foreign Affairs* 97, no. 2 (March–April 2018): 48–59.

Wilder, Ursula M. "Why Spy Now? The Psychology of Espionage and Leaking in the Digital Age." *Studies in Intelligence* 61, no. 2 (June 2017), https://www.cia.gov/library/center-for-the-study-of-intelligence/csi-publications/csi-studies/studies/vol-61-no-2/pdfs/why-spy-why-leak.pdf.

See also: *Bartnicki v. Vopper*; Doxing; Espionage Act; First Amendment; Journalism and the Protection of Sources; Official Secrets Act; Plame Affair; *U.S. Department of Justice v. Reporters Committee*; Whistleblower; WikiLeaks

Next Generation Identification (NGI)

Identification: A national repository and system of biometric identification services maintained by the Criminal Justice Information Services (CJIS) Division of the Federal Bureau of Investigation (FBI).

Over 18,000 local, state, tribal, federal, and international partners use NGI, which built upon the Integrated Automated Fingerprint Identification System (IAFIS) database of 70 million criminal fingerprint records and 34 million civil fingerprint records. NGI contains more than 230 million civil and criminal digital records of biometric, personal, and biographic data. The system represents a $1.2 billion investment by the U.S. federal government. Like IAFIS, NGI was developed by Lockheed Martin and employs MorphoTrak processing software and algorithms. It was deployed in seven increments between 2008 and 2014. In September 2014, NGI reached full operational capability and replaced the IAFIS database with advanced functionality and search capabilities. NGI also introduced additional services: Advanced Fingerprint Identification Technology, Repository for Individuals of Special Concern, Interstate Photo System, Latents and National Palm Print System, Rap Back Service, and Iris Recognition.

Advanced Fingerprint Identification Technology (AFIT) increases accuracy and lowers response times for searches within the fingerprint records database. New algorithms improved ten-print matching accuracy from 92.6 percent to 99.6 percent and decreased the need for manual print review by 90 percent. The system is three times more effective than IAFIS in matching latent prints to ten-print records when matches exist in the national database. Fingerprint examiners no longer need to specify which hand and finger may have created a latent print before conducting a search. Unlike IAFIS, NGI allows search capabilities across the entire repository. Some privacy groups worry that this larger pool of available data increases the risk of implicating innocent civilians as suspects in criminal cases.

The Repository for Individuals of Special Concern (RISC) service is used in conjunction with mobile identification devices to screen individuals quickly. Mobile devices scan an individual's index fingerprints and compare them against records in a repository of Wanted Persons, Sex Offender Registry Subjects, Known and Suspected Terrorists, and others of special interest. Search results are retrieved in under ten seconds and show red-, yellow-, or green-colored flags identifying the probability of a match. If a highly probable match is identified with a red flag, officers may obtain criminal history information about the individual. RISC is used primarily when an individual is unable to provide proper identification or in situations when officers wish to assess the threat level of a situation. The service is free and currently used by over twenty agencies. The FBI estimates that approximately 1,200 RISC transactions occur per day.

The Interstate Photo System (IPS) is a photograph repository with a facial recognition component for image searching. In 2013, the database included 75 million criminal history records with 16 million mug shots, or booking photographs. Two years later, it held approximately 52 million facial images in the following categories: 46 million criminal images, 4.3 million civil images, 215,000 images from the RISC collection, 750,000 images from a Special

Population Cognizant (SPC) category, and 215,000 images attributed to New Repositories. Full criminal records in the NGI system may include mug shots and related ten-prints and arrest records. Civil records may include photographs collected during employment background checks. The FBI has not defined the SPC or New Repositories image categories. Although FBI representative Brian Edgell claimed that IPS will not draw from social media websites, passports, or department of motor vehicle (DMV) photographs, no formal restrictions prevent the FBI from collecting images from these sources. The FBI offers law enforcement agencies access to a free facial recognition toolbox, which can process 55,000 photographs and conduct tens of thousands of searches per day. Agencies may submit a photo image, such as a mug shot, and receive a ranked list of possible facial matches for manual review. The FBI estimates that a matching candidate will be returned in the list of top fifty candidates only 85 percent of the time when the true match exists in the gallery, but it has not clarified what will happen if the true candidate does not exist in the gallery.

The Latents and National Palm Print System (NPPS) improves latent processing services and introduced a palm print database. An estimated one-third of all latent prints may be attributed to palm prints. Millions of palm prints, originating from repositories in at least twenty-five states, are now searchable for the first time through NPPS. Fingerprint examiners can use the processing system to register new latent prints collected at crime scenes, compare these prints against all records in the database, and manually analyze probable matches generated by the system to identify a likely match. With NGI's enhanced processing capability, examiners can now conduct searches throughout the entire repository of all civil and criminal ten-prints, latent fingerprints, and palm prints at one time.

Rap Back Service continuously monitors a specified list of individuals and alerts law enforcement agencies when people in the file have new criminal activity. Monitored individuals include those under criminal investigation or supervision, such as former inmates released on probation or parole. Public servants such as teachers, bank tellers, and people working with the elderly may also be monitored, particularly if the state in which they are employed requires criminal background checks. Rap Back compares inbound arrest records against individuals in the database and automatically notifies state authorities within twenty-four hours if a monitored individual has been arrested before.

The Iris Recognition (IR) pilot program aims to evaluate existing IR technology through tests with agencies, private companies, and states that currently use it in criminal justice and other settings. For example, the New York Police Department has scanned irises of arrestees since 2010, and many correctional facilities use the technology to identify inmates. The Department of Homeland Security and the Department of Defense also collect iris data. The FBI may use findings from the IR pilot program to request additional funding for continuing operations.

Privacy groups have voiced concern about NGI components, particularly facial recognition services and the possible origins of biometric data maintained in criminal and civil files. The Electronic Frontier Foundation (EFF) and Electronic Privacy Information Center (EPIC) each submitted multiple Freedom of Information Act (FOIA) requests for FBI documents related to NGI. After the FBI failed to comply, both groups filed lawsuits to enforce the FOIA requests, compelling the FBI to release documentation, which EFF and EPIC then published online. The privacy impact assessment (PIA) for the NGI project has not been updated since 2008. Federal agencies that collect personally identifiable information are required to perform PIAs for new systems and make the assessments available to the public. PIAs provide notice of new government programs and technology, evaluate risks and privacy protections, and ensure legal and policy compliance as the project develops.

The current PIA does not effectively restrict the types of biometric data that may be collected and who can access it, and does not provide guidelines for how it can be used and shared. In a 2014 letter to the Attorney General, thirty-two organizations, including EFF and EPIC, called for a revised PIA for the NGI program. EPIC states that a centralized database of personally identifiable biometric information operating under unknown restrictions and guidelines presents great risks of security breaches, mission creep, and the possibility for large-scale government tracking and surveillance.

Carey Sias

Further Reading

Electronic Frontier Foundation and Jennifer Lynch. "FBI Plans to Have 52 Million Photos in its NGI Face Recognition Database by Next Year." https://www.eff.org/deeplinks/2014/04/fbi-plans-have-52-million-photos-its-ngi-face-recognition-database-next-year.

Electronic Frontier Foundation. "Transparency Project: FBI's Next Generation Identification Biometrics Database." https://www.eff.org/foia/fbis-next-generatio-nidentification-biometrics-database.

Electronic Privacy Information Center. "EPIC v. FBI—Next Generation Identification." http://epic.org/foia/fbi/ ngi/

Electronic Privacy Information Center. "Next Generation Identification—FBI." https://epic.org/privacy/fbi/ ngi. html.

Electronic Privacy Information Center. "Spotlight on Surveillance—December 2013. The FBI's Next Generation Identification Program: Big Brother's ID System?" https://epic.org/privacy/surveillance/spotlight/ ngi. html.

Federal Bureau of Investigation. "Next Generation Identification (NGI)." https://www.fbi.gov/about-us/cjis/ fingerprints_biometrics/ngi.

Vrankulj, Adam. "NGI: A Closer Look at the FBI's Billion-Dollar Biometric Program." *Biometric Update*. http://www.biometricupdate.com/201311/ngi-a-closer-lookat-the-fbis-billion-dollar-biometric-program.

See also: Electronic Privacy Information Center (EPIC); Integrated Automated Fingerprint Identification System (IAFIS); Repository for Individuals of Special Concern (RISC)

Obscenity

Identification: Speech or expressions of speech that offend the general morals of the community. These works usually contain depictions of sexual activity, graphic nudity, or excretion.

Obscene speech is not protected under the First Amendment, meaning such speech could be subject to prior restraint—as outlined in *Freedman v. Mary-land*—and the individual making the speech may be prosecuted.

Though twenty states had laws prohibiting obscene publications by the end of the Civil War, the Comstock Law of 1873 was the first federal obscenity law and criminalized the distribution of obscene material through the U.S. postal service. Under Comstock, courts initially defined obscenity using the holding of *Regina v. Hicklin,* a British case defining obscene materials as those that "deprave and corrupt those whose minds are open to such immoral influences." However, the Hicklin test began to lose ground following

U.S. vs. One Book Called Ulysses in 1934, when the Court of Appeals for the Second Circuit held that James Joyce's *Ulysses,* when taken as a whole, depicted "the souls of men and women" and did not "promote lust."

The Supreme Court explicitly broke from the Hicklin test when it decided *Roth v. United States* in 1957. In *Roth,* Justice Brennan wrote that obscene materials are not protected by the First Amendment because they are "utterly without redeeming social importance." However,

In 1904, Roland D. Sawyer launched a crusade against obscenity. (By HL Graf.)

the Court also held that "sex and obscenity are not synonymous," and that the test for obscenity would be whether (1) the dominant theme of the material taken as a whole appeals to a "prurient interest" in sex; (2) the material was "patently offensive" and against contemporary community standards regarding sex; and (3) the material was "utterly without redeeming social value." Courts then spent several years further defining "social value," "patently offensive," and "prurient interest" in various cases, including *Jacobellis v. State of Ohio,* where Justice Potter Stewart famously stated, "I shall not today attempt further to define [obscene] material [. . .] But I know it when I see it."

Two years after *Jacobellis*, the Supreme Court held in *Memoirs v. Massachusetts* that for a work to be obscene, it had to violate all three elements discussed in *Roth*, and works containing even a "modicum of social value" should not be considered obscene. *Stanley v. Georgia* also helped to loosen obscenity laws in 1969, when the Supreme Court held that the First and Fourteenth Amendments prohibited making mere private possession of obscene material a crime. This decision was largely based on the high level of constitutional deference the Court gives to the privacy of the home and the right to receive information and ideas.

Not all decisions from this period loosened obscenity standards; in *Ginzburg v. U.S.*, the Supreme Court held that publications that might not qualify as obscene on their own merits could lead to criminal prosecution if their purpose was to pander, with "pandering" meaning that they were an integral part of the "commercial exploitation of erotica solely for the sake of their prurient appeal." For example, in *Ginzburg*, mailed advertisements telling recipients how they could order obscene materials were found to be obscene.

Chief Justice Berger clarified the requirements for obscenity in the 1973 Supreme Court case *Miller v. California*. In that case, the Court specifically rejected the "utterly without redeeming value" test from *Memoirs v. Massachusetts* and created the three-pronged test that still forms the basis of obscenity law today. According to *Miller*, in order for a work to be obscene, a trier of fact would have to determine:

(a) whether "the average person, applying contemporary community standards" would find that the work, taken as a whole, appeals to the prurient interest; (b) whether the work depicts or describes, in a patently offensive way, sexual conduct specifically defined by the applicable state law; and (c) whether the work, taken as a whole, lacks serious literary, artistic, political, or scientific value.

Telecommunications (and the Internet in particular) complicated this standard. In the 1996 case *U.S. v. Thomas*, the defendants argued that the obscene materials technically never left their home and therefore they were protected under *Stanley*. They also argued that the Internet necessitated a "new definition of community." The Court of Appeals for the Sixth Circuit held that the materials had actually left the house when they were sent digitally. The court further held fact finders should judge using the standards of the community where the materials were sent because the defendants could have refused to give passwords to users from "jurisdictions with less tolerant standards for determining obscenity."

Today, the primary materials found to be obscene are those that feature child pornography. In the 1982 case *New York v. Ferber*, the Supreme Court held that works visually depicting children below a state-specified age engaged in sexual activity are categorically obscene and do not need to be evaluated under the *Miller* test because the social costs of child abuse and exploitation are so great and the potential social value in such performances is so small.

Except for child pornography, modern courts are hesitant to label speech as obscene, as can be seen in the 2010 Supreme Court decision *U.S. v. Stevens*. In *Stevens*, the defendant was prosecuted under 18 U.S.C. §48 for selling videos of dog fighting. The legislation had been drafted to prevent "crush" videos, which are sexual fetish videos depicting the torture or killing of small animals. In the case, the government argued that crush videos and depictions of animal fighting were either obscene or analogous to obscenity. However, the Court gave great deference to the protections of the First Amendment and held the language of §48, which could also apply to hunting magazines or videos, was overly broad and therefore unconstitutional. Following this decision, Congress passed the Animal Crush Video Prohibition Act of 2010, which contained much narrower language that specifically defined animal crush videos and labeled those videos as obscene.

Note that obscene speech is legally different from indecent speech, which was defined in *F.C.C. v. Pacifica Foundation*. Under that Supreme Court ruling, the Federal Communications Commission can censor certain speech without that speech meeting the obscenity standard because broadcast media is so pervasive in American life.

Savanna L. Nolan

Further Reading

Beerworth, Andrew A. "*United States v. Stevens:* A Proposal for Criminalizing Crush Videos under Current Free Speech Doctrine." *Vermont Law Review* 35, no. 4 (2011): 901.

Dennis, Donna I. "Obscenity Law and the Conditions of Freedom in the Nineteenth-Century United States." *Law and Social Inquiry* 27, no. 2 (May 2002): 369–399.

Lipschultz, Jeremy Harris. *Broadcast and Internet Indecency: Defining Free Speech*. New York: Routledge, 2008.

MacKinnon, Catharine, and Andrea Dworkin. *In Harm's Way: The Pornography Civil Rights Hearings*. Cambridge, Mass.: Harvard University Press, 1997.

Rembar, Charles. *The End of Obscenity: The Trials of Lady Chatterley, Tropic of Cancer, and Fanny Hill*. New York: Random House, 1968.

See also: Federal Communications Commission (FCC); First Amendment to the U.S. Constitution; Legal evolution of privacy rights in the United States; Pornography; *Stanley v. Georgia*

Official Secrets Act

Identification: The United Kingdom's legislation that protects secret government information relating to national defense, intelligence gathering, and international relations, and penalizes its disclosure.

Originally passed in 1889, the Official Secrets Act was amended multiple times throughout the twentieth century, with its most recent amendment in 1989. Throughout its history, it has been used to punish those who release sensitive state secrets and was considered as a means to prosecute the *Guardian* newspaper's release of Edward Snowden's files, which revealed eavesdropping by the United States and the United Kingdom.

First enacted in 1889, the Official Secrets Act was a response to the failed prosecution of two men who leaked information regarding British negotiations with foreign powers. Because the government lacked a law specifically prohibiting the disclosures, the leakers were acquitted. The government then began work on a new law titled the "Breach of Official Trust Bill," which would punish these sorts of revelations not because of the value of the information but, as the title indicates, because of the offender's breach of the government's trust. Ultimately, after various additions, the Breach of Official Trust Bill was enacted in 1889 as the Official Secrets Act. Twenty-two years later, in response to public concern about German spies, the act was amended as the Official Secrets Act of 1911. While the intent of the 1911 act continued to focus on prosecuting spies, the new act contained controversial amendments. For example, it placed the burden of proof on the accused; the prosecution had no burden to prove guilt.

A 1920 amendment to the act came in the wake of attacks by the Irish Republican Army and the Irish civil war. The act was amended again in 1939 in reaction to the threatened prosecution of Duncan Sandys, a member of Parliament. Sandys had raised a question in the House of Commons about London's inadequate air defenses and refused to disclose his source of information detailing the inadequacies. Throughout the twentieth century, there were various attempts to amend the 1939 version of the act; all proved unsuccessful.

It was not until two scandals rocked the British government in the 1980s that the act was most recently amended. Roger Hollis, a former British spy, wrote a book recounting his time working for the British government, including his attempts to root out Soviet spies. The British government responded by unsuccessfully attempting to ban the book. In addition, Clive Ponting, an employee with the British Ministry of Defense, leaked documents describing the British sinking of an Argentine navy vessel during the Falklands War. Ponting was prosecuted for violating the act. He raised a public interest defense in arguing that revealing the documents were in the public interest and any damage to the state was outweighed by the public's benefit from knowing the information. His defense succeeded and he was acquitted. In response, Parliament amended the act in 1989 and, among other things, removed the public interest defense. As a result, the act places a blanket, unqualified ban on the disclosure of confidential state information except under prior, official authorization.

The act primarily prohibits the disclosure of information pertaining to security and intelligence, military defense, and international relations. The act also prohibits the disclosure of information that results in the commission of a crime, aids the escape of a prisoner, impedes the investigation of crime, or impedes apprehension of a suspect. The act applies not only to a government employee or contractor who might leak information but also to third parties, such as newspapers, that may come to possess the protected information. Those third parties are prohibited from publishing the information and can be prosecuted for doing so. This lack of a public interest defense, along with a prohibition on publication by newspapers, has raised freedom of speech and press concerns as well as concerns about transparency and the public's right to know.

Those concerns were expressed at various times in 2013 when a British newspaper, the *Guardian*, ran an exposé and published classified documents collected by Edward Snowden, a former Central Intelligence Agency (CIA) employee and U.S. government security contractor. Working with Snowden, the *Guardian* published a series of articles exposing the U.S. and British governments' bulk collection of Internet data. In response, a British member of Parliament, Julian Smith, scheduled a parliamentary debate about whether the *Guardian* was guilty of treason and called for the newspaper to be prosecuted under the Official Secrets Act. Those who possessed the Snowden documents were also threatened with prosecution under the act. For example, Glenn Greenwald was one of the main authors of the *Guardian*'s Snowden articles. His partner, David Miranda, was detained at London's Heathrow Airport on his way from Germany to Brazil. Miranda had in his possession some of the Snowden documents and was detained. Miranda was ultimately released, but the British government considered prosecuting him under the Official Secrets Act for his role in transporting the documents.

Most people accept that governments must protect some state secrets and prohibit their distribution if it would be harmful to national security. A tension exists, however, between governments' desire to keep information secret and the public's desire to have access to information. With a lack of a public interest defense and the authority to punish journalists for publishing newsworthy information, governments can rely on legislation like the Official Secrets Act to hide large-scale violations of privacy that are all the more possible in the digital age.

Douglas B. McKechnie

Further Reading

Feuer, Katherine. "Protecting Government Secrets: A Comparison of the Espionage Act and the Official Secrets Act," *Boston College International and Comparative Law Review* Vol. 38, no. 1 (2015).

See also: Greenwald, Glenn; Snowden, Edward; Whistleblowers

Olmstead v. United States, 277 U.S. 438 (1928)

Identification: A 1928 U.S. Supreme Court decision holding that the Fourth Amendment did not require federal law enforcement agents to obtain a warrant prior to wiretapping a telephone line.

The decision in *Olmstead v. United States* applied a limited interpretation of the Fourth Amendment as protecting only physical things, specifically the "persons, houses, papers, and effects" enumerated in the Fourth Amendment's text, from trespassory searches. Although eventually overturned by *Katz v. United States*, 389 U.S. 347 (1967), and the "reasonable expectation of privacy" standard, *Olmstead*'s trespass approach was the governing precedent for wiretaps for nearly forty years, and it served as the impetus for the Wiretap Act, codified as 18 U.S.C. §§ 2510–2577. Furthermore, the recent Supreme Court decision in *United States v. Jones*, 132 S.Ct. 945 (2012), suggested that *Katz* simply expanded upon *Olmstead* and that the trespass approach to Fourth Amendment searches and seizures is still valid.

Olmstead involved a Federal Bureau of Investigation (FBI) investigation into a Prohibition-era alcohol distribution conspiracy, in which warrantless wiretapping was used to monitor the defendant's telephone communications. At the time, telephones and wiretaps were comparatively new technologies, and regulations governing law enforcement wiretaps were sparse. At trial, Olmstead's attorney objected to the admission of evidence obtained by wiretap, claiming that it violated the Fourth and Fifth Amendments. On review, the Supreme Court sought to answer the issue of whether federal law enforcement's warrantless wiretapping was unconstitutional and therefore should be excluded from evidence at trial. Although both Fourth and Fifth Amendment challenges were raised, the Court quickly dismissed the Fifth Amendment challenge, devoting the remainder of the opinion to the more difficult Fourth Amendment question (*Olmstead*, 456–458).

The Fourth Amendment prohibits unreasonable searches and seizures by the government, and prohibits the use of evidence obtained in violation of a defendant's Fourth Amendment rights in that defendant's criminal trial (*Weeks v. United States*, 232 U.S. 383

(1914); *Mapp v. Ohio*, 367 U.S. 643 (1961)). This "reasonableness" requirement usually requires law enforcement agents to obtain a warrant from an impartial magistrate authorizing the search or seizure. Yet a threshold question to Fourth Amendment analysis is whether the law enforcement action qualifies as a "search" or "seizure" (*Kyllo v. United States*, 533 U.S. 27 (2001)). The Fourth Amendment now provides broader protections, but when *Olmstead* was decided, the Fourth Amendment was construed narrowly to protect only searches and seizures involving a trespass—a physical violation. And while seizures almost universally involve a trespass, nontrespassory searches, such as looking through a window or listening through a wall, were generally unprotected.

Applying this trespass standard, the Court held that warrantless wiretaps did not violate the Fourth Amendment, both because wiretaps were not trespassory searches and because the wiretapped telephone line was not among the defendant's person, house, papers, or effects. The installation of a wiretap did not trespass against the defendant's property because the telephone line was not the defendant's property; it was the telephone company's property. More fundamentally, the Court held that wiretaps should not implicate the Fourth Amendment generally because wiretaps are not trespassory searches. As the Court said, "There was no searching. There was no seizure. The evidence was secured by the use of the sense of hearing, and that only. There was no entry of the houses or offices of the defendants" (*Olmstead* at 464). Although the Court did acknowledge the similarity to searching mail, which requires a warrant, it distinguished this on several grounds, including the Constitution's postal clause, and that mail clearly constitutes "papers" or "effects," the search of which requires a trespass to open the envelope and read its contents (*Olmstead* at 464).

Of note in *Olmstead* is the lengthy dissent by Justice Brandeis (co-author of "The Right to Privacy"). Rather than adhering to a strictly textual reading of the Fourth Amendment, Brandeis argued for a more fluid interpretation that protects individuals from governmental invasions of privacy generally. Rejecting the trespass interpretation, Brandeis recognized the potential for technology to circumvent personal liberties with minimal or no physical violation and argued that the Fourth Amendment should extend to all "invasions of the home and the privacies of life" (*Olmstead* at 473). In his conception, the fundamental guarantee of the Fourth Amendment was not a right against government trespass but rather a "right to be let alone." Noting that wiretaps were illegal in Washington, where Olmstead resided, Brandeis went on to assert that evidence obtained in violation of state law should be inadmissible as a matter of both law and policy (*Olmstead* at 482).

Olmstead is useful as an example of the difficulty in applying constitutional protections to novel technologies. When *Olmstead* was decided, the telephone was a relatively recent invention, and the societal expectations around telephones were not well developed. This would change by the time of *Katz,* the decision overturning *Olmstead,* when household phones had become commonplace. This novelty also meant *Olmstead* was one of the Court's first attempts to address the constitutionality of nontrespassory searches, but subsequent technological progress continually forced the Court to grapple with noninvasive methods of searching. By the time of *Katz,* the notion of searches as purely physical was supplanted by a more modern understanding where noninvasive searches may nonetheless implicate substantial privacy concerns.

Technology continues to challenge which details of our lives should be shielded from government scrutiny, as the recent case *United States v. Jones* demonstrated. *Jones* called into question the constitutionality of the constant surveillance and recording of public information, specifically public movements, something typically not protected by *Katz.* Recognizing this potential diminution of the Fourth Amendment

by technology, the Court reverted to *Olmstead*'s trespass approach to invalidate the specific government action in *Jones.* Concurring opinions voiced concerns over the implications of these new technologies. The Court's official position was that *Katz* merely added to the constitutional protections guaranteed by *Olmstead* and the trespass approach, and that the Constitution has always protected against trespassory searches of constitutionally protected areas. This apparent reversion was met with mixed reviews because the Court did not address the more difficult issue of whether this near-constant surveillance would have been legal absent a trespass. Regardless, the Court's decision in *Jones* effectively expanded the Fourth Amendment to include both protections against trespassory searches, as in *Olmstead,* and nontrespassory searches, as in *Katz.*

Scott Russell

Further Reading

Kerr, Orin S. "The Fourth Amendment and New Technologies: Constitutional Myths and the Case for Caution." *Michigan Law Review* 102, no. 5 (March 2004): 801–888.

Simmons, Ric. "From *Katz* to *Kyllo*: A Blueprint for Adapting the Fourth Amendment to Twenty-First-Century Technologies." *Hastings Law Journal* 53, no. 6 (August 2002): 1303–1358.

See also: Brandeis, Louis Dembitz; Fifth Amendment to the U.S. Constitution; Fourth Amendment to the U.S. Constitution; *Katz v. United States*; *Kyllo v. United States*; *Mapp v. Ohio*; Search warrants; *United States v. Jones*; Wiretapping

Online privacy and protection

Identification: Privacy-related laws.

Since 1966, the federal government has enacted several major privacy-related laws, the most important of which, from the standpoint of computer and online activity, are:

- The Freedom of Information Act(Pub. L. No. 89-487, 80 Stat. 250 (1966))

- The Fair Credit Reporting Act(Pub. L. No. 91-508, 84 Stat. 1128 (1970))
- The Family Educational Rights and Privacy Act of 1974 (Pub. L. No. 93-380, 88 Stat. 571(1974))
- The Privacy Act of 1974(Pub. L. No. 93-579, 88 Stat. 1896 (1974))
- The Right to Financial Privacy Act of 1978 (Pub. L. No. 95-630, 92 Stat.3697 (1978))
- The Electronic Funds Transfer Act of 1978 (Pub. L. No. 95-630, 92 Stat. 3728(1978))
- The Cable Television Privacy Act of 1984 (Pub. L. No. 98-549, 98 Stat. 2779 (1984))
- The Video Privacy Protection Act (Pub. L. No.100-618, 102 Stat. 3195 (1988))
- The Electronic Communications Privacy Act(Pub. L. No. 99-508, 100 Stat.1868 (1986))
- The Health Insurance Portability and Accountability Act (HIPAA) (Pub. L. No. 104-191, 110 Stat. 1936 (1996))
- The Children's Online Privacy and Protection Act of 1998 (Pub. L. No. 105-277, 112
- Stat. 2681-728 (1998))
- The Gramm-Leach-Bliley Act (Pub. L. No. 106–102, 113 Stat. 1338(1999))
- The E-Government Act (Pub. L. No. 107-347, 116 Stat. 2899 (2002))

Even with all of these privacy laws, the United States' current privacy infrastructure is largely inadequate to protect the average consumer interacting on the Internet with a business entity. Currently, despite many proposals and bills, no comprehensive federal data security regulation exists; rather, it is a patchwork of related measures. Little or nothing, for example, regulates whether the average company must implement data security measures to protect the mountain of information it collects and maintains on its users. Virtually nothing requires these companies to disclose to users how they secure data.

Arguably the main reason that vast areas of data collection remain unregulated is that Congress tends to enact privacy legislation only in response to significant privacy breaches. This reactive approach tends to lead to narrower laws. An example from recent decades is Judge Robert Bork's list of video rentals printed in the Washington *City Paper,* an alternative weekly serving the Washington D.C. metropolitan area. Many legislators took offense to this breach of privacy and introduced legislation to prohibit the release of private video rentals. The result was the Video Privacy Protection Act ("VPPA"). With a broken law, VPPA prevents the disclosure of a customer's video rentals and provides for a private right of action. The law is narrow, however, in that it does little to regulate businesses such as bookstores or music retailers.

Four of the privacy acts noted above touch on online privacy policies. The Children's Online Privacy and Protection Act (COPPA) guards against unauthorized use of information about children, aged 13 or less. It requires that child-oriented websites post privacy policies. The websites under COPPA must also disclose the data they collect, how they obtained the data (passively or proactively), how they intend to use it if shared with others, and how one can be deleted from the collection or otherwise opt out. The E-Government Act mandates similar disclosures related to citizens' private information.

The Gramm-Leach-Bliley Act requires financial institutions to explain their data collection activities and how they intend to use their customers' data. Financial institutions must disclose any collected information, the names of any affiliates and third parties with shared data, the data shared, and how to opt out. The Health Insurance Portability and Accountability (HIPPA) is specific. Institutions subject to HIPPA must explain the purposes of HIPPA's privacy policy, disclose collected information, and how it is used. The institution must disclose patient's rights regarding their data, how the health care company is expected to protect that data, and whom to contact to get more information. As with the prior three acts mentioned, HIPPA's primary focus has to do with disclosure.

The vast majority of states, like the federal government, have not passed data privacy laws. The exceptions are California, Delaware, and Nevada. California was the first state to enact such a law in 2013, as an amendment to the California Online Privacy Protection Act (CalOPPA). As a result, most privacy policies since 2013 have followed the California requirements. The amendment covers any person or entity that collects or maintains data on California residents. The entity must (1) identify categories of personally identifiable information (PII) that the operator collects; (2) describe the process (if any) to review and change a user's PII; (3) describe the notification process for material changes to the policy; (4) identify the policy's effective date; (5) disclose the operator's response to "do not track" signals (proposed HTTP header field that requests that a web application disable either its tracking or cross-site user tracking of an individual); and (6) disclose third-party rights to collect PII concerning a user's online activities. In California, the notice must be conspicuously posted.

Effective January 1, 2016, Delaware became the second state in the U.S., joining California, to require operators of commercial websites that collect personally identifiable information to post online privacy policies. Like California, coverage applies to any person or entity that collects or maintains data on Delaware residents. The entity must (1) identify categories of PII that the operator collects, (2) describe the process (if any) to review and change a user's PII, (3) describe the notification process for material changes to the policy, (4) identify the effective date, (5) disclose the operator's response to "do not track" signals, and (6) disclose third-party rights to collect PII concerning a user's online activities. The notice must be conspicuously available. The Delaware Online Privacy and Protection Act (DOPPA) enumerates specific ways to display the notice conspicuously.

On October 1, 2017, Nevada became the third state to require operators of commercial websites that collect personally identifiable information to post online privacy policies. Like California and Delaware, the law applies to any person or entity that collects or maintains data on Nevada residents. The entity must (1) identify categories of PII that the operator collects, (2) describe the process (if any) to review and change a user's PII, (3) describe the notification process for material changes to the policy, (4) disclose third-party rights to collect PII concerning a user's online activities, and (5) identify the effective date; waives requirement to post a privacy policy if the operator resides in-state, Internet sales are a minority of the operator's income, or the site has below 20,000 visitors per year. "[A]n operator shall make [its privacy policy] available, in a manner reasonably calculated to be accessible by consumers whose covered information the operator collects." (NV ST 603A.340, Oct.1, 2017).

Data privacy has been a significant concern regarding children's privacy. The Federal Trade Commission (FTC) broadened its rules regarding children's privacy to address smartphone apps and social media, but it does not appear to have the teeth to make mega companies like Apple or Facebook accountable for violating the Children's Online Privacy and Protection Act of 1998 (COPPA). COPPA regulates how companies collect personal data from children, age 13 and less. The FTC has enforcement authority, but privacy concerns still abound with apps automatically capturing user information from mobile devices and sharing it with third parties. Other information that a mobile app can capture data stored or linked to a mobile device includes geolocation, phone numbers, call logs, and contacts, to name a few.

Joseph A. Custer

Further Reading

Cohen, Julie E. *Configuring the Networked Self: Law, Code, and the Play of Everyday Practice*. New Haven, Conn.: Yale University Press, 2012.

Hartzog, Woodrow, *Privacy's Blueprint: the Battle to Control the Design of New Technologies*. Cambridge, Mass.: Harvard University Press, 2018.

Hoofnagle, Chris Jay. *Federal Trade Commission Privacy Law and Policy*. New York, NY: Cambridge University Press, 2016.

MacKie,-Mason, Jeffrey K., and Waterman. *Telephony, the Internet, and the Media*. New York, NY: Routledge, 2000.

Mitnick, Kevin D., Simon, William J., and Wozniak, Steve. *The Art of Deception: Controlling the Human Element of Security*. Indianapolis, Ind.: Wiley, 2007.

Suchman, Lucy A. *Human-Machine Reconfigurations*, 2d. ed. New York, NY: Cambridge University Press, 2007.

See also: Children's Online Privacy and Protection Act; Family Educational Rights and Privacy Act; Freedom of Information Act; Fair Credit Reporting Act; Gramm-Leach-Bliley Act; Health Insurance Portability and Accountability Act (HIPAA); Privacy Act of 1974; Smartphones; Social media; Video Privacy Protection Act

Open data movement

Identification: A concept of net neutrality that encourages innovation, creativity, and the idea that open information stimulates economic growth within entrepreneurs.

Open data is free data that allows for the exploration, exchange, and creation of technology via a public government service. This type of transparency places all the necessary tools for use in any and all ways that any with Internet access can have available online.

President Barack Obama's 2009 memorandum established three basic concepts of the open data movement's purpose: openness, participation, and collaboration. The heart of the memorandum focuses on empowerment by providing a source for public access research and information for an efficient and effective democratic government. As with all open policies or initiatives, there are two sides and, although the presidential memorandum calls on government organizations for compliance, the sources cited holding private or proprietary data require

protection. Central issues include the following: Who is accessing the open data? What impact does this movement have on Americans' privacy? And why is this movement valuable?

Americans can access data from the websites of government agencies; state, local, and county governments; research organizations; nonprofit organizations; and many other sources for cost-free information. These data are available freely, as a way to show the American public the government is transparent and open about activities, discoveries, ideology, policy, and other data that are public-sector information. The government policy written by the president makes a rule to level the technical playing field of information by increasing accessibility for all Americans. The policy was intended for American access only, but it does not specify how it will be protected from foreign sources. The intention is to target Americans with technical knowledge and expertise, researchers, policy analysts, journalists, students, educators, public activists, and nonprofit organizations with unanswered questions or a desire to collaborate by increasing the information that the government has made available to the public. Thus, the information is available to read, reuse, refine, and redistribute; for example, a teacher may use some of the data to form a lesson plan for a public policy course at a local high school. President Obama's intention for this policy is for the people or Americans to use it but to work with the government while accessing this information.

The open data movement affects privacy rights based on the details of the data required, which means tracking to ensure Americans who access the data are not doing so improperly or illegally. The open data initiative is one that can make personal identification information, personal records, and other individual private data searchable when it should be protected by the government. Open sharing comes with the governmental responsibility to minimize access and protect the availability of private information that may be collected for criminal uses. This collaborative government sharing should have a goal of guarding Americans' privacy rights while providing this tool of information to educate and make data accessible to all. The government has a right to collect a variety of types of information that, if the information were to fall into the wrong hands or if it was made virtually available, could be used for criminal activity potentially causing financial, credit reporting issues, or physical harm. A few years after the president's memorandum was distributed, some federal agencies began to take steps to protect private information. One example is the Department of Education, which hired a chief privacy officer to:

". . . serve as a senior advisor to the secretary on all of the Department's policies and programs related to privacy, confidentiality, and data security [and] . . . coordinate technical assistance efforts for states, districts, and other education stakeholders, helping them understand important privacy issues such as minimizing unnecessary collection of personal information."

The open data movement affects Americans' privacy rights because it relinquishes some control over all the data the government collects and then makes available. Accessible and useful data including private or personal information requires awareness of the owner, and may actually mean limited protection by the owner of the data and the government organization giving access to the data.

The open data movement is important because information sharing is useful for educational purposes, business ideas, analysis by policymakers, and general transparency. Cost-free and accessible data are a way to explore, learn, and develop ideas in an open environment for everyone. Some positive outcomes of this are captured in the city of San Francisco's Open Data Policy of 2009: The creation of an open data policy will provide benefits to the city that include creation of social and economic benefits based on innovation in how residents interact with government stemming from increased accessibility to city

data sets. Open data has a potential to support a range of outcomes from increased quality of life, more efficient government services, better decisions, and new businesses.

While there is wide-spread support for the idea of accessibility of data and information, there are current actions attempting to move toward limiting the type of information we have access to. The Federal Communications Commission (FCC), under the direction of its chairman, Ajit Pai, acted in 2018 to place limits on individual access to information on the Internet. According to the American Civil Liberties Union, the (FCC) has moved to end net neutrality, or the principle that internet service providers should treat online content equally in making it available to their customers. The removal of this principle means that some content may now be privileged over other content (based, for example, on revenue streams) or could otherwise be internally "slowed" in a way that challenges the idea of freely accessed information. This issue is now in the hands of Congress, which will be charged with either supporting or reversing the action of the FCC.

One benefit of the innovative open data movement is that Americans are generating a free exchange of information from the government and other sources in support of several positive professional activities with the potential to teach, create, or improve any interested information seeker. The positive impact the open data movement has the potential to have in America could be infinite in terms of social change and a wealth of knowledge sharing.

Shaunté Chácon and Amber Dickinson

Further Reading

The American Civil Liberties Union. https://www.aclu.org/issues/free-speech/internet-speech/what-net-neutrality

Baker, Mary Beth. "Article Title." *Journal Title* 57, no. 3 (2011): 96.

Black, Alissa. "Public Management of Open Data." *Journal Title* 94, no. 6 (2012): 22. City of San Francisco. Open Data Policy of 2009. www.data.sfgov.org/about.

U.S. Department of Education, Office of Education Technology. "Article Title." *Journal Title* 00, no. 00 (2011): 91. www.tech.ed.gov.

See also: Big data; Computers and privacy; Confidential Information Protection and Statistical Efficiency Act; Educational setting, privacy in an; Financial information, privacy right to; Privacy torts

Open source

Identification: Software with source code that anyone is able to modify or enhance because its design is publicly accessible. Source code is the code used to manipulate or change how a program or application functions. Individuals who have access to a computer program's source code can improve that program by adding features to it or adjusting parts with performance issues.

While the term *open source* was not invented until 1989, some of the concepts surrounding it have existed since the early 1980s. The Open Source Initiative (OSI) maintains the Open Source Definition (OSD) and is recognized worldwide as the authority on determining whether a particular software is a truly open source.

Open source software differs from proprietary or closed source software because, with the latter, the person, team, or organization who created it and maintain exclusive control over the software are the individuals that are able to modify the source code. Because the source code of proprietary software is considered the property of its original authors, they are the only individuals legally authorized able to copy or modify it. Microsoft Word and Adobe Photoshop are examples of proprietary software. To use proprietary software, users must agree (usually by signing a license that comes with the software) that they will not modify the software in ways that the software company has not explicitly allowed.

Open source software has been commercially available since the mid-1990s. Currently, open source is being used by many organizations that operate large-scale or critical infrastructure. Open source software differs from proprietary software because its authors make the source code freely available to others. Open source software includes: LibreOffice and the GNU Image Manipulation Program. Like proprietary software, users must accept the terms of a license when they begin using the open source software. The terms of open source licenses, however, differ significantly from those of proprietary licenses. Open source software licenses promote collaboration and sharing by allowing others to modify the source code and incorporate those changes into their own work. Some open source licenses require that any individual who modifies and then shares a particular program must also share the program's source code without imposing a licensing fee on it. Computer users may freely access, view, and modify open source software as long as they allow others the same right when they share their work. Users could violate provisions of some open source licenses if they fail to comply with this stipulation.

Open source software is licensed under terms allowing the users to practice the four so-called freedoms: (1) Use the software without access restrictions and within the terms of the license applied, (2) view the source code, (3) improve and add to the object and source code, and (4) distribute the source code. Because much of the Internet itself is constructed on many open source technologies, including the Linux operating system and the Apache Web server application, anyone using the Internet benefits from open source software.

Open source software has the following current and potential benefits: (1) encourages reuse, (2) enables easy innovation and flexibility; (3) drives the price of software down to nothing; (4) because there is no vendor or service monopoly, there is no reason to hide defects and security vulnerabilities; (5) there is no single vendor, meaning there is no reason to avoid free and open standards; (6) key software is improved through a process analogized to Darwinian evolution; and (7) with lower barriers to entry, there is wider participation

Remote computing is frequently referred to as cloud computing, so-called because it entails functions (including storing files, sharing photos, or watching videos) that incorporate not only local devices but also the global network of remote computers that form an "atmosphere" around them. Cloud computing has grown increasingly popular. Some cloud-computing applications, such as Google Docs, are closed source programs. Others, such as Etherpad, are open source programs.

Cloud-computing applications run over additional software, which helps them operate smoothly and effectively. The software that runs "underneath" cloud-computing applications is a platform for those applications. Cloud-computing platforms may be open source or closed source. OpenStack is one form of an open source cloud-computing platform.

Many users prefer open source software because it gives them more control. They can examine the code to ensure that it is functioning properly and make modifications as needed. Users who are not programmers also benefit from open source software because they can use this software for any purpose they would like. Some software users prefer open source software because it improves their programming skills. Open source code is publicly accessible, so users can learn to make better software by studying what others have written.

Some users favor open source software because they view it as more secure and stable than proprietary software. Anyone can view and modify open source software, and anyone might spot and correct errors or omissions overlooked by the program's original authors. Because so many programmers can work on some open source software without seeking approval from the original authors, open source software is generally fixed, updated, and upgraded quickly.

Many users prefer open source software to proprietary software for significant, long-term projects because the source code for open source software is publicly distributed. Users that rely on software for critical tasks can ensure that their software will remain functional even if the original creators cease their participation in the project.

The term *open source* does not mean that the program is distributed without charge. Programmers may charge for the open source software they create or when they cooperate with others in its creation. However, most open source licenses require users to release their source code when they sell software to others, so many open source software programmers find that charging users money for software services and support (as opposed to the software itself) is more profitable. With this method, their software remains free of charge; instead, they earn money by assisting others install, use, and troubleshoot it.

There is a misconception that open source software is not as secure as proprietary software. Many individuals are concerned that open source software is inherently less secure and riskier than closed source software because the source code is easily available to all. There is, in fact, no particular type of software that is inherently more or less secure than others. Each must be considered on its own merits.

Gretchen Nobahar

Further Reading

DiBona, Chris. *Open Sources Voices from the Open Source Revolution.* Beijing: O'Reilly, 1999.

Dixon, Rod. *Open Source Software Law.* Boston, MA: Artech House, 2004.

Feller, Joseph. *Perspectives on Free and Open Source Software.* Cambridge, MA: MIT Press, 2005.

Kavanagh, Paul. *Open Source Software Implementation and Management.* Amsterdam: Elsevier Digital Press, 2004.

Lerner, Joshua, and Mark Schankerman. *The Comingled Code: Open Source and Economic Development.* Cambridge, MA: MIT Press, 2010.

Weber, Steve. *The Success of Open Source.* Cambridge, MA: Harvard University Press, 2004.

See also: Cloud computing; Computers and privacy.

P

Patient Safety and Quality Improvement Act of 2005 (PSQIA), 42 U.S.C. § 299b-21 to -26

Identification: Enacted July 29, 2005, effective January 19, 2009, a regulation to improve patient safety by creating incentives for healthcare providers to report and analyze patient safety events. PSQIA facilitates providers' being able to share information concerning adverse events with patient safety organizations (PSOs) by allowing them to communicate such information without waiving privilege or violating confidentiality requirements. As of 2015, healthcare providers appear to be working out how to optimize their PSO use, and some providers have invoked PSQIA to protect materials from discovery during legal proceedings.

The Health Insurance Portability and Accountability Act (HIPAA) of 1996, 110 Stat. 1936 (1996), outlines the privacy and security requirements for covered entities. Covered entities, under certain circumstances, may share information with business associates, as defined under HIPAA. Covered entities not complying with HIPAA's requirements may face fines or other penalties; conversely, HIPAA does not confer any privilege on materials shared with a PSO. As a result, a covered entity may be reluctant to share information on adverse events with an entity such as a PSO because doing so may run afoul of HIPAA's confidentiality provisions and may make such information vulnerable to discovery and use against the covered entity.

Congress enacted PSQIA in response to the Institute of Medicine's 1999 report "To Err Is Human: Building a Safer Health System," which estimated that each year preventable medical errors caused between 44,000 and 98,000 deaths in hospitals and between $17 billion and $29 billion in hospital costs. Lawmakers took up one of the report's recommendations, a voluntary reporting system for adverse events to identify and learn from errors, thus encouraging participation by protecting the disclosed information. Congress began debating the law in late 1999, and multiple versions w9ere introduced in subsequent sessions of Congress. Both houses of Congress passed the final version in 2005. The Department of Health and Human Services published the initial Notice of Proposed Rulemaking on February 12, 2008, and promulgated the final rule implementing the act on November 21, 2008.

PSQIA amends Title IX of the Public Health Service Act. PSQIA outlines the requirements for PSO certification and clarifies that, for purposes of applying HIPAA's confidentiality regulations, PSOs will be treated as business associates, and patient safety activities will be treated as healthcare operations of the provider (defined in the act).

PSQIA confers privilege on "patient safety work product," which is defined in the act as including data, reports, records, memoranda, analyses, or written or oral statements that are assembled or developed to report to a PSO, that a PSO develops for patient safety activities or that show that an entity is reporting to a PSO. It does not include patients' medical records, billing and discharge information, or any other original patient or provider record. *Identifiable* patient safety work product is patient safety work product that allows the identification of providers that are the subject of the work product or whose activities are the subject of the work product, individually identifiable health information as defined by HIPAA, or patient safety work product that allows the identification of an individual who reports information. *Nonidentifiable* patient safety work product is patient safety work product that does not fall into those categories.

Under PSQIA, patient safety work product is privileged and confidential. Because it is privileged, it is not subject to federal, state, or local civil, criminal, or administrative subpoena or order; to discovery in connection with federal, state, or local civil, criminal, or administrative proceedings; or to disclosure under the Freedom of Information Act or similar laws. It also cannot be admitted as evidence in federal, state, local, or governmental civil or criminal proceedings or administrative rulemaking or adjudicatory proceedings, nor can it be admitted in a professional disciplinary body's proceedings. Subject to PSQIA's listed exceptions, patient safety work product is confidential and cannot be disclosed.

PSQIA provides limited exceptions to both privilege and confidentiality. These include use in a criminal proceeding after the court has reviewed the patient work safety product and made an in camera determination that it contains evidence of a criminal act where necessary to enforce protection of a reporter (as defined in the act), and when authorized by each provider identified in the work product. Privilege does not apply to voluntary disclosure of nonidentifiable patient safety work product. Work safety product is exempt from confidentiality

when the work product is disclosed to carry out patient safety activities, when nonidentifiable patient safety work product is disclosed, when the secretary of Health and Human Services sanctions the disclosure, for disclosure to the Food and Drug Administration with respect to a product or activity it regulates, for voluntary disclosure to an accrediting body, when the secretary deems it necessary for business operations consistent with the act's goals, to law enforcement authorities when the person reporting reasonably believes disclosure is necessary for criminal law enforcement purposes, and to a non-PSO when the disclosure does not include materials that assess the quality of care of an identifiable provider or do not describe or pertain to actions or failures of an identifiable provider. Disclosure of patient safety work product under these exceptions does *not* waive privilege or confidentiality, so the materials disclosed under PSQIA's exceptions otherwise remain privileged and confidential.

PSQIA contains some additional protections to encourage reporting. Accrediting bodies cannot take an accrediting action against a provider based on the provider's good-faith participation in collecting, developing, reporting, or maintaining patient safety work product, and an accrediting body cannot require a provider to reveal its communications with a PSO. A provider in turn cannot take an adverse employment action (as defined in the act) against an individual who in good faith reports information for the provider to provide to a PSO or who reports it directly to the PSO.

The penalty for disclosing identifiable patient safety work product is $10,000 for each act constituting a knowing or reckless violation of PSQIA's confidentiality provisions, but double fines for the same act cannot be imposed under both HIPAA and PSQIA.

Last, PSQIA states that it will not limit the application of federal, state, or local laws that provide greater privilege or confidentiality protections than those in the act. Because many states have their own statutory schemes for peer review that attach privilege and confidentiality protections, the amount of protection attached to a provider's information may vary by state.

Julie E. Randolph

Further Reading

Levy, Frederick, Darren Mareniss, Corianne Iacovelli, and Jeffrey Howard. "The Patient Safety and Quality Improvement Act of 2005: Preventing Error and Promoting Patient Safety." *Journal of Legal Medicine* 31, no. 4 (2010): 397–422.

Liang, Bryan A. "Regulating for Patient Safety: The Law's Response to Medical Errors: Collaborating on Patient Safety: Legal Concerns and Policy Requirements." *Widener Law Review* 12 (2005): 83–105.

U.S. Department of Health and Human Services. "Patient Safety and Quality Improvement: Final Rule." *Federal Register* 73, no. 226 (November 21, 2008).

See also: Federal Freedom of Information Act (FOIA); Health Insurance Portability and Accountability Act (HIPPA); Medical confidentiality, privacy right to; Privacy laws, state

Personal autonomy

Identification: The branch of the right to privacy that acknowledges the individual's right to make important decisions about one's most intimate relationships, family life, and bodily functions. The other branch of the right to privacy is known as informational privacy, or the right of an individual to control the distribution to others of one's own personal information. In 1977, the U.S. Supreme Court acknowledged both aspects of the constitutionally protected privacy interest.

In the United States, personal autonomy is primarily based on the liberty protections of the federal and state constitutions. The Supreme Court has long acknowledged, however, that the right was also recognized under common law.

In 1891, the U.S. Supreme Court decided *Union Pacific Railway Company v. Botsford*, 141 U.S. 250. In that case, Botsford sued the railroad company for personal injuries that she suffered in a sleeping car when an upper sleeping berth collapsed and fell on her. Shortly before trial, the railroad asked the trial court to order a surgical examination to confirm Botsford's diagnosis. The trial court refused, and the Supreme Court agreed that the trial court lacked authority to require Botsford to undergo a diagnostic examination at the behest of the railroad. The Court reasoned, "No right is held more sacred, or is more carefully guarded by the common law, than the right of every individual to the possession and control of his own person, free from all restraint or interference of others, unless by clear and unquestionable authority of law."

More recently, the privacy right with respect to personal autonomy has been addressed by the courts in cases dealing with reproductive rights, the right to refuse medical treatment, the right of families to make decisions about raising and educating their children, and the right to engage in consensual intimate relationships. The earliest of these was *Griswold v. Connecticut*, 381 U.S. 479, decided in 1965. Officials of the Planned Parenthood League were convicted for violating a Connecticut statute by giving married couples information and medical advice on birth control. The criminal statute prohibited anyone from using contraceptives, including anyone who assisted or counseled another person to do so. The Planned Parenthood officers challenged the constitutionality of the Connecticut criminal statute. The U.S. Supreme Court declared the statute unconstitutional, relying on several constitutional grounds and the "penumbral rights of privacy and repose" emanating from each one. As the Court recognized, a series of its prior decisions illustrated that "the right of privacy which presses for recognition here is a legitimate one," which in turn implicates "a relationship lying within the zone of privacy created by several fundamental constitutional guarantees."

Would we allow the police to search the sacred precincts of marital bedrooms for telltale signs of the use of contraceptives? The very idea is repulsive to the notions of privacy surrounding the marriage relationship. We deal with a right of privacy older than the Bill of Rights—older than our political parties, older than our school system. Marriage is a coming together for better or for worse, hopefully enduring, and intimate to the degree of being sacred. It is an association that promotes a way of life, not causes; a harmony in living, not political faiths; a bilateral loyalty, not commercial or social projects. Yet it is an association for as noble a purpose as any involved in our prior decisions.

In 1967, just two years after *Griswold*, the Supreme Court struck down a Virginia statute that made interracial marriage a criminal offense. In *Loving v. Virginia*, 388 U.S. 1, the Court relied primarily on the equal protection clause of the Fourteenth Amendment, which was adopted after the Civil War specifically for the purpose of removing the authority of state governments to permit "invidious racial discrimination." In addition, the Court held that antimiscegenation statutes also violated the due process clause of the Fourteenth Amendment by infringing on the freedom to marry. Marriage had "long been recognized as one of the vital personal rights essential to the orderly pursuit of happiness by free men, [and] fundamental to our very existence and survival."

In 1972, the Supreme Court extended its reasoning in *Griswold* to strike down a Massachusetts statute that allowed married persons, but not single individuals, to obtain contraceptives (*Eisenstadt v. Baird*, 405 U.S. 438). While *Griswold* relied in part on the traditional respect for privacy associated with the marital relationship, the Court disavowed the government's effort to limit the right to married couples: "[T]he marital couple is not an independent entity with a mind and heart of its own, but an association of

two individuals each with a separate intellectual and emotional makeup. If the right of privacy means anything, it is the right of the individual, married or single, to be free from unwarranted governmental intrusion into matters so fundamentally affecting a person as the decision whether to bear or beget a child."

Griswold was a turning point in Supreme Court jurisprudence on an individual's constitutional right of personal autonomy to make decisions about intimate matters of family life without governmental interference. In later decisions, the Court clarified that the right of personal autonomy recognized in *Griswold* was based on the First Amendment's freedom of association. In particular, the Court has distinguished between the right of intimate association and the right of expressive association, both guaranteed by the First Amendment (*Roberts v. Jaycees*, 468 U.S. 609). The former aspect of freedom of association bars the government from intruding on personal relationships of the kind that have played "a critical role in the culture and traditions of the Nation by cultivating and transmitting shared ideals and beliefs[,] thereby foster[ing] diversity and act[ing] as critical buffers between the individual and the power of the State." Those relationships include marriage, childbirth, family relationships, cohabiting with one's relatives, and educating children.

For example, the Supreme Court has struck down state "compulsory attendance" statutes requiring students to attend public schools, holding that they unreasonably interfere with the liberty of parents and guardians to direct the upbringing and education of children under their control" (*Pierce v. Society of the Sisters of the Holy Names of Jesus & Mary*, 268 U.S. 510 (1925)). In 1972, the Court reaffirmed the same principle in *Wisconsin v. Yoder*, 406 U.S. 205, acknowledging the "fundamental interest of parents, as contrasted with that of the State, to guide the religious future and education of their children. The history and culture of Western civilization reflect a strong tradition of parental concern for the nurture and upbringing of their children. This primary role of the parents in the upbringing of their children is now established beyond debate as an enduring American tradition."

In 1973, the Court applied these constitutional principles of personal autonomy to strike down state statutes that criminalized a woman's decision to terminate her pregnancy. In *Roe v. Wade,* 410 U.S. 113, the Supreme Court held that a woman has an absolute right of privacy to decide, along with her physician, whether to terminate her pregnancy, at least within the first trimester. While the federal Constitution does not explicitly refer to a right of privacy, the Court observed that a series of its decisions had recognized an implied right of personal privacy based on both "the penumbras of the Bill of Rights" and the Fourteenth Amendment's liberty protections. Whatever its constitutional basis, the Court held that the right of privacy extended to "a woman's decision whether or not to terminate her pregnancy."

In 1977, the Supreme Court referred to the "right of personal privacy" as "one aspect of the 'liberty' protected by the Due Process Clause of the Fourteenth Amendment," including "the interest in independence in making certain kinds of important decisions" (*Carey v. Population Services, Int'l.,* 431 U.S. 678). While the Court declined to impose any "outer limits," it reaffirmed that the constitutional right of privacy extended at least to decisions on marriage, procreation, contraception, family relationships, and child rearing and education. In particular, the decision whether or not to bear children holds "a particularly important place in the history of the right of privacy." The Court reaffirmed the constitutional basis for the right, in particular as it applied to "the most intimate of human activities and relationships."

Also in 1977, the Supreme Court extended the constitutional right of personal autonomy to a person's decision to marry (*Zablocki v. Redhail,* 434 U.S. 374). The Court struck down a Wisconsin statute that required an individual to obtain a court order before marrying if that person had children from a prior relationship who were entitled to child support. In doing so, the Court explicitly "reaffirm[ed] the fundamental character of the right to marry" for purposes of constitutional protections.

By the 1980s, several legal controversies revolved around homosexuality and the AIDS epidemic. In 1986, the Supreme Court upheld a state criminal law prohibiting sodomy, even when the result was to criminalize consensual adult same-sex intimate conduct (*Bowers v. Hardwick,* 478 U.S. 186). The Court rejected the argument that homosexuals have a fundamental right to engage in consensual acts of sodomy, even in the privacy of the home. The Court reasoned that the nation had a long tradition of prohibiting sodomy at common law, even before most of the states had enacted criminal sodomy statutes. And the Court was not "inclined to take a more expansive view of [its] authority to discover new fundamental rights imbedded in the Due Process Clause."

In a highly unusual turn of events, the Supreme Court reversed *Bowers v. Hardwick* a mere seventeen years later when the Court decided *Lawrence v. Texas,* 539 U.S. 558 (2003). That case challenged the constitutionality of the Texas criminal sodomy statute. The state government had filed criminal charges against "two adults who, with full and mutual consent from each other, engaged in sexual practices common to a homosexual lifestyle." The Supreme Court struck down the state criminal statute, holding that the couple was constitutionally entitled to protection from state interference with their private, consensual sexual conduct. The Court barred the state from seeking to "control their destiny by making their private sexual conduct a crime." The state failed to convince the Court that criminalizing the couple's private, consensual intimate conduct served any legitimate state interest that could justify its "intrusion into the personal and private life of the individual."

The Supreme Court has also considered the constitutional right of personal autonomy of terminally ill patients and individuals in a persistent vegetative state due to illness or injury. In 1990, the Court held that federal constitutional protections for individual liberty interests extend to a person's right to refuse medical treatment, including the right to refuse life support in the form of hydration and nutrition (*Cruzan by Cruzan v. Director, Missouri Dep't of Health*, 497 U.S. 261). The Court has declined, however, to hold that the constitutional right of personal autonomy overrides the government's interest in prohibiting assisted suicide. In 1997, for example, the Court upheld a Washington statute that made it a crime to assist another person in committing suicide. In reaching its conclusion, the Court relied on the long tradition in the United States of criminalizing suicide, in contrast to the nation's "long legal tradition protecting the decision to refuse unwanted medical treatment" (*Washington v. Glucksberg*, 521 U.S. 702). Therefore, a patient's right to refuse nutrition, water, and medical treatment is constitutionally protected; however, that right to personal autonomy does not bar a state from criminalizing suicide, with or without assistance.

The Supreme Court held in June 2015 that the constitutional right of personal autonomy includes the right of same-sex partners to marry one another. The Court observed that "the reasons marriage is fundamental under the Constitution apply with equal force to same-sex couples" (*Obergefell v. Hodges,* 135 S.Ct. 2071). Writing for the majority, Justice Kennedy relied on the Court's own precedents, beginning with *Loving v. Virginia,* holding that "the right to personal choice regarding marriage is inherent in the concept of individual autonomy." Like other private decisions on "contraception, family relationships, procreation, and childrearing," the Court held that "decisions concerning marriage are among the most intimate that an individual can make." Quoting from *Zablocki*, the majority reasoned that "it would be contradictory 'to recognize a right of privacy with respect to other matters of family life and not with respect to the decision to enter the relationship that is the foundation of the family in our society.'"

The U.S. Constitution, as interpreted by the Supreme Court, is the supreme law of the land. Under the supremacy clause, the U.S. Constitution preempts any state law or state constitutional provision that infringes on the fundamental individual rights guaranteed by the federal Constitution, including the right of personal autonomy. Therefore, the Supreme Court's 1967 decision in *Loving v. Virginia* invalidated several state laws then in existence that prohibited interracial marriage, and the Court's decision in *Obergefell* supersedes and invalidates state laws that refuse to recognize same-sex marriage. After the Supreme Court's *Obergefell* decision, no state statute or constitutional provision can prevent same-sex couples from marrying in the state of their choice.

J. Lyn Entrikin

Further Reading

Ball, Howard. *The Supreme Court in the Intimate Lives of Americans: Birth, Sex, Marriage, Childrearing, and Death.* New York: New York University Press, 2004.

Bartee, Alice Fleetwood. *Privacy Rights: Cases Lost and Causes Won before the Supreme Court.* Lanham, MD: Rowman & Littlefield, 2006.

Johns, Fran Moreland. *Perilous Times: An Inside Look at Abortion before—and after—*Roe v. Wade. New York: YBK, 2013.

Shaman, Jeffrey M. "The Right of Privacy in State Constitutional Law." *Rutgers Law Journal* 37 (2006): 971.

Solove, Daniel J., and Paul M. Schwartz. *Privacy Law Fundamentals,* 3d ed. Portsmouth, NH: International Association of Privacy Professionals, 2015.

Urofsky, Melvin I. *Lethal Judgments: Assisted Suicide and American Law.* Lawrence: University of Kansas Press, 2000.

Wacks, Raymond. *Privacy: A Very Short Introduction,* 2d ed. New York: Oxford University Press, 2015.

See also: Constitutional law, *Cruzan v. Director, Missouri Department of Health; Griswold v. Connecticut; Lawrence v. Texas;* Legal evolution of privacy rights in the United States; The Right to Privacy; Sexual orientation; Supreme Court of the United States; *Washington v. Glucksberg*

Philosophical basis of privacy

Identification: Privacy, whether as a right or something else entirely, is something with which Americans are so familiar that its bases are not often questioned.

While the word *privacy* is never mentioned in the Constitution, its presence in the "penumbras" of the Bill of Rights has been discussed for decades. The word *private* explicitly appears in the Fourth Amendment. In addition to our laws and Constitution, popular literature highlights our fear of the loss of privacy; novels such as *Nineteen Eighty-Four* by George Orwell and *Brave New World* by Aldous Huxley portray futuristic worlds where individuals have all but lost even a recollection of privacy. Debates so often center around what should be kept private and how far one's privacy rights stretch, but one questions less often what the privacy right actually is, why Americans feel entitled to privacy, and the origins and nature of the concept of privacy in and of itself. These questions may be best answered by considering the philosophical bases of privacy.

Modern philosophical discussions of privacy

While there is a plethora of written works on privacy, these writings are not necessarily diverse. One could easily divide the literature into four categories: definitions of privacy, privacy theories (which are similar, but not the same, as attempts to define privacy), arguments on the relationship between privacy and morality, and criticism of the value of privacy. We first turn to how privacy is defined.

To examine the philosophical bases of privacy closely, the commonly accepted definition of privacy must be examined. Classical philosophers stopped short of developing a formal definition of privacy. The English word *private* derives from the Latin words *prīvātus, privo,* or *privus,* all of which are connected to exclusion. The questions surrounding what is meant by

privacy are as numerous as are proffered definitions; take Ruth Gavison's musings on the status of privacy: "[I]s privacy a situation, a right, a claim, a form of control, a value?" And in fact, the terms encompassed by the concept of privacy include, but are not limited to, *reserve, seclusion, autonomy, secrecy, repose, identity/ personality, control, protection, power, liberty, freedom, withdrawal, individuality, self, dignity* and *shame.* Judge Richard Posner has even considered *privacy* as a synonym for *freedom.*

While many definitions exist, perhaps the most fully encompassing definition, especially when considering privacy as a right, would be the definition Richard B. Parker defended in his work, *A Definition of Privacy:* "[P]rivacy is control over when and by whom the various parts of us can be sensed by others." Parker goes on to explain that "'[p]arts of us' also includes objects very closely associated with us." Similarly, Roger Clarke defines privacy as "the interest individuals have in sustaining a personal space, free from interference by other people and organizations." In what is often considered the bedrock work on privacy by many scholars, Samuel Warren and Louis Brandeis identify *privacy* as "being let alone" or free from intrusion. Newer theories included restricted access/control theory, personhood theory, and intimacy theory. Considering all these definitions and theories together best allows for an analysis of what the term, as well as the right, includes and entails.

Control theory

The idea that only when one has control over certain information may one be entitled to privacy regarding it is known as control theory. This theory is endorsed by scholars such as Charles Fried, Arthur Miller, Alan F. Westin, James Rachels, Elizabeth Beardsley, Sisella Bok, and others. This theory does not associate privacy with solitude or liberty. Rather, it centers on the role of the individual in the choice he or she has to enjoy privacy. In other words, a person may grant or deny access to information about him- or herself to others. Such access is that individual's sole choice. This is the exercise of the privacy right under the control theory.

Control theory divides information into nonpublic personal information (NPI) and public personal information (PPI). For example, if you park your car and walk into a health clinic that is visible from the street, the fact that you went to this clinic would be public personal information. However, the information you discuss with the doctor behind closed doors and put onto any forms would be nonpublic personal information. Most, but not all, control theorists use the distinction to show that one has control over nonpublic personal information, but not public personal information. Because the control over the information is at the pinnacle of privacy for control theorists, one could divulge nonpublic personal information to others and still retain his or her privacy with respect to that information. Thus, a criticism of this theory is the fact that one could theoretically divulge all nonpublic personal information about oneself and yet still retain privacy.

Limitation theory

Scholars such as Gavison, Parent, Allen, and others subscribe to the limitation theory of privacy. Under this theory, when information about a person is limited in some contexts, that person has privacy. To preserve one's privacy best, one must set up zones (i.e., contexts) of privacy in order to restrict others' access to the information one wishes to keep private. Thus, the more that information can be kept from others, the more privacy one has.

Nonintrusion theory (or the right to be let alone)

Perhaps the most highly regarded theory of privacy, known as nonintrusion theory, is credited to Samuel Warren and Louis Brandeis. The two are hailed by many scholars as writing the foundational article on privacy law in the United States, "The Right to Privacy," in which the nonintrusion theory was developed. Justice Brennan also articulated this view of privacy in *Olmstead v. U.S.*, 277 U.S. 438 (1928). The theory, as the name implies, describes privacy as being free from intrusion. Critics of this theory cite the confusion of liberty and privacy as a problem of nonintrusion theory. Distinguishing liberty from privacy shows us that liberty allows one to express unpopular ideas, while privacy allows one to disclose or withhold such ideas. Nonintrusion theory does not allow for such a distinction.

Seclusion theory

Seclusion theory, also known as the idea of limiting access to one's self, equates privacy with being alone, as identified by Ruth Gavison and Alan F. Westin. The basic idea of this theory is that the more secluded one is from others, the more privacy one has. As phrased by philosopher Sissela Bok, "[T]he condition of being protected by unwanted access by others—especially physical access, personal access, or attention"—is in fact privacy. Unlike nonintrusion theory, seclusion theory allows for the separation of privacy and liberty but does conflate privacy with solitude. Thus, a critique of this theory questions whether it is necessary to be secluded to have privacy.

Restricted access/limited control theory (and control over personal information)

Moor and Tavani examined a theory of privacy in which privacy needs to be differentiated from the justification and management of the same (Moor originally introduced the theory). The theory further differentiates between the condition of privacy and the right to privacy (the first having a consequence of a loss of privacy while the latter has a consequence of a violation of privacy).

Personhood theory

Yet another theory of privacy centers around protecting personhood, or "those attributes of an individual which are irreducible in his selfhood," as explained by Paul Freund, who coined the term by expanding on the work of Warren and Brandeis. According to Edward Bloustein, it is specifically one's *individuality* that privacy protects. Although a separate theory in its own right, this theory is often used in conjunction with other theories in explaining the importance of privacy.

In landmark privacy cases in the United States, such as *Griswold v. Connecticut,* 381 U.S. 479 (1965); *Roe v. Wade,* 410 U.S. 113 (1973); and *Planned Parenthood v. Casey,* 505 U.S. 833 (1992), the Supreme Court has adopted the personhood theory of privacy. Critics of these cases, as well as personhood theory, often conflate privacy with autonomy and therefore do not think personhood theory correctly identifies and protects the right values. Other critiques include that of Jed Rubenfeld in his significant article, "The Right to Privacy," in which he correctly states that the law could never protect all forms of individuality or self-definition.

Intimacy theory

In discussing other theories of privacy, philosopher Julie Inness suggests ". . . that these apparently disparate areas are connected by the common denominator of intimacy—privacy's content covers intimate information, access, and decisions." Like other subscribers to the intimacy theory, Inness has articulated that privacy consists of limited access or control in some form, but she places the *value* of privacy in the context of personal relationships. Charles Fried and James Rachels also advance a view of privacy that encompasses the intimacy theory. The two suggest that intimate information is the information that one wishes to reveal only to a certain few people. Critics of the intimacy theory view it as too narrow because of the focus on personal relationships.

To best understand how these theories of privacy developed, looking back to classical philosophers can be quite informative.

Classic philosophy and history

The first philosophical references to privacy trace back to Classic Athens and Aristotle's description of the two most basic social units: the private *oikos* (loosely translated to "house," "household," or "family") and the public sphere of *polis.* However, Aristotle stopped short of describing a "right" to privacy or explaining why the *oikos* was desirable; rather such a structure was more a necessity. When a man transitioned from the *polis* role to the *oikos* role, so too did his responsibilities. Within his *oikos,* a man must be a master to his slaves, wife, and children compared to the equal he is with his fellow citizens. While Aristotle emphasizes the differences between these spheres, the two are certainly not entirely separate. For example, Aristotle suggests that the *oikos* is the basic social unit of *polis.* Laws of the *polis* control the rules of forming the *oikos,* as the *polis* did have laws regarding marriage (for example, the law that siblings could not marry.) When necessary, the *polis* would enact laws that infringed directly on the *oikos,* for example, the law 451/0 proposed by Pericles in which the determinate of citizenship became an issue of the *polis* rather than a father betrothing his daughter ("I give this woman for the ploughing of legitimate children") and thereby such children becoming Athens citizens.

Still, the private nature of the *oikos* was honored. Should family disputes arise, the preference was to resolve them out of court. Arbitration-type procedures existed to keep the disputes out of public courts. Courts were provided by the *polis* for such disputes when a solution could not otherwise be reached. Commonly, litigants would argue that the familial dispute should not be settled in court, further emphasizing Classic Athenians regard for the idea of privacy.

The regard for privacy and respect for the individual *oikos* may be most notable by looking at laws that were not enacted. For example, while the *polis* decided that siblings could not marry, the *polis* was silent on the consequences, if any, for sexual relations between siblings. Just as family-planning matters encompass modern American privacy rights, so too were such issues prevalent in Classic Athens. While there is evidence that the Classical populations used what they believed were contraceptives and abortifacients, the *polis* was silent on the use of each. Abortion was practiced, as there is a reference to the practice in the Hippocratic corpus. The laws surrounding abortions in Classic Athens are unclear, but could be brought by any citizen. It appears the only time there was a legal ban to abortion was a case involving a widowed pregnant woman. While the *polis* and *oikos* were separate spheres, the two regularly interacted, often engaged in a delicate tango, and if Aristotle had used such a metaphor, he might have argued that the slightest misstep would have resulted in the loss of both.

Stoic philosopher Epictetus discussed privacy related to what is under our control (thoughts and impulses) and what is not. Epicurus argues for a man to protect his secrets because they are under his control. Without privacy, there can be no secrets.

The Bible contains multiple references to the idea of privacy, and especially the shame associated with a violation of one's privacy. After eating the "sacred fruit," Adam and Eve suddenly became aware of their nakedness and felt the need to cover themselves with fig leaves; while on the ark, when Noah's son found his father laying naked and he thereby violated his privacy.

The social contract

As time progressed, themes of privacy can be seen in a number of great philosopher's works, even if it is not mentioned explicitly. By considering how privacy is connected with liberty (and therefore personal autonomy), it is clear that a degree of privacy is relinquished in Thomas Hobbes's social contract. Considering Hobbes's definition of a contract as "the mutual transferring of right," the social contract can briefly be described as a citizen giving up some autonomy for the benefit of the protections and other advantages that a government provides (for example, roads). Without law and regulations imposed by a government (which derives its power from consent to the social contract,) individual people may dream up and carry out any and all manners of the articles of their individual wills. Upon entering the social contract, however, this personal autonomy (and thereby privacy to some degree) is restricted to varying degrees. The government may deem some activities criminal and subject to penalties beyond the consequences an individual would be subject to in his or her natural state. However, other concepts are granted protections (including privacy in the modern United States) and others that would be unavailable without the social contract, including the ability to participate in rule-making (that is, voting), benefits derived from intellectual property rights, and access to stable sources of common utility, are made obtainable by entering the social contract itself.

Privacy as the United States was born

Throughout the history of Western civilization, a dichotomy between the public and private spheres has been maintained in some way, shape, or form. One of the ways this ideal has manifested itself is in the progression of beliefs about the human body. As stated by the Supreme Court in *Union Pacific Railroad Company v. Botsford*, 141 U.S. 250 (1899) at 141, "[n]o right is held more sacred, or is more carefully guarded by the common law, than the right of every individual to the possession and control of his own person." The deep roots of the connection between the human body and privacy in Western culture can be seen in practices and rituals that have taken place for centuries and are still prevalent today, such as the concealment of certain body parts (which was not practiced in Ancient Greece and Rome), the idea of one's own personal space, confidentiality with respect to health-related information, and so on.

In fact, in *Griswald v. Connecticut*, 381 U.S. 479 (1965), the Court informs us that the idea of privacy as an ideal is one that the colonists brought with them from England. Perhaps the justices were referencing the offense of eavesdropping, which was a common law crime in England and was adopted by the colonists when the entirety of the common law began to regulate the colonies. Without necessarily intending to, Justice Douglas references Aristotle's split of the public (or political) sphere with that of home life: "Certainly the safeguarding of the home does not follow merely from the sanctity of property rights. The home derives its preeminence as the seat of family life. Moreover, the integrity of that life is something so fundamental that it has been found to draw to its protection the principles of more than one explicitly granted Constitutional right. . . . Of this whole 'private realm of family life,' it is difficult to imagine what is more private or more intimate than a husband and wife's marital relations."

According to historian and lawyer Alison La-Croix, however, scholars have not spent much time focusing on privacy ideals of eighteenth-century Americans. There is a dearth of information about the views of our Founding Fathers with respect to privacy, whether as a right or as a concept in general. In fact, LaCroix cites scholars who show that in the colonial United States, both survival and salvation for the Puritans (English settlers of New England) depended on a close-knit community with public monitoring of activities now wholly considered to be in the private sphere, namely child rearing, spirituality, and sexual activity. Suspicion regarding privacy (or the private sphere, at least) was expressed by at least one Founding Father: John Adams. Adams followed Aristotle's view that there is a public sphere and a private one, but his writings show that he believed that the private sphere was only utilized for selfish purposes and exposed human weaknesses.

Still, some privacy violations existed in colonial America. Eavesdropping could be handled with community sanctions or public chastising with a little bit of help from the law, but few took this route in New England because handling the matter privately was often easier and met with more satisfying results for the victim. "Peeping" or "spying" was a different offense, but any litigable offense required a physical intrusion of private space, which is very different from the privacy violations in modern case decisions. As contradictory as all of this information can seem, one ideal that the settlers certainly brought from England was the idea that the home itself was sacred.

The suggestion of a future of privacy rights can easily be extrapolated from the view that early Americans held (and modern Americans hold) about the home: the idea that one's home is one's "castle" and a place where one should be free from government intrusion (a phrase originally penned by Sir Edward Coke in *Semayne's case* (Coke's Rep. 91a, 77 Eng. Rep. 194 (K.B. 1604)). This mirrors Aristotle's view of the *oikos* and *polis*. It can be argued, however, that the United States furthered the separation between the home sphere and the political sphere when the Fourth Amendment was drafted to protect against unreasonable searches and seizures or by protecting the "sanctity of a man's home," as the Supreme Court did in *Boyd v. United States* (116 U.S. 616 (1886) at 327).

If viewed in conjunction with a property right, most of the philosophers who influenced the drafting of the U.S. Constitution would have agreed in strong support of protecting a privacy right. John Locke, for example, believed that the protection of property rights is at the center of the purpose of law. He further agreed that the home is sacred, or a castle, as noted above: "may be opposed as a Thief and a Robber, if he endeavors to break into my house to Execute Writ."

Although Locke wrote more on property rights than an explicit privacy right, as noted below, the two are often entangled, and recognizing the home as a private dwelling for every property owner was certainly a start. Locke's influence very well might have informed the drafters' inclusion of the Fourth Amendment of the Bill of Rights (the freedom from unreasonable searches and seizures.) Adam Smith's description of the "unseen hand" in the philosophy of economics (a theory that argues for a free market with little regulation, stating that the "unseen hand" of the market will regulate itself,) shows his fondness for private actors, if not privacy in and of itself.

How important is privacy?

Because the importance of privacy is very much engrained in the culture of modern America, not everyone questions whether privacy is actually an important virtue. Philosophers often do, and they also question the cultural relativity of privacy. Arguably, if privacy is more important in one culture than it is in another, perhaps it is not inherently valuable at all. Philosophers have found that indifference to privacy in a society is not only possible but it is also considered preferable by some scholars (in principle, if nothing else). The argument for the latter suggests that too much value placed on privacy increases humans' feeling of vulnerability, shame, and embarrassment. Those who argue against this view believe that intimacy requires removing objectivity, which cannot take place with indefinite points of view; that trust necessities self-selected disclosures; and that different relationships compel us to show to different people different versions of our selves. Thereby, privacy is a necessity for humans to flourish.

"On Liberty"

John Stuart Mill, in his landmark essay "On Liberty," suggested that the idea of privacy is very much part of economic thinking. At the heart of Mill's writing is the idea that social control (in other words, when people act on habits as opposed to reason) is problematic: "[W]hen society itself is the tyrant . . . it practices a social tyranny more formidable than many kinds of political oppression." Mill argued for protection from this type of "tyranny." Many have interpreted Locke's work to include individuals exercising their right to privacy.

Privacy as a right

"The right to be let alone is indeed the beginning of all freedom." [*Public Utilities Commission v. Pollak*, 343 U.S. 451, 467 (1952) (dissenting)]
—*William O. Douglas*

Scholars indicate that privacy has evolved in the United States from being associated with physical access (or intrusion) to concerns related to decision making and, most recently, in dealing with information. When looking at privacy as a right, one should note the difference between positive and negative rights. Positive rights are rights that allow a person to do something (for example, a property right in a document might include the positive rights of holding the document, altering the document, even tearing the document.) Negative rights are those by which one can stop another from doing something (for example, the same property rights in a document may include the negative rights of concealing a document from others, disallowing others to alter the document, and so on). With respect to privacy rights, a person not only has the right to take measures to conceal something but also has the specific right that the same something *will not be looked at*. Thus, multiple rights are implicated when one "owns" something. Privacy rights mostly implicate negative rights, although subscribers of the seclusion theory might argue that positive rights are involved as well because one has the right to seek seclusion. Once one actively attempts to exclude others, however, a negative right is again initiated.

When a person alleges that his or her right to privacy has been violated, other rights are usually involved. As the example above highlights, this often includes a property right. Therefore, a question that philosophers have grappled with is whether privacy issues are actually distinctive issues. Some have argued that in cases that are labeled privacy issues are viewed morally, the ultimate justifications employed to resolve such issues can be reached independently of any connection with privacy. Some argue at the most extreme that we could do away with concern over privacy because all issues can be resolved using standard moral or legal categories. On the other hand, many philosophers argue that privacy issues share a unique nature, a uniqueness that exists despite the details or commonalities with other concerns or rights of the individual. However, these philosophers still debate about what that uniqueness is: Some philosophers argue that the inherent connection with human dignity is the common thread binding property right cases; others state that the role privacy plays in forming social relationships is the unique trait of privacy rights cases. One can easily surmise how the privacy theory that a philosopher subscribes to might influence his or her view on the issue.

The Practical Application of Philosophy to Privacy in the Modern Age

Up until the 1950s, it was almost unquestioned that the government could regulate what is now seen as private activities. The government in the United States criminalized homosexuality, contraception, abortion, and other related actions. It is precisely these controversial issues that make up the bulk of cases, most specifically the Supreme Court cases, that deal with privacy rights. Ironically, one must go to the most public of forums in an attempt to keep those things that he or she considers private just that—private. One might question how many violations of privacy are never litigated because the victim would prefer less of an intrusion on his or her private life. There are options, such as changing one's name (many are familiar with the fact that

Roe was not the name of anyone involved in *Roe v. Wade*). However, when charging that privacy rights are violated, does not sharing the story of the violation further the violation? Is showing one's face not deepening the shame that is often associated with privacy violations? What, then, is the answer when one's privacy has been violated? Would Aristotle argue for arbitration of such cases? Would John Stuart Mills suggest that alleged privacy violations deserve a closed courtroom? If a privacy right is at stake, how would Hobbes decide between the rights of the press (and thereby, arguably, society) and the rights of the victim (the individual)? These questions are best left open for modern philosophers, legal scholars, lawyers and judges.

Julie Ann Embler

Further Reading

Aaken, Dominik, Andreas Ostermaier, and Arnold Picot. "Privacy and Freedom: An Economic (Re-)Evaluation of Privacy." *Kyklos* 67, no. 2: 133–155. *Business Source Complete*, EBSCOhost.

Arthur, John, and William H. Shaw. *Readings in the Philosophy of Law*, 4rd ed. Upper Saddle River, NJ: Prentice Hall, 2001.

Gavison, Ruth. "Privacy and the Limits of Law." *An Anthology: Philosophical Dimensions of Privacy* 89, no. 3 (1980): 346–402. http://heinonline.org.

Konvitz, Milton R. "Privacy and the Law: A Philosophical Prelude." *Law and Contemporary Problems*: 272–280. http://0-www.jstor.org.library.law.stetson.edu/stable/1190671.

LaCroix, Allison. "'Bound Fast and Brought Under the Yokes': John Adams and the Regulation of Privacy at the Founding." *Fordham Law Review* 72, no. 6 (2004): 2331–2354. http://ir.lawnet.fordham.edu/cgi/viewcontent.cgi?article=3992&context=flr.

Roy, J. "'Polis' and 'Oikos' in Classical Athens." *Greece & Rome* 46, no. 1 (1999): 1–18. http://www.jstor.org/stable/643032.

Schoeman, Ferdinand. "Privacy: Philosophical Dimensions of the Literature." *An Anthology: Philosophical Dimensions of Privacy* 1–33.

Stein, Joshua B. *Commentary on the Constitution from Plato to Rousseau*. Lanham, MD: Lexington Books, 2011.

Tavani, Herman T. "Philosophical Theories of Privacy: Implications for an Adequate Online Privacy Policy." *Metaphilosophy* 38, no. 1 (2007): 1–22.

Tebbit, Mark. *Philosophy of Law: An Introduction*, 2nd ed. London, England: Routledge Taylor & Francis Group, 2005.

Thomson, Judith Jarvis. "The Right to Privacy." *An Anthology Philosophical Dimensions of Privacy* 272–289. JSTOR.org.

Warren, Samuel D., and Louis D. Brandeis. "The Right to Privacy." *Harvard Law Review 4*, no. 5 (1890): 193–220. http://www.jstor.org/stable/1321160.

See also: Constitutional law; Private sphere; Economic arguments for privacy rights; Right to be let alone

The Plame Affair

Identification: The Plame Affair of 2003 concerned the public disclosure of the identity of an undercover CIA employee, Valerie Plame Wilson, by the U.S. administration for political reasons. The disclosure unleashed a political controversy and a federal investigation that resulted in the temporary detention of a *New York Times* reporter and the conviction of an administration official. It began with a single line in an article by syndicated columnist Robert D. Novak: "Wilson [i.e., Joseph C. Wilson, Plame's husband] never worked for the CIA, but his wife, Valerie Plame, is an agency operative on weapons of mass destruction."

Background: Iraq and African Uranium

In 2002–03, the Republican administration of President George W. Bush was preparing public opinion for an invasion of Iraq. The public case for war was built on frequently flimsy intelligence, arguments that administration officials sincerely believed but could not substantiate with solid evidence, and exaggerations designed to make the case more convincing for the public. After the invasion, which began on March 20, 2003, virtually the entire case was found to be untrue.

A major thread in the justification was a claim that Iraqi dictator Saddam Hussein was actively working to develop nuclear weapons that he might then turn over to Islamist terrorists. During his Jan. 28, 2003, State of the Union address, President Bush asserted, among other things, "The British government has learned that Saddam Hussein recently sought significant quantities of uranium from Africa." Bush was referring to a document that was published by the British government in September 2002 with the intention of supporting Bush's argument for war. Prime Minister Tony Blair had decided to support Bush's policy on Iraq despite the assessment of British intelligence that the Bush administration had already decided for war and that "the intelligence and facts were being fixed around the policy." The September 2002 report was later criticized for being slipshod, and its allegations proved to be false. The ultimate source of the British uranium claim was a set of documents obtained by Italian military intelligence in 2001. The documents stated that Iraq had sought to purchase "yellowcake" (a semi-processed form of uranium) from Niger in the 1999–2001 period. These documents were later turned over to the International Atomic Energy Agency (IAEA), and on March 7, 2003, about two weeks before the invasion of Iraq, the IAEA assessed that they were "in fact not authentic." The U.S. and British governments asserted that they had additional sources verifying the claim, but the IAEA later assessed that those sources appeared to be rooted in the same forged documents.

In fact, behind the scenes, CIA, the State Department, and the Pentagon had already voiced their skepticism as to the documents' authenticity. On July 6, 2003, after the occupation of Iraq, Joseph C. Wilson IV published an op-ed in the *New York Times*, titled "What I Didn't Find in Africa," in which he stated that "some of the intelligence related to Iraq's nuclear weapons program was twisted to exaggerate the Iraqi threat." A retired Foreign Service Officer who had served in Niger and whose wife was a CIA officer, Wilson had been asked by CIA

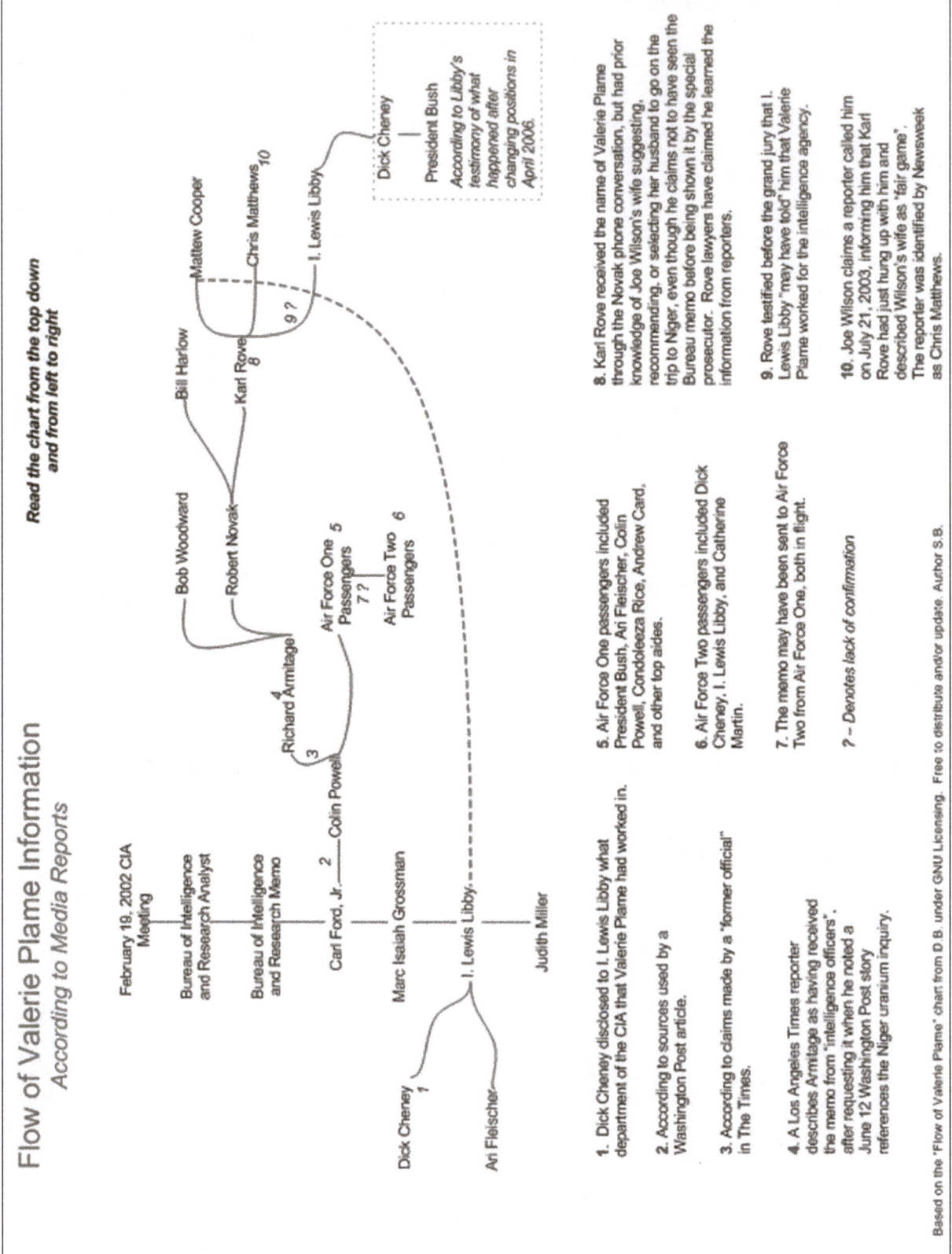

Flow of Valerie Plame Information
According to Media Reports

Read the chart from the top down and from left to right

February 19, 2002 CIA Meeting

Bureau of Intelligence and Research Analyst

Bureau of Intelligence and Research Memo

Carl Ford, Jr. — 2 — Colin Powell

Richard Armitage — 4

3

Bob Woodward

Robert Novak

Air Force One Passengers — 5

7 ?

Air Force Two Passengers — 6

Bill Harlow

Karl Rove — 8

9 ?

Matthew Cooper

Chris Matthews — 10

I. Lewis Libby

Dick Cheney

President Bush

According to Libby's testimony of what happened after changing positions in April 2006.

Marc Isaiah Grossman

I. Lewis Libby

Judith Miller

Dick Cheney — 1

Ari Fleischer

1. Dick Cheney disclosed to I. Lewis Libby what department of the CIA that Valerie Plame had worked in.

2. According to sources used by a Washington Post article.

3. According to claims made by a "former official" in The Times.

4. A Los Angeles Times reporter describes Armitage as having received the memo from "intelligence officers", after requesting it when he noted a June 12 Washington Post story references the Niger uranium inquiry.

5. Air Force One passengers included President Bush, Ari Fleischer, Colin Powell, Condoleezza Rice, Andrew Card, and other top aides.

6. Air Force Two passengers included Dick Cheney, I. Lewis Libby, and Catherine Martin.

7. The memo may have been sent to Air Force Two from Air Force One, both in flight.

? – Denotes lack of confirmation

8. Karl Rove received the name of Valerie Plame through the Novak phone conversation, but had prior knowledge of Joe Wilson's wife suggesting, recommending, or selecting her husband to go on the trip to Niger, even though he claims not to have seen the Bureau memo before being shown it by the special prosecutor. Rove lawyers have claimed he learned the information from reporters.

9. Rove testified before the grand jury that I. Lewis Libby "may have told" him that Valerie Plame worked for the intelligence agency.

10. Joe Wilson claims a reporter called him on July 21, 2003, informing him that Karl Rove had just hung up with him and described Wilson's wife as "fair game". The reporter was identified by Newsweek as Chris Matthews.

to go to Niger in February 2002, nearly a year before Bush's speech, to assess the documents' claim because Vice President Dick Cheney had expressed an interest in the issue. Wilson found the claim to be unlikely. The U.S. ambassador in Niger had already debunked it, and current and former Nigerien government officials denied any knowledge of it. Moreover, the Nigerien uranium industry was controlled not by the Nigerien government but by a multinational consortium and it was closely monitored by the IAEA, making surreptitious sales highly unlikely. Wilson briefed the embassy, the CIA, and the State Department on his findings.

Backlash: The Outing of Valerie Plame

Novak's column, titled "Mission to Niger," was published about a week later, on July 14, 2003. In it, he depicted Wilson's assessment as his opinion alone and asserted that CIA had considered his report to be "less than definitive." Director George Tenet was unlikely to have seen it, Novak continued, much less the president. What drew attention, however, was the naming of Valerie Plame. (Novak, who had been told only of Wilson's wife "Valerie," used her maiden name, which he got from Wilson's *Who's Who* entry, and thus the episode acquired its label.) Novak reported that she had recommended using Wilson and had been the CIA's contact with him. Novak attributed his information to "two senior administration officials." On July 17, Matthew Cooper of *Time* magazine revealed that government officials had also told him that Wilson's wife was a CIA operative. The *Washington Post* later cited a "senior administration official" to the effect that two White House officials had informed at least six journalists of Plame's identity and occupation "simply for revenge" against Wilson for calling the president a liar.

Disclosing the identity of a "covert agent" is a felony under 50 U.S.C. §§3121–3126 (formerly §§421–426), the Intelligence Identities Protection Act(IIPA) of 1982. Yet it is not necessarily easy to prosecute such cases. Specifically, as summarized by the Congressional Research Service, the law "provides criminal penalties in certain circumstances for an intentional, unauthorized disclosure of information identifying a 'covert agent' by a person who knows that the information identifies a covert agent as such and that the United States is taking affirmative measures to conceal the covert agent's foreign intelligence relationship to the United States." The act also details exceptions and defenses to prosecutions. The length of sentence depends on whether the person making the disclosure: 1) had authorized access to the identifying information (up to 15 years), 2) came across the identity as a result of authorized access to other classified information (up to 10 years), or 3) did not have authorized access to classified information but engaged in a pattern of activities intended to identify and expose covert agents (up to 3 years). The law exempts journalists who are not engaged in such a pattern. At the time of the Plame Affair, only one person had ever been convicted under the act, Sharon Scranage, a CIA clerk in Ghana, in 1985. Another, CIA officer John Kiriakou, followed in 2012. Former CIA official Aldrich Ames and former FBI official Robert Hanssen, both of whose disclosures led to the execution of more than a dozen intelligence sources in the Soviet Union/Russia, were each sentenced to life in prison, in 1994 and 2002 respectively, under the Espionage Act, not the IIPA.

The Investigation: A Special Counsel

In late September 2003, the Department of Justice informed the White House that it had opened an investigation into possible unauthorized disclosures concerning the identity of a CIA employee. In December, U.S. attorney Patrick Fitzgerald was named special counsel to investigate whether a crime had been committed. In fact, Novak's primary source had been Deputy

Secretary of State Richard L. Armitage. (Armitage had also mentioned it to the *Washington Post*'s Bob Woodward.) The identity was confirmed to Novak by White House senior adviser Karl Rove. Armitage, who of course was not based in the White House, had voluntarily disclosed his role to the FBI before Fitzgerald's appointment. Nevertheless, Fitzgerald found that Vice President Dick Cheney had in fact organized an effort to counter Wilson's claims. Cheney's chief of staff, I. Lewis "Scooter" Libby, was instructed to reveal details of a national intelligence estimate to several reporters, including Judith Miller of the *New York Times*, to support the claim that Iraq had sought uranium from Niger. Cheney convinced President Bush to declassify portions of the estimate for this purpose. In the process, Cheney reportedly mentioned that Wilson's wife worked at CIA, but he denied that he had instructed Libby to reveal that. Nonetheless, Libby did so on more than one occasion, including to Miller and *Time*'s Cooper.

Miller never wrote an article on the subject and thus never revealed Plame's name. In the course of the investigation, however, Miller was jailed from July 6 to September 29, 2005, for contempt of court after refusing to reveal Libby as her source. (The Supreme Court declined to hear her appeal of the contempt charge.) Miller was released after saying she had received permission from her source to reveal his identity to a grand jury. Libby said that he had released her from any confidentiality pledge a year earlier, but Miller had considered that a generic statement and she wanted a statement from him that she knew to be voluntary and specific to her.

Libby was convicted in 2007 of one count of obstruction of justice, two counts of perjury, and one count of making false statements, all in the course of the investigation itself. He was sentenced to 30 months in prison, 2 years' probation, and a fine of $250,000. He was also disbarred. President Bush commuted his sentence to eliminate the prison time, saying that he considered it excessive, but he did not pardon him,

which became a point of contention between Bush and Cheney. President Donald J. Trump pardoned Libby in April 2018, at a time when Trump was having his own issues with a special counsel. Libby's was the only conviction connected to the Plame Affair. No one was charged under the IIPA, apparently because it was impossible to prove that Libby or any of the others knew that Plame was a covert agent and that the CIA was taking active measures to conceal her relationship. The CIA stated that this was the case at the time of Libby's sentencing, but Libby claimed that her relationship to the CIA was widely known in Washington.

The disclosure of Valerie Plame Wilson's identity ended her career at the CIA, exposed a firm where she had worked as a CIA front operation, and drew suspicion to virtually all the foreign nationals with whom she had had regular contact in the previous two decades as possible CIA agents, informants, or sources. She later wrote a memoir about her time at CIA, *Fair Game*, but the agency redacted it heavily. (All current and former CIA employees must get CIA approval for any publications.) Although the CIA had confirmed at the time of Libby's sentencing that she was a covert agent in 2002 and 2003, it had never explicitly confirmed her status prior to 2002. Therefore, according to the agency's reasoning, any reference in her memoir to her being at the CIA prior to 2002 was considered classified and had to be excised. Plame finally published the memoir with the redactions blacked out but with an "afterword" written by a journalist summarizing the excised portions.

Scott C. Monje

Further Reading

Elsea, Jennifer K. *Intelligence Identities Protection Act*, CRS Report RS21636. Washington, D.C.: Congressional Research Service, April 10, 2013.

Lee, William E. "Deep Background: Journalists, Sources, and the Perils of Leaking," *American University Law Review* 57, no. 5 (June 2008): 1453–1529.

Miller, Judith. *The Story: A Reporter's Journey*. New York: Simon & Schuster, 2015.

Novak, Robert D. "Mission to Niger," *Washington Post* (July 14, 2003),

Wilson, Joseph C., IV. "What I Didn't Find in Africa," *New York Times* (July 6, 2003), https://www.nytimes.com/2003/07/06/opinion/what-i-didn-t-find-in-africa.html.

Wilson, Joseph. *The Politics of Truth: Inside the Lies That Put the White House on Trial and Betrayed My Wife's CIA Identity.* New York: Carroll & Graf, 2005.

Wilson, Valerie Plame. *Fair Game*, with an afterword by Laura Rozen. New York: Simon & Schuster, 2007.

See also: Criminal Justice; Doxing; Foreign Intelligence Surveillance Act; Foreign Intelligence Surveillance Court; Invasion of Privacy; News Leaks; September 11; USA Patriot Act

Poitras, Laura

Identifcation: A filmmaker, journalist, and artist. Her most famous work to date is a trilogy of documentaries on America's post–September 11 war on terror.

Born on February 2, 1964, Poitras grew up near Boston and moved to San Francisco to become a chef. She studied under the experimental filmmaker Ernie Gehr at the San Francisco Art Institute. In 1992, she moved to New York to continue her work in film and took classes in social and political theory at the New School.

The beginnings of Poitras's trilogy of films are described by Peter Maass, writing for the *New York Times*:

On Sept. 11, 2001, Poitras was on the Upper West Side of Manhattan when the towers were attacked. Like most New Yorkers, in the weeks that followed she was swept up in both mourning and a feeling of unity. It was a moment, she said, when "people could have done anything, in a positive sense." When that moment led to the pre-emptive invasion of Iraq, she felt that her country had lost its way. "We always wonder how countries can veer off course," she said. "How do people

Laura Poitras. (By Katy Scoggin at http://www.praxis-films.org)

let it happen, how do people sit by during this slipping of boundaries?"

In June 2004, Poitras went to Iraq by herself and began filming. This film, *My Country, My Country* (2006) was nominated for an Oscar and documented the impact of the Iraq War on ordinary Iraqis. The story is told through Dr. Riyadh, a Sunni doctor and political candidate in Iraq's first democratic election. He was an outspoken critic of the U.S. occupation.

Her second documentary, *The Oath* (2010), was nominated for an Emmy and tells the story of Salim Hamdan, chauffeur to Osama bin Laden, and his brother-in-law, Abu Jandal, bodyguard to Osama bin Laden. The title refers both to Jandal's initial allegiance to al Qaeda and the pledge of loyalty to the United States of an FBI interrogator testifying before Congress against certain interrogation techniques. Hamdan was the first man to face the military tribunal set up to try Guantanamo detainees. His case was heard by the U.S. Supreme Court in *Hamdan v. Rumsfeld*, 548 U.S. 557 (2006), which held the Bush administration did not have the authority to form such tribunals without congressional authorization. Poitras's documentary was filmed in Yemen and Guantanamo Bay.

Poitras's last film in the trilogy, *CITIZEN-FOUR* (2014), earned her a Director's Guild of America Award and an Oscar. The film tells the story of National Security Agency contractor Edward Snowden's 2013 meeting with journalists Poitras and Glenn Greenwald in Hong Kong. Poitras filmed Snowden discussing the thousands of classified National Security Agency (NSA) documents he was leaking to them and his motives for doing so. The film's title echoes the pseudonym Snowden used when he contacted Poitras through encrypted emails. Snowden was eventually able to leave Hong Kong; became stranded in Moscow's Sheremetyevo airport when the United States canceled his passport; and was finally offered political asylum in Russia, where he currently resides. Snowden's leaked documents revealed the NSA's bulk surveillance of American phone records, which civil liberties advocates have condemned. The articles written about the documents have earned Pulitzer Prizes for *the Guardian* and *the Washington Post*.

In August 2015, Poitras, represented by lawyers from the digital rights advocacy group the Electronic Frontier Foundation, filed a lawsuit against the government. The lawsuit claims that Poitras filed several requests for records under the Freedom of Information Act but various government agencies unlawfully withheld the records ("Laura Poitras v. Homeland Security Complaint," *EFF.com*, last modified July 13, 2015, https://www.eff.org/document/poitrasfoia-complaint.) Poitras said that after her work on *My Country, My Country* in 2006, she was repeatedly stopped and questioned when reentering the United States. Although she was never charged with a crime, the stops continued until 2012, when journalist Glenn Greenwald wrote an article about her experience. A coalition of

nonfiction filmmakers, including Albert Maysles, Alex Gibney, and Morgan Spurlock, also signed an open letter protesting Poitras's treatment at borders and calling her "one of America's most important nonfiction filmmakers."

Poitras serves on the board of the Freedom of the Press Foundation, which focuses on exposing government corruption, and is also a founding member of the Intercept, an online publication launched in February 2014. The publication currently focuses on the documents leaked by Edward Snowden and has long-term plans to "produce fearless, adversarial journalism across a broad range of issues."

Poitras received a MacArthur Foundation "genius" grant in 2012 and will have a solo exhibition at the Whitney Museum in 2016. She currently lives in Berlin, Germany.

Noëlle Sinclair

Further Reading

Binney, William, and Laura Poitras. *The Program.* *New York Times* Op-Doc, 8:27. August 22, 2012.

Maass, Peter. "How Laura Poitras Helped Snowden Spill His Secrets." *New York Times*, August 13, 2013.

"MacArthur Fellows Program—Meet the Class of 2012: Laura Poitras." *Macfound.org*, October 2, 2012.

See also: Electronic Frontier Foundation (EFF); Greenwald, Glenn; National Security Agency (NSA); September 11; Snowden, Edward; Terrorism and privacy

Pornography

Identification: Material containing explicit displays of sexual organs or activity, intended to stimulate erotic feelings.

While both pornography and obscenity are commonly considered indecent material, pornography is not synonymous with obscenity. The key legal distinction between the two is that pornographic materials are protected under the freedom of speech clause of the First Amendment, while obscene materials are not. The First Amendment protects pornographic writings, photographs, and movies displaying sexual activity or eroticism that is intended to arouse sexual excitement. The First Amendment does not protect obscenity, however, and the sexual depictions they convey.

In fact, the Supreme Court has consistently held that obscenity and obscene speech is one of the few types of speech not entitled to constitutional protection under the First Amendment: *Miller v. California*, 413 U.S. 15, 24 (1973); *Alliance for Community Media v. FCC*, 56 F.3d 105, 113 (D.C. Cir. 1995). Obscenity, under the *Miller* Supreme Court test, is defined as material, when taken as a whole, which the average person, applying contemporary community standards, would find as appealing to the prurient interests and lacking serious educational or artistic value (*Sable Comm. of California, Inc. v. FCC*, 492 U.S. 115 (1989); *Paris Adult Theatre v. Salon*, 413 U.S. 49, 69 (1973); *Alliance for Community Media*).

Despite the fact that both have sexual content, obscenity differs from pornography (or indecency) because "language or material that, in context, depicts or describes, in terms patently offensive, as measured by contemporary community standards for the broadcast medium, sexual or excretory activities or organs."

In distinguishing between pornography and obscenity, Judge Patricia Wald said that pornography (or indecent material) "is not confined merely to material that borders on obscenity— obscenity lite." Unlike obscenity, indecent material includes literarily, artistically, scientifically, and politically meritorious material. Pornography, by definition, includes all "patently offensive" material deemed to have any of these types of "merit." Therefore, such material is not obscene under the Supreme Court's *Miller* standard. See, for example, *Alliance for Community Media*, 56 F.3d at 130 (Wald, J., dissenting).

Because pornography is protected under the First Amendment, any government regulation of pornography must be by the least restrictive means possible to further a compelling government interest. The regulation must "do so by narrowly drawn regulations designed to serve those interests without unnecessarily interfering with First Amendment freedoms" (*Sable,* at 126).

The Supreme Court's obscenity test has evolved over the years. It is intended to determine whether certain materials involving sexual conduct as forms of expression and speech were entitled to the Constitution's protection for free speech. Notwithstanding, the Supreme Court has had considerable difficulty in formulating and applying specific standards in deciding obscenity cases.

The Supreme Court, in *Roth v. United States,* 354 U.S. 476 (1957), held that obscenity is not constitutionally protected speech and articulated a test that has since been overruled: Material is deemed obscene if, as a whole, its predominant appeal is to the prurient interest (a shameful or morbid interest in nudity, sex, or excretion) and if it goes substantially beyond the customary sensible limits on the description or representation of the matter. In articulating this test, the Court adamantly rejected the argument that the First Amendment protected obscene speech. The Court consequently upheld the defendant's conviction under the federal statute that prohibited individuals from engagin in the unsolicited sending of obscene, lewd, or lascivious circulars or advertising. Because the obscene circulars and advertising depicted individuals engaging in sexual activities that were sent to solicit sales from unwilling recipients of such advertising and depicted individuals engaging in sexual activities and were intended to appeal to a shameful or morbid interest in nudity, sex or excretion that went substantially beyond the customary sensible limits in their description and representation."

A plurality of the justices *in Memoirs v. Attorney General of Massachusetts*, 383 U.S. 413 (1966), added a new prong to the *Roth* obscenity test: "when considered as a whole, the work must be utterly without any redeeming social value to be considered obscene and, accordingly, not constitutionally protected." The Court held that the published memoir was protected speech, regardless of whether it appealed to the prurient interest and was patently offensive, because it had some redeeming value.

Using the obscenity test that had been rejected in *Roth*, the Court, in *Jacobellus v. Ohio*, 378 U.S. 184 (1964), held that an explicit love scene during the last reel of the film in the case was not hardcore pornography because it was so fragmented and fleeting that the audience would have to be explicitly informed that some offensive behavior would occur. Also, the Court held that the film was not without redeeming social value because it received favorable reviews in various national publications.

The Court, in *Stanley v. Georgia*, 394 U.S. 557 (1969), unanimously held that, while the First Amendment does not protect obscenity, the government may not punish the mere private possession of obscene material. The Court held that the First Amendment protected a person's right to possess and view pornography in his own home. Justice Thurgood Marshall wrote, "If the First Amendment means anything, it means that a State has no business telling a man, sitting alone in his own house, what books he may read or what films he may watch." The Court added, however, that the government can still ban the public distribution of such material.

Although obscene material is speech that is not protected by the Constitution, pornography that merely depicts is not necessarily obscene and therefore may have First Amendment protection. In *Jenkins v. Georgia*, 418 U.S. 153 (1974), the Court held that a movie containing scenes of sexual conduct did not appeal to the prurient interest, that it did not constitute patently offensive material, but that it did have social value. The film at issue in *Jenkins* did not visibly display genitalia, the bodies of the actors were not emphasized in the cinematography, and neither the entire film nor the focal points of the movie consisted of sexually explicit scenes.

In *Erznoznik v. City of Jacksonville*, 422 U.S. 205 (1975), the Supreme Court invalidated a city ordinance forbidding drive-in theaters from showing films depicting nudity because the ordinance overinclusively targeted films solely on the basis of nudity. The Court did not analyze the movie under the *Miller* obscenity standard but instead based its decision on the concept that, absent an unacceptable invasion of substantial privacy interests, the government may not stop speech or expression exclusively to protect others from hearing or seeing it. Thus, when not considered obscene, the government may not halt speech or expression exclusively to protect others from hearing or seeing it, and when a work is not deemed obscene under the *Miller* standards, mere nudity as a form of pornography remains constitutionally protected speech.

The Court, in *Reno v. American Civil Liberties Union*, 521 U.S. 844 (1997), invalidated Section 5 of the Communications Decency Act, 110 Stat. 133 (1996), a key anti-indecency provision of the act, as an overboard suppression of speech, but upheld Section 230, which granted legal immunity for Internet service providers (ISPs). The Court, in striking down Section 5, held that private filtering options offered an alternative to a state prohibition on indecent speech.

In *Ashcroft v. American Civil Liberties Union*, 535 U.S. 564 (2002), however, the Court upheld a statute that sought to restrict minors' access to obscene materials on the Internet. The Court declared that, because community standards are used to determine obscene materials under the *Miller* obscenity test, a publisher sending obscene materials to a specific community through the Internet must comply with the contemporary standards of that community. Although certain forms of Internet pornography is protected free speech, revenge pornography is often deemed as obscene and can often be restricted.

In *Nitke v. Gonzales*, 413 F.Supp. 2d 262 (S.D.N.Y., 2005), a New York federal district court held that the right to free speech, including certain forms of pornography, applies to

Internet speech. Obscenity laws nonetheless apply in cases involving the Internet. The types of pornography involved in that case were all fairly unusual sexual activities, including sadomasochism.

Revenge pornography

Revenge pornography entails the posting and distribution of intimate, nude, and sexually erotic photographs of an individual on the Internet without that person's consent. As an especially extreme type of indecent speech, revenge pornography should be found obscene, under the *Miller* obscenity test.

Although revenge pornography websites are generally visited by willing viewers, each displayed individual is an unwilling target in the public distribution of this material when he or she did not give permission to such distribution. Similar to the advertisements in *Miller,* the victim of revenge pornography is depicted as nude and in a sexually erotic position or engaging in sexual activity with his or her genitals or breasts exposed. Cases of revenge pornography differ from *Jenkins v. Georgia,* where the Supreme Court held that the depictions of sexual conduct in the film, in that case, did not appeal to the prurient interests because there was no genitalia visible, and the camera did not focus on the actors' bodies during the sex scenes. Consensual and artistic nudity alone does not make material with such sexual conduct obscenity under *Miller.*

Sexually explicit photographs, however, posted for vengeful or spiteful purposes, such as revenge pornography, use the sexual aspect of the images to embarrass or harass the displayed individual. Therefore, revenge pornography is a far different act than a depiction of mere nudity. The sexually explicit photographs of nude individuals used in revenge pornography are used, then, for a far different purpose than the artistic endeavor of the film in *Jenkins*. The dissemination of revenge pornography over the Internet is principally used to exact revenge and view the victim for warped sexual gratification.

Revenge pornography has no constitutional protection, so Congress and the state legislatures should enact legislation to deter revenge pornography and protect the victims of these acts. The courts could either hold revenge pornography to be obscene or apply tort remedies to address revenge pornography's grave and repugnant breaches of morality and the privacy rights of the victim.

Child pornography

Child pornography is a thriving and technologically advanced industry. The Internet makes child pornography readily accessible, and the computer enables thousands of people throughout the world to communicate with each other while maintaining the secrecy and covert nature of underground networks. For all these reasons, the Internet emerged as the primary means of distributing child pornography.

The state has a compelling interest in eliminating child pornography because it involves the sexual exploitation of a defenseless group of people. The Court, in *Jacobsen v. United States,* 503 U.S. 540 (1992), acknowledged the seriousness of the issue when it stated that "there can be no dispute about the evils of child pornography or the difficulties that the laws and law enforcement have encountered in eliminating it."

Child pornography is often referred to as child abuse because it depicts a child engaged some sexual activity. This activity may involve other children or adults. Child pornography, as abuse, can damage and haunt the child for years. Also, child abusers use child pornography to lure children to engage in sexual activity. The abuser manipulates the child into believing that sexual activity is acceptable because the children shown in pictures are engaged in such acts. Pedophiles also use technology to transmit and receive child pornography anonymously. For all these reasons, legislation has been promoted to fight child pornography.

Many privacy organizations, such as the American Civil Liberties Union (ACLU), EPIC, and CDT, have successfully challenged the constitutionality of legislation restricting Internet speech deemed as harmful to minors by arguing that the availability of self-help alternatives meant that each such statute could not be considered the "least restrictive means" of regulating constitutionally protected speech. With this argument, they opposed the Communications Decency Act of 1996; the Child Online Protection Act (COPA), codified as 47 U.S.C. 231 (COPA should not be confused with the Children's Online Privacy Protection Act of 1998 (COPPA), 129 Stat. 437 and state laws that fulfill purposes similar to COPA. The ACLU and EPIC argued that the user-based filtering software could be used if parents wished to restrict what their children viewed.

Christopher T. Anglim

Further Reading

Bambauer, Derek E. "Exposed." *Minnesota Law Review* 98 (2014): 2025–2092.

Ek, Kaitlin. Note, "Conspiracy and the Fantasy Defense: The Strange Case of the Cannibal Cop." *Duke Law Journal* 64 (2015): 901–945.

Godwin, Mike. *Cyber Rights: Defending Free Speech in the Digital Age,* rev. and updated ed. Cambridge, MA: MIT Press, 2003.

Kinsley, Jennifer M. "Sexual Privacy in the Internet Age: How Substantive Due Process Protects Online Obscenity." *Vanderbilt Journal of Entertainment and Technology Law* 16 (2013): 103–131.

Levendowski, Amanda. "Using Copyright to Combat Revenge Porn." NYU *Journal of Intellectual Property and Entertainment Law* 3 (2014): 422–446.

Wortley, Richard, and Steven Smallbone. *Internet Child Pornography: Causes, Investigation, and Prevention.* Santa Barbara, CA: Praeger, 2012.

See also: Children's Online Privacy Protection Act (COPPA) First Amendment to the U.S. Constitution; Obscenity; *Stanley v. Jackson*; Supreme Court of the Untied States

PRISM

Identification: The code name for a controversial electronic surveillance program conducted by the U.S. government.

Under PRISM, a federal agency— most often the National Security Agency (NSA), (although the Federal Bureau of Investigation and the Central Intelligence Agency also participate)— collects and retains stored electronic information obtained from a variety of Internet companies for foreign intelligence purposes. While the United States Director for National Intelligence (DNI) has asserted that PRISM is actually the name for the computer program that facilitates the government's collection of foreign intelligence, the term is often used to describe the overall surveillance program.

The government's claimed legal authority for PRISM is the FISA Amendments Act of 2008, Section 702, which authorizes foreign intelligence electronic surveillance when certain conditions are met. Among those conditions, the information collection may not intentionally target any person known at the time of acquisition to be located in the United States; may not intentionally target a person reasonably believed to be located outside the United States if the purpose of such acquisition is to target a particular, known person reasonably believed to be in the United States; may not intentionally target a U.S. person reasonably believed to be located outside the United States; may not intentionally acquire any communication as to which the sender and all intended recipients are known at the time of the acquisition to be located in the United States; must include minimization procedures designed to reduce the chance that the government will collect and retain information about U.S. persons; and must be conducted in a manner consistent with the Fourth Amendment to the Constitution of the United States. Under Section 702, when the U.S. government wishes to obtain information on a target, the attorney general and DNI certify to the Foreign Intelligence Surveillance Court (FISC) that, among other things, procedures are in place to ensure that the data collection is targeting only non-U.S. persons outside the United States and that a significant purpose of the collection is foreign intelligence. The FISC reviews the certification for compliance with Section 702, and then a federal agency issues a directive to an Internet company compelling the company to produce information on the target. The directives include demands for information for specific "selectors," such as specific email addresses. The company is then required to produce all its records for those selectors. Once transmitted by the Internet company, the U.S. government stores the communications in several databases to which intelligence agencies have access.

Despite Section 702's requirement that collection may not intentionally target a U.S. person, there are several ways the government might obtain information on U.S. persons under PRISM. For instance, if a U.S. person communicates with a non-U.S. person who has been targeted or if two non-U.S. persons discuss a U.S. person, these are "incidental" collections, and the communications may be retained and used by the government. On the other hand, "inadvertent" collections of information on U.S. persons, such as if a U.S. person is erroneously targeted, or there is a technological malfunction, must be destroyed. If the government is intentionally targeting a U.S. person, it is required first to obtain a court order.

A few specific companies comprise the vast majority of Internet companies that the federal government has used in its PRISM collection program: Microsoft (including its Hotmail and Outlook email programs and subsidiary Skype), Yahoo!, and Google. The type of records the companies might produce includes email; instant messages; text, voice, and video chat; and file transfers of various types. Although the program is not authorized to target persons in the United States, PRISM is able to obtain significant quantities of foreign communications because much of the world's Internet communication uses the companies mentioned above.

The legal status of PRISM has been the subject of debate, with some members of Congress claiming to have been unaware of PRISM's existence or that Section 702 authorized such intelligence gathering. The activities now termed PRISM were initially conducted after 9/11 under the president's Terrorist Surveillance Program, arguably under the legal authority of the initial Foreign Intelligence Surveillance Act. In 2007, Congress specifically codified authorization for the PRISM activities in the Protect America Act. When this temporary legal authority expired, Congress included it in the FISA Amendments Act of 2008. All three branches of the U.S. federal government appear to have participated in authorizing PRISM and related activities, including congressional authorization through Section 702 and ongoing oversight, executive branch approval of Section 702 and implementation of PRISM, and judicial branch oversight through the FISC.

In 2013, details of the previously clandestine PRISM were leaked by NSA contractor Edward Snowden through the *Guardian* and *New York Times* newspapers. PRISM is sometimes confused with another intelligence-gathering program, also revealed by Mr. Snowden, through which the government engages in bulk collection and retention of telephone call metadata from U.S. telephone service providers. Another common misunderstanding is that PRISM gives the government direct access to Internet company servers. The government and such companies have repeatedly insisted that the companies provide copies of records to the government pursuant to lawful directives and orders, but the program does not allow the government to have direct access to the companies' electronic storage systems.

Eric Merriam

Further Reading

Ball, James. "NSA's PRISM Surveillance Program: How It Works and What It Can Do." The *Guardian*, June 2013.

Privacy and Civil Liberties Oversight Board. *Report on the Surveillance Program Operated Pursuant to Section 702 of the Foreign Intelligence Surveillance Act*, July 2, 2014.

Savage, Charlie, Edward Wyatt, and Peter Baker. "U.S. Confirms That It Gathers Online Data Overseas." *New York Times,* June 2013.

See also: Foreign Intelligence Surveillance Act (FISA); Foreign Intelligence Surveillance Court (FISC); National Security Agency (NSA); Protect America Act of 2007; Snowden, Edward; Terrorism and privacy; Wiretapping

Privacy Act of 1974

Identification: A privacy protection and government records access statute (5 U.S.C. § 552a) that was enacted by the U.S. Congress in 1974 as a post-Watergate government reform measure to regulate the federal government's collection, maintenance, use, and dissemination of information about individuals (sometimes referred to as "fair information practices").

The Privacy Act of 1974 took effect on September 27, 1975, and was the first such comprehensive privacy protection law enacted anywhere in the world. With respect to access to government records, it heavily overlaps the Freedom of Information Act (FOIA), though in contrast to that statute, it affords rights only to U.S. citizens (plus persons holding lawful permanent residency [LPR] status), and it applies only to records about such individuals that are located within formal systems of records maintained by federal executive branch agencies; record retrieval according to an individual's name or personal identifier is a key jurisdictional element of it as well. Consequently, if access to a record about an individual is properly requested by him- or herself under the Privacy Act as well as under FOIA, it can be withheld only if it is exempt from disclosure under both statutes. Generally speaking, and apart from the Privacy Act's special system-wide exemptions for all records of the Central Intelligence Agency (CIA) and certain law enforcement files, the Privacy Act's access exemptions are narrower than those of FOIA; they do not include business information, most privileged information, and (ironically)

the disclosure of information that would invade another person's personal privacy interests.

The heart of the Privacy Act, though, is the additional rights and protections that it provides to the individuals to whom agency records pertain. The first of these is a disclosure prohibition that bars agencies from disclosing Privacy Act–protected information—that is, records within systems of records that are retrieved through use of a citizen's or LPR's name or identifier—without that individual's written consent or unless one of several disclosure prohibition exceptions applies. (Note that *disclosure* in this context does not mean just disclosure to the public or disclosure outside the executive branch, as under FOIA; rather, it includes disclosure to another federal agency and even disclosure *within* the agency that is holding the information.) The major such exceptions to this prohibition are disclosure within an agency on an official need-to-know basis; disclosure required by a third-party FOIA request that the agency has received; disclosure to a congressional committee; disclosure in compliance with a federal court order; and disclosure made in accordance with a specific "routine use" of that information, compatible with the purpose for which the information was obtained (for example, routine Justice Department sharing of judicial nominations information with the White House), that formally has been established (i.e., in a published systems notice) for that system of records. (These are highly technical terms of art created exclusively for the Privacy Act as part its unique record-keeping requirements.) In addition, because even intra-agency disclosure is regulated, the Privacy Act calls for the use of strict security measures and training of agency personnel in order to protect the confidentiality of all covered information.

Next is the right to request amendment of records, correction of records, and/or expungement/expunction of records based on a showing that they are not accurate, relevant, timely, or complete. Agencies are required to have formal administrative processes by which individuals can obtain such relief, which usually is preceded by the individual obtaining access to the records (in whole or in part) in order to learn their contents. Also, as an alternative to amendment and correction, a dissatisfied individual is entitled to submit a brief counterstatement to a record, which the agency is required to attach to it (either physically or electronically) so that the challenged record will not be used or disseminated elsewhere without that accompaniment. And an individual can request an accounting of any record dissemination.

Then there are the Privacy Act's "fair information practices" provisions, which largely pertain to the collection and maintenance of personal information. As for the former, agencies are required, wherever practicable, to collect such information from the individual directly, rather than from third-party sources, and to notify individuals before they supply personal information to the government of the consequences of doing so or not doing so, as the case may be. As for record maintenance, the Privacy Act has two provisions that even after forty years remain relatively little known but which nonetheless contain potent agency obligations. The first, found in subsection (e)(5) of the act, requires agencies to "maintain all records which are used by the agency in making any determination about any individual with such accuracy, relevance, timeliness, and completeness as is reasonably necessary to assure [sic] fairness to the individual in the determination." The second, which is found in subsection (e)(7) and is potentially even broader in its sweep, commands that an agency shall "maintain no record describing how any individual exercises rights guaranteed by the First Amendment [to the U.S. Constitution] unless expressly authorized by statute," consented to by that individual, or deemed relevant to "an authorized law enforcement activity." This latter provision means, for example, that when considering an application for a career employment position, a federal hiring official cannot indulge in the now-commonplace

private-sector practice of "doing an Internet search" on the applicant and jotting down on the application any pertinent information found; such a step, taken as part of a corrupt hiring scheme during the George W. Bush administration, became the basis of more than $500,000 in damages and attorney's fees paid by the government in the case of *Gerlich v. Department of Justice* in 2014.

Civil damages are indeed available as an enforcement mechanism under the Privacy Act, wherever a violation of its disclosure prohibition or a fair information practices provision is shown to have been "intentional or willful" and to have had a demonstrable "adverse effect" on an individual. And as with FOIA, court-awarded attorney's fees are available to successful Privacy Act litigants as well. Beyond that, the Privacy Act has an even more powerful enforcement mechanism: It contains criminal penalties, at the misdemeanor level, that can be imposed against federal employees for willful violation of its provisions. There have been more than a dozen such criminal prosecutions over the years, most often where the violator acted with a commercial motive.

Last, the Privacy Act is long overdue for legislative reform and updating, especially considering that it was drafted by Congress quite hurriedly in the wake of President Nixon's resignation in 1974 and contains both inconsistencies and an outdated focus on information in paper (rather than electronic) form. Over the years, it has been amended significantly only once—by the insertion of several "computer matching" provisions in 1988. FOIA, by comparison, has been amended many times. Oversight of the Privacy Act's government-wide implementation has suffered from gross inattention since the mid-1980s. Under subsection (v) of the act, the lead agency responsible for oversight is the U.S. Office of Management and Budget (OMB), which is part of the executive office of the president. But historically that obligation has been honored more in the breach by OMB, leaving it to the U.S. Department of Justice to fill the gap with government-wide guidance and assistance to federal agencies as a function ancillary to its advisory role under FOIA.

Daniel J. Metcalfe

Further Reading

Bloomberg BNA. "DOJ Settles, Turns Page on 'Dark Chapter' in Politicized Honors Program Hiring Dispute." *Daily Labor Report* 53, no. 1 (March 19, 2014).

Coles, Todd R. Comment, "Does the Privacy Act of 1974 Protect Your Right to Privacy? An Examination of the Routine Use Exemption [sic]." *American University Law Review* 40, no. 957 (1991).

Gellman, Robert. "Willis Ware's Lasting Contribution to Privacy: Fair Information Practices." *IEEE Security & Privacy* 12, no. 51 (2014).

Hammitt, Harry A., et al., eds. *Litigation under the Federal Open Government Laws.* Washington, DC: Electronic Privacy Information Center, 2010.

Metcalfe, Daniel J. "The Nature of Government Secrecy." *Government Information Quarterly* 26, no. 305 (2009).

Susman, Thomas M. "The Privacy Act and the Freedom of Information Act: Conflict and Resolution." *Journal of the Marshall Law Review* 21, no. 703 (1988).

See also: Driver's Privacy Protection Act of 1994 (DPPA); Electronic Communications Privacy Act (ECPA); Family Educational Rights and Privacy Act of 1974 (FERPA); Financial information, privacy right to; Freedom of Information Act (FOIA); Health Insurance Portability and Accountability Act (HIPAA); Mug shots

Privacy and Civil Liberties Oversight Board (PCLOB)

Identification: As currently constituted, a five-member, bipartisan, independent agency whose members are appointed by the president and confirmed by the Senate. PCLOB was created by 42 U.S.C. §2000ee in 2007, as part of the executive branch. Other documents that give authority and operations purpose to PCLOB are Executive Order 13636, on Improving Critical Infrastructure Cybersecurity; Presidential Policy Directive 28 (PPD-28); and Section 803 of the Implementing Recommendations of the 9/11 Commission. By statute, the chairperson of PCLOB serves fulltime, while the remaining four members serve part-time. Terms are staggered, six-year terms.

The stated mission of PCLOB is to ensure that "the federal government's efforts to prevent terrorism are balanced with the need to protect privacy and civil liberties." Activities of the board include assessment of proposed policy and implementation of matters involving intelligence activities, collaborating with the Department of Homeland Security to the extent of providing an annual report with updates as needed, and directing the privacy and civil liberties officers of eight federal agencies. At times, PCLOB reports reviews that have been undertaken at agencies regarding the rights of citizens in relation to data collection, exchange of information between agencies, and threats to cybersecurity. PCLOB is authorized to access and audit agency records and any relevant materials, as well as to interview, take statements from or take public testimony from any executive branch employee. The board may request that the Attorney General subpoena parties in order that they produce information.

Much of the current work of PCLOB centers around Section 215 of the 1978 Foreign Intelligence Surveillance Act (FISA). Amended in 2001 and renamed the USA PATRIOT Act, this legislation allowed the Federal Bureau of Investigation (FBI) to apply for an order to produce records, books, phone data, and other items in an investigation against terrorism or clandestine intelligence activities. A January 23, 2014, PCLOB report on the telephone records search and operations of the Foreign Intelligence Surveillance Court (FISC) made the following recommendations: (1) end the National Security Agency (NSA) collection of telephone records and metadata; (2) immediately add privacy safeguards to the bulk telephone records program; (3) revamp FISC to hear independent views, allow opportunities for appellate review, and explore opportunities for outside legal and technical input in FISC matters; (4) release information regarding FISC decisions; (5) publicly report on the operation of the FISC Special Advocate Program; (6) permit companies to disclose information about their receipt of FISA production orders and to disclose more detailed statistics on surveillance; (7) inform PCLOB of FISA activities and provide relevant congressional reports about FISC decisions; (8) revise NSA's procedures for more accurate documentation of the foreign intelligence reason for targeting decisions; (9) update the FBI's procedures to place additional limits on the FBI's use of data; (10) require NSA and Central Intelligence Agency (CIA) personnel to provide a statement explaining their purpose before using identifiers, and develop written guidance on applying this standard; (11) adopt measures to document and publicly release information showing how frequently NSA acquires and uses communications of people within the United States or U.S. citizens located abroad; and (12) develop a methodology for assessing the value of counterterrorism programs.

The PCLOB report of January 2014 was released largely in response to a July 2013 news report by then–NSA contractor Edward Snowden, who made public information about the U.S. government's sweeping efforts to collect and monitor phone calls and other metadata of citizens. PCLOB effectively affirmed at least some of Snowden's concerns. A PCLOB report released in January 2015 revealed that, contrary to their earlier recommendations, NSA had not ended telephone surveillance, although legislation was in progress. Most other recommendations were partially implemented or were accepted and awaiting implementation. The suggestion to take advantage of opportunities outside legal and technical input in FISC matters was consistently implemented. Other activities, reviews, and reports by PCLOB include a May 2015 report to the Department of Homeland Security on cybersecurity, issued in compliance with an executive order that requires federal agencies to develop

and induce participation in a technology-neutral cybersecurity framework, share information on cyber-threats with the private sector in a timely manner, and work with senior agency officials to ensure that privacy and civil liberties protections are incorporated into these activities.

From early 2017 until October 2018, the only PCLOB board member was Elisabeth Collins. Three new board members were approved by the Senate in October 2018, but Collins completed her term in December 2018.

Increasing concerns have been voiced by United States allies in the European Union over the need for the PCLOB to adopt and implement a privacy framework that is compatible with the EU Privacy Shield. At least two deadlines were passed, with the result that the EU is using a call for concern over the status of EU-USA transmissions of data, and whether EU citizens are protected against potential threats to their private information when dealing with US transfers.

In August 2018, watchdog groups called for a shift in the PCLOB's agenda towards the following priorities: 1) review the impact of the call detail records (CDR) program, particularly in light of the use of call detail data in the NSA data breach; 2) review warrantless data searches, and limit searches under Section 702; 3) investigate targeted surveillance of people of color by groups such as the New York Police Department, Homeland Security, the Drug Enforcement Agency (DEA), and the FBI.

For the 2018 annual operating budget, the PCLOB requested $8 million, and no new positions, in order to continue to carry out its mission: to "conduct oversight and provide advice to ensure that efforts taken by the executive branch to protect the nation from terrorism are appropriately balanced with the need to protect privacy and civil liberties, while operating as an established agency with a growing infrastructure and increasingly comprehensive operating policies and procedures."

Paula Collins

Further Reading

Kerry, Cameron. "It's Time for the Senate to Act on PCLOB Nominations." August 27, 2018. Lawfare.com.

Laperruque, Jake. "A Proposed Agenda for a New PCLOB." August 28, 2018. Lawfare.com.

Nelson, Steven. "Privacy Board Will Do 'Deep Dive' on NSA, CIA Practices." *U.S. News and World Report,* April 8, 2015.

Relyea, Harold. *Privacy and Civil Liberties Oversight Board Congressional Refinements.* Washington, DC: Congressional Information Service, Library of Congress,2007.

Relyea, Harold. *Privacy and Civil Liberties Oversight Board New Independent Agency Status.* Washington, DC: Congressional Research Service, Library of Congress, 2008.

Relyea, Harold. *Privacy and Civil Liberties Oversight Board 109th Congress Proposed Refinements.* Washington, DC: Congressional Information Service, Library of Congress, 2005.

See also: Foreign Intelligence Surveillance Act (FISA); Foreign Intelligence Surveillance Court (FISC); Homeland Security, Department of (DHS); National Security Agency (NSA); Snowden, Edward Joseph; USA PATRIOT Act

Privacy laws, federal

Identification: A hodgepodge of federal statutes strewn throughout the U.S. Code, each controlling or protecting private data on individuals held by different agencies or for different purposes. Federal privacy laws are not the single monolith one might expect.

The predominant federal protector of consumer privacy, both on- and offline, is the Federal Trade Commission (FTC). This essay will not attempt to synthesize all of the various federal privacy laws into a contrived single body of laws; instead, this essay identifies and briefly discusses a number of the key federal privacy laws most relevant to data in the digital age; the laws are presented in alphabetical order based on the acronym for each. Note that, although these are all federal privacy laws, many apply to state and even private actors depending on the circumstances. This essay does not address the many state-level privacy laws that endeavor to protect privacy within a state's boundaries.

CAN-SPAM

The Controlling the Assault of Non-Solicited Pornography and Marketing Act restricts collection and use of email addresses to disseminate or market unsolicited pornography and other products and services. CAN-SPAM forbids marketers from transmitting former subscriber information once that subscriber has opted out and forbids email address harvesting.

CFAA

The Computer Fraud and Abuse Act criminalizes acts whereby persons or entities gain unauthorized access without consent to protected data and share those data with others. The CFAA also criminalizes distribution of malicious code, denial-of-service attacks, and trafficking in passwords and related nonpublic user information.

CIPA

The Children's Internet Protection Act requires schools and libraries to take precautions to prevent minors' access to harmful materials online and to take active steps to prevent unauthorized disclosure, use, or dissemination of personal information on minors. CIPA also requires covered entities to ensure the safety and security of children when using the entities' computers.

COPPA

The Children's Online Privacy Protection Act prohibits and penalizes certain online collection of private data on children under thirteen years of age, requires such data-gatherers to secure parental permissions before obtaining the data, and requires them to disclose to parents that they have gathered private data on the parents' children. The protected private data on children include name, address, email address, telephone number, and any other information enabling one to identify or contact a particular child. Private data on children that are tied to individually identifiable information are also protected, including children's hobbies, interests, and other information commonly collected on computer users by way of cookies.

ECPA

The Electronic Communications Privacy Act controls the privacy of electronic communications and prohibits interception of electronic communications unless the interceptor meets the requirements in the act. The act provides a range of protections for electronic communications, with some available subject to a mere subpoena, some available pursuant to a special court order, and others protected to the greatest degree by requiring a search warrant supported by probable cause. Under the ECPA, most, but not all, interceptions of electronic communications must be disclosed to the parties whose communications were intercepted.

FCRA

The Fair Credit Reporting Act limits the manner and circumstances in which persons or entities can collect, disseminate, and use private consumer information, including consumer credit information, rental history information, check-writing information, and certain medical records. The FCRA also requires that those holding private consumer information, including credit bureaus and credit reporting agencies, inform the subject if data they hold is used against the subject, inform the subject the contents of the agencies' files, provide a credit score (where applicable), correct or delete inaccurate or incomplete data, provide a procedure for the subject to challenge the data, provide data to only a limited list of entities, have the subject's consent before releasing data to employers, and so on.

FERPA

The Family Educational Rights and Privacy Act controls student data, including grades, submitted work products, attendance records, and the like. All educational institutions that receive any federal funds are required to adhere to FERPA's student data protection requirements. Teachers and staff members at covered educational institutions cannot share private student data with anyone except the student; with the student's written consent, another teacher or staff person at the same institution for an educational purpose; or to law enforcement or others in an emergency.

FISA

The Foreign Intelligence Surveillance Act authorizes electronic surveillance, physical searches, pen registers, trap-trace devices, access to business and banking records in investigations involving foreign intelligence when and to the degree approved by the FISA court, a separate and quite secretive court created by the FISA statute.

FOIA

The Freedom of Information Act provides a path through which citizens and others can obtain data held or created by the government. Certain data held by the government are not accessible through FOIA, particularly to the extent they are relevant to ongoing national security interests or where disclosure would disseminate private data on individuals.

FTCA

The Federal Trade Commission Act authorizes the FTC to prosecute and punish or fine entities that have inadequate consumer data protection or data security policies, permit unauthorized dissemination of personal data, or fail to adhere to their posted privacy policies. In its role as lead federal watchdog agency over consumer data privacy, the FTC has found all the following data security practices wanting: transporting unencrypted data, retaining data in vulnerable formats, failing to restrict data access to employees with a "need to know," failing to monitor unauthorized computer system intrusions, and failing to destroy or purge personal data no longer needed for bona fide business purposes.

GLBA

The Gramm-Leach-Bliley Act regulates the dissemination by banks, insurance companies, brokerages, and other financial entities of nonpublic data on individuals. The GLBA also requires, in many instances, that such companies prominently disclose their privacy and data dissemination policies, and take extensive precautions to prevent improper and nonconsensual disclosure of private data on individuals.

HIPAA

The Health Information Portability and Accountability Act controls medical, psychiatric, psychological, pharmaceutical, and dental patient records and information. In essence, HIPAA provides that private patient data cannot be released except to the patient or to others with the patient's express written consent. Given the immense growth in the percentage of patient data held electronically, and the susceptibility of much of that data to hackers, new data protections are likely to be imposed on those who hold such information by requiring them to take certain data safety precautions to avoid accidental dissemination and intentional hacking.

HITECH Act

The Health Information Technology for Economic and Clinical Health Act expanded incentives for healthcare providers to migrate patient data to digital platforms. Appreciating the enhanced risk to data privacy in that migration, the HITECH Act also dramatically increased the data privacy protections that had been codified in HIPAA and requires healthcare providers and their associates to notify patients promptly of any data breach.

PPA

The Privacy Protection Act prevents law enforcement officers from obtaining certain material from "publishers" who possess work products or documentary materials. Under the PPA, the investigator would have to give notice of intent to seize such materials prior to seizing them so that the publisher could interpose a motion to quash the request for disclosing those protected materials.

SCA

The Stored Communications Act, which is a subpart of the ECPA, protects electronic communications and other personal data, including IP addresses, subscriber names, and billing records, that are stored on service providers' equipment.

T3

Title III of the Omnibus Crime Control and Safe Street Act of 1968 drastically curtails government interception of wire, oral, and electronic communications, frequently in the form of wiretaps. Title III provides an exhaustive and detailed procedure that prosecutors and investigators must follow before and after installing a wiretap on a subject's telephone or other communications device.

TPA

The Privacy Act is a wide-ranging act controlling federal surveillance and investigation of individuals. The act was a reaction to the growth in the sheer volume of private data on individuals that were maintained by federal agencies, particularly private data that was tracked by a common identifier, such as the subjects' Social Security numbers. The TPA prohibits dissemination of most private data on individuals without a signed consent from the subject.

USA FREEDOM Act

The Uniting and Strengthening America by Fulfilling Rights and Ensuring Effective Discipline Over Monitoring Act was adopted in 2015 in response to concerns about the National Security Agency's (NSA's) cellular telephony metadata program that gathered phone call data involving over 200 million Americans over a period of several years.

USA PATRIOT Act

The Uniting and Strengthening America by Providing Appropriate Tools Required to Intercept and Obstruct Terrorism Act modified the ECPA, T3, and FISA with respect to gathering electronic communications and other private data on individuals during the so-called War on Terror. It was supplanted in 2015 by the USA FREEDOM Act, which, among other things, transferred storage of seized telephone call data from the NSA to the individual private service providers.

Charles E. MacLean

Further Reading

Allen, Anita L. *Unpopular Privacy: What Must We Hide?* Oxford: Oxford University Press, 2011.

Cate, Fred H. *Privacy in the Information Age.* Washington, DC: Brookings Institution Press, 1997. Craig, Terence, and Mary Ludloff. *Privacy and Big Data.* Sebastopol, CA: O'Reilly Media, 2011.

Habte, M. "Federal and State Data Privacy Laws and Their Implications for the Creation and Use of Health Information Databases." *Big Data: A Business and Legal Guide.* 2014, 55–78.

The Information Privacy Law Sourcebook. Chicago, IL: American Bar Association, 2012. Jones, Virginia A. "Protecting Information Privacy per U.S. Federal Law." *Information Management* 48, no. 2 (2014): 18.

Meyer, John. "First Federal Net Privacy Law Approved." *Computers & Security*: 719. "Right to Privacy: Statutes: Partial Invalidity." *Michigan Law Review* 7, (1909): 83.

Samuels, A. "The Rights of Privacy and Freedom of Expression: The Drafting Challenge." *Statute Law Review* 00, no. 00 (1999): 66–73.

Strahilevitz, Lior Jacob. "Toward a Positive Theory of Privacy Law." *Harvard Law Review* (2013).

Woodward, Beverly. "Federal Privacy Legislation." *The Journal of Law, Medicine & Ethics* 26, no. 1 (1998): 80–81.

See also: Children's Online Privacy Protection Act (COPPA); Computer Fraud and Abuse Act (CFA); Data harvesting; Data protection regimes; Electronic Communications Privacy Act (ECPA); Fair Credit Reporting Act (FCRA); Family Educational Rights and Privacy Act (FERPA); Federal Trade Commission (FTC); Foreign Intelligence Surveillance Act (FISA); Freedom of Information Act (FOIA); Fourth Amendment to the U.S. Constitution; GrammLeach-Bliley Act; Health Information Portability and Accountability Act (HIPAA); Privacy laws, state; Privacy Protection Act; Stored Communications Act (SCA); USA FREEDOM Act; USA PATRIOT Act

Privacy laws, state

Identification: Privacy protections emanating from state constitutions, civil codes, and case law. All states recognize an implied right to privacy under their constitution, and the constitution of Alaska, Arizona, Illinois, Louisiana, South Carolina, and Washington expressly recognize a right of privacy.

State privacy law in the United States originated in a seminal article by Samuel D. Warren and Louis D. Brandeis, "The Right to Privacy," written in 1890. Brandeis and Warren articulated the foundations and limitations for the common law right of privacy. During the late 1890s and early 1900s, several states issued decisions that ultimately led to recognition of a tort-based claim arising from the publication of private information. In *Pavesich v. New England Life Insurance Co.*, 50 S.E. 68 (GA, 1905), the Georgia Supreme Court recognized that "a violation of a right of privacy is a direct invasion of a legal right of the individual" and established invasion of privacy as a tort, leading the way for other states to follow. In New York, in *Roberson v. Rochester Folding Box,* 64 N.E. 442 (N.Y. Ct. App. 1902), the New York Court of Appeals found that the right of privacy had not yet been established and that doing so would be contrary to the settled legal principles; however, public uproar against this decision led the New York legislature to pass the first statutory protections of privacy in sections 50 and 51 of its civil rights law.

Another seminal work on privacy rights was a 1960 article by William Prosser in which he analyzed more than 300 tort cases that had been decided since the 1890s. Prosser identified four rights of protected interests: intrusion upon plaintiff's seclusion, public disclosure of embarrassing facts about an individual, publicity that unreasonably places one in a false light before the public, and appropriation of an individual's likeness or name. Following the publication of Prosser's article, these rights have been recognized in the American Law Institute's Restatement of the Law, Second, Torts 2d (1963–1977) and found their way into numerous state laws.

On the constitutional level, three of the most significant decisions that led to the establishment of the right of privacy were *Katz v. United States*, 389 U.S. 347 (1967), which established the right of privacy in the context of search and seizure protections in the Fourth Amendment; *Griswold v. Connecticut*, 381 U.S. 479 (1965), in which the majority of the Supreme Court found the right of privacy in various constitutional protections of the Fifth, Ninth, and Fourteenth Amendments; and *Roe v. Wade*, 410 U.S. 113 (1973), in which the Supreme Court strongly reaffirmed the existence of the constitutional right of privacy.

These cases expanded the right of privacy from a traditional idea of privacy in one's home to a substantive right of privacy grounded in the U.S. Constitution. Several states in the late 1960s and the 1970s included the right of privacy into their constitutions.

The federal case law has allowed for the possibility that states would provide for more stringent privacy protections than the federal government. Since it added the right to privacy to its constitution in 1972, California has been the trendsetter for privacy protections on the state level. Many California laws became models for other states' laws. In 2002 California passed the first data breach notification law in the United States, which required businesses to notify individuals who suffer an unauthorized breach into their personal information (CA SB 1386 (2002)).

Since then, forty-seven states have adopted data breach notifications laws that are widely based on the California standards. They require notifying affected individuals without undue delay if it is believed that their personal information

has been accessed without proper authorization and when this breach likely would compromise the confidentiality of the personal information. These basic standards were also incorporated into the federal data breach notification law.

Following the California example, most of these laws define "personal information" as a resident's first name or initial and a last name, with one or more of the following elements: a Social Security number; a driver's license or state identification card number; or an account number, credit card number or debit card number, with security code, access code, or password.

California has protected Social Security numbers since 2001, when the state legislature enacted section 1798.85 of the California Civil Code. This provision imposed significant restrictions on the commercial use of Social Security numbers. Except for specified exemptions, California law prohibits businesses from publicly displaying Social Security numbers on the documents they send. For example, state law provides that customers may only send Social Security numbers over the Internet using a secured connection, prohibits Social Security numbers from being used to log onto websites, and forbids businesses to print Social Security Numbers on any mail they send to customers. Most states have adopted the California model, with some providing for broader exemptions. Michigan has enacted some of the most stringent standards protecting Social Security numbers in the United States. That state limits not only the entire Social Security number but also the last four digits of the number.

In 2003 California enacted its Online Privacy Protection Act, Cal. Bus. & Prof. Code §§ 22575–22579 (2004), which stipulated that all commercial websites that collect personal information on California residents must post a conspicuous online privacy policy that clearly identifies the type of personal information a website collects and with whom the website operator may share this information. While other states have enacted confidentiality requirements on

Internet service providers, California is the only state that requires all website operators to publish and comply with privacy policies.

Another innovative California privacy law was the Shine the Light law, Cal. Civ. Code 1798.83 (2015). This was one of the first laws on the issue of information sharing and marketing. The act requires businesses to disclose to their customers, upon request and without charge, a list of types of personal information that the business shared with other businesses in the prior calendar year for marketing purposes and the names and addresses of the businesses to whom such information was provided. The law also has a notification requirement that obliges businesses to notify their customers of their privacy rights. This law applies to all businesses that operate in California, have more than twenty employees, and shared personal information about their customers with other businesses for marketing purposes.

California has also been a leader in protecting patient medical records. It enacted its Confidentiality of Medical Information Act in 1980 (Cal. Civ. Code 56–56.07 (2015)).

In 1996 Congress enacted the Health Insurance Portability and Accountability Act (HIPAA), 110 Stat. 1936, which preempts state laws that are less stringent than the HIPAA. California law differs from HIPAA because it has provisions that apply directly to pharmaceutical companies. It requires companies, in their capacity as employers, to formulate procedures to protect the confidentiality of their employees' medical records. It also provides for private right of action for individuals to recover damages if their medical records are breached. California law also goes beyond the federal Genetic Information Nondiscrimination Act of 2008, 122 Stat. 881, in protecting genetic information of California residents. Texas is another state with more expansive health privacy law than the HIPAA. The definition of "covered entity" in the Texas Medical Privacy Act, S.B.11 (2001), goes far beyond that in the federal statute.

The California Consumer Protection Against Computer Spyware Act, Cal. Bus. & Prof. Code §§ 22947 et seq. (2004) prohibits unauthorized individuals from willfully loading spyware onto computers of California residents and using spyware to collect personal information, manipulate computer software, or take control of computers belonging to California residents. This law also served as a model for anti-spyware laws in various other states. Some of these states expanded the reach of their antispyware legislation by providing enforcement provisions, which the California law lacks.

The California Financial Information Protection Act of 1990 (Cal. Fin. Code § 4050, et seq.) amended the Song-Beverly Credit Card Act of 1971 (Civil Code § 1747–1748.95). It serves as a model for protecting personal information in credit card transactions. It prohibits retailers from obtaining personal identification information as part of credit card transactions.

California is a trendsetter in various aspects of state privacy legislation, and the California Supreme Court, in *Hill v. National Collegiate Athletic Association*, 865 P.2d 633 (Cal. 1994) at 35–37, established an "invasion of privacy" standard that has served as a model for those states that recognize the invasion of privacy tort. In its decision, the court created a test for causes of action in invasion of privacy cases. This test contains three elements: identification of a specific privacy interest; reasonable expectation of privacy on the part of the plaintiff; and causes for action on "invasions of privacy must be sufficiently serious in their nature, scope, and actual or potential impact to constitute an egregious breach of the social norms underlying the privacy right" (865 P.2d 633 Cal. (1994)).

Tomasz Kolodziej

Further Reading

Cooper, Scott P., and Kristen J. Mathews. "State Privacy Laws," in *Proskauer on Privacy*, ed. Christopher Wolf. New York: Practicing Law Institute, 2006– .

Hadjipetrova, Ganka, and Hannah G. Poteat. "States Are Coming to the Fore of Privacy in the Digital Era." *Landslide* 6, no. 6 (July/August 2014).

Prosser, William Lloyd. "*Privacy.*" *California Law Review* 48, no. 3 (1960): 383–423.

Sotto, Lisa J. "Privacy and Data Security." *Privacy and Data Security Law Deskbook*. Frederick, MD: Aspen, 2010– .

Spears, Victoria Prussen. "The Case That Started It All: *Roberson v. The Rochester Folding Box Company*." *Privacy & Data Security Law Journal* 3 (November 2008): 1048.

Warren, Samuel D., and Louis D. Brandeis. "The Right to Privacy." *Harvard Law Review* 4, no. 5 (1890): 193–220.

See also: Brandeis, Louis Dembitz; Credit and debit cards; Data breach notification laws; Griswold v. Connecticut; Health Insurance Portability and Accountability Act (HIPAA); Home, Privacy of the; Katz v. United States; Legal evolution of privacy rights; Marketing; Medical Confidentiality; Privacy, Right of; Privacy torts; Prosser, William Lloyd; The Right to Privacy; Social Security Numbers; Spyware

Privacy Protection Act, 42 U.S.C. § 2000aa et seq.

Identification: Legislation enacted on October 13, 1980, to protect the work product and other documents held by persons engaged in public communications from searches and seizures by police and other government officers. The purpose of the act is to prevent the use of search warrants to interfere with the editorial integrity of the news media and other First Amendment actors without providing those actors an opportunity to seek judicial protection for materials to which the government is not entitled. The act also provides civil damages for violations.

The Privacy Protection Act was enacted by Congress in reaction to the Supreme Court decision in *Zurcher v. Stanford Daily*. In April 1971, following a student demonstration against the Vietnam War that included occupation of the Stanford University Hospital in Palo Alto,

California, police obtained a warrant to search the offices of the *Stanford Daily* for the purpose of finding photographs of students who may have beaten police officers and committed other violations. Although nothing was seized in the fifteen-minute search, the newspaper sued for a declaration that use of a search warrant under these circumstances violated the First Amendment and for an injunction against seeking, issuing, or executing such a warrant.

The newspaper argued that, because there was no evidence that anyone on the *Daily* staff had committed a crime, a subpoena *duces tecum*, requiring the newspaper to produce the evidence sought or explain why it need not, should have been used instead of a search warrant. The police argued that the search was lawful in every respect under state law, which provided for the use of search warrants wherever the police had probable cause to believe evidence might be found to show the commission of a felony or to identify the perpetrator.

The U.S. District Court agreed with the newspaper, holding that third parties, that is, persons who were not suspected of criminal conduct, were entitled to greater protection, particularly when First Amendment interests were involved. The court said that, unless the magistrate receives a sworn affidavit establishing proper cause to believe that the evidence in question will be destroyed, or that a subpoena *duces tecum* is otherwise "impractical," a search of a third party for materials in his or her possession is unreasonable per se and therefore violates the Fourth Amendment. The court awarded attorney's fees to the newspapers.

The U.S. Court of Appeals for the Ninth Circuit affirmed, rejecting the government's argument that its good faith in securing what turned out to be an invalid warrant insulated it from liability. While good faith might immunize government officials from liability for money damages, the court said, it did not bar attorney's fees where declaratory and injunctive relief was sought.

In a 5–3 decision on May 31, 1978, however, the U.S. Supreme Court reversed the decisions of the lower courts, holding that nothing in the Fourth Amendment precluded the issuance of a warrant to search for evidence simply because the owner of the premises was not suspected of a crime. The showings required for the proper issuance of a search warrant—which must be applied "with particular exactitude" when First Amendment interests would be endangered— were adequate to protect the ability of the press to gather and disseminate news. Nothing limits the police to using a subpoena *duces tecum* in gathering evidence from third parties, Justice Byron White wrote in the majority opinion. Justices Potter Stewart, Thurgood Marshall, and John Paul Stevens dissented.

Congress reacted to the *Zurcher* decision by introducing several bills to protect First Amendment activity from search warrants. A compromise was reached between House and Senate negotiators in late September 1980 and became law in mid-October. The statute distinguishes between "work product" and "other documents" and establishes somewhat different rules for each.

With respect to "work product," such as notes, drafts, or articles produced for ultimate dissemination to the public, the act provides that it is unlawful for a government officer to search for or seize any work product materials "possessed by a person reasonably believed to have a purpose to disseminate to the public a newspaper, book, broadcast, or other similar form of public communication." An exception is made where there is probable cause that the person who has the material has committed or is committing a crime other than withholding the information sought. Even then, a search warrant can be used where the material involves the national defense, including classified and otherwise restricted documents, or child pornography or exploitation. Another exception is made when there is reason to believe that the immediate seizure of the material is necessary to prevent the death of, or serious bodily injury to, a human being.

With respect to "other documents," the act affords exactly the same protection, but additional exceptions are provided. For example, an additional exception arises when there is reason to believe that the notice one gives of a subpoena would result in the destruction, alteration, or concealment of the materials sought. Another exception arises when the materials have not been produced in response to a court order directing compliance with a subpoena after all administrative remedies have been exhausted and there is reason to believe that further delay would threaten the interest of justice. In that case, however, the person who has the material must be given an opportunity to submit an affidavit explaining why the material should not be subject to seizure.

The act also gives anyone aggrieved by a search or seizure in violation of these provisions a civil cause of action for damages against the government or the officers involved, except that an officer who reasonably believes that the conduct was lawful will not be held personally liable. The successful plaintiff can be awarded $1,000 or actual damages, whichever is greater, and reasonable costs and attorney's fees, but no prejudgment interest.

The act also required the U.S. Attorney General to issue guidelines for procedures to be employed by any federal officer in order to comply with provisions of the law and report the use of search warrants to Congress.

Eric B. Easton

Further Reading

"The Privacy Protection Act of 1980." *Electronic Privacy Information Center. July 25, 2003.* https://epic.org/privacy/ppa/.

Reid, Beth Ann. *A Manual for Complying with the Freedom of Information Act and the Privacy Protection Act.* Richmond, VA: Department of Management Analysis and Systems Development, 1980.

Reporters Committee for Freedom of the Press. "Confidential Sources and Information," in *First Amendment Handbook.* 7th ed. (2011). https://www.rcfp.org/first-amendment-handbook.

Uzelac, Elizabeth B. "Reviving the Privacy Protection Act of 1980." *Northwestern University Law Review* 107, no. 3 (April 2013): 1437.

See also: First Amendment to the U.S. Constitution; Fourth Amendment to the U.S. Constitution; Search warrants; Subpoenas

Privacy settings

Identification: Means by which users of a website or application manipulate and control the amount and type of personal information about them that is collected and disseminated. Forms of privacy settings range from the ability to control what other users see to what information might be passed on to third parties for targeted advertising or other purposes by the company providing the service.

Privacy settings have become essential in the digital world. An option to enable standard privacy settings or the ability to manipulate and personalize privacy settings is available on almost every form of digital platform—from operating systems to applications and websites. Google, Facebook, and even web browsers include options to determine what data users reveal to third parties—to an extent—during their time online.

Privacy settings became important as a way to implement the fair information practice principles (FIPPs) drafted by the Federal Trade Commission (FTC) in May 2000. No company is legally required to have privacy settings that consumers can manipulate or to have privacy settings at all, but companies are required to comply with the principles. Nearly ten years after FIPPs were created, websites began to experiment with more substantial and customizable privacy settings.

Currently, in the digital world, most websites and software provide privacy policies that detail whether a user has the ability to manipulate his or her privacy settings. The most significant and often cited example of privacy policies online is Facebook's policy. Many Facebook users know that the website allows users to manipulate privacy settings to a certain degree. Users may decide with whom to share their posts and information—from a small group of friends to the general public. Because it is so simple to disseminate information online, privacy settings are essential to the preservation of an individual's personal information and online image, which may affect his or her personal and professional life, especially on a site as widely used as Facebook. Privacy settings have been controversial, however, since their inception because the existence of privacy settings does not mean that the settings are actually followed or enforced.

The issue of privacy settings is a largely unregulated area. No government agency is authorized to govern all the areas of cyberspace. In online services such as Google and Facebook, the FTC has the ability only to enforce the privacy settings, which companies disclose to consumers, to alleviate consumer fraud. In some controversial cases, the FTC may enter into legal agreements with companies to preserve consumer privacy and security. Google currently has an agreement with the FTC stating that the company will honor user privacy settings and not circumvent them. Specifically, the FTC ordered Google "not [to] misrepresent in any manner, expressly or by implication . . . the extent to which consumers may exercise control over the collection, use or disclosure of covered information." Although the FTC seems to exert control over one of the world's most significant online companies through this 2011 order, this contract demonstrates the current limit of the FTC's power. The FTC can only ensure that Google and other corporations do not engage in consumer fraud. Beyond this, the FTC is powerless to control how these massive online corporations handle private consumer data.

Privacy settings are also controversial because consumers face many challenges even when privacy settings are in place. First, consumers often ignore privacy settings or do not have the technical skills that may be necessary to take advantage of the available protections. Under current law, privacy settings tend to be opt-in rather than opt-out provisions, which means that, unless requested, users' privacy settings will be off or set to the least restrictive settings. To protect privacy rights, consumers must be proactive and search for additional protection. Each update to a company's privacy policy may result in an individual's personal privacy settings are no longer as active or as restrictive as the user requested prior to the policy change.

Despite the controversy over privacy settings, only one bill is currently pending in Congress that will affect privacy settings. The bill, known as the Do Not Track Kids Act of 2015 (H.R. 2734, 2015), is not the first bill to attempt to regulate privacy settings. In fact, a broader bill, Do Not Track Me Online Act of 2011 (H.R. 654, 2011), was originally introduced in 2011. This previous bill would have required the FTC to "establish standards for the required use of an online opt-out mechanism," which would have been placed within an application or website's privacy settings. This bill did not gain sufficient support in 2011 but was reintroduced in 2015 with a focus on children. The pending bill requires companies to gain verifiable consent from parents before the companies are able to track any of the information within the application regarding children. The parents, via privacy settings, would be able to control exactly what information about their children is collected and how companies may then use the information. However, the Do Not Track Kids Act of 2015 was not enacted, so privacy settings continue to be a largely unregulated area with the potential danger to privacy rights that this entails.

Many of the most ubiquitous web presences in modern society including Facebook, Apple, and Google, continue to have a contentious relationship with users who want their data, browsing habits, and purchasing habits kept private. Turning off location services may prevent some parts of the companies' services from working but can keep people's private information more secure. Apps that use augmented reality or virtual reality rely on location services as well. Many apps, such as Facebook, track users' movements whether or not the app itself is open unless users change their privacy settings to prevent it.

Currently, privacy settings remain a legally murky area. The FTC has little power to regulate the way in which privacy settings are presented or enforced. Consumers must trust that online companies provide users with options to safeguard their privacy while still being able to apprise themselves of the benefits of the various services. As the digital landscape has evolved, privacy settings began and continue to be a point of contention among consumers, government administrations, and online corporations.

Ashley Baker

Further Reading

Datta, Anwitaman, et al. *Social Informatics: Third International Conference, SocInfo, 2011, Singapore, October 2011.* Berlin: Springer-Verlag, 2011.

Trepte, Sabine, and Leonard Reinecke. *Privacy Online: Perspectives on Privacy and Self-Disclosure in the Social Web.* Berlin: Springer-Verlag, 2011.

"Windows 10 privacy settings: How to stop Microsoft from spying on you." *The Star.* February 16, 2019.

Zetlin, Minda. "Want to Make Facebook Stop Tracking Your Location When Not in Use? Here's How." *Inc.* February 22, 2019.

See also: Do-not-track legislation; Facebook; Fair Information Practice Principles (FIPPs); Federal Trade Commission (FTC); Google

Privacy torts

Identification: Appropriation, intrusion, publication of private information, and false light invasion of privacy, the traditional torts for plaintiffs seeking damages for invasion of privacy.

Privacy law had its spiritual beginnings in 1890 when Harvard law professors Samuel Warren and Louis Brandeis, at Warren's instigation, published in the *Harvard Law Review* an article titled "The Right to Privacy." It's difficult to exaggerate the significance of the article on the development of privacy law. Indeed, in the history of legal research on all topics, according to law professor Fred R. Shapiro, only one other law journal article has been cited more than "The Right to Privacy." It is not clear why Professor Warren suggested that the two scholars write the article, but a common theory is that he was dissatisfied with the way his socially prominent family had been treated by the popular media in Boston.

While "The Right to Privacy" was a significant piece of legal literature, privacy law in the United States was slow in developing—many judges were skeptical of claims of psychological damage resulting from invasions of one's privacy. Without being able to make specific physical claims as to harm, plaintiffs in tort actions could not recover damages.

Another law journal article, this one by William Prosser, the dean of the University of California law school, helped break down some of the barriers that were preventing success by privacy plaintiffs. Dean Prosser researched privacy law for the second edition of *The Restatement of the Law of Torts* by the American Law Institute.

The *Restatement* seeks to clarify and synthesize the common law in a particular area of law. Dean Prosser also published the results of his research in a law journal article titled "Privacy," published in 1960 in the *California Law Review*. (Prosser's article is the forty-fifth most-cited article on Shapiro's list.)

In this landmark piece, Dean Prosser posited that there was not a single tort that could be classified as "invasion of privacy." Instead, he wrote, there are four torts that fall under the privacy umbrella: appropriation, intrusion, the publication of private information, and false light invasion of privacy. The identification of these four torts has guided privacy law since.

Appropriation is the use of a person's name, image, or likeness, without permission, for commercial gain. A "use" might be a caricature or silhouette of an individual, a photograph, a description, or an imitation of a person's voice. The use must be designed to provide commercial gain for the user; that is, the purpose of the use is to make money rather than for the dissemination of information of public concern. Appropriation is often associated with celebrities, but the tort is not limited to people who are well known. Indeed, an early case, *Roberson v. Rochester Folding Box Co.* (64 N.E. 442 [NY, 1902]), involved the use of a photograph of a woman who was not a celebrity on boxes of flour. Much more recently, a Virginia man settled out of court with a company that used a photograph of him on a greeting card made to advertise the state fair.

The U.S. Supreme Court has not resolved a case that is purely appropriation but came close in the 1977 case *Zacchini v. Scripps-Howard Broadcasting* (433 U.S. 562). Hugo Zacchini, who performed as "The Human Cannonball," successfully sued a television station for broadcasting his entire performance—which lasted only 15 seconds. The Court upheld the $25,000 verdict, even though the station did not broadcast the performance for commercial gain. The broadcast, however, posed a substantial threat, the Court held, to the economic value of the performance.

Appropriation was one of the first privacy torts to develop because it was, in large part, tied to property rights. Similarly, courts have recognized that individuals have a right of privacy; that is, people have a right to profit from images of themselves. An exception in the law allows the news media to circumvent appropriation suits. Courts have ruled that the media have only their content to sell and therefore they may use their own content—including photographs of individuals—for advertising purposes.

Intrusion is the one privacy tort that is unrelated to publication or publicity. It occurs when a place were a person has a reasonable expectation of privacy is physically invaded, often by the use of cameras or electronic listening devices.

Under common law, people in public places have no expectation of privacy. When those same people are in private places, however, the law protects their rights to be free from exposure to the outside world. Intrusion might involve the use of recording devices, the use of telephoto or infrared lenses, trespassing, or entering a private place under false pretenses. When journalists for *Life* magazine entered the home of self-proclaimed healer A. A. Dietmann, for example, passing themselves off as potential customers, a jury found their actions to be intrusive and, in *Dietmann v. Time, Inc.* (449 F.2d 245 [9th Cir., 1971]) awarded Dietmann $1,000 in damages.

The Supreme Court found a type of intrusion when journalists accompanied law enforcement officers onto private property in two cases. In *Wilson v. Layne* (526 U.S. 603 [1999]), a task force from various law enforcement agencies in the Washington, DC, area made a late-night raid into the home of Charles and Geraldine Wilson, thinking they might find Dominic Wilson, who was wanted by the task force. Dominic was not present, and the journalists watched as Charles was thrown to the floor and handcuffed, and Geraldine looked on in shock. The Court found for the Wilsons when they sued for invasion of privacy. The invasion occurred when the journalists entered the home, even though law enforcement officers allowed the entry.

Similarly, in *Hanlan v. Berger* [526 U.S. 808 (1999)], the Court reprimanded the officials for bringing the journalists along on a raid on a Montana ranch where they suspected that pesticides might be causing the deaths of eagles, which are protected as an endangered species.

The publication of private information is the tort most people think of when they hear the term "invasion of privacy." It is the widespread publication of information that is private, and the publication of which is highly offensive to a reasonable person.

To win a private information case, therefore, a plaintiff must prove that the offensive material was, first, private. Nothing that occurs in public can be considered private. Similarly, nothing that appears on a public document, even if few people know about it, can be considered private. For example, the Supreme Court, in *Cox Broadcasting Co. v. Cohn* [420 U.S. 469 (1975)], ruled that a television station was not liable for publishing the identity of a rape victim because the name appeared on a public document.

The plaintiff must also prove that the private information was disseminated to a large audience, which is generally easy to prove if the material was published in a medium of widespread circulation, broadcast over the airwaves, or posted on the Internet.

Finally, a plaintiff must demonstrate that the material was not simply private but that its publication was highly offensive to a reasonable person. This is a highly subjective criterion, and its determination is based on the finding of a jury. Dorothy Barber, for example, won damages when *Time* magazine published a photograph of Barber in her hospital bed alongside a story identifying her as a "starving glutton." Barber had a rare ailment that caused her to lose weight regardless of how much she ate.

A defense in a private information case is that the published information was a matter of public concern—that is, it was newsworthy. Even if the material is private, is widely disseminated, and is highly offensive to a reasonable person, if it is newsworthy, it is protected. The iconic example of the newsworthy defense came in the case of Hilda Bridges, who was taken hostage in her apartment by her estranged husband. When the abduction became known and police arrived, the husband forced Bridges to take off all her clothes, believing she would not attempt to flee if she were nude. The husband ended up shooting himself; police stormed the apartment, and Bridges did indeed flee. A photograph of her covering herself as best she could with a dish towel was published by the newspaper *Today* of Cocoa Beach, Florida. Bridges sued, but a judge, though expressing sympathy for Bridges, ruled that her story was newsworthy and therefore she could not win a private information case.

False light invasion of privacy occurs with the widespread publication of false information with actual malice, the publication of which is highly offensive to a reasonable person. False light resembles defamation, but the requirement in a false light case is simply that the published material places the plaintiff in a false light, not that the published material is defamatory. Indeed, false light cases have been won because of publications provided glowing reports about a plaintiff that were so greatly exaggerated that the plaintiff found them to be embarrassing, that is, highly offensive.

Because of its resemblance to defamation, plaintiffs have often filed false light claims in conjunction with defamation claims. For that reason, several states (North Carolina and Virginia are two) no longer recognize false light as a tort action. In addition, the Supreme Court, in order to prevent an end-run around defamation, requires all plaintiffs in false light claims to prove actual malice, that is, knowledge of falsity or reckless disregard for the truth. The case was *Time, Inc. v. Hill* [385 U.S. 374 (1967)].

The case began when James Hill and his family were held hostage in their home near Philadelphia by three escaped convicts in 1952. They were released unharmed, but the events received nationwide publicity and became the basis for Joseph Hayes's novel *The Desperate Hours*, which became a Broadway play and a movie starring Humphrey Bogart. *Life* magazine published a story about the events during tryouts for the play that indicated that the Hill events were the sole basis for the play, which was not true. The Hills also objected to the way their relationship with their captors was portrayed in the article.

The Hills sued. Even though it is generally not defamatory to be identified as victims of a crime, the Hills claimed that their portrayal in the magazine article was highly offensive and caused them severe embarrassment, thus the false light claim. They won at trial, but the

Supreme Court overturned the verdict, holding that plaintiffs in false light cases are required to prove that the publication was made with actual malice, as defined by the Court in *New York Times Co. v. Sullivan* [376 U.S. 254 (1964)].

The continuing effectiveness of the classic Prosser torts has come under scrutiny, especially in a world where information can be disseminated instantly over the Internet. Also, scholars, attorneys, and jurists are beginning to examine the foundational premise of privacy law, that is, that if something occurs in public, it cannot be private. When a gaffe can be spread around the world, for example, in a matter of moments, and when that gaffe remains perpetually in the memory of the Internet, some scholars (Daniel Solove is one) are suggesting that an alternative to the traditional view of public and private actions should be considered.

W. Wat Hopkins

Further Reading

Glasser, Charles, ed. *International Libel & Privacy Handbook*. New York: Bloomberg Press, 2006. Prosser, William. "Privacy." *California Law Review* 48 (1960): 383–423.

Richards, Neil M. "The Limits of Tort Privacy." *Journal on Telecommunications & High Technology Law* 9 (2011): 357–384.

Solove, Daniel. *The Future of Reputation: Gossip, Rumor and Privacy on the Internet*. New Haven, CT: Yale University Press, 2007.

Solove, Daniel J. "'I've Got Nothing to Hide' and Other Misunderstandings of Privacy." *San Diego Law Review* 44 (2007): 745–772.

Terilli, Samuel A., Jr., and Sigman Splichal, "Privacy Rights in an Open and Changing Society." In *Communication and the Law,* edited by W. Wat Hopkins, 283–309.

Warren, Samuel D., and Louis D. Brandeis. "The Right to Privacy." Harvard Law Review 4 (1890): 193–220.

See also: *Cox Broadcasting Co. v. Cohn,* 420 U.S. 469 (1975); Invasion of Privacy; *New York Times Co. v. Sullivan, Abernathy, et al.,* 376 U.S. 254; Privacy, Right of; Prosser, William Lloyd; The Right to Privacy; *Time, Inc. v. Hill,* 385 U.S. 374 (1967); *Wilson v. Layne,* 526 U.S. 603 (1999); *Zacchini v. Scripps-Howard Broadcasting,* 433 U.S. 562 (1977).

Private sphere

Identification: As opposed to the public sphere, that is, the part of social life in which the individual may exercise a great deal of authority and autonomy, and is able to exercise a significant amount of freedom from the intrusions of government and other institutions. The most common and most traditional examples of the private sphere are family and home.

The dichotomy of private and public is never absolute because any area in or upon which the law operates becomes public to some extent. In this sense, the public defines the private as that part of society with which it declines to deal. However, some areas of life, such as regulating family and private life, are areas where modern American law does not venture. Drawing a definitive line between the two is difficult. There are definitional ambiguities associated with the public–private dichotomy. Many believe that the dichotomy's existence depends on societal choice. There are, perhaps, many credible ways to distinguish the two. One of the most persuasive arguments is that the private sphere should be those aspects of a person's life and activities that any person has a right to exclude others from. Thus, the private means what the individual chooses to withdraw from public view.

The factors separating public and private spheres have varied greatly in culture and history. The ancient Greeks understood the distinction to indicate a clear demarcation in society. The public sphere (*polis*) and the private sphere (*oikos*) were completely separate: The former described a public sphere based on open interactions between free citizens in the political realm, and the latter designated a private sphere based on hidden interactions between free individuals in the domestic realm.

Traditionally, only matters that could not be dealt with by the household alone entered the public realm of the polis. In contemporary society the public sphere, especially because of the use of advanced technology, permeates the life of the home and family. The distinction between private and public spheres has traditionally been described in gendered terms. Traditionally, the feminine world is considered to be that of the private sphere, that is, household, family, and unpaid domestic work. The public sphere has often been traditionally described in terms of the masculine world of politics and paid employment.

Some feminists have argued that women's historical association with the private sphere undermines and limits them in contemporary society, based on how they view that law as reinforcing that association. They have also observed that men have historically been represented in the public sphere, that is, the workplace and the halls of political power, in far greater numbers than women. Thus, the argument goes, women continue to be politically underrepresented because of their long-time role in the private sphere.

In antiquity, crime and punishment were the concern of kinship groups, a concept challenged only slowly by ideas of public justice. Similarly in medieval Europe, the blood feud was replaced only slowly by legal control. During the medieval era, there existed no separation or distinction between the private and public spheres under the feudal system. In early modern Europe, religion was an important public issue, viewed as essential to the maintenance of the state, so religious matters were controversial and intensely debated in the public sphere. Sexual behavior was also subject to a generally agreed code publicly enforced by both formal and informal social control. In our current postmodern society, both religion and sexual behavior are most often left to individual choice.

By the late eighteenth century, feudal institutions and ecclesiastical rule were eroding. They were giving way to public power, in which the people received greater autonomy. Rulers become public entities. This was also a time when bourgeois became autonomous vis-à-vis the government.

In nineteenth-century American society, the public and private spheres were strictly divided.

The private household was considered a refuge from the commercial world and the world of work. In the home, the domain of the private sphere, the individual was able to cultivate close relationships and to express intense and spontaneous feelings, behavior that was disapproved of in the formal, judgmental public sphere. Society was segmented, and so was the individual self. Both the public self and a private self were both subject to the demands of its respective sphere. Only in the private sphere was one permitted to display one's emotions and "true self." As the philosopher Martin Heidegger said, the private sphere is the only place where one can be authentically him- or herself, as opposed to the impersonal world of the public realm.

By the late nineteenth-century, many popular newspapers invaded what had long been considered the private sphere by publishing sensationalist articles, particularly about the personal behavior of prominent individuals While the low-brow press steadily broadened the concept of what was found to be newsworthy, they also generated a backlash in which many sought to protect personal privacy. By the late nineteenth century, the "right to privacy" was being widely discussed in legal and academic circles. The concept of privacy, then as now, has a wide variety of diverse meanings and connotations. It was also closely connected to intensifying social pressures for public self-presentation.

When the right to privacy began being discussed as a legal concept, it was largely understood as a right to protect one's public image by concealing embarrassing, personal, or private matters from public scrutiny. The private sphere encompassed not only one's home and family life, but also issues involving one's body, physical functions, and emotions. Those who wished to present themselves to society as dignified and respectable thus steadfastly objected to publicity of his or her private life.

Louis Brandeis, the future Supreme Court justice, and his colleague Samuel Warren, a prominent Boston attorney, responded to these concerns by publishing what would become the modern American view of privacy with their article, "The Right to Privacy," which was printed in the *Harvard Law Review*. This article formed the impetus for subsequent statutes, case law, and regulations that sought to limit the intrusion into the private sphere by either government or private actors. Brandeis explained that protecting individual privacy was essential for people being able to function in the public sphere without every private aspect of their lives being subject to scrutiny.

The dichotomy between the public and private spheres is particularly relevant in many legal contexts, and its connotations vary. One of these contexts relates to the free speech doctrine that distinguishes between public discourse and private discourse. Another related context is the privacy torts, with their overarching concern with protecting from public disclosure or exploitation that which invades the individual's personality or psychic space. The third legal context deals with Fourth Amendment search and seizure issues. Warren and Brandeis did not see the public–private dichotomy as entirely incompatible. In their article, they wrote that the right to privacy did not prohibit publication of matters of "public interest" because the latter concept was central to First Amendment philosophy. This compatibility is also similarly reflected in the contemporary law of invasion of privacy. With respect to the publication of private facts, the publication of so-called newsworthy items is considered exempt from liability.

Privacy torts developed in U.S. law to protect the integrity and inviolability of inherently private spheres that a person restricts from "uninvited, unwelcomed, prying persons" (*Cummings v. Walsh Constr. Co.*, 561 F. Supp. 872, 884 (S.D. Ga. 1983)). "Intrusion upon seclusion" has long been a particularly difficult area for the courts to define and apply. Since Prosser articulated the tort in 1960, courts have struggled to strike a judicious balance between protecting an individual's seclusion and protecting "the freedom of action and expression of those who threaten the seclusion of others." Thus, the courts have limited the protection of privacy interests by requiring that a plaintiff prove that (1) he or she had an actual expectation of privacy and that such expectation was objectively reasonable. and (2) the intrusion into this private sphere was highly offensive. Modern technology, however, is making this tort increasingly difficult to establish in several ways.

Another major venue where the issue of the private and public spheres is particularly salient are the Fourth Amendment issues regarding "unreasonable searches and seizures." Defining when a search has occurred is crucial because, in many cases, it distinguishes between when the government may engage in potentially warrantless and suspicionless intrusions into the private sphere and when it must first appear before a neutral and detached magistrate to obtain a warrant issued on probable cause. Accordingly, the Supreme Court has had to strike repeatedly the appropriate balance between individual liberty and law enforcement through its "search" jurisprudence.

On the one hand, the Fourth Amendment is an important check on the government's power, and the Founding Fathers included the provision after the American colonialists felt oppressed by their British rulers' abuse "of general warrants." The Fourth Amendment must also be interpreted so that effective law enforcement, which is an essential function of any government, is not unduly stifled.

Privacy is at the core of American democratic values. Preserving privacy fosters individual autonomy, dignity, and self-determination, and ultimately promotes a more robust, participatory citizenry. A society that is constantly under surveillance is a conformist society. In other words, when people fear unwanted exposure, they censor themselves or withdraw out of concern that full engagement in society will lead to a loss of control over the most intimate details of their lives. People fear that unwanted exposure will result in discrimination, loss of ben-

efits, stigma, and embarrassment. But not only are individuals at risk of harm, but our communities also suffer when people either withdraw from the essential activities of life or are harmed by privacy intrusions.

Another aspect of the dichotomy of the public and private spheres must be stressed. While the spheres have not disappeared in modern society, they have dramatically changed. They no longer denoted as completely independent spheres, one—the public—of coercion, and the other—the private—of mutual exchange. Today, there is a blurring of the traditional boundaries between the two spheres of action, as indicated by the exercise of public power by private interests and concern over what were previously considered private economic circumstances by the state. For example, the privacy of the family has become subject to regulation by child welfare services, and corporations have come to employ market power as a means of dictating public policy.

Further Reading

Alldridge, Peter. *Personal Autonomy, the Private Sphere, and the Criminal Law: A Comparative Study.* Oxford, England: Hart Pubisher, 2001.

Calhoun, Craig J. *Habermas and the Public Sphere.* Cambridge, MA: MIT Press, 1992.

Clapham, Andrew. *Human Rights in the Private Sphere.* Oxford, England: Clarendon Press, 1993.

Emden, Christian. *Changing Perceptions of the Public Sphere.* Oxford, England: Berghahn Books, 2012.

Goode, Luke. *Jürgen Habermas Democracy and the Public Sphere.* London: Pluto Press, 2005.

Gripsrud, Jostein. *The Public Sphere.* Los Angeles, CA: Sage, 2011.

Habermas, Jurgen. *The Structural Transformation of the Public Sphere: An Inquiry into a Category of Bourgeois Society.* Cambridge, MA: MIT Press, 1989.

Keen, Paul. *The Crisis of Literature in the 1790s: Print Culture and the Public Sphere.* New York: Cambridge University Press, 1999.

Machan, Tibor R. *Private Rights and Public Illusions.* New Brunswick, NJ: Transaction Publishers, 1995.

Oliver, Dawn. *Human Rights and the Private Sphere: A Comparative Study.* Abingdon, United Kingdom: Routledge-Cavendish, 2007.

Rosner, Victoria. *Modernism and the Architecture of Private Life*. New York: Columbia University Press, 2005.

Volkmer, Ingrid. The Global Public Sphere: Public Communication in the Age of Reflective Interdependence.

See also: Brandeis, Louis Dembitz; Fourth Amendment to the U.S. Constitution; Legal evolution of privacy rights; Philosophical basis of privacy; Privacy torts; The Right to Privacy

Prosser, William Lloyd (1898–1972)

Identification: The twentieth century's preeminent scholar on U.S. tort law.

William Lloyd Prosser's *Handbook of the Law of Torts,* first published in 1941, was revised three times in his lifetime and updated by others for a fifth edition in 1984. He was also the reporter and principal draftsperson for the American Law Institute's *Restatement 2nd of the Law of Torts*. His work on the torts of invasion of privacy and intentional infliction of emotional distress was especially influential.

Along with the study of contracts and crimes, the course in torts is at the heart of every law student's introduction to the profession. Judges interpret torts according to the law of each jurisdiction, which in the United States usually means a state, although the U.S. Constitution sets certain conditions that bind every state's legal rules.

Prosser, who was born in Indiana, graduated from Harvard University in 1918. After military service, he studied for one year at Harvard Law School before spending several years as a businessman in Minneapolis. He completed law school at the University of Minnesota, practiced law for several years and began teaching at Minnesota in 1931. He left the university in 1942 to work for the Office of Price Administration, then he returned to private practice for four years before resuming his academic career, first from 1947 to 1948 at Harvard and then as dean of the

University of California Berkeley School of Law in 1948. He resigned as dean in 1960 but continued on the Berkeley faculty until 1963. He taught at the University of California Hastings College of Law in San Francisco from 1963 until 1971.

Prosser began intense scholarship on tort law when offered a contract in 1936 to do a volume on torts for St. Paul–based West Publishing's Hornbook series. The project grew to over 1,100 pages, and summarized and categorized the outcomes of thousands of U.S. court decisions, ranging across every aspect of the law of torts. Although the Hornbook series was primarily aimed at students, Prosser's Handbook quickly became a principal resource on tort law for lawyers and judges. *The Restatement 2nd of Torts,* developed under Prosser's leadership until his resignation as a reporter in 1970, largely followed the Handbook's system of categories and definitions. *The Restatement 2nd,* published in four volumes from 1965 to 1979, remains a vital resource to judges and lawyers today. Both the Handbook and the Restatement are cited thousands of times in lawyers' briefs and in court decisions, where both are viewed as objective and compelling authorities.

While Prosser's formulation of the four categories of invasion of privacy was largely set out in the Handbook, he followed up in the California Law Review with a 1960 article entitled simply Privacy, which has become one of the most widely cited of all law review articles.

Prosser described the four categories in these terms:

1. Intrusion upon the plaintiff's seclusion or solitude, or into his private affairs.
2. Public disclosure of embarrassing private facts about the plaintiff.
3. Publicity that places the plaintiff in a false light in the public eye.
4. Appropriation, for the defendant's advantage, of the plaintiff's name or likeness.

For better or worse, Prosser's own work was a principal factor in the survival and independent development of all four categories of privacy invasion.

Prosser's scholarship came at a time when U.S. law, like much else in the world, was becoming increasingly interconnected, sprawling, and complex. He saw the need to categorize and simplify developments across all U.S. jurisdictions to guide practitioners and judges confronted with often contradictory patterns in the judicial decisions and statutes that defined tort actions. This meant many painstaking hours examining and summarizing the written opinions of courts, and stating and describing the prevailing rules by which the cases' outcomes were determined. In some areas, however, the lines of cases were so thin or so contradictory as to leave Prosser room to push the envelope in ways that some believe went beyond the evidence. Such an area was privacy, a concept largely unknown in tort law until the publication of Louis Brandeis and Samuel Warren's famous article on the subject at the end of the nineteenth century, "The Right to Privacy." Prosser's legacy in privacy law is his success in convincing judges and practitioners that he had derived a discernible and principled order to the concept of privacy that could be applied with sensible and predictable results.

Harold W. Fuson, Jr.

Further Reading

Abraham, Kenneth S., and G. Edward White, "Prosser and His Influence." Journal of Tort Law 6, no. 1–2 (2013): 27–74. Virginia Public Law and Legal Theory Research Paper No. 2014–51.

Eldredge, Lawrence H. "William Lloyd Prosser.c California Law Review 60, no. 5 (September 1972): 1245–1251.

"Prosser's *Privacy* at 50." A Symposium on Privacy in the 21st Century at the University of California, Berkeley, School of Law (January 29, 2010).

Richards, Neil M., and Daniel J. Solove. "Prosser's Privacy Law: A Mixed Legacy." *California Law Review* 98, no. 6 (2010): 1887–1924.

See also: Brandeis, Louis Dembitz; Invasion of privacy; Privacy torts, The Right to Privacy

Protect America Act of 2007

Identification: Protect America Act of 2007 (PAA), Public Law 110–55. The federal statute passed in 2007 modifying the Foreign Intelligence Surveillance Act of 1978 (FISA).

The PAA was submitted to Congress by the George W. Bush administration, claiming concerns that FISA needed to be modernized. Remarkably, the bill passed both houses of Congress and was signed by the president just four days after it was first introduced in the Senate. The PAA contained several key modifications to FISA, including narrowing the scope of electronic surveillance that required a warrant or court order, creating a procedure under which the executive branch itself determined whether a warrant was necessary, and reducing the role of the Foreign Intelligence Surveillance Court (FISC) in intelligence-gathering oversight.

The original FISA required the U.S. government to obtain a warrant or court order if foreign intelligence acquisition of the contents of a wire communication to or from a person in the United States occurred in the United States. By contrast, the PAA created a new Section 105A of FISA that excluded from the FISA requirement to obtain a warrant or court order any surveillance "directed at a person reasonably believed to be located outside of the United States." The PAA did this by excluding such surveillance from the definition of electronic surveillance. Because FISA had required a warrant or court order for "electronic surveillance," the exclusion of surveillance directed at persons outside the United States from the definition of electronic surveillance meant that such surveillance, even if conducted by electronic means, would not require a warrant or court order. This development was particularly important because far more electronic information—particularly Internet communication—passed through the United States in 2008 than in 1978 when FISA was first created.

The PAA also created Section 105B of FISA, which established a new procedure by which the national intelligence apparatus could acquire foreign intelligence information without a warrant. Under Section 105B, intelligence acquisition could be conducted without a warrant or court order based solely on certifications by the Director of National Intelligence (DNI) and Attorney General (AG) that the intelligence acquisition concerned a person believed to be outside the United States; the acquisition involves obtaining the foreign intelligence information from or with the assistance of a communications service provider as it is transmitted or stored; a significant purpose of the acquisition is to obtain foreign intelligence information; and procedures are implemented to minimize the risk of targeting U.S. persons.

Finally, the PAA seemed to reduce the power of FISC to oversee a wide array of surveillance activities. Under the procedure established in the PAA, the AG and DNI submitted a copy of their certifications regarding specific acquisition to FISC, but the certifications were kept under seal and reviewed by FISC only if the acquisitions were later challenged, thus limiting FISC's role to an after-the-fact review of specific acquisition decisions. FISC was given a new responsibility of annually assessing whether federal agencies' procedures for determining whether surveillance was "electronic surveillance" were "clearly erroneous." Though this did constitute a new review, its practical oversight of government surveillance was limited for several reasons: Under this procedure, FISC was limited to reviewing the mechanism of government assessment of determining whether surveillance was or was not "electronic surveillance," not specific decisions themselves; the "clearly erroneous" standard of review was very deferential to government agencies; and the annual nature of the review meant significant time could pass before FISC would correct any deficiencies in the government decision-making process.

The PAA codified actions already being conducted under the president's Terrorism Surveillance Program, which itself raised significant questions of legal authority. The PAA's passage thus generated significant controversy, especially among civil liberties groups and constitutional scholars who saw the act as inconsistent with the Fourth Amendment to the U.S. Constitution. Despite being hailed by the government as an important tool in the U.S. fight against terrorism, the expanded warrantless surveillance authority under the PAA was not, in fact, limited to terrorism investigations. In fact, the PAA allowed warrantless intelligence acquisition without any requirement that the target of the intelligence gathering be related to terrorism, criminal activity, or even a foreign agent, as FISA had required. To some who objected, the PAA was thus a blank check for any kind of government surveillance.

Intended to be a temporary solution, the PAA had a sunset provision under which the operative sections expired 180 days after the PAA went into effect. Shortly before the expiration, Congress passed a fifteen-day extension. A replacement for the PAA, the FISA Amendments Act of 2008, was passed soon thereafter. While the FISA Amendments Act included some significant revisions, the PAA served as the first congressional sanction of warrantless electronic surveillance that had been barred by FISA.

Eric Merriam

Further Reading

Addicott, Jeffrey F., and Michael T. McCaul. "The Protect America Act of 2007: A Framework for Improving Intelligence Collection in the War on Terror." *Texas Review of Law and Politics* 13 (2008).

Cohn, Marjorie. "FISA Revised: A Blank Check for Domestic Spying." Huffington Post, August 9, 2007.

CRS Report for Congress. P.L. 110–55, the Protect America Act of 2007: Modifications to the Foreign Intelligence Surveillance Act. February 14, 2008.

See also: Foreign Intelligence Surveillance Act of 1978 (FISA); Foreign Intelligence Surveillance Court (FISC)

Public morality

Identification: The observance and subscription to the moral principles, ethical standards, and fundamental values in which a society enforces or upholds, either by statutory law, police work or social pressure, norms or expectations, and applied to everyday public life, from the regulation of behaviour of individual citizens in public spaces to the control of material appearing in the media.

Public morality includes the words, behaviors and actions regarded as in accordance with community standards of justice, honesty, good morals, and integrity. Crimes against public morality have been otherwise referred to as crimes against public decency, public moral crimes, and crimes of moral turpitude; they may also include some forms of deviancy.

In some cases, these offenses are also commonly known as vice crime—practices or behaviors deemed immoral, sinful or degrading—as they work to contaminate the social well-being of society, and bring to question aspects concerning the perpetrator's character or morality.

Provincial Archives of Alberta.

Attitudes towards public morality may change over time, and they may also vary by country and culture, and thus legal jurisdiction. For example, there may be differences in otherwise mundane behaviors, such as the consumption of food or alcohol on public transportation, while other public moral crimes, such as murder, will continue to remain a capital offense.

In today's society, there are many examples of issues and offenses often regulated by public morality, with some receiving more attention than others. For example, while religious codes have historically forbidden sex offenses such as seduction, adultery, polygamy, fornication, contraception, and homosexuality, tolerance and acceptability of these offenses have come to vary over time and across cultures. The same could be said of prostitution and solicitation of a prostitute, which fluctuate in legal status and acceptability by country and culture. Likewise, society has become more tolerant of some types of legally controlled and less visibly advertised forms of prostitution, such as escorts and sex tourism, and less tolerant of more visible and low-level types, such as the more commonly known street prostitution. A similar case is the consumption and production of pornography, and in particular, the exposure to minors. Cases of child or underage pornography have been regarded as much more serious public morality crimes. Other examples of public moral offenses include drug use, gambling, public intoxication and vulgarity, abortion, suicide and euthanasia, animal cruelty, and corruption, to name a few.

In the United States, the privacy rights and personal autonomy of American citizens are safeguarded by the Constitution, and since being established, the Supreme Court has interpreted these rights through several landmark decisions in relation to many areas surrounding public morality issues, such as marriage, procreation, homosexual activity, and pornography, to name a few. For example, with regard to marital privacy, after the State of Connecticut in 1965 convicted two individuals as accessories for providing information and prescription of contraception to a married couple in the case of *Griswold v. Connecticut*, 381 U.S. 479, the Supreme Court later overturned the ruling as the state law was deemed to be unconstitutional as violating the privacy rights of those in a marital relationship. Later in 1972, in the similar case of *Eisenstadt v. Baird*, 405 U.S. 438, the Supreme Court expanded upon privacy rights to include all procreative sexual intercourse, after reversing a ruling based on a Massachusetts law that banned the selling of contraceptives to unwed couples. With regard to pornography, in deciding *Stanley v. Georgia*, 394 U.S. 557 (1969), the Supreme Court invalidated all state laws prohibiting the private possession of obscene materials for adults. In 1986, a Georgia statute making same-sex sodomy illegal was upheld in *Bowers v. Hardwick*, 478 U.S. 186 (2003). *Bowers* was overturned with the Supreme Court's decision in *Lawrence v. Texas*, 539 U.S. 558 (2003), which upheld adults' rights to engage in private homosexual activity.

Privacy rights are growing increasingly complex in today's digital era, with the risk of violation more common than before. Advances in computer technology have drastically improved the capability and range of real-time communication and sharing of information, which have nonetheless afforded many benefits to global society. Consequently, new privacy vulnerabilities have been created, from identity theft and financial fraud by hackers, to abuses in electronic surveillance and interception by state actors. Over time, these new technologies have consequently established extensive repositories of metadata—telephone calls, e-mails, Internet browsing activity, etc.—and thus potentially evidence of public moral crimes and other information of significance to governments. As such, new types of surveillance programs have been created, which raise the issue of how privacy rights can continue to be protected while being invaded in the digital era. For example, in 2013 former CIA employee Edward Snowden publicly revealed information on several global surveillance and data harvesting programs on American citizens since the early 2000s by the U.S. National Security Agency.

With advances in social media, more individuals begin to shift their personal and private lives into a new technological sphere of public life whereby public morality offenses can easily become known. Consequently, in today's digital world lawmakers and governments have the challenge of ensuring the protection of privacy while continuing to develop new ways to maintain a safe society.

Michael J. Puniskis

Further Reading

Condit, Celeste Michelle. "Crafting Virtue: The Rhetorical Construction of Public Morality." *Quarterly Journal of Speech* 73, no. 1 (1987): 79–97.

George, Robert P. "The Concept of Public Morality." *American Journal of Jurisprudence* 45, no. 1 (2000): 17–31.

Hampshire, Stuart, ed. *Public and Private Morality*. New York: Cambridge University Press, 1978.

Richards, David A. J. "Liberalism, Public Morality, and Constitutional Law: Prolegomenon to a Theory of the Constitutional Right to Privacy." *Law and Contemporary Problems* 51, no. 1 (1988): 123–150.

Willbern, York. "Types and Levels of Public Morality." *Public Administration Review* 44, no. 2 (1984): 102–108.

Wolfe, C. (2000). "Public Morality and the Modern Supreme Court." American Journal of Modern Jurisprudence 45 (1): 66–92.

See also: Constitutional law; Electronic surveillance; *Griswold v. Connecticut*; *Lawrence v. Texas*; Metadata; National Security Agency (NSA); "The Right of Privacy"; Snowden, Edward Joseph; *Stanley v. Georgia*; Supreme Court of the United States

Public records

Identification: An essential journalistic tool promoting public accountability in government decision making.

The first federal FOIA statute was enacted in 1966, taking effect in 1967. It began its life humbly as a clause in the Administrative Procedure Act, which establishes the process for federal agencies to enact regulations. In signing the first FOIA statute into law, President Lyndon Johnson declared, "This legislation springs from one of our most essential principles: a democracy works best when the people have all of the information that the security of the nation will permit." Even then, the president's statement tellingly identified the central tension that underlies every open-records regime – the tension between an informed public and the government's ability to keep secrets in the name of public safety.

Wisconsin is credited with enacting the nation's first open-records statutes in 1848, shortly after it became a state. By the time Congress enacted the federal FOIA statute, a majority of states already had their own freedom-of-information laws; every state and the District of Columbia now has an analog to the federal statute. In a few states, including Florida and Montana, the right of access to public records is so deeply rooted in the culture that it is memorialized in the state constitution.

The Supreme Court has recognized a common-law right of access to public records, including the records of criminal judicial proceedings, in the landmark case of *Nixon v. Warner Communications, Inc.*, 425 U.S. 589 (1978), involving a publisher's request to make duplicates of former President Nixon's incriminating White House tapes. The Court has declined, however, to find that the right of access is of constitutional dimension. Most recently, the Court in *McBurney v. Young*, 133 S. Ct. 1709 (2013) rejected the theory that state public-records statutes giving preference to in-state requesters violate the citizenship protections of the Privileges and Immunities Clause, finding that the preference did not burden any constitutionally recognized right.

"Records" are given a broad interpretation and include any medium in which information is memorialized. In recent years, as the storage of information has migrated from paper to electronic media, requesters have been able to gather such information as records of security access cards swiping the card-reading devices on doorways of government buildings, or – in one memorable Florida case – the records of electronic tollway passes mounted on the dashboards of police cruisers.

Access to public records has enabled journalists to break news stories of national consequence, including the *Detroit Free Press'* 2009 Pulitzer Prize-winning investigative series that led to the removal and corruption conviction of Detroit Mayor Kwame Kilpatrick. Using Michigan's open-records act to obtain some 14,000 text messages sent on city-owned paging devices, *Free Press* reporters demonstrated that Kilpatrick and his aide and lover, Christine Beatty, lied under oath at a 2007 police whistleblower trial.

Although journalists are the most avid and highest-profile users of public records, a requester need not be a journalist or furnish a journalistic justification to obtain public records. Indeed, some of the highest-profile conflicts over access to records have involved citizen activists or industries with a business need to obtain information, such as *NLRB v. Robbins Tire & Rubber Co.*, 437 U.S. 214 (1978), in which a manufacturer sought (ultimately, without success) to compel the National Labor Relations Board to release its files of interviews with witnesses in an impending NLRB enforcement proceeding.

The default assumption of every open-records statute is that the statute must be liberally construed in favor of openness. Accordingly, as a federal appeals court stated in the early FOIA case of *Vaughn v. Rosen*, 484 F.2d 820, 823 (D.C. Cir. 1973), "exemptions from disclosure must be construed narrowly, in such a way as to provide the maximum access consonant with the overall purpose of the Act." With rare exceptions, the exemptions in federal FOIA and its state analogs are permissive, not mandatory, meaning that the custodian has discretion to release more than the bare minimum required by law, as the Supreme Court explained in *Chrysler*

Corp. v. Brown, 441 U.S. 281, 293 (1979). While the federal FOIA statute has nine relatively broad categorical exemptions, state statutes commonly have dozens, often narrowly targeted to satisfy industry lobbyists; the Georgia statute, for instance, has 46 enumerated exemptions (many with multiple parts), including carve-outs for the unpublished data of university researchers and measurements of farmers' water usage. In a June 2012 report, "The state of public records laws: Access denied," the Center for Public Integrity concluded that the proliferation of special-interest exemptions – including a commonplace one allowing government officials to withhold "draft" versions of documents or documents reflecting policymakers' "deliberative process" – has rendered the statutes largely ineffective.

A frequent source of tension between government efficiency and the public's right to know involves the investigative files of police and regulatory agencies. Exemption 7 in the federal FOIA statute, which is mirrored in nearly every state open-records law, originally permitted agencies to withhold all "records or information compiled for law enforcement purposes." In 1974, concerned that agencies were abusing Exemption 7 to forever conceal records no longer of any practical use in ongoing investigations, Congress amended FOIA to clarify that law enforcement records could be withheld only if certain specified harms could be demonstrated, such as compromising an investigation or invading personal privacy. Notwithstanding this clarification, the breadth of the "law enforcement" exemption remains a rich vein of conflict between requesters and the custodians of records.

In an influential 1989 case, *Department of Justice v. Reporters Committee for Freedom of the Press*, 489 U.S. 749, the Supreme Court refused to order the FBI to disclose "rap sheets" consisting of compilations of police and court records from throughout the country. Although the contents of the rap sheets were largely already a matter of public record if a requester were able to physically canvass courthouses nationwide,

the Court reasoned that those records were "practically obscure" and that making the once-inaccessible records readily available for inspection would unreasonably violate the personal privacy of those named in the files.

As the Internet makes public records more readily searchable, and more enduringly accessible beyond a single fleeting broadcast, policymakers are revisiting long-held presumptions about the openness of records that might prove harmful to individuals' reputations or traumatic to families. For instance, in 2005 the Florida legislature rapidly enacted a statutory exemption for autopsy photos after news media organizations sued to obtain records of the autopsy of legendary auto racer Dale Earnhardt, who died in a crash at the Daytona Motor Speedway. The exemption was justified in part by the possibility that a family member might be traumatized by stumbling onto the photos during an Internet search. Similarly, the proliferation of extortionate websites offering to un-publish jailhouse mug-shots for a fee led to a wave of statutory exemptions withdrawing booking photos from the public record.

In addition to the statutory exemptions, various state and federal privacy statutes have been interpreted as overriding the public's right of access. Among them is the Drivers Privacy Protection Act of 1994, 18 U.S.C. § 2721, a federal statute that prohibits the disclosure of personally identifiable information from motor vehicle records maintained by state licensing agencies. Other federal statutes that have been interpreted to override the right of access to otherwise-public documents include the Family Educational Rights and Privacy Act (student educational records) and the Health Insurance Portability and Accountability Act (medical records kept by health care providers or insurers).

In recent years, litigation has arisen around electronic messages exchanged by government employees in the course of their official duties. Access to such ephemeral messages, especially when sent on non-government-controlled devices, presents new challenges in the retrieval, retention and storage of records, to which government agencies are struggling to adapt. In an August 2015 ruling, *Nissen v. Pierce County*, the Washington Supreme Court determined that text messages sent and received by a county prosecutor in the course of doing government business were subject to disclosure under the state Public Records Act even if they were sent on a personally owned device outside of business hours.

Public records statutes almost never extend to the judicial branch of government and rarely to the legislative branch. A number of quasi-governmental entities – such as university fund-raising foundations, public hospital authorities and lobbying associations for city and county governments – exist in a gray zone of accessibility, frequently resulting in litigation. Otherwise-private entities are not typically required to abide by open-records statutes merely because they receive substantial taxpayer money (for example, construction companies that accept government contracts, or private universities that benefit from federal financial aid). However, when a private entity performs a traditional governmental function under state supervision – such as contractually operating a prison – the courts have regarded the private actor as an "arm of the state" subject to disclosing the records of that function.

The federal FOIA statute provides a limit of 10 working days to fulfill a request, though in practice that deadline is aspirational and, due to the delay inherent in bringing a judicial challenge, of little enforceable value. A denial or refusal to respond may be appealed internally within the agency, but there, too, the statutory deadline of 20 days to respond is practically unenforceable and widely ignored. A 2007 study by the National Security Archive at George Washington University found that federal agencies were so backlogged on FOIA compliance that five of them (including the State Department, FBI and CIA) had "pending" requests dating back 15 years or longer. In a May 2015 report, the Justice Department's Office of Information Policy

documented 160,000 unfulfilled federal FOIA requests that were past the statutory deadline, a spike of 70 percent over the previous year. Most state open-records statutes merely require compliance within a "reasonable time," though a minority impose turnaround times as short as three days – which, as with the federal deadline, are seldom observed in practice.

Open-records statutes typically are enforced by way of a private civil action by an aggrieved requester. A handful of states (including Iowa, Maryland and Pennsylvania) provide state administrative remedies short of filing suit, by way of executive-branch "FOI councils" that can render interpretations of the law. But in most states, a requester's only resort is to initiate a civil complaint. Although criminal penalties are theoretically possible, prosecutions are almost unheard-of. The standard penalty for noncompliance is, at most, an order for the agency to pay the prevailing requester's attorney fees (and under many state statutes, attorney fees are awarded only upon proof that records were withheld purposefully in bad faith). Consequently, open-records statutes are widely regarded as "toothless" and easily defied. In a rare exception, the director of the Little Rock, Ark., housing authority was tried and convicted in June 2015 on a misdemeanor count of violating the Arkansas Freedom of Information Act for demanding more than $16,000 to process a newspaper's public-records request with no documentation that the charges had any basis in reality.

The accessibility of public records has increasingly been hampered by unaffordable fees beyond the reach of all but the deepest-pocketed requester. It is not uncommon for requesters to be presented with five-figure invoices – payable in advance – to cover the cost of retrieving and producing records; the scope of costs taxable to the requester varies by state and is a matter of continuing disagreement. Florida Gov. Rick Scott declared upon taking office in 2011 that agencies were to begin assessing the full cost of compliance with requests for public records including a "special service charge" for requests considered especially laborious, a directive denounced by press-rights groups as a blow to transparency. Ironically, Scott accepted an unprecedented $700,000 settlement in August 2015 to resolve a series of seven lawsuits alleging that he and the state's attorney general circumvented the state public-records law by doing state business on private email accounts and then withholding the messages in defiance of a public-records request.

Frank LoMonte

Further Reading

Richard J. Peltz-Steele, *The Law of Access to Government* (Carolina Academic Press 2012)

David Cuillier and Charles N. Davis, The Art of Access: Strategies for Acquiring Public Records (CQ Press 2010)

See also: Educational setting, privacy in an; Family Educational Rights and Privacy Act (FERPA); Freedom of Information Act (FOIA); Health Insurance Portability and Accountability Act (HIPPA); Law enforcement; Medical confidentiality, right to

Publicity, right of

Identification: A tort claim that many states recognize as a derivation of one of the traditional four privacy torts. Broadly defined, the right of publicity recognizes celebrities' economic interest in controlling or limiting the distribution of their public identities or personas. States that recognize the right of publicity often define a person's image or identity quite broadly to include one's name, likeness, voice, or any other identifiable trait that evokes the celebrity's image in the public eye.

Beginning in the early 1900s, courts in several states began to recognize the right of a private person to recover compensation from anyone who violated the right to privacy. The courts recognized the emotional harm suffered by individuals whose privacy was invaded without their consent. Some of the earliest privacy tort claims were filed against advertising companies for using the photographs or sketches of private individuals in commercial advertisements without the subjects' consent. One of the four most widely recognized privacy torts allows a person to sue someone else who uses the person's name or likeness for the other's benefit without authorization. Like all privacy torts, this state law right was designed to provide a legal remedy for the emotional harm that a private person suffers from an invasion or violation of the right to privacy.

Traditionally, the right to privacy was considered waived if a person engaged in actions that the courts considered inconsistent with a desire for privacy. For example, when a celebrity entertainer or a political figure sued for violating the right to privacy, early courts would not recognize the claim because the famous person was considered to have implicitly given up the right to remain unknown and anonymous, out of the public eye.

As the right to privacy evolved, state courts gradually allowed even celebrities to recover compensation from another person, usually a business, for using their names and likenesses for commercial purposes without the celebrity's consent. In effect, the privacy right traditionally known as protection from misappropriation of a person's name or likeness was extended to celebrities. States that have recognized right of publicity claims have implicitly disregarded the fact that celebrities, by definition, have waived their privacy rights by becoming famous personalities.

The policy foundation for the right of publicity is twofold. First, recognizing the right allows a celebrity to seek compensation when someone else exploits the value of a celebrity's well-known identity without sharing the economic gain with the celebrity. Second, the right of publicity recognizes that a celebrity has an economic interest in limiting or controlling how the celebrity's recognizable image is distributed commercially for advertising or other purposes. For example, some commercial uses of a celebrity's identity might harm or otherwise diminish the person's professional reputation. If the celebrity does not consent, the unauthorized use may harm the capacity to earn an income from the celebrity's public identity. When a court recognizes a celebrity's right of publicity claim, the law requires the defending party who exploited that right to compensate the celebrity for the lost economic value of the celebrity's public persona.

Along with the development of mass media, the right of publicity evolved gradually, beginning with the so-called golden age of radio in the 1930s and 1940s. Fred Waring, a famous orchestra conductor, filed a lawsuit against a radio broadcasting company to prevent it from playing a musical recording by his orchestra. The case reached the Pennsylvania Supreme Court in 1937, and the court upheld Waring's right to stop the broadcasting company from playing the record on the radio without his consent.

The Pennsylvania Supreme Court began its opinion by observing the novelty of Waring's claim:

> The problems involved in this case have never before been presented to an American or an English court. They challenge the vaunted genius of the law to adapt itself to new social and industrial conditions and to the progress of science and invention. For the first time in history human action can be photographed and visually reportrayed by the motion picture. Sound can now be mechanically captured and reproduced, not only by means of the phonographs for an audience physically present, but, through broadcasting, for practically all the world as simultaneous auditors. Just as the birth of the printing press made it necessary for equity to inaugurate a protection for literary and intellectual property, so these latter-day

inventions make demands upon the creative and ever-evolving energy of equity to extend that protection so as adequately to do justice under current conditions of life. (*Waring v. WDAS Broad. Station*, 194 A. 631 (Pa. 1937))

The Pennsylvania Supreme Court recognized that Waring's interest in controlling the publication of the musical recording was in the nature of a property right to prevent misappropriation of the orchestra's unique sound. The court also relied on the state's common law right against unfair competition in enforcing Waring's claim against the broadcasting company.

In 1953, a famous professional boxer filed a lawsuit seeking compensation from a television station for airing a movie, without his consent, depicting one of his old prizefights. The lawsuit eventually made its way to the U.S. Court of Appeals for the Third Circuit in *Ettore v. Philco Television Broad. Corp.*, 229 F.2d 481 (3d Cir., 1956). The legal issue was whether the prizefighter had a legal remedy against the television station for airing the movie in four different states without his consent. The Third Circuit Court of Appeals first observed that the right asserted was more akin to a property right than a right to privacy: "The state of the law is still that of a haystack in a hurricane. . . . We read of the right of privacy, of invasion of property rights, of breach of contract, of equitable servitude, of unfair competition; and there are even suggestions of unjust enrichment." In holding for the prizefighter, the court reasoned that broadcasting the boxer's performance without compensating him was a legal wrong that "vitally affect[ed] his livelihood."

One of the most important court cases involving the state right of publicity was *Zacchini v. Scripps-Howard Broadcasting Co.*, 433 U.S. 562 (1977), decided by the U.S. Supreme Court in 1977. The case involved an entertainer who had performed his human cannonball act at a county fair in Ohio. A television reporter videotaped the live performance without the entertainer's consent. Later that day, the video was replayed on a television news program. Hugo Zacchini, the entertainer, sued the news broadcasting company for violating his "right to the publicity value of his performance." The broadcasting company argued that it had a First Amendment constitutional right to air the videotape because it was broadcasting a matter of public interest. In effect, the company argued that its First Amendment privilege to air the news on television prevented the entertainer from filing suit under Ohio law to enforce his right to bar the unauthorized replay of the video recording. The Supreme Court upheld the entertainer's right under Ohio law, rejecting the broadcaster's First Amendment argument. Thus, the Supreme Court disagreed that the broadcasting company's right to disseminate the news outweighed Zacchini's right to protect the economic value of his human cannonball performance.

The right of publicity has since been recognized in one form or another by about half the states. In some states, the courts have interpreted the right to privacy (in the form of misappropriation of one's name or likeness) to extend to celebrities, even though they have willingly become public personalities. In other states, the courts have recognized a distinct right of publicity, acknowledging that the right provides a remedy not for the emotional distress traditionally associated with an invasion of privacy but rather for the reduced economic value of one's public persona or identity. An increasing number of states have enacted statutes that authorize civil claims for violating the right of publicity.

One of the most interesting recent developments with respect to the right of publicity involves the nature of the right as a descendible property interest. The common law has traditionally recognized the right to privacy as a personal right that expires at the end of the individual's life. In contrast, the right of publicity reflects the economic value of the celebrity's public persona. For that reason, many courts have addressed whether the right of publicity survives beyond the lifetime of the celebrity.

Some state courts have been reluctant to interpret the common law right of publicity to extend to the celebrity's heirs. However, an increasing number of states have enacted statutes that allow the right of publicity to survive for a number of years after the death of the celebrity. Indiana's statute is among the most liberal; it provides that the right of publicity continues for 100 years after the celebrity's death. Other states, including Pennsylvania and California, have enacted statutes extending the right of publicity for thirty to seventy years after death. Based on these newly enacted statutes, some courts have retroactively applied them to protect the rights of publicity of long-deceased celebrities, including Dr. Martin Luther King, Marilyn Monroe, Elvis Presley, and "Muppets" creator Jim Henson.

J. Lyn Entrikin

Further Reading

Elder, David A. *Privacy Torts* § 6.7. Westlaw current through June 2015 (descendibility and inheritability of the right of publicity).

Faber Jonathan L. "Indiana: A Celebrity-Friendly Jurisdiction." *Res Gestae: J. Ind. State B. Ass'n* 43 (March 2000). http://www.luminarygroup.com/images/ResGestae_2000–03.pdf.

Richardson, Jeffrey. "Michigan Needs a Statutory Right of Publicity." *Michigan Business Journal* 86, no. 26 (September 2007).

Savare, Matthew, and John Wintermute. "Right of Publicity Issues in Emerging Media." Los Angeles Law 38, no. 10 (May 2015)

See also: Consent; Legal Evolution of Privacy Rights in the United States; The Right to Privacy

R

Reno v. Condon, 528 U.S. 141 (2000)

Identification: A unanimous decision, with a majority opinion by Chief Justice William Rehnquist, in which the U.S. Supreme Court ruled that the Driver's Privacy Protection Act of 1994 (DPPA), 18 U.S.C. 2271–2725, was a constitutional federal statutory scheme.

The DPPA instituted a regulatory framework that limited states' ability to release personal information contained in state motor vehicle department records. The U.S. Congress passed the DPPA in response to a growing trend of women being stalked or harmed after their attackers used vehicle license plate numbers to obtain personal information about them from state motor vehicle departments. In addition, many states were selling drivers' information for commercial purposes. States and others who had benefited from the sale or use of drivers' information challenged the constitutionality of the DPPA in federal court on multiple occasions. In 2000, pursuant to litigation initiated by the state of South Carolina, the Supreme Court held that the DPPA was constitutional.

At the time, South Carolina law permitted the state to sell drivers' information to private parties as long as the information was not used for telephone solicitation. South Carolina and its attorney general filed suit in the U.S. District Court for the District of South Carolina challenging the DPPA's constitutionality. Among other allegations, South Carolina contended that the DPPA effectively required the state to implement a federal regulatory program. South Carolina argued that this violated the U.S. Constitution's Tenth Amendment federalism principles limiting Congress's ability to govern states' behavior.

South Carolina's Tenth Amendment federalism argument was based primarily on principles delineated in two Supreme Court cases, *New York v. United States*, 505 U.S. 144 (1992), and *Printz v. United States*, 521 U.S. 898 (1997). In *New York*, the Supreme Court stated that "[w]hile Congress has substantial powers to govern the Nation directly . . . the Constitution has never been understood to confer upon Congress the ability to require the States to govern according to Congress' instructions" (*New York*, 505 U.S. at 162). That is, Congress cannot compel states to implement and enforce specific laws.

The Supreme Court expanded on the limitations that the Tenth Amendment imposes on congressional regulation of the States in *Printz* (521 U.S. at 935):

We held *in New* York that Congress cannot compel the States to enact or enforce a federal regulatory program. Today we hold that Congress cannot circumvent that prohibition by conscripting the State's officers directly. The federal Government may neither issue directives requiring the States to address particular problems, nor command the States' officers . . . to administer or enforce a federal regulatory program.

The District Court agreed with South Carolina that the DPPA was unconstitutional because, in contravention of *New York* and *Printz*, it "commanded the States to implement federal policy by requiring them to regulate the dissemination and use of these records" [*Condon v. Reno*, 972 F. Supp. 977, 984–85 (D.S.C. 1997), *overruled by Condon*, 528 U.S. 141].

The United States appealed the District Court's ruling to the U.S. Court of Appeals for the Fourth Circuit. On appeal, the United States argued that *New York* and *Printz* federalism principles were inapplicable because the DPPA did not require states to regulate their citizens' behavior. Rather, the United States contended, the DPPA was a generally applicable regulatory scheme that governed both the states' conduct in maintaining a driver information database and private parties' conduct in accessing and using that information. The United States argued that this generally applicable law was passed pursuant to Congress's power to regulate interstate commerce under the commerce clause of the U.S. Constitution. Thus, the United States contended that because the law applied to both states and private parties, the law did not commandeer state legislative processes or officials, and *New York* and *Printz* did not apply. Rejecting this argument, the Fourth Circuit concluded that the DPPA applied only to states and was not generally applicable; therefore, in the court's view, the DPPA was still subject to the strictures outlined in *New York* and *Printz*. Consequently, the Fourth Circuit agreed with the District Court that the DPPA forced South Carolina to administer a federal regulatory program in violation of the Tenth Amendment.

The United States appealed the Fourth Circuit's ruling, and the Supreme Court granted review. In Chief Justice Rehnquist's writing about the unanimous opinion, the Court initially explained that the drivers' information, which the states had offered for sale, was used to solicit drivers within the stream of interstate commerce. Therefore, Congress had authority to regulate the release of drivers' information pursuant to the U.S. Constitution's commerce clause [*Condon v. Reno*, 155 F.3d 453, 462–63 (4th Cir. 1998), *overruled by Condon*, 528 U.S. 141].

The Supreme Court's opinion emphasized that, despite Congress's commerce clause authority to regulate the use of drivers' information, it was still necessary to determine whether the DPPA complied with Tenth Amendment principles. The Court, accepting South Carolina's assertion that the state would have to expend resources complying with the DPPA, concluded that, despite this burden on state resources, *New York* and *Printz* did not apply. The Court based its conclusion on *South Carolina v. Baker*, 485 U.S. 505, 514–15 (1988), a Tenth Amendment case. Explaining that the DPPA did not unconstitutionally commandeer state government, the Court wrote that "[a]ny federal regulation demands compliance. That a State wishing to engage in certain activity must take administrative and sometimes legislative action to comply with federal standards regulating that activity is a commonplace that presents no constitutional defect" (*Condon*, 528 U.S. at 150–51). In accord with *Baker*, the Court reasoned that the DPPA does not require the states to regulate their citizens but rather mandates that if a state chooses to maintain a driver information database, it must do so pursuant to the DPPA's regulations.

Finally, the Court rejected South Carolina's argument that the federalism principles in *New York* and *Printz* must apply in lieu of those in *Baker* because the DPPA regulated only states and not individuals. The Court concluded that the DPPA was generally applicable because it "regulate[d] the universe of entities that participate as suppliers to the market for motor vehicle information," applying to both the states supplying the information and the private parties purchasing and using it (ibid. at 151). Thus, the Court held that principles in *Baker* governed, and the DPPA was constitutionally valid and did not violate the Tenth Amendment.

Paul Riermaier

Further Reading

Chemerinsky, Erwin. "Right Result, Wrong Reasons: *Reno v. Condon.*" *Oklahoma City University Law Review* 25 (2000): 823–841.

Odom, Thomas H., and Gregory S. Feder. "Challenging the Federal Driver's Privacy Protection Act: The Next Step in Developing a Jurisprudence of Process-Oriented Federalism under the Tenth Amendment." *University of Miami Law Review* 53 (1998): 71–167.

See also: Constitutional law; Driver's Privacy Protection Act (DDPA); Privacy laws, federal; Privacy laws, state; Supreme Court of the United States

Repository for Individuals of Special Concern (RISC)

Identification: Implemented throughout the United States on August 25, 2011, as part of the Federal Bureau of Investigation's (FBI's) Next Generation Identification (NGI) system.

The NGI system compares the fingerprints in its database against a registry of 2.5 million sets of fingerprints of people such as wanted persons, known or suspected terrorists, and sex offenders. The database is designed to include individuals who are repeat offenders of the most serious crimes. RISC was tested in several states for two years prior to national implementation. While some jurisdictions have local versions of RISC, RISC is the only national database that can assist in identifying individuals wanted for serious crimes in other states.

RISC is a searchable subset of the NGI database's worst offenders, including high-risk offenders such as wanted persons, sex offenders, known or suspected terrorists, and other persons for which rapid identification is needed. RISC seeks to assist law enforcement officers in quickly identifying possible risks presented by suspects and other individuals encountered during traffic stops and other, similar situations. Using this database allows law enforcement to screen detainees and criminal suspects against the database. Through better and more accurate technology such as RISC, the FBI claims that it is providing a more efficient and more effective service. To use the RISC system, a law enforcement officer using a mobile device takes two fingerprints from a subject and remotely queries the database to retrieve results within ten seconds. RISC currently assists thousands of state and local police officers capture and submit images of fingerprints using mobile devices. RISC is authorized under 28 U.S.C. Sections 533 and 534. Supplemental regulatory authorities include 28 C.F.R. Section 0.85, part 20, and 50.12.

A key benefit of RISC for law enforcement is that it makes the searches of NGI by authorized users in field settings much faster and more efficient. Other important benefits include greater protection for the public and law enforcement personnel, enhanced investigative support, and reduced impact of law enforcement activities on innocent persons with biographic similarities to persons of investigative interest.

Authorized NGI users submit a query to RISC electronically using a maximum of ten fingerprints, usually in interaction with potential suspects or similar encounters. The fingerprints are captured by a mobile fingerprint device and transmitted wirelessly to the user agency's existing criminal justice infrastructure, then on to RISC. The submission results in an automated search of RISC records and a generation of response within seconds of the submission. The response is forwarded to the requestor's mobile device. RISC responses are either red, yellow, green, or reject:

- A *red response* is a hit, indicating an identification of a highly probable individual in RISC. A red response is not viewed as positive identification but rather as a high likelihood of identification. The submitting agency must supplement the RISC response with other information to confirm whether the candidate returned is indeed the person whose prints were submitted.

- A *yellow response* is a possible hit, indicating identification of a possible candidate (or candidates) in RISC, but it is one below the level of confidence established for a highly probable match (red response). Thus, the yellow response may be used only as an investigative tool providing leads for further investigative inquiries.
- A *green response* indicates no hit; that is, the search did not locate a matching candidate in the RISC.
- A *reject response* means that the quality of the RISC submission is too low to be used for a RISC search.

In all cases, the RISC response is based solely on a search of RISC, and a negative response from RISC does not necessarily preclude the possibility of responsive records in other biometric or name-based repositories. Also, RISC users may not rely solely on RISC responses to initiate any law enforcement action. Instead, search responses are intended to provide potential links between submitted images and true identities that must be considered with the totality of information available to officers or investigators.

For several reasons, RISC implicates major privacy concerns. In safeguarding privacy and protecting the public's rights and civil liberties, NGI is subject to the same security protections, access limitations, and quality control standards as currently exists for the Integrated Automated Fingerprint Identification System (IAFIS).

A RISC search submitted from a mobile device is not designed or expected to take the place of customary booking procedures that utilize ten-print submissions. The FBI emphasizes to all system users that RISC responses are not to be considered "positive" identifications and must be used only as investigative aids together with other investigative processes and information. In addition, a RISC search makes available biometric-based searches in time-sensitive situations where previously only name-based searches

were viable. These biometric-based checks can provide more accuracy than name-based checks alone, reducing the number of erroneous identifications in these situations.

One privacy vulnerability is that RISC's enhanced search-and-response capabilities provide an increased ability to locate information about a specific person that might not otherwise be discovered as quickly or as efficiently, or might never be discovered at all. Although information in NGI and NCIC has been lawfully acquired and accessible to authorized NGI and NCIC users, currently that information may be more functionally obscure as a result of users having to check multiple systems separately or encountering longer response times. This risk is mitigated, however, by the advantages of being able to move quickly and accurately to locate responsive information about a specific person. This capability permits more complete and timely investigative analysis, including more effective and efficient identification of perpetrators and persons who may present increased threats to the safety of the public and law enforcement personnel. The privacy risk is also mitigated by facilitating a more rapid means to eliminate misidentifications and/ or rule out concerns that could adversely affect innocent persons.

Another privacy risk could be the intake of records that do not belong in the RISC repository. This risk is mitigated by Criminal Justice Information Services (CJIS) procedures that ensure that fingerprints of wanted KSTs and sex offenders are appropriately flagged as they are entered into IAFIS. RISC extracts records based on those flags.

RISC searches are available only to users authorized to initiate searches of NGI and NCIC for authorized law enforcement or national security purposes. Routine uses for information in NGI are currently promulgated in the system of records notice (SORN) for the FBI Fingerprint Identification Records System (FIRS), and routine uses for information in NCIC are promulgated in NCIC's SORN. In addition to routine use disclosures, this information may be disclosed under other circumstances authorized by the Privacy Act, including disclosures to those Department of Justice (DOJ) personnel who need the information in the performance of their duties.

The results of RISC searches are used by law enforcement officers as leads to determine the identity and relevant history of the subject and take appropriate investigatory action, and, if necessary, precautions for the protection of the investigating law enforcement officer.

The Justice Department may make RISC submissions and receive suspect information similar to other state, local, and federal law enforcement partners. This will primarily encompass the following Justice Department agencies whose missions typically involve interactions in field settings with persons associated with criminal activity or otherwise having a lawful investigative or national security interest: the FBI, the Drug Enforcement Administration (DEA), the Bureau of Alcohol, Tobacco, Firearms and Explosives (ATF), the Federal Bureau of Prisons (BOP), the U.S. National Central Bureau of the International Criminal Police Organization (INTERPOL), and the United States Marshals Service (USMS). In addition, any DOJ component that has previously submitted a latent fingerprint to the NGI ULF file will be notified if a RISC submission hits on that latent fingerprint.

The results of RISC searches are given primarily to authorized NGI and NCIC users to alert a submitting agency's on-scene employees in real time whenever the subject of a RISC submission may be a wanted person, registered sex offender, known or appropriately suspected terrorist, or other person of heightened investigative interest or who may present increased risk to the public and/or to law enforcement personnel.

As RISC searches are being done in the conduct of criminal investigations or issuance of arrest warrants, the affected individuals may not always be specifically aware that personal information is being collected and disseminated. It is the Justice Department's view that individuals planning or engaging in criminal activities may reasonably be charged with constructive knowledge that law enforcement will seek to collect and lawfully disseminate all relevant information to identify them and to deter or prevent them from committing crimes.

Because the information in the RISC subset is collected in connection with law enforcement investigations and/or processing, the suspects involved in these investigations generally do not have the right or opportunity to object to the collection of this information by the source agencies, nor to the forwarding of the collected information for retention in NGI and/or NCIC, nor to the collation of the RISC subset from information in NGI.

Whether certain individuals have the right or opportunity to object to the collection of the fingerprints used to initiate a RISC check, and the consequences for objecting, depends on the location and circumstances of the particular field encounter from which the fingerprints were obtained. All collections must be lawfully obtained under the laws, regulations, and policies to which the agency that obtained the fingerprints may be subject. In many instances, the fingerprints for RISC checks may be collected in connection with law enforcement investigations and/or processing in which the individuals generally may not be accorded the right or opportunity to object to the collection. In other instances, however, a submitting agency may be required under its governing laws, regulations, and/or policies to provide an individual with the right or opportunity to object to the collection; personnel of an encountering agency may, according to their discretion, voluntarily elect to ask an individual to consent to the collection. In some situations where an individual declines to consent to collection, the agency may nonetheless be entitled to proceed with nonconsensual collection based on alternative authority. In other situations, however, an individual's failure to consent may be controlling, and the encountering agency will have to forego the collection and resolve the encounter without the benefit of a RISC check. Even where an individual is able successfully to decline to be subject to a RISC check, the consequences vary. In some circumstances, a RISC check does not affect the eventual outcome of an encounter, so the declination will have no consequences to the individual. In other circumstances, the results of the RISC check could have altered the outcome of an encounter. This might result in an individual's avoiding further law enforcement interest if the encountering agency were aware of derogatory RISC information (e.g., a red, or hit, response), but it could result in an individual's being subjected to prolonged law enforcement interest that might have been avoided if the encountering agency were aware of a nonderogatory RISC response (e.g., a green or no-hit response).

Because of the nature of RISC interactions with suspects, 28 C.F.R. Sections 16.30–16.34 and 20.34 provide the only means for access and amendment of criminal history records. Under these regulations, a subject of an FBI identification record may obtain a copy of his or her own record for review and correction. If the subject thereof believes, after reviewing his or her identification record, that it is incorrect or incomplete in any respect and wishes changes, corrections, or updating, he or she should make application directly to the agency that contributed the questioned information. The subject may also direct his or her challenge to the FBI CJIS Division. The FBI will then forward the challenge to the agency that submitted the data, requesting that agency to verify or correct the challenged entry.

The opportunity to seek access to or redress information in the source records of a contributing federal, state, local, or tribal agency is controlled by the laws and procedures applicable to that agency. To the extent that an agency that contributes information to NGI and/or NCIC has a process in place for access to or correction of the contributing agency's source records, individuals may avail themselves of the process,

and if this results in a correction of the source records, the contributing agency should in turn make appropriate corrections in the information contributed to NGI and/or NCIC.

RISC is subject to the same extensive security protections, access limitations, and quality control standards in existence for NGI. Previously identified risks related to potential misuse of the system have been addressed via training, audits, and sanctions. To mitigate any potential risks in these areas, NGI data and infrastructure (which encompasses RISC) are maintained within FBI-controlled secure, restricted areas and are accessible only by authorized personnel. Wireless transmissions and mobile devices outside FBI control are subject to the CJIS Security Policy.

Data integrity, privacy, and security remain a significant part of the enhanced system and the NGI contract. The developer is required to follow all CJIS Division guidelines, appropriate regulations, and specific statutes. Those agencies and entities with electronic connectivity must comply with requirements of the CJIS Division's security standards and operating policies.

The Justice Department claims that RISC does not constitute a new collection type or collection purpose not already encompassed by NGI or NCIC, nor does it represent any expansion of users authorized to access this information. Instead, the Justice Department asserts that RISC merely collates a subset of existing NGI identity records to permit employment of specialized biometric-based search techniques in field encounters, rapid searches of the collated information, and rapid responses to authorized users. In addition, RISC automatically searches RISC submissions against the existing NGI ULF and searches NCIC for any existing NCIC information appropriate for inclusion in RISC responses.

The Justice Department admits that RISC does present certain privacy risks. However, the agency said that these risks can be appropriately mitigated. Specifically, they are mitigated through long-standing technology protections present in the underlying NGI and NCIC systemsl the existing eligibility limitations and careful vetting of system users; and the existing access policies, training requirements, and audits. Privacy risks are further mitigated by the responsibility imposed on each user agency to ensure that the collection and use of fingerprints obtained for RISC submissions are lawful and permissible under the laws and policies of the governmental jurisdiction to which the user agency is subject.

As appropriately mitigated, any additional privacy impact is outweighed by the RISC advantages, including the added flexibility and simplicity via accommodation of searches using fewer than ten fingerprints; rapid real-time search and response capability in time-critical field encounters; enhanced investigative support and crime solving; enhanced accuracy and privacy protection over mere name-based searching, including reduction of false positives; and greater protection for the public and law enforcement personnel.

Further Reading

Dempsey, John S., and Linda S. Forst. *An Introduction to Policing.* 6th ed. Clifton Park, NY: Delmar Cengage Learning, 2012.

Follow-up Review of the FBI's Progress toward Biometric Interoperability between IAFIS and IDENT. Washington, D.C.: U.S. Dept. of Justice, Office of Inspector General, Evaluations and Inspections Division, 2006.

Kalaf, William M. *Arizona Law Enforcement Biometrics Identification and Information Sharing Technology Framework.* Ft. Belvoir: Defense Technical Information Center, 2010.

Li, Chang. *New Technologies for Digital Crime and Forensics Devices, Applications, and Software.* Hershey, PA: Information Science Reference, 2011.

Wilson, C. L., and C. L. Wilson. *Biometric Data Specification for Personal Identity Verification.* Rockville, MD: NIST, 2013.

Woodward, John D. *Biometrics a Look at Facial Recognition.* Santa Monica, Calif.: RAND, 2003.

See also: Criminal justice (criminal procedure); Integrated Automated Fingerprint Identification System (IAFIS); Law enforcement; Next Generation Identification (NGI); Terrorism and privacy

Right to be forgotten

Identification: A principle that gives a data subject (an individual whose personal data relating to him- or herself is in dispute) the right to demand that search engines delete the data subject's personal data.

The Right to Be Forgotten stems from the European Union's Data Protection Directive labeled 95/46/EC, outlining "the processing of personal data and . . . free movement of such data" and a natural person's particular right to privacy. This directive was enacted in 1995, but a contemporary interpretation was not adopted until a landmark decision in Case C-131/12, *Google Spain SL, Google, Inc. v. Agencia Española de Protección de Datos (AEPD), Mario Costeja González,* CJEU 13 May 2014, that allows data subjects "the right to obtain from the controller the erasure of personal data relating to them and the abstention from further dissemination of such data, and to obtain from third parties the erasure of any links to, or copy, or replication of that data . . ." under certain conditions (Data Protection Directive, art. 17, Oct. 24, 1995, 95/46/EC). Currently, the Right to Be Forgotten is limited to citizens of member countries of the European Union, but it is open to search engines operating outside the European Union.

The original 95/46/EC Directive was proposed in 1990, when the Internet was in its early stage of development. The directive passed in 1995, and the Internet's most popular search engine, Google, made its debut three years later.

Google v. AEPD, González

In the *Google v. AEPD, Gonzalez* case, the European Court of Justice decided the liability of third parties. In this case, Google Spain and Google Inc. lawfully published links to web pages with true information on data subjects, but the information of those data subjects may be prejudicial to them, and the data subjects may wish to be "forgotten" after a certain time.

The current interpretation of Right to Be Forgotten from the March 5, 2010, lawsuit commenced by the AEPD on behalf of Mario Costeja González, a Spanish citizen (Spain is an EU member state). Gonzalez claimed his fundamental right to data protection and dignity was violated after the newspaper *La Vanguardia Ediciones SL* published information and documents with personal debts searchable by his name using Internet search engines. Mr. Gonzalez asserted that the matter of his personal debts was resolved, and the information and documents that resulted from searching his name were no longer relevant to the public proceedings on his debts.

Mr. Gonzalez asked for relief against *La Vanguardia* either to remove or alter pages with his personal data or to use certain tools in the search engines to protect the data. Mr. Gonzalez also asked for relief against Google Spain and Google Inc. to remove or conceal his personal data from its search results and the links to *La Vanguardia*.

On July 30, 2010, AEPD dismissed *La Vanguardia* from the action because a legal nexus existed between the posting of Mr. Gonzalez's information and the Ministry of Labor and Social Affairs's intent to give maximum publicity to the auction of Mr. Gonzalez's debts in order to secure as many bidders as possible. Google Spain and Google Inc. remained as parties in litigation.

To protect privacy, family life, and a balanced necessity for the erasure of data based on its irrelevancy or prejudice against the data subject, the Court interprets 95/46/EC as such:

Per Article 2(b) and (d), "Processing of personal data" is the activity of a search engine consisting of finding information published or placed on the internet by third parties, indexing it automatically, storing it temporarily and, finally, making it available to internet users according to a particular order of preference when that information contains personal data; and "Controller" is the operator of the search engine for processing data.

A "controller of a Member State" under Article 4(1)(a) is an operator of a search engine who sets up a branch or subsidiary in a Member State that intends to promote and sell advertising space offered by that engine that orientates its activity towards the inhabitants of the Member State.

The provisions of Article 12(b) and subparagraph (a) of Article 14, Paragraph 1 require [that] the operator of a search engine is obligated to remove from the displayed list of search results on the basis of:

1. A data subject's name links to web pages with personal data;

2. That is published by third parties and contains information relating to that data subject; and

3. The name or information is not erased beforehand or simultaneously from those web pages, and

4. When the publication in itself on those pages is lawful.

Furthermore, when appraising the conditions for the application of those provisions, it should be examined, among other things, whether:

1. The data subject has a right that the information personally relating to him should, at this point in time, no longer be linked to his name by a list of results displayed following a search made on the basis of his name, where prejudice to the data subject is not a necessary element.

2. The data subject may, under Art. 7 and 8, request that personal data no longer be made available to the general public. Those rights override, as a rule, the economic interest of the operator of the search engine and the interest of the general public in having access to that

information upon a search relating to the data subject's name.

3. Exception: a data subject's role in public life creates a preponderant interest of the general public in maintaining access to the data subject's information and overrides the data subject's fundamental rights.

Companies such as Google, Inc., Microsoft's Bing, and Yahoo! provide an online web form for any data subject who is a citizen of a European Union member state to request the removal of their personal information. Personal information includes, among other things, the name used to search, the urls to be removed, and an explanation about why it pertains to the data subject.

The United States strongly values freedom of expression and freedom of the press as fundamental values. Such values are incompatible with the Right to Be Forgotten as applied in 95/46/EC. Yet practices in U.S. bankruptcy law, credit reporting, and criminal law conceptually recognize the doctrine of the Right to Be Forgotten Private companies such as Twitter are adopting policies mirroring the basic principles of the Right to Be Forgotten.

The U.S. Supreme Court has held that states may not pass laws restricting the media from disseminating truthful but embarrassing information (for example, the name of a rape victim) as long as the information was legally acquired (*Florida Star v. B.J.F.*, 491 U.S. 524 (1989). Particular state laws governing online privacy issues currently exist as well.

Crystal N. Le

Further Reading

Grande, Allison, "EU, Google in Power Struggle Over 'Right to Be Forgotten.'" Law360, July 30, 2014.

"Recent Case: Internet Law—Protection of Personal Data— Court of Justice of the European Union Creates Presumption That Google Must Remove Links to Personal Data upon Request, Case C-131/12, *Google Spain SL v. Agencia Española de Protección de Datos* (May 13, 2014)." *Harvard Law Review* 128 (2014): 735–742.

Toobin, Jeffrey. "The Solace of Oblivion: In Europe, the Right to Be Forgotten Trumps the Internet." *New Yorker,* September 29, 2014.

Walker, Robert Kirk. "Note: The Right to Be Forgotten." *Hastings Law Journal* 64 (2012): 257–286.

See also: Florida Star v. B.J.F.; Financial information, Privacy right to; Privacy torts; Search engines

Right to be let alone

Identification: A foundational principle in the field of privacy law that was introduced in the seminal 1890 *Harvard Law Review* article "The Right to Privacy," by Samuel Warren and Louis Brandeis. The article was written largely as a result of the authors' perception that modern technology, including increasingly portable cameras, and a dearth of ethical behavior among journalists allowed them to commoditize gossip and eroded the private lives of public figures to the detriment of society as a whole.

In "The Right to Privacy," Warren and Brandeis argued that, in the face of technological and cultural developments that revealed to the public matters that were historically personal and private, it was necessary to recognize a common law right for an individual to determine to what extent his or her personal life would be subject to exposure. The article was well received, and the influence of the principle of the right to be let alone increased in 1928, when then–Supreme Court Justice Brandeis wrote a dissenting opinion in the U.S. Supreme Court case *Olmstead v. United States*, 277 U.S. 438 (1928), which outlined a right to privacy from government intrusion founded on the Fourth Amendment to the U.S. Constitution. The popularity and importance of the concept of the right to be let alone has persisted, and its impact on the philosophy and legal field of privacy continues.

In "The Right to Privacy," Warren and Brandeis first examined how the common law, that is, principles of law developed through court decisions as opposed to legislation, evolved to protect changing notions of the principle that a person "shall have full protection in person and in property." Namely, the authors tracked how the common law expanded from protecting only tangible violations to one's person or property to including protection for intangibles like intellectual property or one's reputation.

From there, the authors looked at how changing society, culture, and technology facilitated the publication of gossip that infringed on areas of individuals' lives that had historically been shielded from public scrutiny. In particular, they lamented the use of portable cameras that could photograph a person without permission and the popularity and ubiquity of newspapers' gossip features. In particular, Warren and Brandeis railed against the publication of gossip as a trade, arguing that it injured not only the individual's whose secrets were discussed but also "result[ed] in a lowering of social standards and of morality. Even gossip apparently harmless, when widely and persistently circulated is potent for evil." Thus, they contended that the increasing focus on the private lives of individuals necessitated common law protection of individuals' privacy. In the remainder of the article, the authors review a variety of existing common law protections, looking for an established basis in which to ground their theory of the right to privacy or, as they also referred to it, the right to be let alone.

In searching for a basis for the right to privacy, Warren and Brandeis noted that the publication of gossip, and the accompanying invasion of privacy, "is attained by the use of that which is another's, the facts relating to his private life, which he has seen fit to keep private." They then reviewed the common law and concluded that the historical "protection afforded to thoughts, sentiments, and emotions, expressed through the medium of writing or of the arts" that is common law protection akin to copyright protection "is merely an instance of the enforcement of the more general right of the individual to be let alone." Warren and Brandeis stated that these common law protections historically afforded to private writings should be applied, on the basis of the principle of the right to be let alone, to protect individuals from unauthorized photography and discussion of an individual's private actions.

In having identified a basis for the right to privacy, Warren and Brandeis strove to define how a cause of action for the violation of a person's right to privacy would function. The authors envisioned that a wronged party may sue for damages in all cases—an "injury to feelings" would be sufficient to warrant relief. The right to privacy, however, was limited in many ways. Most substantially, matters that were of interest to the public were not shielded by the right to privacy. As an example, Warren and Brandeis suggested that publication that a private individual could not spell properly would be a privacy invasion, but publication of the same fact when concerning a candidate for political office would not.

"The Right to Privacy" was well received upon publication, and in the years immediately following its publication, court opinions and legislation began to reference and invoke the right to privacy, especially in instances of unauthorized photography. In 1928, Justice Brandeis, writing a dissenting opinion in *Olmstead*, argued that the government's wiretapping of a phone should be seen as a violation of the right to be let alone and should be deemed a violation of the Fourth Amendment (277 U.S. 438, 478 (Brandeis, J., dissenting).

The right to be let alone continued to involve in the common law, and in 1960, William Prosser identified four distinct tort actions for a violation of a privacy:

1. Intrusion upon the plaintiff's seclusion or solitude, or into his private affairs.
2. Public disclosure of embarrassing facts about the plaintiff.

3. Publicity that places the plaintiff in a false light in the public eye.

4. Appropriation, for the defendant's advantage, of the plaintiff's name or likeness.

Undoubtedly, as new technologies emerge and society and culture continue to change, the right to be let alone will evolve and be applied in new situations perhaps unimaginable to Brandeis and Warren, yet their principled arguments will likely remain relevant.

Paul Riermaier

Further Reading

Barbas, Samantha. "Saving Privacy from History." *Depaul Law Review* 61 (Summer 2012): 973–1048.

Bratman, Benjamin E. "Brandeis and Warren's 'The Right to Privacy and the Birth of the Right to Privacy.'" *Tennessee Law Review* 69 (Spring 2002): 638–644.

Glancy, Dorothy J. "The Invention of the Right to Privacy." *Arizona Law Review* 21, no. 1 (1979): 1–39.

Kramer, Irwin R. "The Birth of Privacy Law: A Century Since Warren and Brandeis." *Catholic University Law Review* 39 (Spring 1990): 703–724.

Prosser, William L. "Privacy." *California Law Review* 48, no. 3 (1960): 389. Wilkerson, Jared A. "Battle for the Disclosure Tort." *California Western Law Review* 49 (Spring 2013): 231–268.

See also: Brandeis, Louis Dembitz; Fourth Amendment to the U.S. Constitution; *Olmstead v. United States*; Prosser, William Lloyd; Supreme Court of the United States

The Right to Privacy

Identification: In the United States, a wide variety of legal rights protected by many different laws. In a constitutional sense, for example, a person has a right to privacy against unreasonable government intrusions into the home.

Individuals also have a right to privacy protecting them against certain government restrictions on personal autonomy, such as reproductive decision making, family relationships, and the right to die. For purposes of state tort law (as determined by state courts), the right of privacy is understood as a personal right to recover monetary compensation from anyone, including a corporation, who invades the person's privacy and causes the person emotional distress or anguish. In some instances, even criminal laws seek to protect the personal right to privacy by imposing criminal penalties on persons who violate laws prohibiting activities such as identity theft, eavesdropping, and voyeurism.

The difficulty in defining an individual's right to privacy is identifying the nature of personal privacy interests that the law protects, and the limits of those protected interests. Many other countries protect a much more comprehensive scope of personal privacy than U.S. law protects. European countries, for example, have adopted broad omnibus privacy laws. In contrast, the United States has a patchwork of constitutional, common law, and statutory provisions, both federal and state, which together make up a complex body of sectoral privacy law. For that reason, the right of privacy in the United States has many gaps and exceptions, and the legal remedies for violation of the right are varied and complex.

Some of these exceptions to the right of privacy are designed to balance the individual's right of privacy against other important legal and social interests. For example, the personal right of privacy is sometimes inconsistent with others' rights to freedom of speech and the press, both protected by the First Amendment to the U.S. Constitution and comparable provisions in most state constitutions. The courts, as government actors, are reluctant to enforce one person's right to privacy in a way that intrudes on others' constitutional freedoms. For that reason, the right to privacy as protected by state and federal law is limited in recognition that the public has a First Amendment right to information about public officials and matters of legitimate public interest.

Under some circumstances, a person's right to privacy must yield to important government interests in protecting public safety. For example, criminal statutes prohibit the possession and sale of controlled substances to protect public safety from the negative effects of drug use. For that reason, the government has a limited right to search a person's home or business to enforce those criminal statutes. The law must find a way to balance the government's interests in protecting public safety against the individual's right to privacy. Therefore, the Fourth Amendment to the U.S. Constitution, and similar provisions in most state constitutions, prohibit only "unreasonable" searches of a person or the person's home by law enforcement officers. When a law enforcement officer secures a search warrant beforehand from a judge, the law considers a search of the specific place identified in the warrant to be a reasonable one. Thus, a person's right to privacy against government intrusion is not absolute. The right to privacy is always subject to balancing against other competing legal interests.

The right of privacy in the United States has two major subdivisions. The first is the right of privacy with respect to personal autonomy, which includes the right to make personal decisions about relationships, reproduction, family matters, medical treatment, and end-of-life concerns. The second is informational privacy, which includes the right to control whether and how one's personal information is gathered and disseminated to others. For example, laws that govern how social media websites use subscribers' personal information deal with informational privacy rights. In this broad sense, the right to informational privacy also includes photographs and other images that depict a person and the person's activities.

The personal autonomy branch of privacy law is largely governed by federal and state constitutional law, as that body of law has been interpreted and applied by federal and state courts. The right of privacy in the sense of personal autonomy is also limited in many ways, however, by state and federal criminal statutes. Criminal statutes impose penalties on individuals who engage in certain private conduct or

activities, and the imposition of such penalties is generally meant to advance policies that are considered to be in the best interests of the public safety in carrying out the government's police powers.

Sometimes criminal statutes conflict with the constitutionally protected right to privacy. When those statutes are challenged in court, they may be declared unenforceable. For example, in the 1960s, some states prohibited the sale of contraceptives, even to married couples. In *Griswold v. Connecticut*, 381 U.S. 479 (1965), the U.S. Supreme Court struck down these laws, holding that married couples have a constitutional right to privacy to make their own decisions about whether and when to have children. In another example, several states had statutes criminalizing abortion before 1973. In *Roe v. Wade*, 410 U.S. 113 (1973), the U.S. Supreme Court relied on a woman's implied constitutional right to privacy in holding that state laws criminalizing abortion during the first trimester of a woman's pregnancy were unconstitutional. The Court held that a woman has a constitutionally protected right to privacy to make that decision in consultation with her private physician, and that right is protected from interference by state criminal statutes until the end of the first trimester.

Even when state or federal law protects a person's right to privacy, the right can be given up by an individual's waiver or consent. A person waives the right of privacy by taking actions that are inconsistent with a desire for privacy. For example, a person who seeks a career as a celebrity entertainer or political figure is considered to have implicitly given up the right to remain unknown and anonymous, out of the public eye. Even a private person can yield the right to privacy by consent. Some states require written consent before anyone can lawfully intrude on another's right to privacy. Other states recognize that a person may consent verbally or even by engaging in activities that another person would reasonably interpret to be inconsistent with a desire for privacy. A person may also waive the right to privacy or consent to an invasion of the right by written or electronic agreement. For example, millions of individuals, knowingly or not, have consented to violations of their informational right to privacy by clicking "I agree" when asked to consent to the terms and conditions of social media and other Internet websites.

J. Lyn Entrikin

Further Reading

Alderman, Ellen, and Caroline Kennedy. *The Right to Privacy*. New York: Alfred A. Knopf, 1995, xiii–xvi, 323–332.

European Union Agency for Fundamental Rights and the Council of Europe. *Handbook on European Data Protection Law*. 2014, http://www.echr.coe.int/Documents/Handbook_data_protection_ENG.pdf.

Friedman, Lawrence M. *Guarding Life's Dark Secret*. Stanford, CA: Stanford University Press, 2007, 213–234.

Wacks, Raymond. *Privacy: A Very Short Introduction*. New York: Oxford University Press, 2010, 38–50.

See also: Consent; Constitutional Law; First Amendment to the U.S. Constitution; Fourth Amendment to the U.S. Constitution; *Griswold v. Connecticut,* 381 U.S. 479 (1965); Legal Evolution of Privacy Rights in the United States; Personal Autonomy; Social Media

Riley v. California, 134 S. Ct. 2473 (2014)

Identification: A unanimous decision, with a majority opinion by Chief Justice John Roberts, in which the U.S. Supreme Court held that the police generally may not, without a warrant, search digital information on a cellphone seized from an individual who has been arrested.

This case of *Riley v. California* was a consolidated appeal, meaning that two separate but similar cases were heard at the same time by the U.S. Supreme Court. The decision applied equally to both cases.

In the first case, David Riley was stopped by a police officer for driving with expired vehicle registration tags. Once stopped, the officer

discovered that Riley's driver's license had been suspended. Riley's vehicle was subsequently impounded while a different police officer conducted an inventory search of the vehicle. The search revealed that two handguns had been placed under the vehicle's hood. Riley was then arrested for possession of concealed and loaded firearms, in violation of California state law.

An officer searched Riley incident to the arrest and discovered items associated with a street gang. The officer also took possession of Riley's cellphone, which Riley described as a "smartphone." The officer then accessed the contents of the cellphone, observing additional indications of gang-related signs.

At the police station, two hours after Riley's arrest, a detective continued to investigate the contents of Riley's cellphone, searching for additional signs of gang activity. The detective discovered several photographs of Riley standing in front of a vehicle that authorities suspected was involved in a drive-by shooting that had occurred a few weeks earlier.

Riley was ultimately charged with, in connection with the drive-by shooting, firing at an occupied vehicle, assault with a semiautomatic firearm, and attempted murder. Riley filed a pretrial motion to suppress the evidence obtained from his cellphone, arguing that it violated his Fourth Amendment rights. The trial court rejected his motion, and Riley was convicted on all three counts and received a sentence of fifteen years to life in prison. The California Court of Appeal affirmed Riley's convictions, and the California Supreme Court denied Riley's petition for review.

In the second case, a police officer observed Brima Wurie make an apparent drug sale from a car. The officer arrested Wurie, and he was taken to the police station, where officers seized two cellphones that he was carrying. Officers soon noticed that one of the cellphones, a flip phone, was receiving several calls from the same source. Officers opened the phone and accessed its call log to determine the number associated with the phone calls. The officers then used an online phone directory to trace the phone number to an apartment building. The officers went to the apartment building, discovered Wurie's apartment, and secured the apartment while obtaining a search warrant. After executing the warrant, the officers found and seized 215 grams of crack cocaine, marijuana, drug paraphernalia, a firearm, ammunition, and cash.

Wurie was charged with distributing crack cocaine, possessing crack cocaine with intent to distribute, and being a felon in possession of a firearm and ammunition. Wurie moved to suppress the evidence obtained from the search, arguing that it was discovered based on an unconstitutional search of his cellphone. The district court denied the motion; Wurie was convicted on all three counts and sentenced to 262 months in prison. The U.S. Court of Appeals for the First Circuit reversed the denial of Wurie's motion to suppress and vacated two of his convictions.

The U.S. Supreme Court agreed to review both cases, specifically on the issue of whether the police may, without a warrant, search digital information on a cellphone seized from an individual who had been lawfully arrested.

Chief Justice Roberts first emphasized that the touchstone of Fourth Amendment analysis was reasonableness. Here, the two cases concerned the reasonableness of a warrantless search of a cellphone incident to a lawful arrest. Warrantless searches following a lawful arrest have been held constitutional, subject to the reasonableness standard, as discussed in a trilogy of cases, *Chimel v. California*, 395 U.S. 752 (1969); *United States v. Robinson*, 414 U.S. 218 (1973); and *Arizona v. Gant*, 556 U.S. 332 (2009).

Chief Justice Roberts noted that, although warrantless searches following an arrest have been deemed reasonable, particularly where the officer's safety is at risk or where there is a concern of a loss of evidence, the scope of what is considered reasonable has been debated. In

addition, past cases involved physical searches of objects, whereas the present case involved digital searches.

In deciding whether to exempt the search of cellphones absent a warrant, the Court balanced the degree to which a search intrudes upon an individual's privacy and the degree to which it is needed for a legitimate governmental interest. The Court held that officers must generally secure a warrant before conducting a search of data on a cellphone.

Chief Justice Roberts also noted that the digital data stored on a cellphone cannot itself be used as a weapon to injure an arresting officer or to aid in a suspect's escape. Therefore, the rationale of a warrantless search based on officer safety is not applicable in these circumstances. Moreover, there was no risk of the defendants destroying any evidence in the cellphone because the officers had already secured the cellphones before they were searched. Thus, the officers could have obtained a warrant without risking the loss of evidence.

The government argued, however, that remote destruction of data or encryption methods could hinder an investigation if the cellphones were not immediately searched. The Court rejected this argument, concluding that several alternatives existed to prevent such destruction of evidence.

Chief Justice Roberts also discussed how cellphones differ significantly from other objects, and that an arrestee's diminished expectation of privacy does not foreclose all Fourth Amendment protections. Although "privacy comes at a cost," the Court noted that exigent circumstances for warrantless searches are still available in extreme situations where quickly accessing cellphone data might be necessary.

The judgment of the California Court of Appeal was reversed, and the judgment of the First Circuit was affirmed.

While the Supreme Court unanimously agreed that the warrantless searches of the defendants' cellphones were unreasonable,

Justice Samuel Alito wrote a separate concurrence. Justice Alito voiced some doubts over the majority's approach to analyzing the search of digital evidence, but he also acknowledged that he could not conceive of a more workable alternative. Justice Alito also suggested that legislatures were better equipped to handle privacy concerns than were federal courts using the "blunt instrument" of the Fourth Amendment.

The decision in *Riley* demonstrates the U.S. Supreme Court's reluctance to apply Fourth Amendment rules mechanically to emerging technologies. Prior to *Riley*, nearly all searches incident to a lawful arrest were deemed reasonable. This decision lays an important analytical framework as courts continue to grapple with applying constitutional principles to rapidly evolving technology.

Ethan P. Fallon

Further Reading

"Fourth Amendment—Search and Seizure—Searching Cell Phones Incident to Arrest—*Riley v. California*." *Harvard Law Review* 128 (2014): 251–260.

Pincus, Andrew. "Evolving Technology and the Fourth Amendment: The Implications of *Riley v. California*." *Cato Supreme Court Review* 2014–2015 (2014): 307–336.

Shoebotham, Leslie A. "The Strife of Riley: The Search-Incident Consequences of Making an Easy Case Simple." *Louisiana Law Review* 75 (2014): 29–70.

See also: Cellphones; Constitutional law; Criminal justice (criminal procedure); Fourth Amendment to the U.S. Constitution; Search warrants; Supreme Court of the United States

S

Safe Harbor

Identification: A framework for transatlantic data transfer.

The European Court of Justice ruled on October 6, 2015, that Safe Harbor is invalid because privacy protections in the United States are insufficient, allowing U.S. government authorities to gain routine access to personal information from European Union (EU) citizens stored by U.S. companies. Based on the EU data protection guidelines that went into effect in 1998, transfer of personal data from a member state to a nonmember state may be authorized only if an "adequate" level of privacy protection based on EU standards can be guaranteed. The Safe Harbor framework, developed in 2000 between the U.S. Department of Commerce and the European Commission, however, provided a way to work around these restrictions. The framework allowed U.S. companies to transfer personal data if they committed to a self-certification process to ensure compliance with a set of Safe Harbor privacy principles. Over 4,400 U.S. companies (large companies, such as Google, Inc., Face-book, Inc., Apple, Inc., Microsoft, Corp., Amazon, Com., Time Inc., as well many smaller companies) store data from European customers in the United States. The ruling means that the data protection authorities in individual EU member states are now authorized to review data transfers to the United States on a case-bycase basis.

The case was brought by privacy activist Maximilian Schrems, a lawyer and PhD student from Vienna, Austria, who founded the organization *Europe v. Facebook* and has challenged Facebook's inadequate privacy protections for several years. A Facebook user since 2008, he wrote a paper on Facebook's privacy policies while he was pursuing his legal studies as an exchange student in California. He noted the differences between U.S. and European privacy protections, and in 2011 ventured to get a detailed account of the kind of information Facebook had collected from him over the years. While getting his user information from Facebook was not easy, he persisted, and eventually received a CD from Facebook's headquarters in California. The CD contained a 1,222 page PDF document that contained all the user data the company had collected about him, including a lot of data he had deleted: wall posts, messages, and email addresses from friends. Aiming for greater transparency from the company and the ability for users to control their own information, he lodged a complaint against Facebook with the Irish data protection agency (Facebook's European headquarters are located in Ireland). Schrems argued that, in light of Edward Snowden's revelations about the National Security Agency's (NSA's) surveillance program, U.S. laws do not provide sufficient protections against government surveillance of customer data stored on U.S. servers. The Irish data protection agency rejected the complaint, however, on the ground of the Safe Harbor framework. Schrems then sued the agency in the High Court of Ireland, which subsequently referred the case to the European Court of Justice.

In its ruling, the European Court of Justice followed the opinion of the Advocate General, Yves Bot, which he had delivered on September 23, 2015. The Advocate General of the Court provides an advisory legal opinion on specific legal cases. Bot wrote: "First, personal data transferred by undertakings such as Facebook Ireland to their parent company established in the United States is then capable of being accessed by the NSA and by other U.S. security agencies in the course of a mass and indiscriminate surveillance and interception of such data. Indeed, in the wake of Edward Snowden's revelations, the evidence now available would admit of no other realistic conclusion. Second, citizens of the Union have no effective right to be heard on the question of the surveillance and interception of their data by the NSA and other United States security agencies."

In its judgment, the Court wrote, "legislation permitting the public authorities to have access on a generalized basis to the content of electronic communications must be regarded as compromising the essence of the fundamental right to respect for private life," which is guaranteed by Article 7 of the Charter of Fundamental Rights of the European Union. The Court also referred to Article 8 of the Charter, "Protection of personal data," which guarantees the following: "Everyone has the right to the protection of personal data concerning him or her." The judgment also cites Article 47, "Right to an effective remedy and to a fair trial."

Commentators in Europe called the judgment "spectacular, brave, sensational," and privacy advocates welcomed the ruling as a major victory. Schrems stated on his website: "I very much welcome the judgement of the Court, which will hopefully be a milestone when it comes to online privacy. This judgement draws a clear line. It clarifies that mass surveillances violates our fundamental rights. Reasonable legal redress must be possible." In contrast, U.S. Commerce Secretary Penny Pritzer stated in response to the European Court of Justice decision: "We are deeply disappointed in today's decision from the European Court of Justice, which creates significant uncertainty for both U.S. and EU companies and consumers, and puts at risk the thriving transatlantic digital economy."

It is not entirely predictable at this point what impact the ruling will have on companies that are transferring personal data between Europe and the United States, and the implementation of the ruling will differ from EU member country to member country. Some commentators predict that it might—in some instances— bring data transfer between Europe and the United States to a complete halt. Others see the decision as largely symbolic and predict that big companies in particular will be able to find alternative methods to allow the continuation of data transfer between Europe and the United States. There is no doubt, however, that the ruling significantly strengthened the work of the data protection authorities in the individual EU member countries and that it advanced digital rights for EU citizens.

Katharina Hering

Further Reading

Darcy, Shane. "Battling for the Rights to Privacy and Data Protection in the Irish Courts: *Schrems v. Data Protection Commissioner* [2014] IEHC 213 [2014]." *Utrecht Journal of International and European Law* 31 (2015): 131–135.

European Union, Charter of Fundamental Rights of the European Union. October 26, 2012. 2012/C 326/02. http://perma.cc/LR4G-U4AY.

Initial response to the decision by the CJEU, *Europe v. Facebook* website. http://perma.cc/6PRQ-Q2JE.

Judgment in Case C-362/14 Maximillian Schrems v. Data Protection Commissioner [2015]. *http://perma.cc/HQW4-JBB9. Case C-362/14 Maximillian Schrems v. Data Protection Commissioner* [2015]. *Opinion of Advocate General Yves Bot.* http://perma.cc/6JDQ-ZS7L.

Mouzakiti, Foivi. "Transborder Data Flows 2.0: Mending the Holes of the Data Protection Directive." *European Data Protection Law Review* 1 (2015): 39–51.

Statement from U.S. Secretary of Commerce Penny Pritzker on European Court of Justice Safe Harbor Framework Decision. October 6, 2015. https://perma.cc/6GKFELAL.

Timm, Trevor. "The Snowden Effect: New Privacy Wins Await after Data Transfer Ruling." *The Guardian*, October 8, 2015. http://perma.cc/57MX-NBBY.

See also: Amazon; Apple, Inc.; Big data; Facebook; National Security Agency; The Right to Privacy; Snowden, Edward.

Scientific and medical data sharing

Identification: One of the benefits of modern communication technology is the increased ability of physicians and other scientists to share data in order to cooperate to find solutions to medical and scientific problems. Such sharing leads to greater coordination between researchers, which is a clear benefit when dealing with public health emergencies, such as the Ebola and Zika virus outbreaks. It also helps researchers more easily present their initial findings to organizations that might give them access to funding sources to continue their work. The sharing of individual patient data from clinical trials can improve the quality of research. As researchers cooperate, the understanding of diseases and their treatments can increase dramatically. However, the sharing of such data comes with clear legal and ethical challenges for researchers.

One of the main challenges in medical and scientific data sharing involves the sharing of the data of individual patients or research subjects. While policies aimed at the aggregation of data and the de-identification of individual patient-level data have protected patient privacy, and the Health Insurance Portability and Accountability Act (HIPPA) has provided privacy standards to medical providers in the protection of patient data, such depersonalization can sometimes prove to be a barrier to researchers. Some of these barriers are less stringent when the goal is academic, non-commercial research. However, with the important role that pharmaceutical corporations play in the modern research infrastructure, pure academic research is not always the most feasible route. Another consideration revolves around ownership of the data itself. Again, with the increased role of large pharmaceutical corporations, this is a particular challenge. Whereas many academic research bodies have called for more openness in the sharing of clinical research data, this too can lead to roadblocks for profit-based research.

This is not to say that large pharmaceutical corporations do not bring advantages when it comes to the sharing of data. They, much more than academic research centers, are able to provide the funding required in order to create the secure systems necessary to share data while protecting patient privacy. The associated costs can run up to $50,000 per year per study in order to administer requests for the data, collate the data sets and study documentation, anonymize the data and documents and create the computer infrastructure to allow access to them, and providing other types of support for researchers.

In order to protect patient data, it is necessary for research proposals conducted with patient data be reviewed for scientific merit by an objective, independent review panel. The study's sponsors, whether corporate or academic, should play no role in this determination. Some early efforts in this vein are the Yale University Open Data Access (YODA) project and the Supporting Open Access Research (SOAR) initiative. These types of bodies have been cooperatively formed with pharmaceutical corporations, such as GlaxoSmithKlein (GSK). In 2014, GSK established a public website, clinicalstudydatarequest.com, in order to share data from more than 200 clinical trials, and the requests for such data were governed by an independent review board run by the Wellcome Trust. Other corporations such as Johnson & Johnson and Pfizer have opted to create their own systems for dealing with patient data.

Many academic scientists agree, however, that a single system would be more efficient in helping researchers across institutions share the necessary data to increase the fruitfulness of their research. Further, there is a consensus among many that making such scientific data more broadly available is not only helpful, but ethically and scientifically necessary. The World Health Organization (WHO) has helped lead the charge to create best practices for clinical trials, that include the protection of patient identities, the public disclosure of results from all trials, and the sharing of data. The process to implement this has been slow in developing, however, it brings with it the potential not only to help with actual research, but to increase public awareness and support for research. To that end, in January 2016 the International Committee of Medical Journal Editors (ICMJE) committed to the idea of creating an environment where the sharing of de-personalized clinical data was the expected norm, believing it to be an ethical obligation.

Though technological, financial, and ethical questions remain, the idea of a global research community where de-identified data is shared routinely carries with it the prospect of maximizing the impact of all clinical trials and other types of patient-based scientific research.

Steven L. Danver

Further Reading

Bertino, E., Yang, Y., Ooi, B.C., and Deng, R.H. "Privacy and Ownership Preserving of Outsourced Medical Data." *IEEE Proceedings of the 21st International Conference on Data Engineering*, 2005.

McNutt, M., et al., "Data Sharing." *Science* 351:6277 (March 4, 2006). 1007.

Puebla, I., and Heber, J. "Data sharing in clinical research: challenges and open opportunities." *EveryOne*, May 2, 2017. https://blogs.plos.org/everyone/2017/05/02/data-sharing-in-clinical-research/

Rockhold, F., Nisen, P., and Freeman, A. "Data Sharing at a Crossroads." *New England Journal of Medicine* 375 (September 22, 2016), 1115–1117.

Strom, B.L., Buyse, M.E., Hughes, J., and Knoppers, B.M. "Data Sharing: Is the Juice Worth the Squeeze?"
New England Journal of Medicine 375 (October 27, 2016), 1608–1609.

Taichman, D.B., et al., "Data Sharing Statements for Clinical Trials: A Requirement of the International Committee of Medical Journal Editors." *New England Journal of Medicine* 376 (June 8, 2017), 2277–2279.

Yang, J., Li, J., and Niu, Y. "A hybrid solution for privacy preserving medical data sharing in the cloud environment." *Future Generation Computer Systems* 43 (February 2015). 74–86.

See also: Anonymity and anonymizers; Bioethics; Confidential Information Protection and Statistical Efficiency Act (CIPSEA); Health Insurance Portability and Accountability Act (HIPAA)

Search engines

Identification: Software programs or networks of programs that search the Internet for terms entered by a user and that compile a list of Internet locations at which the term is found.

A search engine appears to users as a search box at the top of the computer page. Many search engines are available, including Google, Bing, Yahoo! Search, Ask, AOL Search, Wow, WebCrawler, and many more. All these search engines serve as users' more or less convenient path to the content on the Internet; however, many search engines also serve as a convenient path for marketers and even less scrupulous persons and groups to learn a great deal about users' formerly private lives.

Google, the world's leading search engine at present, with an estimated 1.1 billion users per month, routinely forwards users' search histories, identities, and shopping patterns—for a fee—to marketers around the world. From one perspective, there is an advantage to that for the users, who receive targeted advertisements and whose search results are returned in a personally relevant order based on the user's browsing history. Even Edward Snowden, who tipped off the world to the National Security Agency's (NSA's) cellphone telephony metadata collection program that captures and retains the phone call history of millions of Americans, has warned us all that users must stop using Google to protect users' privacy in this digital age. And Tim Cook, CEO of Apple Computers, derided Google and other search engines by claiming that at least Apple doesn't "read your email or your messages to get information to market to you."

If the upside of search engines is convenience, the downside is the user privacy that is lost in the process. Search engines operate by applying rather complex search algorithms to interpret users' search queries, then seek information on the Internet that is relevant to those queries. How can search engine companies make any money doing that? Well, they sell priority placements so that entities willing to pay for the service will end up prominently displayed on the first page of the search results on all relevant queries. A business school in Ohio can purchase priority placement from Google to highlight their school whenever a Google user query in Ohio and contiguous states includes the words *business school*. Once a user has searched for, say, a laptop computer, a barrage of ads for laptop computers will appear on that user's screen. Those pop-up targeted ads are bought and paid for by the companies selling the laptop computers. That all sounds convenient—and it is. Each time a targeted ad is clicked in Google, the company that sponsored the ad pays a fee to Google. Google's annual income from its advertising business is estimated to be approximately $50 billion.

Users pay a steep privacy price for that convenience. As disclosed among the fine print of Google's all-encompassing privacy policy,

> When you upload, submit, store, send or receive content to or through our Services, you give Google (and those we work with) a worldwide license to use, host, store, reproduce, modify, create derivative works ..., communicate, publish, publicly perform, publicly display and distribute such content. . . . This license continues even if you stop using our Services. . . . Our automated systems analyze your content (including emails) to provide you personally relevant product features, such as customized search results, tailored advertising, and spam and malware detection. This analysis occurs as the content is sent, received, and when it is stored.

In other words, in exchange for the convenience and robust search features of Google, the user must give up a great deal of privacy. To make matters worse—in fact, much worse—data captured and stored by Google can be retained by Google indefinitely, just as information on the Internet can almost never be removed. That huge store of personal data is a tremendous draw for law enforcement agencies, who can use the third-party doctrine to access that data quite easily and without notice to the user whose data were accessed.

The third-party doctrine provides that (1) only the individual whose constitutional rights were violated has standing to contest violation; (2) a search of data on an individual that is stored by a third-party did not violate the individual's constitutional right to be free from unreasonable searches and seizures (the individual's physical property was not invaded or searched); and therefore, (3) upon a lawful demand from law enforcement, a third-party must turn over to law enforcement the data they seek on the individual. The third-party doctrine may have survived the pre–digital era relatively intact, but in the digital age, with users so freely sharing so much private data with third parties—as a convenience and almost as a necessity—the third-party doctrine can no longer prevail. Until it is abandoned by the courts or rendered impermissible through legislation, however, the third-party doctrine will remain the law of the land, and digital age privacy will be the victim left in its wake.

Some search engines have begun to offer more private services, and that is a sound development. Search engine DuckDuckGo, with monthly users at just two-hundredths of one percent of Google's monthly user rate, offers private web searching that does not use cookies or log IP addresses. Ixquick, touting itself as the most private search engine, does not record users' IP addresses or track cookies, and guarantees that it will not share users' information with any third party. StartPage, too, holds itself out as having "state-of-the-art privacy protection." If these more private search engines can begin to take at least some of the search engine business away from Google and other low-privacy search engines, perhaps Google and the rest will have to add more privacy protections to their search services or at least create different tiers of privacy so that users can select their preferred privacy tier.

Some of these so-called private search engines (PSE) started as direct competitors to Google and Bing but have begun to specialize in providing additional privacy features. StartPage actually uses Google search results, but without the tracking that Google includes. Similarly, DuckDuckGo uses Yahoo search results without the tracking. One PSE, Search Encrypt, uses AES-256 and Secure Sockets Layer (SSL) encryption to secure data being transmitted. Gibiru bills itself as being what Google was in the beginning, avoiding the cookies that track your movements across the Internet. Another PSE called Swisscows offers similar protections but also uses artificial intelligence to learn the context of users' searches. Almost all PSEs do not track users searches or store any information about them. Along with providing security, by offering searches done in isolation from company algorithms, these PSEs return a wider variety of less demographically-targeted results. This can be an advantage in an age where companies like Google and Facebook curate information to present users exactly what they expect and what aligns with their values.

Information once on the Internet seems always to be on the Internet, not susceptible to masking or erasure. Data relevant to a foreclosure process that occurred and was resolved many years before is still on the Internet years later,

with the potential to harm the reputation of the one foreclosed against. That was the actual situation in Spain, and the injured party sued Google Spain and Google Inc. to have that irrelevant entry removed from Google's information stores. The lawsuit was transferred to the Court of Justice of the European Union, which ultimately held that (1) the European Union's (EU's) rules apply wherever Google has a branch or subsidiary that markets its services there; (2) the EU's data protection rules, which had been issued as an EU Directive in 1995, did apply to search engines; and (3) under certain circumstances, Internet users and persons about whom information is placed on the Internet, have a "right to be forgotten" and to have the search engine remove the private information and render it inaccessible. That "right to be forgotten" movement was violently opposed by Google in the EU, and Google is fighting even harder to keep that movement from reaching the United States.

It appears, in the digital age, that the United States has largely abdicated its responsibility to create and administer nationwide privacy determinations and protections, or have delegated those decisions to software engineers or to the entities that hire them and control— and sell— access to so much private data on individuals. That may seem like inertia or it may seem inevitable, but the European Union and its Court of Justice proved otherwise in the case out in Spain. Congress, the courts, and individuals in the United States can take a similar stand and reset the privacy bar. We need not all be victims of the next technology that will decimate our privacy while making the technology designers and search engines a fortune.

Of course, the "right to be forgotten" movement, especially in the United States, has been attacked as a variant of censorship and antithetical to free speech, but the EU has attacked those challenges as myths set up by the movement's opponents but devoid of substance. On opponents' claims that the "right to be forgotten" is a form of censorship, the EU maintains, "The right to be forgotten does not allow governments to decide what can and cannot be online and what should or should not be read. It is a right that citizens will invoke to defend their interests as they see fit. Independent authorities will oversee the assessment carried out by the search engine operators." On opponents' claims that the "right to be forgotten" violates free speech, the EU responds, "the right to be forgotten applies where the information is inaccurate, inadequate, irrelevant or excessive for the purposes of data processing . . . This assessment must balance the interest of the person making the request and the public interest to have access to the data by retaining it in the list of results. [It] does not give the all-clear for people or organizations to have search results removed from the web simply because they find them inconvenient."

It is time for this dialogue in the United States. We need not be victims of technology in the digital age. We can resume control over technology, allowing it to be used in socially responsible and constitutional ways but, in the process, limiting its ability to damage the privacy rights of us all.

Charles E. MacLean

Further Reading

Efrati, Amir. "Google's Data-Trove Dance." *Wall Street Journal,* July 30, 2013. http://www.wsj.com/articles/SB10001424127887324170004578635812623154242.

European Commission. "Myth-Busting: The Court of Justice of the EU and the 'Right to be Forgotten.'" http://ec.europa.eu/justice/data-protection/files/factsheets/factsheet_rtbf_mythbusting_en.pdf.

Goodale, Gloria. "Privacy Concerns? What Google Now Says It Can Do with Your Data." *Christian Science Monitor,* April 16, 2014. http://www.csmonitor.com/USA/2014/0416/Privacy-concerns-What-Google-nowsays-it-can-do-with-your-data-video

Stewart, Christian. "The Best Private Search Engines—Alternatives to Google." *Medium.* February 8, 2018. https://hackernoon.com/untraceable-search-engines-alternatives-to-google-811b09d5a873

See also: Apple; Cookies; Data protection regimes; Fourth Amendment to the U.S. Constitution; Google; Internet service providers; National Security Agency (NSA); Right to be forgotten

Search warrants

Identification: Documents issued by a neutral judicial officer, also known as a magistrate, upon application by a law enforcement officer that, once issued, authorizes the officer to conduct a search of a specifically identified place.

To secure a search warrant, the officer must state, under oath or affirmation, sufficient facts to support a judicial finding of probable cause that contraband or other evidence of criminal activity will be found in the place to be searched. A valid search warrant must specifically identify the place to be searched, and if it authorizes the officer to seize items, the warrant must specifically identify and enumerate them.

The warrant requirement of the Fourth Amendment represents the earliest recognition in the United States of constitutionally protected privacy rights. The federal courts have mapped out the parameters of the constitutional right of privacy primarily by interpreting the Fourth Amendment. Its restrictions on the issuance of warrants protect against unreasonable searches

Secret Service agent trainees practice executing a search warrant. (By U.S. Secret Service.)

and seizures by government officials looking for evidence of criminal activity. In fact, the very purpose of adopting the Fourth Amendment to the U.S. Constitution was in part to protect citizens against general warrants then in common use in England and against writs of assistance used in the colonies [*Steagald v. United States,* 451 U.S. 2014 (1981)].

A writ of assistance was a general warrant that allowed a British customs official holding the document to search any place of his choice and seize any contraband that might be found. The writ often operated indefinitely, and its purpose was to assist customs authorities in enforcing laws against smuggling. British merchants sought to restrict colonial trade with other countries to maximize their profits. To discourage trade with other countries, the British government imposed duties on goods the colonists imported from elsewhere. In colonial times, smuggling was commonplace as a means of avoiding British duties on imported French, Spanish, and Dutch goods. Law-abiding colonists considered these English writs of assistance offensive and intrusive because customs officials could use them indiscriminately against anyone.

In 1761, James Otis, a Massachusetts lawyer, unsuccessfully argued before a Massachusetts colonial court in Boston that writs of assistance violated the unwritten British constitution. John Adams, then a young lawyer, observed Otis's argument before the Massachusetts court. Many years later, Adams declared it a momentous turning point in the founding of our nation, as quoted in *Payton v. New York,* 445 U.S. 573 (1980):

> Vivid in the memory of the newly independent Americans were those general warrants known as writs of assistance under which officers of the Crown had so bedeviled the colonists. The hated writs of assistance had given customs officials blanket authority to search where they pleased for goods imported in violation of British tax laws. They were denounced by James Otis as "the

worst instrument of arbitrary power, the most destructive of English liberty, and the fundamental principles of law, that ever was found in an English law-book," because they placed "the liberty of every man in the hands of every petty officer." The historic occasion of that denunciation, in 1761 at Boston, has been characterized as "perhaps the most prominent event that inaugurated the resistance of the colonies to the oppressions of the mother country. 'Then and there,' said John Adams, 'then and there was the first scene of the first act of opposition to the arbitrary claims of Great Britain. Then and there the child Independence was born.'"

In 1779, John Adams drafted Article 14 of the Massachusetts Declaration of Rights, which later became the model for the Fourth Amendment to the U.S. Constitution. The straightforward words of the Fourth Amendment echo the arguments first made by James Otis in 1761 for restricting the use of general warrants by customs officials:

> The right of the people to be secure in their persons, houses, papers, and effects, against unreasonable searches and seizures, shall not be violated, and no Warrants shall issue, but upon probable cause, supported by Oath or affirmation, and particularly describing the place to be searched, and the persons or things to be seized.

When a government search implicates the Fourth Amendment, the court must balance "the need for effective law enforcement against the [individual's] right of privacy" [*Johnson v. United States,* 333 U.S. 10 (1948)]. Thus, the Fourth Amendment does not prohibit all government searches—only unreasonable ones. As a general rule, a neutral magistrate rather than a law enforcement officer must decide when the government's interest in searching for evidence of criminal activity outweighs the personal right to privacy. If the magistrate considers the facts sufficient to support a finding of probable cause, the judicial officer may issue a search warrant.

The law generally presumes that a law enforcement search conducted in a manner consistent with a search warrant is a reasonable one, which is all the Fourth Amendment requires. That legal presumption may be rebutted in court, however, if a criminal defendant establishes that the facts presented to the magistrate were insufficient, as a matter of law, to qualify as probable cause. If the reviewing court determines that the facts provided to the magistrate did not demonstrate probable cause, the evidence seized in the search may be ruled inadmissible at trial based on the exclusionary rule.

The meaning of probable cause, required by the Fourth Amendment before a search warrant may be issued, is not easy to articulate in precise terms. Generally, the term refers to facts available to a law enforcement officer that would support a belief by a reasonably cautious person that contraband or evidence of a crime is present in the place to be searched [*Florida v. Harris*, 133 S.Ct. 1050 (2013)]. "All [the Court has] required is the kind of 'fair probability' on which 'reasonable and prudent [people,] not legal technicians, act'" (*Florida v. Harris*). The Court considers "the totality of the circumstances" in determining whether the law enforcement officer seeking the warrant has satisfied the probable cause requirement, which the Court has called a "practical and commonsensical standard" (*Florida v. Harris*).

Historically, a person's home has been considered so private that government officials should not be permitted to intrude without a very good reason. The Supreme Court has often acknowledged that a person's home is his castle. "We have, after all, lived our whole national history with an understanding of 'the ancient adage that a man's house is his castle [to the point that t]he poorest man may in his cottage bid defiance to all the forces of the Crown'" [*Georgia v. Randolph*, 547 U.S. 103 (2013)].

It was James Otis himself who first asserted this well-known metaphor in his 1761 argument against writs of assistance. John Adams's contemporaneous notes of Otis's argument recorded that Otis spoke of the "Priviledge of the House" as a "fundamental principle" of the law: "A Man, who is quiet, is as secure in his House, as a Prince in his Castle. . . ."

Therefore, in interpreting the Fourth Amendment, the Court has always considered a person's residence, and the immediately surrounding area known as the curtilage, as deserving special protection against unreasonable government searches [*Florida v. Jardines*, 569 U.S. 1 (2013); *Kyllo v. United States*, 533 U.S. 27 (2001)]. For example, the front porch of a house is considered part of the curtilage of the home and is therefore entitled to the same protections against warrantless searches as the inside of the home.

While the home is entitled to special protection against warrantless searches, the Court has also held that "the Fourth Amendment protects people, not places" [*Katz v. United States*, 389 U.S. 347 (1967)]. In *Katz*, the Court held that the Fourth Amendment prohibited law enforcement officials from making a warrantless tape recording of a telephone conversation in a glassed-in public telephone booth. The government argued that the conversation occurred in a public place, and therefore the defendant had no reasonable expectation that his conversation would remain private. The Court agreed that "[w]hat a person knowingly exposes to the public, even in his own home or office, is not a subject of Fourth Amendment protection" (*Katz v. United States*). Thus, if a person consents to a search or seizure, the Fourth Amendment is not violated.

However, the *Katz* Court reasoned that the constitutional right against unreasonable searches and seizures is not limited to places, like the home, in which courts have historically assumed that individuals have had a reasonable expectation of privacy. By closing the glass door of the telephone booth, the defendant had demonstrated intent to keep his conversation private. Therefore, a search warrant was required before law enforcement officers tape-recorded the telephone conversation (*Katz v. United States*).

The Supreme Court has carved out many exceptions to the warrant requirement. One important example is a search of the interior of an automobile when lawfully stopped by police for a traffic violation. The purpose of this exception is to protect officer safety and to prevent the destruction of evidence of a crime. For that reason, the search of the car's trunk or a closed container inside the car not within easy reach of an occupant is generally not within the scope of the warrant exception. "[A]n automobile search incident to a recent occupant's arrest is constitutional (1) if the arrestee is within reaching distance of the vehicle during the search, or (2) if the police have reason to believe that the vehicle contains 'evidence relevant to the crime of arrest'" [*Davis v. United States*, 131 S.Ct. 2419 (2011)].

Another important exception to the warrant requirement is a search incident to a lawful arrest, which serves the same government interests as the automobile exception: officer safety and preservation of evidence [*Arizona v. Gant*, 556 U.S. 332 (2009)]. On the other hand, the Supreme Court held in 2014 that even when a cellphone is seized by law enforcement incident to lawful arrest, the exception does not apply. Therefore, the Fourth Amendment protection against warrantless searches generally extends to the contents of a person's cellphone [*Riley v. California*, 134 S.Ct. 2473 (2014)]. The Court acknowledged that cellphones are commonly used by individuals to store a wide variety of private information and that the reasons for the warrant exception for searches incident to arrest are not sufficiently served by expanding the scope of that exception to include the contents of cellphones.

Even if one of the many judicially recognized exceptions applies and a warrant is therefore not required, the Fourth Amendment requires that any search must be reasonable. This fundamental constitutional requirement of reasonableness applies to both the scope of the search and the manner in which it is conducted [*Maryland v. King*, 569 U.S. 12 (2013)].

Over the last several decades, the Court has narrowly defined what qualifies as a Fourth Amendment search in the first place. No search warrant is required if the law enforcement activity does not qualify as a "search" as the courts have defined that term (*Kyllo v. United States*). Therefore, even if a person has a subjective expectation of privacy in a place to be searched or the information seized, that does not necessarily mean that the Fourth Amendment applies. The Supreme Court has interpreted the Fourth Amendment to apply only if the person who challenges the search had an expectation of privacy that the society recognizes as objectively reasonable.

For example, the Court has held that a person has no reasonable expectation of privacy in the contents of an opaque garbage bag set out on the curb for collection [*California v. Greenwood*, 486 U.S. (1988)]. Therefore, a search of a garbage bag's contents generally does not amount to a Fourth Amendment search. If a court determines that a particular law enforcement activity does not qualify as a Fourth Amendment search, the officer is not required to obtain a warrant or even to conduct a reasonable search, as that term is defined for purposes of the Fourth Amendment.

The Fourth Amendment is not the only constitutional basis for the search warrant requirement. Many state constitutions include guarantees against unreasonable searches and seizures, and in some cases the state courts have interpreted those constitutional protections to be broader than those guaranteed by the U.S. Constitution. The Supreme Court has repeatedly held that a state, as a matter of its own law, may impose greater restrictions on law enforcement activities than those that the U.S. Constitution imposes, for example, *Oregon v. Hass*, 420 U.S. 714, 719 (1975).

Some states also impose additional restrictions on law enforcement searches by statute. For example, some state statutes restrict the means by which law enforcement officers may conduct strip searches and body cavity searches beyond the minimum requirements of the federal and state constitutions.

J. Lyn Entrikin

Further Reading

Bloom, Robert M. *Searches, Seizures & Warrants: A Reference Guide to the United States Constitution.* Westport, CT: Praeger, 2003.

Burkoff, John. *Search Warrant Law Deskbook.* New York: Clark Boardman Callaghan, 2015.

Clancy, Thomas K. "The Importance of James Otis." *Mississippi Law* Journal 82, no. 2 (2013): 487–524. http://ssrn.com/abstract=2111601.

Solove, Daniel J., and Paul M. Schwartz, *Privacy Law Fundamentals*, 3d ed. Portsmouth, NH: International Association of Privacy Professionals, 2015, pp. 73–78.

See also: Cellphones; Consent; Constitutional law; Fourth Amendment to the U.S. Constitution; Home, privacy of the; *Kyllo v. United States*; Legal Evolution of Privacy Rights; The Right to Privacy; *Riley v. California*

Security flaws, computers

Identification: Computer vulnerabilities, or weaknesses in a computer product that could allow an attacker to compromise the integrity, availability, or confidentiality of that particular computer.

Importance of security flaws

Computer security flaws threaten system security and could exist anywhere in the system. These flaws are considered to be any conditions or circumstances that may result in denial of service, or unauthorized disclosure, destruction, or modification of data.

In our digital world, every organization gathers, maintains, organizes, and stores vast quantities of digitized data, including sensitive personally identifiable information. Organizations cannot function without collecting or holding personally identifying information, such as names and addresses, Social Security numbers, credit card numbers, and other account numbers. While holding this data enables organizations to provide more complete and efficient service to their customers or constituents, such access also opens organizations to significant risk. Every bit of data that enables better and more efficient service may also aid the work of cybercriminals who engage in identity theft, computer hacking, and fraud.

The vulnerability of computer-stored sensitive information has been highlighted by the increasing number of high-profile security breaches, for example, at Target department store, the Department of Defense, the Department of Veterans Affairs, Bank of America, and U.S. Office of Personnel Management. One example helps illustrate both the challenge and the problem. In October 2012, the South Carolina Department of Revenue was informed of a potential cyber-attack that compromised the personal information of taxpayers. The attack was facilitated by a state Department of Revenue employee who clicked on an embedded link in an email and compromised his computer. The subsequent investigation revealed that outdated computers and security flaws at the state's Department of Revenue allowed international hackers to steal 3.8 million tax records. For example, the state had not encrypted Social Security numbers. Once the outer perimeter security was compromised, the hackers were able to log in as tax officials and steal the data.

Legislatures, regulatory agencies, and all organizations are increasingly concerned about safekeeping confidential data. New statutes are being enacted, regulations are being promulgated, and lawsuits and enforcement actions are being filed, all directed at improving the performance of entities whose poor security practices resulted in the disclosure of sensitive data entrusted to them.

Bugs versus vulnerabilities

Both computer bugs and computer vulnerabilities may result from programming flaws, but vulnerabilities differ from bugs, with the former being much more serious than the latter. Any kind of computer weakness can be described as a bug. The difference is in degree of seriousness. A vulnerability is definitely a bug, but a bug is not necessarily a vulnerability.

Bugs may or may not be dangerous to the computer. They are referred to as security bugs or security defects. One example is an unauthorized additional code: It may be a weakness that causes the product to take longer to respond.

A vulnerability, however, must be patched as soon as possible because unauthorized users may gain access to the system with a computer vulnerability for criminal and destructive purposes. It may not be risky to defer actions to fix a mere bug because inaction or delay will not allow unauthorized users to compromise computer equipment. A vulnerability, however, may allow unauthorized access to the product and then to different parts of a computer network, including the database. Thus, a vulnerability must be fixed immediately to protect the integrity and security of the data and the system.

A normal bug fix can be done easily with service packs. If a vulnerability is discovered, Microsoft and other software manufacturers issue a security bulletin and develop a patch.

The danger of computer vulnerabilities

A security risk may be classified as a vulnerability. The use of the word *vulnerability* with the same meaning of risk may lead to confusion. The risk is connected to the potential of a significant loss. Some vulnerabilities are without risk, for example, when the affected asset has no value. A vulnerability with one or more known instances of a working and fully implemented attack is classified as an exploitable vulnerability—a vulnerability that can be exploited.

The following are common examples of criminals exploiting a computer vulnerability:

(1) An attacker finds and uses an overflow weakness to install malware to export sensitive data;

(2) an attacker convinces a user to open an email message with attached malware;

(3) an insider copies a hardened, encrypted program onto a thumb drive and cracks it at home; and

(4) a flood damages computer systems installed at ground floor.

Three conditions are required before a computer security problem is considered a computer vulnerability (or computer flaw):

Integrity (i.e., trustworthiness or reliability). If the weakness is serious enough that it allows exploiters to misuse it, the computer lacks sufficiently integrity.

Availability. If an exploiter is able to gain control over the computer and deny access to it for authorized users, then the bug is a vulnerability.

Confidentiality (i.e., maintaining the security of the data). If the bug in the system allows for unauthorized people to access the system's data, then it is a vulnerability.

Vulnerabilities allows attackers to degrade a system's information assurance. The seriousness of circumstances involving the flaw involve the confluence of three elements: a system susceptibility or flaw, attacker access to the flaw, and attacker capability to exploit the flaw. To exploit a computer vulnerability, an attacker must have at least one applicable tool or technique that can exploit a system weakness.

Vulnerability management is the cyclical practice of identifying, classifying, remediating, and mitigating vulnerabilities. This practice generally refers to software vulnerabilities in computing systems.

Vulnerabilities are related to (1) the physical environment of the system, (2) the personnel management administration procedures and security measures within the organization, (3) business operation and service delivery, (4) hardware, (5) software, (6) communication equipment and facilities, and (7) their combinations.

A bifurcated approach is necessary in dealing with computer vulnerabilities. This approach entails effective use of technical approaches, and administrative action to allow personnel to enter the facilities and people with adequate knowledge of the procedures who can implement them properly.

The law and computer security flaws

Data privacy laws are intended to promote and enforce several fair information practices that give individuals the ability to determine what personal information is being kept and by whom, opportunities to correct or remove such information, assurances that reasonable measures will be implemented to protect such information from disclosure, and to dispose of such information properly when appropriate and may include remedial.

The United States has no single, comprehensive statute for data privacy. Congress, the state legislatures, and federal and state regulatory agencies have enacted several different laws and regulations to protect specific types of information held by various organizations. Several sector-specific federal laws have been enacted to protect particularly sensitive information that is collected and stored by private companies. Forty states have data breach notification statutes. If the entities covered by these laws and regulations fail to comply with these standards, the results can be disastrous for the company, its shareholders, and its consumers.

The Gramm-Leach-Bliley Act (GLBA), and rules pursuant to it, regulate the collection, use, protection, and disposal of nonpublic personal information by financial institutions. The GLBA data security requirements are in a Federal Trade Commission (FTC) regulation called the safeguarding rule (16 C.F.R. 314). Under this rule, financial institutions are required to protect the security, confidentiality, and integrity of customer information by developing a comprehensive written information security program that has reasonable administrative, technical, and physical safeguards. This security program includes, of course, taking due diligence in monitoring for computer vulnerabilities and taking appropriate action when they discovered. The record to date indicates that dealing with computer vulnerabilities is a serious and continuous challenge that will require organizations to be constantly vigilant and committed to safeguarding the information entrusted to them.

Gretchen Nobahar

Further Reading

Burnett, Mark, and James C. Foster. *Hacking the Code ASP.NET Web Application Security*. Rockland, MA: Syngress, 2004.

Foster, James C., and Stephen C. Foster. *Programmer's Ultimate Security Deskref*. Rockland, MA: Syngress, 2004. Harrington, Jan L. *Network Security: A Practical Approach*. Amsterdam: Elsevier, 2005.

Howard, Michael, and David LeBlanc. *24 Deadly Sins of Software Security Programming Flaws and How to Fix Them*. New York: McGraw-Hill, 2010.

Osborne, Mark, and Paul M. Summitt. *How to Cheat at Managing Information Security*. Rockland, MA: Syngress, 2006.

Rittinghouse, John W., and James F. Ransome. *Wireless Operational Security*. Burlington, MA: Elsevier/Digital Press, 2004.

Stuttard, Dafydd, and Marcus Pinto. *The Web Application Hacker's Handbook: Finding and Exploiting Security Flaws,* 2nd ed. Indianapolis, IN: Wiley, 2011.

See also: Big data; Consumer Privacy; Data Collection; Financial information, privacy right to; Gramm-Leach-Bliley Act; Hacking, computers; Identity fraud

September 11

Identification: Or 9/11, the day on which the worst terrorist attack occurred in the United States in 2001. It was carried out by al Qaeda–affiliated jihadist radicals operating in the

United States, who attacked the Twin Towers in New York City and the Pentagon in Washington, DC, with civilian aircraft that they had highjacked. Over 3,000 people were killed in the 9/11 attacks.

The United States reacted to 9/11 in two key ways. First, it increased internal oversight procedures by creating a new balance between human rights and security needs, through legislation such as the PATRIOT Act. Second, it sought to combat terrorism abroad by armed means and other devices. This entry focuses on the first response, especially in relation to how this response affected or had the potential to affect the privacy rights of Americans. However, it is important to note that the American military response to 9/11 led to the Taliban regime in Afghanistan, and a fifteen-year military presence in Afghanistan that may not end anytime soon. America's war against terrorism abroad was fought by enhanced national security actions at home. These actions resulted from certain critical issues that arose after the 9/11 attacks.

In the aftermath of 9/11, policymakers and the general public asked: Why was the United States surprised by this attack? Why were such a large number of conspirators able to travel freely in the United States and plan the attack for several years without U.S. law enforcement or intelligence discovering the conspiracy? These questions led to the conclusion that U.S. immigration, intelligence, and security authorities were inadequate to contend with terrorism because of constitutional restrictions that were intended to protect civil liberties. Therefore, many believed that constitutional and legal changes were necessary to establish a new balance between civil liberties and the national security.

The concerns following 9/11 led the United States to enact the USA PATRIOT Act,, which provided law enforcement with enhanced authority to observe the conduct of individuals through sophisticated and enhanced surveillance, including monitoring, tracking a suspect's computer movements, and eavesdropping on communications with other computer users.

The PATRIOT Act also granted government new authority to search and investigate individuals attempting to gain entrance into the United States, special powers to arrest persons suspected of terrorist activities, and special deportation procedures. The PATRIOT Act strictly limited judicial oversight of security agencies and law enforcement agencies, which were granted new powers. The Bush administration, in particular, wanted law enforcement to exercise its powers as expeditiously as possible, without being delayed by judicial proceedings.

After the PATRIOT Act had become law, many in the privacy rights and civil liberties communities argued that the new law was an example of court stripping, meaning that authority was removed from the judiciary during times of crisis. There had been repeated instances of this in U.S. history. The government has often responded by enacting legislation to reduce or eliminate judicial review and the civil liberties of Americans.

Undoubtedly, the 9/11 attacks, like the Japanese attack on Pearl Harbor, was a devastating surprise attack. However, the U.S. response needed to be reasonable as well as forceful. The issues included the following: Were new government actions in limiting or potentially violating civil liberties constitutional? Were they sufficiently proportional? Did law enforcement and the military receive overly broad authority to scrutinize the lives of citizens under the pretext of protecting national security? Would the government receive powers that were even more intrusive of privacy rights?

In the aftermath of 9/11, the American war on terrorism was widely supported by Americans, but many observers expressed concerns that the PATRIOT Act posed a threat to American privacy rights in particular and to constitutional rights in general. Both those favoring and opposing the act realized that balancing national security, democracy, and civil liberties was difficult, particularly in difficult times. The speed and lack of deliberation with which the reassessment of this balance occurred, however, was particularly worrisome to the privacy rights community. Congress passed the legislation without full deliberations on the PATRIOT Act's ramifications, despite the potential impact of the PATRIOT Act on the civil liberties of Americans. Many civil libertarians objected to what they considered an inordinate and unjustified tilt of the balance to national security combined with failure to address civil liberty concerns.

Despite the immense tragedy of 9/11, principles of rigorous debate and thoughtful legislative process should not be forsaken in this time of crisis. When fundamental individual civil liberties are at stake, including the right to privacy, the American process of public discourse is all the more necessary.

In response to the attacks, President George W. Bush requested anti-terrorism laws and authority to defend the homeland. In late September 2001, several members of Congress were expressing concern that the bill would unduly and unnecessarily expand government power at the expense of privacy and other civil liberties. Despite these concerns, Congress passed and President Bush signed the USA PATRIOT Act in October 2001, purportedly to provide security and law enforcement agencies with new tools to fight terrorism. The major provisions of the statute sought to facilitate efforts of law enforcement in locating and apprehending terrorist suspects.

The PATRIOT Act significantly altered the court system's supervision of the executive in its investigation of routine criminal matters not related to terrorism. Specifically, critics of the PATRIOT Act claimed that various provision of the act infringed on the right of Americans to privacy, in addition to infringement on the freedom of association and on the right to due process.

In any time of crises, various minorities can be victimized by government overreach. The courts exist in the United States in part to protect minority groups and were created because

the Founding Fathers knew that majority groups could very well silence and persecute unpopular group or viewpoint.

Undoubtedly, the threat posed to national security by terrorist organizations is a real and serious threat. This threat is directed concurrently at both the range of democratic values and the freedoms cherished by the people of the United States. Thus, the war waged by a democratic state against terrorism is made more difficult than a war waged by a dictatorship because the democratic state must always refrain from infringing democratic values and the freedoms of the individual.

Enacting appropriate legislation is necessary for nations to confront terrorism. This legislation must be carefully crafted, however, and should include checks and balances against the possibility of state abuse of its powers. The proper balance should be based on the relative weight of the right being violated, which depends on the elements underlying the right, on one hand, and the degree of importance of the clashing interest, to achieve which the right will be violated, on the other. Every measure enacted as U.S. law must meet three criteria if it impinges civil liberties. The test determines whether the legislation had a proper purpose, and the legislation must satisfy the test of proportionality (the legislation must not exceed what was necessary).

A rational connection must exist between the measure adopted and the purpose. It must be the least intrusive measure available (no other alternative that would achieve the objective and infringe the right to any lesser degree), and the benefit derived from infringing the right must exceed the damage ensuing from the violation.

In addition to government action taken after the attacks, changes also occurred in the private sector. Some companies were legally required or adopted policies to use technologically advanced security measures to engage in surveillance of and collect personally identifiable information (PII) from their employees. While private companies have a general right to monitor their employees for legitimate business reasons, the invasiveness of such technologies and the collection of such PII could violate privacy law in the United States *and* the domestic law of other nations.

Further Reading

Diffie, Whitfield, and Susan Eva Landau. *Privacy on the Line: The Politics of Wiretapping and Encryption,* updated and expanded ed. Cambridge, MA: MIT Press, 2010.

Etzioni, Amitai. *How Patriotic Is the Patriot Act?: Freedom versus Security in the Age of Terrorism.* New York: Routledge, 2004.

Freedman, Jeri. *America Debates Privacy versus Security.* New York: Rosen Pubishing Group, 2008.

Grant, Rebecca A. *Visions of Privacy Policy Choices for the Digital Age.* Toronto, Ontario, Canada: University of Toronto Press, 1999.

Klosek, Jacqueline. *The War on Privacy.* Westport, CT: Praeger Publishers, 2007. Lyon, David. *Surveillance after September 11.* Malden, MA: Polity Press, 2003.

Protecting Individual Privacy in the Struggle against Terrorists: A Framework for Program Assessment. Washington, DC: National Academies Press, 2008.

The 9/11 Commission Report: Final Report of the National Commission on Terrorist Attacks upon the United States. New York: Norton, 2004.

Wright, Lawrence. *The Looming Tower: Al-Qaeda and the Road to 9/11.* New York: Knopf, 2006.

See also: Criminal justice (criminal procedure); Fourth Amendment to the U.S. Constitution; Law enforcement; Terrorism and privacy

Sexting

Identification: Any digital transmission of an explicit image created by a sender and sent to a recipient. Sexting involves only two parties, and the images depict either the recipient or the sender.

The most controversial aspects of sexting is when it involves a minor. Most of the discussion in this entry involves sexting as related to teenagers. The "narrow scope of sexting occurs between two teenagers, either as part of courtship or a relationship, and when they act in a flirtatious or romantic manner. The pictures are consensually sent and received within the agreed upon boundaries of the relationship. The "wide scope" of sexting involves those cases when a minor sends an image they made of themselves to multiple recipients or sends an unsolicited sext that is not part of a romantic relationship.

Under current law, sexting poses a difficult legal issue because minors technically violate state and federal law when they sext. Child pornography law prohibits any visual depiction that involves a minor engaging in sexually explicit conduct. No exceptions have been recognized on the context. Child pornography statutes currently prohibit sexting-related images, despite the fact that the statutes are intended to prosecute "sexual exploitation and other abuse of children" by predatory adults. Under current circumstances, prosecutors are punishing minors for intimate sexual decisions, not for conduct that abuses children.

Although sexting is technically a criminal offense, it appears to be common practice among a wide spectrum of individuals, including well-known individuals. Sexting is becoming increasingly common among teenagers. A Pew survey in 2009 found that 15 percent of cellphone users between the ages of twelve and seventeen have received a sexually explicit image of a person they know. The National Campaign to Prevent Teen and Unplanned Pregnancy reported that 19 percent of survey participants aged thirteen to nineteen had sent a sexually suggestive picture or video of themselves through email, cellphone or other medium and 31 percent had received a nude or semi-nude picture. Sexting becomes a legal issue because approximately 20 percent of all teenagers are involved in conduct that could result in imprisonment and sex offender registration.

Despite the potential of harsh punishment, the National Campaign's 2008 survey appears to indicate that sexting has become a "normal" part of life for many teenagers. Usually, the recipient of sexts is a significant other of the sender. Teens most frequently engage in sexting for fun or to be flirtatious. A majority of teen recipients of sexts reported that they were amused or aroused. Less than 10 percent of the respondents reported they were scared, angry, or disappointed, and only 15 percent said they were disgusted. Sexting appears to have also become part of courtship among contemporary American teenagers. After receiving a sext, 22 percent of recipients said were more interested in dating compared to 13 percent that were less interested.

Current criminal statutes, however, associate sexted images with child predators. This could result in the prosecution of minors for creating what is technically "child pornography," when, they view sexting as merely expressing their sexuality through a new medium.

Some teenage sexting has led to serious consequences and tragic results. In 2008, Jessica Logan, a high school senior, took some provocative pictures of herself using her cellphone and transmitted the images to her boyfriend. After the relationship had ended, he sent the photographs to Jessica's classmates, who disseminated both the photos, along with vile comments about her. As a result of this torment, Jessica committed suicide shortly after her graduation.

Opponents of sexting argue that because there are negative consequences when minors are forced into child pornography, there are also dangers when the teenagers produce the pornography themselves. In most cases, however, adult exploitation is absent from teen sexting. It may be a difficult argument to make that teenagers are abused when they created sexual images through their own free will.

There are three commonly made arguments stressing that sexting is harmful. First, the government believes that teen sexual activity is always inherently "abusive" because minors are incapable of consent. This argument would assert that individuals under the age of consent do not accurately perceive all the ramifications of engaging in sexual activities. Children who

engage in sexual intercourse, therefore, are victimized regardless if they perceive themselves as a victim. Privacy rights advocates have criticized this argument because sexting does not result in issues such as pregnancy or sexually transmitted diseases. These privacy advocates also argue that any harms such as bullying and the harmful dissemination are committed by third parties, not by the creators of the sexts.

Another argument is that there is the possibility that embarrassing images may be widely disseminated, beyond what the sender had intended. While this is a potential danger, privacy advocates argue, criminalizing sexting does not answer the actual risk. Cases of bullying or harassment may be dealt with statutes directed at the wrongdoers. Opponents of sexting also argue that sexting is potentially harmful to minors because other individuals might use these images inappropriately. Opponents of sexting offer a rebuttal that it is more effective and efficient for the government to eliminate sexting entirely rather than seeking to identify and punish difficult to find third party disseminators of the images. When an item appears on the Internet, it is almost impossible to stop its spread.

Last, many sexting opponents argue that any production of child pornography is potentially dangerous because it may later be used to encourage predators or entice children into unwanted sexual activity. Privacy advocates, however, argue that just because an activity may have harmful side effects, however, does not necessarily justify a blanket prohibition of an activity that involves fundamental rights. Privacy advocates invoke Justice Kennedy, who wrote a majority opinion that invalidated the Child Pornography Prevention Act of 1996. He wrote that "[t]here are many things innocent in themselves, however, such as cartoons, video games, and candy, that might be used for immoral purposes, yet we would not expect those to be prohibited because they can be misused," *Ashcroft v. Free Speech Coalition*, 535 U.S. 234 (2002). Privacy advocates, thus, argue that the sexual abuse of children should be fought by prosecuting predatory adults as opposed to suppressing of teenage sexting.

Although no court has held that sexting is constitutionally protected speech, some privacy rights advocates argue that courts could consider the rights of privacy raised by prosecuting minors who engage in sexting. Privacy advocates argue that courts should balance governmental regulations against sexting against their costs to individual liberty. These advocates offer *Lawrence v. Texas*, 539 U.S. 558 (2003) as a workable framework to determine whether state interests justify state involvement in the personal decisions involved with teenage sexuality, as exemplified in sexting.

Further Reading

Kreimer, Seth F. "Sex, Laws, and Videophones: The Problem of Juvenile Sexting Prosecutions," in *Children, Sexuality, and the Law*, ed. Sacha M. Coupet and Ellen Marrus, 133–62 (New York: New York University Press, 2015).

Sweeny, Jo Anne, "Sexting and Freedom of Expression: A Comparative Approach," Kentucky Law Journal 102 (2013–2014): 103–46.

See also: Child Online Privacy Protection Act (COPPA); Children's right to privacy; *Lawrence v. Texas*; Obscenity; Pornography

Sexual orientation

Identification: A person's attraction to another person of the same or opposite sex. This attraction is generally labeled as heterosexual, homosexual, or bisexual. *Asexual* refers to someone who is not sexually attracted to others.

The consensus among scientists is that sexual orientation is not a choice. There is no agreement, however, about why an individual develops a particular sexual orientation. A heterosexual person is attracted to a person of the opposite sex. In the United States, a homosexual person is generally considered a lesbian, a woman attracted to other women, or a gay man, a man attracted to other men. A person who is bisexual is a man or a woman attracted to both sexes.

A t-shirt bearing the slogan "Can you notice any difference? I cannot," worn by an activist at the LGBT event "L'amore spiazza" ("Love wrong-foots," with a pun in Italian with the word "piazza," meaning "square") held in Pavia on May 16, 2010, in order to increase awareness about LGBT issues and to fight against homophobia. (By Giovanni Dall'Orto.)

Sexual preference is a person's preference for one sex over another. It is often mentioned when discussing sexual orientation, but it is not synonymous with that phrase. While scientists believe that sexual orientation is not a choice, it has been suggested that there is a degree of choice with sexual preference.

Sexual orientation differs from sexual identity because it includes relationships with others, while sexual identity is a person's perception of his or her sex.

Sexual behavior refers to sexual acts performed by an individual, while sexual orientation refers to the attachments, longings, or fantasies that person might have. A person may not express his sexual orientation in his behaviors. A person who chooses not to accept his or her sexual orientation because it does not align with his or her sexual identity is referred to as closeted. When a person's sexual orientation, behaviors, and identity match, scientists use the term *concordance*. When these do not match, scientists use the term *discordance*. For example, a man who is attracted to other men but calls himself heterosexual and has sex only with women is experiencing discordance between his sexual orientation and his sexual identity and behavior.

In the United States, the U.S. Equal Employment Opportunity Commission has held that claims by homosexual and bisexual individuals that allege sex stereotyping present a sex discrimination claim under Title VII of the Civil Rights Act of 1964 (78 Stat. 241). The Civil Service Reform Act of 1978 (CSRA; 92 Stat. 111) also protects federal government applicants and employees from discrimination in personnel actions based on sex, which can include sexual orientation status. The Office of Special Counsel and the Merit Systems Protection Board enforce the prohibitions against federal employment discrimination codified in the CSRA.

More than thirty states and the District of Columbia provide legal protections against discrimination based on sexual orientation. An additional 185 cities and counties have passed nondiscrimination laws for sexual orientation. Most of these cities and counties are located in states that have statewide nondiscrimination policies in effect.

The Employment Non-Discrimination Act (ENDA) is legislation that has been proposed in the U.S. Congress every year since 1994, except the 109th Congress (2005–2007). This proposed legislation would prohibit discrimination in hiring and employing a person based on sexual orientation by an employer with more than fifteen employees. At the time of publication, ENDA has not been enacted.

Traditionally, sexual orientation has been seen as a private matter; however, incomplete data creates another hole in the well-worn fabric of society. Services cannot be made available unless there is evidence showing that a need

exists. Prejudice and discrimination will continue to dictate how lesbian, gay, bisexual, and transgender (LGBT) individuals live their lives unless the issue of sexual orientation is understood and accepted.

Maureen Halliden Anderson

Further Reading

Anzalone, Christopher A. *Supreme Court Cases on Gender and Sexual Equality, 1787–2001*. Armonk, NY: M.E. Sharpe, 2002.

Bamforth, Nicholas, ed. *Sexual Orientation and Rights*. Burlington, VT: Ashgate, 2014.

Botcherby, Sue, and Chris Creegan. *Moving Forward: Putting Sexual Orientation in the Public Domain*. Manchester, UK: Equality and Human Rights Commission, 2009. [Equality and Human Rights Commission Research Summary 40]. http://www.equalityhuman-rights.com/sites/default/files/documents/research/research40_so_moving_forward.pdf.

Heinze, Eric. *Sexual Orientation: A Human Right: An Essay on International Human Rights Law*. Dordrecht: M. Nijhoff Publishers, 1995.

Wintemute, Robert. *Sexual Orientation and Human Rights: The United States Constitution, the European Convention, and the Canadian Charter*. Oxford, UK: Clarendon Press, 1995.

See also: Constitutional law; Privacy laws, federal; Privacy laws, state

Smart meters

Identification: Installed in 38 million locations nationwide, they gather information on household electricity consumption and transmit it wirelessly at regular intervals to electric companies.

Smart meters are considered a major part in efforts to develop a "smart grid," which would more efficiently distribute electricity in the United States. The electric utilities argue that smart meters are intended to ensure that there are fewer power outages, smaller outages and faster service restoration if an outage occurs. The role of smart meters is to measure and report this data, enabling the grid to balance out fluctuations in supply and demand. Through the processing of

An antenna near residential homes collects data from home smart grid / smart utility meter systems via radio signal. June 11, 2017 near Rice, Minnesota. (By Tony Webster from Minneapolis, Minnesota, United States.)

such data, the smart-grid is then able to regulate the flow of electricity more efficiently and reliably. This will also enable electric utilities to integrate cleaner, local, renewable sources of energy. The electric utilities also claim that smart meters would give greater control of customers over their energy use and monthly bills, greater convenience, and improved customer service.

Several privacy advocates, however, argue that smart meters would allow the government to engage in surveillance and conduct searches that violate the Fourth Amendment right against unreasonable seizure. Some activists have argued that smart meters are surveillance devices that would record such personal information as when an individual is at home, what appliances they are using, and a person's habits.

Critics have expressed concerns that consumers would lose their private data to both electric utilities, and possibly to third-party data aggregators (who could use the information for data harvesting). They argue that very private and sensitive information could be disclosed about the home lives of customers, and thus violate the cherished privacy values associated with the home. Data users could make inferences about people's private lives from detailed energy consumption data, including the number of people living at the house, daily routines, various religious practices, and household appliance use.

Such exhaustive electricity consumption data would also be valuable to marketing analysts and consumer data aggregators, and would greatly assist retailers, who would use such information to plan new products, improve existing products, or open new stores.

In answering these privacy claims, utilities stress that smart meters retrieve the same data that utilities have retrieved through mechanical devices – namely, measuring energy use. Analog meter readings recorded aggregated energy data (kilowatt hours per month), while smart meters report data on a more granular level, and in real-time. The data collected from both types of meters is being used for the same purpose: billing, settlement, forecasting, demand response, and fraud detection.

One major difference between the two meters is that smart meters have a two-way communication capability, allowing the company to not only receive information from the meters, but also send commands, and receive responses in return.

Denying that smart meters are "surveillance devices" or could be used in wiretapping, electric utilities claim that smart meters measure the amount of energy used at a property as part of a customer's service agreement to purchase electricity from the utility. They do not how record energy usage. Nor do they store or transmit any information about the individuals, or their actions.

To answer the privacy concerns of its customers, many electric utilities have issued policies safeguarding their customers' privacy and protecting their networks and customer data from cyber threats. They also claim to support and comply with laws and regulations that prohibit third-party access to individual customer data unless the customer explicitly requests or approves the sharing of their data, it is necessary for the legitimate business needs of the utility, or the law requires it. They further argue that these practices are consistent with how these companies had protected customer data generated by electromechanical meters.

One major privacy involving third-party collection issue is that law enforcement officials have increasingly been seeking subpoenas of utility data to determine if illegal activity is occurring at a given residence.

In addressing concerns over home security, the electric utilities addressed concerns that cyber-savvy thieves could hack into smart meters and steal consumer information and energy. The utility companies argue that smart meters are no more vulnerable to tampering than mechanical meters. Similar to how all equipment that operate on wireless networks, smart meters may be hacked. One problem in the case of smart meters is the data being transmitted are not encrypted.

Utilities and smart grid developers, however, have implemented safeguards to maximize network security. These safeguards include network resiliency, security software on meters, event correlation improvements, identity management and authorization, meter-to-meter authentication and encryption, meter worm prevention. Implementing these measures would ensure grid security and obstruct meter hacking.

Smart grid designers must continue to make privacy an important priority in their development of hardware, software, and services that interact with a network. Utility companies should continue to develop and refine a comprehensive privacy policy that specifies how individual customer usage data will be used, to what it extent and under what circumstances it may be shared with third parties, and how customers can deny data sharing.

In compliance with the Energy Independence and Security Act of 2007, the National Institute of Standards and Technology (NIST) designated a Smart Grid Interoperability Panel to create standards for smart grid deployment. Operating under this panel is the Cyber Security Working Group, which focuses entirely on smart grid cyber security. In 2010, the group issued guidelines on privacy issues.

Data privacy protections must accompany the benefits that wireless networks like the Internet would provide. Similarly, the necessary safeguards may be implemented for smart meter data. Ultimately, this data can revolutionize the way electricity is distributed so that it is more responsive, more efficient, and more reliable.

In January 2015, the U.S. Department of Energy presented a final draft of a voluntary code of conduct governing data privacy from smart meters. A crucial part of the code would be "customer choice and content," which includes the principle that customers should control access to their use data that is provided to third parties. Critics, however, have questioned whether the code of conduct would be robust enough to withstand the temptations that this lucrative "big data" opportunities would offer for third party aggregators. Critics have particularly criticized the consumer "voluntary consent" provision in the code of conduct that would allow consumers to permit access to their consumption data perhaps for a price discount, thus, resulting in a major compromise of privacy rights.

Gretchen Nobahar

Further Reading

Cavoukian, Ann, and Alexander Dix. *Smart Meters in Europe Privacy by Design at Its Best.* Toronto, Ont.: Information and Privacy Commissioner of Ontario, Canada, 2012.

Doris, Elizabeth, and Kim Peterson. *Government Program Briefing Smart Metering.* Golden, CO: National Renewable Energy Laboratory, 2011.

Herold, Rebecca, and Christine Hertzog. *Data Privacy for the Smart Grid.* Reid, Irwin E. *Smart Meters and the Smart Grid: Privacy and Cybersecurity Considerations.* New York: Nova Science Publishers, 2012.

"Smart Meter Data and Privacy." *Data Privacy for the Smart Grid,* 2015, 55–74.

"The Tech Scene: The Know-It-All Smart Card Stirs Privacy Fears." *American Banker,* October 18, 2000.

Toledo, Fabio. *Smart Metering Handbook.* "What Is Privacy?" *Data Privacy for the Smart Grid,* 2015, 43–54.

Wolf, Christopher Maxwell. "Smart Grids and Privacy. (Regulation and Competition)." *Communications & Strategies,* October 1, 2009.

See also: Consumer privacy; Electronic surveillance; Fourth Amendment to the U.S. Constitution

Smartphones

Identification: Mobile phone devices that combine the features of a cellphone with those of a personal computer.

A 128 GB iPhone can contain more data than could be held on an average-sized hard drive on a desktop computer in 2009. In other words, such a smartphone could hold 20 million pages of word documents, or 600 million small emails, or 128,000 four-megapixel color digital photographs. From another perspective, such a smartphone has 2 million times the random access memory (RAM) running at least 800 times faster than the Apollo guidance computer that helped put a human on the moon. And that smartphone fits into your shirt pocket.

Consider what smartphones contain your thoughts and thought processes in written form, Internet web browsing history, phone logs, phone messages, text messages, banking records, bills, correspondence, emails, email attachments, photographs, videos, and so on. Smartphones can send and receive phone calls and Internet service because they transmit signals to and from cell towers, thereby telling those towers the precise location of the smartphone.

In all fairness, when each smartphone user first receives a new smartphone, the software gives the new user an opportunity to read; understand; and, most important, waive the privacy limitations created and detailed by the smartphone Internet and telephone service provider. Let's examine one example, however: Verizon's full privacy policy contains 6,700 words; its FiOS policy, another 4,000 words; its privacy policy summary, chief privacy officer message, tips for guarding your information, mobile analytics privacy notice, and device installment privacy plan, another 3,000 words. It is realistic to believe that almost no new smartphone user has read and understood all 13,700 words of that privacy doublespeak before clicking through Verizon's privacy waiver to get it over with and use the new smartphone.

In spite of all that storage power, smartphones are granted very little privacy indeed. Until very recently, in the case *Riley v. California,* if a person was arrested with a smartphone in a shirt pocket, the arresting officers could search the entire memory contents of that smartphone with a warrant, without probable cause, and without even a minimal standard such as reasonable suspicion. When a person enters the United States across an international border, perhaps from Canada, officers may seize that person's cellphone and hold it for days and even weeks searching it extensively without a warrant and without any probable cause or reasonable suspicion. Any data leaving or entering a smartphone must travel through other people's possession, such as Internet service providers, cell tower companies, phone companies, and so on. And that implicates what is known as the third-party doctrine, which holds that no person can have a reasonable expectation of privacy in anything that the person voluntarily disclosed to a third party. Of course, Internet service providers, cell tower companies, and phone companies are third parties. Thus, instead of getting a search warrant to obtain the contents of a person's smartphone directly from that person, law enforcement officers simply go to those third parties and demand that they turn over to the officers the contents that were sent to and from the person's smartphone. Those third parties must turn over those contents because those third parties have no "standing" to enforce in court the smartphone owner's constitutional right against unreasonable searches and seizures. And the smartphone user has no standing to contest that seizure of data from the third parties because it was not seized directly from the smartphone user.

Imagine the implications of the third-party doctrine in the digital era. By applying the doctrine to smartphones, the officers can trample the smartphone owner's constitutional rights and use that seized data against the smartphone owner in a criminal trial. But if the logical underpinning of the third-party doctrine is that no person can expect privacy in data voluntarily disclosed to third parties, then one must ask how voluntary was it when each smartphone user "agreed" to let the smartphone emanations be transmitted to the Internet service provider or the telephone company. It could be argued that smartphone users could have chosen not to use a smartphone and thereby not disclosed the smartphone data through third parties, but that argument is indefensible in the modern era when nearly everyone is compelled to have and use smartphones for business, recreation, communication, and the like.

Both the indefensible third-party doctrine in the digital age and the amazingly one-sided and verbose smartphone providers' privacy notices are almost outdone by the privacy waivers associated with applications (apps) on smartphones. Think of the last time you downloaded an app for your smartphone. It probably asked you for access to your location in real time while you are using the app and, even when you are not using it, for access to your contacts and Facebook pages, your camera, and all manner of other private information about you. With many of those apps, you cannot access or use the apps if you refuse any of those permissions. So you, like so many others, simply click through the privacy notices and waivers and grant each app almost any access its creators demand. As a result, the Facebook smartphone app accesses each user's location and contacts list; QR Pal accesses each user's calendar; Angry Birds accesses all three and sends user information, for a fee, to at least five different Internet marketers; Pandora sends your personal information, location, and phone identification to multiple data trackers from six companies; YouTube seizes your username and password, and the list continues.

These click-through privacy notices might be better called waivers of adhesion. Their terms are drafted and controlled in their entirety by the app or smartphone companies. The users have no power to redraft or amend those waivers and cannot propose their own waivers or refuse the companies' waivers. This kind of waiver is not a fair fight, is not a freely given waiver, and is a product of unequal bargaining power: It is a waiver of adhesion. If the user wants to use the smartphone or the app, the user must grant the privacy waiver.

Why do the smartphone and app companies collect all these data and what do they do with the data? They sell your private data, or they use your private data for their own purposes such as up-selling or targeting ads based on your web-surfing history or your location, or they charge others to tell them who you are and how to market to you. To have access to the device, the user gives up the privacy and in turn that formerly private data is rendered a public commodity available to the highest bidder.

Perhaps the starkest instance of privacy degradation traced to smartphones is the cellphone bulk telephony collection program maintained in secret for years by the National Security Agency (NSA). Under the mantle of safeguarding our nation during the so-called war on terror, the NSA collects and stores huge quantities of bulk data on our smartphone use. The NSA then reports that it intermittently mines that bulk data for patterns and individual instances that might be traced to terroristic activities. The NSA's program, at its initiation, arose from post-9/11 national security legislation and did not require judge-issued search warrants to collect all those data.

Various federal courts have wrestled with the constitutionality of the NSA bulk telephony collection program, with mixed results. At the time of publication of this essay, however, the highest court that has considered it to date, the U.S. Court of Appeals for the District of Columbia Circuit, has ruled that the program does not violate the Fourth Amendment ban on unreasonable searches and seizures. That circuit court opinion represented a split of authority because a panel of the Second Circuit Court of Appeals recently handed down an opinion in *ACLU v. Clapper* with the opposite holding: that the NSA bulk telephony program was unconstitutional.

In 2018, the US military took action regarding insecure smartphones, when it banned devices manufactured by Chinese makers ZTE and Huawei from being used by American soldiers. The companies, partially owned by the Chinese government, were deemed to be security risks in that they could potentially be used to conduct surveillance on American military operations or even disrupt military communication.

Another more mundane and universal way that smartphones are vulnerable is through the increasing ubiquity of public charging stations. While users may think that they are only accessing electricity to recharge their devices, those charging stations could easily be modified to download all manner of data from unsuspecting users. Though modern iOS and Android-based devices include safeguards against such intrusions, the apps that users place on their phones can create points of vulnerability for this type of attack.

One can scarcely blame law enforcement agencies, particularly federal agencies charged with protecting our nation from terror threats originating around the world, when those agencies use whatever tools, technological and otherwise, that are available to them to get the job done. As the pace of technological change quickens in the digital age, those agencies will be tempted to use each new generation of surveillance technology that engineers can conceive. Therefore, the power to decide which tools are constitutional and permissible cannot lie with the agencies in the executive branch that are charged with enforcing the law and keeping the nation safe. On the contrary, the power—and responsibility—to decide which surveillance tools will be permitted as constitutional rests with the other two branches: the judicial, through the courts, and the legislative through Congress. Without court and legislative intervention, Americans' constitutional rights to be free of unreasonable searches and seizures in the digital age will erode as fast as technology advances.

Charles E. MacLean

Further Reading

Brady, Sasha. "Could your smartphone be at risk when using a public USB charger?" *Lonely Planet*. February 23, 2019. https://www.lonelyplanet.com/news/2019/02/23/smartphone-risk-public-usb-port/

Egelman, Serge, Adrienne Porter Felt, and David Wagner. "Choice Architecture and Smartphone Privacy: There's a Price for That." *The Economics of Information Security and Privacy*: 211–236.

Espejo, Roman. *Smartphones*. Gomez-Martin, Laura E. "Smartphone Usage and the Need for Consumer Privacy Laws." *Tlp Pittsburgh Journal of Technology Law and Policy* 12 (2012).

Swire, Peter P. *Privacy and Surveillance with New Technologies. Wall Street Journal*. "What They Know—Mobile." August 30, 2015.

Woo, S. and Lubold, G. "Pentagon Orders Stores on Military Bases to Remove Huawei, ZTE Phones." *The Wall Street Journal*, May 2, 2018. https://www.wsj.com/articles/pentagon-asking-military-bases-to-remove-huawei-zte-phones-1525262076

See also: American Civil Liberties Union (ACLU); Apps; Cellphones; Fourth Amendment to the U.S. Constitution; National Security Agency (NSA); Privacy laws, federal; *Riley v. California*; USA PATRIOT Act; Wiretapping

Snapchat

Identification: A video-messaging application that allows users to send to other users text, pictures, videos, and drawings, called "snaps," that will be automatically deleted after they are viewed by their recipients. In addition to sending snaps, Snapchat offers a My Story feature, which allows users to post snaps for up to twenty-four hours on their Story. A Story can be viewed by other users an unlimited number of times during that twenty-four hour period. Snapchat also offers text and video chat functions, a multiuser-input Our Story, and an electronic payment system called Snapcash. Snapchat is one of the most popular social media applications available, with estimates of approximately 187 million active daily users.

Snapchat is notable for its prominent use of augmented reality "filters" and "lenses."

Snapchat allows users to modify the subject in the camera by altering their face or providing overlays onto the world "in camera." Popular examples include the addition of animal ears and noses, enlarging the eyes, and smoothing facial features. Although these changes are primarily cosmetic, some offer more practical functionality, such as overlaying the local temperature or the speed at which the user is traveling. The latter, the so-called "speed" filter, has implicated Snapchat in lawsuits where Snapchat users used the filter while traveling at dangerous speeds, resulting in traffic accidents.

Snapchat's central feature is that all snaps are ephemeral and will eventually be deleted. Snapchat therefore allows users to communicate and express themselves through an online medium with the knowledge that they will not create a permanent record that can be subjected to future scrutiny. Snapchat co-creator Evan Spiegel has claimed that Snapchat differs from other social media by removing the requirement to cultivate an idealized online identity, instead allowing for a less inhibited form of expression. This ephemerality of snaps is also perceived to provide more robust privacy and security than more traditional forms of online communication, such as text messaging, although Snapchat cannot ultimately guarantee that the content of snaps will be deleted.

Indeed, Snapchat's ephemeral quality can be undermined through several methods, all allowing users to produce lasting copies of snaps. These include taking a screenshot of the phone while an image is being shown (although Snapchat will notify the sender if a recipient screenshots), taking a picture of the phone with another camera, or using one of several third-party apps designed specifically to store the transient snaps. One of these third-party "Snapchat scraper" apps was the subject of a massive data breach in 2014, dubbed the Snappening, which led to an estimated 100,000 snaps being publicly leaked on the Internet.

Snapchat's claim that it deletes all snaps stored on its servers is also subject to certain limitations, such as law enforcement warrants requesting file retention and the temporary retention of files on redundant backup servers. These shortcomings led the Federal Trade Commission to bring an enforcement action against Snapchat in 2013, claiming that it had misled its users about the privacy and security the app provided. In addition, Snapchat has been frequently criticized for poor privacy and security practices, being voted "most unreliable" by the Electronic Frontier Foundation in its 2014 report on privacy policies.

Notwithstanding these security concerns, Snapchat has proved to be a popular means for sending pictures or videos that are considered privacy-sensitive, such as those called sexting. Sexting (a portmanteau of *sex* and *texting*), refers to sexually explicit personal messages and can include anything from merely suggestive text to actual nude photographs. Sexting is a popular research subject, with particular interest on its prevalence among teenagers. Considering the sexually explicit nature of sexts, sending or receiving sexts often carries serious legal ramifications, particularly if the subject is under the age of consent. And because Snapchat's primary demographic is younger users, sexting among these users may violate child pornography laws. Thus, Snapchat has frequently been criticized for facilitating child pornography. Snapchat refutes these claims, however, pointing out that almost all photo-messaging applications create the potential for underage sexting.

Despite these concerns with teen sexting, research conducted by the University of Washing- ton found that the majority of users claim to use Snapchat primarily for "funny content," such as taking selfies with funny faces or drawn-on mustaches, not for sexting. This usage suggests less a desire for privacy than it does a desire to prevent snaps from being subjected to lasting scrutiny. And indeed many respondents cited not privacy but different social standards as their primary reason for using Snapchat. Online media entails a permanence that can stifle expression, and Snapchat offers a means of recapturing this freedom of expression that other forms of social media inhibit.

Snapchat may be viewed more broadly as an attempt to use technology to solve privacy and security problems created by the digital age. One of the many concerns among social media users is that their actions leave a permanent digital record, and that record is often owned and controlled by a third party. Even social media platforms that provide much control over content still retain records of that user's activity, and this threat of a permanent record for all online activity can seriously stifle free speech and uninhibited expression. Snapchat represents an attempt to circumvent this problem by creating a medium that utilizes the benefits of technology while also limiting some of these perceived negatives. Although Snapchat's technical solution is imperfect, it represents a novel approach to information sharing. Its success suggests that a market for similar privacy-protecting apps may have strong consumer support.

Thus, Snapchat is part of the broader trend in privacy that attempts to regulate data retention. Snapchat's primary appeal is that it inherently limits how long personal data is stored, both by itself and among its users. While Snapchat's data retention limits are integral to its design, some suggest these limitations should be imposed on all companies that manage personal data. Considering the amount of personal data that is shared with and controlled by third parties and the ease of storage, data retention limits are a proposed mechanism to reduce the extent this data can be subjected to lasting scrutiny. While there is currently no federal law limiting data retention by private companies generally, there are some limits for government agencies, and broader regulations are increasingly common abroad, most notably the European Union's "Right to Be Forgotten"

and the corresponding provisions in the General Data Protection Regulation (GDPR).

Scott Russell

Further Reading

Cardoza, Nate, Cindy Cohn, Parker Higgins, Kurt Opsahl, and Rainey Reitman. *Who Has Your Back: Protecting Your Data from Government Request.* Electronic Frontier Foundation, May 15, 2014.

Colao, J. J. "Snapchat: The Biggest No-Revenue Mobile App since Instagram." *Forbes*, November 27, 2012.

Crump, Catherine. "Data Retention: Privacy, Anonymity, and Accountability Online." *Stanford Law Review* 56, no. 1 (2003): 191.

"How Snaps Are Stored and Deleted." *Snapchat Blog*, May 9, 2013.

McBride, Sarah, and Alexei Oreskovic. "Snapchat Breach Exposes Flawed Premise, Security Challenge." Reuters, October 14, 2014.

Meyer, Robinson. "The New Terminology of Snapchat." *The Atlantic*, May 2, 2014.

Roesner, Franziska, Brian T. Gill, and Tadayoshi Kohno. "Sex, Lies, or Kittens? Investigating the Use of Snapchat's Self-Destructing Messages." In *Financial Cryptography and Data Security,* vol. 8437 of the series *Lecture Notes in Computer Science* (November 9, 2014), 64–76.

Shontell, Alyson. "Snap Is a Lot Bigger Than People Realize and It Could be Nearing 200 Million Active Users." *Business Insider*, January 3, 2015.

Strassberg, Donald, Ryan K. McKinnon, Michael A. Sustaíta, and Jordan Rullo. "Sexting by High School Students: An Exploratory and Descriptive Study." *Archives of Sexual Behavior* 42, no. 1 (June 7, 2012): 15–21.

See also: Apps; Mobile devices; Right to be forgotten; Sexting; Social media; Social networking technologies

Snooper's Charter

Identification: Formally known as the Communications Data Bill; draft legislation originally proposed by Britain's Conservative government in 2012.

Snooper's Charter, if passed, would require Internet service providers (ISPs), mobile phone networks, and telecommunications companies in Britain to maintain records of every user's Internet browsing, social media activity, phone calls, text messages, and instant messages. The bill would expand existing communications data retention requirements and grant access to law enforcement to assist intelligence agencies and the police investigating crime and terrorism. Under current law, British ISPs may retain data, when it has been processed for normal business purposes such as billing or marketing, for twelve months, as regulated by the British Data Protection Act 1998 (DPA).

The new proposals would require telecommunications companies to keep data that would not ordinarily be retained for business purposes for up to twelve months, during which time official agencies would able be able to access the data. The original language of the draft bill does not specify what types of information that firms are required to retain. The bill added, however, that this power may be exercised only after a period of consultation with the companies and would be subject to existing data protection safeguards. Prime Minister David Cameron said that British encrypted messaging services could be outlawed unless they provide the government with backdoor access to user data.

In 2012, Cameron's government said that it was seeking passage of the bill to ensure that law enforcement and intelligence agencies have access to vital communications data under strict safeguards to protect the public. Supporters said that the bill would prevent extremists from being able to communicate with each other without being monitored by British intelligence agencies.

The proposed obligations imposed on ISPs, however, raise serious issues for both the ISPs and the British public. Critics of the bill claim that, if enacted, the legislation would grant the government very broad surveillance powers and would legally authorize it to record and store personal data on every person in Britain. Denying allegations that the bill would allow for massive and unfettered surveillance, British home secretary Teresa May claimed that the collected data would not include message contents; however, it could include who they are sent to, their frequency, and where they originated.

Critics of the bill claimed that requirements to retain more data and make it available to a growing number of recipients increase the risk of breaching data protection laws. Critics also expressed concerns that cybercriminals could hack into the database, which would be a potential bonanza for hackers, criminals, and rogue states.

Almost a year after the Conservative–Liberal Democrat coalition government proposed the bill, Deputy Prime Minister Nick Clegg announced in April 2013 that the Liberal Democrats would no longer support the legislation. The Liberal Democrats later blocked the bill. In the 2015 elections, however, Cameron won a majority of seats in Parliament, thus removing a major obstacle to the bill's passage.

Existing data protection laws apply to information about people, for example, from identifiers such as name, address, employment history, and medical records, to subtle identifiers such as social networking content, browser history, or call log. The DPA imposes several principles on organizations that use personal information, including transparency (people must be told how their information is used and by whom); organizations must not collect excessive personal information, and what they do collect should not be kept for longer than is necessary; and citizens have a right to access the data held about them by organizations and to object to processing where it causes damage and distress. These principles appear to clash with the details in the bill.

Further Reading

Draft Communications Data Bill. London: Stationery Office, 2012.

Draft Communications Data Bill: Session 2012–13: Report, Together with Appendices and Formal Minutes. London: Stationery Office, 2012.

Rowe, Heather. "Draft UK Data Protection Bill." *Computer Law & Security Review* 10, no. 5 (1994): 280.

See also: Big data; Electronic surveillance; Metadata

Snowden, Edward Joseph

Identification: An American information technology professional responsible for one of the most significant disclosures of classified U.S. government documents in history.

Edward ("Ed") Joseph Snowden was born June 21, 1983, in Elizabeth City, North Carolina. In May 2004, he enlisted in the U.S. Army Reserve as a special forces candidate. He joined the global communications division of the Central Intelligence Agency (CIA) in 2005, as part of a team charged with the maintenance of CIA computer network security in Geneva, Switzerland. In 2009, he was hired by Dell Inc., a contractor for the National Security Agency (NSA), as an expert in cyber-counterintelligence. He began working for the NSA contractor Booz Allen Hamilton in 2013, for the express purpose of gathering classified data to leak it to the press.

The U.S. Department of Defense estimates that Snowden disclosed a total of 1.7 million classified documents, as well as the existence and structure of several secret NSA surveillance programs. Snowden stated that he carefully evaluated every document that was disclosed to ensure that such disclosure was in the public interest. The disclosures notably revealed the details of three secret global surveillance programs—PRISM, Boundless Informant, and XKeyscore—operated by NSA with the support of the governments of the United Kingdom, Australia, and Canada. The PRISM program granted NSA direct access to the Google and Yahoo accounts of people within the United States. The Boundless Informant program allowed access to worldwide telephonic metadata and provided analytic tools for analyzing them to reveal patterns and connections between callers. The XKeyscore program granted access to nearly everything the average user does on the Internet, including the content of emails, web searches, and websites visited. Snowden further disclosed the existence of NSA's MonsterMind program, which is capable of automatically responding to unusual

In February 2014, Edward Snowden joined the board of Freedom of the Press Foundation, which published this photo under a Creative Commons Attribution 4.0 International License.

patterns of Internet use consistent with cyberattacks and blocking such potential attacks from entering U.S. networks.

Snowden testified before the European Parliament that he had expressed his doubts about the legality of the programs to ten NSA officials, who either took no action or told him to remain silent on the matter. This contention is disputed by NSA, which claims that there is no evidence that Snowden ever made any such reports.

Snowden chose to make his identity public rather than remain anonymous, as had many prior whistleblowers. He did so to protect fellow NSA contractors and employees from being subjected to government scrutiny in a potential hunt for the source of the leaks, as well as to embolden others to step forward with their own disclosures and because he believed that he had done nothing wrong. Snowden initially did not want to appear on camera; however, out of a desire that the press focus on the content of the disclosures rather than their source, he changed his mind.

Eighteen days after the leaks were first published, the U.S. government revoked Snowden's passport while he was en route to Ecuador to seek asylum. As a result, he was forced to stay in Moscow, Russia, where his flight had landed for a layover. He lived in Moscow's Sheremetyevo international airport for thirty-nine days before being granted a temporary one-year asylum in Russia on August 1, 2014, which was extended, upon expiration, into a three-year Russian residency permit.

The U.S. government filed the following criminal charges against Snowden on June 14, 2013: theft of government property, two violations of the Espionage Act, and willful communication of classified intelligence information to an unauthorized person. Snowden's disclosures have contributed to the grounds of two notable lawsuits. In *Klayman v. Obama* (957 F. Supp. 2d 1 (D.D.C., 2013)]), plaintiff Larry Klayman alleged, based on the Snowden leaks, that the U.S. government had unlawfully collected his telephonic metadata in violation of the First, Fourth, and Fifth Amendments to the U.S. Constitution. In *ACLU v. Clapper* (no. 13–3994) (S.D.N.Y, 2013), the American Civil Liberties Union alleged that NSA's mass collection of telephonic metadata, revealed by Snowden, had violated the First Amendment as well as the Fourth Amendment's protection of the right to privacy.

Expressly in response to Snowden's disclosures, the United Nations General Assembly in December 2013 adopted nonbinding Resolution 68/167, which is meant to protect the right of privacy against unlawful surveillance.

Snowden was the subject of Laura Poitras's 2014 documentary *Citizenfour,* which won the 2015 Academy Award for Best Documentary Feature. Among the many awards and honors bestowed upon Snowden in recognition of the disclosures, he was named the *Guardian's* person of the year, was the runner-up for *Time* magazine's person of the year, and was presented with the Sam Adams Award, all in 2013.

Reuben Fuller-Bennett

Further Reading

Greenwald, Glenn. *No Place to Hide: Edward Snowden, the NSA, and the U.S. Surveillance State.* New York: Metropolitan Books/H. Holt, 2014.

Harding, Luke. *The Snowden Files: The Inside Story of the World's Most Wanted Man.* New York: Vintage Books, 2014.

Lyon, David. *Surveillance after Snowden.* Malden, MA: Polity Press, 2015.

Snowden, Edward. *The Snowden Reader,* edited by David P. Fidler. Bloomington: Indiana University Press, 2015.

See also: American Civil Liberties Union (ACLU); Boundless Informant; Electronic Surveillance; Espionage Act; Fifth Amendment to the U.S. Constitution; First Amendment to the U.S. Constitution; Fourth Amendment to the U.S. Constitution; Greenwald, Glenn; Metadata; Poitras, Laura; PRISM; The Right to Privacy; Whistleblowers

Social media

Identification: Evolving technology platforms allowing ordinary people to disseminate ideas and information simply by establishing a social media account.

Social media empowers every person to become a live-streaming news and entertainment source, sharing images and stories that range from the intimately personal to the mundane and the dubious or violent. Items shared on social media are often referred to as "posts" or "postings." Users share information about themselves, others, current events, recipes, parties, sporting events, beverage and food choices, political issues, and seemingly limitless other topics. Some social media platforms only permit users to share (or "post") photos. Social media can compete, and increasingly has competed, with traditional media.

Individuals using social media are not required to provide their real identity or present their actual opinions. Further, individuals can have numerous social media accounts, often cutting across technological platforms. Many individuals will have different social media accounts for their professional and personal lives. Social media is not limited to actual persons. Businesses, restaurants, athletic teams, entertainers, political entities, and universities have all begun capitalizing on the low- to cost-free usage of social media.

Many famous individuals have social media accounts. In fact, both the President of the United States (@realDonaldTrump; also @POTUS) and the Pope (Pope Francis @PONTIFEX) have Twitter accounts. The U.S. Internal Revenue Service also uses social media platforms, including YouTube, Twitter, Tumblr, and Facebook. Overall, the Pew Research Center found that, as of 2018, 73 percent of adults report using social media. This same study indicates that 68 percent of adults utilize Facebook, while more than 25 percent use Twitter, Snapchat, Pinterest, and LinkedIn; 35 percent use Instagram. There is no question that social media usage is expanding across all demographics, even as questions of its abuse by nefarious actors have also increased.

Social media users can "share" information with "friends" and "followers," individuals or entities the user confirms are permitted to access their information. These "friends" and "followers," however, who may not be known acquaintances, can then share that information with other individuals, who can do the same with their "friends" and "followers" until such time that a story goes "viral," or spreads beyond the immediate target audience. Many social media platforms also permit individuals to have their account be entirely public so that any individual or entity can view the information.

Social media primarily differs from traditional media in that the information disseminated is not generally vetted for accuracy or authenticity. In fact, there are many social media accounts that are intended to be fictional or to parody an actual person. One of the more popular social media platforms, Twitter, allows parody but not impersonation. Its website has rules regarding proper usage and how individuals can create "fan" and "parody" accounts that will not be suspended.

Social media posts are generally not censored, except by the individual posting the information. Instead, the only limits placed on social media tend to be after the fact, with a social media platform deleting a post or suspending an account if the post is found to violate usage terms. The most obvious examples have included the deletion of accounts owned by terrorist groups, such as ISIS, that have posted graphic depictions of actual crimes, as well as "bot" accounts (software robot devices) designed to generate interest or activity around a particular post or user by artificial means. The latter method, for example, figured prominently in the 2016 U.S. presidential election. Officials at Twitter and Facebook were criticized, in the media and at Congressional hearings, for not acting swiftly enough to remove fake accounts and quell the dissemination of hate speech and other noxious messages.

Social media platforms are numerous and constantly expanding. Some permit posts that include words, images, audios, and videos. Others may be limited solely to words or images (such as photographs). Each platform tends to have a descriptive focus. For example, Facebook is arguably the most popular social social media platform where users generally share a wide-range of information about themselves, their interests, and their daily lives. Common posts include pictures of what one ate at a particular meal; descriptions of one's exercise regime; requests for advice on particular matters; rants about businesses, entertainers, politicians, or sports; Biblical quotations and other religious or inspirational passages; funny photos or cartoons; and calls for help in funding a particular person or cause. Again, however, fake news and bot activity have plagued Facebook along with other social media in recent years.

Twitter, another highly popular social media network, currently limits its posts to 280 characters or fewer (having doubled the original

140-character limit in 2017). Individuals can post images and words but in very short, often cryptic fashion. Other Twitter users will simply send numerous "tweets" that allow them to expand their message beyond the 280 characters, as a series of "tweets" can accomplish what a single message cannot. Still other social media platforms, such as YouTube, Pinterest, and Instagram, focus on visual mediums to allow users to share photos and video recordings.

Other conventional social media platforms include Google+, LinkedIn, About.me, Foursquare, MySpace, Houseparty, Periscope, Tumblr, Blogger, Vox, Reddit, Scribd, SlideShare, Classmates, Friendster, CaringBridge, MyLife, Flickr, and Snapchat. At the moment this list was typed, it was likely obsolete. Social media is growing and changing at a furious a pace, although the main players continue to dominate the field.

The law relating to technology, in general, and social media, in particular, however, has not grown at the same rate. Few legal restraints are placed on social media users. Instead, most social media platforms provide usage "guidelines" that seek to impose legal norms on users. For example, Twitter (and most other social media platforms, including Houseparty and Periscope) prohibits copyright and trademark infringement, threats and harassment, targeted abuse, "graphic content," and release of "private information." Twitter, along with Facebook and others, reserves the right to remove any content violating its "guidelines" and/or to entirely shut down an account, which is consistent with current social norms and usage practices. While formal rules may impose more restraints than the law itself would, these guidelines tend to steer users away from potential legal violations. Further, these guidelines ensure that the companies hosting the social media platforms do not, themselves, become subject to legal action for many of the violations they prohibit. Facebook, for example, has long claimed that it is not a "publisher" having the responsibilities that go along

with that designation, but rather is a "platform" that simply allows users to publish their own content. This claim has come under increasing pressure in recent years.

Social media platforms run by independent companies can regulate speech and expression in a much more restrictive manner than the United States government can. The First Amendment, like all constitutional provisions, applies only to governmental action. Thus, most social media platforms cannot be found to violate a user's First Amendment rights because the First Amendment does not apply to private restrictions on speech and expression.

To the extent that individuals and companies are subjected to governmental punishment or prosecution for social media usage, that governmental action will be tempered by the First Amendment. Cases involving cyberbullying, for example, may be subject to a First Amendment defense unless the behavior involved a true threat. Under traditional First Amendment jurisprudence, a true threat is considered low-value speech that is not protected by the First Amendment. Similarly, individuals sharing or posting information that is itself criminal in nature—for example, actual child pornography—will not benefit from the First Amendment because it is the very act of sharing or posting such information that constitutes the crime.

Social media platforms also implicate individual privacy concerns. Many individuals constantly provide "status updates" and live-stream stories such that individuals can discern their location and precise activities. It is not uncommon for someone to "check in" on Facebook, which immediately indicates his or her location to "friends"—and, potentially, criminals. Further, an experiment posted on YouTube entitled "The Dangers of Social Media" illustrates the serious risk that social media poses to children. Actor Coby Persin, proceeding with the permission and complicity of several teens' parents, easily lured both male and female teens to meet with him (he was posing as someone else) despite the warnings of their parents about the dangers of social media. The experiment demonstrated some of the risks posed by social media— how do parents monitor their children's usage and protect against predators?

Just as criminals can use social media, so can the police and government. Because social media permits individuals to create accounts using a fictitious name and persona, the police have been able to set up stings to arrest (without entrapment) individuals seeking to commit statutory rape, terroristic crimes, or drug-related offenses. Sometimes police officers, posing as someone else, enter chat rooms and observe other individuals' postings and comments. Alternatively, the police may simply benefit from information posted by a criminal about a crime he or she committed, or such information shared with the police by a "friend" or "follower" of the individual. Moreover, with the live-streaming capacity of Houseparty and Periscope, officers also happen upon criminals who foolishly post their crimes online. Posts on Periscope, which was acquired by Twitter in 2015, have resulted in the arrest of drunk drivers and burglars who live-streamed their respective crimes.

Social media has also been credited with creating an alternate "community" where activists can help spur political change and revolution. In countries where traditional media sources are controlled by the government and Internet access is limited—particularly during periods of political instability—social media can aid ordinary citizens by helping galvanize this alternative community to bring about change at the grassroots level. The Arab Spring is largely believed to have benefited from the presence, and leveraging, of social media.

Those desiring negative change, instability, and chaos also resort to social media. ISIS took to social media to depict, in graphic video and still photography footage, the beheading of its captives. Each time, it was not until after the videos surfaced and were shared that these accounts were suspended and the images taken down.

Similarly, in Myanmar in 2016 and 2017, government military and local militia units made use of Facebook and other social media to coordinate a drive to eliminate the Rohingya ethnic group from their homeland in Rakhine State. That activity, too, came to light mostly after the fact. Also, as noted, the 2016 U.S. presidential race was disrupted by waves of fake news and bot activity on social media, much of it linked to Russian state actors (as was later determined).

The lesson, clearly, is that social media can be used for good and it can be used for evil. It can bring people together and can tear societies apart. Without clear laws in place—particularly obligations that can be enforced transnationally—there is little hope that those seeking to use social media to harm society or others can be effectively deterred. Social media provides every individual with the opportunity to tell his or her story, be it truth, fiction, or opinion. Thus, as the technology expands, serious consideration should be given to the benefits and risks that social media poses to society. Congressional leaders have begun, belatedly, to realize this fact.

Social media remains a new and ever-evolving form of communication. Its achievements, potential, and shortcomings are still being assessed. From an international perspective, social media has opened up the world in a myriad of positive ways—as well as negative ways. Now, without waiting for a traditional media source to filter a story—particularly in a country that depends on state-sponsored media outlets—information can be transmitted literally across the world in seconds. Information is no longer just the property of the traditional media or government. Even in the United States, messages and newsworthy events can be instantaneously shared without waiting for traditional media platforms to vet, package, and present the story.

As social media becomes more entrenched in our daily lives, the law will ultimately need to catch up. There will be increased need to protect the intellectual property rights of business and individuals, through copyright and trademark infringement protections. There will be greater need to protect the vulnerable from predators, whether the vulnerable are our children, the elderly, or citizen-voters seeking information about a political race. There will be an increased need to consider the true privacy implications of what we post and share with others. Libel laws, defamation laws, obscenity laws, and intellectual property laws will all need to be refashioned to consider their application in a social media-driven world. Even those who "like" social media must appreciate both the benefits and risk posed by such expansive communicative opportunities operating almost entirely outside the bounds of the law.

Mary M. Penrose and Michael Shally-Jensen

Further Reading

Albarran, Alan B., ed. *The Social Media Industries*. New York: Routledge, 2013.

Berger, J. M., and Jonathon Morgan. *The ISIS Twitter Census: Defining and Describing the Population of ISIS Supporters on Twitter.* Brookings Project on U.S. Relations with the Islamic World Analysis Paper no. 20 (March 2015).

Hannigan, Robert. *"The Web Is a Terrorist's Command-and-Control Network of Choice,"* Financial Times, November 3, 2014.

Hartley, John, Jean Burgess, and Axel Bruns, eds. *A Companion to New Media Dynamics.* Malden, MA: Wiley, 2013.

Mandiberg, Michael. *The Social Media Reader*. New York: New York University Press, 2012.

Parkinson, Hannah Jane. *"James Foley: How Social Media Is Fighting Back against ISIS Propaganda,"* Guardian, August 20, 2014.

Pew Research Center. "Social Media Use in 2018" Available at: http://www.pewinternet.org/2018/03/01/social-media-use-in-2018/

Pollack, John. "Streetbook: How Egyptian and Tunisian Youth Hacked the Arab Spring," *MIT Technology Review,* August 23, 2011.

Qualman, Erik. *Socialnomics: How Social Media Transforms the Way We Live and Do Business.* 2d ed. Hoboken, NJ: Wiley, 2013.

Warburton, Steven, and Stylianos Hatzipanagos, eds. *Digital Identity and Social Media.* Hershey, PA: Information Science Reference, 2013.

Youngs, Gillian, ed. *Digital World: Connectivity, Creativity, and Rights.* 2013; reprint, New York: Routledge, 2013.

See also: Bots; Election interference and privacy issues; Facebook; First Amendment to the U.S. Constitution; Harassment; Instagram; Law enforcement; Obscenity; Pornography; Snapchat; Twitter

Social media profiling

Identification: The corporate practice of accumulating personal information on social media (and other Internet sites) and using it to compile a detailed portrait of an individual user to be used for a variety of commercial purposes.

Social media began as a way for people to meet new friends and to reconnect with old ones; however, the conversation on the use of social media has turned unfriendly. One reason for that turn is the increase in the number of accusations that information from online users is gathered, stored, and sold to commercial companies. Major players, Google and Facebook, for example, admit to collecting personal user data. Both have online privacy policy websites that provide information on what type of information they collect and how and why it is used. The Google Privacy and Policies website provides extensive details on how it uses information as well as how and with whom the information is shared. Facebook's Data Policy provides users a similar service. The website for Twitter, Twitter Privacy Policy, gives users Twitter's procedures for collecting, issuing, and sharing data.

How have these privacy issues affected users? There has been a change in the way many users view these social media sites. The excitement of being able to express personal opinions on issues and share personal information and intimate details is not as pronounced as it was in the first stage of the social media wave.

What is the profile being created of you? Can you see it? How can you be in control of it? How will it be used and who will use it? Those are just a few of the questions that individuals, governmental agencies, and countries are asking. There are concerns about the use of profiles created by agencies. Online users now realize that information shared on the Internet is also finding its way into employer files and credit agency reports. In spite of the concern over what information is being stored about users of websites, arguments are made that the value of social media outweighs concerns of privacy invasion. The profiling of users can be taken to extremes, and both academic and popular articles address the impact of such profiling on the public.

Employers readily use social media as part of their background checks on prospective employees. Trying to have a conversation about privacy in any form on social media is counterintuitive. Yet users rarely consider the thought that such postings, made in an arguably relaxed and informal social arena, could be subject to the serious process of seeking employment. An issue for many people who viewed social media suspiciously from its outset was what would happen with user data gathered by media site hosts. Its use and impact on the lives of individuals was debated.

Profiling of individuals by gathering data from their time spent on the Internet takes several forms. Major department stores usually claim that they collect data only on what their customers buy, how much they spend, and how often they shop. Profiling of that kind may indeed be benign. There is no way to confirm, however, that companies to whom the information is sold or shared will be as benign in their use of the data. Assumptions about people can be made by analyzing their use of the Internet. Medications bought, magazines read, and sites visited can provide data on individuals that in turn can create profiles used for many unknown reasons. The unknown continues to cause concern.

Online users now realize that information shared on the Internet is also finding its way into many different platforms. Employers use the Internet and social media to profile the activities of those who visit their sites. They also focus on the postings of prospective employees. Credit reporting agencies, some of which may be partners with websites, also share and use information collected from websites.

Arguments are made by Google and Facebook that they gather information to enhance their websites for their users. Supposedly consumers benefit from profiles created from the data gathered on their websites. Nevertheless consumers were not informed that their information was being used. Pharmaceutical companies may send unsolicited letters referencing medications for conditions to persons who sought information from online websites in the privacy of their homes.

One of the early major concerns about establishing a social presence was the lack of certainty on the protection of personal information. Uncertainty and a focus on profiling came later. Now governmental and social agencies and academic institutions routinely collect data that provides profiles of their clients and students. What has changed is that individuals are pushing back against the practice and demanding that these agencies provide information on what they do with the data that they collect.

Sandra Jowers-Barber

See also: Background checks; Credit reporting agencies; Data brokers; Employment Eligibility Verification Systems; Invasion of privacy; Marketing; Social media; Social media technologies; Spam

Social networking technologies

Internet-based platforms that enable individuals and organizations to connect with other user of the platform and share information about themselves. The participant's information, as well as varying degrees of additional identifying information, is displayed as a profile describing the user. Participants can then view, and at times engage with, the information of the other users with whom they have made a formal connection. Participants can also view the information of users whose information is public.

While there is some debate about which Internet-based platform was the first social networking technology, GeoCities and Sixdegrees.com were two of the earliest precursors to the modern concept. GeoCities, which began operating as such in 1995, provided users with the opportunity to create free personalized webpages. Those webpages were located within communities called neighborhoods, which were groupings of webpages that shared similar content. Webpage owners within a community could then search and access the webpages of users who shared similar interests or characteristics.

Sixdegrees.com began in 1997 and took a more intentional approach to connecting users. Members of the website could communicate with other users with whom they formalized a connection and could invite nonmembers to join. Members could also seek out other users on the site and view their relationship to those users. GeoCities ended operations in 2009, ten years after having been acquired by Yahoo!, and Sixdegrees.com ended operations in 2001.

After GeoCities and Sixdegrees.com began the idea of utilizing the Internet to form and maintain relationships between users of a particular platform, Friendster was founded in 2003 with the intent of allowing people to create personalized pages and then to connect and interact more intimately with the personalized pages of others. Friendster took on the form of what is now considered a modern social networking platform because it also allowed users to tailor their profile pages with media and other online content. Friendster was plagued with slow connections, however, which frustrated users and caused them to abandon the service. As Friendster saw its usage decline, MySpace and Facebook, launched in 2003 and 2004, respectively, began to take over and fulfill the public's desire for interconnected relationships on the web. MySpace, however, struggled to keep users because it was ill-equipped and reluctant to accommodate third-party developers; whereas Facebook remained open to their applications.

By 2009, Facebook had more than 200 million users, while MySpace had 100 million users. Facebook continued its success and by 2013 had over 1 billion users. Facebook's initial structure was premised on empowering users by allowing them to accept or reject requests to access each other's profiles. Therefore, the presumption was that users acted as their own gatekeepers by limiting others' access to the information they presented via the platform.

Twitter, another Internet platform founded in 2006, presumed open access to information, which required users to privatize their information sharing affirmatively. Unlike Facebook's initial structure, Twitter users could track the sharing of information by other Twitter users without an affirmative, approved bidirectional relationship. As new platforms come online, they increasingly add new options for more intimate sharing of information. For example, sites like FourSquare and Instagram, as well as some of the more established platforms, have allowed users to share the time and location of their activities. As new means are developed to share an increasing amount of information, new platforms are created to facilitate and capitalize on it.

Social networking technologies have been celebrated for their democratization of the exchange of ideas. They have allowed billions of people to access and contribute to public discourse regardless of notoriety or affluence. While access to the effective means of communication historically resided with powerful and influential public figures, social networking technologies allow users of the same platform to access and engage with each other's social, political, and religious views. Users can instantly approve, share, and respond to other's ideas in a fluid and synchronous manner.

These attributes have led some to credit social networking technologies with facilitating substantial social change. For example, the effective use of social networking technology has been recognized as key to U.S. President Barack Obama's 2008 election. Social networking technology is credited with coordinating and enabling the protests that ultimately pushed the Communist Party from power in Moldova in 2009. Many have also argued that social networking technology played a vital role in the Arab Spring, which was a series of revolutions and civil unrest in the Middle East beginning in 2010 and leading to the overthrow of governments in Tunisia, Egypt, Libya, and Yemen.

The role of social networking technologies in politics is hard to overstate. After the 2016 American election cycle several social networking platforms, including Facebook and Twitter have been forced to reckon with their influence on politics internally, and also to appear before government bodies to help explain that influence. Further, in Myanmar, Facebook partnered with MTP, the state's telecom company, to provide the public with its "free basics" program. Many have blamed Facebook's influence for the ethnic cleansing of Myanmar's Rohingya Muslim minority. The company failed to remove accounts with doctored images and anti-Muslim propaganda.

In addition to acting as a virtual "public square," social networking technologies also facilitate the spread of so-called fake news. Facebook has recently launched a campaign against fake news, removing several prominent conspiracy theorists from its platform. However, as recently as February of 2019, the British Parliament had labeled Facebook a "digital gangster" which fails to adequately police its platform. Often fake news is spread by fraudulent "bot" users on platforms like Facebook and Twitter, with 1 percent of individual accounts making up 80 percent of the fake news stories posted.

While social networking technologies have arguably assisted in ushering in social change, they have also enabled the intentional and unintentional sharing of vast amounts of private information. In some cases, social media technologies have been used to disseminate private information about others without their permission and have resulted in civil lawsuits. For example, a medical clinic worker in Minnesota allegedly accessed embarrassing medical information about a patient without the patient's authorization. The clinic worker then disclosed the information to others, which ultimately resulted in a MySpace page containing the information about the patient. The patient sued the clinic worker and the clinic for, among other things, invasion of privacy. Lawsuits have also resulted from the republication of information shared on personal, private social media pages.

In New Jersey, a paramedic maintained a private Facebook page where others could view her posts only if they had permission. The paramedic had permitted friends and coworkers access yet did not give permission to her employer, an emergency medical service provider. After her employer was informed about the paramedic's controversial Facebook post, the employer allegedly coerced some of the paramedic's coworkers to access her account while a supervisor looked on. The supervisor then copied the post and forwarded it to the state paramedic licensing board, alleging that the post demonstrated unprofessional behavior. The paramedic sued her employer and claimed that sharing her private Facebook post was an invasion of privacy.

Courts are divided, however, on these sorts of civil claims of invasion of privacy. Some courts have determined that privacy is lost when one posts information on a publicly accessible Internet site, even if their privacy settings are highly restrictive. Other courts have found that an invasion of privacy can occur where the user has created a password-protected, private account and limits those who can view it. The question has yet to be resolved.

Criminal charges are also possible where social media technologies have been used to disseminate private information. In 2010, Dharun Ravi, a college student, used his Twitter account to announce that his college roommate, Tyler Clementi, had asked to use their shared room until midnight. In addition, Ravi stated that he had accessed his computer's webcam and observed his roommate becoming intimate with another man. Ravi then live-streamed Clementi's tryst via iChat. Three days later Clementi posted a message on his Facebook page announcing that he was going to commit suicide and did indeed do so. Ravi was charged with, among other things, the crime of invasion of privacy, which makes it illegal to record and disseminate another's sexual encounter without his or her consent. In 2012, Ravi was found guilty and sentenced to thirty days in jail, a $10,000 fine, three years of probation, and 300 hours of community service.

Facebook itself has come under scrutiny for the collection of user data. In 2018 it was revealed that the social networking platform had allowed a third-party app developer and research firm, Cambridge Analytica, to have access to 50 million users' data without informing them. This data was then used for various political enterprises, including as part of Donald Trump's campaign for the U.S. presidency.

While social media technologies often present the appearance of privacy by permitting users to limit access by other users, the government can often access the information shared via social media technologies. If the government is seeking the information, the question arises whether it must obtain a warrant. In *Katz v. United States*, 389 U.S. 347 (1967), the U.S. Supreme Court determined that FBI agents could not record an individual's phone call in a telephone booth without a warrant. The Court determined that the Fourth Amendment protected the individual from unreasonable search, and not just in private places. In his concurrence, Justice John Marshall Harlan II articulated a test that has been used by the Court since. He stated that the government must attain a warrant before a search if the person to be searched

has a reasonable expectation of privacy and the expectation is one that society would recognize as reasonable.

In the 1970s, the Supreme Court decided two cases, *Smith v. Maryland*, 442 U.S. 735 (1979), and *United States v. Miller*, 425 U.S. 435 (1976), that created what is known as the third-party doctrine. Individuals in those cases had transmitted information to a third party, a telephone company and a bank, respectively. The Court determined that the transmittal of information to a third party invalidated an individual's expectation of privacy in the information and that the government could access it without a warrant. Social networking technology users often allow some other users of the platform, however few, to view the information they post. In addition, any information posted to a social media platform is, at the least, shared with the organization that owns the platform. Therefore, most courts have found that the government can lawfully obtain that information without a warrant.

For example, in a case in New York, a defendant's Facebook "friend" allowed the government to access the defendant's Facebook posts through the friend's account. When the defendant challenged the use of the posts against him in his criminal trial, the court found that the government did not need a warrant, had obtained the information from his account legally, and could use it against him in court.

It is not only the government that can take advantage of the lack of privacy protection associated with social networking technologies. Third parties, as well as the social media platforms themselves, can access and use the information that users share. Information that is publicly shared on social media platforms is often collected and aggregated by third-party organizations, including for-profit corporations.

These organizations can then use the information to construct a portrait of the user's likes and dislikes, activities, location, and propensities. The constructed portrait is valuable to companies that would use it for the purposes of marketing their products. It can also be used by companies to anticipate the likelihood that a user will default on a loan or be an insurance risk. Politicians use the information gleaned from social networking technologies to microtarget their messages and get-out-the vote efforts. The social networking platforms also use the information that their users share in similar ways. Users that express interest in a particular product, share their location and activities, or share a major life experience will often see advertisements directed related to those characteristics.

Criminals have also been known to use the lack of privacy in social networking technologies for nefarious purposes. While many social networking platforms allow users to share their location, some rely primarily on users posting their activities and locations so that other users can find recommended businesses and services.

In addition to intentionally sharing one's location and activities, sharing pictures via social networking platforms can unintentionally reveal location through geotagging (geographically identifiable metadata). Whether intentional or otherwise, criminals can use this and other information to their advantage. For instance, users have been burglarized after sharing their location and revealing that they are not home or plan not to be home at a particular time. Cyberstalkers can use information posted on social media platforms to learn their victims' patterns and more easily threaten, harass, or attack them. Criminals can also build a picture of users by collecting available, personal information and ultimately steal the user's identity.

In addition to privacy, hate speech has become an increasing issue on social media platforms, though it has been difficult to police. In 2018, Facebook took to banning users who posted sentences such as "men are trash" but continued allowing white nationalist and other extremist organizations on their platform. Twitter, Tumblr, and Instagram face similar issues,

with extremist content often reported but found to "not violate terms of service."

In response to the inaction of social media platforms like Facebook and Twitter, loosely affiliated, often anarchist groups have taken to "doxing" users who post or participate in white nationalist or right-wing extremist groups. While not a common practice, and certainly not legal, doxing, or exposing names, locations, and other data, has been used against prominent social media users such as journalists and YouTubers. It also presents an issue for social media platforms as the users who post "dox" content are often anonymous and take steps to disguise their point of origin, making the practice hard to effectively combat.

Social media technologies have had a significant impact on societies throughout the world. Since their beginnings, they have served to connect people to one another, facilitate relationships, and foster the sharing of information and ideas. Along with this nearly unfettered freedom to share ideas, however, social media users may find themselves making a trade-off. When users engage with the technology they find themselves, almost necessarily, giving up some of their privacy.

In the digital age, we are faced with a Hobson's choice. We can protect our privacy to the greatest degree possible by avoiding social media technology, thereby missing out on all it has to offer, or we can embrace the technology knowing that, in doing so, we give up a claim to some of the privacy we would otherwise have.

Douglas B. McKechnie and J. N. Manuel

Further Reading

Granville, Kevin. "Facebook and Cambridge Analytica: What You Need to Know as Fallout Widens," *The New York Times*, March 19, 2018.

Grinberg, Nir, et al. "Fake news on Twitter during the 2016 U.S. presidential election," *Science*, Vol. 363, No. 6425 (January 2019), pp. 374–378.

Mozur, Paul. "A Genocide Incited on Facebook, With Posts From Myanmar's Military," *The New York Times*, October 15, 2018.

Reinecke, Leonard, and Sabine Trepete. *Privacy Online: Perspectives on Privacy and Self-Disclosure in the Social Web.* New York: Springer Publishing Company, 2011.

Silverman, Jacob. *Terms of Service: Social Media and the Price of Constant Connection.* New York: HarperCollins, 2015.

Turkle, Sherry. *Alone Together: Why We Expect More from Technology and Less from Each Other.* New York: BasicBooks, 2011.

See also: Doxing; Facebook; Instagram; *Katz v. United States;* Search warrants; Twitter

Social Security numbers (SSNs)

Identification: Identification numbers issued by the U.S. government that have long been required for Americans to engage in a broad range of activities, such as setting up telephone service, obtaining a driver's license, or banking.

Social Security numbers (SSNs) have a vital role in establishing an individual's identity. Indeed, the easiest and most common way for someone to steal the identity of another person is by obtaining that person's SSN. With the SSN, a thief can open up and access the bank accounts of that other person. SSNs are attractive to identity thieves because they provide access to a victim's private information and because SSNs are commonly used as a national identifier for everything from car rentals to credit card applications. Often a thief needs only a name and an SSN to open up a credit card account or to gain access to an existing account. Identity thieves are also able to use another person's SSN for employment purposes or to obtain medical care.

Individuals should limit access to their SSN as much as possible. While the potential sources of SSNs are vast and accessible, people can take prudent and reasonable action to prevent thieves from accessing their SSNs.

Social Security numbers (SSNs) were first issued in 1936, pursuant to the Social Security Act, 49 Stat. 620 (1935). At the time, the federal government said that these numbers would be used only for Social Security programs. Over time, however, the SSN became the de facto national identification number and was used for a broad range of non-Social-Security-related purposes. SSNs are widely used to identify individuals and authenticate information. As an identifier, the SSN answers the question, "Who are you?" As an authenticator, the SSN answers the demand, "Prove who you are."

The SSN is used as an identification number in many computer files, allowing a convenient way of linking databases but also giving access to information that an individual may wish to keep private. The files of utility companies are an example of such usage. In recent years, data breaches in which SSNs are compromised have become increasingly common.

In 2006, the U.S. Government Accountability Office (GAO) described the potential for identity theft posed by SSNs contained in public records. The GAO estimated that 85 percent of the largest, most populated counties surveyed make records that may have SSNs available in bulk sales or online. Frequently SSNs appear in state and local court files and local property ownership records.

Government agencies generally impose no restrictions on the reuse of data included in public records, which means that information may be transferred between individuals multiple times and even be outsourced to foreign service providers. Recently, many states have sought to limit the accessibility of SSNs contained in public records. Nonetheless, millions of SSNs are already available in public records. Some jurisdictions have started redacting SSNs from older public records, a costly and time-consuming process.

The GAO's report found that SSNs were displayed on millions of cards issued by federal agencies, including 42 million Medicare cards, 8 million Department of Defense identification cards and insurance cards, and 7 million Veteran Affairs identification cards.

Because the connection between identity theft and widespread use of SSNs is well established, the federal government has been curtailing its use. In 2007, the Office of Management and Budget (OMB) issued a memorandum that required agencies to review their use of SSNs and identify instances in which collection or use is unnecessary. Thus, federal agencies have been greatly reducing unnecessary SSN use. SSNs have not appeared on military identification cards since 2011. As of 2015, it is required that SSNs be removed from Medicare cards and that they be replaced with randomly generated Medicare beneficiary identifiers. Some government agencies, however, such as tax authorities, welfare offices, and state departments of motor vehicles, still require a person's SSN due to federal law [42 USC 405 (c)(2)(C)(v) and (i)].

The Privacy Act of 1974, as amended at 5 U.S.C. 552a, protects records that can be retrieved from a system of records by personal identifiers such as a name, social security number, or other identifying number or symbol. The Privacy Act of 1974 requires all government agencies (federal, state, and local) that request SSNs to provide a "disclosure" statement that explains whether an individual is required to provide an SSN or, if it is optional, how the SSN will be used and under what statutory or other authority the number is requested (5 USC 552a, note). The Privacy Act states that individuals may not be denied a government benefit or service if they refuse to disclose their SSN unless federal law requires such disclosure or the disclosure is to an agency that had been using SSNs prior to January 1975, when the Privacy Act became effective.

Generally individuals are not legally required to provide their SSNs to private businesses. There is no law, however, that prevents businesses from requesting an individual's SSN, and businesses have few restrictions on what they may do with it once they have it. Even though an individual may not legally be required to disclose his or her SSN, the business is not required to provide the individual with goods or services if the person refuses to release the SSN. In some cases there may be alternate numbers that a person can provide to the company, such as a driver's license number.

Federal law requires private businesses to submit the SSNs of individuals when (1) the individual is involved in a transaction for which the Internal Revenue Service (IRS) requires notification, or (2) the individual is engaged in financial transactions covered by federal Customer Identification Program rules.

Medicaid and Medicare may require that an individual provide an SSN. Commercial insurance companies may request the SSN of an individual client if that individual is covered by group insurance through his or her employer or if he or she purchased an Affordable Care Act (ACA) plan through a state or federal marketplace.

Beginning in the 2015 tax year, health insurance companies are required to provide Form 1095-B to the IRS. The information will be used to verify information on the individual income tax return under the ACA, 124 Stat. 119 through 124 Stat. 1025 (2010). If the information the insured provides on the tax return cannot be verified, the individual may receive a notice from the IRS indicating that he or she is liable for a shared responsibility payment under the ACA.

Credit card applications usually request SSNs. The individual's number is used primarily to verify the identity of a person who has a name similar to or the same as the name of other persons. Most credit grantors will insist that applicants provide their SSN.

Credit-reporting agencies generally require that customers provide their SSN. They claim that the SSN is necessary to retrieve the correct files from among the many records they maintain. These agencies already have customer SSNs. When requesting an annual credit report from any of the established credit bureaus, individuals may request that the SSN be omitted from the document when sent through the mail.

Some websites request an SSN from individuals applying for a credit card or seeking an insurance quote online. Individuals should be cautious about determining that personal data is transmitted securely and that it is stored safely by the online business. Individuals should ensure that the latest antivirus and anti-spyware software is installed on their own computers. Customers should conduct commercial transactions only with well-known, reputable companies. Individuals should read the company's privacy policy, which should indicate how it safeguards personal data. It is not reasonable or prudent to transact business with a company that does not appear to protect customer data.

Customers should not respond to spam (unsolicited email messages) asking for an SSN or other personal information. Individuals may receive many email messages that appear to originate from a government agency such as the Internal Revenue Service or from a bank or company. The message typically says that the company or agency is updating its records or has detected fraudulent activity on an individual's account and needs personal information, such as an SSN, account number, password, or mother's maiden name. It may also direct the customer to an official-looking website through a link in the message. Customers should not respond to such messages because they are phishing scams. Although they appear to be legitimate, these messages and websites are schemes to obtain personal information for fraudulent purposes. No reputable company or government agency sends email messages requesting sensitive personal data.

In many states employers may use an employee's SSN as an employee identification number. Employers should not display SSNs on documents that may be seen by other people—such as badges, parking permits, or lists distributed to employees. Employers do need each employee's SSN, however, to report income and payroll taxes.

In 1961, the Internal Revenue Service began using SSNs as taxpayer identification numbers. Therefore, SSNs are required on transactions in which the IRS has jurisdiction. That includes most banking transactions, the stock market and other investments, real estate purchases, many automobile purchases, many insurance documents, and other financial transactions as well as employment records.

To retain their funding, publicly funded schools and those that receive federal funding must comply with the Family Educational Rights and Privacy Act (FERPA) (1974), codified as 20 USC 1232g. FERPA requires written consent for the release of educational records or personally identifiable information, with some exceptions. The courts have ruled that SSNs are covered in this provision. See *Krebs v. Rutgers,* 797 F. Supp. 1246 (D.N.J. 1992).

FERPA applies to state colleges, universities, and technical schools that receive federal funding. If such a school displays students' SSNs on identification cards or distributes class rosters or grade listings with SSNs, this might violate FERPA. Some schools and universities nevertheless continue to use an SSN as a student identifier.

Public schools, colleges, and universities are also covered by the Privacy Act of 1974, which requires these schools to provide a disclosure statement explaining how SSNs are used. If the school is a private institution, the administration would set the policy and may allow students to use an alternate identification number as a student ID. The U.S. Department of Education and Department of Justice interpret the Privacy Act as prohibiting a public school district from requiring a pupil or parent to provide an SSN or denying admittance because a pupil does not provide an SSN. Many colleges and universities have sought to eliminate the SSN as primary identifiers for students, faculty members, and staff members.

The Intelligence Reform and Terrorism Prevention Act of 2004, 118 Stat. 3638, prohibits states from including SSNs on driver's licenses, state identification cards, or motor vehicle registrations. The law applies to all licenses, registrations, and identification cards issued after 2005. Drivers with licenses that still have the SSN as the ID number may request that this be changed. Although a person's SSN may not be used as the ID number on his or her license, under the Real ID Act of 2005, 119 Stat. 302 (2005), states must require proof of a person's SSN (or verification that the individual is not eligible for an SSN) when issuing a license.

Further Reading

Dwan, Berni. "Identity Theft." *Computer Fraud & Security*, no. 4 (April 2004): 14–17.

Jasper, Margaret C. *Social Security Law*. Dobbs Ferry, NY: Oceana Publications, 1999.

Sorrells, Felipe D. *Social Security Numbers and ID Theft*. New York: Nova Science Publishers, 2010.

"US Government Tackles Identity Theft." *Computer Fraud & Security* no. 5 (May 2007): 4.

See also: Affordable Care Act; Family Educational Rights and Privacy Act of 1974 (FERPA); Financial information, privacy right to; Privacy Act of 1974; Spam

Sorrell v. IMS Health, 131 S. Ct. 2653 (2011)

Identification: A U.S. Supreme Court decision holding that a Vermont statute regulating the use of physician data for advertising violated the First Amendment. The Court found that Vermont was attempting to burden unduly a disfavored viewpoint and disfavored speakers, specifically pharmaceutical manufacturers and their advocates, and that this content-based and speaker-based approach to regulation was unconstitutional. *Sorrell* has been interpreted to represent a broader trend in U.S. constitutional law toward the greater protection of corporate speech, and suggests that the Court may consider elevating the legal standard it applies for commercial speech from intermediate scrutiny to strict scrutiny.

Background

In 2007, Vermont passed the Prescription Confidentiality Law in response to growing concern over pharmaceutical detailing: targeted marketing to physicians by pharmaceutical representatives known as detailers. Detailing provides pharmaceutical manufacturers an opportunity to influence directly the drugs physicians prescribe and is therefore both highly profitable and highly effective. To bolster detailing's efficacy, detailers use data on physicians' prescribing history to craft marketing strategies specific to those physicians. As such, an industry of data miners emerged that would buy prescribing data from pharmacists, aggregate that data, and resell it in the form of physician profiles to pharmaceutical manufacturers, all for more effective detailing (*Sorrell* at 2660).

The Vermont statute in *Sorrell* attempted to regulate detailing by restricting the sale, disclosure, and use of physician data for marketing without the physician's consent. The official purpose of the Vermont statute was to protect the privacy of physicians, although another strong motivating factor was to encourage the use of generic drugs by hindering the more expensive drugs marketed by detailers. The statute also provided several exceptions allowing the data to be used in areas like research and law enforcement. In response to the Vermont statute, pharmaceutical manufacturers and data-mining companies challenged the law, claiming it violated their First Amendment right to free speech (*Sorrell* at 2661).

The Law

Prior to *Sorrell,* the Supreme Court differentiated commercial speech from other categories of protected speech by giving it a weaker standard of review: "intermediate scrutiny." Intermediate scrutiny requires that regulations assert a "substantial government interest," that the regulation must "directly support the government interest," and that it must not be "more extensive than is necessary to serve that interest" (*Central Hudson v. Public Service Commission* at 566). This is to be contrasted with "strict scrutiny," the higher standard typically applied to protected speech, which requires a "compelling government interest" that is "narrowly tailored" and is the "least restrictive means" for achieving the government's interest (see, for example, *United States v. Playboy Entertainment Group*, 529 U.S. 803 (2000)).

Despite this precedent, *Sorrell* moved away from intermediate scrutiny in favor of a nebulous "heightened scrutiny" whenever a regulation imposes content-based or speaker-based restrictions on speech. Rejecting Vermont's contention that the statute was a purely commercial regulation, the Court emphasized that the statute made content-based restrictions by regulating the sale of physician data *for advertising*, and speaker-based restrictions by targeting entities that buy and sell physician data, specifically pharmaceutical manufacturers and data-mining companies (*Sorrell* at 2663).

Although *Sorrell* emphasized the need for "heightened scrutiny," the analysis found that Vermont's interest in protecting physician privacy did not satisfy even intermediate scrutiny, effectively dodging this apparent discrepancy. Vermont's argument that the statute protected physician privacy failed because the data was restricted only for marketing purposes. This didn't advance the government's interest because it didn't prevent the use of physician data for other purposes, like medical research. Essentially, the Court held that the law didn't truly protect the physicians' privacy. The Court does suggest, however, that more comprehensive privacy legislation might be treated differently, and provides as an example the Health Insurance Portability and Accountability Act (HIPAA) (*Sorrell* at 2668). Yet the dissent casts doubt on this point by noting that the Vermont statute's exceptions were modeled on HIPAA's exceptions and that invalidating the Vermont statute could cast serious doubts on the constitutionality of privacy statutes like HIPAA (*Sorrell* at 2684).

The Court went on to dismiss Vermont's second government interest: lowering the costs associated with public health. Detailers advocate newer, more expensive drugs, and Vermont argued that the statute promoted the use of more economical medication, like generics. Although the Court recognized that promoting cheaper drugs was certainly a valid government interest, that interest could not be furthered by silencing the opposing viewpoint. The government cannot silence a disfavored viewpoint, nor can the government unduly burden a disfavored speaker, so Vermont's attempt to restrict detailing was an unconstitutional method of promoting generic drugs and therefore an unconstitutional restriction on free speech (*Sorrell* at 2672).

Sorrell is notable because the Court's distinction between a content-based or speaker-based regulation and a purely commercial regulation, while seemingly simple, is difficult to articulate in practice. Any commercial regulation could be framed as targeting specific content (e.g., advertising) or as targeting specific speakers (e.g., advertisers), and the Court provided little help in determining when to apply intermediate scrutiny and when to apply heightened scrutiny. This ambiguity, coupled with the Court's highly protective language with regard to commercial speech, has led many commentators to suggest that *Sorrell* signifies the Court's willingness to elevate permanently the standard for commercial speech to strict scrutiny. Indeed, Justice Breyer's dissent assumed as much, decrying the majority's opinion as harkening back to the *Lochner* era, a contentious period when the Court policed commercial regulations much more aggressively (*Sorrell* at 2675).

Whether or not the Court abandons the intermediate scrutiny test for commercial speech, *Sorrell* raises concerns for the constitutionality of any statute regulating data held by third parties to protect privacy. If the mere sale of data is speech, then any regulation attempting to limit the sale of data would be a content-based and speaker-based restriction on free speech, warranting heightened scrutiny. Extending these powerful First Amendment protections to data makes regulating how third parties use that data extremely difficult, and considering the significant amount of personal data that is generated and held by third parties, such an expansive reading of the First Amendment may seriously hinder legislative attempts to protect personal privacy.

Scott Russell

Further Reading

Bambauer, Jane. "Is Data Speech?" *Stanford Law Review* 66, no. 57 (2014).

Bhagwat, Ashutosh. "*Sorrell v. IMS Health:* Details, Detailing, and the Death of Privacy." *Vermont Law Review* 36, no. 855 (2012).

See also: Consent; Constitutional law; First Amendment to the U.S. Constitution; Health Insurance Portability and Accountability Act (HIPAA); Marketing; Supreme Court of the United States

Spam

Identification: An abuse of email technology to transmit a large amount of unsolicited junk email in bulk, often for commercial reasons. Spam is often sent by botnets, networks of virus-infected computers, which hinders the prosecution of spammers. Some estimates state that nearly 80 percent of all email sent worldwide is spam.

For computer users, spam can be annoying. Spam is often used to send fraudulent offers or to disseminate malicious software such as viruses. Spammers harvest and compile bulk listings of email address through automated scanning of popularly used websites or by intercepting the transmission of electronic mailing lists.

Spam often has some form of false or misleading information and consistently offends recipients by promoting investment scams, pornography, or medications. The Federal Trade Commission (FTC) found that 66 percent of all spam has false, fraudulent, or misleading infor-

mation somewhere in the email's routing information, subject line, or message content.

Most Americans agree that spam clutters email inboxes with unwanted communication and thus violates the privacy of email users and their "right to be let alone." Current Supreme Court jurisprudence on the right to privacy in one's home also grants email recipients a right to privacy in what they receive in their email inboxes. One origin of this right in this context is from the case of *Rowan v. United States Post Office Department,* 397 U.S. 728 (1970), in which the U.S. Supreme Court recognized an individual's "right to be let alone" and held that a mailer's right to communicate ends at the mailbox of an uninterested addressee. The appellants challenged the constitutionality of a statute that effectively prohibited sexually explicit mailings on free speech grounds. Rejecting this argument, the Court pointed to the necessity that the "right to be let alone" must balance with the right of others to communicate: "Individual autonomy must survive to permit every householder to exercise control over unwanted mail." Accordingly, the statute served to protect individuals' privacy and passed constitutional muster. The Court stated:

> In effect, Congress allows each citizen to erect a wall that no advertiser may penetrate without his acquiescence. The continuing effect of a mailing ban once imposed presents no constitutional issues; the citizen cannot be put to the burden of determining on repeated occasions whether the offending mailer has altered its material so as to make it acceptable. Nor should the householder have to risk that offensive material come into the hands of children before it can be stopped.

Similarly, the right of spammers to solicit others must end at the outer edge of each individual's private domain. The sanctuary of the home in the *Rowan* case included the mailbox. A mailbox and an email inbox serve the same purpose: to send and receive communications. Individuals maintain a higher expectation of privacy in email addresses. Email addresses maintain anonymity and are not a matter of public record. Each recipient must have a password to access an inbox, just as one must have a key to enter a residence. Thus, an inbox must be considered part of the home and enjoy at least the same protected status as the mailbox. It follows that no one has the right to impose ideas on unwilling recipients in the sanctuary of his or her email inbox. Spammers do not have a fundamental right to send unsolicited commercial emails to individuals' inboxes. Consequently, spam encroaches upon the personal space of individuals and violates their "right to be let alone," their right to be free from objectionable intrusion, and their right to privacy.

Because email inboxes are personal space, they receive privacy protection. In *CompuServe Inc. v. Cyber Promotions, Inc.*, 962 F. Supp. 1015 (U.S. Dist., 1997), an Internet service provider (ISP) sought to prevent a spammer from sending unsolicited commercial email to its subscribers based on a "trespass to chattels claim." The ISP argued that the volume of messages generated by mass mailings substantially burdened its equipment and storage capacity. Defendant spammers ignored the ISP's notification that they were prohibited from continuing such activity and disregarded the ISP's request to cease and desist from sending unsolicited email to its subscribers. The spammers also modified their equipment and messages to circumvent the ISP's filtering software. The ISP in CompuServe asserted that this action represented a trespass upon its personal property. The court agreed, holding that "the use of personal property exceeding consent is a trespass." Electronic signals generated and sent by computers have been held to be sufficiently physically tangible to support a trespass cause of action. Given the determination that ISPs maintain private property, email inboxes must therefore constitute personal private property rather than public property.

In *Cyber Promotions, Inc. v. AOL,* 948 F.Supp. 456 (1996), a federal district court found that AOL had the right to prevent spammers from reaching its subscribers over the Internet. The spammers claimed that AOL's conduct constituted state action to support their claim that AOL was required to respect their right to free speech. The court found that AOL did not exercise any "municipal powers or public services traditionally exercised by the State." Even though AOL "technically" availed its email system to the public by connecting to the Internet, it did not open its property to the public by performing functions typically reserved for a municipality or a state. AOL's Internet email connection did not constitute an exclusive public function because several alternatives to email existed for commercial communication, such as the World Wide Web, U.S. mail, telemarketing, television, cable, newspapers, magazines, and leaflets. Email inboxes thus constitute personal, rather than community, space and thus enjoy a right to privacy.

Spam invades the privacy of email recipients by sending objectionable content to them, whether or not they want this type of material. Spam imposes significant costs on email users. By the first decade of the twenty-first century, spam cost both individuals and businesses a considerable amount of time and money. Both the privacy and cost issues contributed to demands that spam be curtailed, including by federal legislation.

Congress recognized the importance of email and the harms caused by spammers. To shift the costs of advertising to the spammer and to enhance the privacy of email users, Congress enacted the Controlling the Assault of Non-Solicited Pornography and Marketing Act of 2003 (CAN-SPAM Act), 117 Stat. 2699. The statute became effective January 1, 2004. Finding that many spammers purposely mislead recipients and often conceal their identity, Congress justified the statute, asserting that there is a substantial government interest in regulating commercial email on a national level, spammers should not mislead recipients about the source or content of electronic messages, and recipients of commercial email have the right to decline additional spam messages. To enforce this statute, the FTC promulgated and enforced protocols for the commercial use of bulk email.

The statute prohibits predatory and abusive commercial email. The law penalizes those who knowingly engage in one or more of the following behaviors: (1) accessing a protected computer without authorization and intentionally initiating the transmission of multiple commercial email messages through that computer; (2) sending several multiple commercial email messages with the intent to deceive or mislead recipients, or any Internet access service, as to the origin of such messages; (3) materially falsifying header information in several commercial emails and intentionally initiating the transmission of such messages; (4) registering for five or more email accounts or online user accounts or two or more domain names using false identification and intentionally sending spam from such accounts or domain names; and (5) falsely representing oneself to be the registrant of five or more Internet protocol addresses and intentionally initiating the transmission of spam. Individuals participating in these activities could be imprisoned for up to five years and be liable for a maximum of $6 million in fines.

The statute's opt-out provision requires commercial email messages to include a functioning return email address that a recipient may use to opt out of future spam from the sender. The email address provided must remain active for at least thirty days after the original message was transmitted. Once a consumer effectively chooses to opt out of future email messages, the sender must respect the decision. After this point, it would be unlawful for the initial sender or anyone acting on such person's behalf to transmit, or to assist in the transmission of, a commercial email message upon the expiration of ten business days after

the receipt of the opt-out notice. The initial sender and any person with knowledge of the opt-out request must refrain from selling, leasing, exchanging, or transferring the recipient's email address. Also, commercial email messages must provide clear and conspicuous identification that the message is an advertisement or solicitation, notice of the opportunity to decline to receive further messages, and a valid physical postal address for the sender.

The CAN-SPAM statute also prohibits harvesting and dictionary attacks, and requires individuals to place warning labels on commercial emails with sexually oriented material. Email messages containing sexually explicit content must include in the subject line the marks or notices prescribed by the FTC. Such messages must further ensure that the message, when initially opened, contains only the content required by the opt-out provision and instructions on how to access the sexually explicit material, unless the sender receives the prior affirmative consent of the recipient. An individual in violation of this provision can face up to five years in jail and/or fines.

The CAN-SPAM Act restricted the role of the states in combating spam, and placed the FTC in charge of enforcement actions. However, the act, permitted state attorneys general to bring civil litigation for injunctions or to obtain damages, but only if the alleged violation threatens the interests of a resident of a particular state. Thus, the CAN-SPAM Act preempts or supersedes state laws that expressly deal with commercial emails (even if the state law is more stringent than CAN-SPAM). States may only prohibit false and deceptive commercial email messages and can regulate issues such as computer crime, tort, and trespass.

This legislative action enjoyed rare overwhelming bipartisan support. This support indicated a substantial legislative commitment to the spam issue and understanding of the severity of this problem. The act was a significant step forward in supporting the individual's "right to be let alone" in balancing privacy with free speech rights. The CAN-SPAM Act will serve to deter spammers from sending fraudulent or misleading email messages, from concealing their identity, and from using intrusive methods to collect email addresses. Email users will be able to identify spam messages as advertisements generally and as pornographic messages specifically due to the provisions of the act. The CAN-SPAM Act has had a valuable role in initiating legislative action, which would restrict spam, increase the privacy of the email inboxes of Americans, and relieve Americans from the financial burdens of unwanted advertising.

Despite the promise of the law, some observers argue that the statute is not effective enough in fighting spam. These critics believe that spam needs to be subject to further restriction through a combination of market-based initiatives and additional restrictive statutes and regulations.

The CAN-SPAM Act did not create an entirely effective solution to the spam problem because it allows spammers to continue to send messages to inboxes with impunity, forced spam recipients to take an affirmative act to curtail future incursions, provided lenient requirements and inadequate enforcement mechanisms, preempted stricter state anti-spam laws, and delayed the need for a global solution. Despite congressional acknowledgment of the spam problem, recognition of the substantial government interest in remedying such a problem, and the bipartisan support for this federal anti-spam legislation, Congress made concessions to several special interest groups and failed to provide consumers adequate protection from intrusive spam marketing techniques. Public opinion against spam helped motivate Congress to enact the CAN-SPAM Act. Even shortly after passage, the act failed to present an entirely effective solution to the expensive and intrusive problem of spam.

The spam law debate shifted into a controversy over two conflicting approaches: the opt-in and the opt-out mechanisms. The opt-in approach requires that all spammers obtain express permission before transmitting any email addresses. The more lenient opt-out approach allows spammers to send messages as long as each message offers a legitimate link from which one can request that the spammer refrain from sending future emails. Congress favored the opt-out approach because it allowed marketers and businesses with the most leeway to conduct their work.

The opt-out method of regulation has failed, however, to protect individual privacy fully. It continues to allow uninvited and unwelcome messages to individual inboxes in homes and businesses. Under current law, to halt unwanted email, individual users must take an affirmative step against each piece of unwanted mail; such a move wastes more time and money than the underlying problem. By implementing the opt-out approach, Congress developed a method that imposed additional costs on individuals because it is a competitive, repetitive, and labor-intensive method to oppose spam.

In terms of privacy, the opt-in approach protects consumers to a significantly greater degree and in a more effective manner. The opt-in approach prohibits unsolicited intrusions and requires that spammers send invited messages only. Like a vaccine prevents a disease, the opt-in approach stops the widespread dissemination of spam. Rather than imposing the costs of the remedy on all email users for each uninvited message like the opt-out approach, the opt-in approach imposes costs on spammers and those interested in receiving spam. In other words, it shifts the burden of sending spam onto spammers. Spammers must ask permission to enter an inbox instead of entering and then being asked to leave. The opt-in approach would ultimately serve to reduce the enormous volume of spam clogging networks and flooding the email system, and would halt the widespread waste of time and money directed at eliminating spam. Congress should adopt the opt-in approach to protect the privacy of email users.

The CAN-SPAM Act delayed efforts to pursue an internationally harmonized solution to spam by calling on the FTC to study the issues relating to the CAN-SPAM Act from 2014 to 2016. The U.S. law hampered efforts to form an international alliance to fight spam because the legislation failed to prohibit spam. The United States and the European Union (EU) ended up with contradictory legislation. The EU Directive, enacted in the fall of 2003, forbade email promotions unless the recipient provided the marketer prior consent. The EU holds the position that an email account must enjoy privacy and thus requires businesses to obtain explicit permission before sending email messages. To stop spam from systematically compromising the privacy of email users, many observers urged Congress to take action to harmonize the U.S. position on spam with that of the EU by supporting the opt-in approach.

The CAN-SPAM Act, in its current form, has ineffectively regulated commercial spam and has not reduced the amount of commercial spam. Internet junk email increased in the years since the legislation was enacted. Critics charge that the opt-out provision continues to be a major weakness of the legislation. One reason is that spammers have no incentive to comply with opt-out requests. Several fixes and compromises were proposed, including one that would provide an opt-out regulation for political spam and an opt-in regulation for commercial spam, which would effectively balance free speech interests with the right to privacy by allowing spammers to send unsolicited emails as long as recipients are able to block future unwanted emails.

Gretchen Nobahar

Further Reading

Beales, J. Howard. *Legislative Efforts to Combat Spam: Joint Hearing before . . . 108th Congress, 1st Session, July 9, 2003.* Washington, DC: US Government Printing Office, 2003.

The Criminal Spam Act of 2003: Report (to Accompany S. 1293). Washington, DC: US Government Printing Office, 2003.

Garfinkel, Simson, and Gene Spafford. *Web Security, Privacy & Commerce,* 2nd ed. Sebastopol, CA: O'Reilly Media, 2011.

Gelman, Robert B., and Stanton McCandlish. *Protecting Yourself Online: The Definitive Resource on Safety, Freedom, and Privacy in Cyberspace.* New York: HarperEdge, 1998.

Himma, Kenneth Einar. *The Handbook of Information and Computer Ethics.* Hoboken, NJ: Wiley, 2008.

Jasper, Margaret C. *The Law of Obscenity and Pornography,* 2nd ed. New York: Oceana, 2009.

Jenkins, Simms. *The Truth about Email Marketing.* Upper Saddle River, NJ: FT Press, 2009.

Manishin, Glenn B. *Complying with the CAN-SPAM Act and Other Critical Business Issues: Staying out of Trouble.* New York: Practicing Law Institute, 2004.

Reduction in Distribution of Spam Act of 2003: Hearing before the Subcommittee on Crime, Terrorism, and Homeland Security of the Committee on the Judiciary, House of Representatives, One Hundred Eighth Congress, First Session, on H.R. 2214, July 8, 2003. Washington, DC: US Government Printing Office, 2003.

Schwabach, Aaron. *Internet and the Law: Technology, Society, and Compromises.* Santa Barbara, CA: ABC-CLIO, 2006.

Smith, Marcia S. *"Junk E-mail": An Overview of Issues and Legislation concerning Unsolicited Commercial Electronic Mail ("Spam").* Washington, DC: Congressional Research Service, Library of Congress, 2001.

See also: Computers and privacy; Consumer privacy; Data harvesting; Federal Trade Commission (FTC); Financial information, privacy right to; Marketing; Right to be left alone

Spyware

Identification: In general, software that performs certain behaviors, generally without appropriately obtaining the user's consent first.

With so many types of malicious software in the Internet, users must be aware of what spyware is and what spyware does. Spyware generally performs certain behaviors, including (1) advertising, (2) collecting personal information, and (3) changing the configuration of the user's computer. Spyware is often associated with software that displays advertisements (known as adware) or software that tracks personal or sensitive information.

Not all software that has advertisements or tracks user online activities is harmful. For example, a user may sign up for a free service and in return for the service, she or he must agree to receive targeted ads. If the user understands these terms and agrees to them, the user may decide that this trade-off is worthwhile. The user may also agree to let the company track his or her online activities to determine which ads to show the individual. For any software program, the user must understand what the software will do and have agreed to install the software on his or her computer.

Detecting spyware can often be difficult process because most spyware is intended to be difficult to remove. Spyware that changes the computer's configuration can be annoying and can cause the computer to slow down or crash.

Spyware can alter the web browser's homepage or search page, or add additional components to the browser that users may not want. Spyware also makes it difficult for the user to change the settings. One common tactic is that spyware is covertly installed along with the software a user may want, such as a music or video file-sharing program.

Whenever a user installs software on a computer, he or she must carefully read all disclosures, including the license agreement and privacy statement. Sometimes the inclusion of unwanted software in a given software installation is documented, but it might appear at the end of a license agreement or privacy statement.

Gretchen Nobahar

Further Reading

Aycock, John Daniel. *Spyware and Adware*. New York: Springer, 2011.

Bennett, Colin J. *The Privacy Advocates: Resisting the Spread of Surveillance*. Cambridge, MA: MIT Press, 2008.

Erbschloe, Michael. *Trojans, Worms, and Spyware: A Computer Security Professional's Guide to Malicious Code*. Amsterdam: Elsevier Butterworth Heinemann, 2005.

Marzolf, Julie Schwab. *Online Privacy*. New York: Gareth Stevens Pub., 2013.

See also: Consent; Malware; Marketing

Stalking

Identification: Harassing or threatening behavior that one individual engages in repeatedly against another. This type of harassment is referred to as either physical stalking or cyberstalking. Both physical stalking and cyberstalking may or may not be accompanied by a "credible threat of serious harm," depending on the facts of the case. Both types of stalking are intended to control or intimidate the victim through instilling fear, stress, and/or anxiety. Both the physical stalker and the cyberstalker intend to cause psychological harm and distress to the victim. Both types of stalking have the potential to escalate and lead to the stalker assaulting and/or killing the victim. Cyberstalking may result in physical stalking.

Physical stalking

The National Institute of Justice describes physical stalking as a series of actions by the stalker against a particular person, which includes repeated instances of the stalker seeking visual or physical proximity to the victim; nonconsensual communication; or verbal, written, or implied threats or a combination of such acts, which would instill fear in a reasonable person. Physical stalking involves repeated harassing or threatening behavior, such as following a person, appearing at one's house or work, sending written messages or objects, or vandalizing another person's property.

In 2012, the Department of Justice (DOJ) reported that an estimated 1.5 percent of persons age eighteen or older were stalking victims. Individuals who were divorced or separated are at the greatest risk of being stalked compared to those who are married, never married, or widowed. While more females were stalked than males, females and males were equally likely to experience harassment. Men reported stalking incidents as often as women. Those less than thirty-five years old were more likely to be stalked than older people.

According to the Privacy Rights Clearinghouse, most victims know their stalker. Slightly more than 30 percent of stalking offenders are a known, intimate partner: a current or former spouse, a cohabiting partner, or a date. Approximately 45 percent of stalking offenders are acquaintances other than intimate partners. Just under 10 percent of all stalkers are strangers. In approximately 15 percent of stalking cases, the victim does not know the identity of the stalker and thus cannot report whether he or she might be an intimate partner, acquaintance, or stranger.

Stalking victims may be required to take time from work to change a phone number, move, replace damaged property, obtain a restraining order, and/or testify in court. In the 2012 DOJ report, almost 13 percent had to take time off from work. Over 100,000 victims reported that they had been terminated from or had been asked to leave their jobs because they were being stalked.

Stalkers may also commit identity theft against victims, including opening or closing accounts, removing money from accounts, or charging purchases to a victim's credit card.

Cyberstalking

The Internet has proven to be a highly efficient way for stalkers to intimidate, terrorize, and harm their victims. Cyberstalking is the repeatd use of an electronic or Internet-capable device to pursue or harass an individual or group of people. Cyberstalking is viewed as the most dangerous type of Internet hasassment because of a credible threat of harm to the victim. Some of the key differences between physical and cyberstalking are that, with the latter, (1) a message communicated online can be sent to anyone with Internet access, is present immediately, and cannot be taken back or deleted; (2) the stalker

could be anywhere in the world; (3) the stalker may easily impersonate another individual to communicate with the victim; and (4) the stalker may use third parties to contact or communicate with the victim.

Cyberharassment differs from cyberstalking because the former does not usually invovle a credible threat. Examples of cyberharassment includes threatening or harassing email messages, instant messages, or blog entries or websits that are intended to harrass a specific person.

Cyberstalkers post messages on various sites using the victim's personal information, including home address, phone number, and/or Social Security number. These posts are often lewd or intended to be embarrassing, and result in the victim receiving several emails, calls, or visits from individuals who read the online posts. The cyberstalkers also sign up for several online mailing lists and services using a victim's personal information.

Stalkers abuse the anonymity provided by the Internet to harass their victims. Because the identity of the stalker is often unknown to the victim, the victim often becomes more fearful. Cyberstalking is difficult to curtail and prosecute because the stalker could be far removed or very close to the victim. Because of the Internet's anonymity, it is difficult to verify a stalker's identity, gather the necessary evidence for an arrest and trace the cyberstalker to a physical location.

Stalkers almost always stalk someone they know or believe they know, as is the case with stalkers of celebrities or other public persons. While stalkers believe they know the celebrity, the celebrity most often does not know a stalker. One drawback of being a celebrity or public figure is having to deal with stalkers, who could be obsessed fans.

Corporate cyberstalking is when a company harasses a person online, or an individual or group of people harasses an organization. Corporate cyberstalking could be motivated by ideology, greed, or revenge.

Cyberstalkers are motivated by many factors: envy; pathological obsession (professional or sexual); unemployment or failures with their own job or life; the desire to intimidate and make others feel inferior; delusion, which makes the stalker believe that he or she knows the target; desire to instill fear in a person to justify the stalker's status; belief in remaining anonymous and thus getting away with it; intimidation for financial advantage or business competition; revenge over perceived or imagined rejection.

Cyberstalking evolves as technology changes. A technologically proficient cyberstalker can cause severe problems for the victim, especially because an increasing number of people use the Internet to pay bills, make social connections, do their work, share ideas, and seek employment.

Cyberstalking victims should attempt to gather as much physical evidence as possible and document each contact from the perpetrator.

While cyberstalking doesn't involve physical contact, it can be more dangerous than physical stalking. A proficient Internet user can easily locate enough of the victim's personal information, such as phone number or place of business, to determine his or her physical location.

Social networking, through websites such as Facebook, Twitter, and LinkedIn, presents security issues for victims of stalking. A social network profile might include a victim's contact information, birthday, legal name, names of family members, and even updates on a victim's location.

If a victim has a public online profile, a stalker could easily access any information posted to the social networking account, according to Privacy Clearinghouse. Even with strong privacy settings or a private profile, a stalker might be able to access a victim's account by:

1. Hacking the victim's bank accounts.
2. Creating a false profile and sending a friend request or follow request. The request may even appear to be from a known friend or family member. Victims should verify with their friends and family members that one of them owns the account before accepting the request.
3. Gaining access to the victim's Facebook account. Stalking victims should consider suspending their social networking accounts until the stalking has been resolved. If the victim continues to use social networking sites, he or she should:

- use privacy settings. Many social networking sites allow the user to make his or her profile completely private simply by checking a box.
- use any available security settings, including two-factor authentication. When a user enables this, the account requires another user to provide something the user knows (such as a password) that goes with something you have (such as a particular device). Therefore, if someone else obtains the password, he or she will be unable to log into the account without the specific code that the service sends to the computer.
- limit how much personal information is posted to the account. For example, the user should not include contact information, birth date, place of birth, or names of family members.
- refrain from accepting friend requests and follow requests from people he or she does not know. If the user recognizes the individual sending the request, contact him or her offline to verify that he or she sent the request.
- warn friends and acquaintances not to post personal information about the victim, especially contact information and location. The victim should also abstain from participating in activities, particularly those requesting personal information.
- refrain from posting photographs of his or her home that might indicate its location. For example, users should

refrain from posting photographs showing a house number or an identifying landmark.

- be cautious when joining online organizations, groups or fan pages.
- be cautious when connecting his or her cellphone to a social networking account.
- always use a strong, unique password for every social networking site.

If the user decides to connect a cellphone to an online account, the user should be cautious in providing live updates on her or his location or activities. The user should avoid posting information about current or future locations or providing information that a stalker may later use locate the user.

Victims most likely will be unaware that a stalker has accessed an online social networking account. Victims should post only information that would not expose them to harm if the stalker should read it.

Cyberstalkers attempt to gather information about the victim. They may approach their victim's friends, family member, and work colleagues to obtain personal information. They may advertise for information on the Internet or hire a private detective, and they often:

- monitor their target's online activities and attempt to trace an IP address to gather more information about their victims.
- encourage others to harass the victim.
- Many cyberstalkers try to involve third parties in the harassment. They may claim the victim has harmed the stalker or his or her family in some way, or they may post the victim's name and telephone number to encourage others to join the pursuit.
- engage in false victimization. The cyberstalker may claim that the victim is harassing the stalker instead of the other way around.
- attack the victim's data and equipment. They may attempt to damage the victim's computer by sending viruses.

- order goods and services or subscribe to magazines in the victim's name. These often involve subscriptions to pornography or the ordering of sex toys, then having them delivered to the victim's workplace.
- attempt to arrange to meet their victims. Young people are particularly at risk of having cyberstalkers attempt to arrange meetings with them.

As new technology has developed, cyberstalkers have developed new strategies to stalk victims. A cyberstalker can be either a stranger to the victim or have a former or present relationship. Cyberstalkers often search websites looking for opportunities to take advantage of people.

Harassment and stalking often include rape threats and other threats of violence, as well as the posting of the victim's personal information. Both activities are blamed for limiting victims' presence online or forcing them offline entirely, thereby impeding their participation in online life and undermining their autonomy, dignity, identity, and opportunities.

Cyberstalking of intimate partners includes the online harassment of a current or former romantic partner. It is a form of domestic violence, and experts say that its purpose is to control the victim by forcing social isolation and creating dependency. Harassers may send repeated insulting or threatening emails to their victims, or disrupt their victims' email use, and use the victim's account to send emails to others posing as the victim or to purchase goods or services the victim does not want. They may also use the Internet to research and compile personal information about the victim and then use that information to harass him or her.

Physical stalking is a relatively new crime. Prior to the passage of antistalking laws, victims had very few remedies. Restraining orders, often the only way to prevent stalking, were effective only after the behavior they were designed to prevent had occurred. Victims relied on assault and battery laws or restraining orders to fight stalking.

Stalking first received widespread public attention in 1980 when an unstable fan murdered John Lennon. In 1981, John Hinckley Jr.'s attempt to assassinate President Ronald Reagan was intended to impress the actress, Jodie Foster.

State antistalking legislation

In 1989, Rebecca Schaeffer, an actress who had appeared on the television show *My Sister Sam,* was murdered by an obsessed fan who had stalked Schaefer for two years. California was the first state to pass an antistalking statute in 1990 in the aftermath of Schaeffer's death. The elements of stalking include: (1) a credible threat, (2) conduct performed with the intent and ability to carry out the threat, and (3) the conduct causes a person to fear for her or his safety and the safety of immediate family members.

By 1993, all fifty states and the District of Columbia had an antistalking statute. The legal definition of stalking varies by jurisdiction. Some state laws require that a person must have made a credible threat of violence against the victim before he or she can be found guilty of being a stalker. Other states require only that the stalker's conduct constitute an implied threat. All legislatures recognized the need to stop stalking before it developed into a more serious threat to the victim's personal safety. Statutes were enacted to respond to behavior that would disrupt normal life for the victim and to prevent such behavior from escalating into violence. These statutes were more preventive and proactive because they were intended to criminalize certain acts of harassment before they escalated into more serious violent conduct by the stalker.

California addresses stalking in both its criminal and civil codes. California criminal law defines a stalker as someone who willfully, maliciously, and repeatedly follows or harasses another individual and who makes a credible threat with the intent to make the victim or

victim's immediate family members fearful for their safety.

In the United States, most states have cyberstalking laws. Also, many law enforcement agencies have cybercrime units. Often Internet stalking is viewed with more seriousness than physical stalking. Cyberstalking is the most dangerous of Internet harassment because of the credible threat of harm it can pose. A conviction of cyberstalking can result in a restraining order, probation, and/or criminal penalties against the accused, which could include incarceration.

Federal antistalking law

The most important federal statutes intended to deter and prosecute cyberstalking are the Interstate Stalking Act, the Interstate Communications Act, the Federal Telephone Harassment Statute, and the Protection of Children from Sexual Predators Act.

Interstate Stalking Act

President Clinton signed the Interstate Stalking Act into law in 1996. Th act made it a federal crime to travel across state lines with "the intent to kill, injure, harass, or place under surveillance with intent to kill, injure, harass, or intimidate another person" (18 U.S.C. 2261A). Several serious stalking cases have been prosecuted under Section 2261A, but the requirement that the stalker physically travel across state lines makes it largely inapplicable to cyberstalking cases. In addition, the travel must result in reasonable fear of death, serious bodily injury, or substantial emotional distress either to a victim or a victim's family member, spouse, or intimate partner. The act was amended in 2006 and 2013.

Section 2261A (2) makes it a federal crime to stalk another person across state, tribal, or international lines, using regular mail, email, or the Internet. The stalker must have the intent to kill, injure, harass, intimidate, and/or cause substantial emotional distress, or to place a victim or a victim's family member, spouse, or intimate partner in fear of death or serious bodily injury.

Interstate Communications Act

Enacted in 1994, the Interstate Communications Act (18 U.S.C. 875 (c)) makes it a federal crime for someone to transmit in interstate or foreign communications any threat to kidnap or injure another person. Under 18 U.S.C. 875(c), it is a federal crime, punishable by up to five years in prison and a fine of up to $250,000, to transmit any communication in interstate or foreign commerce containing a threat to injure the person of another. Section 875(c) includes threats transmitted in interstate or foreign commerce via the telephone, email, beepers, or the Internet. It has been interpreted to apply only to communications of actual threats. The statute would be inapplicable in a situation where the cyberstalker is engaged in a pattern of conduct intended to harass or annoy another without a specific threat. Also, it is unclear that it would apply to situations where a person harasses another person by posting messages on a bulletin board or in a chat room with the intent to encourage others to harass or annoy another person.

Federal Telephone Harassment Statute

Enacted in 1996, this federal statute (47 U.S.C. Section 223(a)(1)(C)) makes it a crime to use a telephone or other telecommunications device anonymously to annoy, abuse, harass, or threaten another person at the called number. This statute is broader than 18 U.S.C. 875 because it covers both threats and harassment. Section 223 applies, however, only to direct communications between the perpetrator and the victim. Thus, it would not apply to a cyberstalking situation where a person harasses or terrorizes the victim by posting messages on a bulletin board or in a chat room encouraging others to harass or annoy another person. In addition, Section 223 is only a misdemeanor, punishable by not more than two years in prison.

Protection of Children from Sexual Predators Act

A federal statute (18 U.S.C. 2425) enacted in October 1998, it protects children against online stalking.

The statute makes it a federal crime to use any means of interstate or foreign commerce (such as a telephone line or the Internet) to communicate with any person with the intent to solicit or entice a child into unlawful sexual activity. While this statute provides important protections for children, it does not cover harassing phone calls to minors that do not include intent to entice or solicit the child for illicit sexual purposes.

While current federal statutes cover many instances of cyberstalking, there remain major inadequacies in federal cyberstalking law, including that the law generally applies only to direct communication between the cyberstalker and the victim. When the cyberstalker persuades other individuals to join the harassment, the current law is grossly inadequate. While a federal stalking law is in place, it applies only to interstate travel. The perpetrator must travel across state lines, which makes the law frequently inapplicable in prosecuting stalkers.

Major cyberstalking cases

There have been several major cyberstalking cases. Some have involved the suicides of young children. In many other cases, charges either weren't brought for cyber-harassment or prosecution failed to obtain convictions.

A fourteen-year-old student in Michigan, for instance, pressed charges against her alleged rapist, which caused her to be cyberstalked and cyberbullied by other students. After she committed suicide in 2010, all charges were dropped against the defendant because the only witness was dead, despite the fact that statutory rape charges could have been pursued.

In another major cyberstalking case, college student Dharun Ravi secretly filmed his roommate's sexual liaison with another man. He then posted it online. After the victim had committed suicide, Ravi was convicted of bias intimidation and invasion of privacy in *New Jersey v. Dharun Ravi*. In 2012, the defendant was imprisoned for thirty days and was required to pay more than $11,000 in restitution and to serve three years of probation.

Conclusion

The federal government and the U.S. states have recognized the impact of technology in the daily lives of everyday Americans and have sought to update legislation to protect citizens against cyberstalking. Significant gaps continue, however, in legal protections and in enacting and implementing legislation against this crime. Inadequate legal protections facilitate the cyberstalker's ability to place a victim in a state of fear and causing the victim to feel defenseless. A cyberstalker can threaten the victim with danger, which empowers the offender. The law in this area is in need of improvement and must be continually revised as technology changes.

Further Reading

Bell, Mary Ann, and Bobby Ezell. *Cybersins and Digital Good Deeds: A Book about Technology and Ethics.* New York: Haworth Press, 2007.

Bocij, Paul. *Cyberstalking: Harassment in the Internet Age and How to Protect Your Family.* Westport, CT: Praeger, 2004.

Curtis, George E. *The Law of Cybercrimes and Their Investigations.* Boca Raton, FL: CRC Press, 2012.

Cyberstalking, a New Challenge for Law Enforcement and Industry a Report from the Attorney General to the Vice President. Washington, DC: Department of Justice, 1999.

Deibert, Ronald. *Black Code: Surveillance, Privacy, and the Dark Side of the Internet.* Hiller, Janine, and Ronnie Cohen. *Internet Law & Policy.* Upper Saddle River, NJ: Prentice Hall, 2002.

Holtzman, David H. *Privacy Lost: How Technology Is Endangering Your Privacy.* San Francisco, CA: Jossey-Bass, 2006.

Reyns, Bradford W. *The Anti-social Network: Cyberstalking Victimization among College Students.* El Paso, TX: LFB Scholarly Publishing, 2012.

The Impact of Recent Cyberstalking and Cyberharassment Cases: Leading Lawyers on Navigating Privacy Guidelines and the Legal Ramifications of Online Behavior. McQuade, Samuel C., and Sarah Gentry. *Cyberstalking and Cyberbullying.* New York: Chelsea House, 2012.

US Department of Justice. *1999 Report on Cyberstalking: A New Challenge for Law Enforcement & Industry.* Washington, DC: Author, 1999.

Yar, Majid. *Cybercrime and Society.* London: SAGE Publications, 2006.

See also: Children's right to privacy; Computers and privacy; Criminal justice (criminal procedure); Hacking, computer; Harrassment; Law enforcement; Telephones

Stanley v. Georgia, 394 U.S. 557 (1969)

Identification: A unanimous Supreme Court opinion upholding the right of an individual to possess, but not produce or distribute, certain obscene materials in the privacy of his home.

The opinion in *Stanley v. Georgia* was written at the end of the Warren Court era, an expansive period for individual rights between 1953 and 1969 when Earl Warren served as Chief Justice. The case, written by Justice Thurgood Marshall, highlights the importance of First Amendment freedoms as protections against criminal prosecution. As we learn in *Stanley*, the First Amendment protects more than just words; it also protects the "right to receive information and ideas," *Stanley v. Georgia*, 394 U.S. 557 (1969), at 564.

Police officers came to Stanley's home to execute a search warrant seeking evidence that Stanley was involved in illegal gambling activities. The officers did not find any evidence of gambling but found three reels of 8 mm film in Stanley's bedroom that allegedly contained obscene materials. Officers used a projector found in Stanley's home to watch the film before leaving. Believing the films violated Georgia's obscenity laws, the police arrested Stanley.

Stanley was tried and convicted of possessing obscene materials. The Georgia state courts upheld his conviction. For this reason, Stanley filed a petition for certiorari with the U.S. Supreme Court seeking permission to appeal his Georgia conviction. Stanley argued that simply possessing obscene materials was protected under the First Amendment. Because the First Amendment has been held to apply to all fifty states through the incorporation doctrine of the Fourteenth Amendment, the Supreme Court granted the requested petition for certiorari and gave Stanley permission to challenge his conviction.

Justice Marshall's opinion agreed with Stanley that the First Amendment protects "mere possession" of obscene materials from criminal prosecution (394 U.S. at 559). Unlike an earlier Supreme Court case involving the mailing of obscene materials to others, *Roth v. United States* (354 U.S. 476 [1957]), Stanley was not accused of distributing or producing obscene materials. Instead, Stanley was convicted of simply possessing obscene films. In a famous quotation from the *Stanley* case, Justice Marshall explained, "[i]f the First Amendment means anything, it means that a State has no business telling a man, sitting alone in his own house, what books he may read or what films he may watch" (394 U.S. at 565).

Georgia sought to criminalize possession of obscenity to protect its citizens against deviant behavior, including sexual violence, and to make it easier to enforce obscenity laws prohibiting distribution of obscene materials (394 U.S. at 566–67). The Supreme Court, however, did not accept either interest as outweighing Stanley's right to possess the obscene films in his own home.

Obscenity, often confused with pornography, is not treated the same as pornography under the law. While pornography may be controversial, only materials that are considered obscene can be outlawed or restricted. In *Roth v. United States*, a case described above, the Supreme Court held that obscenity is low-value speech that falls outside the First Amendment's protection. The first clear test for obscenity was provided in *Miller v. California*, 413 U.S. 15 (1973). Still, as the *Stanley* case demonstrates, certain obscene materials may be possessed in the privacy of one's home under the First Amendment.

While *Stanley* remains a strong First Amendment case, its holding and impact has since been limited. *Stanley* does not protect obscene displays in public. In the 1973 case, *Paris Adult Theatre v. Slaton*, 413 U.S. 49 (1973), the Supreme Court upheld a Georgia law prohibiting public displays of obscene films. The Supreme Court, with Chief Justice Warren Burger writing for the majority, distinguished the right of an individual to view obscenity in private from the right of an individual to do so at a public theater. Both *Miller* and *Slaton* mark a turning point in the Supreme Court as the new Burger Court, led by Chief Justice Warren Burger, sought to constrict many of the broad individual rights established under the Warren Court.

Stanley does not provide protection to individuals who possess child pornography, even in the privacy of their home. In 1990, the Supreme Court, in an opinion written by Justice Byron White, refused to extend *Stanley*'s First Amendment protection to a case involving possession of live child pornography in the home. The case, *Osborne v. Ohio*, 495 U.S. 103 (1990), shows that some governmental interests, such as protection of children, outweigh First Amendment protections even in the privacy of one's home.

Unlike the obscene materials at issue in *Stanley*, where there was no evidence anyone was harmed during filming, videos containing sexual images of live children have been found by the Supreme Court to cause sufficient injury to overcome a First Amendment defense. *New York v. Ferber*, 458 U.S. 747 (1982), was a unanimous Supreme Court opinion holding that child pornography, much like obscenity, is of such low value that it does not merit First Amendment protection. Justice White also authored the Court's opinion in *Ferber*. *Osborne* and *Ferber* provide important limits on the *Stanley* precedence.

The Supreme Court has drawn a line, however, between live depictions of child pornography and virtual depictions of child pornography. In *Ashcroft v. Free Speech Coalition*, 535 U.S. 234 (2002), the Supreme Court, in an opinion written by Justice Anthony Kennedy, found that virtual images of children engaged in pornographic acts was protected under the First Amendment. The Supreme Court distinguished virtual child pornography from actual, live depiction of child pornography by explaining that no crime occurs when virtual images are crafted and therefore there would be no victims in producing such works. Unlike previous obscenity cases that were unanimous, *Ashcroft* included three dissenting Justices who would place virtual child pornography outside the protective reach of the First Amendment.

Obscenity issues continue to raise First Amendment challenges in our society. The vital need to ensure child safety and the rapid advancements of technology suggest that the Supreme Court will continue to refine its reach of *Stanley*.

Mary M. Penrose

Further Reading

Ball, Carlos A. "Privacy, Property, and Public Sex." *Columbia Journal of Gender and Law* 18, no. 1 (2009). Bosmajian, Haig A. *Obscenity and Freedom of Expression*. New York: B. Franklin, 1976.

Devol, Kenneth S. *Mass Media and the Supreme Court: The Legacy of the Warren Years,* 4th ed. Mamaroneck, NY: Hastings House, 1990.

Friedman, Leon. *Obscenity: The Complete Oral Arguments before the Supreme Court in the Major Obscenity Cases,* rev. ed. New York: Chelsea House, 1983.

Harrison, Maureen. *Obscenity and Pornography Decisions of the United States Supreme Court*. Carlsbad, CA: Excellent Books, 2000.

Jasper, Margaret C. *The Law of Obscenity and Pornography,* 2d ed. New York: Oceana, 2009.

Jones v. Alfred H. Mayer Co. (1968); Stanley v. Georgia (1969). Bethesda, MD: University Publications of America, 1975.

"*Karalexis v. Byrne* and the Regulation of Obscenity: 'I Am Curious (Stanley).'" *Virginia Law Review* 56, no. 6 (1970): 1205.

Sumberg, Theodore A. "Privacy, Freedom, and Obscenity." *Journal of Critical Analysis* 3, no. 2 (1971): 84–96.

See also: Criminal justice (criminal procedure), First Amendment to the U.S. Constitution; Law Eenforcement; Obscenity; Pornography

Stop and frisk policy

Identification: A common phrase referring to the Supreme Court's opinion in *Terry v. Ohio* that permits police officers to stop legally an individual, or vehicle, based solely on reasonable suspicion that a crime is occurring or the person is armed and dangerous to conduct a limited search for weapons (a frisk).

A stop and frisk is both a seizure and a search governed by the Fourth Amendment. Stop-and-frisk encounters are a common police tool. Stop and frisks do not require a search warrant or probable cause. Stop and frisks empower police to conduct a brief, pat down of a person and all items immediately associated with the person's body from which a weapon could be drawn, such as a backpack or purse.

Terry v. Ohio, 392 U.S. 1 (1968), was decided by the Warren Court. Chief Justice Earl Warren wrote the majority opinion for an 8–1 decision. A *Terry* stop, also known as a stop and frisk, is an exception to the Fourth Amendment's warrant requirement. Generally, warrantless searches are unreasonable subject to a few well-established exceptions. *Terry* provides one of those exceptions.

A Cleveland detective with nearly 40 years of police experience noticed two individuals near downtown Cleveland that looked, to him, out of place. During the motion to suppress proceedings, Detective McFadden testified that, although he had been patrolling this area of Cleveland for over 30 years, he did not recognize either individual. As Detective McFadden watched the men, he noticed that they appeared to be "casing" a store—something criminals do prior to committing a robbery or theft. Each man would take turns walking past the store, glancing in, and then return to discuss something with the other. Sometime during these numerous, continuous strolls past the store, a third man joined the pair.

His suspicion aroused, Detective McFadden decided he needed to investigate the group. He further testified that "he feared 'they may have a gun.'" He approached the men and told them he was a police officer. He did not arrest the men or advise them they were under arrest. Instead, he asked the men for their names. The men did not provide their names but simply "mumbled something," which further concerned Detective McFadden.

Without first seeking a search warrant, Detective McFadden turned Terry around so he was facing the other men and began an outer-clothes, open-hand pat-down of Terry. This type of search is often called a frisk because the officer does no more than tap, usually with the palms of his or her hands, the outer clothing of a person. This is not an intrusive search that goes inside clothing or even inside a jacket. Rather, it is a very quick, cursory search that seeks solely to discern whether the individual is armed.

While conducting the frisk, Detective McFadden felt what he believed to be a weapon in Terry's coat. He ordered the men inside the store. Upon removing Terry's coat, McFadden found a revolver. He then ordered the men against the wall and conducted a frisk of the other two individuals. One of the other two men, Chilton, also had a gun hidden in his coat. Terry and Chilton were both arrested and charged with carrying concealed weapons.

Terry, believing McFadden's warrantless seizure and search was unconstitutional, filed a motion to suppress. A motion to suppress is a motion, usually filed before a trial or other legal proceeding occurs, to keep otherwise legally relevant evidence out of the proceeding. In this case, had Terry succeeded on his motion to suppress, McFadden's seizure of the group would have been deemed unlawful, and all evidence flowing from that encounter, including the revolver found during the frisk, would have been excluded from the trial. Had Terry won his motion, the charges against him would have been dismissed or, on appeal, his conviction overturned.

The Supreme Court found that, although McFadden had not secured a warrant prior to stopping and engaging the men, he had reasonable, articulable suspicion that they were about to commit a crime and were likely armed and dangerous. Relying on the importance of officer safety, the Court found that an officer has the legal right briefly to stop and investigate (thereby hopefully diffusing) what he or she believes to be a dangerous situation. Chief Justice Warren "emphatically" rejected any claim by the state that a stop is not a seizure and a frisk is not a search. The Fourth Amendment clearly applies to such investigatory encounters between a police officer and citizen.

Relying on a test subsequently used by the Supreme Court in other "special needs" cases, such as *New Jersey v. T.L.O.,* 469 U.S. 325 (1985), the Court indicated the constitutionality of stop-and-frisk encounters will be judged by whether the seizure (the stop) and subsequent search (the outer-clothes frisk) was justified at its inception and justified in its scope. As with other "special needs" cases, the Court dispensed with the warrant requirement for both the stop and the frisk observing that this case illustrated the difficulties that officers face with immediately responding to developing criminal, and potentially dangerous, scenarios. To require a warrant for either the seizure (the stop) or search (the outer-clothes frisk) would delay the proceedings to such an extent as to make the stop and frisk essentially useless. Imagine what would have happened in this case had Officer McFadden not responded to the gentlemen's casing of the store?

Another departure from the Fourth Amendment was the level of suspicion deemed acceptable to initiate a stop and frisk. Emphasizing the brevity of the stop and the lesser intrusiveness of a frisk, the Court held that an officer need only demonstrate, based on the reasonable inferences drawn from his or her own experiences, that he or she had reasonable, articulable suspicion that an individual was engaging in criminal activity or was armed and dangerous. Although a mere hunch that something is wrong or about to go down is a constitutionally insufficient basis for a stop and frisk, probable cause is not required.

Following *Terry,* officers have a strong tool in their arsenal to help prevent crime and keep individuals safe. As the *Terry* doctrine has been broadened, however, some concern has been expressed that warrantless stop and frisks based on mere reasonable suspicion may result in citizens being unduly harassed. In *Illinois v. Wardlow,* 528 U.S. 119 (2000), the Supreme Court expanded *Terry*'s application to permit officers to stop and frisk an individual in a high-crime area that, upon seeing the police, flees.

Wardlow involved the stop and frisk of a man who, without provocation, fled from the police in a high-crime area. The area was known to the officers for drug trafficking. Prior to taking flight, the officers noticed the man holding an opaque bag. When the officers finally caught the man, one of the officers frisked the man and his bag. The officer felt something hard that he believed to be a weapon. The officer opened the bag and found a gun. Wardlow was arrested and convicted of unlawful use of a weapon.

The Illinois trial court denied Wardlow's motion to suppress. The appellate courts of Illinois reversed this ruling, however, and found that officers did not have adequate suspicion—from Wardlow's flight alone—to conduct a *Terry* stop. Illinois appealed to the U.S. Supreme Court, which accepted the case on appeal.

In a 5–4 decision written by Chief Justice William Rehnquist, the Supreme Court held that unprovoked flight from the police plus presence in a high-crime area created the necessary reasonable suspicion that an individual was then engaging in criminal activity or was armed and dangerous. Unprovoked flight or evasive behavior, the majority reasoned, was sufficient to empower officers to investigate further. The Supreme Court reversed the Illinois appellate courts and reinstated Wardlow's conviction.

The *Terry* doctrine, particularly as it relates to high-crime areas, has continued to be controversial. New York City was sued civilly for its stop-and-frisk practices. In the case *Floyd v. City of New York,* 959 F. Supp.2d 540 (2013), the federal district court found that New York City stop and frisks were disproportionately used on racial minorities. The case resulted in court-mandated reforms to the New York City police policies. Still, both *Terry* and *Wardlow* remain legally valid and enable police to stop individuals believed to be engaging in criminal activity or to be armed and dangerous to perform briefly a limited search for weapons.

Mary M. Penrose

Further Reading

Bobis, Charles S. *Terry v. Ohio 30 Years Later: A Symposium on the Fourth Amendment, Law Enforcement, and Police-citizen Encounters.* Brooklyn, N.Y.: St. John's Law Review Association, 1998.

Bradley, Craig M. "The Wicked May Flee, but the Police May Stop Them." *Trial,* April 1, 2000.

Cooper, Frank Rudy. "'Who's the Man?': Masculinities Studies, Terry Stops, and Police Training." *Columbia Journal of Gender and Law* 18 p. 671 (2009).

"Fourth Amendment. Stop and Frisk." *The Journal of Criminal Law and Criminology* 69, no. 4 (1978): 464.

MacIntosh, Susanne M. "Fourth Amendment: The Plain Touch Exception to the Warrant Requirement." *Journal of Criminal Law and Criminology* 84, no. 4 (1994).

Ridgeway, Greg. *Summary of the RAND Report on NYPD's Stop, Question, and Frisk.* Santa Monica, Calif.: RAND, 2009.

Sullum, Jacob. "When Policing Becomes Harassment: Why the NYPD's Stop-and-Frisk Program Is Unconstitutional." *Reason,* July 1, 2013.

Zeidman, Steven. "Whither the Criminal Court: Confronting Stops-and-Frisks." *Albany Law Review* 76, no. 2 (2013): 1187.

See also: Criminal justice (criminal procedure); Fourth Amendment to the U.S. Constitution; Law enforcement; *New Jersey v. TLO*; Warren, Earl

Stored Communications Act (SCA)

Identification: Title II of the Electronic Communications Privacy Act (ECPA), 100 Stat. 1848 (1986). The Stored Communications Act became effective on October 21, 1986. The SCA provisions are codified at 18 U.S.C. Chapter 121 §§ 2701–2712.

The Fourth Amendment to the U.S. Constitution prohibits unreasonable search and seizure of physical property, but the courts have not always agreed on how best to apply these principles to modern information and communication technology. The ECPA extended privacy protections to cellphones and emerging electronic communications of that time, such as email.

The SCA provides privacy protections specifically to stored electronic and wire communications. It prevents service providers from voluntarily disclosing customer communications and requires legal authorization to release communications to the government. The statute does not specify how long an item must be held before it is considered to be in storage. Therefore, the SCA theoretically covers communications stored at any time in the past, from one second to several years ago.

The law applies only to providers of electronic communication service (ECS) and remote computing service (RCS) to the public. An ECS is defined as "any service which provides . . . the ability to send or receive wire or electronic communications" (18 U.S.C. 2510). An RCS provides the public with "computer storage or processing services" (18 U.S.C. 2711). Private providers of these services, such as workplace email providers, are not covered under SCA and can voluntarily disclose communications without restriction.

ECS and RCS providers may not share the contents of customer communications except in the following circumstances:

- with the intended recipient of the communication;
- when authorized by the necessary court order, subpoena, or search warrant;
- with the permission of the sender or intended recipient of the communication;
- to another provider in order to deliver the communication to its intended recipient;
- as needed to provide the service or protect the rights of the service provider;
- to the National Center for Missing and Exploited Children in cases of kidnapping;
- to law enforcement if the communication was accidentally obtained by the provider and appears to relate to a crime; and
- to a government entity in cases of "emergency involving danger of death or serious physical injury to any person" (18 U.S.C. 2702).

To obtain the contents of communications, the government must obtain a court order, subpoena, or search warrant depending on the type of provider, the age of the communication, and whether notice is given to the customer. In cases in which customer notice is required, the government may delay notification if notification could adversely affect the ongoing investigation or put someone in danger (18 U.S.C. 2705). In certain counterintelligence cases, the service provider may be prohibited from disclosing that customer records were requested or obtained (18 U.S.C. 2709). This is commonly known as a gag order.

Information that an ECS or RCS keeps about its customers does not receive as much protection as the content of customer communications. The government can use an administrative subpoena to obtain a customer's name, address, telephone records (including the recipient, date, time, and length of calls), ID numbers, and payment information. Additional customer information may be obtained with the permission of the customer, a court order based on reasonable grounds that the information is relevant to an ongoing criminal investigation, or a warrant. The government is not required to notify the customer that this information has been requested (18 U.S.C. 2703). Noncontent information about customers may be released voluntarily to nongovernment entities such as marketing firms.

The SCA also protects videotape rental and sales records. Customer records of videotape rental and sales may be shared with law enforcement only if a warrant, grand jury subpoena, or court order based on probable cause is issued. The subject area of the video rental or sales may be provided to marketing agencies as long as specific titles are not disclosed (18 U.S.C. 2710). More robust protections for video rental records are found in the Video Privacy Protection Act of 1988, 102 Stat. 3195, codified as, 18 U.S.C. § 2710.

In 2010, the Sixth Circuit Court ruled in *United States v. Warshak,* 631 F.3d 266 (2010), that emails stored on third-party servers are protected under the Fourth Amendment, regardless of their age, and may be obtained only with a warrant. This ruling applies only to investigations conducted in the Sixth Circuit. In *Riley v. California,* 134 S.Ct. 2473 (2014), the U.S. Supreme Court held that a warrant was needed to search the digital information stored on a cellphone.

Although the SCA was written to balance the right for privacy with the needs of law enforcement, privacy advocates argue that the major changes in technology since 1986 have left technology users vulnerable and have given too much power to law enforcement. At the time the ECPA was enacted, commercial email for the public did not exist. Email users downloaded messages from a third-party server and saved them on their own computers. The messages were then deleted from the remote server (ECPA [Part I] 2013). Communications left on the remote server for more than 180 days were considered abandoned (S. Rep 113–34 2013).

The third-party doctrine, affirmed by the Supreme Court in *Katz v. United States,* 389 U.S. 347 (1967), holds that a person who voluntarily provides information to a third party (such as an email or Internet service provider or a phone company) does not have an expectation of privacy for that information. Current electronic communication technology encourages long-term storage of all messages on a third-party server. Therefore, modern technology practices have fewer privacy protections for contemporary electronic communications than when the SCA was enacted.

Legislators and privacy advocates pushing for reform of the SCA and its parent law, the ECPA, believe updated language would reduce confusion for the courts and law enforcement and would better protect the privacy of users of modern communication technologies. Among the proposed changes are elimination of the distinction between ECS and RCS providers because current technology blurs the boundaries between these types of providers. Many, including the Department of Justice, also believe the 180-day rule and provisions for opened versus unopened email are no longer meaningful.

Lissa N. Snyders

Further Reading

Burshnic, Rudolph J. "Applying the Stored Communications Act to the Civil Discovery of Social Networking Sites." *Washington and Lee Law Review* 69 (2012): 1259–1293.

Fox, Christopher. "Checking In: Historic Cell-Site Location Information and the Stored Communications Act." *Seton Hall Law Review* 42 (2012): 769–792.

Horton, David. "The Stored Communications Act and Digital Assets." *Vanderbilt Law Review* 72, no. 6 (2014): 1729–1739.

Kerr, Orin S. "A User's Guide to the Stored Communications Act, and a Legislator's Guide to Amending It." *George Washington Law Review* 72, no. 6 (August 2004): 1208–1243.

Medina, Melissa. "The Stored Communications Act: An Old Statute for Modern Times." *American University Law Review* 63, no. 1 (2013): 267–305.

Robison, William Jeremy. "Free at What Cost?: Cloud Computing Privacy under the Stored Communications Act." *Georgetown Law Journal* 98 (2010): 1195–1239.

See also: Big data; Electronic Communications Privacy Act (ECPA); Email; Fourth Amendment to the U.S. Constitution; *Katz v. United States; Riley v. California;* Video Privacy Protection Act

Subpoenas

Identification: Legal orders requiring an individual to appear, and usually to testify, in a court on a given date and time, and/or to produce certain documents and/or records that a witness has in his or her possession, or is in control of, in a certain place and at a certain time. A subpoena is usually served by a neutral person, who is not a party to the litigation. Usually, a sheriff or process server delivers the subpoena.

The term *Subpoena duces tecum* is a Latin phrase meaning "Bring it with you." Subpoenas are commonly used in investigating civil and criminal cases because they are relatively easy for law enforcement to obtain from a prosecutor. Subpoenas do not usually require court approval or review.

Warrants, which a judge must approve, are required to wiretap phones and to monitor conversations, pursuant to the Fourth Amendment prohibition against unreasonable searches and seizures. Warrants thus require a higher standard than subpoenas. Law enforcement must usually have a warrant to seize letters sent through the postal service. The traditional rule has been applied in the debate about digital communication because there has been greater legal protection granted to a sealed envelope at the post office than to an opened letter on a person's desk. Law enforcement, under current law, can easily obtain the private electronic communications of ordinary Americans and is doing so to a significant and growing degree.

The rules governing the discovery of digital communications are different despite the fact that emails and text messaging have superseded written communication as the primary form of communication. In most cases, government agencies are not required to obtain search warrants to retrieve the private emails or cellphone records of individuals. The Electronic Communications Privacy Act (EPCA), 100 Stat. 1848 (1986), states that a federal prosecutor may issue a subpoena and obtain an individual's emails without a court-approved warrant. The only exception is unopened emails that are less than 180 days old, which do require a warrant. The record of any email that has been opened or is more than 180 days old can be obtained through

Copy of the US District Court-ordered subpoena, made by the Science Education Resource Center (SERC), an office of Carleton College.

a subpoena. Government agencies also obtain cellphone and text message records by subpoenas. Such records could include geographical locating information indicating where a phone was at a given time. Regardless of whether a subpoena or a warrant is used, law enforcement officials can request that the user be informed of the seizure for up to ninety days so the user will know that that her or his private communications are no longer private. In contrast to the EPCA standard used in most of the United States, several western states that comprise the district for the Ninth Circuit Court of Appeals require law enforcement agents to obtain a warrant to access to someone's private electronic communications.

Unlike other businesses that retain customer records, the records held by Internet companies cover an unusually large amount of information about a person's interests, transactions, and social relationships. Computers retain records of all the data they have processed. This data is often disseminated among various companies and their servers.

An IP address and nothing else will not identify an individual user under the current configuration of the Internet. However, an IP address maybe traced to a specific Internet service provider (ISP). If served with a subpoena, the ISP may be compelled to identify the customers associated with a specific IP address at a particular time. This is the method that the recording industry used to identify and prosecute individuals using illegal file-sharing programs. Most log files retained by ISPs are of little interest to anyone; however, some could be very relevant in criminal or civil investigations, or they could provide facts that could embarrass a public figure.

Law enforcement is issuing subpoenas more and more often against social media companies such as Google to retrieve information on users for criminal investigations. The people being investigated may never even realize that an investigation has occurred unless they are indicted with a crime based on the investigation. While information obtained from subpoenas has assisted local authorities in apprehending dangerous criminals, privacy advocates claim that the government has too-easy access to personal communications and other private information without an adequate showing of probable cause. To remedy this problem, they urge Congress to prevent warrantless snooping by modernizing digital privacy laws to accommodate the current realities of cellphones, social media, and email.

Many of the large Internet companies, such as Google and Microsoft, do not release the contents of user emails and electronic messages unless they are served with a warrant. However, Google reported producing other noncontact subscriber information in almost 90 percent of the law enforcement requests.

At least one court has ruled that Tweets may also be subpoenaed under certain circumstances.

During the Occupy Wall Street protests in 2011, 700 protesters were arrested on the Brooklyn Bridge. Prosecutors attempted to subpoena the email addresses, Twitter login information, and all Tweets that one of the protestors sent between September 5, 2011, and December 31, 2011. Manhattan criminal court judge Matthew Sciarrino Jr. ruled that the defendant lacked standing to quash the subpoena because Twitter owned the Tweets. Twitter then challenged the subpoena, arguing that the judge's ruling contradicted the terms of service, which states that a user owns his or her Tweets. The company also argued that the judge's interpretation placed an undue burden on Twitter to defend the users because they would be unable to defend themselves. Twitter finally claimed that law enforcement should be required to obtain a warrant to force the company to disclose users' Tweets. Judge Sciarrino rejected Twitter's claims. "There is no reasonable expectation of privacy," the judge wrote. "There is no proprietary interest in [the] tweets. . . . This is not the same as a private email, a private direct message, a private chat, or any of the other readily available ways to have a private conversation via the internet that now exist."

Privacy advocates have expressed concerns with the unfettered power that law enforcement has to conduct surveillance on the digital communications of Americans without their knowledge and the lack of judicial oversight over this process. They blame this dysfunctional situation on obsolete laws that have not addressed the realities brought about by advances in technology. Privacy groups assert that the Fourth Amendment and the right of Americans to have a legitimate expectation of privacy should preclude, absent probable cause, the type of government surveilliance of email permitted under the EPCA. Privacy groups say that stronger privacy laws will ensure that ISPs are more careful about what information they collect and that the government is more selective about what information it pursues.

Privacy advocates have sought passage of a proposed Electronic Communications Privacy Act Amendments Act of 2013, which was intended to update ECPA. The legislation would have required the government to obtain a search warrant to collect the contents of emails, texts, social media posts, and other communications stored with third-party ISPs. The legislation, which had bipartisan support, also would end the 180-day rule on electronic messages and require the government to inform individuals when it seizes records of their electronic communications. This legislation and subsequent variations of it have failed to pass Congress.

Unless privacy laws are strengthened in the United States, the best way to protect one's privacy is never to send a message through email that you would not want the whole world to see.

Further Reading

Hall, John Wesley. *Search and Seizure,* 3rd ed. Charlottesville, VA: LEXIS Law Pub., 2000.

Hayes, Paul. *Subpoenas.* Melbourne: Leo Cussen Institute, 2001.

How the Health Insurance Portability and Accountability Act (HIPAA) and Other Privacy Laws Affect Public Transportation Operations. Washington, DC: Transportation Research Board, 2014.

Lee, N. Genell. *Legal Concepts and Issues in Emergency Care.* Philadelphia, PA: W.B. Saunders, 2001.

Rosen, Jeffrey. *The Unwanted Gaze: The Destruction of Privacy in America.* New York: Vintage Books, 2001.

Slobogin, Christopher. *Privacy at Risk: The New Government Surveillance and the Fourth Amendment.* Chicago, IL: University of Chicago Press, 2007.

See also: Computers and privacy; Criminal justice (criminal procedure); Electronic Communications Privacy Act (ECPA); Email; Fourth Amendment to the U.S. Constitution; Google; Law enforcement; Social media; Twitter

Supreme Court of the United States

Identification: The highest court in the country and the ultimate interpreter of the Constitution, including the extent to which constitutional law protects, among other things, privacy rights. The U.S. Supreme Court's test for deciding when and where a person is constitutionally protected against government intrusion is called reasonable expectation of privacy.

Like most Americans, U.S. Supreme Court justices understand that modern technologies bring both advantages and disadvantages. On the one hand, these new digital tools aid law enforcement efforts, strengthen our nation's security, and provide certain benefits for civilian use. They also carry information to broad audiences and open up courtrooms far beyond their physical seating capacity. Technological advances make it easier and cheaper to connect Americans to each other, the world, and their government. These advances in technology, however, also threaten to diminish Americans' treasured personal privacy in a way that makes it difficult to regulate from a legal perspective.

Supreme Court justices are entrusted with the job of balancing these competing interests, and their decisions carry potentially long-term consequences. Indeed, they have been assigned the exceedingly difficult and sometimes contradictory roles of being both the guardians of the past and the predictors of the future. As guardians of the past, the justices are duty-bound to apply, with rare exceptions, existing legal concepts and precedents. Legal analysis depends on uniformity and predictability over time. Thus, the justices must honor the decisions of past courts and established legal rules.

As predictors of the future, they are also tasked with writing opinions that will be applied now and in the future. In this role, they must analyze increasingly novel uses of modern technology while remaining mindful of how the legal guidelines they announce today might be applied in future cases. The Court summed up these dual tasks in a 1909 decision, declaring: "In the application of a Constitution . . . our contemplation cannot be only of what has been, but of what may be" (*Weems v. United States,* 217 U.S. 349, 373 (1910)).

When addressing issues of new and evolving technology, the Supreme Court is most comfortable when it can analogize a new technology to an older, more familiar, and time-tested scenario. Finding common ground between modern technology and past situations grounds their decisions in legal precedent. Thus, the justices tend to query whether a new technology is the equivalent of trespassing into someone's home or of recording a suspect's fingerprints, because these are situations that have been definitively been ruled on in the past.

Sometimes the analogy seems like a logical fit- the nature of previous cases fit the details of current cases even though they differ in terms of technology. In other cases, however, the relevant comparisons are less clear. When this happens, the Court's opinions can lead to dead ends, conflicting conclusions, or even arguably absurd arguments. Nonetheless, the justices have continued to approach cases involving privacy interests in digital information through the process of applying old law to new technologies.

The Supreme Court and traditional privacy

Issues about privacy in a digital world have reached the Court through several different legal channels. Digital privacy concerns have appeared in cases involving legal issues such as freedom of speech (*Bartnicki v. Vopper*, 532 U.S. 514 (2001)), rights of press access (*Hollingsworth v. Perry*, 558 U.S. 183 (2010)), questions of standing (whether a particular party may bring certain cases, *Clapper v. Amnesty Int'l USA*, 133 S. Ct. 1138 (2013)), freedom of association (*John Doe No. 1 v. Reed*, 561 U.S. 186 (2010)), federal court jurisdiction (*Mims v. Arrow Fin. Servs., LLC*, 132 S. Ct. 740 (2012)), child pornography (*Paroline v. United States*, 134 S. Ct. 1710 (2014)), compelled disclosure of medical records (*Nat'l Aeronautics & Space Admin. v. Nelson*, 562 U.S. 134 (2011)), and statutory freedom of information claims

(*National Archives and Records Administration v. Favish*, 541 U.S. 157 (2004)). It is, however, the Court's ongoing examination of the Fourth Amendment that protects "the people" from "unreasonable searches and seizures" by the government that has provided most of the justices' insights into privacy in the digital age. The Court's Fourth Amendment jurisprudence pits the individual's interests in personal privacy against the government's interest in effective law enforcement.

From as early as the mid-nineteenth century, the Court has acknowledged the Fourth Amendment's declaration that "the right of the people to be secure in their persons, houses, papers, and effects" included not just physical intrusions but also matters of personal privacy— even though the word *privacy* never appears. In an 1886 decision, for example, the Court held Fourth Amendment rights "apply to all invasions on the part of the government and its employes [sic] of the sanctity of a man's home and the privacies of life" (*Boyd v. United States*, 116 U.S. 616, 630 (1886)).

At the center of the Court's traditional Fourth Amendment jurisprudence is the right of privacy within the home. In a 2013 case, Justice Antonin Scalia wrote that "when it comes to the Fourth Amendment, the home is first among equals. At the Amendment's 'very core' stands 'the right of a man to retreat into his own home and there be free from unreasonable government intrusion'" (*Florida v. Jardines*, 133 S. Ct. 1409, 1414 (2013) [quoting *Silverman v. United States*, 365 U.S. 505, 511 (1961)]). The Court concluded that this right extended to the home's curtilage as well. Thus, when the police brought a drug-sniffing dog onto the porch of a private home without a warrant, the Court held the privacy of the home's residents had been violated. The Court has further extended this protection to other personal spaces in which a person has an expectation of privacy, such as offices, hotel rooms, and telephone booths (*Katz v. United States*, 389 U.S. 347, 359 (1967)).

While the justices have strongly supported an individual's privacy rights in the home, this support drops quickly once the individual leaves his or her house or interacts with the outside world. The Court has held there is no Fourth Amendment protection for that which "a person knowingly exposes to the public" (*Id.* at 351). Thus, once a person exposes any personal information to the public sphere, his or her expectations of privacy diminish or disappear.

The Court has found, for example, that there is no expectation of privacy in the sound of one's voice (*United States v. Dionisio*, 410 U.S. 1 (1973)) or in the visible characteristics of handwriting (*United States v. Mara,* 410 U.S. 19, 21–22 (1973)), explaining that "[n]o person can have a reasonable expectation that others will not know the sound of his voice, any more than he can reasonably expect that his face will be a mystery to the world" (*Dionisio*, 410 U.S. at 14 (1973)).

Over time, the justices extended this concept of "public" space to cover information that can be gleaned with the use of special tools. This means, for example, objects in a person's backyard are not private if they can be seen from an airplane (*California v. Ciraolo*, 476 U.S. 207 (1986); *Florida v. Riley*, 488 U.S. 445 (1989)), even if seeing them required a "precision aerial mapping camera"(*Dow Chem. Co. v. United States*, 476

U.S. 227, 229 (1986)). They likewise decided a driver has no privacy interests in smells emanating from his car, even if only a trained dog can detect them (*Illinois v. Caballes,* 543 U.S. 405, 410 (2005)).

The Court and privacy in the digital age

Airplanes and drug-sniffing dogs do not compare to the capabilities of modern technology. With the right to be free of unreasonable searches and seizures traditionally grounded in physical concepts such as trespassing and actual barriers, it is not obvious how to treat the intangible intrusions made possible by today's powerful electronic technologies. These technological advances have blurred the once clear physical lines and raised new questions about the limits on government invasion of personal spaces and private matters.

The Court first faced questions about privacy and nonphysical intrusions in early cases on government wiretapping of telephone conversations. Initially, the Court applied the concept of physical trespass to the intercepted telephone conversations and concluded there was no privacy right. In a 1928 case, for example, the Court declared there was no constitutional violation with government wiretapping because "[t]here was no searching. There was no seizure. The evidence was secured by the use of the sense of hearing and that only. There was no entry of the houses or offices of the defendants" (*Olmstead v. United States*, 277 U.S. 438, 464 (1928), The Court also applied its concept that there is no privacy interest once a person has reached out to the outside world, explaining "one who installs in his house a telephone instrument with connecting wires [and] intends to project his voice to those quite outside" has no Fourth Amendment protection (*Id.* at 46).

In dissent, Justice Louis Brandeis was less sure if reliance on physical barriers or connections with wires and telephone services was the right approach. He expressed concern that this type of traditional thinking about government intrusion would not suffice in the face of evolving technology. He warned his brethren that "[t]he progress of science in furnishing the government with means of espionage is not likely to stop with wiretapping. Ways may someday be developed by which the government, without removing papers from secret drawers, can reproduce them in court, and by which it will be enabled to expose to a jury the most intimate occurrences of the home" (*Id*. at 474 (Brandeis, J., dissenting)).

In time, the rest of the Court caught up with Justice Brandeis's views. In the key 1967 case of *Katz v. United States*, the Court overruled its earlier opinion on wiretapping and concluded electronically eavesdropping on a confidential conversation did constitute a search even without a physical intrusion (*Katz*, 389 U.S. 347 (1967)). The Court held the Fourth Amendment "protects people—and not simply 'areas'" and "cannot turn upon the presence or absence of a physical intrusion into any given enclosure (*Id*. at 353). In *Katz*, the Court established the crucial inquiry is whether or not the person at that time had a "reasonable expectation of privacy" (*Id*. at 360–61 (Harlan, John Marshall, II, concurring)).

Building on this idea, the justices have found privacy rights do exist when enhanced technologies are used to infiltrate the inner spaces of the home or body. Thus, while law enforcement officers may use (without a warrant) an airplane and sophisticated viewing technology to peer into a person's backyard, the Court has said law enforcement may not use thermal radiation imaging to detect unusual amounts of heat coming from someone's home. The difference, according to the Court, is that the latter allows the government "to explore details of the home that would previously have been unknowable without physical intrusion" (*Kyllo v. United States*, 533 U.S. 27, 40 (2001)).

Digital technologies are unique not just because of their nonphysical nature but also because of the amount and breadth of information they can hold. The Court recognized how these storage capabilities can affect personal privacy recently in the 2014 case of *Riley v. California* (134 S. Ct. 2473 (2014)). The issue in *Riley* was whether police could search the contents of a person's cellphone during an arrest without warrant. In earlier cases, the Court had allowed officers to search items found on a person during

an arrest, such as a wallet or cigarette package (*United States v. Robinson*, 414 U.S. 218, 236 (1973)). In *Riley*, however, the Court unanimously drew a line at cellphones, noting the significant differences in the quantity and quality of information they contained. Chief Justice John Roberts explained, "[p]rior to the digital age, people did not typically carry a cache of sensitive personal information with them as they went about their day. Now it is the person who is not carrying a cellphone, with all that it contains, who is the exception" (*Riley v. California*, 134 S. Ct. at 2490). Noting that cellphones are actually "minicomputers," the Court further held that they "collect in one place many distinct types of information—an address, a note, a prescription, a bank statement, a video—that reveal much more in combination than any isolated record" (*Id*. at 2489).

While broadening its view of personal spaces, however, the Court has continued to embrace the other traditional approach to privacy rights—looking to see whether a person purposely interacts with the public sphere. The Court has applied this concept of willful public disclosure to cases involving electronic information. In a 1979 case, for example, the justices concluded there is no reasonable expectation of privacy in the telephone numbers dialed on a phone because making the call requires the caller to disclose that information to an outside party—the telephone company (*Smith v. Maryland*, 442 U.S. 735, 744–45 (1979)).

In concurrence with another case, Justice Sonia Sotomayor questioned whether this rule makes sense in the digital age. She observed the Court should "reconsider the premise that an individual has no reasonable expectation of privacy in information voluntarily disclosed to third parties" (*United States v. Jones*, 132 S. Ct. 945, 957 (2012) (Sotomayor, J., concurring)). She went on to observe that, in the modern world, people must "reveal a great deal of information about themselves to third parties in the course of carrying out mundane tasks" (*Id*.).

In coming years the Court might also reexamine its earlier view that a person has no privacy interest in anything visibly seen in public. Traditionally, for example, the Court held that there is no privacy right in a person's public movements or activities. The police can follow someone's car (*Cardwell v. Lewis*, 417 U.S. 583, 589–90 (1974); plurality opinion), the justices held, because the driver has "voluntarily conveyed to anyone who wanted to look the fact that he was traveling over particular roads in a particular direction, the fact of whatever stops he made, and the fact of his final destination when he exited from public roads onto private property" (*United States v. Knotts*, 460 U.S. 276, 281–82 (1983)). By this same logic, the Court upheld police use of a radio transmitter to track the movements of a suspect's car (*Id.* at 282).

In a 2012 case, the Court was faced with this question again but this time with a new technological tool—a global positioning system (GPS) device. The issue was whether a constitutional violation occurred when the police placed a GPS device on a person's car and used it to monitor the car's movements twenty-four hours a day for almost a month (*Jones*, 132 S. Ct. at 948). The Court concluded there was a privacy violation. It did so, however, by relying on the concept of a physical trespass, stating the government physically intruded upon the defendant's property by placing the device on the car without permission (*Id.* at 949). It did not decide whether the GPS tracking would have been unlawful without the physical trespass.

In a concurring opinion, Justice Samuel Alito observed that technology was changing the public's expectations of privacy and noted, "[i]n the pre-computer age, the greatest protections of privacy were neither constitutional nor statutory, but practical," with time and money placing limits on government intrusions; "[d]evices like the one used in the present case, however, make long-term monitoring relatively easy and cheap" (*Id.* at 963–64 (Alito, J., concurring)).

Finally, the justices divided on the impact of digital technology on the privacy of the human body. The Court has held that government intrusion into a person's body, like government intrusion on the sanctity of the home, involves important privacy rights, noting "any compelled intrusion into the human body implicates significant, constitutionally protected privacy interests" (*Missouri v. McNeely*, 133 S. Ct. 1552, 1565 (2013)). Based on this principle, the justices have held that forcibly obtaining a blood sample, a urine sample, or a breath test raises constitutional issues and requires a warrant (*Skinner v. Ry. Labor Execs.' Ass'n*, 489 U.S. 602, 616–17 (1989); *Schmerber v. California*, 384 U.S. 757, 769–70 (1966)). They upheld exceptions to this general rule only in "reasonable [and] appropriate circumstances" (*McNeely*, 133 S. Ct. at 1565).

Modern technical advances have again raised issues of the proper analogy to bodily intrusions. New technological tools can extract far more personal information from the testing of bodily material than before. Pondering these developments, the justices have argued over whether the crucial privacy issue is *how* the information was obtained or *what* the information reveals.

The justices agree when the police take a person's photograph for identification purposes, there is no constitutional concern. They have extended this concept to fingerprinting and handwriting samples. They nevertheless drew the line at scraping material from underneath a person's fingernail, concluding that such action involved "severe, though brief, intrusion" on the body (*Cupp v. Murphy*, 412 U.S. 291, 295 (1973) (quoting *Terry v. Ohio*, 392 U.S. 1, 24–25) (1968)).

Recently, however, the justices were faced with the question of whether a police swab of a person's cheek for the purposes of collecting DNA evidence was akin to photographing or fingerprinting an arrestee or whether it was something else entirely. In a 5–4 decision, the Court held the bodily intrusion of a cheek swab was minimal, and the use of DNA for identification purposes was reasonable (*Maryland v. King*, 133 S. Ct. 1958, 1980 (2013)).

Four justices disagreed, however, arguing the information contained in DNA evidence is not used for identification but for the significantly different purpose of trying to solve old cases. This, according to the dissenters, makes it akin to a "general warrant" against all persons (*Id.* at 1980–81 (Scalia, J., dissenting)). In dissent, Justice Scalia warned that the Court's failure to recognize the inherent privacy interest in DNA could lead to a world where "your DNA can be taken and entered into a national DNA database if you are ever arrested, rightly or wrongly, and for whatever reason" (*Id.* at 1989).

As technology advances, so must the law. The Supreme Court has struggled to keep pace with the digital world. Often the justices have turned to old case law and analogies to find answers. Increasingly, however, Supreme Court justices are realizing the limitations of that approach. Until they settle on a new framework regarding how to balance privacy and information in the digital age, however, they will likely continue to take incremental steps on an as-needed basis.

Sonja R. West

Further Reading

Goldfarb, Ronald, et al. *After Snowden: Privacy, Secrecy and Security in the Information Age*. New York: T. Dunne, 2015.

Lind, Nancy S., and Erik Rankin, eds. *Privacy in the Digital Age: 21st-Century Challenges to the Fourth Amendment*. 2 vols. Santa Barbara, CA: Praeger,

Martin, Greg, Rebecca Scott Bray, and Miiko Kumar, eds. *Secrecy, Law, and Society*. New York: Routledge, 2015. Mills, Jon L. *Privacy in the New Media Age*. Gainesville: University Press of Florida, 2015.

Richards, Neil. *Intellectual Privacy: Rethinking Civil Liberties in the Digital Age*. New York: Oxford University Press, 2015.

Sarat, Austin, ed. *A World Without Privacy: What Law Can and Should Do?* New York: Cambridge University Press, 2015.

Schneier, Bruce. *Data and Goliath: The Hidden Battles to Collect Your Data and Control Your World*. New York: W. W. Norton, 2015.

Tunick, Mark. *Balancing Privacy and Free Speech: Unwanted Attention in the Age of Social Media*. New York: Routledge, 2015.

See also: *Bartnicki*; Body, privacy of the; Brandeis, Louis Dembitz; Cellphones; Constitutional law; DNA databases; Fifth Amendment to the U.S. Constitution; First Amendment to the U.S. Constitution; Fourth Amendment to the U.S. Constitution; Global positioning system (GPS) tracking; Home, privacy of the; Invasion of privacy; *Katz v. United States*; *Kyllo v. United States*; Law enforcement; Legal evolution of privacy rights; *National Archives and Records Administration v. Favish*; *Olmstead v. United States*; Privacy laws, federal; Privacy laws, state; Search warrants; Telephones; *United States v. Jones*; Wiretapping

Surveillance cameras

Identification: Video devices used to observe an area. Usually connected to a recording device or Internet Protocol (IP) network, surveillance cameras may be monitored by a security guard or law enforcement officer.

Prior to widespread digitization, surveillance cameras and recording equipment were relatively expensive, and human monitoring of the equipment was necessary. Automated software has made the monitoring process more effective and efficient. This software helps to organize digital video footage into a searchable database, with software that performs video analysis.

Privacy law on surveillance through the capture of visual images has traditionally relied on an analogy between actions visible to passersby and actions captured by cameras. New surveillance technologies have rendered this analogy inapplicable; there is a difference between a passerby and a video surveillance camera. A passerby's observation is restricted to what can be normally observed. The passerby is able to use equipment, such as binoculars, however, because the passerby exists at the same time and in the same space as the subject, the subject is likely to know of the observation and to have an opportunity to react. The subject of video

Privacy may be lessened by surveillance – in this case through CCTV.

surveillance, however, is most likely to be unaware that she or he is under surveillance, what images are being captured, who is monitoring the image and where the individual is located, when the image is being reviewed, or how the image is being modified.

Video surveillance technologies have greatly improved and have become increasingly less expensive. Thus, video surveillance has been increasingly more widespread. This has been accompanied by dramatic changes in how society has viewed security and how Americans view privacy and public spaces; however, privacy laws on video surveillance of public spaces has not kept up with the technology.

Neither the U.S. Constitution nor the Bill of Rights specifically grants an explicit right to privacy. In the absence of applicable legislation, courts decide privacy rights on a case-by-case basis. The traditional tests often used to determine a legitimate expectation of privacy have often not been applied to video surveillance. Currently, there is no legal standard covering citizens who do not wish to have the images captured by either state or private actors. Nevertheless, many

privacy advocates argue that individuals should have the right to control the use of his or her image, even if the image was taken in a public space.

Only in recent times has society had both the technology and interest to conduct wholesale, intensive, visual surveillance of its public spaces. After the 9/11 attacks, however, there was renewed emphasis on technology and security concerns. Because of these factors, new privacy issues arose. Privacy advocates argued that expectations of privacy in the context of video surveillance of public spaces demanded a new definition of "a legitimate expectation of privacy" that reflects the changes in society and technology.

The debate over surveillance cameras is one that focuses on finding the appropriate balance between national security and individual freedom in a democratic nation. Many privacy advocates argue that an over-reliance on surveillance cameras leads to diminished privacy, autonomy, and anonymity. Some commentators believe that the greater use of video surveillance systems with facial recognition technology (FRT) could be used against certain groups. Those favoring the utilization of this technology argue that these devices increase security, decrease crime, and fight terrorism. They also argue that these systems can be used responsibly and to protect legitimate privacy interests.

Government use of surveillance camera systems, along with FRT, involves several serious privacy issues. These systems are commonly used in public spaces (such as streets, parks, business districts, and public land) to investigate or deter crime and to fight terrorism. One initial issue is the extent to which one or more established constitutional provisions forbid the operation of such systems in public places. These constitutional provisions are the Fourth Amendment's proscription "against unreasonable searches and seizures;" the First Amendment's protection of the guarantees of free speech and association, and the right to privacy; the guarantees of freedom of movement and repose under the due process clause of the Fifth and Fourteenth Amendments; and the Fifth Amendment privilege against self-incrimination.

Widespread private-sector use of surveillance cameras has been a reality for several years. For example, retailers have used these systems to control inventory shrinkage. Surveillance cameras are ubiquitous at shopping centers, hospitals, gas stations, subways, and schools. Governments at all levels use surveillance cameras to promote public safety and to prevent crime, whether recording traffic infractions on streets and highways, in bridges and tunnels, and along open sections of the U.S. international borders with Canada and Mexico.

Government use of closed-circuit television cameras in conjunction with FRT is subject to constitutional limitations, including the Fourth Amendment (which prohibits "unreasonable searches and seizures"), the First Amendment (which protects free speech and free association), the due process clause of the Fifth and Fourteenth Amendments, (which protects individuals' right to privacy, guarantees of freedom of movement and repose), and the Fifth Amendment (which prohibits against self-incrimination).

Fourth Amendment protections

The Fourth Amendment protects against "unreasonable searches and seizures." Generally, for a search to be lawful, there must be: (1) a warrant based on probable cause, (2) exception to the warrant requirement, or (3) reasonable articulable grounds of suspicion. To determine whether surveillance cameras with FRT technology violates an individual's Fourth Amendment rights, courts often apply *Katz v. United States,* 369 U.S. 347 (1967), which delineates when government conduct violates an individual's reasonable expectation of privacy and thus represents a unreasonable search. In defining a search, the Court distinguished between those privacy interests protected by the Fourth Amendment and the more general right of privacy. The Court

observed that "the protection of a person's general right to privacy—his right to be let alone by other people—is like the protection of his property and of his very life, left largely to the law of the individual States." The former, the Court found, protected privacy and other interests.

The Court held that the "Fourth Amendment protects people—and not simply 'areas'—against unreasonable searches and seizures." Although the conduct by the government agents occurred in a public place, the Court in *Katz* observed: "What a person knowingly exposes to the public, even in his own home or office, is not a subject of Fourth Amendment protection. But what he seeks to preserve as private, even in an area accessible to the public, may be constitutionally protected."

Many of the cases following and relying on *Katz* discussed the expectations of privacy vis-à-vis the government's use of advanced technology, and they are also useful when assessing the impact, if any, that the Fourth Amendment has on the use in public places of closed-circuit television cameras equipped with FRT.

In view of current case law, the use of surveillance cameras, even those equipped with FRT systems, does not appear to constitute a search (in Fourth Amendment terms) when those cameras are used in public places. First, surveillance cameras and FRT are publicly available. Second, is the principle that the Fourth Amendment largely applies to the extent of "where those people are." Third, *Katz* plainly states that "what a person knowingly exposes to the public, even in his own home or office, is not a subject of Fourth Amendment protection." Thus, the Supreme Court has held that individuals do not possess a reasonable expectation of privacy to physical characteristics, such as voice or facial features, that are exposed to the public. Regarding the degree of privacy protected by the Fourth Amendment for movement on a public street, the Court has ruled that, in terms of travel by car on public roadways, a person "has no reasonable expectation of privacy in his movements from one place to another." Thus, courts have ruled that the use of surveillance cameras in public does not violate the Fourth Amendment, whether these devices are used in public, urban, rural, or public land settings.

First Amendment protections

The First Amendment forbids Congress from passing laws that would abridge freedom of speech. Although the term *association* is not explicitly stated in the First Amendment, the Supreme Court has held that "freedom to engage in association for the advancement of beliefs and ideas is an inseparable aspect of the 'liberty' assured by the Due Process Clause of the Fourteenth Amendment, which embraces freedom of speech."

When the government enacts a law that "tends to have the incidental effect of inhibiting First Amendment rights," this law will pass constitutional muster "if the effect on speech is minor concerning the need for control of the conduct and the lack of alternative means for doing so." The Supreme Court has also made clear that this constitutional provision applies only to some speech-related activity. While there may be some degree of expression in any human activity, such actions do not bring the activity under First Amendment protection.

In the context of public places, even in cases involving First Amendment rights (such as joining in or speaking at a political demonstration), the government's interest in deterring crime or identifying terrorists appears sufficiently important to support the use of surveillance cameras, based on current First Amendment jurisprudence.

Common law privacy rights

In 1960, Dean William Prosser wrote an influential article discussing the four torts that violate an individual's privacy: (1) intrusion upon seclusion or solitude, (2) public disclosure of private facts, (3) false light, and (4) appropriation. Later, the *Restatement (Second) of Torts* incorporated all four categories into its list of actionable privacy torts. The issue then becomes whether the consti-

tutional right to privacy can be invoked to enjoin the use of surveillance cameras in public places.

Analyzing the right to privacy as one that seeks the protection of personhood, some privacy advocates argue that, even in a public setting, individuals should have an expectation of privacy because much of human personality is developed in public venues. Surveillance cameras risk stultifying public conduct and stifling human activity, and thus adversely affect that right.

Under current law, it is highly unlikely that courts will find that surveillance of public places, even if the surveillance cameras are equipped with FRT, infringes on the individual's right to privacy. As to the confidentiality element of the right to privacy, its range of protecting autonomy has not extended beyond prohibiting disclosure of medical, financial, and other intimately personal data. In one case, a court has ruled that the common law right to privacy is not infringed when a video camera is openly used to record persons "walking on a public street as they entered and exited" a clinic because those images "could also be viewed by members of the general public who were standing or walking in the vicinity of the clinic."

Freedom of movement and repose

The freedom to travel within the United States has long been recognized as a fundamental constitutional right for American citizens under the due process clauses of the Fifth and Fourteenth Amendments. Some privacy rights advocate argue that the surveillance of public places may compromise those rights to travel and to repose, which are derived from the due process clause. A definitive judicial issue has not addressed this issue. As discussed previously with respect to the First Amendment, the government's interest in preventing crime and identifying suspected terrorists through the use of surveillance cameras equipped with FRT is reasonable and legitimate, and would outweigh any incidental impairment that such use may have on a person's freedom to travel.

Fifth Amendment Protection

The Fifth Amendment states that "no person . . . shall be compelled in any criminal case to be a witness against himself." The amendment protects an individual from self-incrimination by his or her own compelled, testimonial communications. Generally, the Fifth Amendment does not protect the individual from being compelled to undergo fingerprinting, photographing, or measurements; to write or speak for identification; to appear in court; to stand; to assume a stance; to walk; or to make a particular gesture. In other words, the prohibition against compelling someone in a criminal court to be a witness against him- or herself prohibits using physical or moral compulsion to obtain communications from that person, but it does not exclude the use of his or her body as evidence when it may be material. The use in public places of surveillance cameras in conjunction with FRT does not involve any government compulsion, but even if an argument could be presented that it did, observing a person or comparing his or her face (a physical characteristic easily observable and commonly available to the public) with that found in a database is not a communication that would invoke application of the privilege.

Conclusion

Considering the realities of crime and terrorism, and depending on the public interest involved, the use of surveillance cameras in conjunction with facial recognition technology (FRT) in public places can be a reasonable protective measure that serves critical government interests by helping to identify suspected terrorists and criminals, and to deter crime; however, the implementation of surveillance systems, including those with FRT, raise significant privacy issues. Appropriate regulations and legislation protecting individual privacy should be promulgated to prevent abuse and to ensure proper use of the systems by law enforcement and homeland security agencies. The use of such camera surveillance systems in public places to deter crime or to identify known or suspected terrorists does not appear to be unconstitutional.

Gretchen Nobahar

Further Reading

Doyle, Aaron. *Eyes Everywhere: The Global Growth of Camera Surveillance*. Abingdon, Oxon, England: Routledge, 2012.

Greiffenhagen, Michael. *Engineering, Statistical Modeling and Performance Characterization of a Real-Time Dual Camera Surveillance System*. 2002.

Kruegle, Herman. CCTV *Surveillance: Analog and Digital Video Practices and Technology,* 2nd ed. Amsterdam: Elsevier Butterworth-Heinemann, 2007.

Nouwt, Sjaak. *Reasonable Expectations of Privacy?: Eleven Country Reports on Camera Surveillance and Workplace Privacy*. The Hague, The Netherlands: T.M.C. Asser Press, 2005.

See also: Computers and privacy; Criminal justice (criminal procedure; Electronic Communications Privacy Act (ECPA); Email; Fourth Amendment to the U.S. Constitution; Google; Law enforcement; Social media; Twitter

Telephones

Identification: Devices that can transmit and receive voice communications through the telecommunications network, originally the Bell network in the United States and eventually the Internet. Telephones now encompass mobile devices and a variety of communications equipment.

Alexander Graham Bell invented the telephone in 1876 and received two patents for his work. The following year, he established the Bell Telephone Company, and the year after that he began offering telephone service in what would become a national system for landline voice communications. In the late 1880s and 1890s, Bell Telephone Company subsidiary American Telephone & Telegraph (AT&T) constructed long-distance telephone wires and began completing long-distance calls. Also before the turn of the twentieth century, several smaller companies began offering telephone service. After over a decade of disputes with AT&T, these companies were allowed to interconnect with AT&T's network and therefore complete calls outside their territories. Transatlantic calls began in 1927, initially via radio signals and later through a submerged cable. Underwater cables allowed calls across the Pacific Ocean and eventually worldwide, with the notable exception of Antarctica.

Telephones initially consisted of a limited number of devices, usually consisting of a part that was held to one ear to hear a voice, and a microphone in which to speak. Human operators located at the switch would complete calls by connecting the calling party and the receiving party. Switches were later mechanized, then computerized, allowing calls to complete automatically without human intervention. Also, to place calls independently, users would need to be able to dial the called number on the device. Phones with number dials were developed by the 1910s. They were followed by phones with touchtone number keypads in the 1960s. Gradually, traditional copper wire networks were replaced with fiber optic cable. Fiber optic cable allows faster service due to its greater bandwidth, but it requires electric power to operate, rendering it less reliable during a power outage. Traditional copper wire networks are also more difficult to hack and use for eavesdropping on conversations, but fiber optic cable continues to replace copper to support the growth of data-dependent networks. For approximately 100 years after telephone service was commercially available in the United States, the telephone devices were owned by the telephone company and provided as part of a monthly telephone service, usually with a separate rental fee for the device. This connection between device and service continues today in the relationship between mobile device discounts and service contracts in the mobile telephony market.

The Communications Act of 1934, 48 Stat. 1064 (1934), 47 U.S.C. § 151 et seq., regulated telecommunications and established a new U.S.

Advertisement for dial telephone service available to delegates to the 1912 Republican convention in Chicago. A major selling point of dial telephone service was that it was "secret," in that no operator was required to connect the call.

federal agency, the Federal Communications Commission (FCC). The Communications Act includes the following provision that protects privacy: "Every telecommunications carrier has a duty to protect the confidentiality of proprietary information of, and relating to, other telecommunication carriers, equipment manufacturers, and customers, including telecommunication carriers reselling telecommunications services provided by a telecommunications carrier," with limited exceptions for fraud investigations, law enforcement, and emergencies, 47 U.S. Code § 222. This authority to protect Customer Proprietary Network Information (CPNI) has led the FCC to take the lead in protecting privacy in the telecommunications area, while the Federal Trade Commission (FTC)

covers privacy issues in other industries. CPNI is valuable customer information, and activity associated with "pretexting," or calling a telephone company to attempt to get another person's CPNI under the pretext of being that person, is considered fraud and punishable as a criminal offense. Telephone carriers must take special precautions to make sure the calling party is the customer of record for that CPNI or face sanctions from the FCC. Unless the calling party provides a prearranged password to the telecommunications carrier, the carrier may only provide the requested information by mail to the official address of the customer of record for the relevant account. Customers must opt in to receive marketing information from their carrier beyond information that pertains to services to which they already subscribe, that is, within local services or within long-distance services.

The 911 service (later E911 service, which added location information) is a telephone service that allows telephone users to dial the digits 9, 1, and 1, and be connected to an emergency call center called a public safety answering point (PSAP)—and then to the police or ambulance if necessary. The number was established in the late 1960s as a nationwide standard. Regulators have deemed this an essential service to the extent that carriers are often required to leave a "warm line" to allow access to 911 service even if the customer at that location has fallen behind on his or her payments for telephone service.

In 1984, in the Modified Final Judgment (MFJ), the U.S. Justice Department broke apart AT&T; created seven Regional Bell Operating Companies (RBOCs); and allowed AT&T to continue as a separate long-distance telephone company, to engage in manufacturing equipment like telephones, and to conduct research and development (R&D). The RBOCs provided plain old telephone service (POTS) and related ancillary services such as call forwarding, call waiting, and Caller ID. A large number of companies begin to offer long-distance telephone service following the breakup of AT&T's monopoly. The Telecommunications Act of 1996, 110 Stat. 56 (1996), amended the Communications Act of 1934 and allowed new companies (and old ones like AT&T) into the local exchange telephone market. Companies began to bundle long distance; local service; and eventually wireless mobile communications service, Internet, and cable television service for competitive price discounts.

Telephones have been the center of controversy over privacy rights in the United States since their introduction into the public sphere. Initially, opponents likened the ring of the telephone to the unwanted knock on the door of the user's home or even to an unannounced entry into the home. Even an individual in a telephone booth was granted the right to have a private conversation on the telephone without government agents listening in via wiretap in *Katz v. U.S.* 389 U.S. 347 (1967). Katz was a handicapper for sports who gathered information in phone booths located on Sunset Boulevard in Los Angeles, California, and the Federal Bureau of Investigation (FBI) wanted to stop him. The government asked the telephone company to place the booth out of order. It then put a tape recorder in the air between two remaining booths, and stationed an agent outside Katz's apartment to record his pay phone conversations. Katz was indicted in the Federal District Court in Los Angeles, but the U.S. Supreme Court overruled the lower courts and found that Katz had a reasonable expectation of privacy in his phone conversation in the telephone booth. The Supreme Court applied the Fourth Amendment to the Constitution that protects people from unreasonable searches and seizures, and said that the government could obtain the information from Katz's call, but only with a warrant.

The Telephone Consumer Protection Act (TCPA) of 1991, 105 Stat. 2395 (1991), 47 U.S.C. § 227, and FCC regulations under the TCPA provide some protections for telephone user privacy. The result of these regulations was to reduce the number of unsolicited telephone calls and facsimiles sent via telephone wire. The law provided exceptions for customers with whom the calling party had a preexisting business relationship or for noncommercial calls such as calls for political campaigns or nonprofit social causes. Customers may still consent to receive telemarketing calls, in writing, but later regulation eliminated the preexisting business relationship exception. Prerecorded messages must have an opt-out option for the party receiving the call to opt out of receiving such calls, and the call must be disconnected at that time. Callers choosing the opt-out option would be added to the Do Not Call list. The National Do Not Call Registry is a registry of telephone numbers of consumers who do not wish to be called at a particular number. The FCC also allowed prerecorded calls to residential telephone lines made by healthcare companies who are regulated by the Health Insurance Portability and Accountability Act of 1996 (HIPAA), 110 Stat. 1936 (1996). Automatic dialers, or robocalls, to wireless numbers were not permitted, with a carve-out if the caller did not know that the call was a wireless number.

The use of telephonic equipment in mobile devices, in motor vehicles, and in other communications devices expands the impact of these regulations. Voice communications have gone beyond the telephone into live video chat using Skype, FaceTime, and other products offering real-time voice and video two-way interactions, which have begun to replace traditional telephone calls. On the other hand, voice communications have reduced usage on the Internet network because Voice Over Internet Protocol (VoIP) calls are used less, and data transmissions and Machine to Machine (M2M) communications use greater bandwidth and have greater impact than human interaction with the Internet network.

Jill Bronfman

Further Reading

Diffie, Whitfield, and Susan Eva Landau. *Privacy on the Line: The Politics of Wiretapping and Encryption.* Cambridge, MA: MIT Press, 1998.

Etzioni, Amitai. "Privacy," in *Privacy in a Cyber Age: Policy and Practice.* New York: Palgrave Macmillan, 2015.

Green, Walter L., Randy Seidehamel, and Martha Grace Rich. "Cellular Telephones and Interference with Privacy." *Mayo Clinic Proceedings* 82, no. 7 (2007): 889.

Hayes, David L. "Cellular Telephones and Interference with Privacy–Reply–III." *Mayo Clinic Proceedings* 82, no. 7 (2007): 890.

"Telephone Privacy." *Security Management*, March 1, 2000. Toth, Victor J. "Telephone Privacy—How to Invade It." *Business Communications Review* 24, no. 4 (April 1994): 70.

See also: Caller ID; Customer Proprietary Network Information (CPNI); Federal Communications Commission (FCC); Federal Trade Commission (FTC); Fourth Amendment to the U.S. Constitution; *Katz v. United States*,; Mobile devices; Supreme Court of the United States; Telemarketing; Wiretapping

Tempora

Identification: The code name for a formerly secret mass surveillance computer system used by the British government's Government Communications Headquarters (GCHQ). This system buffers most Internet communications that are extracted from fiber optic cables so that these communications can be processed and searched later. It was tested beginning in 2008 and became operational in late 2011. The British government continues to "neither confirm nor deny" Tempora's existence.

Tempora uses intercepts on the fiber optic cables that compose the backbone of the Internet to access large amounts of personal data on Internet users, without any individualized suspicion or targeting. The intercepts are placed in Great Britain and throughout the world, with the knowledge of companies owning either the cables or landing stations.

Edward Snowden, an ex–U.S. intelligence contractor who worked for the National Security Agency (NSA), leaked information about Tempora to then–*Guardian* journalist Glenn Greenwald in May 2013 as one of his revelations about government-sponsored mass surveillance programs. Snowden revealed documents seeming to indicate that the data collected by Tempora is shared with the NSA.

Snowden claimed that Tempora has two key modules, the Mastering the Internet (MTI) and Global Telecoms Exploitation (GTE), both of which were intended to collate online and telephone traffic. However, this claim appeared to contradict two original documents, which indicated that Tempora is used only for Internet traffic, such as NSA's XKeyscore, parts of which are incorporated in Tempora.

The GCHQ reportedly collects more metadata than NSA. In May 2012, 300 GCHQ analysts and 250 NSA analysts were sifting through the data.

The *Guardian* claims that no distinction was made in the gathering of data between private citizens and targeted suspects. Tempora reportedly includes recordings of telephone calls, the content of email messages, Facebook entries, and the personal Internet history of users. In reflecting on the GCHQ use of programs such as Tempora, Snowden said that the British agency was "worse" than its American counterparts.

Tempora reportedly was possible only because of secret understandings that were entered into with commercial companies, which Snowden's leaked documents described as "intercept partners." The government allegedly paid some companies for their cooperation. Snowden also alleged that GCHQ concealed sources used in its reports out of concern that the companies' cooperation as intercept partners would cause major political embarrassment. The various companies were forbidden to reveal the existence of warrants ordering them to allow GCHQ access to the cables. GCHQ lawyers objected to requests for lists of the total number of individuals targeted by Tempora because it would not be feasible considering the volume involved.

GCHQ conducted a three-year trial period at GCHQ facilities in Cornwall. GCHQ had probes attached to over 200 Internet links by the summer of 2011. Each probe carried ten gigabits of data a second. NSA analysts assisted in these trials. Tempora was subsequently launched in autumn 2011, with data being shared with NSA. Technological work enhanced GCHQ's capacity to collect data from new supercables that carry data at 100 gigabits a second. The data is retained for three days; metadata is retained for thirty days.

Tempora has different components, such as the actual access points to fiber optic cables, a sanitization program codenamed POKERFACE, NSA's XKEYSCORE system, and a Massive Volume Reduction (MVR) capability. In May 2012, GCHQ installed Tempora systems at the following locations: (1) sixteen for 10 gigabit/second cables at the CPC processing center, (2) seven for 10 gigabit/second cables at the OPC processing center, and (3) twenty-three for 10 gigabit/second cables at the RPC1 processing center.

British defense officials issued a confidential DA-Notice to the British media requesting them to refrain from further reporting on surveillance leaks, including the U.S. PRISM program and British involvement with that program. The U.S. army restricted its employees' access to the *Guardian* website after the leaks of the PRISM and Tempora programs "to prevent an unauthorized disclosure of classified information."

Privacy International, Liberty, and Amnesty International sued the British secret services following the Snowden revelations. Britain's Investigatory Powers Tribunal (IPT) considered the matter. IBT is intended to deter the intelligence agencies from abusing their power, and it conducted its investigation "on the basis of assuming the relevant allegations to be derived from Mr. Snowden's leaks to be true." This is standard practice for the tribunal. The claimants did not need to prove that their privacy had been breached for the tribunal to consider the principle of the case. "[This] enables claimants to bring claims without having the kind of arguable case which they would need to pursue a case in the High Court."

In December 2014, IBT ruled that Tempora was "legal in principle" and that the GCHQ could conduct mass surveillance of all fiber optic cables entering or leaving the United Kingdom under the Regulatory of Investigatory Powers Act of 2000 (RIPA). IBT further ruled that "[t]he Snowden revelations . . . have led to the impression that the law permits the intelligence services carte blanche to do what they will. We are satisfied that this is not the case." The tribunal also found no impropriety in sharing intelligence with U.S. NSA or accessing information obtained through NSA's PRISM program. It relied on secret government policies in reaching this decision.

The claimant's vowed to challenge the ruling at the European Court of Human Rights (ECHR) because it usually requires that the rules and procedures be public, although the tribunal found that "signposting" such policies to the general public is sufficient. Privacy International said: "The policies reveal that the government considers it justifiable to engage in mass surveillance of every Facebook, Twitter, YouTube and Google user in the country, even if there is no suspicion that the user has committed any offence, by secretly redefining Britons' use of them as 'external communications.'"

Further Reading

Fidler, David P. *The Snowden Reader*. Steininger, Michael. "Merkel under Fire as Germany Seethes over NSA Spying." *Christian Science Monitor*, July 2, 2013.

"Travels and Travails: Secrecy." *The Economist*, June 29, 2013.

See also: Big data; Electronic surveillance; Government Communications Headquarters; Greenwald, Glen; National Security Agency (NSA); PRISM; Snowden, Edward

Terrorism and privacy

Identification: An ongoing debate regarding the balance between actions to protect the United States from terrorist attacks and infringement on civil liberties.

Following the terrorist attacks of September 11, 2001, the United States was united in wondering how such an attack could have occurred and wanting to ensure that it never happened again. While there were already existing laws to investigate and prosecute terrorists, Congress chose to give law enforcement new tools to help in the war against terror. Increasing the scope and power of surveillance and investigation tools required concessions on the part of civil liberties. The complexity and tensions in determining just where these borders between national security and the right to privacy should be are well illustrated in the discussions surrounding the USA PATRIOT Act, 115 Stat, 272 (2001).

The USA PATRIOT Act became law on October 26, 2001, six weeks after the September 11 terrorist attacks. Its title is an acronym that stands for "Uniting and Strengthening America by Providing Appropriate Tools Required to Intercept and Obstruct Terrorism" (Pub. L. 107–56). Congress moved quickly, and the bill became law without hearings or markup by a congressional committee. The House approved the final bill, which was sponsored by Representative Jim Sensenbrenner (R-WI), in a single day. The Senate followed the next day, and President George W. Bush signed it into law.

The PATRIOT Act was considered a wish list of changes presented by Attorney General John Ashcroft that expanded the ability to detect and prosecute terrorism and other crimes. It amended several existing federal statutes, affecting laws on several issues, including criminal procedure, computer fraud, foreign intelligence, wiretapping, and immigration. Because the PATRIOT Act challenged so many existing laws, it is an extremely complex task to understand its breadth and depth.

In 2001 opponents of the PATRIOT Act were all Democrats, and only one, Wisconsin Senator Russ Feingold, actually voted no. Reluctance to support the law was politically problematic because nobody wanted answer claims that he or she were not helping to prevent another

September 11 attack. At the same time, many civil liberties groups were critical of aspects of the PATRIOT Act and expressed concern that law enforcement would be able to invade the privacy of American citizens unnecessarily and without proper judicial oversight.

Shifting opinions

While there was almost complete unanimity when Congress voted for the PATRIOT Act, there has always been a split of opinion on its provisions. Law enforcement, elected officials, privacy groups, and citizens all have expressed evolving opinions on where the balance between national security and personal privacy lies. The Pew Research Center has conducted extensive polling over time, and its findings illustrate the evolution of public opinion.

In 2001, shortly after the September 11 attacks, when asked if it was "necessary to give up civil liberties to curb terrorism," 55 percent agreed and 35 percent said it was not necessary. By 2004, just three years later, the balance had flipped, with 56 percent saying that giving up civil liberties was not necessary to stop terrorists, and 38 percent saying that it was still necessary. In 2007 opinion was about even, with 50 percent saying that it was not necessary and 43 percent saying that it was. In 2009, the largest disparity was seen, with 65 percent saying that it was not necessary to only 27 percent saying that it was. In 2011, 54 percent said that it was not necessary, with 40 percent saying it was.

What is notable about these results is that every query has a significant minority and illustrates there is by no means a consensus on the issue. There has not been another major terrorist attack on American soil since September 11, but a variety of other events have spurred the public into considering the balance between national security and privacy. The revelations caused by National Security Agency (NSA) contractor Edward Snowden's leaked documents; repeated breaches of security at major retailers and financial institutions, including the Internal

Revenue Service (IRS); and lawsuits contesting many PATRIOT Act provisions have brought the issue of privacy, especially of digital records, into the forefront.

The Pew Research Center and the *Washington Post*, however, administered a national survey in June 2013, shortly after Snowden's leaks on NSA bulk collection of American phone records were published. The survey indicated that 62 percent said that it was more important for the government to investigate terrorist threats, even if it intruded on personal privacy. Only 34 percent said that it was more important for the government not to intrude on privacy, even if that limited its ability to investigate terrorist threats. The numbers in 2013 remained constant from polls taken in 2006 and 2010.

In 2014, 54 percent said they did not approve of the government collecting telephone and internet data to fight terrorism. In 2015, 57 percent said it was not acceptable for the government to monitor the phones and internet of Americans, but it was okay to monitor citizens of other countries. Another Pew survey in February 2017 indicated that 70 percent of Americans believed it was at least somewhat likely that the government monitored their phone calls and emails.

Privacy groups

Several groups with special expertise have joined in the criticism of some PATRIOT Act provisions. Groups such as the American Civil Liberties Union (ACLU) and Electronic Frontier Foundation (EFF) continue to fight against provisions of the act by lobbying Congress, partnering with congressional representatives, trying to educate the public, as well as defending those who were adversely affected by PATRIOT Act.

The ACLU calls itself "the nation's largest public interest law firm," and their mission is to "defend and preserve the individual rights and liberties guaranteed to every person in this country by the Constitution and laws of the United States." When initially founded in 1920, it focused on freedom of speech, but it grew to

address a wide variety of civil liberties issues. It provides legal assistance in cases where it considers civil liberties to be at risk, offering direct legal representation or amicus curiae briefs. The EFF describes itself as "protecting freedom where law and technology collide." It was founded in July 1990 by Mitch Kapor, former president of Lotus Development Corporation; John Perry Barlow, Wyoming cattle rancher and lyricist for the Grateful Dead; and John Gilmore, an early employee of Sun Microsystems. The group believed that technology evolves so quickly that it is difficult for the government, civil liberties groups, and the public in general to understand some of the privacy and legal issues involved. Like the ACLU, it provides legal defense for individuals and technologies, both in the form of direct representation and amicus curiae briefs.

While the ACLU and EFF provide legal assistance for privacy issues, another group that spoke out against PATRIOT Act provisions was the American Library Association (ALA). ALA issued a resolution on the USA PATRIOT Act opposing "any use of governmental power to suppress the free and open exchange of knowledge and information or to intimidate individuals exercising free inquiry . . . ALA considers that sections of the USA PATRIOT ACT are a present danger to the constitutional rights and privacy rights of library users." The ALA advised libraries to retain records only as long as legally required to limit the amount of information the Federal Bureau of Investigation (FBI) might be able to access.

The FBI and other law enforcement agents utilizing the tools provided by the PATRIOT Act are often frustrated by the efforts of these groups. The *New York Times* published an email from a frustrated FBI agent that was obtained through a Freedom of Information Act (FOIA) request. An internal message dated October 2003, it stated in part, "While radical militant librarians kick us around, true terrorists benefit from OIPR's failure to let us use the tools given to us."

Legislative challenges

In 2001 only a single senator voted against the PATRIOT Act, but in the years that followed, many congressional representatives began to express concern about provisions in the act, especially those dealing with surveillance. The privacy groups that had objected to parts of the PATRIOT Act when it was initially passed in 2001 soon found allies in some of these congressional representatives. Several bills were proposed to amend the act. While none of them were passed, they illustrate some of the concerns shared by civil liberties groups, congressional representatives, and citizens. Some of these acts included the Protecting the Rights of Individuals Act of 2003 (S1552), the Benjamin Franklin True Patriot Act of 2003 (H.R. 3171), and the Security and Freedom Ensured Act of 2005 (H.R. 1526). Many of these acts were presented by coalitions of civil rights groups and congressional representatives. For instance, with the Benjamin Franklin True Patriot Act, the ACLU and Representatives Dennis Kucinich (D-OH) and Ron Paul (R-TX) joined forces. The Benjamin Franklin True Patriot Act sought to repeal more than ten sections of the PATRIOT Act, including those authorizing sneak-and-peek searches; surveillance of Internet activities without probable cause; and warrantless searches of library, medical, and financial records. Its name was a reference to Benjamin Franklin's aphorism, "Those who would give up Essential Liberty, to purchase a little temporary Safety, deserve neither Liberty nor Safety."

Sunset struggles

The PATRIOT Act had several provisions that sunset, or expire, unless Congress renewed or replaced them. The initial sunsets were set to expire on December 15, 2005. As this deadline drew near, much had changed. There had been no major terrorist attacks within the United States since September 11, 2001, and Congress and the American public continued to consider whether the appropriate balance had been stuck between law enforcement surveillance authority and civil liberties. In these renewals, parts of the act that had been challenged or overturned by the courts were often rewritten. Support for the act, which was almost unanimous in 2001, gave way to filibusters and negotiations. The dialogue between support for antiterrorism efforts and the protection of privacy rights continued during the debate, amendment, and voting for these various reauthorization acts.

More information about how the September 11 attacks were perpetrated was also available by this time. The 9/11 Commission report was released on July 22, 2004. The 570-page report ultimately concluded that it was a "failure of imagination," or an inability to assemble the intelligence it did have, that prevented law enforcement from predicting the attacks.

In 2005, the first renewal came up in the form of the USA PATRIOT Improvement and Reauthorization Act of 2005 (120 Stat. 192). The act sought to make permanent fourteen of the sixteen expiring PATRIOT Act sections and create a new 2009 sunset for Sections 206 and 215. It also looked to amend various aspects of the PATRIOT Act, such as providing for greater congressional and judicial oversight of Section 215 orders, Section 206 roving wiretaps, and national security letters. It required high-level approval for Section 215 requests for library, bookstore, firearm sale, medical, tax return, and educational records, and enhanced procedural protections and oversight concerning delayed-notice, or sneak-and-peek, search warrants authorized by Section 213. While the act was ultimately passed, it was not without significant discussion and negotiation. Subsequent renewals and revisions would also reflect the variety of viewpoints, with law enforcement, privacy groups, and others participating in the process.

The most recent renewal was in the form of the USA FREEDOM Act (Public Law No. 114–23), passed in June 2015. It restored several provisions of the PATRIOT Act (they had expired the day before). It also limited mass surveillance under Section 215 of the PATRIOT Act. According to the EFF, it was the first time since 1978 that Congress voted to constrain intelligence authorities.

The bill was introduced to Congress in 2013, following the publication of several documents leaked by Edward Snowden on NSA bulk collection of American citizen's telephone data. In 2015 many Republicans, particularly libertarian- minded Sen. Rand Paul of Kentucky, joined liberal Democrats in demanding changes to the law. Rep. Jim Sensenbrenner, who sponsored the PATRIOT Act bill in 2001, advocated passage of the FREEDOM Act to "reform the government's surveillance authorities." He pointed out that the act is the product of a "robust public debate and intense bipartisan negotiations dedicated to finding a way to protect our Constitutional rights without compromising national security."

Sections of the PATRIOT Act

Three sections of the PATRIOT Act receive much attention from both privacy rights groups and the intelligence and law enforcement groups responsible for national security. The issues involved with each illustrate the challenges of balancing counterterrorism efforts with privacy concerns. The interpretation of various statutes, legal challenges, and the need for secrecy in certain circumstances create a complex, organic environment in which to try to understand all the elements involved in finding an appropriate balance.

Section 213—Delayed-Notice Search Warrants: Section 213 allows for an exception to Fourth Amendment privacy protections, permitting federal law enforcement agents to delay giving notice when they conduct searches. This is sometimes referred to as a sneak-and-peek warrant. Agents may enter a home or office with a search warrant, conduct their search when the owner is not there, and inform the owner of the search only after it is completed. This provision

did not have a sunset date and was to be a permanent change in the law.

The Fourth Amendment to the U.S. Constitution provides protection against unreasonable searches and seizures. It requires law enforcement to obtain a warrant and then give notice to the person whose property will be searched before the search may be conducted. All searches and seizures must be reasonable, and all warrants must be based on probable cause. In addition, warrants must be specific about the place to be searched and the items seized. This requirement of notice allows for the assertion of Fourth Amendment rights because it provides opportunity to discover problems with the warrant, such as an incorrect address. It also allows for notice regarding the limits of the warrant. For instance, a warrant to search for a stolen car would not give permission to search dresser drawers.

Perhaps the most important reason for requiring a warrant prior to a search is to ensure that a neutral third party, such as a judge, reviews the warrant to ensure its reasonableness. A covert search warrant removes this third party from the process, which provides law enforcement with greater latitude as far as defining what may be searched.

Delayed-notice search warrants existed prior to the PATRIOT Act. The U.S. Supreme Court has ruled that, while generally police are required by the Fourth Amendment to "knock and announce" their entry prior to a search, there are exceptions. In both *Wilson v. Arkansas*, 514 U.S. 927 (1995), and *Richards v. Wisconsin*, 520 U.S. 385 (1997), the Court said that Fourth Amendment requirements could be circumvented in situations where evidence was under threat of destruction or there were concerns for officer safety. There is debate about whether Section 213 really did anything besides create a legislative equivalent of extant case law. In recognition of this debate and others surrounding the PATRIOT Act, the American Bar Association created a blog prior to the 2005 PATRIOT Act renewal deadline where lawyers discussed these varying viewpoints.

There has been an increase in the use of these types of warrants since Section 213 was passed. According to the ACLU, from 2006 to 2009, sneak-and-peek warrants were used 1,755 times, with fifteen of those cases involving terrorism. The rest were in cases involving fraud or drugs. In 2010, 3,970 sneak-and-peek warrants were issued, with 76 percent drug-related, 24 percent other, and less than 1 percent terror-related. In 2011, of the 6,775 warrants issued, 5,093 were used for drugs and only 31 were used for terrorism. The 2012 statistics indicate only 58 requests were used for terrorism. In 2013, 11,129 requests were issued, with just 51 used for terrorism. The bulk of the requests, 9,401, were used in drug-related cases, causing privacy groups to point out these warrants are not being used to fight terrorism, but as an everyday tool for drug cases.

Both the U.S. Supreme Court cases that allowed for delayed-notice warrants dealt with drug arrests, however, where evidence could have been destroyed if notice had been given in advance. It is unclear whether the increase in the incidence of delayed-notice warrants is due to Section 213, a rise in drug cases, or other factors. *Section 505—National Security Letters*: A national security letter (NSL) is a legal demand for documents that the FBI can issue by itself, without a court order. They are also known as administrative subpoenas and date back to 1978 with the Right to Financial Privacy Act (RFPA), which was part of the Financial Institutions Regulatory and Interest Rate Control Act of 1978 (92 Stat. 3642). This act gave the FBI the power to issue NSLs to obtain financial records in terrorism and espionage investigations, and compliance was optional. In 1986, RFPA was amended to require compliance with the information request, but it still held no penalty for refusing to comply with an NSL.

Though NSLs existed before the PATRIOT Act, a provision of the act enhanced their power. The FBI could demand a variety of records, such as phone records, bank account information, or information from Internet service providers on Internet use. In the PATRIOT Act of 2001, there was also a gag-order provision, and the recipient was prohibited from revealing the receipt or contents of the order to anyone, even an attorney. Violation of the gag order could be punishable by up to five years in prison.

The USA PATRIOT Improvement and Reauthorization Act of 2005, passed in March 2006 after much debate, allowed for some judicial review of an NSL. Other amendments allowed a recipient of an NSL to talk with an attorney about the request, and law enforcement had to utilize the court system to enforce compliance with the request.

According to the Inspector General's 2007 report on NSLs, 8,500 NSLs were issued in 2000, prior to the PATRIOT Act. The number of NSLs issued peaked at 56,507 in 2004. However, the numbers have declined since then, with 19,000 issued in 2013, 16, 348 issued in 2014, 12,870 in 2015 and 12,150 in 2016. EFF estimates that over 300,000 NSLs have been issued since 2001.

There have been several court challenges to NSLs and their accompanying gag orders. In the first legal challenge to an NSL, the ACLU represented Nick Merrill. The case was *Doe v. Ashcroft*, which was subsequently changed to *Doe v. Holder* (S.D.N.Y 04 Civ. 2614). Merrill owned a small Internet service provider and received an NSL in 2004. The FBI eventually withdrew its NSL request; however, Merrill continued to fight the gag order. In 2010 Merrill was allowed to reveal his identity but not the contents of the request. In September 2015, eleven years after the initial NSL, a federal district court judge in New York fully lifted the gag order. The court order goes into effect in December 2015 to allow the government time to appeal if it chooses to do so. In 2005 the FBI used an NSL to request patron records from the Library Connection, a consortium of twenty-six Connecticut libraries. The libraries and the ACLU filed a lawsuit that became known as *Doe v. Gonzales*, 546 U.S.

1301. At the same time, Congress was debating the first reauthorization of the PATRIOT Act. The ACLU sought an emergency court order to lift the gag order so librarians could tell Congress that the FBI had used an NSL to demand library records. The gag order was ruled unconstitutional by a district court judge in September 2005. That same month, the *New York Times* reported that Library Connection was the "Doe" in the case. In April 2006, six weeks after reauthorization of the PATRIOT Act was passed, the government dropped its legal battle to keep the gag order and withdrew its demand for records.

In 2014, Twitter sued the government to remove a gag order that prevented them from publishing NSLs it received (*Twitter v. Sessions*, 263 F.Supp.3d 803). Twitter claimed the government was infringing on its First Amendment rights by not allowing them to publish a transparency report regarding the NSLs it received. In 2017, Twitter won the case and the company was able to publish the two NSLs it received.

Section 215—Access to Business Records ("Libraries Provision"): Section 215 revised the authority under the Foreign Intelligence Surveillance Act (FISA) for seizure of business records. Previously, under FISA, the FBI could apply to the Foreign Intelligence Surveillance Court (FISC) for an order to seize business records of hotels, car rental agencies and storage rental facilities. Section 215 eliminated any restriction on the type of business, so records from *any* business could be seized. It also expanded the scope from "business records" to "any tangible things (including books, records, papers, documents, and other items)." There was also a gag-order provision, so the recipient of the order could not tell anyone about the content of the request or even that one was received. Section 215 also made it easier to obtain an order because judicial review is limited to whether "the application meets the requirements."

In 2011, the *Washington Post* reported that the FBI was changing the types of information requests it issued. While they previously used NSLs to retrieve information on emails and Internet surfing, many Internet service providers were limiting the information they provided to names, addresses, length of service, and phone bill records. FBI officials said that, "beginning in late 2009, certain electronic communications service providers no longer honored" requests for more detailed information. The FBI turned to these Section 215 business record requests to try to obtain more detailed information. In 2010 it made ninety-six requests, compared with the twenty-one issued in 2009.

Section 215 gained additional notoriety in 2013 when NSA contractor Edward Snowden leaked classified documents, which indicated that FISC was interpreting Section 215 in a manner that authorized the NSA's bulk collection of American citizens' phone records. In January 2014, the Privacy and Civil Liberties Oversight Board, an independent panel appointed by the White House, issued a report indicating that bulk surveillance had not prevented any terrorist attacks in the United States. It recommended discontinuation of bulk collection of American phone metadata.

Shortly after Snowden's leaked documents were published, the ACLU filed a lawsuit challenging the program's legality under the First and Fourth Amendments. In May 2015 the Court of Appeals for the Second Circuit ruled that the NSA program violated Section 215 of the Patriot Act. In June 2015 Congress passed the USA Freedom Act, a reauthorization of the PATRIOT Act that amended Section 215 to prohibit the bulk collection of American citizens' phone records.

The discussion surrounding the various elements of the PATRIOT Act illustrates the continuing concern about how to protect the United States from terrorist attacks and to keep safe the ideals and freedoms that the Constitution provides. There has never been a consensus on exactly how to accomplish both goals. While there was little discussion with the initial passage of the PATRIOT Act, there is much within the courts, Congress, and beyond that has contributed to the conversation since the act went into effect.

Noëlle Sinclair

Further Reading

Baker, Stewart A., and John Kavanagh. *Patriot Debates: Experts Debate the USA Patriot Act*. Chicago: American Bar Association, 2005.

Clarke, Richard A. *Cyber War: The Next Threat to National Security and What to Do about It*. New York: Ecco, 2010.

Doherty, Carroll. "Balancing Act: National Security and Civil Liberties in a Post-9/11 Era." Pew Research Center. June 7, 2013. http://www.pewresearch.org/ facttank/2013/06/07/balancing-act-national-securityand-civil-liberties-in-post-911-era/ .

Foerstel, Herbert N. *The PATRIOT Act: A Documentary and Reference Guide*. Westport, CT: Greenwood, 2007.

Geiger, Abigail. "How Americans have viewed government surveillance and privacy since Snowden leaks." Pew Research Center. June 4, 2018. http://www.pewresearch.org/fact-tank/2018/06/04/how-americans-have-viewed-government-surveillance-and-privacy-since-snowden-leaks/.

Goldfarb, Ronald. *After Snowden: Privacy, Secrecy, and Security in the Information Age*. New York: T. Dunne Books, 2015.

Greenwald, Glenn. *No Place to Hide: Edward Snowden, the NSA, and the U.S. Surveillance State*. New York: Picador, 2015.

National Commission on Terrorist Attacks upon the United States. *The 9/11 Commission Report: Final Report of the National Commission on Terrorist Attacks Upon the United States / Thomas H. Kean, Chair, Lee H. Hamilton, Vice-Chair*. Washington, DC: US Government Printing Office, 2004.

Nemeth, Charles P. *Homeland Security: An Introduction to the Principles and Practice,* 2nd ed. Boca Raton, FL: CRC Press, 2013.

Posner, Richard A. *Preventing Surprise Attacks: Intelligence Reform in the Wake of 9/11*. Lanham, MD: Rowman & Littlefield Publishers, 2004.

Posner, Richard A. "Privacy, Surveillance, and Law." *University of Chicago Law Review* 75, no. 1 (2008): 245–260.

Solove, Daniel J. *Nothing to Hide: The False Tradeoff between Privacy and Security*. New Haven, CT: Yale University Press, 2011.

Vladeck, Stephen I. "Big Data before and after Snowden." *Journal of National Security Law and Policy* 7, no. 2 (2014): 333–340.

See also: American Civil Liberties Union (ACLU); Electronic Frontier Foundation (EFF); Electronic surveillance; Fourth Amendment to the U.S. Constitution; Freedom of Information Act (FOIA); Metadata; National Security Agency (NSA); Privacy and Civil Liberties Oversight Board (PCLOP); Search warrants; September 11; Snowden, Edward Joseph; Subpoenas; Twitter; USA FREEDOM Act; USA PATRIOT Act

Text messaging

Identification: Or texting, the composing and sending of brief, electronic messages between two or more mobile phones, or between fixed or portable devices, over a phone network.

The term originally referred to messages sent through the Short Message Service (SMS). It now includes messages with image, video, and sound content, which is known as Multimedia Messaging Service (MMS) messages. Text messages may be used to interact with automated systems for several activities, including ordering products or services. Companies use direct text marketing, instead of mail, email or voicemail, to inform mobile phone users about promotions, payment due dates, and similar matters.

The provider, or carrier, retains records of the customer's cellphone use, including calls, text messages, and pictures sent from the user's phone. Most cellphone carriers provide detailed information on the phone's use in bills sent to the owner. The details include when a text message or image was sent from the user's phone and how much it cost to transmit. If the user is charged for messages and pictures sent to the user's phone, the bill likely will show when it was sent. The bill does not say what was written in a text message nor does it show the images.

Federal privacy laws, such as the Consumer Telephone Records Protection Act of 2006, 120 Stat. 3568, prohibit cellphone carriers from disseminating phone records, even to the phone owner or to the party that pays the bill. The rationale for this regulation is that the records often show that someone else may have sent or received the message and that person's privacy rights must be protected. Exceptions to the rule include the following: If the owner believes that his or her phone is being used for criminal activities, or if the owner is being harassed or threatened through text messages, the phone owner may need a court order requiring the phone carrier to release the records. Some cellphone carriers limit the time period that the text messages and images are stored on their computers.

One of the landmark cases on privacy relevant text messaging is *City of Ontario v. Quon, 560 U.S. 746 (2010)*. The U.S. Supreme Court held in this case that a government employer conducted a legal search of its employee's text messages transmitted on employer-issued pagers. Quon was an employee with the city of Ontario, California, police department. The city issued pagers to its employees, including Quon. Years prior to receiving the pagers, Quon and his coworkers had signed an employee acknowledgment of the city's computer usage, Internet and email policy. This document prohibited personal use of city-issued devices, including computers. The policy also stated, "[employees] should have no expectation of privacy or confidentiality when using [city-issued electronic] resources." The city never formally modified its policy to include pagers; however, it did orally notify its employees that the policy applies to pager use.

According to its service contract with Arch Wireless, the city was required to pay any overage charges in pager use. Recognizing that many of the officers used the pagers for both personal and professional purposes, the city maintained an informal policy whereby if each officer paid the resulting overage charges, the city would not audit the text messages to determine if the overages were for private rather than business use.

Quon's pager usage incurred several months of overage charges. Even though he had paid for the charges, officials decided to audit his text messages. The city requested the transcripts of the text messages from the wireless company.

During the audit, the city discovered several sexually explicit text messages that Quon had sent to his wife and to his girlfriend. After finding these messages, the city terminated Quon. He then sued the city for violations of his right to privacy under the California constitution and the Fourth Amendment to the U.S. Constitution, as well as Arch Wireless for violating the Stored Communications Act, 100 Stat. 1848 (1986).

The Ninth Circuit affirmed the trial court's decision in Quon's favor, holding that he had a reasonable expectation of privacy in his text messages, that the audit was constitutionally unreasonable in scope, and that Arch Wireless had violated the Stored Communications Act by sending the text message transcripts to the city. The city appealed to the U.S. Supreme Court, which granted certiorari only as to the Fourth Amendment claim against the city.

The Supreme Court held that, even assuming Quon had a reasonable expectation of privacy, the search was reasonable because the city had a legitimate, work-related rationale for the search, and it was not overly intrusive. Unlike the Sixth Circuit in *United States v. Warshak*, 631 F.3d 266 (2010), which recognized that interpretation of the Fourth Amendment must change with the times and evolve to be relevant in the digital era, the Supreme Court cautiously stated: "The judiciary risks error by elaborating too fully on the Fourth Amendment implications of emerging technology before its role in society has become clear." Nonetheless, it was significant that the *Quon* Court indicated the following: "employer policies concerning communications will of course shape the reasonable expectations of their employees, especially to the extent that such policies are clearly communicated."

Thus, it would seem that a carefully crafted electronic use policy could eradicate, or at least considerably alter, an employee's reasonable expectation of privacy when using employer-issued electronic devices such as laptops and cellphones. *Quon* was the first of a large number of electronic communication appellate decisions during the 1980s, a time when use of smartphones and social media was expanding rapidly.

Employers learned that it was necessary to be specific when drafting electronic use policies. Employers must decide whether, and under what parameters, to allow limited personal use of not only company computers but also company email and personal web-based email. If employers intend to monitor employee use of company computers and e-mail, language should be included noting that the company may monitor, search, access, inspect and read computer contents and/or email, and that electronic information created, stored, received, or sent on company computers is not private. Individuals, whether in the workplace or not, must realize that password-protected email accounts, even though personal, are usually safe, but privacy rights as to cellphones and text messages, especially involving company-issued devices, are quite tenuous.

Search of texts incident to arrest

A recent California Supreme Court case, *People v. Diaz,* 244 P3rd 5011 (2011), further reduced the Fourth Amendment protection afforded text messages in the context of a lawful arrest. In this case, a deputy sheriff witnessed Diaz participate in the sale of narcotics to a police informant. Once the sale was completed, the deputy stopped Diaz and arrested him for conspiracy in selling drugs. Incident to his arrest, the deputy searched Diaz's person and found drugs and his cellphone. After arriving at the police station, the deputy continued to question Diaz, but Diaz refused to cooperate. A full one and one half hours after arresting Diaz, the deputy searched Diaz's cellphone and found an incriminating text message. Once confronted with the text message, Diaz admitted to his role in the drug deal. Diaz later moved to suppress both the text message and his subsequent confession as resulting from an unlawful, warrantless search.

The California Supreme Court affirmed the decisions of the appellate and lower courts,

finding that the search was a lawful search incident to arrest because the cellphone was immediately associated with [Diaz's] person at the time of arrest, which is an exception to the Fourth Amendment's warrant requirement. The court did not reflect much on the impact of developments in modern technology on searches incident to a lawful arrest, indicating: "If . . . the wisdom of the high court's decisions 'must be newly evaluated' in light of modern technology[,] . . . then that reevaluation must be undertaken by the high court itself." The court then echoed previous U.S.

Supreme Court search and seizure cases, such as *United States v. Ross,* 456 U.S. 798 (1982), in articulating that the character of the searched item should not influence the analysis of whether a warrantless search was lawful, despite the seemingly infinite storage capacity of cellphones. The court noted: "differing expectations of privacy based on the amount of information a particular item contains should . . . be irrelevant."

Text message spamming

In 2002, a dramatical increase in the spamming of mobile phone users through SMS led cellular service carriers to adopt steps to halt these problems before they became widespread. The existence of mobile phone spam was first reported by consumer groups. In 2005, UCAN sued Sprint for spamming its customers and charging them $0.10 per text message. In 2006, the parties reached a settlement, with Sprint agreeing not to send its customers Sprint advertisements via SMS.

In late 2006, SMS expert Acision (formerly LogicaCMG Telecoms) reported the first instances of SMiShing (which is similar to email phishing scams). In SMiShing, users receive SMS messages that claim to be from a company and that entice users to phone premium-rate numbers or reply with personal information. PhonepayPlus, a British consumer group in Britain, reported a similar problem in 2012.

Security concerns

Consumer SMS is not the appropriate media for confidential or secure communication. The network operator's systems and personnel know the contents of ordinary SMS messages. To contend with security issues, many companies use an SMS gateway provider based on SS7 connectivity to route messages. This international termination model has the advantage of routing data directly through SS7, which allows the provider to see the complete path of the SMS. Therefore, SMS messages may be sent directly to and from recipients without going through the SMS-C of other mobile operators. This approach reduces the number of mobile operators that handle the message. It is not a secure end-to-end communication because the message contents travel through the SMS gateway provider.

Failure rates without backward notification can be high between carriers (T-Mobile to Verizon is quite bad in the United States). International texting can be extremely unreliable depending on the country of origin, destination, and respective carriers.

An alternative approach is to use end-toend security software that operates on both the sending and receiving device, where the original text message is transmitted in encrypted form as a consumer SMS. By using key rotation, the encrypted text messages stored under data retention laws at the network operator cannot be decrypted even if one of the devices is compromised. A problem with this approach is that communicating devices need to run compatible software. Key management also requires individual pairing of devices or a central point of trust.

Text messaging and surveilliance

There are two separate standards under current U.S. surveillance law, which provides differing degrees of legal protection for different data types. Communication content (the "what" of the message) generally is more protected than the associated "metadata" records (the receiver of the message, as well as when and where the message is conveyed). Although U.S. surveillance law has many shortcomings, the law is largely neutral in governing particular types of technologies. Therefore, emails, Facebook messages, private Twitter direct messages, and Snapchat photos are all communications content and receive an equal degree of legal protection.

While U.S. law is technology-neutral in terms of communications content, it provides different treatment in terms of metadata because the communications that flow over the telephone network and on the Internet receive different treatment. The federal government can compel the production of Internet communications metadata, such as the "to" and "from" information associated with emails, with either a search warrant or other type of court order, 18 USC 2703(c)(1). In other words, to obtain records on emails or Facebook messages, federal agents must convince a judge to issue an order of production for these records.

The government may also obtain local and long-distance telephone billing records associated with an account only with a subpoena. Thus, the government can obtain a list of the numbers (and names) that the owner called with a subpoena, but determining the names or email addresses of the people that the owner emails requires a court order (18 USC 2703(c)(2)).

Such different standards for metadata surveillance of internet and phone communications is now obsolete. Today, telephone calls and emails are no longer conducted on different devices, connected to different networks, and use services provided by companies in different industries. In the contemporary environment, communications are transmitted over the same device (often a smartphone), and all types of data flow over the same network, that is, the Internet.

Surveillance standards are different for Google's many different text-messaging services. Google includes (or distributes) at least four different text-messaging applications and services for its Android mobile operating system:

- The built-in Android Messaging app, which is an interface to the SMS and MMS services provided by the users' wireless carrier.
- The built-in Google Talk app, which provides text instant-messaging, audio-chat, and video-chat services with other users of Google Talk. These messages are transmitted over the Internet connection to Google's servers.
- The Google+ app, which includes the ability to engage in text-based conversations with other Google+ users. These messages are transmitted over the Internet to Google's servers.
- The Google Voice app, which provides text messaging to other telephone numbers via an Internet connection to Google's servers. When the recipients of the text messages are also users of Google Voice, the messages are delivered by Google's servers to the app on their device via the Internet. However, if the recipient is not using Google Voice, then Google's servers transmit the message to him or her as an SMS via their wireless carrier's telephone network. Whether or not the recipient uses Google Voice, all data transmitted between the Google Voice app on the sending user's phone and Google's servers is transmitted over the Internet.

The Google+ and Talk apps are clearly Internet-based communication services. Therefore, records associated with Google+ or Talk conversations are protected by 18 USC 2703(c)(1), and their disclosure requires a court order, as is the case with government surveillance of email communications.

It is much more difficult to define Google Voice. Messages between two Google Voice subscribers using the Google Voice app on their smartphones are transmitted over the Internet and do not use the SMS functionality provided by the wireless carriers. Because Google Voice is interoperable with the wireless carriers' SMS system, however, messages sent to people not using Google Voice are transmitted by Google through the SMS system. Google Voice is a hybrid system. As such, it is very difficult, just by the letter of the statute to determine what the legal standard should be for the government to obtain metadata records.

The government is, in fact, obtaining Google Voice records without a court order. Although the law remains unclear, Google produces records to the government of SMS messages sent through Google Voice with only a subpoena. Google is considered to be in a difficult position. Obsolete surveillance law provides different treatment for telephone and Internet communications, so hybrid services that communicate over both Internet and communications networks are in a legally ambiguous area. If Google produces Google Voice text message metadata with a mere subpoena, however, will it insist on a court order before providing Google Talk or Google+ text-messaging metadata to law enforcement officers? Google should disclose its decision to its customers.

It seems highly unreasonable to impose differing legal standards for phone and Internet metadata in the current environment. Civil liberties groups, legal scholars, and telecommunications companies have asked Congress to update the Electronic Communications Privacy Act (ECPA) to reflect current circumstances. Congress has much to do to improve the privacy protections for metadata, whether transmitted by the Internet or telephone. The subpoena standard for basic subscriber records (including telephone billing records) means that obtaining these sensitive records are typically the first step in any investigation, long before the state would be able to persuade a judge to issue an order compelling the production of other forms of data. When Congress first passed the ECPA in 1986, and permitted the government to obtain communications metadata with a subpoena, the phone companies did not store vast amounts of customer data, and law enforcement did not make a large number of requests.

This environment has now dramatically changed. The low cost of digital storage, along with increased pressure from law enforcement, has led wireless carriers to create retention policies that last several years. Law enforcement has been requesting larger and larger amounts of phone records. Sprint, the third-largest wireless carrier, alone receives 500,000 subpoenas annually. Many of these likely involve historical call detail records for text messages.

Gretchen Nobahar

Further Reading

Bell, David. *Cyberculture: The Key Concepts*. London: Routledge, 2004.

Bidgoli, Hossein. *Handbook of Information Security*. Hoboken, NJ: Wiley, 2006.

Gilbert, Franc. *Sixteenth Annual Institute on Privacy and Data Security Law.*

Mena, Jesus. *Homeland Security Techniques and Technologies*. Hingham, MA: Charles River Media, 2004.

See also: *City of Ontario v. Quon*; Electronic Communications Privacy Act (ECPA); Facebook; Fourth Amendment to the U.S. Constitution; Google; Metadata; Spam; Stored Communications Act (SCA); Telephones; Workplace, privacy in the

Theoretical basis for privacy

Identification: Pertains to the debate about privacy is often considered a debate about "boundaries": the boundary between the individual and others, often conceived of as a collective that is often defined as including the state, the community. Privacy defines the differences and boundaries between individuals, and between individuals and the collective whole.

When a person asserts their liberty, autonomy, rationality, and privacy, they are assumed to rationally understand their interests. In prevalent western thought, the individual should be allowed to act within a "private sphere," where the individual cannot be coerced or compelled by others, whether the others are acting as individuals or in the collective.

The modern social view of privacy is based on the works of liberal political philosophy, written by John Locke in eighteenth century England. Locke based his ideas on the concept that dynamic forces behind social progress are derived from individual efforts, rather than collective efforts. Building upon the work of Locke, English Utilitarian philosopher John Stuart Mill, sharply distinguished between certain "self-regarding" activities of strictly private concern, as opposed to "other-regarding" activities that are shaped by community interest and regulation. Samuel Warren and Louis Brandeis further developed this concept in their conception of privacy as the "right to be let alone" in their seminal article on privacy for the *Harvard Law Journal* in 1890. In 1956, Edward Shils, a sociologist who taught at the University of Chicago, stressed that privacy is essential to the pluralism and democracy in the United States because it strengthens the boundaries between competing and countervailing centers of powers. Shils also added that it reinforces the boundaries between the individual and the state and within civil society.

Similar to Shils, Alan F. Westin, a Public Law and Government Professor at Columbia University, in 1967, stressed that democracies can be distinguished from totalitarian regimes, in that "a balance that ensures strong citadels of individual and group privacy and limits both disclosure and surveillance is a prerequisite for liberal democratic societies. The democratic society relies on publicity as a control over government, and on privacy as a shield for the group and individual life. . . Liberal democratic theory assumes that a good life for the individual must have substantial areas of interest apart from political participation." Westin also addressed the specific functions and role of privacy in society. Privacy promotes freedom of association. It shields scholarship and science from unnecessary government interference. It permits the use of a secret ballot and protects the voting process by forbidding government surveillance of a citizen's voting behavior. It restrains improper police conduct such as "physical brutality, compulsory self-incrimination and unreasonable searches and seizures." Privacy in a democratic society serves also to protect non-governmental institutions, such as the media, which as the "Fourth Estate," operates to maintain governmental accountability and transparency.

Several contemporary scholars have relied on eighteenth-century thought as the basis for their interpretations on privacy. The philosopher Robert B. Hallborg discussed the evolution of privacy theory from the German philosopher, Immanuel Kant's concept of freedom, as a state that all people are entitled to solely because they are human. Further. This fundamental right of privacy requires the state to allow individuals to make fundamental personal decisions on their own and without government coercion.

Other scholars and writers drew various theories on the correlation between privacy and liberty as a function of personal autonomy and development, which is not possible to achieve unless individuals are able to express themselves in private. Karen Struening, professor of Political Science at Baruch University, relies on Mill's work to develop a concept of a right to privacy that protects individual sexual lifestyle choices. She views Mill's defense of diverse ways of life and experimentation as encouraging individualism vis-a-vis accepted convention. Modern ideas of privacy, then, rest on a notion of a boundary between the individual and other individuals, and between the individual and the state. It is based on the ideas that the private and public spheres are distinct and separate. It is also based on the idea that there is a civil society comprised of relatively autonomous individuals who must have some degree of privacy to make rational self-regarding choices about their lives.

There are four distinct critiques of liberal political theory as a basis for privacy. First, the right of privacy as the "right to be let alone," focuses on negative reasons for why an individual might wish to be left alone, and that privacy rights are largely asserted by those who have the most to hide, which is often illicit information. Heinz W. Arndt, an Australian economist, wrote in 1949 that, "The cult of privacy seems specifically designed as a defense mechanism for the protection of antisocial behavior." Arndt believed that privacy seemed practically pathologically obsessed with possessive individualism: "The cult of privacy rests on an individualist conception of society, not merely in the innocent and beneficial sense of a society in which the welfare of individuals is conceived as the end of all social organization, but in the more specific sense of 'each for himself and the devil take the hindmost.'"

Richard Posner, the leading law and economics theorist, similarly criticized the theory of information privacy. He argued, in 1987, that "the principle of information privacy has a negative corollary, as it allows people to conceal personal information to mislead others and misrepresent their character. Others, including the government, Posner wrote, "have a legitimate interest in unmasking the misrepresentation." Posner rejected the rebuttal argument that the "people have 'the right to be let alone.' Few people want to be let alone. They want to manipulate the world around them by selective disclosure of facts about themselves. Why should others be asked to take their self-serving claims at face value and prevented from obtaining the information necessary to verify or disprove these claims?"

Several scholars view the distinction between the public and the private spheres as inherently problematic. Joseph Bensman, Professor of Sociology at the City University of New York and Robert Lilienfeld, argue that the "private and the public are inextricably intertwined and interlaced. They cannot be treated as separate entities." They can at the very least be considered "complex-structured concepts" that operate on different dimensions. Stanley Benn, a Professor of Political and Social Philosopher at the Australian National University, and Gerald Gaus, Professor of Philosophy at the University of Arizona, contend that the public/private distinction must be qualified according to whether one is analyzing the "allocation of access to information, resources, the capacities in which agents enjoyed that access, and in whose interest it was used." Many feminist scholars view the public/private dichotomy (and, therefore, much theorization about privacy) as being inherently gendered.

Feminists have critiqued liberalism for reifying a distinction between a private, domestic (female) world, and a public sphere that is chiefly the preserve of men. Anita Allen, Law Professor at the University of Pennsylvania Law School, and Erin Mack, an Associate at Gibson, Dunn, and Crutcher, criticize Warren and Brandeis model of privacy for that reason. Allen and Mack argued that Warren and Brandeis seemed blind to the fact that their view of privacy, including, "assertions of masculine personality, and norms of female modesty contributed to women's lacking autonomous decision making and meaningful forms of individual privacy." They advocated "too much of the wrong kinds of privacy—too much modesty, seclusion, reserve and compelled intimacy—and too little individual modes of personal privacy and autonomous private choice." Patricia Boling, a political science professor at Purdue University, praised the work of feminist scholars such as Carole Pateman, a British feminist, and political scientist, and Susan Moller Okin, a feminist political philosopher, who argue that ending state power at the front of the family home merely reinforces patriarchy, and that whoever has public power determines who has power in the "private sphere." Boling argued, however, that these scholars often equivocate on the desire for privacy, and she argues that that respect for privacy can be empower-

ing. Her argument is supported by bioethicists such as Alta Charo, Ruth Faden, Dorothy Roberts, and Karen Rothenberg, who favor keeping women's decisions on abortion and other health matters private.

Thirdly, from a democratic theory perspective, some philosophers argue that the liberalism of Locke and Mill, which form the basis on the theory of information privacy rests, represents only one version of democratic theory. Pateman, for example, has argued that there are essentially two general traditions of democratic theory. One is a liberal tradition based in eighteenth-century natural rights theory. The other is derived from the viewpoint that the test of a democratic society is not the protection of individual or minority rights, or the degree of competition between centers of power. Rather, the test considers factors such as the level of participation, cooperation, and community consciousness, values that are not necessarily promoted by asserting the "right to be let alone." Information privacy is, therefore, a precondition not of democracy per se, however, of a particular form of liberal democracy. The theoretical justifications for this were provided by Locke, Madison, and Mill, rather than by Jean-Jacques Rousseau.

This argument is reflected in the communitarian approach of Amitai Etzioni, sociologist and Director of the Institute for Communitarian Policy Studies, at George Washington University. This view has resonated with both contemporary liberal and conservative political philosophers in both Europe and North America. Etzioni argued that the thought of J.S. Mill, Locke, and Adam Smith must be understood as advocating opposing excessively oppressive and authoritarian social controls. Etzioni argued that the "negative consequences" of advocating privacy as "sacrosanct" were "largely ignored" by the champions of individualism. Highlighting the benefits of encryption and "Megan's Law," while also criticizing "cyberspace anarchists," Etzioni advocates a view of privacy based on communitarianism. This approach recognizes that privacy is based in a sociohistoric context and is not a natural right. He further argues that the power of individual choice may be protected, if, paradoxically, there is less individual privacy, as societal scrutiny lessens the need for governmental control.

The concept of distinct private and public spheres then leads to the issue of how privacy relates or conflicts with social or community values. It often leads to the view that privacy and social values such as internal security, social welfare, and government efficiency, are necessarily antithetical to each other. The issue then becomes whether these concepts are deeply contested and ambiguous, however, also that the promotion of privacy can itself be socially significant. Priscilla Regan, Assistant Professor of Public Affairs at George Mason University, has recognized that the liberal, Lockean tradition continues to provide the background for discussing privacy. She argues, however, that it overemphasizes individual privacy and fails to address the social importance of privacy. She maintains that privacy, is both a commonly held value and public value and collective value, because it is essential to a democratic political system. She wrote that, "Most privacy scholars emphasize that the individual is better off if privacy exists. I argue that society is better off as well when privacy exists. Privacy serves not merely individual interests; it also serves common, public, and collective purposes. If privacy became less important to one individual in one particular context, or even to several individuals in several contexts, it would still be important as a value because it serves other crucial functions beyond those that it performs for a particular individual. Even if the individual interests in privacy became less compelling, social interests in privacy would most likely remain.

Paul Schwartz, Law Professor at the University of California at Berkeley and Director of Berkeley Center of Law and Technology, describes information privacy as an important part of a civil society. Instead of personal choice being the paradigm of information control, society normatively defines standards of privacy, which limit access to information. Because the standards are multidimensional, they impose duties of confidentiality and disclosure for the same piece of information. Schwartz builds on this to suggest a set of obligations for information privacy in cyberspace.

A final critique is presented by those who argue based on post-structuralist assumptions that the essential ontological premise about the central autonomy of the subject is misguided. Jeremy Bentham, an English philosopher and father of utilitarianism, described "Panopticon" as a prison that could efficiently observe prisoners continuously through a central tower or another method. The system was intended to create a state of permanent and constant surveillance to maintain discipline. Michel Foucault, a twentieth-century French philosopher, expanded on the concept of panopticism, arguing that it could be applied in many areas of life, and was not limited to surveillance. However, it could be used when classifying people by many categories. Foucault described the link between knowledge and power, and the tendency by those in power to define and separate those deemed deviant, and create norms that are culturally reinforced. Mark Poster, Professor of History at the University of California at Irvine, transformed Foucault's view of the Panopticon as a contemporary form of routine surveillance and social control. Poster thus, described, the postmodern/post-structuralist argument as follows: Foucault presented new form of power by deciphering discourse/practice formations instead of intentions of a subject or instrumental actions. Such a discourse analysis, when applied to the mode of information, yields the finding that the population participates in its twelve self-constitution as subjects of the normalizing gaze of the Superpanopticon. We view databases not as an invasion of privacy, as a threat to a centered individual, but as the multiplication of the individual, the constitution of an additional self, one that may be acted upon to the detriment of the "real" self without the "real" self ever being aware of what is happening. Poster's analysis places the "mode of information" and especially the surveillance capacity of modern information technology at the heart of contemporary social transformations. For him, the theory and language of information privacy is irrelevant. The more profound issue for the postmodern era is nothing less than "where the human self is located if fragments of personal data constantly circulate within computer systems, beyond any agent's personal control." Poster seeks for a politics of databases that emphasizes not autonomy and individual privacy, but takes into account new forms of identity formation and community in an era of cyberspace and virtual reality. Other critics have also cited Foucault to contend that an individually-based privacy regime locks individuals into standardized identities and arbitrary social restraints and that liberation comes from a refusal to accept such restraints.

Despite these various critiques of privacy, privacy remains often thought of as the public business of the state and public life vis-a-vis the private spheres of individual life. There continues to be a discussion on a deeper philosophical issues on the nature of the "self" in modern on postmodern conditions or about cultural relativity or bias according to class or gender. To some extent, this selective focus may be explained by the fact that most of the philosophical debate about privacy occurs in the political and legal fora. Many European political philosophers view much of U.S. political theory as little more than a footnote to the Constitution. On issues of privacy, there may be some truth in this observation. Much of what has been written on privacy law was intended to describe and interpret the emerging "right to privacy" that the U.S. Supreme Court developed and applied to private decisions about intimate family issues including contraception and abortion. Much of U.S. political philosophy, therefore, was directed toward emerging legal doctrine.

Privacy theory and public policy

The pervasiveness of liberal assumptions within privacy scholarship has had several political and policy results. First, it explains the continuous reference in the privacy literature to the concept of balance. However conceptualized, privacy is not an absolute right. It must be balanced against correlative rights and obligations to the community. Richard Hixson, Professor of Communications Law and Journalism History, Information, and Library Studies, at Rutgers University, views "balance" as the "continuing struggle over the meaning of private and public, the jurisprudential debate over individual autonomy and collective welfare, between the person and the state, the individual and the community." Etzioni also defines communitarianism as an approach that "holds that a good society seeks a careful balance between individual rights and social responsibilities, between liberty and the common good. . . ." David Brin, scientist, author, and tech-futurist, wrote of his view of the need for balance between privacy and transparency. He presents three questions: A) Where do we want to end up? B) Who has the ultimate advantage in each situation? and C) Which situation is robust or stable? He posits regulatory regimes of transparency and secrecy and discusses which one is more likely to reward the powerful or protect the weak, and which is more realistic. Brin examined the advantages of transparency and secrecy along both an accountability and plausibility matrix. He made arguments for and against each system, concluding, "Perhaps we who stand at the extremes, both strong privacy advocates and believers in transparency, underestimate how smart folks are. Over the long haul, people may work their way toward a clear-headed mixture of our purist positions, finding pragmatic ways. . . . [to secure] an enviable curtilage for average citizens and their families. Charles Raab, Professor of Government at the University of Edinburgh, however, states that "balance" is an ambiguous term that has different implications for action depending on who is doing the 'balancing" and for what reasons.

The assumption of "balance" of privacy forms the basis of government investigations or studies into a privacy policy. The U.S. Privacy Protection Study Commission concluded that "the Commission has constantly sought to examine the balance between the legitimate, sometimes competing, interests of the individual, the record-keeping organization, and society in general." The assumption about balance also forms the basis for the doctrine of "fair information principles" (FIPs) for the appropriate collection, retention, use and disclosure of personal information, although the codification of these principles has varied over time and location. They appear either explicitly or implicitly within all national data protection laws (including those in the U.S. and Canada that known as "Privacy" Acts). They also form the basis of international agreements, such as the 1981 Guidelines from the Organization for Economic Cooperation and Development, the 1981 Convention from the Council of Europe, and the more recent Directive on Data Protection from the European Union While the codification may vary, there tend to be six essential principles: 1) openness—the very existence of personal recordkeeping systems should be publicly known; 2) individual access and correction; 3) collection limitation—organizations should only collect and store information that is relevant to accomplish a legitimate task; 4) use limitation—data should only be used for purposes consistent with those tasks; 5) disclosure limitation—personal data should only be disclosed externally for legitimate reasons or with the consent of the individual; and 6) security—against loss, unauthorized access, destruction, use, erasure, or modification of personal data. The development of these statutory principles rests on some basic liberal assumptions about procedural justice. We all have privacy rights and interests, it is assumed, but those concerns can only be subjectively defined.

No paternalistic definitions of the privacy value appear; no attempts are made to second-guess the privacy interests of individual citizens. Implicit is a rational faith in the capacity of longstanding principles of procedural justice to deal with adverse effects of new technologies. The political theory of privacy remains a work in progress. Privacy is an issue that all democratic states are attempting to deal with simultaneously. It provides an opportunity to consider wider theories about politics in advanced industrial states. Unlike some other regulatory issues, privacy raises central and enduring issues on the power of the state, the respect for civil liberties, the relationship between the state and civil society, and the definition of the "subject" within conditions of modernity (or post-modernity).

Further Reading:

Acquisti, Alessandro. *Digital Privacy: Theory, Technologies, and Practices.* New York: Auerbach Publications, 2008.

Barendt, E. M. *Privacy.* Aldershot: Ashgate/Dartmouth, 2001.

Byford, Katrin Schatz. "Privacy in Cyberspace: Constructing a Model of Privacy for the Electronic Communications Environment." *Rutgers Computer & Technology Law Journal* 1998.

Cohen, Julie E. "What Privacy Is For." *Harvard Law Review*, May 1, 2013.

Petronio, Sandra Sporbert. *Boundaries of Privacy Dialectics of Disclosure.* Albany: State University of New York Press, 2002.

Schlabach, Gabriel R. "Privacy in the Cloud: The Mosaic Theory and the Stored Communications Act." *Stanford Law Review*, 2015.

Solove, Daniel J. *Understanding Privacy.* Cambridge, Mass.: Harvard University Press, 2008.

Strahilevitz, Lior Jacob. "Toward a Positive Theory of Privacy Law." *Harvard Law Review*, 2013.

Wacks, Raymond. *Privacy.* New York, NY: New York University Press, 1993.

See also: Brandeis, Louis; Constitutional law; Economic arguments for privacy pights; Legal evolution of privacy rights; Locke, John; Philosophical basis of privacy; Private sphere; Right to be let alone; Supreme Court of the United States

Time, Inc. v. Hill, 385 U.S. 374 (1967)

Identification: The first decision by the United States Supreme Court to balance privacy interests and First Amendment free speech rights by applying the "actual malice" standard of *New York Times Co. v. Sullivan*, 376 U.S. 254 (1964), to a privacy claim.

The *Time, Inc. v. Hill* case stemmed from an article in *Life* magazine about a Broadway production of the novel (and later film) *The Desperate Hours* by Joseph Hayes. The article said that the book and play had be inspired by a 1952 real-life incident in which James J. Hill, his wife Elizabeth, and their five children were held hostage in their home for nineteen hours by escaped convicts. The article primarily consisted of photographs of actors portraying scenes from the play, taken in the Hill's former home.

James and Elizabeth Hill sued *Life* in New York, claiming that the article violated their right of privacy by placing them in a "false light." They claimed that the photos inaccurately portrayed the events of their captivity as more violent and menacing than the actual events, and caused them emotional distress. After eleven years of litigation, the U.S. Supreme Court reversed a trial court verdict for the Hills, holding that the award infringed on the magazine's First Amendment free speech rights to report on a matter of public interest.

The Hills sued under New York's "right of publicity" statute, N.Y. Civil Rights Law §§ 50–51, which creates civil and criminal liability for unauthorized use of an individual's likeness to promote a commercial product. While this is the only privacy claim recognized in New York, courts in the state have applied the statute to other scenarios in which an individual's name and likeness was published in the media without permission. To fit their claim into the statute, the Hills argued that the purpose of the article was to promote the play.

After a two-week trial, the jury awarded James Hill $50,000 in compensatory and $25,000 in punitive damages, and awarded Elizabeth Hill $75,000 in compensatory and $25,000 in punitive damages. Elizabeth Hill then settled, but *Life* appealed the award to James Hill, leading to a 4–1 decision by New York's Appellate Division sustaining the jury verdict of liability, with the majority finding that the article's implication that the photos were accurate re-creations made it commercial speech "to advertise and attract further attention to the play, and to increase present and future magazine circulation as well" (*Hill v. Hayes*, 18 A.D.2d 485, 489, 240 N.Y.S.2d 286, 290 [N.Y. App. Div., 1st Dep't. 1963]). But the appeals court ordered a new trial on damages, holding that jurors were improperly shown the film and other evidence that the appellate court deemed improper.

In a bench retrial, the judge awarded $30,000 compensatory damages to James Hill but no punitive damages. This verdict was affirmed by New York's highest court, the Court of Appeals, by a 5–2 vote (*Hill v. Hayes*, 15 N. Y. 2d 986, 207 N. E. 2d 604, 260 N.Y.S.2d 7 [N.Y. 1965]).

After granting certiorari with the votes of five justices, the U.S. Supreme Court heard arguments in the case on April 27, 1966. Richard M. Nixon, then practicing law after having served as vice president, argued the case for Hill. The initial vote after the argument was 6–3 for the Hills, based on the rationale that the "fictionalized" nature of the *Life* story meant that actual malice did not apply. Justice Abe Fortas was assigned to write the majority opinion. Justice John Marshall Harlan II circulated a concurrence, while Justice William O. Douglas circulated a dissent. Justice Byron White circulated another dissent raising questions regarding interpretation of the New York statute.

According to Leonard Garment, Justice Hugo Black was offended by the tone of Fortas's draft and said that he needed time to respond. Thus, at the end of its 1965–1966 term, the Court ordered re-argument in the case, asking the lawyers to focus on the scope of the New York statute and whether "fictionalization" of a story led to reduced First Amendment protection.

Justice Black finally circulated a memo on the case on the eve of re-argument. The memo blasted Justice Fortas's draft, and it had the intended effect. After the re-argument, held on October 18 and 19, 1967, the initial vote was 7–2 for reversal of the award to the Hills.

The Court eventually reversed the award in a 5–4 decision. The majority opinion by Justice William Brennan, joined by Justice Potter Stewart and Justice Byron White, held that actual malice, which the Court had held to limit libel actions by public officials regarding matters of public concern in *New York Times Co. v. Sullivan*, also applied to the privacy case brought by the Hills. According to the majority, the Hills were public figures involved in a matter of public concern and thus had to show actual malice in order to prevail. Because the jury instructions did not require this, the instructions were unconstitutional and the jury verdict had to be reversed.

Justice Black wrote a concurring opinion, joined by Justice Douglas, agreeing with the majority's application of *Sullivan* but also expressing support for broader protection for free speech. In his own, separate concurrence, Justice Douglas agreed that the First Amendment's protection of free speech should be absolute, and "[when] a private person is catapulted into the news by events over which he had no control[, h]e and his activities are then in the public domain as fully as the matters at issue in *New York Times Co. v. Sullivan*."

Justice Harlan concurred in part and dissented in part, and was joined by Justice Fortas. While he agreed that it was unclear whether the jury based its compensatory award after remand on a finding that *Life* had acted with negligence or actual malice, he diverged from the majority on the significance of this, saying that either basis would pass constitutional muster. He also disagreed with the extension of *Sullivan*'s protection for discussion of public officials to the Hills, whom he characterized as private, not public, figures.

Justice Fortas also authored his own dissent, joined by Chief Justice Warren and Justice Clark, arguing that privacy is a fundamental right, and it should not be outweighed by free speech rights in cases such as the Hills', which he classified as involving private individuals and a matter that is not of public concern. As Garment and Bernard Schwartz have both noted, later cases actually took this view, holding that people such as the Hills should be considered private figures to whom the "actual malice" standard does not apply (*Gertz v. Robert Welch, Inc.*, 418 U.S. 323 [1974]).

After the U.S. Supreme Court's reversal, the case was again remanded to the trial court for a new trial (*Hill v. Hayes*, 20 N.Y.2d 738, 229 N.E.2d 698, 283 N.Y.S.2d 101 [1967]). But the new trial never occurred: According to papers in the Nixon library uncovered by Samantha Barbas, *Life* settled the case with James Hill for $75,000. But the profound effect of the article on the Hill family took its toll, with Elizabeth Hill taking her own life in August 1971.

Eric P. Robinson

Further Reading

Barbas, Samantha. "When Privacy Almost Won: *Time, Inc. v. Hill* (1967)." *University of Pennsylvania Journal of Constitutional Law* http://ssrn.com/abstract=2588870.

Friend, Charles E. "Constitutional Law—Right of Privacy—*Time, Inc. v. Hill*, 87 S. Ct. 534 (1967)." *William & Mary Law Review* 8 (1967): 683–687. http://scholarship.law.wm.edu/wmlr/vol8/iss4/10.

Garment, Leonard. "Annals of Law: The Hill Case." *The New Yorker*, April 17, 1989, 90–110.

Kalven, Jr., Harry. "The Reasonable Man and the First Amendment: Hill, Butts, and Walker," *Supreme Court Review* 1967 (1967): 280–309.

Levine, Lee, and Stephen Wermiel. *The Progeny: Justice William J. Brennan's Fight to Preserve the Legacy of New York Times v. Sullivan*. Chicago, IL: American Bar Association, 2014, pp. 55–64.

Schwartz, Bernard. *The Unpublished Decisions of the Warren Court*. New York: Oxford University Press, 1985, pp. 240–303.

See also: Constitutional law; First Amendment to the U.S. Constitution; Supreme Court of the United States

Twitter

Identification: An online social networking tool that enables registered users send and read messages of up to 140 characters. Unregistered users may read the messages called Tweets, but they may not compose Tweets themselves. Users may access Twitter through a website, Short Message Service (SMS), or mobile device application. As of June 2015, Twitter has more than 300 million active monthly users and has become influential in contemporary society.

Jack Dorsey, then an undergraduate student at New York University, developed the concept of an individual using an SMS service to communicate with a small group. He originally referred to the project as twttr. Work on this idea began in March 2006. Initially, Dorsey and contractor Florian Weber developed the first Twitter prototype as an internal service for the podcasting company Odeo and its employees. The full public version was released on July 15, 2006. When asked about the name, Dorsey explained, "[W]e came across the word 'twitter,' and it was just perfect. The definition was 'a short burst of inconsequential information,' and 'chirps from birds.' And that's exactly what the product was." Twitter's popularity increased at the 2007 South by Southwest Interactive festival. Twitter had placed large television screens in the conference hallways to stream Twitter messages about the conference and thus allow attendees to keep in contact with each other. During that time, Twitter usage increased from 20,000 Tweets per day to 60,000 per day.

Twitter has various features, with the most obvious being the ability to create and read Tweets. The default setting is that they are visible to anyone online, but users can restrict their messages so that only followers can see them. Twitter users can Tweet from the actual Twitter website or through external devices such as apps for a smartphone. Also, users can retweet messages and subscribe to view other users' feed, which is known as following a user. Also, Twitters may place hashtags in their Tweet. A hashtag uses the number symbol (#), and groups words together to indicate the topic of the Tweet. This also allows other users to search for Tweets by topic, and allows Twitter to list trending topics, which are popular topics shown on the sidebar of Twitter. Users may make a topic trend either by a concerted effort or because of recent events.

Users can also use web-based interfaces that allow them to post from multiple accounts, maintain various column views, track activities (like who is following the user), and schedule Tweets to be posted in the future. Users may use Twitter to direct-message one another, as long as both parties are following one another. Only the recipient, and not the general public, may see a direct message. However, the message still restricts the recipient to 140 characters.

Over the years, individuals have begun to use Twitter in various different ways. For example, people have used Twitter to organize protests and social movements, connect with celebrities, receive emergency notifications, and read news. Also, the emergence of live Tweeting has changed the way people sometimes watch television. Live Tweeting usually consists of a television show's actor, producer or director Tweeting about the show as fans are watching it. Similarly, Twitter has changed the way fans interact with celebrities. Many celebrities have started to use Twitter to promote themselves and reach out to fans, posting updates on various topics such as where they are vacationing and promoting a new television show. Most celebrities use a verified account, which shows up as a blue check, signifying that Twitter verifies that they are who they say they are. This is important for various public figures. Holding a verified account also

Live tweets as Secretary Vilsack lays out his 2012 Farm Bill priorities in a speech at the John Deere Des Moines Works. (U.S. Department of Agriculture)

gives the user additional features not available to unverified users, such as the ability to receive direct messages from people they do not follow. You can Tweet at a celebrity, or other user, by using the at sign (@) in front of a username. This also means that celebrities can Tweet back at a fan, which often allows more fan access. Obviously, this can also create security and privacy risks for public figures because the general public has access to greater information about the public figure.

Twitter has also changed how people engage in politics and elections. The 2016 election was the first election that saw the rise of twitter being used for campaigning, as well as "twitter bots" attempting to influence the election. Twitter admitted that more than 50,000 Russian linked accounts used twitter to post automated materials about the 2016 US election. In January 2018, congressional Democrats called on Twitter and

Facebook to investigate the Russian influence, and the use of twitter bots.

Another development in regards twitter and privacy that has come as a result of the 2016 Presidential election, albeit indirectly, is the case of *Knight First Amendment Institute at Columbia University v. Trump*, No. 17 Civ. 5205 (NRB) (S.D.N.Y. May 23, 2018). This case, brought by the Knight First Amendment Institute on behalf of themselves and a group of other plaintiffs, argued that it was unconstitutional for users to be "blocked" from reading the personal account of President Trump, @realDonaldTrump. The lawsuit also named then-White House Press Secretary Sean Spicer and White House Social Media Director Dan Scavino as co-defendants.

The plaintiffs, who had been blocked from viewing the President's account, argued that doing so breached their First Amendment rights, arguing that the account in question is a public forum. The Knight Institute, whilst not themselves banned from the account, argued that depriving them of the views of dissenters who had been blocked was similarly unconstitutional. In doing so, the plaintiffs cited the 2017 case of *Packingham v. North Carolina* where the Supreme Court held that twitter was "the modern public square."

In delivering the judgment, Judge Buchwald stated that:

This case requires us to consider whether a public official may, consistent with the First Amendment, "block" a person from his Twitter account in response to the political views that person has expressed, and whether the analysis differs because that public official is the President of the United States. The answer to both questions is no.

The Judge further held that, in regard to the plaintiff's First Amendment claims, the speech in which they seek to engage is protected by the First Amendment and that the President and Scavino exert governmental control over certain aspects of the @realDonaldTrump account, including the interactive space of the tweets sent from the account. That interactive space is susceptible to analysis under the Supreme Court's forum doctrines, and is properly characterized as a designated public forum. The viewpoint-based exclusion of the individual plaintiffs from that designated public forum 1s proscribed by the First Amendment and cannot be justified by the President's personal First Amendment interests.

The government has subsequently appealed the decision in this case in the United States Court of Appeal for the Second Circuit, but a decision on this appeal has not yet been delivered.

As is true of most online services, however, privacy and the use of data are a concern. Twitter's own website and privacy policy states: "When using any of our Services you consent to the collection, transfer, storage, disclosure, and use of your information as described in this Privacy Policy." Also, most are aware that what you Tweet is for public view. There is an option to make your account private and to choose who

sees your Tweets, but your account name is still visible to the public.

Other serious privacy issues exist. For example, Twitter collects data from you when you Tweet, but it also collects data when you visit other sites. For example, many websites have embedded Tweet buttons, which, even without Tweeting the website, alerts Twitter to the fact that you have visited the website. Twitter has admitted that it uses this information to recommend people to follow in Twitter.

In 2013, Twitter acquired MoPub, a company that places ads within various mobile apps. This creates an advantage for Twitter because it allows advertisers not only to track Internet usage but also to track it across all devices. Data security experts have also raised security concerns about this type of tracking because hackers could obtain a multitude of information through MoPub.

Twitter's track record on privacy, however, has been stellar to date. It allows users to opt out of tracking functions and respects the do-not- track settings in browsers. Also, when government officials have attempted to subpoena Twitter users' data, Twitter has resisted exposing the data. The Electronic Frontier Foundation has even named Twitter the best large technology company for protecting data.

Melissa A. Gill and Ian Gill

Further Reading

Curtis, Craig R., Michael C. Gizzi, and Michael J. Kittleson. "Using Technology the Founders Never Dreamed Of: Cell Phones As Tracking Devices and the Fourth Amendment." *University of Denver Criminal Law Review* 4, no. 61 (2014.

Harkinson, Josh. "Here's How Twitter Can Track You on All of your Devices." *Mother Jones*, September 24, 2013.

https://www.theguardian.com/technology/2018/jan/19/twitter-admits-far-more-russian-bots-posted-on-election-than-it-had-disclosed

Knight First Amendment Institute v. Trump, No. 1:17-cv-05205 (S.D.N.Y.) (2017)

See also: Bots; Social networking technologies

U

U.S. Department of Justice v. Reporters Committee for Freedom of the Press, 489 U.S. 749 (1989)

Identification: A major privacy ruling that expansively construed the personal privacy exemptions in the Freedom of Information Act (FOIA). The *Reporters Committee* decision introduced into FOIA law the concept of "practical obscurity"— the notion that personal information found in criminal court records can be so difficult to locate and access that the law should recognize an individual's privacy interest in not having the collections of those details publicly disclosed.

The decision is also significant for its narrow interpretation of the public interest that may be taken into account in deciding whether the disclosure of private facts about an individual is warranted under FOIA. Together with the Court's later ruling in *National Archives and Records Administration v. Favish*, 541 U.S. 157 (2004), the holding in *Reporters Committee* affords enormous protection to personal information in government files by requiring anyone seeking records under FOIA that contain personal information to demonstrate affirmatively that disclosing those records will provide the public with significant information about government actions.

As amended in 1974, following the Watergate scandal and at a time of great public dissatisfaction with government secrecy surrounding the Vietnam War, FOIA declares that all records held by federal government agencies must be disclosed to the public upon request, unless they fall into one of nine categories of information that Congress specifically chose to exempt from the disclosure mandate. Two of the FOIA exemptions deal with private information about individuals contained in government files. One exemption allows an agency to withhold information in "personnel and medical files and similar files" if disclosure "*would* constitute a *clearly* unwarranted invasion of personal privacy;" the other more broadly allows law enforcement records to be withheld if disclosure "*could reasonably be expected to* constitute an unwarranted invasion of personal privacy" 5 USC 552(b)(6) & (7)(C) (emphasis added). The meaning of these provisions was squarely at issue in *Reporters Committee*.

The case arose out of a 1978 FOIA request by CBS reporter Robert Schakne who, with the help of the Reporters Committee, asked the FBI for the rap sheets of four brothers with alleged ties to organized crime. An FBI rap sheet compiles in one place an individual's arrests, acquittals, convictions and sentences. This information has been voluntarily provided to the FBI by local, state, and federal law enforcement agencies since the 1920s. These rap sheets are used by law enforcement agencies to detect and prosecute criminals and are provided to courts and corrections officers for their use in making decisions about sentencing and parole. As a matter of policy, however, the Justice Department had always treated the FBI rap sheets as confidential and allowed access to them only by other government agencies.

Schakne wanted the rap sheets on William, Phillip, Samuel and Charles Medico for an investigative news report he was preparing. The brothers had well-known ties to organized crime and ran a company that allegedly worked with a "corrupt Congressman" to win defense contracts. The FBI initially invoked the personal privacy exemptions and denied the rap sheet requests saying that disclosure would constitute an unwarranted invasion of privacy. After three of the brothers had died, however, the FBI found the privacy interest diminished and released their rap sheets. The Reporters Committee and Schakne then sued to compel disclosure of the rap sheet on the fourth brother, Charles Medico.

In the lawsuit, the Reporters Committee asserted that disclosing the rap sheet could not be an unwarranted invasion of Medico's personal privacy because there was no privacy to protect. All of the arrest and conviction information in his rap sheet came from public court files, and the common law does not generally recognize a privacy interest in the information contained in public files. The Reporters Committee argued, therefore, neither do the FOIA privacy exemptions. It also asserted a public interest in the disclosure of Medico's rap sheet based on his dealings with the corrupt Congressman and that he was a director of a company with Defense Department contracts.

The district court would have none of this. It agreed completely with the Justice Department that disclosing a summary of Medico's long history of run-ins with the law, including arrests that never led to convictions, would invade his privacy in a manner that was "clearly unwarranted."

Believing that the states generally made summary information like that contained in an FBI rap sheet available to the public, the court of appeals reversed. It recognized that FOIA's

requirement for an "*unwarranted* invasion of personal privacy" required a balancing of Medico's privacy interest against the public interest in disclosure to determine whether an invasion of his privacy was warranted. The court found at best only a minimal privacy interest in information publicly available elsewhere, and it concluded that FOIA's privacy exemptions therefore did not apply. In the process, the court also bemoaned FOIA's failure to provide courts with any standard for deciding when an invasion of privacy should be considered "unwarranted." Was it the general public's interest in the information that should be considered, and how is that to be weighed against a person's interest in keeping information private?

The Justice Department promptly asked for reconsideration, pointing out that the premise of the court's ruling was incorrect—most states actually refuse to make criminal history information public. In response, the court acknowledged the misunderstanding and sent the case back to the district court to determine if the information about Medico being withheld by the FBI was publicly available at its source.

At this interlocutory stage, the Supreme Court surprisingly agreed to review the court of appeals' decision. This case presented the Court with two issues: Can personal information that is available in public records nevertheless be considered private for purposes of the FOIA privacy exemptions? Moreover, how should a court decide when the disclosure of private information is sufficiently "unwarranted" that it can be withheld under FOIA?

Addressing the first issue, Justice Stevens explained for the unanimous Court that a key purpose for the protection of privacy at common law is to enable individuals to control the disclosure of their personal information so that divulging something about yourself in one context did not strip away all privacy protection in all contexts (489 U.S. at 764). Rather, the scope of protection afforded to personal information typically depends on how widely it has been disseminated and on how much time has passed since its disclosure. Even accepting the as-yet untested allegations of the Reporters Committee that the information on an FBI rap sheet was in a public court record at one time or another, the Court found that Medico still had a meaningful privacy interest arising from the "practical obscurity" of the information. The various arrests, charges, and convictions over many decades that would be reflected on his rap sheet were scattered about in different courthouses and would be very hard to locate and compile. In other words, a personal privacy interest can exist for purposes of FOIA in a collection of information, even if the scattered information itself is available in other public files.

The Court found this expansive reading of the personal privacy protected by the FOIA exemptions to be appropriate in light of other actions Congress had recently taken to prevent the disclosure of personal information held in government computers, such as the Privacy Act of 1974, 5 U.S.C. §552a: "Congress' basic policy concern regarding the implications of computerized data banks for personal privacy is certainly relevant in our consideration of the privacy interest affected by dissemination of rap sheets from the FBI computer," Justice Stevens explained (489 U.S. at 767). He also found a broad reading of personal privacy in FOIA to be consistent with earlier court decisions such as *Whalen v. Roe*, 429 U.S. 589 (1977), which addressed the threat to privacy posed by centralized government computers.

Having thus construed the term "personal privacy" very broadly to include a privacy interest in Medico's publicly available rap sheet information, the Court turned to the second issue: What interest in disclosure could justify invading this privacy interest; that is, what makes an invasion of personal privacy warranted under FOIA? Here, the Court narrowly constrained the public interest that can be weighed against personal privacy, making it easier for agencies to withhold personal information under FOIA's privacy exemptions.

Earlier FOIA decisions had held that the issue of whether a disclosure is warranted cannot turn on the purpose for which the information is sought [for example, *Department of Air Force v. Rose*, 425 U.S. 352, 372 (1976)]. That a CBS reporter was seeking the Medico rap sheet for use in a news program was therefore irrelevant to the public interest analysis— a reporter has no greater right to information under FOIA than any member of the public. *Reporters Committee* took things a step further, holding that the *only* public interest that can be balanced against a privacy interest under FOIA is the specific interest in knowing what the government is up to. In other words, a government disclosure of personal information can only be warranted under FOIA if the disclosure will shed significant light on the actions of government. As Justice Stevens put it, the balance of the public interest in disclosure against the personal privacy at stake "must turn on the nature of the requested document and its relationship to the basic purpose of [FOIA] 'to open agency action to the light of public scrutiny'" (489 U.S. at 772).

Medico's past dealings with a corrupt congressman and his status as an officer of a corporate defense contractor thus did nothing to tip the balance in favor of disclosure. That Medico had been charged or convicted of a crime "would tell us nothing about the character of the congressman's behavior," nor would it "tell us anything about the conduct of the Department of Defense." Disclosure of Medico's rap sheet was an unwarranted invasion of his personal privacy, the Court held, because its disclosure would not reveal anything about the actions *of government* (489 U.S. at 774).

Having concluded that Medico's rap sheet could properly be withheld by the FBI, Justice Stevens went one step further still. In the part of the opinion not joined by Justices Brennan and Marshall, he further held that this same analysis would apply to all rap sheets, not just Medico's. The practical obscurity in maintaining the privacy of a rap sheet will always exist, as will the absence of any significant information about government conduct, given the nature of a rap sheet. The Court thus declared rap sheets to be categorically exempt from FOIA disclosure and indicated that this same categorical approach could properly be applied under FOIA for any class of documents where the balance required by the privacy exemptions will characteristically tip in one direction.

Since *Reporters Committee* was decided in March 1989, the personal privacy exemptions have come to be widely understood to reach almost any record that names an individual or discloses personal identifying information, and the notion that practical obscurity may create a protectable privacy interest has become ingrained in FOIA law.

David A. Schulz

Further Reading

Bergman, Hannah. "Out of Sight, Out of Bounds," *The News Media and the Law* 33, no. 2 (Spring 2009): 11. http://www.rcfp.org/browse-media-law-resources/news-media-law/news-media-and-law-spring-2009/out-sight-out-bounds#sthash.RfKWo5cb.dpuf.

Halstuk, Martin E. "When Is an Invasion of Privacy Unwarranted under the FOIA? An Analysis of the Supreme Court's 'Sufficient Reason' and 'Presumption of Legitimacy' Standards." *University of Florida Journal of Law & Public Policy* 16, no. 3 (December 2005): 361–400.

Halstuk, Martin E., and Bill F. Chamberlin, "The Freedom of Information Act 1966–2006: A Retrospective on the Rise of Privacy Protection over the Public Interest in Knowing What the Government's Up To," *Communication Law and Policy* 11, no. 4 (September 2006): 511–564.

Halstuk, Martin E., and Charles N. Davis. "The Public Interest Be Damned: Lower Court Treatment of the Reporters Committeee 'Central Purpose' Reformulation." *Administrative Law Review* 54, no. 3 (2002): 983–1024.

Larson, Robert G., III, "Forgetting the First Amendment: How Obscurity-Based Privacy and a Right to Be Forgotten Are Incompatible with Free Speech," *Communication Law and Policy* 18, no. 1 (2013): 91–120.

Rehnquist, William. "Is an Expanded Right of Privacy Consistent with Fair and Effective Law Enforcement?" *University of Kansas Law Review* 23 (1974–1975): 1. [Based on Chief Justice Rehnquist's two-part Nelson Timothy Stephens Lectures, University of Kansas Law School, September 26–27, 1974.]

Winn, Peter A. "Online Court Records: Balancing Judicial Accountability and Privacy in an Age of Electronic Information." *Washington Law Review* 79, no. 1 (2004): 307–329.

See also: Federal Freedom of Information Act (FOIA); National Archives and Records Administration v. Favish; Federal Privacy Act of 1974

Unenumerated constitutional right, privacy as an

Identification: The established principle that, although the term *privacy* is found nowhere in the text of the U.S. Constitution, the concept of privacy has a firm foundation in U.S. constitutional law.

Privacy is defended as implicit in the constellation of rights and liberties protected by the Constitution and as a necessary corollary to the exercise of many of those rights and liberties. In general, constitutional privacy is recognized in two distinct, but connected, forms: First is the privacy related to freedom from unwanted intrusion in autonomous decision making; second is the privacy related to freedom from unwanted disclosure of personal information. The former is known as decisional privacy, the latter as information privacy. Both concern what famously has been described as the "right to be let alone."

Decisional privacy

The modern origins of decisional privacy may be traced to a U.S. Supreme Court case called *Griswold v. Connecticut*, 381 U.S. 479 (1965). The case involved a challenge to a law that made it more difficult for married couples to obtain contraception. In the lead opinion, Justice William O. Douglas reasoned that individuals enjoy a "zone of privacy" recognized by the various provisions of the Bill of Rights: the First Amendment, which protects anonymous speech and association; the Third, which protects the sanctity of the home; the Fourth, which expressly protects from unwarranted government intrusion in an individual's home, person, and effects; and the Fifth, which protects the right to remain silent during a criminal investigation. Despite expressing doubts about this understanding of privacy, the Court's majority agreed that the Constitution protects a right to decide whether to bear or beget a child without governmental interference.

In *Roe v. Wade,* 410 U.S. 113 (1973), the Court confirmed that, regardless whether there exists a "zone of privacy" or whether due process protects an individual's interest in autonomous decision making about intimate matters, a woman has a constitutional right to determine whether she will bear a child, at least in the first trimester of pregnancy. A plurality of the Court modified *Roe* in *Planned Parenthood v. Casey,* 505 U.S. 833 (1992). The *Casey* plurality held that, prior to the viability of an unborn fetus, a woman has the right to terminate her pregnancy, and the state legitimately may regulate abortion to preserve its interests in maternal and fetal health as long as that regulation places no undue burden on a woman's right to choose.

In a more recent case, *Lawrence v. Texas,* 539 U.S. 558 (2003), a majority of the Court broadly stated that the due process clauses of the Fifth and Fourteenth Amendments protect individuals from "unwarranted government intrusions into a dwelling or other private places" and preserve "an autonomy of self that includes freedom of thought, belief, expression, and certain intimate conduct." This understanding of constitutional privacy limits government interference in personal decision making related to intimate matters such as procreation, marriage, family relationships, and child rearing.

When a law is alleged to undermine decisional privacy interests, courts approach the government's justification for the law critically, often demanding at least a compelling reason for the intrusion. Nonetheless, history shows courts have been sensitive to the legitimate needs of state and local governments to regulate various

activities and conduct to promote the health, safety, and welfare of the citizenry, and thus have sought to limit constitutionally protected decisional privacy interests to those that are not only embedded in the nation's history and legal traditions but are also considered to be, as the Supreme Court put it, "implicit in the concept of ordered liberty" (*Washington v. Glucksberg,* 521 U.S. 702 (1997)).

Information privacy

In contrast to decisional privacy, information privacy concerns the interest of individuals in controlling access to, and dissemination of, information about themselves and their activities. This kind of privacy has been valued as necessary to the formation and maintenance of the personal and commercial relationship, as well as the informed exercise of decisional privacy rights. The Fourth Amendment notably protects individuals from the unwarranted search and seizure by the government of "persons, houses, papers, and effects," but outside the context of criminal investigations, no enumerated right protects personal information from disclosure to the government.

In two cases, the U.S. Supreme Court has suggested that a constitutional right to information privacy exists. In *Whalen v. Roe,* 429 U.S. 589 (1977), the Court assumed that individuals possess a constitutionally based interest "in avoiding disclosure of personal matters" to the government. The case involved a challenge to a state law requiring that the names and addresses of persons who had obtained certain legal pharmaceuticals be recorded. The Court concluded that, assuming the existence of a constitutionally protected interest in the nondisclosure of this kind of information, that interest was not abridged by a law requiring the disclosure of such information as part of modern medical practice.

In a more recent decision, *National Aeronautics and Space Administration v. Nelson,* 131 S. Ct. 746 (2011), the Court again assumed that the Constitution protects an individual's interest in the nondisclosure of certain personal information to the government. On the facts of the case—which involved a challenge to portions of a government background check—the Court concluded there was no constitutional violation. The Court held the government's interests "as employer and proprietor in managing its internal operations," combined with the federal statutory protection afforded personal information in the government's possession, mitigated any threat to an individual's interest in not disclosing personal information.

Although the Constitution does not enumerate a right to privacy per se, the Supreme Court has held that individuals have a constitutional interest in decisional privacy when it comes to certain intimate matters. The Court has also assumed that, in an appropriate case, individuals may have a constitutionally protected interest in not being compelled to disclose personal information to the government. Clarification of the scope of this interest awaits further judicial attention.

Lawrence M. Friedman

Further Reading

Fried, Charles. "Privacy." *Yale Law Journal* 77 (1968): 475. Rubenfeld, Jed. "The Right to Privacy." *Harvard Law Review* 102 (1989): 737.

Warren, Samuel, and Louis Brandeis. "The Right to Privacy." *Harvard Law Review* 4 (1890): 193.

Westin, Alan F. *Privacy and Freedom.* New York: Atheneum, 1967.

See also: Douglas, William Orville; Fifth Amendment to the U.S. Constitution; First Amendment to the U.S. Constitution; Fourth Amendment to the U.S. Constitution; *Griswold v. Connecticut*; *Lawrence v. Texas*; Right to be let alone; "The Right to Privacy"; Supreme Court of the United States; *Washington v. Glucksberg*

United States v. Jones, 132 S. Ct. 945 (2012)

Identification: A unanimous decision, with a majority opinion by Justice Antonin Scalia, in which the U.S. Supreme Court ruled that the government's attachment of a Global Positioning System (GPS) device to a vehicle, and its use to monitor the vehicle's movements, constituted a search under the meaning of the Fourth Amendment.

The Global Positioning System (GPS) is a satellite-based navigation system commissioned by the U.S. Department of Defense. GPS was initially developed for military use, but the U.S. government has now made the system available for civilian and commercial use. A GPS device calculates geographic location by receiving and analyzing satellite data, and it is commonly available for private use in cellphones and other electronic devices.

In this case, Antoine Jones, owner and operator of a Washington, DC, nightclub, came under suspicion of trafficking narcotics. A joint task force, consisting of the Federal Bureau of Investigation (FBI) and local police, investigated Jones by visually monitoring his nightclub, installing a camera focused on the front entrance of his club, and employing a pen register and wiretap over his cellphone. The government subsequently obtained a search warrant authorizing the installation of a GPS tracking device on a vehicle driven by Jones, which was registered to his wife. The warrant authorized the installation of the device in the District of Columbia within ten days of its issuance.

Agents installed the GPS device on the eleventh day, however, and did so in the state of Maryland. The government tracked the vehicle's movements for the next twenty-eight days and once had to replace the device's battery in a public parking lot. The device established the vehicle's location within 50 to 100 feet, and it relayed more than 2,000 pages of data over the twenty-eight days of its use.

The government indicted Jones and his alleged co-conspirators with conspiracy to distribute and possess with intent to distribute five kilograms or more of cocaine and fifty grams or more of cocaine base, in violation of federal law. Jones filed a pretrial motion to suppress the evidence obtained through the GPS device, arguing that his Fourth Amendment rights were violated. The district court granted his motion in part: with regard to the data collected while the vehicle was parked in his garage. The district court held, however, that the rest of the data was admissible because an individual traveling in a vehicle on public roadways had no reasonable expectation of privacy.

After his first trial resulted in a hung jury, the government charged Jones and his co-conspirators with the same conspiracy in a second indictment. The evidence obtained through the GPS device was also permitted in the second trial. This time, however, the jury found Jones guilty and he was sentenced to life imprisonment.

The Court of Appeals for the District of Columbia reversed the conviction, holding that the use of the GPS tracking device violated Jones's Fourth Amendment rights. The U.S. Supreme Court agreed to review the case.

Justice Scalia first explained that a vehicle is an "effect" as the term is used in the text of the Fourth Amendment. Justice Scalia also underscored that the government physically occupied private property for the purpose of obtaining personal information. Such intrusion, he explained, would have undoubtedly been considered a "search" within the meaning of the Fourth Amendment when it was first adopted.

Justice Scalia acknowledged, however, that Fourth Amendment jurisprudence was no longer exclusively tied to common law trespass, noting that Justice Harlan's "reasonable expectation of privacy" approach first enunciated in *Katz v. United States*, 389 U.S. 347 (1967), came to dominate most Fourth Amendment cases. Nonetheless, the Court clarified that *Katz*'s reasonable expectation of privacy approach simply augmented the common law trespassory test rather than displacing it. Therefore, because the government physically intruded into a constitutionally protected area by attaching a GPS device on Jones's vehicle and subsequently monitored

its movements, a "search" occurred within the meaning of the Fourth Amendment.

The government asserted that, even if its acts constituted a Fourth Amendment search, those acts were "reasonable" and therefore permissible. Justice Scalia rejected this argument, stating that the government waived this argument because it did not make it in front of the lower courts. Accordingly, the Supreme Court affirmed the judgment of the court of appeals.

While the Supreme Court was unanimous in affirming the judgment of the court of appeals, two justices wrote concurring opinions. Justice Sonia Sotomayor wrote separately to highlight the difficulties in applying Fourth Amendment principles in the digital age, noting that it may be necessary to reconsider the notion that individuals do not have a reasonable expectation of privacy when information is disclosed to third parties. Justice Sotomayor also suggested that Fourth Amendment jurisprudence should cease to treat secrecy as a prerequisite for having a reasonable expectation of privacy.

Justice Samuel Alito also wrote a separate concurrence, joined by Justices Ruth Bader Gins-burg, Stephen Breyer, and Elena Kagan. Justice Alito rejected the trespassed-based rule and instead analyzed the case under the reasonable expectation of privacy test articulated in *Katz*. Under the *Katz* test, Jones had a reasonable expectation of privacy in the long-term monitoring of the movements of the vehicle he drove. Therefore, Justice Alito agreed that the court of appeals should be affirmed.

Jones is a recent example of the U.S. Supreme Court's struggle to articulate Fourth Amendment standards in the face of emerging technologies. The case revived the old trespass-based rule that looks to whether the government physically intruded into a constitutionally protected area. Justice Sotomayor's concurrence suggests that the Court could begin to rethink some of its prior Fourth Amendment case law to better cope with the digital age.

Ethan P. Fallon

Further Reading

Easton, Richard D., and Eric F. Frazier. *GPS Declassified: From Smart Bombs to Smartphones.* Herndon, VA: Potomac Books, 2013.

Priester, Benjamin J. "Five Answers and Three Questions After *United States v. Jones* (2012), the Fourth Amendment 'GPS Case.'" *Oklahoma Law Review* 65 (2013): 491–532.

Rosen, Jeffrey. "The Deciders: The Future of Privacy and Free Speech in the Age of Facebook and Google." *Fordham Law Review* 80 (2012): 1525–1538.

See also: Constitutional law; Criminal justice (criminal procedure); Fourth Amendment to the U.S. Constitution; *Katz v. United States*; Supreme Court of the United States; Wiretapping

USA FREEDOM Act, Pub. L. No. 114–23

Identification: The federal statute signed by President Barack Obama on June 2, 2015, the day after the expiration of some provisions of the USA PATRIOT Act.

The USA FREEDOM Act's full title is the Uniting and Strengthening America by Fulfilling Rights and Ensuring Effective Discipline Over Monitoring Act of 2015. The USA FREEDOM Act has three significant privacy-related provisions. First, it withdrew a specific legal authority used by the National Security Agency (NSA) to conduct bulk collection of telephone metadata records. Second, it required greater transparency of Foreign Intelligence Surveillance Court (FISC) decisions and authorized appointment of amicus curiae ("friends of the court") to make legal arguments before the FISC to "advance the protection of individual privacy and civil liberties." Third, the USA FREEDOM Act allowed individuals and companies greater freedom to report or disclose their participation or non-participation in bulk data collection by the government.

As its full name suggests, the USA FREEDOM Act's stated purpose was to better control surveillance of American citizens. The primary way in which the USA FREEDOM Act attempted to accomplish this was to impose a sunset on the statutory authority used by the federal government for the bulk collection of information of Americans' telephone calls. This form of surveillance, under which the government required telephone providers to turn over all telephone call metadata, such as the numbers of the caller and recipient, and time, location, and duration of the call, though not the content of the calls themselves, had been authorized controversially under the USA PATRIOT Act's Section 215. The existence of the bulk collection program was confirmed through leaks by former NSA contractor Edward Snowden in June 2013. The first draft of the USA FREEDOM Act was introduced shortly thereafter, in October 2013. The USA FREEDOM Act ultimately ended Section 215 authority for bulk data collection; under the terms of the USA FREEDOM Act, the authority expired six months after the bill became law. Ironically, because Section 215 of the PATRIOT Act had expired the day before the USA FREEDOM Act was signed into law, the USA FREEDOM Act technically served to revive temporarily the authority for bulk collection rather than end it. Some commentators have suggested that because Section 215 expired, it could not be revived by the USA FREEDOM Act. Nevertheless, soon after enactment of the USA FREEDOM Act, the NSA apparently resumed its bulk collection program.

The USA FREEDOM Act also required greater transparency of FISC operations. Specifically, the USA FREEDOM Act requires the FISC to disclose unclassified summaries of significant opinions publicly. These summaries are to include descriptions of the context of the opinion and any significant interpretations of law. The USA FREEDOM Act also authorized appointment of amicus curiae to represent "the public interest" during FISC proceedings as it relates to individual privacy and civil liberties, a development considered by some to be an important step toward greater privacy protection. Because

FISC routinely made legal decisions with only counsel for the government participating, many critics of government surveillance suggested that the court was insufficiently informed of significant privacy concerns. It is unclear how effective amicus participation under the USA FREEDOM Act may be. First, FISC retains control over amici appointments and when and how it will consider their arguments. In addition, the amici may not be privy to all information in a particular case because the USA FREEDOM Act requires them to have access only to materials that FISC determines are relevant to their duties. Perhaps most important, the amicus procedure still does not allow the subjects of FISC orders to have legal representation before FISC. USA FREEDOM Act proponents counter that while it may not offer the same vigor that opposing parties traditionally provide under the U.S. adversarial legal system, the participation of amicus curiae results in a more informed court.

Finally, under the USA FREEDOM Act, individuals and companies who receive bulk collection orders from the government may publicly disclose more information, including the number of selectors requested by the government. Individuals and private companies that do not receive surveillance orders are explicitly permitted to confirm nonparticipation.

Critics have suggested that the USA FREEDOM Act is a failure as a privacy protection tool for several reasons. First, although it eliminated a specific statutory authority on which the government had relied for bulk data collection, it did not affirmatively outlaw the practice. Second, the USA FREEDOM Act requires telephone companies to store and maintain their metadata so that it can later be searched by the government on an individual basis. Finally, many critics argue that the USA FREEDOM Act is a token substitute for meaningful surveillance reform. Notably, the USA FREEDOM Act did not remove the statutory authority for other controversial surveillance activities, including PRISM, under which the government collects Internet-based communications.

Eric Merriam

Further Reading

Etzioni, Amitai. *How Patriotic Is the Patriot Act?: Freedom versus Security in the Age of Terrorism.* New York: Routledge, 2004.

Eyre, William. *The Real ID Act Privacy and Government Surveillance.* El Paso, TX: LFB Scholarly Pub., 2011.

Kiefer, Francine. "With Passage of USA Freedom Act, Congress Tweaks Security-Privacy Balance." *Christian Science Monitor,* June 2, 2015.

Mass, Warren. "USA Freedom Act Fails." *New American,* December 22, 2014. Moore, Adam D. *Information Ethics: Privacy, Property, and Power.* Seattle: University of Washington Press, 2005.

Rackow, Sharon H. "How the USA Patriot Act Will Permit Governmental Infringement upon the Privacy of Americans in the Name of 'Intelligence' Investigations." *University of Pennsylvania Law Review* 150, no. 4 (May 2002): 1651–1696.

Rubel, Alan. "Privacy and the USA Patriot Act: Rights, the Value of Rights, and Autonomy." *Law and Philosophy* 26, no. 2 (2007): 119–159. http://ssrn.com/abstract=881130.

Stone, Geoffrey R. *Perilous Times: Free Speech in Wartime from the Sedition Act of 1798 to the War on Terrorism.* New York: W. W. Norton, 2004.

See also: Foreign Intelligence Surveillance Court (FISC); Metadata; National Security Agency (NSA); PRISM; Snowden, Edward Joseph; USA PATRIOT Act

USA PATRIOT Act, Pub. L. No. 107–52

Identification: A statute expanding the powers of law enforcement to detect and intercept terrorists' communications, enacted by Congress and signed into law by President George W. Bush on October 26, 2001, in the wake of the terror attacks on the World Trade Center Twin Towers and the Pentagon on September 11, 2001. The acronym USA PATRIOT is short for Uniting and Strengthening America by Providing Appropriate Tools Required to Intercept and Obstruct Terrorism.

The USA PATRIOT Act provided American law enforcement with unprecedented peacetime surveillance and law enforcement powers in an effort to prevent subsequent attacks. In summary, the act, among other things:

- allowed the government to search and seize, without notice to the citizen and without a warrant or probable cause, that citizen's financial, travel, and medical records, and Internet activity that are held by third parties such as Internet service providers, banks, and airlines.

- authorized law enforcement to conduct sneak-and-peek searches and wiretaps without any requirement that it be conducted to combat terrorism and without notifying (at least without promptly notifying) the owner or possessor of the area searched.

- allowed law enforcement to collect trap-trace or pen-register data related to telephone calls and Internet activity; these data capture the general description of telephone calls, such as numbers dialed and durations of calls, or Internet URLs, allegedly without capturing the voice content of the calls or the actual content of the visited websites.

- allowed law enforcement to collect, without a particularized warrant, the telephone usage and Internet browsing history of millions of Americans. Subsequent extension of the PATRIOT Act enabled creation of the National Security Agency's (NSA's) bulk telephone metadata collection program.

Some saw the PATRIOT Act as an essential tool for fighting terrorism. Others saw the act as a nonessential tool, ineffective with regard to terrorism but effective with regard to violating constitutional rights. Many commentators claimed that not a single terror attack was thwarted by the PATRIOT Act or its investigative and surveillance tools. If that is true, Americans suffered immense loss of privacy for no national security gain.

It is critical that we all appreciate the pressures that drove Congress to pass the PATRIOT Act and that drive federal law enforcement agencies to protect us from foreign and domestic terrorists even at the expense of some civil liberties. If there were to be another 9/11-style attack on American soil, there would be months of recriminations and congressional hearings to identify those federal officials who should be held accountable. Similarly, if the federal officials cut some constitutional privacy corners to make us all safer, there may be recriminations and hearings, but ideally those extra surveillance powers would have prevented the next attack. Those pressures are real and substantial, and more than that, they are understandable.

Those pressures, or similar ones, will strike again in the future, and decision makers, courts, Congress, and law enforcement will be tempted to go once again go the way of secret courts and unconstitutional surveillance. That is not a condemnation of the government or its officials; it is recognition that government is a human system, fraught with errors, biases, and all infirmities that plague humankind. The PATRIOT Act was certainly not the first such instance of the loss of civil liberties in U.S. history.

The war on terror was not a declared war, but 9/11 was certainly seen as a warlike act, and Congress responded within two months with the PATRIOT Act. The creation of the PATRIOT Act immediately after 9/11 is reminiscent of other overreaches and overreactions by Congress in time of war or when Congress legislates as if the country were at war. Several examples include:

- The Alien and Sedition Acts of 1798 outlawing anti-American speeches and authorizing mass deportations as America nearly went to war with France.

- During the Civil War, President Lincoln declared martial law and suspended writs of habeas corpus.
- During World War I, hundreds were convicted under the Espionage and Sedition Acts, which outlawed speech and writings criticizing the U.S. government; *in Schenck v. United Sta*tes, the Supreme Court upheld convictions for distributing antiwar leaflets, although the Court acknowledged that such behavior would not be criminal had America not been at war.
- In World War II, Congress authorized the internment of Japanese Americans and curfews for German Americans and Italian Americans for the duration of the war. Reparations of $20,000 per World War II Japanese American internee were not paid until 1988 and thereafter.

Countries, including the United States, often restrict human rights and protections in wartime. The PATRIOT Act could be seen as just the latest example. Indeed, governments have not always waited for wartime or international threats to justify curtailment of civil rights. Nor has law enforcement always scrupulously used special investigative and surveillance powers only for the purposes for which they were initially permitted.

The PATRIOT Act empowered law enforcement not just to combat terrorism during the putative war on terror, but it did far more than that by expanding law enforcement powers to investigate all types of crimes without the warrant and particularized probable cause guarantees explicit in the Fourth Amendment to the U.S. Constitution. The Constitution is best viewed as the governance contract between the people and their government. If that contract is to be changed, it must be changed by the amendment procedures within its text. And that contract is to be amended only with the consent or ratification of the people. Legislating loopholes in constitutional protections, as the Congress

did by creating the PATRIOT Act, is itself an unconstitutional act.

Fortunately, cooler heads have prevailed, and in June 2015, in response to Edward Snowden's 2013 leaks regarding the NSA bulk telephony collection program, President Obama signed into law the USA FREEDOM Act, Congress's hard-fought replacement for the USA PATRIOT Act. The USA FREEDOM Act (acronym for Uniting and Strengthening America by Fulfilling Rights and Ensuring Effective Discipline Over Monitoring Act of 2015) is expected to scale back and delimit, but not completely terminate, the NSA bulk phone records program and allow other features of the PATRIOT Act to expire. Many believe it will ultimately result in the destruction of NSA's vast database of American's telephone calls but will transfer the responsibility for storing future call records to the telephone companies themselves. The USA FREEDOM Act appears to be Congress's attempt to right its previous wrong and return to the spirit if not the letter of the Constitution and its Fourth Amendment.

Perhaps the most important and lasting lesson from the USA PATRIOT Act experience is that the government, even in meeting its awesome responsibilities related to national security, must honor the dictates of the Constitution, at least with regard to the privacy rights of U.S. citizens and residents. The Constitution was designed to grant limited powers, such as national defense, interstate commerce, and the like, to the federal government in exchange for detailed and specific limits on the powers of that federal government.

The process of being on guard is a shared responsibility. Government officials must ensure that they are acting within those constitutionally enumerated powers, and must ensure that they are protecting those constitutionally enumerated rights. Conversely, citizens and residents must be vigilant to ensure that the Constitution, the people's contract with its government, is honored at all times. The violation of any of our civil rights are viewed most accurately as the violation of all of our civil rights. It is far too easy to ignore violations of others' rights because "at least it didn't happen to me" or "that would never happen to me." However, governmental power can serve as a one-way ratchet. Power once exercised at the expense of the constitutional rights of others is very difficult to rein in again. Thus, the battle for privacy in the digital age, and the battle to protect individual privacy from congressional, executive, or even judicial overreach is one we all must wage in real time. As Supreme Court Associate Justice Antonin Scalia told University of Hawai'i law students in 2014, "Well, of course, [the Supreme Court's opinion in] *Korematsu* [v. United States, affirming the constitutionality of wartime internment of Japanese-Americans] was wrong . . . But you are kidding yourself if you think the same thing will not happen again." As Justice Scalia notes, wartime leads to many erosions of civil liberties—that is a given—so we must all stay on guard to protect against it no matter what its guise next time.

Charles E. MacLean

Further Reading

Abdolian, Lisa Finnegan Takooshian. "The USA PATRIOT Act: Civil Liberties, the Media, and Public Opinion." *Fordham Urban Law Journal* 30, no. 4 (2002).

Etzioni, Amitai. *How Patriotic Is the Patriot Act?: Freedom versus Security in the Age of Terrorism.* New York: Routledge, 2004.

Kiefer, Francine. "With Passage of USA Freedom Act, Congress Tweaks Security-Privacy Balance." *The Christian Science Monitor,* June 2, 2015.

Lee, Laurie Thomas. "The USA PATRIOT Act and Telecommunications: Privacy under Attack." *Rutgers Computer & Technology Law Journal* (2003, June 22.

Pike, George H. "USA PATRIOT Act Still Raising Questions." *Information Today,* July, 2015.

Rackow, Sharon H. "How the USA Patriot Act Will Permit Governmental Infringement upon the Privacy of Americans in the Name of 'Intelligence' Investigations." *University of Pennsylvania Law Review* 150, no. 5 (2002): 1651, 2012.

Rubel, Alan. "Privacy and the USA Patriot Act: Rights, the Value of Rights, and Autonomy." *Law and Philosophy:* 119–159.

Soma, John T. Nichols. "Balance of Privacy vs. Security: A Historical Perspective of the USA PATRIOT Act." *Rutgers Computer &; Technology Law Journal,* 2005.

Sproule, C. "The Effect of the USA Patriot Act on Workplace Privacy." *The Cornell Hotel and Restaurant Administration Quarterly:* 65–73.

Wills, Nathan J. "A Tripartite Threat to Medical Records Privacy: Technology, HIPAA's Privacy Rule and the USA Patriot Act." *Journal of Law and Health* (2002): 000–000.

See also: Electronic surveillance; Fourth Amendment to the U.S. Constitution; National Security Agency (NSA); Privacy laws, federal; September 11; Smartphones; Snowden, Edward; Terrorism and privacy; USA FREEDOM Act; Wiretapping

V

Video Privacy Protection Act (18 USCA §2710)

Identification: An act passed by the U.S. Congress in 1988 and signed into law by President Ronald Reagan. Essentially it prevents disclosure of videotape rental or sale records and makes any provider that discloses rental or sale information liable for damages.

The impetus for the Video Privacy Protection Act (VPPA) was the nomination of Judge Robert Bork to the U.S. Supreme Court in 1988. Judge Bork's Washington, DC, area video store released his rental records to a reporter for a local paper, the *Washington City Paper*. The newspaper's intentions were most likely to embarrass Bork, but in reality the disclosure only succeeded in alarming Congress sufficiently to pass the VPPA. Patrick Leahy (D-VT) wrote the bill. According to the Senate Report, the bill's purpose was "to preserve personal privacy with respect to the rental, purchase or delivery of video tapes or similar audio visual materials." On the floor, Senator Leahy stressed that the bill was necessary in "an era of interactive television cables, the growth of computer checking and check-out counters, of security systems and telephones, all lodged together in computers. . . ." The legislative history also indicates that this particular act is a natural step in a "long line" of statutes passed by Congress extending privacy protections to records and expanding the meaning of the

"right to privacy." S. Rep. No. 100–599, 100th Cong., 2d Sess. at 6 (1988).

The law creates a general ban on the disclosure of personally identifiable rental information unless the consumer consents specifically to that disclosure and does so in writing. Also, it allows disclosure of records to police officers only if there is a valid warrant or court order. The act also allows disclosure of "genre preferences" with names and addresses for marketing purposes only but must allow customers to opt out. It also requires that video stores destroy rental records no longer than a year after an account has been closed. The act provides for civil remedies, including possible punitive damages and attorney's fees. The VPPA also allows states to enact broader protection for individual's records.

In fact, many states have enacted laws that do just that, including Connecticut, California, Maryland, Rhode Island, Delaware, Iowa, Louisiana, New York and Michigan. The Michigan statute goes beyond the VPPA to protect book purchases, rentals, and borrowing, and the Connecticut and Maryland laws make video rentals in those states confidential, preventing such information from being sold.

There is some question about whether the VPPA applies to just videos, as the name indicates, or whether it extends to things like DVDs and streaming. Although plain meaning of the statute would indicate that it applies only to videos, it seems, given the policy and legislative history, not to mention fairly recent case law, that courts will extend the meaning to more modern technologies.

In 2011, the bill was amended, mostly because of lobbying from companies such as Netflix. Representative Robert Goodlatte (R-VA) introduced H.R. 2471, which eventually became H.R 6671, and was signed into law by President Barack Obama in 2013. The change amended the VPPA's consent provision as follows:

> to any person with the informed, written consent (including through an electronic means using the Internet) in a form distinct and separate from any form setting forth other legal or financial obligations of the consumer given at one or both of the following times—
> (i)   the time the disclosure is sought; and
> (ii) in advance for a set period of time or until consent is withdrawn by such consumer.

This amendment weakens the consent portion of the act by limiting the ability of users to control the disclosure. For example, companies may obtain a one-time blanket consent and post information about the user on a continuous basis. Specifically, this allows Netflix to share users' preferences on Facebook.

Since the VPPA was passed, there has been significant case law. For example, in 1996, an officer conducting an internal affairs investigation asked for, and received, the plaintiff's rental records from a clerk at a video store. There was no warrant or court order, and the video store's employee did not question the request. The plaintiff sued, arguing that his rights were violated under the VPPA. The Court reasoned that the purpose of the statute was to protect privacy as new technology developed, and the Court noted that the plaintiff could sue the video store for the unauthorized release but also allowed for a claim to be brought against the police department. This was a broad reading of the statute and essentially established that any party using wrongfully obtained video records could

be liable. *Dirkes v. Borough of Runnemede*, 936 F. Supp. 235 (D.N.J. 1996).

Another important case is often referred to as the ACLU Tin Drum Case. In 1997, a man in Oklahoma complained that the movie *The Tin Drum* contained child pornography, which violated Oklahoma law. A local judge viewed the film, ruled that it was likely child pornography, and ordered local video stores to remove all copies of the movie. Also, the authorities obtained, without a warrant, lists of the individuals currently renting the movie, and went to their homes and asked for the copies of the movie. The Tenth Circuit court ruled that obtaining the rental records without a warrant was indeed a violation of the VPPA. *Camfield v. City of Oklahoma City*, 248 F.3d 1214 (10th Cir. 2001).

In 2011, Peter Comstock and Jeff Milans both filed suit against Netflix for violating the VPPA, specifically for keeping user information longer than allowed under the act. In response to this, Netflix changed its privacy policies in 2012 so that it no longer retains rental histories of people that have left the site.

A recent suit against Hulu helped to define what constitutes a "knowing disclosure." In a class action lawsuit against the streaming service, plaintiffs alleged that Hulu was disclosing identities and viewing selections to Facebook. Facebook had combined two sets of data, without Hulu's knowledge or permission, allowing Facebook to piece together a user's identity and viewing history. The Court agreed that this did not constitute "knowing" on the part of Hulu.

A question does remain, however about how this act interacts with the USA PATRIOT Act, 115 Stat. 272 (2001), which allows for obtaining records in the course of an ongoing investigation. The latter is a much lower standard than a warrant or court order.

Melissa A. Gill

Further Reading

Farivar, Cyrus. "Class-Action Lawsuit Settlement Forces Netflix Privacy Changes." *Ars Technica,* July 20, 2012.

Hutnik, Alysa Zeltzer, Robyn Mohr, and Matthew P. Sullivan. "Applying the Video Privacy Protection Act to Online Streaming." AD Law Access, June 2, 2015.

Smith, Robert Ellis. "Consumer's Handbook Guide to Privacy Protections." Privacy Journal, September 1, 2010.

See also: American Civil Liberties Union (ACLU); Facebook; Privacy laws, federal; Privacy laws, state; The Right to Privacy; USA PATRIOT Act

Voting and privacy rights

Identification: Broadly speaking, the issue of privacy rights in regards to voting can be separated into two areas. The first is the issue of ensuring the privacy of the voter when casting his or her ballot. The second is the question of what information about a voter is or is not available as a matter of public record in the voter rolls.

Voter Privacy in Casting a Ballot

In the United States, since the late 1800s, the majority of ballots cast have been done so under the so-called "secret ballot" system, where voters are presented with an official ballot produced by the state, which contains the names of all candidates contesting the election, as well as all proposals up for vote, when they arrive at their polling place. They then mark their ballot in private. This system gradually replaced the previously common "oral ballot," whereby voters would vote by voice, or the "open ballot," where people would queue to make their vote. The public nature of both these systems of voting were believed to be open to coercion and corruption. Likewise, giving voters paper ballots only upon their arriving at the polling place was introduced to prevent the possibility of "pre-filled" ballots being cast.

In recent years, however, there has been a large increase in voting by mail, and, indeed, in some states such as Washington and Colorado, all elections are now carried out by mail vote. This may raise questions about potential privacy issues, as mail voting means that the ballot is

A ballot for the New Hampshire primary is entered into a machine at a polling site, Feb. 9, 2016, in Nashua, N.H. (By Voice of America.)

sent out to the voter, rather than being handled only at the polling place, and there is no guarantee that a voter will choose to fill out his or her vote in private.

There are also certain laws in place to ensure that the right to vote is properly extended to Americans with disabilities. Provisions included in the Americans with Disabilities Act (1990), the Voting Rights Act (1965), and the Help America Vote Act (2002), among others, ensure that voters with disabilities have the same right to vote as anyone else. This means that polling places must provide the previously discussed vote by mail, wheelchair-accessible voting booths, voting equipment for blind or visually impaired people, and various other facilities to ensure that voters with disabilities are able to cast their vote.

The Help America Vote Act also created the Election Assistance Commission, which uses federal funds to provide support to both voters and election officials, in an attempt to ensure certain minimum standards are met by all states.

Voter Rolls and Voter Information

Most Americans know the basic information regarding the physical casting of a ballot. What is less commonly known, however, is the amount of information about voters that is a matter of public record. Indeed, in all 50 states, as well as in the District of Columbia, it is possible to obtain voter information through the state voter rolls. Nonetheless, there is no uniform system determining whom the information is available to, what information is contained within a voter list, what (if any) information is to be kept confidential, and how that confidentiality is achieved.

The decision as to who is able to obtain voter lists varies significantly from state to state, and almost every state has a slightly different criteria in place. In some states, such as Florida, Georgia, and Texas, the voter list is available to the public upon request. In other states, such as California, the list is not available to the general public per se, but rather is limited to those involved in political parties, campaigns, or committees or those who can show a journalistic, political, or governmental need for the information, as determined by the Secretary of State. In New York, after the close of registration, the board of elections publishes a complete list of names and addresses of the registered voters in each district and makes these available for public inspection and allows copies to be purchased. The cost of obtaining this information again varies greatly from state to state, ranging from free to several thousand dollars, depending on the state in question.

In terms of what information is contained within voter list files, this too varies greatly by state. Almost all states include some basic information as standard, such as the name and residential address of the registered voter. Many also include the voting history of the voter (not *for whom* they voted but rather *when* they voted), while others also include the party affiliation of voters. Some states contain the date of birth of the voter, though that specific information is often kept as confidential.

As to what other information is kept confidential as a matter of course by states, it varies

again but drivers license numbers and social security numbers (SSNs) are two of the most common pieces of information recorded but kept confidential. SSNs are perhaps one of the most controversial pieces of information recorded by states in regard to voter registration. A number of states, including Georgia, Tennessee, and Virginia, have faced legal challenges in recent years as to whether they have the right to request SSNs when registering voters, and, if the information is registered, to whom it can be disseminated. As a result of this, the vast majority of states keep SSNs confidential.

Finally, there are certain specific policies in place regarding confidentiality in states, specifically in regards to the address of certain voters. In a handful of states, it is possible that all voters can request that their address be kept private. However, this is not common. Over 30 states use Address Confidentiality Programs (ACPs) to help protect the information of certain voters. These programs were created to try to protect the victims of certain crimes—such as domestic violence, stalking, or assault—from offenders who could use the public record to try to trace them.

Melissa A Hale

Further Reading

Greidinger v. Davis United States Court of Appeals, Fourth Circuit. 988 F.2d 1344

McKay v. Thompson United States Court of Appeals, Sixth Circuit. 226 F.3d 752

Schwier v. Cox United States Court of Appeals, Eleventh Circuit. 340 F.3d 1284 www.eac.gov/

www.usa.gov/voting-laws

www.eff.org/deeplinks/2016/02/voter-privacy-what-you-need-know-about-your-digital-trail-during-2016-election

www.ncsl.org/research/elections-and-campaigns/access-to-and-use-of-voter-registration-lists.aspx

W

Warren, Earl

Identification: The fourteenth Chief Justice of the U.S. Supreme Court. During his time as Chief Justice, Warren demonstrated strong leadership and was known for his ability to obtain consensus or majority rulings on major decisions.

Warren was born on March 19, 1891, in Los Angeles, California. He earned his BA in political science in 1912. Two years later, he completed his JD from the University of California Berkeley School of Law. In 1917, he enlisted in the army and earned the rank of first lieutenant before being discharged in 1918 at the end of World War I.

After leaving the army, Warren worked as a clerk for the Judicial Committee of the California State Assembly for one legislative session (1919–1920). He then accepted a position as deputy district attorney for Alameda County and worked in this role for five years. In 1925, Warren received a vacancy appointment for district attorney of Alameda County. After his appointment, Warren married Nina Palmquist Meyers and adopted her son from her first marriage; the couple went on to have five more children. Warren was reelected as district attorney general three times, in part because of his reputation for being tough on crime and corruption.

Earl Warren became the attorney general (AG) for the state of California in 1939 and held the position until 1943. As AG, he continued to fight corruption and organized crime. After the bombing of Pearl Harbor, he initially opposed discrimination against Japanese Americans as unconstitutional. Eventually, however, he became an outspoken and influential proponent of Japanese internment. (He only expressed regret for his actions in his posthumously published memoirs.) Warren then served three consecutive terms as governor of California, from 1943 to 1953. As governor, he reformed California's prison system, increased pensions for the elderly, built numerous schools and hospitals, and developed programs focusing on mental health and disabilities.

Although Warren had no previous experience as a judge, President Dwight D. Eisenhower appointed him Chief Justice of the Supreme Court in 1953, after the death of Chief Justice Fred M. Vinson. The Warren Court proved to be more liberal than Eisenhower had anticipated. Warren oversaw several landmark decisions by the Supreme Court. In 1954, he led the Court to end racial segregation in schools in *Brown v. Board of Education,* 347 U.S. 483 (1954). By obtaining a unanimous decision, Warren hoped to hasten public acceptance of the ruling. He was able to secure unanimous decisions in all subsequent desegregation cases during his tenure as Chief Justice. During the McCarthy era, the Court repeatedly upheld individual rights in cases such as *Sweezy v. New Hampshire*, 354 U.S. 234 (1957), putting Warren further at odds with President Eisenhower.

Through two court cases, the Warren Court promoted equal representation. In *Baker v. Carr* in 1963, the Court determined that federal courts have the authority to rule on state redistricting cases. This was followed by *Reynolds v. Sims,* 377 U.S. 533 (1964), which held that state legislature districts must represent roughly the same proportion of the population. This came to be known as the "one man, one vote" ruling, and it helped ensure that sparsely populated rural areas were not given greater legislative representation than densely populated cities.

Multiple Warren Court rulings protected or expanded the rights of criminal defendants. In 1961, the Court ruled in *Mapp v. Ohio,* 367 U.S. 643 (1961), that state courts cannot admit evidence obtained through unreasonable search and seizure, which is prohibited by the Fourth Amendment. (By this time, such evidence was already inadmissible in federal courts.) The right to an attorney for those who cannot afford one was extended to defendants in state courts in *Gideon v. Wainwright,* 372 U.S. 335 (1963). The 1966 ruling in *Miranda v. Arizona,* 384 U.S. 436 (1966), required that the legal rights of persons being interrogated be clearly explained to them. These rights are now commonly called Miranda rights.

After the death of President John F. Kennedy in 1963, Warren reluctantly joined the Commission on the Assassination of President Kennedy formed by President Lyndon B. Johnson. Under his leadership as chair of the investigation, it became known unofficially as the Warren Commission. The commission determined that Lee Harvey Oswald acted alone and found no evidence of a conspiracy.

In 1965, in *Griswold v. Connecticut,* 381 U.S. 479 (1965), the U.S. Supreme Court ruled that privacy is a constitutional right. Although the right to privacy is not directly mentioned in the Constitution, the Court ruled that the Bill of Rights as a whole protects citizens from governmental intrusion.

Warren retired from the Supreme Court on June 23, 1969. He was succeeded as Chief Justice by Warren E. Burger. Earl Warren died on July 9, 1974, in Washington, DC, and is buried at Arlington National Cemetery.

Lissa N. Snyders

Further Reading

Christman, Henry M., ed. *The Public Papers of Chief Justice Earl Warren,* rev. ed. New York: Capricorn Books, 1966

Cray, *Ed. Chief Justice: A Biography of Earl Warre*n. New York: Simon & Schuster, 1997.

Frantz, Joe B., interviewer. *Transcript, Earl Warren Oral History Intervie*w I. September 21, 1971. Internet Copy, LBJ Library. http://www.lbjlib.utexas.edu/johnson/archives.hom/oralhistory.hom/Warren-E/Warren-e.PDF.

Newton, *Jim. Justice for All: Earl Warren and the Nation He Made.* New York: Riverhead Books, 2006.

Pollack, Jack H. *The Judge Who Changed America.* Englewood Cliffs, NJ: Prentice-Hall, 1979.

Schwartz, Bernard, ed. *The Warren Court: A Retrospective.* New York: Oxford University Press, 1996.

Warren, Earl. *The Memoirs of Earl Warren.* Garden City, NY: Doubleday and Company, Inc., 1977.

See also: Fourth Amendment to the U.S. Constitution; *Griswold v. Connecticut; Mapp v. Ohio*; Supreme Court of the United States

Washington v. Glucksberg, 521 U.S. 702 (1997)

Identification: A case in which no justice of the U.S. Supreme Court found a constitutional right to a physician-assisted suicide. This is one of only two cases in which the Supreme Court has directly addressed the question of whether there is a constitutional right to terminate one's life, commonly referred to as the right to die. Unlike in *Cruzan v. Missouri,* in which the Court had seven years earlier first considered the right to die, in *Glucksberg,* the Court ultimately answered the broader question of whether there was a constitutional right to die.

A Washington State statute criminalized "promoting a suicide attempt." The felony offense, punishable by up to five years' imprisonment and a fine, prohibited knowingly causing or aiding another person to attempt suicide. Four physicians who occasionally treated terminally ill patients, and some patients who requested assistance in ending their lives, challenged the law. The plaintiffs argued that the Washington statute placed an undue burden on the physicians' exercise of a constitutionally protected liberty interest: the personal choice by a mentally competent, terminally ill adult to commit physician-assisted suicide.

Both the District Court and Court of Appeals for the Ninth Circuit (sitting en banc) held that Washington State's assisted suicide ban was unconstitutional. The Ninth Circuit found the issue analogous to the abortion question as it had been answered most recently in *Casey v. Planned Parenthood*. The court noted that both cases involved "the most intimate and personal choices a person may make in a lifetime, choices central to personal dignity and autonomy," and thus a fundamental liberty interest was protected.

In the Supreme Court, however, Chief Justice Rehnquist, writing for the majority, rejected the notion that "all important, intimate, and personal decisions" are protected by the due process clause. The Court noted that the due process clause protects only those rights and liberties that are deeply rooted in the nation's history and "implicit in the concept of ordered liberty such that neither liberty nor justice would exist if they were sacrificed." Pointing to the long history of criminalization of assisted suicide in the United States, the Court concluded that the right to assistance in committing suicide was not a fundamental right protected by the due process clause. Because assisted suicide was not a fundamental right, Washington State's ban only had to be rationally related to a legitimate government interest, a test the Court found was met by the statute.

Glucksberg was the second opportunity for the Court to determine that there was a constitutional right of privacy that protected end-of-life decisions from government intrusion. In *Cruzan*, after listing numerous opinions in which state courts had held there was a constitutional right of privacy protecting the right to terminate one's life, the Court had perfunctorily determined that the right to refuse treatment was more properly analyzed in terms of a Fourteenth Amendment liberty interest rather than a generalized constitutional right to privacy. Similarly, in *Glucksberg*, Chief Justice Rehnquist acknowledged several decisions that have been characterized as recognizing a right to privacy (including *Meyer v. Nebraska*, *Pierce v. Society of Sisters*, *Griswold v. Connecticut*, *Eisenstadt v. Baird*, *Rochin v. California*, and *Casey*) but nevertheless found that the right to die was not constitutionally protected.

Chief Justice Rehnquist distinguished *Cruzan* as being about the right to refuse unwanted medical treatment, which was "not simply deduced from abstract concepts of personal autonomy" but rather was based on long-standing doctrine that treating an unwilling patient is a form of battery. Thus, the majority rejected the idea that *Cruzan* meant people have a fundamental right of autonomy. Rehnquist also insisted that there was a fundamental difference between allowing life to end by withholding treatment and terminating life by proactive means, a distinction Justice Stevens criticized in his concurrence when noting "in both situations, the patient is seeking to hasten a certain, impending death."

In separate concurrences, Justices Souter and Breyer both cited Justice Harlan's dissent in *Poe v. Ullman*, the precursor to *Griswold*, in which Justice Harlan noted that the Constitution protected a right of privacy of the home that included the intimate details of the "marital relation." Their references to Harlan's earlier dissent suggest that they were rejecting Justice Douglas's later approach to privacy in *Griswold*.

Justice Breyer analogized Harlan's approach in finding a right of marital privacy to finding a "right to die with dignity" by identifying other legally protected interests relating to personal dignity, medical treatment, and "freedom from state-inflicted pain." Breyer ultimately concluded that Washington State law did not force a patient to undergo pain, and therefore the right to die with dignity was not infringed.

Despite numerous decisions in lower courts that a privacy right protected patients' end-of-life decisions, not one justice opined that a constitutional right of privacy protected a terminally ill patient's right to assistance in committing suicide. With no justice interpreting *Cruzan* or *Casey* as a right of privacy case, *Glucksberg* may have been the final nail in the coffin for the notion of a general "constitutional right of privacy," or at least one that protects an individual's autonomy in making decisions about their bodies free from government intrusion.

In 2008, eleven years after the Supreme Court's decision in *Glucksberg,* the Washington State legislature accepted several justices' suggestion that legislative power rather than courts should address emerging issues like assisted suicide by passing the Washington Death With Dignity Act, which allows terminally ill adults seeking to end their life to request lethal doses of medication from physicians.

Eric Merriam

Further Reading

Kamisar, Yale. "Against Assisted Suicide—Even a Very Limited Form." *University of Detroit Mercy Law Review* 735 (1995).

Richards, David A. J. "Constitutional Privacy, the Right to Die and the Meaning of Life: A Moral Analysis." *William and Mary Law Review* 22 (1981).

Wolhandler, Steven J. "Voluntary Active Euthanasia for the Terminally Ill and the Constitutional Right to Privacy." *Cornell Law Review* 363 (1984).

See also: *Cruzan v. Director, Missouri Department of Health*; *Griswold v. Connecticut*

"We Are Watching You" Act

Identification: A bill introduced in the U.S. House of Representatives in 2015 to regulate mass, corporate surveillance within the home through consumer electronics and video services.

Because of previous privacy scandals, many Americans are now wary of the activities of the National Security Agency (NSA), which has been collecting information about U.S. residents from their electronic devices. Currently, many Americans are unaware that the government is not alone in its endeavor to collect and analyze the data of the general population. Many private corporations, such as Microsoft and Verizon, not only collect consumer data stored online and on personal devices but also use consumer devices with video capabilities to surveil individuals in their homes. To curtail this practice, some members of Congress have sought to regulate this activity through the introduction of House Bill 1164, known as the "We Are Watching You" Act.

Within the average American household, one can expect to find one or more electronic devices such as a computer, tablet, smartphone, videogame console, or television. It is likely that each device includes a camera and the capability to access the Internet. The ability of devices to create and store data through cameras and the Internet has enhanced the ability of corporations to gather new and different types of data via video surveillance within the home. Microsoft's Kinect, for example, has the capacity to observe and record everything within its view. Thus, when consumers bring this technology into their homes, they have, likely unintentionally, invited Microsoft to observe their habits within that space. Microsoft's privacy policy states, however, that it collects pictures and videos of consumers only while they are engaged with the Kinect, that is, when an individual is actually playing the game or using the Kinect's camera functions to watch movies or complete other entertainment tasks. Although Microsoft's privacy policy does not specifically list continuous video surveillance as something in which it engages, it is clear that the console has the capability to do so. Similarly, in May 2011, Verizon filed for a patent for a DVR that can track the movements of users. Neither of these corporations currently monitor consumers via camera, but according to their current privacy policies, they certainly have the technological and legal capability to do so with a one-sentence revision to their privacy policies. With this reality in mind, Representative Michael E. Capuano (D-MA) introduced the "We Are Watching You" Act in 2013. The bill did not gain any traction initially. Therefore, Representative Capuano reintroduced the bill (H.R. 1164, 2015) on February 27, 2015.

The "We Are Watching You" Act attempts to curtail the ability of corporations to surveil consumers through electronic devices. Specifically, the bill requires companies "to provide for notification to consumers before a video service collects visual or auditory information from the viewing area and to provide consumers with choices that do not involve the collection of such information" (H.R. 1164, 2015). The bill specifies that the notification must read "we are watching you" as an onscreen message continuously while the information is being collected. In addition, companies must provide traditional notifications and descriptions of what and how information is collected as part of the terms and conditions as well as the written instructions for the product or service (H.R. 1164, 2015). The fact that a user knows that his or her information is being collected does not mean, however, that the individual will discontinue use of the service.

Many companies that gather data on consumers have significantly greater bargaining power than consumers. Standard terms and conditions, which detail how and when information is collected, typically condition the use of the service on consent to all of the terms contained therein. If consumers do not wish to have their data collected, they must decline use of the service. Most consumers are not mindful enough of personal privacy concerns to abstain from using the goods or services. Users either disregard or consent to terms because they believe the value of the goods or services is greater than maintaining their personal privacy. Thus, the act's requirement that companies disclose the fact that they are gathering information alone will not likely effect consumer privacy but would only reiterate the Federal Trade Commission's (FTC's) lax requirements, which only prevent consumer fraud. The drafters of this bill, however, anticipated that a disclosure requirement alone would not be enough to quell the potential degradation of privacy in the modern world. Thus, the act seeks to impose a level playing field.

To allow consumers to preserve their privacy without the cost of losing goods or services, the "We Are Watching You" Act prevents companies from requiring consumers to opt-in to surveillance in order to take advantage of their services. The act states that operators must offer an "alternative video service that does not involve the collection of such information, but is otherwise identical" (H.R. 1164, 2015). This provision takes an unprecedented stance in regard to the preservation of consumer privacy because the service provider must not only allow for an alternative service but the alternative service must be equal to the service that consumers who choose to opt in receive. No longer would consumers be forced to choose between privacy and service.

In its 2015 session, Congress has the ability to add new consumer privacy protections through the passage of the "We are Watching You" Act. If enacted, this legislation will authorize reasonable regulation of privacy settings in the United States, which would greatly enhance the privacy rights of American consumers.

Ashley Baker

Further Reading

Brav, Hiawatha. "Would You Let Your TV Watch You?" *The Boston Globe.* June 14, 2013.

Foege, Alec. "Consumer Data Privacy and the Importance of a Social Contract." *Data-Informed.com*. August 6, 2013. http://data-informed.com/consumer-data-privacy-and-the-importance-of-a-social-contract/.

Payton, Theresa, and Ted Claypoole. *Privacy in the Age of Big Data: Recognizing Threats, Defending Your Rights, and Protecting Your Family*. MD: Rowman & Littlefield, 2014.

Roberts, Brian F. 2011. Methods and Systems for Presenting an Advertisement Associated with an Ambient Action of a User. Patent Appl. No. 13/116784, filed May 26, 2011.

Sundar, Sindhu. "Bill Would Regulate Spying Technology Aimed at TV Viewers." *Law360*. June 14, 2013.

See also: Federal Trade Commission (FTC); National Security Agency (NSA)

Wearable technology

Identification: Also known as wearable tech, wearable devices, or simply wearables; electronics incorporated into clothing, wristwatches, eyeglasses, and other familiar and not-so-familiar methodologies of attachment to the human body. They are generally not permanently affixed to the body and may be removed. They may be viewed as the end designs for sensor and communications technology or as segues into more permanent invasive devices, such as cochlear implants that allow the deaf to hear. Wearables now include the potential use of surface tattoo and implanted microchip technology, but these categories may diverge as internal devices proliferate and become a separate category from externally worn devices.

Wearable technology gathers data about the individual wearing it and uploads it to an app or the Internet, or it may gather data from the environment or the Internet and display it for the user. Some wearables may store and process data locally in the device itself, or they may transmit it for analysis. Generally, wearables use wireless/ Wi-Fi and/or cellular service for communication capabilities. Because wearables communicate with a network or the Internet,

they are considered members of the Internet of things (IoT). Like many IoT devices, wearables often lack screens or other interfaces to facilitate notice and consent for privacy communications with the user.

Initial applications of this technology have been successful in the healthcare field. In this context, healthcare is construed broadly, incorporating general wellness concerns such as fitness, weight loss, and safety/location monitoring. Devices such as Fitbit monitor the user's physical activity in multiple dimensions and supersede the one-dimensional mechanical step counter. However, most information generated by fitness trackers is not regulated under the primary U.S. regulatory scheme for healthcare information, the Health Insurance Portability and Accountability Act of 1996 (HIPAA) 42 U.S.C. § 300gg, 29 U.S.C § 1181 et seq., and 42 USC 1320d et seq., unless the data relates to the person's health condition, the provision of health-care, or the payment of healthcare and the data collected is personal health information (PHI). This would be a legal disincentive to integrate unregulated fitness tracker data with regulated health records, even if it makes financial or medical sense.

Fitness wearables may still have some regulatory obligations. Wearable technology companies might incur obligations under the HITECH Act, which amended HIPAA to include business associates of regulated entities, if, for example, they contract with health insurance companies to share their customers' fitness data. The U.S. Food and Drug Administration (FDA) has regulated traditional medical devices and may, as consumer fitness wearables become more mainstream, venture into this field as well. Faulty wearables are subject to review and recall by the Consumer Product Safety Commission (CPSC). In one example, a Fitbit band was associated with skin irritations and approximately 1 million devices were recalled. The Federal Trade Commission (FTC) has launched several initiatives related to IoT, including wearable devices, focusing on concerns about appropriate notices to users under its mandate to seek out unfair and deceptive communications with consumers. The FTC has looked into the security of IoT devices and wearables to determine if companies offering such devices have established protocols guarding against unauthorized sale of consumer data and against breach of databases holding such data.

More traditional medical applications that would fit under FDA and/or HIPAA regulation are wearable insulin-, blood pressure–, heartbeat-, epileptic seizure–, and glucose-monitoring devices provided by medical providers to assist in monitoring patients. While not yet a substitute for medical attention, these devices have been lauded for allowing users to receive early alerts for life-threatening medical conditions and then to obtain the necessary medical treatment. There are concerns that some wearables are still primitive in their ability to measure body data as accurately as clinical devices do, and so research continues into increasing the accuracy and availability of such data. In addition, companies are continually looking at new ways to gather data from the human body. In development for medical and possibly for commercial markets, Google has researched the possibility of smart contact lenses and nanoscale cancer hunters for use in the human body.

A variety of companies have entered the wearables market, such as Google's experiment with Glass, a wearable eyepiece computer that may have failed to gain widespread acceptance because it was both visible and distracting to others. Criticisms of the device included its use to record video and audio of other parties without their knowledge and consent, copyright concerns, and the possibility of distracted driving or biking while wearing the device.

The Apple iWatch was launched with much fanfare, but it remains to be seen whether it will be accepted the way its counterpart has been. Commercials for the Apple iWatch portray users running with the device and checking it for

smartphone messages in situations in which it would be difficult or dangerous to pull a mobile phone from a pocket to examine the screen. A generation of users has moved its time-telling functions from wristwatches to the time management functions of smartphones, so marketers for wearable devices intent on using the wristwatch model may have to reacquaint younger users with this older method of receiving data.

Wearable devices have begun to figure in insurance, employment, and legal cases as the temptation to use gathered data about individuals mounts. Cases may arise in which fitness devices are used to demonstrate that someone was not injured as claimed; an employment disability was not accurate; or, using the devices' Global Positioning System (GPS), a user was not where he or she claimed to be. In each scenario, the user's data would be subpoenaed or otherwise revealed in discovery in a way that the user of the wearable device did not intend on initial purchase or use of the device.

The impact of big data, including information on individuals collected by wearables, may affect insurance rates, potentially allowing fluctuations on a daily or minute-by-minute basis rather than adjustments made solely on renewal of an annual contract. Data aggregators and analysis companies can now look to wearables as one potential source of data that can be collected to create a health profile of an individual or a numerical score for that user. This information can be used to set insurance rates, determine employment, or inform marketing companies looking for individuals for whom certain pharmaceuticals or other medical products might be appropriate. Big data aggregated from wearables can also be used to create data maps of risky neighborhoods or types of individuals, and such data may affect individuals who do not use wearables at all.

Also, employers have begun offering free or low-cost wearable fitness or location trackers as a benefit or condition of employment to employees. These offerings are frequently included as part of an overall corporate wellness program. As a benefit, employee users may receive a discount on insurance or other financial benefit for using the device. As a condition of employment, some employees may be required to wear location trackers to determine if, for example, they are following a prescribed delivery route or taking only authorized breaks. On the rise is the use of body cameras by police officers, a measure that has the potential to increase safety for the police and for the public but may reduce privacy for the police officers and those who may cross their paths, whether suspect or bystander.

This fledgling use of wearables presents many layers of privacy concerns, most of which have been subsumed under the traditional legal methods of notice and consent in a written contract. If the wearable device in question does not fit into one of the usual regulatory frameworks, industry standards prevail, and customer concerns are embedded into privacy policies, terms of use, acceptable use policies, and other physical and digital contractual methods for obtaining consent from users. Employment law may reach this issue and establish some standards beyond voluntary contracts for what employers may do, and union negotiations may include wearable device parameters as part of the next cycle of labor contracts.

The aggregation of wearable data into databases presents a security risk to that data, especially if the data is not encrypted and made anonymous prior to database entry. The sheer volume of such data makes it a target for hackers who seek to discredit particular companies or countries, create valuable portraits of individuals for identity theft purposes, or resell the data to marketers. As with many IoT devices, the wearables market remains dispersed, and there is an opening for products that provide a platform to manage multiple wearables. That product would need to have even stricter security protocols because the stakes increase with the amount, specificity, and individually identifiable

data collected. Risks include profiling by government and private companies, stalking, tracking, ID theft and other digital and physical theft like home burglaries, and miscellaneous and yet to be imagined losses of individual privacy. Additional regulatory plans for data security protocols and other minimum standards on the U.S. federal level may include wearables explicitly or implicitly via the inclusion of provisions for IoT devices, big data, or network security.

Jill Bronfman

Further Reading

Barfield, Woodrow. *Fundamentals of Wearable Computers and Augmented Reality*, 2d ed. Lanham, MD: Rowman and Littlefield, 2015.

Federal Trade Commission. "Consumer Generated and Controlled Health Data." May 7, 2014. https://www.ftc.gov/system/files/documents/public_events/195411/consumer-health-data-webcast-slides.pdf.

Ng, Cindy. "5 Things Privacy Experts Want You to Know about Wearables." Varonis Blog. July 17, 2014. http://blog.varonis.com/5-things-privacy-experts-want-you-to-know-about-wearables/.

Tehrani, Kiana, and Andrew Michael. "Wearable Technology and Wearable Devices: Everything You Need to Know." *Wearable Devices Magazine*. Last modified March 26, 2014. http://www.wearabledevices.com/what-is-a-wearable-device/.

See also: Big data; Federal Communications Commission (FCC); Federal Trade Commission (FTC); Global positioning system (GPS) tracking, Identity theft; Mobile devices; Profiling; Stalking

Whistleblowers

Identification: People who disclose secret or confidential information they believe to be evidence of illegal, unethical, or disreputable institutional activities.

Whistleblowers may exist in the private sector, such as employees who work for corporations and disclose alleged corporate misdeeds. Whistleblowers may also exist in the public sector, such as civil servants who divulge state secrets. Whistleblowers have been instrumental in exposing matters of public concern that would otherwise have remained secret yet, once exposed, have a dramatic effect on politics and public policy. Because whistleblowers are instrumental in exposing corruption and unethical behavior of powerful corporations and/or the government, creating protections for these individuals has been necessary throughout history.

While whistleblowers have exposed what many believe to be corporate and governmental violations of digital privacy, whistleblowing is not a new phenomenon. There is a long history of people with access to confidential information releasing information to expose wrongdoing or to educate the public. The Continental Congress—the governing body of the thirteen colonies during the American Revolution—passed the first whistleblower law in reaction to the dismissal from the navy of two officers who reported the torture of British prisoners of war during the Revolutionary War. Since then, the U.S. government has often reacted to embarrassing revelations of wrongdoing by passing additional whistleblower protections. For example, in reaction to President Richard Nixon's illegalities while in office, the United States passed the Civil Service Reform Act of 1978, which contained, among other things, whistleblower protections for federal employees. The whistleblower protections in the act were then updated by the Whistleblower Protection Act of 1989 and again by the Whistleblower Protection Enhancement Act of 2012, which is considered one of the key whistleblower laws in the United States.

The Whistleblower Protection Enhancement Act of 2012 provides protections for federal employee whistle-blowers who reveal evidence of waste, fraud, and abuse. However, the law protects federal employees only in certain circumstances and only when they reveal certain kinds of information. Other whistleblower laws either at the federal level or at the state level protect people based on the specific industry in which they work or the specific information they

The Office of the Whistleblower (U.S.SEC) Symbol

reveal. It is this ad hoc patchwork of protections that have led some to criticize whistleblower protections laws in the United States as full of loopholes and exceptions.

Whistleblowers have played an instrumental role in exposing the secret collection of data by governments. For example, in 2005, the *New York Times* published an article exposing the George W. Bush administration's secret warrantless wiretapping program. The article reported that, under the authorization of President Bush, the National Security Agency (NSA) monitored the electronic communication and Internet activity between suspected terrorists outside the United States even when the person with whom the suspects were communicating was in the United States. Critics of the program argued that, because the NSA failed to get approval from the Foreign Intelligence Surveillance Act Court, it violated the law. Initially, the *New York Times* withheld the exposé, but when the Bush administration threatened to seek a court order prohibiting the publication of the article, the newspaper immediately published it. It was not until three years later that Thomas Tamm, a lawyer in the U.S. Department of Justice at the time of the surveillance, revealed himself to be the person who leaked the information to the newspaper. Tamm reported that he contacted the *New York Times* to leak the program because it "didn't smell right." Tamm was investigated by the Federal Bureau of Investigation (FBI) and the U.S. Justice Department, but ultimately the investigation was ended in 2011 and the government did not pursue charges.

At times, whistleblowers who have revealed information about government surveillance and the collection of personal data have come from outside of the government. In 2003, Babak Pasdar was hired by a major telecommunications company as a computer security expert. Pasdar's responsibilities were to upgrade and implement a new security infrastructure for the company. While completing the upgrade, Pasdar discovered a hole in the company's security that allowed data to flow out of the company to a third party. The result of the hole in security was that the third party had total access to all of the company's customer data, including text and voice communication, user location, and billing. After reporting the security lapse to the company, Pasdar's attempts to monitor and rectify the situation were rebuffed. Believing the situation posed a significant threat to privacy, Pasdar approached the Government Accountability Project, a government watchdog group, and signed an affidavit detailing his findings. Named the "Quantico Circuit," the conduit for information out of the telecommunication company was so named as a reference to Quantico, Virginia, the home of the FBI. The revelation of the "Quantico Circuit" and Pasdar's whistle-blowing ultimately led to a lawsuit against Verizon Wireless for permitting the transfer of its customers' data.

With the U.S. government's increasing use of contractors for computer security, whistle-blowers in the digital age also straddle the division between government and the private sector. While considered by some a traitor and others a patriot, Edward Snowden is perhaps one of the best known whistleblowers of the twenty-first century. Snowden, a former member of the U.S. Army, worked as a computer security expert for various organizations, including the Central Intelligence Agency (CIA). In 2012, while working for a private contractor assisting the U.S. government and its agencies with computer security,

Snowden began downloading files evidencing and detailing numerous secret surveillance programs conducted by the government along with its European allies. After being transferred to Hawaii, Snowden quit his job and was hired by another private contractor to do very similar computer security work. Snowden reportedly gained even greater access to the government's mass surveillance programs at his new job and continued to collect evidence of their existence. After three months with his new employer, Snowden took a leave of absence and flew to Hong Kong, determined to leak the information he had collected. Snowden eventually made contact with Glenn Greenwald, a journalist for the British newspaper the *Guardian*, and Laura Poitras, a documentary filmmaker. Greenwald and Poitras, along with another reporter from the *Guardian*, met Snowden in Hong Kong. Once they arrived, Greenwald interviewed Snowden over the course of two weeks. Snowden revealed the information that he had collected and that documented the existence of the government's mass surveillance programs. The *Guardian* eventually ran a multi-article exposé describing mass surveillance programs run by the U.S. government with the help of its international partners and private telecommunication companies. Snowden was eventually charged with violating the U.S. Espionage Act, which makes it a crime to communicate classified, national security information without authorization. He fled to Russia, where he was granted temporary asylum and has sought asylum elsewhere ever since. Speculation abounds regarding whether or not Snowden will ever strike a deal with the government and return to the United States. For now, he remains overseas.

Whistleblowers play a unique role in society. While the evidence of wrongdoing they obtain is considered confidential or secret, it is the information's secrecy that compels them to reveal it. They are usually driven by a sense of duty to expose what they believe to be illegal or unethical behavior; driven by a desire to give vital information they believe civilians have a right to know. While some believe whistleblowers to be heroes protecting citizens, others believe them to be traitors defying the government. That conflict often makes being a whistleblower a heavy burden to bear.

Douglas B. McKechnie

Further Reading

Bellia, Patricia L. "Wikileaks and the Institutional Framework for National Security Disclosures." *Yale Law Journal* 121 (2012): 1448–1526.

Vaughn, Robert G. *The Successes and Failures of Whistleblower Laws.* Cheltenham, UK: Edward Elgar Publishing Limited, 2012.

See also: Electronic surveillance; Espionage Act; Foreign Intelligence Surveillance Act (FISA); Foreign Intelligence Surveillance Court (FISC); National Security Agency (NSA); Snowden, Edward; Wiretapping

WikiLeaks

Identification: An online site that publishes secret information, news leaks, and classified media from anonymous sources.

WikiLeaks portrays itself as an international, nonprofit group of journalists and as "an uncensorable system for untraceable mass document leaking." WikiLeaks sees itself as a protection intermediary. Rather than leaking directly to the press, and fearing exposure and retribution, whistleblowers can leak to WikiLeaks, which then leaks the information to the press for them.

Its servers are located throughout Europe and are accessible from any uncensored web connection. The group located its headquarters in Sweden because the country has one of the world's strongest laws to protect confidential source–journalist relationships. The website is available on multiple servers and under different domain names as a result several denial-of-service attacks and its elimination from different Domain Name System (DNS) providers.

Because it seeks to ensure that journalists and whistleblowers are not jailed for emailing sensitive or classified documents, it uses a secure and anonymous drop-box for sources to leak secret information to WikiLeaks. This is particularly important because in so many areas of the world, such as China and parts of Africa and the Middle East, leaking government secrets means even incarceration or even death.

WikiLeaks is a project of the Sunshine Press, which is incorporated in Iceland. It is operated by a mostly anonymous group of contributors operating from several countries worldwide. Julian Assange, WikiLeaks's founder and editor-in-chief, is an Australian citizen who claims to have no permanent address. The current editor-in-chief is Kristinn Hrafnsson, an Icelandic national who has also served as a spokesperson for the organization from 2010-2017.

The Wikileaks website began operating in 2006 and reportedly had a database of more than 1.2 million documents by 2007. The saga of WikiLeaks occurred in three acts: (1) the website's publications, (2) the backlash against leaked U.S. government secrets, and (3) the reaction to that backlash. WikiLeaks claims that its goal is "to bring important news and information to the public . . . One of our most important activities is to publish original source material alongside our news stories so readers and historians alike can see evidence of the truth." Public perception of WikiLeaks has always been mixed, however. The 2016 American election cycle, during which WikiLeaks released hacked emails embarrassing to the Democratic presidential nominee, Hillary Clinton, has focused more negative attention on the organization.

Assange has discussed the limits of free speech, saying, "[It is] not an ultimate freedom; however, free speech is what regulates government and regulates law. That is why in the U.S. Constitution the Bill of Rights says that Congress is to make no such law abridging the freedom of the press." Wikileaks' work has often been compared to Daniel Ellsberg's leak of the Pentagon

Wikileaks Mobile Information Collection Unit - WikiLeaks Truck at *Fox News* Channel

Papers (U.S. Vietnam War–related secrets) to the *New York Times* in 1971. In the United States, the leaking of some documents may be legally protected. The U.S. Supreme Court has ruled that the Constitution recognizes anonymity.

At first, few of Wikileaks' publications were directed at the U.S. government. In 2008, WikiLeaks was awarded the Economist Index on Censorship Freedom of Expression award, and in 2009, it won the Amnesty International Human Rights Reporting award for the New Media category. WikiLeaks revealed the so-called secret bible of Scientology, an internal report by Trafigura discussing the health effects of waste dumping in Africa, emails from the Climate Research Unit at the University of East Anglia in the United Kingdom, and reports of an accident at a nuclear facility in Iran.

Leaks

WikiLeaks began publishing secret U.S. government material in December 2007. The first document was the standard operating procedures for Camp Delta from the prison operated by the U.S. Navy at Guantanamo Bay, Cuba. The manual permitted prisoners to be denied access to the Red Cross for up to four weeks and described how toilet paper could be used as a reward for good behavior. This was followed by publication of emails from

then-vice-presidential candidate Sarah Palin's private email account indicating that Palin was using her private account for official business, supposedly to circumvent Freedom of Information Act requests.

In mid-February 2010, WikiLeaks received a leaked diplomatic cable from the U.S. embassy in Reykjavik relating to the Icesave scandal, which WikiLeaks published on February 18. The cable, known as Reykjavik 13, was the first of the classified documents WikiLeaks published among those allegedly provided to them by U.S. Army private Chelsea Manning (then known as Bradley Manning).

Some of WikiLeaks' early releases included documentation of equipment expenditures and holdings in the Afghanistan war and a report about a corruption investigation in Kenya. In March 2010, WikiLeaks released a secret 32-page U.S. Department of Defense counterintelligence analysis report written in March 2008 discussing the leaking of material by WikiLeaks and how it could be deterred.

In April 2010, WikiLeaks published gunsight footage from the July 12, 2007, Baghdad airstrike in which Iraqi journalists were among those killed by an AH-64 Apache helicopter. In July 2010, WikiLeaks released Afghan War Diary, a compilation of more than 76,900 documents about the war in Afghanistan not previously available to the public.

In October 2010, Wikileaks released nearly 400,000 documents referred to as the Iraq War Logs in coordination with major commercial media organizations. This leak allowed the mapping of 109,032 deaths in "significant" attacks by insurgents in Iraq that had been reported to multinational forces in Iraq, including about 15,000 that had not been previously published.

In April 2011, WikiLeaks began publishing 779 secret files on prisoners detained in the Guantanamo Bay detention camp.

In July 2010, WikiLeaks released 92,000 documents related to the war in Afghanistan between 2004 and the end of 2009 to the *Guardian,* the *New York Times,* and *Der Spiegel.* The documents detail individual incidents including friendly fire and civilian casualties. After the leak of information on the Afghan war, in October2010, around 400,000 documents relating to the Iraq war were released. The U.S. Defense Department referred to this incident as the largest leak of classified documents in its history. Media coverage of the leaked documents emphasized claims that the U.S. government had ignored reports of torture by the Iraqi authorities after the2003 war.

On November 28, 2010, WikiLeaks and five major newspapers from Spain (*El País*), France (*Le Monde*), Germany (*Der Spiegel*), the United Kingdom (the *Guardian*), and the United States (the *New York Times*) started simultaneously publishing the first 220 of 251,287 leaked documents labeled confidential (but not top secret) and dated from December 28, 1966, to February 28, 2010.

In November 2010, WikiLeaks collaborated with several major global media organizations to release U.S. State Department diplomatic cables in redacted format. On September 1, 2011, it became public that an encrypted version of WikiLeaks' large archive of unredacted U.S. State Department cables. The incident resulted in widely expressed fears that the information released could endanger innocent lives. The contents of the diplomatic cables include numerous unguarded comments and revelations regarding: critiques and praises about the host countries of various U.S. embassies, political maneuvering regarding climate change, discussion and resolutions toward ending ongoing tension in the Middle East, efforts and resistance toward nuclear disarmament, actions in the war on terror, assessments of other threats around the world, dealings between various countries, U.S. intelligence and counterintelligence efforts, and other diplomatic actions.

Reactions

Reactions to the U.S. diplomatic cables leak varied. After the WikiLeak site became the target of a denial-of-service attack on its old servers, WikiLeaks moved its website to Amazon.com's servers. Later, however, the website was evicted from the Amazon servers. Amazon claimed that WikiLeaks was not following its terms of service and that Wikileaks was engaged in several violations. For example, Amazon's terms of service state that "you [the user] represent and warrant that you own or otherwise control all of the rights to the content . . . that use of the content you supply does not violate this policy and will not cause injury to any person or entity." In Amazon's view, WikiLeaks neither owned nor controlled the rights to the classified content it held.

WikiLeaks has contended that it has never released a misattributed document and that documents are assessed before release. In response to concerns that the group may publish misleading or fraudulent leaks, WikiLeaks claimed that misleading leaks are already published in the established media. Assange said in 2010 that submitted documents are vetted by five expert reviewers, who also investigate the background of the leaker if his or her identity is known. The editor-in-chief has the final decision in assessing a document.

Several U.S. government officials have criticized WikiLeaks for exposing classified information and claimed that the leaks harm national security and compromise international diplomacy. In March 2008, the U.S. Army counterintelligence center issued a special report on the threat posed to the U.S. Army by WikiLeaks. The document identified WikiLeaks' reliance on trust as the website's major weakness. WikiLeaks relies on insiders and whistleblowers to trust that they will maintain their anonymity.

The report concluded that identifying leakers and exposing them to employment termination or legal action could shake the trust on which WikiLeaks relies. As a result, others would be deterred from leaking documents to WikiLeaks. Although this report existed in 2008, no overt action was taken against WikiLeaks until the publication of the embassy cables.

The reaction to WikiLeaks' publication of the cables was quick and furious. Hillary Clinton, then-U.S. Secretary of State said, "This disclosure is not just an attack on America—it's an attack on the international community." Sarah Palin responded by stating that Assange had "blood on his hands" and asked the rhetorical question, "Why was he not pursued with the same urgency we pursue al Qaeda and Taliban leaders?" Defense secretary Gates, in a more nuanced manner, said, "Is this embarrassing? Yes. Is it awkward? Yes. Consequences for U.S. foreign policy? I think fairly modest."

The U.S. Justice Department launched a criminal investigation of WikiLeaks and Assange soon after the leak of the diplomatic cables. The department had considered bringing charges under the Espionage Act of 1917, 40 Stat. 217 (1917), because of First Amendment protections for the press. Several Supreme Court cases, including *Bartnicki v. Vopper*, 532 U.S. 514 (2001), have established that the U.S. constitution protects the republication of illegally gained information as long as the publishers did not violate any laws in acquiring this material. Federal prosecutors have also considered prosecuting Assange for trafficking in stolen government property. Because the diplomatic cables are intellectual rather than physical property, however, this may be a difficult strategy. Any prosecution of Assange would require extraditing him to the United States, a procedure made more complicated and potentially delayed by any preceding extradition to Sweden.

One of Assange's lawyers said they fought extradition to Sweden because it might result in Assange's extradition to the United States. Several human rights organizations requested with respect to earlier document releases that WikiLeaks adequately redact the names of civilians working with international forces in order to prevent repercussions. Some journalists have also criticized a perceived lack of editorial discretion when releasing thousands of documents at once and without sufficient analysis.

WikiLeaks' credibility as a source of apolitical information has come under increased scrutiny following the 2016 American presidential election cycle. In March of 2016, WikiLeaks released a trove of emails collected from the private Gmail account of former White House chief-of-staff and then-Clinton campaign advisor John Podesta. The FBI alleges that WikiLeaks obtained these emails from the Russian government. In September of 2016, WikiLeaks sent a direct message to Donald Trump Jr. via its Twitter account advising him to investigate a political action committee (PAC) website opposed to then-Republican nominee(and father of Trump Jr.) Donald J. Trump.

In January of 2019, the *New York Times* reported that former Trump campaign official Roger Stone was arrested in connection the investigation of Special Counsel Robert Muller into connections between the Trump campaign (and possibly President Trump) and the Russian government. Additionally, throughout the 2016 election, then-candidate Trump made repeated appeals to both WikiLeaks and the Russian government to release more Clinton campaign-related material.

WikiLeaks has also come under increased scrutiny in the United Kingdom due to connections between Nigel Farage, former head of the UK Independence Party (UKIP), Assange, and Russia. Farage was photographed visiting Assange at the Ecuadorian Embassy in London, where he (Assange) is currently maintaining political asylum; and the relationship between the two men dates to at least 2011. When questioned about his relationship with Assange in an interview with the German paper *Die Zeit*, Farage reportedly walked out of the interview.

According to *El Pais*, Assange also met with several "key ideologues" within the Catalan independence movement, after which WikiLeaks began tweeting in support of Catalan separatism. According to some reports, at Spain's behest, Ecuador limited Assange's internet access after this. Many note, however, that

Assange (and thus WikiLeaks) likely does not support an independent Catalonia as much as a shakeup of the European nation-state order.

Prosecutions

Criminal prosecution against WikiLeaks has not been successful because WikiLeaks is not a criminal enterprise in the same way that terrorist websites are, and private actors do not support the campaign against WikiLeaks in the way they supported the attacks on terrorist websites. U.S. Army Private Chelsea (then Bradley) Manning was accused of passing the "collateral murder" video and other documents to WikiLeaks.

On May 29, 2010, Manning was charged under the Uniform Code of Military Justice (UCMJ), articles 92 and 134, for transferring a classified video to his personal computer, exceeding authorized access on a Secret Internet Protocol Router Network (SIPRnet) computer, and transmitting protected information to someone not entitled to receive it. The UCMJ applies only to current or past members of the military, military cadets, reserve forces, prisoners of war, and people accompanying the armed forces in the field.

In December 2010, a federal grand jury was empanelled in Virginia to investigate whether Assange could be charged under the Espionage Act or the Computer Fraud and Abuse Act (CFAA), 100 Stat. 1213 (1986). The Espionage Act criminalizes several acts related to disclosure of classified material. Since the release of the embassy cables, most calls for prosecution of Assange have focused on the possibility that he could be indicted under the Espionage Act. Specifically, 18 U.S.C. § 793(a) (2011) prohibits knowingly and willfully communicating or making available classified information to an unauthorized person, or publishing such information in any manner prejudicial interests of the United States where the classified information concerns intelligence activities of the U.S. or foreign governments. Further, 18 U.S.C. § 793(b) (2011) outlaws copying any sketch, photograph,

photographic negative, blueprint, plan, map, model, instrument, appliance, document, writing, or note of anything connected with national defense. Subsection (c) proscribes receiving, obtaining, or agreeing to receive or obtain any of the materials from subsection (b) if the receiver knows or has reason to believe the materials were obtained in violation of the act. Subsection (g) makes it a crime to conspire to do something that violates the act. Any violation of these sections is punishable by a maximum of ten years in prison.

Assange almost certainly violated the plain meaning of the Espionage Act. Under subsection (a), Assange published classified information that concerned military intelligence by posting the so-called collateral murder video on WikiLeaks. The very title of the video also demonstrates that the video was prejudicial to U.S. interests because it accuses the U.S. military of killing civilians. Assange received documents and writings that he certainly had reason to believe were classified by the U.S. government.

As such he broke subsection (c) of the act. It could be argued that he also conspired to violate subsection (b) by offering to publish any materials he was given. Through a conspiracy charge, Assange would fall afoul of subsection (g) of the act as well. Although a prima facie case against Assange for violating the Espionage Act is strong, the government faced serious practical problems securing a conviction of Assange using this theory.

In *New York Times Co. v. United States*, 403 U.S. 713 (1971), the U.S. government tried to prosecute the *New York Times* for publishing the Pentagon Papers. The Supreme Court ruled that prior restraint of publication was not valid under the First Amendment. The Court suggested, however, that the government could pursue the newspaper for violations of the Espionage Act without violating freedom of speech. Thus, Assange would probably not be able to make a First Amendment defense against an Espionage Act charge; however, the government must still overcome serious practical and political obstacles to prosecute Assange for violating the Espionage Act. The primary problem arises because WikiLeaks published the embassy cables along with several newspapers.

If WikiLeaks violated the Espionage Act, then every media organization that published material provided by Manning to WikiLeaks also violated the act. Because Assange organized the group of prominent newspapers to publish the embassy cables simultaneously with WikiLeaks, he has set up a public relations trap for the government. The government has taken no steps toward prosecuting the *New York Times* for publishing the embassy cables and seems unlikely to do so.

In another recent Espionage Act prosecution, federal prosecutors did not charge the journalist who received classified information from a source. In that case, James Risen, a *New York Times* writer, was given information about a Central Intelligence Agency (CIA) operation against Iran's nuclear program. When Risen included the information in a 2006 book, *State of War,* the source was prosecuted under the Espionage Act. Although Risen was subpoenaed during the investigation of his source, he has not been charged in connection with the leak. Thus, if Assange is prosecuted for the leaks, he will be able to point out this disparate treatment and claim he is being persecuted. This is not a strong legal defense, but it will make it very hard politically to charge Assange.

Prosecution of WikiLeaks under the Espionage Act would also leave the government vulnerable to a claim that it was the latest in a long line of administrations that had abused the act to suppress political opposition. Parts of the Espionage Act have been used to imprison the leader of the Socialist Party of America, to seize a film that portrayed British soldiers in a negative light, and to convict a leaflet distributor. Even if the government can convict Assange of violating the act, it is quite possible that it would rather not add imprisoning an award-winning journalist to the above list.

The CFAA outlaws a number of activities related to computer hacking. Of particular interest for a potential prosecution of WikiLeaks is 18 U.S.C. § 1030(a)(1) (2006). Specifically, this subsection forbids obtaining from a computer without authorization or in excess of authorization information that has been determined by the U.S. government to require protection against unauthorized disclosure and then willfully communicating, delivering, or transmitting that information to any person who is not entitled to receive the information; in fact, 18 U.S.C. § 371 (2011) outlaws conspiring to commit any crime against the United States. This includes conspiring to violate the CFAA. Conspiracy is punishable by up to five years in prison.

Assange did not violate the CFAA as a principle. Although Assange willfully disclosed the information he received from Manning to persons not entitled to receive the information, Assange did not access any computer without authorization or in excess of authorization to obtain the information. However, Assange may have conspired to violate the CFAA with Manning. To show that Assange conspired to violate Section 1030(a)(1), the government must prove that Assange and Manning agreed to the leak of the information before Manning accessed the computer illegally. There is no publicly available information indicating that Assange and Manning had any contact prior to Manning's access of the computers. Unless there is evidence of this that has not been released, it seems unlikely that the government can secure a CFAA conviction against Assange.

It has been suggested, however, that Assange may be vulnerable to a conspiracy charge because he actively encouraged the leaking of classified information. Conspiracy liability usually extends only to agreements to commit a specific crime and other crimes that are reasonably foreseeable consequences of the original crime. As such, a prosecution of Assange premised on the theory that he generally agreed to receive classified information is unlikely to succeed.

On the other hand, questions have been raised about whether he was perhaps more actively involved in the 2016 U.S. election leaks; and we won't know the answer to this until the various federal investigations wind up and any and all charges are made public.

Gretchen Nobahar and J. N. Manuel

Further Reading

Beauchamp, Zack. "Nigel Farage, the mind behind Brexit, is now an FBI "person of interest" in Trump-Russia," *Vox*, June 1, 2017. https://www.vox.com/world/2017/6/1/15724106/nigel-farage-trump-russia-fbi-interest

Beckett, Charlie, and James Ball. *WikiLeaks*. Cambridge. England: Polity Press, 2012.

_____. *Wikileaks: News in the Networked Era*. Cambridge, England: Polity Press, 2012.

Berg, Daniel, and Tina Klopp. *Inside Wikileaks: My Time with Julian Assange at the World's Most Dangerous Website*. New York: Crown Publishers, 2011.

The End of Secrecy: The Rise and Fall of WikiLeaks. London: Guardian, 2011.

Estulin, Daniel. *Deconstructing Wikileaks*. Chicago, IL: Trine Day, 2012.

Fowler, Andrew. *The Most Dangerous Man in the World: How One Hacker Ended Corporate and Government Secrecy Forever*. New York: Skyhorse, 2011.

Harding, Luke, and David Leigh. *Wikileak,* new. ed. London: Random House UK, 2013.

Leigh, David, and Luke Harding. *Wikileaks: Inside Julian Assange's War on Secrecy*. New York: Public Affairs, 2011.

Miguel, Rafa de, and Lucia Abellan. "Key Catalan ideologue met with Julian Assange in London," *El Pais*, November 13, 2017. https://elpais.com/elpais/2017/11/13/inenglish/1510565565_636373.html Porterfield, Jason. *Julian Assange and Wikileaks*. New York: Rosen Pubishing Group, 2013.

Reuters. "Mueller Says Searches Yielded Evidence of Stone-WikiLeaks Communications," *Reuters*, February 15, 2019. https://www.nytimes.com/reuters/2019/02/15/world/europe/15reuters-usa-trump-russia-stone-wikileaks.html

Thompson, Tamara. *WikiLeaks*. Detroit, MI: Greenhaven Press, 2012.

See also: Assange, Julian; *Bartnicki v. Vopper*; Espionage Act; First Amendment to the U.S. Constitution; Journalism and the protection of sources; Manning, Chelsea Elizabeth; News leaks; Snowden, Edward; Whistleblowers

Wikipedia

Identification: A multilingual, web-based, free-content encyclopedia project supported by the Wikimedia Foundation. This foundation administers and funds Wikipedia but does not exercise editorial control over the encyclopedia.

Wikipedia is based on a model of openly editable content. Its entries are written collaboratively by largely anonymous volunteers, who write without compensation. Anyone with Internet access can write and make changes to the entries, except in limited cases in which editing is deemed necessary, such as to prevent vandalism. Users may contribute anonymously, under a pseudonym, or, if they choose to, with their real identity.

Since it was created in 2001, Wikipedia has become one of the world's largest reference sites, with 374 million unique visitors monthly as of September 2015. Wikipedia has more than 70,000 active contributors who have written more than 35,000,000 entries in 290 languages. Each day, hundreds of thousands of users worldwide make tens of thousands of edits and create thousands of new entries at Wikipedia; individuals of all ages, cultures, and backgrounds are allowed to add or edit article prose, references, images, and other media.

At Wikipedia, the contribution is considered more important than the background of the contributor. What Wikipedia retains as an entry depends on considerations such as copyright issues and whether the entry complies with Wikipedia's policies, such as being verifiable against a published reliable source, thereby notionally excluding the bias of editors and unsupported and unreviewed research. Wikipedia also has software that allows for correction of mistakes, and many experienced editors monitor the entries to ensure the quality of the editing work. Wikipedia invites a large contributor base and attracts a large number of editors from diverse backgrounds. This allows Wikipedia to reduce greatly regional and cultural bias and largely prevents any group from censoring or imposing bias. A large, diverse number of editors also provides access and breadth on subject matter that often is otherwise inaccessible or little documented. Several editors contributing at any given moment also means that Wikipedia can add entries on significant events shortly after they occur. Like any publication, however, Wikipedia may reflect the cultural, age, socioeconomic, and other biases of its contributors.

Currently, Wikipedia is one of the most popular sites for finding information on events or people. In 2009, two German men who killed the actor Walter Sedlmayr in 1990 sued the Wikimedia Foundation (which funds and administers Wikipedia), claiming that their right to privacy was infringed by Wikipedia's inclusion of details about their crimes. The two men each received a life sentence in 1993, but one was released in 2007 and the other in 2008. The attorney representing the two ex-convicts filed lawsuits in German courts to demand that the Wikimedia Foundation remove their names from the English-language article. German Wikipedia editors had removed the killers' names from the German-language version. The lawyer for the convicts cited the suppression of publication of their names in Germany since 2006. He claimed that the German courts, including several courts of appeals, had held that his clients' names and likenesses could no longer be published in connection with Sedlmayr's death.

The debate centered on whether the individuals' German court–determined right to privacy should take preeminence over the First Amendment to the U.S. Constitution. Essentially it involved a conflict between the First Amendment, which guarantees freedom of speech, and German privacy and criminal laws, which stipulate that, after a given period, a crime is "spent" and may not be referred to by the media.

Striking a different balance than U.S. courts between the right to privacy and the public's right to know, German courts allow a convict's name to be withheld in media reports after he

or she has served his or her sentence and a set period has expired. The practice has been justified on the grounds that ex-convicts could return to society and not be publicly stigmatized for their crime. In other words, there is the belief that ex-criminals have a right to privacy, too, and a right to be left alone. The German law is based on a 1973 decision of Germany's highest court, the Federal Court of Justice, which led to German publications referring to people whose convictions are "spent" as, for example, "the perpetrator," or "Mr. G."

The American legal community generally finds the German law highly objectionable because American law holds that people must be allowed to publish truthful information about historical events and because foreign governments should not be able to censor publications in the United States. Under the American justice system, the Wikipedia article would undoubtedly receive First Amendment protection. First Amendment advocates make the "slippery slope" argument that once speech is suppressed, there is pressure to suppress still more speech.

The Wikimedia Foundation responded that it supported its German editors in removing the names of the convicts while also supporting its English-language editors in rejecting the German request. Wikipedia also noted that the ex-convicts were named in several other online sources in Germany. Because of the publicity accorded this case, the efforts of the two German plaintiffs had the opposite of the intended result of maintaining confidentiality. Instead, the controversy fed the publicity.

Despite its commitment to First Amendment freedoms, Wikipedia has restricted editing of the biographies of living individuals after instances of personal details being fabricated to create libelous misinformation. In another set of circumstances, such as when the Taliban seized a *New York Times* journalist in Afghanistan, Wikipedia founder Jimmy Wales personally asked the site's editors not to disseminate information on the incident.

Wikipedia also faced pressure to suppress reporting of stories that might cause embarrassment to prominent individuals. In 2011, Wales announced that he would resist pressure to censor Wikipedia entries in response to the success of an English "family footballer" who had received an injunction from England's High Court to enjoin the media from publicizing an alleged affair with the *Big Brother* contestant Imogen Thomas. Wales said that, as an encyclopedia, Wikipedia seeks to document facts obtained from reputable sources and should not be prevented from recording facts. Wales criticized the injunctions, claiming them to be an infringement of the right to free speech. He added that the public should object to the rich and powerful being able to censor media publications whenever they wanted.

Not all of Wikipedia's privacy clashes occurred overseas. The most prominent of these cases took place in the United States. Among the documents revealed by the whistleblower Edward J. Snowden were those indicating that the National Security Agency (NSA) was surveilling Wikipedia, along with other sites, such as Gmail and Facebook. A leaked slide from a classified PowerPoint presentation stated that monitoring these sites could allow NSA analysts to learn "nearly everything a typical user does on the Internet." On March 10, 2015, the Wikimedia Foundation, along with several human rights and media organizations, responded by filing the lawsuit *Wikimedia Foundation et al. v. National Security Agency* in the U.S. District Court of Maryland, C 1.15-CVv-00662-RDB. Wikimedia said that it was suing NSA to protect the rights of the 500 million people who use Wikipedia monthly, asserting that that this was necessary in order to protect the free exchange of knowledge and ideas.

Specifically, the Wikimedia lawsuit claimed NSA mass surveillance of Internet traffic in the United States (frequently referred to as upstream surveillance) violated both the Fourth Amendment, against unreasonable searches, as well as

the First Amendment, which protects the freedom of expression. Wikimedia also argued that NSA surveillance exceeds the authority granted by the Foreign Intelligence Surveillance Act (FISA), 92 Stat. 1783 (1978), as amended by Congress in 2008. Section 702 of the FISA Amendments Act of 2008 (FAA), 122 Stat. 2436, specifically states that the "Attorney General and the Director of National Intelligence may authorize . . . the targeting of persons reasonably believed to be located outside the United States to acquire foreign intelligence information."

Most people search and read Wikipedia anonymously because an account is not needed to use the service. Many of these users prefer anonymity, especially those who work on controversial issues or who live in countries with repressive governments. User anonymity was frustrated by NSA upstream surveillance that was intercepting and searching almost all of the international text-based traffic flowing across the Internet backbone within the United States (that is, the network that connects Wikipedia with its global community of readers and editors). NSA was tracking the content of what was read or typed, as well as other information that could be linked to the person's physical location and possible identity. Wikipedia maintained that these activities are sensitive and private. They can reveal everything from a person's political and religious beliefs to sexual orientation and medical conditions.

Wikimedia asserted that it and its users were harmed because pervasive surveillance has a chilling effect. It stifles freedom of expression and the free exchange of knowledge that Wikipedia was designed to enable. Specifically, Wikimedia and the plaintiffs say that known NSA surveillance of website users in other countries is discouraging online participation and "undermines their ability to carry out activities crucial to their missions."

Wikimedia, in its lawsuit, asked the court to order NSA to end its unconstitutional dragnet surveillance of Internet traffic, basing its argument on privacy as an essential right. Wales stressed that privacy makes freedom of expression possible and sustains freedom of inquiry and association. It empowers everyone to read, write and communicate in confidence, without fear of persecution. Knowledge flourishes where privacy is protected.

Gretchen Nobahar

Further Reading

Barber, N. W. "A Right to Privacy?" In *Human Rights and Private Law: Privacy as Autonomy*. Portland, edited by Katja S. Ziegler. Portland, OR: Hart, 2007.

Fuchs, Christian. *Social Media: A Critical Introduction*. Thousand Oaks, CA: Sage, 2014.

Greenstein, Shane M., and Feng Zhu. *Collective Intelligence and Neutral Point of View: The Case of Wikipedia*. Cambridge, MA: National Bureau of Economic Research, 2012.

Lee, Newton. *Facebook Nation: Total Information Awareness*, 2d ed. New York: Springer Science + Business Media, 2014.

Lih, Andrew. *The Wikipedia Revolution: How a Bunch of Nobodies Created the World's Greatest Encyclopedia*. New York: Hyperion, 2009.

Palma, Paul. *Computers in Society 09/10*; 15th ed. New York: McGraw-Hill Irwin, 2010. Reagle, Joseph Michael. *Good Faith Collaboration: The Culture of Wikipedia*. Cambridge, MA: MIT Press, 2010.

Rocha, Álvaro, Ana Maria Correa, Tom Wilson, and Karl A. Stroetmann. *Advances in Information Systems and Technologies*. Berlin: Springer, 2013.

Schwartz, John. "Two German Killers Demanding Anonymity Sue Wikipedia's Parent." *New York Times*, November 12, 2009.

See also: Anonymity and anonymizers; First Amendment to the U.S. Constitution; Foreign Intelligence Surveillance Act (FISA); Fourth Amendment to the U.S. Constitution; National Security Agency (NSA); Right to be forgotten; Snowden, Edward Joseph; Whistleblowers

Wilson v. Layne, 526 U.S. 603 (1999)

Identification: A unanimous decision as to Parts I and II, and 8–1 with respect to Part III, with a majority opinion by Chief Justice Rehnquist, in which the U.S. Supreme Court ruled that bringing reporters into a home during the attempted execution of an arrest warrant violated the Fourth Amendment. The Court also held that, notwithstanding the constitutional violation, the officers involved in the case were entitled to qualified immunity.

In this case, the U.S. Attorney General executed a national fugitive apprehension program in which the U.S. Marshals worked with state and local police forces to apprehend dangerous criminals. One such identified fugitive was Dominic Wilson, who had violated his probation on previous felony charges of robbery, theft, and assault. Police computers listed Wilson's residence at an address in Rockville, Maryland, although later it was determined to be the address of his parents.

Marshals and local police officers assembled to execute the warrants issued against Wilson, and they were accompanied by a reporter and photographer from the *Washington Post*. The media representatives were invited at the Marshals' request as part of their ride-along policy. In the early morning, officers entered the Rockville dwelling in search of Wilson. Wilson's parents, Charles and Geraldine Wilson, were still in bed when officers entered their home. Charles ran into the living room and became irate when he discovered armed police officers had entered his home. Geraldine then entered the living room and observed Charles being subdued and restrained. When the officers discovered that Dominic was not in the home, they departed. During the confrontation, the *Washington Post* photographer took several pictures of the event and the reporter observed the event while in the Wilsons' living room.

Charles and Geraldine Wilson subsequently sued law enforcement officials for money damages under *Bivens v. Six Unknown Fed. Narcotics Agents* (403 U.S. 388 (1971)), and 42 U.S.C. § 1983. Under *Bivens* and 42 U.S.C. § 1983, individuals have a right to sue state and federal government officials for alleged violations of their constitutional rights. The Wilsons argued that the officers' conduct in bringing members of the media to observe and record the attempted execution of Dominic Wilson's arrest warrant violated their Fourth Amendment rights. The district court agreed and denied the government's motion for summary judgment on the basis of qualified immunity. Qualified immunity typically shields government officials from liability for constitutional violations if the violation was not clearly established at the time of the violation.

On appeal, a divided U.S. Court of Appeals for the Fourth Circuit concluded that, because no court had held that media presence during a police entry into a residence violated the Fourth Amendment, the right allegedly violated by the Wilsons was not "clearly established," and thus the government officials were entitled to qualified immunity.

Recognizing a split among the circuit courts on this issue, the U.S. Supreme Court agreed to review the case. First, the Supreme Court acknowledged that government officials performing discretionary functions are generally granted qualified immunity and are thus protected from liability for civil damages insofar as their conduct does not violate clearly established statutory or constitutional rights of which a reasonable person would have known.

The Court explained that the first step in evaluating qualified immunity is to determine whether the plaintiff has alleged the deprivation of an actual constitutional right. If so, the next step is to determine whether that right was clearly established at the time of the alleged constitutional violation. The Court underscored the importance of the order of these steps because deciding the constitutional question before addressing the qualified immunity question promotes clarity in legal standards for police conduct, which benefits both the government and the public.

In evaluating the alleged constitutional violation, the Court determined that the officers were authorized to enter the Wilson home to execute the arrest warrant of Dominic Wilson.

That authorization, however, did not automatically sanction the media ride-along. The Court explained that the Fourth Amendment requires that police actions in the execution of an arrest warrant must be related to the objectives of the authorized intrusion, and the presence of reporters inside the home was not related to any objectives of the duly authorized warrant.

The government argued that the reporters served several legitimate law enforcement purposes, including publicizing the government's efforts to combat crime and to facilitate accurate reporting of enforcement activities. The Court rejected this argument, stating that the claim ignores the importance of residential privacy at the core of the Fourth Amendment. In addition, generalized law enforcement objectives do not trump the Fourth Amendment. Justice Rehnquist also noted that the possibility of "good public relations" is simply not enough to justify the ride-along intrusion into a private home. The Court concluded that there was no direct relation between media presence and the constitutional justification for officers to intrude into the home in the execution of an arrest warrant.

The government further argued that the presence of third parties could serve to minimize police misconduct and to protect suspects. Although Chief Justice Rehnquist acknowledged that police officers could videotape home entries as part of a "quality control" effort, that possibility was significantly different from the media presence in this case. Here, private journalists were acting for private purposes.

Thus, the Court held that it is a violation of the Fourth Amendment for officers to bring members of the media or other third parties into a home during the execution of a warrant when the presence of the third parties does not aid in the execution of the warrant.

The Supreme Court next assessed whether the Wilsons' Fourth Amendment rights were clearly established at the time of the search. The Court explained that "clearly established" means that the contours of the right must be sufficiently clear that a reasonable officer would understand that what he was doing violated that right. Here, the appropriate question is whether reasonable officers could have believed that bringing members of the media into a home during the execution of an arrest warrant was lawful, in light of clearly established law and the information possessed by the officers.

First, Chief Justice Rehnquist explained that the constitutional question presented was not an "open and shut case." The officers here had a warrant to enter the home and to arrest Dominic, and it was not obvious to them that inviting media representatives violated general Fourth Amendment principles. Second, at the time of the search, no judicial opinions had held that media ride-alongs were unlawful. Third, the officers in this case relied on institutional policies that explicitly contemplated that media could enter private homes as part of the fugitive apprehension program. Thus, because the state of the law concerning third parties accompanying police on home entries was undeveloped, it was not unreasonable for law enforcement officers to rely on their formal ride-along policies.

Ultimately, the Court held that it was not unreasonable for a police officer to have believed that bringing media observers during the execution of an arrest warrant was lawful. Accordingly, the judgment of the Court of Appeals was affirmed.

Justice John Paul Stevens dissented in part from the majority opinion. Justice Stevens agreed with the majority that a Fourth Amendment violation occurred, but he objected to the majority's holding that the officers were entitled to qualified immunity. Justice Stevens believed that a homeowner's right to protection against this type of trespass was clearly established long before the violation in this case occurred.

Ethan P. Fallon

Further Reading

Ackerman, Caryn J. "Fairness or Fiction: Striking a Balance between the Goals of S 1983 and the Policy Concerns Motivating Qualified Immunity." *Oregon Law Review* 85 (2006): 1027–1062.

Blum, Karen, et. al. "Qualified Immunity Developments: Not Much Hope Left for Plaintiffs." *Touro Law Review* 29 (2013): 633–658.

Catlett, Michael S. "Clearly Not Established: Decisional Law and the Qualified Immunity Doctrine." *Arizona Law Review* 47 (2005): 1031–1063.

Wright, Ashlea. "*Wilson v. Layne:* Increasing the Scope of the Fourth Amendment Right to Privacy." *Pepperdine Law Review* (2000): 163–193.

See also: Constitutional Law; Criminal Justice [Criminal Procedure]; Fourth Amendment to the U.S. Constitution; Supreme Court of the United States

Wiretapping

Identification: The practice of intercepting others' wire, oral, or electronic communications by any means, typically without the consent or knowledge of the parties to the communications.

Since at least the mid-1880s, when telegraph and telephone communication were invented, people have found ways to intercept those communications by tapping the wires that carried the signal transmissions. And before telephones and telegraphs, neighbors leaned up against neighbors' walls to listen or peered through windows to peek. That long history of wiretapping notwithstanding, American courts did not consider its legality until the 1920s, when Roy Olmstead, an alcohol bootlegger, was convicted with evidence obtained in part from a wiretap of his telephone conversations. The U.S. Supreme Court upheld the constitutionality of the Olmstead wiretap because the conversations had been intercepted by investigators without physically entering Olmstead's property. Instead, the investigators had intercepted the conversations by tapping the wires outside Olmstead's property.

In the 1930s, Congress passed the first anti-wiretapping law, making wiretapping a crime and making evidence obtained by wiretapping inadmissible in court. By the 1960s, law enforcement had thought of a new twist:

CrimethInc. sticker on a telephone warning users of phone tapping by the U.S. government. (By David Drexler.)

intercepting telephone conversations at public telephone booths by placing a transmitter that transmitted one side of the conversation to officers listening nearby. That method did not require that any wires be tapped. This issue came before the Supreme Court in the mid-1960s in *Katz v. United States,* a landmark opinion. In *Katz,* the Court held that physical intrusion into a protected space was not required to constitute wiretapping; rather, interception of communications was illegal if the speaker had a reasonable expectation that the conversation was private—the so-called objective and subjective reasonable expectation of privacy principle. That two-pronged principle, that conversations and other tangible and intangible items were private as long as the person claiming the privacy had a subjectively reasonable belief it was private and that the privacy was of a type that society would objectively deem reasonable, continued for decades.

Shortly after the *Katz* opinion, Congress enacted Title III of the Omnibus Crime Control Act of 1968, which controls at the federal level interception of wire, oral, and electronic communications. Title III provides that wiretaps must be supported by a warrant, necessity, and probable cause, and must be executed only in relation to specific predicate acts, within a limited time and topic scope, and in a manner that minimizes the likelihood of intercepting communications beyond the target of the wiretap warrant:

- Wiretaps must be authorized by a judge upon a very detailed and specific showing of facts supporting the need and justifications for the wiretap (the warrant requirement). Some wiretap warrant applications are over 200 pages long! The judge authorizing the wiretap warrant must be neutral and detached; in other words, he or she will not benefit from the wiretap and has no personal interest in the outcome of the wiretap.
- Wiretaps will be issued only if there is a showing that other investigative techniques have been tried and failed, are unlikely to be successful if attempted, or are too dangerous to try (the necessity requirement). All the findings must be supported by probable cause, that is, sufficient to lead a reasonable person in like circumstances to believe there was adequate support for the wiretap and that the wiretap was necessary (the probable cause requirement). The probable cause standard for a wiretap warrant is generally considered much more demanding than the quantum of probable cause needed to support a regular warrant or to support a person's arrest.
- Wiretaps may be granted only for use in investigating a limited number of predicate acts, that is, particular crimes (the predicate act requirement). The list of

applicable predicate acts under Title III are quite extensive and include child pornography, murder, racketeering, robbery, kidnapping, treason, riots, piracy, bribery, use of explosives, sex trafficking, weapons of mass destruction, arson, bank fraud, mail fraud, and counterfeiting. That long list notwithstanding, it was recently estimated that over 90 percent of wiretaps in the United States each year are issued in drug trafficking investigations.

- Wiretaps will be limited in time and scope consistent with the need and justification for the wiretap (the scope requirement). Indeed, wiretaps are issued for the shortest reasonable time consistent with the justifications for the wiretaps.

- Wiretaps must be attended by law enforcement officers in real time, and officers must promptly discontinue listening to each intercepted call if inculpating evidence relevant to the justification for the wiretap does not materialize in each phone call (the minimization requirement).

Once granted, wiretap warrants are often referred to as T3 (Title III) warrants. Phone company personnel who assist in setting up a wiretap may not disclose the existence or target of that wiretap under penalty of federal criminal law. Assuming the phone calls intercepted in a T3 wiretap are otherwise relevant, the calls will be admissible in court as evidence. Note that civilians cannot obtain a T3 wiretap warrant.

Wiretaps are very difficult to obtain because of the very high standards and requirements of Title III, but once obtained, they are a font of prosecution evidence in a criminal case. Indeed, wiretaps should be supremely difficult to obtain. After all, the privacy of our conversations is a right we take seriously, and allowing law enforcement to listen to our calls without limits, requirements, or a warrant is exactly the sort of government intrusion the Fourth Amendment is intended to prevent.

T3 wiretaps are often executed in a listening center staffed by law enforcement officers around the clock. The minimization requirement renders wiretaps very personnel-intensive. The officers listen to intercepted calls in real time—as they are intercepted—listening for whether they must truncate the interception because nothing relevant to the investigation or the warrant has been intercepted. The officers work in shifts, each often assigned to listen to only a single line. When an investigation simultaneously taps multiple phones, the listening center is a very busy place. The listening officers write the time, date, calling phone number, dialed phone number, and topics on a tracking sheet that is passed to the listening center coordinators. Once the judge-approved deadline for the duration of the T3 wiretap has arrived, all interception ceases.

An interesting phenomenon, known as tickling the wire, occurs when officers, who are up on an active wiretap, feed critical but false information related to the crime at issue to the wiretapped persons in an effort to stimulate them to call accomplices and report that false information to them. Tickling the wire often stimulates conversations that are subsequently recorded via the T3 warrant. Whether tickling the wire is permissible has occasionally been litigated in pending criminal cases, but courts have not taken a consistent position on that issue to date.

When wiretapped evidence is offered in a criminal trial, the effect on the jury can be enormous. Although a criminal defendant cannot be compelled to take the witness stand and incriminate him- or herself, a criminal defendant can be compelled to sit at the defense table while his or her own words, on those recorded telephone calls, are played for the jury to hear. Long before those wiretapped conversations are played for the jury, however, the defendant's attorney has had an opportunity to try to suppress those recordings for lack of relevance, lack of proof of identity of the speakers, lack of adherence to the requirements of Title III, lack of proper procedures, among other challenges.

Wiretapping by law enforcement officers can be and often is conducted without any T3 warrant at all, in fact, without consulting any judge at all. If properly conducted, these warrantless wiretaps are perfectly permissible. Let's say that law enforcement officers are investigating a crime, and the victim has agreed to cooperate with the police in gathering evidence in the case. The officers ask the victim to place a call to the alleged perpetrator, and the victim agrees to do so. The victim also agrees to let the officers record both sides of the call that the victim places to the suspect. When the officers record a telephone call with the permission of at least one participant in that call, the officers need not have a T3 wiretap warrant. The officers need no wiretap at all. The logic is that no one engaged in a phone conversation with another person, even with a supposedly close friend or accomplice, has a reasonable expectation that the contents of that call will remain private. Even the best friend, spouse, or accomplice can have a change of heart and turn state's evidence at any point. Because the suspect has no reasonable expectation that the phone conversation will be private, the suspect has no Fourth Amendment right to have a warrant or probable cause support that interception. That call between the suspect and the victim, surreptitiously recorded by the police with the victim's cooperation and consent, is admissible in court against the suspect.

Of course, wiretapping is not always conducted by law enforcement officers. Rather, civilians, spouses, parents, and others sometimes set up devices to record others' conversations. Indeed, the Watergate scandal arose from an attempt to wiretap the offices of the Democratic National Committee headquarters in Washington, DC, an attempt that was later covered up by White House officials loyal to President Richard Nixon. If recorded without the permission of at least one participant in that intercepted conversation, that interception is illegal, as a violation of Title III.

But civilians can record, with impunity, any phone conversation to which they are a party. The theory is identical to the one allowing officers to have one party's consent to record a phone call. The person at the other end of a phone conversation has no reasonable expectation of privacy that the call will not be intercepted and recorded. An exception to this civilian rule applies to attorneys, whose ethical codes preclude them from recording telephone calls to which they are a party unless they give notice of the recording to the other parties to the call.

In sum, our telephone calls are private only if we have a reasonable expectation that they are private. When we place a call to or receive a call from someone we believe to be a friend, we are on notice that that person may be a false friend working with law enforcement. That is, we are aware that anyone can record their own telephone calls without notifying the other parties to the calls. Law enforcement officers can intercept and record telephone calls of others only if they have the consent of at least one party to do so or they have been granted a valid T3 wiretap warrant and abide by all its terms.

Note that Title III, by its terms, applies to wire, oral, and electronic communications. Wire communications include landline telephone calls and other communications transmitted by wires. Oral communications are conversations held by persons within hearing distance of each other. And electronic communications are those transmitted digitally or electronically, such as by cellular phone transmissions, Wi-Fi, or other similar electronic or digital means. Interception of any of these types of communications without consent of at least one party or without a T3 wiretap warrant is illegal. Any evidence seized by illegal means or beyond the scope of a T3 wiretap warrant is inadmissible and cannot be used as evidence in criminal court.

That rather exhaustive list of types of communications is, in reality, not exhaustive at all because many forms of communication do not fall within Title III's requirements. For example, if one has a conversation with another in a crowded restaurant, the parties have no reasonable expectation that the conversation will be private so that conversation is not protected from interception by Title III. Similarly, communications you transmit knowingly through a third person, such as notes on postcards or notes you hand to a third person for delivery to another, are not protected. Communications you send to multiple persons via email or text or post in public chatrooms on Twitter, Instagram, Facebook, and the like, are electronic communications, but they are not private and thus do not fall under Title III or require a wiretap warrant.

Some forms of communication are habitually nonprivate. At the most obvious extreme are cellphone calls, which cannot be completed unless the cellphone pings off a nearby cell tower. That ping tells the cellphone service provider, and anyone who asks the provider the right question, where that phone was and when, what numbers it called, what numbers called it, how long the calls lasted, and where the phone traveled from and when. Officers have increasingly used those cellphone pings, which they obtain through administrative subpoenas and stingrays (cell-site simulators controlled by law enforcement, commonly known as stingrays after the Harris Corporation's widely adopted stingray model), to track suspects in real time with no warrant, no probable cause, and no notice to the tracked person at all. In September 2015, the U.S. Department of Justice (DOJ) adopted regulations requiring its agents to obtain a warrant supported by probable cause and issued by a judge before using a cell-site simulator. Those DOJ regulations, which also allow warrantless use of cell-site simulators but only in exceptional circumstances, apply solely to DOJ's federal agents and not to state and local law enforcement officers. As the digital age progresses and makes communication simpler, it concomitantly reduces the privacy of those very communications.

Implications of these general principles are as follows:

- A suspicious girlfriend cannot lawfully set up a recording device to catch her boyfriend having a phone call with another girl.
- A nosy parent cannot record all calls placed on the family phone or on the children's cellphones.
- Any person, other than an attorney, can record any telephone call to another even without notifying the other that the call is being recorded.
- Law enforcement cannot place listening devices in or on public telephones.
- Law enforcement may record phone calls to which they are not a party only if they have a T3 wiretap warrant or consent from one of the parties to the calls.

Bear in mind that this essay was written with a focus on federal wiretap laws. State laws on interception and wiretapping of communications can very—and quite dramatically—from these federal rules. California law and the laws of up to eleven other states, for example, do not permit civilians, in most circumstances, to record a telephone call to which they are a party unless all parties to the call are notified or a distinct beep tone implicitly notifies all parties that the call is being recorded.

This essay deals with interception of the communications themselves, the words actually spoken. A much lower standard than T3 must be shown to intercept less detailed information such as numbers dialed, durations of telephone calls, and the like.

Charles E. MacLean

Further Reading

Administrative Office for the United States Courts. *Wiretap—Major Offenses for Which Court-Authorized Intercepts Were Granted—During the 12-Month Period Ending December 31, 2013.* http://www.uscourts.gov/statistics/table/wire-3/wiretap/2013/12/31.

Bronk, Chris. "Wiretapping, Surveillance, and the Internet." *SSRN Electronic Journal SSRN Journal.*

Congressional Research Service. *Privacy: An Overview of Federal Statutes Governing Wiretapping and Electronic Wiretapping Prepared for Members and Committees of Congress* (October 9, 2012). http:// congressionalresearch.com/98–326/document.php?s tudy=Privacy+An+Overview+of+Federal+Statutes +Governing+Wiretapping+and+Electronic+Eavesd ropping.

Desai, Anuj C. "Wiretapping before the Wires: The Post Office and the Birth of Communications Privacy." *Stanford Law Review* 60, no. 2 (2007).

Diffie, Whitfield, and Susan Eva Landau. *Privacy on the Line: The Politics of Wiretapping and Encryption.* Cambridge, MA: MIT Press, 1998.

"FBI Outlines a Wiretapping Future." *Network Security* 1995, no. 11 2–3.

Kravets, David. "We Don't Need No Stinking Warrant: The Disturbing, Unchecked Rise of the Administrative Subpoena." *Wired* (August 28, 2012) http://www.wired.com/2012/08/administrative-subpoenas/

Landau, Susan Eva. *Surveillance or Security?: The Risks Posed by New Wiretapping Technologies.* Cambridge, MA: MIT Press, 2010.

Norvell, Blake Covington. "The Constitution and the NSA Warrantless Wiretapping Program: A Fourth Amendment Violation?" *Yale Journal of Law & Technology* 11, no. 1 (2008).

See also: Administrative searches; Cellphones; Electronic surveillance; Fourth Amendment to the U.S. Constitution; *Katz v. United States*; *Olmstead v. United States*; Privacy laws, federal; Privacy laws, state; Smartphones; Telephones; USA PATRIOT Act

Workplace, privacy in the

Identification: Far more limited in the digital age, because interception, audio-recording, video-recording, and other electronic surveillance is easy and inexpensive for employers to conduct, and statutory and judicial protections have been glacially slow to arrive.

Lewis Maltby wrote in 2013, "The battle for workplace privacy is over; privacy lost . . . no employee has ever won a case against his or her employer for computer monitoring." Imagine all the ways employers can spy on their employees today:

- Intercept and read emails and text messages sent and received on company-provided computers and cellular telephones – both at work and while away from work – and even when those emails are sent to or from the employees' private email accounts, so long as the emails were sent or received via company computers
- Track websites visited on company-provided computers – both at work and while away from the workplace
- Install security cameras in public areas in the workplace
- Search employees when leaving work with notice and given particular missing items
- Search work lockers (with notice and proper justification)
- Search work desks and office spaces with adequate work-related justification
- Listen in on incoming and outgoing telephone calls to and from work telephones
- Test employees for drugs and alcohol pre-employment and post-employment in safety-sensitive jobs and with notice
- Require employees to submit to medical exams, psychological exams, personality tests, and polygraphs with notice and adequate work-related need
- Use key-logging software to capture employee use of work computers
- Use keycards, security fobs, thumb or iris scans, or other security approaches to track employees' comings and goings from the place of employment and even from room-to-room or wing-to-wing within the worksite
- Use GPS techniques to track the physical location of company vehicles in real time or historically

Moreover, this is a very abbreviated list. Consider the erosion of workplace privacy when the workplace involves cyber-commuting or work-from-home arrangements! All of this workplace privacy erosion can be tracked to two realities: (1) technology has enabled electronic and surveillance intrusions unimaginable just a short time ago; and (2) legislatures and courts have been slow to respond with appropriate workplace privacy protections.

Clearly, workplace surveillance of employee's computer use has exploded. According to a 2007 American Management Association study, updated through 2014, among all employers: 66% monitor employees' internet activity; 65% block access to specified websites; 45% track keystrokes, content, and time spent on work computers; 43% store and later review computer files; 10% monitor social networking site activity; 48% use video-surveillance to combat theft, sabotage, and violence; 7% use video-surveillance to monitor employee productivity; 8% use GPS to track locations of company vehicles; 3% use GPS to track physical location of work cellphones; 52% use technology to track employee location within work buildings; 2% use fingerprint scans; and less than 1% use facial recognition or iris scan equipment. These percentages will only increase as time passes.

Nor is the erosion of workplace privacy simply a matter of inconvenience for those surveilled or titillation for those conducting the surveillance. Fully 28% of employers have fired one or more workers for email misuse. Moreover, 30% of employers have fired one or more workers for internet misuse.

At first blush, one might think that governmental employers, subject as they are to the Fourth Amendment and its limits on warrantless searches, would be, if anything, even more constrained in their surveillance of employees' computer and cellphone activity than private employers. Not so fast. The leading United States Supreme Court decision on workplace privacy, *City of Ontario v. Quon*, 560 U.S. 746, was decided in 2010. In *Quon*, the employee, Jeff Quon, was a police officer for the City of Ontario, California. The police department had issued Quon and other police officers alphanumeric pagers that were capable of sending text messages. Soon, Officer Quon went over the text message limit, so city officials sought the text message transcripts from the pager service provider to ascertain whether the texts Officer Quon had sent were all work-related. Those transcripts revealed that many of Officer Quon's texts were personal, and some were sexually explicit. After that, Officer Quon was disciplined for violating police department rules regarding permissible uses for department-issued equipment. Those rules had also notified Quon in writing that pager activity could be tracked and intercepted. The police chief later informed Quon that his texts would not be audited in Quon paid the cost for any texts beyond the maximum permissible number of texts. Officer Quon sued the police department and others for violating his Fourth Amendment right to be free from unreasonable and warrantless searches and seizures by the government – his employer, the City of Ontario.

In its decision, the Supreme Court rejected Quon's Fourth Amendment claim, but in that opinion, the Supreme Court also held, Rapid changes in the dynamics of communication and information transmission are evident not just in the technology itself but in what society accepts as proper behavior . . . many employers expect or at least tolerate personal use of such equipment by employees because it often increases worker efficiency . . . [and] the law is beginning to respond to these developments, as some States have recently passed statutes requiring employers to notify employees when monitoring their electronic communications . . . . At present, it is uncertain how workplace norms, and the law's treatment of them, will evolve.

That is precisely the issue. Technology in the workplace and employers' abilities to monitor employees' use of that technology is growing rapidly, dynamically changing the way American companies conduct business, and giving companies a powerful tool they can use to discipline and terminate employees misusing company telephones, computers, and other electronic equipment. Squared off against that technological juggernaut is a legislative process and court system that move at a snail's pace, unable to keep up. The time has come for legislatures and courts to stand up and be counted. Just because employers have the ability to monitor and intercept employees' electronic communication and discipline or terminate them for it, does not mean those employers have the right to do so. Principled legislation and court rulings can restore the proper balance of workplace privacy and employees' rights.

Charles E. MacLean

Further Reading

Alderman, Ellen, and Caroline Kennedy. *The Right to Privacy*. New York: Knopf, 1995.

Espejo, Roman. *Privacy*. Detroit: Greenhaven Press, 2011.

Hudson, David L. *The Right to Privacy*. New York: Chelsea House, 2010.

Jasper, Margaret C. *Employee Rights in the Workplace*. 2nd ed. Dobbs Ferry, N.Y.: Oceana Publications, 2003.

Kennedy, Charles H. *The Business Privacy Law Handbook*. Boston: Artech House, 2008.

Lane, Frederick S. *The Naked Employee How Technology Is Compromising Workplace Privacy*. New York: AMACOM, 2003.

Nouwt, Sjaak. *Reasonable Expectations of Privacy?: Eleven Country Reports on Camera Surveillance and Workplace Privacy*. The Hague: T.M.C. Asser Press, 2005.

Stanton, Jeffrey M., and Kathryn R. Stam. *The Visible Employee Using Workplace Monitoring and Surveillance to Protect Information Assets—without Compromising Employee Privacy or Trust*. Medford, N.J.: Information Today, 2006.

See also: Privacy laws, federal; Fourth Amendment to the U.S. Constitution; Smartphones

Z

Zacchini v. Scripps-Howard Broadcasting Co., 433 U.S. 562 (1977)

Identification: A five to four decision, with a majority opinion by Justice Byron White, in which the U.S. Supreme Court reversed the Ohio Supreme Court and ruled that the First Amendment did not bar a claim for appropriation of a "right of publicity" by a performer whose "entire act" was broadcast by a television station without the performer's consent.

Justice Lewis F. Powell, in a dissent joined by Justices William J. Brennan, Jr. and Thurgood Marshall, argued that the First Amendment did bar the claim. Justice John Paul Stevens also dissented but on the grounds that the Ohio decision was based on state law, not on the First Amendment. News media activists decried the decision as opening the door to liability for factual coverage of public events.

In many respects, Zacchini was much ado about nothing, turning as it did on the unique nature of the plaintiff's act: fifteen seconds beginning with the bang of a carnival cannon and ending with a plop into a net. No published court decision before or since has presented a similar set of facts. Also, never again has the Supreme Court reviewed a case arising out of the category of invasion of privacy torts labeled "appropriation" by the Restatement of Torts 2nd and William Prosser's influential Handbook of the Law of Torts.

The case, however, is a study in the complexities of resolving invasion of privacy and other tort cases, and it served as a warning that some members of the Court felt that the press was pushing too hard for First Amendment protection in contexts the Court was not prepared to sustain.

Zacchini arose when a freelance reporter for a Cleveland television station saw Hugo Zacchini's human cannonball act at the Geauga County Fair. The Zacchini family had been in the cannonball business since the 1920s, when Edmondo Zacchini successfully constructed a pneumatic cannon, and his son Hugo and other family members, some also named Hugo, took the show on the road.

Zacchini noticed the reporter carrying a small camera and asked him not to film the performance. The reporter complied, but on instructions from his producer went back the next night and filmed the act. A fifteen-second clip capturing the act from the firing of the cannon to the landing appeared on the evening newscast with a voiceover urging viewers to see it in person.

Zacchini sued for damages of $25,000 for wrongful appropriation of the property rights in his act. Three years later, after numerous rulings from three Ohio courts and the Supreme Court, and without ever going before a jury, Zacchini accepted a settlement of $13,000, or about half his original demand.

Prior to Zacchini, the law of Ohio—its constitution, statutes, and court decisions—had little to say about the category of privacy invasion that Prosser had labeled appropriation and that included claims for taking an individual's "right to publicity." In 1956, the Ohio Supreme Court, in a case arising out of intrusive and harassing debt-collection practices, none of which could be construed as appropriation, had decided on the basis of decisions of other states that Ohio recognized a right of privacy, which the court in passing said included appropriation.

The complaint in Zacchini characterized the claim as one for appropriation, and the trial judge, while agreeing that Ohio law recognized such a claim, ruled that the First Amendment as applied in *Time, Inc. v. Hill*, 385 U.S. 374 (1967), foreclosed enforcing such a claim against the news media. The claim in *Time, Inc.*, was brought under the theory of "false light" invasion of privacy, not appropriation, and unlike the film in Zacchini, the magazine article in Time, Inc. arguably contained falsehoods. The Ohio court of appeals reversed the dismissal on the grounds that the claim was based on other Ohio theories that were not barred by the First Amendment, specifically, the common law of copyright and the ancient tort of conversion. The Ohio Supreme Court reversed the court of appeals, adopting the trial judge's view that the claim was for appropriation and that it was barred by the free speech rights of the news media. The Ohio Supreme Court, labeling the claim as one for appropriation of Zacchini's "right of publicity," reasoned that "the 'privacy' which the performer seeks is personal control over commercial display and exploitation of his personality and the exercise of his talents."

Justice White's opinion accepted the Ohio Supreme Court's decision that such a claim existed under Ohio law, but he held that the First Amendment did not bar such a claim. Much of Justice White's opinion, however, is devoted to the possibility that the Ohio Supreme Court relied on an independent Ohio doctrine, not on the First Amendment, in concluding that

the claim could not be brought against a news organization. Such a doctrine, if it existed, could be binding in Ohio even if the First Amendment did not require it. The case was sent back to the Ohio Supreme Court to allow it to clarify whether its ruling had been based on the state's own law or on the First Amendment. The Ohio Supreme Court held that Zacchini's claim was not barred by any Ohio rule and that his case could proceed to trial. Instead, the parties chose to settle the claim.

Had there been a trial, the basic premise on which the appeals court's rulings had been based—that the station had aired Zacchini's "entire act"—might have collapsed. The act began with a promotional buildup that started well before the cannon fired and continued until Zacchini climbed out of the net and took the last of many bows. As Justice White acknowledged in a footnote, a jury might well have found the news report increased, not diminished, the value of Zacchini's act.

Despite Zacchini's relative obscurity in the First Amendment canon, the very uniqueness of the fact pattern continues today to lure litigants and scholars to examine the case for assistance in shaping the legal playing field affecting celebrityhood in a world where name and face recognition often produces large fortunes. For example, Zacchini has been cited in the context of athletes whose "acts" allegedly have been appropriated in videogames and in disputes about the rights of news organizations to live-stream athletic events.

Harold W. Fuson Jr.

Further Reading

Baird, Douglas G. "Note: Human Cannonballs and the First Amendment: *Zacchini v. Scripps-Howard Broadcasting Co.*" *Stanford Law Review* 30, no. 6 (July 1978): 1185–1209. http://chicagounbound.uchicago. edu/cgi/viewcontent.cgi?article=2019&context=journal_articles.

Samuelson, Pamela. "Reviving Zacchini: Analyzing First Amendment Defenses in Right of Publicity and

Copyright Cases." *Tulane Law Review* 57, (1982): 836–929. http://scholarship.law.berkeley.edu/facpubs/1231

Smolla, Rodney A. "Court Uses Human Cannonball to Shoot Hole in Gannett's First Amendment Claim." The Media Institute, January 30, 2012. http://www.mediainstitute.org/IPI/2012/013012.php.

Volokh, Eugene. "Freedom of Speech and the Right of Publicity." *Houston Law Review* 40, no. 4 (2003): 903–930. http://www2.law.ucla.edu/volokh/publicity.pdf

See also: First Amendment to the U.S. Constitution; Invasion of privacy; Privacy laws, state; Privacy torts; Prosser, William Lloyd; Publicity, right of

Appendixes

Primary Document: The Privacy Act of 1974

prepare and execute without consideration such instruments as may be appropriate to carry out the purposes of this Act.

Approved December 31, 1974.

Public Law 93-579

December 31, 1974
[S. 3418]

AN ACT

To amend title 5, United States Code, by adding a section 552a to safeguard individual privacy from the misuse of Federal records, to provide that individuals be granted access to records concerning them which are maintained by Federal agencies, to establish a Privacy Protection Study Commission, and for other purposes.

Privacy Act of 1974.
5 USC 552a note.
Congressional findings.
5 USC 552a note.

Be it enacted by the Senate and House of Representatives of the United States of America in Congress assembled, That this Act may be cited as the "Privacy Act of 1974".

SEC. 2. (a) The Congress finds that—

(1) the privacy of an individual is directly affected by the collection, maintenance, use, and dissemination of personal information by Federal agencies;

(2) the increasing use of computers and sophisticated information technology, while essential to the efficient operations of the Government, has greatly magnified the harm to individual privacy that can occur from any collection, maintenance, use, or dissemination of personal information;

(3) the opportunities for an individual to secure employment, insurance, and credit, and his right to due process, and other legal protections are endangered by the misuse of certain information systems;

(4) the right to privacy is a personal and fundamental right protected by the Constitution of the United States; and

(5) in order to protect the privacy of individuals identified in information systems maintained by Federal agencies, it is necessary and proper for the Congress to regulate the collection, maintenance, use, and dissemination of information by such agencies.

Statement of purpose.

(b) The purpose of this Act is to provide certain safeguards for an individual against an invasion of personal privacy by requiring Federal agencies, except as otherwise provided by law, to—

(1) permit an individual to determine what records pertaining to him are collected, maintained, used, or disseminated by such agencies;

(2) permit an individual to prevent records pertaining to him obtained by such agencies for a particular purpose from being used or made available for another purpose without his consent;

(3) permit an individual to gain access to information pertaining to him in Federal agency records, to have a copy made of all or any portion thereof, and to correct or amend such records;

(4) collect, maintain, use, or disseminate any record of identifiable personal information in a manner that assures that such action is for a necessary and lawful purpose, that the information is current and accurate for its intended use, and that adequate safeguards are provided to prevent misuse of such information;

(5) permit exemptions from the requirements with respect to records provided in this Act only in those cases where there is an important public policy need for such exemption as has been determined by specific statutory authority; and

(6) be subject to civil suit for any damages which occur as a result of willful or intentional action which violates any individual's rights under this Act.

88 Stat.]   PUBLIC LAW 93-579—DEC. 31, 1974   1897

Sec. 3. Title 5, United States Code, is amended by adding after section 552 the following new section:

"§ 552a. Records maintained on individuals

5 USC 552a.

"(a) Definitions.—For purposes of this section—

"(1) the term 'agency' means agency as defined in section 552(e) of this title;

Ante, p. 1564.

"(2) the term 'individual' means a citizen of the United States or an alien lawfully admitted for permanent residence;

"(3) the term 'maintain' includes maintain, collect, use, or disseminate;

"(4) the term 'record' means any item, collection, or grouping of information about an individual that is maintained by an agency, including, but not limited to, his education, financial transactions, medical history, and criminal or employment history and that contains his name, or the identifying number, symbol, or other identifying particular assigned to the individual, such as a finger or voice print or a photograph;

"(5) the term 'system of records' means a group of any records under the control of any agency from which information is retrieved by the name of the individual or by some identifying number, symbol, or other identifying particular assigned to the individual;

"(6) the term 'statistical record' means a record in a system of records maintained for statistical research or reporting purposes only and not used in whole or in part in making any determination about an identifiable individual, except as provided by section 8 of title 13; and

"(7) the term 'routine use' means, with respect to the disclosure of a record, the use of such record for a purpose which is compatible with the purpose for which it was collected.

"(b) Conditions of Disclosure.—No agency shall disclose any record which is contained in a system of records by any means of communication to any person, or to another agency, except pursuant to a written request by, or with the prior written consent of, the individual to whom the record pertains, unless disclosure of the record would be—

"(1) to those officers and employees of the agency which maintains the record who have a need for the record in the performance of their duties;

"(2) required under section 552 of this title;

"(3) for a routine use as defined in subsection (a)(7) of this section and described under subsection (e)(4)(D) of this section;

"(4) to the Bureau of the Census for purposes of planning or carrying out a census or survey or related activity pursuant to the provisions of title 13;

"(5) to a recipient who has provided the agency with advance adequate written assurance that the record will be used solely as a statistical research or reporting record, and the record is to be transferred in a form that is not individually identifiable;

"(6) to the National Archives of the United States as a record which has sufficient historical or other value to warrant its continued preservation by the United States Government, or for evaluation by the Administrator of General Services or his designee to determine whether the record has such value;

"(7) to another agency or to an instrumentality of any governmental jurisdiction within or under the control of the United States for a civil or criminal law enforcement activity if the activity is authorized by law, and if the head of the agency or instrumentality has made a written request to the agency which maintains the record specifying the particular portion desired and the law enforcement activity for which the record is sought;

"(8) to a person pursuant to a showing of compelling circumstances affecting the health or safety of an individual if upon such disclosure notification is transmitted to the last known address of such individual;

"(9) to either House of Congress, or, to the extent of matter within its jurisdiction, any committee or subcommittee thereof, any joint committee of Congress or subcommittee of any such joint committee;

"(10) to the Comptroller General, or any of his authorized representatives, in the course of the performance of the duties of the General Accounting Office; or

"(11) pursuant to the order of a court of competent jurisdiction.

"(c) ACCOUNTING OF CERTAIN DISCLOSURES.—Each agency, with respect to each system of records under its control, shall—

"(1) except for disclosures made under subsections (b)(1) or (b)(2) of this section, keep an accurate accounting of—

"(A) the date, nature, and purpose of each disclosure of a record to any person or to another agency made under subsection (b) of this section; and

"(B) the name and address of the person or agency to whom the disclosure is made;

"(2) retain the accounting made under paragraph (1) of this subsection for at least five years or the life of the record, whichever is longer, after the disclosure for which the accounting is made;

"(3) except for disclosures made under subsection (b)(7) of this section, make the accounting made under paragraph (1) of this subsection available to the individual named in the record at his request; and

"(4) inform any person or other agency about any correction or notation of dispute made by the agency in accordance with subsection (d) of this section of any record that has been disclosed to the person or agency if an accounting of the disclosure was made.

"(d) ACCESS TO RECORDS.—Each agency that maintains a system of records shall—

Personal review.

"(1) upon request by any individual to gain access to his record or to any information pertaining to him which is contained in the system, permit him and upon his request, a person of his own choosing to accompany him, to review the record and have a copy made of all or any portion thereof in a form comprehensible to him, except that the agency may require the individual to furnish a written statement authorizing discussion of that individual's record in the accompanying person's presence;

Amendment request.

"(2) permit the individual to request amendment of a record pertaining to him and—

"(A) not later than 10 days (excluding Saturdays, Sundays, and legal public holidays) after the date of receipt of such request, acknowledge in writing such receipt; and

"(B) promptly, either—

"(i) make any correction of any portion thereof which the individual believes is not accurate, relevant, timely, or complete; or

"(ii) inform the individual of its refusal to amend the record in accordance with his request, the reason for the refusal, the procedures established by the agency for the individual to request a review of that refusal by the head of the agency or an officer designated by the head of the agency, and the name and business address of that official;

"(3) permit the individual who disagrees with the refusal of the agency to amend his record to request a review of such refusal, and not later than 30 days (excluding Saturdays, Sundays, and legal public holidays) from the date on which the individual requests such review, complete such review and make a final determination unless, for good cause shown, the head of the agency extends such 30-day period; and if, after his review, the reviewing official also refuses to amend the record in accordance with the request, permit the individual to file with the agency a concise statement setting forth the reasons for his disagreement with the refusal of the agency, and notify the individual of the provisions for judicial review of the reviewing official's determination under subsection (g)(1)(A) of this section;

Review.

"(4) in any disclosure, containing information about which the individual has filed a statement of disagreement, occurring after the filing of the statement under paragraph (3) of this subsection, clearly note any portion of the record which is disputed and provide copies of the statement and, if the agency deems it appropriate, copies of a concise statement of the reasons of the agency for not making the amendments requested, to persons or other agencies to whom the disputed record has been disclosed; and

Notation of dispute.

"(5) nothing in this section shall allow an individual access to any information compiled in reasonable anticipation of a civil action or proceeding.

"(e) AGENCY REQUIREMENTS.—Each agency that maintains a system of records shall—

"(1) maintain in its records only such information about an individual as is relevant and necessary to accomplish a purpose of the agency required to be accomplished by statute or by executive order of the President;

"(2) collect information to the greatest extent practicable directly from the subject individual when the information may result in adverse determinations about an individual's rights, benefits, and privileges under Federal programs;

"(3) inform each individual whom it asks to supply information, on the form which it uses to collect the information or on a separate form that can be retained by the individual—

"(A) the authority (whether granted by statute, or by executive order of the President) which authorizes the solicitation of the information and whether disclosure of such information is mandatory or voluntary;

"(B) the principal purpose or purposes for which the information is intended to be used;

"(C) the routine uses which may be made of the information, as published pursuant to paragraph (4)(D) of this subsection; and

"(D) the effects on him, if any, of not providing all or any part of the requested information;

"(4) subject to the provisions of paragraph (11) of this subsection, publish in the Federal Register at least annually a notice of the existence and character of the system of records, which notice shall include—

Publication in Federal Register.

"(A) the name and location of the system;

1900   PUBLIC LAW 93-579—DEC. 31, 1974   [88 STAT.

"(B) the categories of individuals on whom records are maintained in the system;

"(C) the categories of records maintained in the system;

"(D) each routine use of the records contained in the system, including the categories of users and the purpose of such use;

"(E) the policies and practices of the agency regarding storage, retrievability, access controls, retention, and disposal of the records;

"(F) the title and business address of the agency official who is responsible for the system of records;

"(G) the agency procedures whereby an individual can be notified at his request if the system of records contains a record pertaining to him;

"(H) the agency procedures whereby an individual can be notified at his request how he can gain access to any record pertaining to him contained in the system of records, and how he can contest its content; and

"(I) the categories of sources of records in the system;

"(5) maintain all records which are used by the agency in making any determination about any individual with such accuracy, relevance, timeliness, and completeness as is reasonably necessary to assure fairness to the individual in the determination;

"(6) prior to disseminating any record about an individual to any person other than an agency, unless the dissemination is made pursuant to subsection (b)(2) of this section, make reasonable efforts to assure that such records are accurate, complete, timely, and relevant for agency purposes;

"(7) maintain no record describing how any individual exercises rights guaranteed by the First Amendment unless expressly authorized by statute or by the individual about whom the record is maintained or unless pertinent to and within the scope of an authorized law enforcement activity;

"(8) make reasonable efforts to serve notice on an individual when any record on such individual is made available to any person under compulsory legal process when such process becomes a matter of public record;

Rules of conduct.

"(9) establish rules of conduct for persons involved in the design, development, operation, or maintenance of any system of records, or in maintaining any record, and instruct each such person with respect to such rules and the requirements of this section, including any other rules and procedures adopted pursuant to this section and the penalties for noncompliance;

Confidentiality of records.

"(10) establish appropriate administrative, technical, and physical safeguards to insure the security and confidentiality of records and to protect against any anticipated threats or hazards to their security or integrity which could result in substantial harm, embarrassment, inconvenience, or unfairness to any individual on whom information is maintained; and

Publication in Federal Register.

"(11) at least 30 days prior to publication of information under paragraph (4)(D) of this subsection, publish in the Federal Register notice of any new use or intended use of the information in the system, and provide an opportunity for interested persons to submit written data, views, or arguments to the agency.

"(f) AGENCY RULES.—In order to carry out the provisions of this section, each agency that maintains a system of records shall promulgate rules, in accordance with the requirements (including general notice) of section 553 of this title, which shall—

5 USC 553.

"(1) establish procedures whereby an individual can be notified in response to his request if any system of records named by the individual contains a record pertaining to him;

"(2) define reasonable times, places, and requirements for identifying an individual who requests his record or information pertaining to him before the agency shall make the record or information available to the individual;

"(3) establish procedures for the disclosure to an individual upon his request of his record or information pertaining to him, including special procedure, if deemed necessary, for the disclosure to an individual of medical records, including psychological records, pertaining to him;

"(4) establish procedures for reviewing a request from an individual concerning the amendment of any record or information pertaining to the individual, for making a determination on the request, for an appeal within the agency of an initial adverse agency determination, and for whatever additional means may be necessary for each individual to be able to exercise fully his rights under this section; and

"(5) establish fees to be charged, if any, to any individual for making copies of his record, excluding the cost of any search for and review of the record.

Fees.

The Office of the Federal Register shall annually compile and publish the rules promulgated under this subsection and agency notices published under subsection (e)(4) of this section in a form available to the public at low cost.

Publication in Federal Register.

"(g)(1) CIVIL REMEDIES.—Whenever any agency

"(A) makes a determination under subsection (d)(3) of this section not to amend an individual's record in accordance with his request, or fails to make such review in conformity with that subsection;

"(B) refuses to comply with an individual request under subsection (d)(1) of this section;

"(C) fails to maintain any record concerning any individual with such accuracy, relevance, timeliness, and completeness as is necessary to assure fairness in any determination relating to the qualifications, character, rights, or opportunities of, or benefits to the individual that may be made on the basis of such record, and consequently a determination is made which is adverse to the individual; or

"(D) fails to comply with any other provision of this section, or any rule promulgated thereunder, in such a way as to have an adverse effect on an individual,

the individual may bring a civil action against the agency, and the district courts of the United States shall have jurisdiction in the matters under the provisions of this subsection.

Jurisdiction.

"(2)(A) In any suit brought under the provisions of subsection (g)(1)(A) of this section, the court may order the agency to amend the individual's record in accordance with his request or in such other way as the court may direct. In such a case the court shall determine the matter de novo.

Amendment of record.

"(B) The court may assess against the United States reasonable attorney fees and other litigation costs reasonably incurred in any case under this paragraph in which the complainant has substantially prevailed.

"(3)(A) In any suit brought under the provisions of subsection (g)(1)(B) of this section, the court may enjoin the agency from withholding the records and order the production to the complainant of any agency records improperly withheld from him. In such a case the court shall determine the matter de novo, and may examine the contents of

Injunction.

any agency records in camera to determine whether the records or any portion thereof may be withheld under any of the exemptions set forth in subsection (k) of this section, and the burden is on the agency to sustain its action.

"(B) The court may assess against the United States reasonable attorney fees and other litigation costs reasonably incurred in any case under this paragraph in which the complainant has substantially prevailed.

Damages.

"(4) In any suit brought under the provisions of subsection (g)(1)(C) or (D) of this section in which the court determines that the agency acted in a manner which was intentional or willful, the United States shall be liable to the individual in an amount equal to the sum of—

"(A) actual damages sustained by the individual as a result of the refusal or failure, but in no case shall a person entitled to recovery receive less than the sum of $1,000; and

"(B) the costs of the action together with reasonable attorney fees as determined by the court.

"(5) An action to enforce any liability created under this section may be brought in the district court of the United States in the district in which the complainant resides, or has his principal place of business, or in which the agency records are situated, or in the District of Columbia, without regard to the amount in controversy, within two years from the date on which the cause of action arises, except that where an agency has materially and willfully misrepresented any information required under this section to be disclosed to an individual and the information so misrepresented is material to establishment of the liability of the agency to the individual under this section, the action may be brought at any time within two years after discovery by the individual of the misrepresentation. Nothing in this section shall be construed to authorize any civil action by reason of any injury sustained as the result of a disclosure of a record prior to the effective date of this section.

"(h) RIGHTS OF LEGAL GUARDIANS.—For the purposes of this section, the parent of any minor, or the legal guardian of any individual who has been declared to be incompetent due to physical or mental incapacity or age by a court of competent jurisdiction, may act on behalf of the individual.

"(i)(1) CRIMINAL PENALTIES.—Any officer or employee of an agency, who by virtue of his employment or official position, has possession of, or access to, agency records which contain individually identifiable information the disclosure of which is prohibited by this section or by rules or regulations established thereunder, and who knowing that disclosure of the specific material is so prohibited, willfully discloses the material in any manner to any person or agency not entitled to receive it, shall be guilty of a misdemeanor and fined not more than $5,000.

"(2) Any officer or employee of any agency who willfully maintains a system of records without meeting the notice requirements of subsection (e)(4) of this section shall be guilty of a misdemeanor and fined not more than $5,000.

"(3) Any person who knowingly and willfully requests or obtains any record concerning an individual from an agency under false pretenses shall be guilty of a misdemeanor and fined not more than $5,000.

5 USC 553.

"(j) GENERAL EXEMPTIONS.—The head of any agency may promulgate rules, in accordance with the requirements (including general notice) of sections 553 (b)(1), (2), and (3), (c), and (e) of this title, to exempt any system of records within the agency from any part of this section except subsections (b), (c)(1) and (2), (e)(4)(A) through

(F), (e) (6), (7), (9), (10), and (11), and (i) if the system of records is—

"(1) maintained by the Central Intelligence Agency; or

"(2) maintained by an agency or component thereof which performs as its principal function any activity pertaining to the enforcement of criminal laws, including police efforts to prevent, control, or reduce crime or to apprehend criminals, and the activities of prosecutors, courts, correctional, probation, pardon, or parole authorities, and which consists of (A) information compiled for the purpose of identifying individual criminal offenders and alleged offenders and consisting only of identifying data and notations of arrests, the nature and disposition of criminal charges, sentencing, confinement, release, and parole and probation status; (B) information compiled for the purpose of a criminal investigation, including reports of informants and investigators, and associated with an identifiable individual; or (C) reports identifiable to an individual compiled at any stage of the process of enforcement of the criminal laws from arrest or indictment through release from supervision.

At the time rules are adopted under this subsection, the agency shall include in the statement required under section 553(c) of this title, the reasons why the system of records is to be exempted from a provision of this section.

5 USC 553.

"(k) SPECIFIC EXEMPTIONS.—The head of any agency may promulgate rules, in accordance with the requirements (including general notice) of sections 553(b) (1), (2), and (3), (c), and (e) of this title, to exempt any system of records within the agency from subsections (c) (3), (d), (e) (1), (e) (4) (G), (H), and (I) and (f) of this section if the system of records is—

"(1) subject to the provisions of section 552(b) (1) of this title;

5 USC 552.

"(2) investigatory material compiled for law enforcement purposes, other than material within the scope of subsection (j) (2) of this section: *Provided, however,* That if any individual is denied any right, privilege, or benefit that he would otherwise be entitled by Federal law, or for which he would otherwise be eligible, as a result of the maintenance of such material, such material shall be provided to such individual, except to the extent that the disclosure of such material would reveal the identity of a source who furnished information to the Government under an express promise that the identity of the source would be held in confidence, or, prior to the effective date of this section, under an implied promise that the identity of the source would be held in confidence;

"(3) maintained in connection with providing protective services to the President of the United States or other individuals pursuant to section 3056 of title 18;

"(4) required by statute to be maintained and used solely as statistical records;

"(5) investigatory material compiled solely for the purpose of determining suitability, eligibility, or qualifications for Federal civilian employment, military service, Federal contracts, or access to classified information, but only to the extent that the disclosure of such material would reveal the identity of a source who furnished information to the Government under an express promise that the identity of the source would be held in confidence, or, prior to the effective date of this section, under an implied promise that the identity of the source would be held in confidence;

"(6) testing or examination material used solely to determine individual qualifications for appointment or promotion in the

Federal service the disclosure of which would compromise the objectivity or fairness of the testing or examination process; or

"(7) evaluation material used to determine potential for promotion in the armed services, but only to the extent that the disclosure of such material would reveal the identity of a source who furnished information to the Government under an express promise that the identity of the source would be held in confidence, or, prior to the effective date of this section, under an implied promise that the identity of the source would be held in confidence.

5 USC 553.

At the time rules are adopted under this subsection, the agency shall include in the statement required under section 553 (c) of this title, the reasons why the system of records is to be exempted from a provision of this section.

44 USC 3103.

"(l)(1) ARCHIVAL RECORDS.—Each agency record which is accepted by the Administrator of General Services for storage, processing, and servicing in accordance with section 3103 of title 44 shall, for the purposes of this section, be considered to be maintained by the agency which deposited the record and shall be subject to the provisions of this section. The Administrator of General Services shall not disclose the record except to the agency which maintains the record, or under rules established by that agency which are not inconsistent with the provisions of this section.

Publication in Federal Register.

"(2) Each agency record pertaining to an identifiable individual which was transferred to the National Archives of the United States as a record which has sufficient historical or other value to warrant its continued preservation by the United States Government, prior to the effective date of this section, shall, for the purposes of this section, be considered to be maintained by the National Archives and shall not be subject to the provisions of this section, except that a statement generally describing such records (modeled after the requirements relating to records subject to subsections (e)(4)(A) through (G) of this section) shall be published in the Federal Register.

"(3) Each agency record pertaining to an identifiable individual which is transferred to the National Archives of the United States as a record which has sufficient historical or other value to warrant its continued preservation by the United States Government, on or after the effective date of this section, shall, for the purposes of this section, be considered to be maintained by the National Archives and shall be exempt from the requirements of this section except subsections (e)(4) (A) through (G) and (e)(9) of this section.

"(m) GOVERNMENT CONTRACTORS.—When an agency provides by a contract for the operation by or on behalf of the agency of a system of records to accomplish an agency function, the agency shall, consistent with its authority, cause the requirements of this section to be applied to such system. For purposes of subsection (i) of this section any such contractor and any employee of such contractor, if such contract is agreed to on or after the effective date of this section, shall be considered to be an employee of an agency.

"(n) MAILING LISTS.—An individual's name and address may not be sold or rented by an agency unless such action is specifically authorized by law. This provision shall not be construed to require the withholding of names and addresses otherwise permitted to be made public.

Notice to Congress and OMB.

"(o) REPORT ON NEW SYSTEMS.—Each agency shall provide adequate advance notice to Congress and the Office of Management and Budget of any proposal to establish or alter any system of records in order to permit an evaluation of the probable or potential effect of such proposal on the privacy and other personal or property rights of individuals or the disclosure of information relating to such individuals, and its effect on the preservation of the constitutional principles of federalism and separation of powers.

"(p) Annual Report.—The President shall submit to the Speaker of the House and the President of the Senate, by June 30 of each calendar year, a consolidated report, separately listing for each Federal agency the number of records contained in any system of records which were exempted from the application of this section under the provisions of subsections (j) and (k) of this section during the preceding calendar year, and the reasons for the exemptions, and such other information as indicates efforts to administer fully this section.

    Report to Speaker of the House and President of the Senate.

(q) Effect of Other Laws.—No agency shall rely on any exemption contained in section 552 of this title to withhold from an individual any record which is otherwise accessible to such individual under the provisions of this section.".

    5 USC 552.

Sec. 4. The chapter analysis of chapter 5 of title 5, United States Code, is amended by inserting:

"552a. Records about individuals."

immediately below:

"552. Public information; agency rules, opinions, orders, and proceedings.".

Sec. 5. (a)(1) There is established a Privacy Protection Study Commission (hereinafter referred to as the "Commission") which shall be composed of seven members as follows:

    Privacy Protection Study Commission. Establishment. 5 USC 552a note. Membership.

    (A) three appointed by the President of the United States,

    (B) two appointed by the President of the Senate, and

    (C) two appointed by the Speaker of the House of Representatives.

Members of the Commission shall be chosen from among persons who, by reason of their knowledge and expertise in any of the following areas—civil rights and liberties, law, social sciences, computer technology, business, records management, and State and local government—are well qualified for service on the Commission.

(2) The members of the Commission shall elect a Chairman from among themselves.

(3) Any vacancy in the membership of the Commission, as long as there are four members in office, shall not impair the power of the Commission but shall be filled in the same manner in which the original appointment was made.

    Vacancies.

(4) A quorum of the Commission shall consist of a majority of the members, except that the Commission may establish a lower number as a quorum for the purpose of taking testimony. The Commission is authorized to establish such committees and delegate such authority to them as may be necessary to carry out its functions. Each member of the Commission, including the Chairman, shall have equal responsibility and authority in all decisions and actions of the Commission, shall have full access to all information necessary to the performance of their functions, and shall have one vote. Action of the Commission shall be determined by a majority vote of the members present. The Chairman (or a member designated by the Chairman to be acting Chairman) shall be the official spokesman of the Commission in its relations with the Congress, Government agencies, other persons, and the public, and, on behalf of the Commission, shall see to the faithful execution of the administrative policies and decisions of the Commission, and shall report thereon to the Commission from time to time or as the Commission may direct.

1906   PUBLIC LAW 93-579—DEC. 31, 1974   [88 Stat.

(5) (A) Whenever the Commission submits any budget estimate or request to the President or the Office of Management and Budget, it shall concurrently transmit a copy of that request to Congress.

(B) Whenever the Commission submits any legislative recommendations, or testimony, or comments on legislation to the President or Office of Management and Budget, it shall concurrently transmit a copy thereof to the Congress. No officer or agency of the United States shall have any authority to require the Commission to submit its legislative recommendations, or testimony, or comments on legislation, to any officer or agency of the United States for approval, comments, or review, prior to the submission of such recommendations, testimony, or comments to the Congress.

(b) The Commission shall—

(1) make a study of the data banks, automated data processing programs, and information systems of governmental, regional, and private organizations, in order to determine the standards and procedures in force for the protection of personal information; and

(2) recommend to the President and the Congress the extent, if any, to which the requirements and principles of section 552a of title 5, United States Code, should be applied to the information practices of those organizations by legislation, administrative action, or voluntary adoption of such requirements and principles, and report on such other legislative recommendations as it may determine to be necessary to protect the privacy of individuals while meeting the legitimate needs of government and society for information.

(c) (1) In the course of conducting the study required under subsection (b) (1) of this section, and in its reports thereon, the Commission may research, examine, and analyze—

(A) interstate transfer of information about individuals that is undertaken through manual files or by computer or other electronic or telecommunications means;

(B) data banks and information programs and systems the operation of which significantly or substantially affect the enjoyment of the privacy and other personal and property rights of individuals;

(C) the use of social security numbers, license plate numbers, universal identifiers, and other symbols to identify individuals in data banks and to gain access to, integrate, or centralize information systems and files; and

(D) the matching and analysis of statistical data, such as Federal census data, with other sources of personal data, such as automobile registries and telephone directories, in order to reconstruct individual responses to statistical questionnaires for commercial or other purposes, in a way which results in a violation of the implied or explicitly recognized confidentiality of such information.

(2)(A) The Commission may include in its examination personal information activities in the following areas: medical; insurance; education; employment and personnel; credit, banking and financial institutions; credit bureaus; the commercial reporting industry; cable television and other telecommunications media; travel, hotel and entertainment reservations; and electronic check processing.

(B) The Commission shall include in its examination a study of—

(i) whether a person engaged in interstate commerce who maintains a mailing list should be required to remove an individual's name and address from such list upon request of that individual;

(ii) whether the Internal Revenue Service should be prohibited from transfering individually indentifiable data to other agencies and to agencies of State governments;

(iii) whether the Federal Government should be liable for general damages incurred by an individual as the result of a willful or intentional violation of the provisions of sections 552a (g) (1) (C) or (D) of title 5, United States Code; and

Ante, p. 1897.

(iv) whether and how the standards for security and confidentiality of records required under section 552a (e) (10) of such title should be applied when a record is disclosed to a person other than an agency.

(C) The Commission may study such other personal information activities necessary to carry out the congressional policy embodied in this Act, except that the Commission shall not investigate information systems maintained by religious organizations.

Religious organizations, exception.

(3) In conducting such study, the Commission shall—

Guidelines for study.

(A) determine what laws, Executive orders, regulations, directives, and judicial decisions govern the activities under study and the extent to which they are consistent with the rights of privacy, due process of law, and other guarantees in the Constitution;

(B) determine to what extent governmental and private information systems affect Federal-State relations or the principle of separation of powers;

(C) examine the standards and criteria governing programs, policies, and practices relating to the collection, soliciting, processing, use, access, integration, dissemination, and transmission of personal information; and

(D) to the maximum extent practicable, collect and utilize findings, reports, studies, hearing transcripts, and recommendations of governmental, legislative and private bodies, institutions, organizations, and individuals which pertain to the problems under study by the Commission.

(d) In addition to its other functions the Commission may—

(1) request assistance of the heads of appropriate departments, agencies, and instrumentalities of the Federal Government, of State and local governments, and other persons in carrying out its functions under this Act;

(2) upon request, assist Federal agencies in complying with the requirements of section 552a of title 5, United States Code;

(3) determine what specific categories of information, the collection of which would violate an individual's right of privacy, should be prohibited by statute from collection by Federal agencies; and

(4) upon request, prepare model legislation for use by State and local governments in establishing procedures for handling, maintaining, and disseminating personal information at the State and local level and provide such technical assistance to State and local governments as they may require in the preparation and implementation of such legislation.

(e) (1) The Commission may, in carrying out its functions under this section, conduct such inspections, sit and act at such times and places, hold such hearings, take such testimony, require by subpena the attendance of such witnesses and the production of such books, records, papers, correspondence, and documents, administer such oaths, have such printing and binding done, and make such expenditures as the Commission deems advisable. A subpena shall be issued only upon an affirmative vote of a majority of all members of the Commission. Subpenas shall be issued under the signature of the Chairman or any member of the Commission designated by the Chairman and shall be served by any person designated by the Chairman or any such member. Any member of the Commission may administer oaths or affirmations to witnesses appearing before the Commission.

(2) (A) Each department, agency, and instrumentality of the executive branch of the Government is authorized to furnish to the Commission, upon request made by the Chairman, such information, data, reports and such other assistance as the Commission deems necessary

Reports, transmittal to Commission. *Ante*, p. 1897.

to carry out its functions under this section. Whenever the head of any such department, agency, or instrumentality submits a report pursuant to section 552a (o) of title 5, United States Code, a copy of such report shall be transmitted to the Commission.

(B) In carrying out its functions and exercising its powers under this section, the Commission may accept from any such department, agency, independent instrumentality, or other person any individually indentifiable data if such data is necessary to carry out such powers and functions. In any case in which the Commission accepts any such information, it shall assure that the information is used only for the purpose for which it is provided, and upon completion of that purpose such information shall be destroyed or returned to such department, agency, independent instrumentality, or person from which it is obtained, as appropriate.

(3) The Commission shall have the power to——

(A) appoint and fix the compensation of an executive director, and such additional staff personnel as may be necessary, without regard to the provisions of title 5, United States Code, governing appointments in the competitive service, and without regard

5 USC 5101, 5331.

to chapter 51 and subchapter III of chapter 53 of such title relating to classification and General Schedule pay rates, but at rates not in excess of the maximum rate for GS–18 of the General

5 USC 5332 note.

Schedule under section 5332 of such title; and

(B) procure temporary and intermittent services to the same extent as is authorized by section 3109 of title 5, United States Code.

The Commission may delegate any of its functions to such personnel of the Commission as the Commission may designate and may authorize such successive redelegations of such functions as it may deem desirable.

(4) The Commission is authorized—

Rules and regulations.

(A) to adopt, amend, and repeal rules and regulations governing the manner of its operations, organization, and personnel;

(B) to enter into contracts or other arrangements or modifications thereof, with any government, any department, agency, or independent instrumentality of the United States, or with any person, firm, association, or corporation, and such contracts or other arrangements, or modifications thereof, may be entered into without legal consideration, without performance or other bonds, and without regard to section 3709 of the Revised Statutes, as amended (41 U.S.C. 5);

(C) to make advance, progress, and other payments which the Commission deems necessary under this Act without regard to the provisions of section 3648 of the Revised Statutes, as amended (31 U.S.C. 529); and

(D) to take such other action as may be necessary to carry out its functions under this section.

(f)(1) Each [the] member of the Commission who is an officer or employee of the United States shall serve without additional compensation, but shall continue to receive the salary of his regular position when engaged in the performance of the duties vested in the Commission.

(2) A member of the Commission other than one to whom paragraph (1) applies shall receive per diem at the maximum daily rate for GS–18 of the General Schedule when engaged in the actual performance of the duties vested in the Commission.

(3) All members of the Commission shall be reimbursed for travel, subsistence, and other necessary expenses incurred by them in the performance of the duties vested in the Commission.

(g) The Commission shall, from time to time, and in an annual report, report to the President and the Congress on its activities in carrying out the provisions of this section. The Commission shall make a final report to the President and to the Congress on its findings pursuant to the study required to be made under subsection (b)(1) of this section not later than two years from the date on which all of the members of the Commission are appointed. The Commission shall cease to exist thirty days after the date on which its final report is submitted to the President and the Congress.

(h)(1) Any member, officer, or employee of the Commission, who by virtue of his employment or official position, has possession of, or access to, agency records which contain individually identifiable information the disclosure of which is prohibited by this section, and who knowing that disclosure of the specific material is so prohibited, willfully discloses the material in any manner to any person or agency not entitled to receive it, shall be guilty of a misdemeanor and fined not more than $5,000.

(2) Any person who knowingly and willfully requests or obtains any record concerning an individual from the Commission under false pretenses shall be guilty of a misdemeanor and fined not more than $5,000.

Sec. 6. The Office of Management and Budget shall—

(1) develop guidelines and regulations for the use of agencies in implementing the provisions of section 552a of title 5, United States Code, as added by section 3 of this Act; and

(2) provide continuing assistance to and oversight of the implementation of the provisions of such section by agencies.

Sec. 7. (a)(1) It shall be unlawful for any Federal, State or local government agency to deny to any individual any right, benefit, or privilege provided by law because of such individual's refusal to disclose his social security account number.

(2) the provisions of paragraph (1) of this subsection shall not apply with respect to—

(A) any disclosure which is required by Federal statute, or

(B) the disclosure of a social security number to any Federal, State, or local agency maintaining a system of records in existence and operating before January 1, 1975, if such disclosure was required under statute or regulation adopted prior to such date to verify the identity of an individual.

(b) Any Federal, State, or local government agency which requests an individual to disclose his social security account number shall inform that individual whether that disclosure is mandatory or voluntary, by what statutory or other authority such number is solicited, and what uses will be made of it.

Marginal notes:

Compensation.

Per diem.

5 USC 5332 note.

Travel expenses.

Report to President and Congress.

Penalties.

5 USC 552a note.

Ante, p. 1897.

5 USC 552a note.

1910   PUBLIC LAW 93-580—JAN. 2, 1975   [88 Stat.

Effective date.
5 USC 552a
note.

SEC. 8. The provisions of this Act shall be effective on and after the date of enactment, except that the amendments made by sections 3 and 4 shall become effective 270 days following the day on which this Act is enacted.

Appropriation.
5 USC 552a
note.

SEC. 9. There is authorized to be appropriated to carry out the provisions of section 5 of this Act for fiscal years 1975, 1976, and 1977 the sum of $1,500,000, except that not more than $750,000 may be expended during any such fiscal year.

Approved December 31, 1974.

Public Law 93-580

January 2, 1975
[S. J. Res. 133]

JOINT RESOLUTION

To provide for the establishment of the American Indian Policy Review Commission.

CONGRESSIONAL FINDINGS

25 USC 174
note.

The Congress, after careful review of the Federal Government's historical and special legal relationship with American Indian people, finds that—

(a) the policy implementing this relationship has shifted and changed with changing administrations and passing years, without apparent rational design and without a consistent goal to achieve Indian self-sufficiency;

(b) there has been no general comprehensive review of conduct of Indian affairs by the United States nor a coherent investigation of the many problems and issues involved in the conduct of Indian affairs since the 1928 Meriam Report conducted by the Institute for Government Research; and

(c) in carrying out its responsibilities under its plenary power over Indian affairs, it is imperative that the Congress now cause such a comprehensive review of Indian affairs to be conducted.

DECLARATION OF PURPOSE

Congress declares that it is timely and essential to conduct a comprehensive review of the historical and legal developments underlying the Indians' unique relationship with the Federal Government in order to determine the nature and scope of necessary revisions in the formulation of policies and programs for the benefit of Indians.

American Indian Policy Review Commission.
Establishment.
25 USC 174
note.
Membership.

Resolved by the Senate and House of Representatives of the United States of America in Congress assembled, That—

(a) In order to carry out the purposes described in the preamble hereof and as further set out herein, there is hereby created the American Indian Policy Review Commission, hereinafter referred to as the "Commission".

(b) The Commission shall be composed of eleven members, as follows:

(1) three Members of the Senate appointed by the President pro tempore of the Senate, two from the majority party and one from the minority party;

(2) three Members of the House of Representatives appointed by the Speaker of the House of Representatives, two from the majority party and one from the minority party; and

(3) five Indian members as provided in subsection (c) of this section.

Glossary

Acquittal – A jury verdict that a criminal defendant is not guilty, or the finding of a judge that the evidence is insufficient to support a conviction.

Add-on – A supplement to a piece of software that gives an added layer of functionality: for example, add-ons in Mozilla Firefox can allow the user to take pictures of the screen or remove advertisements.

Address book – Part of the user's email software where the user stores details of friends' and contacts' e-mail addresses so the user don't have to remember them.

Admissible – A term used to describe evidence that may be considered by a jury or judge in civil and criminal cases. Adobe Flash – Creates and plays interactive videos, games and other multimedia items on the Internet. The user may need to install a plug-in to view Flash content on the user's browser.

Adware – A form of spyware which installs programs which generate advertising on the user's computer (often in the form of pop-up windows).

Affiant – The person who makes and subscribes (signs) an affidavit.

Affidavit – 1. A written or printed statement made under oath. 2. A voluntary, written, or printed declaration of facts, confirmed by oath of the party making it before a person with authority to administer the oath.

Affirmation – A solemn and formal declaration that an affidavit is true. This is substituted for an oath in certain cases.

Affirmative defense – A defense raised in a responsive pleading (answer) relating a new matter as a defense to the complaint; affirmative defenses might include contributory negligence or estopped in civil actions; in criminal cases insanity, duress, or self-defense might be used.

Affirmed – In the practice of the court of appeals, it means that the court of appeals has concluded that the lower court decision is correct and will stand as rendered by the lower court.

Alien – A foreign-born person who has not qualified as a citizen of the country. Allegation – A statement of the issues in a written document (pleading or "information") which a person is prepared to prove in court.

Alteration – Changing or making different.

Alternative Dispute Resolution – Settling a dispute without a full, formal trial. Methods include mediation, conciliation, arbitration, and settlement, among others.

America Bar Association – A national association of lawyers whose primary purpose is improvement of lawyers and the administration of justice.

Alternative dispute resolution (ADR) – A procedure for settling a dispute outside the courtroom. Most forms of ADR are not binding, and involve referral of the case to a neutral party such as an arbitrator or mediator.

Amicus curiae – Latin for "friend of the court." It is advice formally offered to the court in a brief filed by an entity interested in, but not a party to, the case.

Android – An operating system developed by Google for mobile phones and other hand-held devices.

Animated GIF – Short for 'Graphics Interchange Format', a GIF is a type of image file. When it is animated it might blink, flash or have moving elements.

Answer – The formal written statement by a defendant in a lawsuit that answers the allegations stated in the complaint.

Answers to Interrogatories – A formal written statement by a party to a lawsuit which answers each question or interrogatory propounded by the other party. These answers must be acknowledged before a notary public or other person authorized to take acknowledgments.

Anti-spyware – Anti-spyware software helps stop malicious programs stealing confidential information from the user's computer.

Anti-virus – Security software that helps protect the user's computer from viruses spread online. AOL – Formerly known as American Online, this company used to be the world's largest Internet Service Provider (ISP).

Appeal – 1. A proceeding brought to a higher court to review a lower court's decision. 2. A request made after a trial by a party that has lost on one or more issues that a higher court review the decision to determine if it was correct. To make such a request is "to appeal" or "to take an appeal." One who appeals is called the "appellant;" the other party is the "appellee."

Appearance – The act of coming into court as a party to a suit either in person or through an attorney. Appendix – Supplementary materials added to the end of a document.

Appellate – About appeals; an appellate court has the power to review the judgment of a lower court (trial court) or tribunal. For example, the U.S. circuit courts of appeals review the decisions of the U.S. district courts.

Appellate Court – A court having jurisdiction to hear appeals and review a trial court's procedure.

Appellant – The party who appeals a district court's decision, usually seeking reversal of that decision.

Appellate Court – A court having jurisdiction to hear appeals and review a trial court's procedure.

Appellee – The party against whom an appeal is taken.

Application – Another word for a computer program. For example, Microsoft Word (which is used for creating text documents) is a word processing application.

Arbitration – The hearing of a dispute by an impartial third person or persons (chose by the parties), whose award the parties agree to accept.

Arbitrator – A private, disinterested person chosen by the parties in arbitration to hear evidence concerning the dispute and to make an award based on the evidence.

Archive – The place on a website where the user fined old news, articles, stories etc.

Arraignment – 1. The hearing at which the accused is brought before the court to plead to the criminal charge in the indictment or information filed. He or she may plead "guilty," "not guilty," or where permitted under the law "nolo contender."
2. A proceeding in which a criminal defendant is brought into court, told of the charges in an indictment or information, and asked to plead guilty or not guilty.

Article III judge – A federal judge who is appointed for life, during "good behavior," under Article III of the Constitution. Article III judges are nominated by the President and confirmed by the Senate.

Assets – Property of all kinds, including real and personal, tangible and intangible. Assume – An agreement to continue performing duties under a contract or lease.

B

Back up – To save files to a CD or USB drive so that they are kept in multiple places.

Bail – The release, prior to trial, of a person accused of a crime, under specified conditions designed to assure that person's appearance in court when required. Also can refer to the amount of bond money posted as a financial condition of pretrial release.

Bandwidth – The amount of data that can be carried per second by the user's Internet connection. Usually measured in kilobytes per second (kBps).

Bankruptcy – A legal procedure for dealing with debt problems of individuals and businesses; specifically, a case filed under one of the chapters of title 11 of the United States Code (the Bankruptcy Code).

Banner – A rectangular shaped advert or heading normally at the top of a web page.

Baud rate – The speed at which the user's modem can transmit and receive information. Nowadays it's more usual to use the term bps (bits per second) or Bps (bytes per second).

Bench – the seat occupied by the judge. More broadly, the court itself.

Bench trial – A trial without a jury, in which the judge serves as the fact-finder.

Blog – Short for 'weblog', a blog is an online personal diary with thoughts and opinions on life as well as links to other websites the author likes.

Booking – The process of photographing, fingerprinting, and recording identifying data of a suspect. This process generally follows an arrest.

Breach – The breaking or violating of a law, right, or duty, either by commission or omission. The failure of one party to carry out any condition of a contract.

Breach of contract – An unjustified failure to perform when performance is due.

Brief – 1. A written statement submitted in a trial or appellate proceeding that explains one side's legal and factual arguments.
2. A written argument by counsel arguing a case, which contains a summary of the facts of the case, pertinent laws, and an argument of how the law applies to the fact situation. Also called a memorandum of law.

Broadband – A permanent high-speed Internet connection. It receives digital information about 100 times faster than an old dial up modem and is always on.

Browser – A software program that allows the user to view files (including web pages, PDFs, images, video and audio) over the Internet.

Burden of proof – The duty to prove disputed facts. In civil cases, a plaintiff generally has the burden of proving his or her case. In criminal cases, the government has the burden of proving the defendant's guilt. In the law of evidence, the necessity or duty of affirmatively proving a fact or facts in dispute on an issue raised between the parties in a lawsuit. The responsibility of proving a point (the burden of proof). It deals with which side must establish a point or points.

Byte – One of the smallest units that data are able to be measured in. Usually, a byte consists of eight 'bits'. A byte is generally measured by the amount of data required to save just one character of text.

C

Cable – a wire insulated with plastic that is used to transfer electricity or information. Also a type of television service that is transmitted via a physical cable into televisions.

Capital crime – A crime punishable by death.

Capacity – Having legal authority or mental ability. Being of sound mind.

Caption – Heading or introductory party of a pleading.

Case file – A complete collection of every document filed in court in a case.

Case law – The law as established in previous court decisions. A synonym for legal precedent. Law established by previous decisions of appellate courts, particularly the United States Supreme Court or state Supreme Courts.

Cases – General term for an action, cause, suit, or controversy, at law or in equity; questions contested before a court of justice.

Cause – A lawsuit, litigation, or action. Any questions, civil or criminal, litigated or contested before a court of justice.

Cause of action – 1. A legal claim. 2. The fact or facts which give a person a right to relief in court.

Certification – 1. Written attestation. 2. Authorized declaration verifying that an instrument is a true and correct copy of the original.

Chat site – A website that allows people to send each other messages in real-time, without having to download any instant messaging software to their computers.

Chip – A small computer component (also known as a microchip) which processes information.

Class action – A lawsuit brought by one or more persons on behalf of a larger group, or class, of individuals or other entities sue on behalf of the entire class. The district court must find that the claims of the class members contain questions of law or fact in common before the lawsuit can proceed as a class action.

Clear and convincing evidence – Standard of proof commonly used in civil lawsuits and in regulatory agency cases. It governs the amount of proof that must be offered in order for the plaintiff to win the case.

Clerk of court – The court officer who oversees administrative functions, especially managing the flow of cases through the court. The clerk's office is often called a court's central nervous system.

Cloud computing – Where the data is stored and accessed by the Internet ('clouds') instead of on a computer: this can include online storage and online applications.

Cloud-based storage – When data the user upload online is kept not on single servers but across several different ones at the same time. If one of the servers breaks, less data is lost as a whole.

CNET – A news website which provides, amongst other things, reviews of computer-related products and services, as well as software downloads and technology stories.

Common law – The legal system that originated in England and is now in use in the United States, which relies on the articulation of legal principles in a historical succession of judicial decisions. Common law principles can be changed by legislation.

Complaint – A written statement that begins a civil lawsuit, in which the plaintiff details the claims against the defendant.

Consent – Agreement; voluntary acceptance of the wish of another.

Constitution – The fundamental law of a nation or state which establishes the character and basic principles of the government.

Constitutional law – Law set forth in the Constitution of the United States and the state constitutions.

Consumer bankruptcy – A bankruptcy case filed to reduce or eliminate debts that are primarily consumer debts.

Consumer debts – Debts incurred for personal, as opposed to business, needs.

Contract – An agreement between two or more people that creates an obligation to do or not to do a particular thing.

Conviction – A judgment of guilt against a criminal defendant.

Cookies – Small files automatically downloaded to a computer by websites that may have information about the user and what the user has done on that website for the website to view next time the user goes online.

Counsel – Legal advice; a term also used to refer to the lawyers in a case.

Court – Government entity authorized to resolve legal disputes. Judges sometimes use "court" to refer to themselves in the third person, as in "the court has read the briefs."

CPU – Stands for 'central processing unit', this is the 'brain' of the computer. The speed of a computer refers to the speed of the CPU.

Crash – When a computer temporarily stops working. It may pause or 'freeze' up, or tell the user to restart or quit.

Crawler – Also known as a bot or robot: a computer program which runs through the Internet collecting data, often for search engines.

Credit counseling – Generally refers to two events in individual bankruptcy cases: (1) the "individual or group briefing" from a nonprofit budget and credit counseling agency that individual debtors must attend prior to filing under any chapter of the Bankruptcy Code; and (2) the "instructional course in personal financial management" in chapters 7 and 13 that an individual debtor must complete before a discharge is entered. There are exceptions to both requirements for certain categories of debtors, exigent circumstances, or if the U.S. trustee or bankruptcy administrator have determined that there are insufficient approved credit counseling agencies available to provide the necessary counseling.

Creditor – A person to whom or business to which the debtor owes money or that claims to be owed money by the debtor.

Crime – An act in violation of the penal laws of a state or of the United States. A positive or negative act in violation of penal law.

Criminal justice system – the network of courts and tribunals which deal with criminal law and its enforcement.

Cross-examination – The questioning of a witness produced by the other side in a trial.

Crumb trail – A series of text links across the top of a page that show the user where he or she has been on a website.

Cursor – The flashing vertical line on the screen that shows the user where is and where the next character the user types will appear.

Custody – Detaining of a person by lawful process or authority to assure his or her appearance to any hearing; the jailing or imprisonment of a person convicted of a crime.

CVV2/CVC – The last part of the code above the signature strip on modern credit and debit cards, which is often required by online vendors to verify that the card is genuine.

Cybercafé – Also known as an Internet café – a real café a customer may to drink coffee and buy Internet access for short periods of time.

Cyberspace – A term often used to describe the Internet/online environment, but which was originally invented to describe an as yet non-existent wholly interactive virtual world.

D

Damages – 1. Money awarded by a court to a person injured by the unlawful act or negligence of another person. 2. Money that a defendant pays a plaintiff in a civil case if the plaintiff has won. Damages may be compensatory (for loss or injury) or punitive (to punish and deter future misconduct).

Data Protection Act – British legislation which says how personal data should be treated, including what information can be kept about people.

Database – A program which allows the storing and organizing of data so that it can be retrieved and used in a variety of different ways.

Default settings – Non-customized settings: usually, when installing a program or signing up to a service the company will make assumptions about how the user would like things to work, based on what the majority of their users choose to do.

Declaratory judgment – A judge's statement about someone's rights. For example, a plaintiff may seek a declaratory judgment that a particular statute, as written, violates some constitutional right.

Decree – An order of the court. A final decree is one that fully and finally disposes of the litigation.

Defamation – That which tends to injure a person's reputation.

Defendant – An individual (or business) against whom a lawsuit is filed. The person defending or denying a suit. In a civil case, the person or organization against whom the plaintiff brings suit; in a criminal case, the person accused of the crime.

Deposition – An oral statement made before an officer authorized by law to administer oaths. Such statements are often taken to examine potential witnesses, to obtain discovery, or to be used later in trial. *See* discovery.

Desktop – A metaphor used to describe the way different programs are laid out on the computer screen, which is similar to how a user may arrange documents and photos on a real desk.

Dial-up – An old-fashioned way of connecting to the Internet through a conventional phone line.

Direct evidence – Proof of facts by witnesses who saw acts done or heard words spoken.

Direct examination – The first questioning of witnesses by the party on whose behalf they are called.

Directory – A folder containing files: this is a way of organizing files into different groups so they are easier to find and navigate.

Discovery – Procedures used to obtain disclosure of evidence before trial.

Docket – A log containing the complete history of each case in the form of brief chronological entries summarizing the court proceedings.

DNS (domain name system) – the method through which human-readable web addresses (such as udc.edu) are re-directed to the IP addresses the websites are hosted on (such as 12.23.34.45).

Domain name – a web address: for example, udc.edu is a domain name.

DoS (denial of service) attack – A malicious attempt to make a website stop functioning, usually by overwhelming it with web traffic.

DOS (disk operating system) – A type of computer operating system (OS) used from the 1980s to around 2000 but which is now rarely used.

Dotcom – A company which operates solely (or mainly) from the Internet.

Download – To transfer a file from the Internet on to the user's computer.

Due process – The right of all persons to receive the guarantees and safeguards of the law and the judicial process. It includes such constitutional requirements as adequate notice, assistance of counsel, and the rights to remain silent, to a speedy and public trial, to an impartial jury, and to confront and secure witnesses. In criminal law, the constitutional guarantee that a defendant will receive a fair and impartial trial. In civil law, the legal rights of someone who confronts an adverse action threatening liberty or property.

E

Elements of a crime – Specific factors that define a crime which the prosecution must prove beyond a reasonable doubt in order to obtain a conviction: (1) that a crime has actually occurred, (2) that the accused intended the crime to happen, and (3) a timely relationship between the first two factors.

Email attachments – Documents and files (such as images and videos) which are sent along with an email.

Encrypt/encryption – To change/scramble information so that it can't be read by anyone who doesn't know the password/key to unscramble it. This makes the information more secure.

Enjoining – An order by the court telling a person to stop performing a specific act.

Entity – A person or legally recognized organization.

Equal protection of the laws – The guarantee by the Fourteenth Amendment to the U.S. Constitution that all persons be treated equally by the law.

Equitable – Pertaining to civil suits in "equity" rather than in "law." In English legal history, the courts of "law" could order the payment of damages and could afford no other remedy (see damages). A separate court of "equity" could order someone to do something or to cease to do something (e.g., injunction). In American jurisprudence, the federal courts have both legal and equitable power, but the distinction is still an important one. For example, a trial by jury is normally available in "law" cases but not in "equity" cases.

Equity – Justice administered according to fairness; the spirit or habit of fairness in dealing with other persons.

Error message – A message letting a user know that something has gone wrong or is not working as it should (often in the form of a pop-up).

Ethics – Of or relating to moral action and conduct; professionally right; conforming to professional standards.

Evidence – Information presented in testimony or in documents that is used to persuade the fact finder (judge or jury) to decide the case in favor of one side or the other.

Ex parte – A proceeding brought before a court by one party only, without notice to or challenge by the other side.

Executable (program) – A computer program which is able to perform tasks when asked to do so. All software which runs off the user's computer hard drive will have an EXE file.

Exclusionary rule – The rule preventing illegally obtained evidence to be used in any trial. Doctrine that says evidence obtained in violation of a criminal defendant's constitutional or statutory rights is not admissible at trial.

Exculpatory evidence – Evidence indicating that a defendant did not commit the crime.

Executory contracts – Contracts or leases under which both parties to the agreement have duties remaining to be performed. If a contract or lease is executory, a debtor may assume it (keep the contract) or reject it (terminate the contract).

F

Family law – Those areas of the law pertaining to families, such as marriage, divorce, child custody, and paternity.

Federal question jurisdiction – Jurisdiction given to federal courts in cases involving the interpretation and application of the U.S. Constitution, acts of Congress, and treaties.

Felony – A serious crime, usually punishable by at least one year in prison. Fiduciary – A person or institution who manages money or property for another and who must exercise a standard care imposed by law, i.e., personal representative or executor of an estate, a trustee, etc.

File – To place a paper in the official custody of the clerk of court to enter into the files or records of a case.

File (computer) – A piece of information which can be opened by a computer program; for example, an image, a text document, or a video.

Finding – Formal conclusion by a judge or regulatory agency on issues of fact. Also, a conclusion by a jury regarding a fact.

File-sharing – Sharing files across the Internet, commonly using software such as BitTorrent.

Firefox – A popular type of Internet browser, made by Mozilla.

Firewall – A piece of hardware or software that controls what information passes from the user's computer to the Internet, and who or what can access the user's computer while the user is connected.

Flame – To send messages through the Internet which are designed to offend or annoy somebody, normally through conversations held on message boards or chat forums.

Flickr – A website where users can upload and share photos and images for free.

Fraud – A false representation of a matter of fact which is intended to deceive another.

Fraudulent transfer – A transfer of a debtor's property made with intent to defraud or for which the debtor receives less than the transferred property's value.

FTP (File Transfer Protocol) – A way of transferring files between a user's computer and a web server.

G

Garnishment – A legal proceeding in which a debtor's money, in the possession of another (called the garnishee) is applied to the debts of the debtor, such as when an employer garnishes a debtor's wages.

Gmail – A webmail service run by Google.

Grand jury – A jury of inquiry whose duty it is to receive complaints and accusations in criminal matters and if appropriate, issue a formal indictment. A body of 16-23 citizens who listen to evidence of criminal allegations, which is presented by the prosecutors, and determine whether there is probable cause to believe an individual committed an offense.

Grooming – Making friends with someone online under false pretenses to lure them into a difficult or dangerous situation.

H

Habeas corpus – Latin, meaning "you have the body." A writ of habeas corpus generally is a judicial order forcing law enforcement authorities to produce a prisoner they are holding, and to justify the prisoner's continued confinement. Federal judges receive petitions for a writ of habeas corpus from state prison inmates who say their state prosecutions violated federally protected rights in some way.

Hacker – Someone who attempts to access secure information over the Internet without permission – or someone who customizes or recycles computer equipment to invent new devices. Hardware – The physical parts of a computer.

Hearing – A formal proceeding (generally less formal than a trial) with definite issues of law or of fact to be heard. History – A record which the browser or file explorer keeps of places a user has visited, either on the Internet or on the user's computer.

Hits – The number of times a web page has been visited by different people on the Internet. Most websites keep a record of who has visited their website so that they can see how popular it is. Homepage – The web page the browser automatically displays when a user starts it up. Most browsers will allow the user to change the user homepage.

Host – A computer or server connected to the Internet. Hotmail – A free webmail service provided by Microsoft. This is one of the first and most popular free webmail services when it began in 1996.

I

Inbox – The part of email program/webmail where users may view all the emails the user has received.

Inculpatory evidence – Evidence indicating that a defendant did commit the crime.

Indictment – The formal charge issued by a grand jury stating that there is enough evidence that the defendant committed the crime to justify having a trial; it is used primarily for felonies. *See* information.

Infect/infection – A computer is 'infected' with a virus is one in which a malicious code has installed itself on the computer and is adversely affecting the way the computer works.

Information – A formal accusation by a government attorney that the defendant committed a misdemeanor. *See* indictment.

Injunction – A court order preventing one or more named parties from taking some action. A preliminary injunction often is issued to allow fact-finding, so a judge can determine whether a permanent injunction is justified.

Install – Transferring software onto the user's computer and setting it up so that it is able to work properly.

Instant messaging (IM) – Sending messages between people 'instantly' using a program on a computer or a website – it is much like very fast text messaging.

Internet – Millions of computers (and the data stored on them) around the world connected together by telephone lines, cables or satellites over which they can exchange information.

Internet café – A real café where customers may go to eat and drink and buy Internet access for short periods of time.

Internet Explorer – One of the most popular and oldest Internet browsers, which is usually set as the standard browser with Microsoft computers.

Interrogatories – A form of discovery consisting of written questions to be answered in writing and under oath. iPad – A touch-screen tablet computer made by Apple, which will only run software approved by Apple and purchased through the iTunes store. iPhone – A touch-screen smartphone made by Apple, Inc.

ISP (Internet Service Provider) – A company which provides access to an Internet connection.

Issue – 1. The disputed point between parties in a lawsuit. 2. To send out officially, as in a court issuing an order.

J

Java – A programming language widely used on the web to run small programs in the browser called applets.

JavaScript – A scripting language developed by Netscape and Sun Microsystems which is used for such actions as make new browser windows 'pop up'.

Judge – An official of the judicial branch with authority to decide lawsuits brought before courts. Used generically, the term judge may also refer to all judicial officers, including Supreme Court justices.

Judgment – The official decision of a court finally resolving the dispute between the parties to the lawsuit submitted to the court for determination.

Junk email – Unsolicited or unwanted email.

Jurisdiction – The legal authority of a court to hear and decide a certain type of case. It also is used as a synonym for venue, meaning the geographic area over which the court has territorial jurisdiction to decide cases.

Jurisprudence – The study of law and the structure of the legal system.

Jury – The group of persons selected to hear the evidence in a trial and render a verdict on matters of fact. *See* grand jury.

Jury instructions – A judge's directions to the jury before it begins deliberations regarding the factual questions it must answer and the legal rules that it must apply.

L

LAN – Local Area Network: a small private network of computers, for example in an office.

Law – The combination of those rules and principles of conduct promulgated by legislative authority, derived from court decisions and established by local custom.

Lawsuit – A legal action started by a plaintiff against a defendant based on a complaint that the defendant failed to perform a legal duty which resulted in harm to the plaintiff.

Lien – A charge on specific property that is designed to secure payment of a debt or performance of an obligation. A debtor may still be responsible for a lien after a discharge.

LinkedIn – A social network used to help people make professional business connections.

Litigant – A party to a lawsuit.

Linux – A type of free, open-source operating system made by the people who use it. It is most frequently used on servers and as an alternative to Microsoft Windows. Popular versions include Ubuntu, Fedora and Mint. Pronounced "LIN-ucks."

Litigation – A case, legal action, controversy, or lawsuit. Participants (plaintiffs and defendants) in lawsuits are called litigants.

M

Macro – A computer script which when run will record a chain of actions and repeat them for the user.

Magistrate judge – A judicial officer of a district court who conducts initial proceedings in criminal cases, decides criminal misdemeanor cases, conducts many pretrial civil and criminal matters on behalf of district judges, and decides civil cases with the consent of the parties.

Mailbox – synonymous for email inbox.

Mailing list – Multiple email addresses collected to send out newsletters or group emails.

Mailwasher – Software which filters out spam emails before they go to the user's email program.

Malware – Malicious software specifically designed to damage the user's computer or corrupt the user's data.

Meta search engine – A site which automatically submits a search to several search engines at the same time and quickly retrieve results. Examples include MetaCrawler, Dogpile and Ask Jeeves.

Media player – A software program that plays audio and video content: RealPlayer, iTunes and Windows Media Player are popular media players.

Mediation – A form of alternative dispute resolution in which the parties bring their dispute to a neutral third party, who helps them agree on a settlement.

Memory – The storage and thinking parts of a computer. More storage memory on the hard disk (ROM) means the user is able to save more files and more thinking memory (RAM) means the computer is able to perform more complex tasks more quickly.

Mental health treatment – Special condition the court imposes to require an individual to undergo evaluation and treatment for a mental disorder. Treatment may include psychiatric, psychological, and sex offense-specific evaluations, inpatient or outpatient counseling, and medication.

Micro browser – An Internet browser scaled down for use on a mobile phone or other mobile devices.

Microsoft – One of the oldest and largest computing companies. It created the hugely popular operating system Microsoft Windows, which comes as standard on most PCs, as well as a great deal of widely-used software (such as Microsoft Office).

Microsoft Office – A suite of software created by Microsoft with software to create text documents, spreadsheets, slide-shows, and emails

Minor – A person under the age of legal competence.

Misdemeanor – An offense punishable by one year of imprisonment or less.

Mistrial – An invalid trial, caused by fundamental error. When a mistrial is declared, the trial must start again with the selection of a new jury.

Moot – Not subject to a court ruling because the controversy has not actually arisen, or has ended

Motion – A request by a litigant to a judge for a decision on an issue relating to the case.

Motion in limine – A pretrial motion requesting the court to prohibit the other side from presenting, or even referring to, evidence on matters said to be so highly prejudicial that no steps taken by the judge can prevent the jury from being unduly influenced.

Mozilla Firefox – A popular type of Internet browser.

N

Navigate/navigation – To move within or between websites which appears on each web page within that website.

Negligence – Failure to use care which a reasonable and prudent person would use under similar circumstances.

Negotiation – The process of submission and consideration of offers until an acceptable offer is made and accepted.

Network – A group of computers communicating together through a server along cables or wirelessly.

Network connections – Connections made from one computer to another as part of a network.

New media – A vague term referring to any new or digital technology, including the Internet, IPTV, digital radio and more.

Notice – Formal notification to the party that has been sued in a civil case of the fact that the lawsuit has been filed. Also, any form of notification of a legal proceeding.

O

Online attackers – Individuals on the Internet who attack the computers of others to gain access to their data.

Operating system – The basic software on the computer which instructs all the different parts of the computer to work together. All computers need an operating system (OS) to work. Popular operating systems include Microsoft Windows, Mac OS X, and Linux.

Opt-in – To choose to do something/be involved with something.

Opt-out – To choose not to do something/be involved with something.

Opinion – A judge's written explanation of the decision of the court. Because a case may be heard by three or more judges in the court of appeals, the opinion in appellate decisions can take several forms. If all the judges completely agree on the result, one judge will write the opinion for all. If all the judges do not agree, the formal decision will be based upon the view of the majority, and one member of the majority will write the opinion. The judges who did not agree with the majority may write separately in dissenting or concurring opinions to present their views. A dissenting opinion disagrees with the majority opinion because of the reasoning and/or the principles of law the majority used to decide the case. A concurring opinion agrees with the decision of the majority opinion, but offers further comment or clarification or even an entirely different reason for reaching the same result. Only the majority opinion can serve as binding precedent in future cases.

Oral argument – An opportunity for lawyers to summarize their position before the court and also to answer the judges' questions.

Order – A mandate, command, or direction authoritatively given. Direction of a court or judge made in writing.

Ordinance – A rule established by authority; may be a municipal statute of a city council regulating such matters as zoning, building, safety, matters of municipality, etc.

Outlook Express – Popular email software made by Microsoft.

Overrule – A judge's decision not to allow an objection. Also, a decision by a higher court finding that a lower court decision was in error.

P

Panel – 1. In appellate cases, a group of judges (usually three) assigned to decide the case. 2. In the jury selection process, the group of potential jurors. 3. The list of attorneys who are both available and qualified to serve as court-appointed counsel for criminal defendants who cannot afford their own counsel.

Parental control software – Software which can help restrict what children or vulnerable people can do and see on a computer and the Internet: for example, parental control software will filter pornography websites.

Party in interest – A party who has standing to be heard by the court in a matter to be decided in the bankruptcy case. The debtor, U.S. trustee or bankruptcy administrator, case trustee, and creditors are parties in interest for most matters.

Password – A secret combination of letters and numbers (and sometimes other characters) which protects personal information.

PayPal – A company which acts as an intermediary between a bank and online retailers, meaning consumers can pay for things online without having to trust retailers with credit card details.

PDF – A file extension by Adobe. PDFs are formatted documents that have been fixed in place, and are difficult to edit. This format is commonly used for brochures and formal documents, so that they can be viewed and printed the way the creator intended.

Per curiam – Latin, meaning "for the court." In appellate courts, often refers to an unsigned opinion.

Periodical – A publication which appears regularly but less often than daily.

Petit jury (or trial jury) – A group of citizens who hear the evidence presented by both sides at trial and determine the facts in dispute. Federal criminal juries consist of 12 persons. Federal civil juries consist of at least six persons.

Petitioner – The person filing an action in a court of original jurisdiction. Also, the person who appeals the judgment of a lower court.

Petty offense – A federal misdemeanor punishable by six months or less in prison.

Phish/phishing – Attempting to get someone to give someone their private data over the Internet/email by posing as a reputable company, commonly a bank or financial institution. Also known as spoofing.

Photoshop – A software program made by Adobe which allows users use to view and edit images.

Plaintiff – A person who brings an action; the party who complains or sues in a civil action.

Plan – A debtor's detailed description of how the debtor proposes to pay creditors' claims over a fixed period of time.

Plea – In a criminal case, the defendant's statement pleading "guilty" or "not guilty" in answer to the charges.

Pleadings – Written statements filed with the court that describe a party's legal or factual assertions about the case.

Precedent – A court decision in an earlier case with facts and legal issues similar to a dispute currently before a court. Judges will generally "follow precedent," meaning that they use the principles established in earlier cases to decide new cases that have similar facts and raise similar legal issues. A judge will disregard precedent if a party can show that the earlier case was wrongly decided, or that it differed in some significant way from the current case.

Preponderance of the proof – Greater weight of the evidence, the common standard of evidence in civil cases.

Prima facie case – A case that is sufficient and has the minimum amount of evidence necessary to allow it to continue in the judicial process.

Privilege – A benefit or advantage to certain persons beyond the advantages of other persons, i.e., an exemption, immunity, power, etc.

Probable cause – A reasonable belief that a crime has or is being committed; the basis for all lawful searches, seizures, and arrests.

Procedure – The rules for conducting a lawsuit; there are rules of civil procedure, criminal procedure, evidence, bankruptcy, and appellate procedure.

Prosecute – To charge someone with a crime. A prosecutor tries a criminal case on behalf of the government.

Prosecutor – A trial lawyer representing the government in a criminal case and the interests of the government in civil matters. In criminal cases, the prosecutor has the responsibility of deciding who and when to prosecute.

Protocol – A set of rules that tell computers how to transfer data between themselves.

Proximate cause – The last negligent act which contributes to an injury. A person generally is liable only if an injury was proximately caused by his or her action or by his or her failure to act when he or she had a duty to act.

Proxy server – A server on the Internet that acts as an intermediary. For example, it can be used to hide the user's real IP address, or to temporarily store information about websites the user visits so that it can be loaded more quickly.

Public defender – Government lawyer who provides legal defense services to an indigent person accused of a crime.

Public domain software – Software which is free to download and use and which comes without any copyright restrictions: similar to Freeware.

R

RAM (random access memory) – temporary space on the computer used for programs which are currently running.

RAW – A type of file format for unprocessed image files (for example, files which are still on a digital camera).

Raw code – Also known as source code: code viewed in its most basic format (text) without being processed by a computer or browser. To view this web page's raw code in Internet Explorer or Firefox, click 'View' in the browser menu and select 'Page source' or 'Source'.

Real property – Land, buildings and whatever is attached or affixed to the land. Generally synonymous with the words "real estate."

Reasonable doubt – An accused person is entitled to acquittal if, in the minds of the jury, his or her guilt has not been proved beyond a "reasonable doubt;" that state of minds of jurors in which they cannot say they feel an abiding conviction as to the truth of the charge.

Reasonable person – A phrase used to denote a hypothetical person who exercises qualities of attention, knowledge, intelligence, and judgment that society requires of its members for the protection of their own interests and the interests of others. Thus, the test of negligence is based on either a failure to do something that a reasonable person, guided by considerations that ordinarily regulate conduct, would do, or on the doing of something that a reasonable and prudent (wise) person would not do.

Rebut – Evidence disproving other evidence previously given or reestablishing the reliability of challenged evidence.

Record – A written account of the proceedings in a case, including all pleadings, evidence, and exhibits submitted in the course of the case.

Register – To sign up for an online service by providing contact details (such as email address, and a password).

Remand – Send back.

Remedy – Legal or judicial means by which a right or privilege is enforced or the violation of a right or privilege is prevented, redressed, or compensated.

Remote attack – When a user's computer is attacked through the Internet by a virus or hacker working on a different computer

Resolution – The amount of detail being displayed: the higher the resolution, the more detailed an image appears.

Re-tweet (RT) – Twitter language for taking a tweet somebody else has posted and posting it again so that a user's followers can see it. It is good netiquette to credit the person who originally tweeted the message by including their username in the tweet.

Reverse – The act of a court setting aside the decision of a lower court. A reversal is often accompanied by a remand to the lower court for further proceedings.

Robot – Also "bot," a piece of software that runs on the Internet performing specific tasks, such as looking for information about web pages (bots made for search engines are also known as spiders).

Router – A piece of hardware that decides the next network point to which a packet of data on the Internet should be sent on its journey towards its final destination.

RSS – Really Simple Syndication: an RSS feed is a list of information taken from a website or service, updated in real-time with any new information added to the website.

Rules – Established standards, guides, or regulations set up by authority.

Rules of evidence – Standards governing whether evidence in a civil or criminal case is admissible.

S

Sanction – A penalty or other type of enforcement used to bring about compliance with the law or with rules and regulations.

Scareware – Useless or dangerous software which is sold by scammers, often by scaring them into thinking they have a computer virus which can be fixed by buying their software.

Search engine – A very large searchable database of links to different websites, created by robots which trawl the Internet searching for information.

Search warrant – A written order issued by a judge that directs a law enforcement officer to search a specific area for a particular piece or pieces of evidence.

Security patch – An update released by the maker of a piece of software to fix small problems or security flaws.

Semantic web – A way of sorting information (like text, videos and images) with metadata or tags which computers can fully understand so that it becomes flexible enough to be used in lots of different ways.

Sentence – The punishment ordered by a court for a defendant convicted of a crime.

Sequester – To separate. Sometimes juries are separated from outside influences during their deliberations.

Server – A very simple, large computer used simply for doing one or two set tasks, such as storing large amounts of information and making it available to the Internet.

Service of process – The delivery of writs or summonses to the party named in the document.

Settlement – Parties to a lawsuit resolve their dispute without having a trial. Settlements often involve the payment of compensation by one party in at least partial satisfaction of the other party's claims, but usually do not include the admission of fault.

Shareware – Free software which users may download and use for free for a set period of time so they can try out some or all of the features before they decide whether or not they wish to pay for it.

Shopping cart – A 'shopping list' a user is able to build on an online store to buy all the items he or she may want at once instead of paying for everything separately.

Skim – To quickly find the basic details of something. Robots skim and compile information taken from websites.

Skype – A software program which allows people to make phone and video calls over the Internet.

SMS (short messaging service) – Also known as text messaging; a way of sending short text messages from one mobile phone to another through a traditional mobile phone network.

Social networking – Using websites (like Facebook, Instagram, SnapChat and Twitter) to connect to and share information with other people.

Social networking website – A website which allows users to meet up with existing friends online, as well as make new ones. Examples include Facebook, Instagram, SnapChat and Twitter.

Software – Code which is run by a user's computer, which tells it what to do. This can be anything from photo-editing programs to browsers that allows the computer to view information over the Internet.

Software firewall – Software that controls what information passes from the computer to the Internet, and who or what can access the computer while the user is connected.

Source code – Code viewed in its most basic format (text) without being processed by a computer or browser. To view this web page's raw code in Internet Explorer or Firefox, the user can click 'View' in the browser menu and select 'Page source' or 'Source'.

Spam – Unsolicited or unwanted email.

Spam filter – Software or code attached to the inbox that filters out spam emails from legitimate emails.

Spambot – A computer robot that automatically sends out spam emails to users, on behalf of a hacker/human spammer.

Spammer – An individual who sends out spam emails, or writes a spambot program to do it on his/her behalf.

Spider – Also known as a robot: a piece of software that trawls the Internet for information to send back to search engines.

Spoofing – Attempting to persuade an individual to release their private data over the Internet/email by posing as a reputable company, commonly a bank or financial institution. Also known as phishing.

Spyware – A type of virus software that conceals itself on computers and gathers user personal data (like credit card details) to send back to a hacker or spammer.

SSID – A code up to 32 characters long that identifies a network, helping the computer to connect to it.

Standard of proof – Degree of proof required. In criminal cases, prosecutors must prove a defendant's guilt "beyond a reasonable doubt." The majority of civil lawsuits require proof "by a preponderance of the evidence" (50 percent plus), but in some instances, the standard is higher and requires "clear and convincing" proof.

Standing – The legal right to bring a lawsuit. Only a person with something at stake has standing to bring a lawsuit.

Statute – A law passed by a legislature. Legislative enactment; it may be a single act of a legislature or a body of acts which are collected and arranged for a session of a legislature.

Statute of limitations – The time within which a lawsuit must be filed or a criminal prosecution begun. The deadline can vary, depending on the type of civil case or the crime charged. It must be done within a specified time period after the occurrence which gives rise to the right to sue or prosecute.

Statutory – Relating to a statute; created or defined by a law.

Streaming – When a sound or video file is played at almost the same time it is being sent from a website. In this way a user doesn't have to wait for a clip to download; he or she just watches it as it downloads.

Strong/secure password – A password that is very difficult to guess or bypass, for example, one which contains a mixture of upper and lower case letters and numbers.

Sua sponte – Latin, meaning "of its own will." Often refers to a court taking an action in a case without being asked to do so by either side.

Subpoena – A command, issued under a court's authority, to a witness to appear and give testimony.

Subpoena duces tecum – A command to a witness to appear and produce documents.

Summary judgment – A judgment given on the basis of pleadings, affidavits, and exhibits presented for the record without any need for a trial. It is used when there is no dispute as to the facts of the case and one party is entitled to a judgment as a matter of law.

Summons – Instrument used to commence a civil action or special proceeding; the means of acquiring jurisdiction over a party.

Suppress – To forbid the use of evidence at a trial because it is improper or was improperly obtained.

Surf/surfing – to use the Internet to go from website to another, often without a specific purpose.

T

TCP/IP – The combination of protocols that make the Internet. TCP deals with the process of dividing data into packets of information. IP deals with the process of passing these packets from one computer to the next until they reach their final destination.

Technical support – A phone number a user calls to receive help from a human being if in case the user encounters problems or needs assistance.

Temporary Relief – Any form of action by a court granting one of the parties an order to protect its interest pending further action by the court.

Temporary restraining order – Akin to a preliminary injunction, it is a judge's short-term order forbidding certain actions until a full hearing can be conducted. Often referred to as a TRO.

Testimony – Evidence presented orally by witnesses during trials or before grand juries.

Text messaging – Also known as SMS, a means of sending short text messages from one mobile phone to another through a traditional mobile phone network.

Thread – A group of messages, often e-mail messages or message board posts, linked by a common subject. A thread is the online equivalent of a conversation. Many message boards present messages on the same subject together, as a thread.

Tort – A civil, not criminal, wrong. A negligent or intentional injury against a person or property, with the exception of breach of contract.

Transcript – A written, word-for-word record of what was said, either in a proceeding such as a trial, or during some other formal conversation, such as a hearing or oral deposition

Transfer – Any mode or means by which a debtor disposes of or parts with his/her property.

Trial – A judicial examination of issues between parties to an action.

Trojan – A program which appears harmless but is carrying inside viruses, worms or even another program that will damage a computer. A trojan is usually an attachment and is often carrying a program which allows someone to hack into a computer.

Troll – A term widely used on the Internet to describe an individual who deliberately posts contentious and inflammatory remarks online to provoke others. These remarks may appear on Internet forums, chat rooms or in comment fields of blog articles.

Twitter – A social networking website where users may only post short messages of 140 characters or less. Users may 'follow' other people, and their messages will appear on user's screen in a time line. Many people use Twitter on their mobile phones, especially smartphones.

U

UNIX – A computer operating system (OS) used by most Internet Service Providers (ISPs) on their 'host' computers as it allows many people to connect to the same resources at any given time.

U.S. Attorney – Lawyers appointed by the President in each judicial district to prosecute and defend cases for the federal government. The U.S. Attorney employs a staff of Assistant U.S. Attorneys who appear as the government's attorneys in individual cases.

Uphold – The appellate court agrees with the lower court decision and allows it to stand.

URL (Uniform Resource Locator) – A web address, e.g., www.udc.edu

Username: An identifying name a user can give him or herself to log into services, which he or she can choose and that does not need to be person's actual name.

V

Vacate – To set aside.

Venire – A writ summoning persons to court to act as jurors.

Venue – Authority of a court to hear a matter based on geographical location. The geographic area in which a court has jurisdiction. A change of venue is a change or transfer of a case from one judicial district to another.

Verdict – The decision of a trial jury or a judge that determines the guilt or innocence of a criminal defendant, or that determines the final outcome of a civil case. A conclusion, as to fact or law that forms the basis for the court's judgment.

Viral – Information which has spread through the Internet via word of mouth.

Viral marketing – When advertisers try to spread information about their products through word of mouth on the Internet. This is commonly done by creating funny or thought-provoking videos.

Virus – A computer program which can copy itself and spread from one computer to another, adversely affecting the way that computer operates.

Vista – An operating system (also known as Windows Vista) by Microsoft. Void – Invalid; a void agreement is one for which there is no remedy.

Voidable – Capable of being declared invalid; a voidable contract is one where a person may avoid his obligation, as a contract between an adult and a minor.

Voir dire – The preliminary examination made in court of a witness or juror to determine his competency or interest in a matter. Literally, to speak the truth.

VPN (Virtual Private Network) – A system where people can access work intranets and private networks over the Internet.

W

Waive – Intentionally give up a right.

Warrant – Court authorization, most often for law enforcement officers, to conduct a search or make an arrest.

Web browser – Software which allows the user to surf the Internet.

Web developer – An individual who writes codes to create a website.

Web page – Any page on the Internet.

Webcam – A small, usually cheap video camera a user may plug into a computer to talk to people over the Internet.

Webcast – A pre-recorded or live video file broadcast over the Internet to several people at once: a type of Internet television.

Webmail – An email service that users may log in to through an Internet browser to send and receive emails online, instead of having to install software on a computer.

Webmaster – The individual in charge of the content on a website, who maintains the files kept on the server. The webmaster also resolves problems on the website.

Windows – A very popular operating system by Microsoft.

Windows Explorer – A file manager that helps users to navigate the files on their computer.

Windows Media Player – A media player by Microsoft which will play video and audio files.

Windows XP – A particular version of a Microsoft operating system.

Wireless – A means of gaining access to a network (such as the Internet) without having to use a cable: the information is transmitted through the atmosphere, such as with mobile phones.

Wireless router – Hardware that takes wired Internet access and makes it wireless. When a user signs up to a broadband Internet service their Internet service provider (ISP) will often provide a wireless router so that the user is able to connect to the Internet with a laptop or smartphone.

Witness – 1. A person called upon by either side in a lawsuit to give testimony before the court or jury. 2. One who personally sees or perceives a thing; one who testifies as to what he has seen, heard, or otherwise observed.

Worm – A program that is able to reproduce itself over a computer network. It usually attaches itself to another software program and then proceeds to cause malicious damage to computer such as shutting it down.

WPA (Wi-Fi Protected Access) – A means of encrypting a wireless connection so that people can't hack into it and steal information.

Writ – A written court order directing a person to take, or refrain from taking, a certain act.

Writ of certiorari – An order issued by the U.S. Supreme Court directing the lower court to transmit records for a case which it will hear on appeal.

Writ of execution – An order of the court evidencing debt of one party to another and commanding the court officer to take property in satisfaction of the debt.

Writ of garnishment – An order of the court whereby property, money, or credits in the possession of another person may be seized and applied to pay a debtor's debt. It is used as an incident to or auxiliary of a judgment rendered in a principal action.

Y

Yahoo! – A company that provides a search engine, free webmail, advertising, and news portal and other services.

Ymail – A webmail service operated by Yahoo!

Z

Zombie computer – A personal computer connected to the Internet which has been unwittingly hijacked by a hacker and used to do what the hacker wants without the owner even noticing, often to run DoS attacks or to send spam emails.

Chronology of Privacy Rights

1600s

Under Puritan law in Massachusetts Bay Colony; it was considered a civic duty to monitor the activities of your neighbors. In many towns, individuals were forbidden to live alone.

1600s

The Puritan clergy, who maintain births, marriages and deaths, seek an increasing amount of information on individual activities in Massachusetts. Tythingmen, working for the government, inspect households to ensure proper moral conduct.

1690

English political philosopher, John Locke, publishes *Two Treatises of Government*, in which he argues that the purpose of government is to preserve natural rights—"lives, liberties and states."

1700s

In the thirteen colonies, private life is seen as a sanctuary from the public sphere. The colonists generally agree with the English adage that "a man's home is his castle."

1700s

Mail is routinely opened as it passes through the colonial postal system.

1776

Virginia adopts a Bill of Rights, which declares that men are "by nature equally free and independent, and have certain inherent rights." Other states soon follow.

1782

Congress begins to enforce confidentiality of mail going through the postal system.

1787

the U.S. Constitution is drafted and sent to the states for ratification. Several of the amendments have provisions pertaining to privacy.

1789

The U.S. Constitution is formally adopted by the states.

December 15, 1791

The states ratify ten of the proposed twelve amendments, thus adding the Bill of Rights to the U.S. Constitution. Throughout the twentieth century, the courts hold that among the rights guaranteed are several protecting certain aspects of privacy, including the right to privacy of belief under the First Amendment and a right to privacy within our homes under the Third Amendment. The Fourth Amendment, guaranteeing the right to be secure in our persons and property against unreasonable searches and seizures, was interpreted by the Supreme Court in 1967 to protect a right to privacy wherever there is a reasonable expectation of privacy.

1830s

The "penny press" emerges, which publishes unfettered gossip about the private lives of public people, under the protection of the First Amendment.

1859

British political philosopher, John Stuart Mill, publishes, *On Liberty*, which he argues that the only reason for government interference with a person's liberty against that individuals will is self-preservation—to prevent harm to others.

July 9, 1868

The Fourteenth Amendment is added to the U.S. Constitution. The Due Process Clause of this amendment becomes the means through which provisions of the Bill of Rights are applied to the states. During the twentieth century, the Supreme Court held that privacy is one of the fundamental liberties protected by the Fourteenth Amendment.

1880

Thomas Cooley, in his A *Treatise of the Law of Torts*, refers to privacy as "a right of complete immunity: to be let alone."

1886

The U.S. Supreme Court recognizes protection for privacy under the Fourth and Fifth Amendment in *Boyd v. United States*. In that case, the court ruled that the seizure or compulsory production of one's personal papers to be used as evidence against that person is the same as compelling self-incrimination.

December 15, 1890

Louis Brandeis and Samuel Warren publish "The Right to Privacy" in the *Harvard Law Review*. The article calls upon the Supreme Court to recognize a specific and independent constitutional right to privacy.

1890s

Law enforcement agencies begin wire-tapping of telephones.

1891

The U.S. Supreme Court specifically enunciates a "the due right to be let alone" in *Union Pacific Railroad v. Botsford*.

1897

The U.S. Supreme Court begins to apply the privacy provisions of the Bill of Rights to the states in *Chicago, Burlington, and Quincy Railroad Company v. Chicago*.

Ca.1900

Fingerprints are available as unique and unchangeable identifiers.

1902

The Court of Appeals of New York, the highest court in the state, refuses to recognize tan independent right of privacy under the state constitution in Roberson v. Rochester Folding Box Company.

1901

The New York Civil Service Commission begins the first systematic use of fingerprint identifiers in the United States.

1905

The Georgia Supreme Court becomes the first court to recognize privacy as a distinct and independent right under ta state constitution in *Pavesich v. New England Life Insurance Company.*

1907

The first dictograph (an early type of telephone bugging apparatus) is invented.

1914

In *Weeks v. United States*, the Supreme Court held that the warrantless seizure of items from a residence violated constitutional protections.

1920

The American Civil Liberties Union (ACLU) is formed.

June 4, 1923

In *Meyer v. Nebraska*, the U.S. Supreme Court acknowledges protection under the Due Process Clause of the Fourteenth Amendment for personal privacy. The Supreme Court rules that a Nebraska law violates the due process clause of the Fourteenth Amendment. The Court holds that the liberties protected under this clause include more than "merely freedom from bodily restraint but also the right of the individual to contract, to engage in any of the common occupations of life, to acquire useful knowledge, to marry, establish a home and bring up children, to worship God according to the dictates of his own conscience, and generally to enjoy those privileges long recognized at common law as essential to the orderly pursuit of happiness by free men." This ruling provides the basis for an expanded right to privacy under the Constitution.

1925

In *Carroll v. United States*, the Supreme Court rules that police may make a warrantless search of an automobile if they have probable cause to suspect that it contains contraband.

June 1, 1925

The U.S. Supreme Court grants constitutional protection to personal privacy in the areas of education and family in *Pierce v. Society of Sisters*. The United States Supreme Court rules that an Oregon law requiring that children ages eight to sixteen attend public schools violates the constitutionally protected right of "parents and guardians to direct the upbringing and education of children under their control." Selecting a school for their children was a parental choice that fell into a zone of privacy into which the government could not tread.

1928

In *Olmstead v. United States*, the court ruled that wiretapped private telephone conversations recorded by authorities without judicial approval did not violate the Fourth or Fifth Amendment rights of the defendant. The Court found that evidence from wiretaps placed by federal officials without judicial approval is permissible and that allowing the wiretaps did not violate the suspected bootlegger's Fourth Amendment rights as the case involved phone conversations and not physical artifacts, nor did the federal agents trespass on the accused's property. This decision was reversed by *Katz v. United States* in 1967. Dissenting in *Olmstead v. United States*, Justice Louis Brandeis, argues that the U.S. Constitution confers upon each individual a general right to privacy.

1934

The Federal Communications Act is passed. This statute was the first statute that addressed wiretapping. Section 605 prohibits a third party from intercepting and using any communication without authorization of the sender. This, however, has very little impact on preventing such practices. It also established the Federal Communications Commission (FCC). The statute does not outlaw wiretapping, but information gathered may not be disclosed.

1938

The House Un-American Activities Committee is commissioned.

1942

Referring to procreation as one to the "basic civil rights of man," the U.S. Supreme Court extends constitutional protection to procreation in *Skinner v. Oklahoma*.

1945

Beginning of the Cold War. Government surveillance of ordinary citizens increases without their knowledge.

1945

The Armed Forces Security Agency (AFSA) initiates project SHAMROCK, an intelligence-gathering program that collects—without warrants—the international telegrams coming through ITT World International, RCA Global, and Western Union to screen for espionage and Soviet spying. The program operates for thirty years.

1947

In *Harris v. United States*, the U.S. Supreme Court affirms the admissibility of evidence of one crime that was found by officers during a proper, but warrantless, search for evidence of another, unrelated crime. The basis for the Court's ruling was subsequently expanded as the test required for the "plain view" doctrine.

1952

President Harry S. Truman establishes the National Security Agency (NSA), which absorbs the AFSA, for national defense. The NSA's current mission includes, "to defeat terrorists and their organizations at home and abroad, consistent with U.S. laws and the protection of privacy and civil liberties."

1953

Senator Joseph McCarthy (R-WI) holds the first of a set of hearings seeking to find and remove Communists from the Federal government.

1956

The first Federal Bureau of Investigation Counter Intelligence (COINTELPRO) program begins.

1957

In *Watkins v. United States*, the U.S. Supreme Court rules that the House Committee on Un-American Activities acted in excess of the scope of congressional power.

1958

In *NAACP v. Alabama*, the Supreme Court first recognizes "freedom of association."

1965

The first electronic mail (e-mail) system is created.

June 7, 1965

The U.S. Supreme Court specifically recognizes an independent and fundamental right to privacy under the U.S. Constitution in *Griswold v. Connecticut*, invalidating a state statute that prohibits the use of contraception as applied to married couples. The Court also applies this right to privacy to the states through the Due Process Clause of the Fourteenth Amendment. In *Griswold*, the United States Supreme Court strikes down a Connecticut law that forbids counseling for and the use of contraceptives. In a 7-2 ruling, the Court holds that the Connecticut law violates a "right to marital privacy." In the opinion, Justice William Douglas argues that in addition to the expressed guarantees of the Bill of Rights, other rights were contained within the "penumbras," (or "zones") existing along the margins of the Bill of Rights. These penumbras were "formed by emanations from those guarantees that help give them life and substance." In other words, the First, Third, Fourth, Fifth, and Ninth Amendments, Douglas argued, protected more than the specific rights contained within each of them; they also established "zones of privacy" that the government was equally bound to protect.

1965

The first U.S. reports emerge of police using surveillance cameras in public places.

1966

Congress passes the Freedom of Information Act (FOIA), which President Lyndon B. Johnson signs into law.

1966

In *Schmerber v. California*, the U.S. Supreme Court held that a blood test ordered by police and introduced as evidence in court did not violate the Fifth Amendment guarantee against self-incrimination

Jun 12, 1967

In *Loving v. Virginia*, the United States Supreme Court rules that a Virginia law prohibiting interracial marriage violates the Equal Protection and Due Process Clauses of the Fourteenth Amendment to the

United States Constitution. In *Loving*, the U.S. Supreme Court characterizes the personal interest in choosing who m to marry as a fundamental privacy right.

1967

In *Warden v. Hayden*, the Supreme Court lets stand a warrantless search by police because there was probable cause and the situation made that course of action imperative.

1967

Congress establishes the National Crime Information Center.

December 18, 1967

In *Katz v. United States*, the United States Supreme Court holds that Fourth Amendment protections against unreasonable search and seizure require that the police obtain a search warrant in order to wiretap a public pay phone. A warrant is required, it says, before the police or other government agency can tap a public phone. Emphasizing that the Fourth Amendment protects people, and not just places, one justice argues that under the Fourth Amendment an individual is guaranteed privacy wherever there is a reasonable expectation of privacy. In *Katz*, the Court overturns the *Olmsted*, finding that the Fourth Amendment protect non-tangible possessions such as phone calls and electronic transmissions as well as the "reasonable expectation of privacy" in places like home, office, hotel room, phone booth. Examination of such places and things now require a warrant.

1968

In *Terry v. Ohio*, the Supreme Court establishes the "stop and frisk" rule, which permits police to temporarily detain someone for questioning if there are specific facts that would lead a reasonable police officer to believe that criminal activity is occurring.

1968

Congress passes the Omnibus Crime Control and Safe Streets Act, the first federal statute to restrict wiretapping, as Title III of the Act specifies when a warrant is required for wiretapping. The statute, however, makes exception for the president's overriding authority to approve wiretaps if in the service of protecting the United States.

1969

In *Davis v. Mississippi*, the Supreme Court holds that an arrest in order to take fingerprint is covered by the Fourth Amendment prohibition against unreasonable searches and seizures.

1970

The Fair Credit Reporting Act becomes law.

1970

The Bank Secrecy Act becomes law.

1971

Referring to divorce as a "precondition to the adjustment of a fundamental human relationship," the U.S. Supreme Court extends constitutional protection to divorce in *Boddie v. Connecticut*.

March 22, 1972

In *Eisenstadt v. Baird*, the U.S. Supreme Court declares unconstitutional a state statute that prohibits the use of contraceptives as applied to unmarried persons, upholding that constitutional guarantees an individual the freedom from unwarranted governmental intrusion in matters so fundamental affecting a person as whether to bear a child. The Court held that single persons possess the same privacy right earlier extended to married couples under *Griswold*. The ruling strikes down a Massachusetts law that made it a felony to distribute contraceptives to unmarried persons. In the ruling, the Court states that "if the right to privacy means anything, it is the right of the individual, married or single, to be free from unwarranted government intrusion into matters so fundamentally affecting a person as the decision whether to bear or begat a child."

January 22, 1973

In *Roe v. Wade*, the Supreme Court holds that a woman's right to an abortion falls within her right to privacy previously recognized in *Griswold v. Connecticut* and protected by the Fourteenth Amendment. The Court strikes down a Texas law that prohibits abortion in all cases except those performed in order to save the mother's life. The Court holds that the constitutionally protected right to privacy was "broad enough to encompass a woman's decision whether or not to terminate her pregnancy." Acknowledging, however, that the state acquires an increasing interest in a woman's pregnancy as it advances, as both the viability of the fetus and the health risks of an abortion to the mother increase, the Court establishes a trimester framework to guide permissible forms of state intervention. During the first three months, a woman can obtain an abortion without any government interference. During the second three months, as the risks posed by an abortion to the mother increase, states can intervene in order to protect the mother's health. And during the last three months, as the fetus reaches viability, states can regulate and even prohibit abortions. In *Roe*, the Court held that constitutional privacy includes a woman's decision whether or not to terminate her pregnancy. Congressional opponents of the constitutional right to abortion propose a Human Life Amendment, which declares that life begins at conception. This proposed amendment, the first of many of this type, fails to receive the necessary votes to be reported out of Congress.

1973

In the case *Paris Adult Theatre I v. Slaton*, the Supreme Court holds that obscene films did not have constitutional protection simply because their display was restricted to consenting adults.

1974

The Family Educational Rights and Privacy Act becomes law.

1974

The Privacy Act becomes law.

1975

Dr. Martin Cooper receives a patent for the first cell phone.

1975

Personal computers become commercially available.

1975–1976

The Church Committee reports are published.

1976

In *South Dakota v. Opperman*, the Supreme Court states that automobiles have less protection under the Fourth Amendment than homes.

1976

The New Jersey Supreme Court holds that the constitutional privacy protects a patient's decision to refuse or withdraw life-sustaining medical treatment and a guardian or family's decisions to authorize the termination of such treatment under certain circumstances in *In re Quinlan*.

1977

The U.S. Supreme Court determines that personal choice in matters of family living arrangements is a fundamental freedom in *Moore v. City of East Cleveland*.

1978

The Foreign Intelligence Surveillance Act (FISA) becomes law. FISA establishes a secret court to hear requests for warrants for "electronic surveillance to obtain foreign intelligence information."

1980

IBM signs a contract with the Microsoft Company to supply an operating system for IBM's new PC model.

1980s

DNA fingerprinting and cellular telephones become increasingly more common.

June 30, 1980

In *Harris v. McRae*, the United States Supreme Court rules that the Hyde Amendment, which imposed severe limitations on the use of federal funds to pay for abortions, does not violate the privacy rights granted under the Constitution. The Court holds that the right to an abortion does not convey to a woman "a constitutional entitlement to the financial resources to avail herself of the full range of protected choices."

1984

In *Hudson v. Palmer*, the Supreme Court holds that the Fourth Amendment proscription against unreasonable searches does not apply within the confines of the prison cell.

January 15, 1985

In *New Jersey v. T.L.O.*, the United States Supreme Court rules that while students are protected under the Fourth Amendment against unreasonable searches by school officials, the standard for conducting a warrantless search is lower. Teachers and administrators need not have "probable cause" that a crime has been committed in order to conduct a search; instead, the search must only meet a standard of "reasonableness, under all of the circumstances." In practice, this means that school officials only need a reasonable suspicion that a school rule or law has been broken before conducting a search, and that the search itself must be reasonably conducted.

1985

The Colorado Supreme Court declares that constitutional privacy encompasses the right of individuals to make legitimate medical or therapeutic use of sexually stimulating devices in *People v. Seven Thirty-Five East Colfax, Inc.* The Kansas Supreme Court makes a similar ruling in 1990.

1986

In *Bowers v. Hardwick*, the U.S. Supreme Court holds that homosexual sodomy is not a fundamental right and thus not protected under the constitutional right to privacy. Therefore, states can continue outlaw such practices.

1989

The World Wide Web service is added to the Internet.

1990s

Jack Kervorkian publicizes his assistance in the death of Janet Atkins in 1990 and dozens, and perhaps hundreds, of patients.

1990s

Increasing instances of identity theft are being reported.

1994

Netscape is credited with inventing the browser cookie, a computer file that allows firms to create a profile of a user by recognizing and tracking his or her Web surfing behavior.

1995

The European Union issues its first major data protection directive on the processing of personal data and its movement.

1995

The term *spyware* is used for the first time.

1997

The Electronic Privacy Information Center (EPIC) reviews 100 of the most frequently visited Internet sites and reports in June 1997 that only 17 have explicit privacy policies. None meet the basic standards for privacy protections, according to EPIC.

1998

An Alaska trail court recognizes a fundamental privacy right to choose one's life partner, irrespective of gender, in *Brause v. Bureau of Vital Statistics*. The decision is later overturned by a state constitutional amendment.

1998

The Vermont Supreme Court rules that state marriage laws denying equal benefits to committed same-sex partners violates the state constitution's guarantee of equal protection. Vermont becomes the first state to authorize civil unions and give same-sex unions all the identical rights and protections that stem from the martial relationship.

1999

The first commercially available GPS phone is launched by mobile phone manufacturer Benefon and sold mainly in Europe, even before such GPS-enabled mobile phones are widely available in the United States.

July 3, 1989

In *Webster v. Reproductive Health Services*, the Supreme Court finds that none of the provisions of Missouri legislation restricting abortions infringe upon the right to privacy or the Equal Protection Clause of the Fourteenth Amendment. In so doing, the Court affirms most parts of a Missouri law written from the premise that the "life of each human being begins at conception." The law forbids state employees to conduct abortions and prohibits the use of public facilities for abortions. The law also requires fetal viability tests at twenty weeks before performing abortions, rather than twenty-four weeks, the requirement established by *Roe v. Wade's* trimester approach. In its ruling, the Court does not overturn the essential guarantee provided in *Roe v. Wade* but it does defend the right of the states to impose these sorts of restrictions and it criticizes the inflexibility of the trimester framework established in the 1973 ruling.

1990

The Supreme Court hears its first "right to die" case in *Cruzan v. Director, Missouri Dep't of Health*, and holds that while individuals enjoy the right to refuse medical treatment, incompetent persons are not able to exercise such rights.

1990

The Human Genome Project is formally initiated.

1992

Tim Berners invents the "World Wide Web" at the European Particle Physics Laboratory in Switzerland.

1992

The first CCTV video surveillance system is installed in Newcastle, England.

Jun 29, 1992

In *Planned Parenthood v. Casey*, the United States Supreme Court eliminates the trimester framework established under *Roe v. Wade* for measuring the constitutionality of state laws on abortion. In reviewing a Pennsylvania statute that imposes several requirements regarding abortions on women and doctors, the Court upholds the basic guarantees established in *Roe v. Wade*. The Court, however, holds that the state possesses an interest in the fetus prior to the third trimester, and therefore states can intervene earlier than the last three months of the pregnancy. A woman still has a privacy right to an abortion, but states can introduce requirements of various sorts so long as they do not pose an "undue burden" or present "substantial obstacles" to this right.

1993

President Bill Clinton implements the "Don't ask, don't tell" policy for homosexuals serving in the military.

1994

The Communications Assistance for Law Enforcement Act becomes law.

1994

The Electronic Privacy Information Center is established.

1994

The Sexually Violent Predator Law (Stephanie's Law) is first applied in Kansas.

1994

The Driver's Privacy Protection Act becomes law.

Jun 26, 1995

In the case *Vernonia School District v. Acton*, the Supreme Court finds that the school's student athlete drug policy does not violate the prohibition against unreasonable search and seizure of the Fourth Amendment. The Court rules that the district's mandatory drug testing program for all student athletes does not violate students' Fourth Amendment rights. Citing the compelling school drug problem, the failure of other forms of intervention, and the peer influence of student athletes, it holds that the drug testing program meets the standard of reasonableness established in *New Jersey v. T.L.O.* The Court also holds that the test itself is not unreasonably invasive of the students' privacy. Athletes, it argues, are accustomed to less privacy than other students as they shower and change in a common locker room.

1995

The Communications Decency Act becomes law.

1996

The Health Insurance Portability Act becomes law.

1996

The Telecommunication Act becomes law.

1997

Carnivore is invented.

1997

Princess Diana's death a car crash, resulted in a debate on a celebrity's right to privacy versus the freedom of the press.

1998

The European Data Protection Directive becomes effective.

1998

The Children's Online Privacy Protection Act becomes law.

1999

The Financial Services Modernization Act is passed into law.

2000

In *Lawrence v. Texas*, the Supreme Court holds that the Texas statute making it a crime for two persons of the same sex to engage in certain sexual conduct violates the Due Process Clause of the Fourteenth Amendment.

June 28, 2000

In *Stenberg v. Carhart*, the United States Supreme Court strikes down a Nebraska law that prohibits partial birth abortions except when necessary to save the life of the mother. The Court holds that the law does not include an allowance for abortions necessary to protect the mother's health. And the Court further holds that the law is ambiguous—it fails to adequately differentiate between the method of abortion being prohibited and other legal late-term methods. This ambiguity, the Court argues, may discourage doctors from performing even legal abortions thereby posing an "undue burden" on women seeking an abortion.

2001

In *Lofton v. Kearney*, a federal judge rules that constitutional privacy does not confer upon homosexual adults a fundamental right to adopt a child.

2001

The U.S. Court of Appeals for the Eleventh Circuit remands a case back to a federal district court, instructing the judge to reconsider a state case involving a state ban on sexually stimulating devices in light of the "important interest in sexual privacy."

2001

In the case *Bartnicki v. Vopper*, the Supreme Court holds that the First Amendment protects the public disclosure of an illegally intercepted cellular telephone call.

2001

The Uniting and Strengthening America by Providing Appropriate Tools Required to Intercept and Obstruct Terrorism Act of 2001 (USA PATRIOT Act) is signed into law by President George W. Bush on October 26, 45 days after the attacks of September 11, and passing both houses of Congress by wide margins. The new statute grants new surveillance powers to law enforcement and intelligence agencies to "identify, to dismantle, to disrupt, and to punish terrorists before they strike." The Patriot Act, which makes significant changes to FISA and ECPA, includes easing wiretapping restrictions (by allowing roving wiretaps for example). Section 215 allows the sharing of "any tangible thing" as part of a foreign intelligence or international terrorism investigation.

2001

In the case *Camfield v. City of Oklahoma City*, the U.S. Supreme Court holds that the city violated a citizen's rights under the Video Privacy Protection Act by obtaining his video rental records without a warrant.

2001

In the case, *United States v. Kyllo*, the U.S. Supreme Court finds that the use of a thermal-imaging device to detect heat emanating from a private home violates Fourth Amendment protections.

2002

The National Joint Terrorist Task Force (NJTTF) is created. A multi-agency collaboration, local task forces (JTTF) consist of "small cells of highly trained, locally based, passionately committed investigators, analysts, linguists, SWAT experts, and other specialists" created to collect intelligence and combat terrorism.

2002

"Total Information Awareness." The news media discloses that the Pentagon is building a "computer system that could create a vast electronic dragnet, searching for personal information as part of the hunt for terrorists around the globe including the United States. Total Information Awareness is designed to use data mining techniques to uncover hidden patterns of activity from Internet mail information, credit card and banking transactions, and government documents. The program is later renamed as "Terrorism Information Awareness."

2002

President George W. Bush secretly authorizes the National Security Agency to eavesdrop on Americans and others inside the United States to search for evidence.

2003

In *Sell v. United States*, the U.S. Supreme Court allows searches of those suspected of terrorist activities without the court approved search warrants normally required for domestic spying. The court also held that the federal government may compel a mentally ill criminal defendant to take antipsychotic drugs make him competent to stand trial.

2003

The National Do-Not-Call Registry becomes effective.

November 2003

Congress passes the Homeland Security Act, which creates the Department of Homeland Security, "a Cabinet-level department to further coordinate and unify national homeland security efforts."

2003

AT&T technician Mark Klein discovers a room at the company's facility in San Francisco that was used to pursue "vacuum-cleaner surveillance" of internet use of millions of Americans, without the consent of other carriers.

2004

Facebook, the popular social-networking Web site, is introduced.

2006

President renews the USA Patriot Act. Congress reauthorizes the USA Patriot Act as permanent statutory law.

September 2006

Facebook launches a News Feed feature that broadcasts changes members to make to their Web profiles to the pages of others in their Facebook social networks. Due to widespread complaints over the invasiveness of feature, Facebook apologizes and allows its users to disable or modify it.

2007

Protect America Act becomes law, and amends the FISA. The Department of Justice asserts that the legislation "restores FISA to its original focus of protecting the rights of persons in the United States, while not acting as an obstacle to gathering foreign intelligence on targets located in foreign countries. By enabling our intelligence community to close a critical intelligence gap that existed before the Act became law, the Protect America Act has already made our Nation safer."

2007

Google launches Street View, a new feature of Google Maps, which allows users to view and navigate within a 360-degree panoramic street-level imagery of various U.S. cities. The remarkably detailed imagery resulted in widespread privacy complaints. It is also revealed that Street View also collected sensitive personal information from wireless home networks.

Apr 18, 2007

In *Gonzales v. Carhart* and *Gonzales v. Planned Parenthood*, the United States Supreme Court upholds the Partial Birth Abortion Ban Act passed by Congress in 2003. The statute prohibits a specific form of abortion in which the fetus is destroyed after being removed from the uterus. The Court holds that the law does not impose an undue burden since the more common method of dilation and extraction, in which the fetus is destroyed before removal, is unaffected by the ban and therefore still available to women. The majority of the Court argues that the essential protections of *Roe v. Wade* are not affected. Justice Ruth Bader Ginsburg, however, argues that the decision signals a new hostility to reproductive rights within the Court.

2008

Congress passes and President Bush signs the FISA Amendments Act in July 2008, which expands the federal surveillance powers and grants immunity for telecom companies that cooperate with governmental information gathering.

2009

The *New York Times* reports that the NSA is involved in "significant and systemic" "overcollection" of domestic communications.

2009

Thousands of Facebook users protests against terms of service changes that allow Facebook to use anything uploaded to the site at any time, even after users have deleted their profiles and left Facebook. After the controversy, the company reverts to its original policy and issues a statement of rights and responsibilities surrounding its relationships with users.

2010

President Barack Obama signs a one-year extension of provisions of the Patriot Act that were due to expire.

November 2010

Secure Flight is established by the DHS to help streamline and make uniform the watch list system and is administered by the Transportation Security Administration (TSA). Prior to the implementation of Secure Flight, individual airlines were responsible for comparing passenger information with the government's watch lists (including the No Fly List (immediate threats) and the Selectee List (enhanced screening required)).

2010

WikiLeaks and other news organizations begin publishing excerpts from classified military documents captured by Private First Class Bradley Manning. Private Manning is arrested in May in Iraq and was eventually tried on 21 counts of the leaking of more than half a million documents, or "cables," related to the wars in Iraq and Afghanistan.

2011

A subpoena is issued for Twitter to release account information for individuals involved in the WikiLeaks disclosure of sensitive and confidential diplomatic cables.

May 2011

Congress passes an extension of the Patriot Act, which President Obama signs into law.

2011

Google agrees to settle the federal trade Commission charges that it used deceptive tactics and violated its own privacy promises to s0oncumers when it launched its social network Google Buzz in 2010. Thousands of users complain to Google about public disclosures of their email contacts that included, in some cases, ex-spouses, patients, students, employers or competitors.

January 2012

Google announces it will integrate user data across its email, video, social-networking and other services.

2012

The *New York Times* reports an unprecedented public accounting of cell phone carriers. They respond to 1.3 million demands by law enforcement for subscriber information such as text messages and caller locations. The reports paint a picture of dramatic increase in cell phone surveillance over the last five years.

2012

Congress extends the FISA Amendments Act for another five years. Obama signs the bill into law.

2012

Google agreed to pay a $ 22.5 million fine to settle allegations that it violated terms of the settlement order it signed in 2011 involving Google Buzz. The Federal Trade Commission imposed the penalty on Google, the largest ever imposed for violating a FTC order, for misleading Apple's Safari Web browser about tracking their online activities.

2013

The *Guardian* reports that FISA court judge Roger Vinson issues a secret order to Verizon to produce "metadata"—time, duration, numbers called (without revealing the actual call content)—to the NSA for a three-month timeframe. The *Wall Street Journal* reports of similar arrangements with AT&T and Sprint.

The *Guardian* and The *Washington Post* simultaneously disclose the existence of the PRISM program, which was launched in 2009. Prism grants NSA access to the personal data of millions of people through Microsoft, Yahoo, Google, Facebook, Apple, and AOL. The Office of the Director of National Intelligence argued that the program is authorized by the FISA Amendments Act of 2008.

June 21, 2013

The U.S. Justice Department files espionage charges against Edward Snowden, a former NSA contractor, for the leak of classified information.

2013

FBI director Robert Mueller admits that the United States employs drones as part of the domestic surveillance program. Speaking before a Senate Judiciary Committee, Mueller agrees that still-uncommon drone usage sparks concerns about personal privacy and is "worthy of debate and perhaps legislation down the road."

December 16, 2013

Ruling against the NSA's surveillance program, Judge Richard Leon of the Federal District Court for the District of Columbia, claimed that the program is "significantly likely" to violate the Fourth Amendment's protection against unreasonable searches. "I cannot imagine a more 'indiscriminate' and 'arbitrary invasion' than this systematic and high tech collection and retention of personal data on virtually every single citizen for purposes of querying and analyzing it without prior judicial approval." The government relied on *Smith v. Maryland* (U.S., 1989) to justify its spying program. The ruling said police may capture information about phone numbers a suspect called without a warrant because suspects cannot expect to keep such information private when using a service of a third party. Leon said that given the changes in technology, the Smith ruling no longer applies to current circumstances.

December 18, 2013

An advisory panel commissioned by President Obama released a 300-page report that recommended 46 changes to the NSA's surveillance program. The recommendations included: handing authority of metadata gleaned from surveillance to a third party, such as a telecommunications company or a private group; requiring that NSA analysts obtain a court order before accessing the data; requiring that the government obtain a court order before issuing national security letters, which force businesses to hand over private customer information; banning the government from using "back door" methods to gain access to hardware or software; and that an advocate should argue in favor of civil liberties in cases that come before the Foreign Intelligence Surveillance Court. Currently, these cases are heard in private and only the government presents a case. The report also said the NSA's surveillance program has not been "essential to preventing attacks."

January 17, 2014,

President Obama announced reforms to the country's surveillance program based on the panel's recommendations. He said that while he believed the activities of the NSA were legal, he acknowledged that some had compromised civil liberties. The reforms he outlined include: requiring NSA analysts to get a court order to access phone data unless in cases of emergencies; an eventual end to the collection of massive amounts of metadata by the government; the NSA will stop eavesdropping on leaders of allied nations; officials can pursue a phone number linked to a terrorist association by two degrees rather than three; and Congress will appoint advocates to argue on the side of civil liberties before the FISA court. He did not implement the recommendation about national security letters.

January 23, 2014

The Privacy and Civil Liberties Oversight Board issues a report stating that NSA program is likely both illegal and unconstitutional and has not proven to be effective in fighting terrorism. The report recommended the collection of the metadata be terminated.

July 2014

Relations between the U.S. and Germany become strained because of reports that the U.S. hired a clerk at Germany's intelligence agency to steal hundreds of documents. Days later, German officials announce they believe they had uncovered a second spy working for the U.S. In response, Germany expels the CIA station chief from Berlin.

May 2015

A three-judge panel of the 2nd U.S. Circuit Court of Appeals in Manhattan rules that Congress never authorized the bulk collection of the phone records of U.S. citizens when it passed the U.S.A. Patriot Act, and therefore the National Security Agency's program that does so is illegal. The panel allowed the program to continue, but called on Congress to amend the law. In the court's opinion, Judge Gerard Lynch wrote "knowledge of the program was intentionally kept to a minimum, both within Congress and among the public." The program was secret until 2013, when it was disclosed by Edward Snowden.

June 2, 2015

The Senate votes, 67 to 32, to pass the USA FREEDOM Act. The House had previously approved the bill, and President Obama signs it into law. The act ends the NSA's bulk collection of phone records of millions of Americans. That responsibility shifts to the phone companies, who can turn the data over to the government only when the Foreign Intelligence Surveillance Court issues a warrant to search the phone records of individuals. The law also reinstates three provisions of the USA Patriot Act, which expired on June 1: roving wiretaps of terror suspects who change devices, surveillance of "lone wolf" suspects who are not affiliated with a terrorist organization, and the seeking of court orders to search business records.

Table of Privacy Rights Cases

Abrams v. United States, 250 U.S. 616 (1919)

ACLU v. Ashcroft, 542 U.S. 656 (2004)

ACLU v. U.S. Dep't of Justice, 750 F.3d 927 (D.C. Cir., 2014)

Almedia v. Amazon.com, 456 F.3d 1316 (11th Cir., 2006)

AT&T Inc. v. FCC, 582 F.3d 490 (3d Cir. 2009), rev'd, 562 U.S. 397 (2011)

Bartnicki v. Vopper, 532 U.S. 514 (2001)

Board of Education v. Earls, 536 U.S. 822, 837 (2002)]

Boyd v. United States, 116 U.S. 616 (1886)

Brown v. Board of Education, 347 U.S. 483 (1954)

California v. Ciraolo, 476 U.S. 207, 106 S.Ct. 1809 (1986)

Camara v. Municipal Court, 387 U.S. 523 (1967)

Cantrell v. Forest City Publishing Company, 310 U.S. 296 (1940)

Cardwell v. Lewis, 419 U.S. 245 (1974)

Carey v. Population Services International, 431 U.S. 678, 97 S.Ct. 2010 (1977)

Castello v. U.S. Postal Service, EEOC Request No. 0520110649 (Dec. 20, 2011)

Citizens United v. FEC, 558 U.S. 310 (2010)

City of Sherman v. Henry, 928 SW2d 464 (TX, 1996)

Clapper v. Amnesty Int'l USA, 667 F.3d 163 (2d Cir., 2011)

Cox Broadcasting Corporation v. Cohn, 420 U.S. 469 (1975)

Cruzan v. Missouri Department of Health, 497 U.S. 261 (1990)

Cupp v. Murphy, 412 U.S. 291 (1973)

Department of Justice v. Reporters Committee for Freedom of the Press, 489 U.S. 749 (1989)

Detroit Free Press, Inc. v. U.S. Dep't of Justice, No. 14-670, 2012 WL _____ (6th Cir. Aug. 12, 2015) (petition for en banc rehearing pending)

Doe v. Chao, 540 U.S. 615 (2004)

Doe v. Gonzales, 546 U.S. 1301 (2005)

Does v. Bolton, 410 U.S. 179 (1973)

Dow Chemical Co. v. United States, 250 F.Supp. 2d 748 (ED Mich., 2003) mod. In part by oth. grds. By Dow Chem Co. v. U.S. , 278 F. Supp. 2d 844 (E.D. Mich., 2003), rev'd in part on oth. Grds by Dow Chem Co. v. United States, 435, 435 F.3d 594 (6th Cir., 2006)

EF Cultural Travel BV v. Explorica, Inc., 274 F.3d 577 (1st Cir. 2001)

Eisenstadt v. Baird, 405 U.S. 438, 453 (1972)

Medicaid Privacy Requirements, 42 USC 1396a(a)(7)

National Security Act of 1947, 61 Stat. 495 (1947)
Occupational Health and Safety Act of 1970, 29 USC § 657
Omnibus Crime Control and Safe Streets Act of 1968, Pub. L. No. 90-351 (1968), 82 Stat. 197 (1968), 18 U.S.C. § 2510 et seq.
Paperwork Reduction Act of 1995
Patient Protection and Affordable Care Act of 2012, P.L. 111-148 (2012)
Patient Safety and Quality Improvement Act of 2005 (PSQUIA), 42 USC § 299b-21 to 229b-26
Pen-Trap Statute, 18 USC § 3121-3127
Preserving American Privacy Act, HR 113-637 (2013)
Privacy Act of 1974, Pub. L. No. 93-579 (1974), 88 Stat. 1896 (1974), 5 USC § 552a
Privacy Protection Act of 1980, Pub. L. No. 96-440 (1980), 94 Stat. 1879 (1980), 42 USC § 2000aa, et seq.
Protect America Act of 2007, Pub. L. No. 110-55 (2007); 121 Stat, 552 (2007)
Protection of Children from Sexual Predators Act, 18 USC 2425
REAL ID Act of 2006, HR 1268, 109 P.L. 13 (2006)
Right to Financial Privacy Act of 1978, 12 USC §§ 3401-3403
Safeguards Rule, 15 U.S.C. § 6801-6809
SAMSHA: Confidentiality of Substance Abuse Patient Records, 42 USC § 290dd
Save America Through Verification and Employment Act (2015), H.R. 2000 (2015)
"Snooper's Charter" [Draft Communications Data Bill, 2012-2013]
Social Security Act of 1935, 49 Stat. 620 (1935)
Social Security Number Confidentiality Act of 2000, Pub. L. No. 106-433 (2000), 114 Stat. 1910 (2000), 31 U.S.C. § 3327
Stored Communications Act, Title III, 100 Stat. 1848 (1986); 18 USC § 2701, et seq.
Tax Reform Act of 1976
Telecommunications Act of 1996, Pub. L No. 104-104 (1996), 110 Stat. 56 (1996); 47 USC § 6501
Telemarketing and Consumer Fraud and Abuse Prevention Act of 1994, 15 U.S.C. § 6101-6108
Telephone Consumer Protection Act of 1991, 47 USC § 615a
Telephone Records Protection Act of 2006, 120 Stat. 3568 (2006)
Truth in Caller ID Act of 2009, Pub. L. 111-331
US Privacy Act, 5 USC § 552a
USA Freedom Act of 2015, Pub. L. No. 114-23 (2015)
USA PATRIOT Act, Pub. L. No. 107-52 (2001), 115 Stat, 272 (2001), codified in various sections of 18, 31, and 42 U.S.C.
USA PATRIOT Act Additional Reauthorizing Amendments Act of 2006, 120 Stat. 278 (2006)
Video Privacy Protection Act of 1988, Pub. L. No. 100-618 (1998), 102 Stat. 3195 (1998), 18 USC § 2710

Video Voyeurism Prevention Act of 2004
Violent Crime Control and Law Enforcement Act of 1994, 108 Stat. 2102 (1994); 18 U.S.C. 2271-2725
"We Are Watching You" Act, HR 1164 (2015)
Whistleblower Protection Act of 1989
Whistleblower Protection Enhancement Act of 2012
Wireless Communications and Public Safety Act of 1991
Wiretap Act of 1968, Title III of the Omnibus Crime Control Act of 1968; codified as 18 USC §§ 2510-2522

Bibliography

A

Aaken, Dominik, Andreas Ostermaier, and Arnold Picot. *"Privacy and Freedom: An Economic (Re-)Evaluation of Privacy." Kyklos* 67, no. 2: 133–155. *Business Source Complete*, EBSCOhost.

Abagnale, Frank W. *Stealing Your Life: The Ultimate Identity Theft Prevention Plan.* New York: Broadway Books, 2008.

Abdolian, Lisa Finnegan Takooshian. "The USA PATRIOT Act: Civil Liberties, the Media, and Public Opinion." *Fordham Urban Law Journal* 30, no. 4 (2002).

Abeyratne, Ruwantissa. "Full Body Scanners at Airports—the Balance between Privacy and State Responsibility." *Journal of Transportation Security*: 73–85.

Ablon, Lillian, Martin C. Libicki, and Andrea A. Golay. *Markets for Cybercrime Tools and Stolen Data.* Santa Monica: RAND Corporation, 2014.

Abraham, Kenneth S., and G. Edward White, "Prosser and His Influence." Journal of Tort Law 6, no. 1–2 (2013): 27–74. Virginia Public Law and Legal Theory Research Paper No. 2014–51.

Abramson, Shelton, and Mali Friedman. "Key Holdings in the In re iPhone Application Dismissal Order." *InsidePrivacy,* June 18, 2012.

Ackerman, Caryn J. "Fairness or Fiction: Striking a Balance between the Goals of S 3 and the Policy Concerns Motivating Qualified Immunity." *Oregon Law Review* 85 (2006): 1027–1062.

Acquisti, Alessandro. *Digital Privacy: Theory, Technologies, and Practices.* New York: Auerbach Publications, 2008.

Addicott, Jeffrey F., and Michael T. McCaul. "The Protect America Act of 2007: A Framework for Improving Intelligence Collection in the War on Terror." *Texas Review of Law and Politics* 13 (2008).

Administrative Office for the United States Courts. *Wiretap—Major Offenses for Which Court-Authorized Intercepts Were Granted—During the 12-Month Period Ending December 31, 2013.*

Agre, Philip. *Technology and Privacy: The New Landscape.* Cambridge, Mass.: MIT Press, 1997.

Ahearn, Eileen M. "Special Education in the New National Educational Data System." *Communication Disorders Quarterly* 29, no. 4 (2008): 236–238.

Akerlof, George A. "The Market for 'Lemons': Quality Uncertainty and the Market Mechanism." *The Quarterly Journal of Economics* 84, no. 3 (1970): 488–500.

Albarran, Alan B., ed. *The Social Media Industries.* New York: Routledge, 2013.

Alderman, Ellen, and Caroline Kennedy. *The Right to Privacy.* 1995; reprint, New York: Vintage Books, 1997.

Alderman, Ellen M. "Dragnet Drug Testing in Public Schools and the Fourth Amendment." *Columbia Law Review* 86, no. 4 (May 1986): 852–875.

Aldrich, Richard J. *GCHQ: The Uncensored Story of Britain's Most Secret Intelligence Agency.* London: HarperPress, 2010.

Alldridge, Peter. *Personal Autonomy, the Private Sphere, and the Criminal Law: A Comparative Study.* Oxford, England: Hart Pubisher, 2001.

Allen, Anita L. *Unpopular Privacy: What Must We Hide?* Oxford: Oxford University Press, 2011.

Allhoff, Fritz. *The Affordable Care Act Decision Philosophical and Legal Implications.* New York: Routledge, Taylor and Francis, 2014.

Anandarajan, M., R. D'ovidio, and A. Jenkins. "Safeguarding Consumers against Identity-Related Fraud: Examining Data Breach Notification Legislation through the Lens of Routine Activities Theory." *International Data Privacy Law* 00, no. 00 (2012): 51–60.

Andreasen, Kristin. "*Lawrence v. Texas:* One Small Step For Gay Rights; One Giant Leap for Liberty." *Journal of Contemporary Legal Issues* 14, no. 1, (2004): 73–82.

Andrews, Lori B. *I Know Who You Are and I Saw What You Did: Social Networks and the Death of Privacy.* New York: Free Press, 2012.

Angelelli, L. *Steve Paul Jobs.* Computer Science Department NSF-Supported Education Infrastructure Project. 2008.

Annas, George J. "Nancy Cruzan and the Right to Die." *New England Journal of Medicine* 323, no. 10 (September 6, 1990): 670–673.Arthur, John. *Morality and Moral Controversies.* 5th ed. Upper Saddle River, N.J.: Prentice Hall, 1999.

Antonopoulos, Andreas M. "Bitcoin Neutrality." Bitcoin 2013 Conference, May 18, 2013, San Jose, CA. YouTube, June 10, 2013.

Anzalone, Christopher A. *Supreme Court Cases on Gender and Sexual Equality, 1787–2001.* Armonk, NY: M.E. Sharpe, 2002.

Ariew, Roger, and Marjorie Grené, eds. *Descartes and His Contemporaries: Meditations, Objections, and Replies.* Chicago, IL: University of Chicago Press, 1995.

Armijo, Lisa Marie. *The Search for Space and Dignity: Using Participatory Action Research to Explore Boundary Management among Homeless Individuals.* 2002.

Armstrong, William M. *E. L. Godkin: A Biography.* Albany: State University of New York Press, 1978.

Arterton, F. Christopher. *Teledemocracy: Can Technology Protect Democracy?* Newbury Park, CA: Sage Publications; 1987.

Arthur, John, and William H. Shaw. *Readings in the Philosophy of Law*, 4rd ed. Upper Saddle River, NJ: Prentice Hall, 2001.

Associated Press. "Pentagon's 'Terror Information Awareness' Program Will End." *USA Today*, September 25, 2003.

Atkin, Michelle Louise. *Balancing Liberty and Security: An Ethical Study of U.S. Foreign Intelligence Surveillance, 2001–2009*. Lanham, MD: Rowman & Littlefield Publishers, 2013.

Aycock, John Daniel. *Spyware and Adware*. New York: Springer, 2011.

Ayday, Erman, Emiliano De Cristofaro, Jean-Pierre Hubaux, and Gene Tsudik. "Whole Genome Sequencing: Revolutionary Medicine or Privacy Nightmare?" *Computer*: 58–66.

Ayenson, Mika, Dietrich James Wambach, Ashkan Soltani, Nathan Good, and Chris Jay Hoofnagle. "Flash Cookies and Privacy II: Now with HTML5 and ETag Respawning," July 29, 2011.

B

Baca, Murtha, and Tony Gill. *Introduction to Metadata*.

Los Angeles, CA: Getty Research Institute, 2008. Bagley, Ian. "Constitutional Law—Search-Incident-to-Arrest Exception to Prohibition against Warrantless Searches Inapplicable to Cell Phone Searches—*Smallwood v. State.*" *Suffolk University Law Review* (2014).

Bailard, Catie Snow. *Democracy's Double-Edged Sword: How Internet Use Changes Citizens' Views of Their Government.*

Bailey, Martha J. " 'Momma's Got the Pill': How Anthony Comstock and *Griswold v. Connecticut* Shaped U.S. Childbearing." *American Economic Review* 100, no. 1 (2010): 98–129.

Baird, Douglas G. "Note: Human Cannonballs and the First Amendment: *Zacchini v. Scripps-Howard Broadcasting Co.*" *Stanford Law Review* 30, no. 6 (July 1978): 1185–1209.

Baker, Mary Beth. "Article Title." *Journal Title* 57, no. 3 (2011): 96.

Baker, Patricia. "Sexual Harassment: High School Girls Speak Out." *Canadian Review of Sociology and Anthropology* 34, no. 1 (February 1997): 114.

Baker, Robert. "A Theory of International Bioethics: The Negotiable and Non-Negotiable." *Kennedy Institute of Ethics Journal* 8, no. 3 (1998): 233–273.

Balasubramani, Venkat. "Judge Koh Whittles Down iPhone App Privacy Lawsuit—In re iPhone Application Litig." Technology and Marketing Law Blog, July 4, 2012.

Balko, Radley. *Overkill: The Rise of Paramilitary Police Raids in America*. Washington, DC: Cato Institute, 2006.

Ball, Carlos A. "Privacy, Property, and Public Sex." *Columbia Journal of Gender and Law* 18, no. 1 (2009).

Ball, Howard. *The Supreme Court in the Intimate Lives of Americans: Birth, Sex, Marriage, Childrearing, and Death*. New York: New York University Press, 2004.

Ball, James. "NSA's PRISM Surveillance Program: How It Works and What It Can Do." The *Guardian*, June 2013.

Bambauer, Derek E. "Exposed." *Minnesota Law Review* 98 (2014): 2025–2092.

Bambauer, Jane. "Is Data Speech?" *Stanford Law Review* 66, no. 57 (2014).

Bamford, James. *Body of Secrets: Anatomy of the Ultra-Secret National Security Agency*. New York: Doubleday, 2001.

Bamforth, Nicholas, ed. *Sexual Orientation and Rights*. Burlington, VT: Ashgate, 2014.

Barbas, Samantha. "Saving Privacy from History." *Depaul Law Review* 61 (Summer 2012): 973–1048.

———. "When Privacy Almost Won: *Time, Inc. v. Hill* (1967)." *University of Pennsylvania Journal of Constitutional Law*.

Barber, N. W. "A Right to Privacy?" In *Human Rights and Private Law: Privacy as Autonomy*. Portland, edited by Katja S. Ziegler. Portland, OR: Hart, 2007.

Barendt, E. M. *Privacy*. Aldershot: Ashgate/Dartmouth, 2001.

Barendt, Eric. "Libel and Invasion of Privacy," in *Freedom of Speech*, 2d ed. New York: Oxford University Press, 2007.

Barfield, Woodrow. *Fundamentals of Wearable Computers and Augmented Reality*, 2d ed. Lanham, MD: Rowman and Littlefield, 2015.

Bargmeyer, Bruce E. and Daniel W. Gillman. "Metadata Standards and Metadata Registries: An Overview." Bureau of Labor Statistics, 2000.

Barker, Adam and Jonathan Stuart Ward, "Undefined By Data: A Survey of Big Data Definitions," *arXiv preprint arXiv:1309.5821*, 2013.

Barker, Katherine, Jackie D'Amato, and Paul Sheridan. "Credit Card Fraud: Awareness and Prevention." *Journal of Financial Crime* 15 (2008): 398.

Barrett Lidsky, Lyrissa. "Silencing John Doe: Defamation and Discourse in Cyberspace." *Duke Law Journal* vol. 49, no. 4 (2000): 855–946.

Bartee, Alice Fleetwood. *Privacy Rights: Cases Lost and Causes Won before the Supreme Court*. Lanham, MD: Rowman & Littlefield, 2006. Print.

Batty, David. "Instagram Acts after BBC Finds Site Users Are Advertising Illegal Drugs." *Guardian,* November 7, 2013.

Beales, J. Howard. *Legislative Efforts to Combat Spam: Joint Hearing before . . . 108th Congress, 1st Session, July 9, 2003*. Washington, DC: US Government Printing Office, 2003.

Beattie, James R., Jr. "Privacy in the First Amendment: Private Facts and the Zone of Deliberation." *Vanderbilt Law Review* 44 (1991): 899–923.

Beckett, Charlie, and James Ball. *Wikileaks: News in the Networked Era*. Cambridge, England: Polity Press, 2012.

Bedi, Monu Singh. "Fourth Amendment Doctrine Mash-Up: The Curious Case of Cell Phone Location Data." *SSRN Electronic Journal SSRN Journal.*

Beerworth, Andrew A. "*United States v. Stevens*: A Proposal for Criminalizing Crush Videos under Current Free Speech Doctrine." *Vermont Law Review* 35, no. 4 (2011): 901.

Belangia, David. "Data Breach Preparation." Master's thesis, SANS Technology Institute, Los Alamos National Laboratory, 2015.

Bell, David. *Cyberculture: The Key Concepts*. London: Routledge, 2004. Bell, Mary Ann, and Bobby Ezell. *Cybersins and Digital Good Deeds: A Book about Technology and Ethics*. New York: Haworth Press, 2007.

Bellia, Patricia L. "Wikileaks and the Institutional Framework for National Security Disclosures." *Yale Law Journal* 121 (2012): 1448–1526.

Bender, Lewis G., et al., eds. *Critical Issues in Police Discipline: Case Studies*. Springfield, IL: C. C. Thomas, 2005.

Bennett, Colin J. *The Privacy Advocates: Resisting the Spread of Surveillance*. Cambridge, MA: MIT Press, 2008.

Bennett, W. Lance. *News: The Politics of Illusion*, 9th ed. Chicago, IL: University of Chicago Press, 2011.

Benson, Kenneth R. *Financial Services Modernization: GLBA of 1999: Law and Explanation*. Chicago, Ill.: CCH, 1999.

Bentzen, Sheila A. "Safe for Work? Analyzing the Supreme Court's Standard of Privacy for Government Employees in Light of *City of Ontario v. Quon*." *Iowa Law Review* 97, no. 4 (May 2012): 1283–1304.

Berg, Candace D. "Widening the Lane: An Argument for Broader Interpretation of Permissible Uses under the Driver's Privacy Protection Act." *Notre Dame Law Review* 90, no. 2 (2014): 847–873.

Berg, Daniel, and Tina Klopp. *Inside Wikileaks: My Time with Julian Assange at the World's Most Dangerous Website*. New York: Crown Publishers, 2011.

Berger, J. M., and Jonathon Morgan. *The ISIS Twitter Census: Defining and Describing the Population of ISIS Supporters on Twitter*. Brookings Project on U.S. Relations with the Islamic World Analysis Paper no. 20 (March 2015).

Bergman, Hannah. "Out of Sight, Out of Bounds," *The News Media and the Law* 33, no. 2 (Spring 2009): 11.

Berleur, Jacques, and Diane Whitehouse. *An Ethical Global Information Society Culture and Democracy Revisited.*

Bernescu, Laura. "When Is a Hack Not a Hack: Addressing the CFAA's Applicability to the Internet Service Context." *University of Chicago Legal Forum* (2013): 633.

Bernstein, Fred. "Glenn Greenwald: Life Beyond Borders." *Out Magazine*, May 2011. Bhagwat, Ashutosh. "*Sorrell v. IMS Health:* Details, Detailing, and the Death of Privacy." *Vermont Law Review* 36, no. 855 (2012).

Bidgoli, Hossein. *Handbook of Information Security*. Hoboken, NJ: Wiley, 2006. Binney, William, and Laura Poitras. *The Program*. New York Times Op-Doc, 8:27. August 22, 2012.

Birnbaum, Michael. "Europeans Seek to Learn Extent of U.S. Agencies' Data Collection." *Washington Post,* June 11, 2013. Bivins, Amy E. "United States: Privacy—House Judiciary Explores Espionage Act's Application to Wikileaks' Net Posts." *World Communications Regulation Report* 6, no. 1 (2011): 16–18.

Blair, J. P. "What Do We Know about Interrogation in the United States?" *Journal of Police and Criminal Psychology* 20, no. 2 (September 2005): 44–57.

Blasi, Vincent. "The Checking Value in First Amendment Theory." *American Bar Foundation Research Journal* 2, no. 3 (1977): 521.

Blatterer, Harry. *Modern Privacy Shifting Boundaries, New Forms*. New York: Palgrave Macmillan, 2010. Bleumer, Gerrit. "Biometric Yet Privacy Protecting Person Authentication." *Information Hiding Lecture Notes in Computer Science*, 99–110.

Bloemraad, Irene. *Becoming a Citizen: Incorporating Immigrants and Refugees in the United States and Canada*. Berkeley: University of California Press, 2006. Bloom, Robert M. *Searches, Seizures & Warrants: A Reference Guide to the United States Constitution*. Westport, CT: Praeger, 2003.

Bloomberg BNA. "DOJ Settles, Turns Page on 'Dark Chapter' in Politicized Honors Program Hiring Dispute." *Daily Labor Report* 53, no. 1 (March 19, 2014). Blum, Karen, et. al. "Qualified Immunity Developments: Not Much Hope Left for Plaintiffs." *Touro Law Review* 29 (2013): 633–658.

Blumenthal, David. "Launching HITECH." *New England Journal of Medicine* 362 (February 2010): 382–85.

Bobis, Charles S. *Terry v. Ohio 30 Years Later: A Symposium on the Fourth Amendment, Law Enforcement, and Police-citizen Encounters*. Brooklyn, N.Y.: St. John's Law Review Association, 1998.

Bocij, Paul. *Cyberstalking: Harassment in the Internet Age and How to Protect Your Family*. Westport, CT: Praeger, 2004.

Boddie, J. "Has Apple Hit the Right Disruptive Notes?" *Strategy & Innovation* (July–August, 2005): 3–4.

Bodenheimer, Thomas and Kevin Grumbach. 2005. Conflict and Change in America's Health Care System. In Understanding Health Policy: A Clinical Approach, eds. Harriet Lebowitz, Shelley Reinhardt and Lester A. Sheinis, 193–203. The McGraw-Hill Companies.

Bollinger, Lee C. *Images of a Free Press*. Chicago, IL: University of Chicago Press, 1991. Bonaci, T. and H. Chizack. Privacy by Design in Brain-Computer Interfaces. University of Washington, Department of EE. website: www.ee.washington.edu/ techsite/ papers/documents/ UWEETR-2013–0001.

Booth, Phil. "The UK Should Take Note of the U.S. Biometric Security Projects Says Privacy Advocate." *Computer Fraud & Security* (2007): 7.

Borgman, Christine L. *Scholarship in the Digital Age: Information, Infrastructure, and the Internet*. Cambridge, MA: MIT Press, 2010.

Borjas, George J. *Immigration Economics*. Cambridge, MA: Harvard University Press, 2014. Bosmajian, Haig A. *Obscenity and Freedom of Expression*. New York: B. Franklin, 1976.

Botcherby, Sue, and Chris Creegan. *Moving Forward: Putting Sexual Orientation in the Public Domain*. Manchester, UK: Equality and Human Rights Commission, 2009. [Equality and Human Rights Commission Research Summary 40].

Botkin, Jeffrey R. "Federal Privacy and Confidentiality." *The Hastings Center Report* 25, no. 5 (September-October 1995).

Bove, Victor M. "HIV Testing of Health Care Workers. (AIDS)." *Physician Executive* 18 (May 1, 1992).

Boyd D., Hargittai E., J. Schultz, and J, Palfrey J. (2011). "Why Parents Help Their Children Lie to Facebook about Age: Unintended Consequences of the 'Children's Online Privacy Protection Act.'" *First Monday* 16, no. 11.

Boyle, David C. "Proposal to Amend the United States Privacy Act to Extend Its Protections to Foreign Nationals and Non-Resident Aliens." *Cornell International Law Journal* 22, no. 2 (1989): 285–305.

Bradley, Craig M. "Reconceiving the Fourth Amendment and the Exclusionary Rule." *Law and Contemporary Problems* 73 (Summer 2010): 211–238.

____. "The Wicked May Flee, but the Police May Stop Them." *Trial*, April 1, 2000. Brandeis, Louis D., and Warren, Samuel D. "The Right to Privacy." *Harvard Law Review* 4, no. 193 (1890)

Brandt, Richard L. *One Click: Jeff Bezos and the Rise of Amazon*. New York: Portfolio/Penguin, 2011. Branscomb, Anne W. *Who Owns Information?: From Privacy to Public Access*. New York: Basic Books, 1994.

Braswell, Michael, John Fuller, and Bo Lozoff. *Corrections, Peacemaking, and Restorative Justice: Transforming Individuals and Institutions*. Cincinnati, OH: Anderson, 2001.

Bratman, Benjamin E. "Brandeis and Warren's 'The Right to Privacy and the Birth of the Right to Privacy.'" *Tennessee Law Review* 69 (Spring 2002): 638–644.

Brav, Hiawatha. "Would You Let Your TV Watch You?" *The Boston Globe*. June 14, 2013. Brazhnik, Tatiana. "Cookies in E-Commerce: Balancing Privacy and Business." *SSRN*, April 29, 2013.

Brehm, Robert P. "What CIOs and CTOs Need to Know About Big Data and Data Intensive Computing." PhD diss., University of Oregon, 2012.

Brinson, Susan L. *The Red Scare, Politics, and the Federal Communications Commission, 1941–1960*. Westport, CT: Praeger, 2004.

Bronk, Chris. "Wiretapping, Surveillance, and the Internet." *SSRN Electronic Journal SSRN Journal*.

Broughton, Janet. *Descartes's Method of Doubt*. Princeton, NJ: Princeton University Press, 2003.

Browdie, Brian. "ATMs May be Top Targets for Crime: Verizon Report." *Payments Source* (October 25, 2012).

Brown, Cecilia Wright, Kevin A. Peters, and Kofi Adofo Nyarko, eds. *Cases on Research and Knowledge Discovery: Homeland Security Centers of Excellence*. Hershey, PA: Information Science Reference, 2014.

Brownell, George A. *The Origin and Development of the National Security Agency*. Laguna Hills, CA: Aegean Park Press, 1981.

Bruno, Andorra, et al. *Immigration Legislation and Issues in the 112th Congress*. Washington, DC: Congressional Research Service, September 30, 2011.

Bryson, Kerry J. "The Naked Truth: Fourth Amendment Lessons from the U.S. Supreme Court: A Review of Recent Home-search Cases from the U.S. Supreme Court, including the Rettele Case from May, Where the Court Ruled That Police Didn't Act Unreasonably When They Forced Search." *Illinois Bar Journal* (2007).

Buchanan, Sarah Alix. "An Evaluation of the FERPA (1974) on Student Records Management and Access." MA thesis, University of California at Los Angeles, 2009.

Buckman, Deborah F. "Validity, Construction, and Application of Federal Driver's Privacy Protection Act, 18 U.S.C.A. §§ 2721 to 2725." *American Law Reports, Federal* 183 (2003).

____. "Validity, Construction, and Application of Health Insurance Portability and Accountability Act of 1996 (HIPAA) and Regulations Promulgated Thereunder." *American Law Reports Annotated*. 194 (2004) Fed. 133.

Buettgens, Mathew and Caitlin Carroll. 2012. Eliminating the Individual Mandate: Effects on Premiums, Coverage, and Uncompensated Care. Urban Institute Health Policy Center and Robert Wood Johnson Foundation.

"Building a Metadata Schema - Where to Start (ISO/ TC 46/SC11N800R1)." National Information Standards Organization (NISO), 2014.

Bureau of Justice Statistics. "Identity Theft." bjs.gov. Last modified February 10, 2015. Burkoff, John. *Search Warrant Law Deskbook*. New York: Clark Boardman Callaghan, 2015.

Burnett, Mark, and James C. Foster. *Hacking the Code ASP.NET Web Application Security*. Rockland, MA: Syngress, 2004.

Burnett, Nicholas F. "*New York Times v. Sullivan*," in *Free Speech on Trial: Communication Perspectives on Landmark Supreme Court Decisions*, ed. Richard A. Parker, 116–129. Tuscaloosa: University of Alabama Press, 2003.

Burshnic, Rudolph J. "Applying the Stored Communications Act to the Civil Discovery of Social Networking Sites." *Washington and Lee Law Review* 69 (2012): 1259–1293.

Buyya, R., Pandey, S. and Vecchiola, C. "Market-Oriented Cloud Computing and the Cloudbus Toolkit." In *Large Scale Network-Centric Distributed Systems*, edited by H. Sarbazi-Azad and A. Y. Zomaya, 319–358. Hoboken, NJ: John Wiley & Sons, Inc., 2013.

Byford, Katrin Schatz. "Privacy in Cyberspace: Constructing a Model of Privacy for the Electronic Communications Environment." *Rutgers Computer & Technology Law Journal* 1998.

Bygrave, Lee A., *Data Privacy Law, an International Perspective*. Oxford: Oxford University Press, 2014.

C

Cackley, Alicia Puente. *Facial Recognition Technology: Commercial Uses, Privacy Issues, and Applicable Federal Law: Report to the Ranking Member, Subcommittee on Privacy, Technology and the Law, Committee on the Judiciary, U.S. Senate*. Washington, DC: United States Government Accountability Office, 2015.

Caldero, Michael A., and John P. Crank. *Police Ethics: The Corruption of Noble Cause*, 3d ed. New York: Routledge, 2010.

Calhoun, Craig J. *Habermas and the Public Sphere*. Cambridge, MA: MIT Press, 1992. California Senate Bill No. 178, California Electronic Communications Privacy Act (signed into law by California Governor Jerry Brown on October 8, 2015).

Calo, M. Ryan. "The Drone as Privacy Catalyst." *Stanford Law Review* 64 (2011): 29–33. Caloyannides, Michael A., and Michael A. Caloyannides. *Privacy Protection and Computer Forensics*. 2nd ed. Boston: Artech House, 2004.

Campbell, James, et al. "Privacy Regulation and Market Structure." *Journal of Economics & Management Strategy* 24 (2015): 47–73.

Cantor, Norman L. *Advanced Directives and the Pursuit of Dying with Dignity*. Bloomberg: Indiana University Press, 1993.

Caplan, Arthur L., James J. McCartney, and Dominic A. Stisi. *The Case of Terri Schiavo: Ethics at the End of Life*. Amherst, NY: Prometheus Books, 2006.

Cappel, James J. "A Study of Individuals' Ethical Beliefs and Perceptions of Electronic Mail Privacy." *Journal of Business Ethics J Bus Ethics*: 819–27.

Capron, Alexander Morgan. "Medical Decision-making and the Right to Die after Cruzan." *The Journal of Law, Medicine & Ethics J Law Med Ethics*: 5–8.

Cardoza, Nate, Cindy Cohn, Parker Higgins, Kurt Opsahl, and Rainey Reitman. *Who Has Your Back: Protecting Your Data from Government Request*. Electronic Frontier Foundation, May 15, 2014.

Carolan, Eoin. "Surveillance and the Individual's Expectation of Privacy Under the Fourth Amendment." *SSRN Electronic Journal SSRN Journal*.

Carpenter, Dale. *Flagrant Conduct: The Story of Lawrence v Texas: How a Bedroom Arrest Decriminalized Gay Americans*. W.W. Norton & Company, 2012.

Carr, Peter F. *Lawfully Managing Student Records without Violating Privacy Rights*. Eau Claire, WI: National Business Institute, 2013.

Carroll, Jamuna. *Privacy*. Detroit, MI: Greenhaven Press, 2006. Carroll, Thomas F. "Freedom of Speech and of the Press in War Time: The Espionage Act." *Michigan Law Review* 17, no. 8 (1919): 621–665.

Carter, Stephen. "A Battlefield of Drones and Privacy in Your Backyard." *Chicago Tribune*, August 3, 2015.

Cate, Fred H. "The Failure of Fair Information Practice Principles." In *Consumer Protection in the Age of the "Information Economy,"* new edition, edited by Jane K. Winn. Burlington, VT: Ashgate, 2006.

____. *Privacy in the Information Age*. Washington, D.C.: Brookings Institution Press, 1997. Cate, Fred. "The Changing Face of Privacy Protections in the European Union and the United States." *Indiana Law Review* 33 (1999): 173–232.

Catlett, Charlie. *Cloud Computing and Big Data*. Amsterdam: IOS Press, 2013. Catlett, Michael S. "Clearly Not Established: Decisional Law and the Qualified Immunity Doctrine." *Arizona Law Review* 47 (2005): 1031–1063.

Cavoukian, Ann, and Alexander Dix. *Smart Meters in Europe Privacy by Design at Its Best*. Toronto, Ont.: Information and Privacy Commissioner of Ontario, Canada, 2012.

Cepeda. Simon. *NSA Intelligence Collection, Leaks, and the Protection of Classified Information: Background and Issues*. New York: Nova Publishers, 2014.

Ceruzzi, Paul E. *Computing: a concise history*. Cambridge, Mass: MIT Press, 2012.

Chander, Anupam. *Securing Privacy in the Internet Age*. Stanford, CA: Stanford Law Books, 2008.

Chee, Brian J. S., and Curtis Franklin. *Cloud Computing: Technologies and Strategies of the Ubiquitous Data Center*. New York: CRC, 2010.

Chemerinsky, Erwin. "Narrowing the Tort of Public Disclosure of Private Facts." *Chapman Law Review* 11 (2008): 423–433.

____. "Right Result, Wrong Reasons: *Reno v. Condon*." *Oklahoma City University Law Review* 25 (2000): 823–841.

Chen, Brian X. *Always On: How the iPhone Unlocked the Anything-Anytime-Anywhere Future—and Locked Us In*. Boston, MA: Da Capo Press, 2012.

Christman, Henry M., ed. *The Public Papers of Chief Justice Earl Warren*, rev. ed. New York: Capricorn Books, 1966.

Christodorescu, Mihai, et al. *Malware Detection*. New York: Springer, 2006.

Clancy, Thomas K. "Spyware, Adware, Malware, Phishing, Spam, and Identity-Related Crime," in *Cyber Crime and Digital Evidence: Materials and Cases,* 2d ed. New Providence, NJ: LexisNexis, 2014.

____. "The Importance of James Otis." *Mississippi Law Journal* 82, no. 2 (2013): 487–524.

____. "The Importance of James Otis." *Mississippi Law Journal* 82, no. 2 (2013): 487–524.

____. *The Fourth Amendment: Its History and Interpretation*. Durham, NC: Carolina Academic Press, 2008.

Clapham, Andrew. *Human Rights in the Private Sphere*. Oxford, England: Clarendon Press, 1993.

Clarke, Richard A. *Cyber War: The Next Threat to National Security and What to Do about It*. New York: Ecco, 2010.

Clarke, Richard A., Michael J. Morell, Geoffrey R. Stone, Cass R. Sunstein, and Peter Swire. *The NSA Report: Liberty and Security in a Changing World*. Princeton, NJ: Princeton University Press, 2014.

Cogan, Neil H., ed. *The Complete Bill of Rights: The Drafts, Debates, Sources, and Origins*.

Cogen, Marc. *Democracies and the Shock of War: The Law as a Battlefield*. New ed. Burlington, VT: Ashgate, 2012.

Cohen, Julie E. "Inverse Relationship Between Secrecy and Privacy." *Social Research* 77.3 (Fall 2010): 883–898. ____. "What Privacy Is For." *Harvard Law Review*, May 1, 2013.

Cohn, Marjorie. "FISA Revised: A Blank Check for Domestic Spying." Huffington Post, August 9, 2007. Colao, J. J. "Snapchat: The Biggest No-Revenue Mobile App since Instagram." *Forbes*, November 27, 2012.

Colby, William H. *Long Goodbye: The Deaths of Nancy Cruzan*. Carlsbad, Calif.: Hay House, 2002. Cole, George F., and Marc G. Gertz, *The Criminal Justice System: Poli-*

tics and Policies, 10th ed. Belmont, CA: Belmont-Cengage, 2012.

Cole, Simon A. "More Than Zero: Accounting for Error in Latent Fingerprint Identification." *Journal of Criminal Law and Criminology* 95, no. 3 (2005): 985–1078.

Coleman, E. Gabriella. *Coding Freedom: The Ethics and Aesthetics of Hacking*. Princeton, NJ: Princeton University Press, 2013.

Colker, Ruth. *Abortion; Dialogue Pro-choice, Pro-life, and American Law*. Bloomington: Indiana University Press, 1992.

Condit, Celeste Michelle. "Crafting Virtue: The Rhetorical Construction of Public Morality." *Quarterly Journal of Speech* 73, no. 1 (1987): 79–97.

Congressional Research Service. *Privacy: An Overview of Federal Statutes Governing Wiretapping and Electronic Wiretapping Prepared for Members and Committees of Congress* (October 9, 2012).

Consumer Financial Protection Bureau, *List of Consumer Reporting Agencies*. Washington, DC: 2015.

"Consumer Watchdog Calls California 'Apps' Privacy Agreement a Step Forward, but Says Do Not Track Legislation Is Necessary to Protect Consumers." Marketing Weekly News, March 10, 2012.

Cooper, Candance. "Preparing for Biometrics and Drones in the 'Post Privacy' Era". *Corporate Legal Times* (November 2014).

Cooper, Frank Rudy. "'Who's the Man?': Masculinities Studies, Terry Stops, and Police Training." *Columbia Journal of Gender and Law* 18 p. 671 (2009).

Cooper, Scott P., and Kristen J. Mathews. "State Privacy Laws," in *Proskauer on Privacy*, ed. Christopher Wolf. New York: Practicing Law Institute, 2006– .

Cornish, Craig M. *Drugs and Alcohol in the Workplace: Testing and Privacy*. Wilmette, Ill.: Callaghan, 1988.

Cottrell, Robert C. *Roger Nash Baldwin and the American Civil Liberties Union*. New York: Columbia University Press, 2000.

Coyle, Erin K. "E. L. Godkin's Criticism of the Penny Press: Antecedents to a Legal Right to Privacy." *American Journalism* 31, no. 2 (2014): 262–282.

Craig, John D. R. *Privacy and Employment Law*. Oxford: Hart, 1999. Craig, Terence, and Mary Ludloff. *Privacy and Big Data*. Sebastopol, CA: O'Reilly Media, 2011.

Crocker, Thomas P. "From Privacy to Liberty: The Fourth Amendment after Lawrence." *SSRN Electronic Journal SSRN Journal*.

CRS Report for Congress. *P.L. 110–55, the Protect America Act of 2007: Modifications to the Foreign Intelligence Surveillance Act*. February 14, 2008.

Crump, Catherine, et al. "You Are Being Tracked: How License Plate Readers Are Being Used to Record Americans' Movements." American Civil Liberties Union (July 2013).

____. "Data Retention: Privacy, Anonymity, and Accountability Online." *Stanford Law Review* 56, no. 1 (2003): 191.

Cuddihy, William J. *The Fourth Amendment*. Oxford University Press, 2009. Cullina, Matt. "Broadband Bullies: Homeowners Insurers Are Being Asked to Pay Damages for Social Media Harassment." *Best's Review*, November 1, 2013.

Currie, Mary Beth. "Intrusion upon Seclusion: The Tort of Invasion of Privacy." *LawNow* 37, no. 2 (November 1, 2012).

Curry, Lynne. *Mapp v. Ohio: Guarding against Unreasonable Searches and Seizures*. Lawrence: University Press of Kansas, 2006.

Curtis, Craig R., Michael C. Gizzi, and Michael J. Kittleson. "Using Technology the Founders Never Dreamed Of: Cell Phones As Tracking Devices and the Fourth Amendment." *University of Denver Criminal Law Review* 4, no. 61 (2014.

Curtis, George E. *The Law of Cybercrimes and Their Investigations*. Boca Raton, FL: CRC Press, 2012.

D

Damon, Joseph P. *Whole Genome Sequencing: Privacy and Security in an Era of Genomic and Advancements*. Daniel J. Solove & Paul Schwartz, Information Privacy Law (2015)

Darcy, Shane. "Battling for the Rights to Privacy and Data Protection in the Irish Courts: *Schrems v. Data Protection Commissioner* [2014] IEHC 213 [2014]." *Utrecht Journal of International and European Law* 31 (2015): 131–135.

Data Quality Campaign. *Student Data Privacy Legislation: What Happened in 2015, and What Is Next?* 2015. Datta, Anwitaman, et al. *Social Informatics: Third International Conference, SocInfo, 2011, Singapore, October 2011*. Berlin: Springer-Verlag, 2011.

David Cuillier and Charles N. Davis, *The Art of Access: Strategies for Acquiring Public Records* (CQ Press 2010)

Davidson, Stephen M. *A New Era in U.S. Health Care Critical next Steps under the Affordable Care Act*. Stanford, CA: Stanford Books, 2013.

Davis, J. J. "Marketing to Children Online: A Manager's Guide to the Children's Online Protection Act." *S.A.M. Advanced Management Journal* 67, no. 4 (2002), 11–21.

Davis, Michelle R., and Wilson, David L. "S.C. Ranks Worst in Guarding Residents' Privacy—Journal Study Gave State Only Negative Score in U.S." *The Charlotte Observer* (Charlotte, North Carolina), October 6, 1999.

De Mauro, Andrea, Marco Greco, and Michele Grimaldi. "What is Big Data? A Consensual Definition and a Review of Key Research Topics." *AIP Conference Proceedings* 1644, no. 97 (2015). doi: 10.1063/1.4907823.

Debt Collection, Privacy, Fair Credit Reporting & Consumer. Conference on Consumer Finance Law, 2000 - Bankruptcy. www.debt.org/credit

Decker, Scott H., Leanne Fiftal Alarid, and Charles M. Katz, eds. *Controversies in Criminal Justice: Contemporary Readings*. New York: Oxford University Press, 2002.

Declan, Keara. Foreign Intelligence Surveillance Courts: Background, Issues, and Proposals. New York: Novinka, 2014.

Deibert, Ronald. *Black Code: Surveillance, Privacy, and the Dark Side of the Internet*. Hiller, Janine, and Ronnie Cohen. *Internet Law & Policy*. Upper Saddle River, NJ: Prentice Hall, 2002.

Del Carmen, Rolando V., and Jeffrey T. Walker. *Briefs of Leading Cases in Law Enforcement*, 9th ed. New York: Routledge, 2015. [United States Supreme Court cases.]

Delaney, E. (2012). "The Children's Online Privacy Protection Act and Rule: An Overview." *Journal of Civil Rights and Economic Development*, 16, no. 3 (2101): 641–648.

Dempsey, John S., and Linda S. Forst. *An Introduction to Policing*. 6th ed. Clifton Park, NY: Delmar Cengage Learning, 2012.

Denham, Elizabeth. *Investigation into the Use of Facial Recognition Technology by the Insurance Corporation of British Columbia*. Victoria: Office of the Information and Privacy Commissioner for British Columbia, 2012.

Denison, Charles M. *Transforming Healthcare with Health Information Technology*. New York: Nova Science Publishers, 2011.

Dennis, Donna I. "Obscenity Law and the Conditions of Freedom in the Nineteenth-Century United States." *Law and Social Inquiry* 27, no. 2 (May 2002): 369–399.

Denno, Deborah W. "The Privacy Rights of Rape Victims in the Media and the Law: Perspectives on Disclosing Rape Victims' Names." *Fordham Law Review* 61 (1993): 1113–1131.

Dershowitz, Alan M. *Is There a Right to Remain Silent?: Coercive Interrogation and the Fifth Amendment after 9/11*. Oxford: Oxford University Press, 2008.

Desai, Anuj C. "Wiretapping before the Wires: The Post Office and the Birth of Communications Privacy." *Stanford Law Review* 60, no. 2 (2007).

Deutschman, A. *The Second Coming of Steve Jobs*. New York: Broadway Books, 2000. Devol, Kenneth S. *Mass Media and the Supreme Court: The Legacy of the Warren Years*, 4th ed. Mamaroneck, NY: Hastings House, 1990.

Dhasarathan, Chandramohan, Vengattaraman Thirumal, and Dhavachelvan Ponnurangam. "Data Privacy Breach Prevention Framework for the Cloud Service." *Security and Communication Networks* 8, no. 6 (April 2015): 982–1005.

DiBona, Chris. *Open Sources Voices from the Open Source Revolution*. Beijing: O'Reilly, 1999.

Dicker, Georges. *Descartes: An Analytical and Historical Introduction*. Oxford, England: Oxford University Press, 1993.

Diffie, Whitfield, and Susan Eva Landau. *Privacy on the Line: The Politics of Wiretapping and Encryption*, updated and expanded ed. Cambridge, MA: MIT Press, 2010.

Dixon, Rod. *Open Source Software Law*. Boston, MA: Artech House, 2004.

Doerner, William G., and M. L. Dantzker, eds. *Contemporary Police Organization and Management: Issues and Trends*. Boston, MA: Butterworth-Heinemann, 2000.

Doherty, Carroll. "Balancing Act: National Security and Civil Liberties in a Post-9/11 Era." Pew Research Center. June 7, 2013.

Donaldson, Molla S. *Health Data in the Information Age: Use, Disclosure, and Privacy*. Washington, DC: National Academy Press, 1994.

Donohue, Laura K. "Anglo-American Privacy and Surveillance." *Journal of Criminal Law and Criminology* 96, no. 3 (Spring 2006): 1059–1208.

Donohue, Laura K. "Bulk Metadata Collection: Statutory and Constitutional Considerations." Harvard Journal of Law and Public Policy 37 (Summer 2014): 757–900.

Doris, Elizabeth, and Kim Peterson. *Government Program Briefing Smart Metering*. Golden, CO: National Renewable Energy Laboratory, 2011.

Dorr, Dieter, and Russell L. Weaver, eds. *The Right to Privacy in the Light of Media Convergence: Perspectives from Three Continents*. Berlin: De Gruyter, 2012.

Douglas, William O. *Go East, Young Man: The Early Years*. New York: Random House, 1974.

____. *The Court Years*. New York: Random House, 1980.

Doyle, Aaron. *Eyes Everywhere: The Global Growth of Camera Surveillance*. Abingdon, Oxon, England: Routledge, 2012.

Doyle, Charles. Terrorism: Section by Section Analysis of the USA PATRIOT Act. Congressional Research Service Report for Congress. Washington, DC: Library of Congress, 2001.

____. *Wiretapping and Electronic Surveillance: The Electronic Communications Privacy Act and Related Matters*. Washington, DC: Congressional Research Service, Library of Congress, 1992.

Doyle, Michael. "False Light, Camera, Action: The Story Joe Eszterhas Forgot to Share." *Slate*, February 25, 2004.

Draft Communications Data Bill. London: Stationery Office, 2012. Drake, Bruce. "Divide between Blacks and Whites on Police Runs Deep." Washington, DC: Pew Research Center, 2015.

Dreisbach, Christopher. *Ethics in Criminal Justice*. New York: McGraw-Hill, 2008.

Dryer, Randy L., and S. Shane Stroud. "Automatic License Plate Readers: An Effective Law Enforcement Tool or Big

Brother's Latest Instrument of Mass Surveillance? Some Suggestions for Legislative Action." *Jurimetrics Journal* 55, no. 2 (Winter 2015): 225–274.

Duda, Nancy Lee. *The Intersection of Privacy Concern and Trust: Beliefs of Privacy Orientation Groups*. 2004.

Dudley, Christie. "Statutory (Re)Interpretation of CPNI: Protecting Mobile Privacy." February 14, 2013.

Duffy, D. Jan. "Tortious Invasion of Privacy." *Employment Relations Today* 10, no. 4 (Winter 1983): 381–390.

Duffy, Gerard J. "The New CPNI Rules." *Rural Telecommunications*, March 1, 2008.

Dumas, M. Barry. *Diving into the Bitstream: Information Technology Meets Society in a Digital World*. New York: Routledge, 2012.

Dumbill, Edd. Volume, Velocity, Variety: What You Need to Know About Big Data. Forbes, January 19, 2012.

Dunham, Wolcott B. *After the Gramm-Leach-Bliley Act: A Road Map for Insurance Companies*. New York, N.Y.: Practicing Law Institute, 2000.

Durga Priya, G., and Soma Prathibha. "Assuring Correctness for Securing Outsourced Data Repository in Cloud Environment." In *2014 IEEE International Conference on Advanced Communications, Control and Computing Technologies*, 1745–1748. IEEE, 2014.

Dwan, Berni. "Identity Theft." *Computer Fraud & Security*, no. 4 (April 2004): 14–17. Dworkin, Gerald. "Access to Medical Records-Discovery, Confidentiality and Privacy." *The Modern Law Review* 42, no. 1 (1979): 88–91.

E

Easton, Eric B. "Ten Years After: *Bartnicki v. Vopper* as a Laboratory for First Amendment Advocacy and Analysis." *University of Louisville Law Review* 50 (2011): 287.

Easton, Richard D., and Eric F. Frazier. *GPS Declassified: From Smart Bombs to* Easttom, Chuck, and Jeff Taylor. *Computer Crime, Investigation and the Law*. Boston, MA: Course Technology Publishers, 2011.

Ebbe, Obi N. I., ed. *Comparative and International Criminal Justice Systems: Policing, Judiciary, and Corrections*, 3d ed. Boca Raton, FL: CRC Press, 2013.

Efrati, Amir. "Google's Data-Trove Dance." *Wall Street Journal*, July 30, 2013.

Egelman, Serge, Adrienne Porter Felt, and David Wagner. "Choice Architecture and Smartphone Privacy: There's a Price for That." *The Economics of Information Security and Privacy*: 211–236.

Eibner Christine, et al. 2010. Establishing state health insurance exchanges: implications for health insurance enrollment, spending, and small businesses. RAND. Santa 105 Monica, CA.

____. 2012. The Effect of the Affordable Care Act on Enrollment and Premiums, With and Without the Individual Mandate. RAND. Santa Monica, CA.

Ek, Kaitlin. Note, "Conspiracy and the Fantasy Defense: The Strange Case of the Cannibal Cop." *Duke Law Journal* 64 (2015): 901–945.

Eldredge, Lawrence H. "William Lloyd Prosser.c California Law Review 60, no. 5 (September 1972): 1245–1251.

Elmendorf, Douglas. "CBO's Analysis of the Major Health Care Enacted in March 2010." Testimony before the Subcommittee on Health, Committee on Energy and Commerce U.S. House of Representatives from Washington, D.C., 2011.

Emden, Christian. *Changing Perceptions of the Public Sphere*. Oxford, England: Berghahn Books, 2012. Emerson, Thomas I. "The Right of Privacy and Freedom of the Press," in vol. 1 of *Privacy*, 2 vols., ed. by Raymond Wacks. New York: New York University Press, 1993. Faculty Scholarship Series. Paper 2776.

Employment Systems Review Guide to the Audit Process: Employment Equity. Ottawa: Employment Equity Branch, Canadian Human Rights Commission, 2002.

The End of Secrecy: The Rise and Fall of WikiLeaks. London: Guardian, 2011.

Engdahl, Sylvia. *Mobile Apps*. Detroit, MI: Greenhaven Press, 2014. Epstein, Richard A. "Privacy, Publication, and the First Amendment: The Dangers of First Amendment Exceptionalism." *Stanford Law Review* 52 (2000): 1003–1048.

Erbschloe, Michael. *Trojans, Worms, and Spyware: A Computer Security Professional's Guide to Malicious Code*. Amsterdam: Elsevier Butterworth Heinemann, 2005.

Erickson, Jon. *Hacking: The Art of Exploitation*, 2nd ed. San Francisco: No Starch Press, 2008.

Esayas, Samson. "Breach Notification Requirements under the European Union Legal Framework: Convergence, Conflicts, and Complexity in Compliance." *John Marshall Journal of Information Technology & Privacy Law* 31, no. 3 (2014): 317–368.

Espejo, Roman. *AIDS*. Detroit, MI: Greenhaven Press, 2012. ____. *Privacy*. Detroit: Greenhaven Press, 2011.

____. *Smartphones*. Gomez-Martin, Laura E. "Smartphone Usage and the Need for Consumer Privacy Laws." *Tlp Pittsburgh Journal of Technology Law and Policy* 12 (2012).

Estlack, Russell W. *Shattered Lives Shattered Dreams: The Disrupted Lives of Families in America's Internment Camps*. Springville, UT: Bonneville Books, 2011.

Estulin, Daniel. *Deconstructing Wikileaks*. Chicago, IL: Trine Day, 2012.

Etzioni, Amitai. "HIV Testing of Infants: Privacy and Public Health." *Health Affairs* 17, no. 4 (July/August 1998): 170–83.

____. "Privacy," in *Privacy in a Cyber Age: Policy and Practice*. New York: Palgrave Macmillan, 2015. ____. *How*

Patriotic Is the Patriot Act?: Freedom versus Security in the Age of Terrorism. New York: Routledge, 2004.

____. *The Limits of Privacy*. New York: Basic Books, 1999.

____. "Seeking Middle Ground on Privacy vs. Security." *Christian Science Monitor*, October 15, 2002: 11.

"EURODAC Fingerprint Database under Fire by Human Rights Activists." Euractiv.com, July 15, 2015. European Commission. "Myth-Busting: The Court of Justice of the EU and the 'Right to be Forgotten.'"

European Union Agency for Fundamental Rights and the Council of Europe. *Handbook on European Data Protection Law*. 2014.

Examination of the GLBA Five Years after Its Passage: Hearing before the Committee on Banking, Housing, and Urban Affairs, United States Senate, One Hundred Eighth Congress, Second Session, on the GLBA(P.L. 106–102), T. Washington: U.S. G.P.O.:, 2006.

Executive Office of the President. *Big Data and Differential Pricing*. The White House. February 2015. Executive Office of the President. *Big Data: Seizing Opportunities, Preserving Values*. The White House. May 1, 2014.

Eyre, William. *The Real ID Act Privacy and Government Surveillance*. El Paso, TX: LFB Scholarly Pub., 2011. Ezor, Jonathan. *Privacy and Data Protection in Business: Laws and Practices*. New Providence, NJ: LexisNexis, 2012.

F

Faber Jonathan L. "Indiana: A Celebrity-Friendly Jurisdiction." *Res Gestae: J. Ind. State B. Ass'n* 43 (March 2000). http://www.luminarygroup.com/images/ResGestae_2000–03.pdf.

Fair Credit Reporting. Boston, MA: National Consumer Law Center, 2013. www.nclc.org/library.org. Farivar, Cyrus. "Class-Action Lawsuit Settlement Forces Netflix Privacy Changes." *Ars Technica*, July 20, 2012.

Fay, John. *Drug Testing*. Boston: Butterworth-Heinemann, 1991. "FBI Outlines a Wiretapping Future." Network Security 1995, no. 11 2–3.

Felderer, Bernhard. "Can Immigration Policy Help to Stabilize Social Security Systems?," in *Economic Aspects of International Migration*, ed. Herbert Giersch. Berlin: Springer-Verlag, 1994.

Feller, Joseph. *Perspectives on Free and Open Source Software*. Cambridge, MA: MIT Press, 2005.

Feng, Yicheng, and Pong C. Yuen. "Biometric Template Protection: Towards A Secure Biometric System." *Handbook of Pattern Recognition and Computer Vision*. 455–476.

Ferguson, Andrew Guthrie. "Personal Curtilage: Fourth Amendment Security in Public." *William and Mary Law Review* 55, no. 4 (2014).

Feser, Edward. *Locke*. London: Oneworld, 2007.

Feuer, Katherine. "Protecting Government Secrets: A Comparison of the Espionage Act and the Official Secrets Act," *Boston College International and Comparative Law Review* Vol. 38, no. 1 (2015).

Fibbe, George H. "Screen-Scraping and Harmful Cyber-trespass after Intel." *Mercer Law Review* 55, no. 1011 (2004).

Fidler, David P. *The Snowden Reader*. Steininger, Michael. "Merkel under Fire as Germany Seethes over NSA Spying." *Christian Science Monitor*, July 2, 2013.

Figliola, Patricia Moloney. *Wireless Privacy and Spam Issues for Congress*. Washington, DC: Congressional Research Service, Library of Congress, 2006.

"Financial Data Safeguards. (GLBA Regulates Financial Institution Security)." Security Management, September 1, 2002.

Financial Services Modernization: Analysis of the GLBA of 1999. New York, N.Y.: Matthew Bender, 2000.

Finkelman, Paul. "German Victims and American Oppressors: The Cultural Background and Legacy of *Meyer v. Nebraska*," in *Law and the Great Plains: Essays on the Legal History of the Heartland*, ed. John R. Wunder. Westport, CT: Greenwood Press, 1996.

Finn, Peter, and Sari Horwitz. "U.S. Charges Snowden with Espionage." *Washington Post*, June 21, 2013.

Fishman, Clifford S. "Electronic Privacy in the Government Workplace and *City of Ontario, California v. Quon*: The Supreme Court Brought Forth a Mouse."

Fishman, Steve. "Bradley Manning's Army of One." *New York*. July 3, 2011.

Foege, Alec. "Consumer Data Privacy and the Importance of a Social Contract." *Data-Informed.com*. August 6, 2013.

Foerstel, Herbert N. *The PATRIOT Act: A Documentary and Reference Guide*. Westport, CT: Greenwood, 2007.

Follow-up Review of the FBI's Progress toward Biometric Interoperability between IAFIS and IDENT. Washington, D.C.: U.S. Dept. of Justice, Office of Inspector General, Evaluations and Inspections Division, 2006.

Forer, Lois G. *A Chilling Effect: The Mounting Threat of Libel and Invasion of Privacy Actions to the First Amendment*. New York: Norton, 1987.

Foster, James C., and Stephen C. Foster. *Programmer's Ultimate Security Deskref*. Rockland, MA: Syngress, 2004.

"Fourth Amendment—Search and Seizure—Searching Cell Phones Incident to Arrest." Harvard Law Review (2014).

"Fourth Amendment. Stop and Frisk." The Journal of Criminal Law and Criminology 69, no. 4 (1978): 464.

Fowler, Andrew. *The Most Dangerous Man in the World: The Explosive True Story of Julian Assange and the Lies,* *Cover-Ups and Conspiracies He Exposed*. New York: Skyhorse Publishing, 2011.

Fox, Christopher. "Checking In: Historic Cell-Site Location Information and the Stored Communications Act." *Seton Hall Law Review* 42 (2012): 769–792.

Francesca M. Brancato, *Fourth Amendment Right to Privacy with Respect to Bank Records in Criminal Cases* 29 Touro Law Review 1241 (2013)

Frankel, Alison. "Why Is DOJ Fighting to Keep Mug Shots Out of Reporters' Hands?" *Reuters* (August 13, 2015).

Frankfurt, Harry. *Demons, Dreamers and Madmen: The Defense of Reason in Descartes' Meditations*. Indianapolis, IN: Bobbs-Merrill, 1970.

Franklin, Cary. "Griswold and the Public Dimension of the Right to Privacy." *Yale Law Journal Forum* 124, 332.

Frantz, Joe B., interviewer. *Transcript, Earl Warren Oral History Interview* I. September 21, 1971. Internet Copy, LBJ Library.

Freedman, Jeri. *America Debates Privacy versus Security*. New York: Rosen Pubishing Group, 2008. Freeman, Lee. *Information Ethics Privacy and Intellectual Property*. Hershey, PA: Information Science Pub., 2005.

Friedland, Steven. "Cell Phone Searches in a Digital World: Blurred Lines, New Realities and Fourth Amendment Pluralism." *SSRN Electronic Journal SSRN Journal*.

Friedman, Lawrence M. *Guarding Life's Dark Secret*. Stanford, CA: Stanford University Press, 2007, 213–234.

Friedman, Leon. *Obscenity: The Complete Oral Arguments before the Supreme Court in the Major Obscenity Cases*, rev. ed. New York: Chelsea House, 1983.

Friend, Charles E. "Constitutional Law—Right of Privacy—*Time, Inc. v. Hill*, 87 S. Ct. 534 (1967)." *William & Mary Law Review* 8 (1967): 683–687.

Fuchs, Christian. *Social Media: A Critical Introduction*. Thousand Oaks, CA: Sage, 2014.

G

Gajda, Amy. "What If Samuel D. Warren Hadn't Married a Senator's Daughter?: Uncovering the Press Coverage That Led to 'The Right to Privacy,'" *Michigan State Law Review*. 2008, 35.

Galbally, Javier, Julian Fierrez, Javier Ortega-Garcia, and Raffaele Cappelli. "Fingerprint Anti-spoofing in Biometric Systems." *Handbook of Biometric Anti-Spoofing Advances in Computer Vision and Pattern Recognition*, 35–64.

Garber, Daniel. *Descartes' Metaphysical Physics*. Chicago, IL: University of Chicago Press, 1992.

Garbin, Brigette, et al. "Tracking Legislative Developments in Relation to 'Do Not Track' Initiatives." *In Uberveillance and the Social Implications of Microchip Implants: Emerging Technologies*, edited by

M. G. Michael and Katina Michael. Hershey, PA: Information Science Reference, 2014.

Garcia, Alfredo. *The Fifth Amendment: A Comprehensive Approach*. Westport, CT: Greenwood Press, 2002.

Gardner, Steven. "Privacy and Debt Collection Implications of the Fair Credit Reporting Act and the 2003 Fact Act." *Consumer Finance Law Quarterly Report* 58, no. 46 (2004).

Garfield, Jay L. *Abortion, Moral and Legal Perspectives*. Amherst: University of Massachusetts Press, 1984.

Garfinkel, Simson, and Gene Spafford. *Web Security, Privacy & Commerce*, 2nd ed. Sebastopol, CA: O'Reilly Media, 2011.

Garrett, Brandon. *The Right to Privacy*. New York: Rosen Pub. Group, 2001.

Garrow, David J. "Human Rights Hero: The Legal Legacy of *Griswold v. Connecticut*." *Human Rights* (2011): 26–25.

_____. *Liberty and Sexuality: The Right to Privacy and the Making of Roe v. Wade*. 1994

Gaukroger, Stephen. *Descartes: An Intellectual Biography*. Oxford, England: Clarendon Press, 1995.

Gavison, Ruth. "Privacy and the Limits of *Law*." An *Anthology: Philosophical Dimensions of Privacy* 89, no. 3 (1980): 346–402.

Gelenbe, Erol. *Information Sciences and Systems 2013: Proceedings of the 28th International Symposium on Computer and Information Sciences.*

Gellman, Robert. "Willis Ware's Lasting Contribution to Privacy: Fair Information Practices." *IEEE Security & Privacy* 12, no. 51 (2014).

Gellman, Robert. *Fair Information Practices: A Basic History*. February 11, 2015.

Gelman, Robert B., and Stanton McCandlish. *Protecting Yourself Online: The Definitive Resource on Safety, Freedom, and Privacy in Cyberspace*. New York: HarperEdge, 1998.

George, Richard T. *The Ethics of Information Technology and Business*. Malden, MA: Blackwell, 2003.

George, Robert P. "The Concept of Public Morality." *American Journal of Jurisprudence* 45, no. 1 (2000): 17–31.

Gilbert, Franc. *Sixteenth Annual Institute on Privacy and Data Security Law.*

Gill, Peter. *Policing Politics: Security Intelligence and the Liberal Democratic State*. Hoboken, NJ: Taylor and Francis, 2012.

Gilliom, John. *Surveillance, Privacy, and the Law: Employee Drug Testing and the Politics of Social Control*. Ann Arbor: University of Michigan Press, 1994.

Gladstone, Julia Alpert. "Data Mines and Battlefields: Looking at Financial Aggregators to Understand the Legal Boundaries and Ownership Rights in the Use of Personal Data." *Journal of Marshall Computer and Information Law* 19, no. 313 (2001).

Glancy, Dorothy J. "Privacy and the Other Miss M." *Northern Illinois University Law Review* 10 401 (1990).

_____. "The Invention of the Right to Privacy." *Arizona Law Review* 21, no. 1 (1979): 1–39.

Glasser, Charles, ed. *International Libel & Privacy Handbook*. New York: Bloomberg Press, 2006. Gluck, Elizabeth Brody. "An Act Worth Balancing: Privacy and Safety on Today's College Campuses." *University Business* 11, no. 11 (November 2008).

Godkin, Edwin Lawrence. *Life and Letters of E. L. Godkin*. Edited by Rollo Ogden. New York: Macmillan, 1907.

_____. *The Gilded Age Letters of E. L. Godkin*. Edited by William M. Armstrong. Albany: State University of New York Press, 1974.

Godwin, Mike. *Cyber Rights: Defending Free Speech in the Digital Age*, rev. and updated ed. Cambridge, MA: MIT Press, 2003.

Goldberg, Suzanne B. "Morals-Based Justifications for *Lawrence*: Before and after *Lawrence v. Texas*." *Minnesota Law Review* 88, no. 5 (2004).

Goldenberg, Suzanne, and Ed Pilkington, eds. "State Conservative Groups Plan US-Wide Assault on Education, Health and Tax." *Guardian* (New York), December 13, 2013.

Goldfarb, Ronald, et al. *After Snowden: Privacy, Secrecy and Security in the Information Age*. New York: T. Dunne, 2015.

Goldstein, Emmanuel. *Best of 2600: A Hacker Odyssey*. Indianapolis, IN: Wiley Publishing, 2008.

Gonzales, Alfonso. *Reform without Justice: Latino Migrant Politics and the Homeland Security State*. New York: Oxford University Press, 2014.

Goodale, Gloria. "Privacy Concerns? What Google Now Says It Can Do with Your Data." *Christian Science Monitor*, April 16, 2014.

Goode, Luke. *Jürgen Habermas Democracy and the Public Sphere*. London: Pluto Press, 2005.

Gottfried, Ted. *Privacy Individual Right v. Social Needs*. Brookfield, CT: Millbrook Press, 1994.

Government Communications Headquarters (GCHQ): New Accommodation Programme: Report. London: Stationery Office, 2003.

Grabell, M. (Jan. 27, 2012). Drive-by Scanning: Officials Expand Use and Dose of Radiation for Security Screening. ProPublica.

Graham, Richard, Richard Hall, and W. Gerry Gilmer. "Connecting the Dots . . .: Information Sharing by Post-Secondary Educational Institutions under the Family

Education Rights and Privacy Act (FERPA)." *Education and the Law* 20, no. 4 (2008): 301–316.

Grama, Joanna Lyn. *Legal Issues in Information Security*, 2d ed. Burlington, MA: Jones & Bartlett Learning, 2015.

Grande, Allison, "EU, Google in Power Struggle Over 'Right to Be Forgotten.'" Law360, July 30, 2014.

Grandinetti, Lucio, Ornella Pisacane, and Mehdi Sheikhalishahi. *Pervasive Cloud Computing Technologies: Future Outlooks and Interdisciplinary Perspectives.* Hershey, PA: Information Science Reference, 2014.

Grant, Joseph Karl. "What the Financial Services Industry Puts Together Let No Person Put Asunder: How the GLBA Contributed to the 2008–2009 American Capital Markets Crisis." *Albany Law Review*, 2010.

Grant, Rebecca A. *Visions of Privacy Policy Choices for the Digital Age.* Toronto, Ontario, Canada: University of Toronto Press, 1999.

Gray, Dahli, and Jessica Ladig, "The Implementation of EMV Chip Card Technology to Improve Cyber Security Accelerates in the U.S. Following Target Corporation's Data Breach." *International Journal of Business Administration* 6 (2015): 60.

Graybeal, J. "Achieving Semantic Interoperability." In *The MMI Guides: Navigating the World of Marine Metadata*, 2009.

Grayling, A. C. *Liberty in the Age of Terror: A Defence of Civil Liberties and Enlightenment Values.* London: Bloomsbury, 2009.

Green, Walter L., Randy Seidehamel, and Martha Grace Rich. "Cellular Telephones and Interference with Privacy." *Mayo Clinic Proceedings* 82, no. 7 (2007): 889.

Greene, Kathryn, Valerian J.Verlega, Gust A. Yep, and Sandra Petronio. *Privacy and Disclosure of HIV in Interpersonal Relationships: A Sourcebook for Researchers and Practitioners.* New York: Routledge, 2003.

Greenhalgh, William W. *The Fourth Amendment Handbook: A Chronological Survey of Supreme Court Decisions.* Chicago: Criminal Justice Section, American Bar Association, 1995.

Greenstein, Shane M., and Feng Zhu. *Collective Intelligence and Neutral Point of View: The Case of Wikipedia.* Cambridge, MA: National Bureau of Economic Research, 2012. Greenwald, Glenn. "On the Espionage Act Charges against Edward Snowden." *Guardian* June 22, 2013.

_____. *No Place to Hide: Edward Snowden, the NSA, and the U.S. Surveillance State.* New York: Metropolitan Books/H. Holt, 2014.

Greiffenhagen, Michael. *Engineering, Statistical Modeling and Performance Characterization of a Real-Time Dual Camera Surveillance System.* 2002.

Griffith, Elwin J. "Credit Reporting, Prescreened Lists, and Adverse Action: The Impact of the Fair Credit Reporting

Act and the Equal Credit Opportunity Act." *California West Law Review* 46, no. 1 (2009).

Gripsrud, Jostein. *The Public Sphere.* Los Angeles, CA: Sage, 2011.

Gun Control Opportunities to Close Loopholes in the National Instant Criminal Background Check System. Washington, D.C.: U.S. General Accounting Office, 2002.

Gun Control: Options for Improving the National Instant Criminal Background Check System: Report to Congressional Requesters. Washington, D.C.: U.S. General Accounting Office, 2002.

Gunning, Jennifer, and Law Ethics. *Ethics, Law and Society.* Aldershot, England: Ashgate, 2009.

Gutnick, Aviva Lucas, Michael Robb, Laurie Takeuchi, and Jennifer Kotler. *Always Connected: The New Digital Media Habits of Young Children.* New York: Joan Ganz Cooney Center at Sesame Workshop, 2011.

H

Habermas, Jurgen. *The Structural Transformation of the Public Sphere: An Inquiry into a Category of Bourgeois Society.* Cambridge, MA: MIT Press, 1989.

Habte, M. "Federal and State Data Privacy Laws and Their Implications for the Creation and Use of Health Information Databases." *Big Data: A Business and Legal Guide.* 2014, 55–78.

Hadjipetrova, Ganka, and Hannah G. Poteat. "States Are Coming to the Fore of Privacy in the Digital Era." *Landslide* 6, no. 6 (July/August 2014).

Hall, John Wesley. *Search and Seizure*, 3rd ed. Charlottesville, VA: LEXIS Law Pub., 2000. Hall, Kermit L., and John J. Patrick. *The Pursuit of Justice: Supreme Court Decisions That Shaped America.* New York: Oxford University Press, 2006.

Halper, T. "Privacy and Autonomy: From Warren and Brandeis to Roe and Cruzan." *Journal of Medicine and Philosophy*, 1996, 121–135.

Halstuk, Martin E. "Shielding Private Lives from Prying Eyes: The Escalating Conflict between Constitutional Privacy and the Accountability Principle of Democracy." *Communications Law Conspectus* 11 (2003): 71.

_____. "When Is an Invasion of Privacy Unwarranted under the FOIA? An Analysis of the Supreme Court's 'Sufficient Reason' and 'Presumption of Legitimacy' Standards." *University of Florida Journal of Law & Public Policy* 16, no. 3 (December 2005): 361–400.

Halstuk, Martin E., and Bill F. Chamberlin, "The Freedom of Information Act 1966–2006: A Retrospective on the Rise of Privacy Protection over the Public Interest in Knowing What the Government's Up To," *Communication Law and Policy* 11, no. 4 (September 2006): 511–564.

_____. "The Public Interest Be Damned: Lower Court Treatment of the Reporters Committeee 'Central Purpose'

Reformulation." *Administrative Law Review* 54, no. 3 (2002): 983–1024.

Hamblen, J. W. "Preservation of Privacy in Testing." *Science* 151, no. 3715 (March 11, 1966): 1174.

Hammitt, Harry A., et al., eds. *Litigation under the Federal Open Government Laws*. Washington, DC: Electronic Privacy Information Center, 2010.

Hampshire, Stuart, ed. *Public and Private Morality*. New York: Cambridge University Press, 1978.

Handley, John. "Prism and Boundless Informant: Is NSA Surveillance a Threat?" *American Diplomacy*, July 17, 2013.

Harding, Luke, and David Leigh. *Wikileak*, new. ed. London: Random House UK, 2013.

____. *The Snowden Files: The Inside Story of the World's Most Wanted Man*. New York: Vintage Books, 2014.

Harkinson, Josh. "Here's How Twitter Can Track You on All of your Devices." *Mother Jones*, September 24, 2013.

Harper, Nick. "FISA's Fuzzy Line between Domestic and International Terrorism." University of Chicago Law Review 81, no. 3 (Summer 2014): 1123–1164.

Harrington, Jan L. *Network Security: A Practical Approach*. Amsterdam: Elsevier, 2005.

Harris, Shane. "TIA Lives On." *National Journal* 38, no. 8 (2006): 66–67.

____. *@War: The Rise of the Military-Internet Complex*. Boston, MA: Houghton Mifflin Harcourt, 2014.

Harrison, Maureen. *Obscenity and Pornography Decisions of the United States Supreme Court*. Carlsbad, CA: Excellent Books, 2000.

Hartley, John, Jean Burgess, and Axel Bruns, eds. *A Companion to New Media Dynamics*. Malden, MA: Wiley, 2013.

Hartman, Scott. Note in "Privacy, Personhood and the Courts: FOIA Exemption 7(C) in Context." 120 *Yale Law Journal* 120, no. 379 (2010).

Harvey, Trevor. "Cookies Part II—Privacy Pirates or Useful Utilities?" *British Journal of Healthcare Management* 5, no. 8 (August 1999): 323.

Hassan, M. Kabir, and Abdullah Mamun. "Global Impact of the Gramm-Leach-Bliley Act: Evidence from Insurance Industries of Developed Countries." *Financial Market Regulation*, 2010, 63–77.

Hastedt, G. P. *Reading in American Foreign Policy: Problems and Responses*. Lanham, MD: Rowman & Littlefield, 2016.

Hastings, Glen, and Richard Marcus. *Identity Theft, Inc.: A Wild Ride with the World's #1 Identity Thief*. New York: The Disinformation Company, 2006.

Hayes, David L. "Cellular Telephones and Interference with Privacy–Reply–III." *Mayo Clinic Proceedings* 82, no. 7 (2007): 890.

Hayes, Paul. *Subpoenas*. Melbourne: Leo Cussen Institute, 2001.

Heffernan, William C. "Fourth Amendment Privacy Interests." *Journal of Criminal Law and Criminology* 92, no. 1 (2001).

Heinze, Eric. *Sexual Orientation: A Human Right: An Essay on International Human Rights Law*. Dordrecht: M. Nijhoff Publishers, 1995.

Henry, Anna. "The Fight to Protect CPNI." *Rural Telecommunications*, November 1, 2009.

Herold, Rebecca, and Christine Hertzog. *Data Privacy for the Smart Grid*. Reid, Irwin E. *Smart Meters and the Smart Grid: Privacy and Cybersecurity Considerations*. New York: Nova Science Publishers, 2012.

Herold, Rebecca. "Privacy Breach Incident Response," in *Information Security Management Handbook*, 6th ed., ed. Harold F. Tipton and Micki Krause. Boca Raton, FL: Auerbach Publications, 2007.

Hersey, Pala. "*Moore v. East Cleveland*: The Supreme Court's Fractured Paean to the Extended Family." *Journal of Contemporary Legal Issues* 14, no. 1, (2004): 57–64.

Heun, David. "Pealing Back Layers of Fraud Protection." *Payments Source* (March 14, 2012)

Hiestand, Todd C. and W. Jesse Weins, eds., Sexting and Youth: A Multidisciplinary Examination

Kreimer, Seth F. "Sex, Laws, and Videophones: The Problem of Juvenile Sexting Prosecutions," in *Children, Sexuality, and the Law*, ed. Sacha M. Coupet and Ellen Marrus, 133–62 (New York: New York University Press, 2015).

Hills, J. "Regulation, Innovation and Market Structure in International Telecommunications: The Case of the 1956 TAT1 Submarine Cable." *Business History* 49, no. 6 (2007): 868–885.

Himma, Kenneth Einar. *The Handbook of Information and Computer Ethics*. Hoboken, NJ: Wiley, 2008. Hinde, Natasha. "Did Instagram Ban This Account Because of a Photo Showing Women's Pubic Hair?" *The Huffington Post UK*, January 21, 2015.

Hinkle, Robert, David McCraw, Daniel Kanstroom, and Eleanor Acer. Conference on Privacy and Internet Access to Court Files, Panel Two: "Should There Be Remote Public Access to Court Filings in Immigration Cases?" *Fordham Law Review* 79, no. 1 (2010): 25–44.

Hinsley, F. H. *Codebreakers: The inside Story of Bletchley Park*. Oxford: Oxford University Press, 1993.

HIPAA in Practice: The Health Information Manager's Perspective. Chicago, IL: AHIMA, 2004.

Hirschey, Jeffrey Kenneth. "Symbiotic Relationships: Pragmatic Acceptance of Data Scraping," *Berkeley Technical Law Journal* 29, no. 897 (2014).

Hodder, Lucy C. *Health Care Reform, a Legal Perspective: Where Are We and Where Are We Going?* Concord, N.H.: New Hampshire Bar Association, 2010.

Hoff, Jessica, *Enhancing Security While Protecting Privacy: The Rights Implicated by Supposedly Heightened Airport Security*, 2014 *Michigan State Law Review*. 1609 (2014)

Holder, Eric Himpton, Laurie O. Robinson, John H. Laub, and National Institute of Justice. *The Fingerprint Source-book*. Washington, DC: U.S. Dept. of Justice, Office of Justice Programs, National Institute of Justice, 2011.

Holland, Stephen. "The Virtue Ethics Approach to Bioethics." *Bioethics* 25, no. 4 (2011): 192–201. Holmes, Burnham. *The Fifth Amendment*. Englewood Cliffs, N.J.: Silver Burdett Press, 1991.

Holtzman, David H. *Privacy Lost: How Technology Is Endangering Your Privacy*. San Francisco, CA: Jossey-Bass, 2006.

Hoofnagle, Chris Jay. "Identity Theft: Making the Known Unknowns Known." *Harvard Journal of Law and Technology* 21, no. 1 (2007): 97–122.

Hopkins, W. Wat. "*Snyder v. Phelps* and the Unfortunate Death of Intentional Infliction of Emotional Distress as a Speech-Based Tort." Journal of Media Law and Ethics, no. 3/4 (Summer/Fall 2012): 1–36.

____. *Actual Malice: Twenty-Five Years After* Times v. Sullivan. New York: Praeger, 1989. Hormozi, Amir M. "Cookies and Privacy." *Information Systems Security* 13, no. 6 (2005): 51–59.

Horne, Felix, and Cynthia Wong. *"They Know Everything We Do": Telecom and Internet Surveillance in Ethiopia.*

Horner, Annie M. Gonzaga v. Doe: *The Need for Clarity in the Clear Statement Test*, 52 S.D.L.Rev 537 (2007).

Horsey, Kirsty, and Erika Rackley. "Invasion of Privacy," in *Tort Law*, 4th ed. New York: Oxford University Press, 2015.

Horton, David. "The Stored Communications Act and Digital Assets." *Vanderbilt Law Review* 72, no. 6 (2014): 1729–1739.

Hosek, Susan D., and Susan G. Straus. *Patient Privacy, Consent, and Identity Management in Health Information Exchange: Issues for the Military Health System.*

Hossain, S. M. E., and G. Chetty. "Human Identity Verification Using Physiological and Behavioral Biometric Traits." *International Journal of Bioscience, Biochemistry and Bioinformatics* 1, no. 3 (2011): 199–205.

Hotaling, A. (2007). Protecting personally identifiable information on the internet: Notice and consent in the age of behavioral targeting. CommLaw Conspectus.

How the Health Insurance Portability and Accountability Act (HIPAA) and Other Privacy Laws Affect Public Transportation Operations. Washington, DC: Transportation Research Board, 2014.

Howard, Michael, and David LeBlanc. *24 Deadly Sins of Software Security Programming Flaws and How to Fix Them*. New York: McGraw-Hill, 2010.

Hsia, Richard. *Cybersecurity*. Kostopoulos, George K. *Cyberspace and Cybersecurity*. Boca Raton, Fl.: CRC Press, 2013.

Hubbartt, William S. *The New Battle over Workplace Privacy: How Far Can Management Go? What Rights Do Employees Have?: Safe Practices to Minimize Conflict, Confusion, and Litigation*. New York: AMACOM, 1998.

Huber, Peter W. *Law and Disorder in Cyberspace: Abolish the FCC and Let Common Law Rule the Telecoms*. New York: Oxford University Press, 1997.

Hudson, David L. *The Right to Privacy*. New York: Chelsea House, 2010.

____. *Let the Students Speak!: A History of the Fight for Free Expression in American Schools*. Boston, MA: Beacon Press, 2011.

Huggins, Maeve E. Note in "Don't Take It Personally: Supreme Court Finds Corporations Lack Personal Privacy under FOIA Exemptions." *Catholic University Journal of Law and Technology* 19, no. 481 (2011).

Hull, N. E. H. *The Abortion Rights Controversy in America: A Legal Reader*. Chapel Hill: University of North Carolina Press, 2004.

Humphries, Stephanie. "Institutes of Higher Education, Safety Swords, and Privacy Shields: Reconciling FERPA and the Common Law." *Journal of College and University Law* 35, no. 1 (2008): 145.

Hunt, Jennifer Nichole. "*Bartnicki v. Vopper:* Another Media Victory or Ominous Warning of a Potential Change in Supreme Court First Amendment Jurisprudence?" *Pepperdine Law Review* 30 (2003): 367.

Hunter, Richard. *World without Secrets: Business, Crime, and Privacy in the Age of Ubiquitous Computing*. New York: Wiley, 2002.

Hutchins, John P. *U.S. Data Breach Notification Law: State by State*. Chicago, IL: American Bar Association, Section of Science & Technology Law, 2007.

Hutnik, Alysa Zeltzer, Robyn Mohr, and Matthew P. Sullivan. "Applying the Video Privacy Protection Act to Online Streaming." AD Law Access, June 2, 2015.

Hyslop, Maitland. *Critical Information Infrastructures: Resilience and Protection*. New York: Springer, 2007.

I

Iannarelli, John. *Information Governance and Security: Protecting and Managing Your Company's Proprietary Information*. Waltham, MA: Elsevier, 2015.

Ignatius, David. "Rules for Spying." *Washington Post*, November 3, 2013. Im Hof, Ulrich. *The Enlightenment*. Tr. by William E. Yuill. Cambridge, MA: Blackwell, 1994.

The Impact of Recent Cyberstalking and Cyberharassment Cases: Leading Lawyers on Navigating Privacy Guidelines and the Legal Ramifications of Online

Behavior. The Information Privacy Law Sourcebook. Chicago, IL: American Bar Association, 2012.

Information Commissioner's Office, United Kingdom. *Guidance on Data Security Breach Management. Information Privacy Law Sourcebook.* Chicago, IL: American Bar Association, 2012.

Inness, Julie C. "The Threatened Downfall of Privacy: Judith Jarvis Thomson's 'The Right to Privacy' and Skepticism about Privacy." In *Privacy, Intimacy, and Isolation.* New York: Oxford University Press, 1996.

International Survey of Privacy Rights and Developments. United States: EPIC, 2006. Isaac, Mike. "Exclusive: Facebook Deal Nets Instagram CEO $400 Million." *Wired*, April 9, 2012.

Israel, Jonathan I. *Democratic Enlightenment: Philosophy, Revolution, and Human Rights 1750–1790.* New York: Oxford University Press, 2011.

J

Jacoby, Nicolle L., Melissa Bergman Squire, and Bureau of National Affairs. *Employee Background Checks: Balancing the Need to Hire Wisely with Employees' Right to Privacy.* Workforce Strategies 29, no. 4 (2011).

Jain, Anil K., and Karthik Nandakumar. "Biometric Authentication: System Security and User Privacy." *Computer* 11, no. 45 (2012): 87–92.

Jenkins, Simms. *The Truth about Email Marketing.* Upper Saddle River, NJ: FT Press, 2009. Jennings, Laurel, and Richard M Eastman. *Wiretaps and Electronic Eavesdropping: Federal Law and Legal Ethics.* New York: Nova Publishers, 2013.

Jensen, Gary F., and Dean G. Rojek. *Delinquency and Youth Crime*, 4th ed. Long Grove, IL: Waveland Press, 2009. Jensen, Tamila C. "From *Belle Terre* to *East Cleveland*: Zoning, the Family, and the Right of Privacy." *Family Law Quarterly* 13, no. 1 (Spring 1979): 1–25.

Jentzsch, Nicola. *The Economics and Regulation of Financial Privacy: An International Comparison of Credit Reporting Systems.* [Electronic resource.] Heidelberg : Physica-Verlag, 2006.

John Pollack, "Streetbook: How Egyptian and Tunisian Youth Hacked the Arab Spring," *MIT Technology Review*, August 23, 2011.

Johns, Fran Moreland. *Perilous Times: An Inside Look at Abortion before—and after—Roe v. Wade.* New York: YBK, 2013.

Johnson, Arthur M. "Theodore Roosevelt and the Bureau of Corporations." *The Mississippi Valley Historical Review* 45, no. 4 (March 1959): 571–590.

Johnson, Emily M. *Legalities of GPS and Cell Phone Surveillance.* New York: Novinka, 2012.

Johnson, John W. *Griswold v. Connecticut: Birth Control and the Constitutional Right of Privacy.* University Press of Kansas, 2005.

Johnson, Johna Till. "Privacy Discussion Overdue." *Network World*, August 28, 2006. Johnson, Kenneth C. "Beast of Burden: Regulatory Compliance and the Small Carrier." *Rural Telecommunications*, January 1, 2008.

Johnson, Michelle. "Of Public Interest: How Courts Handle Rape Victims' Privacy Suits." *Communications Law and Policy*, 4 no. 201 (1999).

Johnson, T. A. *Cybersecurity: Protecting Critical Infrastructures from Cyber-Attack and Cyber Warfare.* Boca Raton, FL: CRC Press, 2015.

Jolls, Christine. "Privacy and Consent over Time: The Role of Agreement in Fourth Amendment Analysis." *William and Mary Law Review* 54, no. 5 (2013).

Jones, Kyle M. L. "Learning Analytics & FERPA: Issues of Student Privacy and New Boundaries of Student Data." *Proceedings of the American Society for Information Science and Technology* 50, no. 1 (2013): 1–5.

Jones, Virginia A. "Protecting Information Privacy per U.S. Federal Law." *Information Management* 48, no. 2 (2014): 18.

Jonsen, Albert R. "The History of Bioethics as a Discipline." *Philosophy and Medicine* 78 (2004): 31–51.

Jonsen, Albert R. *A Short History of Medical Ethics.* New York: Oxford University Press, 2008.

Jung, Donald J. *The Federal Communications Commission, the Broadcast Industry, and the Fairness Doctrine, 1981–1987.* Lanham, MD: University Press of America, 1996.

K

Kahney, L. *Inside Steve's Brain.* New York: Penguin Books Ltd., 2008. Kahney, L. *The Cult of Mac.* San Francisco, CA: No Starch Press Inc., 2004.

Kalaf, William M. *Arizona Law Enforcement Biometrics Identification and Information Sharing Technology Framework.* Ft. Belvoir: Defense Technical Information Center, 2010.

Kalafut, Andrew, Abhinav Acarya, and Minaxi Gupta. "A Study of Malware in Peer-to-Peer Networks." *Proceedings of the Sixth ACM SIGCOMM Conference on Internet Measurement* (2006): 327–332. Kallen, Stuart A. *Are Privacy Rights Being Violated?* Detroit, MI: Greenhaven, 2006.

Kalven, Harry, Jr. "The New York Times Case: A Note on 'The Central Meaning of the First Amendment.'" *Supreme Court Review* 1964 (1964): 191–221.

Kalven, Jr., Harry. "The Reasonable Man and the First Amendment: Hill, Butts, and Walker," *Supreme Court Review* 1967 (1967): 280–309.

Kamisar, Yale. "Against Assisted Suicide—Even a Very Limited Form." *University of Detroit Mercy Law Review* 735 (1995).

Kanstoroom, Marci and Eric C. Osberg, Ed. *A Byte at the Apple: Rethinking Education Data for the Post-NCLB Era.*

Washington D.C.: Thomas B. Fordham Institute Press, 2008.

"Karalexis v. Byrne and the Regulation of Obscenity: 'I Am Curious (Stanley).'" Virginia Law Review 56, no. 6 (1970): 1205.

Karas, Stan. "Privacy, Identity, Databases: Toward a New Conception of the Consumer Privacy Discourse." American University Law Review 52 (December 2002).

Karch, Steven B. Workplace Drug Testing. Boca Raton: CRC Press, 2008. Karimi, Hassan A. Big Data: Techniques and Technologies in Geoinformatics. Boca Raton, FL: CRC Press/Taylor & Francis Group, 2014.

Katz, Lewis R. "Mapp after Forty Years: Its Impact on Race in America." Case Western Reserve Law Review 52 (Winter 2001): 471–487.

Kavanagh, Paul. Open Source Software Implementation and Management. Amsterdam: Elsevier Digital Press, 2004.

Kayastha, Nipendra, Dusit Niyato, Ping Wang, and Ekram Hossain. " Applications, Architectures, and Protocol Design Issues for Mobile Social Networks: a Survey." Proceedings of the IEEE 99, no. 12 (2011): 2130–2158.

Keane, Tom. "Assessing Snowden, Six Months Later." Boston Globe, December 29, 2013.

Keen, Paul. The Crisis of Literature in the 1790s: Print Culture and the Public Sphere. New York: Cambridge University Press, 1999.

Keeton, W. Page, et al. Prosser and Keeton on the Law of Torts § 117, at 85, 5th ed., 1984.

Keiter, Robert B. "Privacy, Children, and Their Parents: Reflections on and beyond the Supreme Court's Approach." Minnesota Law Review 66 (November 1981): 459–468.

Keizer, Garret. Privacy. New York: Picador, 2012.

Keller, Bill. "Is Glenn Greenwald the Future of News?" New York Times, (New York, NY) Oct. 27, 2013.

Kennedy, Charles H. The Business Privacy Law Handbook. Boston, MA: Artech House, 2008.

Kenny, Anthony. Descartes: A Study of His Philosophy. New York: Random House, 1968.

Kent, Stephen T. Who Goes There? Authentication through the Lens of Privacy. Washington, DC: National Academies Press, 2003.

Kerr, Orin S. "A User's Guide to the Stored Communications Act, and a Legislator's Guide to Amending It." George Washington Law Review 72, no. 6 (August 2004): 1208–1243.

____. "Cybercrime's Scope: Interpreting 'Access' and 'Authorization' in Computer Misuse Statutes." New York University Law Review 78 (2003): 1596.

____. "Four Models of Fourth Amendment Protection." Stanford Law Review 60, no. 2 (2007): 503–551.

____. "The Fourth Amendment and New Technologies: Constitutional Myths and the Case for Caution." Michigan Law Review 102, no. 801 (2004).

____. "Vagueness Challenges to the Computer Fraud and Abuse Act." Minnesota Law Review 94 (2010): 1561.

Kettl, Donald F., ed. The Department of Homeland Security's First Year: A Report Card. New York: Century Foundation, 2004.

Kgopa, Alfred Thaga. Information Security Issues Facing Internet Café Users. Kiefer, Francine. "With Passage of USA Freedom Act, Congress Tweaks Security-Privacy Balance." The Christian Science Monitor, June 2, 2015.

Kim, Richard S. Y. "Cyber-Surveillance: A Case Study in Policy and Development." Ph.D. dissertation, City University of New York, 2010.

Kinsley, Jennifer M. "Sexual Privacy in the Internet Age: How Substantive Due Process Protects Online Obscenity." Vanderbilt Journal of Entertainment and Technology Law 16 (2013): 103–131.

Kizza, Joseph Migga. Ethical and Social Issues in the Information Age. 4th ed. London: Springer, 2010. Klein, Mark. Wiring Up the Big Brother Machine—and Fighting It. Charleston, SC: BookSurge, 2009.

Kleinig, John. The Ethics of Policing. New York: Cambridge University Press, 1996.

Klitou, Demetrius. "Technological Threats to Privacy." Part II of Privacy-Invading Technologies and Privacy by Design. The Hague: T.M.C Asser Press, 2014.

Klosek, Jacqueline. Protecting Your Health Privacy: A Citizen's Guide to Safeguarding the Security of Your Medical Information. Santa Barbara, CA: Praeger, 2011.

Knowles, Jeffrey, and Ronald Jacobs. "FCC's CPNI Rule Limits Telecoms." Direct Marketing News, May 21, 2007.

Kobilinsky, Lawrence F., Thomas F. Liotti, and Jamel Oeser-Sweat. DNA: Forensic and Legal Applications. Hoboken, NJ: Wiley-Interscience, 2005.

Kohli, Aarti, Peter L. Markowitz, and Lisa Chavez. "Secure Communities by the Numbers: An Analysis of Demographics and Due Process." Chief Justice Earl Warren Institute on Law and Social Policy, Berkeley Law Center for Research and Administration, October 2011.

Konvitz, Milton R. "Privacy and the Law: A Philosophical Prelude." Law and Contemporary Problems: 272–280.

Koops, Bert-Jaap, "The Trouble with European Data Protection Law." International Data Privacy Law 4, no. 4 (2014): 250–261.

Korjus, Markus. The Foreign Intelligence Surveillance Act. New York: Nova Science Publishers, 2013.

Kostopoulos, George K. Cyberspace and Cybersecurity. Boca Raton, FL: CRC Press, 2013.

Kramer, Irwin R. "The Birth of Privacy Law: A Century Since Warren and Brandeis." Catholic University Law Review 39 (Spring 1990): 703–724.

Kravets, David. "Mug-Shot Industry Will Dig Up Your Past, Charge You to Bury It Again." *Wired.com* (Aug. 2, 2011).

____. "We Don't Need No Stinking Warrant: The Disturbing, Unchecked Rise of the Administrative Subpoena." *Wired* (August 28, 2012)

Kreimer, Seth F. "Sex, Laws, and Videophones: The Problem of Juvenile Sexting Prosecutions," in *Children, Sexuality, and the Law*, ed. Sacha M. Coupet and Ellen Marrus, 133–62 (New York: New York University Press, 2015).

Krishnan, Aishwaria. "Unified Metadata: Key to Reliable, Consistent Information Exchange Between Banks and Regulators." Report, Fintellix Solutions Pvt. Ltd., 2015.

Kristol, David M. "HTTP Cookies: Standards, Privacy, and Politics." *ACM Transaction on Internet Technology* 1, no. 2 (2001).

Kruegle, Herman. *CCTV Surveillance: Analog and Digital Video Practices and Technology*, 2nd ed. Amsterdam: Elsevier Butterworth-Heinemann, 2007.

Kuhn, Betsy. *Prying Eyes: Privacy in the Twenty-first Century*. Minneapolis, MN: Twenty-First Century Books, 2008.

Kulesza, Joanna. "International Law Challenges to Location Privacy Protection." *International Data Privacy Law* 3, no. 3 (2013): 158–169.

L

Lab, Steven G., et al. *Criminal Justice: The Essentials*, 3d ed. New York: Oxford University Press, 2012.

LaCroix, Allison. "'Bound Fast and Brought Under the Yokes': John Adams and the Regulation of Privacy at the Founding." *Fordham Law Review* 72, no. 6 (2004): 2331–2354.

Laer, Tom Van. "The Means to Justify the End: Combating Cyber Harassment in Social Media." *Journal of Business Ethics* 123, no. 1 (August 2014): 85–98.

LaFave, Wayne R. *Search and Seizure: A Treatise on the Fourth Amendment*, 5th ed. St. Paul: West Publishing, 2014.

Lamberg, Lynne. "Confidentiality and Privacy of Electronic Medical Records." *JAMA* 285, no. 24 (June 27, 2001): 3075.

Lamparello, A. (2015). Online Data Breaches, Standing, and the Third-Party Doctrine. Cardozo Law Review de Novo 119–129.

Landau, Susan Eva. *Surveillance or Security?: The Risks Posed by New Wiretapping Technologies*. Cambridge, MA: MIT Press, 2010.

Landree, Eric, et al. *A Delicate Balance: Portfolio Analysis and Management for Intelligence Information Dissemination Programs*. Santa Monica, CA: RAND, 2009.

Lane, Frederick S. *The Naked Employee How Technology Is Compromising Workplace Privacy*. New York: AMACOM, 2003.

Lapets, Andrei. "Machine Involvement in Formal Reasoning: Improving the Usability of Automated Formal Assistance and Verification Systems." Ph.D. diss., Boston University, 2011.

Lapsley, Phil. *Exploding the Phone: The Untold Story of the Teenagers and Outlaws who Hacked Ma Bell*. New York: Grove Press, 2013.

Laptop Computer–Based Facial Recognition System Assessment. Oak Ridge, TN: Oak Ridge Y-12 Plant, 2001.

Larence, Eileen Regen. *Firearm and Explosives Background Checks Involving Terrorist Watch List Records*. Washington, DC: U.S. Government Accountability Office, 2009.

Larson, Robert G., III, "Forgetting the First Amendment: How Obscurity-Based Privacy and a Right to Be Forgotten Are Incompatible with Free Speech," *Communication Law and Policy* 18, no. 1 (2013): 91–120.

Lashinsky, Adam. *Inside Apple: How America's Most Admired—and Secretive—Company Really Works*. New York: Business Plus, 2012.

Lassieur, Allison. *Abortion*. San Diego, Calif.: Lucent Books, 2001.

Lassiter, G. Daniel. *Police Interrogations and False Confessions: Current Research, Practice, and Policy Recommendations*. Washington, D.C.: American Psychological Association, 2010.

Laurie, G. T. *Genetic Privacy a Challenge to Medico-legal Norms*. Cambridge, England: Cambridge University Press, 2002.

Laws, Joseph, and Yang Cai. "A Privacy Algorithm for 3D Human Body Scans." *Computational Science—ICCS 2006 Lecture Notes in Computer Science*: 870–77.

Lazer, David, *ed. DNA and the Criminal Justice System: The Technology of Justice*. Cambridge, MA: MIT Press, 2004.

Lee, Cynthia. *The Fourth Amendment: Searches and Seizures: Its Constitutional History and the Contemporary Debate*. Amherst, N.Y.: Prometheus Books, 2011.

Lee, Ellie. *Abortion Law and Politics Today*. Houndmills, Basingstoke, Hampshire: Macmillan Press, 1998.

Lee, Laurie Thomas, and Robert Larose. "Caller ID and the Meaning of Privacy." *The Information Society*: 247–265.

____. "The USA PATRIOT Act and Telecommunications: Privacy under Attack." *Rutgers Computer & Technology Law Journal* (2003, June 22.

____. *U.S. Telecommunications Privacy Policy and Caller ID: A Study of Anonymity and Solitude Interests in Conflict*. Location of Publisher: Publisher's Name: 1993.

Lee, N. Genell. *Legal Concepts and Issues in Emergency Care*. Philadelphia, PA: W.B. Saunders, 2001.

Lee, Newton. *Counterterrorism and Cybersecurity: Total Information Awareness*. 2nd ed. Cham: Springer, 2015.

_____. *Facebook Nation: Total Information Awareness*, 2d ed. New York: Springer Science + Business Media, 2014.

Lee, Ronald, and Timothy Miller. "Immigration, Social Security, and Broader Fiscal Impacts." *American Economic Review* 90, no. 2 (2000): 350–354.

Leigh, David, and Luke Harding. *Wikileaks: Inside Julian Assange's War on Secrecy*. New York: Public Affairs, 2011.

Leipnik, Mark R. *GIS in Law Enforcement Implementation Issues and Case Studies*. London: Taylor & Francis, 2003.

Leming, Robert S., and Bloomington Education. Indiana v. Jamie L. Curtis: *"The Case of the Questionable Book Bag Search." A Constitution-based Scripted Trial*. Washington, DC: ERIC Clearinghouse, 1992.

Leo, Richard A. *Police Interrogation and American Justice*. Cambridge, Mass.: Harvard University Press, 2008.

_____. *The Miranda Debate: Law, Justice, and Policing*. Boston: Northeastern University Press, 1998.

Leo, Ross. *The HIPAA Program Reference Handbook*. Boca Raton: Auerbach Publications, 2005.

Leonard, Peter. "Customer Data Analytics: Privacy Settings for 'Big Data' Business." *International Data Privacy Law* 4, no. 1 (2014): 53–68

Lerner, Joshua, and Mark Schankerman. *The Comingled Code: Open Source and Economic Development*. Cambridge, MA: MIT Press, 2010.

Lerner, Natan. *Religion, Beliefs, and International Human Rights*. Maryknoll, N.Y.: Orbis Books, 2000.

Levendowski, Amanda. "Using Copyright to Combat Revenge Porn." NYU *Journal of Intellectual Property and Entertainment Law* 3 (2014): 422–446.

Lever, Annabelle. *On Privacy*. New York: Routledge, 2012.
Levin, Avner, and Mary Jo Nicholson. "Privacy Law in the United States, the EU, and Canada: the Allure of the Middle Ground." *University of Ottawa Law & Technology Journal* 2, no. 2 (2005): 357–395.

Levine, Lee, and Stephen Wermiel. *The Progeny: Justice William J. Brennan's Fight to Preserve the Legacy of* New York Times v. Sullivan. Chicago, IL: American Bar Association, 2014, pp. 55–64.

Levmore, Saul. *The Offensive Internet: Speech, Privacy, and Reputation*. Cambridge, Mass.: Harvard University Press, 2010.

Levy, Frederick, Darren Mareniss, Corianne Iacovelli, and Jeffrey Howard. "The Patient Safety and Quality Improvement Act of 2005: Preventing Error and Promoting Patient Safety." *Journal of Legal Medicine* 31, no. 4 (2010): 397–422.

Levy, Leonard W. *Origins of the Fifth Amendment: The Right against Self-incrimination*. New York: Oxford University Press, 1968.

Levy, Steven. *Hackers: Heroes of the Computer Revolution—25th Anniversary Edition*. Sebastopol, CA: O'Reilly Media, 2010.

Lewis, Anthony. *Freedom for the Thought That We Hate*. New York: Basic Books, 2009. Lewis, Sean M. "The Fourth Amendment in the Hallway: Do Tenants Have a Constitutionally Protected Privacy Interest in the Locked Common Areas of Their Apartment Buildings? (Note)." *Michigan Law Review* (2002).

Li, Chang. *New Technologies for Digital Crime and Forensics Devices, Applications, and Software*. Hershey, PA: Information Science Reference, 2011.

Li, Fei, Yogachandran Rahulamathavan, Mauro Conti, and Muttukrishnan Rajarajan. "Robust Access Control Framework for Mobile Cloud Computing Network." *Computer Communications* 68 (2015), 61–72.

Li, Han, Rathindra Sarathy, and Jie Zhang. "The Role of Emotions in Shaping Consumers' Privacy Beliefs about Unfamiliar Online Vendors." *Journal of Information Privacy and Security*: 36–62.

Li, Jin, Zheli Liu, Xiaofeng Chen, Fatos Xhafa, Xiao Tan, and Duncan S. Wong. " L-encdb: a Lightweight Framework for Privacy-Preserving Data Queries in Cloud Computing." *Knowledge-Based Systems* 79 (2015): 18–26.

Li, Joyce H. *The Center for Democracy and Technology and Internet Privacy in the U.S.: Lessons of the Last Five Years*. Lanham, MD: Scarecrow Press, 2003.

Li, Stan Z., and Anil K. Jain. *Handbook of Face Recognition*, 2nd ed. London: Springer London, 2011.

Liang, Bryan A. "Regulating for Patient Safety: The Law's Response to Medical Errors: Collaborating on Patient Safety: Legal Concerns and Policy Requirements." *Widener Law Review* 12 (2005): 83–105.

Liebow, Elliot. *Tell Them Who I Am: The Lives of Homeless Women*. New York: Free Press, 1993.

Lih, Andrew. *The Wikipedia Revolution: How a Bunch of Nobodies Created the World's Greatest Encyclopedia*. New York: Hyperion, 2009.

Lin, Zhen Owen. "Genomic Research and Human Subject Privacy." *Science*, July 9, 2004.

Lind, Nancy S. *Privacy in the Digital Age: 21st-Century Challenges to the Fourth Amendment*.

Lind, Nancy S., and Erik Rankin, eds. *Privacy in the Digital Age: 21st-Century Challenges to the Fourth Amendment*. 2 vols. Santa Barbara, CA: Praeger,

Linnartz, Jean-Paul, and Pim Tuyls. "New Shielding Functions to Enhance Privacy and Prevent Misuse of Biometric Templates." *Lecture Notes in Computer Science Audio- and Video-Based Biometric Person Authentication*. 393–402.

Linzmayer, O. W. *Apple Confidential: The Real Story of Apple Computer, Inc.* New York, 2004.

Lipschultz, Jeremy Harris. *Broadcast and Internet Indecency: Defining Free Speech.* New York: Routledge, 2008.

Liss, Jerald M. "Creative Destruction and Globalization: The Rise of Massive Standardized Education Platforms." *Globalizations* 10, no. 4 (08/01; 2015/10, 2013): 557–570.

Lister, Stuart, and Michael Rowe, eds. *Accountability in Policing.* New York: Routledge, 2015.

Liu, Chengjun, and V. K. Mago. *Cross Disciplinary Biometric Systems.* Berlin: Springer, 2012.

Liu, Ray H. *Handbook of Workplace Drug Testing.* Washington, DC: AACC Press, 1995.

Liu, Yue. "Rational Concerns about Biometric Technology." *Computer Security, Privacy and Politics: Current Issues, Challenges and Solutions* (2008): 94–134.

Looijen, D. (2010). Time for a Change: The Schema of Contract in the Digital Era. Journal on Telecommunications & High Technology Law 8: 547–570.

Lowrance, William W. *Privacy, Confidentiality, and Health Research.* New York: Cambroidge University Press, 2012.

Luber B, Fisher C, Appelbaum PS, Ploesser M, Lisanby SH. Lisanby. Non-invasive Brain Stimulation in the Detection of Deception: Scientific Challenges and Ethical Consequences. *Behavioral Sciences & the Law,* 27(2):191–208, 2009.

Lynch, Jennifer. From Fingerprints to DNA: *Biometric Data Collection in U.S. Immigrant Communities and Beyond.* Special Report for the Electronic Frontier Foundation and the Immigration Policy Center. May 2012.

Lyon, David. *Computers, Surveillance, and Privacy.* Minneapolis: University of Minnesota Press, 1996.

———. *Surveillance after September 11.* Malden, MA: Polity Press, 2003.

———. *Surveillance after Snowden.* Malden, MA: Polity Press, 2015.

M

Maass, Peter. "How Laura Poitras Helped Snowden Spill His Secrets." *New York Times,* August 13, 2013.

"MacArthur Fellows Program—Meet the Class of 2012: Laura Poitras." Macfound.org, October 2, 2012.

MacCormick, Neil. *Enlightenment, Rights, and Revolution: Essays in Legal and Social Philosophy.* Aberdeen, UK: Aberdeen University Press, 1989.

Macdonald, Lynda A. C. *Tolley's Managing Email and Internet Use.* Croydon: LexisNexis UK, 2004.

Machan, Tibor R. *Private Rights and Public Illusions.* New Brunswick, NJ: Transaction Publishers, 1995.

MacIntosh, Susanne M. "Fourth Amendment: The Plain Touch Exception to the Warrant Requirement." *Journal of Criminal Law and Criminology* 84, no. 4 (1994).

MacKinnon, Catharine, and Andrea Dworkin. *In Harm's Way: The Pornography Civil Rights Hearings.* Cambridge, Mass.: Harvard University Press, 1997.

MacKinnon, Rebecca. *Consent of the Networked: The World-wide Struggle for Internet Freedom.* New York: Basic Books, 2012.

MacLean, Charles E., and Adam Lamparello, *Forensic DNA Phenotyping in Criminal Investigations and Criminal Courts: Assessing and Mitigating the Dilemmas Inherent in the Science,* 8(2) Recent Advances in DNA & Gene Sequencing 104–112 (2014).

Maclin, Tracey. *The Supreme Court and the Fourth Amendment's Exclusionary Rule.* New York: Oxford University Press, 2013.

Madden, M., S. Cortesi, U. Gasser, A., Lenhart, and M. Duggan. *Parents, Teens, and Online Privacy.* Pew Internet & American Life Project, 2012.

Madden, Mary, and Lee Rainie. "Americans' Attitudes about Privacy, Security and Surveillance." Pew Research Center. May 20, 2015.

Maginnis, Maureen. "Maintaining the Privacy of Personal Information: The DPPA and the Right of Privacy." *South Carolina Law Review* 51 (2000): 807–822.

Mago, V. K. *Cross-Disciplinary Applications of Artificial Intelligence and Pattern Recognition Advancing Technologies.* Hershey, PA: Information Science Reference, 2012.

Maguire, Mary, and Dan Okada, eds. *Critical Issues in Crime and Justice: Thought, Policy, and Practice,* 2d ed. Los Angeles: Sage, 2015.

Mahmood, Zaigham. *Cloud Computing: Methods and Practical Approaches.* London: Springer, 2013.

"Mainstream Neglect of Sexual Harassment as a Social Problem." Canadian Journal of Sociology 21, no. 2 (March 22, 1996): 185–203.

Mandiberg, Michael. *The Social Media Reader.* New York: New York University Press, 2012.

Manishin, Glenn B. *Complying with the CAN-SPAM Act and Other Critical Business Issues: Staying out of Trouble.* New York: Practicing Law Institute, 2004.

Mank, Bradford. *Suing under §1983: The Future after Gonzaga v. Doe* (2003). Faculty Articles and Other Publications. Paper 123.

Mann, Robert. "The Cypherpunk Revolutionary: On Julian Assange." *The Monthly,* March 1, 2011.

Mantlero, Alessandro. "The EU Proposal for a General Data Protection Regulation and the Roots of the 'Right to Be Forgotten.'" *Computer Law & Security Review* 29, no. 3 (June 2013): 229–235.

Manz, Willaim H., ed. *Civil Liberties in Wartime: Legislative Histories of the Espionage Act 1917 and the Sedition Act of 1918* (vol. 1, Documents 1–57). Buffalo, NY: William S. Hein & Co., Inc., 2007.

Marcel, Se. *Handbook of Biometric Anti-spoofing: Trusted Biometrics under Spoofing Attacks.*

Marion, Nancy E., Kelley A. Cronin, and Williard M. Oliver. *Homeland Security: Policy and Politics.* Durham, NC: Carolina Academic Press, 2015.

Mark, K., and M. Crossan. *Apple Computer, Inc.: iPods and iTunes.* Ivey Case Studies, Richard Ivey School of Business, Ivey Publishing, 2005, 1–14.

Markoff, John. "Pentagon Plans a Computer System That Would Peek at Personal Data of Americans." *New York Times,* November 9, 2002.

Marks, Murray K. *Computer-Graphic Facial Reconstruction.* Burlington, MA: Elsevier Academic Press, 2005.

Marlin-Bennett, Renée. *Knowledge Power: Intellectual Property, Information, and Privacy.* Boulder, CO: Lynne Rienner, 2004.

Marshall, John. *Descartes's Moral Theory.* Ithaca, NY: Cornell University Press, 1998.

Martin, Greg, Rebecca Scott Bray, and Miiko Kumar, eds. *Secrecy, Law, and Society.* New York: Routledge, 2015.

Martin, James P., and Harry Cendrowski. *Cloud Computing and Electronic Discovery.* Hoboken, NJ: Wiley, 2014.

Martínez-Pérez, Borja, Isabel De La Torre-Díez, and Miguel López-Coronado. "Privacy and Security in Mobile Health Apps: A Review and Recommendations." *Journal of Medical Systems* 39, no. 1 (2014): 181.

Martinovic, Ivan, Doug Davies, Mario Frank, Daniele Perito, Tomas Ros, and Dawn Song. On the Feasibility of Side-Channel Attacks with Brain-Computer Interfaces. In *the Proceedings of the 21st USENIX Security Symposium.* USENIX, 2012.

Marzolf, Julie Schwab. *Online Privacy.* New York: Gareth Stevens Pub., 2013.

Mass, Warren. "USA Freedom Act Fails." *New American,* December 22, 2014.

Mathieson, Rick. *The On-demand Brand 10 Rules for Digital Marketing Success in an Anytime, Everywhere World.* New York: AMACOM, 2010.

Maurer, Virginia, and Roger D. Blair. "Statute Law and Common Law: The Fair Credit Reporting Act." *Missouri Law Review* 49, no. 289 (1984)

Maxwell, Bruce, ed. *Homeland Security: A Documentary History.* Washington, DC: CQ Press, 2004.

Maxwell, Lida. "Truth in Public: Chelsea Manning, Gender Identity, and the Politics of Truth-Telling." *Theory & Event* 18, no. 1 (2015)

Mayer-Schönberger, Viktor. "The Internet and Privacy Legislation: Cookies for a Treat?" *Computer Law & Security Review* 14, no. 3 (May 1, 1998): 166–174.

McBride, Sarah, and Alexei Oreskovic. "Snapchat Breach Exposes Flawed Premise, Security Challenge." Reuters, October 14, 2014.

McCall, Ginger. "The Face Scan Arrives." *New York Times* (August 30, 2013).

McCann, E. (June 17, 2015). Medical identity theft hits all-time high. Healthcare IT News.

McClellan, Grant S., ed. *The Right to Privacy.* New York: H.W. Wilson, 1976.

McCullagh, Declan. "Instagram Apologizes to Users: We Won't Sell Your Photos." C/net, December 18, 2012.

McInnis, Thomas N. *The Evolution of the Fourth Amendment.* Lanham, MD: Lexington Books, 2009. McKay, Sinclair. *The Secret Life of Bletchley Park: The History of the Wartime Codebreaking Centre by the Men and Women Who Were There.* London: Aurum, 2010.

McKenna, Brian. "Privacy Advocate Warns Biometric Industry to Stay Clear of Government." *Computer Fraud & Security* 11 (2004): 3.

McKinney, K. D. "Space, Body, and Mind: Parental Perceptions of Children's Privacy Needs." *Journal of Family Issues* (1998): 75–100.

McMurtrie, Jacqueline. "Swirls and Whorls: Litigating Post-Conviction Claims of Fingerprint Misidentification after the NAS Report." *Utah Law Review* 2010, no. 2 (2010): 267–297.

McNally, Megan. *Identity Theft in Today's World.* Santa Barbara, CA: Praeger, 2012.

McQuade, Samuel C., and Sarah Gentry. *Cyber-stalking and Cyberbullying.* New York: Chelsea House, 2012.

McThomas, Mary. *The Dual System of Privacy Rights in the United States.* Hoboken: Taylor and Francis, 2013.

Medina, Melissa. "The Stored Communications Act: An Old Statute for Modern Times." *American University Law Review* 63, no. 1 (2013): 267–305.

Meiklejohn, Alexander. *Free Speech and Its Relation to Self-Government.* The Lawbook Exchange, Ltd., 2011.

Melson, Brent. "Protecting Privacy and Security in Software and Mobile Apps: How to Take Precautions to Keep Your Data Secure." *Wireless Design & Development,* July 1, 2015.

Mena, Jesus. *Homeland Security Techniques and Technologies.* Hingham, MA: Charles River Media, 2004.

Merino, Noe. *Abortion.* Farmington Hills, MI: Greenhaven Press, 2013.

Merkow, Mark S., and Jim Breithaupt. *The E-Privacy Imperative: Protect Your Customers' Internet Privacy and Ensure Your Company's Survival in the Electronic Age.* New York: AMACOM, 2002.

Messenger, Ashley. "What Would a 'Right to Be Forgotten' Mean for Media in the United States?" *Communications Lawyer* 29, no. 1 (June 2012): 12.

Metcalfe, Daniel J. "*Amending the FOIA: Is It Time for a Real Exemption 10?*" *Administration and Regulation Law News* 37, no. 16 (Summer 2012).

_____. "Hillary's E-Mail Defense Is Laughable." *POLITICO Magazine*, March 16, 2015. http://www.politico.com/magazine/story/2015/03/hillary-clinton-email-scandaldefense-laughable-foia-116116.html#.VXw6lvlViko.

_____. "The History of Transparency," in *Research Handbook on Transparency*, edited by Padideh Ala'i and Robert G. Vaughn. Northampton, MA: Edward Elgar, 2014.

_____. *"The Nature of Government Secrecy." Government Information Quarterly* 26, no. 305 (2009)

Meyer, John. "First Federal Net Privacy Law Approved." *Computers & Security*: 719.

Meyer, Robinson. "The New Terminology of Snapchat." *The Atlantic*, May 2, 2014. Meyers, Martin. *"T.L.O. v. New Jersey:* Officially Conducted School Searches and a New Fourth Amendment Balancing Test." *Juvenile and Family Court Journal* 37, no. 1 (February 1986): 25–37.

Michael, John. *Anxious Intellects: Academic Professionals, Public Intellectuals, and Enlightenment Values.* Durham, NC: Duke University Press, 2000.

Michalowski, Sabine. *Medical Confidentiality and Crime.* Aldershot, England: Ashgate, 2003.

Miles, Jason G. *Instagram Power: Build Your Brand and Reach More Customers with the Power of Pictures.* New York: McGraw-Hill Education, 2014.

Miller, Debra A. *Homeland Security.* Detroit, MI: Greenhaven Press, 2009. Mills, Jon L. *Privacy in the New Media Age.* Gainesville: University Press of Florida, 2015.

Mironenko, Olga. "Body Scanners versus Privacy and Data Protection." *Computer Law & Security Review*: 232–44. Mitchell, Ian D. "Third-Party Tracking Cookies and Data Privacy." April 25, 2012.

Mitnick, Kevin. *Ghost in the Wires: My Adventures as the World's Most Wanted Hacker.* New York: Little, Brown and Company, 2011.

Mizell, Louis R. *Invasion of Privacy.* New York: Berkley Books, 1998.

Mohapatra, Manas, Andrew Hasty, et al. *Mobile Apps for Kids Current Privacy Disclosures Are Disappointing.* Washington, DC: U.S. Federal Trade Commission, 2012.

Moisescot, R. *Steve Jobs: A Biography by Romain Moisescot. All About Steve Jobs.* 2008.

Monagle, John F. *Health Care Ethics: Critical Issues.* Gaithersburg, Md.: Aspen Publishers, 1994.

Mooney, Linda A., and David Knox. *Understanding Social Problems*, 6th ed. Belmont, CA: Wadsworth/Cengage Learning, 2009.

Moore, Adam D. *Information Ethics: Privacy, Property, and Power.* Seattle: University of Washington Press, 2005. Moore, Tyler. *Economics of Information Security and Privacy.* New York: Springer, 2010.

Morgan, John S. "Comment, The Junking of the Fourth Amendment: *Illinois v. Krull* and *New York v. Burger.*" *Tulane Law Review* 63, no. 2 (December 1988): 335–378.

Morrow, D. (1995). *Oral History Interview with Jobs.* April 20, 1995.

Mouzakiti, Foivi. "Transborder Data Flows 2.0: Mending the Holes of the Data Protection Directive." *European Data Protection Law Review* 1 (2015): 39–51.

Muller, Max. *The Manager's Guide to HR Hiring, Firing, Performance Evaluations, Documentation, Benefits, and Everything Else You Need to Know*, 2d ed. New York: American Management Association, 2013.

Murphy, Bruce. *Wild Bill: The Legend and Life of William O. Douglas.* New York: Random House, 2003.

Murphy, Daniel Robert. *Educational Records: A Practical Guide for Legal Compliance.* Lanham, MD: Rowman & Littlefield, 2009.

Murphy, Paul L. The Right to Privacy and the Ninth Amendment. New York: Garland Publishing.

Murray, Jim. *Digital Forensics for Network, Internet, and Cloud Computing: A Forensic Evidence Guide for Moving Targets and Data.* Burlington, MA: Syngress, 2010.

Murray, Ryan Patrick. "Myspace-ing Is Not a Crime: Why Breaching Terms of Service Agreements Should Not Implicate the Computer Fraud and Abuse Act Written February 2, 2009," *Loyola of Los Angeles Entertainment Law Review* 29, no. 3 (June 2009): 475.

N

Nash, Richard. "Publishing 2020." *Publishing Research Quarterly* 26, no. 2 (June 2010): 114–118.

Nass, Sharyl J., et al., eds. *Beyond the HIPAA Privacy Rule: Enhancing Privacy, Improving Health through Research.* Washington, DC: National Academies Press, 2009.

Nass, Sharyl J., Laura A Levit, and Lawrence O Gostin. *Beyond the HIPAA Privacy Rule Enhancing Privacy, Improving Health through Research.* Washington, DC: National Academies Press, 2009.

National Research Council. *Strengthening Forensic Science in the United States: A Path Forward.* Washington, DC: The National Academies Press, 2009.

National Security Agency. *The Origins of NSA.* Fort George G. Meade, Md.: Center for Cryptologic History, 1996.

Natoli Jr., Frank. "Biometrics in Banking: Overcoming the Barriers." *American Banker Magazine* (June 2014)

Natter, Raymond. "The Reasons for the Gramm-Leach-Bliley Act." *SSRN Electronic Journal SSRN Journal.*

Negangard, Richard. *Legal Principles for Guiding School Administrators in the Search and Seizure of Public School Students: Protecting Students' Fourth Amendment Rights and Providing for Safe Schools.* Ph.D Diss. University of Miami, 1988

Nelles, Walter, ed. *Espionage Cases: With Certain Others on Related Points.* New York: National Civil Liberties Bureau, 1918.

Nelson, Steven. "Privacy Board Will Do 'Deep Dive' on NSA, CIA Practices." *U.S. News and World Report*, April 8, 2015.

Nemeth, Charles P. *Homeland Security: An Introduction to the Principles and Practice*, 2nd ed. Boca Raton, FL: CRC Press, 2013.

New South Wales Privacy Committee. *Private Lives and Public Health: Privacy Guidelines for HIV Testing*. Sydney: Committee, 1993. New York: Oxford University Press, 1997. Newcombe, Chris, et al. "How Amazon's Web Services Uses Formal Methods." *Communications of the ACM* 58, no. 4 (April 2015): 66–73.

Newell, Bryce Clayton. "Local Law Enforcement Jumps on the Big Data Bandwagon: Automated License Plate Recognition Systems, Information Privacy, and Access to Government Information." *Maine Law Review* 66, (2014): 397–435.

Newton, Jim. *Justice for All: Earl Warren and the Nation He Made*. New York: Riverhead Books, 2006.

Newton, Lee. *Facebook Nation: Total Information Awesomeness*. New York: Springer, 2014.

Ng, Cindy. "5 Things Privacy Experts Want You to Know about Wearables." Varonis Blog. July 17, 2014.

Nichols, Randall K., and Daniel J. Ryan. *Defending Your Digital Assets against Hackers, Crackers, Spies, and Thieves*. New York: McGraw-Hill, 2000.

NICS, National Instant Criminal Background Check System. Clarksburg, WV: U.S. Dept. of Justice, Federal Bureau of Investigation, Criminal Justice Information Services Division, 1998.

Nizan Geslevich Packin & Yafit Lev Aretz, *Big Data and Social Netbanks: Are You Ready to Replace Your Bank?* 53 Houston Law Review.

Noftsinger, John B., Jr., Kenneth F. Newbold, Jr., and Jack K. Wheeler. *Understanding Homeland Security: Policy, Perspectives, and Paradoxes*. New York: Palgrave Macmillan, 2007.

Nolan, Andrew, and Richard M. Thompson II. *Reform of the Foreign Intelligence Surveillance Courts: Procedural and Operational Changes*. Washington, DC: U.S. Library of Congress, Congressional Research Service.

Noll, A. Michael. "An Inquiry into the Privacy Aspects of Caller-ID." *Telecommunications Policy*: 690–693.

Norlin, John W. *Confidentiality in Student Testing: Access and Disclosure Requirements under FERPA and the IDEA*. Horsham, PA: LRP Publications, 2008.

Norris, Cameron T. "Your Right to Look Like an Ugly Criminal: Resolving the Circuit Split over Mug Shots and the Freedom of Information Act." *Vanderbilt Law Review* 66, no. 5 (2013).

Northouse, Clayton. *Protecting What Matters: Technology, Security, and Liberty since 9/11*. Washington, DC: Computer Ethics Institute:, 2006.

Norvell, Blake Covington. "The Constitution and the NSA Warrantless Wiretapping Program: A Fourth Amendment Violation?" *Yale Journal of Law & Technology* 11, no. 1 (2008).

Notestine, Kerry E. *Fundamentals of Employment Law*. Chicago: American Bar Association, 2000.

Notturno, Mark Amadeus. *Privacy and Privacy Rights*. Parkersburg, WV: Interactivity Foundation Press, 2005.

Nouwt, Sjaak. *Reasonable Expectations of Privacy?: Eleven Country Reports on Camera Surveillance and Workplace Privacy*. The Hague, The Netherlands: T.M.C. Asser Press, 2005.

Nowrasteh, Alex Cole. "Open the Gates." *USA Today*, November 1, 2013. NSA Director of Civil Liberties and Privacy Office. *NSA's Civil Liberties and Privacy Protections for Targeted SIGINT Activities under Executive Order 12333*. Washington, DC: NSA Civil Liberties and Privacy Office, October 7, 2014.

O

O'Brien, David M. *Privacy, Law and Public Policy*. New York: Praeger, 1970. O'Neill, Cathy and Rachel Schutt, *Doing Data Science: Straight Talk from Frontline*. O'Reilly Media Inc., 2013.

Odlyzko, Andrew. "Privacy, Economics, and Price Discrimination on the Internet." In *Proceedings of the Fifth International Conference on Electronic Commerce—ICEC*, edited by Norman M. Sadeh et al. New York: ACM Press, 2003.

Odom, Thomas H., and Gregory S. Feder. "Challenging the Federal Driver's Privacy Protection Act: The Next Step in Developing a Jurisprudence of Process-Oriented Federalism under the Tenth Amendment." *University of Miami Law Review* 53 (1998): 71–167.

Office of the Director of National Intelligence, Office of General Counsel. *Intelligence Community Legal Reference Book*, 2d ed. Washington, DC: Office of the Director of National Intelligence, Office of General Counsel/USGPO, 2009.

Office of the Privacy Commissioner of Canada. *Key Steps for Organizations in Responding to Privacy Breaches*.

Olivenbaum, Joseph M. "Ctrl-Alt-Delete: Rethinking Federal Computer Crime Legislation." *Seton Hall Law Review* 27 (1997): 574.

Oliver, Dawn. *Human Rights and the Private Sphere: A Comparative Study*. Abingdon, United Kingdom: Routledge-Cavendish, 2007.

Olson, Parmy. *We Are Anonymous: Inside the Hacker World of LulzSec, Anonymous, and the Global Cyber Insurgency*. New York: Little, Brown and Company, 2012.

Omohundro, Steve. "Cryptocurrencies, Smart Contracts, and Artificial Intelligence." *AI Matters* 1, no. 2 (December 2014): 19–21.

Orr, S. (July 28, 2014). New York knows where your license plate goes. USA Today.

Osborne, Mark, and Paul M. Summitt. *How to Cheat at Managing Information Security*. Rockland, MA: Syngress, 2006.

P

Palma, Paul. *Computers in Society 09/10;* 15th ed. New York: McGraw-Hill Irwin, 2010.

Panos, Linda. "Privacy in Schools: Dogs, Lockers, Bodies, and Backpacks (Human Rights Law)." *LawNow*, March 1, 2009.

Paper, Lewis J. *Brandeis:* Prentice-Hall, 1983.

Paradis, Daniel P. "*Bartnicki v. Vopper:* Cell Phones and Throwing Stones." *New England Law Review* 37 (2003): 1117.

Parkinson, Hannah Jane. "*James Foley: How Social Media Is Fighting Back against ISIS Propaganda,*" *Guardian,* August 20, 2014.

Parry, John T., and L. Song Richardson, eds. *The Constitution and the Future of Criminal Justice in America*. New York: Cambridge University Press, 2013.

Parsons, Kimberly D. *Immigration Policy Proposals and Potential Budgetary Effects*. New York: Nova Science, 2015.

Pasquale, Frank. "The Dark Market for Personal Data." *New York Times*, October 17, 2014.

Pasquale, Frank. *The Black Box Society: The Secret Algorithms That Control Money and* "Patent Issued for Healthcare Privacy Breach Prevention through Integrated Audit and Access Control." Computer Weekly News, April 2, 2015.

Patterson, Kelsey T. "Narrowing It Down to One Narrow View: Clarifying and Limiting the Computer Fraud and Abuse Act." *Charleston Law Review* 7, no. 3 (March 2013): 489.

Pattison, Scott. "Restricting 'Caller ID.'" *Consumers' Research Magazine*, May 1, 1992.

Payne, Bridget Watson, ed. *This Is Happening: Life through the Lens of Instagram*. San Francisco, CA: Chronicle Books, 2013.

Payton, Theresa, and Ted Claypoole. *Privacy in the Age of Big Data: Recognizing Threats, Defending Your Rights, and Protecting Your Family*. MD: Rowman & Littlefield, 2014.

Pellegrino, E. "Toward a Virtue-Based Normative Ethics for the Health Professions." *Kennedy Institute of Ethics Journal 5*, no. 3 (1995): 253–277.

Pence, Gregory. *Elements of Bioethics*. New York: McGraw-Hill, 2007.

Peretti, Kimberly Kiefer. "Data Breaches: What the Underground World of 'Carding' Reveals." *Santa Clara Computer and High Technology Law Journal* 25 (2009): 375.

Persico, Deborah A. New Jersey v. T.L.O.: *Drug Searches in Schools*. Springfield, NJ: Enslow, 1998. Peterson, T.F., Institute Historian. *Nightwork: A History of Hacks and Pranks at MIT* (updated edition). Cambridge, MA: MIT Press, 2011.

Petronio, Sandra Sporbert. *Boundaries of Privacy Dialectics of Disclosure*. Albany: State University of New York Press, 2002.

Pike, George H. "USA PATRIOT Act Still Raising Questions." *Information Today*, July, 2015.

Pincus, Andrew. "Evolving Technology and the Fourth Amendment: The Implications of *Riley v. California*." *Cato Supreme Court Review* 2014–2015 (2014): 307–336.

Pincus, Walter. "NSA Reform Should Proceed Cautiously." *Washington Post*, November 7, 2013.

Pinson, Chad M., and John B. Lawrence. "FCRA Preemption of State Law: A Guide Through Muddy Waters." *Journal of Consumer and Commercial Law* 15, no. 47 (2012)

Poitras, Laura, dir. *Citizenfour*. 2014. New York: Radius-TWC, 2015. Streaming Video. Pollack, Jack H. *The Judge Who Changed America*. Englewood Cliffs, NJ: Prentice-Hall, 1979.

Pollock, Joycelyn M. *Ethical Dilemmas and Decisions in Criminal Justice*, 8th ed. Belmont, CA: Wadsworth, 2014.

Popoli, Anna Rita. "Cookies and Electronic Commerce: A Survey About Actual Knowledge of the Issues Concerning Privacy." December 10, 2012.

Porterfield, Jason. *Julian Assange and Wikileaks*. New York: Rosen Pubishing Group, 2013.

Posner, Richard A. "Orwell versus Huxley: Economics, Technology, Privacy, and Satire." University of Chicago Law School, John M. Olin Law & Economics Working Paper No. 89 (November 1999).

____. *Preventing Surprise Attacks: Intelligence Reform in the Wake of 9/11*. Lanham, MD: Rowman & Littlefield Publishers, 2004.

____. *The Economics of Justice*. Cambridge, MA: Harvard University Press, 1981.

Post, Robert C. "The Constitutional Concept of Public Discourse: Outrageous Opinion, Democratic Deliberation, and Hustler Magazine v. Falwell." Harvard Law Review 103 (1990): 601–686.

Potter, Van Rensselaer. "Bioethics: The Science of Survival." *Perspectives in Biology and Medicine* 14, no. 2 (1970): 127–153.

Poulsen, Kevin and Kim Zetter. "U.S. Intelligence Analyst Arrested in Wikileaks Video Probe." *Wired*. June 6, 2010.

Poulsen, Kevin. *Kingpin: How One Hacker Took Over the Billion-Dollar Cybercrime Underground*. New York: Broadway Paperbacks, 2011.

Powers, Meghan. *The Abortion Rights Movement*. Detroit: Greenhaven Press/Thomson/Gale, 2006.

President's Council of Advisors on Science & Technology. *Big Data and Privacy: A Technological Perspective.* The White House. May 1, 2014.

Price, Ira M. "Torts: Right of Privacy: Invasion of Privacy through Fictional Works." *Michigan Law Review* 45, no. 8 (June 1947): 1064–1066.

Priester, Benjamin J. "Five Answers and Three Questions After *United States v. Jones* (2012), the Fourth Amendment 'GPS Case.'" *Oklahoma Law Review* 65 (2013): 491–532.

Primus, Eve Brensike. "Disentangling Administrative Searches." *Columbia Law Review* 111, no. 2 (March 2011): 254–312.

Privacy and Civil Liberties Oversight Board. *Report on the Surveillance Program Operated Pursuant to Section 702 of the Foreign Intelligence Surveillance Act*, July 2, 2014.

Privacy and Civil Liberties Oversight Board. *Report on the Telephone Records Program Conducted under Section 215 of the USA PATRIOT ACT and on the Operations of the Foreign Intelligence Surveillance Court.* Washington, DC: Publisher, 2015.

Privacy The Lost Right. Oxford Scholarship Online, 2008.

Privacy, Free Speech & the Garden Grove Cyber Café Experiment. Durham, NC: Duke University School of Law, 2004.

Probhakar, S., S. Pankanti, and A. K. Jain. "Biometric Recognition: Security and Privacy Concerns." *IEEE Security and Privacy* 2, no. 1 (2003): 33–42.

Prosser, William Lloyd. *"Privacy." California Law Review* 48, no. 3 (1960): 383–423. "Prosser's Privacy at 50." A Symposium on Privacy in the 21st Century at the University of California, Berkeley, School of Law (January 29, 2010).

Protecting Individual Privacy in the Struggle against Terrorists: A Framework for Program Assessment. Washington, DC: National Academies Press, 2008.

"Protecting Privacy under the Fourth Amendment." The Yale Law Journal 91, no. 2 (1981): 313.

Provost, Foster and Tom Fawcett, *Data Science for Business: What you need to know about data mining.* O'Reilly Media Inc., 2013.

Public Law 104–208,110 Stat. 3009 (September 30, 1996). 15 USC 1692 www.nclc.org/issues/debt-collection.html

Q

Qualman, Erik. *Socialnomics: How Social Media Transforms the Way We Live and Do Business.* 2d ed. Hoboken, NJ: Wiley, 2013.

Quinn, Michael J. *Ethics for the Information Age.* Boston, MA: Pearson/Addison-Wesley, 2005.

R

Rabbany, Ahmed. *Introduction to GPS: The Global Positioning System.* Boston, MA: Artech House, 2002.

Rackow, Sharon H. "How the USA Patriot Act Will Permit Governmental Infringement upon the Privacy of Americans in the Name of 'Intelligence' Investigations." *University of Pennsylvania Law Review* 150, no. 5 (2002): 1651, 2012.

Rakower, Lauren. "Blurred Line: Zooming in on Google Street View and the Global Right to Privacy." *Brooklyn Journal of International Law* 37, no. 1 (2011): 317–347.

Ransom, Harry Howe. *Central Intelligence and National Security.* Cambridge, MA: Harvard University Press, 1958.

Reagan, Leslie J. *When Abortion Was a Crime Women, Medicine, and Law in the United States, 1867–1973.* Berkeley: University of California Press, 1997.

Reagle, Joseph Michael. *Good Faith Collaboration: The Culture of Wikipedia.* Cambridge, MA: MIT Press, 2010.

"Real Estate Roundtable Urges Pro-Growth Immigration Reform with Flexible Visa Caps." Real Estate Weekly News, May 10, 2013.

Reardon, Conor M. "Cell Phones, Police Recording, and the Intersection of the First and Fourth Amendments." *Duke Law Journal* (2013).

"Recent Case: Internet Law—Protection of Personal Data—Court of Justice of the European Union Creates Presumption That Google Must Remove Links to Personal Data upon Request, Case C-131/12, Google Spain SL v. Agencia Española de Protección de Datos (May 13, 2014)." Harvard Law Review 128 (2014): 735–742.

Rees, Mark I. *Challenges and Opportunities of Next-Generation Sequencing for Biomedical Research.* Amsterdam: Elsevier/Academic Press, 2012.

Rehnquist, William. "Is an Expanded Right of Privacy Consistent with Fair and Effective Law Enforcement?" *University of Kansas Law Review* 23 (1974–1975): 1.

Reid, Beth Ann. *A Manual for Complying with the Freedom of Information Act and the Privacy Protection Act.*

Richmond, VA: Department of Management Analysis and Systems Development, 1980. Reinecke, Leonard, and Sabine Trepete. *Privacy Online: Perspectives on Privacy and Self-Disclosure in the Social Web.* New York: Springer Publishing Company, 2011.

Relyea, Harold. *Privacy and Civil Liberties Oversight Board New Independent Agency Status.* Washington, DC: Congressional Research Service, Library of Congress, 2008.

Rembar, Charles. *The End of Obscenity: The Trials of Lady Chatterley, Tropic of Cancer, and Fanny Hill.* New York: Random House, 1968.

Rengel, Alexandra. *Privacy in the 21st Century*. Leiden: Martinus Nijhoff Publishers, 2013. Repa, Barbara Kate. *Your Rights in the Workplace*, 9th ed. Berkeley, CA: Nolo, 2010.

"Report on Whole-Genome Sequencing Concerns Issued; Presidential Commission Worries About Privacy." Biotechnology Law Report: 579.

Reporters Committee for Freedom of the Press. "Confidential Sources and Information," in *First Amendment Handbook*. 7th ed. (2011).

Reyns, Bradford W. *The Anti-social Network: Cyberstalking Victimization among College Students*. El Paso, TX: LFB Scholarly Publishing, 2012.

Rhodes, James Ford. "Edwin Lawrence Godkin." In *Historical Essays*, 1909. Reprint, Port Washington, NY: Kennikat Press, 1966.

Rhodes, Jill D., and Vincent I. Polley. *The ABA Cybersecurity Handbook: A Resource for Attorneys, Law Firms, and Business Professionals*. Chicago, IL: American Bar Association, 2013.

Richard J. Peltz-Steele, *The Law of Access to Government* (Carolina Academic Press 2012)

Richards, David A. J. "Constitutional Privacy, the Right to Die and the Meaning of Life: A Moral Analysis." *William and Mary Law Review* 22 (1981).

Richards, David A. J. "Liberalism, Public Morality, and Constitutional Law: Prolegomenon to a Theory of the Constitutional Right to Privacy." *Law and Contemporary Problems* 51, no. 1 (1988): 123–150.

Richards, Neil M. "The Dangers of Surveillance." Harvard Law Review 126, no. 7 (May 2013): 1934–1965.

____. "The Limits of Tort Privacy." *Journal on Telecommunications & High Technology Law* 9 (2011): 357–384.

____. "Prosser's Privacy Law: A Mixed Legacy." *California Law Review* 98 1887, 1924 (2010)

____. *Intellectual Privacy: Rethinking Civil Liberties in the Digital Age*. New York: Oxford University Press, 2015.

Richardson, Jeffrey. "Michigan Needs a Statutory Right of Publicity." *Michigan Business Journal* 86, no. 26 (September 2007).

Richey, Warren. "Supreme Court: NASA's Intrusive Background Checks OK." *Christian Science Monitor*, January 19, 2011.

Richie, Donald A. *American Journalists: Getting the Story*. Oxford: Oxford University Press, 1997. Ridgeway, Greg. *Summary of the RAND Report on NYPD's Stop, Question, and Frisk*. Santa Monica, Calif.: RAND, 2009.

Rittinghouse, John W., and James F. Ransome. *Wireless Operational Security*. Burlington, MA: Elsevier/Digital Press, 2004.

Robert Hannigan, "*The Web Is a Terrorist's Command-Control Network of Choice*," *Financial Times*, November 3, 2014.

Roberts, Brian F. 2011. Methods and Systems for Presenting an Advertisement Associated with an Ambient Action of a User. Patent Appl. No. 13/116784, filed May 26, 2011.

Roberts, David J., and Meghann Casanova. "Automated License Plate Recognition Systems: Policy and Operation Guidance for Law Enforcement." Washington, DC: U.S.

Robison, William Jeremy. "Free at What Cost?: Cloud Computing Privacy under the Stored Communications Act." *Georgetown Law Journal* 98 (2010): 1195–1239.

Rocha, Álvaro, Ana Maria Correa, Tom Wilson, and Karl A. Stroetmann. *Advances in Information Systems and Technologies*. Berlin: Springer, 2013.

Roderick, Leanne. "Discipline and Power in the Digital Age: The Case of the U.S. Consumer Data Broker Industry." *Critical Sociology* 40, no. 5 (2014): 729–746.

Rodis-Lewis, Genevieve. *Descartes: His Life and Thought*, translated by Jane Marie Todd. Ithaca, NY: Cornell University Press, 1998

Rodriguez, Joshua I. "Note: Interrogation First, Miranda Warnings Afterward: A Critical Analysis of the Supreme Court's Approach to Delayed Miranda Warnings." *Fordham Urban Law Journal* 40 (March 2013): 1091.

Roesner, Franziska, Brian T. Gill, and Tadayoshi Kohno. "Sex, Lies, or Kittens? Investigating the Use of Snapchat's Self-Destructing Messages." In *Financial Cryptography and Data Security*, vol. 8437 of the series *Lecture Notes in Computer Science* (November 9, 2014), 64–76.

Roewe, Brian. "Bill Proposes Sweeping Immigration Reform." *National Catholic Reporter*, April 26, 2013.

Rohrs, Jeffrey K. *Audience: Marketing in the Age of Subscribers, Fans and Followers* Rosen, David J. "Limiting Employee Liability under the CFAA: A Code-Based Approach to 'Exceeds Authorized Access.'" *Berkeley Technology Law Journal* 27 (2012): 737.

Rosen, Jeffrey. *The Supreme Court: The Personalities and Rivalries That Defined America*. New York: Times Books, 2006.

____. *The Unwanted Gaze: The Destruction of Privacy in America*. New York: Vintage Books, 2001.

Rosner, Victoria. *Modernism and the Architecture of Private Life*. New York: Columbia University Press, 2005.

Ross, William G. "A Judicial Janus: *Meyer v. Nebraska* in Historical Perspective." *University of Cincinnati Law Review* 57, no. 1, (1988): 125–204.

Rossow, Lawrence F., and Jacqueline Anne Stefkovich. *Search and Seizure in the Public Schools*, 3rd ed. Dayton, OH: Education Law Association, 2006.

Rotenberg, Marc, *Body Scanners, Pat Downs Violate Law And Privacy*, November 19, 2010

Rothe, Dawn L., and Kevin F. Steinmetz. "The Case of Bradley Manning: State Victimization, Realpolitik and WikiLeaks." *Contemporary Justice Review* 16, no. 2 (June 2013): 280–292.

Rothstein, Mark A. *Genetic Secrets Protecting Privacy and Confidentiality in the Genetic Era*. New Haven, CT: Yale University Press, 1997.

Rowe, Heather. "Draft UK Data Protection Bill." *Computer Law & Security Review* 10, no. 5 (1994): 280.

Roy, J. "'Polis' and 'Oikos' in Classical Athens." *Greece & Rome* 46, no. 1 (1999): 1–18.

Rozemond, Marleen. *Descartes's Dualism*. Cambridge, MA: Harvard University Press, 1998.

Rubel, Alan. "Privacy and the USA Patriot Act: Rights, the Value of Rights, and Autonomy." *Law and Philosophy* 26, no. 2 (2007): 119–159.

Rubenfeld, Jed. "The Right to Privacy." *Harvard Law Review* 102 (1989): 737.

Rubenstein, Ira S. and Nathaniel Good. "Privacy By Design: A Counterfactual Analysis of Google and Facebook Privacy Incidents." *Berkeley Technology Law Journal* 28.2 (Fall 2013): 1333–1413.

Rubin, Aaron. "How Website Operators Use CFAA to Combat Data-Scraping." *Law360*.

Rushin, Steven. "The Judicial Response to Mass Police Surveillance." *University of Illinois Journal of Law, Technology and Policy* 2011, no. 2 (2011): 281–328.

Rusli, Evelyn. "Instagram Pictures Itself Making Money." *Wall Street Journal*, September 8, 2013.

Ruzich, Emily, Carrie Allison, Bhismadev Chakrabarti, Paula Smith, Henry Musto, Howard Ring, and Simon Baron-Cohen. "Sex and STEM Occupation Predict Autism-Spectrum Quotient (AQ) Scores in Half a Million People." *PLoS One* 10, no. 10 (2015): e0141229.

S

Sack, Robert D. "Protection of Opinion under the First Amendment: Reflections on Alfred Hill, 'Defamation and Privacy under the First Amendment.'" *Columbia Law Review* 100, no. 1 (January 2000): 294–330.

Salky, Steven M., and Paul B. Hynes. *The Privilege of Silence Fifth Amendment Protections Against Self Incrimination*. 2nd ed. Lanham: American Bar Association, 2015.

Samuels, A. "The Rights of Privacy and Freedom of Expression: The Drafting Challenge." *Statute Law Review* 00, no. 00 (1999): 66–73.

Samuelson, Pamela. "Reviving Zacchini: Analyzing First Amendment Defenses in Right of Publicity and Copyright Cases." *Tulane Law Review* 57, (1982): 836–929.

_____. *Privacy as Intellectual Property?* In *First Amendment Handbook, edited by* James L. Swanson. New York: C. Boardman, 2002.

Sangarasivam, Yamuna. "Cyber Rebellion: Bradley Manning, WikiLeaks, and the Struggle to Break the Power of Secrecy in the Global War on Terror." *Perspectives On Global Development & Technology* 12, no. 1/2 (January 2013): 69–79.

Sarat, Austin, ed. *A World Without Privacy: What Law Can and Should Do?* New York: Cambridge University Press, 2015.

Sarpu, Bridget A. "Google: The Endemic Threat to Privacy." *Journal of High Technology Law* 15, no. 1 (2014): 97–134.

Savage, Charlie, Edward Wyatt, and Peter Baker. "U.S. Confirms That It Gathers Online Data Overseas." *New York Times*, June 2013.

Savare, Matthew, and John Wintermute. "Right of Publicity Issues in Emerging Media." Los Angeles Law 38, no. 10 (May 2015)

Schein, David D., and James D. Phillips. "Holding Credit Reporting Agencies Accountable: How the Financial Crisis May Be Contributing to Improving Accuracy in Credit Reporting." *Loyola Consumer Law Review* 24, no. 329 (2012).

Schieck, Glenn R. "Undercutting Employee Mobility: The Computer Fraud and Abuse Act in the Trade Secret Context." *Brooklyn Law Review* 79, no. 2 (2014): 831.

Schlabach, Gabriel R. "Privacy in the Cloud: The Mosaic Theory and the Stored Communications Act." *Stanford Law Review*, 2015.

Schlag, Chris. "The New Privacy Battle: How the Expanding Use of Drones Continues to Erode Our Concept of Privacy and Privacy Rights." *Pittsburgh Journal of Technology Law and Policy* 13, no. 2 (Spring 2013).

Schmalleger, Frank. *Criminal Justice Today*, 13th ed. Boston, MA: Pearson, 2015.

Schmitz, Amy J. "Secret Consumer Scores and Segmentations: Separating the 'Haves' from 'Have-Nots.'" *Michigan State Law Review* (2014): 1411.

Schneier, Bruce. *Data and Goliath: The Hidden Battles to Collect Your Data and Control Your World*. New York: W. W. Norton, 2015.

Schneier, Bruce. *Economics of Information Security and Privacy III*. New York: Springer, 2013.

Schoeman, Ferdinand. "Privacy: Philosophical Dimensions of the Literature." *An Anthology: Philosophical Dimensions of Privacy* 1–33.

Schulhofer, Stephen J. *More Essential Than Ever: The Fourth Amendment in the Twenty-First Century*. New York: Oxford University Press, 2012.

Schwabach, Aaron. *Internet and the Law: Technology, Society, and Compromises*. Santa Barbara, CA: ABC-CLIO, 2014.

Schwartz, Bernard, ed. *The Warren Court: A Retrospective*. New York: Oxford University Press, 1996.

_____. *The Unpublished Decisions of the Warren Court*. New York: Oxford University Press, 1985, pp. 240–303.

Schwartz, John. "Two German Killers Demanding Anonymity Sue Wikipedia's Parent." *New York Times*, November 12, 2009.

Secada, Jorge. *Cartesian Metaphysics: The Late Scholastic Origins of Modern Philosophy*. Cambridge, England: Cambridge University Press, 2000.

Setalvad, Ariha. "Instagram Direct Gets a Huge Update Focused on Messaging Your Friends." *The Verge*, September 1, 2015.

Severson, Richard James. *The Principles of Information Ethics*. Armonk, NY: M.E. Sharpe, 1997.

Shaman, Jeffrey M. *Equality and Liberty in the Golden Age of State Constitutional Law*. New York: Oxford UP, 2008. Print.

Shane, Scott. "Ex-Contractor Is Charged in Leaks on NSA Surveillance." *New York Times* June 21, 2013.

Shaughnessy, Perri. *Invasion of Privacy*. New York: Delacorte Press, 1996.

Shear, Bradley. "Ed Tech Must Embrace Stronger Student Privacy Laws." *T H E Journal* (April 2015).

Sheinkopf, Cheryl M. "Balancing Free Speech, Privacy and Open Government: Why Government Should Not Restrict the Truthful Reporting of Public Record Information." *UCLA Law Review* 44 (1997): 1567–1612.

Shelton-Mason County Journal Staff. "Codewords, Secrecy Become Clearer." *Shelton-Mason County Journal* (August 2013).

Shema, Mike. "Browser & Privacy Attacks," in *Hacking Web Apps: Detecting and Preventing Web Application Security Problems*. Boston, MA: Syngress, 2012.

Shmueli, Benjamin, and Ayelet Blecher-Prigat. "Privacy for Children." *Columbia Human Rights Law Review* 42, no. 3 (Spring 2011): 759–795.

Shoebotham, Leslie A. "The Strife of Riley: The Search-Incident Consequences of Making an Easy Case Simple." *Louisiana Law Review* 75 (2014): 29–70.

Shoenberger, Allen. "Privacy Wars." *Indiana International & Comparative Law Review* 17 (2007): 355–393.

Shontell, Alyson. "Snap Is a Lot Bigger Than People Realize and It Could be Nearing 200 Million Active Users." *Business Insider*, January 3, 2015.

Shorts, Edwin. *Civil Liberties: Legal Principles of Individual Freedom*. London: Sweet & Maxwell, 1998.

Siegel, Larry J., and John L. Worrall. *Essentials of Criminal Justice*, 9th ed. Stamford, CT: Cengage Learning, 2015.

Siegel, Neil S., and Reva B. Siegel. *Contraception as a Sex Equality Right*. Yale Law Journal Forum 124, 349.

Sigal, Mark. "You Say You Want a Revolution? It's Called Post-PC Computing." Radar (O'Reilly), October 24, 2011.

Silk, Jennie Vee. "Calling Out *Maryland v. King*: DNA, Cell Phones, and the Fourth Amendment." *SSRN Electronic Journal SSRN Journal*.

Silva, Alberto J. Cerda. "Enforcing Intellectual Property Rights by Diminishing Privacy: How the Anti-Counterfeiting Trade Agreement Jeopardizes the Right to Privacy." *American University International Law Review* 26, no. 3 (2011): 601–643.

Silverman, Jacob. *Terms of Service: Social Media and the Price of Constant Connection*. New York: HarperCollins, 2015.

Simmons, Ric. "From *Katz* to *Kyllo*: A Blueprint for Adapting the Fourth Amendment to Twenty-First-Century Technologies." *Hastings Law Journal* 53, no. 6 (August 2002): 1303–1358.

Simon, James F. *Independent Journey: The Life of William O. Douglas*. New York: Harper & Row, 1980.

Sin, Yvonne Pui Man. *Email Privacy: Legal and Ethical Implication of Workplace Surveillance and Monitoring*. Auckland, New Zealand: Department of Management Science and Information Systems, University of Auckland, 2002.

Singer, Natasha. "A Data Broker Offers a Peek behind the Curtain." *New York Times*, September 1, 2013.

Singer, Peter. *Animal Liberation: A New Ethics for Our Treatment of Animals*. New York: Random House, 1975.

Sipior, Janice C., Burke T. Ward, and Ruben A. Mendoza. "Online Privacy Concerns Associated with Cookies, Flash Cookies, and Web Beacons." *Journal of Internet Commerce* 10, no. 1 (2011): 1–16.

Skeen, Shelly L. "Note & Comment: City of Sherman v. Henry: Is the Texas Constitutional Right of Privacy Still a Source of Protection for Texas Citizens?" *4 Tex. Wesleyan L. Rev.* 99 (1997) 99–122.

Skloot, Rebecca. *The Immortal Life of Henrietta Lacks*. Broadway Books 2011. Sloan, Robert H., and Richard Warner. *Unauthorized Access: The Crisis in Online Privacy and Security*. Boca Raton, FL: CRC Press, 2013.

Slobogin, Christopher. *Privacy at Risk: The New Government Surveillance and the Fourth Amendment*. Chicago, IL: University of Chicago Press, 2007.

Slote, Michael A. *From Enlightenment to Receptivity: Rethinking Our Values*. New York: Oxford University Press, 2013.

Smallwood, Robert F. *Information Governance: Concepts, Practices, and Best Strategies*. Hoboken, NJ: Wiley, 2014.

"Smart Meter Data and Privacy." Data Privacy for the Smart Grid, 2015, 55–74.

Smartphones. Herndon, VA: Potomac Books, 2013.

Smith, Marcia S. *"Junk E-mail": An Overview of Issues and Legislation concerning Unsolicited Commercial Electronic Mail ("Spam")*. Washington, DC: Congressional Research Service, Library of Congress, 2001.

Smith, Michael. *Station X: The Codebreakers of Bletchley Park*. London: Channel 4 Books, 1998.

Smith, Robert Ellis. "Consumer's Handbook Guide to Privacy Protections." Privacy Journal, September 1, 2010.

Smolla, Rodney A. "Court Uses Human Cannonball to Shoot Hole in Gannett's First Amendment Claim." The Media Institute, January 30, 2012.

_____. "Emotional Distress and the First Amendment: An Analysis of *Hustler v. Falwell.*" *Arizona State Law Journal* 20 *(January 1, 1988)*: 423–474.

_____. *Jerry Falwell v. Larry Flynt: The First Amendment on Trial.* New York: St. Martin's Press, 1988.

Snowden, Edward. *The Snowden Reader,* edited by David P. Fidler. Bloomington: Indiana University Press, 2015.

Sobel, Richard. "The HIPAA Paradox: The Privacy Rule That's Not." *The Hastings Center Report,* July 1, 2007.

Solove, Daniel J. *Nothing to Hide: The False Tradeoff between Privacy and Security.* New Haven, CT: Yale University Press, 2011.

____. *The Digital Person: Technology and Privacy in the Information Age.* New York: New York University Press, 2004.

____. *The Future of Reputation Gossip, Rumor, and Privacy on the Internet.* New Haven, CT: Yale University Press, 2007.

____. *Understanding Privacy.* Cambridge, Mass.: Harvard University Press, 2008.

Solove, Daniel J., and Paul M. Schwartz. *Privacy, Law Enforcement and National Security.*

Solove, Daniel J., and Woodrow Hartzog. "The FTC and the New Common Law of Privacy." 584 *Columbia Law Review* 114 (2014): 583–676.

Solove, Daniel. *The Future of Reputation: Gossip, Rumor and Privacy on the Internet.* New Haven, CT: Yale University Press, 2007.

Soltani, Ashkan, et al. "Behavioral Advertising: The Offer You Cannot Refuse., *Harvard Law & Policy Review* 6, no. 273 (2012)

Soma, John T. Nichols. "Balance of Privacy vs. Security: A Historical Perspective of the USA PATRIOT Act." *Rutgers Computer &; Technology Law Journal,* 2005.

Sorokina, Nonna. "Long-Term Impact of GLBA on the Financial Industry." *SSRN Electronic Journal SSRN Journal.*

Sorrells, Felipe D. *Social Security Numbers and ID Theft.* New York: Nova Science Publishers, 2010.

Sotto, Lisa J. "Privacy and Data Security." *Privacy and Data Security Law Deskbook.* Frederick, MD: Aspen, 2010.

Spears, Victoria Prussen. "The Case That Started It All: *Roberson v. The Rochester Folding Box Company.*" *Privacy & Data Security Law Journal* 3 (November 2008): 1048.

Sproule, C. "The Effect of the USA Patriot Act on Workplace Privacy." *The Cornell Hotel and Restaurant Administration Quarterly*: 65–73.

Spurlock, Jefferson Tarter. "The Effects of the *Cox Broadcasting Corp. v. Cohn* Decision: Almost Four Decades Later." *Communications Law Review* no. 14: 48–62.

Stalla-Bourdillon, Sophie, Joshua Phillips, and Mark D. Ryan. *Privacy vs. Security.* New York: Springer, 2015. Springer Briefs in Privacy and Security series.

Stanaland, A. J. S., M. O. Lwin, and S. Leong, (2009). "Providing Parents with Online Privacy Information: Approaches in the U.S. and the UK." *Journal of Consumer Affairs* 43 no. 3 (2009): 474–494.

Stanton, Jeffrey M., and Kathryn R. Stam. *The Visible Employee Using Workplace Monitoring and Surveillance to Protect Information Assets—without Compromising Employee Privacy or Trust.* Medford, N.J.: Information Today, 2006.

Stein, Joshua B. *Commentary on the Constitution from Plato to Rousseau.* Lanham, MD: Lexington Books, 2011.

Steinberg, Robert A. "Defamation, Privacy and the First Amendment." *Duke Law Journal,* no. 5 (December 1976): 1016–1050.

Steininger, Michael. "In Return to Berlin, Obama Finds a Cooler Germany." *Christian Science Monitor,* June 19, 2013.

Steptoe and Johnson. *Comparison of U.S. State and Federal Security Breach Notification Laws.* August 26, 2015.

Stern, Seth, and Stephen Wermiel. *Justice Brennan: Liberal Champion,* 2010. Reprint, Lawrence: University Press of Kansas, 2013.

Sternstein, Aliya. "NSA to Crack Codes with Big Data (National Security Agency)." *NextGov.com,* March 30, 2012.

Stevens, Gina Marie. *Privacy: Total Information Awareness Programs and Latest Developments.* New York: Novinka Books, 2003. Excerpted from CRS Report No. RL31730.

Stevens, Gina Marie. *Privacy: Total Information Awareness Programs and Related Information Access, Collection, and Protection Laws.* Washington, DC: Congressional Research Service, 2003.

Stevens, Gina. *Federal Information Security and Data Breach Notification Laws.* Washington, DC: Congressional Research Service, January 28, 2010.

Stiglitz, Joseph E. "Information and the Change in the Paradigm in Economics." *American* Stone, Brad. *The Everything Store: Jeff Bezos and the Age of Amazon.com.* New York: Little Brown and Company, 2013.

Stone, Geoffrey R. *Perilous Times: Free Speech in Wartime from the Sedition Act of 1798 to the War on Terrorism.* New York: W. W. Norton, 2004.

Strahilevitz, Lior Jacob. "Toward a Positive Theory of Privacy Law." *Harvard Law Review,* 2013.

Strang, Heather, and John Braithwaite, eds. *Restorative Justice and Civil Society*. New York: Cambridge University Press, 2001.

Strassberg, Donald, Ryan K. McKinnon, Michael A. Sustaíta, and Jordan Rullo. "Sexting by High School Students: An Exploratory and Descriptive Study." *Archives of Sexual Behavior* 42, no. 1 (June 7, 2012): 15–21.

Stuart, Gary L. Miranda: *The Story of America's Right to Remain Silent*. Tucson: University of Arizona Press, 2004.

Stuntz, William J. "Privacy's Problem and the Law of Criminal Procedure." *Michigan Law Review* 93, no. 5 (1995): 1057–1062.

Stuttard, Dafydd, and Marcus Pinto. *The Web Application Hacker's Handbook: Finding and Exploiting Security Flaws*, 2nd ed. Indianapolis, IN: Wiley, 2011.

Suber, Peter. *Open Access*. Cambridge, MA: MIT Press, 2012.

Sullum, Jacob. "When Policing Becomes Harassment: Why the NYPD's Stop-and-Frisk Program Is Unconstitutional." *Reason*, July 1, 2013.

Sumberg, Theodore A. "Privacy, Freedom, and Obscenity." *Journal of Critical Analysis* 3, no. 2 (1971): 84–96.

Sundar, Sindhu. "Bill Would Regulate Spying Technology Aimed at TV Viewers." *Law360*. June 14, 2013.

Susman, Thomas M. "The Privacy Act and the Freedom of Information Act: Conflict and Resolution." *Journal of the Marshall Law Review* 21, no. 703 (1988).

Swan, Melanie. *Blockchain: Blueprint for a New Economy*. Sebastopol, CA: O'Reilly Media, 2015.

Sweatt, Brian, Sharon Paradesi, Ilaria Liccardi, Lalana Kagal, and Alex Pentland. "Building Privacy-Preserving Location-Based Apps," in 2014 Twelfth Annual International Conference on Privacy, Security and Trust, Toronto, Ontario, Canada, July 23–24, 2014. New York: IEEE/Wiley, 2014.

Sweeny, Jo Anne, "Sexting and Freedom of Expression: A Comparative Approach," Kentucky Law Journal 102 (2013–2014): 103–46.

Swire, Peter P. *Privacy and Surveillance with New Technologies*. Wall Street Journal. "What They Know— Mobile." August 30, 2015.

T

Talia, Domenico, Paolo Trunfio, and Fabrizio Marozzo. *Data Analysis in the Cloud: Models, Techniques and Applications*. Elsevier, 2015.

Tanner, Adam. Different Customers, Different Prices, Thanks To Big Data. *Frobes,* April 14, 2014.

Taslitz, Andrew E. *Reconstructing the Fourth Amendment: A History of Search and Seizure, 1789–1868*. New York: New York University Press, 2006.

Taufick, Roberto. "Understanding the Federal Trade Commission—An Overview." *Revista de Direito da Concorrência* 14 (2008): 69–106.

Tavani, Herman T. "Philosophical Theories of Privacy: Implications for an Adequate Online Privacy Policy." *Metaphilosophy* 38, no. 1 (2007): 1–22.

Taylor, Simon. "Fraud and Security." *European Voice*. January 15, 2015. www.europeanvoice.com.

Tebbit, Mark. *Philosophy of Law: An Introduction*, 2nd ed. London, England: Routledge Taylor & Francis Group, 2005.

Terilli, Samuel A., Jr., and Sigman Splichal, "Privacy Rights in an Open and Changing Society." In *Communication and the Law*, edited by W. Wat Hopkins, 283–309.

Terry, Nicolas P. "Protecting Patient Privacy in the Age of Big Data." *University of Missouri Kansas City Law Review* 81, no. 2 (2012): 1–31.

Tharp, Marye C. *Transcultural Marketing: Building Customer Relationships in Multicultural America*. New York: Routledge, 2014.

THE Journal Staff. "Keeping Student Data Private: Five CTOs Discuss Their Data Privacy Concerns and Reveal How They Are Working with Teachers, Students and the Community to Safeguard Student Information." *THE Journal* (March 2014): 22–30.

Thibault, Edward A., and Lawrence M. Lynch. *Proactive Police Management*, 9th ed. Boston, MA: Pearson, 2015.

Thompson, Richard M. *Governmental Tracking of Cell Phones and Vehicles: The Confluence of Privacy, Technology, and Law*. Washington, DC: Congressional Research Service, 2011.

Thompson, Tamara. *WikiLeaks*. Detroit, MI: Greenhaven Press, 2012.

Thomson, Aimee. "Cellular Dragnet: Active Cell Site Simulators and the Fourth Amendment." *SSRN Electronic Journal SSRN Journal*.

Thomson, Judith Jarvis. "The Right to Privacy." *An Anthology Philosophical Dimensions of Privacy* 272–289. JSTOR.org.

Tilden, Samuel J. "Health Research and the HIPAA Privacy Rule." *JAMA* 299, no. 11 (March 19, 2008): 1259.

Tillman, Bob. "More Information Could Mean Less Privacy: President Bush Signed the E-Government Act to Enhance Public Access to Information after Authorizing Homeland Security Legislation That May Threaten Privacy. (Capital Edge: Legislative & Regulatory Update)." *Information Management Journal* 37, no. 2 (March–April 2003).

_____. "The Changing Political Landscape: The War on Terrorism Delays Congressional Action on Privacy, the Paperwork Reduction Act, and E-Government. (Capital Edge: Legislative & Regulatory Update)." *Informa-*

tion Management Journal 36, no. 1 (January–February 2002): 14.

Timberg, Craig. "Try as It Might, Anti-Surveillance Group Can't Avoid Washington." *Washington Post*, October 11, 2013.

Timm, Carl, and Richard Perez. "Malware Attacks," in *Seven Deadliest Social Network Attacks*, tech. ed. Adam Ely. Burlington, MA: Syngress/Elsevier, 2010.

Timm, Trevor. "The Snowden Effect: New Privacy Wins Await after Data Transfer Ruling." *The Guardian*, October 8, 2015.

Toledo, Fabio. *Smart Metering Handbook*. "What Is Privacy?" *Data Privacy for the Smart Grid*, 2015, 43–54.

Tomboc, Gmeleen Faye B. "The Lemons Problem in Crowdfunding." *John Marshall Journal of Information Technology & Privacy Law* 30, no. 2 (2013): 253–279.

Toobin, Jeffrey. "The Solace of Oblivion: In Europe, the Right to Be Forgotten Trumps the Internet." *New Yorker*, September 29, 2014.

Torres, Mario S. *The Impact of Demographics and the Political Environment on the Implementation of Fourth Amendment Law in Schools*. 2003.

Toth, Victor J. "Telephone Privacy—How to Invade It (Caller Identification and Automatic Number Identification) (Washington Perspective)." *Business Communications Review*, April 1, 1994.

Townsend, Katherine Novak. *Employee Privacy Challenges & Solutions: Electronic Monitoring, Health Information, Personnel Files, and More*. Brentwood, TN: M. Lee Smith Publishers, 2008.

Trepte, Sabine, and Leonard Reinecke. *Privacy Online: Perspectives on Privacy and Self-Disclosure in the Social Web*. Berlin: Springer-Verlag, 2011.

Tribe, Lawrence H. "Lawrence v. Texas: The 'Fundamental Right' That Dare Not Speak Its Name." *Harvard Law Review* 117, no. 6 (2004).

Trottier, Daniel. *Identity Problems in the Facebook Era*. New York, Routledge, 2014.

True, Michael. "The Passion of Bradley Manning: The Story Behind the Wikileaks Whistleblower." *International Journal On World Peace* 31, no. 3 (September 2014): 84–87

Tsai, Wei-Tek, Guanqiu Qi, and Yinong Chen. "Choosing Cost-Effective Configuration in Cloud Storage." In *2013 IEEE Eleventh International Symposium on Autonomous Decentralized Systems (ISADS)*, 1–8. IEEE, 2013.

Tunick, Mark. *Balancing Privacy and Free Speech: Unwanted Attention in the Age of Social Media*. New York: Routledge, 2015.

Tunnell, Kenneth D. *Pissing on Demand Workplace Drug Testing and the Rise of the Detox Industry*. New York: New York University Press, 2004.

Turow, J., Hennessy, M., & Draper, N. (June 2015). The Tradeoff Fallacy: How Marketers are Misrepresenting American Consumers and Opening Them Up to Exploitation (University of Pennsylvania, Annenberg School for Communication).

U

United States Institute of Peace. "Cyberterrorism: How Real Is the Threat?" December 2004.

Urofsky, Melvin I. *Lethal Judgments: Assisted Suicide and American Law*. Lawrence, Kan.: U of Kansas, 2000. Print.

US Department of Defense. *Report to Congress Regarding the Terrorism Information Awareness Program: In Response to Consolidated Appropriations Resolution, 2003, Pub. L. No. 108–7, Division M, § 111(b)*. Washington, DC: Defense Advanced Research Projects Agency, 2003.

US Department of Justice. *1999 Report on Cyberstalking: A New Challenge for Law Enforcement & Industry*. Washington, DC: Author, 1999.

US Government Printing Office. *Protecting Our Personal Health Information, Privacy in the Electronic Age: Hearings before the Committee on Labor and Human Resources, United States Senate, One Hundred Fifth Congress, First Session Examining Standards with Respect to the Privacy of Individuals*. Washington, DC: Author, 1998.

Uzelac, Elizabeth B. "Reviving the Privacy Protection Act of 1980." *Northwestern University Law Review* 107, no. 3 (April 2013): 1437.

V

Vacca, John R. *Biometric Technologies and Verification Systems*. Boston, MA: Butterworth-Heinemann/Elsevier, 2007.

Vaidhyanathan, Siva. *The Googlization of Everything (And Why We Should Worry)*. Berkeley: University of California Press, 2011.

Van Loo, Rory. "Helping Buyers Beware: The Need for Supervision of Big Retail." *University of Pennsylvania Law Review* 163, no. 5 (April 2015): 1311–1392.

Vaughn, Robert G. *The Successes and Failures of Whistleblower Laws*. Cheltenham, UK: Edward Elgar Publishing Limited, 2012.

Verbeek, Theo. *Descartes and the Dutch: Early Reactions to Cartesian Philosophy 1637–1650*. Carbondale: Southern Illinois University Press, 1994.

Verizon. "2015 Data Breach Investigations Report." Verizonenterprise.com. Last modified February, 2015.

Vermaat, Misty, and Susan L. Sebok. *Discovering Computers 2016: Tools, Apps, Devices, and the Impact of Technology*.

Vile, John R. *Encyclopedia of the Fourth Amendment*. Thousand Oaks, Calif.: CQ Press, 2013.

Villard, Oswald Garrison. "Edwin L. Godkin, Master of Comment and of Style." In *Some Newspapers and Newspaper-Men*. New York: Alfred A. Knopf, 1923.

Vladeck, Stephen I. "Big Data before and after Snowden." *Journal of National Security Law and Policy* 7, no. 2 (2014): 333–340.

Volkmer, Ingrid. *The Global Public Sphere: Public Communication in the Age of Reflective Interdependence.*

Volokh, Eugene. "Freedom of Speech, Cyberspace, Harassment Law, and the Clinton Administration." *Law and Contemporary Problems* 63, nos. 1 and 2 (Winter/Spring 2000): 299–335.

Volonino, Linda, et al. *Computer Forensics: Principles and Practices.* Upper Saddle River, NJ: Pearson/Prentice Hall, 2007.

Vrankulj, Adam. "NGI: A Closer Look at the FBI's Billion-Dollar Biometric Program." *BiometricUpdate.*

W

Wacks, Raymond. *Privacy and Media Freedom.* Oxford, England: Oxford University Press, 2013.

____. *Privacy: A Very Short Introduction*, 2d ed. New York: Oxford University Press, 2015.

Winegarten, Debra L., and Gisela J. Hinkle. *Women, Homelessness and Privacy.* 1990.

Waldron, Jeremy. *God, Locke, and Equality: Christian Foundations in Locke's Political Thought.* Cambridge, England: Cambridge University Press, 2002.

Walker, Robert Kirk. "Note: The Right to Be Forgotten." *Hastings Law Journal* 64 (2012): 257–286.

Walker, Samuel. *In Defense of American Liberties: A History of the ACLU.* 2nd ed. Carbondale: Southern Illinois University Press, 1999.

Wanlund, Bill. "Intelligence Reform: Are U.S. Spy Agencies Prepared for 21st-century Threats?" *CQ Researcher* 25, no. 2 (May 29, 2015).

Warburton, Steven, and Stylianos Hatzipanagos, eds. *Digital Identity and Social Media.* Hershey, PA: Information Science Reference, 2013.

Warren, Earl. *The Memoirs of Earl Warren.* Garden City, NY: Doubleday and Company, Inc., 1977.

Warren, Samuel D., and Louis D. Brandeis. "The Right to Privacy." *Harvard Law Review* 4, no. 5 (1890): 193–220.

Watkins, Tamara E. "Privacy, the Individual, and the 'Good' Society. (Philosophy)." *Michigan Academician,* March 22, 2002.

Wayleith, Paulus R., ed. *Data Security: Laws and Safeguards.* New York: Nova Science Publishers, Inc., 2008.

Wayne, Logan Danielle. "The Data Broker Threat: Proposing Federal Legislation to Protect Post-Expungement Privacy." *Journal of Criminal Law and Criminology* 102, no. 1 (Winter 2012): 253–282.

Weber, Michael. *Invasion of Privacy: Big Brother and the Company Hackers.* Boston, MA: Premier Press, 2004. Weber, Steve. *The Success of Open Source.* Cambridge, MA: Harvard University Press, 2004.

Webster, Warren R., Jr. "DNA Database Statutes & Privacy in the Information Age." *Health Matrix: Journal of Law-Medicine* 10, no. 1 (Winter 2000): 119. *Academic Search Premier,* EBSCOhost (accessed September 26, 2015).

Weil, Nancy. "CDT to File FTC Complaint on Pentium III. (Center for Democracy and Technology)." *Network World,* March 1, 1999.

Weinberg, Louise. "The McReynolds Mystery Solved." *Denver University Law Review* 89, no. 1 (January 2011): 133–160.

Weinstein, Donald D. "Federal Fair Credit Reporting Act—Compliance by Lenders and Other Users of Consumer Credit Information." *Banking Law Journal* 89, no. 410 (1972)

Weir, Robert F., ed. *Ethical Issues in Death and Dying*, 2nd ed. New York: Columbia University Press, 1986.

Wertime, Kent, and Ian Fenwick. *DigiMarketing: The Essential Guide to New Media & Digital Marketing.* Singapore: John Wiley & Sons (Asia), 2008.

West, Nigel. *The SIGINT Secrets: The Signals Intelligence War, 1900 to Today: Including the Persecution of Gordon Welchman.* New York: W. Morrow, 1988.

Western, Bruce. "Criminal Background Checks and Employment among Workers with Criminal Records." *Criminology & Public Policy* 7, no. 3 (August 2008): 413–417.

Westin, Alan F. *Privacy and Freedom.* New York: Athenaeum, 1970.

White House Press Release (Feb. 23, 2012). We Can't Wait: Obama Administration Calls for a Consumer Privacy Bill of Rights for the Digital Age.

White House. *Consumer Data Privacy in a Networked World: A Framework for Protecting Privacy and Promoting Innovation in the Global Digital Economy.*

White, Welsh S. "Miranda's Failure to Restrain Pernicious Interrogation Practices." *Michigan Law Review* 99, no. 5 (March 2001): 1211–1247. (Symposium: Miranda after Dickerson: The Future of Confession Law).

Whitley, Joe D., and Lynne K. Zusman, eds. *Homeland Security: Legal and Policy Issues.* Chicago IL: ABA Section of Administrative Law and Regulatory practice, 2009.

Whitman, James Q. "Two Western Cultures of Privacy: Dignity versus Liberty." *Yale Law Journal* 113, no. 6 (April 2004): 1151–1221.

Wierzel, Kimberly L. "If You Can't Beat Them, Join Them: Data Aggregators and Financial Institutions." *North Carolina Banking Institute* 5, no. 457 (2001).

Wilkerson, Jared A. "Battle for the Disclosure Tort." *California Western Law Review* 49 (Spring 2013): 231–268.

Wilkinson, Francis. *Essential Liberty: First Amendment Battles for a Free Press*. New York: Columbia University Graduate School of Journalism, 1992.

Wilkinson, Nicholas. *Secrecy and the Media: The Official History of the D-notice System. Government Official History Series*. New York: Routledge, 2009.

Willbern, York. "Types and Levels of Public Morality." *Public Administration Review* 44, no. 2 (1984): 102–108.

Williams, Mary E. *Abortion*. Detroit: Greenhaven Press, 2007.

Wills, Nathan J. "A Tripartite Threat to Medical Records Privacy: Technology, HIPAA's Privacy Rule and the USA Patriot Act." *Journal of Law and Health* (2002).

Wilson, C. L., and C. L. Wilson. *Biometric Data Specification for Personal Identity Verification*. Rockville, MD: NIST, 2013.

Winn, Peter A. "Online Court Records: Balancing Judicial Accountability and Privacy in an Age of Electronic Information." *Washington Law Review* 79, no. 1 (2004): 307–329.

____. "Katz and the Origins of the 'Reasonable Expectation of Privacy' Test." *McGeorge Law Review* 40 (2009): 1–9.

Wintemute, Robert. *Sexual Orientation and Human Rights: The United States Constitution, the European Convention, and the Canadian Charter*. Oxford, UK: Clarendon Press, 1995.

Winters, Michael Sean. "Push for Immigration Reform: Negotiation, Compromise Lead to Senators' New Proposal." *National Catholic Reporter*, May 10, 2013.

Wirtz, Brigitte. "Technical Evaluation of Biometric Systems." *Computer Vision—ACCV'98 Lecture Notes in Computer Science*. 499–506.

Wolf, Christopher Maxwell. "Smart Grids and Privacy. (Regulation and Competition)." *Communications & Strategies*, October 1, 2009.

Wolfe, Alan. "The Politics of Privacy, Right and Left." *Harper's Magazine*, May 1, 1993.

Wolfe, C. (2000). "Public Morality and the Modern Supreme Court." *American Journal of Modern Jurisprudence* 45 (1): 66–92.

Wolfe, Gregory Nathaniel. "Smile for the Camera, the World Is Going to See That Mug: The Dilemma of Privacy Interests in Mug Shots." *Columbia Law Review* 133, no. 8 (2013).

Wolhandler, Steven J. "Voluntary Active Euthanasia for the Terminally Ill and the Constitutional Right to Privacy." *Cornell Law Review* 363 (1984).

Woodard, Damon L., and Patrick J. Flynn. "Finger Surface as a Biometric Identifier." *Computer Vision and Image Understanding* 100, no. 3 (2005): 357–384.

Woodward, Beverly. "Federal Privacy Legislation." *The Journal of Law, Medicine & Ethics* 26, no. 1 (1998): 80–81.

Woodward, John D. *Biometrics a Look at Facial Recognition*. Santa Monica, Calif.: RAND, 2003.

Worrall, John, and Craig Hemmens. *Criminal Evidence: An Introduction*. Los Angeles: Roxbury, 2005.

Wortley, Richard, and Steven Smallbone. *Internet Child Pornography: Causes, Investigation, and Prevention*. Santa Barbara, CA: Praeger, 2012.

Wozniak, S., and G. Smith. *iWoz: Computer Geek to Cult Icon: How I Invented the Personal Computer, CoFounded Apple, and Had Fun Doing It*. New York: W. W. Norton & Co., 2006.

Wright, Ashlea. "*Wilson v. Layne:* Increasing the Scope of the Fourth Amendment Right to Privacy." *Pepperdine Law Review* (2000): 163–193.

Wright, Lawrence. *The Looming Tower: Al-Qaeda and the Road to 9/11*. New York: Knopf, 2006.

Wu, Stephen S. *Guide to HIPAA Security and the Law*. Chicago: ABA Section of Science & Technology Law, 2007.

Wugmeister, Miriam. *Global Employee Privacy and Data Security Law*. Arlington, VA: BNA Books, 2009.

Y

Yan, Jean. "Big Data, Bigger Opportunities - Data.gov's Roles: Promote, Lead, Contribute, and Collaborate in the Era of Big Data." 2012 President Management Council Inter-Agency Rotation Program, Cohort 2, April 9, 2013.

Yar, Majid. *Cybercrime and Society*. London: SAGE Publications, 2006.

Yoffie, D. B., and M. Slind. *Apple Inc., 2008*. Harvard Business School Case Studies (708–480). Cambridge, MA: Harvard Business School Publishing, February 2008, 2–32.

Young, J. S., and W. L. Simon. *iCon Steve Jobs: The Greatest Second Act in the History of Business*. Hoboken, NJ: John Wiley and Sons, 2005, 35.

Young, John B. *Privacy*. Chichester, England: Wiley, 1978. Youngs, Gillian, ed. *Digital World: Connectivity, Creativity, and Rights*. 2013; reprint, New York: Routledge, 2013.

Z

Zeidman, Steven. "Whither the Criminal Court: Confronting Stops-and-Frisks." *Albany Law Review* 76, no. 2 (2013): 1187.

Zelermyer, William. *Invasion of Privacy*. Syracuse, NY: Syracuse University Press, 1959.

Zemer, Lior. "The Making of a New Copyright Lockean." *Harvard Journal of Law & Public Policy, no. 3*, 29 (2006): 891–947.

Zeng, Marcia. "Metadata Basics." Kent State University, 2015.

Zero to Eight: Children's Media Use in America 2013. San Francisco, CA: Common Sense Media, 2013.

Zetter, Kim. *Countdown to Zero Day: Stuxnet and the Launch of the World's First Digital Weapon.* New York: Broadway Books, 2014.

Zheng, Zibin, Jieming Zhu, and Michael R. Lyu. "Service-generated Big Data and Big Data-As-a-Service: an Overview." In *2013 IEEE International Congress on Big Data (BigData Congress)*, 403–410. IEEE, 2013.

Zimmerman, Diane. "False Light Invasion of Privacy: The Light That Failed." *New York University Law Review* 64, no. 2 (May 1989): 364–453.

Zittrain, Jonathan. "What the Publisher Can Teach the Patient: Intellectual Property and Privacy in an Era of Trusted Privication." *Stanford Law Review* 52, no. 5 (May 2000): 1201–1250. [Symposium: Cyberspace and Privacy: A New Legal Paradigm?]

Zotti, Priscilla H. Machado. *Injustice for All: Mapp v. Ohio and the Fourth Amendment.* New York: Peter Lang Publishing, 2005.

Subject Index